BIBLIOGRAPHY OF LAW AND ECONOMICS

BIBLIOGRAPHY OF LAW AND ECONOMICS

Edited by

BOUDEWIJN BOUCKAERT

and

GERRIT DE GEEST

Law School,
University of Ghent,
Belgium

KLUWER ACADEMIC PUBLISHERS

DORDRECHT / BOSTON / LONDON

Library of Congress Cataloging-in-Publication Data

Bibliography of law and economics / edited by Boudewijn Bouckaert and Gerrit de Geest.
p. cm.
Includes indexes.
ISBN 0-7923-1645-2 (HB : printed on acid free paper)
1. Law--Bibliography. 2. Law--Europe--Bibliography.
3. Economics--Bibliography. 4. Economics--Europe--Bibliography.
I. Bouckaert, Boudewijn. II. Geest, Gerrit de.
K38.B525 1992
016.34--dc20 92-250

ISBN 0-7923-1645-2

Published by Kluwer Academic Publishers,
P.O. Box 17, 3300 AA Dordrecht, The Netherlands.

Kluwer Academic Publishers incorporates
the publishing programmes of
D. Reidel, Martinus Nijhoff, Dr W. Junk and MTP Press.

Sold and distributed in the U.S.A. and Canada
by Kluwer Academic Publishers,
101 Philip Drive, Norwell, MA 02061, U.S.A.

In all other countries, sold and distributed
by Kluwer Academic Publishers Group,
P.O. Box 322, 3300 AH Dordrecht, The Netherlands.

Printed on acid-free paper

Printed in the Netherlands

FOREWORD

It is with some envy that, as an American, I write this foreword to the landmark *Bibliography of Law & Economics*, edited by Professor B. Bouckaert and Lecturer G. De Geest. Although the modern approach to "law and economics" essentially started in the United States in the early 1960s with the publication of Ronald Coase's famous article "The Problem of Social Cost" and Guido Calabresi's early writings on the cost of accidents, this volume suggests that the field has been taken over by the Europeans. (Actually, it may even be accurate to say that the field was started by Europeans, since Coase is an Englishman by birth, and Calabresi an Italian by birth!) Geographic rivalries aside, law and economics scholars from throughout the world owe a great debt to the editors and their colleagues for this monumental undertaking.

The magnitude of this project can be conveyed by some simple statistics. The bibliography lists approximately 7,000 publications in law and economics, covering both methodological and substantive topics. The methodological topics include the philosophical and normative foundations of the economic approach to law. The substantive topics include property, bankruptcy, contract, insurance, tort law, criminal law, regulation, corporation law, and procedure. The bibliography also includes over 700 entries in several country-specific surveys.

This bibliography far exceeds in breadth and depth every bibliographic effort related to law and economics that has preceded it. Even scholars immersed in law and economics will be amazed at how far our field has progressed in a relatively short time. More importantly, we now have a way to introduce new scholars to the richness of our discipline.

A. Mitchell Polinsky
Josephine Scott Crocker Professor
of Law and Economics
School of Law - Stanford University - U.S.A.

CONTENTS

PART II: LAW & ECONOMICS IN EUROPE: NATIONAL SURVEYS OF NON-ENGLISH PUBLICATIONS

SCIENTIFIC COMMITTEE

INTRODUCTION

Boudewijn Bouckaert and Gerrit De Geest

This book is the result of a long-term project. It started in 1986 with a short bibliographical list of 10 Kilobyte on a Commodore 64 and ended in November 1991 with a 4 Megabyte database on a Macintosh (encompassing more than 7000 references from within the field and about 500 references from related disciplines). In the beginning, we had only very modest ambitions: organizing our library and providing our law & economic students with references they could use when writing a paper. In the following years, we added more and more references, partly as a by-product of our research in the fields of contract and property law. In July 1990, we decided to publish our data as a reference work, and invited 19 European specialists to complete a specific part of our database. Their task was not only to add additional references, but also to refine the classification system.

To guarantee high quality, we used a 'double security' system. There has been, for example, a close co-operation between the authors of the subject-related bibliographies and those of the national bibliographies. Moreover, independently of these contributors, we have done some additional research on all topics and have more particularly scanned systematically all specialized law & economics journals, most American law journals and many economic journals. To avoid important omissions and to verify the references once more, we additionally consulted 7 databases.

In principle, we have tried to list all publications in the field. However, the literature on some topics (especially in the field of old law & economics) is so immense that a complete survey was impossible. This was the case for '5400 Labor Law' (especially for 5410 and 5450), '5700 Antitrust Law', '5800 Regulation of Natural Monopolies & Public Utilities', '5900 Regulation of Other Sectors', '6100 Social Security', and '9200 Legislation' (the latter including most of the public choice literature). For '0600 Fundamental Concepts' too a selection had to be made (most law & economics concepts being borrowed from economic science in general).

With this work, we all hope to fill a gap that certainly exists. 'Law & Economics' is without any doubt a separate field of research. But because it is an interdisciplinary science, the literature is spread over a large number of economic journals and law reviews. The existing bibliographies are very incomplete in the sense that they only cover part of the publications in which law & economics articles may appear. In legal databases it is quite difficult to find out whether an author has used a law & economics approach. In addition, the traditional legal classification systems are not logical from an economic point of view. For European scholars, it is a difficult and timeconsuming task to find the references of recent American and international publications. For

American scholars, finding and consulting European publications is an even bigger problem.

Without a bibliographical instrument, finding the relevant literature was a timeconsuming task. This may explain some of the resistance of many lawyers to the economic approach. By reducing the 'barrier of entry' we hope to contribute to the further development of the discipline.

One practical problem we had to face was the choice of the quotation style. As every scholar can experience every day, there is no uniformity concerning the quotation style in law & economics, nor in economic or legal science. In an early stage of the project, we started to make a study of quotation styles but we gave up when we had found...12 different styles! It was certainly not our task to decide once and for all how scholars should quote in the future. To make this bibliography useful for as many scholars and students as possible, it has been our policy to provide a maximum of information, but within certain limits. More specifically the references of articles contain in principle: both the volume number of the journal and the year of publication, both the first and the last page of an article. References of books contain (amongst other things) the number of pages and the name of the publisher.

The subject index system was another hard case for two reasons. Firstly, the traditional legal structure differs from economic logic. Secondly, there are important differences between the legal structure of the different countries, especially between common law and civil law countries. We have finally opted for an economic logic. Thus we have divided the law in (a) the property question (b) several forms (voluntary and involuntary) of transfer of property and (c) meta-aspects such as procedure, the enforcement of law and the production of legal rules. Property in a wide sense does not only include '2000 property' ff. but also family law (which defines the property rights on children - although it has to be admitted that marriage law is rather concerned with the regulation of contracts) and human rights (most human rights rules, e.g. privacy and free speech, are further definitions of one's own domain). Tort law (3000 ff.) is mainly about forms of involuntary transfer between individuals (although partly also a further property definition). Contracts (4000) are voluntary transfers, and regulations (5000) are governmental limitations on this form of transfer. Tax law (6000), social security (6100), takings (6200) and administrative law (6300) all deal with the problem of involuntary transfer between individuals and the government.
In spite of this economic structure, lawyers will easily find their way, because of the subject index at the end of the book.

Part II gives a survey of law & economics publications in Europe. These publications have also been listed under the relevant headings of Part I. Nevertheless we thought it would be interesting to list them a second time: never before has such a systematic bibliographical survey of law & economics in Europe been made. This interesting material is begging for some first conclusions. Therefore, we invited Roger Van den Bergh, President of the European Association for Law and Economics, to write an introductory article, in which he gives an outline of the present state and future aspects of Law & Economics in Europe.

We are indebted to many people for their help and encouragement. Without the European Association of Law and Economics and the contact network it has created in Europe, this work could never have been made. Therefore, our first thanks go to the actual president, Roger Van den Bergh and the former, Göran Skogh. We owe a lot to Luit Bakker and Gérard Hertig, whose personal databases were the starting point for our surveys on respectively antitrust law and Switzerland. We also would like to thank Vern Da Re, Ingrid Remmery, Inge Van Brabant, Frieda Van Caneghem, Jan Vereeken, Patrick Wallaert, Bengt-Arne Wickström and last but not least Marie M. Stratta for stimulating and supporting the project from its early stages.

Finally we would like to thank even now all readers who will provide us with suggestions for the second edition of this work.

LAW AND ECONOMICS IN EUROPE: PRESENT STATE AND FUTURE PROSPECTS

Roger Van den Bergh

Introduction

1. Law and Economics can be considered the most exciting development in legal scholarship in recent decades. The application of economic methodology to legal concepts and institutions has become a major issue in North America, but the importance of the economic approach to law is also steadily growing in Europe. One could not think of better evidence for the existence of a growing European Law and Economics movement than this bibliography, which lists more than 700 publications in languages other than English. In this introductory essay I consider the ways in which the European Law and Economics movement differs from its American counterpart.

What is European in the European Law and Economics movement? To answer this question a brief overview of the development of Law and Economics in Europe seems appropriate. This overview, to be given in the first part, will clarify the major achievements of the economic approach to law. In the second part the major remaining challenges for Law and Economics in Europe will be addressed.

A. The growth of Law and Economics in Europe

2. Although there was no European Law and Economics movement at the time of its rapid and spectacular growth in the United States of America in the seventies and eighties, attention to the economic aspects of the law was not totally absent. There are two traditional areas in which the economic consequences of legal rules have always been debated: the public supervision of some sectors of the economy[1], and the area of competition law[2].

---

1 See e.g. BALDWIN, G.R. and VELJANOVSKI, Cento G., *Regulation and Cost-Benefit Analysis - The U.S. Experience and U.K. Potential*, Oxford, Centre for Socio-Legal Studies, 1982.; VAN DEN BERGH, Roger, 'Belgian Public Policy Towards the Retailing Trade', in GRAF VON DER SCHULENBURG, J.-Matthias and SKOGH, Göran (eds.), *Law and Economics and The Economics of Legal Regulation*, Dordrecht, Kluwer, 1986, 185-205.

2 The economic approach is mentioned in the introductory chapters of some European handbooks on Competition Law. See e.g.: BAUMBACH, A. and HEFERMEHL, W., *Wettbewerbsrecht*, 16th ed., München, Beck, 27-30 and VAN DEN BERGH, Roger and DIRIX, Eric, *Handels- en economisch recht in hoofdlijnen*, Antwerpen, Maklu, 1989,

One should, however, not overestimate the importance of economic criteria in these fields. State intervention has been justified on "social" grounds when the economic rationales were not convincing. In the area of competition law most European countries distinguish between antitrust law, which should guarantee the free functioning of the market system, and the law of unfair competition, which bans competitive behaviour deemed to be "unfair"[3]. In practice, competition law is often applied with more attention to "good faith" considerations than to economic theories of competition[4].

182-189. These references remain exceptions. However, many articles and books devoted to particular problems of competition law make use of economic methodology and concepts. See e.g. HOPPMAN, Erich, *Die Abgrenzung des relevanten Marktes im Rahmen der Mißbrauchsaufsicht über marktbeherrschende Unternehmen*, Baden-Baden, Nomos, 1974; LEHMANN, M., 'Verkauf unter Einstandspreis und Lockvogelwerbung. Eine rechtsvergleichende Untersuchung', *Gewerblicher Rechtsschutz und Urheberrecht - Internationaler Teil*, 1977, 135-151; MESTMäCKER, E.-J., *Der verwaltete Wettbewerb*, Tübingen, Mohr, 1984; SCHLUEP, W., *"Wirksamer Wettbewerb" Schlüssel-begriff des neuen schweizerischen Wettbewerbsrecht*, Bern, Huber, 1987; VAN DEN BERGH, Roger, *Inkoopmacht en Prijsconcurrentie*, Antwerpen, Kluwer, 1982.

3 To illustrate this point it is useful mentioning that e.g. both in Belgium and in Germany freedom of competition is protected by antitrust law (in Germany the "Gesetz gegen Wettbewerbsbeschrankungen", which contains a prohibition of cartel agreements and abuse of dominant position as well as a merger control; in Belgium the "Wet tot beteugeling van het misbruik van economische machtspositie", which only applies if the existence of a dominant position can be proven), whereas at the same time this freedom of competition is limited by rules prohibiting "unfair competition" (in Germany the "Gesetz gegen den unlauteren Wettbewerb"; in Belgium the "Wet betreffende de handelspraktijken"). About the difficulties resulting from the co-existence of both types of law, see e.g. LEHMANN, Michael, 'Wettbewerbspolitik, Strukturpolitik und Mittelstandsschutz', *Gewerblicher Rechtsschutz und Urheberrecht*, 1977, 580-588 and 633-642.

4 See e.g. VAN DEN BERGH, Roger, 'Over de mededingingsbeperkende werking van de Wet Handelspraktijken of het verhaal van concurrenten die tegen de concurrentie beschermd willen worden' [On the Competition Limiting Effect of the Law on Trade Practices or the Story of Competitors Who Want to Be Protected Against Competition], **34** *Economisch en Sociaal Tijdschrift*, 1980, 421-446; MESTMäCKER, E.-J., cited note 2; LEHMANN, Michael, 'Die UWG-Neuregelungen 1987 - Erläuterungen und Kritik' [The New UWG Unfair Competition Rules - Explanations and Critique], **89** *Gewerblicher Rechtsschutz und Urheberrecht*, 1987, 199-214.

In the civil law area (contracts, torts), the first signs of an economic approach, apart from a few early and admirable exceptions [5], emerged only in the second half of the eighties. The "new" economic analysis of law has mainly been imported into Europe by scholars who studied at the most important university centers of Law and Economics in North America (e.g. Chicago, Yale, Berkeley).

The establishment of the *European Association of Law and Economics* (EALE) has been the institutional response to the increasing importance of the economic analysis of law in Europe. The EALE was founded in 1984. The purpose of the Association is to provide assistance for scholars embarking on this new field of research. The annual conference of the EALE has become an important forum for the exchange of information and ideas [6]. The EALE also arranges seminars jointly with other organizations and locally in different countries. Several conference volumes have been published [7], and the EALE has a periodical newsletter.

3. In many European countries (especially Germany, France, Belgium and the Netherlands) the introduction of the new economic approach encountered

---

5 TRIMARCHI, Pietro, *Rischio e responsabilità oggettiva*, Milano, Giuffrè, 1961; TRIMARCHI, Pietro, 'Sul significato economico dei criteri di responsabilità contrattuale' [On the economic significance of the Criterions for Contractual Liability], *Rivista trimestriale di diritto e procedura civile*, 1970, 512 ff.; COUSY, Herman, 'Produktenaansprakelijkheid. Proeve van een juridisch-economische analyse' [Product Liability. Attempt of a Legal-Economic Analysis], *Tijdschrift voor Privaatrecht*, 1976, 995-1035.

6 Those interested in obtaining more information about the EALE may contact Dr. Michael FAURE, Secretary EALE, METRO, PO Box 616, 6200 MD Maastricht, The Netherlands.

7 SCHULENBURG, J.-Matthias Graf von der and SKOGH, Göran (eds.), *Law and Economics and the Economics of Legal Regulation*, Dordrecht, Kluwer, 1986, 230 p.; SKOGH, Göran (ed.), *Liability, Insurance and Safety Regulation*, Special Issue of the Geneva Papers on Risk and Insurance, Vol. 12, April 1987; FAURE, Michael and VAN DEN BERGH, Roger (eds.), *Essays in Law and Economics. Corporations, Accident Prevention and Compensation for Losses*, Antwerpen, Maklu, 1989, 232 p; WHELAN, C. (ed.), *The Law and Economics of Professional Liability Insurance*, Special Issue of the Geneva Papers on Risk and Insurance, Vol. 14, October 1989; PARDOLESI, Roberto and VAN DEN BERGH, Roger (eds.), *Law and Economics: Some further Insights*, Milano, Giuffrè, 1991, 205 p.

hostility[8]. Cultural and legal traditions, as well as misunderstandings about the ambitions of Law and Economics in the legal discipline, created a serious entry barrier for the economic approach. Although this entry barrier has now been overcome in some countries, it seems useful to clarify the methodology and the real ambitions of Law and Economics, especially for those countries where (misinformed) opposition has not yet been stilled. Starting with the cultural problems, the European cultural tradition is certainly different from the American. The utilitarian cost-benefit analysis, a major influence in the United States, contrasts with the dominant view of European philosophers. In the tradition of Kant, autonomous individuals may not be used to social ends. The European cultural tradition therefore does not provide a firm basis for the instrumental use of the law. Such an instrumental use becomes especially problematic when so-called "external values" are said to infiltrate an autonomous legal order. Allocative efficiency is an example of such an external value. German opponents call it a "Fremdkörper". The use of allocative efficiency as a device to explain and evaluate the law, they say, would be a misplaced manifestation of economic imperialism. According to the dominant view of European lawyers, the goal of the law is justice, not efficiency.

In response to this criticism proponents of the economic approach have belittled justice as a "fuzzy" concept which needs specificity in order to be useful in resolving concrete legal disputes. This objection may be more powerful in the United States of America than in Europe. Indeed, many European lawyers seem to attach value to vague norms, precisely because of their vagueness. When these lawyers try to specify "justice" they merely replace it by other vague norms. A long list of examples can be given: fairness, good faith, decency, correction of unequal bargaining power, protection of the "weaker party", weaker parties being consumers, victims and even middle class

8 Belgium: KRUITHOF, Robert, 'Leven en dood van het contract' [Life and Death of Contract], **49** *Rechtskundig Weekblad*, 1985-86, 2761-2768; VAN DEN BERGH, Roger and HEREMANS, Dirk, 'Over krommen en rechten. Een reactie op de kritiek van Kruithof ten aanzien van de economische analyse van het recht' [On Curves and Lines: A Reaction on the Critique of Kruithof on Economic Analysis of Law], **50** *Rechtskundig Weekblad*, 1986-87, 1649-1668; KRUITHOF, Robert, 'Naschrift' [Afterword], **50** *Rechtskundig Weekblad*, 1986-87, 1669-1680.

Germany: FEZER, Karl-Heinz, 'Aspekte einer Rechtskritik an der economic analysis of law und am property rights approach' [Aspects of a Legal Critique on Law & Economics and the Property Rights Approach], *Juristenzeitung*, 1986, 817-824; OTT, Claus and SCHÄFER, Hans-Bernd, 'Die ökonomische Analyse des Rechts. Irrweg oder Chance wissenschaftlicher Rechtserkenntnis?' [The Economic Analysis of Law. Wrong Track or Chance for a Scientific Legal Knowledge?], *Juristenzeitung*, 1988, 213-223; FEZER, Karl-Heinz, 'Nochmals: Kritik an der ökonomischen Analyse des Rechts' [Once More: Critique on the Economic Analysis of Law], *Juristenzeitung*, 1988, 223-228.

The Netherlands: NIEUWENHUIS, J.H., 'Ieder het zijne' [Each His Own], *RMThemis*, 1988, Nr.2, 73-84.

retailers[9]. The vagueness of these norms allows the judge to decide each case differently, depending upon its merits. In many cases the decision of the judge is more influenced by "social" considerations than by economic arguments.

4. Also differences in legal traditions are advanced as a major obstacle to the reception of Law and Economics in Europe. In a legal structure of codified law there is less freedom for the judge to use economic criteria than in a common law system based upon precedents. In the United States, the judiciary gains strength by adopting the economic approach. One of the reasons for its success was the ability of Law and Economics to "reconstruct" American Law[10]. The economic analysis provides a framework to think about law in broad theoretical terms and to reconstruct case law.

In a European tradition of legal positivism it is the legislator who balances the relevant value judgements and decides what is "just". Judges must stick to the legal formulation and may only interpret the statutes within limits. However, the differences between the American and the European legal tradition should not be overestimated. Many cases can not be solved by the mere application of statute law. Many statutes use vague concepts and, therefore, increase the importance of case law.

The misunderstandings which have somewhat delayed the reception of Law and Economics in Europe relate both to the economic methodology and to the ambitions of the economic approach with respect to legal policy making.

Much confusion has been caused by not drawing a clear distinction between the different forms of Law and Economics: predictive, explanatory and normative analysis. The former two forms of analysis contain positive statements, which should not be confused with normative statements. When assumptions which are part of the positive analysis, such as rational behaviour, are falsely taken to be normative devices dramatic misunderstandings arise. Human beings are then not simply assumed to behave rationally but the claim is made that they *ought* to do so as well[11]. Therefore, to prevent confusion about the contents of the books and articles mentioned in this bibliography, the distinction between the three different types of economic analysis must be made very clear. The *predictive* economic analysis uses economic models to explore the

---

9 See e.g. VON HIPPEL, E., *Verbraucherschutz,* Tübingen, Mohr, 1986; LEHMANN, Michael, Wettbewerbspolitik, Strukturpolitik und Mittelstandsschutz', *Gewerblicher Rechtsschutz und Urheber- recht*, 1977, 580-588 and 633-642.

10 ACKERMAN, Bruce A., *Reconstructing American Law*, Cambridge (Mass.), Harvard University Press, 1984, 118 p.

11 This is the basic failure of the criticisms made by KRUITHOF, R., cited, note 8.

behavioural effects of the law. It contains no value judgements and only aims at predicting the effects of regulation and legal rule making by judges[12]. The *explanatory* economic analysis tries to explain how the law evolves towards efficiency. It contains an economic reconstruction of the legal decision process. Its claim is that many legal rules can be understood as efficiency enhancing devices[13]. The *normative* economic analysis evaluates the law by reference to economic arguments. It is not value free, since it considers efficiency as an important criterion for policy making. Efficiency is, however, not seen as the only relevant criterion. The fact that other values may play a more important role is acknowledged[14].

6. This clarification brings us to the continuing reluctance of lawyers to use economic analysis as an instrument of policy making. Most European lawyers view the law as a provider of justice. They regard efficiency aspects of the law with skepticism, if not with hostility. How can this reluctance be overcome?

In the first place, the objection that the law must be "just" should be limited to its proper proportions. A great part of the economic analysis is free from value judgements and does, therefore, not affect traditional notions about justice. This is true for economic analyses which predict the consequences of legal rules. Predicting whether the number of accidents will increase or decrease in response to a change from a negligence rule to a rule of strict

---

12 See e.g. PELTZMAN, Sam, 'An Evaluation of Consumer Protection Legislation: The 1962 Drug Amendments', **81** *Journal of Political Economy*, 1973, 1049-1091; EHRLICH, Isaac, 'The Deterrent Effect of Capital Punishment: A Question o Life and Death', **65** *American Economic Review*, 1975, 397-417; CURRAN, Christopher and DWYER, Gerald, 'The Effect of the Double Nickel Speed Limit on Death Rates', in FAURE, Michael and VAN DEN BERGH, Roger (eds.), *Essays in Law and Economics. Corporations, Accident Prevention and Compensation for Losses*, Antwerpen, Maklu, 1989, 117-156; LANDES, Elisabeth M., 'Insurance, Liability, and Accidents: A Theoretical and Empirical Investigation of the Effect of No-Fault Accidents', **2 5** *Journal of Law and Economics*, 1982, 49-65.

13 This is the central claim with respect to the common law, made in the writings of the so-called *Chicago School of Law and Economics*. See POSNER, Richard A., *Economic Analysis of Law*, Boston, Little Brown, 1973, 415 p. (1st ed.), 1977, 572 p. (2nd ed.), 1986, 666 p. (3rd ed.); COOTER, Robert D. and ULEN, Thomas S., *Law and Economics*, Glenview, Scott, Foresman, 1988, 644 p.

14 Very clearly on this point: POSNER, R. -A., cited note 13, at p. 25: “There is more to notions of justice than a concern with efficiency”.

liability[15] or predictions about investments in safety and their relative costs as a result of a change in product liability law[16] are studies which will also be appreciated by traditional lawyers.

The claim to be value free can no longer be upheld when the law is examined from the viewpoint of efficiency. This is certainly true for normative economic analyses which emphasise efficiency as a goal to be reached, but - to a certain extent - also for analyses which explain the law as efficient. A scholar who explains that the existing legal rule is more efficient than the alternative legal rules, which were not approved during the parliamentary debate, comes very close to a value judgement. But in policy making no one can escape from value judgements, and efficiency is, it can well be argued, a desirable property of the law. The problems in the dialogue with traditional European lawyers result from two misunderstandings. The first misunderstanding is that economists are supposed not to bother at all about justice; the second misunderstanding is that lawyers often feel that economists make an absolute value of efficiency.

7. As far as the first misunderstanding is concerned, it should be stressed that different notions of justice or fairness can be found in the literature. In the utilitarian tradition there is the notion of Pareto-efficiency[17]. In order to allow cost-benefit analyses the notion of Pareto-efficiency is replaced by the concept of Kaldor-Hicks-efficiency[18]. There is, of course, also the seminal work of Rawls[19]; many scholars devote attention to the Rawlsian concept of fairness

---

15 See, on the economic analysis of accident law, especially: SHAVELL, Steven, *Economic Analysis of Accident Law*, Cambridge, Harvard University Press, 1987, 312 p.

16 E.g. FINSINGER, Jörg and SIMON, Jürgen, 'An Economic Assessment of the EC Product Liability Directive and the Product Liability Law of the Federal Republic of Germany', in FAURE, Michael and VAN DEN BERGH, Roger (eds.), *Essays in Law and Economics. Corporations, Accident Prevention and Compensation for Losses*, Antwerpen, Maklu, 1989, 185-214.

17 See for further comments: MISHAN, J., *Welfare Economics, New York Random House*, 1964, 11-86; NATH, *A Perspective of Welfare Economics*, London, Mc Millan, 1973.

18 POSNER, R.-A., cited, note 13, p. 12-13.

19 RAWLS, John, *A Theory of Justice*, Cambridge, The Belknop Press of Harvard University Press, 1971.

and its relevance to legal concepts[20].

The latter notions are debated, Pareto-efficiency because it would not be a useful guide for policy making and Kaldor-Hicks-efficiency because many might lose if it were to be used by legal decision makers. At first glance the notion of Pareto-improvement is an attractive guide for policy making. Changes in the law are Pareto-improvements if they make nobody worse off and at least one person better off. It contains only very weak value judgements. People are supposed to prefer more to less, and they may get what they want under the condition that no one else is made worse off. Only paternalists, claiming that individuals are not the best judges of their own interests will disagree when changes in the law would be inspired by Pareto-improvements. In contrast with Pareto-efficiency the concept of Kaldor-Hicks-efficiency is not neutral with respect to distributive ideals. A change in the law is said to be efficient when the winners are able to compensate the losers, even when there is no actual compensation.

Despite these criticisms, these notions should not be discarded too quickly. An example may illustrate their usefulness in policy making. Lawyers usually explain consumer law as an instrument to correct the unequal bargaining power of producers and consumers, so that the bargains struck would become more "fair"[21]. Unequal bargaining power is an empty notion as long as the causes of the alleged inequality are not explained. Economic analysis can fill this gap. The market may fail due to asymmetric information; legal rules which remedy this market failure may be Pareto-improvements. If all consumers are willing to pay a higher price for safer products but are unable to recognise the safer products, a rule of strict liability increasing the safety of the products offered on the market will be a Pareto-improvement. Consumers are better off because they prefer the mix high quality /high price to the mix low quality/ low price. Producers are not worse off: although they will be strictly liable they can pass on the costs of their increased liability to the consumers by charging higher market prices. If only a minority of the consumers prefer lower prices (and less safety) the losses for society by introducing strict liability will be minimal and hence Kaldor-Hicks efficient. In both cases a normative economic analysis seems superior to the use of vague notions about "unequal bargaining power", that do not clarify the causes of the unequality and postulate solutions which are

---

20 BARRY, B., "Reflections on Justice as Fairness", in: BEDAV, H., ed., *Justice and Equality,* Englewood Cliffs, Prentice Hall, 1971; FRANK, R., *Choosing the Right Pond: Human Behavior and the Quest for Status,* New York, Oxford University Press, 1985; FRANK, R., *Passions within Reason: The Strategic Role of the Emotions*, New York, W.W. Norton, 1988.

21 REICH, N., *Markt und Recht,* Neuwied, 1977; VON HIPPEL, E., *Verbrauchersschutz,* Tübingen, Mohr, 1986; BOURGOIGNIE, T., *Eléments pour une theorie du droit de la consommation*, Brussel, Story, 1988.

ineffective. Ineffectiveness occurs whenever the attempts at the correction of "unequal bargaining power" result in higher market prices which pass on the costs of the increased protection to the consumers.

8. The second misunderstanding, that Law and Economics scholars only care about efficiency and neglect justice considerations in their final decisions, can also be very easily put aside. The distributional consequences of various legal rules are examined in the literature and the trade-offs between efficiency and justice are therefore illuminated. This contrasts with the view of lawyers who advocate fairness on the basis of vague concepts. These vague notions about fairness are often a cover for arbitrary solutions. Despite its shortcomings, a value judgement based upon a trade-off between efficiency and justice is certainly to be preferred to arbitrariness. A related point is that Law and Economics research may show that goals inspired by justice considerations are in fact not achieved and that in this respect the legal rules may even have adverse effects[22]. An example is appropriate. Strict liability is often defended by lawyers as a means to provide "just" compensation to victims. This tendency puts great pressure on insurance markets and may even cause an insurance crisis. The victims of such a crisis will be the poorest members of society. This is a redistribution in the wrong direction[23]. To conclude: economic analysis offers a major, although not conclusive, contribution to policy making.

B. Major challenges for Law and Economics in Europe

9. The first major challenge for the European Law and Economics movement is to assert its own European identity. Sometimes the opinion is advanced that European Law and Economics is nothing more than a copy of the dominant American literature. It is obvious that European Law and Economics researchers should devote their time to European legal rules and problems, and not to the American substantive law and procedure. A translation and a summary of the leading American articles and books into a continental European language is not yet "European" Law and Economics research[24].

---

22 See e.g. FAURE, Michael and VAN DEN BERGH, Roger, 'Liability for Nuclear Accidents in Belgium from an Interest Group Perspective', **10** *International Review of Law and Economics*, 1990, 241-254.

23 PRIEST, George L., 'The Current Insurance Crisis and Modern Tort Law', **96** *The Yale Law Journal*, 1987, 1521-1590.

24 On the other hand it should be acknowledged that these translations have had a significant impact on the reception of Law and Economics in Europe. See: ASSMANN, Heinz-Dieter, KIRCHNER, Christian and SCHANZE, Erich (eds.), *Ökonomische Analyse des Rechts* [Economic Analysis of Law], Kronberg, Athenäum,

Nevertheless the relevance of American research should not be underestimated. This relevance is even greater than is regularly thought. First, the basic economic models of the American literature also apply to the European legal system. For instance, both societies are confronted with the problem of minimising accident costs. European scholars active in the field of economic analysis of tort law do not have to reinvent the wheel, although they can of course refine the existing models[25] and adapt them to the European legal environment. Second, common law doctrines and civil law concepts resemble one another more than is usually acknowledged. Comparative legal research shows a discernible convergence between the common law and the civil law[26]. Although the procedure is markedly different, the substantive rules of the two traditions exhibit an increasing similarity. This implies that the American economic analysis has a direct application to many fields of the civil law, such as tort law and contract law.

Although it is certainly valuable to use the American models as a starting point in developing an economic analysis of European legal problems, one should be cautious for two reasons. First, European law may be less coherent than American law. Cultural differences do also exist across European countries and may cause differences in the way legal problems are addressed. Second, due to the predominance of legislation the positive economic analysis of law should profit from theories which focus on decision making by the legislator. This second point merits further attention.

10. Among lawyers there is a growing dissatisfaction with the effects of statute law. This dissatisfaction creates a demand for changes in the law. Economic analysis provides important insights into both the effects of legal rule-making and the origin and evolution of legal rules. Not only the question, of whether statutes reach their publicly pronounced goals may be investigated, but the side effects, which were not meant or are not yet recognized, may be disclosed as well. Whereas lawyers were for a long time indifferent and even ignorant about the effects of statute law, economists are pre-eminently trained

---

1978, 369 p; PARDOLESI, Roberto, *Una introduzione all' analisi economica del diritto con postfazione (Translation of A. Mitchell Polinsky's book)*, Bologna, Zanichelli, 1986, 149 p.

25 See e.g. ADAMS, Michael, 'New Activities and the Efficient Liability Rules', in FAURE, Michael and VAN DEN BERGH, Roger (eds.), *Essays in Law and Economics. Corporations, Accident Prevention and Compensation for Losses*, Antwerpen, Maklu, 1989, 103-106.

26 See e.g. *International Encyclopedia of Comparative Law, XI, Torts*, Tübingen, Mohr, 1982.

in the analysis of these processes. The deregulation debate has created a growing interest among lawyers in the effects and side effects of statute law. It has also made clear that much research remains to be done. Law and Economics has much to offer in this area and cross-fertilisation of related research strategies will increase the relevance of the analysis. The insights offered by Law and Economics should be enriched by lessons from the Public Choice approach. The inefficiencies created by regulations may indeed be explained as succesful attempts at "rent seeking"[27].

This approach to legal issues, which borrows tools from different types of analysis, distinguishes many European Law and Economics papers from orthodox American Law and Economics research, which is built upon a limited set of paradigms: utility, maximization and equilibrium. The combination of different approaches (orthodox Law and Economics, transaction cost analysis and Public Choice) gives European Law and Economics a less conservative and a more progressive character[28].

11. In asserting its own identity the European Law and Economics movement should take full advantage of the long standing European tradition in the field of comparative law. Comparative legal analysis is often the only available - and at the same time the least used - way of empirically testing the positive theories developed by American Law and Economics scholars. If the famous Chicago hypothesis, that the common law evolves towards efficiency, is correct, European scholars will have to find similar rules in European countries with a similar degree of industrial development. Comparative law is not only a major instrument to test the positive theories empirically; it is also a major method of finding answers to the fundamental questions raised in the normative branch of Law and Economics. Comparing different legal solutions in several European countries will provide important insights into the features of the most efficient solution. Comparative legal analysis may also show that a first-best solution is not available due to technical legal problems, so that only second-best solutions can be reached.

Once more examples are appropriate to clarify this crucial point. Legal

---

27 For a general introduction to the theory of rent seeking, see TOLLISON, Robert D., 'Rent-Seeking: a Survey', **35** *Kyklos*, 1982, 575-602. For an application see FAURE, M. and VAN DEN BERGH, R., cited, note 22.

28 Compare ROSE-ACKERMAN, Susan, 'Law and Economics: Paradigm, Politics, or Philosophy', in MERCURO, Nicholas (ed.), *Law and Economics*, Boston, Kluwer Academic Publishers, 1989, 233-258 and in German translation in OTT, Claus and SCHÄFER, Hans-Bernd (eds.), *Allokationseffizienz in der Rechtsordnung. Beiträge zum Travemünder Symposium zur ökonomischen Analyse des Zivilrechts 23.-26. März 1988* [Allocative Efficiency in Legal Order. Contributions to the Travemünder Symposium on Economic Analysis of Civil Law], Berlin, Springer, 1989, 269-292.

doctrine deals in very different ways with the loss of entitlements if a person by his words or conduct wilfully causes another to believe the existence of a certain state of affairs. Under the common law, estoppel by representation is the legal remedy; in civil law countries, the roman law-based concept *venire contra factum proprium* may be used [29]. These verbal distinctions in the law are often underestimated by economists. Although both remedies deal with the same problem and reach a similar solution, the verbal distinctions usually point at important practical problems which are not always fully taken into account in the economic models. Economic analysis of law has not yet fully explored the consequences of the differences in legal categories dealing with the same problem. Comparative legal research will reveal these differences across countries and raise the interesting question, of which of the legal remedies, either the common law or the civil law oriented solution, is preferable from an efficiency viewpoint.

The legal remedies for the classic problem of externalities may differ considerably. Limited liability for corporations offers a good example. It is generally acknowledged that the rule of limited liability provides excessive incentives for cost externalization[30]. To internalise these externalities, the liability of founders of corporations, the liability of directors, the piercing of the corporate veil, dismissal of bankruptcy proceedings and compulsory insurance may be used separately or in combination[31].

These examples show that it is most appealing to examine the different remedies, to compare their legal characteristics and their ability to cure the externality problem. To accomplish this job the use of sophisticated economic models and a thorough comparative legal analysis will be necessary. In a complex world there is a need for researchers who make the existing analysis more complicated.

---

29 See HOUWING, Ph. A.N., *Rechtsverwerking*, s.l., 1968.

30 HALPERN, Paul J., TREBILCOCK, Michael J. and TURNBULL, Stuart M., 'An Economic Analysis of Limited Liability in Corporation Law', **30** *University of Toronto Law Journal*, 1980, 117-150; EASTERBROOK, Frank H. and FISCHEL, Daniel R., 'Limited Liability and the Corporation', **52** *University of Chicago Law Review*, 1985, 89-117.

31 See ADAMS, Michael, 'Ownership, Control and Limited Liability' and HANSMANN, Henry and KRAAKMAN, Reinier, 'The Uneasy Case for Limiting Shareholder Liability for Corporate Torts', Papers presented at the Lugano Symposium on Law and Economics, organised by the Centre d'Etudes Juridiques Européennes and EALE, *International Review of Law and Economics*, 1991, forthcoming.

These "complexifiers"[32] will have a busy working agenda. In the literature few articles fully use the powerful tools of comparative legal research. The relevance of detailed comparative legal analyses is sometimes underestimated by economists, because the link with the - often too simple - economic model is not obvious. These analyses may, however, point to important differences in legal traditions which are not contemplated by the assumptions of the economic models and therefore undermine the attractiveness of the economic approach to lawyers. To overcome the criticism of overly simplistic economic models, Law and Economics scholars should give the best of themselves by complexifying these models and attuning them to the wide variety of legal categories revealed by comparative legal research.

12. The next major challenge of the European Law and Economics movement is the application of the new theories to problems of European integration, especially the evolution toward the European internal market without national borders to be achieved before the end of 1992. European Law and Economics scholars should fully realize that the insights following from the combined use of Law and Economics and theories of rent-seeking are especially significant for the European integration process, as it is embodied in the 1992 programme. The abolition of the physical, technical and fiscal obstacles to the free internal market requires a substantial deregulation programme. The EEC has thus created the legal environment for a peaceful revolution in legislation. An internal market calls for legal rules which are sensitive to efficiency considerations. Herein lies an important task for Law and Economics scholars. They should evaluate the existing national rules and the proposed European rules from an efficiency viewpoint. Because inefficiencies and detrimental side effects were the reason for the deregulation programme itself, this research will facilitate the work of the European legislator. It has been firmly established in the community law that national regulations limiting the free flow of goods and services within the EC member states can only survive if they serve the "public interest"[33]. Law and Economics researchers should investigate whether the rules which are said to be in the public interest really will improve the quality of the products and services offered on the market.

The instrumental use of Law and Economics is noteworthy. Precisely this instrumental use has been criticised by opponents of the economic approach because it would make an absolute value of efficiency. However, in the EC-context this criticism is weak because the EEC-Treaty itself regards legal rules as instruments to achieve economic ends. A large body of legal rules is

32 The terminology is from PARDOLESI, Roberto, 'Un moderno minotauro: law and economics' [A Modern Minotaur: Law and Economics], *Economia, società e istituzioni*, 1989, 519 ff.

33 See e.g. LASOK, D., *The Professions and Services in the European Economic Community*, Deventer, Kluwer, 1986, with further references.

established to further the economic development of the community, as specified in articles 2 and 3 of the EEC-Treaty. Therefore, thanks to the instrumental use of the law and the aim of abolishing inefficient regulations, the EEC-deregulation programme is a major entry point for Law and Economics research. Studying the European integration process is extremely important for bringing Law and Economics into contact with the law of the European Community and speeding its acceptance in the European courts. Many EEC Regulations and Directives have an obvious link with economic analysis. They concern not only economic law, but cover the entire research field of the new economic analysis of law, ranging from contract to liability and crime. In this field, the EALE has an enormous research potential which has not yet been fully tapped.

13. If European scholars profit from the increased interest among lawyers in the effects of the law, the opportunities for Law and Economics research in the European community will be farreaching. Analysis of the consequences of legal rules is important not only for legislation but for the entire process of legal decision making. Also the consequences of developments in the courts should be analysed and Law and Economics scholars should particularly draw the lawyers' attention to the cost implications of certain developments in the courts. This can best be illustrated by means of an example.

European courts are often biased against the wealthier party in litigation. In the field of liability law there is a tendency to hold that party liable who has purchased insurance coverage[34].

The welfare losses of this approach are significant. It reduces the incentives of both injurers and victims to take efficient care. It also makes the calculation of premiums hazardous: the risk no longer depends on the behaviour of the insured but on the fact that the injurer has covered his liability with an insurance company. A related problem is the advocated solidarity between good and bad risks. This concept, moreover, is inspired by distributional considerations. The principle of solidarity again neutralizes the incentive function of tort law and creates impediments to reducing costs by pooling appropriately defined risks. Law and Economics scholars can empirically establish these costs. These studies of alternative legal rules will make both the legislator and the judges aware of the cost implications of their actions.

14. There is little doubt that the fall of communism in Eastern Europe is the

---

34 VAN DEN BERGH, Roger and FAURE, Michael G., 'De invloed van verzekering op de civiele aansprakelijkheid, een rechtseconomische analyse' [The Influence of Insurance on Tort Liability, an Economic Analysis], in *Preadviezen uitgebracht voor de Vereniging voor Burgerlijk Recht*, Lelystad, Vermande, 1990, 9-53. Compare with respect to the common law: TREBILCOCK, Michael J., 'The Role of Insurance Considerations in the Choice of Efficient Civil Liability Rules', 4 *Journal of Law, Economics, & Organization*, 1988, 243-265.

most significant event of 1989. The transition from a communist to a capitalist system also represents the final significant challenge for Law and Economics in Europe. In the former communist countries there is an urgent need for knowledge of the institutions of the market economy and of modern parliamentary democracy. Law and Economics scholars are pre-eminently capable of explaining the way in which legal institutions guarantee or impede the functioning of the market economy. Traditional economists start their analysis with the assumption of an existing, well-functioning market, taking the necessary legal institutions of the market as given. The shortcoming of this approach, of course, is that the former communist countries lack these underlying institutions of the free market economy. Traditional lawyers are able to teach the existing legal rules in different Western countries, but do not have the competence to teach the economics of the legal rules. Here the problem lies in the purely normative approach, which is unable to explain why legal rules are necessary to guarantee the functioning of a free market economy. For these reasons, Law and Economics scholars are the right teachers to meet the Eastern European demand for education in market economics. The economics of the constitution, the role of property rights, the necessity of contract law, tort law and competition law are among the principal topics of interest for Eastern Europe. Although, in the first coming years the European Law and Economics movement will have to devote considerable energy in teaching, the fall of communism in Eastern Europe also offers new research opportunities, of which the economics of transition is the most challenging one.

PART I:

SUBJECT-RELATED SURVEYS

0000 LAW & ECONOMICS: GENERAL WORKS
Roger Van den Bergh

0000 Introductory Books

BEHRENS, Peter, *Die ökonomischen Grundlagen des Rechts* [The Economic Foundations of Law], Tübingen, Mohr, 1986, 386 p.

BOUCKAERT, Boudewijn, *Recht op Zoek naar Economie? Prolegomena tot een Economische Analyse van het Recht* [Law in Search for Economics? Introduction to Economic Analysis of Law], Gent, Story-Scientia, 1984, 49 p.

BOWLES, Roger A., *Law and the Economy*, Oxford, Martin Robertson, 1982, 239p.

COOTER, Robert D. and ULEN, Thomas S., *Law and Economics*, Glenview, Scott, Foresman, 1988, 644 p.

HIRSCH, Werner Z., *Law and Economics: An Introductory Analysis*, San Diego, Academic Press, 1979 (1st ed), 1988 (2nd ed), 275 p. (1st ed.), 434 p. (2nd ed).

HOLZHAUER, Rudi W., TEIJL, Rob et al., *Inleiding Rechtseconomie* [Introduction to Law-and-Economics], Gouda Quint, Arnhem, 1989, 345 p.

LEMENNICIER, Bertrand, *Economie du Droit* [Economics of Law], Paris, Ed. Cujas, 1991, 177 p.

MACKAAY, Ejan J.P., *Economics of Information and Law*, Dordrecht, Kluwer Nijhoff, 1982, 293 p.

MALLOY, Robin Paul, *Law and Economics. A Comparative Approach to Theory and Practice*, St. Paul, West, 1990, 166 p.

MARKOVITS, Richard S., *Law and Economic Theory*, Oxford, Centre for Socio-Legal Studies, 1982.

MERCURO, Nicolas and RYAN, Tim, *Law, Economics, and Public Policy*, New York, JAI Press, 1984.

MURPHY, Jeffrie G. and COLEMAN, Jules L., *The Philosophy of Law: An Introduction to Jurisprudence*, Totowa NJ, Rowman-Allenheld, 1984, 211-278 (ch.5).

OLIVER, J.M., *Law and Economics*, London, George Allen & Unwin, 1979, 108 p.

PARDOLESI, Roberto, *Una introduzione all' analisi economica del diritto con postfazione (Translation of A. Mitchell Polinsky' s "Introduction")*, Bologna, Zanichelli, 1986, 149 p.

POLINSKY A. Mitchell, *An Introduction to Law and Economics*, Boston, Little Brown, 1983, 183 p. (1st ed.), 1989 (2nd ed.).

POSNER, Richard A., *Economic Analysis of Law*, Boston, Little Brown, 1973, 415 p. (1st ed.), 1977, 572 p. (2nd ed.), 1986 666 p. (3rd ed.).

SCHÄFER, Hans-Bernd and OTT, Claus, *Lehrbuch der ökonomischen Analyse des Zivilrechts* [Handbook of Economic Analysis of Civil Law], Berlin, Springer, 1986, 367 p.

STEPHEN, Frank H., *The Economics of the Law*, Ames, Iowa State University

Press, 1988, 224 p.

TORRES, Juan, *Análisis económico del derecho. Panorama doctrinal* [Economic Analysis of Law: An Overview], Madrid, Tecnos, 1987.

TULLOCK, Gordon, *The Logic of the Law*, New York, Basic Books, 1971, 278 p.

VELJANOVSKI, Cento G., *The New Law-and-Economics. A Research Review*, Oxford, Centre for Socio-Legal Studies, 1982, 169 p.

VELJANOVSKI, Cento G., *The Economics of Law - An Introductory Text*, London, Institute of Economic Affairs, Hobart Paperback, 1990, 95 p.

WERIN, Lars, Ekonomi och rättssystem [Economy and Legal System], Malmö, Liber, 1982 (2nd ed.).

0010 Introductory Articles

ADAMS, Michael, 'Der Irrtum über "künftige Sachverhalte": Anwendungsbeispiel und Einführung in die ökonomische Analyse des Rechts' [The Mistake on Future States: Example and Introduction into the Economic Analysis of Law], 4 *Recht*, 1986, 14-23.

ALBERT, Hans, 'Law as an Instrument of Rational Choice', in DAINTITH, Terence and TEUBNER, Gunther (eds.), *Contract and Organization*, Berlin, Walter de Gruyter, 1986, 25-51.

ALPA, Guido, 'Interpretazione economica del diritto' [Economic Interpretation of Law], *voce del Novissimo digesto italiano*, Appendice IV, Torino, UTET, 1983, 315-324.

ALPA, Guido, 'Diritto e analisi economica (a proposito di un recente libro di R. Bowles)' [Law and Economic Analysis, With Regard to a Recent Book by R. Bowles], *Diritto dell'impresa*, 1984, 111-120.

APRILE, Ercole, 'Regolamentazione dei fenomeni economici e analisi economica degli strumenti giuridici: spunti per una riflessione' [Regulation of Economic Phenomena and Economic Analysis of Legal Instruments: Hints for a Reflection], *Nuovo diritto*, 1989, 505-521.

ASSMANN, Heinz-Dieter, 'Kommentar' [Comment] (on Ott, Allokationseffizienz, Rechtsdogmatik und Rechtsprechung), in OTT, Claus and SCHÄFER, Hans-Bernd (eds.), *Allokationseffizienz in der Rechtsordnung*, Berlin, Springer, 1989, 45-49.

BARBERA, Salvador, 'Los derechos individuales en el análisis económico' [Individual Rights and Economic Analysis], **38** *Economistas*, 1989.

BEHRENS, Peter, 'Aspekte einer ökonomischen Theorie des Rechts' [Aspects of an Economic Theory of Law], **12** *Rechtstheorie*, 1981, 472-490.

BEHRENS, Peter, 'Über das Verhältnis der Rechtswissenschaft zur Nationalökonomie: Die ökonomischen Grundlagen des Rechts' [On the Interrelationship between Law and Economics: The Economic Foundations of Law], in BOETTCHER, Erik, HERDER-DORNEICH, Philipp and SCHENK, Karl-Ernst (eds.), **7** *Jahrbuch für neue politische Ökonomie*, Tübingen, J.C.B. Mohr, 1988, 209-228.

BIENAYME, A., 'Défense et illustration d'une réflexion juridique intégrant l'économie' [Defense and Illustration of a Legal Reflexion Integrating Economics], **64(6)** *La Semaine Juridique*, 33-35.

BONGAERTS, Jan C., 'Inleiding tot de economische analyse van het recht met toepassing op het contractenrecht en het aansprakelijkheidsrecht, inzonderheid de milieuramp te Bhopal' [Introduction to Economic Analysis of Law, with Applications to Contract and Tort Law, and in Particular to the Environmental Disaster in Bhopal], in VAN DEN BERGH, Roger (ed.), *Verslagboek Eerste Werkvergadering recht en Economie*, Antwerpen, Handelshogeschool, 1986, 5-20.

BOUCKAERT, Boudewijn, 'Efficiëntie of rechtvaardigheid: het onvermijdelijk dilemma?' [Efficiency or Justice: the Unavoidable Dilemma?], **29** *Tijdschrift voor Sociale Wetenschappen*, 1984, 101-133.

BOUCKAERT, Boudewijn, 'L'analyse économique du droit: vers un renouveau de la science juridique?' [Economic Analysis of Law: Towards a Renewal of Legal Science?], **18** *Revue interdisciplinaire d'études juridiques*', 1987-88, 47-61.

BRUNT, Maureen, 'The Economics of Law: Economic Imperialism in Negligence Law, No Fault Insurance, Occupational Licensing and Criminology: Comment', **67** *Australian Economic Review*, 1984, 113-119.

BULCHA, Mekuria, KIBREAB, Gaim and NOBEL, Peter, 'Sociology, Economy and Law: Views in Common', in NOBEL, Peter (ed.), *Refugees and Development in Africa*, Stockholm, Almqvist and Wiksell International, 1987, 93-103.

CABRILLO, Francisco, '¿Por qué un análisis económico del derecho?' [Why an Economic Analysis of Law?], *Revista de Occidente*, 1987, 58.

CABRILLO, Francisco, 'Una nueva frontera: el análisis económico del Derecho' [A New Border: The Economic Analysis of Law], *Información Comercial Española*, 1990, n. 687, 9-22.

CAMPBELL, C. and WILES, P., 'The Study of Law in Society', **10** *Law and Society Review*, 1976, 547-578.

CHEROT, Jean-Yves, 'Trois thèses sur l'analyse économique du droit - Quelques usages de l'approche économique des règles juridiques' [Three Theses on Economic Analysis of Law - Some Uses of the Economic Approach to Legal Rules], *Revue de la Recherche Juridique*, 1987, nr.2, réédité *Problèmes économiques*, La Documentation française, 10 février 1988, nr. 2061.

COOTER, Robert D., 'Law and the Imperialism of Economics: An Introduction to the Economic Analysis of Law and a Review of the Major Books', **29** *UCLA Law Review*, 1982, 1260-1269.

COSENTINO, Fabrizio, 'Analisi economica del diritto: ritorno al futuro?' [Economic Analysis of Law: Back to the Future?], *Foro it.*, 1990, V, 153-156.

DE GEEST, Gerrit, 'Public Choice en rechtseconomie' [Public Choice and Law & Economics], **39** *Ars Aequi*, 1990, 666-673.

EGER, Thomas, 'Einführung in die Ökonomische Analyse des Rechts' [Introduction to the Economic Analysis of Law], in NAGEL, B. (ed.), *Wirtschaftsrecht II*, München, Oldenborg, 1989, 18-35 (Eigentumsrecht), 51-62 (Deliktrecht), 150-158 (Vertragsrecht)

FIELD, A.J., 'Do Legal Systems Matter?', **28(1)** *Explorations in Economic History*,

1991, 1-35.

FLUET, C., 'L'analyse économique du droit' [Economic Analysis of Law], **43(3)** *Economie Appliquée*, 1990, 53-66.

GUEST, Stephen F.D., 'The Economics of Law', *Current Legal Problems*, 1984, 233-245.

HEYNE, Paul, 'The Economics of Law: Economic Imperialism in Negligence Law, No Fault Insurance, Occupational Licensing and Criminology: Comment', **67** *Australian Economic Review*, 1984, 109-112.

HONDIUS, E.H., SCHIPPERS, J.J. and SIEGERS, J.J. (eds.), 'Rechtseconomie: Brug tussen twee disciplines' [Law-and-Economics: Bridge between two Disciplines], in *Rechtseconomie en Recht*, Tjeenk Willink, Zwolle, 1991, 1-7.

HOTZ, Beat, 'Ökonomische Analyse des Rechts - eine skeptische Betrachtung' [Economic Analysis of Law - A Sceptical Reflection], **34** *Wirtschaft und Recht*, 1982, 293-314.

KIRBY M.D., 'Economics and Law: Symbiosis', **23** *Reform*, 1981, 86-90.

KLEINEWEFERS, Henner, 'Ökonomische Theorie des Rechts, Über Unterschiede zwischen dem ökonomischen und dem juristischen Denken' [Economic Theory of Law, On the Differences between Economic and Legal Thinking], in *Staat und Gesellschaft, Festschrift für Leo Schürmann zum 70. Geburtstag*, Fribourg, Universitätsverlag, 1987, 83-116.

KORNHAUSER, Lewis A., L'analyse économique du droit' [The Economic Analysis of Law], *Revue de Synthese*, 1985, Nr.118-119, 313 ff.

LLEWELLYN, Karl N., 'The Effect of Legal Institutions Upon Economics', **15** *American Economic Review*, 1925, 665-683.

MACKAAY, Ejan, 'La règle juridique observée par le prisme de l'économiste. Une histoire stylisée du mouvement de l'analyse économique du droit' [The Legal Rule Seen Through and Economist's Eyes], *Revue internationale de droit économique*, 1986, 43-88.

MACKAAY, Ejan J.P., 'Het recht bezien door de bril van de economist - Een gestyleerd overzicht van de rechtseconomie' [Law Seen Through Economist's Glasses: An Overview of Law-and-economics], *Rechtsgeleerd Magazijn Themis*, 1988, 411-452.

MACKAAY, Ejan J.P., 'L'ordre spontané comme fondement du droit - un survol des modèles de l'émergence des règles dans une société civile' [Spontaneous Order as Foundation of Law - A Survey of Models of the Emergence of Rules in a Civil Society], **22** *Revue Juridique Themis*, 1988, 347-383.

MACKAAY, Ejan J.P., 'Verschuivingen in de rechtseconomie' [Shifts in Law-and-Economics], **66** *Nederlands Juristenblad*, 1991, 1505-1521. (Subject Code: 0010, 0500)

MENGARONI, F., 'Analisi economica del diritto' [Economic Analysis of Law], *Enciclopedia giuridica*, Roma, Treccani, 1988, vol. I, 1-9.

MERCURO, Nicholas, 'Contributions to Law and Economics: A Survey of Recent Books', **17** *Journal of Economic Education*, 1986, 295-306.

NENTJES, Andries, *De economie van het recht* [The Economy of the Law], oratie Groningen, s.l., 1987, 18 p.

OGUS, Anthony I., 'Economics, Liberty and the Common Law', **18** *Journal of Society of Public Teachers of Law*, 1980, 42-57.

OTT, Claus, 'Allokationseffizienz, Rechtsdogmatik und Rechtsprechung - die immanente ökonomische Rationalität des Zivilrechts' [Allocative Efficiency, Legal Dogmatics and Jurisprudence - The Implicit Economic Rationality of Civil Law], in OTT, Claus and SCHÄFER, Hans-Bernd (eds.), *Allokationseffizienz in der Rechtsordnung*, Berlin, Springer, 1989, 25-44.

OTT, Claus and SCHÄFER, Hans-Bernd, 'Die ökonomische Analyse des Rechts. Irrweg oder Chance wissenschaftlicher Rechtserkenntnis?' [The Economic Analysis of Law. Wrong Track or Chance for a Scientific Legal Knowledge?], *Juristenzeitung*, 1988, 213-223.

PARDOLESI, Roberto, 'Luci ed ombre nell'analisi economica del diritto (appunti in margine ad un libro recente)' [Lights and Shadows in Law and Economics - Notes about a Recent Book], *Rivista di diritto civile*, 1982, II, 718-728.

PARDOLESI, Roberto, 'Analisi economica del diritto' [Economic Analysis of Law], *Digesto civile*, vol. I, Torino, UTET, 1987, 309-320.

PARDOLESI, Roberto, 'Tutela specifica e tutela per equivalente nella prospettiva dell'analisi economica del diritto' [Specific Performance and Damages: An EAL Perspective], *Quadrimestre*, 1988, 76-97.

PARDOLESI, Roberto, 'Un moderno Minotauro: Law and Economics' [A Modern Minotaur: Law and Economics], *Economia, Società e Instituzioni*, 1989, 519-534.

PASQUINI, Nello, 'Interpretazione giuridica e analisi economica - In margine ad un "reading" recente' [Legal Interpretation and Economic Analysis with Regard to a Recent "Reading"], *Rivista trimestrale di diritto e procedura civile*, 1983, 288-300.

PASTOR, Santos, *Economía y Sistema Jurídico. Una Introducción al Anàlisis Económico del Derecho* [Economics and the Legal System. An Introduction to Economic Analysis of Law], Madrid, Tecnos, 1989.

PAZ-ARES, Cándido, 'La Economía Política como Jurisprudencia racional. Aproximación a la Teoría Económica del Derecho' [The Political Economy as Rational Jurisprudence. An Introduction to Law and Economics], *Anuario de Derecho Civil*, 1981, julio/septiembre.

PAZ-ARES, Cándido, 'Seguridad jurídica y seguridad del tráfico' [Legal Certainty and Exhange Certainty], *Revista de Derecho Mercantil*, 1985.

POLINSKY, A. Mitchell, 'Economic Analysis as a Potentially Defective Product: A Buyer's Guide to Posner's Economic Analysis of Law', **87** *Harvard Law Review*, 1974, 1655-1681.

POSNER, Richard A., 'The Economic Approach to Law', **53** *Texas Law Review*, 1975, 757-782.

POSNER, Richard A., 'Some Uses and Abuses of Economics in Law', **46** *University of Chicago Law Review*, 1979, 281-306.

POSNER, Richard A., 'The Law and Economics Movement', **77** *American Economic review (Papers and Proceedings)*, 1987, 1-13.

PRISCHING, Manfred, 'Ökonomische Rechtslehre? Über die Prämissen und Grenzen des "Economic Approach" im Recht' [Economic Jurisprudenz? On the Premisses and Limits of the Economic Approach to Law], in FREISITZER, Kurt, HOLZER, Hans Ludwig, MANTL, Wolfgang and HÖFLECHNER, Walter (eds.), *Reformen des Rechts. Festschrift zur 200-Jahr-Feier der Rechtswissenschaftlichen Fakultät der Universität Graz*, Graz, Akademische Druck u.Verlagsanstalt, 1979, 995-1020.

PULITINI, Francesco, 'Regole giuridiche e teoria economica' [Law and Economic Theory], *Politica del diritto*, 1967, 297-310.

RAHMSDORF, Detlev W. and SCHÄFER, Hans-Bernd, 'Ökonomische Analyse des Rechts - Ein Gegentrend? [Economic Analysis of Law - A Controversy?]', in VOIGT, R. (ed.), *Verrechtlichung*, Köningstein/Ts., Athenäum, 1980, 94-108.

RAITERI, Monica, 'Giustizia distributiva e funzione giudiziaria: qualche osservazione nella prospettiva della analisi economica del diritto' [Distributive Justice and the Judicial Function, Some Observations in an EAL Perspective], *Materiali storia cultura giur.*, 1988, 209-228.

RODANO, Giorgio, 'Il giudice e l' efficienza del mercato. Riflessioni di un economista su un libro di diritto comparato' [The Judge and the Efficiency of the Market. An Economist's Thoughts about an Essay in Comparative Law], *Rivista critica del diritto privato*, 1989, 293-312.

ROWLEY, Charles K., 'Social Sciences and the Law: The Relevance of Economic Theories', **1** *Oxford Journal of Legal Studies*, 1981, 1, 391-405.

SAJó, András, 'Közgazdaságtani vizsgálódások a jogról' [Analysis of Law from an Economic Point of Vieuw], in SáRKÖZY, Tamás, *Gazdasági Jogi Tanulmányok II*, Budapest, Közgazdasági és Jogi Könyvkiadó, 1984, 5-42.

SAJó, András, 'A jog a gazdaság szabályozástechnikái közt' [Law as One of the Regulating Means of the Economy], **3** *Jogtudományi Közlöny*, 1987, 126-132.

SAJó, András, 'Allami változásipar és a jog stabilizáló ereje' [The State Changing Industry and the Stabilizing Effort of the Law], in HOPPAL, Mihály and SZECSKó, Tamás (eds.), *Értékek és változások I*, Budapest, Tömegkommunikációos Kutató Központ, 1987, 91-102.

SALJE, Peter, *Ökonomische Analyse des Rechts aus deutscher Sicht* [Economic Analysis of Law from a German Point of View], **15 (3)** *Rechtstheorie*, 1984, 277-312.

SAMUELS, Warren J., 'Interrelations between Legal and Economic Processes', **14** *Journal of Law and Economics*, 1971, 435-450. Reprinted in SAMUELS, Warren J. and SCHMID, A. Allen (eds.), *Law and Economics: An Institutional Perspective*, Boston, Nijhoff, 1981, 95-110.

SAMUELS, Warren J., 'The Coase Theorem and the Study of Law and Economics', **14** *Natural Resources Journal*, 1974, 1-33.

SANTINI, G., *I servizi. Saggio di economia del diritto* [The Services. An Example of an Economic Approach to Law], Il Mulino, Bologna, 1987.

SCHANZE, Erich, 'Ökonomische Analyse des Rechts in den U.S.A. / Verbindungslinien zur realistischen Tradition' [Economic Analysis of Law in the U.S.A. - Origins and Relations to Legal Realism], in ASSMANN, Heinz-Dieter, KIRCHNER, Christian and SCHANZE, Erich (eds.), *Ökonomische Analyse des Rechts*, Kronberg, 1978, 3-19.

SCHANZE, Erich, 'Rechtsnorm und ökonomisches Kalkül' [Legal Norm and

Economic Calculus], **138** *Zeitschrift für die gesamte Staatswissenschaft*, 1982, 297-312.

SKOGH, Göran, 'Den osynliga handen och lagens långa arm' [The Invisible Hand and the Law's Long Arm], *Ekonomisk Debatt*, 1982, No. 8.

STOLZ, Peter, 'Das wiedererwachte Interesse der Ökonomie an rechtlichen und politischen Institutionen. [The Renewed Interest of Economics in Legal and Political Institutions. With English summary.]', **119** *Schweizerische Zeitschrift fur Volkswirtschaft und Statistik*, 1983, 49-67.

STRASSER, Kurt A., BARD, Robert L. and ARTHUR, H. Thomas, 'A Reader's Guide to the Uses and Limits of Economic Analysis with Emphasis on Corporation Law', **33** *Mercer Law Review*, 1982, 571-593.

STROWEL, Alain, 'Utilitarisme et approche économique dans la théorie du droit. Autour de Bentham et de Posner' [Utilitarianism and Economic Approach in Legal Theory. On Bentham and Posner], **18** *Revue Interdisciplinaire d'Etudes Juridiques*, 1987, 1-45.

SUPPER, Meinhard, ' Das niederösterreichische Landesrecht und die ökonomische Analyse des Rechts' [The Law of the Province of Lower Austria and the Economic Analysis of Law], in FUNK, Bernd-Christian (project management), *Deregulierung und Entbürokratisierung am Beispiel von Niederösterreich*, Vienna, Austrian economic Publishing Comp., 1988, 43-48.

SWAN, Peter L., 'The Economics of Law: Economic Imperialism in Negligence Law, No Fault Insurance, Occupational Licensing and Criminology?', **(67)** *Australian Economic Review*, 1984, 92-108.

TORRES, Juan, 'Tradición y resultados de una disciplina novedosa: la Economía del Derecho. Una orientación bibliográfica' [Tradition and Outcome of a New Discipline: The Economics of Law. A Guide to the Literature], **5** *Revista de la Facultad de Derecho de la Universidad de Granada*, 1987.

TRIMARCHI, Pietro, 'L'analisi economica del diritto: tendenze e prospettive' [Economic Analysis of Law: Tendencies and Perspectives], *Quadrimestre*, 1987, 563-582.

VAN DEN BERGH, Roger, 'Le droit civil face à l'analyse économique du droit' [Civil Law Facing Economic Analysis of Law], *Revue internationale de droit économique*, 1988, 229-254.

VAN DEN BERGH, Roger, 'Wat is rechtseconomie?' [What is Law and Economics?], in HONDIUS, E.H., SCHIPPERS, J.J. and SIEGERS, J.J. (eds.), *Rechtseconomie en Recht,* Zwolle, Tjeenk Willink, 1991, 9-49.

VAN DEN BERGH, Roger and HEREMANS, Dirk, 'Recht en economie' [Law and Economics], **32** *Tijdschrift voor Economie en Management*, 1987, 139-164.

VAN DEN BERGH, Roger and HEREMANS, Dirk, 'Over krommen en rechten. Een reactie op de kritiek van Kruithof ten aanzien van de economische analyse van het recht' [On Curves and Lines: A Reaction on the Critique of Kruithof on Economic Analysis of Law], **50** *Rechtskundig Weekblad*, 1986-87, 1649-1668.

VELJANOVSKI, Cento G., 'The Economic Approach to Law - A Critical Introduction', **7** *British Journal of Law and Society*, 1980, 158-193.

VELJANOVSKI, Cento G., 'Cost-Benefit and Law Reform in Australia', **32** *New Law Journal*, 1982, 893-897.

VERLOREN VAN THEMAAT, Pieter, 'Economie, gezien door juristen' [Economics, Seen by Lawyers], *Koninklijke Nederlandse Akademie van Wetenschappen*, Noord-Hollandsche Uitgevers Maatschappij, 1988, 229-258. Reprinted as 'L'économie à travers le prisme du juriste', *Revue internationale de droit économique*, 1989, 133-162.

WEIGEL, Wolfgang, 'Ökonomie und Recht - Eine Einführung' [Economics and Law - An Introduction], **31(3/4)** *Das öffentliche Haushaltswesen in Österreich*, 1990, 169-198.

WEIGEL, Wolfgang, 'Ökonomie und Recht - Eine Einführung' [Law and Economics, a Primer], in WEIGEL, Wolfgang (project management) and AUSTRIAN ECONOMIC CHAMBER (ed.), *Economic Analysis of Law - a Collection of Applications*, Vienna, Austrian Economic Publishing Compl., 1991, 13-37.

WILBERFORCE, Lord, 'Law and Economics' in HARVEY, B.W. (ed.) *The Lawyer and Justice*, London, Sweet and Maxwell, 1978.

WILLIAMS, A., 'Collaboration between Economists and Lawyers in Policy Analysis', **13** *Journal of Society of Public Teachers of Law*, 1975, 212-218.

0020 Monographies

ABRAHAM, Kenneth S., *Distributing Risk: Insurance, Legal Theory and Public Policy (in American Insurance Law)*, New Haven, Yale University Press, 1986, 254 p.

ADAMS, Michael, *Ökonomische Analyse des Sicherungsrechte* [Economic Analysis of Security Law], Königstein/Ts, Athenäum, 1980, 322 p.

ADAMS, Michael, *Ökonomische Analyse des Zivilprozesses* [Economic Analysis of Civil Procedure], Königstein/Ts, Athenäum, 1981, 130 p.

ADAMS, Michael, *Ökonomische Analyse des Gefährdungs- und Verschuldenshaftung* [Economic Analysis of Strict and Fault Liability], Heidelberg, R.v Decker's/C.F. Müller, 1985, 310 p.

ALPA, Guido, PULITINI, Francesco, RODOTA', Stefano and ROMANI, Franco, *Interpretazione giuridica e analisi economica* [Legal Interpretation and Economic Analysis], Milano, Giuffrè, 1982, 662 p.

ANDERSON, Martin, *Welfare. The Political Economy of Welfare Reform in the United States*, Stanford, Hoover Press, 1978, 251 p.

ANDERSON, R.W ., *The Economics of Crime*, London, Macmillan, 1976, 71 p.

ARMENTANO, Dominick T., *Antitrust and Monopoly: Anatomy of a Policy Failure*, New York, Wiley, 1982, 292 p.

BAIRD, Charles W., *Rent Control: The Perennial Folly*, San Francisco, Cato Institute, 1980, 101 p.

BALDWIN, G.R. and VELJANOVSKI, Cento G., *Regulation and Cost-Benefit Analysis - The U.S. Experience and U.K. Potential*, Oxford, Centre for Socio-Legal Studies, 1982.

BARZEL, Yoram, *Economic Analysis of Property Rights*, Cambridge, Cambridge

University Press, 1989, 122 p.

BAUMOL, William J. and OATES, Wallace E., *The Theory of Environmental Policy*, Cambridge, Cambridge University Press, 1988, 299 p.

BAXTER, William F., *People or Penguins: The Case for Optimal Pollution*, New York, Columbia University Press, 1974, 110 p.

BECKER, Gary S., *The Economics of Discrimination*, Chicago, University of Chicago Press, 1957, 137 p.

BECKER, Gary S., *The Economic Approach to Human Behavior*, University of Chicago Press, Chicago, 1976, 314 p.

BECKER, Gary S., *A Treatise on the Family*, Cambridge, Harvard University Press, 1981, 288 p.

BECKERMAN, Wilfred, *Pricing for Pollution: An Analysis of Market Pricing and Government Regulation in Environment Consumption and Policy*, London, Institute of Economic Affairs, Hobart Paper, no. 66, 1990, 80 p.

BERLANT, J.L., *Profession and Monopoly: A Study of Medicine in the United States and Great Britain*, Berkeley, University of California Press, 1975.

BLAIR, Roger D. and KASERMAN, David L., *Law and Economics of Vertical Integration and Control*, New York, Academic Press, 1983, 211 p.

BLAIR, Roger D. and KASERMAN, David L., *Law and Economics of Vertical Integration and Control*, Harcourt Brace Jovanovich, New York, 1983, 211 p.

BLUMSTEIN, J. et al. (eds.), *Deterrence and Incapacitation: Estimating the Effects of Criminal Sanctions on Crime Rates*, Washington, National Academy of Science, 1978.

BORK, Robert H., *The Antitrust Paradox: A Policy at War with Itself*, New York, Basic Books, 1978, 468 p.

BOWMAN, Ward S., Jr., *Patent and Antitrust Law: A Legal and Economic Appraisal*, Chicago, University of Chicago Press, 1973.

BREYER, Stephen G., *Regulation and its Reform*, Cambridge Mass., Harvard University Press, 1982, 472 p.

BURROWS, Paul, *The Economic Theory of Pollution Control*, Oxford, Martin Robertson, 1979, 192 p.

BUTTON, Kenneth J., *Airline Deregulation: International Experiences*, New York, New York University Press, 1990, 191 p.

CALABRESI, Guido, *The Costs of Accidents: A Legal and Economic Analysis*, New Haven, Yale University Press, 1970, 340 p.

CALABRESI, Guido and BOBBITT, Philip, *Tragic Choices: The Conflicts Society Confronts in the Allocation of Tragically Scarce Resources*, New York, W.W. Norton, 1978, 252 p.

CAMPBELL, Rita Ricardo, *Food Safety Regulations: A Study of the Use and Limitations of Cost-Benefit Analysis*, Washington, A.E.I.P.P.R., 1976.

CASPER, Gerhard and POSNER, Richard A., *The Workload of the Supreme Court*, Chicago, American Bar Foundation, 1976.

CHEUNG, Steven N.S., *A Theory of Share Tenancy*, Chicago, University of Chicago Press, 1969, 188 p.

CHEUNG, Steven N.S., *The Myth Of Social Costs: A Critique of Welfare Economics and the Implications for Public Policy*, London, Institute of Economic Affairs, 1978, 93 p.

COLEMAN, Jules L., *Markets, Morals and the Law*, Cambridge, Cambridge University Press, 1988, 393 p.

CRAIN, W. Mark, *Vehicle Safety Inspection Systems - How Effective?*, Washington D.C., A.E.I., 1980.

CRANDALL, Robert W., *Controlling Industrial Pollution: The Economics and Politics of Clean Air*, Washington, Brookings Institution, 1983, 199 p.

CRANDALL, Robert W. et al., *Regulating the Automobile*, Washington, Brookings Institution, 1986, 202 p.

CREW, Michael A. and KLEINDORFER, Paul R., *The Economics of Public Utility Regulation*, Cambridge, MIT Press, 1986, 304 p.

CULYER, A.J., *The Economics of Social Policy*, London, Martin Robertson, 1973, 268 p.

DAHLMAN, Carl J., *The Open Field System and Beyond: A Property Rights Analysis of an Economic Institution*, Cambridge, Cambridge University Press, 1980, 234 p.

DALES, J.H., *Pollution, Property and Prices: An Essay in Policy-Making and Economics*, Toronto, University of Toronto Press, 1968, 111 p.

DANZON, Patricia M., *Medical Malpractice: Theory, Evidence, and Public Policy*, Cambridge, Harvard University Press, 1985, 264 p.

DE CLERCQ, Marc and NAERT, Frank, *De politieke markt* [The Political Market], Antwerpen, Kluwer, 1985, 163 p.

DEMSETZ, Harold, *Economic, Legal and Political Dimensions of Competition*, Amsterdam, North-Holland, 1982, 125 p.

DERTHICK, Martha and QUIRK, Paul J., *The Politics of Deregulation*, Washington D.C., The Brookings Institution, 1985, 265 p.

DEWEES, Donald N., EVERSON, C.K. and SIMS, W.A., *Economic Analysis of Environmental Policies*, Toronto, University of Toronto Press, 1975, 175 p.

DILNOT, Andrew, *The Economics of Social Security*, Oxford, Oxford University Press, 1989, 287 p.

DOUGLAS, G.W. and MILLER, J.C., *Economic Regulation of Domestic Air Transport: Theory and Policy*, Washington, Brookings Institution, 1974.

ECKERT, Ross D., *The Enclosure of Ocean Resources: Economics and the Law of the Sea*, Stanford, Hoover Institute Press, 1979, 390 p.

EGGERTSSON, Thrainn, *Economic Behaviour and Institutions*, Cambridge, Cambridge University Press, 1990, 385 p.

EINHORN, Michael A., *Price Caps and Incentive Regulation in Telecommunications*, Dordrecht, Kluwer Academic Publishers, 1991, 256 p.

EMONS, Winand, *On the Economic Theory of Warranties*, Bonn, 1987, 84 p.

FAURE, Michael and VAN DEN BERGH, Roger, *Objectieve aansprakelijkheid, verplichte verzekering en veiligheidsregulering* [Strict Liability, Mandatory Insurance and Safety Regulation], Antwerpen, Maklu, 1989, 386 p.

FISCHEL, William A., *The Economics of Zoning Laws: A Property Rights Approach to American Land Use Controls*, Baltimore, John Hopkins University Press, 1985, 372 p.

FLEISHER, B., *The Economics of Delinquency*, New York, Quadrangle, 1966.

FREY, Bruno S., *Ökonomie ist Sozialwissenschaft. Die Anwendung der Ökonomie auf neue Gebiete* [Economics is a Social Science. The Use of Economics in New Domains], München, Vahlen, 1990.

GAAY FORTMAN, Bastiaan de, *Theory of Competition Policy: A Confrontation of Economic, Political and Legal Principles*, Amsterdam, North-Holland, 1966, 341 p.

GELLHORN, Ernest A., *Antitrust Law and Economics*, St. Paul, West Pub., 1976, 472 p.

GHOSH, D., LEES, D. and SEAL, W., *The Economics of Personal Injury*, Westmead, Saxon House, 1976 p.

GIBBS, J., *Crime, Punishment and Deterrence*, New York, Elsevier, 1975.

GRABOWSKI, Henry G., *Drug Regulation and Innovation: Empirical Evidence and Policy*, Washington, American Enterprise Institute, 1976, 82 p.

GRETHER, David M., ISAAC, R. Mark and PLOTT, Charles R., *The Allocation of Scarce Resources. Experimental Economics and the Problem of Allocating Airport Slots*, Boulder, Westview Press, 1989, 333 p.

HAHN, Robert, *A Primer on Environmental Policy Design*, New York, Harwood Academic, 1989, 135 p.

HALPERN, Paul J. and CARR, Jack L., *Liability Rules and Insurance Markets*, Ottawa, Consumer and Corporate Affairs Canada, 1981.

HARRIS, Richard A. and MILKIS, Sidney M., *The Politics of Regulatory Change: A Tale of Two Agencies*, New York, Oxford University Press, 1989, 331 p.

HARTLEY, K. and MAYNARD, A., *The Costs and Benefits of Regulating New Product Development in the UK Pharmaceutical Industry*, London, Office of Health Economics, 1982.

HELLAMAN, D.A., *The Economics of Crime*, New York, St. Martins Press, 1980.

HELLMAN, Daryl A. and ALPER, Neil O., *Economics of Crime: Theory and Practice*, Needham Heights, Simon and Schuster, Ginn Press, 1990, 226 p.

HESS, James D., *The Economics of Organisation*, Amsterdam, North-Holland, 1983, VIII, 284 p.

HODGSON, Geoffrey M., *Economics and Institutions*, Cambridge, Polity Press, 1988, 365 p.

HUBER, Peter W., *Liability. The Legal Revolution and Its Consequences*, 1988, New York, Basic Books, 260 p.

IPPOLITO, Richard A., *The Economics of Pension Insurance*, Homewood, Irwin for the University of Pennsylvania, Wharton School, Pension Research Council, 1989, 270 p.

JACKSON, Thomas H., *The Logic and Limits of Bankruptcy Law*, Cambridge, Harvard University Press, 1986, 287 p.

JOHNSON, Burce M., *Taking Care of Business: The Economics of Crime by Heroin*

Abusers, Lexington, Lexington Books, 1985, 278 p.

JOSKOW, Paul L. and SCHMALENSEE, Richard, *Markets for Power: An Analysis of Electric Utility Deregulation*, Cambridge, MIT Press, 1983, 269 p.

KAHN, Alfred E., *The Economics of Regulation: Principles and Institutions*, Cambridge, Mass., MIT Press, 1988, 199 p. (Volume 1) + 360 p. (Volume 2).

KAUFER, Erich, *The Economics of the Patent System*, Chur, Harwood Academic, 1989, 66 p.

KAUFMANN, Peter J., *Passing Off and Misappropriation: An Economic and Legal Analysis of the Law of Unfair Competition in the U. S. and Continental Europe*, Max Planck Institute for Foreign and International Patent, Copyright and Competition Law, VCH-Weinheim, Reerfield Beach, 1986, 198 p.

KAYSEN, Carl and TURNER, Donald F., *Antitrust Policy: An Economic and Legal Analysis*, Cambridge, Harvard University Press, 1959, 345 p.

KLEIMAN, Mark A.R., *Marijuana: Costs of Abuse, Costs of Control*, Westport, Greenwood Press, 1989, 197 p.

KLITGAARD, Robert, *Controlling Corruption*, Berkeley, University of California Press, 1988, 220 p.

KNEESE, Allan V. and SCHULTZE, Charles L., *Pollution, Prices and Public Policy*, Brookings, Washington D.C., 1975, 125 p.

LABAND, David N. and HEINBUCH, Deborah Hendry, *Blue Laws: The History, Economics, and Politics of Sunday Closing Laws*, Lexington, Lexington Books, 1987, 232 p.

LANDES, William M. and POSNER, Richard A., *The Economic Structure of Tort Law*, Cambridge (Mass.) Harvard University Press, 1987, 330 p.

LEHMANN, Michael, *Bürgerliches Recht und Handelsrecht - eine juristische und ökonomische Analyse ausgewählter Probleme für Wirtschaftswissenschaftler und interdisziplinär interessierte Juristen unter besonderer Berücksichtigung der "Ökonomischen Analyse des Rechts" und der "Theorie der Property Rights"* [Civil Law and Commercial Law - a Legal and Economic Analysis of Selected Problems for Lawyers with an Economic and Interdisciplinary Interest with a Special Attention for the "Economic Analysis of Law" and the "Theory of Property Rights"], Stuttgart, Poeschel, 1983, 329 p.

LEPAGE, Henri, *Pourquoi la propriété* [Why Property?], Paris, 1984. (Subject Code: 0020, 2000)

LEUBE, Kurt R. and MOORE, Thomas Gale, *The Essence of Stigler*, Stanford, Hoover Institution Press, 1986, 377 p.

LIBECAP, Gary D., *Contracting for Property Rights*, Cambridge, Cambridge University Press, 1989, 132 p.

LUKEN, Ralph A., *Efficiency in Environmental Regulation*, Dordrecht, Kluwer Academic Publishers, 1991, 400 p.

LUKSETICH, William and WHITE, Michael, *Crime and Public Policy: An Economic Approach*, 1982.

MACAULEY, Molly K., and PORTNEY, Paul R., *Property Rights in Orbit Regulation*, American Enterprise Institute for Public Policy Research, Washington D.C., Vol. 7, 1984

MALLOY, Robin Paul, *Planning for Serfdom - A Contextual Theory of Law, Economics, and the State*, University of Pennsylvenia Press, 1990.

MATAJA, Victor, *Das Recht des Schadenersatzes vom Standpunkte der Nationalökonomie* [The Law of Compensation from the Standpoint of Economics], Leipzig, 1888.

MEIER, Kenneth J., *The Political Economy of Regulation: The Case of Insurance*, Albany, State University of New York Press, 1988, 230 p.

MENDELOFF, John M., *The Dilemma of Toxic Substance Regulation: How Overregulation Causes Underregulation at OSHA*, Cambridge, MIT Press, 1988, 321 p.

MILLER, James C., III., *The Economist as Reformer: Revamping the FTC, 1981-1985*, Washington D.C., American Enterprise Institure for Public Policy Research, 1989, 110 p.

MOORE, Thomas G., *Trucking Regulation. Lessons from Europe*, Washington, A.E.I.P.P.R., 1976, 148 p.

MORRISON, Steven and WINSTON, Clifford, *The Economic Effects of Airline Deregulation*, Washington D.C., Brookings, 1986, 84 p.

MUNCH, Patricia, *Costs and Benefits of the Tort System if Viewed as a Compensation System*, Santa Monica, Rand Corp., 1977.

MYHRMAN, Johan, PETRÉN, Gustav and STRÖMHOLM, Stig, *Marknadsekonomins rättsliga grundvalar* [The Legal Foundations of the Market Economy], Timbro, 1987.

NEEDHAM, Douglas, *The Economics and Politics of Regulation: A Behavioral Approach*, Boston, Little Brown, 1983, 482 p.

NEELY, Richard, *The Product Liability Mess: How Business Can Be Rescued From the Politics of State Courts*, New York, Free Press/Macmillan, 1988, 181 p.

OLSON, Walter (ed.), *New Directions in Liability Law*, New York, The Academy of Political Science, 1988, 214 p.

OTTO, Hans-Jochen, *Generalprävention und externe Verhaltenskontrolle, Wandel vom sociologischen zum ökonomischen Paradigma in der Nordamerikanischen Kriminologie?* [General Prevention and External Control of Behavior, Evolution from Sociological to Economic Paradigm in the North American Criminology?], Freiburg, Max-Planck-Institut für ausländisches internationales Strafrecht, 1982, 323 p.

OWEN, Bruce M. and BRAEUTIGAN, Ronald R., *The Regulation Game: Strategic Use of the Administrative Process*, Cambridge, Ballinger, 1978, 271 p.

PAPPS, Ivy, *For Love or Money? A Preliminary Economic Analysis of Marriage and the Family*, London, Institute of Economic Affairs (Hobart Paperback No.86), 1980, 63 p.

PELTZMAN, Sam, *Regulation of Pharmaceutical Innovation: The 1962 Amendments*, Washington, A.E.I.P.P.R., 1974, 118 p.

PENROSE, E.T., *The Economics of the International Patent System*, Baltimore, John Hopkins University Press, 1951.

PEJOVICH, Svetozar, *The Economics of Property Rights: Towards a Theory of Comparitive Systems*, Dordrecht, Kluwer Academic Publishers, 1990, 224 p.

PETERSON, Wallace C., *Transfer Spending, Taxes, and the American Welfare State*, Dordrecht, Kluwer Academic Publishers, 1991, 192 p.

PIGOU, A.C., *The Economics of Welfare*, Macmillan, London, 1932, 876 p.

POOLE, Robert W., Jr., *Instead of Regulation*, Lexington Mass., D.C. Heath, 1982, 404 p.

POOLE, Robert W., Jr. (ed.), *Unnatural Monopolies: The Case for Deregulating Public Utilities*, Lexington, Lexington Books, 1985, 224 p.

POSNER, Richard A., *Antitrust Law: An Economic Perspective*, Chicago, University of Chicago Press, 1976, 262 p.

POSNER, Richard A., *The Economics of Justice*, Cambridge (Mass.), Harvard University Press, 1981, 415 p.

POSNER, Richard A., *The Federal Courts: Crisis and Reform*, Harvard University Press, Cambridge, 1985, 365 p.

PYLE, David J., *The Economics of Crime and Law Enforcement*, London, Macmillan, 1983, 216 p.

PYLE, David J., *Tax Evasion and the Black Economy*, New York, St. Martin's Press, 1989, 212 p.

RAUFER, Roger K. and FELDMAN, Stephen L., *Acid Rain and Emissions Trading: Implementing a Market Approach to Pollution Control*, Totowa, Littlefield, 1987, 161 p.

REUTER, Peter, *Disorganized Crime: The Economics of the Visible Hand*, London, MIT Press, 1983, 233 p.

RINGEN, Stein, *The Possibility of Politics: A Study in the Political Economy of the Welfare State*, Oxford, Clarendon, 1987, 303 p.

ROBERT, Philippe and GODEFROY, Thierry, *Le coût du crime ou l'économie poursuivant le crime* [The Cost of Crime or Economics Prosecuting Crime], Genève, Masson, 1977, 225 p.

ROGERS, A.J., *The Economics of Crime*, Illinois, Dryden Press, 1973.

ROWLEY, Charles K., *Antitrust and Economic Efficiency*, London, Macmillan, 1973, 95 p.

RUBIN, Paul H., *Business Firms and the Common Law. The Evolution of Efficient Rules*, New York, Praeger, 1983, 189 p.

SAGOFF, Mark, *The Economy of the Earth: Philosophy, Law, and the Environment*, Cambridge, Cambridge University Press, 1988, 271 p.

SANTINI, Gerardo, *Il commercio* [Trading], Bologna, Il Mulino, 1979, 364 p.

SANTINI, Gerardo, *I servizi. Saggio di economia del diritto* [The Services: An Essay in Economics of Law], Bologna, Il Mulino, 1987, 562 p.

SCHENK, Karl-Ernst, *"Institutional Choice" und Ordnungstheorie* ["Institutional Choice" and Theory of Order], Walter Eucken Institut, Vorträge und Aufsätze, Tübingen, J.C.B. Mohr, Bd. 82, 1982, 39 p.

SCHEPPELE, Kim Lane, *Legal Secrets, Equality and Efficiency in the Common Law*, Chicago, University of Chicago Press, 1988, 363 p.

SCHERER, Frederic M., *The Economic Effects of Compulsory Patent Licensing*,

New York, New York University, 1977.

SCHMID, A. Allan, *Property, Power, and Public Choice: An Inquiry into Law and Economics*, Westport, Greenwood Press, 1987, 332 p.

SCHMIDT, Ingo L.O. and RITTALER, Jan B., *A Critical Evaluation of the Chicago School of Antitrust Analysis*, Dordrecht, Kluwer Academic Press, 1989, 132 p.

SCHMIDT, Peter and WITTE, Ann D., *An Economic Analysis of Crime and Justice: Theory, Methods, and Applications*, New York, Academic Press, 1984, 416 p.

SHAVELL, Steven, *Economic Analysis of Accident Law*, Cambridge, Harvard University Press, 1987, 312 p.

SHENFIELD, Arthur, *Myth and Reality in Antitrust*, London, 1983.

SHEPHERD, William G., *Public Policies Toward Business*, Homewoo, Irwin, 1985, 541 p.

SIMONICH, William L., *Government Antismoking Policies*, New York, Peter Lang, 1991, 300 p.

SMITH, Peter and SWANN, Dennis, *Protecting the Consumer - An Economic and Legal Analysis*, Oxford, Martin Robertson, 1979, 286 p.

SNOW, Marcellus S., *Marketplace for Telecommunications: Regulation and Deregulation in Industrialized Democracies*, New York, Longman, 1986.

SWANN, Dennis, *The Retreat of the State: Deregulation and Privatization in the U.K. and U.S.*, Ann Arbor, University of Michigan Press, 1988, 344 p.

TABAAZ, T.F., *Toward an Economics of Prisons*, Lexington, Heath, 1975.

TAYLOR, Charles T. and SILBERTSON, Z.A., *The Economic Impact of the Patent System*, Cambridge, Cambridge University Press, 1973.

THOMPSON, Howard E., *Regulatory Finance: Finacial Foundations of Rate of Return Regulation*, Dordrecht, Kluwer Academic Publishers, 1991, 256 p.

TILLMAN, Georg, *Equity, Incentives, and Taxation*, Berlin, Springer, 1989, 132 p.

TRIMARCHI, Pietro, *Rischio e responsabilità oggettiva* [Risk and Strict Liability], Milano, Giuffrè, 1961, 383 p.

TULLOCK, Gordon, *Trials on Trial - The Pure Theory of Legal Procedure*, New York, Columbia University Press, 1980, 255 p.

TULLOCK, Gordon, *Economics of Income Redistribution*, Boston, Kluwer-Nijhoff, 1983, 208 p.

TULLOCK, Gordon, *The Economics of Wealth and Poverty*, Brighton, Wheatsheaf, 1986, 210 p.

TULLOCK, Gordon, *The Economics of Special Privilege and Rent Seeking*, Boston, Kluwer, 1989, 104 p.

UTTON, M.A., *The Economics of Regulating Industry*, Oxford, Blackwell, 1986, 243 p.

VANBERG, Viktor, *Verbrechen, Strafe und Abschreckung, die Theorie der Generalprävention im Lichte der neueren sozialwissenschaftslichen Diskussion* [Crime, Sanction and Deterrence: The Theory of General Prevention in the Light of the New Discussion in Social Science], Tübingen, J.C.B. Mohr, 1982, 50 p.

VISCUSI, W. Kip, *Welfare for the Elderly: An Economic Analysis and Policy*

Prescription, New York, Wiley, 1979, 251 p.

VISCUSI, W. Kip, *Regulating Consumer Product Safety*, Washington, American Enterprise Institute, 1984.

VOUSDEN, Neil, *The Economics of Trade Protection*, Cambridge, Cambridge University Press, 1990, 305 p.

WAGSTAFF, Adam and MAYNARD, Alan, *Economic Aspects of the Illicit Drug Market and Drug Enforcement Policies in the United Kingdom*, London, Her Majesty's Stationary Office, 1988, 156 p.

WALDMAN, D.E., *The Economics of Antitrust: Cases and Analysis*, Boston, Little Brown, 1986.

WATERSON, Michael, *Regulation of the Firm and Natural Monopoly*, Oxford, Blackwell, 1988, 164 p.

WEITZMAN, Lenore J., *The Marriage Contract: Spouses, Lovers and the Law*, New York, Free Press, 1981, 536 p.

WHYNES, David K. and BOWLES, Roger A., *The Economic Theory of the State*, Martin Robertson, Oxford, 1981, 236 p.

WILLIAMSON, Oliver E., *Markets and Hierarchies: Analysis and Antitrust Implication: A Study in the Economics of Internal Organization*, New York, Free Press, 1975, 286 p.

WILLIAMSON, Oliver E., *The Economic Institutions of Capitalism: Firms, Markets, Relational Contracting*, New York, Free Press, 1985, 450 p.

WILLIAMSON, Oliver E., *Antitrust Economics: Mergers, Contracting and Strategic Behavior*, Oxford, Blackwell, 1989, 363 p.

YANDLE, Bruce, *The Political Limits of Environmental Regulation: Tracking the Unicorn*, Westport, Greenwood Press, 1989, 180 p.

0030 Books with a Strong L&E Influence

ACKERMAN, Bruce A., *Reconstructing American Law*, Cambridge (Mass.), Harvard University Press, 1984, 118 p.

ATIYAH, Patrick S., *Accidents, Compensation and the Law*, London, Weidenfeld and Nicholson, 1977 (2nd ed.), 1980 (3rd).

BAIRD, Douglas G. and JACKSON, Thomas H., *Cases, Problems, and Materials on Security Interests in Personal Property*, Mineola, Foundation Press, 1987, 889 p.

BAYLES, Michael D., *Principles of Law. A Normative Analysis*, Dordrecht, Reidel (Law and Philosophy Library), 1987, 398 p.

BUTLER, Henry N., *The Legal Environment of Business: Government Regulation and Public Policy Analysis*, Cincinatti, South Western, 1987, 911 p.

EISENBERG, Melvin Aron, *The Nature of the Common Law*, Cambridge (Mass.), Harvard University Press, 1988, 204 p.

EPSTEIN, Richard, *Modern Product Liability Law*, Westport, Quorum Books, 1980,

211 p.

EPSTEIN, Richard A., *Takings: Private Property and the Power of Eminent Domain*, Cambridge, Harvard University Press, 1985, 362 p.

FEJØ, Jens, *Monopoly Law and Market: Studies of EC Competition Law with US American Antitrust Law as a Frame of Reference and Supported by Basic Market Economics*, Deventer, Kluwer, 1990, 416 p.

HARRIS, Donald, *Remedies in Contract and Tort*, London, Weidenfeld & Nicolson, 1988, 411 p.

SUNSTEIN, Cass R., *After the Rights Revolution: Reconceiving the Regulatory State*, Cambridge, Harvard University Press, 1990, 284 p.

0040 Symposia

18de Vlaams Wetenschappelijk Economisch Congres, Brussel 8 en 9 mei 1987, Sociaal-economische Deregulering, Brussel, V.E.H.U.B., 1987, 892 p.

ARNOTT, Richard J. and MINTZ, Jack M. (eds.), *Rent Control: The Internation Experience. Proceedings of a Conference Held at Queen's University, 31 August-4 September 1987*, Kingston, Queen's University, John Deutsch Institute for the Study of Economic Policy, 1987, 176 p.

BEBCHUCK, Lucian Ayre (ed.), *Corporate Law and Economic Analysis*, Cambridge, Cambridge University Press, 1990, 320 p.

BLAIR, Roger D. and RUBIN, Stephen (eds.), *Regulating the Professions: A Public-Policy Symposium*, Lexington, Lexington Books, 1980, 328 p.

CARMICHAEL, H. Lorne, 'Incentives in Academics: Why Is There Tenure?', **96** *Journal of Political Economy*, 1988, 453-472.

CHAMBERLIN, Edward H. (ed.), *Monopoly, and Competition and Their Regulation*, New York, 1954, 549 p.

CONFERENCE : 'Private Alternatives to the Judicial Process. Proceedings of a seminar sponsored by the Liberty Fund and administered by the Law and Economics Center of the University of Miami School of Law', **8** *Journal of Legal Studies*, 1979, 231-415.

CONFERENCE : 'Catastrophic Personal Injuries - A Conference Sponsored by The Hoover Institution', **13** *Journal of Legal Studies*, 1984, 415-622.

CONFERENCE : 'Critical Issues in Tort Law Reform: A Search for Principles. A Conference Sponsored by the Program in Civil Liability, Yale Law School', **14** *Journal of Legal Studies*, 1985, 459-818.

CONFERENCE : 'Conference on the Law and Economics of Procedure', **3** *Journal of Law, Economics, & Organization*, 1987, 143-372.

CONFERENCE : 'The Organization of Political Institutions', **6** *Journal of Law, Economics, & Organization*, 1990, S1-S332.

CONFERENCE : 'The Law and Economics of Risk', **19** *Journal of Legal Studies*, 1990, 531-849.

CRANSTON, Ross and SCHICK, Anne (eds.), *Law and Economics*, Canberra, Australian National University Press, 1982, 220 p.

DALE, Richard (ed.), *Financial Deregulation: The Proceedings of a Conference Held by the David Hume Institute in May 1986*, Cambridge, Woodhead-Faulkner, 1986, 1-12.

DORN, James A. and MANNE, Henry G. (eds.), *Economic Liberties and the Judiciary*, Fairfax, George Mason University Press, 1987, 392 p.

FAURE, Michael and VAN DEN BERGH, Roger (eds.), *Essays in Law and Economics. Corporations, Accident Prevention and Compensation for Losses*, Antwerpen, Maklu, 1989, 232 p.

IPPOLITO, Pauline M. and SCHEFFMAN, David T. (eds.), *Empirical Approaches to Consumer Protection Economics: Proceedings of a Conference Sponsored by the Bureau of Economics, Federal Trade Commission, April 26-27, 1984*, Washington D.C., Federal Trade Commission, 1986.

LITAN, Robert E. and WINSTON, Clifford (eds.), *Liability - Perspectives and Policy*, Washington, Brookings Institute, 1988.

MATHEWSON, G. Frank, TREBILCOCK, Michael J. and WALKER, Michael (eds.), *The Law and Economics of Competition Policy*, Vancouver, Fraser Institute, 1990, 443 p.

NUTZINGER, Hans G. and BACKHAUS, Jürgen (eds.), *Codetermination: A Discussion of Different Approaches*, Berlin, Springer, 1989, 309 p.

OTT, Claus and SCHÄFER, Hans-Bernd (eds.), *Allokationseffizienz in der Rechtsordnung. Beiträge zum Travemünder Symposium zur ökonomischen Analyse des Zivilrechts 23.-26. März 1988* [Allocative Efficiency in Legal Order. Contributions to the Travemünder Symposium on Economic Analysis of Civil Law], Berlin, Springer, 1989, 306 p.

OTT, Claus and SCHÄFER, Hans-Bernd (eds.), *Ökonomische Probleme des Zivilrechts. Beiträge zum 2. Travemünder Symposium zur ökonomischen Analyse des Rechts, 21. - 26. März 1990* [Economic Problems of Civil Law. Contributions to the Second Travemünder Symposium on Economic Analysis of Law], Berlin, Springer, 1991, 347 p.

PALMER, John P. (Guest ed.), *The Economics of Patents and Copyrights*, in ZERBE, Richard O. Jr. (Series ed.), *Research in Law and Economics*, Greenwich, Jai Press, **8**, 1986, 287 p.

PARDOLESI, Roberto and VAN DEN BERGH, Roger (eds.), *Law and Economics: Some further Insights*, Milano, Giuffrè, 1991, 205 p.

PETHIG, Rudiger and SCHLIEPER, Ulrich (eds.), *Efficiency, Institutions, and Economic Policy: Proceedings of a Workshop Held by the Sonderforschungsbereich 5 at the University of Mannheim*, New York, Springer, 1987, 225 p.

RIZZO, Mario J. (ed.), 'Symposium: Change in the Common Law: Legal and Economic Perspectives. A Symposium Sponsored by The Institute for Humane Studies and the Liberty Fund', **9** *Journal of Legal Studies*, 1980, 189-427.

RIZZO, Mario J. (Ed.), *Symposium on Causation in the Law of Torts*, in **63** *Chicago-Kent Law Review*, 1987, 397-680.

RUBIN, Paul H. (ed.), 'Symposium: Evolutionary Models in Economics and Law', **4**

Research in Law and Economics, 1982, 218 p.

SCHULENBURG, J.-Matthias Graf von der and SKOGH, Göran (eds.), *Law and Economics and the Economics of Legal Regulation*, Dordrecht, Kluwer, 1986, 230 p.

SEMINAR : 'Private Alternatives to the Judicial Process', **8(2)** *Journal of Legal Studies*, 1979, 231-418.

SKOGH, Göran (ed.), *Law and Economics. Report from a Symposium in Lund, 24-26 augustus 1977*, Lund, Juridiska Föreningen i Lund, 1978, 231 p.

SLAYTON, Philip and TREBILCOCK, Michael J., (eds.), *The Professions and Public Policy*, Toronto, University of Toronto Faculty of Law, 1978, 346 p.

STEWART, Marion B. (ed.), *Energy Deregulation and Economic Growth: Proceedings of the First Annual Conference on Energy Policy in the Middle Atlantic States*, New Brunswick, Rutgers, Bureau of Economic Research, 1987, 27-32.

SYMPOSIUM : 'Products Liability: Economic Analysis and the Law', **38** *University of Chicago Law Review*, 1970, 1-141.

SYMPOSIUM : 'Deregulation', **57** *Indiana Law Journal*, 1976, 682-755.

SYMPOSIUM : 'The Economics of Bankruptcy Reform', **41(4)** *Law and Contemporary Problems*, 1977, 206 p.

SYMPOSIUM : 'Symposium on Posner's Theory of Privacy', *Georgia Law Review*, Spring 1978.

SYMPOSIUM : 'Regulation and Innovation', **43(1)** *Law and Contemporary Problems*, 1979.

SYMPOSIUM : 'Symposium on Efficiency as a Legal Concern', **8** *Hofstra Law Review*, 1980, 485-972.

SYMPOSIUM : 'The Law and Economics of Privacy. A Conference Sponsored by The Center for the Study of the Economy and the State', **9** *Journal of Legal Studies*, 1980, 621-842.

SYMPOSIUM : 'Managing the Transition to Deregulation', **44(1)** *Law and Contemporary Problems*, 1981.

SYMPOSIUM : 'The Implications of Social Choice Theory For Legal Decision-making', **9** *Hofstra Law Review*, 1981.

SYMPOSIUM : 'The Place of Economics in Legal Education', **33** *Journal of Legal Education*, 1983, 183-376.

SYMPOSIUM : 'Redistribution of Income Through Regulation in Housing', **32** *Emory Law Journal*, Summer 1983, 767-819.

SYMPOSIUM : 'The ALI's Corporate Governance Proposals: Law and Economics', **8** *Delaware Journal of Corporate Law*, Fall 1984.

SYMPOSIUM : 'Attorney Fees Shifting', **47(1)** *Law and Contemporary Problems*, 1984, 1-354.

SYMPOSIUM : 'Alternative Compensation Schemes and Tort Theory', **73(3)** *California Law Review*, 1985, 548-1042.

SYMPOSIUM : 'Symposium on Law and Economics', **85** *Columbia Law Review*, 1985, 899-1119.

SYMPOSIUM : 'Medical Malpractice: Can the Private Sector Find Relief?', **49 (2)** *Law and Contemporary Problems*, 1986, 1-348.

SYMPOSIUM : 'Conference on the Law and Economics of Procedure', **3** *Journal of Law, Economics, and Organization*, 1987, 143-447.

SYMPOSIUM : 'The Crisis in Legal Theory and the Revival of Classical Jurisprudence', **73** *Cornell Law Review*, 1988, 281-446.

SYMPOSIUM : 'Rent Control and the Theory of Efficient Regulation', **54** *Brooklyn Law Review*, 1988, 729-739.

SYMPOSIUM : 'Symposium on Takings', **88** *Columbia Law Review*, 1988, 1581-1794.

SYMPOSIUM : 'Symposium on Post-Chicago Law and Economics', **65** *Chicago-Kent Law Review*, 1989, 1-191.

SYMPOSIUM : 'Non-Posnerian Law and Economics', **12** *Hamline Law Review*, 1989, 197-410.

SYMPOSIUM : 'Issues in Civil Procedure: Advancing the Dialogue', **69** *Boston University Law Review*, 1989, 467-779.

SYMPOSIUM : 'Empirical Approaches to Market Power', **32** *Journal of Law and Economics*, 1989, S1-S275.

SYMPOSIUM : 'Different Approaches to the Economics of Institutions', **146** *Journal of Institutional and Theoretical Economics*, 1990, 1-235.

SYMPOSIUM : 'Symposium on New Views on Antitrust', **147(1)** *Journal of Institutional and Theoretical Economics*, 1991, 1-239.

SYMPOSIUM (MEURER, Michael (ed.)): 'Economics of Contract Law', **52(1)** *Law and Contemporary Problems*, 1989, 209 p.

SYMPOSIUM: 'The Economics of Liability', **5(3)** *Journal of Economic Perspectives*, 1991, 3-136.

VAN DEN BERGH, Roger (ed.), *Verslagboek Eerste Werkvergadering recht en Economie* [Conference Volume First Workshop in Law and Economics], Antwerpen, Leerstoel A. Van Melkebeke, Handelshogeschool, 1986, 72 p.

WEIGEL, Wolfgang (project management) and AUSTRIAN ECONOMIC CHAMBER (ed.), *Economic Analysis of Law - a Collection of Applications*, Vienna, Austrian Economic Publishing Compl., 1991, 295 p.

ZERBE, Richard O., Jr. (ed.), 'Symposium: Antitrust and Regulation', **6** *Research in Law and Economics*, 1984, 292 p.

0050 Collections of (New) Articles

ALBON, Robert P. (ed.), *Rent Control. Costs & Consequences. Essays on the History, and the Economic and Social Consequences of Rent Control in Australia and Overseas*, St.Leonards, Centre for Independent Studies, 1980.

ANDREANO, Ralph and SIEGFRIED, John J. (eds.), *The Economics of Crime*, Cambridge, Schenkman, 1980, 426 p.

AOKI, Masahiko et al. (eds.), *The Firm as a Nexus of Treaties*, London, Sage, 1989, 358 p.

ARS AEQUI, 'Special Issue on Law-and-Economics', **39(10)** *Ars Aequi*, October 1990, 603-804.

ASSMANN, Heinz-Dieter, KIRCHNER, Christian and SCHANZE, Erich (eds.), *Ökonomische Analyse des Rechts* [Economic Analysis of Law], Kronberg, Athenäum, 1978, 369 p.

BAILEY, Elizabeth E. (ed.), *Public Regulation: New Perspectives on Institutions and Policies*, Cambridge, MIT Press, 1987, 404 p.

BAILY, Mary Ann and CIKINS, Warren I. (eds.), *The Effects of Litigation on Health Care Costs*, Washington, Brookings Institution, 1985, 1-10.

BAILY, Mary Ann and CIKINS, Warren I. (eds.), *The Effects of Litigation on Health Care Costs*, Washington, Brookings Institution, 1985.

BECKER, Gary S. and LANDES, William M. (eds.), *Essays in the Economics of Crime and Punishment*, New York, Columbia University Press, 1974, 268 p.

BLOCK, Walter E. (ed.), *Economics and the Environment: A Reconciliation*, Vancouver, Fraser Institure, 1990, 332 p.

BLOCK, Walter and OLSON, Edgar (eds.), *Rent Control. Myths and Realities. International Evidence of the Effects of Rent Control in Six Contries*, Vancouver, Fraser Institute, 1981, 335 p.

BLOCK, Walter E. and WALKER, Michael A. (eds.), *Discrimination, Affirmative Action, and Equal Opportunity - An Economic and Social Perspective*, Vancouver, Fraser Institute, 1982, 271 p.

BOLLARD, Alan and BUCKLE, Robert (eds.), *Economic Liberalisation in New Zealand*, Wellington, Allen and Unwin, 1987, 364 p.

BUCHANAN, James M., TOLLISON, Robert D. and TULLOCK, Gordon (eds.), *Toward a Theory of the Rent Seeking Society*, College Station, Texas A & M University Press, 1980.

BURROWS, Paul and VELJANOVSKI, Cento G. (eds.), *The Economic Approach to Law*, London, Butterworths, 1981, 343 p.

BUTTON, Kenneth J. and SWANN, Dennis (eds.), *The Age of Regulatory Reform*, Oxford, Oxford University Press, 1989, 339 p.

CALVANI, Terry and SIEGFRIED, John (eds.), *Economic Analysis and Antitrust*, Boston, Little Brown, 1979.

CLARCKSON, Kenneth W. and MARTIN, Donald L. (eds.), *The Economics of Nonproprietary Institutions*, Greenwich, JAI Press, *Supplement 1 to Research in Law and Economics*, 1979, 330 p.

COFFEE, John C., Jr., LOWENSTEIN, Louis and ROSE-ACKERMAN, Susan (eds.), *Knights, Raiders, and Targets: The Impact of the Hostile Takeover*, Oxford, Oxford University Press, 1988, 547 p.

COLLARD, David (ed.), *Fiscal Policy: Essays in Honour of Cedric Sandford*, Aldershot, Gower, Avebury, 1989, 173 p.

COMANOR, William, et al., *Competition Policy in Europe and North America: Economic Issues and Institutions*, New York, Harwood, 1991, 260 p.

CREW, Michael A. (ed.), *Analyzing the Impact of Regulatory Change in Public Utilities*, Lexington, Lexington Books, 1985.

CREW, Michael A. (ed.), *Regulating Utilities in an Era of Deregulation*, New York, St. Martin's Press, 1987, 201 p.

CREW, Michael A. (ed.), *Deregulation and Diversification of Utilities*, Dordrecht, Kluwer Academic, 1989, 206 p.

CREW, Michael A. (ed.), *Competition and the Regulation of Utilities*, Dordrecht, Kluwer Academic Publishers, 1991, 224 p.

CREW, Michael A. and KLEINDORFER, Paul R. (eds.), *Competition and Innovation in Postal Services*, Dordrecht, Kluwer Academic Publishers, 1991, 304 p.

DAINTITH, Terence (ed.), *Law as an Instrument of Economic Policy: Comparative and Critical Approaches*, Berlin, Walter de Gruyter, 1988, 432 p.

DAINTITH, Terence and TEUBNER, Gunther (eds.), *Contract and Organisation. Legal Analysis in the Light of Economic and Social Theory*, Berlin, Walter de Gruyter, 1986, 299 p.

EATWELL, John, MILGATE, Murray and NEWMAN, Peter (eds.), *The New Palgrave: A Dictionary of Economics*, London, Macmillan, 1987, 4 volumes (949 + 1044 + 1085 + 1025 p.).

EATWELL, John, MILGATE, Murray and NEWMAN, Peter (eds.), *The New Palgrave: Invisible Hand*, London, Macmillan, 1989, 283 p.

ECONOMISTAS (Journal), *Los derechos de propriedad en el análisis económico* [Property Rights in Economic Analysis], **38** *Economistas*, Special Issue, 1989.

EINHORN, Michael A. (ed.), *Price Caps and Incentive Regulation in Telecommunications*, Dordrecht, Kluwer Academic, 1991, 244 p.

FINSINGER, Jörg and PAULY, Mark V. (eds.), *The Economics of Insurance Regulation: A Cross-National Study*, New York, St. Martin's Press, 1986, 300 p.

GUSTAFSSON, B.A. and KLEVMARKEN, N. Anders (eds.), *The Political Economy of Social Security*, Amsterdam, North-Holland, 1989, 240 p.

HARDIN, Garrett and BADEN, John, (eds.), *Managing the Commons*, San Francisco, Freeman, 1977, 294 p.

HEINEKE, J.M. (ed.), *Economic Models of Criminal Behaviour*, Amsterdam, North Holland, 1978, 391 p.

LANGE, Peter and REGINI, Marino (eds.), *State, Market, and Social Regulation: New Perspectives on Italy*, Cambridge, Cambridge University Press, 1989, 295 p.

LITAN, Robert E. and WINSTON, Clifford (eds.), *Liability: Perspectives and Policy*, Washington D.C., Brookings Institution, 1988, 248 p.

MACKAY, Robert J., MILLER, James C., III and YANDLE, Bruce (eds.), *Public Choice and Regulation: A View form Inside the Federal Trade Commission*, Stanford, Hoover Institution Press, 1987, 363 p.

MAGOULAS, Georgios and SIMON, Jürgen (eds.), *Recht und Ökonomie beim Konsumentenschutz und Konsumentenkredit. Interdisziplinäre Studien zu den Problemen und Konzepten des Verbraucherschutzes* [Law and Economics of

Consumer Protection and Consumer Credit. Interdisciplinary Studies on the Problems and Concepts of Consumer Protection], Baden-Baden, Nomos, 1985, 436 p.

MARTIN, Donald L. and SCHWARTZ, Warren F. (eds.), *Deregulating American Industry: Legal and Economic Problems*, Lexington, Lexington Books, 1977, 120 p.

McKEE, David L. (ed.), *Hostile Takeovers: Issues in Public and Corporate Policy*, New York, Greenwood Press, 1989, 179 p.

McPETERS, L.R. and STRANGE, W.B. (eds.), *The Economics of Crime and Law Enforcement*, Springfield, Charles R. Thomas, 1976.

MERCURO, Nicholas (ed.), *Law and Economics*, Boston, Kluwer Academic Publishers, 1989, 264 p.

MEYER, J.R. and OSTER, C.V. (eds.), *Airline Deregulation: The Early Experience*, Boston, Auburn House, 1981.

MILLER, James C., III and YANDLE, Bruce (eds.), *Benefit-Cost Analysis of Social Regulation*, Washington, American Enterprise Institute, 1979.

MINTZ, Jack and WHALLEY, John (eds.), *The Economic Impacts of Tax Reform*, Toronto, Canadian Tax Foundation, 1989, 463 p.

MOORHOUSE, John C. (ed.), *Electric Power: Deregulation and the Public Interest*, San Francisco: Pacific Research Institute for Public Policy, 1986.

MOSES, Leon N. and SAVAGE, Ian (eds.), *Transportation Safety in an Age of Deregulation*, Oxford, Oxford University Press, 1989, 368 p.

NICKLISCH, Fritz (ed.), *Der Komplexe Langzeitvertrag. Strukturen und Internationale Schiedsgerichtsbarkeit. The Complex Long-Term Contract. Structures and International Arbitration*, Heidelberg, Müller Juristischer Verlag, 1987, 597 p.

NOLL, Roger G. (ed.), *Regulatory Policy and the Social Sciences*, Berkely, University of California Press, 1985, 400 p.

PEACOCK, Alan and FORTE, Francesco (eds.), *The Political Economy of Taxation*, Oxford, Blackwell, 1981, 211 p.

PENNOCK, J. Roland and CHAPMAN, John W., (eds.), *Ethics, Economics and the Law*, (NOMOS 24), New York, New York University Press, 1982, 323 p.

PERETZ, Paul (ed.), *The Politics of American Economic Policy Making*, Armonk, Sharpe, 1987, 454 p.

PESKIN, Henry M., PORTNEY, Paul R. and KNEESE, Allan V. (eds.), *Environmental Regulation and the U.S. Economy*, Baltimore, John Hopkins University Press, 1981, 163 p.

PRICHARD, J. Robert S., STANBURY, W.T. and WILSON, T.A. (eds.), *Canadian Competition Policy - Essays in Law and Economics*, Toronto, Butterworth, 1979.

ROTTENBERG, Simon (ed.), *The Economics of Crime and Punishment*, Washington, American Enterprise Institute for Public Policy Research, 1973, 232p.

ROTTENBERG, Simon (ed.), *The Economics of Medical Malpractice*, Washington, American Enterprise Institute for Public Policy Research, 1978, 293 p.

ROTTENBERG, Simon (ed.), *Occupational Licensure Regulation*, Washington, American Entreprise Institute for Public Policy Research, 1980, 354 p.

ROTTENBERG, Simon (ed.), *The Economics of Legal Mininum Wages*, Washington, American Entreprise Institute for Public Policy Research, 1981, 534p.

SCHÄFER, Hans-Bernd and WEHRT, Klaus (eds.), *Die Ökonomisierung der Sozialwissenschaften: Sechs Wortmeldungen* [Economics in Social Sciences: Six Contributions], Frankfurt am Main, Campus Verlag, 1989, 182 p.

SCHELLING, Thomas C. (ed.), *Incentives for Environmental Protection*, Cambridge (Mass.), MIT Press, 1983, 355 p.

SHOGREN, Jason F. (ed.), *The Political Economy of Government Regulation*, Dordrecht, Kluwer Academic, 1989, 210 p.

SIEGAN, Bernard H. (ed.), *The Interactions of Economics and the Law*, Lexington, Lexington Books, 1977, 171 p.

SIRKIN, Gerald (ed.), *Lexeconomics - The Interactions of Law and Economics*, Boston, Martinus Nijhoff, 1981, 271 p.

SKOGH, Göran (ed.), *Law and Economics*, Lund, Juridiska Foreningen i Lund, 1970.

THEEUWES, Jules J.M., VAN VELTHOVEN, B.C.J., WINTERS, J.K. e.a., *Recht en Economie* [Law and Economics], Amsterdam, Addison-Wesley, 1989, 294 p.

WEIDENBAUM, Murray L. and CHILTON, Kenneth W. (eds.), *Public Policy toward Corporate Takeovers*, New Brunswick, Transaction Books, 1988, 176 p.

WEISBROD, Burton A. (ed.) in collaboration with HANDLER, Joel F. and KOMESAR, Neil K., *Public Interest Law: An Economic and Institutional Analysis*, Berkeley, University of California Press, 1978, 580 p.

WEISS, Leonard W. and KLASS, Michael W. (ed.), *Regulatory Reform: What Actually Happened*, Boston, Little Brown, 1986.

WEISS, Leonard W. and KLASS, Michael W. (eds.), *Regulatory Reform: What Actually Happened*, Boston, Little Brown, 1986.

WILLS, Robert L., CASWELL, Julie A. and CULBERTSON, John D. (eds.), *Issues after a Century of Federal Competition Policy*, Lexington, Lexington Books, 1987, 387 p.

0060 Readers

ACKERMAN, Bruce A. (ed.), *Economic Foundations of Property Law*, Boston, Little Brown and Company, 1975, 332 p.

ALEXANDER, Larry (ed.), *Contract Law. Volumes I&II*, Aldershot, Dartmouth, 1991, 1140 p.

COASE, Ronald H., *The Firm, the Market and the Law*, Chicago, University of Chicago Press, 1988, 217 p.

DEMSETZ, Harold, *Ownership, Control, and the Firm. The Organization of Economic Activity. Volume I*, Oxford, Blackwell, 1988, 300 p.

FURUBOTN, Eirik G. and PEJOVICH, Svetozar (eds.), *The Economics of Property Rights*, Cambridge, Ballinger, 1974, 367 p.

GOETZ, Charles J., *Law and Economics: Cases and Materials*, St. Paul, West, 1984.

GOLDBERG, Victor P. (ed.), *Readings in the Economics of Contract Law*, Cambridge, Cambridge University Press, 1989, 252 p.

KAPLAN, L.J. and KESSLER, P. (eds.), *An Economic Analysis of Crime: Selected Readings*, Springfield, Charles Thomas, 1976.

KRONMAN, Anthony T. and POSNER, Richard A. (eds.), *The Economics of Contract Law*, Boston, Little Brown, 1979, 274 p.

KUPERBERG, Mark and BEITZ, Charles R. (eds.), *Law, Economics and Philosophy - A Criticial Introduction; With Applications to the Law of Torts*, Totowa (NJ), Rowman and Allenheld, 1983, 284 p.

MANNE, Henry G. (ed.), *The Economics of Legal Relationships: Readings in the Theory of Property Rights*, St. Paul, West, 1977, 660 p.

OGUS, Anthony I. and VELJANOVSKI, Cento G. (eds.), *Readings in the Economics of Law and Regulation*, Oxford, Clarendon Press, 1984, 361 p.

POSNER, Richard A. (ed.), *Tort Law: Cases and Economic Analysis*, Boston, Little Brown, 1977 (1st ed.), 1983, 891 p. (2nd ed.).

POSNER, Richard A. and SCOTT, Kenneth E. (eds.), *Economics of Corporation Law and Securities Regulation*, Boston, Little Brown, 1980, 384 p.

RABIN, Robert L. (ed.), *Perspectives on Tort Law*, Boston, Little Brown, 1976 (1st ed.), 1983, 332 p. (2nd ed.).

SAMUELS, Warren J. (ed.), *The Chicago School of Political Economy*, East Lansing, Division of Research, Graduate School of Business Administration, Michigan State University, 1976.

SAMUELS, Warren J. and SCHMID, A. Alan (eds.), *Law and Economics: An Institutional Perspective*, Boston, Nijhoff, 1981, 268 p.

STIGLER, George J., *The Citizen and the State. Essays on Regulation*, Chicago, University of Chicago Press, 1975, 209 p.

STIGLER, George J. (ed.), *Chicago Studies in Political Economy*, Chicago, University of Chicago Press, 1988, 641 p.

TEIJL, Rob and HOLZHAUER, Rudi W. (eds.), *Teksten Rechtseconomie* [Readings in Law-and-Economics], Arnhem, Gouda Quint, 1990/1991, 549 p.

0070 Bibliographies

BUCHANAN, James M., 'Bibliography of James M. Buchanan's Publications, 1949-1986', **89** *Scandinavian Journal of Economics*, 1987, 17-37.

CHIORAZZI, Michael et al., 'Empirical Studies in Civil Procedure: A Selected Annotated Bibliography', **51(3)** *Law and Contemporary Problems*, 1988, 87-207.

FOLEY, Patrick, SHAKED, Avner and SUTTON, John, *The Economics of the*

Professions. An Introductory Guide to the Literature, London, London School of Economics, 1981, 107 p.

GOEHLERT, Robert and GUNDERSON, Nels, *Government Regulation of Business: An Information Sourcebook*, Phoenix, Oryx Press, 1987, 425 p.

HOFFMAN, Elizabeth and SPITZER, Matthew L., 'Experimental Law and Economics: An Introduction', **85** *Columbia Law Review*, 1985, 991-1036.

PYLE, David J., *The Economics of Crime and Law Enforcement: A Selected Bibliography*, SSRC Public Sector Study Group, Bibliography Series No. 1, 1979, 216 p. (Supplement 1980)

SAMUELS, Warren J., 'Law and Economic Policy: A Bibliographical Survey', **58** *Law Library Journal*, 1965, 230-52.

SAMUELS, Warren J., 'Law and Economics: A Bibliographical Survey 1965-72', **66** *Law Library Journal*, 1972, 96-110.

SINDER, Janet, 'Economists as Judges: A Selective, Annotated Bibliography', **50 (4)** *Law and Contemporary Problems*, 1987, 279-286.

SNOW, Marcellus S. and JUSSAWALLA, Meheroo, *Telecommunication Economics and Internation Regulatory Policy: An Annotated Bibliography*, New York, Greenwood Press, 1986, 216 p.

STANBURY, W.T. and TRETHEWAY, Michael W., 'Airline Deregulation: A Bibliography', **22** *Logistics and Transportation Review*, 1986, 449-489.

TEMPLETON, Virginia Evans and TAUBENFELD, Howard J., *World Environment Law Bibliography: Non Periodical Literature in Law and the Social Sciences Published Since 1970 in Various Languages with Selected Reviews and Annotations from Periodicals*, Littleton, Rothman, 1987, 480 p.

VELJANOVSKI, Cento G., *The New Law-and-Economics. A Research Review*, Oxford, Centre for Socio-Legal Studies, 1982, 169 p.

VELJANOVSKI, Cento G., *Economics of the Common Law: A Bibliography*, Oxford, Centre for Socio-Legal Studies, 1984, 59 p.

0100 Organization of Research and Teaching

ACKERMAN, Bruce A., 'Comment: The Marketplace of Ideas', **90** *Yale Law Journal*, 1981, 1131-1148.

BECKER, Edward R., 'The Uses of "Law and Economics" by Judges', **33** *Journal of Legal Education*, 1983, 306-310.

BEVERIDGE, W., 'Economics as a Liberal Education', **1** *Economica*, 1921, 2-19.

BREYER, Stephen G., 'Economics for Lawyers and Judges', **33** *Journal of Legal Education*, 1983, 294-305.

BRIETZKE, Paul H., 'Another Law and Economics', **9** *Research in Law and Economics*, 1986, 57-109.

CALABRESI, Guido, 'On the General State of Law and Economics Research Today and Its Current Problems and Prospects', in SKOGH, Göran (ed.), *Law and Economics. Report from a Symposium in Lund, Sweden, 24-26 August 1977*, Lund, Juridiska Föreningen, 1978, 9-16.

CALABRESI, Guido, 'Thoughts on the Future of Economics in Legal Education', **33** *Journal of Legal Education*, 1983, 359-364.

COOTER, Robert D., 'Comment', **33** *Journal of Legal Education*, 1983, 237-238.

DOYLE, D.A., 'Alternative Teaching Strategies in Law and Economics Courses: Compression, Thematization and the Corporate Field', in CRANSTON, Ross and SCHICK, Anne (eds.), *Law and Economics*, Canberra, Australian National University, 1982, 208-220.

GELHORN, Ernest and ROBINSON, Glen O., 'The Role of Economic Analysis in Legal Education', **33** *Journal of Legal Education*, 1983, 247-273.

HANSMANN, Henry B., 'The Current State of Law-and-Economics Scholarship', **33** *Journal of Legal Education*, 1983, 217-236.

HOLZHAUER, Rudi W. and TEIJL, Rob, 'Rechtseconomie in Nederland' [Law-and-Economics in the Netherlands], **38(4)** *Ars Aequi*, 1989, 248-252.

KITCH, Edmund W., 'The Law and Economics Programme', **26** *University of Chicago Law School Record*, 1980, 42-44.

KLEVORICK, Alvin K., 'Reflections on "The Current State of Law-and-Economics Scholarship"', **33** *Journal of Legal Education*, 1983, 239-246.

KRIER, J., 'Economics in the Law School', **22** *University of Pennsylvania Law Review*, 1974, 1664-1705.

LOVETT, W.A., 'Economic Analysis and its Role in Legal Education', **26** *Journal of Legal Education*, 1974, 385-421.

MICHELMAN, Frank I., 'Reflections on Professional Education, Legal Scholarship, and thc Law-and-Economics Movement', **33** *Journal of Legal Education*, 1983, 197-216.

POSNER, Richard A., 'The Present Situation in Legal Scholarship', **90** *Yale Law Journal*, 1981, 1113-1130.

POSNER, Richard A., 'The Future of Law and Economics: A Comment on Ellickson', **65** *Chicago-Kent Law Review*, 1989, 57-62.

PRIEST, George L., 'The New Scientism in Legal Scholarship: A Comment on Clark and Posner', **90** *Yale Law Journal*, 1981, 1284-1295.

PRIEST, George L., 'Social Science Theory and Legal Education: The Law School as University', **33** *Journal of Legal Education*, 1983, 437-441.

PRIEST, George, 'Preface: Law and Economics after Europe's Revolution', in WEIGEL, Wolfgang (ed.), *Economic Analysis of Law - A Collection of Applications*, Vienna, Österreichischer Wirtschaftsverlag, 1991, 5-7.

ROWLEY, Charles K., 'Supreme Court Economic Review', **5** *International Review of Law and Economics*, 1985, 107-119.

SALOP, Steven C., 'Evaluating Uncertain Evidence with Sir Thomas Bayes: A Note for Teachers: Response', **2** *Journal of Economic Perspectives*, 1988, 178-179.

SCHÄFER, Hans-Bernd and STRUCK, Gerhard, 'Schlammbeseitigung auf der Bundesstraße. Geschäftsführung ohne Auftrag, Deliktsrecht, negatorische Haftung. Ökonomische Analyse des Rechts' [The Case of the Mud Removal at the Federal Highway], in WALZ, W. Rainer and RASCHER-FRIESENHAUSEN, Heinrich (eds.), *Sozialwissenschaften im Zivilrecht: Fälle und Lösungen in Ausbildung und Prüfung*, Neuwied, Luchterhand, 1983, 119-132.

SCHWARTZ, Murray L., 'Economics in Legal Education', **33** *Journal of Legal Education*, 1983, 365-368.

SCHWARTZ, Warren F., 'The Future of Economics in Legal Education: The Prospects for a New Model Curriculum', **33** *Journal of Legal Education*, 1983, 314-336.

SHEEHAN, Michael F., 'Institutionalists Before Regulatory Commissions: The Value of Doing in Thinking, Teaching, and Writing', **22** *Journal of Economic Issues*, 1988, 1169-1178.

STEVENS, Robert, *Law School. Legal Education in America from the 1850's to the 1980's*, Chapel Hill, University of North Carolina Press, 1983, 334 p.

STIGLER, George J., 'Economists and Public Policy', **13** *Regulation*, 1982, 13-17.

SUMMERS, Robert S., 'The Future of Economics in Legal Education: Limits and Constraints', **33** *Journal of Legal Education*, 1983, 337-358.

SYMPOSIUM : 'The Place of Economics in Legal Education', **33** *Journal of Legal Education*, 1983, 183-376.

TREBILCOCK, Michael J., 'The Prospects of "Law and Economics": A Canadian Perspective', **33** *Journal of Legal Education*, 1983, 288-293.

ULEN, Thomas S., 'Law and Economics: Settled Issues and Open Questions', in MERCURO, Nicholas (ed.), *Law and Economics*, Boston, Kluwer Academic Publishers, 1989, 201-231.

VELJANOVSKI, Cento G., *The New Law-and-Economics. A Research Review*, Oxford, Centre for Socio-Legal Studies, 1982, 169 p.

WALZ, W. Rainer (ed.), *Sozialwissenschaften im Zivilrecht, Fälle und Lösungen in Ausbildung und Prüfung* [Social Science in Civil Law, Cases and Answers in Education and Examination], Neuwied, 1983.

WALZ, W. Rainer and WIENSTROH, Claas, 'Die Fehlgeschlagene Investition' [The Case of the Investment Failure], in WALZ, W. Rainer and RASCHER-

FRIESENHAUSEN, Heinrich (eds.), *Sozialwissenschaften im Zivilrecht: Fälle und Lösungen in Ausbildung und Prüfung*, Neuwied, Luchterhand, 1983, 52-75.

WIEGANG, Wolfgang, ' Die Rezeption amerikanischen Rechts' [The Reception of American Law], in *Die schweizerische Rechtsordung in ihren internationalen Bezügen*, Bern, Haupt, 1988, 229-262.

WILLS, Robert L., 'Economists and Competition Policy: A Case Study', in WILLS, Robert L. and CASWELL, Julie A. and CULBERTSON, John D. (eds.), *Issues after a Century of Federal Competition Policy*, Lexington, Lexington Books, 1987, 3-8.

WILSON, G., *Socio-Legal Research in Germany*, London, Social Science Research Council, 1980.

X, 'Foreword: Chicago Economics, the FTC, and the Education of the Federal Judiciary', **15** *Antitrust Law and Economics Review*, 1983, 1-8.

X, 'No Anti-Antitrust 'Bias' at the Law and Economics Center: Federal Judges Can't Be 'Brainwashed'', **14** *Antitrust Law and Economics Review*, 1982, 15-70.

0200 History of Law & Economics

BOWLER, Clara Ann, 'The Papers of Henry C. Simons', **17** *Journal of Law and Economics*, 1974, 7-11.

BREMS, Hans, 'Marshall on Mathematics', **18** *Journal of Law and Economics*, 1975, 583-585.

CARSTENSEN, Peter C., 'Prophets of Regulation: Charles Francis Adams, Louis D. Brandeis, James M. Landis, Alfred F. Kahn',, **6** *American Bar Foundation Research Journal*, 1986, 881-902.

COASE, Ronald H., 'The Appointment of Pigou as Marshall's Successor', **15** *Journal of Law and Economics*, 1972, 473-485.

COATS, A.W., 'The Appointment of Pigou as Marshall's Successor: Comment', **15** *Journal of Law and Economics*, 1972, 487-495.

DE GEEST, Gerrit, 'James Buchanan, Nobelprijswinnaar economie 1986' [James Buchanan, Nobel Laureate Economics 1986], *De Vlaamse Gids*, 1987, 44-49.

DEMSETZ, Harold, *Ownership, Control, and the Firm. The Organization of Economic Activity. Volume I*, Oxford, Blackwell, 1988, 1-11 (ch. 1: 'Autobiographical Sketch)'.

DURDEN, Garey C., 'Determining the Classics in Social Choice', **69** *Public Choice*, 1991, 265-277.

DURDEN, Garey C. and MARLIN, James, 'An Analysis of Contributions and Contributors to Public Choice and the Journal of Law and Economics and 1973-1987', **65** *Public Choice*, 1990, 101-141.

ENGLARD, Izhak, 'Victor Mataja's *Liability for Damages from an Economic Viewpoint*: A Centennial to an Ignored Economic Analysis of Tort', **10** *International Review of Law and Economics*, 1990, 173-191.

EPSTEIN, Richard A., 'Professor, Now Judge - A Tribute to Richard A. Posner', **12** *Journal of Legal Studies*, 1983, 1-2.

GOETZ, Charles J., 'Public Choice and the Law: The Paradox of Tullock', in ROWLEY, Charles K. (ed.), *Democracy and Public Choice: essays in Honor of Gordon Tullock*, Oxford, Blackwell, 1987, 171-180.

HOLLANDER, Samuel, 'Adam Smith and the Self-Interest Axiom', **20** *Journal of Law and Economics*, 1977, 133-152.

HOVENKAMP, Herbert J., 'Derek Bok and the Merger of Law and Economics', **21** *University of Michigan Journal of Law Reform*, 1988, 515-539.

HOVENKAMP, Herbert J., 'The First Great Law & Economics Movement', **47** *Stanford Law Review*, 1990, 993-1058.

HUTTER, Michael, 'Early Contributions to Law and Economics - Adolf Wagner's *Grundlegung*', **16** *Journal of Economic Issues*, 1982, 131-147.

JONES, Trevor W., 'The Appointment of Pigou as Marshall's Successor: The Other Side of the Coin', **21** *Journal of Law and Economics*, 1978, 235-243.

KAHN, Alfred E., 'I Would Do It Again', **12(2)** *Regulation*, 1988, 22-28.

KITCH, Edmund W. (ed.), 'The Fire of Truth: A Remembrance of Law and Economics at Chicago, 1932-1970', **26** *Journal of Law and Economics*, 1983,

163-233.

LANDES, William M., CARLTON, Dennis W. and EASTERBROOK, Frank H., 'On the Resignation of Ronald H. Coase', **26** *Journal of Law and Economics*, 1983, iii-viii.

LEVI, Edward H., 'Aaron Director and the Study of Law and Economics', **9** *Journal of Law and Economics*, 1966, 3-4.

MACKAAY, Ejan J.P., 'La règle juridique observée par le prisme de l'économiste. Une histoire stylisée du mouvement de l'analyse économique du droit' [The Legal Rule Observed Through the Glasses of the Economist. A History of the Law & Economics Movement], *Revue Internationale de Droit Economique*, 1986, 43-83.

MELTZER, Bernard D., 'Aaron Director: A Personal Appreciation', **9** *Journal of Law and Economics*, 1966, 5-6.

MITCHELL, W.C., 'Virginia, Rochester and Bloomington: Twenty-five Years of Public Choice and Political Science', **56** *Public Choice*, 1988, 101-119.

PATINKIN, Don, 'Keynes and Chicago', **22** *Journal of Law and Economics*, 1979, 213-232.

POSNER, Richard A., 'Volume One of *Journal of Legal Studies* - an Afterword', **1** *Journal of Legal Studies*, 1972, 437-440.

POSNER, Richard A., 'Final Remarks', in SKOGH, Göran (ed.), *Law and Economics. Report from a Symposium in Lund, Sweden, 24-26 August 1977*, Lund, Juridiska Föreningen, 1978, 227-231.

POSNER, Richard A., 'The Law and Economics Movement', **77** *American Economic review (Papers and Proceedings)*, 1987, 1-13.

POSNER, Richard A., 'Foreword', in FAURE, Michael and VAN DEN BERGH, Roger (eds.), *Essays in Law and Economics. Corporations, Accident Prevention and Compensation for Losses*, Antwerpen, Maklu, 1989, 5-6

PRIEST, George, 'Preface: Law and Economics after Europe's Revolution', in WEIGEL, Wolfgang (ed.), *Economic Analysis of Law - A Collection of Applications*, Vienna, Österreichischer Wirtschaftsverlag, 1991, 5-7.

SCHANZE, Erich, 'Ökonomische Analyse des Rechts in den U.S.A. / Verbindungslinien zur realistischen Tradition' [Economic Analysis of Law in the U.S.A. - Origins and Relations to Legal Realism], in ASSMANN, Heinz-Dieter, KIRCHNER, Christian and SCHANZE, Erich (eds.), *Ökonomische Analyse des Rechts*, Kronberg, 1978, 3-19.

SCHANZE, Erich, 'Der Beitrag von Coase zu Rechte und Ökonomie des Unternehmens' [Coase's Contribution to Law and Economics of Business Organizations], **137** *Zeitschrift für die gesamte Staatswissenschaft*, 1981, 694-701.

SCHERER, Frederic M., 'Efficiency, Fairness, and the Early Contributions of Economists to the Antitrust Debate', **29** *Washburn Law Journal*, 1990, 243-255.

SCHMIDTCHEN, Dieter, 'Jenseits von Maximierung, Gleichgewicht und Effizienz: Neuland für die ökonomische Analyse des Rechts?' [Beyond Maximization, Balance and Efficiency: New Land for the Economic Analysis of Law?], in OTT, Claus and SCHÄFER, Hans-Bernd (eds.), *Ökonomische Probleme des*

Zivilrechts, Berlin, Springer, 1991, 316-343.

SCHWARTZ, Warren F., 'The Logic of the Law Revisited', in ROWLEY, Charles K. (ed.), *Democracy and Public Choice: essays in Honor of Gordon Tullock*, Oxford, Blackwell, 1987, 186-190.

STIGLER, George J., 'Henry Calvert Simons', **17** *Journal of Law and Economics*, 1974, 1-5.

STIGLER, George J., *Memoirs of an Unregulated Economist*, New York, Basic Books, 1988, 228 p.

THE SECRETARY, 'The Sumptuary Manifesto', **2** *Journal of Law and Economics*, 1959, 120-123.

VELJANOVSKI, Cento G., *The New Law-and-Economics. A Research Review*, Oxford, Centre for Socio-Legal Studies, 1982, 169 p.

WAGNER, Richard E., 'James M. Buchanan: Constitutional Political Economist', **11(1)** *Regulation*, 1987, 13-17.

WHITFORD, William C., 'Ian Macneil's Contribution to Contracts Scholarship', *Wisconsin Law Review*, 1985, 545-560.

WILLIAMSON, Oliver E., 'An Autobiographical Sketch', in WILLIAMSON, Oliver E., *Economic Organization: Firms, Markets and Policy Control*, New York, New York University Press, 1986, xi-xviii.

X, 'Note: The Rule of Law in Residential Associations', **99** *Harvard Law Review*, 1985, 472-490.

0300 LAW & ECONOMICS: METHODOLOGY AND FUNDAMENTAL CONCEPTS
Rob Teijl

0300 Methodology: General

ACKERMAN, Bruce A., 'Deux sortes de recherche "en droit et économie"' [Two Sorts of Research in Law & Economics], *Revue de la Recherche Juridique*, 1986, Nr. 1.

ACKERMAN, Bruce A., *Reconstructing American Law*, Cambridge (Mass.), Harvard University Press, 1984, 118 p.

ACKERMAN, Bruce A., 'Foreword: Talking and Trading', **85** *Columbia Law Review*, 1985, 899-904.

ACKERMAN, Bruce A., 'Law, Economics and the Problem of Legal Culture', *Duke Law Journal*, 1986, 929-947.

ADAMS, Michael, 'Ist die Ökonomie eine imperialistische Wissenschaft? Über Nutz und Frommen der Ökonomische Analyse des Rechts' [Is Economics an Imperialistic Science? On the Utility of Economic Analysis of Law], in *Juristische Ausbildung*, 1984 (Heft 7), 337-349.

ALLOTT, Anthony N., 'Attempting the Impossible: A Plea for Legal Economy', *Denning Law Journal*, 1989, 1-13.

AREEDA, Phillip, 'Comment: Always a Borrower: Law and Other Disciplines', *Duke Law Journal*, 1988, 1029-1043.

ARUP, Christopher, 'Accounting for the Social Costs of Technology Through the Legal Process', in CRANSTON, Ross and SCHICK, Anne (eds.), *Law and Economics*, Canberra, Australian National University, 1982, 25-38.

ASSMANN, Heinz-Dieter, 'Kommentar' (on Ott, Allokationseffizienz, Rechtsdogmatik und Rechtsprechung), in OTT, Claus and SCHÄFER, Hans-Bernd (eds.), *Allokationseffizienz in der Rechtsordnung*, Berlin, Springer, 1989, 45-49.

BACKHAUS, Jürgen G., 'Lawyers' Economics vs. the Economic Analysis of Law: A Critique of Professor Posner's "Economic Approach to Law with Reference to a Case Concerning Damages for Loss of Earning Capacity"', **3** *Munich Social Science Review*, 1978, 57-80.

BACKHAUS, Jürgen G., 'De eis tot correctie van ondoelmatig recht' [The Need to Correct Inefficient Law], **39(10)** *Ars Aequi*, 1990, 660-665.

BAKER, C. Edwin, 'Posner's Privacy Mystery and the Failure of Economic Analysis of Law', **12** *Georgia Law Review*, 1978.

BARNEY, J.B. and OUCHI, W.G., 'Introduction: The Search for New Microeconomic and Organization Theory Paradigms', in BARNEY, J.B. and OUCHI, W.G. (eds.), *Organizational Economics*, San Francisco, 1986, 1-17.

BAUER, P.T. and WALTERS, A.A., 'The State of Economics', **18** *Journal of Law and Economics*, 1975, 1-23.

BEHRENS, Peter, 'Aspekte einer ökonomischen Theorie des Rechts' [Aspects of an Economic Theory of Law], **12** *Rechtstheorie*, 1981, 472-490.

BLACK, Robert A., KREIDE, Rosalie S. and SULLIVAN, Mark, 'Critical Legal Studies, Economic Realism, and the Theory of the Firm', **43** *University of Miami Law Review*, 1988, 343-360.

BRAUCHER, Jean, 'Toward a Broader Perspective on the Role of Economics in Legal Policy Analysis: A Retrospective and an Agenda from Albert O. Hirschman', *Law and Social Inquiry*, 1988, 741-771.

BRENNAN, Geoffrey and BUCHANAN, James M., 'The Normative Purpose of Economic 'Science': Rediscovery of an Eighteenth Century Method', **1** *International Review of Law and Economics*, 1981, 155-166.

BRENNER, Reuven, 'Economics - An Imperialist Science ?', **9** *Journal of Legal Studies*, 1980, 179-188.

BREYER, Stephen G., 'Economics and Judging: An Afterword on Cooter and Wald', **50(4)** *Law and Contemporary Problems*, 1987, 245-252.

BRUCE, Christopher J., 'A Positive Analysis of Methodology in the Law and Economics Literature', **12** *Hamline Law Review*, 1989, 197-228.

BUCHANAN, James M., 'Positive Economics, Welfare Economics, and Political Economy', **2** *Journal of Law and Economics*, 1959, 124-138.

BUCHANAN, James M., 'Is Economics the Science of Choice?' in STREISSLER, E. (ed.), *Roads to Freedom. Essays in honour of F. A. Hayek*, London, Kegan Paul, 1964, 315 p.

BUCHANAN, James M., 'Good Economics, Bad Law', **60** *Virginia Law Review*, 1974, 483-492.

BUCHANAN, James M., *What Should Economists Do?*, Indianapolis, Liberty Press, 1979, 292 p.

BURROWS, Paul and VELJANOVSKI, Cento G., 'Introduction: The Economic Approach to Law', in BURROWS, Paul and VELJANOVSKI, Cento G. (eds.), *The Economic Approach to Law*, London, Butterworths, 1981, 1-34.

BYDLINSKI, Franz, *Fundamentale Rechtsgrundsätze* [Fundamental Principles of Law], Vienna-New York, Springer Publishers, 1988, 133-290 (ch.III).

CALABRESI, Guido, 'On the General State of Law and Economics Research Today and Its Current Problems and Prospects', in SKOGH, Göran (ed.), *Law and Economics. Report from a Symposium in Lund, Sweden, 24-26 August 1977*, Lund, Juridiska Föreningen, 1978, 9-16.

CALABRESI, Guido, *The New Economic Analysis of Law: Scholarship, Sophistry or Self-Indulgence?*, London, British Academy, 1981.

CHUBB, Larry L., 'Economic Analysis in the Courts: Limits and Constraints', **64** *Indiana Law Journal*, 1989, 769-801.

COASE, Ronald H., 'Economics and Contiguous Disciplines', **7** *Journal of Legal Studies*, 1978, 201-211.

COASE, Ronald H., *How Should Economists Choose? The Warren G. Nutter Lectures in Political Economy*, Washington D.C., American Enterprise Institute, 1982.

COHEN, George M., 'Posnerian Jurisprudence and Economic Analysis of Law: The

View from the Bench', **133** *University of Pennsylvania Law Review*, 1985, 1117-1166.

COLEMAN, James S., 'Introducing Social Structure into Economic Analysis', **74** *American Economic Review. Papers and Proceedings*, 1984, 84-88.

COLEMAN, Jules L., 'Efficiency, Exchange and Auction: Philosophic Aspects of the Economic Approach to Law', **68** *California Law Review*, 1980, 221-249.

COLEMAN, Jules L., 'The Economic Analysis of Law', in PENNOCK, J. Roland and CHAPMAN, John W. (eds.), *Nomos XXIV: Ethics, Economics and the Law*, New York, New York University Press, 1982, 83-103.

COLEMAN, Jules L., 'Economics and the Law: A Critical Review of the Foundations of the Economic Approach to Law', **94** *Ethics*, 1984, 649-679.

COLEMAN, Jules L., *Markets, Morals and the Law*, Cambridge, Cambridge University Press, 1988, 393 p.

COLEMAN, Jules L., 'Afterword: The Rational Choice Approach to Legal Rules', **65** *Chicago-Kent Law Review*, 1989, 177-191.

COMMONS, John R., 'Law and Economics', **34** *Yale Law Journal*, 1925, 371-382.

COOTER, Robert D., 'Law and the Imperialism of Economics: An Introduction to the Economic Analysis of Law and a Review of the Major Books', **29** *UCLA Law Review*, 1982, 1260-1269.

COOTER, Robert D., 'The Best Right Laws: Value Foundations of the Economic Analysis of Law', **64** *Notre Dame Law Review*, 1989, 817-837.

CORDATO, Roy E., 'Subjective Value, Time Passage, and the Economics of Harmful Effects', **12** *Hamline Law Review*, 1989, 229-244.

CRANSTON, Ross, 'Creeping Economism: Some Thoughts on Law and Economics', **4** *British Journal of Law and Society*, 1977, 103-115.

CRANSTON, Ross, 'Comment', in CRANSTON, Ross and SCHICK, Anne (eds.), *Law and Economics*, Canberra, Australian National University, 1982, 39-41.

DAINTITH, Terence and TEUBNER, Gunther, 'Sociological Jurisprudence and Legal Economics: Risks and Rewards', in DAINTITH, Terence and TEUBNER, Gunther (eds.), *Contract and Organisation: Legal Analysis in the Light of Economic and Social Theory*, Berlin, Walter de Gruyter, 1986, 3-22.

DAYNARD, Richard A., 'Use of Social Policy in Judicial Decision-Making', **56** *Carnell Law Review*, 1971, 919-950.

DE ALESSI, Louis, 'Nature and Methodological Foundations of Some Recent Extensions of Economic Theory', in RADNITZKY, Gerard and BERNHOLZ, Peter (eds.), New York, Paragon House Publishers, 1987, 51-76.

DE ALESSI, Louis, 'Form, Substance, and Welfare Comparisons in the Analysis of Institutions', **146** *Journal of Institutional and Theoretical Economics*, 1990, 5-23.

DE ALESSI, Louis and STAAF, Robert J., 'Property Rights and Choice', in MERCURO, Nicholas (ed.), *Law and Economics*, Boston, Kluwer Academic Publishers, 1989, 175-200.

DE GEEST, Gerrit, 'Public Choice, mensbeeld en ideologie' [Public Choice, Model of Man and Ideology], **19** *Rechtsfilosofie en Rechtstheorie*, 1990, 109-122.

DE GEEST, Gerrit, 'Public Choice en rechtseconomie' [Public Choice and Law & Economics], **39** *Ars Aequi*, 1990, 666-673.

DeBOW, Michael E. and LEE, D.R., 'Understanding (and Misunderstanding) Public Choice: A Response to Farber and Frickey', **66** *Texas Law Review*, 1988, 993-1012.

DIAMOND, Peter A., 'Posner's Economic Analysis of Law', **5** *Bell Journal of Economics*, 1974, 294-300.

DIONNE, Georges and GAGNE, Robert, 'Models and Methodologies in the Analysis of Regulation Effects in Airline Markets', **15** *International Journal of Transport Economics*, 1988, 291-312.

DONOHUE, John J. III, 'Law and Economics: The Road not Taken', **22** *Law & Society Review*, 1988, 903-926.

DUGGAN, Tony, 'New Directions in Legal Theory: Law and Economics', **63** *Law Institute Journal*, 1989, 852-853.

EASTERBROOK, Frank H., 'Method, Result and Authority: A Reply', **98** *Harvard Law Review*, 1985, 622-629.

EASTERBROOK, Frank H., 'Afterword: Knowledge and Answers', **85** *Columbia Law Review*, 1985, 1117-1119.

EASTERBROOK, Frank H., 'Workable Antitrust Policy', **84** *Michigan Law Review*, 1986, 1696 ff.

ELLICKSON, Robert C., 'Bringing Culture and Human Frailty to Rational Actors: A Critique of Classical Law and Economics', **65** *Chicago-Kent Law Review*, 1989, 23-55.

ENGLARD, Izhak, 'Law and Economics in American Tort Cases: A Critical Assessment of the Theory's Impact on Courts', **41** *University of Toronto Law Journal*, 1991, 359-430.

FAITH, Roger L., McCORMICK, Robert E., and TOLLISON, Robert D., 'Economics and Metrology: Give 'Em an Inch and They'll Take a Kilometre', **1** *International Review of Law and Economics*, 1981, 207-221.

FARBER, Daniel A., 'From Plastic Trees to Arrow's Theorem', *University of Illinois Law Review*, 1986, 337 ff. Reprinted in **19** *Cardozo Law Review*, 1987, 643-683.

FARBER, Daniel A. and FRICKEY, Philip P., 'The Jurisprudence of Public Choice', **65** *Texas Law Review*, 1987, 873-927.

FEZER, Karl-Heinz, 'Aspekte einer Rechtskritik an der economic analysis of law und am property rights approach' [Aspects of a Legal Critique on Law & Economics and the Property Rights Approach], *Juristenzeitung*, 1986, 817-824.

FEZER, Karl-Heinz, 'Nochmals: Kritik an der ökonomischen Analyse des Rechts' [Once More: Critique on the Economic Analysis of Law], *Juristenzeitung*, 1988, 223-228.

FISHER, F.M., 'Multiple Regression in Legal Proceedings', **80** *Columbia Law Review*, 1980, 702-736.

FISS, Owen M., 'The Law Regained', **74** *Cornell Law Review*, 1989, 245-255.

FOX, Eleanor M., 'Consumer Beware Chicago', **84** *Michigan Law Review*, 1986, 1714-1720.

FRANK, Jürgen, 'Die "Rationalität" einer ökonomischen Analyse des Rechts' [The "Rationality" of an Economic Analysis of Law], **2** *Zeitschrift für Rechtssoziologie*, 1986, 191-211.

GALLHORN, Ernest A., 'The Practical Uses of Economic Analysis: Hope vs. Reality', **56** *Antitrust Law Journal*, 1987, 933-945.

GATES, Henry Louis, 'Statistical Stigmata (Deconstruction and the Possibility of Justice)', **11** *Cardozo Law Review*, 1990, 1275-1289.

GELLHORN, Ernest A., 'The Practical Uses of Economic Analysis: Hope vs. Reality', **56** *Antitrust Law Journal*, 1987, 933-945.

GOETZ, Charles J., 'The Courtship of Law and Economics', **12** *Hamline Law Review*, 1989, 245-259.

GOLDRING, John, 'Consumer Law and Legal Theory: Reflections of a Common Lawyer', **13** *Journal of Consumer Policy*, 1990, 113-132.

GRAMM, Warren S., 'Chicago Economics: From Individualism True to Individualism False', in SAMUELS, Warren J. (ed.), *The Chicago School of Political Economy*, East Lansing, Division of Research, Graduate School of Business Administration, Michigan State University, 1976, 167-190.

GRAY, John H., 'The Economic Approach to Human Behaviour: The Prospects and Limitations', in RADNITZKY, Gerard and BERNHOLZ, Peter (eds.), *Economic Imperialism*, New York, Paragon House, 1987, 33-49.

GRBICH, Y., 'Is Economics of Any Use to Tax Lawyers? Towards a more Substantial Jurisprudence to Replace Legalism', **12** *Melbourne University Law Review*, 1980, 340-355.

GUEST, Stephen F.D., 'The Economics of Law', *Current Legal Problems*, 1984, 233-245.

HAMLIN, Alan P., 'Rights, Indirect Utilitarianism, and Contractarianism, **5** *Economics and Philosophy*, 1989, 167-189

HANSMANN, Henry B., 'The Current State of Law-and-Economics Scholarship', **33** *Journal of Legal Education*, 1983, 217-236.

HARRIS, Donald and VELJANOVSKI, Cento G., 'The Use of Economics to Elucidate Legal Concepts: The Law of Contract', in DAINTITH, Terence and TEUBER, Gunther (eds.), *Law and the Social Sciences*, Florence, European University Institute, 1984, 740 p.

HARRISON, Jeffrey L., 'Egoism, Altruism, and Market Illusions: the Limits of Law and Economics', **33** *UCLA. Law Review*, 1986, 1309-1363.

HEALD, Paul J., 'A Lost Episode of "Meeting of the Minds": Posner, Kelman, Holmes, and Pascal', **6** *Journal of Law and Religion*, 1988, 279-295.

HENNING, J.A. and MANN, H.M., 'An Appraisal of Model Building in Industrial Organization', **3** *Research in Law and Economics*, 1981, 1-14.

HESS, James D., 'A Comparison of Alternative Approaches to Economic Organization: Comment', **146** *Journal of Institutional and Theoretical Economics*, 1990, 72-75.

HESSEL, B., 'De mogelijke rol van de rechtseconomie in een moderne rechtsstaat' [The Possible Role of Law-and-Economics in a Modern Constitutional State], **39(10)** *Ars Aequi*, 1990, 645-653.

HEYNE, Paul, 'The Foundations of Law and of Economics: Can the Blind Lead the Blind?', **11** *Research in Law and Economics*, 1988, 53-71.

HOFFMAN, Elizabeth and SPITZER, Matthew L., 'Experimental Law and Economics: An Introduction', **85** *Columbia Law Review*, 1985, 991-1036.

HORN, Norbert, 'Zur ökonomischen Rationalität des Privatrechts. Die privatrechts theoretische Verwertbarkeit der "Economics Analysis of Law"' [On the Economic Rationality of Private Law. On the Utility of the Economic Analysis of Law for Private Law Theory], **176** *Archiv für die Civilistiche Praxis*, 1976, 307-333.

HORWITZ, Morton J., 'Law and Economics: Science or Politics?', **8** *Hofstra Law Review*, 1980, 905-912.

HOTZ, Beat, 'Ökonomische Analyse des Rechts - eine skeptische Betrachtung' [Economic Analysis of Law - A Sceptical Reflection], **34** *Wirtschaft und Recht*, 1982, 293-314.

HOVENKAMP, Herbert J., 'Rhetoric and Skepticism in Antitrust Argument', **84** *Michigan Law Review*, 1986, 1721-1729.

HOVENKAMP, Herbert J., 'Positivism in Law and Economics', **78** *California Law Review*, 1990, 815-851.

HUTTER, Michael, 'Über eine Alternative zur neoklassischen ökonomischen Analyse des Rechts' [On An Alternative for Neo-classical Economic Analysis of Law], **144** *Zeitschrift für das gesamte Handels- und Wirtschaftsrecht*, 1980, 642-651.

JACKSON, Nick, 'The Economic Explanation of Legal Phenomena',**4** *International Review of Law and Economics*, 1984, 163-183.

JOHNSON, Conrad D., 'The Idea of Autonomy and the Foundations of Contractual Liability', **2** *Law and Philosophy*, 1983, 271-303.

KELMAN, Mark G., 'Misunderstanding Social Life: A Critique of the Core Premises of "Law and Economics"', **33** *Journal of Legal Education*, 1983, 274-284.

KELMAN, Mark, 'Trashing', **36** *Stanford Law Review*, 1984, 293-348.

KELMAN, Mark, 'On Democracy-Bashing: A Skeptical Look at the Theoretical and 'Empirical' Practice of the Public Choice Movement', **74** *Virginia Law Review*, 1988, 199-273.

KITCH, Edmund W., 'The Intellectual Foundations of "Law and Economics"', **33** *Journal of Legal Education*, 1983, 184-196.

KLEINEWEFERS, Henner, 'Ökonomische Theorie des Rechts, Über Unterschiede zwischen dem ökonomischen und dem juristischen Denken' [Economic Theory of Law, On the Differences between Economic and Legal Thinking], in *Staat und Gesellschaft, Festschrift für Leo Schürmann zum 70. Geburtstag*, Fribourg, Universitätsverlag, 1987, 83-116.

KLEVORICK, Alvin K., 'Law and Economic Theory : An Economist's View', **65** *American Economic Review*, 1975, 237-243.

KLEVORICK, Alvin K., 'Legal Theory and the Economic Analysis of Torts and Crimes', **85** *Columbia Law Review*, 1985, 905-920.

KOCH, Harald, 'Die Ökonomie der Gestaltungsrechte. Möglichkeiten und Grenzen der ökonomische Analyse des Rechts am Beispiel von Kündiging und Anfechtung' [The Economics of Dispositive Right. Possibilities and Limits of the Economic Analysis of Law by the Example of Notion of Termination and Dispute], in

BERNSTEIN, H., DROBNIG, U. and KÖTZ, H. (eds.), *Festschrift für Konrad Zweigert zum 70. Geburtstag*, Tübingen, J.C.B. Mohr, 1981, 851-877.

KOMESAR, Neil K., 'In Search of a General Approach to Legal Analysis: A Comparitive Institutional Approach', **79** *Michigan Law Review*, 1981, 1350-1392.

KORNHAUSER, Lewis A., 'The New Economic Analysis of Law: Legal Rules as Incentives', in MERCURO, Nicholas (ed.), *Law and Economics*, Boston, Kluwer Academic Publishers, 1989, 27-55.

KRUITHOF, Robert, 'Leven en dood van het contract' [Life and Death of Contract], **49** *Rechtskundig Weekblad*, 1985-86, 2761-2768.

KRUITHOF, Robert, 'Naschrift' [Afterword], **50** *Rechtskundig Weekblad*, 1986-87, 1669-1680.

KÜBLER, Friedrich, 'Schlußwort: Vergleichende Überlegungen zur rechtspraktischen Bedeutung der ökonomischen Analyse' [Closing Word; Comparitive Considerations on the Meaning of Economic Analysis for Legal Practice], in OTT, Claus and SCHÄFER, Hans-Bernd (eds.), *Allokationseffizienz in der Rechtsordnung*, Berlin, Springer, 1989, 293-306.

KUHN, T., *The Structure of Scientific Revolutions*, Chicago, University of Chicago Press, 1962.

LACHMAN, Judith A., 'Knowing and Showing Economics and Law - Book Review: MICHEL POLINSKY: An Introduction to Law & Economics', **93** *Yale Law Journal*, 1984, 1587-1624.

LATIN, Howard, 'Activity Levels, Due Care, and Selective Realism in Economic Analysis of Tort Law', **39** *Rutgers Law Review*, 1987, 487-514. Reprinted in *Personal Injury Review Ann.*, 1988, 956-990.

LEFF, Arthur A., 'Economic Analysis of Law: Some Realism about Nominalism', **60** *Virginia Law Review*, 1974, 451-482.

LEMPERT, Richard, 'Statistics in the Courtroom: Building on Rubinfeld', **85** *Columbia Law Review*, 1985, 1098-1116.

LIEBELER, Wesley J., 'What Are the Alternatives to Chicago?', *Duke Law Journal*, 1987, 879-898.

LIEBHAFSKY, Harold H., 'Price Theory as Jurisprudence: Law and Economics Chicago Style', **10** *Journal of Economic Issues*, 1976, 23-43. Reprinted in SAMUELS, Warren J. (ed.), *The Chicago School of Political Economy*, East Lansing, Division of Research, Graduate School of Business Administration, Michigan State University, 1976, 237-258.

LIEBHAFSKY, Harold H., 'Law and Economics from Different Perspectives', **21** *Journal of Economic Issues*, 1987, 1809-1836.

LIVINGSTON, Marie Leigh, 'Evaluating the Performance of Environmental Policy: Contributions of Neoclassical, Public Choice, and Institutional Models', **21** *Journal of Economic Issues*, 1987, 281-294.

MACKAAY, Ejan J.P., 'Het recht bezien door de bril van de economist - Een geleerd overzicht van de rechtseconomie' [Law Seen Through Economist's Glasses: An Overview of Law-and-economics], *Rechtsgeleerd Magazijn Themis*, 1988, 411-452.

MAGOULAS, Georgios, 'Privatrechtlicher Immissionsschutz, Wucher und ökonomische Analyses des Rechts' [Civil Law Protection against Harmfull Effects on the Environment, Usury and Economic Analysis of Law], in SIMON, Jürgen (ed.), *Regulierungsprobleme im Wirtschaftsrecht*, Neuwied und Darmstadt, Luchterhand, 1986, 1-24.

MAKGETLA, Neva Seidman and SEIDMAN, Robert B., 'The Applicability of Law and Economics to Policymaking in the Third World', **23** *Journal of Economic Issues*, 1989, 35-78.

MALLOY, Robin Paul, 'The Limits of Science in Legal Discourse - A Reply to Posner', **24** *Valparaiso University Law Review*, 1990, 175-181.

MANNE, Henry G., 'Intellectual Styles and the Evolution of American Corporation Law', in RADNITZKY, Gerard and BERNHOLZ, Peter (eds.), *Economic Imperialism: The Economic Approach Applied Outside the Field of Economics*, New York, Paragon House, 1987, 219-241.

MARKOVITS, Richard S., 'A Basic Structure for Microeconomic Policy Analysis in our Worse-Than-Second-Best World: A Proposal and Related Critique of the Chicago Approach to the Study of Law and Economics', *Wisconsin Law Review*, 1975, 950-1080.

MARKOVITS, Richard S., 'Duncan's Do Nots: Cost-Benefit Analysis and the Determination of Legal Entitlements', **36** *Stanford Law Review*, 1984, 1169 ff.

McCLOSKEY, Donald N., 'The Rhetoric of Law and Economics', **86** *Michigan Law Review*, 1988, 752-767.

McKENZIE, Richard B., 'On the Methodological Boundaries of Economic Analysis', **12** *Journal of Economic Issues*, 1978, 627-645.

MELTON, Gary B., 'Law, Science, and Humanity: The Normative Foundation of Social Science in Law', **14** *Law and Human Behavior*, 1990, 315-332.

MERCURO, Nicholas, 'Toward a Comparative Institutional Approach to the Study of Law and Economics', in MERCURO, Nicholas (ed.), *Law and Economics*, Boston, Kluwer Academic Publishers, 1989, 1-26.

MICHELMAN, F.J., 'Microeconomic Appraisal of Constitutional Law: A Methodological Preface', in RUBINFELD, Daniel (ed.), *Essays on the Law and Economics of Local Governments*, 1979.

MICHELMAN, Frank I., 'A Comment on Some Uses and Abuses of Economics in Law', **46** *University of Chicago Law Review*, 1979, 307-315.

MINDA, Gary, 'The Law and Economics and Critical Legal Studies Movement in American Law', in MERCURO, Nicholas (ed.), *Law and Economics*, Boston, Kluwer Academic Publishers, 1989, 87-122.

MINDA, Gary, 'The Jurisprudential Movements of the 1980s', **50** *Ohio State Law Journal*, 1989, 599-662.

MISHAN, Ezra J., 'The Folklore of the Market: An Inquiry into the Economic Doctrines of the Chicago School', in SAMUELS, Warren J. (ed.), *The Chicago School of Political Economy*, East Lansing, Division of Research, Graduate School of Business Administration, Michigan State University, 1976, 95-166.

MOORHOUSE, John C., 'The Mechanistic Foundations of Economic Analysis', **4** *Reason Papers*, 1978, 49-67.

NAGELKERKE, J.J., 'Beschouwingen over economische wetenschap en haar betekenis voor de rechtsvorming' [Considerations about Economic Science and its Use in the Formation of Law], *RMThemis*, 1979, 356-385.

NIEUWENHUIS, J.H., 'Blinddoek en balans in het milieurecht. Drie manieren om belangen af te wegen' [Blindfold and Balance in Environmental Law. Three Ways of Balacing Interests], in *Dilemma's van aansprakelijkheid*, Zwolle, Tjeenk Willink, 1991, 37-51. (Subject Code: 0300)

O'DRISCOLL, Gerald P., Jr. and RIZZO, Mario J., 'Subjectivism, Uncertainty, and Rules', in KIRZNER, Israel M. (ed.), *Subjectivism, Intelligibility and Economic Understanding. Essays in Honor of Ludwig M. Lachmann on his Eightieth Birthday*, London, Macmillan, 1986, 252-267.

OTT, Claus, 'Allokationseffizienz, Rechtsdogmatik und Rechtsprechung - die immanente ökonomische Rationalität des Zivilrechts' [Allocative Efficiency, Legal Dogmatics and Jurisprudence - The Implicit Economic Rationality of Civil Law], in OTT, Claus and SCHÄFER, Hans-Bernd (eds.), *Allokationseffizienz in der Rechtsordnung*, Berlin, Springer, 1989, 25-44.

OTT, Claus and SCHÄFER, Hans-Bernd, 'Die ökonomische Analyse des Rechts. Irrweg oder Chance wissenschaftlicher Rechtserkenntnis?' [The Economic Analysis of Law. Wrong Track or Chance for a Scientific Legal Knowledge?], *Juristenzeitung*, 1988, 213-223.

PARKMAN, A.M., 'The Multiplier in English Fatal Accident Cases: What Happens when Judges Teach Judges Economics', **5** *International Review of Law and Economics*, 1985, 187-197.

POLINSKY, A. Mitchell, 'Economic Analysis as a Potentially Defective Product: A Buyer's Guide to Posner's Economic Analysis of Law', **87** *Harvard Law Review*, 1974, 1655-1681.

POLLOCK, Stewart G., 'Economic Analysis at Work in Judicial Decision-Making', *Annual Survey of American Law*, 1988, 133-136.

POSNER, Richard A., 'Some Uses and Abuses of Economics in Law', **46** *University of Chicago Law Review*, 1979, 281-306.

POSNER, Richard A., 'The Law and Economics Movement', **77** *American Economic review (Papers and Proceedings)*, 1987, 1-13.

POSNER, Richard A., 'Conventionalism: The Key to Law as an Autonomous Discipline?', **38** *University of Toronto Law Journal*, 1988, 333-354.

POSNER, Richard A., 'Comment on Donohue', **22** *Law and Society Review*, 1988, 927-929.

POSNER, Richard A., 'The Future of Law and Economics: A Comment on Ellickson', **65** *Chicago-Kent Law Review*, 1989, 57-62.

POSNER, Richard A., 'Rebuttal to Malloy', **24** *Valparaiso University Law Review*, 1990, 183-184.

PRISCHING, Manfred, 'Ökonomische Rechtslehre? Über die Prämissen und Grenzen des "Economic Approach" im Recht' [Economic Jurisprudenz? On the Premisses and Limits of the Economic Approach to Law], in FREISITZER, Kurt, HOLZER, Hans Ludwig, MANTL, Wolfgang and HÖFLECHNER, Walter (eds.), *Reformen des Rechts. Festschrift zur 200-Jahr-Feier der Rechtswissenschaftlichen Fakultät der Universität Graz*, Graz, Akademische Druck u.Verlagsanstalt, 1979, 995-1020.

PRISCHING, Manfred, 'Über die Karriere einer Handlungstheorie. Der ökonomische Weg auf dem Weg durch die Sozialwissenschaften' [On the Career of a Behavioral Theory. The Economic Way on the way through the Social Sciences], **37** *Zeitschrift für philosophische Forschung*, 1983, 256 -274.

PRISCHING, Manfred, 'Regeln für das Handeln. Soziale Entscheidungsmechanismen im Modernisierungsprozeß' [Rules for Behavior. Social Decision Mechanisms in Modernization Process], **18** *Rechtstheorie. Zeitschrift für Logik, Methodenlehre, Kybernetik und Soziologie des Rechts*, 1987, Heft 2, 151-181.

PRYCHITKO, David L., 'Methodological Individualism and the Austrian School', **1** *Journal des Economistes et des Etudes Humaines*, 1989-1990, 171-179.

RAES, Koen, 'Onrechtmatige daad en de markt van pijn en smart' [Tort and the Market for Pain and Sorrow], *Recht en Kritiek*, 1988, 102-125.

RAES, Koen, 'Recht en neo-klassieke economie' [Law and Neo-classical Economics], **17** *Rechtsfilosofie en Rechtstheorie*, 1988, 29-30.

RAES, Koen, 'Het recht van de schaarste' [The Law of Scarcity], *Recht en kritiek*, 1990, 380-394.

RIZZO, Mario J., 'Uncertainty, Subjectivity and the Economic Analysis of Law', in RIZZO, Mario J. (ed.), *Time, Uncertainty and Disequilibrium*, Lexington, Lexington Books, 1979, 71-89.

RIZZO, Mario J., 'Law amid Flux: The Economics of Negligence and Strict Liability in Tort', **9** *Journal of Legal Studies*, 1980, 291-318.

RIZZO, Mario J., 'Can There Be a Principle of Explanation in Common Law Decisions? A Comment on Priest', **9** *Journal of Legal Studies*, 1980, 423-427.

RIZZO, Mario J., 'Rules versus Cost-Benefit Analysis in the Common Law', **4** *Cato Journal*, 1985, 865-884. Reprinted in DORN, James A. and MANNE, Henry G. (eds.), *Economic Liberties and the Judiciary*, Fairfax, George Mason University Press, 1987, 225-244.

ROBINSON, Glen O., 'Comment: Simplicity versus Complexity in the Law', **4** *Cato Journal*, 1985, 885-891. Reprinted in DORN, James A. and MANNE, Henry G. (eds.), *Economic Liberties and the Judiciary*, Fairfax, George Mason University Press, 1987, 249-255.

ROSE-ACKERMAN, Susan, 'Progressive Law and Economics - and the New Administrative Law', **98** *Yale Law Journal*, 1988, 341-368.

ROSE-ACKERMAN, Susan, 'Law and Economics: Paradigm, Politics, or Philosophy', in MERCURO, Nicholas (ed.), *Law and Economics*, Boston, Kluwer Academic Publishers, 1989, 233-258.

ROWLEY, Charles K., 'Social Sciences and the Law: The Relevance of Economic Theories', **1** *Oxford Journal of Legal Studies*, 1981, 1, 391-405.

ROWLEY, Charles K., 'Public Choice and the Economic Analysis of Law', in MERCURO, Nicholas (ed.), *Law and Economics*, Boston, Kluwer Academic Publishers, 1989, 123-173.

RUBIN, Paul H., 'Predictability and the Economic Approach to Law: A Comment on Rizzo', **9** *Journal of Legal Studies*, 1980, 319-334.

RUBIN, Paul H., 'Some Notes on Methodology in Law and Economics', **7** *Research* *in Law and Economics*, 1985, 29-39.

RUBINFELD, Daniel L., 'Econometrics in the Courtroom', **85** *Columbia Law Review*, 1985, 1048-1097.

SAMUELS, Warren J., 'The Chicago School of Political Economy: A Constructive Critique', in SAMUELS, Warren J. (ed.), *The Chicago School of Political Economy*, East Lansing, Division of Research, Graduate School of Business Administration, Michigan State University, 1976, 1-18.

SAMUELS, Warren J., 'Chicago Doctrine as Explanation and Justification', in SAMUELS, Warren J. (ed.), *The Chicago School of Political Economy*, East Lansing, Division of Research, Graduate School of Business Administration, Michigan State University, 1976, 363-396.

SAMUELS, Warren J., 'Further Limits to Chicago School Doctrine', in SAMUELS, Warren J. (ed.), *The Chicago School of Political Economy*, East Lansing, Division of Research, Graduate School of Business Administration, Michigan State University, 1976, 397-458.

SAMUELS, Warren J., 'Normative Premises in Regulatory Theory', **1** *Journal of Post Keynesian Economics*, 1978, 100-114. Reprinted in SAMUELS, Warren J. and SCHMID, A. Allen (eds.), *Law and Economics: An Institutional Perspective*, Boston, Nijhoff, 1981, 128-142.

SAMUELS, Warren J., 'Maximization of Wealth as Justice: An Essay on Posnerian Law and Economics as Policy Analysis', **60** *Texas Law Review*, 1981, 147-172.

SAMUELS, Warren J., 'Interrelations between Legal and Economic Processes', **14** *Journal of Law and Economics*, 1971, 435-450. Reprinted in SAMUELS, Warren J. and SCHMID, A. Allen (eds.), *Law and Economics: An Institutional Perspective*, Boston, Nijhoff, 1981, 95-110.

SAMUELS, Warren J., 'Ecosystem Policy and the Problem of Power', **2** *Environmental Affairs*, 1972, 580-596. Reprinted in SAMUELS, Warren J. and SCHMID, A. Allen (eds.), *Law and Economics: An Institutional Perspective*, Boston, Nijhoff, 1981, 111-127.

SAMUELS, Warren J., 'The Legal-Economic Nexus', **57** *George Washington Law Review*, 1989, 1556-1578.

SAMUELS, Warren J. and MERCURO, Nicholas, 'Posnerian Law and Economics on the Bench', **4** *International Review of Law and Economics*, 1984, 107-130.

SAMUELS, Warren J. and MERCURO, Nicholas, 'Wealth Maximization and Judicial Decision-Making: The Issues Further Clarified', **6** *International Review of Law and Economics*, 1986, 133-137.

SCHANZE, Erich, 'Rechtsnorm und ökonomisches Kalkül' [Legal Norm and Economic Calculus], **138** *Zeitschrift für die gesamte Staatswissenschaft*, 1982, 297-312.

SCHANZE, Erich, 'Potential and Limits of Economic Analysis: The Constitution of the Firm', in DAINTITH, Terence and TEUBNER, Gunther (eds.), *Contract and Organisation. Legal Analysis in the Light of Economic and Social Theory*, Berlin, Walter de Gruyter, 1986, 204-218.

SCHANZE, Erich, 'Research Perspectives of the Economic Approach to Institutions', in COLJEE, P.D., FRANKEN, H., HEERTJE, A. and KANNING, W. (eds.),

Law and Welfare - Op het Raakvlak van Economie en Recht, Amsterdam, 1991, 27-37.

SCHLAG, Pierre, 'The Problem of Transaction Costs', **62** *Southern California Law Review*, 1989, 1661-1699.

SCHMID, A. Allan, *Property, Power, and Public Choice: An Inquiry into Law and Economics*, Westport, Greenwood Press, 1987, 332 p.

SCHMID, A. Allan, 'Law and Economics: An Institutional Perspective', in MERCURO, Nicholas (ed.), *Law and Economics*, Boston, Kluwer Academic Publishers, 1989, 57-85.

SCHMIDTCHEN, Dieter, 'Jenseits von Maximierung, Gleichgewicht und Effizienz: Neuland für die ökonomische Analyse des Rechts?' [Beyond Maximization, Balance and Efficiency: New Land for the Economic Analysis of Law?], in OTT, Claus and SCHÄFER, Hans-Bernd (eds.), *Ökonomische Probleme des Zivilrechts*, Berlin, Springer, 1991, 316-343.

SCHWAB, Stewart J., 'Coase Defends Coase: Why Lawyers Listen and Economists Do Not', **87** *Michigan Law Review*, 1989, 1171-1198.

SCHWARTZ, Louis, 'On the Uses of Economics: A Review of the Antitrust Treatises (Book Reviews)', **128** *University of Pennsylvania Law Review*, 1979, 244 ff.

SCHWEITZER, Serge, 'De "l'ancienne" à la "nouvelle" économie: Comment passe-t-on d'un paradigme à l'autre' [From "Old" to "New" Economics: How One Goes From One Paradigm to Another], in *De "l'ancienne" à la "nouvelle" économie. Essais à l'occasion de la dixième université d'été de la nouvelle économie. Aix-en-Provence 1978-87*, Aix-en-Provence, Librairie de l'université, 1987, 257-274.

SCOTT, Kenneth E., 'Answers Are More Needed than Perspectives', **33** *Journal of Legal Education*, 1983, 285-287.

SEITA, Alex Y., 'Common Myths in the Economic Analysis of Law', *Brigham Young University Law Review*, 1989, 993-1112.

SHAVELL, Steven, *Economic Analysis of Accident Law*, Cambridge, Harvard University Press, 1987, 291-298 (ch.13).

SODERNAUM, Peter, 'Environmental Management: A Non-Traditional Approach', **21** *Journal of Economic Issues*, 1987, 139-165.

SPROULE-JONES, Mark (ed.), *Methodological Individualism and Public Choice*, London, Sage, 1984. Reprinted from **28** *American Behavioral Scientist*, 1984, 163-287.

STIGLER, George J., 'The Nature and Originality in Scientific Progress', **22** *Economica*, 1955, 1-15.

STIGLER, George J., 'The Law and Economics of Public Policy: A Plea to the Scholars', **1** *Journal of Legal Studies*, 1972, 1-12.

STIGLER, George J., 'What Does an Economist Know?', **33** *Journal of Legal Education*, 1983, 311-313.

STOLJAR, Samuel, 'Comment', in CRANSTON, Ross and SCHICK, Anne (eds.), *Law and Economics*, Canberra, Australian National University, 1982, 99-104.

STRASSER, Kurt A., BARD, Robert L. and ARTHUR, H. Thomas, 'A Reader's Guide to the Uses and Limits of Economic Analysis with Emphasis on

Corporation Law', **33** *Mercer Law Review*, 1982, 571-593.

SYMPOSIUM : 'The Crisis in Legal Theory and the Revival of Classical Jurisprudence', **73** *Cornell Law Review*, 1988, 281-446.

TREBILCOCK, Michael J. and HARTLE, D.G., 'The Choice of Governing Instrument', **2** *International Review of Law and Economics*, 1982, 29-46.

TRIBE, Laurence H., 'Trial by Mathematics Precision and Ritual in the Legal Process', **84** *Harvard Law Review*, 1971, 1329-1393.

TRIBE, Laurence H., 'Technology Assessment and the Fourth Discontinuity: The Limits of Instrumental Rationality', **46** *Southern California Law Review*, 1973, 617-660.

TULLOCK, Gordon, 'Economic Imperialism', in BUCHANAN, James M. and TOLLISON, Robert D. (eds.), *Theory of Public Choice: Political Applications of Economics*, Ann Arbor, University of Michigan Press, 1973.

TULLOCK, Gordon, 'Wanted: New Public-Choice Theories', In ANDERSON, Martin J. (ed.), *The Unfinished Agenda: Essays on the Political Economy of Government Policy in honour of Arthur Seldon*, London, I.E.A., 1986, 13-27.

TURK, Jeremy, 'Power, Efficiency and Institutions: Some Implications of the Debate for the Scope of Economics', in FRANCIS, Arthur, et al. (eds.), *Power, Efficiency and Institutions*, London, Heinemann, 1983, 189-204.

ULEN, Thomas S., 'Law and Economics: Settled Issues and Open Questions', in MERCURO, Nicholas (ed.), *Law and Economics*, Boston, Kluwer Academic Publishers, 1989, 201-231.

ULVAN DEN BERGH, Roger and HEREMANS, Dirk, 'Recht en economie' [Law and Economics], **32** *Tijdschrift voor Economie en Management*, 1987, 139-164.

VAN DEN BERGH, Roger and HEREMANS, Dirk, 'Over krommen en rechten. Een reactie op de kritiek van Kruithof ten aanzien van de economische analyse van het recht' [On Curves and Lines: A Reaction on the Critique of Kruithof on Economic Analysis of Law], **50** *Rechtskundig Weekblad*, 1986-87, 1649-1668.

VAN DUN, Frank, 'Economics and the Limits of Value-Free Science', **11** *Reason Papers*, 1986, 17-32.

VANBUGGENHOUT, Willy, 'De economische benadering van het recht. Haar nut en grenzen voor de praktijk(bedrijfs)jurist' [The Economic Approach of Law: Its Use and Limits for a (Company) Lawyer], *Vlaamse Jurist Vandaag*, 1987, Nr.1, 27-30.

VELJANOVSKI, Cento G., *The New Law-and-Economics. A Research Review*, Oxford, Centre for Socio-Legal Studies, 1982, 169 p.

VELJANOVSKI, Cento G., 'Economic Theorizing about Tort', *Current Legal Problems*, 1985, 117-140.

WALD, Patricia M., 'Limits on the Use of Economic Analysis in Judicial Decisionmaking', **50(4)** *Law and Contemporary Problems*, 1987, 225-244.

WALZ, W. Rainer and WIENSTROH, Claas, 'Die Fehlgeschlagene Investition' [The Case of the Investment Failure], in WALZ, W. Rainer and RASCHER-FRIESENHAUSEN, Heinrich (eds.), *Sozialwissenschaften im Zivilrecht: Fälle und Lösungen in Ausbildung und Prüfung*, Neuwied, Luchterhand, 1983, 52-75.

WEIGEL, Wolfgang, 'Ökonomie und Recht - Eine Einführung' [Economics and Law -

An Introduction], **31(3/4)** *Das öffentliche Haushaltswesen in Österreich*, 1990, 169-198.

WHICHARD, Willis P., 'A Common Law Judge's View of the Appropriate Use of Economics in Common Law Adjudication', **50(4)** *Law and Contemporary Problems*, 1987, 253-263.

WHITE, Barbara, 'Coase and the Courts: Economics for the Common Man.' **72** *Iowa Law Review*, 1987, 577-635..

WILBER, Charles K. and WISMAN, Jon D., 'The Chicago School: Positivism or Ideal Type', in SAMUELS, Warren J. (ed.), *The Chicago School of Political Economy*, East Lansing, Michigan State University, 1976, 79-94.

WILLIAMSON, Oliver E., 'Intellectual Foundations of Law and Economics: The Need for a Broader View', **33** *Journal of Legal Education*, 1983, 210-216.

WILLIAMSON, Oliver E., 'A Comparison of Alternative Approaches to Economic Organization', **146** *Journal of Institutional and Theoretical Economics*, 1990, 61-71.

WILLIAMSON, Oliver E. and OUCHI, William G., 'The Markets and Hierarchies Programme of Research: Origins, Implications, Prospects', in FRANCIS, Arthur, et al. (eds.), *Power, Efficiency and Institutions*, London, Heinemann, 1983, 13-34.

WLADIMIROFF, M., 'Rechtseconomie en strafrecht: enige kritische kanttekeningen' [Law-and-Economics and Criminal Law: Some Critical Remarks], in *Rechtseconomie en Recht*, Tjeenk Willink, Zwolle, 1991, 181-186.

WONNELL, Christopher T., 'Contract Law and the Austrian School of Economics', **54** *Fordham Law Review*, 1986, 507-543.

X, 'Note: Efficiency and the Rule of "Free Contract": A Critique of Two Models of Law and Economics', **97** *Harvard Law Review*, 1984, 978-996.

ZEISEL, Hans, 'Reflections on Experimental Techniques in the Law', **2** *Journal of Legal Studies*, 1973, 107-124.

0400 Norms and Values in Law & Economics

ADAMS, Michael, 'Ist die Ökonomie eine imperialistische Wissenschaft? Über Nutz und Frommen der Ökonomische Analyse des Rechts' [Is Economics an Imperialistic Science? On the Utility of Economic Analysis of Law], in *Juristische Ausbildung*, 1984 (Heft 7), 337-349.

ARMENTANO, Dominick T., 'Comment: Efficiency, Liberty, and Antitrust Policy', in DORN, James A. and MANNE, Henry G. (eds.), *Economic Liberties and the Judiciary*, Fairfax, George Mason University Press, 1987, 309-316.

ARUP, Christopher, 'Accounting for the Social Costs of Technology Through the Legal Process', in CRANSTON, Ross and SCHICK, Anne (eds.), *Law and Economics*, Canberra, Australian National University, 1982, 25-38.

AULT, David E. and RUTMAN, Gilbert L., 'Comment on Bilmes' Paper', **7** *Research in Law and Economics*, 1985, 149-156.

BAKER, C. Edwin, 'Utility and Rights: Two Justifications for State Action Increasing Inequality', **84** *Yale Law Journal*, 1974, 39-59.

BAKER, C. Edwin, 'The Ideology of the Economic Analysis of Law', **5** *Philosophy and Public Affairs*, 1975, 3-48. Reprinted in KRONMAN, Anthony T. and POSNER, Richard A. (eds.), *The Economics of Contract Law*, Boston, Little Brown, 1979, 233-239.

BAKER, C. Edwin, 'Starting Points in the Economic Analysis of Law', **8** *Hofstra Law Review*, 1980, 939-972.

BANDOW, Doug, 'The Conservative Judicial Agenda: A Critique', in DORN, James A. and MANNE, Henry G. (eds.), *Economic Liberties and the Judiciary*, Fairfax, George Mason University Press, 1987, 257-271.

BEBCHUK, Lucian Arye, 'The Pursuit of a Bigger Pie: Can Everyone Expect a Bigger Slice?', **8** *Hofstra Law Review*, 1980, 671-709.

BILMES, Jack, 'Freedom and Regulation: An Anthropological Critique of Free Market Ideology', **7** *Research in Law and Economics*, 1985, 123-147.

BILMES, Jack, 'Rejoinder to Ault and Rutman's Comment', **7** *Research in Law and Economics*, 1985, 157-158.

BLOUSTEIN, E.J., 'Privacy is Dear at any Price: A Response to Professor Posner's Economic Theory', **12** *Georgia Law Review*, 1978, 421-495.

BLUM, Walter J. and KALVEN, Harry, Jr., 'The Empty Cabinet of Dr. Calabresi: Auto Accidents and General Deterrence', **34** *University of Chicago Law Review*, 1967, 239-273. Reprinted in RABIN, Robert L. (ed.), *Perspectives on Tort Law*, Boston, Little Brown, 1983, 178-190.

BOUCKAERT, Boudewijn, 'Efficiëntie of rechtvaardigheid: het onvermijdelijk dilemma?' [Efficiency or Justice: the Unavoidable Dilemma?], **29** *Tijdschrift voor Sociale Wetenschappen*, 1984, 101-133.

BOVENS, M.A.P. and WITTEVEEN, W.J., 'Bruce Ackerman over sociale rechtvaardigheid, de rol van de rechter en "Law and Economics"' [Bruce Ackerman on Social Justice, the Role of the Judiciary and "Law and Economics"] (interview), *Staatkundig Jaarboek*, Nijmegen, Ars Aequi Libri, 1987, 255-278.

BRENNAN, Geoffrey and BUCHANAN, James M., 'The Normative Purpose of

Economic 'Science': Rediscovery of an Eighteenth Century Method', **1** *International Review of Law and Economics*, 1981, 155-166.

BRENNAN, Geoffrey and BUCHANAN, James M., 'Is Public Choice Immoral? The Case for the 'Nobel' Lie', **74** *Virginia Law Review*, 1988, 179-189.

BREYER, Stephen G., 'Economics and Judging: An Afterword on Cooter and Wald', **50(4)** *Law and Contemporary Problems*, 1987, 245-252.

BROMLEY, Daniel W., 'The Ideology of Efficiency: Searching for a Theory of Policy Analysis', **19** *Journal of Environmental Economics and Management*, 1990, 86-107.

BUCHANAN, James M., 'The Relevance of Pareto Optimality', **6** *Journal of Conflict Resolution*, 1962, 341-354.

CALABRESI, Guido, 'An Exchange about Law and Economics: A Letter to Ronald Dworkin', **8** *Hofstra Law Review*, 1980, 553-562.

CASS, Ronald A., 'Coping With Life, Law, and Markets: A Comment on Posner and the Law-and-Economics Debate', **67** *Boston University Law Review*, 1987, 73-97.

CENTI, Jean-Pierre, 'Quel critère d'efficience pour l'analyse économique du droit' [Which Efficiency Criterion for Economic Analysis of Law], *Revue de la Recherche Juridique*, 1987, Nr. 2.

COHEN, Jane Maslow, 'Posnerism, Pluralism, Pessimism', **67** *Boston University Law Review*, 1987, 105-175.

COLEMAN, James S., 'Norms as Social Capital', in RADNITZKY, Gerard and BERNHOLZ, Peter (eds.), *Economic Imperialism*, New York, Paragon House, 1987, 133-155.

COLEMAN, Jules L., 'Efficiency, Exchange and Auction: Philosophic Aspects of the Economic Approach to Law', **68** *California Law Review*, 1980, 221-249.

COLEMAN, Jules L., 'Efficiency, Utility, and Wealth Maximization', **8** *Hofstra Law Review*, 1980, 509-552.

COLEMAN, Jules L., 'The Economic Analysis of Law', in PENNOCK, J. Roland and CHAPMAN, John W. (eds.), *Nomos XXIV: Ethics, Economics and the Law*, New York, New York University Press, 1982, 83-103.

COLEMAN, Jules L., 'Corrective Justice and Wrongful Gain', **11** *Journal of Legal Studies*, 1982, 421-440.

COLEMAN, Jules L., 'Economics and the Law: A Critical Review of the Foundations of the Economic Approach to Law', **94** *Ethics*, 1984, 649-679.

COLEMAN, Jules L., *Markets, Morals and the Law*, Cambridge, Cambridge University Press, 1988, 393 p.

COMMONS, John R., 'The Problem of Correlating Law, Economics and Ethics', **8** *Wisconsin Law Review*, 1932, 3-26.

COOTER, Robert D., 'Liberty, Efficiency, and Law', **50 (4)** *Law and Contemporary Problems*, 1987, 141-163.

COOTER, Robert D., 'Torts as the Union of Liberty and Efficiency: An Essay on Causation', **63** *Chicago-Kent Law Review*, 1987, 523-551.

COOTER, Robert D., 'The Best Right Laws: Value Foundations of the Economic

Analysis of Law', **64** *Notre Dame Law Review*, 1989, 817-837.

COSENTINO, Fabrizio, 'Autonomia privata e paternalismo del legislatore nella prospettiva dell'analisi economica del diritto' [Individual Autonomy and the Paternalism of the Legislator: An EAL Perspective], *Riv. critica dir. priv.*, 1988, 473-511.

DE GEEST, Gerrit, 'Public Choice, mensbeeld en ideologie' [Public Choice, Model of Man and Ideology], **19** *Rechtsfilosofie en Rechtstheorie*, 1990, 109-122.

DEMSETZ, Harold, 'Ethics and Efficiency in Property Rights Systems', in RIZZO, Mario J. (ed.), *Time, Uncertainty and Disequilibrium*, Lexington, Lexington Books, 1979, 97-116.

DEMSETZ, Harold, 'Professor Michelman's Unnecessary and Futile Search for the Philosopher's Touchstone', **24** *NOMOS*, 1982, 41-47.

DOBBS, I., 'Externality, Efficiency and the Pareto Principle', **1** *International Review of Law and Economics*, 1981, 167-181.

DONOHUE, John J. III, 'Law and Economics: The Road not Taken', **22** *Law & Society Review*, 1988, 903-926.

DWORKIN, Ronald M., 'Why Efficiency?', **8** *Hofstra Law Review*, 1980, 563-590. Reprinted in DWORKIN, Ronald M., *A Matter of Principle*, Oxford, Clarendon, 1986, 267-289.

DWORKIN, Ronald M., 'Is Wealth a Value?', **9** *Journal of Legal Studies*, 1980, 191-226. Reprinted in DWORKIN, Ronald M., *A Matter of Principle*, Oxford, Clarendon, 1986, 237-266.

EGGER, J.B., 'Efficiency Is Not a Substitute for Ethics', in RIZZO, Mario J. (ed.) *Time, Uncertainty and Disequilibrium*, Heath, Lexington, 1979, 117-125.

EHRLICH, Isaac, 'On Positive Methodology, Ethics, and Polemics in Deterrence Research', **22** *British Journal of Criminology*, 1982, 124-139.

ENGLARD, Izhak, 'The Failure of Economic Justice', **45** *Harvard Law Review*, 1982, 1162-1178.

ESCHENBURG, Rolf, 'Vertragstheoretisches Denken in der Ökonomie' [Contractual Theory in Economics], **23** *Hamburger Jahrbuch zur Wirtschafts- und Gesellschaftspolitik*, 1978, 221-236.

FARBER, Daniel A., 'Review Essay: Environmentalism, Economics and the Public Interest', **41** *Stanford Law Review*, 1989, 1021-1043.

FEINMAN, Jay M., 'Practical Legal Studies and Critical Legal Studies', **87** *Michigan Law Review*, 1988, 724-731.

FLETCHER, George P., 'Fairness and Utility in Tort Theory', **85** *Harvard Law Review*, 1972, 537-573. Reprinted in RABIN, Robert L. (ed.), *Perspectives on Tort Law*, Boston, Little Brown, 1983, 239-255.

FLETCHER, George P., 'Why Kant', **87** *Columbia Law Review*, 1987, 421-432.

FREEMAN, Donald, 'Value Maximization and Welfare Theory', **10** *Journal of Legal Studies*, 1981, 409-419.

FRIEDMAN, Lawrence M., 'Two Faces of Law', *Wisconsin Law Review*, 1984, 13-35.

GORDON, S., *Welfare, Justice and Freedom*, New York, 1980.

GRANT, Robin F., 'Judge Richard Posner's Wealth Maximization Principle: Another Form of Utilitarianism?', **10** *Cardozo Law Review*, 1989, 815-845.

GUEST, Stephen F.D., 'Utilitarianism, Economics and the Common Law', **5** *Otago Law Review*, 1984, 656-663.

HAMMOND, 'The Economics of Justice and the Criterion of Wealth Maximization' (Book Review), **91** *Yale Law Journal*, 1982, 1493-1507.

HANAK, András, 'Neoklasszicista Justitia' [Neo-classicist Justitia], **12** *Jogtudományi Közlöny*, 1979, 855-859.

HARSANYI, John C., 'Morality and the Theory of Rational Behaviour', **44** *Social Research*, 1977.

HEERTJE, A., 'Conflictstof voor juristen en economen' [Conflict Material for Lawyers and Economists], **15** *Ars Aequi*, 1966, 14-16.

HEERTJE, A., 'Conflictstof voor juristen en economen' [Conflict Material for Lawyers and Economists], **15** *Ars Aequi*, 1966, 14-16.

HELLER, Thomas C., 'The Importance of Normative Decisionmaking: The Limitations of Legal Economics as a Basis for a Liberal Jurisprudence', *Wisconsin Law Review*, 1976, 385-502.

HOL, A.M., 'Efficiëntie als instrument en als norm. Enkele rechtstheoretische kanttekeningen bij de economische analyse van het recht' [Efficiency as Instrument and Norm: Some Remarks from Legal Theory on the Economic Analysis of Law], **39(10)** *Ars Aequi*, 1990, 632-644.

HOL, A.M., 'Rechten en doeleinden. Enkele morele aspecten van juridische aansprakelijkheid' [Rights and Goals. Some Moral Aspects of Legal Liability], in *Dilemma's van aansprakelijkheid*, Zwolle, Tjeenk Willink, 1991, 127-142. (Subject Code: 0400)

HORWITZ, Morton J., 'Law and Economics: Science or Politics?', **8** *Hofstra Law Review*, 1980, 905-912.

HOVENKAMP, Herbert, 'Legal Policy and the Endowment Effect', **20** *Journal of Legal Studies*, 1991, 225-247.

JOHNSEN, D. Bruce, 'Wealth Is Value', **15** *Journal of Legal Studies*, 1986, 263-288.

KEENAN, Donald, 'Value Maximization and Welfare Theory', **10** *Journal of Legal Studies*, 1981, 409-419.

KELMAN, Mark, 'Consumption Theory, Production Theory and Ideology in the Coase Theorem', **52** *Southern California Law Review*, 1979, 669-698.

KELMAN, Mark, 'Choice and Utility', *Wisconsin Law Review*, 1979, 769-797.

KELMAN, Mark G., 'Misunderstanding Social Life: A Critique of the Core Premises of "Law and Economics"', **33** *Journal of Legal Education*, 1983, 274-284.

KELMAN, Mark, 'The Necessary Myth of Objective Causation Judgments in Liberal Political Theory', **63** *Chicago-Kent Law Review*, 1987, 579-637.

KENNEDY, Duncan, 'Form and Substance in Private Law Adjudication', **89** *Harvard Law Review*, 1976, 1685-1778. Reprinted in KRONMAN, Anthony T. and POSNER, Richard A. (eds.), *The Economics of Contract Law*, Boston, Little Brown, 1979, 100-107.

KENNEDY, Duncan, 'Cost-Benefit of Entitlement Problems: A Critique', **33** *Stanford Law Review*, 1981, 387-445.

KORNHAUSER, Lewis A., 'A Guide to the Perplexed Claims of Efficiency in the Law', **8** *Hofstra Law Review*, 1980, 591-639.

KRONMAN, Anthony T., 'Wealth Maximization as a Normative Principle', **9** *Journal of Legal Studies*, 1980, 227-242.

LEE, Dwight R., 'Politics, Ideology, and the Power of Public Choice', **74** *Virginia Law Review*, 1988, 191-198.

MALLOY, Robin Paul, 'Equating Human Rights and Property Rights - The Need for Moral Judgment in an Economic Analysis of Law and Social Policy', **47** *Ohio State Law Journal*, 1986, 163-177.

MALLOY, Robin Paul, 'The Invisible Hand or the Sleight of Hand? Adam Smith, Richard Posner and the Philosophy of Law and Economics', **36** *University of Kansas Law Review*, 1988, 209 ff.

MALLOY, Robin Paul, 'The Merits of the Smithian Critique: A Final Word on Smith and Posner', **36** *University of Kansas Law Review*, 1988, 266-274.

MALLOY, Robin Paul, 'Market Philosophy in the Legal Tension Between Children's Autonomy and Parental Authority', **21** *Ind. Law Review*, 1988, 889 ff.

MALLOY, Robin Paul, 'Is Law and Economics Moral? - Humanistic Economics and a Classical Liberal Critique of Posner's Economic Analysis', **24** *Valparaiso University Law Review*, 1990, 147-161.

MALLOY, Robin Paul, 'The Limits of Science in Legal Discourse - A Reply to Posner', **24** *Valparaiso University Law Review*, 1990, 175-181.

MARKOVITS, Richard S., 'Legal Analysis and the Economic Analysis of Allocative Efficiency: A Response to Professor Posner's Reply', **11** *Hofstra Law Review*, 1983, 667-689.

MICHELMAN, Frank I., 'Property, Utility and Fairness: Comments on the Ethical Foundations of "Just Compensation" Law', **80** *Harvard Law Review*, 1967, 1165-1258. Reprinted in ACKERMAN, Bruce A., *Economic Foundations of Property a Law*, Boston, Little Brown, 1975, 100 ff.

MICHELMAN, Frank I., 'Norms and Normativity in the Economic Theory of Law', **62** *Minnesota Law Review*, 1978, 1015-1048.

MICHELMAN, Frank I., 'A Comment on Some Uses and Abuses of Economics in Law', **46** *University of Chicago Law Review*, 1979, 307-315.

MICHELMAN, Frank I., 'Ethics, Economics, and the Law of Property', in PENNOCK, J. Roland and CHAPMAN, John W. (eds.), *Nomos XXIV: Ethics, Economics and the Law*, New York, New York University Press, 1982, 3-40.

MILLER, Edythe S., 'Economic Efficiency, thc Economics Discipline, and the "Affccted-with-a-Public-Interest" Concept', **24** *Journal of Economic Issues*, 1990, 719-732.

MILLER, Jeremy M., 'Economic Analysis of Legal Method and Law: The Danger in Valueless Values', **21** *Gonzaga Law Review*, 1985-86, 425-455.

NG, Yew Kwang, 'Economic Efficiency versus Egalitarian Rights', **41** *Kyklos*, 1988, 215-237.

NIEUWENHUIS, J.H., 'Recht en belang' [Law and Interests], *Flores Debitorem*,

Zwolle, Tjeenk Willink, 1984, 65-74.

NIEUWENHUIS, J.H., 'Ieder het zijne' [Each His Own], *RMThemis*, 1988, Nr.2, 73-84.

NUTTER, Warren G., 'Economic Welfare and Welfare Economics', **2** *Journal of Economic Issues*, 1968, 166-172.

O'DRISCOLL, Gerald P., Jr., 'Justice, Efficiency, and the Economic Analysis of Law: A Comment on Fried', **9** *Journal of Legal Studies*, 1980, 355-366.

OGUS, Anthony I., 'Economics, Liberty and the Common Law', **18** *Journal of Society of Public Teachers of Law*, 1980, 42-57.

PENNOCK, J. Roland and CHAPMAN, John W., (eds.), *Ethics, Economics and the Law*, (NOMOS 24), New York, New York University Press, 1982, 323 p.

POSNER, Richard A., 'Utilitarianism, Economics, and Legal Theory', **8** *Journal of Legal Studies*, 1979, 103-140.

POSNER, Richard A., 'Some Uses and Abuses of Economics in Law', **46** *University of Chicago Law Review*, 1979, 281-306.

POSNER, Richard A., 'The Value of Wealth: A Comment on Dworkin and Kronman', **9** *Journal of Legal Studies*, 1980, 243-252.

POSNER, Richard A., 'The Ethical and Political Basis of the Efficiency Norm in Common Law Adjudication', **8** *Hofstra Law Review*, 1980, 487-507.

POSNER, Richard A., *The Economics of Justice*, Cambridge (Mass.), Harvard University Press, 1981, 415 p.

POSNER, Richard A., 'The Concept of Corrective Justice in Recent Theories of Tort Law', **10** *Journal of Legal Studies*, 1981, 187-206.

POSNER, Richard A., 'Wealth Maximization and Judicial Decision-Making', **4** *International Review of Law and Economics*, 1984, 131-135.

POSNER, Richard A., 'Wealth Maximization Revisited', **2** *Notre Dame Journal of Law, Ethics and Public Policy*, 1985, 1378-1401.

POSNER, Richard A., 'The Ethical Significance of Free Choice: A Reply to Professor West', **99** *Harvard Law Review*, 1986, 1431-1448.

POSNER, Richard A., 'Comment on Donohue', **22** *Law and Society Review*, 1988, 927-929.

POSNER, Richard A., 'On Theory and Practice: Reply to "Richard Posner's *Praxis*"' **49** *Ohio State Law Journal*, 1989, 1077-1084.

POSNER, Richard A., 'Law and Economics *is* Moral', **24** *Valparaiso University Law Review*, 1990, 163-173.

POSNER, Richard A., 'Rebuttal to Malloy', **24** *Valparaiso University Law Review*, 1990, 183-184.

RADIN, Margaret Jane, 'Market-Inalienability', **100** *Harvard Law Review*, 1987, 1849-1937.

RAHMSDORF, Detlev W., 'Ökonomische Analyse des Rechts, Utilitarismus und die klassische deutsche Philosophie' [Economic Analysis of Law, Utilitarianism and the Classical German Philosophy], in *Rechtstheorie*, 1987, Heft 4, 487-501.

RAHMSDORF, Detlev W. and SCHÄFER, Hans-Bernd (eds.), *Ethische Fragen der*

Wirtschaftspolitik und des Rechts [Ethical Questions of Political Economics and Law], Berlin, Dietrich-Reimer-Verlag, 1988, 219 p.

RAITERI, Monica, 'Giustizia distributiva e funzione giudiziaria: qualche osservazione nella prospettiva della analisi economica del diritto' [Distributive Justice and the Judicial Function, Some Observations in an EAL Perspective], *Materiali storia cultura giur.*, 1988, 209-228.

RIZZO, Mario J., 'The Mirage of Efficiency', **8** *Hofstra Law Review*, 1980, 641-658.

ROSE-ACKERMAN, Susan, 'Law and Economics: Paradigm, Politics, or Philosophy', in MERCURO, Nicholas (ed.), *Law and Economics*, Boston, Kluwer Academic Publishers, 1989, 233-258.

SAGER, Lawrence G., 'Pareto Superiority, Consent, and Justice', **8** *Hofstra Law Review*, 1980, 913-937.

SAMUELS, Warren J., 'Maximization of Wealth as Justice: An Essay on Posnerian Law and Economics as Policy Analysis', **60** *Texas Law Review*, 1981, 147-172.

SCHÄFER, Hans-Bernd, 'Allokationseffizienz als Grundprinzip des Zivilrechts' [Allocative Efficiency as Basic Principle of Civil Law], in OTT, Claus and SCHÄFER, Hans-Bernd (eds.), *Allokationseffizienz in der Rechtsordnung*, Berlin, Springer, 1989, 1-24.

SCHLAG, Pierre, 'An Appreciative Comment on Coase's The Problem of Social Cost: A View from the Left', *Wisconsin Law Review*, 1986, 919-962.

SCHMALBECK, Richard, 'The Justice of Economics: An Analysis of Wealth Maximization as a Normative Goal', **83** *Columbia Law Review*, 1983, 488-525.

SCHWARTZ, Gary T., 'Economics, Wealth Distribution and Justice', *Wisconsin Law Review*, 1979, 799-813.

SCHWARTZ, Gary T., 'The Vitality of Negligence and the Ethics of Strict Liability', **15** *Georgia Law Review*, 1981, 963-1005. Reprinted in RABIN, Robert L. (ed.), *Perspectives on Tort Law*, Boston, Little Brown, 1983, 71-79.

SEITA, Alex Y., 'Common Myths in the Economic Analysis of Law', *Brigham Young University Law Review*, 1989, 993-1112.

SPITZER, Matthew L. and HOFFMAN, Elizabeth, 'A Reply to Consumption Theory, Production Theory and Ideology in the Coase Theorem', **53** *Southern California Law Review*, 1980, 1187-1223.

STEINER, J.M., 'Economics, Morality and the Law of Torts', **26** *University of Toronto Law Journal*, 1976, 227-252.

STROWEL, Alain, 'Utilitarisme et approche économique dans la théorie du droit. Autour de Bentham et de Posner' [Utilitarianism and Economic Approach in Legal Theory. On Bentham and Posner], **18** *Revue Interdisciplinaire d'Etudes Juridiques*, 1987, 1-45.

SYMPOSIUM : 'Symposium on Efficiency as a Legal Concern', **8** *Hofstra Law Review*, 1980, 485-972.

THUROW, L., 'Equity vs. Efficiency in Law Enforcement', **18** *Public Policy*, 1970, 451-459.

TRIBE, Laurence H., 'Constitutional Calculus: Equal Justice or Economic Efficiency', **98** *Harvard Law Review*, 1985, 592-621.

TRIMARCHI, Pietro, 'Sul significato economico dei criteri di responsabilità contrattuale' [On the economic significance of the Criterions for Contractual Liability], *Rivista trimestriale di diritto e procedura civile*, 1970, 512 ff. (Subject Code: 4400)

TULLOCK, Gordon, 'Two Kinds of Legal Efficiency', **8** *Hofstra Law Review*, 1980, 659 ff.

TULLOCK, Gordon, 'Welfare and the Law', **2** *International Review of Law and Economics*, 1982, 151-163.

VARAT, Jonathan D., 'Review Essay: Economic Ideology and the Federal Judicial Task (Review of The Federal Courts: Crisis and Reform by Richard A. Posner), **74** *California Law Review*, 1986, 649-674.

VELJANOVSKI, Cento G., 'Wealth Maximization, Law and Ethics - On the Limits of Economic Efficiency', **1** *International Review of Law and Economics*, 1981, 5-28.

VELJANOVSKI, Cento G., 'The Economic Theory of Tort Liability - Toward a Corrective Justice Approach', in BURROWS, Paul and VELJANOVSKI, Cento G. (eds.), *The Economic Approach to Law*, London, Butterworths, 1981, 125-150.

WALDRON, Jeremy, 'Criticizing the Economic Analysis of Law (Book Review of Jules L. Coleman, Markets, Morals, and the Law)', **99** *Yale Law Journal*, 1990, 1441-1471.

WEINRIB, Ernest J., 'Utilitarianism, Economics and Legal Theory', **30** *University of Toronto Law Journal*, 1980, 307-332.

WHITE, Barbara, 'Coase and the Courts: Economics for the Common Man.' **72** *Iowa Law Review*, 1987, 577-635..

WHITE, James Boyd, 'Economics and Law: Two Cultures in Tension' (Alumni Distinguished Lecture in Jurisprudence), **54** *Tennessee Law Review*, 1987, 161-202.

ZWIER, Paul J., 'The Consequentialist/Nonconsequentialist Ethical Distinction: A Tool for the Formal Appraisal of Traditional Negligence and Economic Tort Analysis', **26** *Boston College Law Review*, 1985, 905-944.

0500 History of Thought

BACKHAUS, Jürgen G., 'Pareto on Public Choice', **33** *Public Choice*, 1978, 5-17.

BAIRD, Charles W., 'James Buchanan and the Austrians: The Common Ground', **9** *Cato Journal*, 1989, 201 ff.

BARNETT, Randy E., 'Foreword: Chicago Law and Economics', **65** *Chicago-Kent Law Review*, 1989, 3 ff.

BARRY, Norman P., 'The 'Austrian' Perspective', in WHYNES, David K. (ed.), *What Is Political Economy?*, Blackwell, New York, 1984, 33-58.

BITTLINGMAYER, George, 'Chicago Credo', **143** *Journal of Institutional and Theoretical Economics*, 1987, 658-667.

BOOIJ, H., 'Nieuwe institutionele economie' [Neo-Institutional Economics], *Van alle markten thuis. Opstellen aangeboden aan J.R. Zuidema*, Universitaire Pers, Rotterdam, 1987, 90-96.

BREMS, Hans, 'Marshall on Mathematics', **18** *Journal of Law and Economics*, 1975, 583-585.

COASE, Ronald H., 'Marshall on Method', **18** *Journal of Law and Economics*, 1975, 25-31.

COASE, Ronald H., 'The New Institutional Economics ', **140** *Journal of Institutional and Theoretical Economics*, 1984, 229-232.

DEVINE, Donald J., 'Adam Smith and the Problem of Justice in Capitalist Society', **6** *Journal of Legal Studies*, 1977, 399-409.

DUGGER, William M., 'The Transaction Cost Analysis of O.E. Williamson: A New Synthesis?', **17** *Journal of Economic Issues*, 1983, 95-114.

DUGGER, William M., 'A Research Agenda for Institutional Economics', **22** *Journal of Economic Issues*, 1988, 983-1002.

DUGGER, William M., 'The New Institutionalism: New But Not Institutonalist', **24** *Journal of Economic Issues*, 1990, 423-431

DUXBURY, Neil, 'Is There a Dissenting Tradition in Law and Economics?', **54** *Modern Law Review*, 1990, 300-311.

EGGERTSSON, Thrainn, 'The Role of Transaction Costs and Property Rights in Economic Analysis', **34** *European Economic Review*, 1990, 450-457.

ELLIOT, John E., 'The Institutionalist School of Political Economy', in WHYNES, David K. (ed.) *What Is Political Economy? Eight Perspectives*, New York, Blackwell, New 1984, 59-89.

FURUBOTN, Eirik G., 'Different Approaches to the Economic Analysis of Institutions: Some Concluding Remarks', **146** *Journal of Institutional and Theoretical Economics*, 1990, 226-232.

GOLDBERG, Victor P., 'Commons Clark, and the Emerging Post-Coasian Law-and-Economics', **10** *Journal of Economic Issues*, 1976, 877-893.

GOLDBERG, Victor P., 'Production Functions, Transaction Costs and the New Institutionalism', in FEIWEL, George (ed.), *Issues in Contemporary Microeconomics*, New York, Macmillan, 1984, 395-402. Reprinted in GOLDBERG, Victor P. (ed.), *Readings in the Economics of Contract Law*,

Cambridge, Cambridge University Press, 1989, 21-23.

GONCE, R.A., 'The New Property Rights Approach and Commons' Legal Foundations of Capitalism', **10** *Journal of Economic Issues*, 1976, 765-769.

GRANT, Robin F., 'Judge Richard Posner's Wealth Maximization Principle: Another Form of Utilitarianism?', **10** *Cardozo Law Review*, 1989, 815-845.

GRUCHY, A.G. 'Three Different Approaches to Institutional Economics: An Evaluation', **24** *Journal of Economic Issues*, 1990, 361-369.

HUTTER, Michael, 'Early Contributions to Law and Economics - Adolf Wagner's *Grundlegung*', **16** *Journal of Economic Issues*, 1982, 131-147.

LEVINSON, Sanford, 'Strolling Down the Path of the Law (and Toward Critical Legal Studies?): The Jurisprudence of Richard Posner' (Book Review of *The Problems of Jurisprudence*, Richard A. Posner), **91** *Columbia Law Review*, 1991, 1221-1252.

LIEBELER, Wesley J., 'What Are the Alternatives to Chicago?', *Duke Law Journal*, 1987, 879-898.

LIVINGSTON, Marie Leigh, 'Evaluating the Performance of Environmental Policy: Contributions of Neoclassical, Public Choice, and Institutional Models', **21** *Journal of Economic Issues*, 1987, 281-294.

MACKAAY, Ejan J.P., 'Verschuivingen in de rechtseconomie' [Shifts in Law-and-Economics], **66** *Nederlands Juristenblad*, 1991, 1505-1521.

McKINNEY, John, 'Frank H. Knight and Chicago Libertarianism', in SAMUELS, Warren J. (ed.), *The Chicago School of Political Economy*, East Lansing, Division of Research, Graduate School of Business Administration, Michigan State University, 1976, 191-214.

MEDEMA, Steven G., 'Discourse and the Institutional Approach to Law and Economics: Factors That Separate the Institutional Approach to Law and Economics From Alternative Approaches', **23** *Journal of Economic Issues*, 1989, 417-425.

MILLER, Edythe S., 'Economic Efficiency, the Economics Discipline, and the "Affected-with-a-Public-Interest" Concept', **24** *Journal of Economic Issues*, 1990, 719-732.

MITCHELL, W.C., 'Virginia, Rochester and Bloomington: Twenty-five Years of Public Choice and Political Science', **56** *Public Choice*, 1988, 101-119.

PAQUÉ, Karl-Heinz, 'How Far Is Vienna From Chicago? An Essay on the Methodology of Two Schools of Dogmatic Liberalism', **38** *Kyklos*, 1985, 412-434.

POSNER, Richard A., 'Blackstone and Bentham', **19** *Journal of Law and Economics*, 1976, 569-606.

POSNER, Richard A., 'The Law and Economics Movement', **77** *American Economic review (Papers and Proceedings)*, 1987, 1-13.

POSNER, Richard A., 'The Crisis in Legal Theory and the Revival of Classical Jurisprudence: Jurisprudential Responses to Legal Realism', **73** *Cornell Law Review*, 1988, 326 ff.

RAHMSDORF, Detlev W., 'Ökonomische Analyse des Rechts, Utilitarismus und die klassische deutsche Philosophie' [Economic Analysis of Law, Utilitarianism and the Classical German Philosophy], in *Rechtstheorie*, 1987, Heft 4, 487-501.

REDER, Melvin W., 'Chicago Economics: Permanence and Change', **20** *Journal of Economic Literature*, 1982, 1-38.

ROSE-ACKERMAN, Susan, 'Progressive Law and Economics - and the New Administrative Law', **98** *Yale Law Journal*, 1988, 341-368.

ROSE-ACKERMAN, Susan, 'Law and Economics: Paradigm, Politics, or Philosophy', in MERCURO, Nicholas (ed.), *Law and Economics*, Boston, Kluwer Academic Publishers, 1989, 233-258.

ROWLEY, Charles K., 'Public Choice and the Economic Analysis of Law', in MERCURO, Nicholas (ed.), *Law and Economics*, Boston, Kluwer Academic Publishers, 1989, 123-173.

SAMUELS, Warren J., 'Introduction: Commons and Clark on Law and Economics', **10** *Journal of Economic Issues*, 1976, 743-749.

SAMUELS, Warren J., 'The Old versus the New Institutionalism', **2** *Review of Political Economy*, 1990, 83-86.

SAMUELS, Warren J. and SCHMID, A. Alan (eds.), *Law and Economics: An Institutional Perspective*, Boston, Nijhoff, 1981, 268 p.

SCHWEIKHARDT, David B., 'The Role of Values in Economic Theory and Policy: A Comparison of Frank Knight and John R. Commons', **22** *Journal of Economic Issues*, 1988, 407-414.

SODERBAUM, Peter, 'Neoclassical and Institutional Approaches to Environmental Economics', **24** *Journal of Economic Issues*, 1990, 481-192.

SPANN, Girardeau A., 'A Critical Legal Studies Perspective on Contract Law and Practice', *Annual Survey of American Law*, 1988, 223-292.

STROWEL, Alain, 'A la recherche de l'intérêt en économie. De l'utilitarisme à la science économique néo-classique' [Searching for Interest in Economics. From Utilitarianism to Neo-Classical Economics], in GERARD, Philippe, OST, François, et VAN DE KERCHOVE, Michel (eds.), *Droit et intérêt*, Bruxelles, Fac. Univ. St-Louis, 1990, Vol. I, 37-87.

SWANEY, James A., 'Elements of a Neoinstitutional Environmental Economics', **21** *Journal of Economic Issues*, 1987, 1739-1779.

SYMPOSIUM : 'Different Approaches to thc Economics of Institutions', **146** *Journal of Institutional and Theoretical Economics*, 1990, 1-235.

TEIJL, Rob and HOLZHAUER, Rudi W., 'Pluriformiteit in de rechtseconomie: een verkenning van scholen' [Multiformity in Law-and-economics: an Exploration of Schools], **39(10)** *Ars Aequi*, 1990, 617-631.

TODT, Horst, 'Freiheit und Utilitarismus' [Freedom and Utilitarianism], in OTT, Claus and SCHÄFER, Hans-Bernd (eds.), *Ökonomische Probleme des Zivilrechts*, Berlin, Springer, 1991, 1-17.

ULEN, Thomas S., 'Law and Economics: Settled Issues and Open Questions', in MERCURO, Nicholas (ed.), *Law and Economics*, Boston, Kluwer Academic Publishers, 1989, 201-231.

WILLIAMSON, Oliver E., 'A Comparison of Alternative Approaches to Economic Organization', **146** *Journal of Institutional and Theoretical Economics*, 1990, 61-71.

WONNELL, Christopher T., 'Contract Law and the Austrian School of Economics', **54** *Fordham Law Review*, 1986, 507-543.

0600 Fundamental Concepts

0600 Fundamental Concepts: General

BECKER, Gary S., *Human Capital*, New York, National Bureau of Economic Research, 1964.

BONNER, John, *Introduction to the Theory of Social Choice*, Baltimore, Hopkins, 1986, 205 p.

COWEN, Tyler (ed.), *The Theory of Market Failure: A Critical Examination*, Fairfax, George Mason University Press, 1988, 384 p.

EATWELL, John, MILGATE, Murray and NEWMAN, Peter (eds.), *The New Palgrave: A Dictionary of Economics*, London, Macmillan, 1987, 4 volumes (949 + 1044 + 1085 + 1025 p.).

EATWELL, John, MILGATE, Murray and NEWMAN, Peter (eds.), *The New Palgrave: Invisible Hand*, London, Macmillan, 1989, 283 p.

HESS, James D., *The Economics of Organisation*, Amsterdam, North-Holland, 1983, VIII, 284 p.

MISHAN, Ezra J., *Cost-benefit Analysis. An Informal Introduction*, London, Allen and Unwin, 1984, 447 p.

MUELLER, Dennis C., 'Public Choice: A Survey', **14** *Journal of Economic Literature*, 1976, 395-433.

MUELLER, Dennis C., *Public Choice*, Cambridge, Cambridge University Press, 1979.

MUELLER, Dennis C., *Public Choice II*, Cambridge, Cambridge University Press, 1989, 518 p.

PHLIPS, L., *The Economics of Imperfect Information*, Cambridge, Cambridge University Press, 1989, 281 p.

RHOADS, Steven E., *The Economist's View of the World: Governments, Markets, and Public Policy*, Cambridge, Cambridge University Press, 1985, 331 p.

SUGDEN, Robert, *The Economics of Rights, Co-operation and Welfare*, New York, Blackwell, 1986, 191 p.

TULLOCK, Gordon, *Private Wants and Public Means*, New York, Basic Books, 1970.

0610 Rationality Assumption. Homo Oeconomicus. Altruism. Bounded Rationality

ANTONIDES, Gerrit, 'An Attempt at Integration of Economic and Psychological Theories of Consumption', **10** *Journal of Economic Psychology*, 1989, 77-99.

ARANSON, Peter H., 'Rational Ignorance in Politics, Economics and Law', **1**

Journal des Economistes et des Etudes Humaines, 1989, 25-42.

ATTANASIO, John B., 'The Principle of Aggregate Autonomy and the Calabresian Approach to Products Liability', **74** *Virginia Law Review*, 1988, 677-750.

BARTHOLD, Thomas A. and HOCHMAN, Harold M., 'Addiction as Extreme Seeking', **26** *Economic Inquiry*, 1988, 89-106.

BAXTER, J.L., *Social and Psychological Foundations of Economic Analysis*, New York, Simon and Schuster, 1988, 288 p.

BECKER, Gary S. and MURPHY, Kevin M., 'A Theory of Rational Addiction', **96** *Journal of Political Economy*, 1988, 675-700.

BECKER, Gary S. and STIGLER, George J., 'De Gustibus Non Est Disputandum', **67** *American Economic Review*, 1977, 76-90.

BERNHEIM, B. Douglas and STARK, Oded, 'Altruism Within the Family Reconsidered: Do Nice Guys Finish Last?', **78** *American Economic Review*, 1988, 1034-1045.

BURT, Robert A., 'Commentary on Schelling's Enforcing Rules on Oneself', **1** *Journal of Law, Economics & Organization*, 1985, 381-383.

COOK, Karen Schweers and LEVI, Margaret (eds.), *The Limits of Rationality*, Chicago, Chicago University Press, 1990, 434 p.

COURSEY, Don L. and STANLEY, L.R., 'Pretrial Bargaining Behavior within the Shadow of the Law: Theory and Experimental Evidence', **8** *International Review of Law and Economics*, 1988, 161-179.

DAVID, Wilfred L., *The Political Economy of Economic Policy: The Quest for Human Betterment*, New York, Greenwood Press, 1988, 266 p.

EGER, Thomas, NAGEL, Bernhard, and WEISE, Peter, 'Effizienz und Menschenwürde - Ein Gegensatz?' [Efficiency and Human Dignity - An Opposition?], in OTT, Claus and SCHÄFER, Hans-Bernd (eds.), *Ökonomische Probleme des Zivilrechts*, Berlin, Springer, 1991, 18-34.

ELLICKSON, Robert C., 'Bringing Culture and Human Frailty to Rational Actors: A Critique of Classical Law and Economics', **65** *Chicago-Kent Law Review*, 1989, 23-55.

ELSTER, Jon, *Sour Grapes: Studies in the Subversion of Rationality*, Cambridge, Cambridge University Press, 1985, 177 p.

ELSTER, Jon, *Solomic Judgements: Studies in the Limitations of Rationality*, Cambridge, Cambridge University Press, 1989, 232 p.

ETZIONI, Amitai, 'Toward a Kantian Socio-economics', **45(1)** *Review of Social Economy*, 1987, 37-47.

ETZIONI, Amitai, *The Moral Dimension: Toward a New Economics*, New York, Macmillan, 1988, 314 p.

FRANK, Robert H., 'If *Homo Economicus* Could Choose His Own Utility Function, Would He Want One with a Conscience?', **77** *American Economic Review*, 1987, 593-604.

FRANK, Robert H., *Passions within Reason: The Strategic Role of the Emotions*, New York, Norton, 1988, 304 p.

FRANK, Robert H., 'If Homo Economicus Could Choose His Own Utility

Function, Would He Want One With a Conscience? Reply', **79** *American Economic Review*, 1989, 594-596.

FREY, Bruno S. and EICHENBERGER, Reiner, 'Anomalies and Institutions', **145** *Journal of Institutional and Theoretical Economics*, 1989, 423-437.

FREY, Bruno and STROEBE, Wolfgang, 'In Defense of Economic Man: Towards an Integration of Economics and Psychology', **116** *Schweizerische Zeitschrift für Volkswirtschaft und Statistik*, 1980, 119-148.

FREY, Bruno and STROEBE, Wolfgang, 'Ist das Modell des Homo Oeconomicus "unpsychologisch"?', **136** *Journal of Institutional and Theoretical Economics*, 1980, 82-97.

HARRINGTON, Joseph E., Jr., 'If Homo Economicus Could Choose His Own Utility Function, Would He Want One with a Conscience?: Comment', **79** *American Economic Review*, 1989, 588-593.

HARRISON, Jeffrey L., 'Egoism, Altruism, and Market Illusions: the Limits of Law and Economics', **33** *UCLA. Law Review*, 1986, 1309-1363.

HART, Oliver D., 'Is "Bounded Rationality" an Important Element of a Theory of Institutions?', **146** *Journal of Institutional and Theoretical Economics*, 1990, 696-702.

HIGGS, Robert, 'Identity and Cooperation. A Comment on Sen's Alternative Program', **3** *Journal of Law, Economics, & Organization*, 1987, 140-142.

HODGSON, Geoffrey M., 'The Rationalist Conception of Action', **19** *Journal of Economic Issues*, 1985, 825-851.

HOGARTH, Robin M. and REDER, Mevin W. (eds.), *Rational Choice: The Contrast Between Economics and Psychology*, Chicago, University of Chicago Press, 1987, 332 p.

HOLLANDER, Samuel, 'Adam Smith and the Self-Interest Axiom', **20** *Journal of Law and Economics*, 1977, 133-152.

HOLLIS, Martin, *The Cunning of Reason*, Cambridge, Cambridge University Press, 1987, 222 p.

KIRCHNER, Christian, 'Kommentar' [Comment] (On Eger, Nagel and Weise, Effizienz und Menschenwürde), in OTT, Claus and SCHÄFER, Hans-Bernd (eds.), *Ökonomische Probleme des Zivilrechts*, Berlin, Springer, 1991, 35-38.

KURZ, Mordecai, 'Altruism as an Outcome of Social Interaction', **68** *American Economic Review. Papers and Proceedings*, 1978, 216-222.

LANDES, William H. and POSNER, Richard A., 'Salvors, Finders, Good Samaritans, and Other Rescuers: An Economic Study of Law and Altruism', **7** *Journal of Legal Studies*, 1978, 83-128.

LANDES, William M. and POSNER, Richard A., 'Altruism in Law and Economics', **68** *American Economic Review. Papers and Proceedings*, 1978, 417-421.

LANGLOIS, Richard N., 'Bounded Rationality and Behavioralism: A Clarification and Critique', **146** *Journal of Institutional and Theoretical Economics*, 1990, 691-695.

LINDENBEG, Siegwart, 'Homo Socio-oeconomicus: The Emergence of a General Model of Man in the Social Sciences', **146** *Journal of Institutional and Theoretical Economics*, 1990, 727-748.

MANSBRIDGE, Jane J. (ed.), *Beyond Self-Interest*, Chicago, University of Chicago Press, 1990, 402 p.

OSTMANN, Axel, 'On Rationality Issues in the Bargaining Context', **146** *Journal of Institutional and Theoretical Economics*, 1990, 673-683.

POSNER, Richard A., 'The Ethical Significance of Free Choice: A Reply to Professor West', **99** *Harvard Law Review*, 1986, 1431-1448.

RUSSELL, Thomas and THALER, Richard, 'The Relevance of Quasi Rationality in Competitive Markets', **75** *American Economic Review*, 1985, 1075-1082.

SCHELLING, Thomas C., 'Enforcing Rules on Oneself', **1** *Journal of Law, Economics, & Organization*, 1985, 357-374.

SCHLICHT, Ekkehart, 'Rationality, Bounded or not, and Institutional Analysis', **146** *Journal of Institutional and Theoretical Economics*, 1990, 703-719.

SCOTT, Robert E., 'Error and Rationality in Individual Decisionmaking: An Essay on the Relationship Between Cognitive Illusions and the Management of Choices', **59** *Southern California Law Review*, 1986, 329-362.

SELTEN, Reinhard, 'Bounded Rationality', **146** *Journal of Institutional and Theoretical Economics*, 1990, 649-658.

SEN, Amartya K., 'Goals, Commitment, and Identity', **1** *Journal of Law, Economics, & Organization*, 1985, 341-355.

SHAVELL, Steven, 'An Economic Analysis of Altriusm and Deferred Gifts', **20** *Journal of Legal Studies*, 1991, 401-421.

SIMON, Herbert A., *Administrative Behaviour*, New York, MacMillan (2nd ed.) 1961.

SIMON, Herbert A., 'Rationality as Process and as Product of Thought', **68** *American Economic Review. Papers and Proceedings*, 1978, 1-16.

SIMON, Herbert A., 'Bounded Rationality', in EATWELL, John, MILGATE, Murray and NEWMAN, Peter (eds.), *The New Palgrave: A Dictionary of Economics*, London, Macmillan, 1987, Volume 1, 266-268.

TIETZ,, Reinhard, 'On Bounded Rationality: Experimental Work at the University of Frankfurt/Main', **146** *Journal of Institutional and Theoretical Economics*, 1990, 659-672.

TIETZEL, Manfred, 'Die Rationalitätsannahme in den Wirtschaftswissenschaften oder Der homo oeconomicus und seine Verwandten' [The Rationality Assumption in Economics or the Homo Oeconomicus and his Relatives], **32** *Jahrbuch für Sozialwissenschaften*, 1981, 115-136.

ULEN, Thomas S., 'Cognitive Imperfections and the Economic Analysis of the Law', **12** *Hamline Law Review*, 1989, 385-410.

WEST, Robin, 'Authority, Autonomy, and Choice: The Role of Consent in the Moral and Political Visions of Franz Kafka and Richard Posner', **99** *Harvard Law Review*, 1985, 384-428.

WEST, Robin, 'Submission, Choice, and Ethics: A Rejoinder to Judge Posner', **99** *Harvard Law Review*, 1986, 1449-1456.

WINSTON, Gordon C., 'The Reasons for Being of Two Minds: A Comment on Schelling's Enforcing Rules on Oneself', **1** *Journal of Law, Economics, & Organization*, 1985, 375-379.

0620 Efficiency

ALCHIAN, Armen A., 'The Meaning of Utility Measurement', **43** *American Economic Review*, 1953, 26 ff.

ARMENTANO, Dominick T., 'Comment: Efficiency, Liberty, and Antitrust Policy', in DORN, James A. and MANNE, Henry G. (eds.), *Economic Liberties and the Judiciary*, Fairfax, George Mason University Press, 1987, 309-316.

BAKER, C. Edwin, 'Counting Preferences in Collective Choice Situations', **25** *UCLA. Law Review*, 1978.

BEAVIS, Brian and ROWLEY, Charles K., 'Evaluating Choice: A Note', **3** *International Review of Law and Economics*, 1983, 79-83.

BROMLEY, Daniel W., 'The Ideology of Efficiency: Searching for a Theory of Policy Analysis', **19** *Journal of Environmental Economics and Management*, 1990, 86-107.

BUCHANAN, James M., 'The Relevance of Pareto Optimality', **6** *Journal of Conflict Resolution*, 1962, 341-354.

CALABRESI, Guido, 'The Pointlessness of Pareto: Carrying Coase Further', **100** *Yale Law Journal*, 1991, 1211-1237.

CENTI, Jean-Pierre, 'Quel critère d'efficience pour l'analyse économique du droit' [Which Efficiency Criterion for Economic Analysis of Law], *Revue de la Recherche Juridique*, 1987, Nr. 2.

COLEMAN, Jules L., 'Efficiency, Exchange and Auction: Philosophic Aspects of the Economic Approach to Law', **68** *California Law Review*, 1980, 221-249.

COLEMAN, Jules L., 'Efficiency, Utility, and Wealth Maximization', **8** *Hofstra Law Review*, 1980, 509-552.

COOTER, Robert D., 'The Best Right Laws: Value Foundations of the Economic Analysis of Law', **64** *Notre Dame Law Review*, 1989, 817-837.

DEMSETZ, Harold, 'Information and Efficiency: Another Viewpoint', **12** *Journal of Law and Economics*, 1969, 1-22.

DOBBS, I., 'Externality, Efficiency and the Pareto Principle', **1** *International Review of Law and Economics*, 1981, 167-181.

EGER, Thomas, NAGEL, Bernhard, and WEISE, Peter, 'Effizienz und Menschenwürde - Ein Gegensatz?' [Efficiency and Human Dignity - An Opposition?], in OTT, Claus and SCHÄFER, Hans-Bernd (eds.), *Ökonomische Probleme des Zivilrechts*, Berlin, Springer, 1991, 18-34.

EGGER, J.B., 'Efficiency Is Not a Substitute for Ethics', in RIZZO, Mario J. (ed.) *Time, Uncertainty and Disequilibrium*, Heath, Lexington, 1979, 117-125.

FRIEDMAN, David D., 'Does Altruism Produce Efficient Outcomes ? Marshall versus Kaldor', **17** *Journal of Legal Studies*, 1988, 1-13.

FRISCH, R., 'On Welfare Theory and Pareto Regions', **9** *International Economic Review*, 1959, 39-92.

GLASNER, David, 'On the Difference Between Wealth and Liberty', **2** *International Review of Law and Economics*, 1982, 227-233.

GRANT, Robin F., 'Judge Richard Posner's Wealth Maximization Principle: Another Form of Utilitarianism?', **10** *Cardozo Law Review*, 1989, 815-845.

HAMMOND, 'The Economics of Justice and the Criterion of Wealth Maximization' (Book Review), **91** *Yale Law Journal*, 1982, 1493-1507.

HANKS, John L., 'On a Just Measure of the Efficiency of Law and Governmental Politics', **8** *Cardozo Law Review*, 1986, 1-38.

HOVENKAMP, Herbert J., 'Legislation, Well-Being, and Public Choice', **57** *University of Chicago Law Review*, 1990, 63-116.

HOVENKAMP, Herbert J., 'Exchange on Public Choice', **57** *University of Chicago Law Review*, 1990, 840-843.

HOVENKAMP, Herbert, 'Legal Policy and the Endowment Effect', **20** *Journal of Legal Studies*, 1991, 225-247.

JOHNSEN, D. Bruce, 'Wealth Is Value', **15** *Journal of Legal Studies*, 1986, 263-288.

JONES, Peter and SUGDEN, Robert, 'Evaluating Choice', **2** *International Review of Law and Economics*, 1982, 47-65.

JONES, Peter and SUGDEN, Robert, 'Evaluating Choice: A Reply', **3** *International Review of Law and Economics*, 1983, 85-87.

JUHNJUHNWALA, Bharat, 'Kaldor-Hicks-Scitovsky Criteria: A Postmortem', **40** *Southern Economic Journal*, 1974, 493-496.

KALDOR, N., 'Welfare Propositions of Economics and Interpersonal Comparisons of Utility', **49** *Economic Journal*, 1939, 549-552.

KEENAN, Donald, 'Value Maximization and Welfare Theory', **10** *Journal of Legal Studies*, 1981, 409-419.

KIRCHNER, Christian, 'Kommentar' [Comment] (On Eger, Nagel and Weise, Effizienz und Menschenwürde), in OTT, Claus and SCHÄFER, Hans-Bernd (eds.), *Ökonomische Probleme des Zivilrechts*, Berlin, Springer, 1991, 35-38.

KNETSCH, Jack L., 'Legal Rules and the Basis for Evaluating Economic Losses', **4** *International Review of Law and Economics*, 1984, 5-13.

KNETSCH, Jack L., 'Environmental Policy Implications of Disparities between Willingness to Pay and Compensation Demanded Measures of Values', **18** *Journal of Environmental Economics and Management*, 1990, 227-237.

KORNHAUSER, Lewis A., 'A Guide to the Perplexed Claims of Efficiency in the Law', **8** *Hofstra Law Review*, 1980, 591-639.

KRONMAN, Anthony T., 'Wealth Maximization as a Normative Principle', **9** *Journal of Legal Studies*, 1980, 227-242.

KÜBLER, Friedrich, ' Effizienz als Rechtsprinzip - Überlegungen zum rechtspraktischen Gebrauch ökonomischer Argumente' [Efficiency als Legal Principle - Considerations for the Legal Practice Use of Economic Arguments], in BAUR, Jürgen F., HOPT, Klaus J. and MAILÄNDER, Peter K. (eds.), *Festschrift für Ernst Steindorff*, 1990, Berlin, de Gruyter, 687-704.

LIPSEY, Richard G. and LANCASTER, K., 'On the General Theory of the Second

Best', **24** *Review of Economic Studies*, 1956, 11-32.

MACEY, Jonathan R. and MILLER, Geoffrey P., 'Good Finance, Bad Economics: An Analysis of the Fraud-on-the-Market Theory', **42** *Stanford Law Review*, 1990, 1059-1092.

MARGOLIS, Stephen E., 'Two Definitions of Efficiency in Law and Economics', **16** *Journal of Legal Studies*, 1987, 471-482.

MARKOVITS, Richard S., 'A Basic Structure for Microeconomic Policy Analysis in our Worse-Than-Second-Best World: A Proposal and Related Critique of the Chicago Approach to the Study of Law and Economics', *Wisconsin Law Review*, 1975, 950-1080.

MARKOVITS, Richard S., 'Legal Analysis and the Economic Analysis of Allocative Efficiency', **8** *Hofstra Law Review*, 1980, 811-903.

MISHAN, Ezra J., 'Pareto Optimality and the Law', **19** *Oxford Economic Papers*, 1967, 255-287.

O'DRISCOLL, Gerald P., Jr., 'Justice, Efficiency, and the Economic Analysis of Law: A Comment on Fried', **9** *Journal of Legal Studies*, 1980, 355-366.

RIZZO, Mario J., 'The Mirage of Efficiency', **8** *Hofstra Law Review*, 1980, 641-658.

ROTHBARD, Murray N., 'Comment: The Myth of Efficiency', in RIZZO, Mario J. (ed.), *Time, Uncertainty and Disequilibrium*, Lexington, Lexington Books, 1979, 91-95.

ROWLEY, Charles K. and WALKER, Martin, 'Pareto-optimality and Gains-from-trade: a Public Choice Interpretation', **34** *Public Choice*, 1979, 123-127.

ROZEN, Marvin E., 'Maximizing Behavior: Reconciling Neoclassical and X-Efficiency Approaches', **19** *Journal of Economic Issues*, 1985, 661-685.

SAGER, Lawrence G., 'Pareto Superiority, Consent, and Justice', **8** *Hofstra Law Review*, 1980, 913-937.

SCITOVSKI, T., 'The State of the Welfare Economics', **41** *American Economic Review*, 1951.

SHAVELL, Steven, 'A Note on Efficiency Vs. Distributional Equity in Legal Rulemaking: Should Distributional Equity Matter Given Optimal Income Taxation?', **71** *American Economic Review. Papers and Proceedings*, 1981, 414-418.

SHAVIRO, Daniel N., 'Exchange on Public Choice', **57** *University of Chicago Law Review*, 1990, 834-843.

STIGLER, George J., 'The Xistence of X-Efficiency', **66** *American Economic Review*, 1976, 213-216.

STIGLER, George J., 'Wealth, and Possibly Liberty', **7** *Journal of Legal Studies*, 1978, 213-217.

SYMPOSIUM : 'Symposium on Efficiency as a Legal Concern', **8** *Hofstra Law Review*, 1980, 485-972.

TULLOCK, Gordon, 'Two Kinds of Legal Efficiency', **8** *Hofstra Law Review*, 1980, 659 ff.

VELJANOVSKI, Cento G., 'Wealth Maximization, Law and Ethics - On the Limits of Economic Efficiency', **1** *International Review of Law and Economics*, 1981, 5-28.

0630 Externalities and the Coase Theorem

AIVAZIAN, Varouj A. and CALLEN, Jeffrey L., 'Uncertain Externalities, Liability Rules and Resource Allocation: Comment', **70** *American Economic Review*, 1980, 1058-1059.

AIVAZIAN, Varouj A. and CALLEN, Jeffrey L., 'The Coase Theorem and the Empty Core', **24** *Journal of Law and Economics*, 1981, 175-181.

BESEN, Stanley M., MANNING, Willard G. Jr. and MITCHELL, Bridger M., 'Copyright Liability for Cable Television: Compulsory Licensing and the Coase Theorem', **21** *Journal of Law and Economics*, 1978, 67-95.

BUCHANAN, James M., 'The Coase Theorem and the Theory of the State', **13** *Natural Resources Journal*, 1973, 579-594.

BUCHANAN, James M., 'The Institutional Structure of Externality', **28** *Public Choice*, 1973, 69-82.

BUCHANAN, James M., 'Rights, Efficiency ad Exchange: The Irrelevance of Transaction Costs', in NEUMANN, M. (ed.), *Ansprüche, Eigentums- und Verfügungsrechte*, Schriften des Vereins für Socialpolitik, 1983, 9 ff. Reprinted in *Liberty, Market and State*, Harvester Press, 1986, 97-107.

BUCHANAN, James M. and FAITH, Roger L., 'Entrepreneurship and the Internalization of Externalities', **24** *Journal of Law and Economics*, 1981, 95-111.

BUCHANAN, James M. and STUBBLEBINE, W. Graig, 'Externality', **29** *Economica*, 1962, 371-384.

BURROWS, Paul, 'On External Costs and the Visible Arm of the Law', **22** *Oxford Economic Papers*, 1970, 39-56.

CALABRESI, Guido, 'Transaction Costs, Resource Allocation and Liability Rules: A Comment', **11** *Journal of Law and Economics*, 1968, 67-73.

CALABRESI, Guido, 'The Pointlessness of Pareto: Carrying Coase Further', **100** *Yale Law Journal*, 1991, 1211-1237.

CHEUNG, Steven N.S., *The Myth Of Social Costs: A Critique of Welfare Economics and the Implications for Public Policy*, London, Institute of Economic Affairs, 1978, 93 p.

COASE, Ronald H., 'The Federal Communications Commission', **2** *Journal of Law and Economics*, 1959, 1-40.

COASE, Ronald H., 'The Problem of Social Cost', **3** *Journal of Law and Economics*, 1960, 1-44. Reprinted in COASE, Ronald H., *The Firm, the Market and the Law*, Chicago, University of Chicago Press, 1988. Reprinted in ACKERMAN, Bruce A. (ed.), *Economic Foundations of Property Law*, Boston, Little Brown, 1975, 17-22.

COASE, Ronald H., 'The Choice of the Institutional Framework: A Comment', **17**

Journal of Law and Economics, 1974, 493-496.

COASE, Ronald H., 'The Coase Theorem and the Empty Core: A Comment', **24** *Journal of Law and Economics*, 1981, 183-187.

COASE, Ronald H., *The Firm, the Market and the Law*, Chicago, University of Chicago Press, 1988, 217 p.

COASE, Ronald H., 'Blackmail' (The 1987 Mc Corkle Lecture), **74** *Virginia Law Review*, 1988, 655-676.

COELHO, Philip R.P., 'Externalities, Separability and Resource Allocation: Comment', **65** *American Economic Review*, 1975, 721-723.

COOTER, Robert D., 'How the Law Circumvents Starret's Nonconvexity', **22** *Journal of Economic Theory*, 1980, 499-504.

COOTER, Robert D., 'The Cost of Coase', **11** *Journal of Legal Studies*, 1982, 1-33.

COOTER, Robert D., MARKS Stephen and MNOOKIN, Robert, 'Bargaining in the Shadow of the Law: A Testable Model of Strategic Behavior', **11** *Journal of Legal Studies*, 1982, 225-251.

COURSEY, Don L. and STANLEY, L.R., 'Pretrial Bargaining Behavior within the Shadow of the Law: Theory and Experimental Evidence', **8** *International Review of Law and Economics*, 1988, 161-179.

COURSEY, Don L., HOFFMAN, Elisabeth and SPITZER, Matthew L., 'Fear and Loathing in the Coase Theorem: Experimental Tests Involving Physical Discomfort', **16** *Journal of Legal Studies*, 1987, 217-248.

CRAIN, W. Mark, SAWMAN, D. and TOLLISON, Robert D., 'The Coase Theorem and Quasi Rents: Correcting the Record', **6** *Public Finance Quarterly*, 1978, 259-264.

DAHLMAN, Carl J., 'The Problem of Externality', **22** *Journal of Law and Economics*, 1979, 141-162.

DALY, George, 'The Coase Theorem: Assumptions, Applications and Ambiguities', **12** *Economic Inquiry*, 1974, 203-213.

DALY, George and GIERTZ, J. Fred,' Externalities, Extortion and Efficiency', **65** *American Economic Review*, 1975, 997-1001.

DAVIS, Otto A. and WHINSTON, Andrew, 'Externalities, Welfare and the Theory of Games', **70** *Journal of Political Economy*, 1962, 241-262.

DAVIS, Otto A. and WHINSTON, Andrew B., 'Some Notes on Equating Private and Social Cost', **32** *Southern Economic Journal*, 1965, 113-126.

DE SHERPA, Allan C., 'The Coase Theorem: A Diagrammatic Presentation', **15** *Economic Inquiry*, 1977, 600-604.

DEMSETZ, Harold, 'Theoretical Efficiency in Pollution Control: Comments on Comments', **9** *Western Economic Journal*, 1971, 444-446.

DEMSETZ, Harold, 'When Does the Rule of Liability Matter ?', **1** *Journal of Legal Studies*, 1972, 13-28.

DEMSETZ, Harold, 'On Extortion: A Reply', **68** *American Economic Review*, 1978, 417-418.

DICK, Daniel T., 'The Voluntary Approach to Externality Problems: A Survey of the Critics', **2** *Journal of Environmental Economy and Management*, 1976,

185-195.

DOLBEAR, F. Trenery, Jr., 'On the Theory of Optimum Externality', **57** *American Economic Review*, 1967, 90-103.

DOLBEAR, F. Trenery, Jr., 'Externalities as Commodities: Comment', **64** *American Economic Review*, 1974, 341-343.

DONOHUE, John J. III, 'Law and Economics: The Road not Taken', **22** *Law & Society Review*, 1988, 903-926.

DONOHUE, John J. III, 'Diverting the Coasian River: Incentive Schemes to Reduce Unemployment Spells', **99** *Yale Law Journal*, 1989, 549-609.

DONOHUE, John J. III, 'Reply', **99** *Yale Law Journal*, 1989, 635-636.

ELLICKSON, Robert C., 'Of Coase and Cattle: Dispute Resolution among Neighbors in Shasta County; ' **38** *Stanford Law Review* 1986, 623-687. Reprinted in **18** *Land Use and Environment Law Review*, 1987, 79-143.

ELLICKSON, Robert C., 'The Case for Coase and Against "Coaseanism"', **99** *Yale Law Journal*, 1989, 611-630.

ENDRES, Alfred, 'Das Coase-Theorem bei langfristiger Betrachtung' [The Coase Theorem in a Long Term Perspective], **27** *Jahrbuch für Sozialwissenschaft*, 1976, 430-433.

ENDRES, Alfred, 'Die Coase-Kontroverse' [The Coase Controversy], **133** *Zeitschrift für die gesamte Staatswissenschaft*, 1977, 637-651.

FARRELL, Joseph, 'Information and the Coase Theorem', **1(2)** *Journal of Economic Perspectives*, 1987, 113-129.

FAURE, Michael, 'Commentaar bij de paper van Dr.Jan C. Bongaerts: Coase en Produktenaansprakelijkheid' [Comment on the paper of Dr. Jan C. Bongaerts: Coase and Product Liability], in VAN DEN BERGH, Roger (ed.), *Verslagboek Eerste Werkvergadering recht en Economie*, Antwerpen, Handelshogeschool, 1986, 31-37.

FRECH, H. Edward III, 'Pricing of Pollution: The Coase Theorem in the Long Run', **4** *Bell Journal of Economics*, 1973, 316-319.

FRECH, H. Edward III, 'The Extended Coase Theorem and Longrun Equilibrium. The Nonequivalence of Liability Rules and Property Rights', **17** *Economic Inquiry*, 1979, 254-268.

FELDMAN, Robert, 'Liability Rules and the Transfer of Economic Rent', **3** *Journal of Legal Studies*, 1974, 499-508.

GIFFORD, Adam, Jr., 'Externalities and the Coase Theorem: A Graphical Analysis', **14** *Quarterly Review of Economics and Business*, 1974, 7-22.

GIFFORD, Adam, Jr., 'Externalities, Liability, Separability and Resource Allocation: Comment', **65** *American Economic Review*, 1975, 724-727.

GIFFORD, Adam, Jr. and STONE, Courtney C., 'Externalities, Liability and the Coase Theorem: A Mathematical Analysis', **11** *Western Economic Journal*, 1973, 260-269.

GJERDINGEN, Donald H., 'The Coase Theorem and the Psychology of Common-Law Thought', **56** *Southern California Law Review*, 1983, 711-760.

GJERDINGEN, Donald H., 'The Politics of the Coase Theorem and Its Relationship to Modern Legal Thought', **35** *Buffalo Law Review*, 1986, 871-935.

GOLDBERG, Victor P., 'Institutional Change and the Quasi-Invisible Hand', **17** *Journal of Law and Economics*, 1974, 461-492. Reprinted in GOLDBERG, Victor P. (ed.), *Readings in the Economics of Contract Law*, Cambridge, Cambridge University Press, 1989, 169-173.

GOULD, John P., 'Mohring and Boyd's Objection to the Coase Theorem: A Note', **42** *Economica*, 1975, 203-206.

GOULD, J.R., 'Meade on External Economies: Should the Beneficiaries Be Taxed?' **16** *Journal of Law and Economics*, 1973, 53-66.

GRADY, Mark F., 'Common Law Control of Strategic Behavior: Railroad Sparks and the Farmer', **17** *Journal of Legal Studies*, 1988, 15-42.

GREENWOOD, Peter H., INGENE, Charles A. and HORSFIED, James, 'Externalities, Separability and Resource Allocation', **65** *American Economic Review*, 1975, 728-729.

GREENWOOD, Peter H. and INGENE, Charles A., 'Uncertain Externalities, Liability Rules and Resources Allocation', **68** *American Economic Review*, 1978, 300-310.

GREENWOOD, Peter H. and INGENE, Charles A., 'Reply', **70** *American Economic Review*, 1980, 1060-1063.

HAMILTON, Jonathan H., SHESHINSKI, Eytan and SLUTSKY, Steven M., 'Production Externalities and Long-Run Equilibria: Bargaining and Pigovian Taxation', **27** *Economic Inquiry*, 1989, 453-471.

HANSMANN, Henry B., 'The Coase Proposition, Information Constraints, and Long-Run Equilibrium: Comment', **67** *American Economic Review*, 1977, 459-461.

HARRIS, Frederick H., 'Economic Negligence, Moral Hazard, and the Coase Theorem', **56** *Southern Economic Journal*, 1990, 698-704.

HARRISON, Glenn W. et al., 'Coasian Solutions to the Externality Problem in Experimental Markets', **97** *Economic Journal*, 1987, 388-3402.

HARRISON, Glenn W. and McKEE, Michael, 'Experimental Evaluation of the Coase Theorem', **28** *Journal of Law and Economics*, 1985, 653-670.

HEAD, John G., 'Public Policies and Pollution Problems', **33** *Finanzarchiv*, 1974, 1-29.

HELLNER, Jan, *Rättsekonomi, avbeställning och Coase-teorem* [Law and Economics, Cancellation and Coase Theorem], Juridiska föreningen i Lund, No. 24, 1978, 101 p.

HOFFMAN, Elizabeth and SPITZER, Matthew L., 'The Coase Theorem: Some Experimental Tests', **25** *Journal of Law and Economics*, 1982, 73-98.

HOFFMAN, Elizabeth and SPITZER, Matthew L., 'Entitlements, Rights, and Fairness: An Experimental Examination of Subjects' Concepts of Distributive Justice', **14** *Journal of Legal Studies*, 1985, 259-297.

HOFFMAN, Elizabeth and SPITZER, Matthew L., 'Experimental Tests of the Coase Theorem with Large Bargaining Groups', **15** *Journal of Legal Studies*, 1986, 149-171.

HOLDERNESS, Clifford G., 'The Assignment of Rights, Entry Effects, and the Allocation of Resources', **18** *Journal of Legal Studies*, 1989, 181-189.

HOMA, M., 'Tentative Note on Liability Rules under the Coase System', **24** *Osaka Economic Papers*, 1974, 86-97.

HOVENKAMP, Herbert J., 'Marginal Utility and the Coase Theorem', **75** *Cornell Law Review*, 1990, 783-810.

INADA, Ken I. and KUGA, Kigoshi, 'Limitations of the 'Coase Theorem' on Liability Rules', **6** *Journal of Economic Theory*, 1973, 606-613.

JAFEE, Jeffrey F., 'The 'Coase Theorem': A Re-examination and Comment', **89** *Quarterly Journal of Economics*, 1975, 660-667.

JOHNSON, David B., 'Meade, Bees, and Externalities', **16** *Journal of Law and Economics*, 1973, 35-52.

KANNING, W., 'Een non-cooperatieve benadering van het Coase-theorema' [A Non Co-operative Approach to the Coase Theorem]', in COLJEE, P.D., FRANKEN, H., HEERTJE, A. and KANNING, W. (eds.), *Law and Welfare Economics*, Symposium 24 October, VU Amsterdam, 39-48.

KELMAN, Mark, 'Consumption Theory, Production Theory and Ideology in the Coase Theorem', **52** *Southern California Law Review*, 1979, 669-698.

KELMAN, Mark, 'Spitzer and Hoffman on Coase: A Brief Rejoinder', **53** *Southern California Law Review*, 1980, 1215-1223.

KELMAN, Mark, 'Comment on Hoffman and Spitzer's Experimental Law and Economics', **85** *Columbia Law Review*, 1985, 1037-1047.

KESSEL, Reuben A., 'Transfused Blood, Serum Hepatitis, and The Coase Theorem', **17** *Journal of Law and Economics*, 1974, 265-289.

KNEESE, Allan V. and MALLER, Koran G., 'Bribes and Charges in Pollution Control : An Aspect of the Coase Controversy', **13** *Natural Resources Journal*, 1973, 677-704.

LEDEBUT, L.C., 'The Problem of Social Cost', **26** *American Journal of Economy and Sociology*, 1967, 399-415.

LIEBERMANN, Yehoshua, 'The Coase Theorem in Jewish Law', **10** *Journal of Legal Studies*, 1981, 293-303.

LIEBHAFSKY, Harold H., 'The Problem of Social Cost: An Alternative Approach', **13** *Natural Resources Journal*, 1973, 615-76.

LINDGREN, James, 'Blackmail: On Waste, Morals and Ronald Coase', **36** *UCLA Law Review*, 1989, 597-608.

LINDOREN, James, ' "Ol' Man River,... He Keeps On Rollin' Along": A Reply to Donohue's Diverting the Coasean River', **78** *Georgetown Law Journal*, 1990, 577-591.

LITTLECHILD, Stephen C., 'The Problem of Social Cost', in SPADARO, Louis M. (ed.), *New Directions in Austrian Economics*, Kansas City, Sheed. Andres & McMeel, 1978, 77-93.

MACEY, Jonathan R., 'Transaction Costs and the Normative Elements of the Public Choice Model: An Application to Constitutional Theory', **74** *Virginia Law Review*, 1988, 471-518.

MAGNAN DE BORNIER, Jean, 'The Coase Theorem and the Empty Core: A Re-examination', **6** *International Review of Law and Economics*, 1986, 265-271.

MALONEY, Michael T., 'Coase Theorem and Longrun Industry Equilibrium', **17** *Quartery Review of Economics and Business*, 1977, 113-118.

McEWIN, R.I., 'Liability Rules, Insurance and the Coase Theorem', **6** *Australian Journal of Management*, 1981, 103-117.

MISHAN, Ezra J., 'Pareto Optimality and the Law', **19** *Oxford Economic Papers*, 1967, 255-287.

MISHAN, Ezra J., 'The Post-war Literature on Externalities: An Interpretative Essay', **9** *Journal of Economic Literature*, 1971, 1-28.

MORE, Daniel, 'The Coase Theorem and the Reciprocal Nature of Land-Use Conflicts in Pollution Cases', **4** *Studies in Law, Tel Aviv University*, 1978-79, 4, 84-114.

MUMEY, George A., 'The Coase Theorem: A Re-examination', **85** *Quarterly Journal of Economics*, 1971, 718-723.

NG, Yew Kwang, 'Recent Developments in the Theory of Externality and the Pigovian Solution', **47** *Economic Record*, 1971, 169-185.

NG, Yew Kwang, 'Coase's Theorem and First-party Priority Rule: Reply', **51** *Economic Record*, 1975, 272-274.

NG, Yew Kwang, 'Again on Externalities and Liability Rules: A Reply', **53** *Economic Record*, 1977, 542-544.

NORTON, Seth W., 'The Coase Theorem and Suboptimization in Marketing Channels', **6** *Marketing Science*, 1987, 268-285.

NUTTER, Warren G., 'The Coase Theorem on Social Cost: A Footnote', **11** *Journal of Law and Economics*, 1968, 503-507.

OGUS, Anthony I., 'Comment' [on Staaf and Yandle, Collective and Private Choice; Constitutions, Statutes and the Common Law], in WEIGEL, Wolfgang (ed.), *Economic Analysis of Law - A Collection of Applications*, Vienna, Österreichischer Wirtschaftsverlag, 1991, 267-269.

POLINSKY, A. Mitchell, 'Controlling Externalities and Protecting Entitlements: Property Right, Liability Rule, and Tax-Subsidy Approaches', **8** *Journal of Legal Studies*, 1979, 1-48.

PRUDENCIO, Yves C., 'The Voluntary Approach to Externality Problems: An Experimental Test', **9** *Journal Environmental Economy and Management*, 1982, 213-228.

RANDALL, Allan, 'Market Solutions to Externality Problems: Theory and Practice', **54** *American Journal of Agricultural Economics*, 1972, 175-183.

RANDALL, Allan, 'Coasian Externality Theory in a Policy Context', **14** *Natural Resources Journal*, 1974, 35-54.

REGAN, Donald H., 'The Problem of Social Cost Revisited', **15** *Journal of Law and Economics*, 1972, 427-437.

SAMUELS, Warren J., 'The Coase Theorem and the Study of Law and Economics', **14** *Natural Resources Journal*, 1974, 1-33.

SARAYDAR, Edward, 'Bargaining Power, Dissimilation and the Coase Theorem', **139** *Zeitsschrift für die gesamte Staatswissenschaft*, 1983, 599-611.

SCHLAG, Pierre, 'An Appreciative Comment on Coase's The Problem of Social

Cost: A View from the Left', *Wisconsin Law Review*, 1986, 919-962.

SCHLAG, Pierre, 'The Problem of Transaction Costs', **62** *Southern California Law Review*, 1989, 1661-1699.

SCHULZE, William D. and D'ARGE, Ralph C., 'The Coase Proposition, Information Costs and Long-run Equilibrium', **64** *American Economic Review*, 1974, 763-772.

SCHULZE, William D. and D'ARGE, Ralph C., 'The Coase Proposition, Information Constraints, and Long-Run Equilibrium: Reply', **67** *American Economic Review*, 1977, 462-463.

SCHWAB, Stewart J., 'Collective Bargaining and the Coase Theorem', **72** *Cornell Law Review*, 1987, 245-287.

SCHWAB, Stewart J., 'A Coasean Experiment on Contract Presumptions', **17** *Journal of Legal Studies*, 1988, 237-268.

SCHWAB, Stewart J., 'Coase Defends Coase: Why Lawyers Listen and Economists Do Not', **87** *Michigan Law Review*, 1989, 1171-1198.

SCHWEIZER, Urs, 'Externalities and the Coase Theorem: Hypothesis or Result?', **144** *Journal of Institutional and Theoretical Economics*, 1988, 245-266.

SHAPIRO, David L. 'A Note on Rent and the Coase Theorem', **7** *Journal of Economic Theory*, 1984, 125-128.

SHEA, Koon-Iam, 'Coase Theorem, Liability Rules and Social Optimum', **114** *Weltwirtschaftliches Archiv*, 1978, 540-550.

SILBERBERG, Eugene, *The Structure of Economics. A Mathematical Analysis*, New York, McGraw-Hill, 1978, 494-501.

SPITZER, Matthew L. and HOFFMAN, Elizabeth, 'A Reply to Consumption Theory, Production Theory and Ideology in the Coase Theorem', **53** *Southern California Law Review*, 1980, 1187-1223.

STAAF, Robert and YANDLE, Bruce, 'Collective and Private Choice: Constitutions, Statutes and the Common Law', in WEIGEL, Wolfgang (ed.), *Economic Analysis of Law - A Collection of Applications*, Vienna, Österreichischer Wirtschaftsverlag, 1991, 254-265.

STIGLER, George J., 'Two Notes on the Coase Theorem', **99** *Yale Law Journal*, 1989, 631-636.

SWAN, Peter L., 'The Coase Theorem and 'Sequential' Pareto Optimality', **51** *Economic Record*, 1975, 268-271.

TYBOUT, Richard A., 'Pricing Pollution and Other Negative Externalities', **3** *Bell Journal of Economics*, 1972, 252-266.

TYBOUT, Richard A., 'Pricing of Pollution: Reply', **4** *Bell Journal of Economics*, 1973, 320-321.

VELJANOVSKI, Cento G., 'The Coase Theorem: The Say's Law of Welfare Economics ?', **53** *Economic Record*, 1977, 535-541.

VELJANOVSKI, Cento G., 'The Coase Theorems and the Economic Theory of Markets and Law', **35** *Kyklos*, 1982, 53-74.

VOGEL, Kenneth R., 'The Coase Theorem and California Animal Trespass Law', **16** *Journal of Legal Studies*, 1987, 149-187.

WALSH, Cliff, 'First-Party-Priority Revisited', **51** *Economic Record*, 1975, 275-277.

WEGEHENKEL, Lothar, *Coase Theorem und Marktsystem* [Coase Theorem and the Market System], Tübingen, J.C.B. Mohr, 1980, 138 p.

WELD, John, 'Coase, Social Cost and Stability: An Integrative Essay', **13** *Natural Resources Journal*, 1973, 595-613.

WHITE, Barbara, 'Coase and the Courts: Economics for the Common Man.' **72** *Iowa Law Review*, 1987, 577-635..

WOHAR, Mark, 'Alternative Versions of the Coase Theorem and the Definition of Transaction Costs', **27(1)** *Quarterly Journal of Business and Economics*, 1988, 3-19.

WOJ, Carolyn, 'Property Rights Disputes: Current Fallacies and a New Approach', **14** *Journal of Legal Studies*, 1985, 411-422.

X (editors Journal), 'A Note on Rent and the Coase Theorem by David Shapiro', **14** *Journal of Economic Theory*, 1977, 221-222.

ZERBE, Richard O., Jr., 'The Problem of Social Cost: Fifteen Years Later', in SAY, Lin, (ed.), *Theory and Measurement of Economic Externalities*, New York, Academia Press, 1976, 29-36.

ZERBE, Richard O., Jr., 'The Problem of Social Cost in Retrospect', **2** *Research in Law and Economics*, 1980, 83-102.

ZUPAN, Mark A., 'On Cream Skimming, Coase and the Sustainability of Natural Monopolies', **22** *Applied Economics*, 1990, 487-492.

0640 Transaction Costs (Approach)

ALCHIAN, Armen A., 'Some Implications of Recognition of Property Right Transaction Costs', in BRUNNER, K. (ed.), *Economics and Social Institutions*, Boston, 1979, 233-252.

BARZEL, Yoram, 'Measurement Cost and the Organisation of Markets', **25** *Journal of Law and Economics*, 1982, 27-48.

BARZEL, Yoram, 'Transaction Costs: Are They Just Costs?', **141** *Journal of Institutional and Theoretical Economics*, 1985, 4-16.

BREEDEN, Charles H. and TOUMANOFF, Peter G., 'Transaction Costs and Economic Institutions', in LEUBE, K.R. and ZLABINGER, A.H. (eds.), *The Political Economy of Freedom*, München, Philosophia Verlag, 1984, 161-177.

CHEUNG, Steven N.S., *The Myth Of Social Costs: A Critique of Welfare Economics and the Implications for Public Policy*, London, Institute of Economic Affairs, 1978, 93 p.

COASE, Ronald H., 'The Nature of the Firm', **4** *Economica*, 1937, 386-405. Reprinted in KRONMAN, Anthony T. and POSNER, Richard A. (eds.), *The Economics of Contract Law*, Boston, Little Brown, 1979, 31-32.

COASE, Ronald H., *The Firm, the Market and the Law*, Chicago, University of Chicago Press, 1988, 217 p.

COHEN, Lloyd, 'Holdouts and Free Riders', **20** *Journal of Legal Studies*, 1991, 351-362.

DEMSETZ, Harold, 'The Cost of Transacting', **82** *Quarterly Journal of Economics*, 1968, 33-53.

DUGGER, William M., 'The Transaction Cost Analysis of O.E. Williamson: A New Synthesis?', **17** *Journal of Economic Issues*, 1983, 95-114.

EGGERTSSON, Thrainn, *Economic Behaviour and Institutions*, Cambridge, Cambridge University Press, 1990, 385 p.

EGGERTSSON, Thrainn, 'The Role of Transaction Costs and Property Rights in Economic Analysis', **34** *European Economic Review*, 1990, 450-457.

FREY, Bruno S., 'Comment' [On Barzel, Transaction Costs: Are They Just Costs?], **141** *Journal of Institutional and Theoretical Economics*, 1985, 17-20.

GOLDBERG, Victor P., 'Production Functions, Transaction Costs and the New Institutionalism', in FEIWEL, George (ed.), *Issues in Contemporary Microeconomics*, New York, Macmillan, 1984, 395-402. Reprinted in GOLDBERG, Victor P. (ed.), *Readings in the Economics of Contract Law*, Cambridge, Cambridge University Press, 1989, 21-23.

HESS, James D., 'A Comparison of Alternative Approaches to Economic Organization: Comment', **146** *Journal of Institutional and Theoretical Economics*, 1990, 72-75.

HIRSHLEIFER, Jack, 'Exchange Theory: The Missing Chapter', **11** *Western Economic Journal*, 1973, 129-146.

HUTTER, Michael, 'Transaction Cost and Communication', in GRAF VON DER SCHULENBURG, J.-Matthias and SKOGH, Göran (eds.), *Law and Economics and The Economics of Legal Regulation*, Dordrecht, Kluwer, 1986, 113-129.

MASTEN, Scott E., MEEHAN, James W., Jr. and SNYDER, Edward A., 'The Costs of Organization', **7** *Journal of Law, Economics, & Organization*, 1991, 1-25.

OTT, Claus, 'Vorvertragliche Aufklärungspflichten im Recht des Güter- und Leistungsaustausches' [Precontractual Obligation to Provide Information in the Sale of Goods and Services Act], in OTT, Claus and SCHÄFER, Hans-Bernd (eds.), *Ökonomische Probleme des Zivilrechts*, Berlin, Springer, 1991, 142-162.

SCHLAG, Pierre, 'The Problem of Transaction Costs', **62** *Southern California Law Review*, 1989, 1661-1699.

SCHMIDTCHEN, Dieter, 'Evolutorische Ordnungstheorie oder: die Transaktionskosten und das Unternehmertum' [The Theory of Evolutionary Order, or: Transaction Costs and Entrepreneurship], *ORDO (Jahrbuch für die Ordnung von Wirtschaft und Gesellschaft)*, Stuttgart, G. Fischer Verlag, 1989, 161-182.

ULPH, A.M. and ULPH, D.T., 'Transaction Costs in General Equilibrium Theory - A Survey', **42** *Economica*, 1975, 355-372.

WEGEHENKEL, Lothar, *Transaktionskosten, Wirtschaftssystem und Unternehmertum* [Transaction Costs, Economic System and Entrepreneurship], 1980, Tübingen, J.C.B. Mohr, 1980, 77 p.

WILLIAMSON, Oliver E., 'Transaction-Cost Economics: The Governance of Contractual Relations', **22** *Journal of Law and Economics*, 1979, 233-261.

WILLIAMSON, Oliver E., 'Contract Analysis: The Transaction Cost Approach', in

BURROWS, Paul and VELJANOVSKI, Cento G. (eds.), *The Economic Appraoch to Law*, London, Butterworths, 1981, 39-60.

WOHAR, Mark, 'Alternative Versions of the Coase Theorem and the Definition of Transaction Costs', **27(1)** *Quarterly Journal of Business and Economics*, 1988, 3-19.

0650 Property Rights (Approach)

ALCHIAN, Armen A., 'Some Economics of Property Rights', Santa Monica: Rand Corporation, *Rand Paper* No. 2316, 1961. Reprinted in **30** *Il Politico*, 1965, 816-829. Reprinted in ALCHIAN, Armen A., *Economic Forces at Work*, Indianapolis, Liberty Press, 1977.

ALCHIAN, Armen A., 'Economic Laws and Political Legislation', in SIEGAN, Bernard H. (ed.), *The Interaction of Economics and the Law*, Lexington, Lexington Books, 1978, 139-148.

ALCHIAN, Armen A. and DEMSETZ, Harold, 'The Property Right Paradigm', **33** *Journal of Economic History*, 1973, 16-27.

ARROW, Kenneth J., 'The Property Rights Doctrine and Demand Revelation under Incomplete Information', in BOSKIN, M.J. (ed.), *Economics and Human Welfare*, New York, 1979, 23-39.

BARZEL, Yoram, 'A Theory of Rationing by Waiting', **17** *Journal of Law and Economics*, 1974, 73-95.

BARZEL, Yoram, 'An Economic Analysis of Slavery', **20** *Journal of Law and Economics*, 1977, 87-110.

BARZEL, Yoram, *Economic Analysis of Property Rights*, Cambridge, Cambridge University Press, 1989, 122 p.

BLÜMEL, Wolfgang, PETHIG, Rüdiger and VON DEM HAGEN, Oskar, 'The Theory of Public Goods: A Survey of Recent Issues', **142** *Journal of Institutional and Theoretical Economics*, 1986, 241 ff.

BÖBEL, Ingo, *Eigentum, Eigentumsrechte und Institutioneller Wandel* [Property, Property Rights and Institutional Change], Berlin, Springer Verlag, 1988, 360 p.

BÖHM, Stephan, 'Handlungsrechte, Wettbewerb und Privatisierung' [Property Rights, Competition and Privatization], **34** *Wirtschaftspolitische Blätter*, 1987, 576-583.

BOTTOMLEY, Anthony, 'The Effect of Common Ownership of Land upon Resource Allocation in Tripolitania', **39** *Land Economics*, 1963, 91-95.

BUHBE, Matthes, *Ökonomische Analyse von Eigentumsrechten - Der Beitrag der economics of property rights zur Theorie der Institutionen* [Economic Analysis of Property Rights - The Contribution of the Property Rights Approach to the Theory of Institutions], Frankfurt am Main, Peter D. Lang, 1980, 185 p.

BYDLINSKI, Franz, *Fundamentale Rechtsgrundsätze* [Fundamental Principles of Law], Vienna-New York, Springer Publishers, 1988, 133-290 (ch.III).

CHEUNG, Steven N.S., 'The Enforcement of Property Rights in Children, and the Marriage Contract', **82** *Economic Journal*, 1972, 641-657.

CLARKSON, Kenneth W., 'Some Implications of Property Rights in Hospital Management', **15** *Journal of Law and Economics*, 1972, 363-384.

COASE, Ronald H., 'The Federal Communications Commission', **2** *Journal of Law and Economics*, 1959, 1-40.

COPES, Parzival, 'The Market as an Open Access Commons: A Neglected Aspect of Excess Capacity', **132** *De Economist*, 1984, 49-60.

CRAIN, W. Mark and TOLLISON, Robert D., 'Attenuated Property Rights and the Market for Governors', **20** *Journal of Law and Economics*, 1977, 205-211.

CRAIN, W. Mark, and ZARDKOOHI, Asghar, 'A Test of the Property-Rights Theory of the Firm: Water Utilities in the United States', **21** *Journal of Law and Economics*, 1978, 395-408.

DAVIES, David G., 'Property Rights and Economic Behavior in Private and Government Enterprises: The Case of Australia's Banking System', **3** *Research in Law and Economics*, 1981, 111-142.

DE ALESSI, Louis, 'The Economics of Property Rights: A Review of the Evidence', **2** *Research in Law and Economics*, 1980, 1-47.

DE ALESSI, Louis, 'Property Rights, Transaction Costs, and X-Efficiency: An Essay in Economic Theory', **73** *American Economic Review*, 1983, 64-81.

DE ALESSI, Louis, 'Property Rights and X-Efficiency: Reply', **73** *American Economic Review*, 1983, 843-845.

DE ALESSI, Louis, 'Form, Substance, and Welfare Comparisons in the Analysis of Institutions', **146** *Journal of Institutional and Theoretical Economics*, 1990, 5-23.

DE ALESSI, Louis and STAAF, Robert J., 'Property Rights and Choice', in MERCURO, Nicholas (ed.), *Law and Economics*, Boston, Kluwer Academic Publishers, 1989, 175-200.

DEMSETZ, Harold, 'Some Aspects of Property Rights', **9** *Journal of Law and Economics*, 1966, 61-70.

DEMSETZ, Harold, 'Toward a Theory of Property Rights', **57** *American Economic Review, Papers and Proceedings*, 1967, 347-359.

DEMSETZ, Harold, 'The Structure of Ownership and the Theory of the Firm', **26** *Journal of Law and Economics*, 1983, 375-390.

DiLORENZO, T.J., 'Property Rights, Information Costs, and the Economics of Rent Seeking', **144** *Journal of Institutional and Theoretical Economics*, 1988, 318-322.

DRAGUN, A.K., 'Property Rights in Economic Theory', **21** *Journal of Economic Issues*, 1987, 859-868.

EGGERTSSON, Thrainn, *Economic Behaviour and Institutions*, Cambridge, Cambridge University Press, 1990, 385 p.

EGGERTSSON, Thrainn, 'The Role of Transaction Costs and Property Rights in Economic Analysis', **34** *European Economic Review*, 1990, 450-457.

ELDER, Harold W., 'Property Rights Structures and Criminal Courts: An Analysis of State Criminal Courts', **7** *International Review of Law and Economics*, 1987, 21-32.

EPSTEIN, Richard A., 'Private Property and the Public Domain: The Case of Antitrust', in PENNOCK, J. Roland and CHAPMAN, John W. (eds.), *Nomos XXIV: Ethics, Economics and the Law*, New York, New York University Press, 1982, 48-82.

ESCHENBURG, Rolf, 'Mikroökonomische Aspekte von Property Rights' [Microeconomic Aspects of Property Rights], in SCHENK, K.E. (ed.), *Ökonomische Verfügungsrechte und Allokationsmechanismen in Wirtschaftssystemen*, Schriften des Vereins für Socialpolitik, Vol. 97, N.F., 1978, 9-27.

FEZER, Karl-Heinz, 'Aspekte einer Rechtskritik an der economic analysis of law und am property rights approach' [Aspects of a Legal Critique on Law & Economics and the Property Rights Approach], *Juristenzeitung*, 1986, 817-824.

FLEISHER, Arthur A. III, SHUGHART, William F. II and TOLLISON, Robert D., 'Ownership Structure in Professional Sports', **12** *Research in Law and Economics*, 1989, 71-75.

FRECH, H. Edward III, 'Property Rights, The Theory of the Firm, and Competitive Markets for Top Decision Makers', **2** *Research in Law and Economics*, 1980, 49-63.

FRECH, H. Edward III and GINSBURG, Paul B., 'Property Rights and Competition in Health Insurance: Multiple Objectives for Nonprofit Firms', **3** *Research in Law and Economics*, 1981, 155-171.

FREY, Bruno S. and BUHOFER, Heinz, 'Prisoners and Property Rights', **31** *Journal of Law and Economics*, 1988, 19-46.

FURUBOTN, Eirik G. and PEJOVICH, Svetozar, 'Property Rights and Economic Theory: A Survey of Recent Literature', **10** *Journal of Economic Literature*, 1972, 1137-1162.

FURUBOTN, Eirik G. and PEJOVICH, Svetozar, 'Property Rights, Economic Decentralization and the Evolution of the Yugoslav Firm, 1965-1972', **16** *Journal of Law and Economics*, 1973, 275-302.

FURUBOTN, Eirik G. and PEJOVICH, Svetovar (eds.), *The Economics of Property Rights*, Cambridge, Ballinger, 1974, 367 p.

GÄFGEN, Gérad, 'Entwicklung und Stand der Theorie der Property Rights. Eine kritische Bestandsaufnahme' [Development and Actual Situation of the Property Rights Theory. A Critical Element], in NEUMANN, M. (ed.), *Ansprüche, Eigentums- und Verfügungsrechte*, Schriften des Vereins für Socialpolitik, Vol. 140, 1983, 43-62.

GOLDBERG, Victor P., 'Fishing and Selling', **15** *Journal of Legal Studies*, 1986, 173-180.

GORDON, Scott and STEGEMANN, Klaus, 'The Market as a Commons: Is Catching Customers Like Catching Fish?', **133** *De Economist*, 1985, 218-231.

GOTTHOLD, Jürgen, 'Zur ökonomischen "Theorie des Eigentums". Eine kritische Einfuhrung' [The Economic Theory of Property - A Critical Introduction], **144** *Zeitschrift für das gesamte Handels- und Wirtschaftsrecht*, 1980, 545-562.

HAFNER, Gerhard, *Seerechtliche Verteilung von Nutzungsrechten* [The Assignment of Property Rights on the Sea], Vienna-New York, Springer Publishers, 1987,

533 p.

HANNER, John, 'Governement Response to the Buffalo Hide Trade, 1871-1883', **24** *Journal of Law and Economics*, 1981, 239-271.

HARDIN, Garrett, 'The Tragedy of the Commons', **162** *Science*, 1968, 1243-1248.

HARDIN, Garrett and BADEN, John, (eds.), *Managing the Commons*, San Francisco, Freeman, 1977, 294 p.

HESSE, Günter, 'Der Property-Rights-Ansatz. Eine ökonomische Theorie der Veränderung des Rechts?' [The Property Rights Approach. An Economic Theory of Legal Evolution?], **195** *Jahrbuch für Nationalökonomie und Statistik*, 1980, 481 ff.

HESSE, Günter, 'Zur Erklärung der Änderung von Handlungsrechten mit Hilfe der ökonomischen Theorie' [The Explanation of the Change of Property Rights with the Help of the Economic Theory], in SCHÜLLER, A. (ed.), *Property Rights und ökonomische Theorie*, München, Vahlen, 1983, 79-109.

HUTTER, Michael, 'The Property Rights Paradigm: A Comment', **188** *Jahrbuch für Nationaliökonomie und Statistik*, 1975, 552-556.

HUTTER, Michael, *Die Gestaltung von Property Rights als Mittel gesellschaftlich-wirtschaftlicher Allokation* [The Structure of Property Rights as a Means of Social-Economic Allocation], Göttingen, Vandenhoeck & Ruprecht, 1979, 245 p.

JOHNSEN, D. Bruce, 'Property Rights to Cartel Rents: The *Socony-Vacuum* Story', **34** *Journal of Law and Economics*, 1991, 177-203.

KÖHLER, Helmut, 'Vertragsrecht und "Property Rights"-Theorie, Zur Integration ökonomischer Theorien in das Privatrecht' [Contract Law and Property Rights Theory - On the Integration of Economic Theory into Private Law], **144** *Zeitschrift für das gesamte Handels- und Wirtschaftsrecht*, 1980, 589-607.

KRÜSSELBERG, Hans-Günter, 'Property Rights-Theorie und Wohlfartsökonomik' [Property Rights Theory and Welfare Economics], in SCHÜLLER, Alfred (ed.), *Property Rights und ökonomische Theorie*, München, Vahlen, 1983, 45-75.

KÜBLER, Friedrich, 'Was leistet die Konzeption der Property Rights für aktuelle rechtspolitische Probléme?' [What is the Use of the Conception of Property Rights for Actual Legal-Political Problems?], in NEUMANN, M. (ed.), *Ansprüche, Eigentums- und Verfügungsrechte*, Schriften des Vereines für Socialpolitik, Vol. 140, 1983, 105-122.

LEHMANN, Michael, 'Patentrecht und Theory der Property Rights, eine ökonomische und juristische Analyse' [Patent Law and Property Rights Theory, an Economic and Legal Analysis], in *Festschrift für R. Franceschelli*, Mailand, 1983, 35-51.

LEHMANN, Michael, 'Eigentum, geistiges Eigentum, gewerbliche Schutzrechte, Property Rights als Wettbewerbsbeschränkungen zur Förderung des Wettbewerbs' [Property, Intellectual Property, Commercial Rights of Protection, Property Rights as Restraints of Competition to Promote the Competition], in *Gewerblicher Rechtsschutz und Urheberrecht, Internationaler Teil (Festschrift für E.Ulmer)*, 1983, 356-362.

LEHMANN, Michael, 'Theorie der Property Rights und Schutz des geistigen und gewerblichen Eigentums - Wettbewerbsbeschränkungen zur Förderung des Wettbewerbs' [Property Rights Theory and the Protection of Intellectual and Commercial Property], in *Ansprüche, Eigentums- und Verfügungsrechte Schriften des Vereins für Socialpolitik*, Band 140, Berlin, Duncker & Humblot, 1984, 519-535.

LEHN, Kenneth, 'Property Rights, Risk Sharing, and Player Disability in Major League Baseball', **25** *Journal of Law and Economics*, 1982, 343-366.

LEIBENSTEIN, Harvey, 'Property Rights and X-Efficiency: Comment', **73** *American Economic Review*, 1983, 831-842.

LIBECAP, Gary D., 'Property Rights in Economic History: Implications for Research', **23** *Explorations in Economic History*, 1986, 227-252.

LIEBERMANN, Yehoshua and SYRQUIN, M., 'On the Use and Abuse of Rights: An Economic View', **4** *Journal of Economic Behavior and Organization*, 1983, 25-40.

LUECK, Dean, 'The Economic Nature of Wildlife Law', **18** *Journal of Legal Studies*, 1989, 291-324.

LUNN, John, 'The Roles of Property Rights and Market Power in Appropriating Innovative Output', **14** *Journal of Legal Studies*, 1985, 423-433.

MARTIN, Donald L., 'Job Property Rights and Job Defections', **15** *Journal of Law and Economics*, 1972, 385-410.

MAYHEW, Anne, 'Dangers in Using the Idea of Property Rights: Modern Property Rights Theory and the Neo-Classical Trap', **19** *Journal of Economic Issues*, 1985, 959-966.

McCHESNEY, Fred S., 'Government Prohibitions on Volunteer Fire Fighting in Nineteenth-Century America: A Property Rights Perspective', **15** *Journal of Legal Studies*, 1986, 69-92.

McCORMICK, Robert E. and MEINERS, Roger E., 'University Governance: A Property Rights Perspective', **31** *Journal of Law and Economics*, 1988, 423-442.

McKEAN, Roland N., 'Products Liability: Implications of Some Changing Property Rights', **84** *Quarterly Journal of Economics*, 1970, 611-626.

MORTENSEN, Dale T., 'Property Rights and Efficiency in Mating, Racing and Related Games', **72** *American Economic Review*, 1982, 968-979.

NUTZINGER, Hans G., 'The Economics of Property Rights - A New Paradigm in Social Science?', in STIGMULLER, W. (ed.), *Philosophy of Economics*, Berlin, Springer-Verlag, 1982.

O'HARA, Maureen, 'Property Rights and the Financial Firm', **24** *Journal of Law and Economics*, 1981, 317-332.

OSTROM, Elinor, *Governing the Commons. The Evolution of Institutions for Collective Action*, New York, Cambridge University Press, 1990.

PEJOVICH, Svetozar, 'Karl Marx, Property Rights School and the Process of Social Change', **35** *Kyklos*, 1982, 383-397.

PEJOVICH, Svetozar, *Fundamentals of Economics: A Property Rights Approach*, Dallas, Fisher Institute, 1984, 258 p.

PEJOVICH, Svetovar, *The Economics of Property Rights: Towards a Theory of Comparitive Systems*, Dordrecht, Kluwer Academic Publishers, 1990, 224 p.

REYNOLDS, R. Larry, 'Institutionally Determined Property Claims', **19** *Journal of Economic Issues*, 1985, 941-949.

ROSE-ACKERMAN, Susan, 'Inalienability and the Theory of Property Rights', **85** *Columbia Law Review*, 1985, 931-969.

ROWLEY, Charles K. and YARROW, G.K., 'Property Rights, Regulation and Public Enterprise: The Case of the British Steel Industry 1957-1975', **1** *International Review of Law and Economics*, 1981, 63 ff.

RUNGE, Carlisle Ford, 'The Innovation of Rules and the Structure of Incentives in Open Access Resources', **67** *American Journal of Agricultural Economics*, 1985, 368-372.

SAMUELS, Warren J., 'Welfare Economics, Power, and Property', in WUNDERLICH, G. and GILSON, W.L. (eds.), *Perspectives of Property*, University Park, Institute for Research on Land and Water Resources, 1972, 61-127. Reprinted in SAMUELS, Warren J. and SCHMID, A. Allen (eds.), *Law and Economics: An Institutional Perspective*, Boston, Nijhoff, 1981, 9-75.

SCHAP, David, 'Pricing and Property Rights in Government Enterprises: Some Dynamic Aspects', **11** *Research in Law and Economics*, 1988, 113-127.

SCHENK, Karl-Ernst, 'Property Rights und Theorie der Institutionen' [Property Rights and Theory of Institutions], in **17(4)** *Das Wirtschaftsstudium*, 1988, 226-231.

SCHMID, A. Allan, 'The Economics of Property Rights: A Review Article', in SAMUELS, Warren J. (ed.), *The Chicago School of Political Economy*, East Lansing, Division of Research, Graduate School of Business Administration, Michigan State University, 1976, 469-478.

SCHMID, A. Allan, 'Predicting the Performance of Alternative Institutions', in SAMUELS, Warren J. and SCHMID, A. Allen (eds.), *Law and Economics: An Institutional Perspective*, Boston, Nijhoff, 1981, 76-94.

SCHMIDTCHEN, Dieter, *Property Rights, Freiheit und Wettbewerbspolitik* [Property Rights, Freedom and Competition Policy], Tübingen, J.C.B. Mohr, 1983, 71 p.

SCHÜLLER, Alfred, 'Property Rights, Unternehmerische Legitimation und Wirtschaftsordnung. Zum vermögenstheoretischen Ansatz einer allgemeinen Theorie der Unternehmung' [Property Rights, Entrepreneurial Legitimation and Economic System. On the Property Rights Approach of a General Theory of the Enterprise], in SCHENK, K.E. (ed.), *Ökonomische Verfügungsrechte und Allokationsmechanismen in Wirtschaftssystemen*, Schriften des Vereins für Socialpolitik, Vol. 97, N.F., 1978, 29-87.

SCHÜLLER, Alfred, 'Eigentumsrechte, Unternehmenskontrollen und Wettbewerbsordnung' [Property Rights, Corporate Control and Competition], **30** *ORDO, Jahrbuch für die Ordnung von Wirtschaft und Gesellschaft*, 1979, Stuttgart, G. Fischer Verlag, 325-364.

SCHÜLLER, Alfred, 'Zur Ökonomik der Property Rights' [On the Economics of Property Rights], **14(5)** *Das Wirtschaftsstudium*, 1985, 259-265.

SCHUMANN, Joachim, '"Neue Mikroökonomik" und Theorie des Eigentumsrechte. Ansätze zur Ergänzung der mikroökonomischen Theorie' ['New Microeconomics' and Property Rights Theory. An Introduction to the Completion of Microeconomic Theory], **7** *Wirtschaftswissenschaftliches Studium*, 1978, 307-

311.

SCHWARTZ, Pedro, 'The Market and the Metamarket: A Review of the Contributions of the Economic Theory of Property Rights', in PEJOVICH, Svetozar (ed.), *Socialism: Institutional, Philosophical and Economic Issues*, Dordrecht, Kluwer Academic, 1987, 11-32.

SWANEY, James A., 'Common Property, Reciprocity, and Community', **24** *Journal of Economic Issues*, 1990, 451-462.

SWEENEY, Richard James, TOLLISON, Robert D. and WILLETT, Thomas D., 'Market Failure, The Common-Pool Problem, and Ocean Resource Exploitation', **17** *Journal of Law and Economics*, 1974, 179-192.

TIETZEL, Manfred 'Die Ökonomie der Property Rights: Ein Überblick' [The Economics of Property Rights: A Survey], **30** *Zeitschrift für Wirtschaftspolitik*, 1981, 207-243.

von WEIZSÄCKER, Carl-Christian, 'Was leistet die Property Rights Theorie für aktuelle wirtschaftspolitische Fragen?' [What Brings the Property Rights Theory for Economic Policy Questions?], in NEUMANN, M. (ed.), *Ansprüche, Eigentums- und Verfügungsrechte*, Schriften des Vereins für Socialpolitik, Vol. 140, Berlin, Dunker u. Humblot, 1984, 123-152.

WILLIAMSON, Oliver E., 'A Comparison of Alternative Approaches to Economic Organization', **146** *Journal of Institutional and Theoretical Economics*, 1990, 61-71.

WINIECKI, J., 'Buying Out Property Rights to the Economy from the Ruling Stratum: The Case of Soviet-Type States', **9** *International Review of Law and Economics*, 1989, 79-85.

YANG, Xiaokai and WILLS, Ian R., 'A Model Formalizing the Theory of Property Rights', **14** *Journal of Comparative Economics*, 1990, 177-198.

0660 Public Goods. Club goods

BONUS, Holger, 'Offentliche Güter und der Öffentlichkeitsgrad von Gütern' [Public Goods and the Publicness of Goods], **136** *Journal of Institutional and Theoretical Economics*, 1980, 50-81.

BORCHERDING, Thomas E., 'Competition, Exclusion, and the Optimal Supply of Public Goods', **21** *Journal of Law and Economics*, 1978, 111-132.

BRUBAKER, Earl D., 'Free Ride, Free Revelation, or Golden Rule ?', **18** *Journal of Law and Economics*, 1975, 147-161.

BUCHANAN, James M., 'An Economic Theory of Clubs', **32** *Economica*, 1965, 1-14.

BUCHANAN, James M., 'Public Goods in Theory and Practice: A Note on the Minasian-Samuelson Discussion', **10** *Journal of Law and Economics*, 1967, 193-197.

CHEUNG, Steven N.S., 'The Fable of the Bees: An Economic Investigation', **16** *Journal of Law and Economics*, 1973, 11-33.

COASE, Ronald H., 'The Lighthouse in Economics', **17** *Journal of Law and Economics*, 1974, 357-376.

COHEN, Lloyd, 'Holdouts and Free Riders', **20** *Journal of Legal Studies*, 1991, 351-362.

CORNES, Richard and SANDLER, Todd, *The Theory of Externalities, Public Goods and Club Goods*, Cambridge, Cambridge University Press, 1986, 303 p.

DE JASAY, Anthony, *Social Contract, Free Ride: A Study on the Public Goods Problem*, Oxford, Oxford University Press, 1989, 256 p.

DEMSETZ, Harold, 'The Private Production of Public Goods', **13** *Journal of Law and Economics*, 1970, 293-306.

DEMSETZ, Harold, 'Joint Supply and Price Discrimination', **16** *Journal of Law and Economics*, 1973, 389-405.

DEMSETZ, Harold, 'Reply to Professor Thompson', **16** *Journal of Law and Economics*, 1973, 413-415.

DUBIN, Jeffrey A. and NAVARRO, Peter, 'How Markets for Impure Public Goods Organize: The Case of Household Refuse Collection', **4** *Journal of Law, Economics, & Organization*, 1988, 217-241.

EKELUND, Robert B., Jr. and HULETT, Joe R., 'Joint Supply, the Taussig-Pigou Controversy, and the Competitive Provision of Public Goods', **16** *Journal of Law and Economics*, 1973, 369-387.

GOLDIN, Kenneth D., 'Equal Access versus Selective Access: A Critique of Public Goods Theory', **29** *Public Choice*, 1977, 53-71.

HANSMANN, Henry B., 'A Theory of Status Organizations', **2** *Journal of Law, Economics, & Organization*, 1986, 119-130.

HARTOG, Hendrik, 'Property as Government in Eighteenth-Century America: The Case of New York City', **10** *Journal of Legal Studies*, 1981, 305-341.

HEAD, John G ., *Public Goods and Public Policy*, Durham, Duke University Press, 1974.

HUMMEL, Jeffrey Rogers, 'National Goods Versus Public Goods: Defense, Disarmament, and Free Riders', **4** *Review of Austrian Economics*, 1990, 88-122.

KIM, O. and WALKER, M., 'The Free Rider Problem: Experimental Evidence', **43** *Public Choice*, 1984, 3 ff.

KORMENDI, Roger C., 'A New Remedy for the Free Rider Problem? - Flies in the Ointment', **1** *Research in Law and Economics*, 1979, 115-130.

KORMENDI, Roger C., 'Further Thought on the Free Rider Problem and Demand Revealing Processes', **2** *Research in Law and Economics*, 1980, 219-225.

LA CROIX, Sumner J., 'Homogeneous Middleman Groups. What Determines the Homogeneity?', **5** *Journal of Law, Economics, & Organization*, 1989, 211-222.

LEE, Dwight R., 'Discrimination and Efficiency in the Pricing of Public Goods', **20** *Journal of Law and Economics*, 1977, 403-420.

MARCHAND, James R. and RUSSEL, Keith P., 'Externalities, Liability and Resource Allocation', **63** *American Economic Review*, 1973, 611-620.

MEADE, J.E., 'External Economies and Diseconomies in a Competitive Situation',

62 *Economic Journal*, 1952, 54-67. Reprinted in ARROW, Kenneth J. and SCITOVSKY, Tibor (eds.), *Readings in Welfare Economics*, London, 1969.

MINASIAN, Jora R., 'Public Goods in Theory and Practice Revisited', **10** *Journal of Law and Economics*, 1967, 205-207.

MINASIAN, Jora R., 'Indivisibility, Decreasing Cost, and Excess Capacity: The Bridge', **22** *Journal of Law and Economics*, 1979, 385-397.

O'DRISCOLL, Gerald P., Jr., 'The American Express Case: Public Good or Monopoly ?', **19** *Journal of Law and Economics*, 1976, 163-175.

OLSON, Mancur, *The Logic of Collective Action. Public Goods and the Theory of Groups*, Cambridge, Harvard University Press, 1965, 186 p.

ROTHENBERG, Jerome, 'The Economics of Congestion and Pollution: An Integrated View', **60** *American Economic Review (Papers and Proceedings)*, 1970, 114-121.

SAMUELSON, Paul A., 'Pitfalls in the Analysis of Public Goods', **10** *Journal of Law and Economics*, 1967, 199-204.

SHOUP, D. Carl, 'Theoretical Efficiency in Pollution Control: Comment', **9** *Western Economic Journal*, 1971, 310-313.

THOMPSON, Earl A., 'The Private Production of Public Goods: A Comment', **16** *Journal of Law and Economics*, 1973, 407-412.

TIDEMAN, Nicolaus T., 'The Evaluation of Rules for Making Collective Decisions: A Reply to Kormendi', **2** *Research in Law and Economics*, 1980, 213-217.

WILLIAMS, Stephen F., 'Running Out: The Problem of Exhaustible Resources', **7** *Journal of Legal Studies*, 1978, 165-199.

WOLF, Charles Jr., 'A Theory of Nonmarket Failure: Framework for Implementation Analysis', **22** *Journal of Law and Economics*, 1979, 107-139.

0670 Other Concepts

ABRAHAM, Kenneth S., *Distributing Risk: Insurance, Legal Theory and Public Policy (in American Insurance Law)*, New Haven, Yale University Press, 1986, 254 p.

AKERLOF, George A., 'The Markets for "Lemons": Qualitative Uncertainty and the Market Mechanism', **84** *Quarterly Journal of Economics*, 1970, 488-500. Reprinted in GOLDBERG, Victor P. (ed.), *Readings in the Economics of Contract Law*, Cambridge, Cambridge University Press, 1989, 24-28.

ALCHIAN, Armen A. and DEMSETZ, Harold, 'Production, Information Costs, and Economic Organization', **62** *American Economic Review*, 1972, 777-795.

ALCHIAN, Armen A., 'Uncertainty, Evolution, and Economic Theory', **58** *Journal of Political Economy*, 1950, 211 ff.

APPELBAUM, E. and KATZ, E., 'Transfer Seeking and Avoidance: On the Full Social Costs of Rent Seeking', **48** *Public Choice*, 1986, 175 ff.

ARANSON, Peter H., 'Rational Ignorance in Politics, Economics and Law', **1**

Journal des Economistes et des Etudes Humaines, 1989, 25-42.

ARROW, Kenneth J., 'The Economics of Moral Hazard: Further Comment', **58** *American Economic Review*, 1968, 537-538. Reprinted in GOLDBERG, Victor P., *Readings in the Economics of Contract Law*, Cambridge, Cambridge University Press, 1989, 33-34.

ARROW, Kenneth J., *Essays in the Theory of Risk-Bearing*, Amsterdam, North-Holland, 1971, 278 p.

BAIRD, Douglas G. and JACKSON, Thomas H., 'Information, Uncertainty, and the Transfer of Property', **13** *Journal of Legal Studies*, 1984, 299-320.

BARZEL, Yoram, 'Some Fallacies in the Interpretation of Information Costs', **20** *Journal of Law and Economics*, 1977, 291-307.

BARZEL, Yoram, 'Measurement Cost and the Organisation of Markets', **25** *Journal of Law and Economics*, 1982, 27-48.

CAMERER, Colin F., 'Comment on Noll and Krier, "Some Implications of Cognitive Psychology for Risk Regulation"', **19** *Journal of Legal Studies*, 1990, 791-799.

CARTER, R.L., 'Public Policy and Insurability', **11** *Geneva Papers on Risk and Insurance*, 1986, 145-156.

COASE, Ronald H., 'The Market for Goods and the Market for Ideas', **64** *American Economic Review. Papers and Proceedings*, 1974, 384-391.

COOTER, Robert D., MARKS Stephen and MNOOKIN, Robert, 'Bargaining in the Shadow of the Law: A Testable Model of Strategic Behavior', **11** *Journal of Legal Studies*, 1982, 225-251.

DEMSETZ, Harold, 'Information and Efficiency: Another Viewpoint', **12** *Journal of Law and Economics*, 1969, 1-22.

DiLORENZO, Thomas J., 'Property Rights, Information Costs, and the Economics of Rent Seeking', **144** *Journal of Institutional and Theoretical Economics*, 1988, 318-322.

RETHER, David M., SCHWARTZ, Alan, and WILDE, Louis L., 'The Irrelevance of Information Overload: An Analysis of Search and Disclosure', **59** *Southern California Law Review*, 1986, 277 ff.

GROSSMAN, Herschel I., 'Adverse Selection, Dissembling, and Competitive Equilibrium', **10** *Bell Journal of Economics*, 1979, 336-343.

HARDY, Charles O., *Risk and Risk Bearing*, Chicago, University of Chicago Press, 1923. Reprinted in KRONMAN, Anthony T. and POSNER, Richard A. (eds.), *The Economics of Contract Law*, Boston, Little Brown, 1979, 26-28.

HARRIS, Milton and TOWNSEND, Robert, 'Resource Allocation under Asymmetric Information', **49** *Econometrica*, 1981, 33-64.

HART, Oliver D., 'The Market Mechanism as an Incentive Scheme', **14** *Bell Journal of Economics*, 1983, 366-382.

HAYEK, Friedrich A. von, 'The Pretence of Knowledge', **77** *Swedish Journal of Economics*, 1975, 433-442.

HAYEK, Friedrich A. von, 'The Use of Knowledge in Society', **35** *American Economic Review*, 1945, 519-530.

HEERTJE, A., 'Speltheorie als economische analyse van het recht' [Game Theory as Economic Analysis of Law], in MARIS, C.W. et al. (eds.), *Recht, Rechtvaardigheid en Doelmatigheid*, Arnhem, Gouda Quint, 1990, 90-100.

HEINER, Ronald A., 'Imperfect Choice and the Origin of Institutional Rules', **146** *Journal of Institutional and Theoretical Economics*, 1990, 720-726.

HIRSHLEIFER, Jack and RILEY, John G., 'The Analysis of Uncertainty and Information - An Expository Survey', **17** *Journal of Economic Literature*, 1979, 1375-1421.

HIRSHLEIFER, Jack and RILEY, John G., 'The Analysis of Uncertainty and Information - An Expository Survey', **17** *Journal of Economic Literature*, 1979, 1375-1421.

HOLMSTRÖM, Bengt, 'Moral Hazard in Teams', **13** *Bell Journal of Economics*, 1982, 324-340.

HOLMSTRÖM, Bengt, 'Moral Hazard and Observability', **10** *Bell Journal of Economics*, 1979, 74-91.

HURWICZ, L. and SHAPIRO, L., 'Incentive Structures Maximizing Residual Gain under Incomplete Information', **9** *Bell Journal of Economics*, 1978, 180-191.

KNETSCH, Jack L., 'Legal Rules and the Basis for Evaluating Economic Losses', **4** *International Review of Law and Economics*, 1984, 5-13.

KOBOLDT, Christian, ' Kommentar' [Comment] (On Schanze, Stellvertretung und ökonomische Agentur-Theorie), in OTT, Claus and SCHÄFER, Hans-Bernd (eds.), *Ökonomische Probleme des Zivilrechts*, Berlin, Springer, 1991, 76-86.

KRIER, James E., 'Risk and Design', **19** *Journal of Legal Studies*, 1990, 781-790.

KUNZ, Harald, 'Kommentar' [Comment] (on Tietzel, Probleme der asymmetrischen Informationsverteilung beim Güter- und Leistungstausch), in OTT, Claus and SCHÄFER, Hans-Bernd (eds.), *Allokationseffizienz in der Rechtsordnung*, Berlin, Springer, 1989, 64-69.

LAFFONT, Jean-Jacques, 'Analysis of Hidden Gaming in a Three-Level Hierarchy', **6** *Journal of Law, Economics, & Organization*, 1990, 301-324.

LELAND, Hayne E., 'Quacks, Lemons, and Licensing: A Theory of Minimum Quality Standards', **87** *Journal of Political Economy*, 1979, 1325-1346.

LEMPERT, Richard, 'Statistics in the Courtroom: Building on Rubinfeld', **85** *Columbia Law Review*, 1985, 1098-1116.

MACHINA, Mark J. and ROTHSCHILD, Michael, 'Risk', in EATWELL, John, MILGATE, Murray and NEWMAN, Peter (eds.), *The New Palgrave: A Dictionary of Economics*, London, Macmillan, 1987, Volume 3, 201-206.

MACKAAY, Ejan J.P., *Economics of Information and Law*, Dordrecht, Kluwer Nijhoff, 1982, 293 p.

MARSHALL, John M., 'Moral Hazard', **66** *American Economic Review*, 1976, 880-890.

MELODY, William H., 'Information: An Emerging Dimension of Institutional Analysis', **21** *Journal of Economic Issues*, 1987, 1313-1339.

MILGROM, Paul R. and ROBERTS John, 'Relying on the Information of Interested Parties', **17** *Rand Journal of Economics*, 1986, 18-32.

MOORE, John H., 'Agency Costs, Technological Change, and Soviet Central Planning', **24** *Journal of Law and Economics*, 1981, 189-214.

MOORE, Peter G., *The Business of Risk*, Cambridge, Cambridge University Press, 1983, 244 p.

NOLL, Roger G. and KRIER, James E., 'Some Implications of Cognitive Psychology for Risk Regulation', **19** *Journal of Legal Studies*, 1990, 747-779.

PAULY, Mark V., 'The Economics of Moral Hazard', **58** *American Economic Review*, 1968, 531-537. Reprinted in GOLDBERG, Victor P. (ed.), *Readings in the Economics of Contract Law*, Cambridge, Cambridge University Press, 1989, 31-32.

PAULY, Mark V. and SATTERTHWAITE, M.A., 'Test of the Role of Consumer Information', **12** *Bell Journal of Economics*, 1981, 488 ff.

RASMUSEN, Eric, 'Moral Hazard in Risk-Averse Teams', **18** *Rand Journal of Economics*, 1987, 428-435.

REED, Robert W., 'Information in Political Markets. A Little Knowledge Can Be a Dangerous Thing', **5** *Journal of Law, Economics, & Organization*, 1989, 355-374.

ROSS, Stephen A., 'The Economic Theory of Agency: The Principal's Problem', **63** *American Economic Review. Papers and Proceedings*, 1973, 134-139.

RUBINFELD, Daniel L., 'Econometrics in the Courtroom', **85** *Columbia Law Review*, 1985, 1048-1097.

SCHÄFER, Hans-Bernd, 'Ökonomische Analyse von Aufklärungspflichten' [Economic Analysis of the Duty to Provide Information], in OTT, Claus and SCHÄFER, Hans-Bernd (eds.), *Ökonomische Probleme des Zivilrechts*, Berlin, Springer, 1991, 117-141.

SCHANZE, Erich, 'Notes on Models of Choice, Incomplete Contracting, and the Agency Framework', **146** *Journal of Institutional and Theoretical Economics*, 1990, 684-690.

SCHANZE, Erich, 'Stellvertretung und ökonomische Agentur-Theorie - Probleme und Wechselbezüge' [The Law of Agency and Agency Theory - Problems and Relations], in OTT, Claus and SCHÄFER, Hans-Bernd (eds.), *Ökonomische Probleme des Zivilrechts*, Berlin, Springer, 1991, 60-75.

SCHMIT, Joan T., 'A New View of the Requisites of Insurability', **53** *Journal of Risk & Insurance*, 1986, 320-329.

SHAVELL, Steven, 'Risk Sharing and Incentives in the Principal and Agent Relationship', **10** *Bell Journal of Economics*, 1979, 55-73.

SPITZER, Matthew L., 'Comment on Noll and Krier, "Some Implications of Cognitive Psychology for Risk Regulation"', **19** *Journal of Legal Studies*, 1990, 801-808.

STIGLER, George J., 'The Economics of Information', **69** *Journal of Political Economy*, 1961, 213-225.

STIGLITZ, Joseph E., 'Principal and Agent (ii)', in EATWELL, John, MILGATE, Murray and NEWMAN, Peter (eds.), *The New Palgrave: A Dictionary of Economics*, London, Macmillan, 1987, Volume 3, 966-972.

STRYDOM, P.D.F., 'The Economics of Information: a Sujectivist View', in

KIRZNER, Israel M. (ed.), *Subjectivism, Intelligibility and Economic Understanding. Essays in Honor of Ludwig M. Lachmann on his Eightieth Birthday*, London, Macmillan, 1986, 288-294.

THOMSON, J.J., 'Rights, Restitution and Risk', in PARENT, W. (ed.), Cambridge (Mass.), Harvard University Press, 1986.

TIETZEL, Manfred, 'Kommentar' [Comment] (on Schäfer, Ökonomische Analyse von Aufklärungspflichten and Ott, Vorvertragliche Aufklärungspflichten), in OTT, Claus and SCHÄFER, Hans-Bernd (eds.), *Ökonomische Probleme des Zivilrechts*, Berlin, Springer, 1991, 163-166.

TIETZEL, Manfred, 'Probleme der asymmetrischen Informationsverteilung beim Güter- und Leistungstausch' [Problems of Asymmetric Information in the Trade of Goods and Services], in OTT, Claus and SCHÄFER, Hans-Bernd (eds.), *Allokationseffizienz in der Rechtsordnung*, Berlin, Springer, 1989, 52-63.

TISDELL, Clem, 'Law, Economics and Risk-Taking', **36** *Kyklos*, 1983, 3-20.

VILLA, Gianroberto, 'Errore riconosciuto, annullamento del contratto ed incentivi alla ricerca di informazioni' [Known Mistake, Contract Avoidance and Incentives To Gathering Information], *Quadrimestre*, 1988, 286-300.

WACHTER, Michael L. and WILLIAMSON, Oliver E., 'Obligational Markets and the Mechanics of Inflation', **9** *Bell Journal of Economics*, 1978, 549-571.

1000 FAMILY LAW
Bertrand Lemennicier

1000 Family Law: General

ALEXANDER, L. and O'DRISCOLL, L., 'Stork Markets: An Analysis of "Baby Selling"', *Journal of Libertarian Studies*, 1980.

BECKER, Gary S., 'On the Relevance of the New Economics of the Family', **64** *American Economic Review. Papers and Proceedings*, 1974, 317-319.

BECKER, Gary S., 'A Theory of Social Interactions', **82** *Journal of Political Economy*, 1974, 1063-1093.

BECKER, Gary S., *The Economic Approach to Human Behavior*, University of Chicago Press, Chicago, 1976, 314 p.

BECKER, Gary S., *A Treatise on the Family*, Cambridge, Harvard University Press, 1981, 288 p.

BECKER, Gary S., 'Human Capital, Effort, and the Sexual Division of Labor', **3** *Journal of Labor Economics*, 1985, S33-ff.

BECKER, Gary S., 'Family Economics and Macro Behavior', **78** *American Economic Review*, 1988, 1-13.

BEN-PORATH, Y., 'The F-Connection: Families, Friends, and Firms and the Organization of Exchange', **6** *Population Development Review*, 1980, 1-30.

BENNETT, Belinda, 'The Economics of Wifing Services: Law and Economics on the Family', **18** *Journal of Law and Society*, 1991, 206-218.

CASS, Ronald A., 'Coping With Life, Law, and Markets: A Comment on Posner and the Law-and-Economics Debate', **67** *Boston University Law Review*, 1987, 73-97.

CHEUNG, Steven N.S., 'The Enforcement of Property Rights in Children, and the Marriage Contract', **82** *Economic Journal*, 1972, 641-657.

CHISWICK, Barry R., 'Minimum Schooling Legislation, Externalities and a "Child Tax', **15** *Journal of Law and Economics*, 1972, 353-361.

CIGNO, Alessandro, *Economics of the Family*, Oxford, Clarendon, 1991, 212 p.

COELEN, Stephen P. and McINTYRE, Robert J., 'An Econometric Model of Pronatalist and Abortion Policies', **94** *Journal of Political Economy*, 1986, 1077-1101.

COHEN, Jane Maslow, 'Posnerism, Pluralism, Pessimism', **67** *Boston University Law Review*, 1987, 105-175.

EDWARDS, Linda N., 'An Empirical Analysis of Compulsory Schooling Legislation, 1940-1960', **21** *Journal of Law and Economics*, 1978, 203-222.

HORTON, Paul and ALEXANDER, Lawrence, 'Freedom of Contract and the Family: A Skeptical Appraisal', in PEDEN, Joseph R. and GLAHE, Fred R. (eds.), *The American Family and the State*, San Francisco, Pacific Research Institute for Public Policy, 1986, 229-255.

KEELEY, Michael C., 'The Economics of Family Formation', **15** *Economic Inquiry*, 1977, 238-250.

LAMBERT, Richard A., 'Executive Effort and Selection of Risky Projects', **17** *Rand Journal of Economics*, 1986, 77-88.

LANDES, Elisabeth M. and POSNER, Richard A., 'The Economics of Baby Shortage', **7** *Journal of Legal Studies*, 1978, 323-348.

LEMENNICIER, Bertrand, *Le Marché du Mariage et de la Famille* [The Marriage Market and the Family], Collection Libre Echange, Paris, PUF, 1988.

LEMENNICIER, Bertrand, 'Bioéthique et liberté' [Bio-Ethics and Liberty], **13** *Droits: revue française de théorie juridique*, 1990, 111-122.

MALLOY, Robin Paul, 'Market Philosophy in the Legal Tension Between Children's Autonomy and Parental Authority', **21** *Ind. Law Review*, 1988, 889 ff.

MANSER, Marilyn and BROWN, Murray, 'Marriage and Household Decision-Making: A Bargaining Analysis', **21** *International Economic Review*, 1980, 31-44.

OLSEN, Frances E., 'The Family and the Market: A Study of Ideology and Legal Reform', **96** *Harvard Law Review*, 1983, 1497-1578.

PALMER, John, 'The Social Cost of Adoption Agencies', **6** *International Review of Law and Economics*, 1986, 189-203.

PAPPS, Ivy, *For Love or Money? A Preliminary Economic Analysis of Marriage and the Family*, London, Institute of Economic Affairs (Hobart Paperback No.86), 1980, 63 p.

POLLAK, R.A., 'A Transaction Cost Approach to Families and Households', **23** *Journal of Economic Literature*, 1985.

POSNER, Richard A., 'The Regulation of the Market in Adoptions', **67** *Boston University Law Review*, 1987, 59-72.

POSNER, Richard A., 'The Ethics and Economics of Enforcing Contracts of Surrogate Motherhood', **6** *Journal of Contemporary Health Law and Policy*, 1989, 21-31.

RAMSEYER, J. Mark, 'Indentured Prostitution in Imperial Japan: Credible Commitments in the Commercial Sex Industry', **7** *Journal of Law, Economics, & Organization*, 1991, 89-116.

RIBOUD, M., 'Altruisme au sein de la famille, croissance économique et démographie' [Altruism in the Family, Economic Growth and Demography], *Revue Economique*, 1988, janvier..

SCHOEMAN, Ferdinand, 'Childhood Competence and Autonomy', **12** *Journal of Legal Studies*, 1983, 267-287.

SCHULTZ, Theodore W. (ed.), *Economics of the Family: Marriage, Children and Human Capital*, Chicago, University of Chicago Press, 1974, 584 p.

SMITH, Vernon L., 'Economic Theory and Its Discontents', **64** *American Economic Review. Papers and Proceedings*, 1974, 320 ff.

TULLOCK, Gordon, 'The Transitional Gains Trap', **6** *Bell Journal of Economics*, 1975, 671-678.

WEISS, Yoram and WILLIS, Robert J., 'Children as Collective Goods and Divorce

Settlements', **3** *Journal of Labor Economics*, 1985, 268 ff.

1100 Marriage Law

ALLEN, Douglas W., 'An Inquiry into the State's Role in Marriage', **13** *Journal of Economic Behavior and Organization*, 1990, 171-191.

BAYLES, Michael D., 'Marriage as a Bad Business Deal: Distribution of Property on Divorce', **17** *Florida State University Law Review*, 1989, 95-106.

BECKER, Gary S., 'A Theory of Marriage: Part 1', **81** *Journal of Political Economy*, 1973, 813-846.

BECKER, Gary S., LANDES, Elisabeth M. and MICHAEL, Robert T., 'An Economic Analysis of Marital Instability', **85** *Journal of Political Economy*, 1977, 1141-1187.

BECKER, Gary S. and MURPHY, Kevin M., 'The Family and the State', **31** *Journal of Law and Economics*, 1988, 1-18.

BISHOP, William, '"Is He Married?" Marriage as a Market Signal' in KNETSCH, Jack L. (ed.), *Economic Aspects of Family Law*, Toronto, Butterworths.

BORENSTEIN, Severin and COURANT, Paul N., 'How To Carve a Medical Degree: Human Capital Assets in Divorce Settlements', **79** *American Economic Review*, 1989, 992-1009.

BRINING, Margaret F., 'Rings and Promises', **6** *Journal of Law, Economics, & Organization*, 1990, 203-215.

BROUDE, Donna L., 'The Effect of the Tax Reform Act of 1984 on Divorce Financial Planning', **21** *Journal of Family Law*, 1986, 283-300.

CARBONE, June, 'Economics, Feminism, and the Reinvention of Alimony: A Reply to Ira Ellman', **43** *Vanderbilt Law Review*, 1990, 1463-1501.

CHEUNG, Steven N.S., 'The Enforcement of Property Rights in Children, and the Marriage Contract', **82** *Economic Journal*, 1972, 641-657.

COHEN, Lloyd, 'Marriage, Divorce, and Quasi-Rents; or, "I Gave Him the Best Years of My Life"', **16** *Journal of Legal Studies*, 1987, 267-303.

FAIR, R.C., 'A Theory of Extramarital Affairs', **86** *Journal of Political Economy*, 1978, 45-61.

FREIDEN, A., 'The United States Marriage Market', **82** *Journal of Political Economy*, 1974, S34-S53.

FRIEDMAN, Lawrence M. and PERCIVAL, Robert V., 'Who Sues for Divorce? From Fault through Fiction to Freedom', **5** *Journal of Legal Studies*, 1976, 61-82.

FUCHS, Maximilian, 'Die Behandlung von Ehe und Scheidung in der "Ökonomischen Analyse des Rechts"' [The Treatment of Marriage and Divorce in the "Economic Analysis of Law"], **7** *Zeitschrift für das gesamte Familienrecht*, 1979, 553-557.

GROSSBARD, Amyra, 'Towards a Marriage between Economics and Anthropology and a General Theory of Marriage', **68** *American Economic Review. Papers and Proceedings*, 1978, 33-37.

GROSSBARD-SHECHTMAN, Amyra, 'A Theory of Allocation of Time in Markets for Labour and Marriage', **94** *Economic Journal*, 1984, 863-882.

HUTCHENS, Robert M., 'Welfare, Remarriage and Market Search', **69** *American Economic Review*, 1979, 369-379.

KING, Allan G., 'Human Capital and the Risk of Divorce: An Asset in Search of a Property Right', **49** *Southern Journal of Economics*, 1982, 536-541.

LANDES, Elisabeth M, 'Economics of Alimony', **7** *Journal of Legal Studies*, 1978, 35-63.

LEMENNICIER, Bertrand, 'La spécialisation des rôles conjugaux, les gains du mariage et la perspective du divorce', *Consommation*, 1980, n. 1.

LEMENNICIER, Bertrand, *Le Marché du Mariage et de la Famille* [The Marriage Market and the Family], Collection Libre Echange, Paris, PUF, 1988.

LEMENNICIER, Bertrand, 'Les déterminants de la mobilité matrimoniale' [The Determinants of Matrimonial Mobility], *Consommation*, 1982, n. 2.

LEMENNICIER, Bertrand et LEVY-GARBOUA, 'L'arbitrage autarcie-marché: une explication du travail féminin' [Arbitration Autarchy-Market: An Explanation of Female Labour], *Consommation*, 1981, n. 2.

LICHTENSTEIN, Norman B., 'Marital Misconduct and the Allocation of Financial Resources at Divorce: A Farewell to Fault', **51** *UMRC Law Review*, 1985, 1-18.

MICHAEL, R., 'Determinants of Divorce', in LEVY GARBOUA, *Sociological Economics*, London, Sage, 1979.

MNOOKIN, Robert H. and KORNHAUSER, Louis, 'Bargaining in the Shadow of the Law: The Case of Divorce', **88** *Yale Law Journal*, 1979, 950-997.

PAPPS, Ivy, *For Love or Money? A Preliminary Economic Analysis of Marriage and the Family*, London, Institute of Economic Affairs (Hobart Paperback No.86), 1980, 63 p.

PENNINGTON, Joan, 'The Economic Implications of Divorce for Older Women', **23** *Clearinghouse Review*, 1989, 488-493.

PETERS, H. Elizabeth, 'Marriage and Divorce: Informational Constraints and Private Contracting', **76** *American Economic Review*, 1986, 437-454.

SCHULTZ, Theodore W. (ed.), *Economics of the Family: Marriage, Children and Human Capital*, Chicago, University of Chicago Press, 1974, 584 p.

SOFER, C., *La Division du Travail entre Hommes et Femmes* [The Division of Labour Between Men and Women], Paris, Economica, 1985.

WEISS, Yoram and WILLIS, Robert J., 'Children as Collective Goods and Divorce Settlements', **3** *Journal of Labor Economics*, 1985, 268 ff.

WEITZMAN, Lenore J., *The Marriage Contract: Spouses, Lovers and the Law*, New York, Free Press, 1981, 536 p.

WEITZMAN, Lenore J., 'The Economics of Divorce: Social and Economic Consequences of Property, Alimony and Child Support Awards', **28** *UCLA Law Review*, 1981, 1181-1268.

WISHIK, Heather Ruth, 'Economics of Divorce: An Explanatory Study', **20** *Family Law Quarterly*, 1986, 79-107.

1500 HUMAN RIGHTS
Gerrit De Geest

1500 Human Rights: General

BADE, Karl, 'Scylla, Charybdis & Adam Smith: An Economic Analysis of the Religion Clauses', **39** *De Paul Law Review*, 1990, 1235-1279.

BARTON, Stephen E., 'Property Rights and Human Rights: Efficiency and Democracy as Criteria for Regulatory Reform', **17** *Journal of Economic Issues*, 1983, 915-930.

DORN, James A., 'Judicial Protection of Economic Liberties', in DORN, James A. and MANNE, Henry G. (eds.), *Economic Liberties and the Judiciary*, Fairfax, George Mason University Press, 1987, 1-28.

DORN, James A. and MANNE, Henry G. (eds.), *Economic Liberties and the Judiciary*, Fairfax, George Mason University Press, 1987, 392 p.

HECKMAN, James J. and PAYNER, Brook S., 'Determining the Impact of Federal Antidiscrimination Policy on the Economic Status of Blacks: A Study of South Carolina', **79** *American Economic Review*, 1989, 138-177.

LUCAS, Jo Desha, 'Constitutional Law and Economic Liberty', **11** *Journal of Law and Economics*, 1968, 5-33.

MALLOY, Robin Paul, 'Equating Human Rights and Property Rights - The Need for Moral Judgment in an Economic Analysis of Law and Social Policy', **47** *Ohio State Law Journal*, 1986, 163-177.

McCONNELL, Michael W. and POSNER, Richard A., 'An Economic Approach to Issues of Religious Freedom', **56** *University of Chicago Law Review*, 1989, 1-60.

NAUDET, Jean-Yves and SERMENT, Laurent, 'Le droit de propriété garanti par la Convention européenne des droits de l'homme face à l'analyse économique' [Property Law Guaranteed by the European Convention of Human Rights, in the Light of Economic Analysis], **15** *Revue de la Recherche Juridique Droit Perspectif*, 1990, 15-50.

PASTOR, Santos, 'Derechos de propriedad y análisis económico: ¿nuevas luces a viejas sombras?' [The Economics of Property Rights: Enlightening Old Shades?], **38** *Economistas*, 1989.

POSNER, Richard A., 'The Law and Economics Movement', **77** *American Economic Review (Papers and Proceedings)*, 1987, 1-13.

POWERS BERTEN, David, 'An Econolegal Opinion' (Case Note), *Wisconsin Law Review*, 1989, 589-605.

SIEGAN, Bernard H., 'Economic Liberties and the Constitution: Protection at the State Level', in DORN, James A. and MANNE, Henry G. (eds.), *Economic Liberties and the Judiciary*, Fairfax, George Mason University Press, 1987, 137-150.

SOFAER, Abraham D., 'The Change-of-Status Adjudication: A Case Study of the

Informal Agency Process', **1** *Journal of Legal Studies*, 1972, 349-421.

SUNSTEIN, Cass R., 'Three Civil Rights Remedies', **79** *California Law Review*, 1991, 751-774.

1600 Prohibition of Slavery

BARZEL, Yoram, 'An Economic Analysis of Slavery', **20** *Journal of Law and Economics*, 1977, 87-110.

1700 Prohibition of Discrimination

SEE ALSO: 5430

ASHENFELTER, Orley and OAXACA, Ronald, 'The Economics of Discrimination: Economists Enter the Courtroom', **77** *American Economic Review. Papers and Proceedings*, 1987, 321-325.

BECKER, Gary S., *The Economics of Discrimination*, Chicago, University of Chicago Press, 1957, 137 p.

BELLER, Andrea H., 'The Economics of Enforcement of an Antidiscrimination Law: Title VII of the Civil Rights Act of 1964', **21** *Journal of Law and Economics*, 1978, 359-380.

BLOCK, Walter E. and WALKER, Michael A. (eds.), *Discrimination, Affirmative Action, and Equal Opportunity - An Economic and Social Perspective*, Vancouver, Fraser Institute, 1982, 271 p.

FARBER, Daniel A. and FRICKEY, Philip P., 'Is *Carolene Products* Dead? Reflections on Affirmative Action and the Dynamics of Civil Rights Legislation', **79** *California Law Review*, 1991, 685-727.

FARRELL, Claude H., HYMAN, David N. and IHNEN, Loren A., 'Forced Busing and the Demand for Private Schooling', **6** *Journal of Legal Studies*, 1977, 363-372.

FISHBACK, Price V., 'Can Competition among Employers Reduce Governmental Discrimination? Coal Companies and Segregated Schools in West Virginia in the Early 1900s', **32** *Journal of Law and Economics*, 1989, 311-328.

FOGEL, Robert William and ENGERMAN, Stanley L., 'Philanthropy at Bargain Prices: Notes on the Economics of Gradual Emancipation', **3** *Journal of Legal Studies*, 1974, 377-401.

JONES, Ethel B., 'ERA Voting: Labor Force Attachment, Marriage, and Religion', **12** *Journal of Legal Studies*, 1983, 157-168.

LAYCOCK, Douglas, 'Statistical Proof and Theories of Discrimination', **49(4)** *Law and Contemporary Problems*, 1986, 97-106.

NORRIS, Barbara A., 'Multiple Regression Analysis in Title VII Cases: A Structural

Approach to Attacks of "Missing Factors" and "Pre act Discrimination."', **49(4)** *Law and Contemporary Problems*, 1986, 63-96.

OLMSTEAD, Alan L. and SHEFFRIN, Steven M., 'Affirmative Action in Medical Schools: Econometric Evidence and Legal Doctrine', **3** *Research in Law and Economics*, 1981, 207-223.

PHELPS, 'The Statistical Theory of Racism and Sexism', **62** *American Economic Review*, 1972, 659 ff.

POSNER, Richard A., 'The Efficiency and the Efficacy of Tittle VII', **136** *University of Pennsylvania Law Review*, 1987, 513-521.

POSNER, Richard A., 'An Economic Analysis of Sex Discrimination Laws', **56** *University of Chicago Law Review*, 1989, 1311-1335.

ROSSELL, Christine H., 'Applied Social Science Research: What Does It Say About the Effectiveness of School Desegregation Plans ?', **12** *Journal of Legal Studies*, 1983, 69-107.

SCHWAD, 'Is Statistical Discrimination Efficient?', **76** *American Economic Review*, 1986, 228 ff.

VOGEL, Kenneth, 'Discrimination on the Basis of HIV Infection: An Economic Analysis', **49** *Ohio State Law Journal*, 1989, 965-998.

1800 Free Speech

HAMMER, Peter J., 'Free Speech and the "Acid Bath": An Evaluation and Critique of Judge Richard Posner's Economic Interpretation of the First Amendment', **87** *Michigan Law Review*, 1988, 499-536.

POSNER, Richard A., 'Free Speech in an Economic Perspective', **20** *Suffolk University Law Review*, 1986, 1-54.

1900 Privacy

BECKER, Gary S., 'Privacy and Malfeasance', **9** *Journal of Legal Studies*, 1980, 823-826.

COLLINS, H., 'The Decline of Privacy in Private Law', **14** *Journal of Law and Society*, 1987.

EASTERBROOK, Frank H., 'Privacy and the Optimal Extent of Disclosure under the Freedom of Information Act', **9** *Journal of Legal Studies*, 1980, 775-800.

EPSTEIN, Richard A., 'A Taste for Privacy? Evolution and the Emergence of a Naturalistic Ethic', **9** *Journal of Legal Studies*, 1980, 665-681.

GOULD, John P., 'Privacy and the Economics of Information', **9** *Journal of Legal Studies*, 1980, 827-842.

HARTMANN, C.J. and RENAS, S.M., 'Anglo-American Privacy Law: An Economic Analysis', **5** *International Review of Law and Economics*, 1985, 133-

152.

HIRSHLEIFER, Jack, 'Privacy: Its Origin, Function and Future', **9** *Journal of Legal Studies*, 1980, 649-664.

KOHL, Helmut, 'Das Allgemeine Persönlichkeitsrecht als Ausdruck oder Grenze des Effizienzdenkens im Zivilrecht?' [The General Right of Privacy as Expression or Limitation of Efficiency Thinking in Civil Law?], in OTT, Claus and SCHÄFER, Hans-Bernd (eds.), *Ökonomische Probleme des Zivilrechts*, Berlin, Springer, 1991, 41-51.

KRONMAN, Anthony T., 'The Privacy Exemption to the Freedom of Information Act', **9** *Journal of Legal Studies*, 1980, 727-774.

POSNER, Richard A., 'Privacy, Secrecy and Reputation', **28** *Buffalo Law Review*, 1979, 1-55.

POSNER, Richard A., 'Rethinking the Fourth Amendment', *Supreme Court Review*, 1981, 49-80.

POSNER, Richard A., 'The Economics of Privacy', **71** *American Economic Review. Papers and Proceedings*, 1981, 405-409.

SCHEPPELE, Kim Lane, *Legal Secrets, Equality and Efficiency in the Common Law*, Chicago, University of Chicago Press, 1988, 363 p.

SEIDL, Christian, 'Kommentar' [Comment] (On Kohl, Das Allgemeine Persönlichkeitsrecht als Ausdruck oder Grenze des Effizienzdenkens im Zivilrecht), in OTT, Claus and SCHÄFER, Hans-Bernd (eds.), *Ökonomische Probleme des Zivilrechts*, Berlin, Springer, 1991, 52-57.

STIGLER, George J., 'An Introduction to Privacy in Economics and Politics', **9** *Journal of Legal Studies*, 1980, 623-644.

SYMPOSIUM : 'Symposium on Posner's Theory of Privacy', *Georgia Law Review*, Spring 1978.

SYMPOSIUM : 'The Law and Economics of Privacy. A Conference Sponsored by The Center for the Study of the Economy and the State', **9** *Journal of Legal Studies*, 1980, 621-842.

2000 PROPERTY LAW
Boudewijn Bouckaert

2000 Property Law: General

ACKERMAN, Bruce A. (ed.), *Economic Foundations of Property Law*, Boston, Little Brown and Company, 1975, 332 p.

ALCHIAN, Armen A., 'Some Economics of Property Rights', Santa Monica: Rand Corporation, *Rand Paper* No. 2316, 1961. Reprinted in **30** *Il Politico*, 1965, 816-829. Reprinted in ALCHIAN, Armen A., *Economic Forces at Work*, Indianapolis, Liberty Press, 1977.

ALCHIAN, Armen A. and DEMSETZ, Harold, 'The Property Right Paradigm', **33** *Journal of Economic History*, 1973, 16-27.

ALEXANDER, Gregory S., 'The Concept of Property in Private and Constitutional Law: The Ideology of the Scientific Turn in Legal Analysis', **82** *Columbia Law Review*, 1982, 1545-1599.

BARZEL, Yoram, *Economic Analysis of Property Rights*, Cambridge, Cambridge University Press, 1989, 122 p.

BÖBEL, Ingo, *Eigentum, Eigentumsrechte und Institutioneller Wandel* [Property, Property Rights and Institutional Change], Berlin, Springer Verlag, 1988, 360 p.

BOUCKAERT, Boudewijn, 'Eigendomsrechten vanuit rechtseconomisch perspectief' [Property Rights from an Economic Perspective], **39** *Ars Aequi*, 1990, 777-786.

BOUCKAERT, Boudewijn, 'What is Property?', **13** *Harvard Journal of Law & Public Policy*, 1990, 775-816.

BOWLES, Roger A., 'Property and the Legal System', in WHYNES, D.K. (ed.) *What is Political Economy?*', Blackwell, New York, 1984, 243 p.

BUCHANAN, James M., 'Politics, Property, and the Law: An Alternative Interpretation of Miller et al. v. Schoene', **15** *Journal of Law and Economics*, 1972, 439-452.

BUHBE, Matthes, *Ökonomische Analyse von Eigentumsrechten - Der Beitrag der economics of property rights zur Theorie der Institutionen* [Economic Analysis of Property Rights - The Contribution of the Property Rights Approach to the Theory of Institutions], Frankfurt am Main, Peter D. Lang, 1980, 185 p.

CHAN, Arthur H., 'To Market or Not to Market: Allocation of Interstate Waters', **29** *Natural Resources Journal*, 1989, 529-547.

COOTER, Robert D., 'Unity in Tort, Contract, and Property: The Model of Precaution', **73** *California Law Review*, 1985, 1-51. Reprinted in GOLDBERG, Victor P. (ed.), *Readings in the Economics of Contract Law*, Cambridge, Cambridge University Press, 1989, 53-60.

CORNES, Richard and SANDLER, Todd, 'On Commons and Tragedies', **73** *American Economic Review*, 1983, 787-792.

CROCKER, Thomas D., 'Externalities, Property Rights, and Transactions Costs: An

Empirical Study', **14** *Journal of Law and Economics*, 1971, 451-464.

DASGUPTA, Partha S. and HEAL, Geoffrey M., *Economic Theory and Exhaustible Resources*, Cambridge, Cambridge University Press, 1979, 501 p.

DAVIS, Lance E. and NORTH, Douglass C., *Institutional Change and American Economic Growth*, Cambridge, Cambridge University Press, 1971, 283 p.

DE ALESSI, Louis, 'The Economics of Property Rights: A Review of the Evidence', **2** *Research in Law and Economics*, 1980, 1-47.

DE ALESSI, Louis, 'Property Rights, Transaction Costs, and X-Efficiency: An Essay in Economic Theory', **73** *American Economic Review*, 1983, 64-81.

DE ALESSI, Louis, 'Property Rights and X-Efficiency: Reply', **73** *American Economic Review*, 1983, 843-845.

DE ALESSI, Louis, 'Property Rights and the Judiciary', **4** *Cato Journal*, 1985, 805-811. Reprinted in DORN, James A. and MANNE, Henry G. (eds.), *Economic Liberties and the Judiciary*, Fairfax, George Mason University Press, 1987, 175-181.

DEGENKAMP, J.Th. and HEYNEN, H.M., 'Juridische en economische eigendom. Een formele analyse' [Legal and Economic Ownership. A Formal Analysis],in *Tolvrije gedachten*, Deventer, Kluwer, 1980, 117-129.

DEMSETZ, Harold, 'Toward a Theory of Property Rights', **57** *American Economic Review, Papers and Proceedings*, 1967, 347-359.

DEMSETZ, Harold, 'Professor Michelman's Unnecessary and Futile Search for the Philosopher's Touchstone', in PENNOCK, J. Roland and CHAPMAN, John W. (eds.), *Nomos XXIV: Ethics, Economics and the Law*, New York, New York University Press, 1982, 41-47.

ESCHENBURG, Rolf, 'Mikroökonomische Aspekte von Property Rights' [Microeconomic Aspects of Property Rights], in SCHENK, K.E. (ed.), *Ökonomische Verfügungsrechte und Allokationsmechanismen in Wirtschaftssystemen*, Schriften des Vereins für Socialpolitik, Vol. 97, N.F., 1978, 9-27.

FIORENTINI, Gianluca, 'Externalities and Property Rights: Some Policy Implications', *Economic Notes*, 1989, 343-361.

FURUBOTN, Eirik G. and PEJOVICH, Svetozar, 'Property Rights and Economic Theory: A Survey of Recent Literature', **10** *Journal of Economic Literature*, 1972, 1137-1162.

FURUBOTN, Eirik G. and PEJOVICH, Svetovar (eds.), *The Economics of Property Rights*, Cambridge, Ballinger, 1974, 367 p.

GAMBARO, Antonio, *La legittimazione passiva alle azioni possessorie* [Standing to Be Sued in Ownership Litigation], Milano, Giuffrè, 1979, 163 p. 7000)

GORDON, Scott, 'Economics and the Conservation Question', **1** *Journal of Law and Economics*, 1958, 110-121.

GOTTHOLD, Jürgen, 'Zur ökonomischen "Theorie des Eigentums". Eine kritische Einfuhrung' [The Economic Theory of Property - A Critical Introduction], **144** *Zeitschrift für das gesamte Handels- und Wirtschaftsrecht*, 1980, 545-562.

GRUNEBAUM, James O., *Private Ownership*, London, Routledge & Kegan Paul, 1987, 213 p.

HARDIN, Garrett, 'The Tragedy of the Commons', **162** *Science*, 1968, 1243-1248.

HARTMAN, Raymond S., 'A Note on Externalities and the Placement of Property Rights: An Alternative Formulation to the Standard Pigouvian Results', **2** *International Review of Law and Economics*, 1982, 111-118.

HOLSWORTH, Robert D., 'Recycling Hobbes: the Limits to Political Ecology', **20** *The Massachusetts Review*, 1979, 9-40.

HUNT, E.K., *Property and Prophets - The Evolution of Economic Institutions and Ideologies*, Cambridge, New York, Harper & Row, 1981, 217 p.

HUTTER, Michael, *Die Gestaltung von Property Rights als Mittel gesellschaftlich-wirtschaftlicher Allokation* [The Structure of Property Rights as a Means of Social-Economic Allocation], Göttingen, Vandenhoeck & Ruprecht, 1979, 245 p.

JOHNSON, Ronald N., 'Restraint under Open Access: Are Voluntary Incentives Sufficient or Is Coercion Required?: Discussion', **67** *American Journal of Agricultural Economics*, 1985, 373-376.

KÖHLER, Helmut, 'Vertragsrecht und "Property Rights"-Theorie, Zur Integration ökonomischer Theorien in das Privatrecht' [Contract Law and Property Rights Theory - On the Integration of Economic Theory into Private Law], **144** *Zeitschrift für das gesamte Handels- und Wirtschaftsrecht*, 1980, 589-607.

LEHMANN, Michael, 'Eigentum, geistiges Eigentum, gewerbliche Schutzrechte, Property Rights als Wettbewerbsbeschränkungen zur Förderung des Wettbewerbs' [Property, Intellectual Property, Commercial Rights of Protection, Property Rights as Restraints of Competition to Promote the Competition], in *Gewerblicher Rechtsschutz und Urheberrecht, Internationaler Teil (Festschrift für E.Ulmer)*, 1983, 356-362.

LEIBENSTEIN, Harvey, 'Property Rights and X-Efficiency: Comment', **73** *American Economic Review*, 1983, 831-842.

LEPAGE, Henri, *Pourquoi la propriété* [Why Property?], Paris, 1984. (Subject Code: 0020, 2000)

LEVIN, Harvey J., 'Regulating the Global Commons: A Case Study', **12** *Research in Law and Economics*, 1989, 247-266.

LIBECAP, Gary D., 'Property Rights in Economic History: Implications for Research', **23** *Explorations in Economic History*, 1986, 227-252.

LIBECAP, Gary D., *Contracting for Property Rights*, Cambridge, Cambridge University Press, 1989, 132 p.

LUNDGREN, Nils and LÖNN, H., 'Gör hyresrätt till bostadsrätt' [Transform Rent Contract to Ownership], *Ekonomisk Debatt*, 1980, Nr. 4.

MANNE, Henry G. (ed.), *The Economics of Legal Relationships: Readings in the Theory of Property Rights*, St. Paul, West, 1977, 660 p.

MEIJS, Paul and JANSEN, Wim, *Eigendom tussen politiek en economie* [Ownership between Politics and Economy], Groningen, Wolters-Noordhoff, 1989, 195 p.

MICHELMAN, Frank I., 'Ethics, Economics, and the Law of Property', in PENNOCK, J. Roland and CHAPMAN, John W. (eds.), *Nomos XXIV: Ethics, Economics and the Law*, New York, New York University Press, 1982, 3-40.

MORRIS, John Richard, 'Enforcement of Property Rights and the Provision of Public Good Attributes', **3(2)** *Information Economics and Policy*, 1988,

91-108.

MYHRMAN, Johan, 'Äganderätt och samhällssystem' [Property Rights and Social Structure], in *Äganderätt och egendomsskydd* [Property Right and Property Protection], Svenska Arbetsgivareföreningen, 1985.

NAUDET, Jean-Yves and SERMENT, Laurent, 'Le droit de propriété garanti par la convention européenne des droits de l'homme face à l'analyse économique' [Property Law Guaranteed by the European Convention of Human Rights, in the Light of Economic Analysis], **15** *Revue de la Recherche Juridique Droit Perspectif*, 1990, 15-50.

NORTH, Douglass C. and THOMAS, Robert P., *The Rise of the Western World: A New Economic History*, Cambridge, Cambridge University Press, 1973.

PASTOR, Santos, 'Derechos de propriedad y análisis económico: ¿nuevas luces a viejas sombras?' [The Economics of Property Rights: Enlightening Old Shades?], **38** *Economistas*, 1989.

PEJOVICH, Svetozar, 'Liberty, Property Rights, and Innovation in Eastern Europe', **9** *Cato Journal*, 1989, 57-71.

PEJOVICH, Svetozar, 'Liberman's Reforms and Property Rights in the Soviet Union', **12** *Journal of Law and Economics*, 1969, 155-162.

PEJOVICH, Svetozar, 'Towards an Economic Theory of the Creation and Specification of Property Rights', *Review of Social Economics*, 1972.

PISANI, Donald J., 'Conflict over Conservation: The Reclamation Service and the Tahoe Contract', **10** *The Western Historical Quarterly*, 1979, 167-190.

POSNER, Richard A., *The Economics of Justice*, Cambridge (Mass.), Harvard University Press, 1981, 415 p.

QUIGGIN, John, 'Common Property, Private Property and Regulation: The Case of Dryland Salinity', **30(2-3)** *Australian Journal of Agricultural Economics*, 1986, 103-117.

QUIGGIN, John, 'Private and Common Property Rights in the Economics of the Environment', **22** *Journal of Economic Issues*, 1988, 1071-1087.

ROSE, Carol M., 'The Comedy of the Commons: Custom, Commerce, and Inherently Public Property', **53** *University of Chicago Law Review*, 1984, 711-781.

ROSE, Carol M., 'Property as Storytelling: Perspectives from Game Theory, Narrative Theory, Feminist Theory', **2** *Yale Journal of Law & the Humanities*, 1990, 37-57.

ROSENBERG, Nathan, *How the West Grew Rich: The Economic Transformation of the Industrial World*, New York, Basic Books, 1986, 353 p.

ROTH, Gabriel, 'The Role of Property Rights in Development', **7** *Cato Journal*, 1987, 117-120.

SAMUELS, Warren J., 'Welfare Economics, Power and Property', in WUNDERLICH, G. and GIBSON, W.L. (eds.), *Perspectives of Property*, Pennsylvania State University Press, 1972.

SCHEIBER, Harry N., 'Law and the Imperatives of Progress: Private Rights and Public Values in American Legal History', in PENNOCK, J. Roland and CHAPMAN, John W. (eds.), *Nomos XXIV: Ethics, Economics and the Law*,

New York, New York University Press, 1982, 303-320.

SCHMID, A. Allan, 'The Economics of Property Rights: A Review Article', in SAMUELS, Warren J. (ed.), *The Chicago School of Political Economy*, East Lansing, Division of Research, Graduate School of Business Administration, Michigan State University, 1976, 469-478.

SIMON, Peter N., 'Economic Analysis of Liberty and Property: A Critique', **57** *University of Colorado Law Review*, 1986, 747-757.

SKOGH, Göran, 'Äganderättens ekonomi och politik' [The Economics and Politics of Property Rights], *Politiskt-Filosofiska Sällskapets årsskrift*, 1988.

SLAGTER, Wiek J., *Juridische en economische eigendom* [Legal and Economic Ownership], Deventer, Kluwer, 1968, 66 p.

SLAGTER, Wiek J., *Schaarse rechten. Afscheidscollege Rotterdam* [Scarce Rights], Deventer, Kluwer, 1989, 42 p.

STROUP, Richard and BADEN, John, 'Externality, Property Rights, and the Management of Our National Forests', **16** *Journal of Law and Economics*, 1973, 303-312.

STROUP, Richard and BADEN, John, 'Property Rights and Natural Resource Management', **2** *Literature of Liberty*, 1979, 5-44.

TIETZEL, Manfred 'Die Ökonomie der Property Rights: Ein Überblick' [The Economics of Property Rights: A Survey], **30** *Zeitschrift für Wirtschaftspolitik*, 1981, 207-243.

TREBILCOCK, Michael J., 'Customary Land Law Reform in Papua New Guinea: Law, Economics and Property Rights in a Traditional Culture', **9** *Adelaide Law Review*, 1983, 191-228.

TREBILCOCK, Michael J., 'Communal Property Rights: The Papua New Guinean Experience', **34** *University of Toronto Law Journal*, 1984, 377-420.

TREBILCOCK, Michael J. and KNETSCH, Jack L., 'Land Policy and Economic Development in Papua New Guinea', **9** *Melanesian Law Journal*, 1981, 102-115.

VANDEVELDE, Kenneth J., 'The New Property of the Nineteenth Century: The Development of the Modern Concept of Property', **29** *Buffalo Law Review*, 1980, 325-367.

WALZ, W. Rainer, 'Sachenrecht für Nichtsachen? Kritik einer Systemanalogie' [Property Law for Immaterial Goods? Critique on a System Analogy], **1** *Kritische Vierteljahresschrift für Gesetzgebung und Rechtswissenschaft*, 1986, 131-164.

WALZ, W. Rainer, 'Sachenrechtliches Systemdenken im Wandel - Die ökonomischen Determinanten des Verfügungstatbestandes' [Property Law System Thinking in Change - The Economic Determinants of the Disposition General Findings], **5** *Kritische Vierteljahresschrift für Gesetzgebung und Rechtswissenschaft*, 1990, 374-405.

WIJKMAN, P.M., 'Kampen om jordens allmänningar' [The Struggle for the Common Land on Earth], *Ekonomisk Debatt*, 1974, No. 6.

WILLIAMS, Stephen F., 'Liberty and Property: The Problem of Government Benefits', **12** *Journal of Legal Studies*, 1983, 3-40.

YANG, Xiaokai and WILLS, Ian R., 'A Model Formalizing the Theory of Property Rights', **14** *Journal of Comparative Economics*, 1990, 177-198.

2100 Private Property vs. Common Property

ALLEN, Douglas W., 'Homesteading and Property Rights; or "How the West Was Really Won"', **34** *Journal of Law and Economics*, 1991, 1-23.

ANDERSON, Terry L. and HILL, Peter J., 'The Evolution of Property Rights: A Study of the American West', **18** *Journal of Law and Economics*, 1975, 163-179.

ANDERSON, Terry L. and HILL, Peter J., 'An American Experiment in Anarcho-Capitalism: The *Not* So Wild, Wild West', **2** *Journal of Libertarian Studies*, 1978, 9-29.

ANDERSON, Terry L. and HILL, Peter J., 'Privatizing the Commons: Comment', **52** *Southern Economic Journal*, 1986, 1162-1167.

ANDERSON, Terry L. and HILL, Peter J., 'Privatizing the Commons: Reply', **54** *Southern Economic Journal*, 1987, 225-226.

AULT, David E. and RUTMAN, Gilbert L., 'The Development of Individual Rights to Property in Tribal Africa', **22** *Journal of Law and Economics*, 1979, 163-182.

AULT, David E. and RUTMAN, Gilbert L., 'Land Scarcity, Economic Efficiency and African Common Law', **12** *Research in Law and Economics*, 1989, 33-54.

BELL, Frederick W., 'Mitigating the Tragedy of the Commons', **52** *Southern Economic Journal*, 1986, 653-664.

BERCK, Peter and PERLOFF, Jeffrey M., 'The Commons as a Natural Barrier to Entry: Why There Are So Few Fish Farms', **67** *American Journal of Agricultural Economics*, 1985, 360-363.

BÖHM, Stephan, 'Handlungsrechte, Wettbewerb und Privatisierung' [Property Rights, Competition and Privatization], **34** *Wirtschaftspolitische Blätter*, 1987, 576-583.

BOLLE, Friedel, 'On the Oligopolistic Extraction of Non-Renewable Common-Pool Resources', **53** *Economica*, 1986, 519-527.

BOTTOMLEY, Anthony, 'The Effect of Common Ownership of Land upon Resource Allocation in Tripolitania', **39** *Land Economics*, 1963, 91-95.

BROMLEY, Daniel W., *Economic Interests and Institutions: The Conceptual Foundations of Public Policy*, New York, Blackwell, 1989, 274 p.

CLARK, J. Stephen and CARLSON, Gerald A., 'Testing for Common versus Private Property: The Case of Pesticide Resistance', **19** *Journal of Environmental Economics and Management*, 1990, 45-60.

DAHLMAN, Carl J., *The Open Field System and Beyond: A Property Rights Analysis of an Economic Institution*, Cambridge, Cambridge University Press, 1980, 234 p.

DE MEZA, David and GOULD, J.R., 'Free Access vs. Private Ownership: A Comparison', **36** *Journal of Economic Theory*, 1985, 387-391.

DE MEZA, David and GOULD, J.R., 'Free Access Versus Private Property in a Resource: Income Distributions Compared', **95** *Journal of Political Economy*, 1987, 1317-1325.

DEMSETZ, Harold, 'The Exchange and Enforcement of Property Rights', **7** *Journal* *of Law and Economics*, 1964, 11-26.

DEMSETZ, Harold, 'Some Aspects of Property Rights', **9** *Journal of Law and Economics*, 1966, 61-70.

DEMSETZ, Harold, 'Toward a Theory of Property Rights', **57** *American Economic Review, Papers and Proceedings*, 1967, 347-359.

FIELD, Barry C., 'The Optimal Commons', **67** *American Journal of Agricultural Economics*, 1985, 364-367.

FIELD, Barry C., 'The Evolution of Property Rights', **42** *Kyklos*, 1989, 319-345

FREYFOGLE, Eric T., 'Land Use and the Study of Early American History', **94** *Yale Law Review*, 1985, 717-742.

FRIEDMAN, David D., 'Private Creation and Enforcement of Law: A Historical Case', **8** *Journal of Legal Studies*, 1979, 399-415.

FURUBOTN, Eirik G., 'Privatizing the Commons: Comment', **54** *Southern Economic Journal*, 1987, 219-224.

FURUBOTN, Eirik G., 'Distributional Issues in Contracting for Property Rights: Comment', **145** *Journal of Institutional and Theoretical Economics*, 1989, 25-31.

GORDON, H.S., 'The Economic Theory of a Common Property Resource: The Fishery', **62** *Journal of Political Economy*, 1954, 124-142.

JOHNSEN, D. Bruce, 'The Formation and Protection of Property Rights among the Southern Kwakiutl Indians', **15** *Journal of Legal Studies*, 1986, 41-67.

LIBECAP, Gary D., *The Evolution of Private Mineral Rights: Nevada's Comstock Lode*, 1978.

LIBECAP, Gary D., 'Economic Variables and the Development of the Law: The Case of Western Mineral Rights', **38** *Journal of Economic History*, 1978, 338-362.

LIBECAP, Gary D., 'Government Support of Private Claims to Public Minerals: Western Mineral Rights', **5** *Business History Review*, 1979, 364-385.

LUECK, Dean, 'The Economic Nature of Wildlife Law', **18** *Journal of Legal Studies*, 1989, 291-324.

PEJOVICH, Svetozar, 'Towards an Economic Theory of the Creation and Specification of Property Rights', *Review of Social Economics*, 1972.

ROSENBERG, Nathan, *How the West Grew Rich: The Economic Transformation of the Industrial World*, New York, Basic Books, 1986, 353 p.

SCHANZE, Erich, 'Distributional Issues in Contracting for Property Rights: Comment', **145** *Journal of Institutional and Theoretical Economics*, 1989, 32-37.

SMITH, Vernon L., 'The Primitive Hunter Culture, Pleistocene Extinction, and the Rise of Agriculture', **83** *Journal of Political Economy*, 1975, 727-755.

SUTINEN, Jon G. and ANDERSEN, Peder, 'The Economics of Fisheries Law Enforcement', **61** *Land Economics*, 1985, 387-397.

UMBECK, John, 'Might Makes Right: A Theory of the Formation and Initial Distribution of Property Rights', **19** *Economic Inquiry*, 1981, 38-59.

WANDSCHNEIDER, Philip R., 'Neoclassical and Institutionalist Explanations of

Changes in Northwest Water Institutions', **20** *Journal of Economic Issues*, 1986, 87-107.

WATERS, Alan Rufus, 'Economic Growth and the Property Rights Regime', **7** *Cato Journal*, 1987, 99-115.

2200 Property Rule vs. Liability Rule vs. Inalienable Rights

ATIAS, Christian, 'La distinction du patrimonial et de l'extra-patrimonial et l'analyse économique du droit: un utile face à face' [The Distinction Between Patrimonial and Extra-Patrimonial Rights and the Economic Analysis of Law], *Revue de la Recherche Juridique*, 1986, Nr. 1.

BROMLEY, Daniel W., 'Property Rules, Liability Rules, and Environmental Economics', **12** *Journal of Economic Issues*, 1978, 43-60.

BUCHANAN, James M. and FAITH, Roger L., 'Entrepreneurship and the Internalization of Externalities', **24** *Journal of Law and Economics*, 1981, 95-111.

CALABRESI, Guido and MELAMED, A. Douglas, 'Property Rules, Liability Rules and Inalienability: One View of the Cathedral', **85** *Harvard Law Review*, 1972, 1089-1128. Reprinted in ACKERMAN, Bruce A., *Economic Foundations of Property Law*, Boston, Little Brown, 1975, 31-48.

COLEMAN, Jules L., 'Property, Wrongfulness and the Duty to Compensate', **63** *Chicago-Kent Law Review*, 1987, 451-470.

COLEMAN, Jules L. and KRAUS, Jody, 'Rethinking the Theory of Legal Rights', **95** *Yale Law Journal*, 1986, 1335-1371.

COOTER, Robert D., 'Economic Theories of Legal Liability', **5(3)** *Journal of Economic Perspectives*, 1991, 11-30.

EPSTEIN, Richard A., 'Why Restrain Alienation?', **85** *Columbia Law Review*, 1985, 970-990.

FRIEDMAN, David D., 'Efficient Institutions for the Private Enforcement of Law', **13** *Journal of Legal Studies*, 1984, 379-397.

HADDOCK, David D., McCHESNEY, Fred S. and SPIEGEL, Menahem, 'An Ordinary Economic Rationale for Extraordinary Legal Sanctions', **78** *California Law Review*, 1990, 1-51.

KNETSCH, Jack L., *Property Rights and Compensation. Compulsory Acquisition and Other Losses*, Toronto, Butterworth, 1983, ch.10.

LANDES, William M. and POSNER, Richard A., 'The Private Enforcement of Law', **4** *Journal of Legal Studies*, 1975, 1-46.

McCHESNEY, Fred S., 'Government as Definer of Property Rights: Indian Lands, Ethnic Externalities, and Bureaucratic Budgets', **19** *Journal of Legal Studies*, 1990, 297-335.

PARDOLESI, Roberto, 'Azione reale e azione di danni nell'art. 844 c.c. Logica economica e logica giuridica nella composizione del conflitto tra usi incompatibili delle proprietà vicine' [Property Rule and Liability Rule in Article 844 Codice Civile: Economic Arguments, Legal Arguments and Litigation for Inconsistent Uses of Neighbours' Lands], *Foro italiono*, 1977, I, 1144-1154.

POLINSKY, A. Mitchell, 'Controlling Externalities and Protecting Entitlements: Property Right, Liability Rule, and Tax-Subsidy Approaches', **8** *Journal of Legal Studies*, 1979, 1-48.

POLINSKY, A. Mitchell, 'Resolving Nuisance Disputes: The Simple Economics of

Injunctive and Damage Remedies', **33** *Stanford Law Review*, 1980, 1075-1112.

POSNER, Richard A., 'Killing or Wounding to Protect a Property Interest', **14** *Journal of Law and Economics*, 1971, 201-232.

RADIN, Margaret Jane, 'Market-Inalienability', **100** *Harvard Law Review*, 1987, 1849-1937.

ROSE-ACKERMAN, Susan, 'Inalienability and the Theory of Property Rights', **85** *Columbia Law Review*, 1985, 931-969.

ROSE-ACKERMAN, Susan, 'Efficiency, Equity and Inalienability', in GRAF VON DER SCHULENBURG, J.-Matthias and SKOGH, Göran (eds.), *Law and Economics and The Economics of Legal Regulation*, Dordrecht, Kluwer, 1986, 11-37.

ROSE-ACKERMAN, Susan, 'I'd Rather Be Liable Than You: A Note on Property Rules and Liability Rules', **6** *International Review of Law and Economics*, 1986, 255-263.

SAMUELS, Warren J. and MERCURO, Nicholas, 'The Role of the Compensation Principle in Society', in SAMUELS, Warren J. and SCHMID, A. Allen (eds.), *Law and Economics: An Institutional Perspective*, Boston, Kluwer-Nijhoff, 1981, 210-247.

SCHAP, David, 'The Nonequivalence of Property Rules and Liability Rules', **6** *International Review of Law and Economics*, 1986, 125-132.

STAAF, Robert J., 'Liability Rules, Property Rights, and Taxes', **5** *Research in Law and Economics*, 1983, 225-231.

STEPHEN, Frank H., 'Property Rules and Liability Rules in the Regulation of Land Development: An Analysis of Development Control in Great Britain and Ontario', **7** *International Review of Law and Economics*, 1987, 33-49.

THOMPSON, Barton H., 'Injunction Negotiations: An Economic, Moral and Legal Analysis', **27** *Stanford Law Review*, 1975, 1563-1595.

2300 Original Assignment of Private Property. Homesteading. Possession. Adverse Possession. Wealth Effects

ALLEN, Douglas W., 'Homesteading and Property Rights; or "How the West Was Really Won"', **34** *Journal of Law and Economics*, 1991, 1-23.

ANDERSON, Terry L. and HILL, Peter J., 'Privatizing the Commons: An Improvement?', **50** *Southern Economic Journal*, 1983, 438 ff.

ANDERSON, Terry L. and HILL, Peter J., 'The Race for Property Rights', **33** *Journal of Law & Economics*, 1990, 177-197.

BRAUNSTEIN, Michael, 'Natural Environments and Natural Resources: An Economic Analysis and New Interpretation of the General Mining Law', **32** *UCLA Law Review*, 1985, 1133-1202.

DEMSETZ Harold, 'Wealth Distribution and the Ownership of Rights', **1** *Journal of Legal Studies*, 1972, 223-232.

DENNEN, R. Taylor, 'Some Efficiency Effects of Nineteenth-Century Federal Land Policy: A Dynamic Analysis', **44** *Agric. Hist.*, 1977, 718 ff.

EPSTEIN, Richard A., 'Past and Future: The Temporal Dimension in the Law of Property', **64** *Washington University Law Quarterly*, 1986, 667 ff.

FURUBOTN, Eirik G., 'Distributional Issues in Contracting for Property Rights: Comment', **145** *Journal of Institutional and Theoretical Economics*, 1989, 25-31.

GRETHER, David M., ISAAC, R. Mark and PLOTT, Charles R., *The Allocation of Scarce Resources. Experimental Economics and the Problem of Allocating Airport Slots*, Boulder, Westview Press, 1989, 333 p.

HADDOCK, David D., 'First Possession versus Optimal Timing: Limiting the Dissipation of Economic Value', **64** *Washington University Law Quarterly*, 1986, 775 ff.

HAYHURST, William L., '"Dreamers" and the Patent System', *European Intellectual Property Review*, 1983, 263-265.

LEVMORE, Saul, 'Variety and Uniformity in the Treatment of the Good-Faith Purchaser', **16** *Journal of Legal Studies*, 1987, 43-65.

LIBECAP, Gary D., 'Distributional Issues in Contracting for Property Rights', **145** *Journal of Institutional and Theoretical Economics*, 1989, 6-24.

McCHESNEY, Fred S., 'Government as Definer of Property Rights: Indian Lands, Ethnic Externalities, and Bureaucratic Budgets', **19** *Journal of Legal Studies*, 1990, 297-335.

NETTER, Jeffry M., HERSCH, Philip L. and MANSON, William D., 'An Economic Analysis of Adverse Possession Statutes', **6** *International Review of Law and Economics*, 1986, 217-228.

ROLPH, Elizabeth S., 'Government Allocation of Property Rights: Who Gets What?', **3** *Journal of Policy Analysis and Management*, 1983, 45-61.

ROSE, Carol M., 'Possession as the Origin of Property', **52** *University of Chicago Law Review*, 1985, 73-88.

SCHANZE, Erich, 'Distributional Issues in Contracting for Property Rights:

Comment', **145** *Journal of Institutional and Theoretical Economics*, 1989, 32-37.

TREBILCOCK, Michael J., 'The Role of Insurance Considerations in the Choice of Efficient Civil Liability Rules', **4** *Journal of Law, Economics, & Organization*, 1988, 243-265.

ZIMMERMAN, Martin B., 'Regulatory Treatment of Abandoned Property: Incentive Effects and Policy Issues', **31** *Journal of Law and Economics*, 1988, 127-144.

2400 Title Systems.Personal and Real Property

BAIRD, Douglas G., 'Notice Filing and the Problem of Ostensible Ownership', **12** *Journal of Legal Studies*, 1983, 53-67.

BAIRD, Douglas G. and JACKSON, Thomas H., 'Information, Uncertainty, and the Transfer of Property', **13** *Journal of Legal Studies*, 1984, 299-320.

BOWLES, Roger A. and PHILLIPS, Jennifer, 'Solicitors' Renumeration: A Critique of Recent Developments in Conveyancing', **40** *Modern Law Review*, 1977, 639-650.

EPSTEIN, Richard A., 'Possession as the Root of Title', **13** *Georgia Law Review*, 1979, 1221 ff.

GOLDBERG, Michael A. and HORWOOD, Peter J., 'The Costs of Buying and Selling Houses: Some Canadian Evidence', **10** *Research in Law and Economics*, 1987, 143-159.

JANCZYK, Joseph T., 'An Economic Analysis of the Land Title Systems for Transferring Real Property', **6** *Journal of Legal Studies*, 1977, 213-233.

JANCZYK, Joseph T., 'Land Title Systems, Scale of Operations, and Operating and Conversion Costs', **8** *Journal of Legal Studies*, 1979, 569-583.

JOSEPH, M., *The Conveyancing Fraud*, London, M. Joseph, 1976.

KENNEDY, Duncan, 'Cost-Benefit of Entitlement Problems: A Critique', **33** *Stanford Law Review*, 1981, 387-445.

SCHECHTER, Dan S., 'Judicial Lien Creditors Versus Prior Unrecorded Transferees of Real Property: Rethinking the Goals of the Recording System and Their Consequences', **62** *Southern California Law Review*, 1988, 105-186.

2500 Droits Réels (Usufruct, Long Lease, Building Rights, Easements, Covenants, Renting, ...)

ACKERMAN, Bruce A., 'Regulating Slum Housing Markets on Behalf of the Poor: Of Housing Codes, Housing Subsidies and Income Redistribution Policy', **80** *Yale Law Journal*, 1971, 1093-1197. Reprinted in ACKERMAN, Bruce A. (ed.), *Economic Foundations of Property Law*, Boston, Little Brown, 1975, 160-212.

ALBON, Robert, 'Lawyers and the Rental Market for Housing: a Critical Appraisal or A Conversation Between two Academics in a Hotel Bar', in CRANSTON, Ross and SCHICK, Anne (eds.), *Law and Economics*, Canberra, Australian National University, 1982, 105-111.

ANAS, Alex, et al., *The Economics of a Regulated Housing Market: Policy Perspectives and Modeling Methods* , Stockholm, Swedish Council for Building Research, 1987, 114 p.

BASU, Kaushik, 'Technological Stagnation, Tenurial Laws, and Adverse Selection', **79** *American Economic Review*, 1989, 251-255.

DUNHAM, Allison, 'Promises Respecting the Use of Land', **8** *Journal of Law and Economics*, 1965, 133-165.

EPSTEIN, Richard A., 'Notice and Freedom of Contract in the Law of Servitudes', **66** *Southern California Law Review*, 1982, 1353-1368.

FLATH, David, 'The Economics of Short-Term Leasing', **18** *Economic Inquiry*, 1980, 247-259.

GROSSMAN, Sanford J. and HART, Oliver D., 'The Costs and Benefits of Ownership: A Theory of Vertical and Lateral Integration', **94** *Journal of Political Economy*, 1986, 691-719.

HEADY, Earl, 'Economics of Farm Leasing', **29** *Journal of Farm Economics*, 1947, 659-678.

HIRSCH, Werner Z., 'Habitability Laws and the Welfare of Indigent Tenants', **63** *Review of Economics and Statistics*, 1980, 263-274.

HIRSCH, Werner Z., 'Landlord-Tenant Relations Law', in BURROWS, Paul and VELJANOVSKI, Cento G. (eds.), *The Economic Approach to Law*, London, Butterworths, 1981, 277-306.

HIRSCH, Werner Z., 'Effects of Habitability and Anti-Speedy Eviction Laws on Black and Aged Indigent Tenant Groups: An Economic Analysis', **3** *International Review of Law and Economics*, 1983, 121-135.

HIRSCH, Werner Z., 'Comment: From "Food for Thought" to "Empirical Evidence" About Consequences of Landlord-Tenant Laws', **69** *Cornell Law Review*, 1984, 604 ff.

HIRSCH, Werner Z., 'Landlord-Tenant Laws and Indigent Black Tenants', **10** *Research in Law and Economics*, 1987, 129-141.

HIRSCH, Werner Z., HIRSCH, Joel G. and MARGOLIS, S., 'Regression Analysis of the Effects of Habitability Laws upon Rent: An Empirical Observation on the Ackerman-Komesar Debate', **63** *California Law Review*, 1975, 1095-1143.

JOHNSON, Alex M., Jr., 'Correctly Interpreting Long-Term Leases Pursuant to Modern Contract Law: Toward a Theory of Relational Leases', **74** *Virginia Law Review*, 1988, 751-808.

JOHNSON, Omotunde E.G., 'Economic Analysis, The Legal Framework and Land Tenure Systems', **15** *Journal of Law and Economics*, 1972, 259-276.

KORNGOLD, Gerald, 'Privately Held Conservation Servitudes: A Policy Analysis in the Context of in Gross Real Covenants and Easements', **63** *Texas Law Review*, 433-495.

KORNGOLD, Gerald, 'Resolving the Flaws of Residential Servitudes and Owners Association: For Reformation not Termination', *Wisconsin Law Review*, 1990, 513-535.

LIANOS, Theodore P. and PARLIAROU, Despina, 'Land Tenure in Greek Agriculture', **63** *Land Economics*, 1987, 237-248.

LIVINGSTON, Marie Leigh and MILLER, Thomas A., 'A Framework for Analyzing the Impact of Western Instream Water Rights on Choice Domains: Transferability, Externalities, and Consumptive Use', **62** *Land Economics*, 1986, 269-277.

MARKOVITS, Richard S., 'The Distributive Impact, Allocative Efficiency, and Overall Desirability of Ideal Housing Codes: Some Theoretical Clarifications', **89** *Harvard Law Review*, 1976, 1815-1846.

MOODY, C.E. Jr. and KRUVANT, W.J., 'OCS Leasing Policy and Lease Prices', **66** *Land Economics*, 1990, 30-39.

REICHMAN, Uriel, 'Judicial Supervision of Servitudes', **7** *Journal of Legal Studies*, 1978, 139-164.

ROBINSON, Glen O., 'Explaining Contingent Rights: The Puzzle of "Obsolete" Covenants', **91** *Columbia Law Review*, 1991, 546-580.

SCHWALLIE, Daniel P., 'Note: The Implied Warranty of Habitability as a Mechanism for Redistributing Income: Good Goal, Bad Policy', **40** *Case Western Reserve Law Review*, 1990, 525 ff.

STAKE, Jeffrey E., 'Toward an Economic Understanding of Touch and Concern', *Duke Law Journal*, 1988, 925-974.

VOGEL, Kenneth R., 'The Coase Theorem and California Animal Trespass Law', **16** *Journal of Legal Studies*, 1987, 149-187.

WILLIAMS, Stephen F., 'Implied Covenants in Oil and Gas Leases: Some General Principles', **29** *University of Kansas Law Review*, 1981, 153 p.

WINOKUR, James L., 'The Mixed Blessings of Promissory Servitudes: Toward Optimizing Economic Utility, Individual Liberty, and Personal Identity', *Wisconsin Law Review*, 1989, 1-97.

WINOKUR, James L., 'Rejoinder: Reforming Servitude Regimes: Toward Associational Federalism and Community', *Wisconsin Law Review*, 1990, 537-552.

2600 Co-ownership and Condominium

DE GEEST, Gerrit, 'Public Choice en rechtseconomie' [Public Choice and Law & Economics], **39** *Ars Aequi*, 1990, 666-673.

DE GEEST, Gerrit, 'Co-ownership Rules in Apartment Buildings: An Economic Analysis', in WEIGEL, Wolfgang (ed.), *Economic Analysis of Law - A Collection of Applications*, Vienna, Österreichischer Wirtschaftsverlag, 1991, 197-205.

HANSMANN, Henry B., 'Condominium and Co-operative Housing: Transactional Efficiency, Tax Subsidies, and Tenure Choice', **20** *Journal of Legal Studies*, 1991, 25-71.

VAN DE VELDE, Jacqueline, 'Comment' [on De Geest, Co-ownership Rules in Apartment Buildings: An Economic Analysis], in WEIGEL, Wolfgang (ed.), *Economic Analysis of Law - A Collection of Applications*, Vienna, Österreichischer Wirtschaftsverlag, 1991, 206-209.

2700 Applications. New Forms of Property

ADELSTEIN, Richard P., 'Comment' [on Pearson, Common Property, Privatisation and Environmental Policy], in WEIGEL, Wolfgang (ed.), *Economic Analysis of Law - A Collection of Applications*, Vienna, Österreichischer Wirtschaftsverlag, 1991, 102-103.

AGNELLO, Richard J. and DONNELLEY, Lawrence P., 'Price and Property Rights in the Fisheries', **4** *Southern Economic Journal*, 1975, 253-262.

AGNELLO, Richard J. and DONNELLEY, Lawrence P., 'Property Rights and Efficiency in the Oyster Industry', **18** *Journal of Law and Economics*, 1975, 521-533.

AGNELLO, Richard J. and DONNELLEY, Lawrence P., 'Regulation and the Structure of Property Rights: The Case of the U.S. Oyster Industry', **6** *Research in Law and Economics*, 1984, 267-281.

AGNEW, Carson E. and GOULD, Richard G., 'Frequency Coordination and Spectrum Economics', **9** *Research in Law and Economics*, 1986, 167-184.

ANDERSON, Lee G. and LEE, Dwight R., 'Optimal Governing Instrument, Operation Level, and Enforcement in Natural Resource Regulation: The Case of the Fishery', **68** *American Journal of Agricultural Economics*, 1986, 678-690.

ATKINSON, Glen, 'Airspace Regulation: Redefining the Public Domain', **24** *Journal of Economic Issues*, 1990, 473-480.

BADEN, John and FORT, Rodney D., 'Natural Resources and Bureaucratic Predators', **11** *Policy Review*, 1980, 69-82.

BAGLEY, Edgar S., 'Water Rights Law and Public Policies Relating to Ground Water "Mining" in the Southwestern States', **4** *Journal of Law and Economics*, 1961, 144-174.

BARNES, David W., 'Enforcing Property Rights: Extending Property Rights Theory to Congestible and Environmental Goods', **10** *Boston College Environmental Affairs Law Review*, 1982, 583-638.

BORENSTEIN, Severin, 'On the Efficiency of Competitive Markets for Operating Licenses', **103** *Quarterly Journal of Economics*, 1988, 357-385.

BRAJER, Victor et al., 'The Strengths and Weaknesses of Water Markets as They Affect Water Scarcity and Sovereignty Interests in the West', **29** *Natural Resources Journal*, 1989, 489-509.

BRAY, Michelle Bourianoff, 'Note: Personalizing Personality: Toward a Property Right in Human Bodies', **69** *Texas Law Review*, 1990, 209-244.

BULKLEY, I.G., 'Property Rights and the Efficient Development of Minerals on the Ocean Floor', **3** *Research in Law and Economics*, 1981, 143-153.

BURNESS, H. Stuart and QUIRCK, James P., 'Appropriative Water Rights and the Efficient Allocation of Resources', **69** *American Economic Review*, 1979, 25-37.

BURNESS, H. Stuart and QUIRK, James P., 'Water Laws, Water Transfers, and Economic Efficiency: The Colorado River', **23** *Journal of Law and Economics*, 1980, 111-134.

CAMPBELL, H.F. and LINDNER, R.K., 'The Production of Fishing Effort and the

Economic Performance of Licence Limitation Programs', **66** *Land Economics*, 1990, 56-66.

CHAN, Arthur H., 'Adapting Natural Resources Management to Changing Societal Needs through Evolving Property Rights', **46** *Review of Social Economy*, 1988, 46-60.

CHAN, Arthur H., 'Policy Impacts of Sporhase v. Nebraska', **22** *Journal of Economic Issues*, 1988, 1153-1167.

CLARKSON, Kenneth W., 'International Law, U.S. Seabeds Policy and Ocean Resource Development', **17** *Journal of Law and Economics*, 1974, 117-142.

CLYDE, Steven E., 'Adapting to the Changing Demand for Water Use through Continued Refinement of the Prior Appropriation Doctrine: An Alternative Approach to Wholesale Reallocation', **29** *Natural Resources Journal*, 1989, 435-455.

COLBY, Bonnie G., 'Estimating the Value of Water in Alternative Uses', **29** *Natural Resources Journal*, 1989, 511-527.

COLIJN, P.J. et al. (ed.), *Economische eigendom* [Economic Ownership], Deventer, Kluwer, Stichting tot bevordering der notariële wetenschap, 1981, 92 p.

CRANDALL, Robert W., 'The Economic Effect of Television-Network Program "Ownership"', **14** *Journal of Law and Economics*, 1971, 385-412.

CRUTCHFIELD, James A., 'An Economic Evaluation of Alternative Methods of Fishery Regulation', **4** *Journal of Law and Economics*, 1961, 131-143.

CUZAN, Alfred G., 'A Critique of Collectivist Water Resources Planning', **32** *The Western Political Quarterly*, 1979, 320-326.

DAM, Kenneth W., 'Oil and Gas Licensing and the North Sea', **8** *Journal of Law and Economics*, 1965, 51-75.

DAM, Kenneth W., 'The Evolution of North Sea Licensing Policy in Britain and Norway', **17** *Journal of Law and Economics*, 1974, 213-263.

DE VANY, Arthur S., ECKERT, Ross D., MEYERS, C., O'HARA, D. and SCOTT, R., 'A Property System Approach for Market Allocation of the Electromagnetic Spectrum: A Legal-Economic Study', **21** *Stanford Law Review*, 1969, 1499 ff.

DUMARS, Charles T. and TARLOCK, A. Dan, 'New Challenges to State Water Allocation Sovereignty: Symposium Introduction', **29** *Natural Resources Journal*, 1989, 331-346.

ECKERT, Ross D., 'Exploitation of Deep Ocean Minerals: Regulatory Mechanisms and United States Policy', **17** *Journal of Law and Economics*, 1974, 143-177.

ECKERT, Ross D., *The Enclosure of Ocean Resources: Economics and the Law of the Sea*, Stanford, Hoover Institute Press, 1979, 390 p.

ELLICKSON, Robert C., 'A Hypothesis of Wealth-Maximizing Norms: Evidence from the Whaling Industry', **5** *Journal of Law, Economics, & Organization*, 1989, 83-97.

FLEISHER, Arthur A. III, SHUGHART, William F. II and TOLLISON, Robert D., 'Ownership Structure in Professional Sports', **12** *Research in Law and Economics*, 1989, 71-75.

GAFFNEY, Mason, 'Economic Aspects of Water Resource Policy', **28** *American*

Journal of Economics and Sociology, 1969, 131-144.

GELLER, Henry, 'The Role of Future Regulation: Licensing, Spectrum Allocation, Content, Access, Common Carrier and Rates', in NOAM, Eli H. (ed.), *Video Media Competition: Regulation, Economics, and Technology*, New York, Columbia University Press, 1985, 283-310.

GORDON, H.S., 'The Economic Theory of a Common Property Resource: The Fishery', **62** *Journal of Political Economy*, 1954, 124-142.

GOULD, George A., 'Transfer of Water Rights', **29** *Natural Resources Journal*, 1989, 457-477.

GRETHER, David M., ISAAC, R. Mark and PLOTT, Charles R., *The Allocation of Scarce Resources. Experimental Economics and the Problem of Allocating Airport Slots*, Boulder, Westview Press, 1989, 333 p.

HAHN, Robert W., 'A New Approach to the Design of Regulation in the Presence of Multiple Objectives', **17** *Journal of Environmental Economics and Management*, 1989, 195-211.

HAHN, Robert W. and HESTER, Gordon L., 'The Market for Bads: EPA's Experience with Emissions Trading', **11(3/4)** *Regulation*, 1987, 48-53.

HANDLEY, Norris Jr., 'The Dark and Bloody Ground of Indian Water Rights: Confusion Elevated to Principal', **9** *The Western Historical Quarterly*, 1978, 455-482.

HANNESSON, Rögnvaldur, 'Varför fiskegränserna bör utvidgas' [Why the Fishing Borders Have to Be Expanded], *Ekonomisk Debatt*, 1974, Nr. 5.

HANNESSON, Rögnvaldur, 'Extending Fishing Limits: In Whose Interest?', in SKOGH, Göran (ed.), *Law and Economics. Report from a Symposium in Lund, Sweden, 24-26 August 1977*, Lund, Juridiska Föreningen, 1978, 31-36.

HAZLETT, Thomas W., 'The Rationality of U.S. Regulation of the Broadcast Spectrum', **33** *Journal of Law & Economics*, 1990, 133-175.

HOLAHAN, William L., 'The Long-Run Effects of Abolishing the Baseball Player Reserve System', **7** *Journal of Legal Studies*, 1978, 129-137.

JOHNSON, Norman K. and DUMARS, Charles T., 'A Survey of the Evolution of Western Water Law in Response to Changing Economic and Public Interest Demands', **29** *Natural Resources Journal*, 1989, 347-387.

JOHNSON, Ronald N., GISSER, Micha and WERNER, Michael, 'The Definition of a Surface Water Right and Transferability', **24** *Journal of Law and Economics*, 1981, 273-288.

JOHNSON, Ronald D. and LIBECAP, Gary D., 'Contracting Problems and Regulation: The Case of the Fishery', **72** *American Economic Review*, 1982, 1005-1022.

JONUNG, Christina, 'Comments on Hannesson's Paper', in SKOGH, Göran (ed.), *Law and Economics. Report from a Symposium in Lund, Sweden, 24-26 August 1977*, Lund, Juridiska Föreningen, 1978, 37-42.

KARPOFF, Jonathan M., 'Suboptimal Controls in Common Resource Management: The Case of the Fishery', **95** *Journal of Political Economy*, 1987, 179-194.

KARPOFF, Jonathan M., 'Characteristics of Limited Entry Fisheries and the Option Component of Entry Licenses', **65** *Land Economics*, 1989, 386-393.

KOENIG, Evan F., 'Fisheries Regulation under Uncertainty: A Dynamic Analysis', **1** *Marine Resource Economics*, 1984, 193-208.

KORNGOLD, Gerald, 'Privately Held Conservation Servitudes: A Policy Analysis in the Context of in Gross Real Covenants and Easements', **63** *Texas Law Review*, 433-495.

KOSLOWSKI, Peter, 'Grenzen der Verkehrsfähigkeit und der Privatrechtsautonomie in der Verfügung über den menschlichen Leib - Kommentar' [Limits of the Marketability and Private Autonomy in the Disposition over the Human Body - Comment], in OTT, Claus and SCHÄFER, Hans-Bernd (eds.), *Allokationseffizienz in der Rechtsordnung*, Berlin, Springer, 1989, 115-119.

LEVIN, Harvey J., 'The Radio Spectrum Resource', **11** *Journal of Law and Economics*, 1968, 433-501.

LEVIN, Harvey J., 'Trading Orbit Spectrum Assignments in the Space Satellite Industry', **81** *American Economic Review. Papers and Proceedings*, 1991, 42-45.

LEVINE, Michael E., 'Landing Fees and the Airport Congestion Problem', **12** *Journal of Law and Economics*, 1969, 79-108.

LIBECAP, Gary D. and JOHNSON, Ronald N., 'Property Rights, Nineteenth-Century Timber Policy, and the Conservation Movement', **39** *Journal of Economic History*, 1979, 129-142.

LIBECAP, Gary D. and WIGGINS, Steven N., 'Contractual Responses to the Common Pool: Prorationing of Crude Oil Production', **74** *American Economic Review*, 1984, 87-98.

LOTHROP, Robert C., 'The Misplaced Role of Cost-Benefit Analysis in Columbia Basing Fishery Mitigation', **16** *Environmental Law*, 517 ff.

MACAULEY, Molly K., 'Out of Space? Regulation and Technical Change in Communications Satellites', **76** *American Economic Review. Papers and Proceedings*, 1986, 280-284.

MACAULEY, Molly K., and PORTNEY, Paul R., *Property Rights in Orbit Regulation*, American Enterprise Institute for Public Policy Research, Washington D.C., Vol. 7, 1984

MALONEY, Michael T. and BRADY, Gordon L., 'Capital Turnover and Marketable Pollution Rights', **31** *Journal of Law and Economics*, 1988, 203-226.

MANNE, Alan S. and RICHELS, Richard G., 'CO2 Emission Limits: An Economic Cost Analysis for the USA', **11(2)** *Energy Journal*, 1990, 51-74.

MANNE, Alan S. and RICHELS, Richard G., 'International Trade in Carbon Emission Rights: A Decomposition Procedure', **81** *American Economic Review. Papers and Proceedings*, 1991, 135-139.

MEAD, Walter J., 'The Performance of Government in Energy Regulation', **69** *American Economic Review*, 1979, 352-365.

MILLIMAN, J.W., 'Water Law and Private Decision-making: A Critique', **2** *Journal of Law and Economics*, 1959, 41-63.

MINASIAN, Jora R., 'Property Rights in Radiation: An Alternative Approach to Radio Frequency Allocation', **18** *Journal of Law and Economics*, 1975, 221-272.

MITCHELL, Robert Cameron and CARSON, Richard T., 'Property Rights, Protest, and the Siting of Hazardous Waste Facilities', **76** *American Economic Review. Papers and Proceedings*, 1986, 285-290.

NELSON, Forrest D. and NOLL, Roger D., 'Policymakers' Preferences for Alternative Allocations of the Broadcast Spectrum', in FISHER, Franklin M. (ed.), *Antitrust and Regulation: Essays in Memory of John J. McGowan*, Cambridge, MIT Press, 1985, 241-262.

PAGANELLI, Maurizio, 'Alla volta di Frankenstein: Biotecnologie e proprietà (di parti) del corpo' [Toward Frankenstein: Biotechnology and Property Rights in Body Parts], *Foro italiano*, 1989, IV, 417-441.

PEARSON, Peter J.G., 'Common Property, Privatisation and Environmental Policy: The Case of Natural Resource Degradation in the Third World', in WEIGEL, Wolfgang (ed.), *Economic Analysis of Law - A Collection of Applications*, Vienna, Österreichischer Wirtschaftsverlag, 1991, 90-100.

POWER, G., 'More About Oysters Than You Wanted to Know', **30** *Maryland Law Review*, 1970, 199 ff.

PULITINI, Francesco, 'Le "new properties" e il decentramento delle scelte pubbliche' [New Properties and Decentralization of Public Choices], in AA.VV., *Dalle res alle new properties*, Minalo, 1991, 67-80.

PULVER, Robert A., 'Liability Rules as a Solution to the Problem of Waste in Western Water Law: An Economic Analysis', **76** *California Law Review*, 1988, 671-726.

RAMSEYER, J. Mark, 'Water Law in Imperial Japan: Public Goods, Private Claims, and Legal Convergence', **18** *Journal of Legal Studies*, 1989, 51-77.

RASSENTI, S.J., SMITH, V.L. and BULFIN, R.L., 'A Combinatorial Auction Mechanism for Airport Time Slot Allocation', **13** *Bell Journal of Economics*, 1982, 402-417.

REECE, D.K., 'Competitive Bidding for Offshore Petroleum Leases', **9** *Bell Journal of Economics*, 1978, 369-384.

REECE, D.K., 'An Analysis of Alternative Bidding Systems for Leasing Offshore Oil', **10** *Bell Journal of Economics*, 1979, 659-669.

ROSE, Carol M., 'Energy and Efficiency in the Realignment of Common-Law Water Rights', **19** *Journal of Legal Studies*, 1990, 261-296.

SCHERAGA, Joel D., 'Establishing Property Rights in Outer Space', **6** *Cato Journal*, 1987, 889-903.

SHUPE, Steven J. and WEATHERFORD, Gary D. and CHECCHIO, Elizabeth, 'Western Water Rights: The Era of Reallocation', **29** *Natural Resources Journal*, 1989, 413-434.

SIEGEL, Daniel R., 'Estimating Potential Social Losses from Market Failure: Oil Exploration in Alberta', **16** *Rand Journal of Economics*, 1985, 537-552.

SKOGH, Göran (ed.), *Vem skall bestämma över skog och mark?* [Who is Going to Decide Over Forest and Land?], Lund, Distr. Dialogos, 1984.

SKOGH, Göran, 'Äganderätten och Lagstiftningen om Markresurserna' [The Property Right and the Legislation on the Land Resources], *Svensk Juristtidning*, February 1985.

SMITH, Paula K., 'Coercion and Groundwater Management: Three Case Studies and a "Market" Approach', **16** *Environmental Law*, 1986, 797 ff.

SMITH, V. Kerry, 'Legislating Open Access to a Scarce Resource: A Shortcoming of Policy on Nuclear Waste', **7** *Journal of Policy Analysis and Management*, 1988, 367-372.

SWAN, Peter, 'Is Law Reform Too Important to be Left to the Lawyers?: a Critique of Two Law Reform Commission Reports, *Human Tissue Transplants* and *Insurance Agents and Brokers*', in CRANSTON, Ross and SCHICK, Anne (eds.), *Law and Economics*, Canberra, Australian National University, 1982, 10-24.

SWEENEY, Richard James, TOLLISON, Robert D. and WILLETT, Thomas D., 'Market Failure, The Common-Pool Problem, and Ocean Resource Exploitation', **17** *Journal of Law and Economics*, 1974, 179-192.

TEEGUARDEN, Dennis E., 'Symposium on Federal Forest Law and Policy: Principles of Decision Making: Benefit-Cost Analysis in National Forest System Planning: Policy, Uses, and Limitations', **17** *Environmental Law Review*, 1987, 393 ff.

TEMPLE SWING, J., 'Who Will Own the Oceans?', **58** *Foreign Affairs*, 1976.

WELCH, W., 'The Political Feasibility of Full Ownership Property Rights: The Cases of Pollution and Fisheries', **16** *Policy Sciences*, 1983, 165-180.

WIHLBORG, Clas G. and WIJKMAN, Per Magnus, 'Outer Space Resources in Efficient and Equitable Use: New Frontiers for Old Principles', **24** *Journal of Law and Economics*, 1981, 23-43.

WILLIAMS, Stephen F., 'Solar Access and Property Rights: A Maverick Analysis', **11** *Connecticut Law Review*, 1979, 430 ff.

WILLIAMS, Stephen F., 'The Requirement of Beneficial Use as a Cause of Waste in Water Resource Development', **23** *Natural Resources Journal*, 1983, 7-23.

YOHE, Gary W., 'Regulation under Uncertainty: An Intuitive Survey and Application to Fisheries', **1** *Marine Resource Economics*, 1984, 171-192.

ZIADEH, Farhat J., 'Land Law and Economic Development in Arab Countries', **33** *American Journal of Comparative Law*, 1985, 93-106.

2800 SECURITY & BANKRUPTCY PRIORITY RIGHTS
Gerrit De Geest

ADAMS, Michael, *Ökonomische Analyse des Sicherungsrechte* [Economic Analysis of Security Law], Königstein/Ts, Athenäum, 1980, 322 p.

BAIRD, Douglas G. and JACKSON, Thomas H., 'Possession and Ownership: An Examination of the Scope of Article 9', **35** *Stanford Law Review*, 1983, 175-212.

BAIRD, Douglas G. and JACKSON, Thomas H., 'Corporate Reorganizations and the Treatment of Diverse Ownership Interests: A Comment on Adequate Protection of Secured Creditors in Bankruptcy', **51** *University of Chicago Law Review*, 1984, 97-130.

BAIRD, Douglas G. and JACKSON, Thomas H., *Cases, Problems, and Materials on Security Interests in Personal Property*, Mineola, Foundation Press, 1987, 889 p.

BISDAL, Joaquím, *La empresa en crisis y el derecho de quiebras* [The Crisis of the Firm and Bankruptcy Law], Bolonia, Real Colegio de España, 1986, 383 p.

BRATTON, Dale, 'Note: The California Agricultural Producer's Lien, Processing Company Insolvencies, and Federal Bankruptcy Law: An Evaluation and Alternative Methods of Protecting Farmers', **36** *Hastings Law Journal*, 1985, 609-644.

BUCKLEY, F.H., 'The Bankruptcy Priority Puzzle', **72** *Virginia Law Review*, 1986, 1393-1470.

CARLSON, David Gray, 'Rationality, Accident, and Priority Under Article 9 of the Uniform Commercial Code', **71** *Minnesota Law Review*, 1986, 207 ff.

CUELENAERE, L.M. and LEEN, A.R., 'Een rechtseconomisch aspect van de positie van de crediteur in een faillissement. Is afschaffing van de maximum rente een oplossing?' [A Law-and-economics Aspect of the Creditors Position in Bankruptcy. Is Abolishing the Maximum Interest Rate a Solution?], **38(10)** *Ars Aequi*, 1989, 834-836.

DALE-JOHNSON, David, DIETRICH, J. Kimball and LANGETIEG, Terence G., 'A Legal and Economic Analysis of the Due-on-Sale Clause: A Retrospective Examination', **10** *Research in Law and Economics*, 1987, 105-127.

ESKRIDGE, William N., Jr., 'One Hundred Years of Ineptitude: The Need for Mortgage Rules Consonant with the Economic and Psychological Dynamics of the Home Sale and Loan Transaction', **70** *Virginia Law Review*, 1984, 1083-1218.

HARRIS, Frederick H., 'Security and Penalty in Debt Contracts: Comment', **143** *Journal of Institutional and Theoretical Economics*, 1987, 168-174.

HESS, James D. and KNOEBER, Charles R., 'Security and Penalty in Debt Contracts', **143** *Journal of Institutional and Theoretical Economics*, 1987, 149-167.

JACKSON, Thomas H., *The Logic and Limits of Bankruptcy Law*, Cambridge, Harvard University Press, 1986, 287 p.

JACKSON, Thomas H. and KRONMAN, Anthony T., 'Secured Financing and

Priorities Among Creditors', **88** *Yale Law Journal*, 1979, 1143-1182.

JACKSON, Thomas H. and SCHWARTZ, Alan, 'Vacuum of Fact or Vacuous Theory: A Reply to Professor Kripke', **133** *University of Pennsylvania Law Review*, 1985, 987-1001.

JACKSON, Thomas H. and SCOTT, Robert E., 'On the Nature of Bankruptcy: An Essay on Bankruptcy Sharing and the Creditors' Bargain', **75** *Virginia Law Review*, 1989, 155-204.

KAHN, Charles and HUBERMAN, Gur, 'Default, Foreclosure, and Strategic Renegotiation', **52(1)** *Law and Contemporary Problems*, 1989, 49-61.

KEATING, Daniel, 'Pension Insurance, Bankruptcy, and Moral Hazard', *Wisconsin Law Review*, 1991, 65-108.

KOROBKIN, Donald R., 'Rehabilitating Values: A Jurisprudence of Bankruptcy', **91** *Columbia Law Review*, 1991, 717-789.

KRIPKE, Homer, 'Law and Economics: Measuring the Economic Efficiency of Commercial Law in a Vacuum of Fact', **133** *University of Pennsylvania Law Review*, 1985, 929-985. Reprinted in **28** *Corporate Practice Commentator*, 1986, 153-210.

LAWRENCE, William H., 'Lender Control Liability: An Analytical Model Illustrated with Applications to the Relational Theory of Secured Financing', **62** *Southern California Law Review*, 1989, 1387-1447.

McCOID, John C. II, 'Setoff: Why Bankrupcty Priority', **75** *Virginia Law Review*, 1989, 15-43.

ROE, Mark J., 'Commentary on "On the Nature of Bankruptcy": Bankruptcy, Priority, and Economics', **75** *Virginia Law Review*, 1989, 219-240.

SCHUMANN, Jochen, 'Security and Penalty in Debt Contracts: Comment', **143** *Journal of Institutional and Theoretical Economics*, 1987, 175-179.

SCHWARTZ, Alan, 'Security Interests and Bankruptcy Priorities: A Review of Current Theories', **10** *Journal of Legal Studies*, 1981, 1-37.

SCHWARTZ, Alan, 'The Enforceability of Security Interests in Consumer Goods', **26** *Journal of Law and Economics*, 1983, 117-162.

SCHWARTZ, Alan, 'The Continuing Puzzle of Secured Debt', **37** *Vanderbilt Law Review*, 1984, 1051-1069. Reprinted in **27** *Corporate Practice Commentator*, 1985, 294-312.

SCHWARTZ, Alan, 'A Theory of Loan Priorities', **18** *Journal of Legal Studies*, 1989, 209-261.

SCHWARTZ, Alan and WILDE, Louis L., 'Imperfect Information in Markets for Contract Terms: The Examples of Warranties and Security Interests', **69** *Virginia Law Review*, 1983, 1387-1485.

SCOTT, James H. Jr., 'Bankruptcy, Secured Debt, and Optimal Capital Structure', **32** *Journal of Finance*, 1977, 1-19.

SCOTT, James H. Jr., 'Bankruptcy, Secured Debt, and Optimal Capital Structure: Reply', **34** *Journal of Finance*, 1979, 253-260.

SCOTT, Robert E., 'A Relational Theory of Secured Financing', **86** *Columbia Law Review*, 1986, 901-977.

SHUPACK, Paul M., 'Solving the Puzzle of Secured Transactions', **41** *Rutgers Law Review*, 1989, 1067-1129.

SLAIN, John J. and KRIPKE, Homer, 'The Interface between Securities Regulation and Bankruptcy: Allocating the Risk of Illegal Securities Issuance between Securityholders and the Issuer's Creditors', **48** *New York University Law Review*, 1973, 261-300.

SMITH, Clifford W., Jr. and WARNER, Jerold B., 'Bankruptcy, Secured Debt, and Optimal Capital Structure: Comment', **34** *Journal of Finance*, 1979, 247-251.

SWARD, Ellen E., 'Resolving Conflicts between Bankruptcy Law and the State Police Power', *Wisconsin Law Review*, 1987, 403-453.

WALSH, Cliff, 'First-Party-Priority Revisited', **51** *Economic Record*, 1975, 275-277.

WASSENAER VAN CATWIJCK, A.J.O. Baron van, 'Op zeker spelen. Invloeden van zekerheden in het NBW op het financieringsbedrijf' [Play it Safe. Influence of Dutch New Civil Code Security on Financing Practice], in COLJEE, P.D., FRANKEN, H., HEERTJE, A. and KANNING, W. (eds.), *Law and Welfare Economics*, Symposium 24 October, VU Amsterdam, 133-150.

WHITE, James J., 'Efficiency Justifications for Personal Property Security', **37** *Vanderbilt Law Review*, 1984, 473 ff.

WHITE, Michelle J., 'Public Policy toward Bankruptcy: Me-First and Other Priority Rules', **11** *Bell Journal of Economics*, 1980, 550-564.

2900 INTELLECTUAL PROPERTY
Rudi W. Holzhauer

2900 General Works - Intellectual Property

ARROW, Kenneth J., 'Economic Welfare and the Allocation of Resources for Invention', in NELSON, R.R. (ed.), *The Rate and Direction of Inventive Activity: Economic and Social Factors*, New York, Princeton University Press, 1962.

BEIER, F.-K. and SHRICKER, G., 'GATT or WIPO? New Ways in the International Protection of Intellectual Property', **11** *IIC Studies*, Weinheim, VCH-Verlagsgesellschaft, 1989.

BESEN, Stanley M. and KIRBY, Sheila N., 'Compensating Creators of Intellectual Property: Collectives That Collect', *The Rand Corporation*, R-3751-MF, November 1989.

BESEN, Stanley M. and RASKIND, Leo J., 'An Introduction to the Law and Economics of Intellectual Property', **5** *Journal of Economic Perspectives*, 1991, 3-27.

BRAUN, Fernand, 'The Economic Role of Industrial Property', **1** *European Intellectual Property Review*, 1979, 265-273.

BRAUNSTEIN, Y.M., FISCHER, D.M., ORDOVER, Janusz A. and BAUMOL, William J., 'Economics of Property Rights as Applied to Computer Software and Data Bases', United States Department of Commerce: PB-268 787, 1977.

DANSBY, Robert E., 'Comment: Liability and Compensation in the Sale of Quasi-Public Goods', **8** *Research in Law and Economics*, 1986, 175-179.

DREYFUSS, Rochelle C., 'The Creative Employee and the Copyright Act of 1976', **54** *University of Chicago Law Review*, 1987, 590-647.

EVENSON, Robert E. and PUTNAM, Jonathan D., 'Institutional Change in Intellectual Property Rights', **69** *American Journal of Agricultural Economics*, 1987, 403-409.

FEINBERG, Robert M. and ROUSSLANG, Donald J., 'The Economic Effects of Intellectual Property Right Infringements', **63** *Journal of Business*, 1990, 79-90.

GOMEZ-POMAR, Fernando, 'Reglas de transacción y derechos de propriedad intelectual'[Transaction Rules and Intellectual Property Rights], **38** *Economistas*, 1989.

HAY, Fenton, 'Canada's Role in International Negotiations Concerning Intellectual Property Laws', **8** *Research in Law and Economics*, 1986, 239-263.

HIRSHLEIFER, Jack, 'The Private and Social Value of Information and the Reward to Innovative Activity', **61** *American Economic Review*, 1971, 561-574.

HIRSHLEIFER, Jack, 'Where Are We in the Theory of Information?', **63** *American Economic Review, Papers and Proceedings*, 1973, 31-39.

HUMMEL-BERGER, *Die volkswirtschaftliche Bedeutung von Kunst und Kultur* [The Economic Significance of Art and Culture], München, 1988.

KINGSTON, William, 'Who Should Protect Intellectual Property?', *European Intellectual Property Review*, 1985, 75-77.

KITCH, Edmund W., 'The Law and Economics of Rights in Valuable Information', **9** *Journal of Legal Studies*, 1980, 683-723.

KOOPMANS, T., 'Mini-monopolies' [Mini-monopolies], *Rechtsgeleerd Magazijn Themis*, 1983, 342-344.

KRAUSS, Michael I., 'Property, Monopoly, and Intellectual Rights', **12** *Hamline Law Review*, 1989, 305-320.

LEHMANN, Michael, 'Theorie der Property Rights und Schutz des geistigen und gewerblichen Eigentums - Wettbewerbsbeschränkungen zur Förderung des Wettbewerbs' [Property Rights Theory and the Protection of Intellectual and Commercial Property], in *Ansprüche, Eigentums- und Verfügungsrechte Schriften des Vereins für Socialpolitik*, Band 140, Berlin, Duncker & Humblot, 1984, 519-535.

LEHMANN, Michael, 'The Theory of Property Rights and the Protection of Intellectual and Industrial Property', 16 *IIC*, 1985, 525-540.

LEHMANN, Michael, 'La teoría de los "Property Rights" y la protección de la propriedad intelectual e industrial' [The Property Rights Theory and the Protection of Intellectual and Industrial Property], *Revista General de Derecho*, 1990, n. 544-545, 265-281.

MACKAAY, Ejan J.P., *Economics of Information and Law*, Dordrecht, Kluwer Nijhoff, 1982, 293 p.

MACKAAY, Ejan J.P., 'De hersenschim als rustig bezit. Moet alle informatie voorwerp van eigendom zijn?' [Chimera as Quiet Possession. Should All Information Be Owned?], *Computerrecht*, 1985, 12-16.

MACKAAY, Ejan J.P., 'Les droits intellectuels - entre propriété et monopole' [Intellectual Property Rights - Between Property and Monopoly], **1** *Journal des Economistes et des Etudes Humaines*, 1989-1990.

MACKAAY, Ejan J.P., 'Economic Incentives in Markets for Information and Innovation', **13** *Harvard Journal of Law and Public Policy*, 1990, 867-909.

MANNE, Henry G., 'Insider Trading and Property Rights in New Information', in DORN, James A. and MANNE, Henry G. (eds.), *Economic Liberties and the Judiciary*, Fairfax, George Mason University Press, 1987, 317-327.

McKEE, Michael, 'You Can't Always Get What You Want: Lessons from the Paris Convention Revision Exercise', **8** *Research in Law and Economics*, 1986, 265-272.

MELVILLE, Leslie, 'A Law of Activities - The Choice of Words and Their Limiting Effect', *European Intellectual Property Review*, 1982, 63-66.

OBERENDER, Peter and RUTER, Georg, 'Innovationsforderung: Einige grundsätzliche ordnungspolitische Bemerkungen' [The Promotion of Innovation: Some Basic Remarks on Policies], in LENEL, Hans Otto at al. (ed.), *ORDO: Jahrbuch fur die Ordnung von Wirtschaft und Gesellschaft*, Band 38, Stuttgart, Fischer, 1987, 143-54.

PALMER, Tom G., 'Intellectual Property: A Non-Posnerian Law and Economics Approach', **12** *Hamline Law Review*, 1989, 261-304.

PRAGER, F.D., 'The Early Growth and Influence of Intellectual Property', *Journal of the Patent Office Society,* 1952, 106-110.

PRIEST, George L., 'What Economists Can Tell Lawyers about Intellectual Property: Comment on Cheung', **8** *Research in Law and Economics*, 1986, 19-24.

SHENG CHENG HU, 'On the Incentive to Invent: A Clarificatory Note', **16** *Journal of Law and Economics*, 1973, 169-177.

TEIJL, Rob and HOLZHAUER, Rudi W., 'De toenemende complexiteit van het intellectuele eigendomsrecht. Een economische analyse' [The Growing Complexity of Intellectual Property Law. An Economic Analysis], in *Rechtseconomische Verkenningen Deel 1*, Arnhem, Gouda Quint, 1991.

TERRELL, Timothy P. and SMITH, Jane S., 'Publicity, Liberty, and Intellectual Property: A Conceptual and Economic Analysis of the Inheritability Issue', **34** *Emory Law Journal*, 1985, 1 ff.

TULLOCK, Gordon, 'Intellectual Property', in KINGSTON, William (ed.), *Direct Protection of Innovation*, Dordrecht, Kluwer Academic for the Commission of the European Communities, 1987, 171-199.

WICHERS HOETH, L., 'Mini-monopolies: Een reactie' [Mini-monopolies: A Response], *Rechtsgeleerd Magazijn Themis*, 1984, 356-357.

2905 General Works - Innovation (R&D, Technology, Technical Productivity) & Competition (Monopoly, Market Power)

BARZEL, Yoram, 'Optimal Timing of Innovations', **50** *Review of Economics and Statistics*, 1968, 348-355.

BOUJU, Andre, 'Direct Protection of Innovation: The "Critical" Chapters', in KINGSTON, William (ed.), *Direct Protection of Innovation*, Dordrecht, Kluwer Academic for the Commission of the European Communities, 1987, 247-256.

BOWMAN, Ward S., Jr., 'The Incentive to Invent in Competitive as Contrasted to Monopolistic Industries', **20** *Journal of Law and Economics*, 1977, 227-228.

BRAGA, C.A., 'The Economics of Intellectual Property Rights and the GATT', **22** *Vanderbilt Journal of Transnational Law*, 1989, 243-264.

BRESNAHAN, Timothy F., 'Post-entry Competition in the Plain Paper Copying Market', **75** *American Economic Review*, 1985, 15-19.

COHEN JEHORAM, Herman, 'Industriële eigendom en innovatie' [Industrial Property and Innovation], *Nederlands Juristen Blad*, 1979, 609-612.

CONRAD, C.A., 'The Advantage of Being First and Competition between Firms', **1** *International Journal of Industrial Organization*, 1983, 353-364.

DASGUPTA, Partha S. and STIGLITZ, Joseph E., 'Uncertainty, Industrial Structure, and the Speed of R&D', **11** *Bell Journal of Economics*, 1980, 1-28.

DASGUPTA, Partha S. and STIGLITZ, Joseph E., 'Industrial Structure and the Nature of Inventive Activity', **90** *Economic Journal*, 1986, 266-293.

DE JONG, Henk Wouter, 'Direct Protection of Innovation: The "Critical" Chapters', in KINGSTON, William (ed.), *Direct Protection of Innovation*, Dordrecht, Kluwer Academic for the Commission of the European Communities, 1987, 215-226.

DEPARTMENT of TRADE and INDUSTRY, *Intellectual Property and Innovation*, London, Her Majesty's Stationary Office, 1986, Cmnd. 9712, 78 p.

DIXIT, A.K. and STIGLITZ, Joseph E., 'Monopolistic Competition and Optimum Product Diversity', **67** *American Economic Review*, 1977, 297-308.

DREYFUSS, Rochelle C., 'Dethroning Lear: Licensee Estoppel and the Incentive to Innovate', **72** *Virginia Law Review*, 1986, 677-765.

FARRELL, Joseph, 'Standardization and Intellectual Property', **30** *Jurimetrics*, 1989, 35-50.

FEINBERG, Robert M., 'Intellectual Property, Injury, and International Trade', **22(2)** *Journal of World Trade Law*, 1988, 45-56.

GILBERT, Richard J., 'Comment: Uncertain Innovation and the Persistence of Monopoly', **74** *American Economic Review*, 1984, 238-242.

GLAZER, A., 'The Advantage of Being First', **75** *American Economic Review*, 1985, 473-480.

GRABOWSKI, Henry G., *Drug Regulation and Innovation: Empirical Evidence and Policy*, Washington, American Enterprise Institute, 1976, 82 p.

GRABOWSKI, Henry G. and MÜLLER, D.C., 'Industrial Research and Development, Intangible Capital Stocks, and Firm Profit Rates', **9** *Bell Journal of Economics*, 1978, 328-343.

GRILICHES, Zvi, 'Issues in Assessing the Contribution of Research and Development to Productivity Growth', **10** *Bell Journal of Economics*, 1979, 92-116.

GRILICHES, Zvi (ed.), *R&D, Patents, and Productivity*, Chicago, University of Chicago Press, 1984.

GROSSMAN, Sanford J. and STIGLITZ, Joseph E., 'Information and Competitive Price Systems', **66** *American Economic Review. Papers and Proceedings*, 1976, 246-253.

HOLCOMBE, Randall G. and MEINERS, Roger E., 'Market Arrangements Versus Government Protection of Innovative Activity', **5** *The Social Science Review*, 1983, 1 ff.

KAMIEN, Morton I. and SCHWARTZ, Nancy L., 'Market Structure, Elasticity of Demand and Incentive to Invent', **13** *Journal of Law and Economics*, 1970, 241-252.

KAMIEN, Morton I. and SCHWARTZ, Nancy L., 'Market Structure and Innovation: A Survey', **13** *Journal of Economic Literature*, 1975, 1-37. Reprinted: Cambridge, Cambridge University Press, 1982.

KAPLOW, Louis, 'The Patent-Antitrust Intersection: A Reappraisal', **97** *Harvard Law Review*, 1984, 1815-1892.

KATZ, M.L. and SHAPIRO, Carl, 'R&D Rivalry with Licensing or Imitation', 77 *American Economic Review*, 1987, 402-420.

KINGSTON, William, 'Recession and Intellectual property', *European Intellectual Property Review*, 1981, 131-133.

KINGSTON, William, *The Political Economy of Innovation*, The Hague, 1984.

KINGSTON, William, 'The Innovation Warrant', in KINGSTON, William (ed.), *Direct Protection of Innovation*, Dordrecht, Kluwer Academic for the Commission of the European Communities, 1987, 59-86.

KINGSTON, William, 'Advantages of Protecting Innovation Directly', in KINGSTON, William (ed.), *Direct Protection of Innovation*, Dordrecht, Kluwer Academic for the Commission of the European Communities, 1987, 87-123.

KINGSTON, William, 'Direct Protection of Innovation: Response', in KINGSTON, William (ed.), *Direct Protection of Innovation*, Dordrecht, Kluwer Academic for the Commission of the European Communities, 1987, 277-337.

KLEIN, Christopher C., 'Strategic Sham Litigation: Economic Incentives in the Context of the Case Law', **6** *International Review of Law and Economics*, 1986, 241-253.

KLEIN, D., 'Tie-ins and the Market Provision of Collective Goods', 10 *Harvard Journal of Law & Public Policy*, 1987, 452 ff.

LEHMANN, Michael, 'Property and Intellectual Property - Property Rights as Restrictions on Competition in Furtherance of Competition', 20 *IIC*, 1989, 1-15.

LEVIN, Richard C., 'Technical Change, Barriers to Entry and Market Structure', **45** *Economica*, 1978, 347-362.

LEVIN, Richard C., COHEN, W.M. and MOWERY, D.C., 'R&D Appropriability, Opportunity, and Market Structure: New Evidence on Some Schumpeterian Hypotheses', **75** *American Economic Review, Papers and Proceedings*, 1985, 20-24.

LEVIN, Richard C., KLEVORICK, Alvin K., NELSON, Richard R. and WINTER, Sidney G., 'Appropriating the Returns from Industrial R&D', **3** *Brookings Papers on Economic Activity: Microelectronics*, 1987, 783-820.

LLOYD OF KILGERRAN, 'The Patent System - A Tool in the Marketing Strategy for the Creation of Wealth and New Jobs', *European Intellectual Property Review*, 1980, 67-69.

LOURY, G.C., 'Market Structure and Innovation', **93** *Quarterly Journal of Economics*, 1979, 395-409.

LUNN, John, 'The Roles of Property Rights and Market Power in Appropriating Innovative Output', **14** *Journal of Legal Studies*, 1985, 423-433.

MACHLUP, Fritz, *The Political Economy of Monopoly*, Baltimore, John Hopkins Press, 1952.

MACHLUP, Fritz, 'The Optimum Lag of Imitation Behind Innovation', **96** *Nationalokonomisk Tidsskrift*, Festskrift til Frederic Zeuthen, 1958, 239-256.

MANDEVILLE, Thomas and MACDONALD, Stuart, 'Innovation Protection Viewed from an Information Perspective', in KINGSTON, William (ed.), *Direct Protection of Innovation*, Dordrecht, Kluwer Academic for the Commission of the European Communities, 1987, 157-169.

MANSFIELD, Edwin, 'Rates of Return from Industrial Development', **55** *American Economic Review, Papers and Proceedings*, 1965, 310-322.

MANSFIELD, Edwin, 'How Rapidly Does New Industrial Technology Leak Out?',

Journal of Industrial Economics, 1985, 217-223.

MANSFIELD, Edwin, 'The R&D Tax Credit and Other Technology Policy Issues', **76** *American Economic Review. Papers and Proceedings*, 1986, 191-197.

MANSFIELD, Edwin, RAPOPORT, J., ROMEO, A., WAGNER, S. and BEARDSLEY, G., 'Social and Private Rates of Return from Industrial Innovations', **71** *Quarterly Journal of Economics*, 1977, 221-240.

MARKHAM, J.W., 'The Joint Effect of Antitrust and Patent Laws upon Innovation', **56** *American Economic Review. Papers and Proceedings*, 1966, 291-300.

McFETRIDGE, D.G., *Government Support of Scientific Research and Development: An Economic Analysis*, Toronto, University of Toronto Press, 1977.

MERGES, Robert P., 'Commercial Success and Patent Standards: Economic Perspectives on Innovation', **76** *California Law Review*, 1988, 803-876.

MOSSINGHOFF, G.J., 'The Importance of Intellectual Property Protection in International Trade', **7** *Boston College International and Comparative Law Review*, 1984, 235-249.

NELSON, Richard R., (ed.), *The Rate and Direction of Inventive Activity*, Princeton, Princeton University Press, 1962.

NELSON, Richard R. and WINTER, S.G., *An Evolutionary Theory of Economic Change*, Cambridge (Mass.), Belknap of Harvard University Press, 1982.

NORDHAUS, W.D., *Invention, Growth, and Welfare: A Theoretical Treatment of Technological Change*, Cambridge (Mass.), MIT Press, 1969.

ORDOVER, Janusz A. and WILLIG, R.D., 'On the Optimal Provisions of Journals qua Sometimes Shared Goods', **68** *American Economic Review*, 1978, 324-339.

ORKIN, Neal, 'A Proposal to Increase Technical Productivity in the United States', *European Intellectual Property Review*, 1982, 331-335.

OSTER, Sharon M., 'The Diffusion of Innovation among Steel Firms: the Basic Oxygen Furnace', **13** *Bell Journal of Economics*, 1982, 45-56.

PENDLETON, Michael, 'Intellectual Property, Information-based Society and a New International Economic Order - The Policy Options?', *European Intellectual Property Review*, 1985, 31-34.

POSNER, Richard A., 'The Social Costs of Monopoly and Regulation', **83** *Journal of Political Economy*, 1975, 807-827.

RAHN, Guntram, 'The Role of Industrial Property in Economic Development: The Japanese Experience', **14** *International Review of Industrial Property*, 1983, 449-592.

RASKIND, Leo J., 'The Misappropriation Doctrine as a Competitive Norm of Intellectual Property Law', **75** *Minnesota Law Review*, 1991.

REINGANUM, Jennifer F., 'Market Structure and the Diffusion of New Technology', **12** *Bell Journal of Economics*, 1981, 618-624.

REINGANUM, Jennifer F., 'Uncertain Innovation and the Persistence of Monopoly', **73** *American Economic Review*, 1983, 741-748.

REINGANUM, Jennifer F., 'Technology Adoption under Imperfect Information', **14** *Bell Journal of Economics*, 1983, 57-69.

ROZEK, Richard P., 'Protection of Intellectual Property Rights: Research and

Development Decisions and Economic Growth', **5(3)** *Contemporary Policy Issues*, 1987, 54-65.

RUSHING, Francis W. and BROWN, Carole Ganz (eds.), *Intellectual Property Rights in Science, Technology, and Economic Performance*, Boulder, Westview, 1990, 354 p.

SAPPINGTON, D., 'Optimal Regulation of Research and Development under Imperfect Information', **13** *Bell Journal of Economics*, 1982, 354-368.

SCHERER, Frederic M., *Industrial Market Structure and Economic Performance*, Chicago, Rand McNally, 1980 (2nd ed.), 632 p.

SCHERER, Frederic M., 'Firm Size, Market Structure, Opportunity and the Output of Patented Invention', **55** *American Economic Review*, 1965, 1097-1125.

SCHERER, Frederic M., 'Research and Development Resource Allocation under Rivalry', **81** *Quarterly Journal of Economics*, 1967, 359-394.

SCHIFF, E., *Industrialization without Patents - The Netherlands 1869-1912 and Switzerland 1850-1907*, Princeton University Press, Princeton, 1971.

SHENG CHENG HU, 'On the Incentive to Invent: A Clarificatory Note', **16** *Journal of Law and Economics*, 1973, 169-177.

SIEGHART, Paul, 'Information Technology and Intellectual Property', *European Intellectual Property Review*, 1982, 187-188.

SILBERSTON, Z.A., 'Direct Protection of Innovation: The "Critical" Chapters', in KINGSTON, William (ed.), *Direct Protection of Innovation*, Dordrecht, Kluwer Academic for the Commission of the European Communities, 1987, 201-213.

SPENCE, A. Michael, 'Product Selection, Fixed Costs, and Monopolistic Competition', **43** *Review of Economic Studies*, 1976, 217-235.

STALSON, Helena, *Intellectual Property Rights and U.S. Competitiveness in Trade*, Washington D.C., National Planning Association, 1987, 106 p.

STILLERMAN, R., 'Resistance to Change', **48** *Journal of the Patent Office*, 1966, 484-499.

TANDON, P., 'Rivalry and the Excessive Allocation of Resources to Research', **14** *Bell Journal of Economics*, 1983, 152-165.

TELSER, Lester G., 'A Theory of Innovation and Its Effects', **13** *Bell Journal of Economics*, 1982, 69-92.

TULLOCK, Gordon, 'The Welfare Costs of Tariffs, Monopolies and Theft', **5** *Western Economic Review*, 1967, 224-232.

USHER, Dan, 'The Welfare Economics of Invention', 31 *Economica*, 1964, 279-287.

WALKER, Charles E. and BLOOMFIELD, Mark A., (eds.), *Intellectual Property Rights and Capital Formation in the Next Decade*, Lanham, University Press of America, 1988, 189 p.

WILSON, R.W., 'The Effect of Technology Environment and Product Rivalry on R&D Effort and Licensing of Inventions', **59** *Review of Economics and Statistics*, 1977, 171-178.

WRIGHT, Brian D., 'The Economics of Invention Incentives: Patents, Prizes and Research Contracts', **73** *American Economic Review*, 1983, 691-707.

WRIGHT, Brian D., 'On the Design of a System to Improve the Production of

Innovations', in KINGSTON, William (ed.), *Direct Protection of Innovation*, Dordrecht, Kluwer Academic for the Commission of the European Communities, 1987, 227-246.

YAMEY, B.S., 'Monopoly, Competition and the Incentive to Invent: A Comment', **13** *Journal of Law and Economics*, 1970, 253-256.

YU, Ben T., 'Potential Competition and Contracting in Innovation', **24** *Journal of Law and Economics*, 1981, 215-238.

ZIMMERMAN, Martin B., 'Learning Effects and the Commercialization of New Energy Technologies: the Case of Nuclear Power', **13** *Bell Journal of Economics*, 1982, 297-310.

2910 Copyright

ADELSTEIN, Richard P. and PERETZ, Steven I., 'The Competition of Technologies in Markets for Ideas: Copyright and Fair Use in Evolutionary Perspective', **5** *International Review of Law and Economics*, 1985, 209-238.

ALAI, *The Economic Importance of Copyright*, Paris, ALAI, 1989, 19-58.

ALCHIAN, Armen A., 'Comment on Robert M. Hurt and Robert M. Schuchmann, "The Economic Rationale of Copyright"', **56** *American Economic Review*, 1966, 438-439.

BESEN, Stanley M., 'Private Copying, Reproduction Costs, and the Supply of Intellectual Property', **2(1)** *Information Economics and Policy*, 1986, 5-22.

BESEN, Stanley M. and KIRBY, Sheila Nataraj, 'Private Copying, Appropriability, and Optimal Copying Royalties', **32** *Journal of Law and Economics*, 1989, 255-280.

BESEN, Stanley M., MANNING, Willard G. Jr. and MITCHELL, Bridger M., 'Copyright Liability for Cable Television: Compulsory Licensing and the Coase Theorem', **21** *Journal of Law and Economics*, 1978, 67-95.

BREYER, Stephen, 'The Uneasy Case for Copyright: A Study of Copyright in Books, Photocopies, and Computer Programs', **84** *Harvard Law Review*, 1970, 281-351.

BREYER, Stephen, 'Copyright: A Rejoinder', **2O** *UCLA Law Review*, 1972, 75 ff.

BROWN, Vance Franklin, 'Comment: The Incompatibility of Copyright and Computer Software: An Economic Evaluation and a Proposal for a Marketplace Solution', **66** *North Carolina Law Review*, 1988, 977 ff.

CLAPES, A.L., LYNCH, P. and STEINBERG, M.R., 'Silicon Epics and Binary Bards: Determining the Proper Scope of Copyright Protection for Computer Programs', **34** *UCLA Law Review*, 1987, 1493-1594.

COHEN JEHORAM, Herman, 'Het economisch belang van het auteursrecht en de gevaren daarvan' [The Economic Importance of Copyright and Its Dangers], **13** *Informatierecht AMI*, 1989, 91-95.

CRAMER-MEIJERING-NIJSSEN, *De economische betekenis van het auteursrecht 1* [The Economic Importance of Copyright 1], Amsterdam, Stichting voor

Economisch Onderzoek Universiteit van Amsterdam, 1986.

DREYFUSS, Rochelle C., 'The Creative Employee and the Copyright Act of 1976', **54** *University of Chicago Law Review*, 1987, 590-647.

ERKKILA, John, 'Copyright Law, Photocopying, and Price Discrimination: Comment', **8** *Research in Law and Economics*, 1986, 201-203.

EUROPEAN COMMISSION, *Green Paper on Copyright and the Challenge of Technology*, Brussels, 1988.

FINNISH COPYRIGHT SOC., *A study of the economic importance of copyright--related industries in Finland*, 1988.

FRASE, R., 'Comments on Hurt and Schuchman. The Economic Rationale of Copyright', **56** *American Economic Review. Papers and Proceedings*, 1966, 435-439.

GHERING, M., PUFFELEN, F. van and SCHILTHUIS, F., *De economische betekenis van het auteursrecht 2* [The Economic Importance of Copyright 2], Amsterdam, Stichting voor Economisch Onderzoek Universiteit van Amsterdam, 1989, 58 p.

GOMEZ-POMAR, Fernando, 'La producción de copias y los derechos de autor: el caso de la fotocopiadora' [Copy Production and Copyright: The Photocopy-Machine Case], *Información comercial Española*, 1990, n. 687, 43-50.

GOMEZ-POMAR, Fernando, 'Copias, fotocopias y derechos de autor' [Copies, Photocopies and Copyrights], *Revista de la Facultad de Derecho de la Universidad Complutense*, 1990.

GORDON, Wendy J., 'Fair Use as Market Failure: A Structural and Economic Analysis of the Betamax Case and Its Predecessors', **82** *Columbia Law Review*, 1982, 1600-1659.

GULDBERG, H. and CANDI, E., *Copyright: An Economic Perspective*, Sidney, Australian Copyright Council, 1987. Reprinted in *GRUR Int.* 1988, 720 ff.

HARDY, I.T., 'An Economic Understanding of Copyright Law's Work-Made-for-Hire Doctrine', **12** *Columbia - VLA Journal of Law and the Arts*, 1988, 181-227.

HOLLANDER, Abraham, 'Comments on Douglas Smith', **8** *Research in Law and Economics*, 1986, 153-155.

JOHNSON, W.R., 'The Economics of Copying', **93** *Journal of Political Economy*, 1985, 158-174.

KEON, Jim, 'Audio Home Recording: Canadian Copyright Implications', **8** *Research in Law and Economics*, 1986, 157-173.

LADD, David, 'The Harm of the Concept of Harm in Copyright', **8** *Auteursrecht*, 1984, 3-6.

LANDES, William M. and POSNER, Richard A., 'An Economic Analysis of Copyright Law', **18** *Journal of Legal Studies*, 1989, 325-363. Reprinted in **22** *Intellectual Property Law Review*, 1990, 447-485.

LIEBOWITZ, S.J., 'Copying and Indirect Appropriability: Photocopying of Journals', **93** *Journal of Political Economy*, 1985, 945-957.

LIEBOWITZ, S.J., 'Copyright Law, Photocopying, and Price Discrimination', **8** *Research in Law and Economics*, 1986, 181-200.

LIEBOWITZ, S.J., 'Comments on Whalley and Hay', **8** *Research in Law and Economics*, 1986, 285-287.

MANNI-LOUKKOLA and ESALA, *A study of the economic importance of copyright-related industries in Finland*, Finnish Copyright Society, 1988.

MARGOLIS, Stephen E., 'Comments on "Copyright and Computer Software"', **8** *Research in Law and Economics*, 1986, 227-231.

MITCHELL, B.M. and SMILEY, R.H., 'Cable, Cities, and Copyrights', **5** *Bell Journal of Economics*, 1974.

NOVOS, Ian E. and WALDMAN, Michael, 'The Effects of Increased Copyright Protection: An Analytic Approach', **92** *Journal of Political Economy*, 1984, 236-246.

O'HARE, Michael, 'Copyright: When Is Monopoly Efficient?', **4** *Journal of Policy Analysis and Management*, 1985, 407-418.

OETHIG, R., 'Copyrights and Copying Costs: A New Price-Theoretic Approach', **144** *Journal of Institutional and Theoretical Economics*, 1988, 462 ff.

OLSSON, Henry, 'Copyright in the National Economy', *Copyright*, 1982, 130 ff.

OLSSON, Henry, 'Copyright and the National Economy, *European Intellectual Property Review*, 1984, 179-181.

OLSSON, Henry, 'The Economic Impact of Copyright Law', in *Internationales Urheberrechtsymposium*, München, 1986, 71 ff.

PALMER, John P. (Guest ed.), *The Economics of Patents and Copyrights*, in ZERBE, Richard O. Jr. (Series ed.), *Research in Law and Economics*, Greenwich, Jai Press, **8**, 1986, 287 p.

PALMER, John P., 'Copyright and Computer Software', **8** *Research in Law and Economics*, 1986, 205-225.

PETHIG, Rudiger, 'Copyrights and Copying Costs: A New Price Theoretic Approach', **144** *Journal of Institutional and Theoretical Economics*, 1988, 462-495.

PEYTON, David, 'A New View of Copyright', **6** *Journal of Policy Analysis and Management*, 1986, 92-98.

PHILLIPS, *The Economic Importance of Copyright*, London, 1985.

PLANT, Arnold, 'The Economic Aspects of Copyright in Books', **1** *Economica*, 1934, 167-195. Reprinted in PLANT, Arnold, *Selected Economic Essays and Addresses*, 1974, 64-65.

PROSI, G., *Ökonomische Theorie des Buches. Volkswirtschaftliche Aspekte des Urheber- und Verlegerschutzes* [The Economic Theory of Books, Copyright and Publisher's Rights], Düsseldorf, 1971.

RASKIND, Leo J., 'A Functional Interpretation of Fair Use', **31** *Journal of the Copyright Society*, 1984, 601-639.

RASKIND, Leo J., 'Reverse Engineering, Unfair Competition, and Fair Use', **70** *Minnesota Law Review*, 1985, 385-415.

RASKIND, Leo J., 'The Continuing Process of Refining and Adapting Copyright Principles', *Columbia - VLA Journal of Law and the Arts*, 1990.

RUBIN, 'The Copyright Industries in the United States', *An Economic Report*

Prepared for the American Copyright Council, 1985.

SCHEUCH, F. and HOLZMUKKER, H., *The Economic Importance of the Copyright Industries in Austria*, Vienna, Vienna University of Economics and Business Administration, 1989.

SEO, *De economische betekenis van het auteursrecht 2: Rapportage 1989* [The Economic Importance of Copyright in the Netherlands 2: Report 1989], Amsterdam, Stichting voor Economisch Onderzoek, 1989.

SKILBECK, *The Economic Importance of Copyright*, International Publishers Association, 1988.

SMITH, Douglas A., 'Collective Administration of Copyright: An Economic Analysis', **8** *Research in Law and Economics*, 1986, 137-151.

SPIVACK, Peter G., 'Does Form Follow Function? The Idea/Expression Dichotomy in Copyright Protection of Computer Software', **35** *UCLA Law Review*, 1988, 723-778.

TYERMAN, 'The Economic Rationale for Copyright Protection for Published Books: A Reply to Professor Breyer', **18** *UCLA Law Review*, 1971, 1100 ff.

US COPYRIGHT OFFICE, 'Report to the Subcommittee on Patents, Copyrights and Trademarks Committee on the Judiciary. United States Senate on the Size of the Copyright Industries in the United States', *GRUR Int.*, 1985, 393 ff.

WHALLEY, John, 'International Aspects of Copyright Legislation in Canada: Economic Analysis of Policy Options', **8** *Research in Law and Economics*, 1986, 273-283.

WILEY, John Shepard, Jr., 'Copyright at the School of Patent', **58** *University of Chicago Law Review*, 1991, 119-185.

2920 Copyright Related rights

BOLCH, Ben W., DAMON, William W. and HINSHAW, C. Elton, 'Visual Artists' Rights Act of 1987: A Case of Misguided Legislation', **8** *Cato Journal*, 1988, 71-78.

GROSHEIDE, F.W. and FREQUIN, M.J., 'Uitgeversrecht' [Publishers Right], **14** *Informatierecht AMI*, 1990, 43-47.

KREVELEN, D.W. van, 'The Information Society and the Right of the Publisher', Internationales Urheberrechtsymposium, *SGRUM*, 1986, 15.

LADD, David, 'The Utility of a Publisher's Right', Internationales Urheberrechtsymposium, *SGRUM*, 1986, 15.

LINNEMAN, M.J.T., 'Sportrechten, artikel 15 en marktopdeling' [Sports Rights, Section 15 and Splitting up the Market], **14** *Informatierecht AMI*, 1990, 63-66.

NEDERLANDS ECONOMISCH INSTITUUT, *Verhuur- en leenrecht EG. Commentaar op het SEO-rapport "Naar een verhuur- en leenrecht in de Europese Gemeenschap* [EC Rental and Lending Rights. Commentary on the SEO-report "Towards a Rental and Lending Right in the European Community], Rotterdam, Nederlands Economisch Instituut, 1991, 24 p.

PIATIER, Andre, 'Innovation Patent, Invention Patent, or Both? Towards a Radical Reform of the Patent System', in KINGSTON, William (ed.), *Direct Protection of Innovation*, Dordrecht, Kluwer Academic for the Commission of the European Communities, 1987, 125-155.

PROSI, G., *Ökonomische Theorie des Buches. Volkswirtschaftliche Aspekte des Urheber- und Verlegerschutzes* [The Economic Theory of Books, Copyright and Publisher's Rights], Düsseldorf, 1971.

RESIUS, F.J., 'Uitgeversbescherming' [The Protection of Publishers], 14 *Informatierecht AMI*, 1990, 67-69.

SEO, *De economische betekenis van het auteursrecht in Nederland: 1982* [The Economic Importance of Copyright in the Netherlands: 1982], Amsterdam, Stichting voor Economisch Onderzoek, 1986.

SEO, *De economische betekenis van de professionele kunsten in Amsterdam* [The Economic Importance of Professional Art in Amsterdam], Amsterdam, Stichting voor Economisch Onderzoek, 1989, 241 p.

SEO, *Naar een verhuur- en leenrecht in de Europese gemeenschap* [Towards a Rental and Lending Rights in the European Community], Amsterdam, Stichting voor Economisch Onderzoek, 1989, 203 p.

SOETENHORST, W.J., 'Wettelijke bescherming van de uitgeefprestatie in Nederland, Duitsland, Zwitserland en Groot-Brittannië' [Legal Protection of Publishers Activities in the Netherlands, Germany, Switzerland and Great-Britain], **13** *Informatierecht*, 1989, 55-57.

X, 'Dutch Publishers Seek Neighbouring Rights', **4(1)** *Rights*, 1990.

X, 'News form the 2nd IPA International Copyright Symposium, Strengthening Publishers' Rights', **4(2)** *Rights*, 1990.

2930 Patents

ABN, *Octrooien in het midden- en kleinbedrijf* [Patents in Middle Size and Small Companies], Alg. Bank Nederland, 1990, 11 p.

ANDERSEN, Cecilia, 'Het Octrooirecht ten dienste van Kleine en Middelgrote Ondernemingen' [Patent Law to the Use of Small and Middle Size Companies], **40** *Economisch en Sociaal Tijdschrift*, 1986, 613-629.

ASSELT, Henk Th. van, 'Octrooiduur & innovatie in de geneesmiddelenindustrie' [Patent Term and Innovation in the Pharmaceutical Industry], **32** *Management Report Series, Rotterdam School of Management*, 1989, 17 p.

ASSELT, Henk Th. van, 'Balanceren tussen innovatie en monopolie: octrooiduur en innovatie in de Geneesmiddelenindustrie' [Balancing Innovation and Monopoly: The Patent Term and Innovation in the Pharmaceutical Industry], **57** *Bijblad Intellectuele Eigendom*, 1989, 143-147.

BAARSLAG, A.D., 'Octrooibeleid van de onderneming' [Patent Policy of the Firm], in *Octrooien in Nederland en Europa*, Kamer van Koophandel en Fabrieken voor Rotterdam en de Beneden-Maas, 22 mei 1990.

BECK, Roger L., 'Patents, Property Rights and Social Welfare: Search for a

Restricted Optimum', **43** *Southern Economic Journal,* 1976, 10511055.

BECK, Roger L., 'Patents and Over-Investment in Process Innovations: Reply', **45** *Southern Economic Journal,* 1978, 289-292.

BECK, Roger L., 'Competition for Patent Monopolies', **3** *Research in Law and Economics,* 1981, 91-110.

BECK, Roger L., 'The Prospect Theory of the Patent System and Unproductive Competition', **5** *Research in Law and Economics,* 1983, 193-209.

BECK, Roger L., 'Does Competitive Dissipation Require A Short Patent Life?', **8** *Research in Law and Economics,* 1986, 121-129.

BEIER, Friedrich-Karl, 'Die Bedeutung des Patentsystems für den technischen, wirtschaftlichen und sozialen Fortschritt' [The Significance of Patent Law for the Technical, Economic and Social Evolution], *Gewerblicher Rechtsschutz und Urheberrecht - Internationaler Teil,* 1979, 227-235.

BENEDETTI, Fabrizio de, 'An Economic and Political Analysis of Changes in the Patent System', **5** *European Intellectual Property Review,* 1983, 295-297.

BERKOWITZ, M.K. and KOTOWITZ, Y., 'Patent Policy in an Open Economy', **15** *Canadian Journal of Economics,* 1982, 1-17.

BITTLINGMAYER, George, 'Property Rights, Progress, and the Aircraft Patent Agreement', **31** *Journal of Law and Economics,* 1988, 227-248.

BOWMAN, Ward S., Jr., *Patent and Antitrust Law: A Legal and Economic Appraisal,* Chicago, University of Chicago Press, 1973.

BRASTOW, Raymond and RYSTROM, David, 'Wealth Effects of the Drug Price Competition and Patent Term Restoration Act of 1984', **32(2)** *American Economist,* 1988, 59-65.

BRETT, Hugh, 'The Patent System - What Future Role in the Creation of Wealth?', **5** *European Intellectual Property Review,* 1983, 83-85.

BRINKHOF, Jan J., 'Over octrooirecht en economie' [On Patent Law and the Economy], **39(10)** *Ars Aequi,* 1990, 794-802.

CAVE, J.A.K., 'A Further Comment on Preemptive Patenting and the Persistence of Monopoly', **75** *American Economic Review,* 1985, 256-258.

CHEUNG, Steven N.S., 'Property Rights and Invention', **8** *Research in Law and Economics,* 1986, 5-18.

COCKBURN, Iain and GRILICHES, Zvi, 'Industry Effects and Appropriability Measures in the Stock Market's Valuation of R&D and Patents', **78** *American Economic Review. Papers and Proceedings,* 1988, 419-423.

DeBROCK, Lawrence M., 'Market Structure, Innovation, and Optimal Patent Life', **28** *Journal of Law and Economics,* 1985, 223-244.

EISENBERG, Rebecca S., 'Patents and the Progress of Science: Exclusive Rights and Experimental Use', **56** *University of Chicago Law Review,* 1989, 1017-1086.

GILBERT, Richard J., 'Preemptive Patenting and the Persistence of Monopoly: Reply', **74** *American Economic Review,* 1984, 251-253.

GILBERT, Richard J. and NEWBERY, David M.G., 'Preemptive Patenting and the Persistence of Monopoly', **72** *American Economic Review,* 1982, 514-526.

GILBERT, Richard J. and SHAPIRO, Carl, 'Optimal Patent Length and Breadth', **21**

Rand Journal of Economics, 1990, 106-112.

GOODMAN, Jeffery S., 'Note: The Policy Implications of Granting Patent Protection to Computer Software: An Economic Analysis', **37** *Vanderbilt Law Review*, 1984, 147 ff.

GRABOWSKI, Henry G. and VERNON, John M., 'Longer Patents for Lower Imitation Barriers: The 1984 Drug Act', **76** *American Economic Review. Papers and Proceedings*, 1986, 195-198.

GREER, D., 'The Case Against the Patent System in Less-Developed Countries', **8** *Journal of International Law and Economics*, 1973, 223-226.

HALL, Bronwyn H., GRILICHES, Zvi and HAUSMAN, Jerry A., 'Patents and R&D: Is There a Lag?', **27** *International Economic Review*, 1986, 265-283.

HARRIS, Christopher J. and VICKERS, John S., 'Patent Races and the Persistence of Monopoly', **33** *Journal of Industrial Economics*, 1985, 461-481. Reprinted in GEROSKI, P.A., PHLIPS, L. and ULPH, A. (eds.), *Oligopoly, Competition and Welfare*, Oxford, Blackwell, 1985, 93-113.

HAUSMAN, Jerry A. and MACKIE-MASON, Jeffrey K., 'Price Discrimination and Patent Policy', **19** *Rand Journal of Economics*, 1988, 253-265.

HODKINSON, Keith and QUEST, Barry, 'Further Reform of the Patent Laws? The Case Against Petty Patents', *European Intellectual Property Review*, 1985, 108-112.

HOLCOMBE, Randall G. and MEINERS, R.E., 'The Contractual Alternative to Patents', **1** *International Review of Law and Economics*, 1981, 227-231.

HUTTER, Michael, *Die Produktion von Recht. Eine selbstreferentielle Theorie der Wirtschaft, angewandt auf den Fall des Arzneimittelpatentrechts* [The Production of Law. A Selfreferential Theory of the Economy, applied to the Case of Pharmaceutical Patent Law], Tübingen, Mohr, 1989, 213 p.

ISAY, H., *Die Funktion der Patente im Wirtschaftskampf* [Patent Functions in Economic Battle], Franz Vahlen Verlag, Berlin, 1927.

JOHNSON, H.G., 'Aspects of Patents and Licenses as Stimuli to Innovation', **112** *Weltwirtschaftliches Archiv*, 1976, 417-428.

JUDLOWE, Stephen B., 'The Worth of Patents - With a Not Very Limiting View towards the Electronics Industry', **10** *APLA Quarterly Journal*, 1982, 50-59.

KAMIEN, Morton I. and SCHWARTZ, Nancy L., 'Patent Life and R&D Rivalry', **64** *American Economic Review*, 1974, 183-187.

KAMIEN, Morton I. and TAUMAN, Yair, 'The Private Value of a Patent: A Game Theoretic Analysis', *Zeitschrift fur Nationalökonomie*, 1984, 93-118.

KAMIEN, Morton I. and TAUMAN, Yair, 'Fees versus Royalties and the Private Value of a Patent', **101** *Quarterly Journal of Economics*, 1986, 471-491.

KAPLOW, Louis, 'The Patent-Antitrust Intersection: A Reappraisal', **97** *Harvard Law Review*, 1984, 1815-1892.

KAUFER, Erich, 'The Incentives to Innovate under Alternative Property Rights Assignments with Special Reference to the Patent System', **142** *Journal of Institutional and Theoretical Economics*, 1986, 210-226.

KAUFER, Erich, *The Economics of the Patent System*, Chur, Harwood Academic, 1989, 66 p.

KINGSTON, William (ed.), 'The Unexploited Potential of Patents', in KINGSTON, William (ed.), *Direct Protection of Innovation*, Dordrecht, Kluwer Academic for the Commission of the European Communities, 1987, 1-34.

KINGSTON, William, 'Kronz's "Innovation Patent"', in KINGSTON, William (ed.), *Direct Protection of Innovation*, Dordrecht, Kluwer Academic for the Commission of the European Communities, 1987, 33-58.

KIRIM, Arman S., 'Reconsidering Patents and Economic Development: A Case Study of the Turkish Pharmaceutical Industry', **13** *World Development*, 1985, 219-236.

KITCH, Edmund W., 'The Nature and Function of the Patent System', **20** *Journal of Law and Economics*, 1977, 265-290.

KITCH, Edmund W., 'Patents, Prospects, and Economic Surplus: A Reply', **23** *Journal of Law and Economics*, 1980, 205-207.

KITCH, Edmund W., 'Patents: Monopolies or Property Rights?', **8** *Research in Law and Economics*, 1986, 31-49.

KLEMPERER, P., 'How Broad Should the Scope of Patent Protection Be?', **21** *Rand Journal of Economics*, 1990, 113-130.

KRONZ, Hermann, 'Patent Protection for Innovations: A Model', *European Intellectual Property Review*, 1983, 178-183, 206-209.

KRONZ, Hermann, 'Response in Defence of the Innovation Patent Concept', in KINGSTON, William (ed.), *Direct Protection of Innovation*, Dordrecht, Kluwer Academic for the Commission of the European Communities, 1987, 257-276.

LA MANNA, Manfredi, MACLEOD, Ross and DE MEZA, David, 'The Case for Permissive Patents', **33** *European Economic Review*, 1989, 1427-443.

LANDAU, D.L., 'Patents and Over-Investment in Process Innovations? Comment', 45 *Southern Economic Journal*, 1978, 285-288.

LEHMANN, Michael, 'Patentrecht und Theory der Property Rights, eine ökonomische und juristische Analyse' [Patent Law and Property Rights Theory, an Economic and Legal Analysis], in *Festschrift für R. Franceschelli*, Mailand, 1983, 35-51.

LEONTIEF, W., 'On Assignment of Patent Rights on Inventions Made under Government Research Contracts', **77** *Harvard Law Review*, 1964, 492-497.

LEVIN, Richard C., 'A New Look at the Patent System', **76** *American Economic Review. Papers and Proceedings*, 1986, 199-202.

LITTLECHILD, Stephen C., 'The Incentives to Innovate under Alternative Property Rights Assignments with Special Reference to the Patent System: Comment', **142** *Journal of Institutional and Theoretical Economics*, 1986, 227-229.

LLOYD OF KILGERRAN, 'The Patent System - A Tool in the Marketing Strategy for the Creation of Wealth and New Jobs', *European Intellectual Property Review*, 1980, 67-69.

MACHLUP, Fritz, *An Economic Review of the Patent System*, Study No. 15 of the Subcommittee on Patents, Trademarks, and Copyrights of the Committee on the Judiciary, U.S. Senate, 85th Congress, 2nd Session, Government Printing Office, Washington, D.C., 1958.

MACHLUP, Fritz and PENROSE. E.T., 'The Patent Controversy in the Nineteenth

Century', **10** *Journal of Economic History*, 1950, 1-29.

MANSFIELD, Edwin, 'Patents and Innovation: An Empirical Study', *Management Science*, 1985.

MANSFIELD, Edwin, SCHWARTZ, M. and WAGNER, S., 'Imitation Costs and Patents: An Empirical Study', **91** *Economic Journal*, 1981, 907-918.

MARKHAM, J.W., 'The Joint Effect of Antitrust and Patent Laws upon Innovation', **56** *American Economic Review. Papers and Proceedings*, 1966, 291-300.

McFETRIDGE, D.G. and RAFIQUZZAMAN, M., 'The Scope and Duration of the Patent Right and the Nature of Research Rivalry', **8** *Research in Law and Economics*, 1986, 91-120.

McFETRIDGE, D.G., and SMITH, D.A., 'Patents, Prospects, and Economic Surplus: A Comment', **23** *Journal of Law and Economics*, 1980, 197-203.

McGEE, John S., 'Patent Exploitation: Some Economic and Legal Problems', **9** *Journal of Law and Economics*, 1966, 135-162.

MELMAN, S., *The Impact of the Patent System on Research*, Study No. 11 of the Subcommittee on Patents, Trademarks, and Copyrights of the Committee on the Judiciary, U.S. Senate, 85th Congress, 2nd Session, Government Printing Office, Washington, D.C., 1958.

NELSON, Richard R., 'The Economics of Invention: A Survey of the Literature', **32** *Journal of Business*, 1959, 101-127.

NEUMEYER, F., 'Patent und Beschränkung des Wettbewerbs' [Patent and Limitation of Competition], **12** *Wirtschaft und Recht*, 1969, 240-251.

NORDHAUS, W.D., *The Optimal Life of a Patent*, Cowles Foundation Discussion Paper N. 241, Cowles Foundation for Research in Economics, New Haven, 1967.

OPPENHEIM, Charles, 'The Information Function of Patents, *European Intellectual Property Review*, 1979, 344-349.

OPPENLÄNDER, K.H., (ed.), *Patentwesen, technischer Fortschritt und Wettbewerb* [Patents, Technical Progress and Competition], Göttingen, Verlag Otto Schwartz, 1974.

OPPENLÄNDER, K.H., 'The Influence of the Patent System on the Readiness of Industry to Invest - An Empirical Analysis', *Industrial Property*, 1986, 494-507.

ORDOVER, Janusz A., 'A Patent System for Both Diffusion and Exclusion', **5** *Journal of Economic Perspectives*, 1991, 43-60.

PALMER, John P. (Guest ed.), *The Economics of Patents and Copyrights*, in ZERBE, Richard O. Jr. (Series ed.), *Research in Law and Economics*, Greenwich, Jai Press, **8**, 1986, 287 p.

PENROSE, E., 'International Patenting and the Less-Developed Countries', **83** *Economic Journal*, 1973, 768-786.

PENROSE, E.T., *The Economics of the International Patent System*, Baltimore, John Hopkins University Press, 1951.

PLANT, Arnold, 'The Economic Theory Concerning Patents and Inventions', 1 *Economica*, 1934, 30-51.

PRUSAK, Leonard, 'Does the Patent System Have Measurable Economic Value?',

10 *APLA Quarterly Journal*, 1982, 50-59.

RAFIQUZZAMAN, M., 'The Optimal Patent Term under Uncertainty', **5** *International Journal of Industrial Organization*, 1987, 233-246.

RAFIQUZZAMAN, M., 'Invention, Market Structure, Cost Reduction Uncertainty and the Optimal Patent Term', **48** *Journal of Economics (Zeitschrift für Nationalökonomie)*, 1988, 303-312.

SALANT, Stephen W., 'Preemptive Patenting and the Persistence of Monopoly: Comment', **74** *American Economic Review*, 1984, 247-250.

SANDERS, B.S., ROSSMAN, J. and HARRIS, L.J., 'The Economic Impact of Patents', **2** *Patent Trademark and Copyright Journal of Research and Education*, 1958, 340-362.

SANDERS, B.S., 'Speedy Entry of Patented Inventions into Commercial Use', **6** *Patent Trademark and Copyright Journal of Research and Education*, 1962, 87-116.

SANDERS, B.S., 'Patterns of Commercial Exploitation of patented Inventions by Large and Small Corporations', **8** *Patent Trademark and Copyright Journal of Research and Education*, 1964, 51-93.

SANDOR, R.L., 'Some Empirical Findings on the Legal Costs of Patenting', **45** *Journal of Business*, 1972, 375-378.

SCHANKERMAN, Mark and PAKES, Ariel, 'Estimates of the Value of Patent Rights in European Countries during the Post 1950 Period', **96** *Economic Journal*, 1986, 1052-1076.

SCHERER, Frederic M., (ed.), *Patents and the Corporation: A Report on Industrial Technology under Changing Public Policy*, Boston, J.J. Galvin, 1958.

SCHERER, Frederic M., 'Firm Size, Market Structure, Opportunity and the Output of Patented Invention', **55** *American Economic Review*, 1965, 1097-1125.

SCHERER, Frederic M., 'Nordhaus' Theory of Optimal Patent Life: A Geometric Reinterpretation', **62** *American Economic Review*, 1972, 422-427.

SCHERER, Frederic M., 'Nordhaus Theory of Optimal Patent Life: A Geometric Reinterpretation', in SCHERER, Frederic M. (ed.), *Innovation and Growth: Schumpeterian Perspectives*, Cambridge, MIT Press, 1984, 130-141.

SCHERER, Frederic M., 'The Propensity to Patent', **1** *International Journal of Industrial Organisation*, 1983, 107-128.

SCHERER, Frederic M., 'Comment on Edmund Kitch', **8** *Research in Law and Economics*, 1986, 51-58.

SCHIFF, E., *Industrialization without Patents - The Netherlands 1869-1912 and Switzerland 1850-1907*, Princeton University Press, Princeton, 1971.

SCHMOOKLER, J., *Patents, Invention, and Economic Change*, Cambridge, Harvard University Press, 1972.

SCOTCHMER, Susanne, 'Standing on the Shoulders of Giants: Cumulative Research and the Patent Law', **5** *Journal of Economic Perspectives*, 1991, 29-41.

SHENG CHENG HU, 'On the Incentive to Invent: A Clarificatory Note', **16** *Journal of Law and Economics*, 1973, 169-177.

SILBERTSON, Aubrey, 'The Patent System', **84** *Lloyds Bank Review*, 1967, 32-44.

SILBERTSON, Aubrey, *The Economic Importance of Patents*, London, Common Law Institute of Intellectual Property, 1989, 38 pp.

SMITH, Douglas A. and McFETRIDGE, Donald G., 'Patents, Prospects, and Economic Surplus: A Comment', **23** *Journal of Law and Economics*, 1980, 197-203.

STILLERMAN, R., 'Resistance to Change', **48** *Journal of the Patent Office*, 1966, 484-499.

TAEGER, U.C., 'Untersuchung der Aussagefähigkeit von Patentstatistiken hinsichtlich technologischer Entwicklungen' [Research into the Informal Value of Patent Statistics with Respect to Technological Developments], **17** *Ifo-Studien zur Industriewirtschaft*, München, Ifo-Institut, 1979.

TANDON, P., 'Rivalry and the Excessive Allocation of Resources to Research', **14** *Bell Journal of Economics*, 1983, 152-165.

TAYLOR, Charles T. and SILBERTSON, Z.A., *The Economic Impact of the Patent System*, Cambridge, Cambridge University Press, 1973.

TURNER, D.F., 'The Patent System and Competitive Policy', **44** *New York University Law Review*, 1969, 450-476.

UNCTAD, *The Role of the Patent System in the Transfer of Technology to Developing Countries*, New York, United Nations, 1975.

UNCTAD, *The International Patent System: The Revision of the Paris Convention for Protection of Industrial Property*, United Nations, New York, 1977.

USHER, Dan, 'The Welfare Economics of Invention', 31 *Economica*, 1964, 279-287.

VAUGHAN, F.L., *The United States Patent System: Legal and Economic Conflicts in American Patent History*, Norman, University of Oklahoma Press, 1956.

WATERSON, Michael, 'The Economics of Product Patents', **80** *American Economic Review*, 1990, 860-869.

WILEY, John Shepard, Jr., 'Copyright at the School of Patent', **58** *University of Chicago Law Review*, 1991, 119-185.

WRIGHT, Brian D., 'The Economics of Invention Incentives: Patents, Prizes and Research Contracts', **73** *American Economic Review*, 1983, 691-707.

YAMEY, B.S., 'Monopoly, Competition and the Incentive to Invent: A Comment', **13** *Journal of Law and Economics*, 1970, 253-256.

2940 Trademarks

BURGUNDER, Lee R., 'An Economic Approach to Trademark Genericism', **23** *American Business Law Journal*, 1985, 391 ff.

CARTER, Stephen L., 'The Trouble with Trademark', **99** *Yale Law Journal*, 1990, 759-800.

DAM, Kenneth W., 'Trademarks, Price Discrimination and the Bureau of Customs', **7** *Journal of Law and Economics*, 1964, 45-60.

ECONOMIDES, Nicholas S., 'The Economics of Trademarks', **78** *Trademark*

Reporter, 1988, 523-539.

FEINBERG, Robert M., 'Trademarks, Market Power, and Information', **2** *Review of Industrial Organization*, 1986, 376-385.

FLETCHER, Patricia Kimball, 'Comment: Joint Registration of Trademarks and the Economic Value of a Trademark System', **36** *University of Miami Law Review*, 1982, 297-335.

FOLSOM, Ralph H. and TEPLY, Larry L., 'Trademark Generic Words', **89** *Yale Law Journal*, 1980, 1323-1359.

HENNING-BODEWIG, Frauke, 'Die Qualitätsfunktion der Marke im Amerikanischen Recht' [The Quality Function of Trademarks in American Law], **7** *GRUR Int.*, 1985, 445-453.

HENNING-BODEWIG, Frauke, *Marke und Verbraucher* [Trademark and Consumer], Weinheim, VCH Verlagsgesellschaft, 1988, 127-168, 258-268.

HURWITZ, Mark A. and CAVES, Richard E., 'Persuasion or Information? Promotion and the Shares of Brand Name and Generic Pharmaceuticals', **31** *Journal of Law and Economics*, 1988, 299-320.

KAUFMANN, Peter J., *Passing Off and Misappropriation: An Economic and Legal Analysis of the Law of Unfair Competition in the U. S. and Continental Europe*, Max Planck Institute for Foreign and International Patent, Copyright and Competition Law, VCH-Weinheim, Reerfield Beach, 1986, 119-161.

KAUFMANN, Peter J., 'Verwarringsgevaar of verwateringsgevaar in het Europese merkenrecht anno 1991: artikel 13 A.1 Benelux Merkenwet mag niet blijven!' [Confusion or Dilution in European Trademark Law 1991: Section 13 A.1 Benelux Trademark Act Cannot Continue to Exist!], *Qui Bene Distinguit Bene Docet*, Arnhem, Gouda Quint, 1991, 175-190.

LANDES, William M. and POSNER, Richard A., 'Trademark Law: An Economic Perspective', **30** *Journal of Law and Economics*, 1987, 265-309. Reprinted in **21** *Intellectual Property Law Review*, 1989, 229-273.

LANDES, William M. and POSNER, Richard A., 'The Economics of Trademark Law', **78** *Trademark Reporter*, 1988, 267-306.

LANE, Walter J., 'Compulsory Trademark Licensing', **54** *Southern Economic Journal*, 1988, 643-655.

LEHMANN, Michael, 'Unfair Use and Damage to the Reputation of Well-Known Marks, Names and Indications of Source in Germany. Some Aspects of Law and Economics', **17** *IIC*, 1986, 746-767.

LIEBELER, Lars H., 'Trademark Law, Economics and Grey-Market Policy', **62** *Indiana Law Journal*, 1986, 753-777.

MIMS, Peter E., 'Promotional Goods and the Functionality Doctrine: An Economic Model of Trademarks', **63** *Texas Law Review*, 1984, 639-669.

MITCHELL, Mark L., 'The Impact of External Parties on Brand Name Capital: The 1982 Tylenol Poisonings and Subsequent Cases', **27** *Economic Inquiry*, 1989, 601-618.

PAGENBERG, Jochen, 'Trademark Rights at a Discount - Is Trademark Law Still Effective?', **19** *IIC*, 1988, 639-646.

PALLADINO, Vincent N., 'The Real Trouble with Trademarks', **81** *Trademark*

Reporter, 1991, 150-168.

PAPANDREOU, A.G., 'The Economic Effects of Trademarks', **44** *California Law Review*, 1956, 503 ff.

PATTISHALL, Beverly W., 'Trademarks and the Monopoly Phobia', **50** *Michigan Law Review*, 1952, 967 ff.

PERRY, Martin K. and GROFF, Robert H., 'Trademark Licensing in a Monopolistically Competitive Industry', **17** *Rand Journal of Economics*, 1986, 189-200.

SHANAHAN, 'The Trademark Right: Consumer Protection or Monopoly?', **72** *Trademark Reporter*, 1982, 233 ff.

SULLIVAN, Lawrence A., 'Warenzeichen und Behinderungspratiken in den USA: Eine vorläufige Analyse' [Product Marks and Hindrance Practices in the USA: A Preliminary Analysis], **9** *GRUR int.*, 1983, 714-721.

2950 Other Rights

ABN, *Kwekersrecht* [Plant Breeders Right], Alg. Bank Nederland, 1989, 12 p.

CARR, Jack L. and LANDA, Janet T., 'The Economics of Symbols, Clan Names, and Religion', **12** *Journal of Legal Studies*, 1983, 135-156.

EISENBERG, Rebecca S., 'Proprietary Rights and the Norms of Science in Biotechnology Research', **97** *Yale Law Journal*, 1987, 177-231.

RISBERG, R., 'Five Years Without Infringement Litigation under the Semiconductor Chip Act: Unmasking the Spectre of Chip Piracy in an Era of Diverse and Incompatible Process Technologies', *Wisconsin Law Review*, 1990, 241-277.

SCHMID, A. Alan, 'Intellectual Property Rights in Bio-Technology and Computer-Technology ', **141** *Journal of Institutional and Theoretical Economics*, 1985, 127-141.

WHEATON, J.J., 'Generic Competition and Pharmaceutical Innovation: The Drug Price Competition and Patent Term Restoration Act of 1984', **35** *Catholic University Law Review*, 1986, 433-487.

X, 'Dutch Publishers Seek Neighbouring Rights', **4(1)** *Rights*, 1990.

X, 'News from the 2nd IPA International Copyright Symposium, Strengthening Publishers' Rights', **4(2)** *Rights*, 1990.

YU, Ben T., 'The Delineation of Rights on Technology Transfer', **12** *Research in Law and Economics*, 1989, 267-278.

2960 Licensing

BESEN, Stanley M. and KIRBY, Sheila N., 'Compensating Creators of Intellectual Property: Collectives That Collect', *The Rand Corporation*, R-3751-MF, November 1989.

CAVES, R.E., CROOKELL, H. and KILLING, J.P., 'The Imperfect Market for Technology Licenses', **45** *Oxford Bulletin of Economics and Statistics*, 1983, 249-267.

CONTRACTOR, F.J., *International Technology Licensing: Compensation, Costs, and Negotiation*, Lexington, Lexington Books, 1981.

GALLINI, Nancy T. and WINTER, Ralph A., 'Licensing in the theory of innovation', **16** *Rand Journal of Economics*, 1985, 237-252.

KATZ, M.L. and SHAPIRO, Carl, 'On the Licensing of Innovations', **16** *Rand Journal of Economics*, 1985, 504-520.

McRAE, James J. and TAPON, Francis, 'Compulsory Licensing as a Policy Instrument', **10** *Canadian Public Policy*, 1984, 74-77.

PERRY, Martin K. and GROFF, Robert H., 'Trademark Licensing in a Monopolistically Competitive Industry', **17** *Rand Journal of Economics*, 1986, 189-200.

ROZEK, Richard P., 'Protection of Intellectual Property through Licensing: Efficiency Considerations', **22(5)** *Journal of World Trade Law*, 1988, 27-34.

2965 Licensing - Patents

ABN, *Octrooien en licenties* [Patents and Licences], Alg. Bank Nederland, 1989, 35p.

DULUDE, Louise Séguin, 'Comments on Hall's Study', **8** *Research in Law and Economics*, 1986, 87-89.

FRANCO, Joseph A., 'Limiting the Anticompetitive Prerogative of Patent Owners: Predatory Standards in Patent Licensing', **92** *Yale Law Journal*, 1983, 831-861.

GREIPEL, E. und TAEGER, U., *Auswirkungen des Patentschutzes und der Lizenzvergabepraxis auf den Wettbewerb in ausgewählten Wirtschaftsbereichen unter besonderer Berücksichtigung der Marktsituation kleiner und mittlerer Unternehmen* [Effects of Patent Protection and License Practice Activity on Competition in Specific Areas of Economic Activity with Special Reference to the Market Position of Small and Middle Size Companies], Gutachten erstellt für das Bundeswirtschaftsministerium in Bonn, München, Ifo-Institut, 1981.

HALL, Christopher D., 'Patents, Licensing, and Antitrust', **8** *Research in Law and Economics*, 1986, 59-86.

JOHNSON, H.G., 'Aspects of Patents and Licenses as Stimuli to Innovation', **112** *Weltwirtschaftliches Archiv*, 1976, 417-428.

PRIEST, George L., 'Cartels and Patent License Arrangements', **20** *Journal of Law and Economics*, 1977, 309-377.

SCHERER, Frederic M., *The Economic Effects of Compulsory Patent Licensing*, New York, New York University, 1977.

SHAPIRO, Carl, 'Patent Licensing and R&D Rivalry', **75** *American Economic Review. Papers and Proceedings*, 1985, 25-30.

TAEGER, U.C., 'Untersuchung der Aussagefähigkeit von Patentstatistiken hinsichtlich technologischer Entwicklungen' [Research into the Informal Value of Patent Statistics with Respect to Technological Developments], **17** *Ifo-Studien zur Industriewirtschaft*, München, Ifo-Institut, 1979.

TANDON, P., 'Optimal Patents with Compulsory Licensing', 90 *Journal of Political Economy*, 1982, 470-486.

WILSON, R.W., 'The Effect of Technology Environment and Product Rivalry on R&D Effort and Licensing of Inventions', **59** *Review of Economics and Statistics*, 1977, 171-178.

2970 Empirical Studies

LUNN, John, 'An Empirical Analysis of Firm Process and Product Patenting', **19** *Applied Economics*, 1987, 743-751.

MANSFIELD, Edwin, SCHWARTZ, M. and WAGNER, S., 'Imitation Costs and Patents: An Empirical Study', **91** *Economic Journal*, 1981, 907-918.

OPPENLÄNDER, K.H., 'The Influence of the Patent System on the Readiness of Industry to Invest - An Empirical Analysis', *Industrial Property*, 1986, 494-507.

SANDOR, R.L., 'Some Empirical Findings on the Legal Costs of Patenting', **45** *Journal of Business*, 1972, 375-378.

SCHERER, Frederic M., 'Time-Cost Tradeoffs in Uncertain Empirical Research Projects', **13** *Naval Research Logistics Quarterly*, 1966, 71-82.

US COPYRIGHT OFFICE, 'Report to the Subcommittee on Patents, Copyrights and Trademarks Committee on the Judiciary. United States Senate on the Size of the Copyright Industries in the United States', *GRUR Int.*, 1985, 393 ff.

2980 Trade Secrets

ADELSTEIN, Richard P., 'Comment' [on Mlikotin-Tomic, Economic Analysis Required for New Liability Rules in Commercial Know-How Contracts]', in WEIGEL, Wolfgang (ed.), *Economic Analysis of Law - A Collection of Applications*, Vienna, Österreichischer Wirtschaftsverlag, 1991, 250-252.

CHEUNG, Steven N.S., 'Property Rights in Trade Secrets', **20** *Economic Inquiry*, 1982, 40-52.

FRIEDMAN, David D., LANDES, William M. and POSNER, Richard A., 'Some Economics of Trade Secret Law', **5** *Journal of Economic Perspectives*, 1991, 61-72.

MILLER, Elizabeth, 'Note: Antitrust Restrictions on Trade Secret Licensing: A Legal Review and Economic Analysis', **52(1)** *Law and Contemporary Problems*, 1989, 183-209.

MLIKOTIN-TOMIC, Desa, 'Economic Analysis Required for New Liability Rules in Commercial Know-How Contracts', in WEIGEL, Wolfgang (ed.), *Economic Analysis of Law - A Collection of Applications*, Vienna, Österreichischer

Wirtschaftsverlag, 1991, 236-249.

2990 Unfair Competition - Monopoly

EPSTEIN, Richard A., 'Private Property and the Public Domain: The Case of Antitrust', in PENNOCK, J. Roland and CHAPMAN, John W. (eds.), *Nomos XXIV: Ethics, Economics and the Law*, New York, New York University Press, 1982, 48-82.

MILLER, J.P., (ed.), *Competition, Cartels and Their Regulation*, Amsterdam, North-Holland, 1962.

POSNER, Richard A., 'The Social Costs of Monopoly and Regulation', **83** *Journal of Political Economy*, 1975, 807-827.

2995 Unfair Competition - Passing Off

HAYHURST, William L., '"Dreamers" and the Patent System', *European Intellectual Property Review*, 1983, 263-265.

HIGGINS, Richard S. and RUBIN, Paul H., 'Counterfeit Goods', **29** *Journal of Law and Economics*, 1986, 211-230.

HILLMAN, Arye L. and KATZ, E., 'Excise Taxes, Import Restrictions, and the Allocation of Time to Illegal Income-Earning Activity', **4** *International Review of Law and Economics*, 1984, 213-222.

KAUFMANN, Peter J., *Passing Off and Misappropriation: An Economic and Legal Analysis of the Law of Unfair Competition in the U. S. and Continental Europe*, Max Planck Institute for Foreign and International Patent, Copyright and Competition Law, VCH-Weinheim, Reerfield Beach, 1986, 198 p.

KAUFMANN, Peter J. and WIJNBERG, N.M., 'Het Decca arrest: bescherming van prestatie en imitatie' [The Decca Case: Protecting Activities and Imitation], *Intellectuele eigendom en reclamerecht*, 1990, 77-81.

RASKIND, Leo J., 'The Misappropriation Doctrine as a Competitive Norm of Intellectual Property Law', **75** *Minnesota Law Review*, 1991.

STERN, R.H. and HOFFMAN, J., 'Public Injury and the Public Interest: Secondary Meaning in the Law of Unfair Competition', **110** *University of Pennsylvania Law Review*, 1962, 935-971.

3000 TORT LAW & ENVIRONMENTAL REGULATION
Gerrit De Geest

3000 Tort Law: General

ABEL, Richard L., 'A Critique of American Tort Law', **8** *British Journal of Law and Society*, 1981, 199-231.

ABEL, Richard L., 'Should Tort Law Protect Property Against Accidental Loss?', **23** *San Diego Law Review*, 1986, 79-123.

ABRAMSON, Elliott M., 'The Medical Malpractice Imbroglio: A Non-Adversarial Suggestion', **78** *Kentucky Law Journal*, 1990, 293 ff.

ADAMS, Michael, *Ökonomische Analyse des Gefährdungs- und Verschuldenshaftung* [Economic Analysis of Strict and Fault Liability], Heidelberg, R.v Decker's/C.F. Müller, 1985, 310 p.

ADAMS, Michael, 'Zur Aufgabe des Haftungsrechts im Umweltschutz' [On the Task of Liability Law for the Protection of the Environment], **99** *Zeitschrift für Zivilprozeß*, 1986, 129-165.

ADAMS, Michael, 'New Activities and the Efficient Liability Rules', in FAURE, Michael and VAN DEN BERGH, Roger (eds.), *Essays in Law and Economics. Corporations, Accident Prevention and Compensation for Losses*, Antwerpen, Maklu, 1989, 103-106.

ALPA, Guido, 'Colpa e responsabilità oggettiva nella prospettiva dell'analisi economica del diritto' [Negligence and Strict Liability in an EAL Perspective], *Politica del diritto*, 1976, 431-448.

ANDERSON, Dan R., 'Financing Asbestos Claims: Coverage Issues, Manville's Bankruptcy and the Claims Facility', **54** *Journal of Risk and Insurance*, 1987, 429-451.

ARLEN, Jennifer H., 'Re-Examining Liability Rules When Injurers as well as Victims Suffer Losses', **10** *International Review of Law and Economics*, 1990, 233-239.

ASSAF, George B., 'The Shape of Reaction Functions and the Efficiency of Liability Rules: A Correction', **13** *Journal of Legal Studies*, 1984, 101-111.

BAILY, Mary Ann and CIKINS, Warren I. (eds.), *The Effects of Litigation on Health Care Costs*, Washington, Brookings Institution, 1985.

BAKKER, B.B. and STERKS, C.G.M., 'Optimal Legal Standards in Negligence Based Liability Rules', **136** *De Economist*, 1988, 383-400.

BARNES, David W. and BAERVERSTAD, Mark, 'Social Choices and Comparative Negligence', **31** *De Paul Law Review*, 1982, 273-306.

BERGER, Robert G., 'The Impact of Tort Law Development on Insurance: The Availability/Affordability Crisis and Its Potential Solutions', **37** *American University Law Review*, 1988, 285 ff.

BIRMINGHAM, Robert L., 'The Theory of Economic Policy and the Law of Torts', **55** *Minnesota Law Review*, 1970, 1-13.

BISBAL, Joaquím, 'La Responsabilidad Extracontractual y la Distribución de los Costes del Progreso' [Liability Rules and Development Cost Allocation], *Rivista de Derecho Mercantil*, 1983, enero-junio.

BISHOP, William, 'Negligent Misrepresentation through the Economists' Eyes', **96** *Law Quarterly Review*, 1980, 360-379.

BISHOP, William, 'Negligent Misrepresentation: An Economic Reformulation', in BURROWS, Paul and VELJANOVSKI, Cento G. (eds.), *The Economic Appraoch to Law*, London, Butterworths, 1981, 167-186.

BISHOP, William, 'Economic Loss: A Reply to Professor Rizzo', **2** *Oxford Journal of Legal Studies*, 1982, 207-210.

BISHOP, William, 'The Contract-Tort Boundary and the Economics of Insurance', **12** *Journal of Legal Studies*, 1983, 241-266. Reprinted in GOLDBERG, Victor P. (ed.), *Readings in the Economics of Contract Law*, Cambridge, Cambridge University Press, 1989, 86-91.

BLOEMBERGEN, *Duizend botsingen: Een kwantitatieve analyse van civiele rechtbankvonnissen in verkeerszaken* [Thousand Accidents: A Quantitative Analysis of Civil Court Decisions on Traffic Matters], Deventer, Kluwer, 1972, 74 p.

BLOMQUIST, Robert F., 'Goals, Means, and Problems for Modern Tort Law: A Reply to Professor Priest', **22** *Valparaiso University Law Review*, 1988, 621-642.

BLUM, Walter J. and KALVEN, Harry, Jr., 'The Empty Cabinet of Dr. Calabresi: Auto Accidents and General Deterrence', **34** *University of Chicago Law Review*, 1967, 239-273. Reprinted in RABIN, Robert L. (ed.), *Perspectives on Tort Law*, Boston, Little Brown, 1983, 178-190.

BLUM, Walter J. and KALVEN, Harry, Jr., 'Ceilings, Costs and Compulsion in Auto Compensation Legislation', *Utah Law Review*, 1973, 341 ff. Reprinted in RABIN, Robert L. (ed.), *Perspectives on Tort Law*, Boston, Little Brown, 1983, 287-314.

BOUCKAERT, Boudewijn, 'Het aansprakelijkheidsrecht tussen rechtvaardigheid en efficiëntie' [Liability Law between Justice and Efficiency], *Vlaams Jurist Vandaag*, 1987, Nr. 1, 23-26.

BROWN, John Prather, 'Toward an Economic Theory of Liability', **2** *Journal of Legal Studies*, 1973, 323-349.

BROWN, John Prather, 'Alternatives to the Present System of Litigation for Personal Injury', in BAILY, Mary Ann and CIKINS, Warren I. (eds.), *The Effects of Litigation on Health Care Costs*, Washington, Brookings Institution, 1985, 69-79.

BRUCE, Christopher, 'The Deterrent Effects of Automobilc Insurance and Tort Law: A Survey of the Empirical Literature', **6** *Law & Policy*, 1984, 67-100.

BRUCE, Christopher J., 'Testing the Hypothesis of Common Law Efficiency: The Doctrine of Informed Consent', **6** *Research in Law and Economics*, 1984, 227-265.

BURROWS, Paul, *The Economic Theory of Pollution Control*, Oxford, Martin Robertson, 1979, 192 p.

BURROWS, Paul, 'Idealised Negligence, Strict Liability and Deterrence', **2**

International Review of Law and Economics, 1982, 165-172.

BURROWS, Paul, 'Tort and Tautology: The Logic of Restricting the Scope of Liability', **13** *Journal of Legal Studies*, 1984, 399-414.

BUTLER, Ann M. and DOHERTY, Neil A., 'Torts and Orbits: The Allocation of the Costs of Accidents Involving Spacecraft', **81** *American Economic Review. Papers and Proceedings*, 1991, 46-49.

CALABRESI, Guido, 'Some Thoughts on Risk Distribution and the Law of Torts', **70** *Yale Law Journal*, 1961, 499-553.

CALABRESI, Guido, 'The Decision for Accidents: An Approach to Non-Fault Allocation for Costs', **78** *Harvard Law Review*, 1965, 713-745.

CALABRESI, Guido, 'Views and Overviews', *Illinois Law Forum*, 1967, 600-611.

CALABRESI, Guido, *The Costs of Accidents: A Legal and Economic Analysis*, New Haven, Yale University Press, 1970, 340 p.

CALABRESI, Guido, 'Optimal Deterrence and Accidents', **84** *Yale Law Journal*, 1975, 656-671.

CALABRESI, Guido, 'The Problem of Malpractice: Trying to Round out the Circle', **27** *University of Toronto Law Journal*, 1977, 131-141.

CALABRESI, Guido, 'Torts - the Law of a Mixed Society', **56** *Texas Law Review*, 1978, 519-536.

CALABRESI, Guido and BOBBITT, Philip, *Tragic Choices: The Conflicts Society Confronts in the Allocation of Tragically Scarce Resources*, New York, W.W. Norton, 1978, 252 p.

CALABRESI, Guido and HIRSCHOFF, Jon T., 'Toward a Test for Strict Liability in Tort', **81** *Yale Law Journal*, 1972, 1054-1085. Reprinted in RABIN, Robert L. (ed.), *Perspectives on Tort Law*, Boston, Little Brown, 1983, 192-212.

CALABRESI, Guido and KLEVORICK, Alvin K., 'Four Tests for Liability in Torts', **14** *Journal of Legal Studies*, 1985, 585-627.

CALFEE, John and CRASWELL, Richard, 'Some Effects of Uncertainty on Compliance with Legal Standards', **70** *Virginia Law Review*, 1984, 965-1003.

CAMPBELL, Charles F., 'An Economic View of Developments in the Harmless Error and Exclusionary Rules', **42** *Baylor Law Review*, 1990, 499-534.

CARLSON, David Gray, 'Successor Liability in Bankruptcy: Some Unifying Themes of Intertemporal Creditor Priorities Created by Running Covenants, Products Liability, and Toxic Waste Cleanup', **50(2)** *Law and Contemporary Problems*, 1987, 119-171.

CARSTENSEN, Peter C., 'Explaining Tort Law: The Economic Theory of Landes and Posner', **86** *Michigan Law Review*, 1988, 1161-1184.

CASTRONOVO, Carlo, 'Inattuazione della prestazione di lavoro e responsabilità del danneggiante' [Employee's Non-Performance and Tortfeasor's Liability], *Massimario di giurisprudenza del lavoro*, 1981, 370-377.

CHAO-DUYVIS, M.A.B., 'Vergelding als schadevergoeding' [Retribution as Damages], *Nederlands Juristen Blad*, 1990, 513-520.

CHELIUS, James R., 'Liability for Industrial Accidents: A Comparison of Negligence and Strict Liability Systems', **5** *Journal of Legal Studies*, 1976, 293-

309.

CHOLLET, Deborah J., 'Liability Rules and Health Care Costs', in BAILY, Mary Ann and CIKINS, Warren I. (eds.), *The Effects of Litigation on Health Care Costs*, Washington, Brookings Institution, 1985, 22-27.

CONARD, A.F., et al., *Automobile Accidents Costs and Payments - Studies in the Economics of Injury Reparation*, Ann Arbor, University of Michigan Press, 1964.

CONFERENCE : 'Critical Issues in Tort Law Reform: A Search for Principles. A Conference Sponsored by the Program in Civil Liability, Yale Law School', **14** *Journal of Legal Studies*, 1985, 459-818.

COOTER, Robert D., 'Unity in Tort, Contract, and Property: The Model of Precaution', **73** *California Law Review*, 1985, 1-51. Reprinted in GOLDBERG, Victor P. (ed.), *Readings in the Economics of Contract Law*, Cambridge, Cambridge University Press, 1989, 53-60.

COOTER, Robert, 'Towards a Market in Unmatured Tort Claims', **75** *Virginia Law Review*, 1989, 383-411.

COOTER, Robert D., 'Economic Theories of Legal Liability', **5(3)** *Journal of Economic Perspectives*, 1991, 11-30.

COOTER, Robert D., KORNHAUSER, Lewis A. and LANE, D., 'Liability Rules, Limited Information, and the Role of Precedent', **10** *Bell Journal of Economics*, 1979, 366-373.

COOTER, Robert D. and ULEN, Thomas S., 'An Economic Case for Comparitive Negligence', **81** *New York University Law Review*, 1986, 1067-1110.

COYTE, Peter C., DEWEES, Donald N. and TREBILCOCK, Michael J., 'Medical Malpractice in Canada, 1971-1987', **15** *Geneva Papers on Risk and Insurance*, 1990, 55-80.

CRANDALL, Robert W., *Controlling Industrial Pollution: The Economics and Politics of Clean Air*, Washington, Brookings Institution, 1983, 199 p.

CROYLE, James L., 'Industrial Accident Liability Policy of the Early Twentieth Century', **7** *Journal of Legal Studies*, 1978, 279-297.

DAM, C.C. van, *Zorgvuldigheidsnorm en aansprakelijkheid* [The Duty of Care and Liability] (diss. Utrecht), Kluwer, Deventer, 1989, 333 p.

DANZON, Patricia M., 'The Frequency and Severity of Medical Malpractice Claims', **27** *Journal of Law and Economics*, 1984, 115-148.

DANZON, Patricia M., 'Tort Reform and the Role of Governement in Private Insurance Markets', **13** *Journal of Legal Studies*, 1984, 517-549.

DANZON, Patricia M., *Medical Malpractice: Theory, Evidence, and Public Policy*, Cambridge, Harvard University Press, 1985, 264 p.

DANZON, Patricia M., 'The Medical Malpractice System: Facts and Reforms', in BAILY, Mary Ann and CIKINS, Warren I. (eds.), *The Effects of Litigation on Health Care Costs*, Washington, Brookings Institution, 1985, 28-35.

DANZON, Patricia M., 'Liability and Liability Insurance for Medical Malpractice', **4** *Journal of Health Economics*, 1985, 309-331.

DANZON, Patricia M., 'The Frequency and Severity of Medical Malpractice Claims: New Evidence', **49(2)** *Law and Contemporary Problems*, 1986.

DANZON, Patricia M., 'Alternative Liability Regimes for Medical Injuries', **15** *Geneva Papers on Risk and Insurance*, 1990, 3-21.

DANZON, Patricia M., 'Liability for Medical Malpractice', **5(3)** *Journal of Economic Perspectives*, 1991, 51-69.

DANZON, Patricia M. and LILLARD, Lee A., 'Settlement out of Court: The Disposition of Medical Malpractice Claims', **12** *Journal of Legal Studies*, 1983, 345-377.

DANZON, Patricia M., PAULY, Mark V. and KINGSTON, Raynard S., 'The Effects of Malpractice Litigation on Physicians' Fees and Income', **80** *American Economic Review. Papers and Proceedings*, 1990, 122-127.

DE ALESSI, Louis and STAAF, Robert J., 'Liability, Control and the Organization of Economic Activity', **7** *International Review of Law and Economics*, 1987, 5-20.

DE MEZA, David, 'The Efficiency of Liability Law', **6** *International Review of Law and Economics*, 1986, 107-113.

DIAMOND, Peter A., 'Single Activity Accidents', **3** *Journal of Legal Studies*, 1974, 107-164.

DIAMOND, Peter A., 'Accident Law and Resource Allocation', **5** *Bell Journal of Economics*, 1974, 366-405.

DIAMOND, Peter A. and MIRRLEES, J.A., 'On the Assignment of Liability: the Uniform Case', **6** *Bell Journal of Economics*, 1975, 487-516.

DONOHUE, John J. III, 'The Law and Economics of Tort Law: The Profound Revolution' (Book Review of William M. Landes and Richard A. Posner, The Economic Structure of Tort Law and of Steven Shavell, Economic Analysis of Accident Law), **102** *Harvard Law Review*, 1989, 1047-1073.

DUNLOP, Bruce, 'Personal Injury, Tort Law, and Compensation', **41** *University of Toronto Law Journal*, 1991, 431-446.

EGER, Thomas, 'Kommentar' [Comment] (On Finsinger and von Randow, Neue Akivitäten und Haftungsregeln), in OTT, Claus and SCHÄFER, Hans-Bernd (eds.), *Ökonomische Probleme des Zivilrechts*, Berlin, Springer, 1991, 109-114.

ELLIS, Dorsey D., Jr., 'An Economic Theory of Intentional Torts: A Comment', **3** *International Review of Law and Economics*, 1983, 45-57.

EMONS, Winand, 'Efficient Liability Rules for an Economy with Non identical Individuals', **42** *Journal of Public Economics*, 1990, 89-104.

EMONS, Winand, 'Some Recent Developments in the Economic Analysis of Liability Law: An Introduction', **146** *Journal of Institutional and Theoretical Economics*, 1990, 237-248.

ENDRES, Alfred, 'Allokationswirkungen des Haftungsrechts' [Allocative Effects of Liability Law], in **40(1)** *Jahrbuch für Sozialwissenschaft*, 1989, 115-129.

ENDRES, Alfred, 'Liability and Information', **145** *Journal of Institutional and Theoretical Economics*, 1989, 249-274.

ENGLARD, Izhak, 'The System Builders: A Critical Appraisal of Modern Tort Theory', **9** *Journal of Legal Studies*, 1980, 27-69.

ENGLARD, Izhak, 'Law and Economics in American Tort Cases: A Critical Assessment of the Theory's Impact on Courts', **41** *University of Toronto Law*

Journal, 1991, 359-430.

EPSTEIN, Richard A., 'A Theory of Strict Liability', **2** *Journal of Legal Studies*, 1973, 151-204.

EPSTEIN, Richard A., 'Defenses and Subsequent Pleas in a System of Strict Liability', **3** *Journal of Legal Studies*, 1974, 165-215.

EPSTEIN, Richard A., 'Intentional Harms', **4** *Journal of Legal Studies*, 1975, 391-442.

EPSTEIN, Richard A., 'The Legal and Insurance Dynamics of Mass Tort Litigation', **13** *Journal of Legal Studies*, 1984, 475-506.

EPSTEIN, Richard A., 'Medical Malpractice, Imperfect Information, and the Contractual Foundation for Medical Services', **49(2)** *Law and Contemporary Problems*, 1986, 201-212.

EPSTEIN, Richard A., 'The Risks of Risk Utility', **48** *Ohio State Law Journal*, 1987, 469 ff.

EPSTEIN, Richard A., 'Market and Regulatory Approaches to Medical Malpractice: The Virginia Obstetrical No-Fault Statute', **74** *Virginia Law Review*, 1988, 1451-1474.

FARBER, Daniel A., 'Recurring Misses', **19** *Journal of Legal Studies*, 1990, 727-737.

FAURE, Michael G., 'Rechtseconomie en privaatrecht: Kunnen rechtsregels bijdragen tot de reductie van ongevalskosten' [Law-and-economics and Private Law: Can Legal Rules Contribute to Reducing Accident Costs], in *Rechtseconomie en Recht*, Zwolle, Tjeenk Willink, 1991, 51-93.

FAURE, Michael and VAN DEN BERGH, Roger, 'Negligence, Strict Liability and Regulation of Safety under Belgian Law: An Introductory Economic Analysis', **12** *Geneva Papers on Risk and Insurance*, 1987, 95-114.

FAURE, Michael and VAN DEN BERGH, Roger, 'Efficiënties van het foutcriterium in het Belgisch aansprakelijkheidsrecht' [Efficiencies of the Fault Criterion in Belgian Liability Law], **51** *Rechtskundig Weekblad*, 1987-88, 1105-1119.

FAURE, Michael and VAN DEN BERGH, Roger, *Objectieve aansprakelijkheid, verplichte verzekering en veiligheidsregulering* [Strict Liability, Mandatory Insurance and Safety Regulation], Antwerpen, Maklu, 1989, 386 p.

FAURE, Michael and VAN DEN BERGH, Roger, 'Liability for Nuclear Accidents in Belgium from an Interest Group Perspective', **10** *International Review of Law and Economics*, 1990, 241-254.

FELDMAN, Robert, 'Liability Rules and the Transfer of Economic Rents', **3** *Journal of Legal Studies*, 1974, 499-508.

FENN, Paul, 'Evaluating Irreplaceable Loss: Some Implications for Insurance and Liability Rules', **12** *Geneva Papers on Risk and Insurance*, 1987, 158-167.

FINE, Max W. and SUNSHINE, Jonathan H., 'Malpractice Reform through Consumer Choice and Consumer Education: Are New Concepts Marketable?', **49(2)** *Law and Contemporary Problems*, 1986, 213-222.

FINSINGER, Jörg, 'Liability and the Incentive for Innovations', in WEIGEL, Wolfgang (ed.), *Economic Analysis of Law - A Collection of Applications*, Vienna, Österreichischer Wirtschaftsverlag, 1991, 184-195.

FINSINGER, Jörg, 'The Choice of Risky Technologies and Liability', **11** *International Review of Law and Economics*, 1991, 11-22.

FINSINGER, Jörg and VON RANDOW, Phillip, 'Neue Aktivitäten und Haftungsregeln - Zugleich ein Beitrag zur ökonomischen Analyse des privaten Nachbarrechts' [New Activities and Liability Rules - Also a Contribution to the Economic Analysis of Private Neighbour Law], in OTT, Claus and SCHÄFER, Hans-Bernd (eds.), *Ökonomische Probleme des Zivilrechts*, Berlin, Springer, 1991, 87-108.

FLANIGAN, G.B. et al., 'Experience from Early Tort Reforms: Comparitive Negligence Since 1974', **56** *Journal of Risk and Insurance*, 1989, 525-534.

FLETCHER, George P., 'Fairness and Utility in Tort Theory', **85** *Harvard Law Review*, 1972, 537-573. Reprinted in RABIN, Robert L. (ed.), *Perspectives on Tort Law*, Boston, Little Brown, 1983, 239-255.

GOETZ, Charles J., 'Commentary on "Towards a Market in Unmatured Tort Claims": Collateral Implications', **75** *Virginia Law Review*, 1989, 413-422.

GOMEZ-POMAR, Fernando, 'Tutela de la apariencia y reglas de responsabilidad: los arts. 1164 y 1527 del código civil' [Protection of Appearance and Liability Rules: Articles 1164 and 1527 of the Civil Code], *Rivista de Derecho Privado*, 1990.

GOMEZ-POMAR, Fernando and PASTOR, Santos, 'El derecho de accidentes y la responsabilidad civil: Un análisis jurídico y económico' [Accident Law and Liability Rules: A Legal and Economic Analysis], *Anuario de Derecho Civil*, 1989.

GRADY, Mark F., 'A New Positive Economic Theory of Negligence', **92** *Yale Law Journal*, 1983, 799-829.

GRADY, Mark F., 'Why Are People Negligent? Technology, Nondurable Precautions, and the Medical Malpractice Explosion', **82** *Northwestern University Law Review*, 1988, 293-334.

GRADY, Mark F., 'Common Law Control of Strategic Behavior: Railroad Sparks and the Farmer', **17** *Journal of Legal Studies*, 1988, 15-42.

GRADY, Mark F., 'Discontinuities and Information Burdens: A Review of the Economic Structure of Tort Law', **56** *George Washington Law Review*, 1988, 658-678.

GRADY, Mark F., 'Untaken Precautions', **18** *Journal of Legal Studies*, 1989, 139-156.

GRADY, Mark F., 'Multiple Tortfeasors and the Economy of Prevention', **19** *Journal of Legal Studies*, 1990, 653-678.

GRAVELLE, Hugh S.E., 'Medical Negligence: Evaluating Alternative Regimes', **15** *Geneva Papers on Risk and Insurance*, 1990, 22-26.

GREEN, Jerry, 'On the Optimal Structure of Liability Laws', **7** *Bell Journal of Economics*, 1976, 553-574.

GRIGALUNAS, Thomas A. and OPALUCH, James J., 'Assessing Liability for Damages under CERCLA: A New Approach for Providing Incentives for Pollution Avoidance?', **28** *Natural Resources Journal*, 1988, 509-533.

HADDOCK, David and CURRAN, Christopher, 'An Economic Theory of

Comparative Negligence', **14** *Journal of Legal Studies*, 1985, 49-72.

HALPERN, Paul J. and CARR, Jack L., *Liability Rules and Insurance Markets*, Ottawa, Consumer and Corporate Affairs Canada, 1981.

HAVIGHURST, Clark C., 'Altering the Applicable Standard of Care', **49(2)** *Law and Contemporary Problems*, 1986, 265-275.

HENDERSON, James A., 'The New Zealand Accident Compensation Reform', **48** *University of Chicago Law Review*, 1981, 781-801. Reprinted in RABIN, Robert L. (ed.), *Perspectives on Tort Law*, Boston, Little Brown, 1983, 316-331.

HEYERDAHL, H. Cristopher, *En Økonomisk Analyse av de Ulovfestede Ansvarsreglene i Erstatningsretten, for Risikonøytrale Aktører* [An Economic Analysis of Common Law Liability Rules in Tort Law for Risk-Neutral Agents], Unpublished thesis, Department of Economics, University of Bergen, 1991.

HINDLEY, B. and BISHOP, B., 'Accident Liability Rules and Externality', **3** *International Review of Law and Economics*, 1983, 59-68.

HORVITZ, S.A. and STERN, L.H., 'Liability Rules and the Selection of a Socially Optimal Production Technology', **7** *International Review of Law and Economics*, 1987, 121-126.

HUBER, Peter W., *Liability. The Legal Revolution and Its Consequences*, 1988, New York, Basic Books, 260 p.

HUGHES, James W., 'The Effect of Medical Malpractice Reform Laws on Claim Disposition', **9** *International Review of Law and Economics*, 1989, 57-78.

HUGHES, James W. and SNYDER, Edward A., 'Evaluating Medical Malpractice Reforms', **7(2)** *Contemporary Policy Issues*, 1989, 83-498.

HUGHES, James W. and SNYDER, Edward A., 'Policy Analysis of Medical Malpractice Reforms: What Can We Learn from Claims Data?', **7** *Journal of Business and Economic Statistics*, 1989, 423-431.

HUNSAKER, Ann T., 'The Federal Government's Perspective on Litigation and Health Care Costs', in BAILY, Mary Ann and CIKINS, Warren I. (eds.), *The Effects of Litigation on Health Care Costs*, Washington, Brookings Institution, 1985, 11-21.

HYLTON, Keith N., 'The Influence of Litigation Costs on Deterrence under Strict Liability and under Negligence', **10** *International Review of Law and Economics*, 1990, 161-171.

HYLTON, Keith N., 'Costly Litigation and Legal Error under Negligence', **6** *Journal of Law, Economics, & Organization*, 1990, 433-452.

JOHNSTON, Jason S., 'Bayesian Fact-Binding and Efficiency: Toward an Economic Theory of Liability Under Uncertainty', **61** *Southern California Law Review*, 1987, 137 ff.

KAHAN, Marcel, 'Causation and Incentives to Take Care under the Negligence Rule', **18** *Journal of Legal Studies*, 1989, 427-447.

KITABATAKE, Yoshifusa, 'Backward Incidence of Pollution Damage Compensation Policy', **17** *Journal of Environmental Economics and Management*, 1989, 171-180.

KLEVORICK, Alvin K., 'Legal Theory and the Economic Analysis of Torts and Crimes', **85** *Columbia Law Review*, 1985, 905-920.

KNOEBER, Charles R., 'Penalties and Compensation for Auto Accidents', **7** *Journal of Legal Studies*, 1978, 263-278.

KORNHAUSER, Lewis, A., 'An Economic Analysis of the Choice Between Enterprise and Personal Liability for Accidents', **70** *California Law Review*, 1982, 1345-1392.

KORNHAUSER, Lewis A. and REVESZ, Richard L., 'Sharing Damages Among Multiple Tortfeasors', **98** *Yale Law Journal*, 1989, 831-884.

KORNHAUSER, Lewis A. and REVESZ, Richard L., 'Apportioning Damages among Potentially Insolvent Actors', **19** *Journal of Legal Studies*, 1990, 617-651.

KORNHAUSER, Lewis A. and REVESZ, Richard L., 'Sequential Decisions by a Single Tortfeasor', **20** *Journal of Legal Studies*, 1991, 363-380.

KORNHAUSER, Lewis A. and SCHOTTER, Andrew, 'An Experimental Study of Single-Actor Accidents', **19** *Journal of Legal Studies*, 1990, 203-233.

KÖTZ, Hein, 'Zivilrechtliche Haftung aus ökonomischer Sicht' [Civil Liability from an Economic Perspective], in SCHÄFER, Hans-Bernd and WEHRT, Klaus (eds.), *Die Ökonomisierung der Sozialwissenschaften: Sechs Wortmeldungen*, 1989, 149-167.

KÖTZ, Hein, 'Ziele des Haftungsrechts' [Purposes of Civil Liability], in BAUR, Jürgen F., HOPT, Klaus J. and MAILÄNDER, Peter K. (eds.), *Festschrift für Ernst Steindorff*, Berlin, de Gruyter, 1990, 643-666.

KÖTZ, Hein and SCHÄFER, Hans-Bernd, 'Schadensverhütung durch ökonomische Anreize. Eine empirische Untersuchung' [Damage Prevention by Economic Incentives. An Empirical Investigation], **189** *Archiv für die civilistische Praxis*, 1989, 501-525.

KRAAKMAN, Reinier H., 'The Economic Functions of Corporate Liability', in HOPT, Klaus J. and TEUBNER, Gunther (eds.), *Corporate Governance and Directors' Liabilities: Legal, Economic and Sociological Responsibility*, New York, de Gruyter, 1984, 178-207.

KRAAKMAN, Reinier H., 'Gatekeepers: The Anatomy of a Third-Party Enforcement Strategy', **2** *Journal of Law, Economics, & Organization*, 1986, 53-104.

KUPERBERG, Mark and BEITZ, Charles R. (eds.), *Law, Economics and Philosophy - A Criticial Introduction; With Applications to the Law of Torts*, Totowa (NJ), Rowman and Allenheld, 1983, 284 p.

LANDES, Elisabeth M., 'Insurance, Liability, and Accidents: A Theoretical and Empirical Investigation of the Effect of No-Fault Accidents', **25** *Journal of Law and Economics*, 1982, 49-65.

LANDES, Elisabeth M., 'Compensation for Automobile Accident Injuries: Is the Tort System Fair ?', **11** *Journal of Legal Studies*, 1982, 253-259.

LANDES, William M., 'Insolvency and Joint Torts: A Comment', **19** *Journal of Legal Studies*, 1990, 679-690.

LANDES, William M. and POSNER, Richard A., 'Joint and Multiple Tortfeasors: An Economic Analysis', **9** *Journal of Legal Studies*, 1980, 517-555.

LANDES, William M. and POSNER, Richard A., 'An Economic Theory of Intentional Torts', **1** *International Review of Law and Economics*, 1981, 127-154.

LANDES, William M. and POSNER, Richard A., 'The Positive Economic Theory of Tort Law', **15** *Georgia Law Review*, 1981, 851-924.

LANDES, William M. and POSNER, Richard A., 'Tort Law as a Regulatory Regime for Catastrophic Personal Injuries', **13** *Journal of Legal Studies*, 1984, 417-434.

LANDES, William M. and POSNER, Richard A., *The Economic Structure of Tort Law*, Cambridge (Mass.) Harvard University Press, 1987, 330 p.

LATIN, Howard, 'Activity Levels, Due Care, and Selective Realism in Economic Analysis of Tort Law', **39** *Rutgers Law Review*, 1987, 487-514. Reprinted in *Personal Injury Review Ann.*, 1988, 956-990.

LEE, Gary L., 'Strict Liability versus Negligence: An Economic Analysis of the Law of Libel', *Brigham Young University Law Review*, 1981, 398-406.

LEHMANN, Michael, 'Die mißglückte Probefahrt. Vertragsrecht, Quasivertragsrecht, Deliktrecht. Ökonomische Analyse des Rechts' [The Failed Excursion. Contract Law, Quasi-Contract Law, Economic Analysis of Law], in WALZ, W. Rainer and RASCHER-FRIESENHAUSEN, Heinrich (eds.), *Sozialwissenschaften im Zivilrecht: Fälle und Lösungen in Ausbildung und Prüfung*, Neuwied, Luchterhand, 1983, 35-51.

LEHMANN, Michael, 'Umwelthaftungsrecht dient der Internalisierung negativer Externalitäten, Kommentar' [Environmental Liability Law Is to Internalize Negative Externalities. A Comment] (on Panther, Zivilrecht und Umweltschutz), in OTT, Claus and SCHÄFER, Hans-Bernd (eds.), *Ökonomische Probleme des Zivilrechts*, Berlin, Springer, 1991, 290-294.

LEONG, A.K., 'Liability Rules When Injurers as well as Victims Suffer Losses', **9** *International Review of Law and Economics*, 1989, 105-111.

LEVMORE, Saul, 'Waiting for Rescue: An Essay on the Evolution and Incentive Structure of the Law', **72** *Virginia Law Review*, 1986, 879 ff.

LEVMORE, Saul and STUNTZ, William J., 'Rechtsfolgen im Privatrecht und im öffentlichen Recht: Rechtsvergleichung unter einem Law-and-Economics Blickwinkel' [Legal Consequences in Private and Public Law: Comparitive Law from a Law and Economics Viewpoint], in OTT, Claus and SCHÄFER, Hans-Bernd (eds.), *Ökonomische Probleme des Zivilrechts*, Berlin, Springer, 1991, 297-314.

LIPNOWSKI, Irwin and SHILONY, Yuval, 'The Design of a Tort Law to Control Accidents', **4(2)** *Mathematical Social Sciences*, 1983, 103-115.

LITAN, Robert E. and WINSTON, Clifford (eds.), *Liability - Perspectives and Policy*, Washington, Brookings Institute, 1988.

MACKAAY, Ejan J.P., 'Veranderingen in het stelsel van vergoeding en verhaal van schade' [Changes in the System of Compensation and Recoupment of Damages], **55** *Nederlands Juristen Blad*, 1980, 813-825. Reprinted in *Schade lijden en schade dragen*, Zwolle, Tjeenk Willink, Nederlands Juristenblad Boekenreeks No. 6, 1981.

MACKAAY, Ejan J.P., 'Le droit relatif aux accidents: une interpretation économique' [Accident Law: An Economic Interpretation], **15** *Revue Juridique Themis*, 1981,

383-415.

MACKAAY, Ejan J.P., 'Het aansprakelijkheidsrecht' [Liability Law], **39(10)** *Ars Aequi*, 1990, 743-749.

MARINER, Wendy K., 'The Potential Impact of Pharmaceutical and Vaccine Litigation', in BAILY, Mary Ann and CIKINS, Warren I. (eds.), *The Effects of Litigation on Health Care Costs*, Washington, Brookings Institution, 1985, 43-68.

MATAJA, Victor, *Das Recht des Schadenersatzes vom Standpunkte der Nationalökonomie* [The Law of Compensation from the Standpoint of Economics], Leipzig, 1888.

MATTEI, Ugo, *Tutela inibitoria e tutela risarcitoria* [Inhibited Protection and Compensatory Protection], Milano, Giuffrè, 1987, 419 p.

McEWIN, R.I., 'No-Fault and Road Accidents: Some Australasian Evidence', **9** *International Review of Law and Economics*, 1989, 13-24.

McINTYRE, David C., 'Note: Tortfeasor Liability for Disaster Response Costs: Accounting for the True Cost of Accidents', **55** *Fordham Law Review*, 1987, 1001 ff.

MICELI, Thomas J. and SEGERSON, Kathleen, 'Contingent Fees for Lawyers: The Impact on Litigation and Accident Prevention', **20** *Journal of Legal Studies*, 1991, 381-399.

MICHELMAN, Frank I., 'Pollution as a Tort: A Non-accidental Perspective on Calabresi's Costs', **80** *Yale Law Journal*, 1971, 647-686.

MISHAN, Ezra J., 'The Effects of Externalities on Individual Choice', **1** *International Review of Law and Economics*, 1981, 97 ff.

MUNCH, Patricia, *Costs and Benefits of the Tort System if Viewed as a Compensation System*, Santa Monica, Rand Corp., 1977.

NEWMAN, Harry A. and WRIGHT, David W., 'Strict Liability in a Principal-Agent Model', **10** *International Review of Law and Economics*, 1990, 219-231.

O'CONNELL, J., *The Injury Industry*, Urbana, University Illinois Press, 1971.

O'CONNELL, Jeffrey, 'Pragmatic Constraints on Market Approaches: A Response to Professor Epstein', **74** *Virginia Law Review*, 1988, 1475-1483.

O'DRISCOLL, Gerald P., Jr., 'The Liability Crisis: A Law and Economics Analysis', **0(11)** *Federal Reserve Bank of Dallas Economic Review*, 1987, 1-13.

OGUS, Anthony I., 'Do We Have a General Theory of Compensation', **36** *Current Legal Problems*, 1984.

OLSON, Walter (ed.), *New Directions in Liability Law*, New York, The Academy of Political Science, 1988, 214 p.

ORDOVER, Janusz A., 'Costly Litigation in the Model of Single Activity Accidents', **7** *Journal of Legal Studies*, 1978, 243-261.

ORDOVER, Janusz A., 'On the Consequences of Costly Litigation in the Model of Single Activity Accidents: Some New Results', **10** *Journal of Legal Studies*, 1981, 269-291.

ORR, Daniel, 'The Superiority of Comparitive Negligence: Another Vote', **20** *Journal of Legal Studies*, 1991, 119-129.

OTA, S., 'The Fairness and the Efficiency of the Compensation System: An Economic Analysis of the Tort Theories', **7** *International Review of Law and Economics*, 1987, 229-239.

PAGE, Talbot, 'On Strict Liability: Reply to Hausman and to Schwartz', **97** *Ethics*, 1987, 817-820.

PANTHER, Stephan, 'Zivilrecht und Umweltschutz' [Civil Law and Environmental Protection], in OTT, Claus and SCHÄFER, Hans-Bernd (eds.), *Ökonomische Probleme des Zivilrechts*, Berlin, Springer, 1991, 267-289

PARKMAN, A.M., 'The Multiplier in English Fatal Accident Cases: What Happens when Judges Teach Judges Economics', **5** *International Review of Law and Economics*, 1985, 187-197.

PARTLETT, David, 'Economic Analysis in the Law of Torts', in CRANSTON, Ross and SCHICK, Anne (eds.), *Law and Economics*, Canberra, Australian National University, 1982, 59-98.

PERRY, Stephen R., 'The Impossibility of General Strict Liability', **1** *Canadian Journal of Law and Jurisprudence*, 1988, 147-171.

PNG, Ivan P.L., 'Litigation, Liability, and Incentives for Care', **34** *Journal of Public Economics*, 1987, 61-85.

POLINSKY, A. Mitchell, 'Strict Liability Versus Negligence in a Market Setting', **70** *American Economic Review*, 1980, 363-367.

POLINSKY, A. Mitchell, 'Optimal Liability When the Injurer's Information about the Victim's Loss Is Imperfect', **7** *International Review of Law and Economics*, 1987, 139-147.

PORTER, John E., 'The Effects of Litigation on Health Care Costs: A Congressional Perspective', in BAILY, Mary Ann and CIKINS, Warren I. (eds.), *The Effects of Litigation on Health Care Costs*, Washington, Brookings Institution, 1985, 36-42.

POSNER, James R., 'Trends in Medical Malpractice Insurance, 1970-1985', **49(2)** *Law and Contemporary Problems*, 1986, 37-156.

POSNER, Richard A., 'A Theory of Negligence', **1** *Journal of Legal Studies*, 1972, 29-96.

POSNER, Richard A., 'Strict Liability: A Comment', **2** *Journal of Legal Studies*, 1973, 205-221.

POSNER, Richard A., 'Epstein's Tort Theory: A Critique', **8** *Journal of Legal Studies*, 1979, 457-475.

POSNER, Richard A., 'The Concept of Corrective Justice in Recent Theories of Tort Law', **10** *Journal of Legal Studies*, 1981, 187-206.

POSNER, Richard A. (ed.), *Tort Law: Cases and Economic Analysis*, Boston, Little Brown, 1977 (1st ed.), 1983, 891 p. (2nd ed.).

POSNER, Richard A., 'Can Lawyers Solve the Problems of the Tort System?', **73** *California Law Review*, 1985, 747-754.

PRICHARD, J. Robert S., 'Professional Civil Liability and Continuing Competence', in SLAYTON, P. and TREBILCOCK, Michael J., *The Professions and Public Policy*, Toronto, University of Toronto Faculty of Law, 1978.

PRIEST, George L., 'Modern Tort Law and Its Reform', **22** *Valparaiso University Law Review*, 1987, 1-38.

PRIEST, George L., 'The Current Insurance Crisis and Modern Tort Law', **96** *The Yale Law Journal*, 1987, 1521-1590.

PRIEST, George L., 'Puzzles of the Tort Crisis', **48** *Ohio State Law Journal*, 1987, 497-502.

PRIEST, George L., 'Satisfying the Multiple Goals of Tort Law', **22** *Valparaiso University Law Review*, 1988, 643-650.

PRIEST, George L., 'The Modern Expansion of Tort Liability: Its Sources, Its Effects, and Its Reform', **5(3)** *Journal of Economic Perspectives*, 1991, 31-50.

PULVER, Robert A., 'Liability Rules as a Solution to the Problem of Waste in Western Water Law: An Economic Analysis', **76** *California Law Review*, 1988, 671-726.

QUAM, Lois, 'Comment: Medical Malpractice in Canada, 1971-1987', **15** *Geneva Papers on Risk and Insurance*, 1990, 81-83.

RABIN, Robert L. (ed.), *Perspectives on Tort Law*, Boston, Little Brown, 1976 (1st ed.), 1983, 332 p. (2nd ed.).

RABIN, Robert L., 'The Historical Development of the Fault Principle: A Reinterpretation', **15** *Georgia Law Review*, 1981, 925 ff. Reprinted in RABIN, Robert L. (ed.), *Perspectives on Tort Law*, Boston, Little Brown, 1983, 44-70.

RABIN, Robert L., 'Indeterminate Risk and Tort Reform: Comment on Calabresi and Klevorick', **14** *Journal of Legal Studies*, 1985, 633-643.

REA, Samuel A., Jr., 'Inflation and the Law of Contracts and Torts', **14** *Ottawa Law Review*, 1982, 465-480.

REA, Samuel A., Jr., 'The Economics of Comparitive Negligence', **7** *International Review of Law and Economics*, 1987, 149-162.

REDER, M.W., 'An Economic Analysis of Medical Malpractice', **5** *Journal of Legal Studies*, 1976, 267-292.

RINGLEB, Al H. and WIGGINS, Steven N., 'Liability and Large-Scale, Long-Term Hazards', **98** *Journal of Political Economy*, 1990, 574-595.

RIZZO, Mario J., 'Law amid Flux: The Economics of Negligence and Strict Liability in Tort', **9** *Journal of Legal Studies*, 1980, 291-318.

ROBERTS, E.F., 'Negligence: Blackstone to Shaw to? - An Intellectual Escapade in a Tory Vein', **50** *Cornell Law Quarterly*, 1965, 191-216.

ROBINSON, Glen O., 'The Medical Malpractice Crisis of the 1970's: A Retrospective', **49(2)** *Law and Contemporary Problems*, 1986, 5-35.

ROBINSON, Glen O., 'Rethinking the Allocation of Medical Malpractice Risks between Patients and Providers', **49(2)** *Law and Contemporary Problems*, 1986, 173-199.

ROE, Mark J., 'Corporate Strategic Reaction to Mass Tort', **72** *Virginia Law Review*, 1986, 1-59.

ROOS, Carl Martin, *Ersättningsrätt och ersättningssystem* [Compensation Right and Compensation System], Nordstedts, Stockholm, 1990.

ROSE-ACKERMAN, Susan, 'Dikes, Dams, and Vicious Hogs: Entitlement and

Efficieny in Tort Law', **18** *Journal of Legal Studies*, 1989, 25-50.

ROSE-ACKERMAN, Susan, 'Market-Share Allocations in Tort Law: Strengths and Weaknesses', **19** *Journal of Legal Studies*, 1990, 739-746.

ROTTENBERG, Simon, 'Liability in Law and Economics', **55** *American Economic Review*, 1965, 107 ff.

ROTTENBERG, Simon (ed.), *The Economics of Medical Malpractice*, Washington, American Enterprise Institute for Public Policy Research, 1978, 293 p.

RUBINFELD, Daniel L., 'On Determining the Optimal Magnitude and Length of Liability in Torts', **13** *Journal of Legal Studies*, 1984, 551-563.

RUBINFELD, Daniel L., 'The Efficiency of Comparative Negligence', **16** *Journal of Legal Studies*, 1987, 375-394.

SCHÄFER, Hans-Bernd and STRUCK, Gerhard, 'Schlammbeseitigung auf der Bundesstraße. Geschäftsführung ohne Auftrag, Deliktsrecht, negatorische Haftung. Ökonomische Analyse des Rechts' [The Case of the Mud Removal at the Federal Highway], in WALZ, W. Rainer and RASCHER-FRIESENHAUSEN, Heinrich (eds.), *Sozialwissenschaften im Zivilrecht: Fälle und Lösungen in Ausbildung und Prüfung*, Neuwied, Luchterhand, 1983, 119-132.

SCHÄFER, Hans-Bernd and WEHRT, Klaus, 'Ökonomische Analyse des Schadensrechts. Ein Überblick' [Economic Analysis of Tort Law. A Survey], **34** *Hamburger Jahrbuch für Wirtschaft und Gesellschaftspolitik*, 1989, 81-106.

SCHILFGAARDE, E. van, 'Economische analyse van het Nederlands aansprakelijkheidsrecht uit onrechtmatige daad' [Economic Analysis of Dutch Tort Liability Law], **39(10)** *Ars Aequi*, 1990, 750-758.

SCHMALZ, Richard A., 'On the Financing of Compensation Systems', **14** *Journal of Legal Studies*, 1985, 807-818.

SCHULZ, Andreas, 'Überlegungen zur ökonomischen Analyse des Haftungsrechts' [Considerations on the Economic Analysis of Liability Law], **35** *Versicherungsrecht*, 1984, 608-618.

SCHWARTZ, Alan, 'Commentary on "Towards a Market in Unmatured Tort Claims": A Long Way Yet to Go', **75** *Virginia Law Review*, 1989, 423-430.

SCHWARTZ, Alan and WILLARD, Richard K., 'Responses to George L. Priest', **24** *Houston Law Review*, 1987, 71-80.

SCHWARTZ, Gary T., 'Contributory and Comparative Negligence: A Reappraisal', **87** *Yale Law Review*, 1978, 697-727.

SCHWARTZ, Gary T., 'The Vitality of Negligence and the Ethics of Strict Liability', **15** *Georgia Law Review*, 1981, 963-1005. Reprinted in RABIN, Robert L. (ed.), *Perspectives on Tort Law*, Boston, Little Brown, 1983, 71-79.

SCHWARTZ, Gary T., 'Tort Law and the Economy in the Nineteenth Century America: A Reinterpretation', **90** *Yale Law Journal*, 1981, 1717-1775.

SCHWARTZ, Gary T., 'Tort Scholarship', **73** *California Law Review*, 1985, 548-554.

SCHWARTZ, Gary T., 'Objective and Subjective Standards of Negligence: Defining the Reasonable Person to Induce Optimal Care and Optimal Populations of Injurers and Victims', **78** *Georgetown Law Journal*, 1989, 241-279.

SCHWARTZ, Gary T., 'The Character of Early American Tort Law', **36** *UCLA Law Review*, 1989, 641-718.

SCHWARTZ, Gary T., 'The Ethics and the Economics of Tort Liability Insurance', **75** *Cornell Law Review*, 1990, 313-365.

SCHWARTZ, Warren F., 'Objective and Subjective Standards of Negligence: Defining the Reasonable Person to Induce Optimal Care and Optimal Populations of Injurers and Victims', **76** *Georgetown Law Journal*, 1988, 241 ff.

SEMKOW, B.W., 'Social Insurance and Tort Liability', **5** *International Review of Law and Economics*, 1985, 153-171.

SHANLEY, Michael G., 'The Distribution of Posttrial Adjustements to Jury Awards', **20** *Journal of Legal Studies*, 1991, 463-481.

SHAVELL, Steven, 'Theoretical Issues in Medical Malpractice', in ROTTENBERG, S. (ed.), *The Economics of Medical Malpractice*, Washington, American Enterprise Institute, 1978, 35-64.

SHAVELL, Steven, 'Strict Liability versus Negligence', **9** *Journal of Legal Studies*, 1980, 1-25.

SHAVELL, Steven, 'On Liability and Insurance', **13** *Bell Journal of Economics*, 1982, 120-132.

SHAVELL, Steven, 'Torts in Which Victim and Injurer Act Sequentially', **26** *Journal of Law and Economics*, 1983, 589-612.

SHAVELL, Steven, 'The Judgment Proof Problem', **6** *International Review of Law and Economics*, 1986, 45-58.

SHAVELL, Steven, *Economic Analysis of Accident Law*, Cambridge, Harvard University Press, 1987, 312 p.

SHAVELL, Steven, 'Comment' [on Finsinger, Liability and the Incentive for Innovations], in WEIGEL, Wolfgang (ed.), *Economic Analysis of Law - A Collection of Applications*, Vienna, Österreichischer Wirtschaftsverlag, 1991, 196.

SHEER, Alain and ZARDKOOHI, Asghar, 'An Analysis of the Economic Efficiency of the Law of Defamation', **80** *Northwestern University Law Review*, 1985, 364-475.

SHUKAITIS, Marc J., 'A Market in Personal Injury Tort Claims', **16** *Journal of Legal Studies*, 1987, 329-349.

SILICIANO, John A., 'Corporate Behavior and the Social Efficiency of Tort Law', **85** *Michigan Law Review*, 1987, 1820-1864.

SILICIANO, John A., 'Wealth, Equity, and the Unitary Medical Malpractice Standard', **77** *Virginia Law Review*, 1991, 439-487.

SIMPSON, A.W.B., 'Legal Liability for Bursting Reservoirs: The Historical Context of *Rylands v. Fletcher*', **13** *Journal of Legal Studies*, 1984, 209-264.

SKOGH, Göran, 'Comments on von Hippel's Paper', in SKOGH, Göran (ed.), *Law and Economics. Report from a Symposium in Lund, Sweden, 24-26 August 1977*, Lund, Juridiska Föreningen, 1978, 222-226.

SMITH, Steven D., 'Rhetoric and Rationality in the Law of Negligence', **69** *Minnesota Law Review*, 1984, 277 ff.

SMITH, Steven D., 'Rhetoric and Rationality in the Law of Negligence', **69** *Minnesota Law Review*, 1984, 277-323.

SPITZER, Matthew L., 'An Economic Analysis of Sovereign Immunity in Tort', **50** *Southern California Law Review*, 1977, 515-548.

STEINER, J.M., 'Economics, Morality and the Law of Torts', **26** *University of Toronto Law Journal*, 1976, 227-252.

STEPHEN, Frank H., 'Decision Making under Uncertainty: In Defence of Shackle', **13(5)** *Journal of Economic Studies*, 1986, 45-57.

STOLJAR, Samuel, 'Comment', in CRANSTON, Ross and SCHICK, Anne (eds.), *Law and Economics*, Canberra, Australian National University, 1982, 99-104.

SULLIVAN, Arthur M., 'Victim Compensation Revisited: Efficiency versus Equity in the Siting of Noxious Facilities', **41** *Journal of Public Economics*, 1990, 211-225.

SUMMERS, John, 'The Case of the Disappearing Defendant: An Economic Analysis', **132** *University of Pennsylvania Law Review*, 1983, 145-185.

SUNDAKOV, Alex, 'Accident Compensation Law: An Economic View', **21** *New Zealand Economic Papers*, 1987, 57-73.

SYKES, Alan O. (Student Note), 'An Efficiency Analysis of Vicarious Liability Under the Law of Agency', **91** *Yale Law Journal*, 1981, 168-206.

SYKES, Alan O., 'The Economics of Vicarious Liability', **93** *Yale Law Journal*, 1984, 1231-1280.

SYKES, Alan O., 'The Boundaries of Vicarious Liability: An Economic Analysis of the Scope of Employment Rule and Related Legal Doctrines', **101** *Harvard Law Review*, 1988, 563-609.

SYMPOSIUM : 'Alternative Compensation Schemes and Tort Theory', **73(3)** *California Law Review*, 1985, 548-1042.

SYMPOSIUM : 'Medical Malpractice: Can the Private Sector Find Relief?', **49 (2)** *Law and Contemporary Problems*, 1986, 1-348.

SYMPOSIUM: 'The Economics of Liability', **5(3)** *Journal of Economic Perspectives*, 1991, 3-136.

TALBOTT, W.J., 'Cost Spreading and Benefit Spreading in Tort Law', **11** *Research in Law and Economics*, 1988, 25-51.

THOMAS, Ewart A. C., 'On Calculating Optimal Contributory Negligence Rules', **2** *Social Choice and Welfare*, 1985, 65-85.

TIETENBERG, Tom H., 'Indivisible Toxic Torts: The Economics of Joint and Several Liability', **65** *Land Economics*, 1989, 305-319.

TREBILCOCK, Michael J., 'The Social-Insurance-Deterrence Dilemma of Modern North American Tort Law: A Canadian Perspective on the Liability Insurance Crisis', **24** *San Diego Law Review*, 1987, 929-1002.

TREBILCOCK, Michael J., 'The Role of Insurance Considerations in the Choice of Efficient Civil Liability Rules', **4** *Journal of Law, Economics, & Organization*, 1988, 243-265.

TREBILCOCK, Michael J., 'The Future of Tort Law: Mapping the Contours of the Debate', **15** *Canadian Business Law Journal*, 1989, 471-488.

TRICOLI, Clara, 'Per una teoria economica dell' espropriazione e dell' indennizzo' [An Economic Theory of Takings and Compensation], *Rivista di diritto commerciale*, 1981, I, 335-357.

TRIMARCHI, Pietro, *Rischio e responsabilità oggettiva* [Risk and Strict Liability], Milano, Giuffrè, 1961, 383 p.

TULLOCK, Gordon, 'Negligence Again', **1** *International Review of Law and Economics*, 1981, 51 ff.

VAN DEN BERGH, Roger and FAURE, Michael G., 'De invloed van verzekering op de civiele aansprakelijkheid, een rechtseconomische analyse' [The Influence of Insurance on Tort Liability, an Economic Analysis], in *Preadviezen uitgebracht voor de Vereniging voor Burgerlijk Recht*, Lelystad, Vermande, 1990, 9-53.

VAN OEVELEN, Aloïs, 'Enige bedenkingen van een jurist bij de economische analyse van het aansprakelijkheidsrecht' [Some Considerations of a Jurist on Economic Analysis of Tort Law], in VAN DEN BERGH, Roger (ed.), *Verslagboek Eerste Werkvergadering recht en Economie*, Antwerpen, Handelshogeschool, 1986, 21-30.

VANDALL, Frank J., 'Applying Strict Liability to Professionals: Economic and Legal Analysis', **59** *Indiana Law Journal*, 1983, 25-64.

VANDALL, Frank J., 'Judge Posner's Negligence-Efficiency Theory: A Critique', **35** *Emory Law Journal*, 1986, 383-418.

VELJANOVSKI, Cento G., 'The Economic Theory of Tort Liability - Toward a Corrective Justice Approach', in BURROWS, Paul and VELJANOVSKI, Cento G. (eds.), *The Economic Appraoch to Law*, London, Butterworths, 1981, 125-150.

VENEZIAN, E.C., NYE, B.F. and HOFFLANDER, A.E., 'The Distribution of Claims for Professional Malpractice: Some Statistical and Public Policy Aspects', **56** *Journal of Risk and Insurance*, 1989, 686-701.

VER STEEG, John C., 'Strict Liability and Judicial Resources', **3** *Journal of Legal Studies*, 1974, 217-248.

VON HIPPEL, Eike, 'Prevention of Accidents and Compensation of Accident Victims', in SKOGH, Göran (ed.), *Law and Economics. Report from a Symposium in Lund, Sweden, 24-26 August 1977*, Lund, Juridiska Föreningen, 1978, 211-221.

VON RANDOW, Philipp and WEHRT, Klaus, 'Comment: New Technologies, Liability Rules and Adaptive Behaviour', in FAURE, Michael and VAN DEN BERGH, Roger (eds.), *Essays in Law and Economics. Corporations, Accident Prevention and Compensation for Losses*, Antwerpen, Maklu, 1989, 107-116.

WARD, John O., 'Origins of the Tort Reform Movement', **6(3)** *Contemporary Policy Issues*, 1988, 97-107.

WASSENAER VAN CATWIJCK, A.J.O. Baron van, *Verkeersverzekering* [Traffic Insurance], Zwolle, Tjeenk Willink, 1977, 78 p.

WASSENAER VAN CATWIJCK, A.J.O. Baron van, 'Verkeersverzekering in Noord--Amerika' [Traffic Insurance in North-America: No-fault in Action], *Het Verzekerings-Archief*, 's-Gravenhage, Verbond van Verzekeraars in Nederland, 1988, 321-377.

WELLISZ, Stanislaw, 'On External Diseconomies and the Governement - Assisted

Invisible Hand', **31** *Economica*, 1964, 345-362.

WENDEL, Heidi, 'Restoration as the Economically Efficient Remedy for Damage to Publicly Owned Natural Resources', **91** *Columbia Law Review*, 1991, 430-455.

WHITE, Michelle J., 'The Economics of Accidents', **86** *Michigan Law Review*, 1988, 1217-1231.

WHITE, Michelle J., 'An Empirical Test of the Comparitive and Contributory Negligence Rules in Accident Law', **20** *Rand Journal of Economics*, 1989, 308-330.

WILLIAMSON, Oliver E., OLSON, Douglas and RALSTON, August, 'Externalities, Insurance, and Disability Analysis', **34** *Economica*, 1967, 235-253.

WITT, Robert C. and URRUTIA, Jorge, 'A Comparative Economic Analysis of Tort Liability and No Fault Compensation Systems in Automobile Insurance', **50** *Journal of Risk and Insurance*, 1983, 631-669.

WITTMAN, Donald, 'The Price of Negligence under Differing Liability Rules', **29** *Journal of Law and Economics*, 1986, 151-163.

X, 'Note: Imposing Tort Liability on Real Estate Brokers Selling Defective Housing', **99** *Harvard Law Review*, 1986, 1861-1875.

ZUCKERMAN, Stephen and KOLLER, Christopher F. and BOVBJERG, Randall R., 'Information on Malpractice: A Review of Empirical Research on Major Policy Issues', **49(2)** *Law and Contemporary Problems*, 1986, 85-111.

ZWIER, Paul J., 'The Consequentialist/Nonconsequentialist Ethical Distinction: A Tool for the Formal Appraisal of Traditional Negligence and Economic Tort Analysis', **26** *Boston College Law Review*, 1985, 905-944.

3100 Causation

ASSMANN, Heinz-Dieter, 'Multikausale Schäden im deutschen Haftungsrecht' [Multicausal Injuries in German Tort Law], in FENYVES, Attila and WEYERS, Hans-Leo (eds.), *Multikausale Schäden im modernen Haftungsrechten*, Frankfurt a.M., Metzner, 1988, 99-151.

BORGO, John, 'Causal Paradigms in Tort Law', **8** *Journal of Legal Studies*, 1979, 419-455.

CALABRESI, Guido, 'Concerning Cause and the Law of Torts', **43** *University of Chicago Law Review*, 1975, 69-108.

CALABRESI, Guido, 'Concerning Cause and the Law of Torts: An Essay for Harry Kalven', **43** *University of Chicago Law Review*, 1976, 69-100.

CELLI, Andrew G., Jr., 'Toward a Risk Contribution Approach to Tortfeasor Identification and Multiple Causation Cases', **65** *New York University Law Review*, 1990, 635-692.

COOTER, Robert D., 'Torts as the Union of Liberty and Efficiency: An Essay on Causation', **63** *Chicago-Kent Law Review*, 1987, 523-551.

CULP, Jerome M., 'Causation, Economists, and the Dinosaur: A Response to [Causal Judgment in Attributive and Explanatory Contexts]', **49(3)** *Law and Contemporary Problems*, 1986, 23-46.

EPSTEIN, Richard A., 'Causation and Corrective Justice: A Reply to Two Critics', **8** *Journal of Legal Studies*, 1979, 477-504.

EPSTEIN, Richard A., 'Causation - In Context: An Afterword', **63** *Chicago-Kent Law Review*, 1987, 653-680.

FARBER, Daniel A., 'Recurring Misses', **19** *Journal of Legal Studies*, 1990, 727-737.

GRADY, Mark, 'Proximate Cause and the Law of Negligence', **69** *Iowa Law Review*, 1984, 537-573.

KELMAN, Mark, 'The Necessary Myth of Objective Causation Judgments in Liberal Political Theory', **63** *Chicago-Kent Law Review*, 1987, 579-637.

KRUSKAL, William, 'Terms of Reference: Singular Confusion about Multiple Causation', **15** *Journal of Legal Studies*, 1986, 427-436.

LANDES, William M. and POSNER, Richard A., 'Causation in Tort Law: An Economic Approach', **12** *Journal of Legal Studies*, 1983, 109-134.

LEVMORE, Saul, 'Probabilistic Recoveries, Restitution, and Recurring Wrongs', **19** *Journal of Legal Studies*, 1990, 691-726.

MOORE, Michael S., 'Thomson's Preliminaries about Causation and Rights', **63** *Chicago-Kent Law Review*, 1987, 497-521.

POLINSKY, A. Mitchell, 'Probabilistic Compensation Criteria', **86** *Quarterly Journal of Economics*, 1972, 407-425.

POSNER, Richard A., 'Epstein's Tort Theory: A Critique', **8** *Journal of Legal Studies*, 1979, 457-475.

RIZZO, Mario J., 'The Imputation Theory of Proximate Cause: An Economic Framework', **15** *Georgia Law Review*, 1981, 1007-1038.

RIZZO, Mario J., 'Foreword: Fundamentals of Causation', **63** *Chicago-Kent Law Review*, 1987, 397-406.

RIZZO, Mario J. (Ed.), *Symposium on Causation in the Law of Torts*, in **63** *Chicago-Kent Law Review*, 1987, 397-680.

RIZZO, Mario J. and ARNOLD, Frank S., 'Causal Apportionment in Tort Law: An Economic Theory', **85** *Columbia Law Review*, 1980, 1399-1429.

RIZZO, Mario J. and ARNOLD, Frank S., 'Causal Apportionment: Reply to the Critics', **15** *Journal of Legal Studies*, 1986, 219-226.

ROBINSON, Glen O., 'Probabilistic Causation and Compensation for Tortious Risk', **14** *Journal of Legal Studies*, 1985, 779-798.

ROSE-ACKERMAN, Susan, 'Market-Share Allocations in Tort Law: Strengths and Weaknesses', **19** *Journal of Legal Studies*, 1990, 739-746.

ROSSELLO, Carlo, *Il danno evitabile. La misura della responsabilità tra diligenza ed efficienza* [Avoidable Damage: The Measure of Liability Between Due Care and Efficiency], Padova, CEDAM, 1990, 320 p.

SCHWARTZ, Alan, 'Causation in Private Tort Law: A Comment on Kelman', **63** *Chicago-Kent Law Review*, 1987, 639-651.

SHAVELL, Steven, 'An Analysis of Causation and the Scope of Liability in the Law of Torts', **9** *Journal of Legal Studies*, 1980, 463-516.

SHAVELL, Steven, 'Uncertainty over Causation and the Determination of Civil Liability', **28** *Journal of Law and Economics*, 1985, 587-609.

THOMSON, Judith Jarvis, 'Causality and Rights: Some Preliminaries', **63** *Chicago-Kent Law Review*, 1987, 471-496.

WEINRIB, Ernest J., 'Causation and Wrongdoing', **63** *Chicago-Kent Law Review*, 1987, 407-450.

WITTMAN, Donald, 'Optimal Pricing of Sequential Inputs: Last Clear Chance, Mitigation of Damages, and Related Doctrines in the Law', **10** *Journal of Legal Studies*, 1981, 65-91.

WRIGHT, Richard W., 'Actual Causation vs. Probabilistic Linkage: The Bane of Economic Analysis', **14** *Journal of Legal Studies*, 1985, 435-456.

WRIGHT, Richard W., 'The Efficiency Theory of Causation and Responsibility: Unscientific Formalism and False Semantics', **63** *Chicago-Kent Law Review*, 1987, 553-578.

3200 Computing of Damages

ADAMS, Michael, 'Warum kein Ersatz von Nichtvermögensschäden?' [Why No Damages for Nonpecuniary Losses?], in OTT, Claus and SCHÄFER, Hans-Bernd (eds.), *Allokationseffizienz in der Rechtsordnung*, Berlin, Springer, 1989, 210-217.

ANDERSON and ROBERTS, 'Economic Theory and the Present Value of Future Lost Earnings: An Integration, Unification, and Simplification of Court Adopted Methodologies', **39** *University of Miami Law Review*, 1985, 723 ff.

ARLEN, Jennifer H. (Note), 'An Economic Analysis of Tort Damages for Wrongful Death, **60** *New York Law Review*, 1985, 1113-1136.

BACKHAUS, Jürgen G., 'Lawyers' Economics vs. the Economic Analysis of Law: A Critique of Professor Posner's "Economic Approach to Law with Reference to a Case Concerning Damages for Loss of Earning Capacity"', **3** *Munich Social Science Review*, 1978, 57-80.

BEN-ZION, Barry and REDDALL, Ronald G., 'Life Expectancy and Actuarial Present Values: A Note to Forensic Economists', **7** *Research in Law and Economics*, 1985, 160-171.

BISHOP, William, 'Economic Loss in Tort', **2** *Oxford Journal of Legal Studies*, 1982, 1-30.

BISHOP, William and SUTTON, John, 'Efficiency and Justice in Tort Damages: The Shortcomings of the Pecuniary Loss Rule', **15** *Journal of Legal Studies*, 1986, 347-370.

BRENZA, Lindley J., 'Asbestos in Schools and the Economic Loss Doctrine', **54** *University of Chicago Law Review*, 1987, 277-311.

BRUCE, Christopher J., 'An Efficient Technique for Determining the Compensation of Lost Earnings', **13** *Journal of Legal Studies*, 1984, 375-378.

CARTER, R.A.L. and PALMER, John P., 'Real Rates, Expected Rates, and Damage Awards', **20** *Journal of Legal Studies*, 1991, 439-462.

CHAPMAN, Bruce, 'Pensions, Sex Discrimination, and the Value of Life after Death', **7** *International Review of Law and Economics*, 1987, 193-214.

COHEN, Lloyd, 'Toward an Economic Theory of the Measurement of Damages in a Wrongful Death Action', **34** *Emory Law Journal*, 1985, 295 ff.

CONFERENCE : 'Catastrophic Personal Injuries - A Conference Sponsored by The Hoover Institution', **13** *Journal of Legal Studies*, 1984, 415-622.

COOTER, Robert D., 'Prices and Sanctions', **84** *Columbia Law Review*, 1984, 1523-1560.

CREEDY, J., 'Taxation and Compensation to Dependents of Accident Victims', **8** *International Review of Law and Economics*, 1988, 85-95.

DARBIS, Rachel, 'The Value of a Life: New Evidence from the Marketplace', **70** *American Economic Review*, 1980, 1077-1082.

DARVISH, Tikva and KAHANA, Nava, 'The Nature of Utility in Jewish Law', **7** *International Review of Law and Economics*, 1987, 127-131.

EIDE, Erling, 'Kapitaliseringsrente ved Personskadeerstatning. Kritikk av en Dom i

Høyesterett' [Capitalization Interest Rates in Personal Injury Compensation. A Critique of a Supreme Court Verdict], *Lov og Rett. Norsk Juridisk Tidsskrift*, 1982, 30-42.

EIDE, Erling, 'Renter og Verdisikring av Pengekrav' [Interest Rates and Security against Inflation in Monetary Claims], **97** *Tidsskrift for Rettsvitenskap*, 1984, 477-533.

EIDE, Erling, 'Ekspropriasjonserstatning i en Inflasjonstid: Valg av Kapitaliseringsrente' [Compensation for Expropriation in Inflationary Times: The Choice of Capitalization Interest Rates], *Lov og Rett. Norsk Juridisk Tidsskrift*, 1987, 165-177.

FISHER, Ann and CHESTNUT, Lauraine G. and VIOLETTE, Daniel M., 'The Value of Reducing Risks of Death: A Note on New Evidence', **8** *Journal of Policy Analysis and Management*, 1989, 88-100.

FRASER, Clive D., 'What is 'Fair Compensation' for Death or Injury?', **4** *International Review of Law and Economics*, 1984, 83-88.

FRIEDMAN, David D., 'What is 'Fair Compensation' for Death or Injury ?', **2** *International Review of Law and Economics*, 1982, 81-93.

FUCHS, Victor R. and ZECKHAUSER, Richard, 'Valuing Health - A "Priceless" Commodity', **77** *American Economic Review. Papers and Proceedings*, 1987, 263-268.

GHOSH, D., LEES, D. and SEAL, W., *The Economics of Personal Injury*, Westmead, Saxon House, 1976 p.

GOLDBERG, Victor P., 'Recovery for Pure Economic Loss in Tort: Another Look at *Robins Dry Dock v. Flint*', **20** *Journal of Legal Studies*, 1991, 249-275.

KIDNER, R. and RICHARDS, K., 'Compensation to Dependants of Accident Victims', **84** *Economic Journal*, 1974, 130-142.

KNETSCH, Jack L., 'Legal Rules and the Basis for Evaluating Economic Losses', **4** *International Review of Law and Economics*, 1984, 5-13.

KOMESAR, Neil K., 'Toward a General Theory of Personal Injury Loss', **3** *Journal of Legal Studies*, 1974, 457-486.

KÖNDGEN, Johannes, 'Ökonomische Aspekte des Schadensproblems. Bemerkungen zur Kommerzialisierungsmethode des Bundesgerichtshofes' [Economic Aspects of the Damage Problem. Remarks on the 'Commercializing Method' of the Bundesgerichtshofes], **177** *Archiv für civilistische Praxis*, 1977, 1-34.

LEHMANN, Michael, 'Juristisch-ökonomische Kriterien zur Berechnung des Verletzergewinns bzw. des entgangenen Gewinns' [Legal-economic Criteria for the Calculation of the Profit of the Injurer Respectively the Lost Profit], **25** *Der Betriebs-Berater*, 1988, 1680-1687.

LIPNOWSKI, I.F., 'The Economist's Approach to Assessing Compensation for Accident Victims', **9** *Manitoba Law Journal*, 1979, 319-333.

MINISTERIE VAN JUSTITIE, *Rapport van de Studiegroep Verkeersaansprakelijkheid, Deel I, Vergoeding van schade door dood en letsel* [Report of the Commission Traffic Liability, Part I, Compensation of Damages through Death and Injury], 's-Gravenhage, Staatsuitgeverij, 1978.

MINISTERIE VAN JUSTITIE, *Rapport van de Studiegroep Verkeersaansprakelijk-*

heid, Deel II, Vergoeding van zaakschade [Report of the Commission Traffic Liability, Part I, Compensation of Damages Caused to Things], 's-Gravenhage, Staatsuitgeverij, 1980.

MOONEY, G., *The Valuation of Human Life*, London, Macmillan, 1977.

O'CONNELL, J. and SIMON, R.J., *Payment for Pain and Suffering*, Illinois, Insurors Press, 1972.

OTT, Claus and SCHÄFER, Hans-Bernd, 'Begründung und Bemessung des Schadensersatzes wegen entganger Sachnutzung' [Foundation and Rating of the Compensation for Damage Because of Lost Utility of Property], **7** *Zeitschrift für Wirtschaftsrecht*, 1986, 613-624.

PNG, Ivan P.L. and ZOLT, Eric M., 'Efficient Deterrence and the Tax Treatment of Monetary Sanctions', **9** *International Review of Law and Economics*, 1989, 209-217.

QUAH, Euston and RIEBER, William J., 'Value of Children in Compensation for Wrongful Death', **9** *International Review of Law and Economics*, 1989, 165-179.

RAES, Koen, 'Onrechtmatige daad en de markt van pijn en smart' [Tort and the Market for Pain and Sorrow], *Recht en Kritiek*, 1988, 102-125.

REA, Samuel A., Jr., 'Inflation, Taxation and Damage Assessment', **58** *Canadian Bar Review*, 1980, 280-298.

REA, Samuel A., Jr., 'Taxation, the Standard of Care and Damage Awards', **10** *International Review of Law and Economics*, 1990, 285-292.

RIZZO, Mario J., 'A Theory of Economic Loss in the Law of Torts', **11** *Journal of Legal Studies*, 1982, 281-310.

ROSSELLO, Carlo, *Il danno evitabile. La misura della responsabilità tra diligenza ed efficienza* [Avoidable Damage: The Measure of Liability Between Due Care and Efficiency], Padova, CEDAM, 1990, 320 p.

SCHÄFER, Hans-Bernd and OTT, Claus, 'Schmerzengeld bei Körperverletzungen. Eine Ökonomische Analyse' [Damages for Pain and Suffering], *Juristenzeitung*, 1990, 563-573.

SCHWARTZ, Gary T., 'Economic Loss in American Tort Law: The Examples of J Aire and of Products Liability', **23** *San Diego Law Review*, 1986, 37-78.

SMITH, V. Kerry, 'Can We Measure the Economic Value of Environmental Amenities?', **56** *Southern Economic Journal*, 1990, 856-878.

von RANDOW, Philipp, 'Kommentar' [Comment] (On Adams, Warum kein Ersatz von Nichtvermögensschäden), in OTT, Claus and SCHÄFER, Hans-Bernd (eds.), *Allokationseffizienz in der Rechtsordnung*, Berlin, Springer, 1989, 218-225.

WITTMAN, Donald, 'Should Compensation Be Based on Costs or Benefits?', **5** *International Review of Law and Economics*, 1985, 173-185.

ZECKHAUSER, Richard A., 'Procedures for Valuing Lives', **23** *Public Policy*, 1975, 419-464.

3300 Punitive Damages

ABRAHAM, Kenneth S. and JEFFRIES, John C. Jr., 'Punitive Damages and the Rule of Law: The Role of Defendant's Wealth', **18** *Journal of Legal Studies*, 1989, 415-425.

CHAPMAN, Bruce and TREBILCOCK, Michael J., 'Punitive Damages: Deterrence in Search of a Rationale', **40** *Alabama Law Review*, 1989, 741-829.

COOTER, Robert D., 'Economic Analysis of Punitive Damages', **56** *Southern California Law Review*, 1982, 79-101.

DANIELS, Stephen and MARTIN, Joanne, 'Myth and Reality in Punitive Damages', **75** *Minnesota Law Review*, 1990, 1-64.

ELLIS, Dorsey D., Jr., 'Fairness and Efficiency in the Law of Punitive Damages', **56** *Southern California Law Review*, 1 ff.

JOHANSSON, Per Olov, 'Valuing Environmental Damage', **6** *Oxford Review of Economic Policy*, 1990, 34-50.

JOHNSTON, Jason S., 'Punitive Liability: A New Paradigm of Efficiency in Tort Law', **87** *Columbia Law Review*, 1987, 1385 ff.

LANDES, William M. and POSNER, Richard A., 'New Light on Punitive Damages', **10(1)** *Regulation*, 1986, 33-36, 54.

LEVMORE, Saul and STUNTZ, William J., 'Rechtsfolgen im Privatrecht und im öffentlichen Recht: Rechtsvergleichung unter einem Law-and-Economics Blickwinkel' [Legal Consequences in Private and Public Law: Comparitive Law from a Law and Economics Viewpoint], in OTT, Claus and SCHÄFER, Hans-Bernd (eds.), *Ökonomische Probleme des Zivilrechts*, Berlin, Springer, 1991, 297-314.

PNG, Ivan P.L., 'Optimal Subsidies and Damages in the Presence of Judicial Error', **6** *International Review of Law and Economics*, 1986, 101-105.

PRIEST, George L., 'Punitive Damages and Enterprise Liability', **56** *Southern California Law Review*, 1982, 123-132.

PRIEST, George L., 'Insurability an Punitive Damages', **40** *Alabama Law Review*, 1989, 1009-1035.

SCHEINER, Alan Howard, 'Judicial Assessment of Punitive Damages, the Seventh Amandment, and the Politics of Jury Power', **91** *Columbia Law Review*, 1991, 142-226.

SCHMIT, Joan T., PRITCHETT, S.T. and FIELDS, P., 'Punitive Damages: Punishment or Further Compensation?', **55** *Journal of Risk and Insurance*, 1988, 453-466.

SCHWARTZ, Gary T., 'Deterrence and Punishment in the Common Law of Punitive Damages: A Comment', **56** *Southern California Law Review*, 1982, 133-153.

WALDEN, Alyssa, 'Note: The Publicly Held Corporation and the Insurability of Punitive Damages', **53** *Fordham Law Review*, 1985, 1383-1408.

3400 Nuisance

ATIYAH, Patrick S., 'Liability for Railway Nuisance in the English Common Law: A Historical Footnote', **23** *Journal of Law and Economics*, 1980, 191-196.

BERGSTROM, John C. and CENTNER, Terence J., 'Agricultural Nuisances and Right to Farm Laws: Implications of Changing Liability Rules', **19(1)** *Review of Regional Studies*, 1989, 23- 30.

BRENNER, Joel Franklin, 'Nuisance Law and the Industrial Revolution', **3** *Journal of Legal Studies*, 1974, 403-433.

BURROWS, Paul, 'Nuisance, Legal Rules and Decentralized Decisions: A Different Ciew of the Cathedral Crypt', in BURROWS, Paul and VELJANOVSKI, Cento G. (eds.), *The Economic Appraoch to Law*, London, Butterworths, 1981, 151-166.

BURROWS, Paul, 'Efficiency Levels, Efficiency Gains and Alternative Nuisance Remedies', **5** *International Review of Law and Economics*, 1985, 59-71.

EPSTEIN, Richard A., 'Nuisance Law: Corrective Justice and Its Utilitarian Constraints', **8** *Journal of Legal Studies*, 1979, 49-102.

LEWIN, Jeff L., 'Compensated Injunctions and the Evolution of Nuisance Law', **71** *Iowa Law Review*, 1986, 777-832.

MERRILL, Thomas W., 'Trespass, Nuisance, and the Costs of Determining Property Rights', **14** *Journal of Legal Studies*, 1985, 13-48.

OGUS, Anthony I. and RICHARDSON, G., 'Economics and the Environment: A Study of Private Nuisance', **36** *Cambridge Law Journal*, 1977, 284-325.

PARDOLESI, Roberto, 'Azione reale e azione di danni nell'art. 844 c.c. Logica economica e logica giuridica nella composizione del conflitto tra usi incompatibili delle proprietà vicine' [Property Rule and Liability Rule in Article 844 Codice Civile: Economic Arguments, Legal Arguments and Litigation for Inconsistent Uses of Neighbours' Lands], *Foro italiono*, 1977, I, 1144-1154.

POLINSKY, A. Mitchell, 'Resolving Nuisance Disputes: The Simple Economics of Injunctive and Damage Remedies', **33** *Stanford Law Review*, 1980, 1075-1112.

POSNER, Richard A., 'Epstein's Tort Theory: A Critique', **8** *Journal of Legal Studies*, 1979, 457-475.

RABIN, Edward H., 'Nuisance Law: Rethinking Fundamental Assumptions', **63** *Virginia Law Review*, 1977, 1299-1348.

SPITTJE, Petra J., 'De hinderwetgeving' [Nuisance Legislation], in COLJEE, P.D., FRANKEN, H., HEERTJE, A. and KANNING, W. (eds.), *Law and Welfare Economics*, Symposium 24 October, VU Amsterdam, 115-132.

TROMANS, Stephen, 'Nuisance-Prevention or Payment?', **41** *Camb. Law Journal*, 1982, 87-109.

WHITE, Lawrence H., 'Economics and Nuisance Law: Comment on Manson', **8** *Harvard Journal of Law & Public Policy*, 1985, 213-223.

WITTMAN, Donald, 'First Come, First Served: An Economic Analysis of "Coming to the Nuisance"', **9** *Journal of Legal Studies*, 1980, 557-568.

X, 'Note: Internalizing Externalities: Nuisance Law and Economic Efficiency', **53**

New York University Law Review, 1978, 219-240.

3500 Environmental Regulation: General

ABBOTT, Alden F. and BRADY, Gordon L., 'Tollison Costs and Technological Innovation: The Case of Environmental Regulation', **65** *Public Choice*, 1990, 157-165.

ACKERMAN, Bruce A., 'Reforming Environmental Law: The Democratic Case for Market Incentives', **13** *Columbia Journal of Environmental Law*, 1988, 171-199.

ADAMS, Michael, 'Das Verursacherprinzip als Leerformel' [The Polluter Pays Principe as Empty Formula], *Juristenzeitung*, 1989, 789-790.

APPLEGATE, John S., 'The Perils of Unreasonable Risk: Information, Regulatory Policy, and Toxic Substances Control', **91** *Columbia Law Review*, 1991, 261-333.

ARCHIBALD, R. and GILLINGHAM, R., 'The Distributional Impact of Alternative Gasoline Conservation Policies', **12** *Bell Journal of Economics*, 1981, 426-444.

ASHFORD, Nicholas A. and HEATON, George R., Jr., 'Regulation and Technological Innovation in the Chemical Industry', **46(3)** *Law and Contemporary Problems*, 1983, 109-157.

ASHWORTH, John, PAPPS, Ivy and STOREY, David J., 'Assessing The Effectiveness of Economic Efficiency of an E.E.C. Pollution Control Directive: The Control of Discharges of Mercury to the Aquatic Environment', in GRAF VON DER SCHULENBURG, J.-Matthias and SKOGH, Göran (eds.), *Law and Economics and The Economics of Legal Regulation*, Dordrecht, Kluwer, 1986, 207-225.

ASHWORTH, John and PAPPS, Ivy, 'Should Environmental Legislation Set the Rules Constraining Polluters?', in WEIGEL, Wolfgang (ed.), *Economic Analysis of Law - A Collection of Applications*, Vienna, Österreichischer Wirtschaftsverlag, 1991, 83-88.

ASSMANN, Heinz-Dieter, 'Privatrechtliche Tatbestände der Umwelthaftung in ökonomischer Analyse' [Economic Analysis of Civil Liability for Pollution], in WAGNER, Gerd Rainer (ed.), *Unternehmung und ökologische Umwelt*, München, Vahlen, 1990, 201-219.

AWAD, A. Safi El Din, 'Islamic Jurisprudence and Environmental Planning: Comments', **3** *Journal of Research in Islamic Economics*, 1985, 83-86.

BAIRD, Douglas G., 'Environmental Regulation, Bankruptcy Law, and the Problem of Limited Liability', **18** *Environmental Law Reporter*, 1988, 10352-10355.

BARBERA, Anthony J. and McCONNELL, Virginia D., 'The Impact of Environmental Regulations on Industry Productivity: Direct and Indirect Effects', **18** *Journal of Environmental Economics and Management*, 1990, 50-65.

BARON, David P., 'Noncooperative Regulation of a Nonlocalized Externality', **16** *Rand Journal of Economics*, 1985, 553-568.

BARTIK, Timothy J., 'The Effects of Environmental Regulation on Business Location in the United States', **19(3)** *Growth and Change*, 1988, 22-44.

BAUMOL, William J. and OATES, Wallace E., *The Theory of Environmental Policy*, Cambridge, Cambridge University Press, 1988, 299 p.

BAXTER, William F., *People or Penguins: The Case for Optimal Pollution*, New York, Columbia University Press, 1974, 110 p.

BEAVIS, Brian and DOBBS, Ian M., 'The Dynamics of Optimal Environmental Regulation', **10** *Journal of Economic Dynamics and Control*, 1986, 415-423.

BEAVIS, Brian and DOBBS, Ian M., 'Firm Behaviour under Regulatory Control of Stochastic Environmental Wastes by Probabilistic Constraints', **14** *Journal of Environmental Economics and Management*, 1987, 112-127.

BEILOCK, Richard and BURKHART, Jeffrey and WELSH, Richard, 'Risk Permits: An Alternative Approach to Transportation Safety Regulations', **25** *Logistics and Transportation Review*, 1989, 195-207.

BERGLAS, Eita,, 'Pollution Control and Intercommunity Trade', **8** *Bell Journal of Economics*, 1977, 217-233.

BERNSTEIN, Mark A. and FELDMAN, Stephen L. and SCHINNAR, Arie P., 'Impact of Pollution Controls on the Productivity of Coal Fired Power Plants', **12(1)** *Energy Economics*, 1990, 11-17.

BESANKO, David A., 'Performance versus Design Standards in the Regulation of Pollution', **34** *Journal of Public Economics*, 1987, 19-44.

BLOCK, Walter E. (ed.), *Economics and the Environment: A Reconciliation*, Vancouver, Fraser Institure, 1990, 332 p.

BONGAERTS, Jan C. and HEINRICHS, Dirk, 'Deutsche Umweltschutzgesetze und Umweltschutzinvestitionen des produzierenden Gewerbes' [German Environmental Protection Legislation and Environmental Investment by West German Manufacturing Industries], **32(3)** *Konjunkturpolitik*, 1986, 151-163.

BONGAERTS, Jan C., MEYERHOFF, Jürgen, THOMASBERGER, Claus and WITTKE, Anja, *Lösungsansätze für ein ganzheitliches System von Umweltsteuern und Sonderabgaben in der Bundesrepublik Deutschland* [A Solution for a Total Environmental System and Special Taxes in the Federal Republic of Germany], Berlin, Schriftenreihe des Instituts für Oekologische Wirtschaftsforschung Nr. 31, 1989.

BRADY, Gordon L., MALONEY, Michael T. and ABBOTT, Alden F., 'Political Limits and the Market for "BAT Medallions"', **13(1)** *Regulation*, 61-64.

BRESNAHAN, Timothy F. and YAO, Dennis A., 'The Nonpecuniary Costs of Automobile Emissions Standards', **16** *Rand Journal of Economics*, 1985, 437-455.

BRESSERS, Hans and KLOK, Pieter Jan, 'Fundamentals for a Theory of Policy Instruments', **15(3/4)** *International Journal of Social Economics*, 1988, 22-41.

BROEK, Jan H.G. van den, 'Nieuwe instrumenten voor energiebesparing' [New Instruments for Energy Savings], in COLJEE, P.D., FRANKEN, H., HEERTJE, A. and KANNING, W. (eds.), *Law and Welfare Economics*, Symposium 24 October, VU Amsterdam, 59-76.

BRUMM, Harold J., Jr. and DICK, Daniel T., 'Federal Environmental Policy and R&D on Water Pollution Abatement', **66** *American Economic Review. Papers and Proceedings*, 1976, 454-458.

BUCKLEY, Colin Hugh, 'Note: A Suggested Remedy for Toxic Injury: Class Actions, Epidemiology, and Economic Efficiency', **26** *William & Mary Law Review*, 1985, 497 ff.

CARLSON, J. Lon, JOHNSTON, Gary V. and ULEN, Thomas S., 'An Economic Analysis of Illinois' New Hazardous Waste Law - P.A. 82-572', **21** *Natural Resources Journal*, 1981, 869-885.

CHILTON, Kenneth and SHOLTZ, Anne, 'A Primer on Smog Control', **13(1)** *Regulation*, 1990, 31-40.

COGGINS, George Cameron and HARRIS, Anne Fleishel, 'The Greening of American Law?: The Recent Evolution of Federal Law for Preserving Floral Diversity', **27** *Natural Resources Journal*, 1987, 247-307.

COHEN, Mark A., 'Optimal Enforcement Strategy to Prevent Oil Spills: An Application of a Principal-Agent Model with Moral Hazard', **30** *Journal of Law and Economics*, 1987, 23-51.

CONRAD, Klaus, 'The Use of Standards and Prices for Environment Protection and Their Impact on Costs', **141** *Zeitschrift für die gesamte Staatswissenschaft*, 1985, 390-400.

CONRAD, Klaus, 'An Incentive Scheme for Optimal Pricing and Environmental Protection', **143** *Journal of Institutional and Theoretical Economics*, 1987, 402-421.

COOK, B.J., EMEL, J.L. and KASPERSON, R.E., 'Organizing and Managing Radioactive Waste Disposal as an Experiment', **9** *Journal of Policy Analysis and Management*, 1990, 339-366.

DALES, J.H., *Pollution, Property and Prices: An Essay in Policy-Making and Economics*, Toronto, University of Toronto Press, 1968, 111 p.

DASGUPTA, Partha S. and HEAL, Geoffrey M., *Economic Theory and Exhaustible Resources*, Cambridge, Cambridge University Press, 1979, 501 p.

DE CLERCQ, Marc, 'Liberaal milieubeleid' [Liberal Environmental Policy], **69** *Economisch-Statistische Berichten*, 1984, 488-493.

DE KOCK, S., 'De vervuiler betaalt: slogan of noodzaak?' [The Polluter Pays: Slogan or Necessity?], **23** *Tijdschrift voor Economie en Management*, 1978, 99-124.

DEGADT, J., 'Het Leefmilieu: relevantie van economische analyses voor een doelmatig overheidsbeleid in het geregionaliseerde België' [The Environment: Relevance of Economic Analyses for an Effective Governmental Policy in Federalized Belgium], **30** *Tijdschrift voor Economie en Management*, 1985, 367-386.

DEWEES, Donald N., EVERSON, C.K. and SIMS, W.A., *Economic Analysis of Environmental Policies*, Toronto, University of Toronto Press, 1975, 175 p.

DORFMAN, Robert, 'The Political Economy of Environmental Protection: A Conversation', **14** *Eastern Economic Journal*, 1988, 205-209.

DUDENHOFFER, Ferdi, 'The Regulation of Intensities and Productivities: Concepts in Environmental Policy', **140** *Zeitschrift für die gesamte Staatswissenschaft*, 1984, 276-287.

ELLIOTT, E. Donald, ACKERMAN, Bruce A. and MILLIAN, John C., 'Toward a Theory of Statutory Evolution: The Federalization of Environmental Law', **1** *Journal of Law, Economics, & Organization*, 1985, 313-340.

ENDRES, Alfred, 'Nonseparability and the Voluntary Approach to Externality

Problems', **4** *Journal of Environmental Economics and Management*, 1977, 209-213.

ENDRES, Alfred, 'Monopoly Power as a Means for Pollution Control?', **27** *Journal of Industrial Economics*, 1978, 185-187.

ENDRES, Alfred, 'Environmental Policy with Pollutant Interactions', in PETHIG, R. (ed.), *Public Goods and Public Allocaton Policy*, Bern, 1985, 165-199.

ENDRES, Alfred, *Umwelt- und Ressourcenökonomie* [Environmental and Resources Economics], Darmstadt, 1985, 193 p.

ENDRES, Alfred, 'Market Incentives for Pollution Control', **39** *Ricerche Economiche*, 1985, 526-539.

ENDRES, Alfred, 'The Search for Effective Pollution Control Policies', in BOTKIN, D.H. (ed.), *Man's Impact on the Global Environment*, New York, 1989, 437-454.

ENDRES, Alfred and SCHWARZE, Reimund, 'Allokationswirkungen einer Umwelt-Haftpflichtversicherung' [Allocative Effects of an Environmental Liability Insurance], in **14** *Zeitschrift für Umweltpolitik und Umweltrecht*, 1991, 1-25.

EPPLE, Dennis and VISSCHER, Michael, 'Environmental Pollution: Modelling Occurrence, Detection, and Deterrence', **27** *Journal of Law and Economics*, 1984, 29-60.

EVANS, David S., 'The Differential Effect of Regulation across Plant Size: Comment on Pashigian', **29** *Journal of Law and Economics*, 1986, 187-200.

FARBER, Daniel A., 'From Plastic Trees to Arrow's Theorem', *University of Illinois Law Review*, 1986, 337 ff. Reprinted in **19** *Cardozo Law Review*, 1987, 643-683.

FARBER, Daniel A., 'Review Essay: Environmentalism, Economics and the Public Interest', **41** *Stanford Law Review*, 1989, 1021-1043.

FARE, Rolf, GROSSKOPF, S. and PASURKA, C., 'The Effect of Environmental Regulations on the Efficiency of Electric Utilities: 1969 versus 1975', **21** *Applied Economics*, 1989, 225-235.

FAURE, Michael and VAN DEN BERGH, Roger, 'Negligence, Strict Liability and Regulation of Safety under Belgian Law: An Introductory Economic Analysis', **12** *Geneva Papers on Risk and Insurance*, 1987, 95-114.

FEINSTEIN, Jonathan S., 'The Safety Regulation of U.S. Nuclear Power Plants: Violations, Inspections, and Abnormal Occurrences', **97** *Journal of Political Economy*, 1989, 115-154.

FELDER, St., 'Sind Externalitäten in jeden Fall zu internalisieren?' [Are Externalities Always to Internalize?], **125** *Schweizerische Zeitschrift für Volkswirtschaft und Statistik*, 1989, 189-193.

FISHER, Anthony C., *Resource and Environmental Economics*, Cambridge, Cambridge University Press, 1981, 284 p.

FRAAS, Arthur and McGARTLAND, Albert, 'Alternative Fuels for Pollution Control: An Empirical Evaluation of Benefits and Costs', **8(1)** *Contemporary Policy Issues*, 1990, 62-74.

FRANK, Jürgen, Kollektive oder Individuelle Steuerung der Umwelt?' [Collective or Individual Control of the Environment?], *Kritische Justiz*, 1989, Heft 1, 36-55.

FREY, Rene L., 'Wirtschaftswachstum und Umweltqualitat: Auf der Suche nach einer neuen Wachstumspolitik' [Economic Growth and Environmental Quality: In Search of a New Growth Policy], **123** *Schweizerische Zeitschrift fur Volkswirtschaft und Statistik*, 1987, 289-315.

FREY, René L. and LEU, Robert E., 'Waldsterben: von der naturwissenschaftlichen Analyse zur Umweltpolitik' [The Death of the Forest: From a Natural Sciences Analysis to Environmental Policy], **39** *Wirtschaft und Recht*, 1987, 58-72.

FULLER, Dan A., 'Compliance, Avoidance, and Evasion: Emissions Control Under Imperfect Enforcement in Steam-Electric Generation', **18** *Rand Journal of Economics*, 1987, 124-137.

GOLLOP, Frank M. and ROBERTS, Mark J., 'Cost-minimizing Regulation of Sulfur Emissions: Regional Gains in Electric Power', **67** *Review of Economics and Statistic*, 1985, 81-90.

GORDON, Roberta G., 'Legal Incentive for Reduction, Reuse, and Recycling: A New Approach to Hazardous Waste Management', **95** *Yale Law Journal*, 1986, 810-831.

HAFNER, Gerhard, *Seerechtliche Verteilung von Nutzungsrechten* [The Assignment of Property Rights on the Sea], Vienna-New York, Springer Publishers, 1987, 533 p.

HAHN, Robert W., 'Jobs and Environmental Quality: Some Implications for Instrument Choice', **20** *Policy Sciences*, 1988, 289-306.

HAHN, Robert, *A Primer on Environmental Policy Design*, New York, Harwood Academic, 1989, 135 p.

HAHN, Robert W., 'Economic Prescriptions for Environmental Problems: How the Patient Followed the Doctor's Orders', **3(2)** *Journal of Economic Perspectives*, 1989, 95-114.

HAHN, Robert W., 'The Political Economy of Environmental Regulation: Towards a Unifying Framework', **65** *Public Choice*, 1990, 21-47.

HAHN, Robert W., 'Regulatory Constraints on Environmental Markets', **42** *Journal of Public Economics*, 1990, 149-175.

HARRIS, Richard A. and MILKIS, Sidney M., *The Politics of Regulatory Change: A Tale of Two Agencies*, New York, Oxford University Press, 1989, 331 p.

HARTMAN, Raymond S., BOZDOGAN, Kirkor and NADKARNI, Ravindra M., 'The Economic Impacts of Environmental Regulations on the U.S. Copper Industry', **10** *Bell Journal of Economics*, 1979, 589-618.

HAWKINS, Keith O., *Environment and Enforcement*, Oxford, Oxford University Press, 1982, 253 p.

HAYES, Douglas L., 'Police and Regulatory Power vs. Pecuniary Interests: The Bankrupt Hazardous Waste Site Owner Faces the Music. United States v. Nicolet, Inc., 857 F.2d 202 (3d Cir. 1988)', **30** *Natural Resources Journal*, 1990, 423-437.

HAZILLA, Michael and KOPP, Raymond J., 'Social Cost of Environmental Quality Regulations: A General Equilibrium Analysis', **98** *Journal of Political Economy*, 1990, 853-873.

HENDRICKSON, Christina, 'Abandonment of Hazardous Waste Sites in the Course of Bankruptcy Proceedings', **28** *Natural Resources Journal*, 1988, 189-198.

HOGAN, William W., 'CO2 Emission Limits: An Economic Analysis for the USA: Comments', **11(2)** *Energy Journal*, 1990, 75-85.

HREZO, Margaret S. and HREZO, William E., 'Judicial Regulation of the Environment under Posner's Economic Model of the Law', **18** *Journal of Economic Issues*, 1984, 1071-1091.

HUBER, Peter K., 'Mistaken Transfers and Profitable Infringement on Property Rights: An Economic Analysis', **49** *Louisiana Law Review*, 1988, 49-109.

HUPPES, Gjalt, 'New Instruments for Environmental Policy: A Perspective', **15(3/4)** *International Journal of Social Economics*, 1988, 42-50.

INGENE, Charles A. and YU, Eden S. H., 'Optimal Intervention Policies for a Region Facing Pollution Induced Uncertainty', **23(1)** *Annals of Regional Science*, 1989, 3-18.

ITEN, R., MAGGI, R., SCHELBERT-SYFRIG, Heidi and ZIMMERMAN, Andreas J., 'There is no such thing as a free lunch', **125** *Schweizerische Zeitschrift für Volkswirtschaft und Statistik*, 1989.

JOHNSON, Ronald D. and LIBECAP, Gary D., 'Contracting Problems and Regulation: The Case of the Fishery', **72** *American Economic Review*, 1982, 1005-1022.

JOHNSTON, George M., FRESHWATER, David and FAVERO, Philip (eds.), *Natural Resource and Environmental Policy Analysis: Cases in Applied Economics*, Boulder, Westview; 1988, 282 p.

JOYCE, Theodore J. and GROSSMAN, Michael and GOLDMAN, Fred, 'An Assessment of the Benefits of Air Pollution Control: The Case of Infant Health', **25** *Journal of Urban Economics*, 1989, 32-51.

KLAUS, J., ' Umweltökonomie und Umweltpolitik' [Environmental Economics and Environmental Politics], in WENZ, E., ISSING, O. and HOFMANN, H. (eds.), *Oekologie, Oekonomie und Jurisprudenz*, München, Florentz, 1987.

KNEESE, Allan V. and SCHULTZE, Charles L., *Pollution, Prices and Public Policy*, Brookings, Washington D.C., 1975, 125 p.

KOCH, Hans-Joachim, 'Die wirtschaftliche Vertretbarkeit nachträglicher Anordnungen' [The Economic Justification of Additional Orders], *Wirtschaft und Verwaltung*, 1983, 158-173.

KOLB, J.A. and SCHERAGA, J.D., 'Discounting the Benefits and Costs of Environmental Regulations', **9** *Journal of Policy Analysis and Management*, 1990, 381-390.

KOLSTAD, Charles D., 'Uniformity versus Differentiation in Regulating Externalities', **14** *Journal of Environmental Economics and Management*, 1987, 386-399.

KRIER, James E., 'Risk and Design', **19** *Journal of Legal Studies*, 1990, 781-790.

KULP, J. Laurence, 'Acid Rain: Causes, Effects, and Control', **13(1)** *Regulation*, 1990, 41-50.

KUNREUTHER, Howard and EASTERLING, Douglas, 'Are Risk-Benefit Tradeoffs Possible in Siting Hazardous Facilities?', **80** *American Economic Review. Papers and Proceedings*, 1990, 252-256.

LANDY, Marc K., ROBERTS, Marc J. and THOMAS, Stephen R., *The Environmental Protection Agency: Asking the Wrong Questions*, Oxford, Oxford University Press, 1990, 309 p.

LANG, Winfried, 'Comment' [on Swanson, Enforcement of Environmental Regulation], in WEIGEL, Wolfgang (ed.), *Economic Analysis of Law - A Collection of Applications*, Vienna, Österreichischer Wirtschaftsverlag, 1991, 80-82.

LEHMANN, Michael, 'Umwelthaftungsrecht dient der Internalisierung negativer Extemalitäten, Kommentar' [Environmental Liability Law Is to Internalize Negative Externalities. A Comment] (on Panther, Zivilrecht und Umweltschutz), in OTT, Claus and SCHÄFER, Hans-Bernd (eds.), *Ökonomische Probleme des Zivilrechts*, Berlin, Springer, 1991, 290-294.

LICHTENBERG, Erik, PARKER, Douglas D. and ZILBERMAN, David, 'Marginal Analysis of Welfare Costs of Environmental Policies: The Case of Pesticide Regulation', **70** *American Journal of Agricultural Economics*, 1988, 867-874.

LICHTENBERG, Erik and ZILBERMAN, David, 'Efficient Regulation of Environmental Health Risks: The Case of Groundwater Contamination in California', **39** *Ricerche Economiche*, 1985, 540-549.

LICHTENBERG, Erik and ZILBERMAN, David, 'Efficient Regulation of Environmental Health Risks', **103** *Quarterly Journal of Economics*, 1988, 167-178.

LICHTENBERG, Erik and ZILBERMAN, David and BOGEN, Kenneth T., 'Regulating Environmental Health Risks under Uncertainty: Groundwater Contamination in California', **17** *Journal of Environmental Economics and Management*, 1989, 22-34.

LIEU, T.S., 'Impacts of Air Pollution Control Costs: An Input Output Approach', **20(2)** *Annals of Regional Science*, 1986, 55-65.

LIVINGSTON, Marie Leigh, 'Evaluating the Performance of Environmental Policy: Contributions of Neoclassical, Public Choice, and Institutional Models', **21** *Journal of Economic Issues*, 1987, 281-294.

LUKEN, Ralph A., *Efficiency in Environmental Regulation*, Dordrecht, Kluwer Academic Publishers, 1991, 400 p.

LYNDON, Mary L., 'Information Economics and Chemical Toxicity: Designing Laws to Produce and Use Data', **87** *Michigan Law Review*, 1989, 1795-1861.

MAGAT, Wesley A. and VISCUSI, W. Kip, 'Effectiveness of the EPA's Regulatory Enforcement: The Case of Industrial Effluent Standards', **33** *Journal of Law & Economics*, 1990, 331-360.

MAGOULAS, Georgios, 'Privatrechtlicher Immissionsschutz, Wucher und ökonomische Analyses des Rechts' [Civil Law Protection against Harmfull Effects on the Environment, Usury and Economic Analysis of Law], in SIMON, Jürgen (ed.), *Regulierungsprobleme im Wirtschaftsrecht*, Neuwied und Darmstadt, Luchterhand, 1986, 1-24.

MALER, Karl Goran and OLSSON, Clas, 'The Cost Effectiveness of Different Solutions to the European Sulpher Problem', **17** *European Review of Agricultural Economics*, 1990, 153-166.

MALFAIT, Jean-Jacques and MOYES, Patrick, 'La gestion de la qualité de l'eau par les agences de bassin. Une tentative d'evaluation empirique' [Water Pollution

Control by the Basin Agencies: An Empirical Analysis], **41(2)** *Revue Economique*, 1990, 395-410.

MALONEY, Michael T. and BRADY, Gordon L., 'Capital Turnover and Marketable Pollution Rights', **31** *Journal of Law and Economics*, 1988, 203-226.

MALONEY, Michael T. and McCORMICK, Robert E., 'A Positive Theory of Environmental Quality Regulation', **25** *Journal of Law and Economics*, 1982, 99-123.

MALONEY, Michael T. and YANDLE, Bruce, 'Estimation of the Cost of Air Pollution Control Regulation', **11** *Journal of Environmental Economics and Management*, 1984, 244-263.

MATTEI, Ugo, 'I modelli nella tutela dell'ambiente' [The Models for the Protection of the Environment], *Rivista di diritto civile*, 1985, II, 389-427.

McCONNELL, Virginia D. and SCHWAB, Robert M., 'The Impact of Environmental Regulation on Industry Location Decisions: The Motor Vehicle Industry', **66** *Land Economics*, 1990, 67-81.

McGARITY, Thomas O., 'Media Quality, Technology, and Cost Benefit Balancing Strategies for Health and Environmental Regulation', **46(3)** *Law and Contemporary Problems*, 1983, 159-233.

McKEAN, Roland N., 'Enforcement Costs in Environmental and Safety Regulation', **6** *Policy Analysis*, 1980, 261-290.

McSWEENY, William T. and SHORTLE, James S., 'Probabilistic Cost Effectiveness in Agricultural Nonpoint Pollution Control', **22** *Southern Journal of Agricultural Economics*, 1990, 95-104.

MEINBERG, Volker, 'Empirische Erkentnissen zum Vollzug des Umweltstrafrechts' [Empirical Insights Concerning the Enforcement of Environmental Criminal Law], **100** *Zeitschrift für die gesamte Strafrechtswissenschaft*, 1988, 112-157.

MENDELSOHN, Robert, 'Regulating Heterogeneous Emissions', **13** *Journal of Environmental Economics and Management*, 1986, 301-312.

MENELL, Peter S., 'The Limitations of Legal Institutions for Addressing Environmental Risks', **5(3)** *Journal of Economic Perspectives*, 1991, 93-113.

MERAN, Georg and SCHWALBE, Ulrich, 'Pollution Control and Collective Penalties', **143** *Journal of Institutional and Theoretical Economics*, 1987, 616-629.

MEYER, Richard and YANDLE, Bruce, 'The Political Economy of Acid Rain', **7** *Cato Journal*, 1987, 527-545.

MILLS, Edwin S. (ed.), *Economic Analysis of Environmental Problems*, New York, National Bureau of Economic Research, 1975, 472p.

MISHAN, Ezra J., 'The Economics of Disamenity', **14** *Natural Resources Journal*, 1974, 55-86.

MITCHELL, Robert Cameron and CARSON, Richard T., 'Property Rights, Protest, and the Siting of Hazardous Waste Facilities', **76** *American Economic Review. Papers and Proceedings*, 1986, 285-290.

MOHR, Ernst, 'Courts of Appeal, Bureaucracies and Conditional Project Permits: The Role of Negotiating Non-Exclusive Property Rights Over the Environment', **146** *Journal of Institutional and Theoretical Economics*, 1990, 601-616.

NAUGHTON, Michael and SEBOLD, Frederick and MAYER, Thomas, 'The Impacts of the California Beverage Container Recycling and Litter Reduction Act on Consumers', **24** *Journal of Consumer Affairs*, 1990, 190-1220.

NENTJES, A., 'Van wie is het milieu?' [Who Owns the Environment?], **39(10)** *Ars Aequi*, 1990, 706-713.

NENTJES, Andries, 'Enforcement of Environmental Regulation', in WEIGEL, Wolfgang (ed.), *Economic Analysis of Law - A Collection of Applications*, Vienna, Österreichischer Wirtschaftsverlag, 1991, 54-65.

NG, Lawrence, 'A DRASTIC Approach to Controlling Groundwater Pollution', **98** *Yale Law Journal*, 1989, 773-791.

NICHOLS, Elizabeth and WILDAVSKY, Aaron, 'Nuclear Power Regulation: Seeking Safety, Doing Harm?', **11(1)** *Regulation*, 1987, 45-53.

NOLL, Roger G. and KRIER, James E., 'Some Implications of Cognitive Psychology for Risk Regulation', **19** *Journal of Legal Studies*, 1990, 747-779.

OATES, Wallace E., PORTNEY, Paul R. and McGARTLAND, Albert M., 'The Net Benefits of Incentive-Based Regulation: A Case Study of Environmental Standard Setting', **79** *American Economic Review*, 1989, 1233-1242.

OLSON, Lars J., 'The Search for a Safe Environment: The Economics of Screening and Regulating Environmental Hazards', **19** *Journal of Environmental Economics and Management*, 1990, 1-18.

PANTHER, Stephan, 'Zivilrecht und Umweltschutz' [Civil Law and Environmental Protection], in OTT, Claus and SCHÄFER, Hans-Bernd (eds.), *Ökonomische Probleme des Zivilrechts*, Berlin, Springer, 1991, 267-289

PASHIGIAN, B. Peter, 'The Effect of Environmental Regulation on Optimal Plant Size and Factor Shares', **27** *Journal of Law and Economics*, 1984, 1-28.

PASHIGIAN, B. Peter, 'Reply to Evans', **29** *Journal of Law and Economics*, 1986, 201-209.

PATE-CORNELL, M.E., 'Risk Analysis and Relevance of Uncertainties in Nuclear Safety Decisions', in BAILEY, Elizabeth E. (ed.), *Public Regulation: New Perspectives on Institutions and Policies*, Cambridge (Mass.), MIT Press, 1987, 227-53.

PEARCE, D.W., *Environmental Economics*, London, Langman, 1976, 202p.

PERSKY, Allan, 'Abatement of Pollution in Models with Stochastic Penalties', **55** *Southern Economic Journal*, 1988, 463-471.

PERSKY, Allan, 'An Uncertain Fine for Pollution as a Fixed Cost that Affects Output', **33(1)** *American Economist*, 1989, 24-27.

PESKIN, Henry M., PORTNEY, Paul R. and KNEESE, Allan V. (eds.), *Environmental Regulation and the U.S. Economy*, Baltimore, John Hopkins University Press, 1981, 163 p.

POINT, Patrick, 'Entreprises, normes d'environnement et incitations à reduire les delais de mise en conformité' [Firms, Environmental Standards and Incentives to Promote Compliance], **100** *Revue d'économique politique*, 1990, 260-282.

PRIEST, W. Curtiss, *Risks, Concerns, and Social Regulation: Forces that Led to Laws on Health, Safety, and the Environment*, Boulder, Westview Press, 1988, 204 p.

QUINN, Robert and YANDLE, Bruce, 'Expenditures on Air Pollution Control under Federal Regulation', **16(3)** *Review of Regional Studies*, 1986, 11-16.

RICHARDSON, Genevra, BURROWS, Paul and OGUS, Anthony I., *Policing Pollution: A Study of Regulation and Enforcement*, Oxford, Clarendon, 1982, 204 p.

ROB, Rafael, 'Pollution Claim Settlements under Private Information', **47** *Journal of Economic Theory*, 1989, 307-333.

ROSS, H. Laurence, 'Law, Science and Accidents: The British Road Safety Act of 1967', **2** *Journal of Legal Studies*, 1973, 1-78.

ROUMASSET, James A. and SMITH, Kirk R., 'Exposure Trading: An Approach to More Efficient Air Pollution Control', **18** *Journal of Environmental Economics and Management*, 1990, 276-291.

RUNGE, Carlisle Ford, 'Induced Agricultural Innovation and Environmental Quality: The Case of Groundwater Regulation', **63** *Land Economics*, 1987, 249-258.

TRIBE, Laurence H., 'Ways Not to Think About Plastic Trees: New Foundations For Environmental Law', **83** *Yale Law Journal*, 1974, 1315-1348.

SAGOFF, Mark, 'Economic Theory and Environmental Law', **79** *Michigan Law Review*, 1981, 1393 ff.

SAGOFF, Mark, *The Economy of the Earth: Philosophy, Law, and the Environment*, Cambridge, Cambridge University Press, 1988, 271 p.

SAJó, András, 'A környezetszennyezés leküzdését célzó gazdasági jogi eszközök' [The Economic Law Devices in Order to Defeat the Pollution], **4** *Allam- és Jogtudomány*, 1986, 545-568.

SAJó, András, 'Környezetvédelmi jogunk továbbfejlesztéséröl' [On the Improvement of Our Laws on the Protection of the Environment], **5** *Jogtudományi Közlöny*, 1987, 213-220.

SALAZAR, Debra J., 'Regulatory Policies and Environment: State Regulation of Logging Practices', **12** *Research in Law and Economics*, 1989, 95-117.

SAMUELS, Warren J., 'Ecosystem, Policy and the Problem of Power', **2** *Environmental Affairs*, 1973, 580-596.

SCHELBERT-SYFRIG, Heidi, LANG, Th., BUSE, I., HENZMAN, J., MAGGI, R., ITEN, R. and NIELSEN, C., *Wertvolle Umwelt* [Valuable Environment], Zurich, Schriftenreihe Wirtschaft und Gesellschaft der Zürcher Kantonalbank, September 1988.

SCHELBERT-SYFRIG, Heidi and ZIMMERMANN, Andreas J., 'Konkurrenz und Umweltschutz. Wald und Holzwirtschaft zwischen Okonomie und Okologie' [Competition and Environment Protection. Forest and Forestry Between Economics and Ecology], **124** *Schweizerische Zeitschrift fur Volkswirtschaft und Statistik*, 1988, 289-302.

SCHELLING, Thomas C. (ed.), *Incentives for Environmental Protection*, Cambridge (Mass.), MIT Press, 1983, 355 p.

SHORTLE, James S. and DUNN, James W., 'The Relative Efficiency of Agricultural Source Water Pollution Control Policies', **68** *American Journal of Agricultural Economics*, 1986, 668-677.

SHORTLE, James S. and WILLETT, Keith D., 'The Incidence of Water Pollution

Control Costs: Partial vs. General Equilibrium Computations', **17(2)** *Growth and Change*, 1986, 32-43.

SIMONICH, William L., *Government Antismoking Policies*, New York, Peter Lang, 1991, 300 p.

SINGER, S. Fred, 'Environmental Strategies with Uncertain Science', **13(1)** *Regulation*, 1990, 65-70.

SJONES, Carol Adaire and SCOTCHMER, Suzanne, 'The Social Cost of Uniform Regulatory Standards in a Hierarchical Government', **19** *Journal of Environmental Economics and Management*, 1990, 61-72.

SMITH, Douglas A. and VODDEN, Keith, 'Global Environmental Policy: The Case of Ozone Depletion', **15** *Canadian Public Policy*, 1989, 413-423.

SMITH, V. Kerry and DESVOUSGES, William H., 'The Valuation of Environmental Risks and Hazardous Waste Policy', **64** *Land Economics*, 1988, 211-219.

SOLOMON, Lewis D. and FREEDBERG, Bradley S., 'The Greenhouse Effect: A Legal and Policy Analysis', **20** *Environmental Law*, 1990, 83 ff.

SPULBER, Daniel F., 'Optimal Environmental Regulation under Asymmetric Information', **35** *Journal of Public Economics*, 1988, 163-181.

STROUP, Richard L., 'Environmental Policy', **12(3)** *Regulation*, 1988, 43-49.

SWANSON, Timothy M., 'Enforcement of Environmental Regulation', in WEIGEL, Wolfgang (ed.), *Economic Analysis of Law - A Collection of Applications*, Vienna, Österreichischer Wirtschaftsverlag, 1991, 67-78.

TYBOUT, Richard A., 'Pricing Pollution and Other Negative Externalities', **3** *Bell Journal of Economics*, 1972, 252-266.

TYBOUT, Richard A., 'Pricing of Pollution: Reply', **4** *Bell Journal of Economics*, 1973, 320-321.

ULEN, Thomas S., HESTER, Mark A. and JOHNSON, Gary V., 'Minnesota's Environmental Response and Liability Act: An Economic Justification', **15** *Environmental Law Reporter*, 1985, 10109-10119.

VANWILDEMEERSCH, J., 'Industrie en milieu' [Industry and Environment], in *18de Vlaams Wetenschappelijk Economisch Congres, Brussel 8 en 9 mei 1987, Sociaal-economische Deregulering*, Brussel, V.E.H.U.B., 1987, 399-405.

VISCUSI, W. Kip, 'Frameworks for Analyzing the Effects of Risk and Environmental Regulations on Productivity', **73** *American Economic Review*, 1983, 793-7801.

WALLACE, Myles S. and WATSON, Sharon B. and YANDLE, Bruce, 'Environment Regulation: A Financial Markets Test', **28(1)** *Quarterly Review of Economics and Business*, 1988, 69-87.

WALZ, W. Rainer, ' Marktbezogener Umweltschutz und privatrechtlicher Immissionsschutz - Kann Umweltökonomie einen Beitrag zur Funktionsbestimmung privatrechtlicher Immissionsschutzregeln leisten?' [Market Related Environmental Protection and Private Law Protection against Noxious Substances - Can Environmental Economics Offer a Contribution concerning the Function of Private Law Protection against Noxious Substances Rules?], in BAUR, P., ESSER, J., KÜBLER, F. and STEINDORFF, E.(eds.),

Funktionswandel der Privatrechtsinstitutionen, Festschrift für Ludwig Raiser, Tübingen, 1974, 185-222.

WIERSMA, D., *De efficiëntie van een marktconform milieubeleid* [The Efficiency of an Environmental Policy in Accordance with Market Principles], diss. Groningen, 1989.

WIRL, Franz, 'Impact of Environmental Regulation on Economic Activity Austria', **16** *Empirica*, 1989, 209-233.

WITTMAN, Donald, 'Efficient Rules in Highway Safety and Sports Activity', **72** *American Economic Review*, 1982, 78-90.

WORTHEN, Kevin J., 'The Last Shall Be First, and the First Last: Ruminations on the Past, Present and Future Course of Government Regulation of Hazardous Pollutants', *Brigham Young University*, 1989, 1113-1154.

X, 'Note: Liability of Parent Corporations for Hazardous Waste Cleanup and Damages', **99** *Harvard Law Review*, 1986, 986-1003.

YANDLE, Bruce, *The Political Limits of Environmental Regulation: Tracking the Unicorn*, Westport, Greenwood Press, 1989, 180 p.

YAO, Dennis A., 'Strategic Responses to Automobile Emissions Control: A Game Theoretic Analysis', **15** *Journal of Environmental Economics and Management*, 1988, 419-438.

3600 Zoning. Land Use Regulation

AMANDES, Christopher B., 'Comment: Controlling Land Surface Subsidence: A Proposal for a Market-Based Regulatory Scheme', **31** *UCLA Law Review*, 1984, 1208 ff.

ATWOOD, James R., 'An Economic Analysis of Land Use Conflicts', **21** *Stanford Law Review*, 1969, 293-315.

AULT, Richard W. and EKELUND, Robert B., Jr., 'Rent Seeking in a Static Model of Zoning', **16(1)** *American Real Estate and Urban Economics Association Journal*, 1988, 69-76.

BARTON, Stephen E., 'Property Rights and Human Rights: Efficiency and Democracy as Criteria for Regulatory Reform', **17** *Journal of Economic Issues*, 1983, 915-930.

BECK, Roger L. and HUSSEY, Donald, 'Politics, Property Rights, and Cottage Development', **15** *Canadian Public Policy*, 1989, 25-33.

BEEN, Vicki, '"Exit" as a Constraint of Land Use Exactions: Rethinking the Unconstitutional Conditions Doctrine', **91** *Columbia Law Review*, 1991, 473-545.

BIGELOW, Ronald J., 'Selection of Wilderness Areas: An Economic Framework for Decision-Making', **11** *Land Use and Environmental Law Review*, 1980, 329-354.

BLACK, Renee Allee, 'State Control of Mining on Federal Land: Environmental or Land Use Regulation?', **28** *Natural Resources Journal*, 1988, 873-881.

BOUCKAERT, Boudewijn, 'Economische analyse van het stadsverval in België: naar een geïntegreerd stadsrenovatiebeleid?' [Economic Analysis of City Decline in Belgium: Towards an Integrated City Renovation Policy?], *Planologische Discussiebijdragen*, 1988, 53-61.

BOUCKAERT, Boudewijn, 'Zin of Onzin van Planning' [Sense or Nonsense of Planning], *Ruimtelijke Planning*, 1990, Afl. 25, II.D.1.b., 19 p.

BOUCKAERT, Boudewijn, 'Eigendomsrechten vanuit rechtseconomisch perspectief' [Property Rights from an Economic Perspective], **39** *Ars Aequi*, 1990, 777-786.

BROWN, Jennifer G., 'Note: Concomitant Agreement Zoning: An Economic Analysis', *University of Illinois Law Review*, 1985, 89 ff.

BUTTLER, Hans Jurg, 'Equilibrium of a Residential City, Attributes of Housing, and Land Use Zoning', **18** *Urban Studies*, 1981, 23-39.

CHANDLER, Cleveland A. and DAVID, Wilfred L., 'Alternative Economic Policies for the Revitalization of U.S. Central Cities', **69** *American Economic Review, Papers and Proceedings*, 1979, 288-297.

CHRESSANTHIS, George A., 'The Impact of Zoning Changes on Housing Prices: A Time Series Analysis', **17(3)** *Growth and Change*, 1986, 49-70.

CLAPP, John M., 'The Impact of Inclusionary Zoning on the Location and Type of Construction Activity', **9** *American Real Estate and Urban Economics Association Journal*, 1981, 436-456.

CRECINE, John P., DAVIS, Otto A., and JACKSON, John E., 'Urban Property Markets: Some Empirical Results and Their Implications Municipal Zoning',

10 *Journal of Law and Economics*, 1967, 79-99.

CRONE, Theodore M., 'Elements of an Economic Justification for Municipal Zoning', **14** *Journal of Urban Economics*, 1983, 168-183.

DANIELSON, Michael N., 'The Politics of Exclusionary Zoning in Suburbia', **91** *Political Science Quarterly*, 1976, 1-18.

DE LEEUW, Frank, LEAMAN, Sam H. and BLANK, Helen, *The Design of a Housing Allowance*, Urban Institute, 1970. Reprinted in ACKERMAN, Bruce A. (ed.), *Economic Foundations of Property a Law*, Boston, Little Brown, 1975, 218-236.

DEYAK, Timothy A. and SMITH, V. Kerry, 'Residential Property Values and Air Pollution: Some New Evidence', **14** *Quarterly Review of Economics & Business*, 1974, 93 ff.

DUNHAM, Allison, 'City Planning: An Analysis of the Content of the Master Plan', **1** *Journal of Law and Economics*, 1958, 170-186.

ELLICKSON, Robert C., 'Alternatives to Zoning: Covenants, Nuisance Rules and Fines as Land Use Controls', **40** *University of Chicago Law Review*, 1973, 681-781. Reprinted in ACKERMAN, Bruce A., *Economic Foundations of Property a Law*, Boston, Little Brown, 1975, 265-301.

ELLICKSON, Robert C., 'Suburban Growth Controls: An Economic and Legal Analysis', **86** *Yale Law Journal*, 1977, 385-511.

ELLICKSON, Robert C., 'The Irony of Inclusionary Zoning', **54** *Southern California Law Review*, 1981, 1167-1216. Reprinted in **11** *Land Use and Environment Law Review*, 1983, 197-216.

ELLICKSON, Robert C., 'The Effect of Growth Controls on Housing Prices on the San Francisco Peninsula', **4** *Stanford Environmental Annual*, 1982, 3-20.

ELLICKSON, Robert C., 'Three Systems of Land-Use Control', **13** *Harvard Journal of Law & Public Policy*, 1990, 67-71.

ELLIS, Neil R. (Student Note), 'Zoning for the Regional Welfare', **89** *Yale Law Journal*, 1980, 748-768.

ELLSON, Richard W. and MCDERMOTT, John, 'Zoning Uncertainty and the Urban Land Development Firm', **22** *Journal of Urban Economics*, 1987, 209-222.

EPPLE, Dennis and ROMER, Thomas and FILIMON, Radu, 'Community Development with Endogenous Land Use Controls', **35** *Journal of Public Economics*, 1988, 133-162.

ERVIN, David E. and FITCH, James B., 'Evaluating Alternative Compensation and Recapture Techniques for Expanded Public Control of Land Use: A Reply to Dr. Scholvinck', **20** *Natural Resources Journal*, 1980, 551-554.

FISCH, Oscar, 'Optimal City Size, the Economic Theory of Clubs and Exclusionary Zoning', **24** *Public Choice*, 1975, 59-70.

FISCHEL, William A., 'A Property Rights Approach to Municipal Zoning', **54** *Land Economics*, 1978, 64-81.

FISCHEL, William A., 'Equity and Efficiency Aspects of Zoning Reform', **27** *Public Policy*, 1979, 301-331.

FISCHEL, William A., 'Externalities and Zoning', **35** *Public Choice*, 1980, 37-43.

FISCHEL, William A., 'Zoning and the Exercise of Monopoly Power: A Reevaluation', **8** *Journal of Urban Economics*, 1980, 283-293.

FISCHEL, William A., *The Economics of Zoning Laws: A Property Rights Approach to American Land Use Controls*, Baltimore, John Hopkins University Press, 1985, 372 p.

FISCHEL, William A., 'The Economics of Land Use Exactions: A Property Rights Analysis', **50(1)** *Law and Contemporary Problems*, 1987, 101-113.

FUJITA, Masahisa, *Urban Economic Theory. Land Use and City Size*, New York, Cambridge University Press, 1989, 366 p.

GIERTZ, J. Fred, 'A Note on Zoning and Monopoly', **8(1)** *Growth and Change*,- 1977, 50-52.

GOETZ, Michael L. and WOFFORD, Larry E., 'The Motivation for Zoning: Efficiency or Wealth Redistribution?', **55** *Land Economics*, 1979, 472-485.

GOLDBERG, Fred, 'Equalization of Municipal Services: The Economics of Serrano and Shaw', **82** *Yale Law Journal*, 1972, 89-122. Reprinted in ACKERMAN, Bruce A. (ed.), *Economic Foundations of Property a Law*, Boston, Little Brown, 1975, 247-263.

GRIESON, Ronald E. and WHITE, James R., 'The Effects of Zoning on Structure and Land Markets', **10** *Journal of Urban Economics*, 1981, 271-285.

GURR, Ted Robert and KING, Desmond S., 'The Post-Industrial City in Transition from Private to Public', in LANE, Jan-Erik (ed.), *State and Market. The Politics of the Public and the Private*, London, Sage, 1985, 271-293.

HAMILTON, Bruce W., 'Zoning and Property Taxation in a System of Local Governments', **12** *Urban Studies*, 1975, 205-211.

HAMILTON, Bruce W., 'Zoning and the Exercise of Monopoly Power', **5** *Journal of Urban Economics*, 1978, 116-130.

HANUSHEK, Eric A. and QUIGLEY, John M., 'Commercial Land Use Regulation and Local Government Finance', **80** *American Economic Review. Papers and Proceedings*, 1990, 176-180.

HEIKKILA, Eric and HUTTON, Thomas A., 'Toward an Evaluative Framework for Land Use Policy in Industrial Districts of the Urban Core: A Qualitative Analysis of the Exclusionary Zoning Approach', **23** *Urban Studies*, 1986, 47-60.

HELPMAN, Elhanan and PINES, David, 'Land and Zoning in a Urban Economy: Further Results', **67** *American Economic Review*, 1977, 982-986.

HENDERSON, J. Vernon, 'The Impact of Zoning Policies Which Regulate Housing Quality', **18** *Journal of Urban Economics*, 1985, 302-312.

HENNEBERRY, David M. and BARROWS, Richard L., 'Capitalization of Exclusive Agricultural Zoning into Farmland Prices', **66** *Land Economics*, 1990, 249-258.

JAAKSON, Reiner, 'Zoning to Regulate On Water Recreation', **47** *Land Economics*, 1971, 382-388.

JAFFE, Austin J., 'Introduction to the Economics of Urban Property Rights', **10** *Research in Law and Economics*, 1987, 1-4.

JOHNSON, Michael W., 'Mobility, Market Failure and Zoning Laws', **12(2)** *Atlantic Economic Journal*, 1984, 71.

JUD, G. Donald, 'The Effects of Zoning on Single Family Residential Property Values: Charlotte, North Carolina', **56** *Land Economics*, 1980, 142-154.

KATZ, Lawrence and ROSEN, Kenneth T., The Interjurisdictional Effects of Growth Controls on Housing Prices', **30** *Journal of Law and Economics*, 1987, 149-160.

KAU, James B. and RUBIN, Paul H., 'The Political Economy of Urban Land Use', **10** *Research in Law and Economics*, 1987, 5-26.

KIRP, David L., '"Growth Management" Zoning, Public Policy, and the Courts', **2** *Policy Analysis*, 1976, 431-458.

KOMESAR, Neil K., 'Housing, Zoning, and the Public Interest', in WEISBROD, Burton A., et al. (eds.), *Public Interest Law. An Economic and Institutional Analysis*, Berkeley, University of California Press, 1978, 218-250.

KONUKIEWITZ, Manfred, 'Taming the Housing Market', in LANE, Jan-Erik (ed.), *State and Market. The Politics of the Public and the Private*, London, Sage, 1985, 181-198.

LAFFERTY, Ronald N. and FRECH, H.E. III, 'Community Environment and the Market Value of Single-Family Homes: the Effect of the Dispersion of Land Uses', **21** *Journal of Law and Economics*, 1978, 381-394.

LEVIN, Martin A., 'Urban Politics and Judicial Behavior', **1** *Journal of Legal Studies*, 1972, 193-221.

LODISE, John P., 'Retroactive Compensation and the Illusion of Economic Efficiency: An Analysis of the First English Decision', **35** *UCLA Law Review*, 1988, 1267-1290.

MARK, Jonathan H. and GOLDBERG, Michael A., 'Land Use Controls: The Case of Zoning in the Vancouver Area', **9** *American Real Estate and Urban Economics Association Journal*, 1981, 418-435.

MARK, Jonathan H. and GOLDBERG, Michael A., 'A Study of the Impacts of Zoning on Housing Values over Time', **20** *Journal of Urban Economics*, 1986, 257-273.

MASER, Steven M., RIKER, William H. and ROSETT, Richard N., 'The Effects of Zoning and Externalities on the Price of Land: An Empirical Analysis of Monroe County, New York', **20** *Journal of Law and Economics*, 1977, 111-132.

McMILLEN, Daniel P. and McDONALD, John F., 'A Two-Limit Tobit Model of Suburban Land-Use Zoning', **66** *Land Economics*, 1990, 272-282.

MILLS, David E., 'Is Zoning a Negative-Sum Game?', **65** *Land Economics*, 1989, 1-12.

MILLS, David E., 'Zoning Rights and Land Development Timing', **66** *Land Economics*, 1990, 283-293.

MILLS, Edwin S. and MACKINNON, Robert H., 'Notes on the New Urban Economics', **4** *Bell Journal of Economics*, 1973, 235-263.

MOSS, William G., 'Large Lot Zoning, Property Taxes, and Metropolitan Area', **4** *Journal of Urban Economics*, 1977, 408-427.

MUTH, Richard, *Cities and Housing*, Chicago, University of Chicago Press, 1969, 106-112. Reprinted in ACKERMAN, Bruce A., *Economic Foundations of*

Property a Law, Boston, Little Brown, 1975, 302 ff.

NATOLI, Salvatore J., 'Zoning and the Development of Urban Land Use Patterns', **47** *Economic Geography*, 1971, 171-184.

NEIMAN, Max, 'Zoning Policy, Income Clustering and Suburban Change', **61** *Social Science Quarterly*, 1980, 666-675.

NIEMI, Ernest G., 'Oregon's Land Use Program and Industrial Development: How Does the Program Affect Oregon's Economy?', **14** *Environmental Law*, 1984, 707-711.

ORON, Y., PINES, D. and SHESHINSKI, E., 'Optimum vs. Equilibrium Land Use Pattern and Congesbon Toll', **4** *Bell Journal of Economics*, 1973, 619-636.

PINES, David and SADKA, Efraim, 'Zoning, First Best, Second Best, and Third Best Criteria for Allocating Land for Roads', **17** *Journal of Urban Economics*, 1985, 167-183.

POGODZINSKI, J. Michael and SASS, Tim R., 'The Economic Theory of Zoning: A Critical Review', **66** *Land Economics*, 1990, 294-314.

POLLAKOWSKI, Henry O. and WACHTER, Susan M., 'The Effects of Land-Use Constraints on Housing Prices', **66** *Land Economics*, 1990, 315-324.

RICKETTS, M., 'Housing Policy: Towards a Public Choice Perspective', **1** *Journal of Public Policy*, 1981, 501-527.

ROLLESTON, Barbara Sherman, 'Determinants of Restrictive Suburban Zoning: An Empirical Analysis', **21** *Journal of Urban Economics*, 1987, 1-21.

ROSE, Louis A., 'Urban Land Supply: Natural and Contrived Restrictions', **25** *Journal of Urban Economics*, 1989, 325-345.

ROSIERS, Marc, 'De Effecten van Leegstand op de Huisvesting' [The Effects of Unoccupied Houses on Housing], **40** *Economisch en Sociaal Tijdschrift*, 1986, 67-85.

RUBINFELD, Daniel L., 'Suburban Employment and Zoning: A General Equilibrium Analysis', **18** *Journal of Regional Science*, 1978, 33-44.

RUETER, Frederick H., 'Externalities in Urban property Markets: An Empirical Test of the Zoning Ordinance of Pitssburgh', **16** *Journal of Law and Economics*, 1973, 313-349.

SCHELLING, Thomas C., 'A Process of Residential Segregation: Neighborhood Tipping', in ACKERMAN, Bruce A. (ed.), *Economic Foundations of Property a Law*, Boston, Little Brown, 1975, 307-328.

SCHOLVINCK, Johan B.W., 'Evaluating Alternative Compensation and Recapture Techniques for Expanded Public Control of Land Use: A Comment', **20** *Natural Resources Journal*, 1980, 153-158.

SIEGAN, Bernard H., 'Non-zoning in Houston', **13** *Journal of Law and Economics*, 1970, 71-147.

SIEGAN, Bernard H., *Land Use Without Zoning*, 1972.

SIEGAN, Bernard H., 'Land Use Regulations Should Preserve Only Vital and Pressing Governmental Interests', **10** *Cato Journal*, 1990, 127-158.

SOLOW, R.M., 'Congestion Cost and the Use of Land for Streets', **4** *Bell Journal of Economics*, 1973, 602-618.

STEPHEN, Frank H. and YOUNG, E., 'An Economic Insight on the Judicial Control of Planning Authorities Discretion', *Urban Law and Policy*, 1985.

STULL, William J., 'Land Use and Zoning in an Urban Economy', **64** *American Economic Review*, 1974, 337-347.

STULL, William J., 'Community Environment, Zoning, and the Market Value of Single-Family Homes', **18** *Journal of Law and Economics*, 1975, 535-557.

SULLIVAN, Arthur M., 'Land Use and Zoning in the Central Business District', **14** *Regional Science and Urban Economics*, 1984, 521-532.

SULLIVAN, Arthur M., 'Large Lot Zoning as Second Best Policy', **24** *Journal of Regional Science*, 1984, 581-589.

TOPHAM, Neville, 'A Note on Zoning and Property Taxation in a System of Local Governments', **19** *Urban Studies*, 1982, 197-199.

VAILLANCOURT, Francois and MONTY, Luc, 'The Effect of Agricultural Zoning on Land Prices, Quebec, 1975 1981', **61** *Land Economics*, 1985, 36-42.

VOGEL, Kenneth R., 'Exclusionary Zoning and the Provision of Education: An Effect of Southern Burlington County N.A.A.C.P. v. Township of Mount Laurel', **8** *Journal of Urban Economics*, 1980, 294-2312.

WALLACE, Nancy E., 'The Consistency Doctrine and the Market Effects of Zoning Undeveloped Land', **10** *Research in Law and Economics*, 1987, 27-52.

WALLACE, Nancy E., 'The Market Effects of Zoning Undeveloped Land: Does Zoning Follow the Market?', **23** *Journal of Urban Economics*, 1988, 307-326.

WEGNER, Judith Welch, 'Moving Toward the Bargaining Table: Contract Zoning, Development Agreements, and the Theoretical Foundations of Government Land Use Deals', **65** *North Carolina Law Review*, 1987, 957 ff.

WHIPPLE, William, Jr., 'Optimizing Investment in Flood Control and Floodplain Zoning', **5** *Water Resources Research*, 1969, 761-766.

WHITE, James R., 'Large Lot Zoning and Subdivision Costs: A Test', **23** *Journal of Urban Economics*, 1988, 370-384.

WHITE, Michelle J., 'Self Interest in the Suburbs: The Trend toward No Growth Zoning', **4** *Policy Analysis*, 1978, 185-203.

WHITE, Michelle J., 'Job Suburbanization, Zoning and the Welfare of Urban Minority Groups', **5** *Journal of Urban Economics*, 1978, 219-240.

WHITE, Michelle J., 'Suburban Growth Controls: Liability Rules and Pigovian Taxes', **8** *Journal of Legal Studies*, 1979, 207-230.

WHITE, Michelle J. and WITTMAN, Donald, 'Optimal Spatial Location under Pollution: Liability Rules and Zoning', **10** *Journal of Legal Studies*, 1981, 249-268.

WILLIAMS, Oliver P., 'Governmental Intervention into Local Economies under Market Conditions: The Case of Urban Renewal', in LANE, Jan-Erik (ed.), *State and Market. The Politics of the Public and the Private*, London, Sage, 1985, 142-157.

WIZARD, K.F., 'Air Pollution and Property Values: A Study of the St. Louis Area', **13** *J. Regional Sci.*, 1973, 91 ff.

WOLFRAM, Gary, 'The Sale of Development Rights and Zoning in the Preservation of Open Space: Lindahl Equilibrium and a Case Study', **57** *Land Economics*, 1981, 398-3413.

X, 'Note: Zoning for the Regional Welfare', **89** *Yale Law Journal*, 1980, 748-768.

3700 Pollution Tax

BISHOP, John A., 'Pigovian Taxes and "Full" Property Rights', **14** *Eastern Economic Journal*, 1988, 193-196.

BONGAERTS, Jan C., MEYERHOFF, Jürgen, THOMASBERGER, Claus and WITTKE, Anja, *Lösungsansätze für ein ganzheitliches System von Umweltsteuern und Sonderabgaben in der Bundesrepublik Deutschland* [A Solution for a Total Environmental System and Special Taxes in the Federal Republic of Germany], Berlin, Schriftenreihe des Instituts für Oekologische Wirtschaftsforschung Nr. 31, 1989.

BRAULKE, M. and ENDRES, Alfred, 'On the Economics of Affluent Charges', **18** *Canadian Journal of Economics*, 1985, 891-897.

BRITO, Dagobert L. and INTRILIGATOR, Michael D., 'Stock Externalities, Pigovian Taxation and Dynamic Stability', **33** *Journal of Public Economics*, 1987, 59-72.

BROOKS, Michael A. and HEIJDRA, Ben J., 'Rent Seeking and Pollution Taxation: An Extension', **54** *Southern Economic Journal*, 1987, 335-342.

BROWN, Gardner M., Jr. and JOHNSON, Ralph W., 'Pollution Control by Effluent Charges: It Works in the Federal Republic of Germany, Why Not in the U.S.?', **24** *Natural Resources Journal*, 1984, 929-966.

BROWN, John Prather and HOLAHAN, William L., 'Taxes and Legal Rules for the Control of Externalities When There Are Strategic Responses', **9** *Journal of Legal Studies*, 1980, 165-178.

CARLSON, J. Lon and BAUSELL, Charles W., Jr., 'Financing Superfund: An Evaluation of Alternative Tax Mechanisms', **27** *Natural Resources Journal*, 1987, 103-122.

CARLTON, Dennis W. and LOURY, Glenn C., 'The Limitation of Pigouvian Taxes as a Long-run Remedy for Externalities: An Extension of Results', **101** *Quarterly Journal of Economics*, 1986, 631-634.

CONRAD, Klaus, 'Taxes on Emissions, Conjectural Variations and Overinvestment in Abatement Capital', **146** *Journal of Institutional and Theoretical Economics*, 1990, 281-297.

DE MEZA, David, 'The Efficacy of Effluent Charges', **21** *Canadian Journal of Economics*, 1988, 182-186.

ENDRES, Alfred, 'Do Effluent Charges (Always) Reduce Environmental Damage?', **35** *Oxford Economic Papers*, 1983, 254-261.

ENDRES, Alfred, 'Effluent Charges and Environmental Damage: Comment', **37** *Oxford Economic Papers*, 1985, 703-704.

ETHRIDGE, D., 'User Charges as a Means for Pollution Control: the Case of Sewer Surcharges', **3** *Bell Journal of Economics*, 1972, 346-353.

FRANKEL, Marvin, 'Taxes, Pollution, and Optimal Abatement in an Urban Economy', **22(2)** *Journal of Urban Economics*, 1987, 117-135.

GERMAIN, Marc , 'Externalités, taxation et traitement de la pollution dans le cadre d'un duopole de Cournot' [Externalities, Taxation and Dealing with Pollution in the Case of a Cournot Duopoly], **55** *Recherches Economiques de Louvain*,

1989, 273-292.

GRABITZ, Eberhard and ZACKER, Christian, 'Scope for Action by the EC Member States for the Improvement of Environmental Protection Under EEC Law: The Example of Environmental Taxes and Subsidies', **26** *Common Market Law Review*, 1989, 423-447.

HADDOCK, David D., McCHESNEY, Fred S. and SPIEGEL, Menahem, 'An Ordinary Economic Rationale for Extraordinary Legal Sanctions', **78** *California Law Review*, 1990, 1-51.

HAMILTON, Jonathan H., SHESHINSKI, Eytan and SLUTSKY, Steven M., 'Production Externalities and Long-Run Equilibria: Bargaining and Pigovian Taxation', **27** *Economic Inquiry*, 1989, 453-471.

HRUBOVCAK, James, LEBLANC, Michael and MIRANOWSKI, John, 'Limitations in Evaluating Environmental and Agricultural Policy Coordination Benefits', **80** *American Economic Review. Papers and Proceedings*, 1990, 208-212.

KOHN, Robert E., 'The Limitations of Pigouvian Taxes as a Long-run Remedy for Externalities: Comment', **101** *Quarterly Journal of Economics*,1986, 625-630.

LEE, Dwight R. and MISIOLEK, Walter S., 'Substituting Pollution Taxation for General Taxation: Some Implications for Efficiency in Pollutions Taxation', **13** *Journal of Environmental Economics and Management*, 1986, 338-347.

MISIOLEK, Walter S., 'Pollution Control Through Price Incentives: The Role of Rent Seeking', **15** *Journal of Environmental Economics and Management*, 1988, 1-8.

PIGOU, A.C., *The Economics of Welfare*, Macmillan, London, 1932, 876 p.

POLINSKY, A. Mitchell, 'Controlling Externalities and Protecting Entitlements: Property Right, Liability Rule, and Tax-Subsidy Approaches', **8** *Journal of Legal Studies*, 1979, 1-48.

SHIBATA, Hirofumi, 'Pareto-optimality and Trade and the Pigovian Tax', **39** *Economica*, 1972, 190-202.

SHIBATA, Hirofumi, 'Pareto-optimality and Gains-from-trade: a Further Elucidation', **41** *Economica*, 1974, 71-78.

SMITH, J.B. and SIMS, W.A., 'The Impact of Pollution Charges on Productivity Growth in Canadian Brewing', **16** *Rand Journal of Economics*, 1985, 410-423.

STARRET, David and ZECKHAUSER, Richard, 'Treating External Diseconomies - Markets or Taxes?', in PRATT, J.W. (ed.), *Statistical and Mathematical Aspects of Pollution Problems*, New York, Dekker, 1974, 65-84.

WENDERS, John T., 'Corrective Taxes and Pollution Abatement', **16** *Journal of Law and Economics*, 1973, 365-368.

WHITE, Michelle J., 'Suburban Growth Controls: Liability Rules and Pigovian Taxes', **8** *Journal of Legal Studies*, 1979, 207-230.

WHITE, Michelle J. and WITTMAN, Donald, 'A Comparison of Taxes, Regulation, and Liability Rules under Imperfect Information', **12** *Journal of Legal Studies*, 1983, 413-425.

YOHE, Gary W., 'More on the Properties of a Tax cum Subsidy Pollution Control Strategy', **31** *Economic Letters*, 1989, 193-198.

3800 Combined Approaches

BARNES, David W., 'Enforcing Property Rights: Extending Property Rights Theory to Congestible and Environmental Goods', **10** *Boston College Environmental Affairs Law Review*, 1982, 583-638.

BECKERMAN, Wilfred, *Pricing for Pollution: An Analysis of Market Pricing and Government Regulation in Environment Consumption and Policy*, London, Institute of Economic Affairs, Hobart Paper, no. 66, 1990, 80 p.

BISHOP, John A., 'Pigovian Taxes and "Full" Property Rights', **14** *Eastern Economic Journal*, 1988, 193-196.

BONGAERTS, Jan C., 'Milieubeleid : Regulering of Aansprakelijkheidsregel?' [Environmental Policy: Regulation or Liability?], *Vlaams Jurist Vandaag*, 1987, nr. 1, 17-22.

BUTLER, Ann M. and DOHERTY, Neil A., 'Torts and Orbits: The Allocation of the Costs of Accidents Involving Spacecraft', **81** *American Economic Review. Papers and Proceedings*, 1991, 46-49.

COELHO, Philip R.P., 'Polluters' Profits and Political Response: Direct Control versus Taxes: Comment', **66** *American Economic Review*, 1976, 976-978.

DEWEES, Donald N., 'Instrument Choice in Environmental Policy', **21** *Economic Inquiry*, 1983, 53-71.

DEWEES, Donald N., *Controlling Asbestos in Buildings: An Economic Investigation*, 1986.

DEWEES, Donald N., 'Economic Incentives for Controlling Industrial Disease: The Asbestos Case', **15** *Journal of Legal Studies*, 1986, 289-319.

FAURE, Michael G., 'Milieubescherming door aansprakelijkheidsrecht of regulering' [Protecting the Environment through Liability Law or Regulation], **39(10)** *Ars Aequi*, 1990, 759-769.

FAURE, Michael and VAN DEN BERGH, Roger, *Objectieve aansprakelijkheid, verplichte verzekering en veiligheidsregulering* [Strict Liability, Mandatory Insurance and Safety Regulation], Antwerpen, Maklu, 1989, 386 p.

FAURE, Michael and VAN DEN BERGH, Roger, 'Liability for Nuclear Accidents in Belgium from an Interest Group Perspective', **10** *International Review of Law and Economics*, 1990, 241-254.

GARDNER, Richard L. and YOUNG, Robert A., 'Assessing Strategies for Control of Irrigation Induced Salinity in the Upper Colorado River Basin', **70** *American Journal of Agricultural Economics*, 1988, 37-49.

HAHN, Robert W., 'A New Approach to the Design of Regulation in the Presence of Multiple Objectives', **17** *Journal of Environmental Economics and Management*, 1989, 195-211.

HARTMAN, Raymond S., 'A Note on Externalities and the Placement of Property Rights: An Alternative Formulation to the Standard Pigouvian Results', **2** *International Review of Law and Economics*, 1982, 111-118.

HELM, Dieter and PEARCE, David W., 'Assessment: Economic Policy towards the Environment', **6** *Oxford Review of Economic Policy*, 1990, 1-16.

HENDERSON, James A., 'The New Zealand Accident Compensation Reform', **48**

University of Chicago Law Review, 1981, 781-801. Reprinted in RABIN, Robert L. (ed.), *Perspectives on Tort Law*, Boston, Little Brown, 1983, 316-331.

HRUBOVCAK, James, LEBLANC, Michael and MIRANOWSKI, John, 'Limitations in Evaluating Environmental and Agricultural Policy Coordination Benefits', **80** *American Economic Review. Papers and Proceedings*, 1990, 208-212.

KAMBHU, John, 'Direct Controls and Incentives Systems of Regulation', **18** *Journal of Environmental Economics and Management*, 1990, S72-85.

KATZMAN, Martin T., 'Environmental Risk Management Through Insurance', **6** *Cato Journal*, 1987, 775-799.

KATZMAN, Martin T., 'Pollution Liability Insurance and Catastrophic Environmental Risk', **55** *Journal of Risk & Insurance*, 1988, 75-100.

KEETON, William R. and KWEREL, Evan, 'Externalities in Automobile Insurance and the Underinsured Driver Problem', **27** *Journal of Law and Economics*, 1984, 149-179.

KEHNE, Jeffrey, 'Encouraging Safety Through Insurance-Based Incentives: Financial Responsibility for Hazardous Wastes', **96** *Yale Law Journal*, 1986, 403-427.

KOLSTAD, Charles D., 'Empirical Properties of Economic Incentives and Command-and-Control Regulations for Air Pollution Control', **62** *Land Economics*, 1986, 250-268.

KOLSTAD, Charles D., ULEN, Thomas S. and JOHNSON, Gary V., 'Ex Post Liability for Harm vs. Ex Ante Safety Regulation: Substitutes or Complements?', **80** *American Economic Review*, 1990, 888-901.

KUNZMAN, Steven A., 'The Insurer as Surrogate Regulator of the Hazardous Waste Industry: Solution or Perversion?', **20** *Forum*, 1985, 169-188.

LEVMORE, Saul and STUNTZ, William J., 'Remedies and Incentives in Private and Public Law: A Comparitive Essay', *Wisconsin Law Review*, 1990, 483-499.

MANNE, Alan S. and RICHELS, Richard G., 'International Trade in Carbon Emission Rights: A Decomposition Procedure', **81** *American Economic Review. Papers and Proceedings*, 1991, 135-139.

MERAN, Georg, 'Zur Kontroverse uber die Wettbewerbswirkungen eines Umweltlizenzmarktes' [The Controversy on the Competition on a Market for Environmental Licenses], **108** *Zeitschrift fur Wirtschafts und Sozialwissenschaften*, 1988, 439-450.

MILLIMAN, Scott R. and PRINCE, Raymond, 'Firm Incentives to Promote Technological Change in Pollution Control', **17** *Journal of Environmental Economics and Management*, 1989, 247-265.

MUSGER, Gottfried, 'Ökonomische Analyse der Umwelthaftung' [Economic Analysis of Environmental Liability], in HAUREICH, Hanspeter and SCHWARZER, Stephan (project management), *Umwelthaftung*, Vienna, Austrian Economic Publishers, 1991, 22-41.

POLINSKY, A. Mitchell, 'Controlling Externalities and Protecting Entitlements: Property Right, Liability Rule, and Tax-Subsidy Approaches', **8** *Journal of Legal Studies*, 1979, 1-48.

QUIGGIN, John, 'Private and Common Property Rights in the Economics of the Environment', **22** *Journal of Economic Issues*, 1988, 1071-1087.

ROSE-ACKERMAN, Susan, 'Tort Law in the Regulatory State', in SCHUCK, J. (ed.), *Tort law and the Public Interest: Competition, Innovation, and Consumer Welfare*, New York, North, 1991.

ROSE-ACKERMAN, Susan, 'Regulation and the Law of Torts', **81** *American Economic Review. Papers and Proceedings*, 1991, 54-58.

SCHWARTZ, Gary T., 'A Proposal for Tort Reform: Reformulating Uninsured Motorist Plans', **48** *Ohio State Law Journal*, 1987, 419-442.

SHAVELL, Steven, 'On Liability and Insurance', **13** *Bell Journal of Economics*, 1982, 120-132.

SHAVELL, Steven, 'A Model of the Optimal Use of Liability and Safety Regulation', **15** *Rand Journal of Economics*, 1984, 271-280.

SHAVELL, Steven, 'Liability for Harm versus Regulation of Safety', **13** *Journal of Legal Studies*, 1984, 357-374.

SHAVELL, Steven, 'The Judgment Proof Problem', **6** *International Review of Law and Economics*, 1986, 45-58.

SHAVELL, Steven, 'The Optimal Use of Nonmonetary Sanctions as a Deterrent', **77** *American Economic Review*, 1987, 584-592.

SKOGH, Göran, 'Public Insurance and Accident Prevention', **2** *International Review of Law and Economics*, 1982, 67-80.

SKOGH, Göran, 'The Combination of Private and Public Regulation of Safety', in FAURE, Michael and VAN DEN BERGH, Roger (eds.), *Essays in Law and Economics. Corporations, Accident Prevention and Compensation for Losses*, Antwerpen, Maklu, 1989, 87-101.

SKOGH, Göran and STUART, Charles, 'Liability, Insurance, and the Regulation of Traffic Accidents', in SKOGH, Göran (ed.), *Law and Economics. Report from a Symposium in Lund, Sweden, 24-26 August 1977*, Lund, Juridiska Föreningen, 1978, 203-210.

STARRET, David and ZECKHAUSER, Richard, 'Treating External Diseconomies - Markets or Taxes?', in PRATT, J.W. (ed.), *Statistical and Mathematical Aspects of Pollution Problems*, New York, Dekker, 1974, 65-84.

STROUP, Richard L., 'Environmental Policy', **12(3)** *Regulation*, 1988, 43-49.

SWANEY, James A., 'Response-Ability of Environmental Controls', **21** *Journal of Economic Issues*, 1987, 911-919.

THOMPSON, Russell G. and SINGLETON, F. D., Jr., 'Wastewater Treatment Costs and Outlays in Organic Petrochemicals: Standards versus Taxes with Methodology Suggestions for Margin al CostPricing and Analysis', **22** *Water Resources Research*, 1986, 467-474.

TIETENBERG, Tom H., 'Economic Instruments for Environmental Regulation', **6** *Oxford Review of Economic Policy*, 1990, 17-33.

TREBILCOCK, Michael J., 'Incentive Issues in the Design of No-Fault Compensation Systems', **39** *University of Toronto Law Journal*, 1989, 19-54.

VISCUSI, W. Kip, 'Structuring an Effective Occupational Disease Policy: Victim Compensation and Risk Regulation', **2** *Yale Journal on Regulation*, 1984, 53-

81.

VISCUSI, W. Kip, 'Toward a Diminished Role for Tort Liability: Social Insurance, Government Regulation, and Contemporary Risks to Health and Safety', **6** *Yale Journal on Regulation*, 1989, 65-107.

WHITE, Michelle J., 'Suburban Growth Controls: Liability Rules and Pigovian Taxes', **8** *Journal of Legal Studies*, 1979, 207-230.

WHITE, Michelle J. and WITTMAN, Donald, 'A Comparison of Taxes, Regulation, and Liability Rules under Imperfect Information', **12** *Journal of Legal Studies*, 1983, 413-425.

WITTMAN, Donald, 'Prior Regulation versus Post Liability: The Choice Between Input and Output Monitoring', **6** *Journal of Legal Studies*, 1977, 193-211.

WITTMAN, Donald, 'Liability for Harm or Restitution for Benefit ?', **13** *Journal of Legal Studies*, 1984, 57-80.

YOHE, Gary W., 'Polluters' Profits and Political Response: Direct Control versus Taxes: Comment', **66** *American Economic Review*, 1976, 981-982.

3900 Other Approaches

ATKINSON, Scott E. and TIETENBERG, T.H., 'Economic Implications of Emissions Trading Rules for Local and Regional Pollutants', **20** *Canadian Journal of Economics*, 1987, 370-386.

BOYD, Roy G. and HYDE, William F., *Forestry Sector Intervention: The Impacts of Public Regulation on Social Welfare*, Ames, Iowa State University Press, 1989, 295 p.

HAHN, Robert W. and HESTER, Gordon L., 'Where Did All the Markets Go? An Analysis of EPA's Emission Trading Program', **6** *Yale Journal on Regulation*, 1989, 109-153.

HAHN, Robert W. and McRAE, G., 'Applications of Market Mechanisms to Pollution', **1** *Policy Studies Review*, 1982, 470-476.

HAHN, Robert W. and NOLL, Roger G., 'Designing a Market for Tradable Emissions Permits', in MAGAT, Wesley A. (ed.), *Reform of Environmental Regulation*, Cambridge (Mass.), Ballinger, 1982.

HAHN, Robert W. and NOLL, Roger G., 'Barriers to Implementing Tradable Air Pollution Permits: Problems of Regulatory Interactions', **1** *Yale Journal on Regulation*, 1983, 63-91.

LIROFF, R., *Reforming Air Pollution Regulation: The Toil and Trouble of EPA's Bubble*, Washington, The Conservation Foundation, 1986.

LYON, Randolph M., 'Transferable Discharge Permit Systems and Environmental Management in Developing Countries', **17** *World Development*, 1989, 1299-1312.

MALIK, Arun S., 'Markets for Pollution Control When Firms Are Noncompliant', **18(1)** *Journal of Environmental Economics and Management*, Part 1, 1990, 97-106.

MALUEG, David A., 'Emission Credit Trading and the Incentive to Adopt New Pollution Abatement Technology', **16** *Journal of Environmental Economics and Management*, 1989, 52-57.

MALUEG, David A., 'Welfare Consequences of Emission Credit Trading Programs', **18** *Journal of Environmental Economics and Management*, 1990, 66-77.

MANNE, Alan S. and RICHELS, Richard G., 'CO2 Emission Limits: An Economic Cost Analysis for the USA', **11(2)** *Energy Journal*, 1990, 51-74.

McGARTLAND, Albert, 'A Comparison of Two Marketable Discharge Permits Systems', **15** *Journal of Environmental Economics and Management*, 1988, 35-44.

MENELL, Peter S., 'The Limitations of Legal Institutions for Addressing Environmental Risks', **5(3)** *Journal of Economic Perspectives*, 1991, 93-113.

MISIOLEK, Walter S. and ELDER, Harold W., 'Exclusionary Manipulation of Markets for Pollution Rights', **16** *Journal of Environmental Economics and Management*, 1989, 156-166.

RAUFER, Roger K. and FELDMAN, Stephen L., *Acid Rain and Emissions Trading: Implementing a Market Approach to Pollution Control*, Totowa, Rowman and Littlefield, 1987, 161 p.

RAUFER, Roger K. and FELDMAN, Stephen L., *Acid Rain and Emissions Trading: Implementing a Market Approach to Pollution Control*, Totowa, Littlefield, 1987, 161 p.

SHORTLE, James S. and WILLETT, Keith D., 'A Computable Market Equilibrium Model with Markets for Transferable Discharge Permits', **8** *Managerial and Decision Economics*, 1987, 263-270.

WALBERT, Mark S. and BIERMA, Thomas J., 'The Permits Game: Conveying the Logic of Marketable Pollution Permits', **19** *Journal of Economic Education*, 1988, 383-389.

WELCH, W., 'The Political Feasibility of Full Ownership Property Rights: The Cases of Pollution and Fisheries', **16** *Policy Sciences*, 1983, 165-180.

YANDLE, Bruce, 'Taxation, Political Action, and Superfund', **8** *Cato Journal*, 1989, 751-764.

4000 CONTRACT LAW
Gerrit De Geest

4000 Contract Law: General

AGHION, Philippe and HERMALIN, Benjamin, 'Legal Restrictions on Private Contracts Can Enhance Efficiency', **6** *Journal of Law, Economics, & Organization*, 1990, 381-409.

ALEXANDER, Larry (ed.), *Contract Law. Volumes I&II*, Aldershot, Dartmouth, 1991, 1140 p.

ATIYAH, Patrick S., 'The Theoretical Basis of Contract Law - An English Perspective', **1** *International Review of Law and Economics*, 1981, 183-205.

AYRES, Ian and GERTNER, Robert, 'Filling Gaps in Incomplete Contracts: An Economic Analysis of Default Rules', **99** *Yale Law Journal*, 1989, 87-130.

BARNETT, Randy E., 'Foreword: Chicago Law and Economics', **65** *Chicago-Kent Law Review*, 1989, 3 ff.

BENDOR, Jonathan and MOOKHERJEE, Dilip, 'Norms, Third-Party Sanctions, and Cooperation', **6** *Journal of Law, Economics, & Organization*, 1990, 33-63.

BIRMINGHAM, Robert L., 'Legal and Moral Duty in Game Theory: Common Law Contract and Chinese Analogies', **18** *Buffalo Law Review*, 1968, 99-117. Reprinted in KRONMAN, Anthony T. and POSNER, Richard A. (eds.), *The Economics of Contract Law*, Boston, Little Brown, 1979, 16-21.

BIRMINGHAM, Robert L., 'The Consumer as King: The Economics of Precarious Sovereignty Case', **20** *Case Western Reserve Law Review*, 1969, 354-377.

BISHOP, William, 'The Contract-Tort Boundary and the Economics of Insurance', **12** *Journal of Legal Studies*, 1983, 241-266. Reprinted in GOLDBERG, Victor P. (ed.), *Readings in the Economics of Contract Law*, Cambridge, Cambridge University Press, 1989, 86-91.

BUCKLEY, F.H., 'Paradox Lost', **72** *Minnesota Law Review*, 1988, 775-827.

CHEUNG, Steven N.S., 'Transaction Costs, Risk Aversion, and the Choice of Contractual Arrangements', **12** *Journal of Law and Economics*, 1969, 23-42.

CHEUNG, Steven N.S., 'The Structure of a Contract and the Theory of a Non-exclusive Resource', **13** *Journal of Law and Economics*, 1970, 49-70.

COLEMAN, J., HEKATHORN, Douglas D. and MASER, Steven M., 'A Bargaining Theory Approach to Default Provisions and Disclosure Rules in Contract Law', **12** *Harvard Journal of Law and Public Policy*, 1989, 639 ff.

COLEMAN, Jules, HECKATHON, Douglas and MASER, Steven, 'A Bargaining Theory Approach to Default Provisions and Disclosure Rules in Contract Law', **12** *Harvard Journal of Law and Public Policy*, 1989, 639 ff.

COOTER, Robert D., 'Unity in Tort, Contract, and Property: The Model of Precaution', **73** *California Law Review*, 1985, 1-51. Reprinted in GOLDBERG, Victor P. (ed.), *Readings in the Economics of Contract Law*, Cambridge, Cambridge University Press, 1989, 53-60.

CRASWELL, Richard, 'Contract Law, Default Rules, and the Philosophy of Promising', **88** *Michigan Law Review*, 1989, 489-529.

D'URSEL, Laurent, 'L'analyse économique du droit des contrats' [Economic Analysis of Contract Law], **14** *Revue interdisciplinaire d'études juridiques*, 1985, 45-88.

DE ALESSI, Louis and STAAF, Robert J., 'Property Rights and Choice', in MERCURO, Nicholas (ed.), *Law and Economics*, Boston, Kluwer Academic Publishers, 1989, 175-200.

DE ALESSI, Louis and STAAF, Robert J., 'Subjective Value in Contract Law', **145** *Journal of Institutional and Theoretical Economics*, 1989, 561-577.

DOWIE, J., 'The Risks of Contract Law', **2** *International Review of Law and Economics*, 1982, 193-204.

EISENBERG, Melvin Aron, 'The Bargain Principle and Its Limits', **95** *Harvard Law Review*, 1982, 741-801.

EPSTEIN, Richard A., 'Toward a Revitalization of the Contract Clause', **51** *University of Chicago Law Review*, 1984, 703-751.

EPSTEIN, Richard A., 'Inducement of Breach of Contract as a Problem of Ostensible Ownership', **16** *Journal of Legal Studies*, 1987, 1-41.

FARBER, Daniel A., 'Contract Law and Modern Economic Theory', **78** *Northwestern University Law Review*, 1983, 303-339.

FEINMAN, Jay M., 'Critical Approaches to Contract Law', **30** *UCLA Law Review*, 1983, 829 ff.

FEINMAN, Jay M., 'The Significance of Contract Theory', **58** *University of Cincinnati Law Review*, 1990, 1283-1318.

FERRARINI, G., *La locazione finanziaria* [Leasing], Milano, Giuffrè, 1977, 261 p.

FINE, Benjamin L., 'Comment: An Analysis of the Formation of Property Rights Underlying Tortious Interference with Contracts and Other Economic Relations', **50** *University of Chicago Law Review*, 1983, 1116-1145.

GOETZ, Charles J. and SCOTT, Robert E., 'Enforcing Promises: An Examination of the Basis of Contract', **89** *Yale Law Journal*, 1980, 1261-1322.

GOETZ, Charles J. and SCOTT, Robert E., 'The Limits of Expanded Choice: An Analysis of the Interactions between Express and Implied Contract Terms', **73** *California Law Review*, 1985, 261-322.

GOLDBERG, Victor P., 'Toward an Expanded Economic Theory of Contract', **10** *Journal of Economic Issues*, 1976, 45-61. Reprinted in SAMUELS, Warren J. (ed.), *The Chicago School of Political Economy*, East Lansing, Division of Research, Graduate School of Business Administration, Michigan State University, 1976, 259-276.

GOLDBERG, Victor P. (ed.), *Readings in the Economics of Contract Law*, Cambridge, Cambridge University Press, 1989, 252 p.

HARRIS, Donald, 'Contract as Promise - A Review Article Based on *Contract as Promise: A Theory of Contractual Obligation* by Charles Fried', **3** *International Review of Law and Economics*, 1983, 69-77.

HARRIS, Donald and VELJANOVSKI, Cento G., 'The Use of Economics to Elucidate Legal Concepts: The Law of Contract', in DAINTITH, Terence and TEUBER, Gunther (eds.), *Law and the Social Sciences*, Florence, European

University Institute, 1984, 740 p.

HARRISON, Jeffrey L., 'Trends and Traces: A Preliminary Evaluation of Economic Analysis in Contract Law', **1988** *Annual Survey of American Law*, 1989, 73-114 (Followed by Panel Discussion 115-130).

HILLMAN, Robert A., 'The Crisis in Modern Contract Theory', **67** *Texas Law Review*, 1988, 103-136.

HOLDERNESS, Clifford G., 'A Legal Foundation for Exchange', **14** *Journal of Legal Studies*, 1985, 321-344.

HORWITZ, Morton J., 'The Historical Foundations of Modern Contract Law', **87** *Harvard Law Review*, 1974, 917-956.

HURST, Thomas R., 'Freedom of Contract in an Unstable Economy: Judicial Reallocation of Contractual Risks under UOC' Section 2-615', **54** *North Carolina Law Review*, 1976, 545-583.

KIDWELL, John, 'A Caveat', *Wisconsin Law Review*, 1985, 615-622.

KÖHLER, Helmut, 'Vertragsrecht und "Property Rights"-Theorie, Zur Integration ökonomischer Theorien in das Privatrecht' [Contract Law and Property Rights Theory - On the Integration of Economic Theory into Private Law], **144** *Zeitschrift für das gesamte Handels- und Wirtschaftsrecht*, 1980, 589-607.

KÖHLER, Helmut, 'Zur ökonomischen Analyse der Regeln über die Geschäftsgrundlage' [On the Economic Analysis of the Rules of the Implicit Basis of a Contract], in OTT, Claus and SCHÄFER, Hans-Bernd (eds.), *Allokationseffizienz in der Rechtsordnung*, Berlin, Springer, 1989, 148-162.

KOSLOWSKI, Peter, 'Grenzen der Verkehrsfähigkeit und der Privatrechtsautonomie in der Verfügung über den menschlichen Leib - Kommentar' [Limits of the Marketability and Private Autonomy in the Disposition over the Human Body - Comment], in OTT, Claus and SCHÄFER, Hans-Bernd (eds.), *Allokationseffizienz in der Rechtsordnung*, Berlin, Springer, 1989, 115-119.

KROLL, Heidi, 'Property Rights and the Soviet Enterprise: Evidence from the Law of Contract', **13** *Journal of Comparative Economics*, 1989, 115-133.

KRONMAN, Anthony T., 'Contract Law and Distributive Justice', **89** *Yale Law Journal*, 1980, 472-511.

KRONMAN, Anthony T., 'Paternalism and the Law of Contracts', **92** *Yale Law Journal*, 1983, 763-798.

KRONMAN, Anthony T., 'Contract Law and the State of Nature', **1** *Journal of Law, Economics & Organization*, 1985, 5-32.

KRONMAN, Anthony T. and POSNER, Richard A. (eds.), *The Economics of Contract Law*, Boston, Little Brown, 1979, 274 p.

LANDO, Ole, 'The Scope and Application of Statutes on Unfair Contract Clauses', in SKOGH, Göran (ed.), *Law and Economics. Report from a Symposium in Lund, Sweden, 24-26 August 1977*, Lund, Juridiska Föreningen, 1978, 165-184.

LEFF, Arthur A., 'Injury, Ignorance and Spite - The Dynamics of Coercive Collection', **80** *Yale Law Journal*, 1970, 1-46. Reprinted in KRONMAN, Anthony T. and POSNER, Richard A. (eds.), *The Economics of Contract Law*, Boston, Little Brown, 1979, 175-181.

LINZER, Peter, 'On the Amorality of Contract Remedies - Efficiency, Equity and the

Second Restatement', **81** *Columbia Law Review*, 1981, 111-139.

LINZER, Peter, 'Is Consent the Essence of Contract? Replying to Four Critics', *Annual Survey of American Law*, 1988, 213-220.

LOWRY, S. Todd, 'Bargain and Contract Theory in Law and Economics', **10** *Journal of Economic Issues*, 1976, 1-22. Reprinted in SAMUELS, Warren J. (ed.), *The Chicago School of Political Economy*, East Lansing, Division of Research, Graduate School of Business Administration, Michigan State University, 1976, 215-236.

MARINI, Giovanni, *Promessa ed affidamento nel diritto dei contratti*, [Promise and Reliance in Contract Law], Napoli, Jovene, 1990, 317 p.

MEURER, Michael J., 'Foreword', **52(1)** *Law and Contemporary Problems*, 1989, 1-7.

MEYERSON, Michael I., 'The Efficient Consumer Form Contract: Law and Economics Meets the Real World', **24** *Georgia Law Review*, 1990, 583-627.

MURIS, Timothy J., 'Opportunistic Behaviour and the Law of Contracts', **65** *Minnesota Law Review*, 1981, 521-590.

NARASIMHAN, Subha, 'Of Expectations, Incomplete Contracting, and the Bargain Principle', **74** *California Law Review*, 1986, 1123-1202.

PERRON, Edgar du, 'De rechtseconomische analyse van het verbintenissenrecht' [A Law-and-economics Analysis of the Law of Obligations], **39(10)** *Ars Aequi*, 1990, 770-776.

POUGHON, Jean-Michel, 'Une constante doctrinale: l'approche économique du contract', **12** *Droits. Revue française de théorie juridique*, 1990, 47-59.

REA, Samuel A., Jr., 'Inflation and the Law of Contracts and Torts', **14** *Ottawa Law Review*, 1982, 465-480.

RHEINSTEIN, Max (ed.), *Max Weber on Law in Economy and Society*, Cambridge, Harvard University Press, 1954. Reprinted in KRONMAN, Anthony T. and POSNER, Richard A. (eds.), *The Economics of Contract Law*, Boston, Little Brown, 1979, 230-233.

ROMANI, Franco, 'Appunti sull' analisi economica dei contratti' [Notes about the Economic Analysis of Contract Law], *Quadrimestre*, 1985, 15-29.

SCHWAB, Stewart J., 'A Coasean Experiment on Contract Presumptions', **17** *Journal of Legal Studies*, 1988, 237-268.

SCHWARTZ, Alan, 'Justice and the Law of Contracts: A Case for the Traditional Approach', **9** *Harvard Journal of Law & Public Policy*, 1986, 107 ff.

SCOTT, Robert E., 'A Relational Theory of Default Rules for Commercial Contracts', **19** *Journal of Legal Studies*, 1990, 597-616.

SEITA, Alex Y., 'Uncertainty and Contract Law', **46** *University of Pittsburgh Law Review*, 1984, 75-148.

SEUROT, François, 'Analyse économique de la liberté des contrats' [Economic Analysis of Freedom of Contracts], in *De "l'ancienne" à la "nouvelle" économie. Essais à l'occasion de la dixième université d'été de la nouvelle économie. Aix-en-Provence 1978-87*, Aix-en-Provence, Librairie de l'université, 1987, 275-281.

SIMPSON, A.W.B., 'The Horwitz Thesis and the History of Contracts', **46** *University of Chicago Law Review*, 1979, 533-601.

SKOGH, Göran, 'Kontraktsteoretisk översikt' [Contractual-theoretical Survey], *Statsökonomisk tidskrift*, 1979, No. 1.

SPANN, Girardeau A., 'A Critical Legal Studies Perspective on Contract Law and Practice', *Annual Survey of American Law*, 1988, 223-292.

SPERGEL, Rochelle, 'Paternalism and Contract: A Critique of Anthony Kronman', **10** *Cardozo Law Review*, 1988, 593-634.

SYMPOSIUM (MEURER, Michael (ed.)): 'Economics of Contract Law', **52(1)** *Law and Contemporary Problems*, 1989, 209 p.

TAYLOR, John B., 'Aggregate Dynamics and Staggered Contracts', **88** *Journal of Political Economy*, 1980, 1-23.

TOLLISON, Robert D., 'A Note on the Equivalence of Contracting and Regulation', **9** *Atlantic Economic Journal*, 1981, 57-59.

WALZ, W. Rainer, 'Ökonomische und rechtssystematische Überlegungen zur Verkehrsfähigkeit von Gegenständen' [Economic and Legal Dogmatic Considerations in Marketability of Objects], in OTT, Claus and SCHÄFER, Hans-Bernd (eds.), *Allokationseffizienz in der Rechtsordnung*, Berlin, Springer, 1989, 93-114.

WANG, William K.S., 'Reflections on Contract Law and Distribution Justice: A Reply to Kronman', **34** *Hastings Law Journal*, 1982, 513-527.

WILLIAMSON, Oliver E., 'Corporate Governance', **93** *Yale Law Journal*, 1984, 1197-1230.

WILLIAMSON, Oliver E., 'Assessing Contract', **1** *Journal of Law, Economics & Organization*, 1985, 177-208.

WITT, Ulrich, 'Evolution and Stability of Cooperation without Enforceable Contracts', **39** *Kyklos*, 1986, 245-266.

WONNELL, Christopher T., 'Contract Law and the Austrian School of Economics', **54** *Fordham Law Review*, 1986, 507-543.

X, 'Note: Efficiency and the Rule of "Free Contract": A Critique of Two Models of Law and Economics', **97** *Harvard Law Review*, 1984, 978-996.

4100 Contractual Choice and Long-Term Contracts

4100 Contractual Choice: General

ALCHIAN, Armen A. and DEMSETZ, Harold, 'Production, Information Costs, and Economic Organization', **62** *American Economic Review*, 1972, 777-795.

BACKHAUS, Jürgen G., 'A Transaction Cost Approach to Explaining Historical Contract Structures', **9** *International Review of Law and Economics*, 1989, 223-226.

BALBIEN, J. and WILDE, L.L., 'A Dynamic Model of Research Contracting', **13** *Bell Journal of Economics*, 1982, 107-119.

BARON, David P. and BESANKO, David, 'Monitoring, Moral Hazard, Asymmetric Information, and Risk Sharing in Procurement Contracting', **18** *Rand Journal of Economics*, 1987, 509-532.

BEALE, H. and DUGDALE, T., 'Contracts Between Businessmen: Planning and the Use of Contractual Remedies', **2** *British Journal of Law and Society* 1975, 45-60.

BOWLES, Roger A. and SKOGH, Göran, 'Reputation, Monitoring and the Organisation of the Law Firm', in FAURE, Michael and VAN DEN BERGH, Roger (eds.), *Essays in Law and Economics. Corporations, Accident Prevention and Compensation for Losses*, Antwerpen, Maklu, 1989, 33-47.

BROWN, D.J. and ATKINSON, J.H., 'Cash and Share Renting: an Empirical Test of the Link between Entrepreneurial Ability and Contractual Choice', **12** *Bell Journal of Economics*, 1981, 296-299.

BUCOBETSKY, Sam and CHILTON, John, 'Concurrent Renting and Selling in a Durable-Goods Monopoly under Threat of Entry', **17** *Rand Journal of Economics*, 1986, 261-278.

BUTLER, Henry N., 'Restricted Distribution Contracts and the Opportunistic Pursuit of Treble Damages', **59** *Washington Law Review*, 1983, 27-60.

CANTOR, Richard, 'Firm Specific Training and Contract Length', **57** *Economica*, 1990, 1-14.

CHEUNG, Steven N. S., 'The Contractual Nature of the Firm', **26** *Journal of Law and Economics*, 1983, 1-21.

COOTER, Robert D. and LANDA, Janeth T., 'Personal versus Impersonal Trade: The Size of Trading Groups and Contract Law', **4** *International Review of Law and Economics*, 1984, 15-22.

COOTER, Robert D. and RUBIN, Edward L., 'A Theory of Loss Allocation for Consumer Payments', **66** *Texas Law Review*, 1987, 63-130.

CRéMER, Jacques and RIORDAN, Michael H., 'On Governing Multilateral Transactions with Bilateral Contracts', **18** *Rand Journal of Economics*, 1987, 436-451.

CREW, Michael A., 'Royalty Contracts: An Efficient Form of Contracting?', **50** *Southern Economic Journal*, 1984, 724-733.

CROCKER, Thomas D., 'Contractual Choice', **13** *Natural Resources Journal*, 1973, 561-577.

CUMMINS, J. Michael, 'Incentive Contracting for National Defense: a Problem of Optimal Risk Sharing', **8** *Bell Journal of Economics*, 1977, 168-185.

DEMOUGIN, Dominique M., 'A Renegotiation-Proof Mechanism for a Principal-Agent Model with Moral Hazard and Adverse Selection', **20** *Rand Journal of Economics*, 1989, 256-267.

DEMSETZ, Harold, 'The Cost of Transacting', **82** *Quarterly Journal of Economics*, 1968, 33-53.

DOMBERGER, Simon and SHERR, Avrom, 'Economic Efficiency in the Provision of Legal Services: The Private Practitioner and the Law Centre', **1** *International Review of Law and Economics*, 1981, 29-49.

DYE, Ronald A., 'Costly Contract Contingencies', **26** *International Economic Review*, 1985, 233-250.

DYE, Ronald A., 'Optimal Monitoring Policies in Agencies', **17** *Rand Journal of Economics*, 1986, 339-350.

FAITH, Roger L. and TOLLISON, Robert D., 'Contractual Exchange and the Timing of Payment', **1** *Journal of Economic Behavior and Organization*, 1980, 325-342.

FELDMAN, Roger, SLOAN, F. and PARINGER, L., 'Compensation Arrangements between Hospitals and Physicians', **12** *Bell Journal of Economics*, 1983, 155-170.

GEMMELL, Norman, 'Is There a Conflict between Authors and Publishers over Royalty Terms?', **29** *Economic Letters*, 1989, 7-11.

HALL, Edward C. and PARSONS, John E., 'The Efficient Design of Contracts to Purchase Cogenerated Power', **11** *Energy Journal*, 1990, 105-116.

HALPERN, Paul J. and TURNBULL, Stuart M., 'Legal Fees Contracts and Alternative Cost Rules: An Economic Analysis', **3** *International Review of Law and Economics*, 1983, 3-26.

HARRIS, Milton and RAVIV, Artur, 'Some Results on Incentive Contracts with Applications to Education and Employment, Health Insurance, and Law Enforcement', **68** *American Economic Review*, 1978, 20-30.

HART, Oliver D. and HOLMSTRÖM, Bengt, 'The Theory of Contracts', in BEWLEY, T. (ed.), *Advances in Economic Theory, Fifth World Congress*, 1987, 71 ff.

HENDERSON, J.V. and IONNIDES, Y.M., 'A Model of Housing Tenure Choice', **73** *American Economic Review*, 1983, 98-113.

HENNART, Jean-François, 'The Transaction-Cost Rationale for Countertrade', **5** *Journal of Law, Economics, & Organization*, 1989, 127-153.

HILLER, John R. and TOLLISON, Robert D., 'An Economic Model of Performance Contracting in Education', **29** *Public Finance*, 1974, 36-48.

JACOB, Nancy L. and PAGE, Alfred N., 'Production, Information Costs, and Economic Organization: The Buyer Monitoring Case', **70** *American Economic Review*, 1980, 476-478.

JESSE, Edward V. and JOHNSON, Aaron C., Jr., 'An Analysis of Vegetable Contracts', **52** *American Journal of Agricultural Economics*, 1970, 545-554.

KAHN, Charles and HUBERMAN, Gur, 'Two-sided Uncertainty and "Up-or-Out" Contracts, **6** *Journal of Labor Economics*, 1988, 423-444.

KAHN, Charles and HUBERMAN, Gur, 'Default, Foreclosure, and Strategic Renegotiation', **52(1)** *Law and Contemporary Problems*, 1989, 49-61.

KANEMOTO, Yoshitsugu and MACLEOD, W. Bentley, 'Optimal Labor Contracts with Non contractible Human Capital', **3** *Journal of the Japanese and International Economy*, 1989, 385-3402.

KLEIN, Benjamin, 'Transaction Cost Determinants of "Unfair" Contractual Arrangements', **70** *American Economic Review. Papers and Proceedings*, 1980, 356-362. Reprinted in GOLDBERG, Victor P. (ed.), *Readings in the Economics of Contract Law*, Cambridge, Cambridge University Press, 1989, 139-146.

KLEIN, Benjamin and LEFFLER, Keith B., 'The Role of Market Forces in Assuring Contractual Performance', **89** *Journal of Political Economy*, 1981, 615-641.

KLEIN, Benjamin and MURPHY, Kevin M., 'Vertical Restraints as Contract Enforcement Mechanisms', **31** *Journal of Law and Economics*, 1988, 265-297.

KNAPP, Charles L., 'Judgment Call: Theoretical Approaches to Contract Decision-Making', *Annual Survey of American Law*, 1988, 307-351.

KNOEBER, Charles R., 'An Alternative Mechanism to Assure Contractual Reliability', **12** *Journal of Legal Studies*, 1983, 333-343.

KNOEBER, Charles R., 'A Real Game of Chicken: Contracts, Tournaments, and the Production of Broilers', **5** *Journal of Law, Economics, & Organization*, 1989, 271-292.

KNOLL, Michael S., 'Uncertainty, Efficiency, and the Brokerage Industry', **31** *Journal of Law and Economics*, 1988, 249-263.

KOLLER, Ingo, *Die Risikozurechnung bei Vertragsstörungen in Austauschverträgen* [The Risk Allocation of Contract Disturbances in Bilateral Contracts], München, C.H. Beck, Münchener Universitätsschriften, Vol. 39, 1979, 474 p.

KORNHAUSER, Lewis A., 'Reliance, Reputation, and Breach of Contract', **26** *Journal of Law and Economics*, 1983, 691-706.

LANDA, Janet T., 'An Exchange Economy with Legally Binding Contracts: A Public Choice Approach', **10** *Journal of Economic Issues*, 1976, 905-922.

LANDA, Janet T., 'A Theory of the Ethnically Homogeneous Middleman Group: An Institutional Alternative to Contract Law', **10** *Journal of Legal Studies*, 1981, 349-362.

LANDA, Janet T., 'The Enigma of the *Kula Ring*: Gift-Exchanges and Primitive Law and Order', **3** *International Review of Law and Economics*, 1983, 137-160.

LEFFLER, Keith, 'Toward a Reasonable Rule of Reason: Comments', **28** *Journal of Law and Economics*, 1985, 381-386.

LEHMANN, Michael, 'Just in time: Handels- und ABG-rechtliche Probleme' [Just in Time: Problems in the Law of Commerce and of Unfair Contract Terms], **27** *Der Betriebs-Berater*, 1990, 1849-1855.

LEITZEL, Jim, 'The New Institutional Economics and a Model of Contract', **11** *Journal of Economic Behavior and Organization*, 1989, 75-89.

LEITZEL, Jim, 'Damage Measures and Incomplete Contracts', **20** *Rand Journal of Economics*, 1989, 92-101.

LEONARD, Herman B. and ZECKHAUSER, Richard J., 'Financial Risk and the Burdens of Contracts', **75** *American Economic Review. Papers and Proceedings*, 1985, 375-380.

LEWIS, Tracy R., 'Bonuses and Penalties in Incentive Contracting', **11** *Bell Journal of Economics*, 1980, 292-301.

MANNE, Henry G., 'Some Perspectives on Contractual Relations: Concluding Remarks', **144** *Journal of Institutional and Theoretical Economics*, 1988, 237-241.

MASTEN, Scott E., 'Minimum Bill Contracts: Theory and Policy', **37** *Journal of Industrial Economics*, 1988, 85-97.

MASTEN, Scott E., 'Equity, Opportunism, and the Design of Contractual Relations', **144** *Journal of Institutional and Theoretical Economics*, 1988, 180-195.

McAFEE, R. Preston and McMILLAN, John, 'Bidding for Contracts: A Principal-Agent Analysis', **17** *Rand Journal of Economics*, 1986, 326-338.

MILLER, Robert S., 'The Sale of Horses and Horse Interests: A Transactional Approach', **78** *Kentucky Law Journal*, 1990, 517 ff.

MURTHA, Thomas P., 'Surviving Industrial Targeting: State Credibility and Public Policy Contingencies in Multinational Subcontracting', **7** *Journal of Law, Economics, & Organization*, 1991, 117-143.

PALAY, Thomas M., 'Comparative Institutional Economics: The Governance of Rail Freight Contracting', **13** *Journal of Legal Studies*, 1984, 265-287.

PALAY, Thomas M., 'Avoiding Regulatory Constraints: Contracting Safeguards and the Role of Informal Agreements', **1** *Journal of Law, Economics, & Organization*, 1985, 155-175.

PALAY, Thomas M., 'A Contract Does not a Contract Make', *Wisconsin Law Review*, 1985, 561-579.

PALAY, Thomas M., 'Diversifying Physician Risk Through Contract', **52(1)** *Law and Contemporary Problems*, 1989, 161-181.

PATTERSON, Edwin W., 'The Apportionment of Business Risks through Legal Devices', **24** *Columbia Law Review*, 1924, 335-359.

POLINSKY, A. Mitchell, 'Fixed Price versus Spot Price Contracts: A Study in Risk Allocation', **3** *Journal of Law, Economics, and Organization*, 1987, 27-46.

POWERS, Mark J., 'Effects of Contract Provisions on the Success of a Future Contract', **49** *Journal of Farm Economics*, 1967, 833-843.

PRYOR, J.H., 'Commenda: The Operation of the Contract in Long Distance Commerce at Marseilles during the Thirteenth Century', **13** *Journal of European Economic History*, 1984, 397-440.

RIORDAN, Michael H., 'Contracting in an Idiosyncratic Market', **14** *Bell Journal of Economics*, 1983, 338-350.

ROB, Rafael, 'The Design of Procurement Contracts', **76** *American Economic Review*, 1986, 378-389.

SANDOR, Richard L., 'Innovation by an Exchange: A Case Study of the Development of the Plywood Futures Contract', **16** *Journal of Law and Economics*, 1973, 119-136.

SAPPINGTON, David E.M., 'Limited Liability Contracts between Principal and Agent', **29** *Journal of Economic Theory*, 1983, 1-21.

SCHANZE, Erich, 'Notes on Models of Choice, Incomplete Contracting, and the Agency Framework', **146** *Journal of Institutional and Theoretical Economics*, 1990, 684-690.

SCHERER, Frederic M., 'The Theory of Contractual Incentives For Cost Reduction', **78** *Quarterly Journal of Economics*, 1964, 257-280.

SEBENIUS, J.K. and STAN, P.J.E., 'Risk-Spreading Properties of Common Tax and Contract Instruments', **13** *Bell Journal of Economics*, 1982, 555-560.

SHAVELL, Steven, 'The Design of Contracts and Remedies for Breach', **99** *Quarterly Journal of Economics*, 1984, 121-148.

SHELTON, John, 'The Cost of Renting Versus Owning a Home', **44** *Land Economics*, 1968, 59-72.

SMITH, Janet Kiholm and COX, Steven R., 'The Pricing of Legal Services: A Contractual Solution to the Problem of Bilateral Opportunism', **14** *Journal of Legal Studies*, 1985, 167-183.

SPULBER, Daniel F., 'Auctions and Contract Enforcement', **6** *Journal of Law, Economics, & Organization*, 1990, 325-344.

TELSER, Lester C., 'A Theory of Self-enforcing Agreements', **53** *Journal of Business*, 1980, 27-44.

TELSER, Lester G., 'Why There Are Organized Futures Markets', **24** *Journal of Law and Economics*, 1981, 1-22.

TOWNSHEND, Robert M., 'Optimal Contracts and Competitive Markets with Costly State Verification', **21** *Journal of Economic Theory*, 1979, 265-293.

TREBILCOCK, Michael J., 'Restrictive Covenants in the Sale of a Business: An Economic Perspective', **4** *International Review of Law and Economics*, 1984, 137-161.

UMBECK, John, 'A Theory of Contract Choice and the California Gold Rush', **20** *Journal of Law and Economics*, 1977, 421-437.

VELJANOVSKI, Cento G., 'An Institutional Analysis of Futures Contracting', in GOSS, B.A. (ed.), *Future Markets: Their Establishment and Performance*, London, Croom Helm, 1984.

VELJANOVSKI, Cento G., 'Organized Futures Contracting', **5** *International Review of Law and Economics*, 1985, 25-38.

VELJANOVSKI, Cento G. and WHELAN, Christopher J., 'Professional Negligence and the Quality of Legal Services - An Economic Perspective', **46** *Modern Law Review*, 1983, 700-718.

VORST, Ton, 'The Relation between the Rent and Selling Price of a Building under Optimal Maintenance with Uncertainty', **10** *Journal of Economic Dynamics and Control*, 1986, 315-320.

WIGGINS, Steven N., 'The Comparitive Advantage of Long-Term Contracts and Firms', **6** *Journal of Law, Economics, & Organization*, 1990, 155-170.

WILLIAMSON, Oliver E., 'The Economics of Defense Contracting: Incentives and Performance', in McKEAN, R.N. (ed.), *Issues in Defense Economics*, New York, Columbia University Press, 1967, 217-256.

WILLIAMSON, Oliver E., *Markets and Hierarchies: Analysis and Antitrust Implication: A Study in the Economics of Internal Organization*, New York, Free Press, 1975, 286 p.

WILLIAMSON, Oliver E., 'Transaction-Cost Economics: The Governance of Contractual Relations', **22** *Journal of Law and Economics*, 1979, 233-261.

WILLIAMSON, Oliver E., 'Contract Analysis: The Transaction Cost Approach', in BURROWS, Paul and VELJANOVSKI, Cento G. (eds.), *The Economic Appraoch to Law*, London, Butterworths, 1981, 39-60.

WILLIAMSON, Oliver E., *The Economic Institutions of Capitalism: Firms, Markets, Relational Contracting*, New York, Free Press, 1985, 450 p.

YARBROUGH, Beth V. and YARBROUGH, Robert M., 'Institutions for the Governance of Opportunism in International Trade', **3** *Journal of Law, Economics, & Organization*, 1987, 129-139.

4110 Long-Term Contracts. Relational Contracts

ACHESON, James M., 'The Maine Lobster Market: Between Market and Hierarchy', **1** *Journal of Law, Economics, & Organization*, 1985, 385-398.

ADAMS, Michael, 'Franchising - A Case of Long-Term Contracts: Comment', **144** *Journal of Institutional and Theoretical Economics*, 1988, 145-148.

ARVAN, L. and LEITE, A.P.N., 'Cost Overruns in Long Term Projects', **8** *International Journal of Industrial Organization*, 1990, 443-467.

AZARIADIS, Costas, 'Human Capital and Self-Enforcing Contracts', **90** *Scandinavian Journal of Economics*, 1988, 507-528.

BAIRD, Douglas G., 'Self-Interest and Cooperation in Long-Term Contracts', **19** *Journal of Legal Studies*, 1990, 583-596.

BENDOR, Jonathan and MOOKHERJEE, Dilip, 'Norms, Third-Party Sanctions, and Cooperation', **6** *Journal of Law, Economics, & Organization*, 1990, 33-63.

BESTER, Helmut, 'Incentive-Compatible Long-Term Contracts and Job Rationing', **7** *Journal of Labor Economics*, 1989, 238-255.

BISHOP, William and PRENTICE, D.D., 'Some Legal and Economic Aspects of Fiduciary Remuneration', **46** *Modern Law Review*, 1983, 289 ff.

BLAIR, Roger D. and KASERMAN, David L., 'A Note on Bilateral Monopoly and Formula Price Contracts', **77** *American Economic Review*, 1987, 460-463.

BOUDREAUX, Don and EKELUND, Robert B., Jr., 'Regulation as an Exogenous Response to Market Failure: A Neo-Schumpeterian Response', **143** *Journal of Institutional and Theoretical Economics*, 1987, 537-554.

BROADMAN, Harry G. and TOMAN, Michael A., 'Non-Price Provisions in Long-Term Natural Gas Contracts', **62** *Land Economics*, 1986, 111-118.

BUTLER, Henry N. and BAYSINGER, Barry D., 'Vertical Restraints of Trade as Contractual Integration: a Synthesis of Relational Contracting Theory, Transaction-Cost Economics and Organization Theory', **32** *Emory Law Journal*, 1983, 1009-1109.

CAMPBELL, David, 'The Social Theory of Relational Contract: Macneil as the Modern Proudhon', **18** *International Journal of the Sociology of the Law*, 1990, 75-95.

CANES, Michael E. and NORMAN, Donald A., 'Long-term Contracts and Market Forces in the Natural Gas Market', **10(1)** *Journal of Energy and Development*, 1984, 73-96.

CRAWFORD, Vincent P., 'Long-Term Relationships Governed by Short-Term Contracts', **78** *American Economic Review*, 1988, 485-499.

CRéMER, Jacques, 'On the Economics of Repeat Buying', **15** *Rand Journal of Economics*, 1984, 396-403.

CREW, Michael A., 'Equity, Opportunism and the Design of Contractual Relations: Comment', **144** *Journal of Institutional and Theoretical Economics*, 1988, 196-199.

CROCKER, Keith J. and MASTEN, Scott E., 'Mitigating Contractual Hazards: Unilateral Options and Contract Length', **19** *Rand Journal of Economics*, 1988, 327-343.

CROCKER, Keith J. and MASTEN, Scott E., 'Pretia ex Machina? Prices and Process in Long-Term Contracts', **34** *Journal of Law and Economics*, 1991, 69-99.

CRYSTAL, Nathan M., 'An Empirical View of Relational Contracts under Article Two of the Uniform Commercial Code', *Annual Survey of American Law*, 1988, 293-306.

CUKIERMAN, Alex and SHIFFER, Zalman F., 'Contracting for Optimal Delivery Time in Long-Term Projects', **7** *Bell Journal of Economics*, 1976, 132-149.

DEWATRIPONT, Mathias, 'Renegotiation and Information Revelation over Time: The Case of Optimal Labor Contracts', **103** *Quarterly Journal of Economics*, 1989, 589-619.

EKELUND, Robert B., Jr. and HIGGINGS, Richard S., 'Capital Fixity, Innovations, and Long-Term Contracting: An Intertemporal Economic Theory', **72** *American Economic Review*, 1982, 32-46.

GAMBETTA, Diego (ed.), *Trust: Making and Breaking Cooperative Relations*, Oxford, Blackwell, 1988, 246 p.

GILLETTE, Clayton P., 'Commercial Rationality and the Duty to Adjust Long-Term Contracts', **69** *Minnesota Law Review*, 1985, 521 ff.

GILLETTE, Clayton P., 'Commercial Relationships and the Selection of Default Rules for Remote Risks', **19** *Journal of Legal Studies*, 1990, 535-581.

GOETZ, Charles J. and SCOTT, Robert E., 'Principles of Relational Contracts', **67** *Virginia Law Review*, 1981, 1089-1150.

GOLDBERG, Victor P., 'Toward an Expanded Economic Theory of Contract', **10** *Journal of Economic Issues*, 1976, 45-61. Reprinted in SAMUELS, Warren J. (ed.), *The Chicago School of Political Economy*, East Lansing, Division of Research, Graduate School of Business Administration, Michigan State University, 1976, 259-276.

GOLDBERG, Victor P., 'Regulation and Administered Contracts', **7** *Bell Journal of Economics*, 1976, 426-448.

GOLDBERG, Victor P., 'Relational Exchange: Economics and Complex Contracts', **23** *American Behavioral Scientist*, 1980, 337-352. Reprinted in GOLDBERG, Victor P. (ed.), *Readings in the Economics of Contract Law*, Cambridge, Cambridge University Press, 1989, 16-20.

GOLDBERG, Victor P., 'Pigou on Complex Contracts and Welfare Economics', **3** *Research in Law and Economics*, 1981, 39-51.

GOLDBERG, Victor P., 'A Relational Exchange Perspective on the Employment Relationship', in STEPHENS, Frank (ed.), *Organization and Labor*, 1984. Reprinted in GOLDBERG, Victor P. (ed.), *Readings in the Economics of Contract Law*, Cambridge, Cambridge University Press, 1989, 147-151.

GOLDBERG, Victor P., 'Price Adjustment in Long-Term Contracts', *Wisconsin Law Review*, 1985, 527-543. Reprinted in GOLDBERG, Victor P. (ed.), *Readings in the Economics of Contract Law*, Cambridge, Cambridge University Press, 1989, 225-235.

GOLDBERG, Victor P., 'Relational Exchange, Contract Law, and the *Boomer* Problem', **141** *Journal of Institutional and Theoretical Economics*, 1985, 570-575. Reprinted in GOLDBERG, Victor P. (ed.), *Readings in the Economics of Contract Law*, Cambridge, Cambridge University Press, 1989, 67-71 and 126-127.

GOLDBERG, Victor P. and ERICKSON, John R., 'Quantity and Price Adjustment in Long-Term Contracts: A Case Study of Petroleum Coke', **30** *Journal of Law and Economics*, 1987, 369-398.

GORDON, Robert W., 'Macaulay, Macneil, and the Discovery of Solidarity and Power in Contract Law', *Wisconsin Law Review*, 1985, 565-579.

GRANDY, Christopher, 'Can Government Be Trusted to Keep Its Part of a Social Contract?: New Jersey and the Railroads, 1825-1888', **5** *Journal of Law, Economics, & Organization*, 1989, 249-269.

HARRIS, Milton and HOLMSTROM, Bengt, 'On the Duration of Agreements', **28** *International Economic Review*, 1987, 389-406.

HART, Oliver D., 'Incomplete Contracts', in EATWELL, John, MILGATE, Murray and NEWMAN, Peter (eds.), *The New Palgrave: A Dictionary of Economics*, London, Macmillan, 1987, Volume 2, 752-759.

HART, Oliver and MOORE, John, 'Incomplete Contracts and Renegotation', **56** *Econometrica*, 1988, 755 ff.

HELLWIG, Martin F., 'Equity, Opportunism, and the Design of Contractual Relations: Comment', **144** *Journal of Institutional and Theoretical Economics*, 1988, 200-207.

HUBBARD, R. Glenn and WEINER, Robert J., 'Regulation and Long-term Contracting in U.S. Natural Gas Markets', **35** *Journal of Industrial Economics*, 1986, 71-79.

HUBBARD, R. Glenn and WEINER, Robert J., 'Efficient Contracting and Market Power: Evidence from the U.S. Natural Gas Industry', **34** *Journal of Law and Economics*, 1991, 25-67.

HUBERMAN, Gur and KAHN, Charles M., 'Strategic Renegotiation', **28** *Economic Letters*, 1988, 117-121.

HUBERMAN, Gur and KAHN, Charles W., 'Limited Contract Enforcement and

Strategic Renegotiation', **78** *American Economic Review*, 1988, 471-484.

JOHNSON, Alex M., Jr., 'Correctly Interpreting Long-Term Leases Pursuant to Modern Contract Law: Toward A Theory of Relational Leases', **74** *Virginia Law Review*, 1988, 751-808.

JOSKOW, Paul L., 'Vertical Integration and Long-Term Contracts: The Case of Coal-Burning Electric Generating Plants', **1** *Journal of Law, Economics & Organization*, 1985, 33-80.

JOSKOW, Paul L., 'Long Term Vertical Relationships and the Study of Industrial Organization and Government Regulation', **141** *Zeitschrift für die gesamte Staatswissenschaft*, 1985, 586-593.

JOSKOW, Paul L., 'Contract Duration and Relationship-Specific Investments: Empirical Evidence from Coal Markets', **77** *American Economic Review*, 1987, 168-185.

JOSKOW, Paul L., 'Price Adjustment in Long-Term Contracts: The Case of Coal', **31** *Journal of Law and Economics*, 1988, 47-83.

JOSKOW, Paul L., 'The Performance of Long-term Contracts: Further Evidence from Coal Markets', **21** *Rand Journal of Economics*, 1990, 251-274.

KAUFMANN, Patrick J. and STERN, Louis W., 'Relational Exchange Norms, Perceptions of Unfairness, and Retained Hostility in Commercial Litigation', **32** *Journal of Conflict Resolution*, 1988, 534-552.

KLEIN, Benjamin, CRAWFORD, Robert G. and ALCHIAN, Armen A., 'Vertical Integration, Appropriable Rents, and the Competitive Contracting Process', **21** *Journal of Law and Economics*, 1978, 297-326.

LAMBERT, Richard A., 'Long-Term Contracts and Moral Hazard', **14** *Bell Journal of Economics*, 1983, 441-451.

LAWRENCE, William H., 'Lender Control Liability: An Analytical Model Illustrated with Applications to the Relational Theory of Secured Financing', **62** *Southern California Law Review*, 1989, 1387-1447.

LEWIS, T., LINDSEY, R. and WARE, R., 'Long-Term Bilateral Monopoly: The Case of an Exhaustible Resource', **17** *Rand Journal of Economics*, 1986, 89-104.

LEWIS, Tracy R., 'Reputation and Contractual Performance in Long-Term Projects', **17** *Rand Journal of Economics*, 1986, 141-157.

LINDENBERG, Siegwart and DE Vos, Henk, 'The Limits of Solidarity: Relational Contracting in Perspective and Some Criticism of Traditional Sociology', **141** *Zeitschrift für die gesamte Staatswissenschaft*, 1985, 558-569.

LINZER, Peter, 'Uncontracts: Context, Contorts and the Relational Approach', *Annual Survey of American Law*, 1988, 139-198.

MACAULAY, Stewart, 'Non-Contractual Relations in Business: A Preliminary Study', **25** *American Sociological Review*, 1963, 55-70. Reprinted in GOLDBERG, Victor P. (ed.), *Readings in the Economics of Contract Law*, Cambridge, Cambridge University Press, 1989, 4-15.

MACAULAY, Stewart, 'Elegant Models, Empirical Pictures and the Complexities of Contract', **11** *Law and Society Review*, 1977, 507-528.

MACAULAY, Stewart, 'An Empirical View of Contract', *Wisconsin Law Review*,

1985, 465-482.

MACNEIL, Ian R., 'The Many Futures of Contracts', **47** *Southern California Law Review*, 1974, 691-816.

MACNEIL, Ian R., 'A Primer of Contract Planning', **48** *Southern California Law Review*, 1975, 627-704.

MACNEIL, Ian R., 'Contracts: Adjustments of Long-Term Economic Relations under Classical, Neoclassical and Relational Contract Law', **72** *Northwestern University Law Review*, 1978, 854-905.

MACNEIL, Ian R., *The New Social Contract: An Inquiry Into Modern Contractual Relations*, New Haven, Yale University Press, 1980, 164 p.

MACNEIL, Ian R., 'Power, Contract and the Economic Model', **14** *Journal of Economic Issues*, 1980, 909-923.

MACNEIL, Ian R., 'Economic Analysis of Contractual Relations', in BURROWS, Paul and VELJANOVSKI, Cento G. (eds.), *The Economic Appraoch to Law*, London, Butterworths, 1981, 61-92.

MACNEIL, Ian R., 'Economic Analysis of Contractual Relations: Its Shortfalls and the Need for a "Rich Classificatory Apparatus"', **75** *Northwestern University Law Review*, 1981, 1018-1063.

MACNEIL, Ian R., 'Values in Contract: Internal and External', **78** *Northwestern University Law Review*, 1983, 340-418.

MACNEIL, Ian R., 'Relational Contract: What We Do and Do Not Know', *Wisconsin Law Review*, 1985, 483-525.

MACNEIL, Ian R., 'Reflections on Relational Contract', **141** *Zeitschrift für die gesamte Staatswissenschaft*, 1985, 541-546.

MACNEIL, Ian R., 'Exchange Revisited: Individual Utility and Social Solidarity', **96** *Ethics*, 1986, 567-593.

MACNEIL, Ian R., 'Barriers to the Idea of Relational Contracts', in NICKLISCH, Fritz (ed.), *Der Komplexe Langzeitvertrag. Strukturen und Internationale Schiedsgerichtsbarkeit. The Complex Long-Term Contract. Structures and International Arbitration*, Heidelberg, Müller Juristischer Verlag, 1987, 31-46.

MACNEIL, Ian R., 'Relational Contract Theory as Sociology: A Reply', **143** *Journal of Institutional and Theoretical Economics*, 1987, 272-290.

MASTEN, Scott E. and CROCKER, Keith J., 'Efficient Adaptation in Long-Term Contracts: Take-or-Pay Provisions for Natural Gas', **75** *American Economic Review*, 1985, 1083-1093.

MULHERIN, J. Harold, 'Complexity in Long-Term Contracts: An Analysis of Natural Gas Contractual Provisions', **2** *Journal of Law, Economics, & Organization*, 1986, 105-117.

MULLER GRAFF, Peter Christian, 'Franchising: A Case of Long-term Contracts', **144** *Journal of Institutional and Theoretical Economics*, 1988, 122-144.

MULLOCK, Philip, 'The New Paradigm of Contract: A Hermeneutical Approach', **17** *Valparaiso University Law Review*, 1983, 677-704.

NARASIMHAN, Subha, 'Of Expectations, Incomplete Contracting, and the Bargain Principle', **74** *California Law Review*, 1986, 1123-1202.

NARASIMHAN, Subha, 'Relationship or Boundary? Handling Successive Contracts', **77** *California Law Review*, 1989, 1077-1122.

NICKLISCH, Fritz (ed.), *Der Komplexe Langzeitvertrag. Strukturen und Internationale Schiedsgerichtsbarkeit. The Complex Long-Term Contract. Structures and International Arbitration*, Heidelberg, Müller Juristischer Verlag, 1987, 597 p.

PAULY, Mark V., 'Relational Contracting, Transaction Cost Economics and the Governance of HMOs', **59** *Temp. Law Quarterly*, 1986, 927 ff.

PAULY, Mark V., 'The Rational Nonpurchase of Long-Term Insurance', **98** *Journal of Political Economy*, 1990, 153-168.

RAMSEYER, J. Mark, 'Indentured Prostitution in Imperial Japan: Credible Commitments in the Commercial Sex Industry', **7** *Journal of Law, Economics, & Organization*, 1991, 89-116.

RAMSEYER, J. Mark, 'Legal Rules in Repeated Deals: Banking in the Shadow of Defection in Japan', **20** *Journal of Legal Studies*, 1991, 91-117.

SCHANZE, Erich, 'Symbiotic Contracts: Exploring Long-Term Agency Structures between Contract and Corporation', in JOERGES, Ch. (ed.), *Regulating the Franchise Relationship: Comparative and European Aspects*, Baden-Baden, Nomos, 1991.

SCOTT, Robert E., 'Risk Distribution and Adjustment in Long-Term Contracts', in NICKLISCH, Fritz (ed.), *Der Komplexe Langzeitvertrag. Strukturen und Internationale Schiedsgerichtsbarkeit. The Complex Long-Term Contract. Structures and International Arbitration*, Heidelberg, Müller Juristischer Verlag, 1987, 51-100.

SCOTT, Robert E., 'Conflict and Cooperation in Long-Term Contracts', **75** *California Law Review*, 1987, 2005-2054.

SCOTT, Robert E., 'A Relational Theory of Default Rules for Commercial Contracts', **19** *Journal of Legal Studies*, 1990, 597-616.

SPEIDEL, Richard E., 'Court-Imposed Price Adjustements Under Long-Term Supply Contracts', **76** *Northwestern University Law Review*, 1981, 369-422.

STRASSER, Kurt A., 'Contract's "Many Features" after Death: Unanswered Questions of Scope and Purpose', **32** *South Carolina Law Review*, 1981, 501-546.

VAN PELT, Mark H., 'Introduction', *Wisconsin Law Review*, 1985, 461-463.

WHITFORD, William C., 'Ian Macneil's Contribution to Contracts Scholarship', *Wisconsin Law Review*, 1985, 545-560.

WILLIAMSON, Oliver E., 'Credible Commitments: Using Hostages to Support Exchange', **73** *American Economic Review*, 1983, 519-540.

WILLIAMSON, Oliver E., 'Credible Commitments: Further Remarks', **74** *American Economic Review*, 1984, 488-490.

WILLIAMSON, Oliver E., *The Economic Institutions of Capitalism: Firms, Markets, Relational Contracting*, New York, Free Press, 1985, 450 p.

WILLIAMSON, Oliver E., *Antitrust Economics: Mergers, Contracting and Strategic Behavior*, Oxford, Blackwell, 1989, 363 p.

ZOLT, Eric M. and BERKOWITZ, Jeffrey I., 'An Economic Perspective on the Law of Excessive Profit Recovery', **45** *University of Chicago Law Review*, 1978, 882-905.

4120 Sharecropping

ALLEN, F. 'On Share Contracts and Screening', **13** *Bell Journal of Economics*, 1982, 541-547.

BARDHAN, P.K. and SRINIVASAN, T.N., 'Cropsharing Tenancy in Agriculture: A Theoretical and Empirical Analysis', **61** *American Economic Review*, 1971, 48-64.

BARDHAN, P.K. and SRINIVASAN, T.N., 'Cropsharing Tenancy in Agriculture: Comment', **64** *American Economic Review*, 1974, 1067-1069.

BELL, Clive and ZUSMAN, Pinhas, 'A Bargaining Theoretic Approach to Cropsharing Contracts', **66** *American Economic Review*, 1976, 578-588.

BRAVERMAN, Avishay and STIGLITZ, Joseph E., 'Sharecropping and the Interlinking of Agrarian Markets', **72** *American Economic Review*, 1982, 695-715.

CHEUNG, Steven N.S., 'Private Property Rights and Share Cropping', **76** *Journal of Political Economy*, 1968, 1107-1122.

CHEUNG, Steven N.S., *A Theory of Share Tenancy*, Chicago, University of Chicago Press, 1969, 188 p.

DATTA, Samar K., O'HARA, Donald J. and NUGENT, Jeffrey B., 'Choice of Argicultural Tenancy in the Presence of Transaction Costs', **62** *Land Economics*, 1986, 145-156.

HALLAGAN, William S., 'Self-Selection by Contractual Choice and the Theory of Sharecropping', **9** *Bell Journal of Economics*, 1978, 344-354.

HALLAGAN, William S., 'Share Contracting for California Gold', **15** *Explorations in Economic History*, 1978, 196-210.

JOHNSON, D. Gale, 'Resource Allocation under Share Contracts', **58** *Journal of Political Economy*, 1950, 111-123.

KHAN, Shahrukh Rafi, 'Henry George and an Alternative Islamic Land Tenure System', **36** *Economic Development & Cultural Change*, 1988, 721-739.

MURRELL, Peter, 'The Economics of Sharing: a Transactions Cost Analysis of Contractual Choice in Farming', **14** *Bell Journal of Economics*, 1983, 283-293.

NEWBERY, D.M.G., 'Cropsharing Tenancy in Agriculture: Comment', **64** *American Economic Review*, 1974, 1060-1066.

SNABAN, Radwan Ali, 'Testing Between Competing Models of Sharecropping', **95** *Journal of Political Economy*, 1987, 893-920.

STIGLITZ, Joseph E., 'Sharecropping', in EATWELL, John, MILGATE, Murray and NEWMAN, Peter (eds.), *The New Palgrave: A Dictionary of Economics*, London, Macmillan, 1987, Volume 4, 320-323.

WARR, Peter G., 'Share Contracts, Limited Information and Production Uncertainty',

17 *Australian Economic Papers*, 1978, 110-123.

4130 Warranties

CENTNER, Terence J. and WETZSTEIN, Michael E., 'Reducing Moral Hazard Associated with Implied Warranties of Animal Health', **69** *American Journal of Agricultural Economics*, 1987, 143-150.

CHAPMAN, Kenneth and MEURER, Michael J., 'Efficient Remedies for Breach of Warranty', **52(1)** *Law and Contemporary Problems*, 1989, 107-131.

COOPER, Russell and ROSS, Thomas W., 'Product Warranties and Double Moral Hazard', **16** *Rand Journal of Economics*, 1985, 103-113.

COOPER, Russell and ROSS, Thomas W., 'An Intertemporal Model of Warranties', **21** *Canadian Journal of Economics*, 1988, 72-286.

COURVILLE, Léon and HAUSMAN, Warren H., 'Warranty Scope and Reliability under Imperfect Information and Alternative Market Structures', **52** *Journal of Business*, 1979, 361-378.

CROCKER, Keith J., 'A Reexamination of the "Lemons" Market When Warranties Are Not Prepurchase Quality Signals', **2** *Information Economics and Policy*, 1986, 147-162.

EISENACH, Jeffrey A., HIGGINS, Richard S. and SHUGHART, William F. II, 'Warranties, Tie-ins, and Efficient Insurance Contracts: A Theory and Three Case Studies', **6** *Research in Law and Economics*, 1984, 167-185.

EMONS, Winand, *On the Economic Theory of Warranties*, Bonn, 1987, 84 p.

EMONS, Winand, 'Warranties, Moral Hazard and the Lemons Problem', **46** *Journal of Economic Theory*, 1988, 16-33.

EMONS, Winand, 'The Theory of Warranty Contracts', **3** *Journal of Economic Surveys*, 1989, 43-57.

GILL, Harley Leroy and ROBERTS, David C., 'New Car Warranty Repair: Theory and Evidence', **55** *Southern Economic Journal*, 1989, 662-678.

GROSSMAN, Sanford J., 'The Informational Role of Warranties and Private Disclosure about Product Quality', **24** *Journal of Law and Economics*, 1981, 461-483.

HEAL, Geoffrey, 'Guarantees and Risk Sharing', **44** *Review of Economic Studies*, 1977, 549-560.

KUBO, Yuji, 'Quality Uncertainty and Guarantee', **30** *European Economic Review*, 1986, 1063-1079.

LELAND, Hayne E., 'Comments on Grossman', **24** *Journal of Law and Economics*, 1981, 485-489.

LOWENTHAL, Franklin, 'Product Warranty Period: A Markovian Approach to Estimation and Analysis of Repair and Replacement Costs: A Comment', **58** *Accounting Review*, 1983, 837-838.

LUTZ, Nancy A., 'Warranties as Signals Under Consumer Moral Hazard', **20** *Rand*

Journal of Economics, 1989, 239-255.

MANN, Duncan P., 'Money-Back Warranties vs. Replacement Warranties: A Simple Comparison', **80** *American Economic Review. Papers and Proceedings*, 1990, 432-436.

MANN, Duncan P. and WISSINK, Jennifer P., 'Money-Back Contracts with Double Moral Hazard', **19** *Rand Journal of Economics*, 1988, 285-292.

PALFREY, Thomas R., 'An Experimental Study of Warranty Coverage and Dispute Resolution in Competitive Markets', in IPPOLITO, Pauline M. and SCHEFFMAN, David T. (eds.), *Empirical Approaches to Consumer Protection Economics*, Washington, Federal Trade Commission, 1986, 307-372.

PALFREY, Thomas R. and ROMER, Thomas, 'Warranties, Performance, and the Resolution of Buyer-Seller Disputes', **14** *Bell Journal of Economics*,1983, 97-117.

PRIEST, George L., 'A Theory of the Consumer Product Warranty', **90** *Yale Law Journal*, 1981, 1297-1352. Reprinted in GOLDBERG, Victor P. (ed.), *Readings in the Economics of Contract Law*, Cambridge, Cambridge University Press, 1989, 174-184.

SCHWARTZ, Alan and WILDE, Louis L., 'Warranty Markets and Public Policy', **1(1)** *Information Economics and Policy*, 1983, 55-67.

SCHWARTZ, Alan and WILDE, Louis L., 'Imperfect Information in Markets for Contract Terms: The Examples of Warranties and Security Interests', **69** *Virginia Law Review*, 1983, 1387-1485.

SHOGREN, Jason F., 'Reducing Moral Hazard Associated with Implied Warranties of Animal Health: Comment', **70** *American Journal of Agricultural Economics*, 1988, 410-412.

WEHRT, Klaus, 'Die Qualitätshaftung des Verkäufers aus ökonomischer Sicht' [The Quality Liability of Sellers from an Economic Point of View], in OTT, Claus and SCHÄFER, Hans-Bernd (eds.), *Ökonomische Probleme des Zivilrechts*, Berlin, Springer, 1991, 235-259.

WHITFORD, William C., 'Comment on a Theory of the Consumer Product Warranty', **91** *Yale Law Journal*, 1982, 1371-1385.

4140 Franchising

ADAMS, Michael, 'Franchising - A Case of Long-Term Contracts: Comment', **144** *Journal of Institutional and Theoretical Economics*, 1988, 145-148.

BARRON, John M. and UMBECK, John R., 'The Effects of Different Contractual Arrangements: The Case of the Retail Gasoline Markets', **27** *Journal of Law and Economics*, 1984, 313-328.

BRICKLEY, James A. and DARK, Frederick N., 'The Choice of Organizational Form: The Case of Franchising', **18** *Journal of Financial Economics*, 1987, 401 ff.

BRICKLEY, James A., DARK, Frederick H. and WEISBACH, Michael S., 'The Economic Effects of Franchise Termination Laws', **34** *Journal of Law and*

Economics, 1991, 101-132.

CAVES, Richard E. and MURPHY, William F. II, 'Franchising: Firms, Markets and Intangible Assets', **42** *Southern Economic Journal*, 1976, 572-586.

HADFIELD, Gilliam K., 'Problematic Relations: Franchising and the Law of Incomplete Contracts', **42** *Stanford Law Review*, 1990, 927-992.

INABA, Frederick S., 'Franchising: Monopoly by Contract', **47** *Southern Economic Journal*, 1980, 65-72.

KLEIN, Benjamin and SAFT, Lester F., 'The Law and Economics of Franchise Tying Contracts', **28** *Journal of Law and Economics*, 1985, 345-361.

KNEPPERS-HEYNERT, E.M., *Een economische en juridische analyse van franchising tegen de achtergrond van een property rights- en transactiekosten benadering* [An Economic and Legal Analysis of Franchising in the Light of a Property and Transaction Costs Approach] (diss. Groningen), Groningen, Van Denderen, 1988, 268 p.

MARTIN, Robert E., 'Franchising and Risk Management', **78** *American Economic Review*, 1988, 954-968.

MATHEWSON, G. Frank and WINTER, Ralph A., 'The Economics of Franchise Contracts', **28** *Journal of Law and Economics*, 1985, 503-526.

MULLER GRAFF, Peter Christian, 'Franchising: A Case of Long-term Contracts', **144** *Journal of Institutional and Theoretical Economics*, 1988, 122-144.

NORTON, Seth W., 'Franchising, Labor Productivity, and the New Institutional Economics', **145** *Journal of Institutional and Theoretical Economics*, 1989, (Nr.4.), 578-596.

RUBIN, Paul H., 'The Theory of the Firm and the Structure of the Franchise Contract', **21** *Journal of Law and Economics*, 1978, 223-233.

WIGGINS, Steven N., 'Franchising - A Case of Long term Contracts: Comment', **144** *Journal of Institutional and Theoretical Economics*, 1988, 149-151.

4200 Contract Formation

ADAMS, Michael, 'Ökonomische Analyse des Gesetzes zur Regelung des Rechts der Allgemeinen Geschäftsbedingungen' [Economic Analysis of Laws on Standard Term Clauses], in NEUMANN, M. (ed.), *Ansprüche, Eigentums- und Verfügungsrechte*, Schriften des Vereins für Socialpolitik, Vol. 140, 1983, 655-680.

ADAMS, Michael, 'Zur Behandlung von Irrtümern und Offenbarungspflichten im Vertragsrecht' [On Mistake and Information Revelation Duties in Contract Law], **186** *Archiv für die civilistische Praxis*, 1986, 453-489.

BARNETT, Randy E. and BECKER, Mary E., 'Beyond Reliance: Promissory Estoppel, Contract Formalities, and Misrepresentation', **15** *Hofstra Law Review*, 1987, 443 ff.

BAUDENBACHER, Carl, *Wirtschafts- schuld- und verfahrens-rechtliche Grundprobleme der Allgemeinen Geschäftsbedingungen* [Standard Term Clauses: Basic Problems of Economic, Liability and Procedural Law], Zurich, Schulthess, 1983.

BESSONE, Mario, 'Gli "standards" dei contratti di impresa e l'analisi economica del diritto' [The "Standards" in Contracts and Economic Analysis of Law], *Giurisprudenza di merito*, 1984, 982-987.

BIRMINGHAM, Robert L., 'The Duty to Disclose and the Prisoner's Dilemma: *Laidlaw v. Organ*', **29** *William and Mary Law Review*, 1988, 249-283.

BISHOP, William, 'Negligent Misrepresentation through the Economists' Eyes', **96** *Law Quarterly Review*, 1980, 360-379.

BISHOP, William, 'Negligent Misrepresentation: An Economic Reformulation', in BURROWS, Paul and VELJANOVSKI, Cento G. (eds.), *The Economic Appraoch to Law*, London, Butterworths, 1981, 167-186.

BRAUNSTEIN, Michael, 'Remedy, Reason, and the Statute of Frauds: A Critical Economic Analysis', *Utah Law Review*, 1989, 383-431.

CASTERMANS, A.G., 'Schadevergoeding bij dwaling' [Damages for Misrepresentation], *Rechtsgeleerd Magazijn Themis*, 1989, 136-146.

CASTERMANS, A.G. and NOTERMANS, R., 'Naar een economische analyse van de mededelingsplicht bij dwaling' [Towards an Economic Analysis of the Duty to Inform in Misrepresentation Law], *BW-krant jaarboek 1985, BW-NBW: twee sporen, één weg*, Leiden, Rijksuniversiteit Leiden, 1985, 141-155.

COLEMAN, Jules, HECKATHON, Douglas and MASER, Steven, 'A Bargaining Theory Approach to Default Provisions and Disclosure Rules in Contract Law', **12** *Harvard Journal of Law and Public Policy*, 1989, 639 ff.

CRASWELL, Richard, 'Precontractual Investigation as an Optimal Precaution Problem', **17** *Journal of Legal Studies*, 1988, 401-436.

CURNES, Ellen J., 'Protecting the Virginia Homebuyer: A Duty to Disclose Defects', **73** *Virginia Law Review*, 1987, 459-481.

DALZELL, John, 'Duress by Economic Pressure', **20** *North Carolina Law Review*, 1942, 237-277. Reprinted in KRONMAN, Anthony T. and POSNER, Richard A. (eds.), *The Economics of Contract Law*, Boston, Little Brown, 1979, 67-72.

Reprinted in GOLDBERG, Victor P. (ed.), *Readings in the Economics of Contract Law*, Cambridge, Cambridge University Press, 1989, 188-193.

DIAMOND, Peter A. and MASKIN, Eric, 'An Equilibrium Analysis of Search and Breach of Contract, I: Steady States', **10** *Bell Journal of Economics*, 1979, 282-316

DIAMOND, Peter A. and MASKIN, Eric, 'An Equilibrium Analysis of Search and Breach of Contract II: A Nonsteady State Example', **25** *Journal of Economic Theory*, 1981, 165-195.

DUGGAN, A.J., 'Economic Analysis of Standard Form Contracts: An Exposition and A Critique' in CRANSTON, Ross and SCHICK, Anne (eds.), *Law and Economics*, Canberra, Austraalian National University, 1982, 145-162.

EISENBERG, Melvin Aron, 'Donative Promises', **47** *University of Chicago Law Review*, 1979, 1-33.

EPSTEIN, Richard A., 'Unconscionability: A Critical Reappraisal', **18** *Journal of Law and Economics*, 1975, 293-315.

FISHMAN, Michael J. and HAGERTY, Kathleen M., 'The Optimal Amount of Discretion to Allow in Disclosure', **104** *Quarterly Journal of Economics*, 1990, 427-444.

FULLER, Lon L., 'Consideration and Form', **41** *Columbia Law Review*, 1941, 799 ff. Reprinted in KRONMAN, Anthony T. and POSNER, Richard A. (eds.), *The Economics of Contract Law*, Boston, Little Brown, 1979, 40-45.

GOLDBERG, Victor P., 'Competitive Bidding and the Production of Precontract Information', **8** *Bell Journal of Economics*, 1977, 250-261.

JOHNSTON, Jason S., 'Strategic Bargaining and the Economic Theory of Contract Default Rules', **100** *Yale Law Journal*, 1990, 615-664.

KATZ, Avery, 'The Strategic Structure of Offer and Acceptance: Game Theory and the Law of Contract Formation', **89** *Michigan Law Review*, 1990, 215-295.

KOBOLDT, Christian, ' Kommentar' [Comment] (On Schanze, Stellvertretung und ökonomische Agentur-Theorie), in OTT, Claus and SCHÄFER, Hans-Bernd (eds.), *Ökonomische Probleme des Zivilrechts*, Berlin, Springer, 1991, 76-86.

KOCH, Harald, 'Die Ökonomie der Gestaltungsrechte. Möglichkeiten und Grenzen der ökonomische Analyse des Rechts am Beispiel von Kündiging und Anfechtung' [The Economics of Dispositive Right. Possibilities and Limits of the Economic Analysis of Law by the Example of Notion of Termination and Dispute], in BERNSTEIN, H., DROBNIG, U. and KÖTZ, H. (eds.), *Festschrift für Konrad Zweigert zum 70. Geburtstag*, Tübingen, J.C.B. Mohr, 1981, 851-877.

KOSTRITSKY, Juliet P., 'Illegal Contracts and Efficient Deterrence: A Study in Modern Contract Theory', **74** *Iowa Law Review*, 1989, 115-163.

KRONMAN, Anthony T., 'Mistake, Disclosure, Information, and the Law of Contracts', **7** *Journal of Legal Studies*, 1978, 1-34.

LEHMANN, Michael, 'Die Untersuchungs- und Rügepflicht des Käufers in BGB und HGB. Rechtsvergleichender Überblick - ökonomische Analyse' [The Duty to Examine and Notify a Defect in the German Civil and Commercial Code. A Comparitive Survey - Economic Analysis],in *Wertpapiermitteilungen*, 1980, Bd.II, 1162-1169.

LEHMANN, Michael, *Vertragsanbahnung durch Werbung* [Contract Preparing through Promotion], München, C. H. Beck, 1981.

MACNEIL, Ian R., 'Bureaucracy and Contracts of Adhesion', **22** *Osgoode Hall Law Journal*, 1984, 5-28.

MATHER, Henry, 'Contract Modification under Duress', **33** *North Carolina Law Review*, 1982, 615-658.

OTT, Claus, 'Vorvertragliche Aufklärungspflichten im Recht des Güter- und Leistungsaustausches' [Precontractual Obligation to Provide Information in the Sale of Goods and Services Act], in OTT, Claus and SCHÄFER, Hans-Bernd (eds.), *Ökonomische Probleme des Zivilrechts*, Berlin, Springer, 1991, 142-162.

POSNER, Richard A., 'Gratuitous Promises in Economic and Law', **6** *Journal of Legal Studies*, 1977, 411-426. Reprinted in GOLDBERG, Victor P. (ed.), *Readings in the Economics of Contract Law*, Cambridge, Cambridge University Press, 1989, 194-198.

ROBINSON, Thorton, 'Enforcing Extorted Contract Modifications', **68** *Iowa Law Review*, 1983, 699-707.

ROTH, G., 'Der Schutzzweck richterlicher Kontrolle von AGB' [The Protection Goal of the Judicial Control of Standard Term Clauses], **4(2)** *Österreichische Zeitschrift für Wirtschaftsrecht*, 1977, 32-37.

ROTTENBERG, Simon, 'Mistaken Judicial Activism: Proposed Constraints on Creditor Remedies', **4** *Cato Journal*, 1985, 335-350. Reprinted in DORN, James A. and MANNE, Henry G. (eds.), *Economic Liberties and the Judiciary*, Fairfax, George Mason University Press, 1987, 335-349.

SCHANZE, Erich, 'Stellvertretung und ökonomische Agentur-Theorie - Probleme und Wechselbezüge' [The Law of Agency and Agency Theory - Problems and Relations], in OTT, Claus and SCHÄFER, Hans-Bernd (eds.), *Ökonomische Probleme des Zivilrechts*, Berlin, Springer, 1991, 60-75.

SCHEPPELE, Kim Lane, *Legal Secrets, Equality and Efficiency in the Common Law*, Chicago, University of Chicago Press, 1988, 363 p.

SCHWARTZ, Alan, 'A Re-examination of Nonsubstantive Unconscionability', **63** *Virginia Law Review*, 1977, 1053-1083.

SHAVELL, Steven, 'An Economic Analysis of Altriusm and Deferred Gifts', **20** *Journal of Legal Studies*, 1991, 401-421.

SMITH, Janet Kiholm and SMITH, Richard L., 'Contract Law, Mutual Mistake, and Incentives to Produce and Disclose Information', **19** *Journal of Legal Studies*, 1990, 467-488.

TREBILCOCK, Michael J., 'The Doctrine of Inequality of Bargaining Power: Post--Benthamite Economics in the House of Lords', **26** *University of Toronto Law Journal*, 1976, 359-385. Reprinted in KRONMAN, Anthony T. and POSNER, Richard A. (eds.), *The Economics of Contract Law*, Boston, Little Brown, 1979, 78-92.

TREBILCOCK, Michael J., 'An Economic Approach to the Doctrine of Unconscionability', in REITER, Barry J. and SWAN, John (eds.), *Studies in Contract Law*, Toronto, Butterworths, 1980, 467 p.

TREBILCOCK, Michael J., 'The Role of Insurance Considerations in the Choice of Efficient Civil Liability Rules', **4** *Journal of Law, Economics, & Organization*,

1988, 243-265.

TREBILCOCK, Michael J. and DEWEES, Donald N., 'Judicial Control of Standard Form Contracts', in BURROWS, Paul and VELJANOVSKI, Cento G. (eds.), *The Economic Appraoch to Law*, London, Butterworths, 1981, 93-119.

VILLA, Gianroberto, 'Errore riconosciuto, annullamento del contratto ed incentivi alla ricerca di informazioni' [Known Mistake, Contract Avoidance and Incentives To Gathering Information], *Quadrimestre*, 1988, 286-300.

4300 Performance. Implied Terms

AIVAZIAN, Varouj A., TREBILCOCK, Michael J. and PENNY, Michael, 'The Law of Contract Modifications: The Uncertain Quest for a Benchmark of Enforceability', **22** *Osgood Hall Law Journal*, 1984, 173-212. Reprinted in GOLDBERG, Victor P. (ed.), *Readings in the Economics of Contract Law*, Cambridge, Cambridge University Press, 1989, 201-207.

ASHLEY, Stephen S., 'The Economic Implications of the Doctrine of Impossibility', **26** *Hastings Law Journal*, 1975, 1251-1276.

BIRMINGHAM, Robert L., 'A Second Look at Suez Canal Cases: Excuse for Nonperformance of Contractual Obligations in the Light of Economic Theory', **20** *Hastings Law Journal*, 1969, 1393-1416.

BRUCE, Christopher J., 'An Economic Analysis of the Impossibility Doctrine', **11** *Journal of Legal Studies*, 1982, 311-323.

BURTON, Steven J., 'Breach of Contract and the Common Law Duty to Perform in Good Faith', **94** *Harvard Law Review*, 1980, 369-403.

BURTON, Steven J., 'Good Faith Performance of a Contract within Article 2 of the Uniform Commercial Code', **67** *Iowa Law Review*, 1981, 1-30.

GILLETTE, Clayton P., 'Commercial Rationality and the Duty to Adjust Long-Term Contracts', **69** *Minnesota Law Review*, 1985, 521 ff.

GILLETTE, Clayton P., 'Commercial Relationships and the Selection of Default Rules for Remote Risks', **19** *Journal of Legal Studies*, 1990, 535-581.

GOETZ, Charles J. and SCOTT, Robert E., 'The Mitigation Principle: Toward a General Theory of Contractual Obligation', **69** *Virginia Law Review*, 1983, 967-1024. Reprinted in GOLDBERG, Victor P. (ed.), *Readings in the Economics of Contract Law*, Cambridge, Cambridge University Press, 1989, 61-68 and 199-200.

GOETZ, Charles J. and SCOTT, Robert E., 'The Limits of Expanded Choice: An Analysis of the Interactions between Express and Implied Contract Terms', **73** *California Law Review*, 1985, 261-322.

GOLDBERG, Victor P., 'Relational Exchange, Contract Law, and the *Boomer* Problem', **141** *Journal of Institutional and Theoretical Economics*, 1985, 570-575. Reprinted in GOLDBERG, Victor P. (ed.), *Readings in the Economics of Contract Law*, Cambridge, Cambridge University Press, 1989, 67-71 and 126-127.

GOLDBERG, Victor P., 'Impossibility and Related Excuses', **144** *Journal of Institutional and Theoretical Economics*, 1988, 100-116. Reprinted in GOLDBERG, Victor P. (ed.), *Readings in the Economics of Contract Law*, Cambridge, Cambridge University Press, 1989, 221-224.

GRAHAM, Daniel A. and PEIRCE, Ellen R., 'Contract Modification: An Economic Analysis of the Hold-Up Game', **52(1)** *Law and Contemporary Problems*, 1989, 9-32.

HART, Oliver D. and MOORE, John, 'Incomplete Contracts and Renegotiation', **56** *Econometrica*, 1988, 755-785.

JOSKOW, Paul L., 'Commercial Impossibility, the Uranium Market and the

Westinghouse Case', **6** *Journal of Legal Studies*, 1977, 119-176.

KAHN, Charles and HUBERMAN, Gur, 'Default, Foreclosure, and Strategic Renegotiation', **52(1)** *Law and Contemporary Problems*, 1989, 49-61.

KOLLER, Ingo, *Die Risikozurechnung bei Vertragsstörungen in Austauschverträgen* [The Risk Allocation of Contract Disturbances in Bilateral Contracts], München, C.H. Beck, Münchener Universitätsschriften, Vol. 39, 1979, 474 p.

MURIS, Timothy J., 'Opportunistic Behaviour and the Law of Contracts', **65** *Minnesota Law Review*, 1981, 521-590.

NARASIMHAN, Subha, 'Of Expectations, Incomplete Contracting, and the Bargain Principle', **74** *California Law Review*, 1986, 1123-1202.

PERLOFF, Jeffrey M., 'The Effects of Breaches of Forward Contracts Due to Unanticipated Price Changes', **10** *Journal of Legal Studies*, 1981, 221-235.

PHILLIPS, Jenny, 'Comments on Posner's and Rosenfield's Paper', in SKOGH, Göran (ed.), *Law and Economics. Report from a Symposium in Lund, Sweden, 24-26 August 1977*, Lund, Juridiska Föreningen, 1978, 95-96.

POSNER, Richard A. and ROSENFIELD, Andrew M., 'Impossibility and Related Doctrines in Contract Law: An Economic Analysis', **6** *Journal of Legal Studies*, 1977, 83-118. Reprinted in SKOGH, Göran (ed.), *Law and Economics. Report from a Symposium in Lund, Sweden, 24-26 August 1977*, Lund, Juridiska Föreningen, 1978, 57-94. Reprinted in GOLDBERG, Victor P. (ed.), *Readings in the Economics of Contract Law*, Cambridge, Cambridge University Press, 1989, 212-220.

SCHWARTZ, Alan, 'Sales Law and Inflations', **50** *Southern California Law Review*, 1976, 1 ff. Reprinted in KRONMAN, Anthony T. and POSNER, Richard A. (eds.), *The Economics of Contract Law*, Boston, Little Brown, 1979, 138-142.

SCHWARTZE, Andreas, 'Die Beseitigung des Wegfalls der Geschäftsgrundlage: Zur wirtschaftlichen Effizienz und zur juristischen Konsistenz eines ökonomischen Modells' [The Abolition of the Frustration of Contract: On Economic Efficiency and Legal Consistency of an Economic Model], in FINSINGER, Jörg and SIMON, Jürgen (eds.), *Recht und Risiko*, München, Florentz, 1988, 155-170.

SNYDERMAN, Mark, 'What's So Good About Good Faith? The Good Faith Performance Obligation in Commercial Lending', **55** *University of Chicago Law Review*, 1988, 1335-1370.

SPEIDEL, Richard E., 'Court-Imposed Price Adjustements Under Long-Term Supply Contracts', **76** *Northwestern University Law Review*, 1981, 369-422.

SYKES, Alan O., 'The Doctrine of Commercial Impracticability in a Second-best World', **19** *Journal of Legal Studies*, 1990, 43-94.

TRIMARCHI, Pietro, 'Der Wegfall der Geschäftsgrundlage aus allokativer Sicht - Kommentar' [The Frustration of Contract from an Allocative Sight], in OTT, Claus and SCHÄFER, Hans-Bernd (eds.), *Allokationseffizienz in der Rechtsordnung*, Berlin, Springer, 1989, 163-167.

TRIMARCHI, Pietro, 'Commercial Impracticability in Contract Law: An Economic Analysis', **11** *International Review of Law and Economics*, 1991, 63-82.

VELJANOVSKI, Cento G., 'Impossibility and Related Excuses: Comment', **144** *Journal of Institutional and Theoretical Economics*, 1988, 117-121.

WHITE, Michelle J., 'Contract Breach and Contract Discharge due to Impossibility: A Unified Theory', **17** *Journal of Legal Studies*, 1988, 353-376.

WILLIAMSON, Oliver E., 'Assessing Contract', **1** *Journal of Law, Economics & Organization*, 1985, 177-208.

WLADIS, John D., 'Impracticability as Risk Allocation: The Effect of Changed Circumstances Upon Contract Obligations for the Sale of Goods', **22** *Georgia Law Review*, 1988, 503 ff.

4400 Remedies

4400 Remedies: General

BARTON, John H., 'The Economic Basis of Damages for Breach of Contract, **1** *Journal of Legal Studies*, 1972, 277-304.

BEVIER, Lillian R., 'Reconsidering Inducement', **76** *Virginia Law Review*, 1990, 877-936.

BIRMINGHAM, Robert L., 'Breach of Contract, Damage Measures, and Economic Efficiency', **24** *Rutgers Law Review*, 1970, 273-292.

BISHOP, William, 'The Choice of Remedy for Breach of Contract', **14** *Journal of Legal Studies*, 1985, 299-320. Reprinted in GOLDBERG, Victor P. (ed.), *Readings in the Economics of Contract Law*, Cambridge, Cambridge University Press, 1989, 122-125.

CARROLL, David W., 'Four Games and the Expectancy Theory', **54** *Southern California Law Review*, 1981, 503-526.

CHAPMAN, Bruce, 'Punitive Damages as Aggravated Damages: The Case of Contract', **16** *Canadian Business Law Journal*, 1990, 269-280.

CHAPMAN, Kenneth and MEURER, Michael J., 'Efficient Remedies for Breach of Warranty', **52(1)** *Law and Contemporary Problems*, 1989, 107-131.

CRASWELL, Richard, 'Contract Remedies, Renegotiation, and the Theory of Efficient Breach', **61** *Southern California Law Review*, 1988, 629-670.

CRASWELL, Richard, 'Performance, Reliance, and One-sided Information', **18** *Journal of Legal Studies*, 1989, 365-401.

CRASWELL, Richard, 'Insecurity, Repudiation, and Cure', **19** *Journal of Legal Studies*, 1990, 399-434.

DIAMOND, Peter A. and MASKIN, Eric, 'An Equilibrium Analysis of Search and Breach of Contract, I: Steady States', **10** *Bell Journal of Economics*, 1979, 282-316

DIAMOND, Peter A. and MASKIN, Eric, 'An Equilibrium Analysis of Search and Breach of Contract II: A Nonsteady State Example', **25** *Journal of Economic Theory*, 1981, 165-195.

ENDRES, Alfred, 'Allokationswirkungen des Haftungsrechts' [Allocative Effects of Liability Law], in **40(1)** *Jahrbuch für Sozialwissenschaft*, 1989, 115-129.

FARBER, Daniel A., 'Reassessing the Economic Efficiency of Compensatory Damages for Breach of Contract', **66** *Virginia Law Review*, 1980, 1443-1484.

FENN, Paul and WHELAN, Christopher J., 'Remedies for Dismissed Employees in the U.K.: An Economic Analysis', **2** *International Review of Law and Economics*, 1982, 205-225.

FINSINGER, Jörg and SIMON, Jürgen, 'Vertragsbruch und Schadensersatz' [Breach of Contract and Damages], **2** *Kritische Vierteljahresschrift für Gesetzgebung und Rechtswissenschaft*, 1987, 262-274.

FRIEDMANN, Daniel, 'The Efficient Breach Fallacy', **18** *Journal of Legal Studies*, 1989, 1-24.

GOETZ, Charles J., 'Comment: Contractual Remedies and the Normative Acceptability of State Imposed Coercion', **4** *Cato Journal*, 1985, 975-980. Reprinted in DORN, James A. and MANNE, Henry G. (eds.), *Economic Liberties and the Judiciary*, Fairfax, George Mason University Press, 1987, 351-356.

GROSSFELD, Bernhard, 'Money Sanctions for Breach of Contract in a Communist Economy', **72** *Yale Law Journal*, 1963, 1326 ff. Reprinted in KRONMAN, Anthony T. and POSNER, Richard A. (eds.), *The Economics of Contract Law*, Boston, Little Brown, 1979, 220-223.

HARRIS, Donald, OGUS, Anthony I. and PHILLIPS Jennifer, 'Contract Remedies and the Consumer Surplus', **95** *Law Quarterly Review*, 1979, 581-610.

HARRIS, Donald and VELJANOVSKI, Cento G., 'Remedies For Breach Under Contract Law: Designing Rules to Facilitate Out-of-Court Settlements', **5** *Law and Policy Quarterly*, 1983, 97-127.

HARTZLER, H. Richard, 'The Business and Economic Functions of the Law of Contract Damages', **6** *American Business Law Journal*, 1968, 387-407.

JACKSON, Thomas H., '"Anticipating Repudiation" and the Temporal Element in Contract Law: An Economic Inquiry into Contract Damages in Cases of Prospective Nonperformance', **31** *Stanford Law Review*, 1978, 69-119.

KNOEBER, Charles R., 'An Alternative Mechanism to Assure Contractual Reliability', **12** *Journal of Legal Studies*, 1983, 333-343.

KÖNDGEN, Johannes and VON RANDOW, Philipp, 'Sanktionen bei Vertragsverletzung' [Sanctions for Breach of Contract], in OTT, Claus and SCHÄFER, Hans-Bernd (eds.), *Allokationseffizienz in der Rechtsordnung*, Berlin, Springer, 1989, 122-140.

KORNHAUSER, Lewis A., 'Reliance, Reputation, and Breach of Contract', **26** *Journal of Law and Economics*, 1983, 691-706.

KORNHAUSER, Lewis A., 'An Introduction to the Economic Analysis of Contract Remedies', **57** *Colorado Law Review*, 1986, 683-725.

KROLL, Heidi, 'Breach of Contract in the Soviet Economy', **16** *Journal of Legal Studies*, 1987, 119-148.

KROLL, Heidi, 'Reform and Damages for Breach of Contract in the Soviet Economy', **5** *Soviet Economy*, 1989, 276-297.

LEHMANN, Michael, 'Die bürgerlich-rechtliche Haftung für Werbeangaben. Culpa in contrahendo als Haftungsgrundlage für vertragsanbahnende Erklärungen' [Civil Liability for Advertising Statements. Culpa in Contrahendo as Liability Ground for Statements which Precede a Contract], *Neue Juristische Wochenschrift*, 1981, 1233-1242.

LEHMANN, Michael, 'Die mißglückte Probefahrt. Vertragsrecht, Quasivertragsrecht, Deliktrecht. Ökonomische Analyse des Rechts' [The Failed Excursion. Contract Law, Quasi-Contract Law, Economic Analysis of Law], in WALZ, W. Rainer and RASCHER-FRIESENHAUSEN, Heinrich (eds.), *Sozialwissenschaften im Zivilrecht: Fälle und Lösungen in Ausbildung und Prüfung*, Neuwied, Luchterhand, 1983, 35-51.

LEVMORE, Saul and STUNTZ, William J., 'Remedies and Incentives in Private and Public Law: A Comparitive Essay', *Wisconsin Law Review*, 1990, 483-499.

MACNEIL, Ian R., 'Efficient Breach of Contract: Circles in the Sky', **68** *Virginia Law Review*, 1982, 947-969.

MACNEIL, Ian R., 'Contract Remedies: A Need for Better Efficiency Analysis', **144** *Journal of Institutional and Theoretical Economics*, 1988, 6-30.

MATTEI, Ugo, 'Diritto e rimedio nell'esperienza italiana ed in quella statunitense: un primo approccio' [Law and Remedies Related to Italian and American Experiences: A First Approach], *Quadrimestre*, 1987, 341-359.

MONATERI, Pier Giuseppe, *Cumulo di responsabilità contrattuale ed extracontrattuale* [Overlap of Contractual and Extracontractual Liability], Padova, CEDAM, 1989, 315 p.

POLINSKY, A. Mitchell, 'Risk Sharing through Breach of Contract Remedies', **12** *Journal of Legal Studies*, 1983, 427-444.

PRIEST, George L., 'Breach and Remedy for the Tender of Nonconforming Goods Under the Uniform Commercial Code: An Economic Approach', **91** *Harvard Law Review*, 1978, 960-1001. Reprinted in KRONMAN, Anthony T. and POSNER, Richard A. (eds.), *The Economics of Contract Law*, Boston, Little Brown, 1979, 167-175.

QUILLEN, Gwyn D., 'Note: Contract Damages and Cross-Subsidization', **61** *Southern California Law Review*, 1988, 1125-1141.

ROBINSON, Glen O., 'Explaining Contingent Rights: The Puzzle of "Obsolete" Covenants', **91** *Columbia Law Review*, 1991, 546-580.

ROTTENBERG, Simon, 'Mistaken Judicial Activism: Proposed Constraints on Creditor Remedies', **4** *Cato Journal*, 1985, 335-350. Reprinted in DORN, James A. and MANNE, Henry G. (eds.), *Economic Liberties and the Judiciary*, Fairfax, George Mason University Press, 1987, 335-349.

SADANAND, Asha, 'Protection of Seller's Interests under Buyer's Breach', **22** *Canadian Journal of Economics*, 1989, 910-916.

SCHWARTZ, Alan, 'The Myth That Promisees Prefer Supracompensatory Remedies: An Analysis of Contracting for Damage Measures', **100** *Yale Law Journal*, 1990, 376 ff.

SCOTT, Kenneth E., 'Contract Remedies: A Need for Better Efficiency Analysis: Comment', **144** *Journal of Institutional and Theoretical Economics*, 1988, 31-34.

SCOTT, Robert E., 'Rethinking the Regulation of Coercive Creditor Remedies', **89** *Columbia Law Review*, 1989, 730-788.

TRIMARCHI, Pietro, 'Sul significato economico dei criteri di responsabilità contrattuale' [Economic Meaning of Contract-Liability Criteria], *Rivista trimestrale di diritto e procedura civile*, 1970, 512-531.

TRIMARCHI, Pietro, 'Die Regelung der Vertragshaftung aus ökonomischer Sicht' [The Regulation of Contractual Liability from an Economic Point of View], **136** *Zeitschrift fur das gesamte Handelsrecht und Wirtschaftsrecht*, 1972, 118-138.

VASGERAU, Hans Jürgen, 'Contract Remedies: A Need for Better Efficiency

Analysis: Comment', **144** *Journal of Institutional and Theoretical Economics*, 1988, 35-38.

WEGEHENKEL, Lothar, 'Kommentar' [Comment] (on Köndgen and van Randow, Sanktionen bei Vertragsverletzung), in OTT, Claus and SCHÄFER, Hans-Bernd (eds.), *Allokationseffizienz in der Rechtsordnung*, Berlin, Springer, 1989, 141-145.

4410 Specific Performance vs. Damages

AGHION, Philippe and HERMALIN, Benjamin, 'Legal Restrictions on Private Contracts Can Enhance Efficiency', **6** *Journal of Law, Economics, & Organization*, 1990, 381-409.

DE ALESSI, Louis and STAAF, Robert J., 'Subjective Value in Contract Law', **145** *Journal of Institutional and Theoretical Economics*, 1989, 561-577.

GOLDBERG, Victor P., 'Relational Exchange, Contract Law, and the *Boomer* Problem', **141** *Journal of Institutional and Theoretical Economics*, 1985, 570-575. Reprinted in GOLDBERG, Victor P. (ed.), *Readings in the Economics of Contract Law*, Cambridge, Cambridge University Press, 1989, 67-71 and 126-127.

HARMAN, Steven G., 'Alleviating Hardship Arising from Inflation and Court Congestion: Toward the Use of the Conditional Specific Performance Decree', **56** *Southern California Law Review*, 1983, 795-823.

KRONMAN, Anthony T., 'Specific Performance', **45** *University of Chicago Law Review*, 1978, 351-382. Reprinted in KRONMAN, Anthony T. and POSNER, Richard A. (eds.), *The Economics of Contract Law*, Boston, Little Brown, 1979, 181-194.

LEWIS, Tracy R., PERRY, Martin K. and SAPPINGTON, David E.M., 'Renegotiation and Specific Performance', **52(1)** *Law and Contemporary Problems*, 1989, 33-48.

LINZER, Peter, 'On the Amorality of Contract Remedies - Efficiency, Equity and the Second Restatement', **81** *Columbia Law Review*, 1981, 111-139.

MURIS, Timothy J., 'Comment: The Costs of Freely Granting Specific Performance', *Duke Law Journal*, 1982, 1053-1069.

NARASIMHAN, Subha, 'Modification: The Self-Help Specific Performance Remedy', **97** *Yale Law Journal*, 1987, 61-95.

PARDOLESI, Roberto, 'Tutela specifica e tutela per equivalente nella prospettiva dell'analisi economica del diritto' [Specific Performance and Damages: An EAL Perspective], *Quadrimestre*, 1988, 76-97.

ROGERSON, William P., 'Efficient Reliance and Damage Measures for Breach of Contract', **15** *Rand Journal of Economics*, 1984, 39-53.

RUBIN, Paul H., 'Unenforceable Contracts: Penalty Clauses and Specific Performance', **10** *Journal of Legal Studies*, 1981, 237-247.

SADANAND, Asha, 'Lost Profits, Market Damages, and Specific Performance: An Economic Analysis of Buyer's Breach', **20** *Canadian Journal of Economics*,

1987, 750-773.

SCHWARTZ, Alan, 'The Case for Specific Performance', **89** *Yale Law Journal*, 1979, 271-306.

SCHWARTZ, Alan, 'The Myth That Promisees Prefer Supracompensatory Remedies: An Analysis of Contracting for Damage Measures', **100** *Yale Law Journal*, 1990, 369-407.

SHAVELL, Steven, 'Damage Measures for Breach of Contract', **11** *Bell Journal of Economics*, 1980, 466-490.

SHAVELL, Steven, 'The Design of Contracts and Remedies for Breach', **99** *Quarterly Journal of Economics*, 1984, 121-148.

ULEN, Thomas S., 'The Efficiency of Specific Performance: Toward a Unified Theory of Contract Remedies', **83** *Michigan Law Review*, 1984, 341-403.

X, 'Note: Alleviating Hardship Arising from Inflation and Court Congestion: Toward the Use of the Conditional Specific Performance Decree', **56** *Southern California Law Review*, 1983, 795-823.

YORIO, Edward, 'In Defense of Money Damages for Breach of Contract', **82** *Columbia Law Review*, 1982, 1365-1424.

4420 Penalty Clauses. Liquidated Damages. Exemption Clauses

ANDERSON, James E. and GOLLOP, Frank M., 'The Effect of Warranty Provisions on Used Car Prices', in IPPOLITO, Pauline M. and SCHEFFMAN, David T. (eds.), *Empirical Approaches to Consumer Protection Economics*, Washington, Federal Trade Commission, 1986, 67-102.

CLARKSON, Kenneth W., MILLER, Roger LeRoy and MURIS, Timothy J., 'Liquidated Damages v. Penalties: Sense or Nonsense?', *Wisconsin Law Review*, 1978, 351-390. Reprinted in GOLDBERG, Victor P. (ed.), *Readings in the Economics of Contract Law*, Cambridge, Cambridge University Press, 1989, 152-160.

COOPERSMITH, Jeffrey B., 'Comment: Refocusing Liquidated Damages Law for Real Estate Contracts: Returning to the Historical Roots of the Penalty Doctrine', **39** *Emory Law Journal*, 1990, 267 ff.

DE ALESSI, Louis and STAAF, Robert J., 'Subjective Value in Contract Law', **145** *Journal of Institutional and Theoretical Economics*, 1989, 561-577.

GOETZ, Charles J. and SCOTT, Robert E., 'Liquidated Damages, Penalties and the Just Compensation Principle: Some Notes on an Enforcement Model and a Theory of Efficient Breach', **77** *Columbia Law Review*, 1977, 554-594. Reprinted in KRONMAN, Anthony T. and POSNER, Richard A. (eds.), *The Economics of Contract Law*, Boston, Little Brown, 1979, 194-207.

GROSS, Leonard E., 'Contractual Limitations on Attorney Malpractice Liability: An Economic Approach', **75** *Kentucky Law Journal*, 1986, 793 ff.

HARRIS, Frederick H., 'Security and Penalty in Debt Contracts: Comment', **143** *Journal of Institutional and Theoretical Economics*, 1987, 168-174.

HESS, James D. and KNOEBER, Charles R., 'Security and Penalty in Debt Contracts', **143** *Journal of Institutional and Theoretical Economics*, 1987, 149-167.

JARRELL, Greg A. and PELTZMAN, Sam, 'The Impact of Product Recalls on the Wealth of Sellers', in IPPOLITO, Pauline M. and SCHEFFMAN, David T. (eds.), *Empirical Approaches to Consumer Protection Economics*, Washington, Federal Trade Commission, 1986, 377-409.

KAPLAN, Philipp R., 'A Critique of the Penalty Limitation on Liquidated Damages', **50** *Southern California Law Review*, 1977, 1055-1090.

KOLLER, Ingo, 'Die Verteilung des Scheckfälschungsrisikos zwischen Kunde und Bank' [The Division of the False Cheque Risk Between Client and Bank], *Neue Juristische Wochenschrift*, 1981, 2433 ff.

KORNHAUSER, Lewis A., 'Reliance, Reputation, and Breach of Contract', **26** *Journal of Law and Economics*, 1983, 691-706.

KÖTZ, Hein, 'Haftungsausschlussklauseln, Eine juristisch-ökonomische Analyse' [Exemption Clauses, a Legal-Economic Analysis], *25 Jahre Karlsruher Forum. Beiheft zu Versicherungsrecht*, 1983, 145-152.

KÖTZ, Hein, 'Haftungsausschluß der Chemischreiniger' [Exemption Clauses in Cleaning Contracts, Legal Validity and Economic Efficiency], in WALZ, W. Rainer and RASCHER-FRIESENHAUSEN, Heinrich (eds.), *Sozialwissenschaften im Zivilrecht: Fälle und Lösungen in Ausbildung und Prüfung*, Neuwied, Luchterhand, 1983, 76-88.

KÖTZ, Hein, 'Zur Effizienz von Haftungsausschlußklauseln' [On the Efficiency of Exemption Clauses], in OTT, Claus and SCHÄFER, Hans-Bernd (eds.), *Allokationseffizienz in der Rechtsordnung*, Berlin, Springer, 1989, 189-200.

LANGENFELD, James, 'The Effect of Warranty Provisions on Used Car Prices: Comments', in IPPOLITO, Pauline M. and SCHEFFMAN, David T. (eds.), *Empirical Approaches to Consumer Protection Economics*, Washington, Federal Trade Commission, 1986, 105-107.

MASTEN, Scott E. and SNYDER, Edward A., 'The Design and Duration of Contracts: Strategic and Efficiency Considerations', **52(1)** *Law and Contemporary Problems*, 1989, 63-85.

MILNER, Alan, 'Liquidated Damages: An Empirical Study in the Travel Industry', **42** *Modern Law Review*, 1979, 508-532.

MURIS, Timothy J., 'Opportunistic Behaviour and the Law of Contracts', **65** *Minnesota Law Review*, 1981, 521-590.

NAGEL, Bernhard, 'Kommentar' [Comment] (On Wehrt, Die Qualitätshaftung des Verkäufers aus ökonomischer Sicht), in OTT, Claus and SCHÄFER, Hans-Bernd (eds.), *Ökonomische Probleme des Zivilrechts*, Berlin, Springer, 1991, 260-264.

REA, Samuel A., Jr., 'Efficiency Implications of Penalties and Liquidated Damages', **13** *Journal of Legal Studies*, 1984, 147-167.

REA, Samuel A., Jr., 'Arm-breaking, Consumer Credit and Personal Bankruptcy', **22** *Economic Inquiry*, 1984, 188-208.

RUBIN, Paul H., 'Unenforceable Contracts: Penalty Clauses and Specific Performance', **10** *Journal of Legal Studies*, 1981, 237-247.

SAPPINGTON, David E.M., 'Limited Liability Contracts between Principal and Agent', **29** *Journal of Economic Theory*, 1983, 1-21.

SCHUMANN, Jochen, 'Security and Penalty in Debt Contracts: Comment', **143** *Journal of Institutional and Theoretical Economics*, 1987, 175-179.

SEIDL, Christian, 'Kommentar' [Comment] (On Kötz, Zur Effizienz von Haftungsausschlußklauseln), in OTT, Claus and SCHÄFER, Hans-Bernd (eds.), *Allokationseffizienz in der Rechtsordnung*, Berlin, Springer, 1989, 201-207.

X, 'Note: Liquidated Damages and Penalties Under the Uniform Commercial Code and Common Law: An Economic Analysis of Contract Damages', **72** *Northwestern University Law Review*, 1978, 1055-1094.

4430 Expectation Losses vs. Reliance Losses vs. Restitution

BARNETT, Randy E. and BECKER, Mary E., 'Beyond Reliance: Promissory Estoppel, Contract Formalities, and Misrepresentation', **15** *Hofstra Law Review*, 1987, 443 ff.

BIRMINGHAM, Robert L., 'Damage Measures and Economic Rationality: The Geometry of Contract Law', **49** *Duke Law Journal*, 1969, 49-71.

BIRMINGHAM, Robert, 'Notes on the Reliance Interest', **60** *Washington Law Review*, 1985, 217-266. Reprinted in GOLDBERG, Victor P. (ed.), *Readings in the Economics of Contract Law*, Cambridge, Cambridge University Press, 1989, 92-98.

BURTON, Steven J., 'Breach of Contract and the Common Law Duty to Perform in Good Faith', **94** *Harvard Law Review*, 1980, 369-403.

CASSY, Robert M., 'An Economic View of the U.C.C. Seller's Damage Measures and the Identification of the Lost-Volume Seller', **19** *Albany Law Review*, 1985, 889-925.

COOTER, Robert D. and EISENBERG, Melvin Aron, 'Damages for Breach of Contract', **73** *California Law Review*, 1985, 1432-1481.

CURTIS, Linda, 'Note: Damage Measurements for Bad Faith Breach of Contract: An Economic Analysis', **39** *Stanford Law Review*, 1986, 161-185.

FRIEDMAN, David D., 'An Economic Analysis of Alternative Damage Rules for Breach of Contract', **32** *Journal of Law and Economics*, 1989, 281-310.

FULLER, Lon L. and PERDUE, William, 'The Reliance Interest in Contract Damages', **46** *Yale Law Journal*, 1936, 52-98. Reprinted in GOLDBERG, Victor P. (ed.), *Readings in the Economics of Contract Law*, Cambridge, Cambridge University Press, 1989, 77-79.

GOETZ, Charles J. and SCOTT, Robert E., 'Measuring Sellers' Damages: The Lost Profits Puzzle', **31** *Stanford Law Review*, 1979, 323-373.

GOLDBERG, Victor P., 'An Economic Analysis of the Lost-Volume Retail Seller', **57** *Southern California Law Review*, 1984, 283-298. Reprinted in GOLDBERG, Victor P. (ed.), *Readings in the Economics of Contract Law*, Cambridge, Cambridge University Press, 1989, 106-113.

KATZ, Avery, 'Reflections on Fuller and Perdue's "The Reliance Interest in Contract Damages": A Positive Economic Framework', **21** *University of Michigan Journal of Law Reform*, 1988, 541-560.

KONAKAYAMA, Akira, MITSUI, Toshihide and WATANABE, Shinichi, 'Efficient Contracting with Reliance and a Damage Measure', **17** *Rand Journal of Economics*, 1986, 450-457.

KORNHAUSER, Lewis A., 'Reliance, Reputation, and Breach of Contract', **26** *Journal of Law and Economics*, 1983, 691-706.

LANDA, Janet T. and GROFMAN, Bernard, 'Games of Breach and the Role of Contract Law in Protecting The Expectation Interest', **3** *Research in Law and Economics*, 1981, 67-90.

LEITZEL, Jim, 'Reliance and Contract Breach', **52(1)** *Law and Contemporary Problems*, 1989, 87-105.

LEITZEL, Jim, 'Damage Measures and Incomplete Contracts', **20** *Rand Journal of Economics*, 1989, 92-101.

MATHER, Henry, 'Restitution as a Remedy for Breach of Contract: The Case of the Partially Performing Seller', **92** *Yale Law Journal*, 1982, 14-48.

MURIS, Timothy J., 'Cost of Completion or Diminution in Market Value: The Relevance of Subjective Value', **12** *Journal of Legal Studies*, 1983, 379-400. Reprinted in GOLDBERG, Victor P. (ed.), *Readings in the Economics of Contract Law*, Cambridge, Cambridge University Press, 1989, 128-132.

NUGENT, Peter E. (NOTE), 'Measuring Contract Damages Policy and the Advantage of Breach', **87** *Notre Dame Lawyer*, 1972, 1335-1348.

OWEN, Marc, 'Some Aspects of the Recovery of Reliance Damages in the Law of Contracts', **4** *Oxford Journal of Legal Studies*, 1984, 393-420.

PETTIT, Mark Jr., 'Private Advantage and Public Power: Reexamining the Expectation and Reliance Interests in Contract Damages', **38** *Hastings Law Journal*, 1987, 417-469.

REA, Samuel A., Jr., 'Damages for Buyer Breach', **6** *International Review of Law and Economics*, 1986, 77-86.

REA, Samuel A., Jr., 'An Economic Analysis of Buyer's Breach: A Comment', **22** *Canadian Journal of Economics*, 1989, 904-909.

ROGERSON, William P., 'Efficient Reliance and Damage Measures for Breach of Contract', **15** *Rand Journal of Economics*, 1984, 39-53.

SADANAND, Asha, 'Lost Profits, Market Damages, and Specific Performance: An Economic Analysis of Buyer's Breach', **20** *Canadian Journal of Economics*, 1987, 750-773.

SHAVELL, Steven, 'Damage Measures for Breach of Contract', **11** *Bell Journal of Economics*, 1980, 466-490.

SIMON, David and NOVACK, Gerald A., 'Limiting the Buyer's Market Damages to Lost Profits: A Challenge to the Enforceability of Market Contracts', **92** *Harvard Law Review*, 1979, 1395-1438.

SPEIDEL, Richard E. and CLAY, Kenneth O., 'Sellers Recovery of Overhead Under UCC Section 2-708(2): Economic Cost Theory and Contract Remedial Policy', **57** *Cornell Law Review*, 1972, 681-718. Reprinted in KRONMAN, Anthony

T. and POSNER, Richard A. (eds.), *The Economics of Contract Law*, Boston, Little Brown, 1979, 208-213.

X, 'Note: Microeconomics and the Lost-Volume Seller', **24** *Case Western Reserve Law Review*, 1973, 712 ff. Reprinted in KRONMAN, Anthony T. and POSNER, Richard A. (eds.), *The Economics of Contract Law*, Boston, Little Brown, 1979, 213-220.

4440 Valuation of Losses: Economic Loss, Physical Injury, Value of Life

ENGELHARDT, Günther, 'Strafzuschlag zum Schadensersatz, Kommentar' [Punitive Damages, Comment] (On Köndgen, Immaterialschadensersatz, Gewinnabschöpfung oder Genugtuung in Geld bei vorsätzlichen Vertragsbruch?), in OTT, Claus and SCHÄFER, Hans-Bernd (eds.), *Ökonomische Probleme des Zivilrechts*, Berlin, Springer, 1991, 183-190.

KNETSCH, Jack L., 'Legal Rules and the Basis for Evaluating Economic Losses', **4** *International Review of Law and Economics*, 1984, 5-13.

KÖNDGEN, Johannes, 'Immaterialschadenersatz, Gewinnabschöpfung oder Genugtuung in Geld bei vorsätzlichen Vertragsbruch?' [Damages for Nonpecuniary Losses, Skimming-off of Extra-Profits or Satisfaction in Money in Case of Intentional Breach of Contract?], in OTT, Claus and SCHÄFER, Hans-Bernd (eds.), *Ökonomische Probleme des Zivilrechts*, Berlin, Springer, 1991, 169-182.

REA, Samuel A., Jr., 'Lump-sum versus Periodic Damage Awards', **10** *Journal of Legal Studies*, 1981, 131-154.

REA, Samuel A., Jr., 'Nonpecuniary Loss and Breach of Contract', **11** *Journal of Legal Studies*, 1982, 35-53.

VISCUSI, W. Kip, 'The Determinants of the Disposition of Product Liability Claims and Compensation for Bodily Injury', **15** *Journal of Legal Studies*, 1986, 321-346.

4450 Causation. Precaution. Foreseeability. Mitigation

COOTER, Robert D., 'Unity in Tort, Contract, and Property: The Model of Precaution', **73** *California Law Review*, 1985, 1-51. Reprinted in GOLDBERG, Victor P. (ed.), *Readings in the Economics of Contract Law*, Cambridge, Cambridge University Press, 1989, 53-60.

DANZIG, Richard, 'Hadley v. Baxendale: A Study in the Industrialization of the Law', **4** *Journal of Legal Studies*, 1975, 249-284.

EPSTEIN, Richard A., 'Beyond Foreseeability: Consequential Damages in the Law of Contract', **18** *Journal of Legal Studies*, 1989, 105-138.

FENN, Paul, 'Mitigation and the 'Correct' Measure of Damage', **1** *International Review of Law and Economics*, 1981, 223-226.

GOETZ, Charles J. and SCOTT, Robert E., 'The Mitigation Principle: Toward a General Theory of Contractual Obligation', **69** *Virginia Law Review*, 1983, 967-1024. Reprinted in GOLDBERG, Victor P. (ed.), *Readings in the Economics of Contract Law*, Cambridge, Cambridge University Press, 1989, 61-68 and 199-200.

LANDA, Janet T., '*Hadley v. Baxendale* and the Expansion of the Middleman Economy', **16** *Journal of Legal Studies*, 1987, 455-470.

LEITZEL, Jim, 'Reliance and Contract Breach', **52(1)** *Law and Contemporary Problems*, 1989, 87-105.

MACINTOSH, Jeffrey G. and FRYDENLUND, David C., 'An Investment Approach to a Theory of Contract Mitigation', **37** *University of Toronto Law Journal*, 1987, 113-182.

PERLOFF, Jeffrey M., 'Breach of Contract and the Foreseeability Doctrine of *Hadley v. Baxendale*', **10** *Journal of Legal Studies*, 1981, 39-63.

RIZZO, Mario J. and ARNOLD, Frank S., 'Causal Apportionment: Reply to the Critics', **15** *Journal of Legal Studies*, 1986, 219-226.

WOLCHER, Louis E., 'Price Discrimination and Inefficient Risk Allocation Under the Rule of *Hadley v.Baxendale*', **12** *Research in Law and Economics*, 1989, 9-31.

4500 Quasi-contracts. Restitution. Unjust Enrichment

KRAUSS, Michael I., 'L'Affaire Lapierre: vers une theorie économique de l'obligation quasi-contractuelle' [The Lapierre Case: Toward An Economic Theory of Quasi-Contractual Obligation], **31** *McGill Law Journal*, 1986, 683-721.

LANDES, William H. and POSNER, Richard A., 'Salvors, Finders, Good Samaritans, and Other Rescuers: An Economic Study of Law and Altruism', **7** *Journal of Legal Studies*, 1978, 83-128.

LANDES, William M. and POSNER, Richard A., 'Altruism in Law and Economics', **68** *American Economic Review. Papers and Proceedings*, 1978, 417-421.

LEVMORE, Saul, 'Explaining Restitution', **71** *Virginia Law Review*, 1985, 65-124.

LEVMORE, Saul, 'Waiting for Rescue: An Essay on the Evolution and Incentive Structure of the Law of Affirmative Obligations', **72** *Virginia Law Review*, 1986, 879 ff.

LONG, Robert A. Jr. (Student Note), 'A Theory of Hypothetical Contract', **94** *Yale Law Journal*, 1984, 415-434.

WITTMAN, Donald, 'Should Compensation Be Based on Costs or Benefits?', **5** *International Review of Law and Economics*, 1985, 173-185.

X, 'Note: Calculating and Allocating Salvage Liability', **99** *Harvard Law Review*, 1986, 1896-1917.

4600 INSURANCE
Göran Skogh

ABRAHAM, Kenneth S., 'Efficiency and Fairness in Insurance Risk Classification', **71** *Virginia Law Review*, 1985, 403-451.

ABRAHAM, Kenneth S., *Distributing Risk: Insurance, Legal Theory and Public Policy (in American Insurance Law)*, New Haven, Yale University Prcss, 1986, 254 p.

ABRAHAM, Kenneth S., 'Products Liability Law and Insurance Profitability', **19** *Journal of Legal Studies*, 1990, 837-844.

ADAMS, Michael, 'An Economic Analysis of Law-Suit Insurance', in FINSINGER, Jörg (ed.), *Economic Analysis of Regulated Markets*, London, Macmillan, 1983, 134-151.

ADAMS, Michael, 'Eine wohlfahrtstheoretische Analyse des Zivilprozesses und der Rechtsschutzversicherungen' [An Economic Analysis of Civil Procedure and Legal Aid Insurance], **139** *Zeitschrift für Schweizerisches Recht*, 1983, 187-208.

ANDERSON, Elizabeth, CHROSTOWSKI, Paul and VREELAND, Judy, 'Risk Assessment Issues Associated with Cleaning up Inactive Hazardous Waste Sites', **14** *Geneva Papers on Risk and Insurance*, 1989, 104-119.

ANGOFF, Jay, 'Insurance against Competition: How the McCarran Ferguson Act Raises Prices and Profits in the Property Casualty Insurance Indus try', **5** *Yale Journal on Regulation*, 1988, 397-415.

ARNOTT, Richard and STIGLITZ, Joseph, 'The Welfare Economics of Moral Hazard', in LOUBERGé, Henri (ed.), *Risk, Information and Insurance. Essays in the Memory of Karl H. Borch*, Boston, Kluwer Academic Publishers, 1990, 91-121.

ARROW, Kenneth J., 'Optimal Insurance and Generalized Deductibles', *Scandinavian Actuarial Journal*, 1974, 1-42.

ATIYAH, Patrick S., *Accidents, Compensation and the Law*, London, Weidenfeld and Nicholson, 1977 (2nd ed.), 1980 (3rd).

BECKER, Gary S. and EHRLICH, Isaac, 'Market Insurance, Self-insurance, and Self-protection', **80** *Journal of Political Economy*, 1972, 623-648.

BEENSTOCK, Michael and BRASSE, Valerie, *Insurance for Unemployment*, London, Allen & Unwin, 1986, 107 p.

BENSTON, G.J. and SMITH, C.W., Jr., 'A Transactions Cost Approach to the Theory of Financial Intermediation', **31** *Journal of Finance*, 1976, 215-231.

BERGER, Robert G., 'The Impact of Tort Law Development on Insurance: The Availability/Affordability Crisis and Its Potential Solutions', **37** *American University Law Review*, 1988, 285 ff.

BISHOP, William, 'The Contract-Tort Boundary and the Economics of Insurance', **12** *Journal of Legal Studies*, 1983, 241-266. Reprinted in GOLDBERG, Victor P. (ed.), *Readings in the Economics of Contract Law*, Cambridge, Cambridge University Press, 1989, 86-91.

BLACKMON, B. Glenn, Jr. and ZECKHAUSER, Richard, 'Mispriced Equity:

Regulated Rates for Auto Insurance in Massachusetts', **81** *American Economic Review. Papers and Proceedings*, 1991, 65-69.

BONGAERTS, Jan C. and DE BIVRE, Aline, 'Insurance for Civil Liability for Marine Oil Pollution Damages', **12** *Geneva Papers on Risk and Insurance*, 1987, 145-157.

BORENSTEIN, Severin, 'The Economics of Costly Risk Sorting in Competitive Insurance Markets', **9** *International Review of Law and Economics*, 1989, 25-39.

BREYER, F. and SCHULENBURG, J. Matthias Graf von der, 'Voting on Social Security: The Family as Decision-Making Unit', **40** *Kyklos*, 1987, 529-547.

BREYER, F. and SCHULENBURG, J. Matthias Graf von der, 'Family Ties and Social Security in a Democracy', **67** *Public Choice*, 1990, 155-167.

BROWN, Craig, 'A Choice of Choice: Adding Postaccident Choice to the Menu of No-Fault Models', **26** *San Diego Law Review*, 1989, 1095-1108.

BROWN, John Prather, 'Toward an Economic Theory of Liability', **2** *Journal of Legal Studies*, 1973, 323-349.

BRUCE, Christopher, 'The Deterrent Effects of Automobile Insurance and Tort Law: A Survey of the Empirical Literature', **6** *Law & Policy*, 1984, 67-100.

BUTLER, Richard J. and WORRALL, John D., 'The Costs of Workers' Compensation Insurance: Private versus Public', **29** *Journal of Law and Economics*, 1986, 329-356.

CALABRESI, Guido, 'Some Thoughts on Risk Distribution and the Law of Torts', **70** *Yale Law Journal*, 1961, 499-553.

CALABRESI, Guido, *The Costs of Accidents: A Legal and Economic Analysis*, New Haven, Yale University Press, 1970, 340 p.

CAMERER, Colin, 'Do Biases in Probability Judgment Matter in Markets: Experimental Evidence', **77** *American Economic Review*, 1987, 981-997.

CANE, Peter, 'Liability Rules and the Cost of Professional Indemnity Insurance', **14** *Geneva Papers on Risk and Insurance*, 1989, 347-359.

CARR, Jack L., 'Giving Motorists a Choice Between Fault and No-Fault Insurance: An Economic Critique', **26** *San Diego Law Review*, 1989, 1087-1094.

CHAMBERLIN, John R., 'Assessing the Fairness of Insurance Classifications', **7** *Research in Law and Economics*, 1985, 65-87.

CHAPMAN, C.B. and COOPER, Dale F., 'Contract Risk Analysis for Turnkey Project Bid: a Case Study', **10** *Geneva Papers on Risk and Insurance*, 1985, 293-305.

CHEEK, Leslie, 'Insurance Issues Associated with Cleaning up Inactive Hazardous Waste Sites', **14** *Geneva Papers on Risk and Insurance*, 1989, 120-148.

COASE, Ronald H., 'The Choice of the Institutional Framework: A Comment', **17** *Journal of Law and Economics*, 1974, 493-496.

COOK, Philip J. and GRAHAM, D.A., 'The Demand for Insurance and Protection: The Case of Irreplaceable Commodities', **91** *Quarterly Journal of Economics*, 1977, 143-156.

CUMMINS, David J. and WEISS, Mary A., 'The Effects of No Fault on Automobile Insurance Loss Costs', **16** *Geneva Papers on Risk and Insurance*, 1991, 20-38.

CUMMINS, J.D. and VANDERHEI, J., 'A Note on the Relative Efficiency of Property-Liability Insurance Distribution Systems', **10** *Bell Journal of Economics*, 1979, 709-719.

DANZON, Patricia M., 'Tort Reform and the Role of Governement in Private Insurance Markets', **13** *Journal of Legal Studies*, 1984, 517-549.

DANZON, Patricia M., 'Liability and Liability Insurance for Medical Malpractice', **4** *Journal of Health Economics*, 1985, 309-331.

DANZON, Patricia M., 'The Frequency and Severity of Medical Malpractice Claims: New Evidence', **49(2)** *Law and Contemporary Problems*, 1986.

DANZON, Patricia M., 'The Political Economy of Workers' Compensation: Lessons for Product Liability', **78** *American Economic Review. Papers and Proceedings*, 1988, 305-310.

DANZON, Patricia M., 'Alternative Liability Regimes for Medical Injuries', **15** *Geneva Papers on Risk and Insurance*, 1990, 3-21.

DANZON, Patricia M., 'On "Bargaining Behavior by Defendant Insurers: An Economic Model"', **15** *Geneva Papers on Risk and Insurance*, 1990, 53-54.

DANZON, Patricia M., PAULY, Mark V. and KINGSTON, Raynard S., 'The Effects of Malpractice Litigation on Physicians' Fees and Income', **80** *American Economic Review. Papers and Proceedings*, 1990, 122-127.

DEERE, Donald R., 'On the Potential for Private Insurers to Reduce the Inefficiencies of Moral Hazard', **9** *International Review of Law and Economics*, 1989, 219-222.

DEVLIN, Rose Anne, 'Some Welfare Implications of No-Fault Automobile Insurance', **10** *International Review of Law and Economics*, 1990, 193-205.

DIAMOND, D.W. and DYBVIG, P.H., 'Banking Theory, Deposit Insurance and Bank Regulation', **59** *Journal of Business*, 1986, 55-68.

DOHERTY, Neil A. and GARVEN, James R., 'Price Regulation in Property Liability Insurance: A Contingent Claims Approach', **41** *Journal of Finance*, 1986, 1031-050.

DRUKARCZYK, Jochen, *Unternehmen und Insolvenz - Zur effizienten Gestaltung des Kreditsicherungs- und Insolvenzrechts* [Entrepreneurship and Insolvency - On the Efficient Shape of Safeguarding of Credits Law and Insolvency Law], Wiesbaden, Gabler Verlag, 1987, 424 p.

EGGERSTEDT, Harald, 'Wettbewerb and Regulierung auf Versicherungsmarkten' [Competition and Regulation in Insurance Markets], **107** *Zeitschrift fur Wirtschafts und Sozialwissenschaften*, 1987, 397-416.

EGGERSTEDT, Harald, 'Uber Regulierung und Deregulierung von Versicherungsmarkten. Eine Replik' [On Regulation and Deregulation of Insurance Markets. A Reply], **58** *Zeitschrift fur Betriebswirtschaft*, 1988, 704-707.

EISEN, Roland, 'Wettbewerb und Regulierung in der Versicherung Die Rolle asymmetrischer Information' [Competition and Regulation in Insurance: The Role of Asymmetrical Information], **122** *Schweizerische Zeitschrift fur Volkswirtschaft und Statistik*, 1986, 339-358.

EISENACH, Jeffrey A., HIGGINS, Richard S. and SHUGHART, William F. II,

'Warranties, Tie-ins, and Efficient Insurance Contracts: A Theory and Three Case Studies', **6** *Research in Law and Economics*, 1984, 167-185.

ENDRES, Alfred and GAFGEN, Gerard, 'Wettbewerb und Regulierung auf dem bundesdeutschen Lebensversicherungsmarkt' [Competition and Regulation in the W. German Life Insurance Market], **205** *Jahrbucher fur Nationalokonomie und Statistik*, 1988, 11-29.

ENDRES, Alfred and GÄFGEN, Gerard, 'Regulierung und Versicherungswirtschaft - Die ökonomische Perspektive' [Regulation and the Insurance Industry - The Economic Perspective], in Forschungsgesellschaft für Wettbewerb und Unternehmensorganisation - FWU (eds.), *Versicherungsmärkte im Wettbewerb*, Baden-Baden, 1989, 11-42.

ENDRES, Alfred and SCHWARZE, Reimund, 'Allokationswirkungen einer Umwelt-Haftpflichtversicherung' [Allocative Effects of an Environmental Liability Insurance], in **14** *Zeitschrift für Umweltpolitik und Umweltrecht*, 1991, 1-25.

EPSTEIN, Richard A., 'The Legal and Insurance Dynamics of Mass Tort Litigation', **13** *Journal of Legal Studies*, 1984, 475-506.

EPSTEIN, Richard A., 'Shooting the Messenger', **47** *Insurance Review*, 1986, 46-47.

FAIRLEY, W.B., 'Investment Income and Profit Margins in Property-Liability Insurance - Theory and Empirical Results', **10** *Bell Journal of Economics*, 1979, 192-210.

FAMA, Eugene F., 'Contract Costs and Financing decision', *Journal of Business*, 1990, S75-S91.

FARNY, Dieter, 'Uber Regulierung und Deregulierung von Versicherungsmarkten' [On Regulating and Deregulating Insurance Markets], **57** *Zeitschrift fur Betriebswirtschaft*, 1987, 1001-023.

FAURE, Michael G., 'De verzekering van geldboeten bij zeewaterverontreiniging door olie' [The Insurance of Fines with Respect to the Oil-Pollution of Seawater], in *Grensoverschrijdend strafrecht. Opstellen*, Arnhem, Gouda Quint, 1990, 203-221.

FAURE, Michael and HEINE, Günter, 'The Insurance of Fines: the Case of Oil Pollution', **16** *Geneva Papers on Risk and Insurance*, 1991, 39-58.

FAURE, Michael and SKOGH, GÖran, 'Liability at Nuclear Accident: A New Convention as Insurance', Departement of Economics, University of Lund, memo, 1991.

FAURE, Michael and VAN DEN BERGH, Roger, 'Negligence, Strict Liability and Regulation of Safety under Belgian Law: An Introductory Economic Analysis', **12** *Geneva Papers on Risk and Insurance*, 1987, 95-114.

FAURE, Michael and VAN DEN BERGH, Roger, 'Compulsory Insurance for Professional Liability?', **14** *Geneva Papers on Risk and Insurance*, 1989, 308-330.

FAURE, Michael and VAN DEN BERGH, Roger, 'Liability for Nuclear Accidents in Belgium from an Interest Group Perspective' **10** *International Review of Law and Economics*, 1990, 241-254.

FELDMAN, P.H., 'The Impact of Third-Party Payment on Professional Practice: Lessons from the Medical Profession', in BLAIR, Roger D. and RUBIN,

Stephen (eds.), *Regulating the Professions: A Public-Policy Symposium*, Lexington, Lexington Books, 1980.

FENN, Paul, 'Evaluating Irreplaceable Loss: Some Implications for Insurance and Liability Rules', **12** *Geneva Papers on Risk and Insurance*, 1987, 158-167.

FENN, Paul and VLACHONIKOLIS, Ioannis, 'Bargaining Behaviour by Defendant Insurers: An Economic Model', **15** *Geneva Papers on Risk and Insurance*, 1990, 41-52.

FINSINGER, Jörg, *Verbraucherschutz auf Versicherungsmärkten* [Consumer Protection in Insurance Markets], München, Florentz, 1988, 219 p.

FINSINGER, Jörg, 'Zur Deregulierung von Versicherungsmarkten' [On the Deregulation of Insurance Markets], **58** *Zeitschrift fur Betriebswirtschaft*, 1988, 698-703.

FINSINGER, Jörg, HAMMOND, Elizabeth and TRAPP, Julian, *Insurance: Competition or Regulation?*, London, Institute for Fiscal Studies, 1985.

FINSINGER, Jörg and PAULY, Mark V. (eds.), *The Economics of Insurance Regulation: A Cross-National Study*, New York, St. Martin's Press, 1986, 300 p.

FINSINGER, Jörg and PAULY, Mark V., 'The Double Liability Rule', **15** *Geneva Papers on Risk and Insurance Theory*, 1990, 159-170.

FLEMING, John G., 'The Insurance Crisis', **24** *University of British Columbia Law Review*, 1990, 1-18.

FRECH, H. Edward III, 'Market Power in Health Insurance: Effects on Insurance and Medical Markets', Journal of Industrial Economics, Vol. 27, 55-72.

FRECH, H. Edward III, 'Health Insurance: Private, Mutual or Government', **Suppl. 1** *Research in Law and Economics*, 1980, 61-73.

FRECH, H. Edward III (ed.), *Health Care in America: The Political Economy of Hospitals and Health Insurance*, San Francisco, Pacific Research Institute for Public Policy, 1988, 293-322.

FRECH, H. Edward III and GINSBURG, Paul B., 'Property Rights and Competition in Health Insurance: Multiple Objectives for Nonprofit Firms', **3** *Research in Law and Economics*, 1981, 155-171.

FRECH, H. Edward III and SAMPRONE, Joseph C., Jr., 'The Welfare Loss of Excess Nonprice Competition: The Case of Property-Liability Insurance Regulation', **23** *Journal of Law and Economics*, 1980, 429-440.

FRIEDMAN, David D., 'What is 'Fair Compensation' for Death or Injury ?', **2** *International Review of Law and Economics*, 1982, 81-93.

GATELY, D. and GEEHAN, R., 'Returns to Scale in the Life Insurance Industry', **8** *Bell Journal of Economics*, 1977, 497-514.

GEEHAN, Randall, 'Economies of Scale in Insurance: Implications for Regulation', in WASOW, Bernard and HILL, Raymond D. (ed.), *The Insurance Industry in Economic Development*, New York, New York University Press, 1986, 137-159.

GEORGE, William C., 'Whither No-Fault in California: Is There Salvation After Proposition 103?', **26** *San Diego Law Review*, 1989, 1065-1085.

GOLDBERG, Victor P., 'Institutional Change and the Quasi-Invisible Hand', **17**

Journal of Law and Economics, 1974, 461-492. Reprinted in GOLDBERG, Victor P. (ed.), *Readings in the Economics of Contract Law*, Cambridge, Cambridge University Press, 1989, 169-173.

GOLDBERG, Victor P., 'Tort Liability for Negligent Inspection by Insurers', **2** *Research in Law and Economics*, 1980, 65-81.

GOLDBERG, Victor P., 'Accountable Accountants: Is Third-Party Liability Necessary ?', **17** *Journal of Legal Studies*, 1988, 295-312.

GRABOWSKI, Henry G., VISCUSI, W. Kip and EVANS, William N., 'Price and Availability Tradeoffs of Automobile Insurance Regulation', **56** *Journal of Risk & Insurance*, 1989, 275-299.

GRAVELLE, Hugh S.E., 'Insurance and Corrective Taxes in the Health Care Market', *Journal of Economics (Zeitschrift für Nationalkonomie)*, 1986, Suppl. 5, 114-130.

GRAVELLE, Hugh S.E., 'Accidents, Taxes, Liability Rules and Insurance', **12** *Geneva Papers on Risk and Insurance*, 1987, 115-131.

GRAVELLE, Hugh S.E., 'Accidents and the Allocation of Legal Costs with an Uninformed Court', **14** *Geneva Papers on Risk and Insurance*, 1989, 11-25.

GRAVELLE, Hugh S.E., 'Medical Negligence: Evaluating Alternative Regimes', **15** *Geneva Papers on Risk and Insurance*, 1990, 22-26.

GRAVELLE, Hugh S.E., 'The Welfare Implications of Controls on Brokers' Commissions', **16** *Geneva Papers on Risk and Insurance*, 1991, 3-19???.

GRAVELLE, Hugh S.E., 'Insurance Law and Adverse Selection', **11** *International Review of Law and Economics*, 1991, 23-45.

HALPERN, Paul J. and CARR, Jack L., *Liability Rules and Insurance Markets*, Ottawa, Consumer and Corporate Affairs Canada, 1981.

HANSEN, Ronald W., MACAVOY, Paul W. and SMITH, Clifford W., Jr., 'Compensation Alternatives for Occupational Disease and Disability' **56** *Journal of Risk and Insurance*, 1989, 252-274.

HANSMANN, Henry B., 'The Organization of Insurance Companies: Mutual versus Stock', **1** *Journal of Law, Economics, & Organization*, 1985, 125-153.

HANSSON, Ingemar, LYTTKENS, C.H. and SKOGH, Göran, 'The Excess Burden of Public Insurance: Some Results from Swedish Data', **4** *International Review of Law and Economics*, 1984, 23-28.

HANSSON, Ingemar and SKOGH, Göran, 'Moral Hazard and Safety Regulation', **12** *Geneva Papers on Risk and Insurance*, 1987, 132-144.

HARRINGTON, Scott E., 'The Relationship Between Voluntary and Involuntary Market Rates and Rate Regulation in Automobile Insurance', **57** *Journal of Risk & Insurance*, 1990, 9-27.

HIGGINS, Richard S., 'Products Liability Insurance, Moral Hazard, and Contributory Negligence', **10** *Journal of Legal Studies*, 1981, 111-130.

HILL, Raymond D., 'Profit Regulation in Property-Liability Insurance', **10** *Bell Journal of Economics*, 1979, 172-191.

HOLDERNESS, Clifford G., 'Liability Insurers as Corporate Monitors', **10** *International Review of Law and Economics*, 1990, 115-129.

HOLMSTRÖM, Bengt, 'Moral Hazard and Observability', **10** *Bell Journal of Economics*, 1979, 74-91.

HUBERMAN, Gur, MAYERS, David and SMITH, Clifford, 'Optimal Insurance Policy Indemnity Schedules', **14** *Bell Journal of Economics*, 1983, 415-426.

JONES-LEE, Michael, 'Natural Disaster: A Comparison of Alternative Methods for Evaluating Preventive Measures', **9** *Geneva Papers on Risk and Insurance*, 1984, 188-205.

JONES-LEE, Michael, 'The Value of Life and Safety: A Survey of Recent Developments', **10** *Geneva Papers on Risk and Insurance*, 1985, 141-173.

JOOST, Robert H., 'Choosing the Best Auto Insurance Choice System', **26** *San Diego Law Review*, 1989, 1033-1064.

KALB, Paul E., 'Controlling Health Care Costs by Controlling Technology: A Private Contractual Approach', **99** *Yale Law Journal*, 1990, 1109-1126.

KARRER, H., *Elements of Credit Insurance. An International Survey*, London, Sir Isaac Pitman, 1957.

KARTEN, Walter, 'Do Shares in Other Insurance Companies Reduce the Solvency Margin of an Insurer?', LOUBERGé, Henri (ed.), *Risk, Information and Insurance. Essays in the Memory of Karl H. Borch*, Boston, Kluwer Academic Publishers, 1990, 257-267.

KATZMAN, Martin T., 'Environmental Risk Management Through Insurance', **6** *Cato Journal*, 1987, 775-799.

KATZMAN, Martin T., 'Pollution Liability Insurance and Catastrophic Environmental Risk', **55** *Journal of Risk & Insurance*, 1988, 75-100.

KEETON, William R. and KWEREL, Evan, 'Externalities in Automobile Insurance and the Underinsured Driver Problem', **27** *Journal of Law and Economics*, 1984, 149-179.

KEHNE, Jeffrey, 'Encouraging Safety Through Insurance-Based Incentives: Financial Responsibility for Hazardous Wastes', **96** *Yale Law Journal*, 1986, 403-427.

KLINGMÜLLER, E., 'Liability Insurance in the Federal Republic of Germany', **15** *Geneva Papers on Risk and Insurance*, 1990, 330-336.

KOCHANOWSKI, Paul S. and YOUNG, Madelyn V., 'Deterrent Aspects of No Fault Automobile Insurance: Some Empirical Findings', **52** *Journal of Risk and Insurance*, 1985, 269-288.

KRAFT, K. and SCHULENBURG, J. Matthias Graf von der, 'Co-Insurance and Supplier-induced Demand in Medical Care: What do we Have to Expect as the Physicians' Response to Increased Out-of-Pocket Payments?', **142** *Journal of Institutional and Theoretical Economics*, 1986, 360-379.

KRONMAN, Anthony T., 'Mistake, Disclosure, Information, and the Law of Contracts', **7** *Journal of Legal Studies*, 1978, 1-34.

KUNREUTHER, Howard, 'The Case for Comprehensive Disaster Insurance', **11** *Journal of Law and Economics*, 1968, 133-163.

KUNREUTHER, Howard, 'Causes of Underinsurance against Natural Disasters', **9** *Geneva Papers on Risk and Insurance*, 1984, 206-220.

KUNREUTHER, Howard, 'Problems and Issues of Environmental Liability Insurance', **12** *Geneva Papers on Risk and Insurance*, 1987, 180-197.

KUNREUTHER, Howard, 'Towards an Integrated Waste Management Program', **14** *Geneva Papers on Risk and Insurance*, 1989, 99-103.

KUNREUTHER, Howard and KLEINDORFER, Paul and PAULY, Mark, 'Insurance Regulation and Consumer Behavior in the United States: The Property and Liability Industry', **139** *Zeitschrift für die gesamte Staatswissenschaft*, 1983, 452-472.

KUNZMAN, Steven A., 'The Insurer as Surrogate Regulator of the Hazardous Waste Industry: Solution or Perversion?', **20** *Forum*, 1985, 169-188.

LACEY, N.J., 'Recent Evidence on the Liability Crisis', **55** *Journal of Risk and Insurance*, 1988, 499-508.

LANDES, Elisabeth M., 'Insurance, Liability, and Accidents: A Theoretical and Empirical Investigation of the Effect of No-Fault Accidents', **25** *Journal of Law and Economics*, 1982, 49-65.

LANDES, William M. and POSNER, Richard A., *The Economic Structure of Tort Law*, Cambridge (Mass.) Harvard University Press, 1987, 330 p.

LEFKIN, Peter A., 'Shattering Some Myths on the Insurance Liability: A Comment', **5** *Yale Journal on Regulation*, 1988, 417-425.

LEMENNICIER, Bertrand, 'Indemnités de licenciement: assurances tous risques, réparation d'un préjudice ou impït sur la liberté de contracter' [Damages of Licensing: All Risk Insurance, Retrieving a Loss or Taxation on the Freedom of Contract], in *Droit Prospectif Revue de la Recherche Juridique*, Aix-Marseille, PUF, 1987.

LITAN, Robert E. and WINSTON, Clifford (eds.), *Liability: Perspectives and Policy*, Washington D.C., Brookings Institution, 1988, 248 p.

LOUBERGé, Henri (ed.), *Risk, Information and Insurance. Essays in the Memory of Karl H. Borch*, Boston, Kluwer Academic Publishers, 1990, 274 p.

MANOVE, M., 'Provider Insurance', **14** *Bell Journal of Economics*, 1983, 489-496.

MARSHALL, John M., 'Insurance as a Market in Contingent Claims: Structure and Performance', **5** *Bell Journal of Economics*, 1974, 670-682.

MAYERS, David and SMITH, Clifford W., Jr., 'Contractual Provision, Organizational Structure, and Conflict Control in Insurance Markets', **54** *Journal of Business*, 1981, 407-434.

MAYERS, David and SMITH, Clifford W., Jr., 'On the Corporate Demand for Insurance', **55** *Journal of Business*, 1982, 281-95.

MAYERS, David and SMITH, Clifford W., Jr., 'Corporate Insurance and the Underinvestment Problem', **54** *Journal of Risk and Insurance*, 1987, 45-54.

MAYERS, David and SMITH, Clifford W., Jr., 'Ownership Structure across Lines of Property-Casualty Insurance', **31** *Journal of Law and Economics*, 1988, 351-378.

MAYERS, David and SMITH, Clifford W., Jr., 'On the Corporate Demand for Insurance: Evidence from the Reinsurance Market', **63** *Journal of Business*, 1990, 19-40.

McDOWELL, Banks, 'Competition as a Regulatory Mechanism in Insurance', **19** *Connecticut Law Review*, 1987, 287-310.

McNEELY, M., 'Illegality as a Factor in Liability Insurance', **41** *Columbia Law*

Review, 1941, 26-60.

MEIER, Kenneth J., *The Political Economy of Regulation: The Case of Insurance*, Albany, State University of New York Press, 1988, 230 p.

MOORE, Peter G., *The Business of Risk*, Cambridge, Cambridge University Press, 1983, 244 p.

MUNCH, Patricia and SMALLWOOD, D., 'Solvency Regulation in the Property-Liability Insurance Industry: Empirical Evidence', **11** *Bell Journal of Economics*, 1980, 261-279.

O'CONNELL, Jeffrey, 'No-Fault Auto Insurance: Back by Popular (Market) Demand?', **26** *San Diego Law Review*, 1989, 993-1015.

O'CONNELL, Jeffrey and GUINIVAN, James, 'An Irrational Combination: the Relative Expansion of Liability Insurance and Contraction of Loss Insurance', **19** *Ohio State Law Journal*, 1988, 757-771.

O'CONNELL, Jeffrey and JOOST, Robert H., 'Giving Motorists a Choice Between Fault and No-Fault Insurance', **72** *Virginia Law Review*, 1986, 61-89.

O'DRISCOLL, Gerald P., Jr., 'The Liability Crisis: A Law and Economics Analysis', **0(11)** *Federal Reserve Bank of Dallas Economic Review*, 1987, 1-13.

OLSON, Walter (ed.), *New Directions in Liability Law*, New York, The Academy of Political Science, 1988, 214 p.

OUTREVILLE, J. François, 'Price Regulation and Segmented Insurance Markets', in LOUBERGé, Henri (ed.), *Risk, Information and Insurance. Essays in the Memory of Karl H. Borch*, Boston, Kluwer Academic Publishers, 1990, 221-229.

PALFREY, Thomas R. and SPATT, C.S., 'Repeated Insurance Contracts and Learning', **16** *Rand Journal of Economics*, 1985, 356-367.

PAULY, Mark V., 'The Rational Nonpurchase of Long-Term Insurance', **98** *Journal of Political Economy*, 1990, 153-168.

PRIEST, George L., 'A Theory of the Consumer Product Warranty', **90** *Yale Law Journal*, 1981, 1297-1352. Reprinted in GOLDBERG, Victor P. (ed.), *Readings in the Economics of Contract Law*, Cambridge, Cambridge University Press, 1989, 174-184.

PRIEST, George L., 'The Invention of Enterprise Liability: A Critical History of the Intellectual Foundations of Modern Tort Law', **14** *Journal of Legal Studies*, 1985, 461-527.

PRIEST, George L., 'The Current Insurance Crisis and Modern Tort Law', **96** *The Yale Law Journal*, 1987, 1521-1590.

PRIEST, George L., 'Products Liability Law and the Accident Rate in Liability: Perspectives and Policy', in LITAN, Robert E. and WINSTON, Clifford (eds.), Washington D.C., Brookings Institution, 1988, 184-222.

PRIEST, George L., 'Antitrust Suits and the Public Understanding of Insurance', **63** *Tulane Law Review*, 1989, 999-1044.

PRIEST, George L., 'Insurability an Punitive Damages', **40** *Alabama Law Review*, 1989, 1009-1035.

RIZZO, John A., 'The Impact of Medical Malpractice Insurance Rate Regulation', **56** *Journal of Risk & Insurance*, 1989, 482-500.

ROOS, Carl Martin, 'On Insurer Generosity', *Scandinavian Studies in Law*, 1981.

ROOS, Carl Martin, 'Analysis and Evaluation of Compensation Systems. The Example of Pollution Damage', *Scandinavian Studies in Law*, 1990, 213-234.

ROOS, Carl Martin, SKOGH, Göran and STUART, Charles, 'The Swedish Property and Liability Insurance Market. An Industry Study', Department of Economics, School of Economics and Management, University of Lund, Memo 1980:72.

ROSETT, Richard N. and FELDSTEIN, Martin S. (eds.), *The Role of Health Insurance in the Health Services Sector*, Universities-National Bureau Conference Series, No. 27, New York, National Bureau of Economic Research, 1976, 156-160

ROTHSCHILD, Michael and STIGLITZ, Joseph E., 'Equilibrium in Competitive Insurance Markets: An Essay on the Economics of Imperfect Information', **90** *Quarterly Journal of Economics*, 1976, 629-649.

ROTTENBERG, Simon, 'Unintended Consequences: The Probable Effects of Mandated Medical Insurance', **13(2)** *Regulation*, 1990, 21-28.

SCHLESINGER, H. and SCHULENBURG, J. Matthias Graf von der, 'Risk Aversion and the Purchase of Risky Insurance', **47** *Journal of Economics*, 1987, 309-314.

SCHMIT, Joan T., 'A New View of the Requisites of Insurability', **53** *Journal of Risk & Insurance*, 1986, 320-329.

SCHULENBURG, J.-Matthias Graf von der, 'Moral Hazard and its Allocative Effects under Market Insurance and Compulsory Insurance', **4** *Munich Social Science Review*, 1978, 83-97.

SCHULENBURG, J.-Matthias Graf von der, 'Optimal Insurance Purchasing in the Presence of Compulsory Insurance and Uninsurable Risks', **11** *Geneva Papers on Risk and Insurance*, 1986, 5-16.

SCHWARTZ, Gary T., 'A Proposal for Tort Reform: Reformulating Uninsured Motorist Plans', **48** *Ohio State Law Journal*, 1987, 419-442.

SCHWEBLER, Robert, 'Market Development and Market Structure of Legal Expense Insurance in Germany', **10** *Geneva Papers on Risk and Insurance*, 1985, 120-133.

SHAVELL, Steven, 'On Moral Hazard and Insurance', **93** *Quarterly Journal of Economics*, 1979, 541-562.

SHAVELL, Steven, 'Strict Liability versus Negligence', **9** *Journal of Legal Studies*, 1980, 1-25.

SHAVELL, Steven, 'On Liability and Insurance', **13** *Bell Journal of Economics*, 1982, 120-132.

SHAVELL, Steven, *Economic Analysis of Accident Law*, Cambridge, Harvard University Press, 1987, 186-261 (ch.8,9,10).

SHAVELL, Steven, 'A Note on the Incentive to Reveal Information', **14** *Geneva Papers on Risk and Insurance*, 1989, 66-74.

SKOGH, Göran, 'Public Insurance and Accident Prevention', **2** *International Review of Law and Economics*, 1982, 67-80.

SKOGH, Göran, 'Professional Liability Insurance in Scandinavia. The Liability of Accountants, Barristers and Estate Agents', **14** *Geneva Papers on Risk and*

Insurance, 1989, 360-370.

SKOGH, Göran, 'The Transactions Costs of Insurance: Contracting Impediments and Costs', **4** *The Journal of Risk and Insurance*, 1989, 726-732.

SKOGH, Göran, 'The Future Insurance Market' in WIHLBORG, C., FRATIANNI, M. and WILLETS, T. (ed.), *Financial Regulation and Monetary Arrangements after 1992. Contributions to Economic analysis*, Elsevier Publishers, 1991.

SKOGH, Göran, 'Insurance and the Institutional Economics of Financial Intermediation', **16** *Geneva Papers on Risk and Insurance*, 1991, 59-72.

SKOGH, Göran and STUART, Charles, 'Liability, Insurance, and the Regulation of Traffic Accidents', in SKOGH, Göran (ed.), *Law and Economics. Report from a Symposium in Lund, Sweden, 24-26 August 1977*, Lund, Juridiska Föreningen, 1978, 203-210.

SKOGH, Göran and SAMUELSSON, Per, *Splittring eller sammanhållning i svensk försäkring? En ekonomisk och rättslig analys av marknadsföringsöverenskommelse m.m* [Disruption or Unity in Swedish Insurance? An Economic and Legal Analysis of the Marketing Agreements etc], Lund, Dialogos, 1985.

SMITH, Clifford W., Jr. and WARNER, Jerold B., 'On Financial Contracting: An Analysis of Bond Covenants', **7** *Journal of Financial Economics*, 1979, 117-61.

SWAN, Peter, 'Is Law Reform Too Important to be Left to the Lawyers?: a Critique of Two Law Reform Commission Reports, *Human Tissue Transplants* and *Insurance Agents and Brokers*', in CRANSTON, Ross and SCHICK, Anne (eds.), *Law and Economics*, Canberra, Australian National University, 1982, 10-24.

SZÖLLÖSY, P., 'Regional Variations of Compensation Awards: The Quantum of Damages in Personal Injury and Wrongful Death Claims in Western Europe', **15** *Geneva Papers on Risk and Insurance*, 1990, 337-343.

TREBILCOCK, Michael J., 'The Social-Insurance-Deterrence Dilemma of Modern North American Tort Law: A Canadian Perspective on the Liability Insurance Crisis', **24** *San Diego Law Review*, 1987, 929-1002.

TREBILCOCK, Michael J., 'Comment on Viscusi, "The Performance of Liability Insurance in States with Different Products-Liability Statutes"', **19** *Journal of Legal Studies*, 1990, 845-849.

VAN DEN BERGHE, Lutgart, 'Financiële instellingen en markten: 3. Verzekeringen' [Financial Institutions and Markets: Insurance], in *18de Vlaams Wetenschappelijk Economisch Congres, Brussel 8 en 9 mei 1987, Sociaal-economische Deregulering*, Brussel, V.E.H.U.B., 1987, 665-692.

VAN DEN BERGHE, Lutgart, '(De)regulation of Insurance Markets', in LOUBERGé, Henri (ed.), *Risk, Information and Insurance. Essays in the Memory of Karl H. Borch*, Boston, Kluwer Academic Publishers, 1990, 199-220.

VERBON, Harrie, *The Evolution of Public Pension Scemes*, Berlin/Heidelberg, Springer-Verlag, 1988, 287 p.

VISCUSI, W. Kip, 'Product Liability Litigation with Risk Aversion', **17** *Journal of Legal Studies*, 1988, 101-121.

VISCUSI, W. Kip, 'The Performance of Liability Insurance in States with Different Products-Liability Statutes', **19** *Journal of Legal Studies*, 1990, 809-836.

VISCUSI, W. Kip, 'The Dimensions of the Product Liability Crisis', **20** *Journal of Legal Studies*, 1991, 147-177.

WADE, John W., 'An Evaluation of the "Insurance Crisis" and Existing Tort Law', **24** *Houston Law Review*, 1987, 81-96.

WALDEN, Alyssa, 'Note: The Publicly Held Corporation and the Insurability of Punitive Damages', **53** *Fordham Law Review*, 1985, 1383-1408.

WANSINK, J.W., Salomons, R.A. and Kremer, F.T. (1990) 'Some Characteristics of the Dutch System for Compensation of Damage', **15** *Geneva Papers on Risk and Insurance Issues and Practices*, 1990, 276-291.

WASSENAER VAN CATWIJCK, A.J.O. Baron van, *Verkeersverzekering* [Traffic Insurance], Zwolle, Tjeenk Willink, 1977, 78 p.

WASSENAER VAN CATWIJCK, A.J.O. Baron van, 'Verkeersverzekering in Noord--Amerika' [Traffic Insurance in North-America: No-fault in Action], *Het Verzekerings-Archief*, 's-Gravenhage, Verbond van Verzekeraars in Nederland, 1988, 321-377.

WEBER, Nathan, *Product Liability: The Corporate Response*, New York, Conference Board, 1987.

WHELAN, Christopher and McBARNET, Doreen, 'The 'Crisis' in Professional Liability Insurance', **14** *Geneva Papers on Risk and Insurance*, 1989, 296-307.

WILHELMSEN, Trine-Lise, *Egenrisiko i Skadeforsikring* [Residual Risk in Accident Insurance], Oslo, Sjørettsfondet, 1989.

WILLIAMSON, Oliver E., OLSON, Douglas and RALSTON, August, 'Externalities, Insurance, and Disability Analysis', **34** *Economica*, 1967, 235-253.

WINTER, Ralph A., 'The Liability Insurance Market', **5(3)** *Journal of Economic Perspectives*, 1991, 115-136.

WITT, Robert C. and URRUTIA, Jorge, 'A Comparative Economic Analysis of Tort Liability and No Fault Compensation Systems in Automobile Insurance', **50** *Journal of Risk and Insurance*, 1983, 631-669.

WORTHAM, Leah, 'The Economics of Insurance Classification: The Sound of One Invisible Hand Clapping', **47** *Ohio State Law Journal*, 1986, 835-890.

ZYCHER, Benjamin, 'Automobile Insurance Regulation, Direct Democracy, and the Interests of Consumers', **13(2)** *Regulation*, 1990, 67-77.

4700 INHERITANCE LAW
Gerrit De Geest

ANDERSON, Gary M. and BROWN, P.J. 'Heir Pollution: A Note on Buchanan's 'Law of Succession' and Tullock's 'Blind Spot'', **5** *International Review of Law and Economics*, 1985, 15-23.

BRACEWELL-MILNES, Barry, *The Wealth of Giving: Every One in his Inheritance*, London, Institute of Economic Affairs, 1989, 112 p.

BRENNER, G.A., 'Why Did Inheritance Laws Change?', **5** *International Review of Law and Economics*, 1985, 91-106.

BROUGH, Wayne T., 'Liability Salvage - by Private Ordering', **19** *Journal of Legal Studies*, 1990, 95-111.

BUCHANAN, James M., 'Rent Seeking, Noncompensated Transfers, and Laws of Succession', **26** *Journal of Law and Economics*, 1983, 71-85.

GREENE, Kenneth V., 'Inheritance Unjustified?', **16** *Journal of Law and Economics*, 1973, 417-419.

IRELAND, Thomas R., 'Inheritance Justified: A Comment', **16** *Journal of Law and Economics*, 1973, 421-422.

KOLLER, Roland H. II, 'Inheritance Justified : A Comment', **16** *Journal of Law and Economics*, 1973, 423-424.

SCHÄFER, Hans-Bernd and STRUCK, Gerhard, 'Schlammbeseitigung auf der Bundesstraße. Geschäftsführung ohne Auftrag, Deliktsrecht, negatorische Haftung. Ökonomische Analyse des Rechts' [The Case of the Mud Removal at the Federal Highway], in WALZ, W. Rainer and RASCHER-FRIESENHAUSEN, Heinrich (eds.), *Sozialwissenschaften im Zivilrecht: Fälle und Lösungen in Ausbildung und Prüfung*, Neuwied, Luchterhand, 1983, 119-132.

SHAMMAS, Carole, SALMON, Marylynn and DAHLIN, Michel, *Inheritance in America from Colonial Times to the Present*, New Brunswick, Rutgers University Press, 1987, 320 p.

TULLOCK, Gordon, 'Inheritance Justified', **14** *Journal of Law and Economics*, 1971, 465-474.

TULLOCK, Gordon, 'Inheritance Rejustified', **16** *Journal of Law and Economics*, 1973, 425-428.

5000 REGULATION OF CONTRACTUAL RELATIONS

5000 REGULATION: GENERAL
Gerrit De Geest

18de Vlaams Wetenschappelijk Economisch Congres, Brussel 8 en 9 mei 1987, Sociaal-economische Deregulering, Brussel, V.E.H.U.B., 1987, 892 p.

ABRAMS, Burton A. and LEWIS, Kenneth A., 'A Median Voter Model of Economic Regulation', **52** *Public Choice*, 1987, 125-142.

AGHION, Philippe and HERMALIN, Benjamin, 'Legal Restrictions on Private Contracts Can Enhance Efficiency', **6** *Journal of Law, Economics, & Organization*, 1990, 381-409.

AMACHER, Ryan C. et al., 'The Behavior of Regulatory Activity over the Business Cycle: An Empirical Test' [Previously published in 1985], in MACKAY, Robert J., MILLER, James C., III and YANDLE, Bruce (eds.), *Public Choice and Regulation: A View from Inside the Federal Trade Commission*, Stanford, Hoover Institution Press, 1987, 145-53.

ANTON, James J. and GERTLER, Paul J., 'External Markets and Regulation', **37** *Journal of Public Economics*, 1988, 243-260.

AVERCH, H. and JOHNSON, L.L., 'Behaviour of the Firm under Regulatory Constraints', **52** *American Economic Review*, 1962, 1052-1069.

BAECK, L., ONGENA, H. and COOLS, J.P., 'Begripsbepaling en situering van het dereguleringsverschijnsel in de geschiedenis van het economisch denken' [Definition and Sketch of the Deregulation Phenomenon in the History of Economic Thought], in *18de Vlaams Wetenschappelijk Economisch Congres, Brussel 8 en 9 mei 1987, Sociaal-economische Deregulering*, Brussel, V.E.H.U.B., 1987, 29-47.

BAILEY, Elizabeth E. (ed.), *Public Regulation: New Perspectives on Institutions and Policies*, Cambridge, MIT Press, 1987, 404 p.

BALDWIN, G.R. and VELJANOVSKI, Cento G., *Regulation and Cost-Benefit Analysis - The U.S. Experience and U.K. Potential*, Oxford, Centre for Socio-Legal Studies, 1982.

BARON, David P., 'Regulation and Legislative Choice', **19** *Rand Journal of Economics*, 1988, 467-477.

BEALES, J. Howard, III, 'The Economics of Regulating the Professions', in BLAIR, Roger D. and RUBIN, Stephen (eds.), *Regulating the Professions: A Public-Policy Symposium*, Lexington, Lexington Books, 1980.

BECKER, Gilbert, 'The Public Interest Hypothesis Revisited: A New Test of Peltzman's Theory of Regulation', **49** *Public Choice*, 1986, 223-234.

BELL, Joe A., 'The Disinterest in Deregulation: Comment', **78** *American Economic Review*, 1988, 282-283.

BENSTON, George J., 'Party Realignments and the Growth of Federal Economic Regulation, 1861-1986: Comments', **2** *Journal of Financial Services Research*,

1989, 227-229.

BOLLARD, Alan, 'More Market: The Deregulation of Industry', in BOLLARD, Alan and BUCKLE, Robert (eds.), *Economic Liberalisation in New Zealand*, Wellington, Allen and Unwin, 1987, 25-45.

BOLLARD, Alan and BUCKLE, Robert (eds.), *Economic Liberalisation in New Zealand*, Wellington, Allen and Unwin, 1987, 364 p.

BOUDREAUX, Don and EKELUND, Robert B., Jr., 'Regulation as an Exogenous Response to Market Failure: A Neo-Schumpeterian Response', **143** *Journal of Institutional and Theoretical Economics*, 1987, 537-554.

BRACKE, F., 'Deregulering en algemeen belang: 1. Bronnen en doelstellingen' [Deregulation and General Interest: Sources and Purposes], in *18de Vlaams Wetenschappelijk Economisch Congres, Brussel 8 en 9 mei 1987, Sociaal-economische Deregulering*, Brussel, V.E.H.U.B., 1987, 101-122.

BREYER, Stephen G., 'Analysing Regulatory Failure: Mismatches, Less Restrictive Alternatives, and Reform', **92** *Harvard Law Review*, 1979, 549-609. Reprinted in OGUS, Anthony I. and VELJANOVSKI, Cento G. (eds), *Readings in the Economics of Law and Regulation*, Clarendon Press, Oxford, 1984, 234-239.

BREYER, Stephen G., *Regulation and its Reform*, Cambridge Mass., Harvard University Press, 1982, 472 p.

BREYER, Stephen G., 'Reforming Regulation', **59** *Tulane Law Review*, 1984, 4-23.

BREYER, Stephen G., 'Economists and Economic Regulation', **47** *University of Pittsburgh Law Review*, 1985, 205-218.

BROCK, William A. and EVANS, David S., 'The Economics of Regulatory Tiering', **16** *Rand Journal of Economics*, 1985, 398-409.

BUTTON, Kenneth J. and SWANN, Dennis (eds.), *The Age of Regulatory Reform*, Oxford, Oxford University Press, 1989, 339 p.

CAILLAUD, B., GUESNERIE, R., REY, P. and TIROLE, J., 'Government Intervention in Production and Incentives Theory: A Review of Recent Contributions', **19** *Rand Journal of Economics*, 1988, 1-26.

CAMPOS, Jose Edgardo L., 'Legislative Institutions, Lobbying, and the Endogenous Choice of Regulatory Instrument: A Political Economy Approach to Instrument Choice', **5** *Journal of Law, Economics, & Organization*, 1989, 333-353.

CASTLES, Francis G., *Australian Public Policy and Economic Vulnerability: A Comparative and Historical Perspective*, Winchester, Allen and Unwin, 1988, 184 p.

CHERKES, Martin, FRIEDMAN, Joseph and SPIVAK, Avia, 'The Disinterst in Deregulation: Comment', **76** *American Economic Review*, 1986, 559-563.

CHEROT, Jean-Yves, 'Elements pour une théorie de la réglementation' [Elements for a Theory of Regulation], *Revue de la Recherche Juridique*, 1987, Nr. 2.

CHESNEY, James D., 'The Politics of Regulation: An Assessment of Winners and Losers', **19** *Inquiry*, 1982, 235-245.

COOTER, Robert D. and RUBIN, Edward L., 'Orders and Incentives as Regulatory Methods: The Expedited Funds Availability Act of 1987', **35** *UCLA Law Review*, 1988, 1115-1186.

CRANDALL, Robert W., 'Deregulation: The U.S. Experience', **139** *Zeitschrift für* *die gesamte Staatswissenschaft*, 1983, 419-434.

CRANDALL, Robert W., 'Economic Rents as a Barrier to Deregulation', **6** *Cato Journal*, 1986, 173-194.

CREW, Michael A. and ROWLEY, Charles K., 'Deregulation as an Instrument in Industrial Policy', **142** *Journal of Institutional and Theoretical Economics*, 1986, 52-70.

CREW, Michael A. and ROWLEY, Charles K., 'The Myth of Disinterest in Deregulation', in ROWLEY, Charles K., TOLLISON, Robert D. and TULLOCK, Gordon (eds.), *The Political Economy of Rent-Seeking*, Norwell, Kluwer Academic Publishers, 1987, 163-178.

DAEMS, H. and DE GRAUWE, Paul, 'Determinanten van de overheidsreglementering' [Determinants of Government Regulation], in, *Overheidsinterventies, Effectiviteit en Efficiëntie. Vijftiende Vlaams wetenschappelijk Economisch Congres*, Leuven, Departement Toegepaste Economische Wetenschappen, 1981, 25-41.

DEMSKI, Joel S. and SAPPINGTON, David E.M., 'Hierarchical Regulatory Control', **18** *Rand Journal of Economics*, 1987, 369-383.

DERTHICK, Martha and QUIRK, Paul J., *The Politics of Deregulation*, Washington D.C., The Brookings Institution, 1985, 265 p.

DERTHICK, Martha and QUIRCK, Paul J., 'Why the Regulators Chose to Deregulate', in NOLL, Roger G. (ed.), *Regulatory Policy and the Social Sciences*, Berkeley, University of California Press, 1985, 200-231.

DIVER, Colin S., 'A Theory of Regulatory Enforcement', **28** *Public Policy*, 1980, 257-299.

DUHARCOURT, Pierre, '"Théories" et "concept" de la régulation' [Regulation as a Theory and as a Concept], **22(5)** *Economies et Sociétés*, 1988, 135-161.

EADS, George C., 'A.E. Kahn: The Economics of Regulation', **2** *Bell Journal of Economics*, 1971, 678-682.

EKELUND, Robert B., Jr. and TOLLISON, Robert D., *Mercantilism as a Rent Seeking Society: Economic Regulation in Historical Perspective*, College Station, Texas A&M University Press, 1981, 169 p.

ESCARMELLE, Jean Francois and HUJOEL, Luc, 'Privatization and Deregulation. Its Implementation in Belgium', **57** *Annals of Public and Co-operative Economy*, 1986, 253-273.

FREY, Bruno S. and RAMSER, Hans Jürgen, 'Where Are the Limits of Regulation?', **142** *Journal of Institutional and Theoretical Economics*, 1986, 571-580.

GEY, Steven G., 'The Political Economy of the Dormant Commerce Clause', **17** *New York University Review of Law & Social Change*, 1989-90, 1-80.

GIFFORD, Adam, Jr., 'Rent Seeking and Nonprice Competition', **27(2)** *Quarterly Review of Economics and Business*, 1987, 63-70.

GILLIGAN, Thomas W., MARSHALL, William J. and WEINGAST, Barry R., 'Regulation and the Theory of Legislative Choice: The Interstate Commerce Act of 1887', **32** *Journal of Law and Economics*, 1989, 35-61.

GOLBERT, J.P. and LOWENSTEIN, Paul, 'The Court and the Marketplace: Who

Should Regulate Whom?', **34** *Baylor Law Review*, 1982, 39-65.

GOLDBERG, Victor P., 'Regulation and Administered Contracts', **7** *Bell Journal of Economics*, 1976, 426-448.

GOODMAN, John C. and PORTER, Philip K., 'Theory of Competitive Regulatory Equilibrium', **59** *Public Choice*, 1988, 51-166.

GUESNERIE, Roger, 'Regulation as an Adverse Selection Problem: An Introduction to the Literature', **32** *European Economic Review*, 1988, 473-481.

HADDOCK, David D. and MACEY, Jonathan R., 'Regulation on Demand: A Private Interest Model, with an Application to Insider Trading Regulation' **30** *Journal of Law and Economics*, 1987, 311-352.

HALEY, John O., 'Administrative Guidance versus Formal Regulation: Resolving the Paradox of Industrial Policy', in SAXONHOUSE, Gary R. and YAMAMURA, Kozo (eds.), *Law and Trade Issues of the Japanese Economy: American and Japanese Perspectives*, Seattle, University of Washington Press, 1986, 107-128.

HANNEQUART, Achille and GREFFE, Xavier, *Economie des interventions sociales* [Economics of Social Interventions], Paris, Economica, 1985, 264 p.

HARMATHY, Attila, 'A gazdasági szabályozók és a Szerzödések kapcsolata' [The Connection between Economic Regulation and Contracts], **12** *Jogtudományi Közlöny*, 1979, 906-813.

HARRIS, Richard A. and MILKIS, Sidney M., *The Politics of Regulatory Change: A Tale of Two Agencies*, New York, Oxford University Press, 1989, 331 p.

HARTLE, Douglas and TREBILCOCK, Michael J., 'Regulatory Reform and the Political Process', **20** *Osgoode Hall Law Journal*, 1982, 643-677.

HEKATHORN, Douglas D. and MASER, Steven M., 'Bargaining and the Sources of Transaction Costs: The Case of Government Regulation', **3** *Journal of Law, Economics, & Organization*, 1987, 69-98.

HIGH, Jack, 'Can Rents Run Uphill? A Note on the Theory of Regulation', **65** *Public Choice*, 1990, 229-237.

HILLMAN, Arye L. and SCHNYTZER, Adi, 'Illegal Economic Activities and Purges in a Soviet-Type Economy: A Rent-Seeking Perspective', **6** *International Review of Law and Economics*, 1986, 87-99.

HÖGLUND, Bengt, *Spelet om Resurserna i den Svenska Blandekonomin* [The Swedish Mixed Economy], Lund, Dialogos, 1984.

HOLCOMBE, Randall G. and HOLCOMBE, Lora P., 'The Market for Regulation', **142** *Journal of Institutional and Theoretical Economics*, 1986, 684-696.

HOUSTON, Douglas A., 'The Mixed Interest in Regulation and Deregulation', **63** *Land Economics*, 1987, 403-405.

HUYSE, Luc, 'Deregulering en algemeen belang: 2. Deregulering als maatschappelijke reconstructie' []Deregulation and General Interest: Deregulation as Social Reconstruction], in *18de Vlaams Wetenschappelijk Economisch Congres, Brussel 8 en 9 mei 1987, Sociaal-economische Deregulering*, Brussel, V.E.H.U.B., 1987, 123-140.

JARRELL, Gregg A., 'Change at the Exchange: The Causes and Effects of Deregulation', **27** *Journal of Law and Economics*, 1984, 273-312.

JORDAN, William A., 'Producer Protection, Prior Market Structure and the Effects of Government Regulation', **15** *Journal of Law and Economics*, 1972, 151-176.

KAHN, Alfred E., 'Comment: Deregulatory Schizophrenia', **75** *California Law Review*, 1987, 1059-1068.

KAHN, Alfred E., *The Economics of Regulation: Principles and Institutions*, Cambridge, Mass., MIT Press, 1988, 199 p. (Volume 1) + 360 p. (Volume 2).

KAHN, Alfred E., 'Deregulation: Looking Backward and Looking Forward', **7** *Yale Journal on Regulation*, 1990, 325-354.

KATZMANN, Robert A., 'Comments on Levine and Forrence, "Regulatory Capture, Public Interest, and the Public Agenda: Toward a Synthesis', **6** *Journal of Law, Economics, & Organization*, 1990, S199-S202.

KEELER, Theodore E., 'Theories of Regulation and the Deregulation Movement', **44** *Public Choice*, 1984, 103-145.

KEMP, Kathleen A., 'Party Realignments and the Growth of Federal Economic Regulation, 1861-1986', **2** *Journal of Financial Services Research*, 1989, 213-225.

KEYSERLING, Leon H., 'The New Deal and Its Current Significance in the National Economic and Social Policy', **59** *Washington Law Review*, 1984, 795 ff.

KIRCHNER, Christian, 'Deregulation as an Instrument in Industrial Policy: Comment', **142** *Journal of Institutional and Theoretical Economics*, 1986, 75-78.

KIRZNER, Israel M., 'The Perils of Regulation: A Market-Process Approach', in KIRZNER, Israel M., *Discovery and Capitalist Process*, Chicago, University of Chicago Press, 1985, 119-149.

KLING, Robert W., 'Building an Institutionalist Theory of Regulation', **22** *Journal of Economic Issues*, 1988, 197-209.

LATIN, Howard, 'Ideal versus Real Regulatory Efficiency: Implementation of Uniform Standards and "Fine-Tuning" Regulatory Reforms', **37** *Stanford Law Review*, 1985, 1267-1332.

LEVINE, Michael E. and FORRENCE, Jennifer L., 'Regulatory Capture, Public Interest, and the Public Agenda: Toward a Synthesis', **6** *Journal of Law, Economics, & Organization*, 1990, S167-S198.

LIBECAP, Gary D., 'Deregulation as an Instrument in Industrial Policy: Comment', **142** *Journal of Institutional and Theoretical Economics*, 1986, 71-74.

MACKAAY, Ejan J.P., 'Le paradoxe des droits acquis' [The Paradox of Acquired Rights], in *De "l'ancienne" à la "nouvelle" économie. Essais à l'occasion de la dixième université d'été de la nouvelle économie. Aix-en-Provence 1978-87*, Aix-en-Provence, Librairie de l'université, 1987, 205-219.

MACKAY, Robert J., MILLER, James C., III and YANDLE, Bruce, 'Public Choice and Regulation: An Overview', in MACKAY, Robert J., MILLER, James C., III and YANDLE, Bruce (eds.), *Public Choice and Regulation: A View from Inside the Federal Trade Commission*, Stanford, Hoover Institution Press, 1987, 3-12.

MALONEY, Michael T., McCORMICK Robert E. and TOLLISON, Robert D., 'Economic Regulation, Competitive Governments, and Specialised Resources',

27 *Journal of Law and Economics*, 1984, 329-338.

MARTIN, Donald L. and SCHWARTZ, Warren F. (eds.), *Deregulating American Industry: Legal and Economic Problems*, Lexington, Lexington Books, 1977, 120 p.

McCHESNEY, Fred S., 'Rent Extraction and Interest-Group Organization in a Coasean Model of Regulation', **20** *Journal of Legal Studies*, 1991, 73-90.

McCORMICK, Robert E., SHUGHART, William F., II and TOLLISON, Robert D., 'The Disinterest in Deregulation', **74** *American Economic Review*, 1984, 1075-1079.

McCORMICK, Robert E., SHUGHART, William F., II and TOLLISON, Robert D., 'The Disinterest in Deregulation: Reply', **76** *American Economic Review*, 1986, 564-565.

McCORMICK, Robert E., SHUGHART, William F., II and TOLLISON, Robert D., 'Reply', **78** *American Economic Review*, 1988, -284.

McCORMICK, Robert E. and TOLLISON, Robert D., *Politicians, Legislation, and the Economy*, Boston, Martinus Nijhof, 1981, 134 p.

McCUBBINS, Mathew D., NOLL, Roger G. and WEINGAST, Barry R., 'Slack, Public Interest, and Structure-Induced Policy', **6** *Journal of Law, Economics, & Organization*, 1990, S203-S212.

McKIE, James W., 'Regulation and the Free Market: The Problem of Boundaries', **1** *Bell Journal of Economics*, 1970, 6-26.

McNALLY, David, *Political Economy and the Rise of Capitalism: A Reinterpretation*, Berkely, University of California Press, 1988, 329 p.

MEIER-SCHATZ, Christian, *Wirtschaftsrecht und Unternehmenspublizität* [Economic Legislation and Enterprise Publicity], Zurich, Schulthess, 1989.

MENTRE, Paul, 'Regulation and Deregulation: An Economic Viewpoint', in VAN DE KAR, Hans M. and WOLFE, Barbara L. (eds.), *The Relevance of Public Finance for Policy-Making: Proceedings of the 41st Congress of the International Institute of Public Finance, Madrid, Spain, 1985*, Detroit, Wayne State University Press, 1987, 293-305.

MEYER, Dirk, 'Rent Seeking durch Rationalisierungsschutz oder die Wohlfahrtsverluste einer Kostensenkungssteuer' [Rent Seeking through Regulations Protecting Human Capital from Devaluation Due to Technological Innovation], **35** *Konjunkturpolitik*, 1989, 188-1200.

MEYERS, Jan and STEENBERGEN, Jacques, 'Deregulering, Europese eenmaking en bescherming van het nationaal belang' [Deregulation, European Unification and Protection of National Interest], in *18de Vlaams Wetenschappelijk Economisch Congres, Brussel 8 en 9 mei 1987, Sociaal-economische Deregulering*, Brussel, V.E.H.U.B., 1987, 51-75.

MIGUÉ, Jean-Luc, 'Controls versus Subsidies in the Economic Theory of Regulation', **20** *Journal of Law and Economics*, 1977, 213-221.

MOORE, Thomas Gale, 'An Agenda for Regulatory Reform', in BOAZ, David and CRANE, Adward H. (eds.), *Beyond the Status Quo: Policy Proposals for America*, Washington, Cato Institute, 1985, 145-63.

MUELLER, Dennis C., 'Anarchy, the Market, and the State', **54** *Southern Economic*

Journal, 1988, 821-830.

NEEDHAM, Douglas, *The Economics and Politics of Regulation: A Behavioral Approach*, Boston, Little Brown, 1983, 482 p.

NISKANEN, William A., 'Economic Deregulation in the United States: Lessons for America, Lessons for China', **8** *Cato Journal*, 1989, 657-668.

NOLL, Roger G., 'The Political Foundations of Regulatory Policy', **139** *Zeitschrift fur die gesamte Staatswissenschaft*, 1983, 377-3404.

NOLL, Roger G. (ed.), *Regulatory Policy and the Social Sciences*, Berkely, University of California Press, 1985, 400 p.

NOLL, Roger G., 'The Political Foundations of Regulatory Policy', in McCUBBINS, Mathew D. and SULLIVAN, Terry (eds.), *Congress: Structure and Policy*, Cambridge, University Press, 1987, 462-492.

NOLL, Roger G., 'Regulation After Reagan', **12(3)** *Regulation*, 1988, 13-20.

OLSON, C. Vincent and TRAPANI III, John M., 'Who Has Benefited from Regulation of the Airline Industry ?', **24** *Journal of Law and Economics*, 1981, 75-93.

ORDOVER, Janusz A. and WEISS, Andrew, 'Information and the Law: Evaluating Legal Restrictions on Competitive Contracts', **71** *American Economic Review. Papers and Proceedings*, 1981, 399-404.

OWEN, Bruce M., 'Interest Groups and the Political Economy of Regulation', in MEYER, Jack A. (ed.), *Incentives vs. Controls in Health Policy: Broadening the Debate*, Washington, American Enterprise Institute for Public Policy Research, 1985, 26-52.

OWEN, Bruce M. and BRAEUTIGAN, Ronald R., *The Regulation Game: Strategic Use of the Administrative Process*, Cambridge, Ballinger, 1978, 271 p.

PALAY, Thomas M., 'Avoiding Regulatory Constraints: Contracting Safeguards and the Role of Informal Agreements', **1** *Journal of Law, Economics, & Organization*, 1985, 155-175.

PASTOR, Santos, 'Estado, mercado, eficiencia y equidad' [The Market, the State, Efficiency and Equity], in CORCUERA, J. and GARCIA HERRERA, M.A. (eds.), *Derecho y economía en el estado social*, Tecnos & Gobierno Vasco, 1988.

PAUL, Chris and SCHOENING, Niles, 'Regulation and Rent-Seeking: Prices, Profits, and Third-Party Transfers', **68** *Public Choice*, 1991, 185-194.

PEACOCK, Alan (ed.), *The Regulation Game: How British and West German Companies Bargain with Government*, Oxford, Basil Blackwell, 1984, 170 p.

PELTZMAN, Sam, 'Toward A More General Theory of Regulation', **19** *Journal of Law and Economics*, 1976, 211-240.

POSNER, Richard A., 'Taxation by Regulation', **2** *Bell Journal of Economics*, 1971, 22-50.

POSNER, Richard A., 'Theories of Economic Regulation', **5** *Bell Journal of Economics* 1974, 335-358.

REAGAN, Michael D., *Regulation: The Politics of Policy*, Boston, Little Brown, 1986, 241 p.

RICKETTS, Martin and PEACOCK, Alan, 'Bargaining and the Regulatory System',

6 *International Review of Law and Economics*, 1986, 3-16.

ROBERTSON, L.S., 'A Critical Analysis of Peltzman's "The Effects of Automobile Safety Regulation"', **11** *Journal of Economic Issues*, 1977, 587-600.

ROGERSON, William P., 'The Social Costs of Monopoly and Regulation: a Game-Theoretic Analysis', **13** *Bell Journal of Economics*, 1982, 391-401.

ROMER, Thomas and ROSENTHAL, Howard, 'Modern Political Economy and the Study of Regulation', in BAILEY, Elizabeth E. (ed.), *Public Regulation: New Perspectives on Institutions and Policies*, Cambridge (Mass.), MIT Press, 1987, 73-116.

ROSA, J.J., 'Derégiementation et théorie du droit' [Deregulation and Legal Theory], *Politique Economique*, 1984, Nr. 33.

ROSE-ACKERMAN, Susan, 'Deregulation and Reregulation: Rhetoric and Reality', **6** *Journal of Law & Politics*, 1990, 287-309.

ROSE-ACKERMAN, Susan, 'Defending the State: A Skeptical Look at "Regulatory Reform" in the Eighties', **61** *University of Colorado Law Review*, 1990, 517-535.

ROSS, Thomas W., 'Uncovering Regulators' Social Welfare Weights', **15** *Rand Journal of Economics*, 1984, 152-155.

ROUSSLANG, D.J., 'Import Injury in U.S. Trade Law: An Economic View', **8** *International Review of Law and Economics*, 1988, 117-122.

ROWLEY, Charles K., 'The Relationship between Economics, Politics and the Law in the Formation of Public Policy', in MATTHEWS, R.C.O. (ed.), *Economy and Democracy*, New York, St. Martin's Press, 1985, 127-150.

SAGOFF, Mark, 'Must Regulatory Reform Fail?', **4** *Journal of Policy Analysis and Management*, 1985, 433-436.

SAMUEL, Warren J., SCHMID, A. Allan and SHAFFER, James D., 'Regulation and Regulatory Reform: Some Fundamental Conceptions', in SAMUELS, Warren J. and SCHMID, A. Allen (eds.), *Law and Economics: An Institutional Perspective*, Boston, Nijhoff, 1981, 248-266.

SAMUELS, Warren J., 'Normative Premises in Regulatory Theory', **1** *Journal of Post Keynesian Economics*, 1978, 100-114. Reprinted in SAMUELS, Warren J. and SCHMID, A. Allen (eds.), *Law and Economics: An Institutional Perspective*, Boston, Nijhoff, 1981, 128-142.

SAPPINGTON, David E.M. and STIGLITZ, Joseph E., 'Information and Regulation', in BAILEY, Elizabeth E. (ed.), *Public Regulation: New Perspectives on Institutions and Policies*, Cambridge (Mass.), MIT Press, 1987, 3-43.

SCHMALENSEE, Richard, 'Comments on Beales, Craswell, and Salop', **24** *Journal of Law and Economics*, 1981, 541-544.

SCHMALENSEE, Richard, 'Good Regulatory Regimes', **20** *Rand Journal of Economics*, 1989, 417-436.

SCHWARTZ, Louis B., 'Some Additional Safeguards for the Newly Liberated Marketplace: Deregulatory Schizophrenia', **75** *California Law Review*, 1987, 1049-1057.

SCHWERT, G. William, 'Using Financial Data to Measure Effects of Regulation',

24 *Journal of Law and Economics*, 1981, 121-158. Reprinted in POSNER, Richard A. and SCOTT, Kenneth E. (eds.), *Economics of Corporation Law and Securities Regulation*, Boston, Little Brown, 1980.

SHOGREN, Jason F. (ed.), *The Political Economy of Government Regulation*, Dordrecht, Kluwer Academic, 1989, 210 p.

SHUGHART, William F., II and TOLLISON, Robert D., 'The Cyclical Character of Regulatory Activity', **45** *Public Choice*, 1985, 303-311.

SIEBER, Hugo, 'Wirtschaftsfreiheit und Wirtschaftspolitik' [Economic Freedom and Economic Policy], in *Recht als Prozess und Gefüge* (Festschrift für Hans Huber zum 80. Geburtstag), Bern, 1981, 447-465.

SIGLER, Jay A. and MURPHY, Joseph E., *Interactive Corporate Compliance: An Alternative to Regulatory Complusion*, Westport, Greenwood Press, 1988, 211 p.

SKOGH, Göran, *Marknadens villkor* [The Terms of the Market], Stockholm, Timbro, 1982.

SLAYTON, Philip and TREBILCOCK, Michael J., (eds.), *The Professions and Public Policy*, Toronto, University of Toronto Faculty of Law, 1978, 346 p.

SPILLER, Pablo T., 'Politicians, Interest Groups, and Regulators: A Multi-Principals Agency Theory of Regulation, or "Let Them Be Bribed"', **33** *Journal of Law & Economics*, 1990, 65-101.

STEWART, Richard B., 'Madison's Nightmare', **57** *University of Chicago Law Review*, 1990, 335-356.

STIGLER, George J., 'The Theory of Economic Regulation', **2** *Bell Journal of Economics*, 1971, 3-21.

STIGLER, George J., 'Free Riders and Collective Action: an Appendix to Theories of Economic Regulation', **5** *Bell Journal of Economics*, 1974, 359-365.

STIGLER, George J., *The Citizen and the State. Essays on Regulation*, Chicago, University of Chicago Press, 1975, 209 p.

STIGLER, George J., 'The Goals of Economic Policy', **18** *Journal of Law and Economics*, 1975, 283-292.

STIGLER, George J. and FRIEDLAND, Claire, 'What Can Regulators Regulate? The Case of Electricity', **5** *Journal of Law and Economics*, 1962, 1-16.

SUNSTEIN, Cass R., *After the Rights Revolution: Reconceiving the Regulatory State*, Cambridge, Harvard University Press, 1990, 284 p.

SUNSTEIN, Cass R., 'Paradoxes of the Regulatory State', **57** *University of Chicago Law Review*, 1990, 407-441.

SWANN, Dennis, *The Retreat of the State: Deregulation and Privatization in the U.K. and U.S.*, Ann Arbor, University of Michigan Press, 1988, 344 p.

SYMPOSIUM : 'Deregulation', **57** *Indiana Law Journal*, 1976, 682-755.

SYMPOSIUM : 'Regulation and Innovation', **43(1)** *Law and Contemporary Problems*, 1979.

SYMPOSIUM : 'Managing the Transition to Deregulation', **44(1)** *Law and Contemporary Problems*, 1981.

THÉRET, B., 'La place de l'État dans les théories économiques françaises de la régulation: éléments critiques et repositionnement à la lumière de l'histoire' [The Place of the State in French Economic Theories of Regulation; Critical Arguments and New Posture Brought to Light by History], **43(2)** *Économie Appliquée*, 1990, 43-81.

THIEMEYER, Theo, 'Deregulation in the Perspective of the German Gemeinwirtschaftslehre', **139** *Zeitschrift für die gesamte Staatswissenschaft*, 1983, 405-418.

TOOL, Marc R., 'Some Reflections on Social Value Theory and Regulation', **24** *Journal of Economic Issues*, 1990, 535-544.

TREBILCOCK, Michael J. and HARTLE, D.G., 'The Choice of Governing Instrument', **2** *International Review of Law and Economics*, 1982, 29-46.

TREBILCOCK, Michael J. and PRICHARD, J.Robert S., 'Economic Analysis of Commercial Law', in ZIEGAL, J.S. (ed.) *Proceedings of the Seventh Annual Workshop on Commercial and Consumer Law*, Toronto, Canada Law Book, 1979.

TREBILCOCK, Michael J., WEAVERMAN, L. and PRICHARD, J.Robert S., 'Markets for Regulation: Implications for Performance Standards and Institutional Design', in *Government Regulation - Issues and Alternatives*, Toronto, Ontario Economic Council, 1978.

TREBING, Harry M., 'Regulation of Industry: An Institutionalist Approach', **21** *Journal of Economic Issues*, 1987, 1707-1737.

TULLOCK, Gordon, 'Concluding Thoughts on the Politics of Regulation', in MACKAY, Robert J., MILLER, James C., III and YANDLE, Bruce (eds.), *Public Choice and Regulation: A View from Inside the Federal Trade Commission*, Stanford, Hoover Institution Press, 1987, 333-343.

UTTON, M.A., *The Economics of Regulating Industry*, Oxford, Blackwell, 1986, 243 p.

VAN GERVEN, Walter, 'Herijken van economische wetgeving (over reguleren en dereguleren)' [Re-Stamping of Economic Regulation (on Regulating and Deregulating)], **49** *Rechtskundig Weekblad*, 1985-86, 289-308.

VAN HULLE, K., 'Informatie en markttransparantie' [Information and Market Transparency], in *18de Vlaams Wetenschappelijk Economisch Congres, Brussel 8 en 9 mei 1987, Sociaal-economische Deregulering*, Brussel, V.E.H.U.B., 1987, 79-97.

VASQUEZ, Pablo, 'Grupos de interés en la Comunidad Económica Europea. Apuntes sobre un regulación actual' [The Regulation of Interest Groups in the European Community], *Información Comercial Española*, 1990, n. 689, 89-102.

VELJANOVSKI, Cento G., 'Regulatory Enforcement - An Economic Case Study of the British Factory Inspectorate', **4** *Law and Policy Quarterly*, 1982.

VELJANOVSKI, Cento G., 'The Economics of Regulatory Enforcement', in HANKINS, Keith and THOMAS, John M. (eds.), *Enforcing Regulation*, Boston, Kluwer-Nijhoff, 1984, 169-188.

VELJANOVSKI, Cento G., *Selling the State: Privatisation in Britain*, London, Weidenfeld and Nicolson, 1987, 239 p.

VESENKA, Mary H., 'Economic Interests and Ideological Conviction: A Note on PACs and Agricultural Acts', **12** *Journal of Economic Behavior and*

Organization, 1989, 259-263.

WATERS, Melissa and MOORE, William J., 'The Theory of Economic Regulation and Public Choice and the Determinants of Public Sector Bargaining Legislation', **66** *Public Choice*, 1990, 161-175.

WEISBROD, Burton A. (ed.) in collaboration with HANDLER, Joel F. and KOMESAR, Neil K., *Public Interest Law: An Economic and Institutional Analysis*, Berkeley, University of California Press, 1978, 580 p.

WEISS, Leonard W. and KLASS, Michael W. (eds.), *Regulatory Reform: What Actually Happened*, Boston, Little Brown, 1986.

WOOD, Stephen G., FLETCHER, Don C. and HOLLEY, Richard F., 'Regulation, Deregulation and Re-Regulation: An American Perspective', *Brigham Young University*, 1987, 381-465.

YANDLE, Bruce, 'Regulatory Reform in the Realm of the Rent Seekers', in MACKAY, Robert J., MILLER, James C., III and YANDLE, Bruce (eds.), *Public Choice and Regulation: A View from Inside the Federal Trade Commission*, Stanford, Hoover Institution Press, 1987, 121-42.

YANDLE, Bruce and YOUNG, Elizabeth, 'Regulating the Function, Not the Industry', **51** *Public Choice*, 1986, 59-70.

ZERBE, Richard O., Jr. and URBAN, Nicole, 'Including the Public Interest in Theories of Regulation', **11** *Research in Law and Economics*, 1988, 1-23.

5100 PRICE REGULATION
Gerrit De Geest

5100 Price Regulation: General

ACKLEY, Gardner, 'Observations on Phase II Price and Wage Controls', **1** *Brookings Papers on Economic Activity*, 1972, 173-190.

AMES, Edward, 'The Firm and Price Control', **29(1)** *Journal of Economics and Business*, 1976, 10-15.

AMES, Edward, 'The Consumer and Wage Price Controls', **30** *Journal of Economics and Business*, 1977, 15-22.

ARAGON, George, 'Mandatory Price Controls: Managing a Response', **15(3)** *Business Economics*, 1980, 25-31.

ARNOULD, Richard J., 'Pricing Professional Services : A Case Study of the Legal Services Industry', **38** *Southern Economic Journal*, 1972, 38, 495-507.

BARCELLA, Mary L., 'In Defense of Price Controls for "Old" Natural Gas', **19(4)** *Business Economics*, 1984, 24-33.

BAUM, Herbert, 'Das Stabilisierungspotential staatlich administrierter Preise' [On the Stabilization Effects of Public Regulated Prices], **190** *Jahrbucher fur Nationalokonomie und Statistik*, 1976, 349-376.

BAUM, Herbert, 'Verteilungswirkungen der staatlichen Preispolitik' [Effects of Public Regulated Prices on Distribution of Income], **193** *Jahrbucher fur Nationalokonomie und Statistik*, 1978, 220-243.

BAUMOL, William J., 'Minimum and Maximum Pricing Principles for Residual Regulation', in BAUMOL, William J., *Microtheory: Applications and Origins*, Cambridge, MIT Press, 1986, 151-164.

BLACKMON, B. Glenn, Jr. and ZECKHAUSER, Richard, 'Mispriced Equity: Regulated Rates for Auto Insurance in Massachusetts', **81** *American Economic Review. Papers and Proceedings*, 1991, 65-69.

BOEHM, E.A., 'Prices and Incomes Policies in the United States', **18** *Australian Economic Review*, 1972, 37-46.

BOURGOIGNIE, Th., 'Overheid en bedrijfsleven/3 La reglementation des prix en Belgique' [Price Regulation in Belgium], **27** *Economisch en Sociaal Tijdschrift*, 1973, 387-400.

BOWLES, Roger A. and PHILLIPS, Jennifer, 'Solicitors' Renumeration: A Critique of Recent Developments in Conveyancing', **40** *Modern Law Review*, 1977, 639-650.

BOYER, Kenneth D., 'The Costs of Price Regulation: Lessons from Railroad Deregulation', **18** *Rand Journal of Economics*, 1987, 408-416.

BRADLEY, Ian and PRICE, Catherine, 'The Economic Regulation of Private Industries by Price Constraints', **37** *Journal of Industrial Economics*, 1988, 99-106.

BRAEUTIGAM, Ronald R. and PANZAR, John C., 'Diversification Incentives Under "Price-Based" and Cost-Based" Regulation', **20** *Rand Journal of Economics*, 1989, 373-391.

BROWN, Donald J. and HEAL, Geoffrey M., 'The Optimality of Regulated Pricing: A General Equilibrium Analysis', in ALISPRANTIS, C.D., BURKINSHAW, O. and ROTHMAN, N.J. (eds.), *Advances in Equilibrium Theory: Proceedings of the Conference on General Equilibrium Theory held at Indiana University-Purdue University at Indianapolis, USA, February 10-12, 1984*, New York, Springer, 1985, 43-54.

BROWNING, Edgar K. and CULBERTSON, William Patton, Jr., 'A Theory of Black Markets under Price Control: Competition and Monopoly', **12** *Economic Inquiry*, 1974, 175-189.

BRUNNER, Karl and MELTZER, Allan H., 'The Economics of Price and Wage Controls: An Introduction', **2** *Journal of Monetary Economics*, 1976, 1-6.

CANDLER, Wilfred and KENNEDY, George, 'Food Cost Stabilization Using Food Coupons', **23** *Canadian Journal of Agricultural Economics*, 1975, 33-45.

CHEUNG, Steven N.S., 'A Theory of Price Control', **17** *Journal of Law and Economics*, 1974, 53-71.

COCHRANE, James L. and GRIEPENTROG, Gary L., 'Sulphur and the U.S. Government: Price Fighting in the 1960s', **16** *Economic Inquiry*, 1978, 360-384.

COLANDER, David, 'Galbraith and the Theory of Price Control', **7** *Journal of Post Keynesian Economics*, 1984, 30-42.

COTTLE, Rex L. and WALLACE, Myles S., 'Economic Effects of Non Binding Price Constraints', **31** *Journal of Industrial Economics*, 1983, 469-474.

COURSEY, Don L. and SMITH, Vernon L., 'Price Controls in a Posted Offer Market', **73** *American Economic Review*, 1983, 218-221.

COUSINEAU, Jean Michel and LACROIX, Robert, 'L'impact de la politique canadienne de controle des prix et des revenus sur les ententes salariales' [The Effect of Canadian Price and Income Control Policy on the Wages], **4** *Canadian Public Policy*, 1978, 88-100.

COX, Charles C., 'The Enforcement of Public Price Controls', **88** *Journal of Political Economy*, 1980, 887-8916.

CSIKOS Nagy, Bela, 'The New Path of Hungarian Price Policy', **118** *Nationalokonomisk Tidsskrift*, 1980, 201-211.

CUKIERMAN, Alex and LEIDERMAN, Leonardo, 'Price Controls and the Variability of Relative Prices', **16** *Journal of Money, Credit, and Banking*, 1984, 271-284.

CURWEN, P.J., 'The Price Commission Report on Books A Short Critique', **27** *Journal of Industrial Economics*, 1979, 295-299.

DARBY, Michael R., 'Price and Wage Controls: The First Two Years', **2** *Journal of Monetary Economics*, 1976, 235-263.

DARBY, Michael R., 'Price and Wage Controls: Further Evidence', **2** *Journal of Monetary Economics*, 1976, 269-271.

DAUGHETY, Andrew F. and FORSYTHE, Robert, 'The Effects of Industry-Wide

Price Regulation on Industrial Organization', **3** *Journal of Law, Economics, & Organization*, 1987, 397-434.

DE BONDT, Raymond, 'Industrial Economic Aspects of Belgian Price Regulation', **23** *Tijdschrift voor Economie en Management*, 1978, 249-264.

DE BONDT, R. and VAN HERCK, G., 'Prijsbeleid en economische efficiëntie' [Price Policy and Economic Efficiency], in *15de Vlaams Wetenschappelijk Economisch Congres*, Leuven, Universitaire Pers, 1981, 253-278.

DEACON, Robert T., 'An Economic Analysis of Gasoline Price Controls', **18** *Natural Resources Journal*, 1978, 801-814.

DEACON, Robert T. and SONSTELIE, Jon, 'The Welfare Costs of Rationing by Waiting', **27** *Economic Inquiry*, 1989, 179-196.

DEACON, Robert T. and SONSTELIE, Jon, 'Price Controls and Rent Seeking Behavior in Developing Countries', **17** *World Development*, 1989, 1945-1954.

DEATON, Thomas and TOLLISON, Robert D. and CRAFTON, Steven, 'A Note on the Theory of Black Markets under Price Controls', **14** *Economic Inquiry*, 1976, 300-3304.

DeGRABA, Patrick J., 'The Effects of Price Restrictions on Competition Between National and Local Firms', **18** *Rand Journal of Economics*, 1987, 333-347.

DOHERTY, Neil A. and GARVEN, James R., 'Price Regulation in Property Liability Insurance: A Contingent Claims Approach', **41** *Journal of Finance*, 1986, 1031-050.

EDWARDS, Clark, 'Exchangeable Coupon Gas Rationing', **26(3)** *Agricultural Economics Research*, 1974, 55-68.

EHEMANN, Christian, 'General Disequilibrium, Fiscal Policy, and a Wage Price Freeze', **12** *Economic Inquiry*, 1974, 35-52.

ERICKSON, Edward W., et al., 'The Political Economy of Crude Oil Price Controls', **18** *Natural Resources Journal*, 1978, 787-780.

EVELY, Richard W., 'The Effects of the Price Code', **77** *National Institute Economic Review*, 1976, 50-59.

FENILI, Robert N. and LANE, William C., 'Thou Shalt Not Cut Prices! Sales-Below-Cost Laws for Gas Stations', **9(5)** *Regulation*, 1985, 31-35.

FIEDLER, Edgar R., 'The Price Wage Stabilization Program', **1** *Brookings Papers on Economic Activity*, 1972, 199-1206.

FLOWERS, Marilyn R. and STROUP, Richard, 'Coupon Rationing and Rent Seeking Bureaucrats', **34** *Public Choice*, 1979, 473-479.

GHALI, Moheb A., 'The Effect of Controls on Wages, Prices, and Strike Activity', **30** *Journal of Economics and Business*, 1977, 23-30.

GITLOW, Abraham L., 'Are Peacetime Wage Price Controls Effective?', **23** *Rivista Internazionale di Scienze Economiche e Commerciali*, 1976, 722-739.

GORDON, Daniel V., 'The Effect of Price Deregulation on the Competitive Behaviour of Retail Drug Firms', **20** *Applied Economics*, 1988, 641-652.

GORDON, Robert J., 'Wage Price Controls and the Shifting Phillips Curve', **2** *Brookings Papers on Economic Activity*, 1972, 385-421.

GORDON, Robert J., 'The Response of Wages and Prices to the First Two Years of

Controls', **3** *Brookings Papers on Economic Activity*, 1973, 765-778.

GRANZIOL, Markus J., 'Direct Price Controls as a Source of Instability in the Interest Rate/Inflation Rate Relationship', **9** *Journal of Banking and Finance*, 1985, 275-288.

GRECO, Anthony J., 'State Fluid Milk Regulation: Antitrust and Price Controls', **32** *Antitrust Bulletin*, 1987, 165-188.

GRIBBIN, J.D., 'The United Kingdom 1977 Price Commission Act and Competition Policy', **23** *Antitrust Bulletin*, 1978, 405-439.

HAMILTON, Mary T., 'Price Controls in 1973: Strategies and Problems', **64** *American Economic Review*, 1974, 100-104.

HELPMAN, Elhanan, 'Macroeconomic Effects of Price Controls: The Role of Market Structure', **98** *Economic Journal*, 1988, 340-354.

HEMPEL, George H., 'Wage and Price Controls for State and Local Governments: Their Effectiveness and the Potential Effects of Phase III', **21** *Public Policy*, 1973, 425-436.

HILL, Raymond D., 'Profit Regulation in Property-Liability Insurance', **10** *Bell Journal of Economics*, 1979, 172-191.

HORWICH, George, 'Disasters and Market Response', **9** *Cato Journal*, 1990, 531-555.

HOUTHAKKER, Hendrik S., 'Are Controls the Answer?', **54** *Review of Economics and Statistics*, 1972, 231-233.

IPPOLITO, Richard A., 'The Effects of Price Regulation in the Automobile Insurance Industry', **22** *Journal of Law and Economics*, 1979, 55-89.

ISAAC, R. Mark and PLOTT, Charles R., 'Price Controls and the Behavior of Auction Markets: An Experimental Examination', **71** *American Economic Review*, 1981, 448-459.

JENNY, F., 'From Price Controls to Competition Policy in France: The Uneasy Alliance of Economical and Political Considerations', **52** *Annals of Public and Co-operative Economy*, 1981, 477-490.

JOHNSON, Ronald N., 'Retail Price Controls in the Diary Industry: A Political Coalition Argument', **28** *Journal of Law and Economics*, 1985, 55-75.

JONES, Clifton T. and BREMMER, Dale S., 'Regional Impacts of Petroleum Price Regulation: The Case of Texas, 1973 1983', **11** *Energy Journal*, 1990, 135-154.

KALT, Joseph P. and LEONE, Robert A., 'Regional Effects of Energy Price Decontrol: The Roles of Interregional Trade, Stockholding, and Microeconomic Incidence', **17** *Rand Journal of Economics*, 1986, 201-213.

KARP, Gordon and YOHE, Gary W., 'The Optimal Linear Alternative to Price and Quantity Controls in the Multifirm Case', **3** *Journal of Comparative Economics*, 1979, 56-65.

KELLER, Robert R., 'Inflation, Monetarism, and Price Controls', **19** *Nebraska Journal of Economics and Business*, 1980, 30-40.

KELLER, Robert R. and GRAY, S. Lee, 'A Neo Classical Argument for Wage Price Controls', **6(2)** *Intermountain Economic Review*, 1975, 46-54.

LANZILLOTTI, Robert F. and ROBERTS, Blaine, 'The Legacy of Phase II Price

Controls', **64** *American Economic Review*, 1974, 82-87.

LE PEN, Claude, 'Reglementation des prix et formes de la concurrence dans l'industrie pharmaceutique' [Price Regulation and Competition Patterns in the Ethical Drug Industry], **39** *Revue Economique*, 1988, 1159-1191.

LEE, Dwight R., 'The Firm's Response to an Input Quota Constraint: Some Price Control Implications', **16(4)** *Quarterly Review of Economics and Business*, 1976, 35-45.

LEE, Dwight R., 'Price Controls, Binding Constraints, and Intertemporal Economic Decision Making', **86** *Journal of Political Economy*, 1978, 293-2301.

LEE, Dwight R., 'Price Controls on Non Renewable Resources: An Intertemporal Analysis', **46** *Southern Economic Journal*, 1979, 179-188.

LEVI, Maurice and DEXTER, Albert, 'Regulated Prices and Their Consequences', **9** *Canadian Public Policy*, 1983, 24-31.

LEVY, Santiago, 'Efectos macroecónomicos del control de precios: un análisis de equilibrio general a corto plazo' [The Macroeconomic Effects of Price Controls: A Short run General Equilibrium Analysis. With English summary]', **3** *Estudios Economicos*, 1988, 27-56.

LIPSEY, Richard G., 'Wage Price Controls: How to do a Lot of Harm by Trying to do a Little Good', **3** *Canadian Public Policy*, 1977, 1-13.

LOTT, John R., Jr. and FREMLING, Gertrud M., 'Time Dependent Information Costs, Price Controls, and Successive Government Intervention', **5** *Journal of Law, Economics, & Organization*, 1989, 293-306.

LOTT, John R., Jr. and ROBERTS, Russell D., 'Why Comply: One-sided Enforcement of Price Controls and Victimless Crime Laws', **18** *Journal of Legal Studies*, 1989, 403-414.

MARTENS, B., 'Effectiveness and Efficiency of Price Controls in Belgium', **22** *Tijdschrift voor Economie en Management*, 1977, 405-418.

MCGRAW, Thomas K., 'Discussion [The Response of the Giant Corporations to Wage and Price Controls in World War II] 1[Planning for Peace: The Surplus Property Act of 1944].', **41(1)** *Journal of Economic History*, 1981, 136-137.

MENDERSHAUSEN, H., 'Prices, Money and the Distribution of Goods in Postwar Germany', **39** *American Economic Review*, 1949, 646 ff.

MICHIELSSEN, F. and VAN HECKE, M., 'Prijsbeleid' [Price Policy], in *11de Vlaams Wetenschappelijk Economische Congres. De overheid in de gemengde economie*, Leuven, Universitaire Pers, 1973, 189-223.

MILLS, D. Quinn, 'Some Lessons of Price Controls in 1971-1973', **6** *Bell Journal of Economics*, 1975, 3-49.

MIRANDA, Mario J. and HELMBERGER, Peter G., 'The Effects of Commodity Price Stabilization Programs', **78** *American Economic Review*, 1988, 46-58.

MIRER, Thad W., 'The Distributive Impact on Purchasing Power of Inflation during Price Controls', **15** *Quarterly Review of Economics and Business*, 1975, 93-96.

MITCHELL, Daniel J.B. and AZEVEDO, Ross E., 'Price Controls and Shortages: A Note', **48** *Journal of Business*, 1975, 571-574.

MUKHERJI, Badal and PATTANAIK, Prasanta K. and SUNDRUM, R.M., 'Rationing, Price Control and Black Marketing', **15** *Indian Economic Review*,

1980, 99-118.

MURPHY, Michael M., 'Price Controls and the Behavior of the Firm', **21** *International Economic Review*, 1980, 285-291.

OI, Walter Y., 'On Measuring the Impact of Wage Price Controls: A Critical Appraisal', **2** *Journal of Monetary Economics*, 1976, 7-64.

ORDOVER, Janusz A. and WEISS, Andrew, 'Information and the Law: Evaluating Legal Restrictions on Competitive Contracts', **71** *American Economic Review. Papers and Proceedings*, 1981, 399-404.

OSTRY, Sylvia, 'Industrial Relations after Wage and Price Control: Panel Discussion', **4** *Canadian Public Policy*, 1978, 425-430.

OUTREVILLE, J. François, 'Price Regulation and Segmented Insurance Markets', in LOUBERGé, Henri (ed.), *Risk, Information and Insurance. Essays in the Memory of Karl H. Borch*, Boston, Kluwer Academic Publishers, 1990, 221-229.

PASOUR, E.C., Jr., 'Information: A Neglected Aspect of the Theory of Price Regulation', **3** *Cato Journal*, 1984, 855-867.

PAUKERT, Felix, 'Price Policies as a Form of Incomes Policy in Developing Countries: 1. Objectives and Instruments', **127** *International Labour Review*, 1988, 135-151.

PAUKERT, Felix, 'Price Policies as a Form of Incomes Policy in Developing Countries: 2. Instruments and Effects', **127** *International Labour Review*, 1988, 293-316.

PENCAVEL, John H., 'A Comment on the Papers at the Conference on Wage Price Controls', **2** *Journal of Monetary Economics*, 1976, 303-304.

PHELPS, C.E., 'Kalt's The Economics and Politics of Oil Price Regulation: Federal Policy in the Post-Embargo Era', **13** *Bell Journal of Economics*, 1982, 289-295.

POLLEFLIET, E., 'Prijsvorming en mededingingsbeleid: 1. Economische aspecten' [Price Formation and Competition Policy: Economic Aspects], in *18de Vlaams Wetenschappelijk Economisch Congres, Brussel 8 en 9 mei 1987, Sociaal-economische Deregulering*, Brussel, V.E.H.U.B., 1987, 145-170.

POOLE, William, 'Wage Price Controls: Where Do We Go from Here?', **1** *Brookings Papers on Economic Activity*, 1973, 285-299.

POSSEN, Uri M., 'Wage and Price Controls in a Dynamic Macro Model', **46** *Econometrica*, 1978, 105-125.

PUSTAY, Michael W. and ZARDKOOHI, Asghar, 'An Economic Analysis of Liquor Price Affirmation Laws: Do They Burden Interstate Commerce?', **48** *Louisiana Law Review*, 1988, 649-676.

QUADEN, Guy, 'Price Control Policy in Belgium', **52** *Annals of Public and Co-operative Economy*, 1981, 465-476.

RAMOS TERCERO, Raul, 'Monopolistic Competition, Credibility and the Output Costs of Disinflation Programs: An Analysis of Price Controls: Comments', **29** *Journal of Development Economics*, 1988, 399-401.

ROCKOFF, Hugh, 'The Response of the Giant Corporations to Wage and Price Controls in World War II', **41** *Journal of Economic History*, 1981, 123-128.

ROCKOFF, Hugh, *Drastic Measures: A History of Wage and Price Controls in the United States*, Cambridge, Cambridge University Press, 1984, 289 p.

SALANT, Walter S., 'Effects of Price Control on Output and the Price Level', in COLANDER, David C. (ed.), *Incentive based incomes policies: Advances in TIP and MAP*, Cambridge, Mass., Harper and Row, 1986, 58-70.

SCHLAGENHAUF, Don E. and SHUPP, Franklin R., 'Inflation and Price Controls in a Flexprice Fixprice Model', **6** *Annals of Economic and Social Measurement*, 1977, 501-519.

SCHULTZ, George P. and DAM, Kenneth W., 'Reflections on Wage and Price Controls', **30** *Industrial and Labor Relations Review*, 1977, 139-151.

SILBERTSON, Aubrey, 'Should Prices be Controlled?', **19** *Australian Economic Review*, 1972, 41-43.

SMITH, Rodney T., BRADLEY, Michael and JARRELL, Greg, 'Studying Firm-Specific Effects of Regulation with Stock Market Data: An Application to Oil Price Regulation', **17** *Rand Journal of Economics*, 1986, 467-489.

SMITH, Vernon L. and WILLIAMS, Arlington W., 'On Nonbinding Price Controls in a Competitive Market', **71** *American Economic Review*, 1981, 467-474.

STIGLER, George J., 'The Theory of Economic Regulation', **2** *Bell Journal of Economics*, 1971, 3-21.

STOLLERY, Kenneth R., 'Price Controls on Nonrenewable Resources When Capacity Is Constrained', **48** *Southern Economic Journal*, 1981, 490-498.

SWAAN, Wim, 'Price Regulation in Hungary: Indirect but Comprehensive Bureaucratic Control', **31(4)** *Comparative Economic Studies*, 1989, 10-52.

UITERMARK, P.J., 'Maximumprijzen: een vergeten hoofdstuk?' [Maximum Prices: A Forgotten Chapter?], **36** *Maandschrift Economie*, 1972, 465-484.

VAN WIJNBERGEN, Sweder, 'Monopolistic Competition, Credibility and the Output Costs of Disinflation Programs: An Analysis of Price Controls', **29** *Journal of Development Economics*, 1988, 375-398.

VARTIKAR, V.S., 'Inflationary Price Controls', **37** *Rivista Internazionale di Scienze Economiche e Commerciali*, 1990, 1-6.

WARREN-BOULTON, Frederick R., 'Maricopa and Maximum Price Agreements: Time for a New Legal Standard? Editorial', **7** *Journal of Health Economics*, 1988, 185-190.

WEBER, Arnold R., 'A Wage Price Freeze as an Instrument of Incomes Policy: Or the Blizzard of '71', **62** *American Economic Review*, 1972, 251-257.

WEIDENBAUM, Murray L., 'New Initiatives in National Wage and Price Policy', **54** *Review of Economics and Statistics*, 1972, 213-217.

WEIGEL, Wolfgang, 'Grenzen der Wettbewerbspolitik' [The Limits of Competition Policy], **37(6)** *Wirtschaftspolitische Blätter*, 1990, 560-566.

WEILER, Paul, 'Industrial Relations after Wage and Price Control: Panel Discussion', **4** *Canadian Public Policy*, 1978, 433-442.

WHITWORTH, Alan, 'Monopoly and the Case for Price Control in Poor Countries', **17** *Journal of Development Studies*, 1980, 80-95.

WHITWORTH, Alan, 'Price Control Techniques in Poor Countries: The Tanzanian

Case', **10** *World Development*, 1982, 475-488.

WILTON, David A., 'An Evaluation of Wage and Price Controls in Canada', **10** *Canadian Public Policy*, 1984, 167-176.

YOHE, Gary W., 'Comparisons of Price and Quantity Controls: A Survey', **1** *Journal of Comparative Economics*, 1977, 213-233.

ZORN, Thomas S., 'The Allocative Effect of Non-binding Price Controls', **22** *Economic Inquiry*, 1984, 136-141.

ZYCHER, Benjamin, 'Automobile Insurance Regulation, Direct Democracy, and the Interests of Consumers', **13(2)** *Regulation*, 1990, 67-77.

5110 Rent Control

ALBON, Robert P., 'Rent Control, a Costly Redistributive Device? The Case of Canberra', **54** *Economic Record*, 1978, 303-313.

ALBON, Robert P., 'The Value of Tenancies Due to Rent Control in Post War New South Wales', **18** *Australian Economic Papers*, 1979, 222-228.

ALBON, Robert P. (ed.), *Rent Control. Costs & Consequences. Essays on the History, and the Economic and Social Consequences of Rent Control in Australia and Overseas*, St.Leonards, Centre for Independent Studies, 1980.

ALBON, Robert and STAFFORD, David C., *Rent Control*, London, Croom Helm, 1987, 128 p.

ALBON, Robert P. and STAFFORD, David C., 'Rent Control and Housing Maintenance', **27** *Urban Studies*, 1990, 233-240.

ANAS, Alex, et al., *The Economics of a Regulated Housing Market: Policy Perspectives and Modeling Methods* , Stockholm, Swedish Council for Building Research, 1987, 114 p.

APPELBAUM, R.P. and GILDERBLOOM, John I., 'The Redistributional Impact of Modern Rent Control', **22** *Environment and Planning*, 1990, 601-614.

ARNAULT, E. Jane, 'Optimal Maintenance under Rent Control with Quality Constraints', **3(2)** *American Real Estate and Urban Economics Association Journal*, 1975, 67-82.

ARNOTT, Richard J. and MINTZ, Jack M. (eds.), *Rent Control: The Internation Experience. Proceedings of a Conference Held at Queen's University, 31 August-4 September 1987*, Kingston, Queen's University, John Deutsch Institute for the Study of Economic Policy, 1987, 176 p.

BAAR, Kenneth K., 'Peacetime Municipal Rent Control Laws in the United States: Local Design Issues and Ideological Policy Debates', in VAN VLIET, William, et al. (eds.), *Housing and Neighborhoods: Theoretical and Empirical Contributions*, London, Greenwood Press, 1987, 257-276.

BAIRD, Charles W., *Rent Control: The Perennial Folly*, San Francisco, Cato Institute, 1980, 101 p.

BERGER, Curtis J., 'Commentary on Redistribution of Income through Regulation in Housing', **32** *Emory Law Journal*, 1983, 733-744.

BERNHARDT, Robin M., 'A Misapplication of the Sherman Act to Rent Control: Fisher v. City of Berkeley', **24** *San Diego Law Review*, 1987, 181-197.

BLOCK, Walter and OLSON, Edgar (eds.), *Rent Control. Myths and Realities. International Evidence of the Effects of Rent Control in Six Contries*, Vancouver, Fraser Institute, 1981, 335 p.

BULL, Clive and TEDESHI, Piero, 'Optimal Probation for New Hires', **145** *Journal of Institutional and Theoretical Economics*, 1989, 627-642.

CHEUNG, Steven N.S., 'Rent Control and Housing Reconstruction: The Postwar Experience of Prewar Premises in Hong Kong', **22** *Journal of Law and Economics*, 1979, 27-53.

CIRACE, John, 'Response: Housing Market Instability and Rent Stabilization', **54** *Brooklyn Law Review*, 1989, 1275 ff.

CLARK, William A.V. and HESKIN, Allan D., 'The Impact of Rent Control on Tenure Discounts and Residential Mobility', **58** *Land Economics*, 1982, 109-117.

EPSTEIN, Richard A., 'Rent Control and the Theory of Efficient Regulation', **54** *Brooklyn Law Review*, 1988, 741-774.

EPSTEIN, Richard A., 'Rent Control Revisited: One Reply to Seven Critics' **54** *Brooklyn Law Review*, 1989, 1281-1304..

FALLIS, George and SMITH, Lawrence B., 'Rent Control in Toronto: Tentant Rationing and Tenant Benefits', **11** *Canadian Public Policy*, 1985, 543-550.

FALLIS, George and SMITH, Lawrence B., 'Price Effects of Rent Control on Controlled and Uncontrolled Rental Housing in Toronto: A Hedonic Index Approach', **18** *Canadian Journal of Economics*, 1985, 652-659.

FALLIS, George and SMITH, Lawrence B., 'Uncontrolled Prices in a Controlled Market: The Case of Rent Controls', **78** *American Economic Review*, 1988, 193-200.

FRANKENA, Mark, 'Alternative Models of Rent Control', **12** *Urban Studies*, 1975, 303-308.

FRIEDMAN, Milton and STIGLER, George J., *Roofs or Ceilings?*, Irvington-on-Hudson, Foundation of Economic Education, 1946.

GOETZ, Charles J., 'Wherefore the Landlord-Tenant Law "Revolution"? - Some Comments', **69** *Cornell Law Review*, 1984, 592-603.

GYOURKO, Joseph, Peter, 'Equity and Efficiency Aspects of Rent Control: An Empirical Study of New York City', **26(1)** *Linneman Journal of Urban Economics*, 1989, 54-74.

HARLE, Jakob S., 'Challening Rent Control: Strategies for Attack', **34** *UCLA Law Review*, 1986, 149-174.

HIRSCH, Werner Z., 'An Inquiry into Effects of Mobile Home Park Rent Control', **24** *Journal of Urban Economics*, 1988, 212-226.

HIRSCH, Werner Z. and HIRSCH, Joel G., 'Legal-economic Analysis of Rent Controls in A Mobile Home Context: Placement Values and Vacancy Decontrol', **35** *UCLA Law Review*, 1988, 399-466.

HOHM, Charles F., 'The Reaction of Landlords to Rent Control', **11** *American Real Estate and Urban Economics Association Journal*, 1983, 504-520.

JOHNSON, George W., 'Introduction: Is the United States Supreme Court Ready for the Question?', **54** *Brooklyn Law Review*, 1988, 729-739.

JOHNSON, M. Bruce, 'Commentary on Redistribution of Income through Regulation in Housing', **32** *Emory Law Journal*, 1983, 761-766.

KAISH, Stanley, 'What Is "Just and Reasonable' in Rent Control? Why Historic Cost Is More Rational Than Current Value', **40** *American Journal of Economics and Sociology*, 1981, 129-137.

KIEFER, David, 'Housing Deterioration, Housing Codes and Rent Control', **17** *Urban Studies*, 1980, 53-62.

KOCHANOWSKI, Paul S., 'The Rent Control Choice: Some Empirical Findings', **6** *Policy Analysis*, 1980, 171-186.

KRISTOF, Frank S., 'Rent Control within the Rental Housing Parameters of 1975', **3(3)** *American Real Estate and Urban Economics Association Journal*, 1975, 47-60.

LETT, Monica R., 'Rent Control: The Potential for Equity', **4(1)** *American Real Estate and Urban Economics Association Journal*, 1976, 57-81.

LINNEMAN, Peter, 'The Effect of Rent Control on the Distribution of Income among New York City Renters', **22** *Journal of Urban Economics*,1987, 14-34.

LOIKKANEN, Heikki A., 'On Availability Discrimination under Rent Control', **87** *Scandinavian Journal of Economics*, 1985, 500-5520.

LUGER, Michael I., 'The Rent Control Paradox: Explanations and Prescriptions', **16(3)** *Review of Regional Studies*, 1986, 25-41.

MARKS, Denton, 'Public Choice and Rent Control', **11(3)** *Atlantic Economic Journal*, 1983, 63-69.

MARKS, Denton, 'The Effect of Rent Control on the Price of Rental Housing: An Hedonic Approach', **60** *Land Economics*, 1984, 81-94.

MARKS, Denton, 'The Effects of Partial Coverage Rent Control on the Price and Quantity of Rental Housing', **16** *Journal of Urban Economics*, 1984, 360-369.

MARKS, Denton, 'The Effect of Rent Control on the Price of Rental Housing: Reply', **62** *Land Economics*, 1986, 106-109.

MARKS, Denton, 'More on Rent Control: A Response to Yang and Dennis, Public Choice and Rent Control', **16(2)** *Atlantic Economic Journal*, 1988, 78-79.

MIRON, J.R., 'Security of Tenure, Costly Tenants and Rent Regulation', **27** *Urban Studies*, 1990, 167-183.

MOORHOUSE, John C., 'Optimal Housing Maintenance Under Rent Control', **39** *Southern Economic Journal*, 1972, 93-106.

MOORHOUSE, John C., 'Long-Term Rent Control and Tenant Subsidies', **27** *Quarterly Review of Economics & Business*, 1987, 6-24.

MUTH, Richard P., 'Redistribution of Income through Regulation in Housing', **32** *Emory Law Journal*, 1983, 691-720.

OLSEN, Edgar O., 'An Econometric Analysis of Rent Control', **80** *Journal of Political Economy*, 1972, 1081-1100.

PENA, Daniel and RUIZ Castillo, Javier, 'Distributional Aspects of Public Rental Housing and Rent Control Policies in Spain', **15** *Journal of Urban Economics*,

1984, 350-370.

PRIEMUS, Hugo, 'Rent and Subsidy Policy in the Netherlands During the Seventies', **1** *Urban Law and Policy*, 1981, 299-355.

SANTERRE, Rexford E., 'The Effect of Rent Control on the Price of Rental Housing: Comment', **62** *Land Economics*, 1986, 104-105.

SHULMAN, David, 'Real Estate Valuation under Rent Control: The Case of Santa Monica', **9(1)** *American Real Estate and Urban Economics Association Journal*, 1981, 38-53.

SIEGAN, Bernard H., 'Commentary on Redistribution of Income through Regulation in Housing', **32** *Emory Law Journal*, 1983, 721-731.

STRUYK, Raymond J., 'The Distribution of Tenant Benefits from Rent Control in Urban Jordan', **64** *Land Economics*, 1988, 125-134.

SYMPOSIUM : 'Redistribution of Income Through Regulation in Housing', **32** *Emory Law Journal*, Summer 1983, 767-819.

SYMPOSIUM : 'Rent Control and the Theory of Efficient Regulation', **54** *Brooklyn Law Review*, 1988, 729-739.

VITALIANO, Donald F., 'The Short run Supply of Housing Services under Rent Control', **22** *Urban Studies*, 1985, 535-542.

VITALIANO, Donald F., 'Measuring the Efficiency Cost of Rent Control', **14(1)** *American Real Estate and Urban Economics Association Journal*, 1986, 61-71.

WEITZMAN, Phillip, 'Economics and Rent Regulation: A Call for a New Perspective', **13** *New York University Review of Law & Social Change*, 1985, 975-988.

WILLIS, Kenneth G. and MALPEZZI, Stephen and TIPPLE, A. Graham, 'An Econometric and Cultural Analysis of Rent Control in Kumasi, Ghana', **27** *Urban Studies*, 1990, 241-257.

X, 'Note: Reassessing Rent Control: Its Economic Impact in a Gentrifying Housing Market', **101** *Harvard Law Review*, 1988, 1835-1855.

YANG, Chin Wei and DENNIS, Enid, 'Elasticities and Rent Control Revisited', **12(4)** *Atlantic Economic Journal*, 1984, 59-61.

5200 CONSUMER PROTECTION REGULATION
Gerrit De Geest

5200 Consumer Protection Regulation: General

BEALES, Howard, CRASWELL, Richard and SALOP, Steven, 'The Efficient Regulation of Consumer Information', **24** *Journal of Law and Economics*, 1981, 491-539.

BRAUCHER, Jean, 'Defining Unfairness: Empathy and Economic Analysis at the Federal Trade Commission', **68** *Boston University Law Review*, 1988, 349-430.

BREYER, Stephen G., 'Analysing Regulatory Failure: Mismatches, Less Restrictive Alternatives, and Reform', **92** *Harvard Law Review*, 1979, 549-609. Reprinted in OGUS, Anthony I. and VELJANOVSKI, Cento G. (eds), *Readings in the Economics of Law and Regulation*, Clarendon Press, Oxford, 1984, 234-239.

DARBY, Michael R. and KARNI, Edi, 'Free Competition and the Optimal Amount of Fraud', **16** *Journal of Law and Economics*, 1973, 67-88.

DARDIS, Rachel, 'Risk Regulation and Consumer Welfare', **22** *Journal of Consumer Affairs*, 1988, 303-318.

DINGWALL, R. and FENN, Paul, '"A Respectable Profession"? Sociological and Economic Perspectives on the Regulation of Professional Services', **7** *International Review of Law and Economics*, 1987, 51-64.

DUGGAN, A.J., 'The Economics of Consumer Protection: A Critique of the Chicago School Case Against Intervention', *Adelaide Law Review - Research Paper No. 2*, 1982.

FALLS, Gregory A. and WORDEN, Debra Drecnik, 'Consumer Valuation of Protection from Creditor Remedies', **22(1)** *Journal of Consumer Affairs*, 1988, 20-37.

FELDMAN, Roger and BEGUN, James W., 'The Welfare Cost of Quality Changes Due to Professional Regulation', **34** *Journal of Industrial Economics*, 1985, 17-32.

FINSINGER, Jörg, *Verbraucherschutz auf Versicherungsmärkten* [Consumer Protection in Insurance Markets], München, Florentz, 1988, 219 p.

GRETHER, David M., SCHWARTZ, Alan, and WILDE, Louis L., 'The Irrelevance of Information Overload: An Analysis of Search and Disclosure', **59** *Southern California Law Review*, 1986, 277 ff.

GRETHER, David M. and WILDE, Louis L., 'Consumer Choice and Information: New Experimental Evidence', **1(2)** *Information Economics and Policy*, 1983, 115-144.

HANCHER, Leigh, *Regulating for Competition. Government, Law, and the Pharmaceutical Industry in the United Kingdom and France*, Oxford, Oxford University Press, 1990, 384 p.

HANREICH, Hanspeter, 'Verbraucherpolitik durch Wettbewerbsrecht' [Consumer Policy By Competition Law], in KORINEK, Karl (ed.), *Beiträge zum*

Wirtschaftsrecht, Vienna, Orac Publishers, 1983, 539-560.

IPPOLITO, Pauline M., 'Consumer Protection Economics: A Selective Survey', in IPPOLITO, Pauline M. and SCHEFFMAN, David T. (eds.), *Empirical Approaches to Consumer Protection Economics*, Washington D.C., Federal Trade Commission, 1986, 1-33.

IPPOLITO, Pauline M. and SCHEFFMAN, David T. (eds.), *Empirical Approaches to Consumer Protection Economics: Proceedings of a Conference Sponsored by the Bureau of Economics, Federal Trade Commission, April 26-27, 1984*, Washington D.C., Federal Trade Commission, 1986.

KLEIN, Benjamin, 'Transaction Cost Determinants of "Unfair" Contractual Arrangements', **70** *American Economic Review. Papers and Proceedings*, 1980, 356-362. Reprinted in GOLDBERG, Victor P. (ed.), *Readings in the Economics of Contract Law*, Cambridge, Cambridge University Press, 1989, 139-146.

KRAMER, Ernst A., 'Konsumentenschutz als neue Dimension des Privat- und Wirtschaftsrecht' [Consumer Protection as a New Dimension of Private and Economic Law], **98** *Zeitschrift für schweizerisches Recht*, 1979, I, 49-92.

LEES, D.S., *The Economic Consequences of the Professions*, London, Institute of Economic Affairs, 1966, 48 p.

LERNER, A.P., 'The Economics ans Politics of Consumer Sovereignty', **62** *American Economic Review. Papers and Proceedings*, 1972, 258 ff.

LLOYD, P.J., 'The Economics of Regulation of Alcohol Distribution and Consumption in Victoria', **69)** *Australian Economic Review*, 1985, 16-29.

LYNCH, Michael et al., 'Product Quality, Consumer Information and "Lemons" in Experimental Markets', in IPPOLITO, Pauline M. and SCHEFFMAN, David T. (eds.), *Empirical Approaches to Consumer Protection Economics*, Washington, Federal Trade Commission, 1986, 251-306.

MACKAY, Robert J., MILLER, James C., III and YANDLE, Bruce (eds.), *Public Choice and Regulation: A View form Inside the Federal Trade Commission*, Stanford, Hoover Institution Press, 1987, 363 p.

MAGOULAS, Georgios, 'Zur ökonomischen Analyse des Konsumentenschutzes - unter besonderer Berücksichtigung informations- und risikobezogener Probleme von Konsumentenmärkten' [On the Economic Analysis of Consumer Protection - With Special Attention for Information and Risk-Related Problems of Consumer Markets], in MAGOULAS, Georgios and SIMON, Jürgen (eds.), *Recht und Ökonomie beim Konsumentenschutz und Konsumentenkredit*, Baden-Baden, Nomos, 23-57.

MAGOULAS, Georgios, 'Ökonomische Probleme und Funktionen finanzierter Abzahlungsgeschäfte und vermittelter Konsumentenkredite' [Economic Problems and Functions of Instalment Sales and Mediated Consumer Loans], in MAGOULAS, Georgios and SIMON, Jürgen (eds.), *Recht und Ökonomie beim Konsumentenschutz und Konsumentenkredit*, Baden-Baden, Nomos, 1985, 265-292.

MAGOULAS, Georgios, 'Ökonomische Bemerkungen zum Problem eines "Sondermarktes" im Rahmen rechtlicher Sittenwidrigkeitsprüfung' [Economic Remarks on the Problem of a "Special Market" in the Context of the Legal Rule of Public Policy], in MAGOULAS, Georgios and SIMON, Jürgen (eds.), *Recht und Ökonomie beim Konsumentenschutz und Konsumentenkredit*, Baden-Baden,

Nomos, 1985, 293-308.

MAGOULAS, Georgios, 'Verbraucherschutz als Problem asymmetrischer Informationskosten' [Consumer Protection as a Problem of Asymmetric Information Costs], in OTT, Claus and SCHÄFER, Hans-Bernd (eds.), *Allokationseffizienz in der Rechtsordnung*, Berlin, Springer, 1989, 70-80.

MAGOULAS, Georgios and SIMON, Jürgen (eds.), *Recht und Ökonomie beim Konsumentenschutz und Konsumentenkredit. Interdisziplinäre Studien zu den Problemen und Konzepten des Verbraucherschutzes* [Law and Economics of Consumer Protection and Consumer Credit. Interdisciplinary Studies on the Problems and Concepts of Consumer Protection], Baden-Baden, Nomos, 1985, 436 p.

MOORE, A.P., 'Measuring the Economic Impact of Consumer Legislation', in CRANSTON, Ross and SCHICK, Anne (eds.), *Law and Economics*, Canberra, Australian National University, 1982, 163-174.

NADEL, M., 'Economic Power and Public Policy: The Case of Consumer Protection', **1** *Politics & Society*, 1971, 313 ff.

OSTER, Sharon M. and QUIGLEY, John M., 'Regulatory Barriers to the Diffusion of Innovation - Some Evidence from Building Codes', **8** *Bell Journal of Economics*, 1977, 361-377.

REICH, B.B., 'Toward a New Consumer Protection', **28** *University of Pennsylvania Law Review*, 1979, 1-40.

RICE, David A., 'Consumer Unfairness at the FTC: Misadventures in Law and Economics', **52** *George Washington Law Review*, 1983, 1-66.

RICHARDSON, William and MORRIS, David, 'Towards More Effective Consumer Market-Place Interventions - A Model for the Improvement of O.F.T. Codes of Practice', **11** *Journal of Consumer Policy*, 1988, 315-334.

SCHMALENSEE, Richard, 'Comments on Beales, Craswell, and Salop', **24** *Journal of Law and Economics*, 1981, 541-544.

SCHOPPE, Gunter, 'Consumer Protection by Law and Information: A View of Western German Practice and Experience', **139** *Zeitschrift fur die gesamte Staatswissenschaft*, 1983, 545-567.

SCHULENBURG, J.-Matthias Graf von der, 'Regulatory Measures to Enforce Quality Production of Self-Employed Professionals - a Theoretical Study of a Dynamic Market Process', in SCHULENBURG, J.-Matthias Graf von der and SKOGH, Göran (eds.), *Law and Economics and The Economics of Legal Regulation*, Dordrecht, Kluwer, 1986, 133-147.

SCHWARTZ, Alan, 'Justice and the Law of Contracts: A Case for the Traditional Approach', **9** *Harvard Journal of Law & Public Policy*, 1986, 107-116.

SCHWARTZ, Alan and WILDE, Louis L., 'Intervening in Markets on the Basis of Imperfect Information: A Legal and Economic Analysis?', **127** *University of Pennsylvania Law Review*, 1979, 630-682.

SHAPIRO, Carl, 'Consumer Protection Policy in the United States', **139** *Zeitschrift für die gesamte Staatswissenschaft*, 1983, 527-544.

SINN, Hans-Werner, 'Kommentar' [Comment] (on Magoulas, Verbraucherschutz als Problem asymmetrischer Informationskosten), in OTT, Claus and SCHÄFER, Hans-Bernd (eds.), *Allokationseffizienz in der Rechtsordnung*, Berlin, Springer,

1989, 81-90.

SKOGH, Göran, *En samhällsekonomisk mål-medel-analys av butikssnatterier* [An Economic Analysis of Shop-liftings], Statens offentliga utredning 'Snatteri', SOU 1971:10, suppl. 9.

SKOGH, Göran, 'Konsumentlagstiftningen i Rättsekonomisk Belysning' [The Consumer Legislation from a Law and Economics Perspective], in *Festskrift till Per Stiernquist*, Juridiska Föreningen i Lund, No. 24, 1978.

SKOGH, Göran, 'The Economics of Trade Laws', in *Conference on Legal Theory and Philosophy of Science*, Lund, Reidels, 1984.

SKOGH, Göran and SAMUELSSON, Per, *Konsumentpolitik* [Consumer Policy], Stiftelsen Marknadsekonomiskt Alternativ för Sverige, 1985.

SMITH, Peter and SWANN, Dennis, *Protecting the Consumer - An Economic and Legal Analysis*, Oxford, Martin Robertson, 1979, 286 p.

SOERIA-ATMADJA, S., 'Handlar konsumentombudsmannen alltid i konsumenternas intresse?' [Do the Consumers' Representatives Always Protect the Consumers' Interests?], *Ekonomisk Debatt*, 1982, No. 4.

STUART, Charles, 'Consumer Protection in a Market Where Sellers Have Better Information than Buyers', in SKOGH, Göran (ed.), *Law and Economics. Report from a Symposium in Lund, Sweden, 24-26 August 1977*, Lund, Juridiska Föreningen, 1978, 155-164.

TOMA, Eugenia Froedge, 'State Liquor Licensing, Implicit Contracting, and Dry/Wet Counties', **26** *Economic Inquiry*, 1988, 507-524.

VAN DEN BERGH, Roger, 'Economische analyse van het consumentenrecht' [Economic Analysis of Consumer Protection Law], **39** *Ars Aequi*, 1990, 787-793.

VINING, Aidan R. and WEIMER, David L., 'Information Asymmetry Favoring Sellers: A Policy Framework', **21** *Policy Sciences*, 1988, 281-303.

X, 'Note: Consumer Protection and Payment Systems: Policy for the Technological Era', **98** *Harvard Law Review*, 1985, 1870-1889.

5210 Product Safety and Health Regulation

ALEXANDER, Donald L., 'An Empirical Investigation of Lawn Mower Safety Regulation', **22** *Applied Economics*, 1990, 795-804.

ANDERSON, Gary M., 'Parasites, Profits, and Politicians: Public Health and Public Choice', **9** *Cato Journal*, 1990, 557-578.

ANDERSON, Richard K. and ENOMOTO, Carl E., 'Product Quality Regulation: A General Equilibrium Analysis', **20** *Canadian Journal of Economics*, 1987, 735-749.

ARNOULD, Richard J. and GRABOWSKI, Henry, 'Automobile Safety Regulation: A Review of the Evidence', **5** *Research in Law and Economics*, 1983, 233-267.

ASCH, Peter, 'Automobile Safety: Is Government Regulation Really Our Savior?', **3** *Yale Journal on Regulation*, 1986, 383-389.

ASCH, Peter, 'Food Safety Regulation: Is the Delaney Clause the Problem or Symptom?', **23(2)** *Policy Sciences*, 1990, 97-110.

ASHFORD, Nicholas A. and HEATON, George R., Jr., 'Regulation and Technological Innovation in the Chemical Industry', **46(3)** *Law and Contemporary Problems*, 1983, 109-157.

BACKHAUS, Jürgen G., 'Competition, Innovation and Regulation in the Pharmaceutical Industry', **4(2)** *Managerial and Decision Economics*, 1983, 107-121.

BEALES, J. Howard, III, 'The Economics of Regulating the Professions', in BLAIR, Roger D. and RUBIN, Stephen (eds.), *Regulating the Professions: A Public-Policy Symposium*, Lexington, Lexington Books, 1980.

BLAIR, Roger D. and KASERMAN, David L., 'Preservation of Quality and Sanctions within the Professions', in BLAIR, Roger D. and RUBIN, S. (eds.), *Regulating the Professions: A Public-Policy Symposium*, Lexington, Lexington Books, 1980.

BOCKSTAEL, Nancy E., 'Economic Efficiency Issues of Grading and Minimum Quality Standards', in KILMER, Richard L. and ARMBRUSTER, Walter J. (eds.), *Economic Efficiency in Agricultural and Food Marketing*, Ames, Iowa State University Press, 1987, 231-250.

CAMPBELL, Rita Ricardo, *Food Safety Regulations: A Study of the Use and Limitations of Cost-Benefit Analysis*, Washington, A.E.I.P.P.R., 1976.

CLAYBROOK, Joan and BOLLIER, David, 'The Hidden Benefits of Regulation: Disclosing the Auto Safety Payoff', **3** *Yale Journal on Regulation*, 1985, 87-131.

CRAIN, W. Mark, *Vehicle Safety Inspection Systems - How Effective?*, Washington D.C., A.E.I., 1980.

CRANDALL, Robert W., 'The Market for Housing Quality: Comments', in IPPOLITO, Pauline M. and SCHEFFMAN, David T. (eds.), *Empirical Approaches to Consumer Protection Economics*, Washington, Federal Trade Commission, 1986, 103-104.

CRANDALL, Robert W. et al., *Regulating the Automobile*, Washington, Brookings Institution, 1986, 202 p.

CRANDALL, Robert W. and GRAHAM, John D., 'Automobile Safety Regulation and Offsetting Behavior: Some New Empirical Estimates', **74** *American Economic Review. Papers and Proceedings*, 1984, 328-331.

CRANDALL, Robert W. and GRAHAM, John D., 'The Effect of Fuel Economy Standards on Automobile Safety', **32** *Journal of Law and Economics*, 1989, 97-118.

DICKENS, William T., 'Safety Regulation and "Irrational" Behavior', in GILAD, Benjamin and KAISH, Stanley (eds.), *Handbook of Behavioral Economics. Volume A. Behavioral Microeconomics*, Greenwich, JAI Press, 1986, 325-348.

DILLMAN, John Patrick, 'Prescription Drug Approval and Terminal Diseases: Desperate Times Require Desperate Measures', **44** *Vanderbilt Law Review*, 1991, 925-951.

DONOHUE, John J. III, 'Using Market Incentives to Promote Auto Occupant Safety', **7** *Yale Law & Policy Review*, 1989, 449-488.

DRANOVE, David, 'Medicaid Drug Formulary Restrictions', **32** *Journal of Law and Economics*, 1989, 143-162.

ECKERT, Ross D., 'AIDS and the Blood Bankers', **10(1)** *Regulation*, 1986, 15-24, 54.

EVANS, W.N. and GRAHAM, J.D., 'An Estimate of the Lifesaving Benefit of Child Restraint Use Legislation', **9** *Journal of Health Economics*, 1990, 121-142.

FUCHS, Victor R. and LEVESON, Irving, 'Motor Accident Mortality and Compulsory Inspection of Vehicles', in FUCHS, Victor R., *The Health Economy*, Cambridge, Harvard University Press, 1986, 169-180.

GARBACZ, C., 'Estimating Seat Belt Effectiveness with Seat Belt Usage Data from the Centers for Disease Control', **34** *Economic Letters*, 1990, 83-88.

GARBACZ, Christopher and KELLY, J. Gregory, 'Automobile Safety Inspection: New Econometric and Benefit/Cost Estimates', **19** *Applied Economics*, 1987, 763-771.

GIERINGER, Dale H., 'The Safety and Efficacy of New Drug Approval', **5** *Cato Journal*, 1985, 177-201.

GOLBE, Devra L., 'Product Safety in a Regulated Industry: Evidence from the Railroads', **21** *Economic Inquiry*, 1983, 39-52.

GRABOWSKI, Henry G., *Drug Regulation and Innovation: Empirical Evidence and Policy*, Washington, American Enterprise Institute, 1976, 82 p.

GRABOWSKI, Henry G., VERNON, John M. and THOMAS, Lacy Glenn, 'Estimating the Effects of Regulation on Innovation: An International Comparative Analysis of the Pharmaceutical Industry', **21** *Journal of Law and Economics*, 1978, 133-163.

GRAHAM, John D., 'Technology, Behavior, and Safety: An Empirical Study of Automobile Occupant Protection Regulation', **17** *Policy Sciences*, 1984, 141-151.

GRAHAM, John D. and GARBER, Steven, 'Evaluating the Effects of Automobile Safety Regulation', **3** *Journal of Policy Analysis and Management*, 1984, 206-224.

GRAHAM, John D. and LEE, Younghee, 'Behavioral Response to Safety Regulation: The Case of Motorcycle Helmet Wearing Legislation', **19** *Policy Sciences*, 1986, 253-273.

GREGORSKY, Frank, 'Oversteer: Twenty Years of Federal Auto Policy', **9(6)** *Regulation*, 1985, 35-41.

HARTLEY, K. and MAYNARD, A., *The Costs and Benefits of Regulating New Product Development in the UK Pharmaceutical Industry*, London, Office of Health Economics, 1982.

HARVEY, A.C. and DURBIN, J., 'The Effects of Seat Belt Legislation on British Road Casualties: A Case Study in Structural Time Series Modelling', **149** *Journal of Royal Statistical Society, Series A*, 1986, 187-210.

HEINRICHS, Dirk, 'Chemical Substances Regulation and the Propensity to Innovate in West Germany', in VAN DEN BERGH, Roger (ed.), *Verslagboek Eerste Werkvergadering recht en Economie*, Antwerpen, Handelshogeschool, 1986, 50-66.

HOFFER, George E., PRUITT, Stephen W. and REILLY, Robert J., 'The Impact of Product Recalls on the Wealth of Sellers: A Reexamination', **96** *Journal of Political Economy*, 1988, 663-670.

IPPOLITO, Richard A. and MASSON, Robert T., 'The Social Cost of Government Regulation of Milk', **21** *Journal of Law and Economics*, 1978, 33-65.

IRWIN, Alan, 'Technical Expertise and Risk Conflict: An Institutional Study of the British Compulsory Seat Belt Debate', **20** *Policy Sciences*, 1987, 339-364.

KEENAN, D. and RUBIN, P.H., 'Shadow Interest Groups and Safety Regulation', **8** *International Review of Law and Economics*, 1988, 21-36.

KESSEL, Reuben A., 'Economic Effects of Federal Regulation of Milk Markets', **10** *Journal of Law and Economics*, 1967, 51-78.

KLUGER, Brian D., 'Implications of Quality Standard Regulation for Multiproduct Monopoly Pricing', **10** *Managerial and Decision Economics*, 1989, 61-67.

KRAMER, Carol S., 'Food Safety: The Consumer Side of the Environmental Issue', **22** *Southern Journal of Agricultural Economics*, 1990, 33-40.

KRIER, James E., 'Risk and Design', **19** *Journal of Legal Studies*, 1990, 781-790.

KRUPNICK, Alan J., 'Reducing Bay Nutrients: An Economic Perspective', **47** *Maryland Law Review*, 1988, 452 ff.

KWEREL, Evan, 'Economic Welfare and the Production of Information by a Monopolist: The Case of Drug Testing', **11** *Bell Journal of Economics*, 1980, 505 ff.

LEWIT, Eugene M., COATE, Douglas and GROSSMAN, Michael, 'The Effects of Government Regulation on Teenage Smoking', **24** *Journal of Law and Economics*, 1981, 545-569.

LINNEMAN, Peter, 'The Effects of Consumer Safety Standards: The 1973 Mattress Flammability Standard', **23** *Journal of Law and Economics*, 1980, 461-479.

LOEB, Peter D., 'The Efficacy and Cost Effectiveness of Motor Vehicle Inspection Using Cross Sectional Data An Econometric Analysis', **52** *Southern Economic Journal*, 1985, 500-509.

LOEB, Peter D., 'The Determinants of Automobile Fatalities, with Special Consideration to Policy Variables', **21** *Journal of Transport Economics and Policy*, 1987, 279-287.

MARCUS, Alfred and BROMILEY, Philip, 'The Rationale for Regulation: Shareholder Losses under Various Assumptions about Managerial Cognition', **4** *Journal of Law, Economics, & Organization*, 1988, 357-372.

MARINO, Anthony M., 'Monopoly, Liability and Regulation', **54** *Southern Economic Journal*, 1988, 913-927.

MASHAN, Jerry L. and HARFST, David L., *The Struggle for Auto Safety*, Cambridge, Harvard University Press, 1990, 285 p.

MASHAW, Jerry L. and HARFST, David L., 'Regulation and Legal Culture: The Case of Motor Vehicle Safety', **4** *Yale Journal on Regulation*, 1987, 257-316.

MAYER, Robert N. and ZICK, Cathleen D., 'Mandating Behavioral or Technological Change: The Case of Auto Safety', **20** *Journal of Consumer Affairs*, 1986, 1-18.

McCARTHY, Patrick S., 'Consumer Demand for Vehicle Safety: An Empirical Study', **28** *Economic Inquiry*, 1990, 530-543.

McKAY, Niccie L., 'Industry Effects of Medical Device Regulation: The Case of Diagnostic Imaging Equipment', **6** *Journal of Policy Analysis and Management*, 1986, 35-44.

METZGER, Michael R., 'Cherries, Lemons, and the FTC: Minimum Quality Standards in the Retail Used Automobile Industry', **21** *Economic Inquiry*, 1983, 129-139.

METZGER, Michacl R., 'Corporate Criminal Liability for Defective Products: Policies, Problems, and Prospects', **73** *Georgetown Law Journal*, 1984, 1-88.

MITCHELL, Mark L. and MALONEY, Michael T., 'Crisis in the Cockpit? The Role of Market Forces in Promoting Air Travel Safety', **32** *Journal of Law and Economics*, 1989, 329-355.

MORRALL, John F. III, 'A Review of the Record', **10(2)** *Regulation*, 1986, 25-34.

NICHOLS, Albert L. and ZECKHAUSER, Richard J., 'The Perils of Prudence: How Conservative Risk Assessments Distort Regulation', **10(2)** *Regulation*, 1986, 13-24.

NICHOLS, John P., 'Economic Efficiency Issues of Grading and Minimum Quality Standards: A Discussion', in KILMER, Richard L. and ARMBRUSTER, Walter J. (eds.), *Economic Efficiency in Agricultural and Food Marketing*, Ames, Iowa State University Press, 1987, 251-55.

NOLL, Roger G. and KRIER, James E., 'Some Implications of Cognitive Psychology for Risk Regulation', **19** *Journal of Legal Studies*, 1990, 747-779.

NYMAN, John A., 'Improving the Quality of Nursing Homes: Regulation or Competition?', **6** *Journal of Policy Analysis and Management*, 1987, 247-251.

PELTZMAN, Sam, 'An Evaluation of Consumer Protection Legislation: The 1962 Drug Amendments', **81** *Journal of Political Economy*, 1973, 1049-1091.

PELTZMAN, Sam, *Regulation of Pharmaceutical Innovation: The 1962 Amendments*, Washington, A.E.I.P.P.R., 1974, 118 p.

PELTZMAN, Sam, 'The Effects of Automobile Safety Regulation', *Journal of Political Economy*, **83**, 677-725, 1978.

PELTZMAN, Sam, 'By Prescription Only ... Or Occasiobally', **11(3/4)** *Regulation*, 1987, 23-28.

PRATT, Michael D. and HOFFER, George E., 'The Efficacy of State Mandated Minimum Quality Certification: The Case of Used Vehicles', **24** *Economic Inquiry*, 1986, 313-318.

PRIEST, W. Curtiss, *Risks, Concerns, and Social Regulation: Forces that Led to Laws on Health, Safety, and the Environment*, Boulder, Westview Press, 1988, 204 p.

ROBERTSON, L.S., 'A Critical Analysis of Peltzman's "The Effects of Automobile Safety Regulation"', **11** *Journal of Economic Issues*, 1977, 587-600.

ROSE-ACKERMAN, Susan, 'Unintended Consequences: Regulating the Quality of Subsidized Day Care', **3** *Journal of Policy Analysis and Management*, 1983, 14-30.

RUBIN, Paul H., MURPHY, R. Dennis and JARRELL, Gregg, 'Risky Products,

Risky Stocks', **12(1)** *Regulation*, 1988, 35-39.

SAGOFF, Mark, *The Economy of the Earth: Philosophy, Law, and the Environment*, Cambridge, Cambridge University Press, 1988, 271 p.

SANDS, Paul E., 'How Effective is Safety Legislation ?', **11** *Journal of Law and Economics*, 1968, 165-179.

SEXTON, Thomas R. and ZILZ, Ulrike, 'On the Wisdom of Mandatory Drug Testing', **7** *Journal of Policy Analysis and Management*, 1988, 542-547.

SIMON, Marilyn J. and WOLF, Robert G. and PERLOFF, Jeffrey M., 'Product Safety, Liability Rules and Retailer Bankruptcy', **51** *Southern Economic Journal*, 1985, 1130-1141.

SIMONICH, William L., *Government Antismoking Policies*, New York, Peter Lang, 1991, 300 p.

STIGLER, George J., 'The Theory of Economic Regulation', **2** *Bell Journal of Economics*, 1971, 3-21.

TEMIN, Peter, 'The Origin of Compulsory Drug Prescriptions', **22** *Journal of Law and Economics*, 1979, 91-105.

THOMAS, Lacy Glenn, 'Revealed Bureaucratic Preference: Priorities of the Consumer Product Safety Commission', **19** *Rand Journal of Economics*, 1988, 102-113.

VANBUGGENHOUT, Willy, 'Comments on the paper of Dirk Heinrichs', in VAN DEN BERGH, Roger (ed.), *Verslagboek Eerste Werkvergadering recht en Economie*, Antwerpen, Handelshogeschool, 1986, 67-72.

VISCUSI, W. Kip, 'A Note on Lemons' Markets with Quality Certification', **9** *Bell Journal of Economics*, 1978, 277-279.

VISCUSI, W. Kip, *Regulating Consumer Product Safety*, Washington, American Enterprise Institute, 1984.

VISCUSI, W. Kip, 'The Lulling Effect: The Impact of Child Resistant Packaging on Aspirin and Analgesic Ingestions', **74** *American Economic Review. Papers and Proceedings*, 1984, 324-327.

VISCUSI, W. Kip, 'Regulatory Economics in the Courts: An Analysis of Judge Scalia's NHTSA Bumper Decision', **50(4)** *Law and Contemporary Problems*, 1987, 17-31.

VISCUSI, W. Kip, MAGAT, Wesley A. and HUBER, Joel, 'An Investigation of the Rationality of Consumer Valuations of Multiple Health Risks', **18** *Rand Journal of Economics*, 1987, 465-479.

WARDELL, William M. and SHECK, Lorraine E., 'Is Pharmaceutical Innovation Declining? Interpreting Measures of Pharmaceutical Innovation and Regulatory Impact in the USA, 1950-1980', in LINDGREN, Bjorn (ed.), *Pharmaceutical Economics: Papers Presented at the 6th Arne Ryde Symposium, Helsingborg, Sweden 1982*, Malmo, Liber, 1984, 177-189.

WEICHER, John C., 'The Market for Housing Quality', in IPPOLITO, Pauline M. and SCHEFFMAN, David T. (eds.), *Empirical Approaches to Consumer Protection Economics*, Washington, Federal Trade Commission, 1986, 39-65.

WEISS, Roger W., 'The Case for Federal Meat Inspection Examined', **7** *Journal of Law and Economics*, 1964, 107-120.

WHEELER, Malcolm E., 'The Use of Criminal Statutes to Regulate Product Safety',

13 *Journal of Legal Studies*, 1984, 593-618.

WIGGINGS, Steven N., 'The Effect of U.S. Pharmaceutical Regulation on New Introductions', in LINDGREN, Bjorn (ed.), *Pharmaceutical Economics: Papers Presented at the 6th Arne Ryde Symposium, Helsingborg, Sweden 1982*, Malmo, Liber, 1984, 191-205.

WINSTON, Clifford and MANNERING, Fred, 'Consumer Demand for Automobile Safety', **74** *American Economic Review*, 1984, 316-319.

ZECKHAUSER, Richard A., 'Measuring Risks and Benefits of Food Safety Decisions', **38** *Vanderbilt Law Review*, 1985, 539 ff.

ZLATOPER, Thomas J., 'Factors Affecting Motor Vehicle Deaths in the USA: Some Cross sectional Evidence', **19** *Applied Economics*, 1987, 753-761.

5220 Information Regulation. Regulation of Advertising

ASSMANN, Heinz-Dieter, 'Entwicklungstendenzen der Prospekthaftung' [Tendencies of Liability for Misleading Information Included in Prospectuses], *WM*, 1983, 138-144.

ASSMANN, Heinz-Dieter, *Prospekthaftung* [Liability for Misleading Information Included in Prospectuses], Köln, Heymann, 1985, 456 p.

AYANIAN, Robert, 'Advertising and Rate of Return', **18** *Journal of Law and Economics*, 1975, 479-506.

BEALES, Howard, CRASWELL, Richard and SALOP, Steven, 'Information Remedies for Consumer Protection', **71** *American Economic Review. Papers and Proceedings*, 1981, 410-413.

BEALES, Howard, CRASWELL, Richard and SALOP, Steven, 'The Efficient Regulation of Consumer Information', **24** *Journal of Law and Economics*, 1981, 491-539.

BEALES, J. Howard, III, 'Comments [The Effects of the Advertising Substantiation Program on Advertising Agencies] [An Economic Analysis of the FTC's Ad Substantiation Program]', in IPPOLITO, Pauline M. and SCHEFFMAN, David T. (eds.), *Empirical Approaches to Consumer Protection Economics*, Washington, Federal Trade Commission, 1986, 213-216.

BENHAM, Lee, 'The Effect of Advertising on the Price of Eyeglasses', **15** *Journal of Law and Economics*, 1972, 337-352.

BENHAM, Lee and BENHAM, Alexandra, 'Regulating Through the Professions: A Perspective on Information Control', **18** *Journal of Law and Economics*, 1975, 421-447.

BENHAM, Lee and BENHAM, Alexandra, 'Prospects for Increasing Competition in the Professions', in SLAYTON, P. and TREBILCOCK, Michael J., *The Professions and Public Policy*, Toronto, University of Toronto Faculty of Law, 1978.

CALFEE, John E., 'The Ghost of Cigarette Advertising Past', **10(2)** *Regulation*, 1986, 35-45.

CALVANI, Terry, LANGENFELD, James and SHUFORD, Gordon, 'Attorney Advertising and Competition at the Bar', **41** *Vanderbilt Law Review*, 1988, 761-788.

COASE, Ronald H., 'Advertising and Free Speech', **6** *Journal of Legal Studies*, 1977, 1-34.

COOTER, Robert D., 'Defective Warnings, Remote Causes, and Bankruptcy: Comment on Schwartz', **14** *Journal of Legal Studies*, 1985, 737-750.

COSTLEY, Carolyn L. and BRUCKS, Merrie, 'The Roles of Product Knowledge and Age on Children's Responses to Deceptive Advertising', in BLOOM, Paul N. (ed.), *Advances in Marketing and Public Policy*, Greenwich, JAI Press, 1987, 41-63.

CRASWELL, Richard, 'Interpreting Deceptive Advertising', **65** *Boston University Law Review*, 1985, 657-732.

DE TURCK, Mark A. and GOLDHABER, Gerald M., 'Effectiveness of Product Warning Labels: Effects of Consumers' Information Processing Objectives', **23** *Journal of Consumer Affairs*, 1989, 111-126.

DEMSETZ, Harold, 'More on Collusion and Advertising: A Reply', **19** *Journal of Law and Economics*, 1976, 205-209.

ELZINGA, K.G., 'The Compass of Competition for Professional Services', in BLAIR, Roger D. and RUBIN, Stephen, *Regulating the Professions: A Public-Policy Symposium*, Lexington, Lexington Books, 1980.

FERGUSON, James M., 'Daily Newspaper Advertising Rates, Local Media Cross-Ownership, Newspaper Chains, and Media Competition', **26** *Journal of Law and Economics*, 1983, 635-654.

FINSINGER, Jörg, 'Kommentar' [Comment] (on Lehmann, Die Zivilrechtliche Haftung für Werbeangaben bei der Vertragsanbahnung als Problem der Allokationseffizienz), in OTT, Claus and SCHÄFER, Hans-Bernd (eds.), *Allokationseffizienz in der Rechtsordnung*, Berlin, Springer, 1989, 185-187.

GOLDBERG, Victor P., 'Fishing and Selling', **15** *Journal of Legal Studies*, 1986, 173-180.

HAZARD, Geoffrey C., Jr., PEARCE, Russell G. and STEMPEL, Jeffrey W., 'Why Lawyers Should Be Allowed to Advertise: A Market Analysis of Legal Services', **58** *New York University Law Review*, 1983, 1084-1113.

HEALD, Paul, 'Money Damages and Corrective Advertising: An Economic Analysis', **55** *University of Chicago Law Review*, 1988, 629-658.

HIGGINS, Richard S. and McCHESNEY, Fred S., 'An Economic Analysis of the FTC's Ad Substantiation Program', in IPPOLITO, Pauline M. and SCHEFFMAN, David T. (eds.), *Empirical Approaches to Consumer Protection Economics*, Washington, Federal Trade Commission, 1986, 197-211.

HIGGINS, Richard S. and McCHESNEY, Fred S., 'Truth and Consequences: The Federal Trade Commission's Ad Substantiation Program', **6** *International Review of Law and Economics*, 1986, 151-168.

HILKE, John C., 'Early Mandatory Disclosure Regulations', **6** *International Review of Law and Economics*, 1986, 229-239.

HUDEC, Albert J. and TREBILCOCK, Michael J., 'Lawyer Advertising and the

Supply of Information in the Market for Legal Services', **20** *University of Western Ontario Law Review*, 1982, 53-99.

HURWITZ, Mark A. and CAVES, Richard E., 'Persuasion or Information? Promotion and the Shares of Brand Name and Generic Pharmaceuticals', **31** *Journal of Law and Economics*, 1988, 299-320.

JORDAN, Ellen R. and RUBIN, Paul H., 'An Economic Analysis of the Law of False Advertising', **8** *Journal of Legal Studies*, 1979, 527-553.

KASSARJIAN, Harold H. and KASSARJIAN, Waltraud M., 'The Impact of Regulation on Advertising: A Content Analysis', **11** *Journal of Consumer Policy*, 1988, 269-285.

KELLEY, Craig A. and GAIDIS, William C. and REINGEN, Peter H., 'The Use of Vivid Stimuli to Enhance Comprehension of the Content of Product Warning Messages', **23** *Journal of Consumer Affairs*, 1989, 243-266.

KOHL, Helmut, KÜBLER, Friedrich, WALZ, W. Rainer and WÜSTRICH, Wolfgang, 'Abschreibungsgesellschaften, Kapitalmarkteffizienz und Publizitätszwang - Plädoyer für ein Vermögensanlagegesetz' [Tax Shelter Companies, Efficiency of Capital Markets and Information Regulation? - A Pleade for a Law Regulating the Public Offer of Investment Opportunities], **138** *Zeitschrift für das gesamte Handels- und Wirtschaftsrecht*, 1974, 1-49.

KOTOWITZ, Y. and MATHEWSON, F., 'Advertising, Consumer Information, and Product Quality', **10** *Bell Journal of Economics*, 1979, 566-588.

LEFFLER, Keith B., 'Persuasion of Information? The Economics of Prescription Drug Advertising', **24** *Journal of Law and Economics*, 1981, 45-74.

LEHMANN, Michael, *Vertragsanbahnung durch Werbung* [Contract Preparing through Promotion], München, C. H. Beck, 1981.

LEHMANN, Michael, 'Die Zivilrechtliche Haftung für Werbeangaben bei der Vertragsanbahnung als Problem der Allokationseffizienz' [Civil Liability for Advertising as a Problem of Allocative Efficiency], in OTT, Claus and SCHÄFER, Hans-Bernd (eds.), *Allokationseffizienz in der Rechtsordnung*, Berlin, Springer, 1989, 169-184.

LYNDON, Mary L., 'Information Economics and Chemical Toxicity: Designing Laws to Produce and Use Data', **87** *Michigan Law Review*, 1989, 1795-1861.

MASSON, Alison and RUBIN, Paul H., 'Plugs for Drugs', **10(1)** *Regulation*, 1986, 37-43, 53.

MATHIOS, Alan and PLUMMER, Mark, 'The Regulation of Advertising by the Federal Trade Commission: Capital Market Effects', **12** *Research in Law and Economics*, 1989, 77-93.

MATTHEWS, Steven and POSTLEWAITE, Andrew, 'Quality Testing and Disclosure', **16** *Rand Journal of Economics*, 1985, 328-340.

MENSCH, Elizabeth and FREEMAN, Alan, 'Efficiency and Image: Advertising as an Antitrust Issue', *Duke Law Journal*, 1990, 321 ff.

MITCHELL, Mark L. and MULHERIN, J. Harold, 'Finessing the Political System: The Cigarette Advertising Ban', **54** *Southern Economic Journal*, 1988, 855-862.

MURIS, Timothy J. and McCHESNEY, Fred S., 'Advertising and the Price and Quality of Legal Services: The Case for Legal Clinics', **1** *American Bar*

Foundation Research Journal, 1979, 179-207.

NAGLE, Thomas T., 'Do Advertising-Profitability Studies Really Show That Advertising Creates a Barrier to Entry ?', **24** *Journal of Law and Economics*, 1981, 333-349.

O'REILLY, James T., 'The Risks of Assumptions: Impacts of Regulatory Label Warning upon Industrial Products Liability', **37** *Catholic University Law Review*, 1987, 85-117.

PELTZMAN, Sam, 'The Effects of FTC Advertising Regulation', **24** *Journal of Law and Economics*, 1981, 403-448.

PELTZMAN, Sam, 'The Health Effects of Mandatory Prescriptions', **30** *Journal of Law and Economics*, 1987, 207-238.

RIZZO, John A. and ZECKHAUSER, Richard J., 'Advertising and Entry: The Case of Physician Services', **98** *Journal of Political Economy*, 1990, 476-500.

SAUER, Raymond D. and LEFFLER, Keith B., 'Did the Federal Trade Commission's Advertising Substantiation Program Promote More Credible Advertising?', **80** *American Economic Review*, 1990, 191-203.

SAUNDERS, Robert S., 'Replacing Skepticism: An Economic Justification for Competitors' Actions for False Advertising Under Section 43(a) of the Lanham Act', **77** *Virginia Law Review*, 1991, 563-601.

SCHNEIDER, Lynne, KLEIN, Benjamin and MURPHY, Kevin M., 'Governmental Regulation of Cigarette Health Information', **24** *Journal of Law and Economics*, 1981, 575-612.

SHAPIRO, Carl, 'Advertising and Welfare: Comment', **11** *Bell Journal of Economics*, 1980, 749-752.

SINGDAHLSEN, Jeffrey P., 'Note: Risk of Chill: A Cost of the Standards Governing the Regulation of False Advertising Under Section 43(a) of the Lanham Act', **77** *Virginia Law Review*, 1991, 339-395.

SPILLER, Pablo T., 'Comments' [The Effects of the Advertising Substantiation Program on Advertising Agencies] [An Economic Analysis of the FTC's Ad Substantiation Program], in IPPOLITO, Pauline M. and SCHEFFMAN, David T. (eds.), *Empirical Approaches to Consumer Protection Economics*, Washington, Federal Trade Commission, 1986, 217-220.

THOMAS, Lacy Glenn, 'Advertising in Consumer Goods Industries: Durability, Economies of Scale, and Heterogeneity', **32** *Journal of Law and Economics*, 1989, 163-193.

URBAN, Raymond and MANCKE, Richard, 'Federal Regulation of Whiskey Labelling: From the Repeal of Prohibition to the Present', **15** *Journal of Law and Economics*, 1972, 411-426.

VISCUSI, W. Kip, MAGAT, Wesley A. and HUBER, Joel, 'Informational Regulation of Consumer Health Risks: An Empirical Evaluation of Hazard Warnings', **17** *Rand Journal of Economics*, 1986, 351-365.

WILKIE, W.L., 'The Impact of Professional Advertising on Consumers', in BLAIR, Roger D. and RUBIN, Stephen (eds.), *Regulating the Professions: A Public-Policy Symposium*, Lexington, Lexington Books, 1980.

WILLNER, Kenneth M., 'Failures to Warn and the Sophisticated User Defense', **74**

Virginia Law Review, 1988, 579-607.

5230 Trade Practices

BLAKENEY, Michael, 'Comment [on Williams]', in CRANSTON, Ross and SCHICK, Anne (eds.), *Law and Economics*, Canberra, Australian National University, 1982, 122-128.

DENNISON, S.R., 'The British Restrictive Trade Practices Act of 1956', **2** *Journal of Law and Economics*, 1959, 64-83.

HESSELBORN, Per-Ove, 'Comments on Stuyck's Paper', in SKOGH, Göran (ed.), *Law and Economics. Report from a Symposium in Lund, Sweden, 24-26 August 1977*, Lund, Juridiska Föreningen, 1978, 152-154.

KNUTSON, Ronald D., 'The Economic Consequences of the Minnesota Dairy Industry Unfair Trade Practices Act', **12** *Journal of Law and Economics*, 1969, 377-389.

LEHMANN, Michael, 'Die UWG-Novelle sollte nicht sterben. Zur wirschaftlichen Bedeutung der Bereitstellung von ökonomisch relevanten Sanktionen' [The UWG-Novelle Should Not Die. The Economic Importance of Relevant Civil Sanctions from an Economic Point of View], **36** *Der Betriebsberater*, 1981, 1717-1726.

LEHMANN, Michael, 'Die UWG-Neuregelungen 1987 - Erläuterungen und Kritik' [The New UWG Unfair Competition Rules - Explanations and Critique], **89** *Gewerblicher Rechtsschutz und Urheberrecht*, 1987, 199-214.

MAGOULAS, Georgios, 'Ökonomische Funktionen und Probleme der Haustürgeschäfte als Instrument direkter Vertriebsstrategien' [Economic Functions and Problems of Door-to-Door Selling as an Instrument of Direct Sales Strategies], in MAGOULAS, Georgios and SIMON, Jürgen (eds.), *Recht und Ökonomie beim Konsumentenschutz und Konsumentenkredit*, Baden-Baden, Nomos, 1985, 391-401.

MAGOULAS, Georgios and SCHWARTZE, Andreas, 'Das Gesetz über den Widerruf von Haustürgeschäften und ähnlichen Geschäften: Eine rechtliche und ökonomische Analyse' [The Law Regarding Revocation of Door-to-Door Dealings and Similar Transactions: A Legal and Economic Analysis], **18(5)** *Jüristische Arbeitsblätter*, 1986, 225-235.

MURRAY, Tracy and ROUSSLANG, Donald J., 'A Method for Estimating Injury Caused by Unfair Trade Practices', **9** *International Review of Law and Economics*, 1989, 149-164.

STUYCK, Jules, 'Six Years of Experience with some Aspects of the Belgian Trade Practices Act 1971 as an Instrument of Consumer Protection', in SKOGH, Göran (ed.), *Law and Economics. Report from a Symposium in Lund, Sweden, 24-26 August 1977*, Lund, Juridiska Föreningen, 1978, 133-151.

VAN DEN BERGH, Roger, 'Over de mededingingsbeperkende werking van de Wet Handelspraktijken of het verhaal van concurrenten die tegen de concurrentie beschermd willen worden' [On the Competition Limiting Effect of the Law on Trade Practices or the Story of Competitors Who Want to Be Protected Against Competition], **34** *Economisch en Sociaal Tijdschrift*, 1980, 421-446.

WARREN, Elizabeth, 'Trade Usage and Parties in the Trade: An Economic Rationale for an Inflexible Rule', **42** *University of Pittsburg Law Review*, 1981, 515 ff.

WILLIAMS, Philip L., 'The Problem of Proving 'Arrangement or Understanding' under Section 45 A of the Trade Practices Act', in CRANSTON, Ross and SCHICK, Anne (eds.), *Law and Economics*, Canberra, Australian National University, 1982, 112-121.

WILLIAMSON, Oliver E., 'Assessing Contract', **1** *Journal of Law, Economics & Organization*, 1985, 177-208.

5240 Licensing. Market Entry Regulation

ARROW, Kenneth J., 'Uncertainty and the Welfare Economics of Medical Care', **53** *American Economic Review*, 1963, 941-973.

BARRON, J.F., 'Restrictive Hiring Practices in Institutions of Higher Learning in California', **4** *Journal of Law and Economics*, 1961, 186-193.

BEALES, J. Howard, III, 'The Economics of Regulating the Professions', in BLAIR, Roger D. and RUBIN, Stephen (eds.), *Regulating the Professions: A Public-Policy Symposium*, Lexington, Lexington Books, 1980.

BENHAM, Lee, MAURIZI, Alex R. and REDER, M.W., 'Migration, Location and Remuneration of Medical Personnel: Physicians and Dentists', **50** *Review of Economics and Statistics*, 332-347.

CAIRNS, J., 'Overprovision and the Licensing (Scotland) Act 1976', **7** *International Review of Law and Economics*, 1987, 215-228.

CARROLL, Sidney L. and GASTON, Robert J., 'State Occupational Licensing Provisions and Quality of Service: The Real Estate Business', **1** *Research in Law and Economics*, 1979, 1-13.

CORGEL, John B., 'Occupational Boundary Setting and the Unauthorized Practice of Law by Real Estate Brokers', **10** *Research in Law and Economics*, 1987, 161-175.

DAVIS, Anthony and THIESSEN, Victor, 'Public Policy and Social Control in the Atlantic Fisheries', **14** *Canadian Public Policy*, 1988, 66-77.

DeVANY, Arthur S., GRAMM, Wendy L., SAVING, Thomas R. and SMITHSON, Charles W., 'The Impact of Input Regulation: The Case of the U.S. Dental Industry', **25** *Journal of Law and Economics*, 1982, 367-381.

DOLAN, A.K., 'Occupational Licensure and Obstruction of Change in the Health Care Delivery System: Some Recent Developments', in BLAIR, Roger D. and RUBIN, Stephen (eds.), *Regulating the Professions: A Public-Policy Symposium*, Lexington, Lexington Books, 1980.

DORSEY, S., 'The Occupational Licensure Queue', **15** *Journal of Human Resources*, 424-433.

EDWARDS, Linda N. and EDWARDS, Franklin R., 'Measuring the Effectiveness of Regulation: The Case of Bank Entry Regulation', **17** *Journal of Law and Economics*, 1974, 445-460.

EVANS, R.G., 'Does Canada Have Too Many Doctors? - Why Nobody Loves an Immigrant Physician', **11** *Canadian Public Policy*, 1976, 147-159.

EVANS, R.G., 'Universal Access: the Trojan Horse', in SLAYTON, P. and TREBILCOCK, Michael J., *The Professions and Public Policy*, Toronto, University of Toronto Faculty of Law, 1978.

FAITH, Roger L. and TOLLISON, Robert D., 'The Supply of Occupational Regulation', **21** *Economic Inquiry*, 1983, 232-240.

FEIN, Rashi, *The Doctor Shortage: An Economic Diagnosis*, Washington, The Brookings Institution, 1967, 199 p.

FELDSTEIN, P.J., *Health Associations and the Demand for Legislation: The Political Economy of Health*, Cambridge Mass., Ballinger Publishing, 1977.

FRECH, H. Edward III, 'Occupational Licensure and Health Care Productivity: The Issues and the Literature', in RAFFERTY, J. (ed.), *Health Manpower and Productivity*, Lexington, Lexington Books, 1974, chapter 6.

FRIEDMAN, Milton, *Capitalism and Freedom*, Chicago, University of Chicago Press, 1962, chapter 9.

FRIEDMAN, Milton and KUZNETS, S., *Income from Independent Professional Practice*, New York, National Bureau of Economic Research, 1945.

GAHVARI, Firouz, 'Licensing and Nontransferable Rents: Comment', **79** *American Economic Review*, 1989, 906-909.

GRADDY, Elizabeth and NICHOL, Michael B., 'Public Members on Occupational Licensing Boards: Effects on Legislative Regulatory Reforms', **55** *Southern Economic Journal*, 1989, 610-625.

HAAS-WILSON, Deborah, 'The Effect of Commercial Practice Restrictions: The Case of Optometry', **29** *Journal of Law and Economics*, 1986, 165-186.

HALL, Thomas D. and LINDSAY, Cotton M., 'Medical Schools: Producers of What? Sellers to Whom?', **23** *Journal of Law and Economics*, 1980, 55-80.

HOLEN, Arlene S., 'Effects of Professional Licensing Arrangements on Interstate Labor Mobility and Resource Allocation', **73** *Journal of Political Economy*, 1965, 492-498.

JULIN, J.R., 'The Legal Profession: Education and Entry', in BLAIR, Roger D. and RUBIN, Stephen (eds.), *Regulating the Professions: A Public-Policy Symposium*, Lexington, Lexington Books, 1980, ???-???

KESSEL, Reuben A., 'The A.M.A. and the Supply of Physicians', **35** *Law and Contemporary Problems*, 1970, 267-283.

KIRP, David L. and SOFFER, Eileen M., 'Taking Californians to the Cleaners', **9(5)** *Regulation*, 1985, 24-26.

LEFFLER, Keith B., 'Physician Licensure: Competition and Monopoly in American Medicine', **21** *Journal of Law and Economics*, 1978, 165-186.

LELAND, Hayne E., 'Quacks, Lemons, and Licensing: A Theory of Minimum Quality Standards', **87** *Journal of Political Economy*, 1979, 1325-1346.

LEUNIS, J. and DE VOS, G., 'De Wet betreffende de Handelsvestigingen: De Eerste 10 Jaar' [The Licensing Law: The First 10 Years], **31** *Tijdschrift voor Economie en Management*, 1986, 309-333.

LEVIN, Harvey J., 'Federal Control of Entry in the Broadcast Industry', **5** *Journal of Law and Economics*, 1962, 49-67.

LEWISCH, Peter, *Erwerbsfreiheit und Bedarfsprüfung* [The Freedom to Earn one's Living as Subjected to Regulations Concerning Needs], Vienna, Marktwirtschaftliche Schriften des Carl Menger Institutes, 1989, 47 p.

LEWISCH, Peter, 'The Political Economy of Barriers to Entry: The Example of the Amendment for Taxicab Regulation in Austria', in WEIGEL, Wolfgang (ed.), *Economic Analysis of Law - A Collection of Applications*, Vienna, Österreichischer Wirtschaftsverlag, 1991, 222-234.

LINDSAY, C.M., 'Real Returns to Medical Education', **8** *Journal of Human Resources*, 1973, 331-348.

LOTT, John R., Jr., 'Licensing and Nontransferable Rents', **77** *American Economic Review*, 1987, 453-455.

LOTT, John R., Jr., 'Licensing and Nontransferable Rents: Reply', **79** *American Economic Review*, 1989, 910-912.

MATHEWSON, G. Frank and WINTER, Ralph A., 'The Economic Effects of Automobile Dealer Regulation', **0(15** 16) *Annales d'Economie et de Statistique*, 1989, 409-426.

MAURIZI, Alex R., 'Occupational Licensing and the Public Interest', **82** *Journal of Political Economy*, 1974, 399-413.

MAURIZI, Alex R., MOORE, Ruth L. and SHEPARD, Lawrence, 'Competing for Professional Control: Professional Mix in the Eyeglasses Industry', **24** *Journal of Law and Economics*, 1981, 351-364.

MENNEMEYER, S.T., 'Really Great Returns to Medical Education?', **13** *Journal of Human Resources*, 1978, 75-90.

MOORE, Thomas G., 'The Purpose of Licensing', **4** *Journal of Law and Economics*, 1961, 93-117.

MUZONDO, Timothy R. and PAZDERKA, Bohumir, 'Income-Enhancing Effects of Professional Licensing', **28** *Antitrust Bulletin*, 1983, 397-415.

NOETHER, Monica, 'The Effect of Government Policy Changes on the Supply of Physicians: Expansion of a Competitive Fringe', **29** *Journal of Law and Economics*, 1986, 231-262.

PASHIGIAN, B. Peter, 'The Market for Lawyers: The Determinants of the Demand for and Supply of Lawyers', **20** *Journal of Law and Economics*, 1977, 53-85.

PASHIGIAN, B. Peter, 'Occupational Licensing and the Interstate Mobility of Professionals', **22** *Journal of Law and Economics*, 1979, 1-25.

PERLOFF, Jeffrey M., 'The Impact of Licensing Laws on Wage Changes in the Construction Industry', **23** *Journal of Law and Economics*, 1980, 409-428.

PFEFFER, J., 'Some Evidence on Occupational Licensing and Occupational Incomes', **53** *Social Forces*, 1974, 102-111.

PSACHAROPOULOS, G., *Earnings and Education in OECD Countries*, Paris, OECD, 1975, Chapter 5 ('Monopoly Elements in Earnings from Education').

ROTTENBERG, Simon, 'The Economics of Occupational Licensing', in X (no editor), *Aspects of Labour Economics*, New York, NBER, 1962.

ROTTENBERG, Simon (ed.), *Occupational Licensure Regulation*, Washington, American Entreprise Institute for Public Policy Research, 1980, 354 p.

RUBIN, Stephen, 'The Legal Web of Professional Regulation', in BLAIR, Roger D. and RUBIN, Stephen (eds.), *Regulating the Professions: A Public-Policy Symposium*, Lexington, Lexington Books, 1980.

SHAKED, Avner and SUTTON, John, 'Heterogeneous Consumers and Product Differentiation in a Market for Professional Services', **15** *European Economic Review*, 1981, 159-177.

SHAKED, Avner and SUTTON, John, 'The Self-Regulating Profession', **47** *Review of Economic Studies*, 1981, 217-234.

SHEPARD, Lawrence, 'Licensing Restrictions and the Cost of Dental Care', **21** *Journal of Law and Economics*, 1978, 187-201.

SLAYTON, Philip, 'Professional Education and the Consumer Interest: a Framework for Inquiry', in SLAYTON, Philip and TREBILCOCK, Michael J. (eds.), *The Professions and Public Policy*, Toronto, University of Toronto Faculty of Law, 1978.

SMITH, Janet Kiholm, 'Production of Licensing Legislation: An Economic Analysis of Interstate Differences', **11** *Journal of Legal Studies*, 1982, 117-137.

SMITH, Janet Kiholm, 'An Analysis of State Regulations Governing Liquor Store Licensees', **25** *Journal of Law and Economics*, 1982, 301-319.

STIGLER, George J., 'The Theory of Economic Regulation', **2** *Bell Journal of Economics*, 1971, 3-21.

SWAN, Peter, 'Is Law Reform Too Important to be Left to the Lawyers?: a Critique of Two Law Reform Commission Reports, *Human Tissue Transplants* and *Insurance Agents and Brokers*', in CRANSTON, Ross and SCHICK, Anne (eds.), *Law and Economics*, Canberra, Australian National University, 1982, 10-24.

TAMAN, L., 'The Emerging Legal Paraprofessionals', in SLAYTON, Philip and TREBILCOCK, Michael J. (eds.), *The Professions and Public Policy*, Toronto, University of Toronto Faculty of Law, 1978.

ULRICH, Alvin, FURTAN, William H. and SCHMITZ, Andrew, 'The Cost of a Licensing System Regulation: An Example from Canadian Prairie Agriculture', **95** *Journal of Political Economy*, 1987, 160-178.

VAN DEN BERGH, Roger, 'De economische reguleringstheorie en de Belgische vestigingswetgeving voor kleine en middelgrote handels- en ambachtsondernemingen' [The Economic Theory of Regulation and the Belgian Licensing Law for Small and Middle Size Companies], in VAN DEN BERGH, Roger (ed.), *Verslagboek Eerste Werkvergadering recht en Economie*, Antwerpen, Handelshogeschool, 1986, 38-49.

VAN DEN BERGH, Roger, 'Belgian Public Policy Towards the Retailing Trade', in GRAF VON DER SCHULENBURG, J.-Matthias and SKOGH, Göran (eds.), *Law and Economics and The Economics of Legal Regulation*, Dordrecht, Kluwer, 1986, 185-205.

WEINGAST, Barry R., 'Physicians, DNA Research Scientists, and the Market for Lemons', in BLAIR, Roger D. and RUBIN, Stephen (eds.), *Regulating the Professions: A Public-Policy Symposium*, Lexington, Lexington Books, 1980.

WHITE, William D., 'The Impact of Occupational Licensure of Clinical Laboratory Personnel', **13** *Journal of Human Resources*, 1978, 91-102.

WHITE, William D., 'Dynamic Elements of Regulation: The Case of Occupational Licensure', **1** *Research in Law and Economics*, 1979, 15-33.

WHITE, William D., 'The Introduction of Professional Regulation and Labor Market Conditions Occupational Licensure of Registered Nurses', **20** *Policy Sciences*, 1987, 27-51.

WRIGHT, D.T., 'The Objectives of Professional Education', in SLAYTON, Philip and TREBILCOCK, Michael J. (eds.), *The Professions and Public Policy*, Toronto, University of Toronto Faculty of Law, 1978.

X, 'Note: Restrictive Licensing of Dental Paraprofessionals', **83** *Yale Law Journal*, 1974, 806-826.

ZARDKOOHI, Asghar and PUSTAY, Michael W., 'Does Transferability Affect the Social Costs of Licensing?', **62** *Public Choice*, 1989, 187-190.

5250 Shop Opening Hours

CLEMENZ, Gerhard and INDERST, Alfred, *Ökonomische Analyse der Ladenöffnungszeiten* [Economic Analysis of Shop Opening Hours], Vienna, Manz Publishers, 1989, 128 p.

FERRIS, J. Stephen, 'Time, Space, and Shopping: The Regulation of Shopping Hours', **6** *Journal of Law, Economics, & Organization*, 1990, 171-187.

FINSINGER, Jörg and SCHULENBURG, J. Matthias Graf von der, 'Der Sonntagsverkauf' [The Effects of Sunday Trading], **109** *Zeitschrift fur Wirtschafts und Sozialwissenschaften*, 1989, 119-128.

JAFFER, Susan M. and KAY, John A., 'The Regulation of Shop Opening Hours in the United Kingdom', in GRAF VON DER SCHULENBURG, J.-Matthias and SKOGH, Göran (eds.), *Law and Economics and The Economics of Legal Regulation*, Dordrecht, Kluwer, 1986, 169-183.

KAY, J.A. and MORRIS, C.N., 'The Economic Efficiency of Sunday Trading Restrictions', **36** *Journal of Industrial Economics*, 1987, 113-129.

LABAND, David N. and HEINBUCH, Deborah Hendry, *Blue Laws: The History, Economics, and Politics of Sunday Closing Laws*, Lexington, Lexington Books, 1987, 232 p.

ROTTENBERG, Simon, 'Legislated Early Shop Closing in Britain', **4** *Journal of Law and Economics*, 1961, 118-130.

5300 PRODUCT LIABILITY
Gerrit De Geest

ABRAHAM, Kenneth S., 'Products Liability Law and Insurance Profitability', **19** *Journal of Legal Studies*, 1990, 837-844.

ADAMS, Michael, 'Produkthaftung - Wohltat oder Plage - Eine ökomische Analyse' [Product Liability - Benefit or Plague - An Economic Analysis], *Der Betriebsberater*, 1987, Beilage 20 zu Heft 31, 24 p.

ADAMS, Michael, 'Ökonomische Analyse der Produkthaftung' [Economic Analysis of Product Liability], *Der Betriebs- Berater*, 1987, Beilage 20, 11/87.

ADAMS, Michael, 'Ökonomische Begründung des AGB-Gesetzes - Verträge bei asymetrischer Information' [The Economic Basis of the German Unfair Contract Terms Act in Case of Asymmetric Information], in *Der Betriebs-Berater*, 1989, 781-788.

ARMSTRONG, Dwight L., 'Products Liability, Comparative Negligence and the Allocation of Damages among Multiple Defendants', **50** *Southern California Law Review*, 1976, 73-108.

ATTANASIO, John B., 'The Principle of Aggregate Autonomy and the Calabresian Approach to Products Liability', **74** *Virginia Law Review*, 1988, 677-750.

BELL, John W., 'Averting a Crisis in Product Liability : An Evolutionary Process of Socioeconomic Justice', **65** *Illinois Bar Journal*, 1977, 640-648.

BLIGHT, Catherine, '"What if that Snail had been in a Bottle of Milk?" or Product Liability in the UK - The Special Case of Agricultural Products', in FAURE, Michael and VAN DEN BERGH, Roger (eds.), *Essays in Law and Economics. Corporations, Accident Prevention and Compensation for Losses*, Antwerpen, Maklu, 1989, 215-232.

BONNEY, Paul R., 'Manufacturers' Strict Liability for Handgun Injuries: An Economic Analysis', **73** *Georgetown Law Journal*, 1985, 1437-1463.

BROWN, John Prather, 'Product Liability: The Case of an Asset with Random Life', **64** *American Economic Review*, 1974, 149-161.

BRÜGGEMEIER, Gert, 'Die Gefährdungshaftung der Produzenten nach der EG-Richtlinie - ein Fortschritt der Rechtsentwicklung?' [Strict Liability of Producers according to the EC-Directive - An Improvement in Legal Development?], in OTT, Claus and SCHÄFER, Hans-Bernd (eds.), *Allokationseffizienz in der Rechtsordnung*, Berlin, Springer, 1989, 228-247.

BUCHANAN, James M., 'In Defense of Caveat Emptor', **38** *University of Chicago Law Review*, 1970, 64-73.

BUTTERS, Gerard R., 'The Impact of Product Recalls on the Wealth of Sellers: Comments', in IPPOLITO, Pauline M. and SCHEFFMAN, David T. (eds.), *Empirical Approaches to Consumer Protection Economics*, Washington, Federal Trade Commission, 1986, 411-413.

CALABRESI, Guido, 'First Party, Third Party, and Product Liability Systems: Can Economic Analysis of Law Tell Us Anything About Them?', **69** *Iowa Law Review*, 1984, 833 ff.

CALABRESI, Guido and BASS, Kenneth C. III, 'Right Approach, Wrong

Implications: A Critique of McKean on Products Liability', **38** *University of Chicago Law Review*, 1970, 74-91.

CASS, Ronald A. and GILLETTE, Clayton P., 'The Government Contractor Defense: Contractual Allocation of Public Risk', **77** *Virginia Law Review*, 1991, 257-336.

COOTER, Robert D., 'Defective Warnings, Remote Causes, and Bankruptcy: Comment on Schwartz', **14** *Journal of Legal Studies*, 1985, 737-750.

COSENTINO, Fabrizio, 'Responsabilità da prodotto difettoso: appunti di analisi economica del diritto (nota a U.S. Supreme Court California, 31 marzo 1988, Brown c. Abbott Laboratories)' [Liability for Defective Products: An Economic Analysis of Law], *Foro Italiano*, 1989, IV, 137-143.

COUSY, Herman, 'Produktenaansprakelijkheid. Proeve van een juridisch-economische analyse' [Product Liability. Attempt of a Legal-Economic Analysis], *Tijdschrift voor Privaatrecht*, 1976, 995-1035.

DANZON, Patricia M., 'The Political Economy of Workers' Compensation: Lessons for Product Liability', **78** *American Economic Review. Papers and Proceedings*, 1988, 305-310.

DE ALESSI, Louis and STAAF, Robert J., 'Liability, Control and the Organization of Economic Activity', **7** *International Review of Law and Economics*, 1987, 5-20.

DORFMAN, Robert, 'The Economics of Product Liability: A Reaction to McKean', **38** *University of Chicago Law Review*, 1970, 92-102.

EISMAN, Deborah E., 'Product Liability: Who Should Bear the Burden?', **27** *American Economist*, 1983, 54-57.

EPPLE, Dennis and RAVIV, Artur, 'Product Safety: Liability Rules, Market Structure, and Imperfect Information', **68** *American Economic Review*, 1978, 80-95.

EPSTEIN, Richard, *Modern Product Liability Law*, Westport, Quorum Books, 1980, 211 p.

EPSTEIN, Richard A., 'Products Liability as an Insurance Market', **14** *Journal of Legal Studies*, 1985, 645-669.

EPSTEIN, Richard A., 'The Temporal Dimension in Tort Law', **53** *University of Chicago Law Review*, 1986, 1175-1218.

EPSTEIN, Richard A., 'The Political Economy of Product Liability Reform', **78** *American Economic Review. Papers and Proceedings*, 1988, 311-315.

EPSTEIN, Richard A., 'The Unintended Revolution in Product Liability Law', **10** *Cardozo Law Review*, 1989, 2193-2222.

FAURE, Michael, 'Commentaar bij de paper van Dr.Jan C. Bongaerts: Coase en Produktenaansprakelijkheid' [Comment on the paper of Dr. Jan C. Bongaerts: Coase and Product Liability], in VAN DEN BERGH, Roger (ed.), *Verslagboek Eerste Werkvergadering recht en Economie*, Antwerpen, Handelshogeschool, 1986, 31-37.

FAURE, Michael and VAN BUGGENHOUT, Willy, 'Produktenaansprakelijkheid. De Europese richtlijn: harmonisatie en consumentenbescherming? (tweede deel en slot)' [The European Directive Concerning Product Liability, Harmonization and

Consumer Protection?], **51** *Rechtskundig Weekblad*, 1987-88, 33-49.

FINSINGER, Jörg and SIMON, Jürgen, *Eine ökonomische Bewertung der EG-Produkthaftungsrichtlinie und des Produkthaftungsgesetzes* [An Economic Appreciation of the EC-Product Liability Directive and the Product Liability Laws], Arbeitsbericht Hochschule Lüneburg, Fachbereich Wirtschafts- und Sozialwissenschaften, 1988, 44 p.

FINSINGER, Jörg and SIMON, Jürgen, 'An Economic Assessment of the EC Product Liability Directive and the Product Liability Law of the Federal Republic of Germany', in FAURE, Michael and VAN DEN BERGH, Roger (eds.), *Essays in Law and Economics. Corporations, Accident Prevention and Compensation for Losses*, Antwerpen, Maklu, 1989, 185-214.

GALITSKY S., 'Manufacturers' Liability: An Examination of the Policy and Social Cost of a New Regime', **3** *University of New South Wales Law Journal*, 1979, 145-174.

GILMORE, Grant, 'Products Liability: A Commentary', **38** *University of Chicago Law Review*, 1970, 103-116.

GOLDBERG, Victor P., 'The Economics of Product Safety and Imperfect Information', **5** *Bell Journal of Economics*, 1974, 683-688.

GOLDBERG, Victor P., 'Accountable Accountants: Is Third-Party Liability Necessary ?', **17** *Journal of Legal Studies*, 1988, 295-312.

GRAHAM, Daniel A. and PRICE, Ellen R., 'Contingent Damages for Products Liability', **13** *Journal of Legal Studies*, 1984, 441-468.

HAMADA, Koichi, 'Liability Rules and Income Distribution in Products Liability', **66** *American Economic Review*, 1976, 228-234.

HAMADA, Koichi, ISHIDA, Hidetoh and MURAKAMI, Masahiro, 'The Evolution and Economic Consequences of Product Liability Rules in Japan', in SAXONHOUSE, Gary R. and YAMAMURA, Kozo (eds.), *Law and Trade Issues of the Japanese Economy: American and Japanese Perspectives*, Seattle, University of Washington Press, 1986, 83-106.

HAMMITT, James K., CARROLL, Stephen J. and RELLES, Daniel A., 'Tort Standards and Jury Decisions', **14** *Journal of Legal Studies*, 1985, 751-762.

HEINKEL, R., 'Uncertain Product Quality: the Market for Lemons with an Imperfect E Testing Technology', **12** *Bell Journal of Economics*, 1981, 625-636.

HIGGINS, Richard S., 'Producers' Liability and Product Related Accidents', **7** *Journal of Legal Studies*, 1978, 299-321.

HIGGINS, Richard S., 'Products Liability Insurance, Moral Hazard, and Contributory Negligence', **10** *Journal of Legal Studies*, 1981, 111-130.

HOFFER, George E., PRUITT, Stephen W. and REILLY, Robert J., 'The Impact of Product Recalls on the Wealth of Sellers: A Reexamination', **96** *Journal of Political Economy*, 1988, 663-670.

JARRELL, Greg A. and PELTZMAN, Sam, 'The Impact of Product Recalls on the Wealth of Sellers', in IPPOLITO, Pauline M. and SCHEFFMAN, David T. (eds.), *Empirical Approaches to Consumer Protection Economics*, Washington, Federal Trade Commission, 1986, 377-409.

JARRELL, Gregg and PELTZMAN, Sam, 'The Impact of Product Recalls on the

Wealth of Sellers', **93** *Journal of Political Economy*, 1985, 512-536.

KAMBHU, John, 'Optimal Product Quality under Asymmetric Information and Moral Hazard. **13** *Bell Journal of Economics*, 1982, 483-492.

KAPRELIAN, Mark A., 'Privity Revisited: Tort Recovery by a Commercial Buyer for a Defective Product's Self-Inflicted Damage', **84** *Michigan Law Review*, 1985, 517-540.

KEENAN, D. and RUBIN, P.H., 'Shadow Interest Groups and Safety Regulation', **8** *International Review of Law and Economics*, 1988, 21-36.

KIRCHNER, Christian, 'Kommentar' [Comment] (On Brüggemeier, Die Gefährdungshaftung der Produzenten nach der EG-Richtlinie), in OTT, Claus and SCHÄFER, Hans-Bernd (eds.), *Allokationseffizienz in der Rechtsordnung*, Berlin, Springer, 1989, 248-253.

LACEY, N.J., 'Recent Evidence on the Liability Crisis', **55** *Journal of Risk and Insurance*, 1988, 499-508.

LAMKEN, Jeffrey A., 'Note: Efficient Accident Prevention as a Continuing Obligation: The Duty to Recall Defective Products', **42** *Stanford Law Review*, 1989, 103 ff.

LANDES, William M. and POSNER, Richard A., 'A Positive Economic Analysis of Products Liability', **14** *Journal of Legal Studies*, 1985, 535-567.

LANDES, William M. and POSNER, Richard A., 'New Light on Punitive Damages', **10(1)** *Regulation*, 1986, 33-36, 54.

LARSEN, Kim D., 'Note: Strict Products Liability and the Risk-Utility Test for Design Defect: An Economic Analysis', **84** *Columbia Law Review*, 1984, 2045-2067.

LAWRENCE, William H. and MINON, John H., 'The Effect of Abrogating the Holder-in-Due-Course Doctrine on the Commercialization of Innovative Consumer Products', **64** *Boston University Law Review*, 1984, 325-374.

LETSOU, Peter V., 'A Time-Dependent Model of Products Liability', **53** *University of Chicago Law Review*, 1986, 209-231.

LITAN, Robert E., 'The Safety and Innovation Effects of U.S. Liability Law: The Evidence', **81** *American Economic Review. Papers and Proceedings*, 1991, 59-64.

MANNE, Henry G., 'Edited Transcript of AALS-AEA Conference on Products Liability', **38** *University of Chicago Law Review*, 1970, 117-141.

MANTELL, Edmund H., 'Allocative and Distributive Efficiency of Products Liability Law in a Monopolistic Market', **7** *Journal of Products Liability*, 1984, 143-152.

MARINO, Anthony M., 'Products Liability and Scale Effects in a Long-Run Competitive Equilibrium', **8** *International Review of Law and Economics*, 1988, 97-107.

MARINO, Anthony M., 'Monopoly, Liability and Regulation', **54** *Southern Economic Journal*, 1988, 913-927.

McKEAN, Roland N., 'Products Liability: Trends and Implications', **38** *University of Chicago Law Review*, 1970, 3-63.

McKEAN, Roland N., 'Products Liability: Implications of Some Changing Property Rights', **84** *Quarterly Journal of Economics*, 1970, 611-626.

NAKAO, Takeo, 'Product Quality and Market Structure', **13** *Bell Journal of Economics*, 1982, 133-142.

NEELY, Richard, *The Product Liability Mess: How Business Can Be Rescued From the Politics of State Courts*, New York, Free Press/Macmillan, 1988, 181 p.

O'REILLY, James T., 'The Risks of Assumptions: Impacts of Regulatory Label Warning upon Industrial Products Liability', **37** *Catholic University Law Review*, 1987, 85-117.

OI, Walter Y., 'The Economics of Product Safety', **4** *Bell Journal of Economics*, 1973, 3-28.

OI, Walter Y., 'The Economics of Product Safety: a Rejoinder', **5** *Bell Journal of Economics*, 1974.

ORDOVER, Janusz A., 'Products Liability in Markets with Heterogeneous Consumers', **8** *Journal of Legal Studies*, 1979, 505-525.

ORDOVER, Janusz A. and WEISS, Andrew, 'Information and the Law: Evaluating Legal Restrictions on Competitive Contracts', **71** *American Economic Review. Papers and Proceedings*, 1981, 399-404.

OWEN, David G., 'The Intellectual Development of Modern Products Liability Law: A Comment on Priest's View of the Cathedral's Foundations', **14** *Journal of Legal Studies*, 1985, 529-533.

POLINSKY, A. Mitchell and ROGERSON, William P., 'Products Liability, Consumer Misperceptions, and Market Power', **14** *Bell Journal of Economics*, 1983, 581-589.

PRIEST, George L., 'The Best Evidence of the Effect of Products Liability Law on the Accident Rate: Reply', **91** *Yale Law Journal*, 1982, 1386-1401.

PRIEST, George L., 'The Invention of Enterprise Liability: A Critical History of the Intellectual Foundations of Modern Tort Law', **14** *Journal of Legal Studies*, 1985, 461-527.

PRIEST, George L., 'Strict Products Liability: The Original Intent', **10** *Cardozo Law Review*, 1989, 2301-2327.

PRIEST, George L., 'The Modern Expansion of Tort Liability: Its Sources, Its Effects, and Its Reform', **5(3)** *Journal of Economic Perspectives*, 1991, 31-50.

REA, Samuel A., Jr., 'Contingent Damages, Negligence, and Absolute Liability: A Comment on Graham and Peirce', **13** *Journal of Legal Studies*, 1984, 469-474.

ROGERSON, Carol and TREBILCOCK, Michael J., 'Products Liability and the Allergic Consumer: A Study in the Problems of Framing an Efficient Liability Regime', **36** *University of Toronto Law Journal*, 1986, 52-103.

ROGERSON, William P., 'Reputation and Product Quality', **14** *Bell Journal of Economics*, 1983, 508-516.

SAGE, William M., 'Drug Product Liability and Health Care Delivery Systems', **40** *Stanford Law Review*, 1988, 989-1026.

SCHWARTZ, Alan, 'Products Liability, Corporate Structure, and Bankruptcy: Toxic Substances and the Remote Risk Relationship', **14** *Journal of Legal Studies*, 1985, 689-736.

SCHWARTZ, Alan, 'Proposals for Products Liability Reform: A Theoretical Synthesis', **97** *Yale Law Journal*, 1988, 353-419.

SCHWARTZ, Gary T., 'Foreword: Understanding Products Liability', **67** *California Law Review*, 1979, 435-496.

SCHWARTZ, Gary T., 'New Products, Old Products, Evolving Law, Retroactive Law', **58** *New York University Law Review*, 1983, 796-852.

SCHWARTZ, Gary T., 'Directions in Contemporary Products Liability Scholarship', **14** *Journal of Legal Studies*, 1985, 763-777.

SCHWARTZ, Gary T., 'Economic Loss in American Tort Law: The Examples of J Aire and of Products Liability', **23** *San Diego Law Review*, 1986, 37-78.

SCHWARTZ, Victor, 'The Post-Sale Duty to Warn: Two Unfortunate Forks in the Road to a Reasonable Doctrine', **58** *New York University Law Review*, 1983, 892-905.

SHAPIRO, Carl, 'Consumer Information, Product Quality, and Seller Reputation', **13** *Bell Journal of Economics*, 1982, 20-35.

SHAVELL, Steven, *Economic Analysis of Accident Law*, Cambridge, Harvard University Press, 1987, 51-72.

SIMON, Marilyn J., 'Imperfect Information, Costly Litigation, and Product Quality', **12** *Bell Journal of Economics*, 1981, 171-184.

SIMON, Marilyn J. and WOLF, Robert G. and PERLOFF, Jeffrey M., 'Product Safety, Liability Rules and Retailer Bankruptcy', **51** *Southern Economic Journal*, 1985, 1130-1141.

SMITHSON, Charles W. and THOMAS, Christopher R., 'Measuring the Cost to Consumers of Product Defects: The Value of "Lemon Insurance"', **31** *Journal of Law and Economics*, 1988, 485-502.

SPENCE, A. Michael, 'Consumer Misperception, Product Failure and Product Liability', **44** *Review of Economic Studies*, 1978, 561-572.

SYMPOSIUM : 'Products Liability: Economic Analysis and the Law', **38** *University of Chicago Law Review*, 1970, 1-141.

TREBILCOCK, Michael J., 'Comment on Viscusi, "The Performance of Liability Insurance in States with Different Products-Liability Statutes"', **19** *Journal of Legal Studies*, 1990, 845-849.

TWERSKI, Aaron D., 'The Role of the Judge in Tort Law: From Risk-Utility to Consumer Expectations: Enhancing the Role of Judicial Screening in Product Liability Litigation', **11** *Hofstra Law Review*, 1983, 861 ff.

VISCUSI, W. Kip, *Regulating Consumer Product Safety*, Washington, American Enterprise Institute, 1984.

VISCUSI, W. Kip, 'Consumer Behavior and the Safety Effects of Product Safety Regulation', **28** *Journal of Law and Economics*, 1985, 527-553.

VISCUSI, W. Kip, 'The Determinants of the Disposition of Product Liability Claims and Compensation for Bodily Injury', **15** *Journal of Legal Studies*, 1986, 321-346.

VISCUSI, W. Kip, 'Product Liability Litigation with Risk Aversion', **17** *Journal of Legal Studies*, 1988, 101-121.

VISCUSI, W. Kip, 'Pain and Suffering in Product Liability Cases: Systematic Compensation or Capricious Awards?', **8** *International Review of Law and Economics*, 1988, 203-220.

VISCUSI, W. Kip, 'Product Liability and Regulation: Establishing the Appropriate Institutional Division of Labor', **78** *American Economic Review. Papers and Proceedings*, 1988, 300-304.

VISCUSI, W. Kip, 'The Interaction between Product Liability and Workers' Compensation as Ex Post Remedies for Workplace Injuries', **5** *Journal of Law, Economics, & Organization*, 1989, 185-210.

VISCUSI, W. Kip, 'The Performance of Liability Insurance in States with Different Products-Liability Statutes', **19** *Journal of Legal Studies*, 1990, 809-836.

VISCUSI, W. Kip, 'Product and Occupational Liability', **5(3)** *Journal of Economic Perspectives*, 1991, 71-91.

VISCUSI, W. Kip, 'The Dimensions of the Product Liability Crisis', **20** *Journal of Legal Studies*, 1991, 147-177.

WADE, John W., 'On the Effect in Product Liability of Knowledge Unavailable Prior to Marketing', **58** *New York University Law Review*, 1983, 734-764.

WARD, John O., 'Origins of the Tort Reform Movement', **6(3)** *Contemporary Policy Issues*, 1988, 97-107.

WEBER, Nathan, *Product Liability: The Corporate Response*, New York, Conference Board, 1987.

WEICHER, John C., 'Product Quality and Value in the New Home Market: Implications for Consumer Protection Regulation', **24** *Journal of Law and Economics*, 1981, 365-397.

WEINRIB, Ernest J., 'The Insurance Justification and Private Law', **14** *Journal of Legal Studies*, 1985, 681-687.

WHEELER, Malcolm E., 'The Use of Criminal Statutes to Regulate Product Safety', **13** *Journal of Legal Studies*, 1984, 593-618.

WINTER, Ralph A., 'The Liability Insurance Market', **5(3)** *Journal of Economic Perspectives*, 1991, 115-136.

X (P.M.K. and W.J.S.), 'Note: Enforcing Waivers in Products Liability', **69** *Virginia Law Review*, 1983, 1111-1152.

X, 'Note: Designer Genes That Don't Fit: A Tort Regime for Commercial Releases of Genetic Engineering Products', **100** *Harvard Law Review*, 1987, 1086-1105.

5400 LABOR LAW & EMPLOYMENT REGULATION
Gerrit De Geest

5400 Labor Law & Employment Regulation: General

ALLEN, Steven G., 'Much Ado about Davis-Bacon: A Critical Review and New Evidence', **26** *Journal of Law and Economics*, 1983, 707-736.

BEHRENS, Peter, 'Die Bedeutung der ökonomischen Analyse des Rechts für das Arbeitsrecht' [The Importance of Economic Analysis of Law for Labour Law], **20** *Zeitschrift für Arbeitsrecht*, 1989, 209-238.

BIERMAN, Leonard, 'Judge Posner and the NLRB: Implications for Labor Law Reform', **69** *Minnesota Law Review*, 1985, 881 ff.

BOORMAN, S.A., 'A Combinatorial Optimization Model for Transmission of Job Information through Contact Networks', **6** *Bell Journal of Economics*, 1975, 216-249.

BRUCE, Christopher J., 'The Adjudication of Labor Disputes as a Private Good', **8** *International Review of Law and Economics*, 1988, 3-19.

BRYN, Brenda Greenberg, 'Case Comment: Refusals to Cross Stranger Picket Lines and the Wealth Maximization Principle: An Economic Analysis of the Views of the NLRB and Judge Posner', **41** *University of Miami Law Review*, 1987, 533 ff.

BURKHAUSER, Richard V., 'Morality and the Cheap: The Americans with Disability Act', **13(2)** *Regulation*, 1990, 47-56.

CULYER, A.J., *The Economics of Social Policy*, London, Martin Robertson, 1973, 268 p.

DANZON, Patricia M., 'The Political Economy of Workers' Compensation: Lessons for Product Liability', **78** *American Economic Review. Papers and Proceedings*, 1988, 305-310.

DUNG, Tran Huu and PREMUS, Robert, 'Do Socioeconomic Regulations Discriminate against Small Firms?', **56** *Southern Economic Journal*, 1990, 686-697.

EHRENBERG, Ronald G. and SCHUMANN, Paul L., 'Compliance with the Overtime Pay Provisions of the Fair Labor Standards Act', **25** *Journal of Law and Economics*, 1982, 159-181.

EPSTEIN, Richard A., 'Common Law, Labor Law, and Reality: A Rejoinder to Professors Getman and Kohler', **92** *Yale Law Journal*, 1983, 1435-1441.

EPSTEIN, Richard A., 'Toward a Revitalization of the Contract Clause', **51** *University of Chicago Law Review*, 1984, 703-751.

EPSTEIN, Richard A., 'In Defense of the Contract at Will', **51** *University of Chicago Law Review*, 1984, 947-982.

EPSTEIN, Richard A. and PAUL, Jeffrey, 'Introduction', **51** *University of Chicago Law Review*, 1984, 945-946.

ERVEN, Bernard L., 'Impact of Labor Laws and Regulations on Agricultural Labor Markets', in EMERSON, Robert D. (ed.), *Seasonal Agricultural Labor Markets in the United States*, Ames, Iowa State University Press, 1984, 376-405.

FEINSTEIN, Jonathan S., 'Detection Controlled Estimation', **33** *Journal of Law & Economics*, 1990, 233-276.

FENN, Paul and WHELAN, Christopher J., 'Remedies for Dismissed Employees in the U.K.: An Economic Analysis', **2** *International Review of Law and Economics*, 1982, 205-225.

FISCHEL, Daniel R., 'Labor Markets and Labor Law Compared with Capital Markets and Corporate Law', **51** *University of Chicago Law Review*, 1984, 1061-1077.

FISCHEL, Daniel R. and LAZEAR, Edward P., 'Comparable Worth and Discrimination in Labor Markets', **53** *University of Chicago Law Review*, 1986, 891-918.

FLANAGAN, Robert J., *Labor Relations and the Litigation Explosion*, Washington D.C., Brookings Institution, 1987, 122 p.

FOX, Alan, *Beyond Contract: Work, Power and Trust Relations*, London, Faber & Faber, 1974, 408 p.

FRANK, Robert H., 'Interdependent Preferences and the Competitive Wage Structure', **15** *Rand Journal of Economics*, 1984, 510-520.

FREEMAN, Andrew D., 'Note: A Critique of Economic Consistency', **39** *Stanford Law Review*, 1987, 1259-1270.

GENSER, Bernd (ed.), *Abfertigungsregeln im Spannungsfeld der Wirtschaftspolitik* [Rules of Indemnification as a Current Problem in Economic Policy], Vienna, Manz Publishers, 1987, 272 p.

GETMAN, Julius G. and KOHLER, Thomas C., 'The Common Law, Labor Law, and Reality: A Response to Professor Epstein', **92** *Yale Law Journal*, 1983, 1415-1434.

GIER, H.G. de, 'Heeft het arbeidsrecht een toekomst? Een verhandeling over de invloed van de economie op het arbeidsrecht' [Has Labour Law a Future? An Essay on the Influence of Economics on Labour Law], in COLJEE, P.D., FRANKEN, H., HEERTJE, A. and KANNING, W. (eds.), *Law and Welfare Economics*, Symposium 24 October, VU Amsterdam, 101-113.

GOLDFARB, Robert S. and HEYWOOD, John S., 'An Economic Evaluation of the Service Contract Act', **36** *Industrial and Labor Relations Review*, 1982, 56-72.

GOLDIN, Claudia, 'Maximum Hours Legislation and Female Employment: A Reassessment', **96** *Journal of Political Economy*, 1988, 189-205.

GOODWIN, William B. and CARLSON, John A., 'Job Advertising and Wage Control Spillovers', **16** *Journal of Human Resources*, 1981, 80-93.

GROENEWEGEN, J., 'Transactiekosten' [Transactions Costs], *Tijdschrift voor politieke economie*, 1990, 50-76.

HANSON, Charles G., 'Economic Significance of British Labor Law Reform', **6** *Cato Journal*, 1987, 851-868.

HARRISON, Jeffrey L., 'The "New" Terminable-at-Will Employment Contract: An Interest and Cost-Incidence Analysis', **69** *Iowa Law Review*, 1984, 327-363.

HART, P.E. (ed.), *Unemployment and Labour Markets Policies*, Aldershot, Gower, 1986, 198 p.

HENDRICKS, Walter, 'Regulation and Labor Earnings', **8** *Bell Journal of Economics*, 1977, 483-496.

HILL, Andrew D., *"Wrongful Discharge" and the Derogation of the At Will Employment Doctrine*, Philadelphia: University of Pennsylvania, Wharton School, Industrial Research Unit, 1987, 246 p.

HILL, John K. and PEARCE, James E., 'The Incidence of Sanctions against Employers of Illegal Aliens', **98** *Journal of Political Economy*, 1990, 28-44.

HIRSCH, Werner Z. and RUFOLO, Anthony M., 'Economic Effects of Residence Laws on Municipal Police', **17** *Journal of Urban Economics*, 1985, 335-348.

HOLDERBEKE, F., PERNOT, A. and DENYS, J., 'Inkomensvorming en deregulering van de arbeidsmarkt: 3. Arbeidsvoorwaarden' [Income Formation and Deregulation of the Labour Market: Labour Conditions], in *18de Vlaams Wetenschappelijk Economisch Congres, Brussel 8 en 9 mei 1987, Sociaal-economische Deregulering*, Brussel, V.E.H.U.B., 1987, 265-303.

HOLLAND, D.M., 'An Evaluation of Tax Incentives for on-the-Job Training of the Disadvantaged', **2** *Bell Journal of Economics*, 1971, 293-327.

JOHNSON, George E. and SOLON, Gary R., 'Estimates of the Direct Effects of Comparable Worth Policy', **76** *American Economic Review*, 1986, 1117-1125.

KESSEL, Reuben A. and ALCHIAN, Armen A., 'Real Wages in the North during the Civil War : Mitchell's Data Reinterpreted', **2** *Journal of Law and Economics*, 1959, 95-113.

KOCH, Harald, 'Die Ökonomie der Gestaltungsrechte. Möglichkeiten und Grenzen der ökonomische Analyse des Rechts am Beispiel von Kündiging und Anfechtung' [The Economics of Dispositive Right. Possibilities and Limits of the Economic Analysis of Law by the Example of Notion of Termination and Dispute], in BERNSTEIN, H., DROBNIG, U. and KÖTZ, H. (eds.), *Festschrift für Konrad Zweigert zum 70. Geburtstag*, Tübingen, J.C.B. Mohr, 1981, 851-877.

KOSTERS, Marvin H., 'Mandated Benefits - On the Agenda', **12(3)** *Regulation*, 1988, 21-27.

KRUSE, Douglas L., 'The Economic Implications of Employment Rights and Practices in the United States', **14** *Journal of Comparative Economics*, 1990, 221-253.

KUHN, Peter J., 'Reply', **80** *American Economic Review*, 1990, 290-297.

LANDES, William M., 'The Economics of Fair Employment Laws', **76** *Journal of Political Economy*, 1968, 507-559.

LINDER, Mark, 'Employees not-so-independent Contractors and the Case of Migrant Farmworkers: a Challenge to the "Law and Economics" Agency Doctrine', **15** *New York University Review of Law & Social Change*, 1987, 435-475.

MENDELOFF, John M., 'Regulatory Reform and OSHA Policy', **5** *Journal of Policy Analysis and Management*, 1986, 440-468.

MEYER, Dirk, 'Rent Seeking durch Rationalisierungsschutz oder die Wohlfahrtsverluste einer Kostensenkungssteuer' [Rent Seeking through Regulations Protecting Human Capital from Devaluation Due to Technological

Innovation], **35** *Konjunkturpolitik*, 1989, 188-1200.

MILLER, James C., III and YANDLE, Bruce (eds.), *Benefit-Cost Analysis of Social Regulation*, Washington, American Enterprise Institute, 1979.

MIYAZAKI, Hajime, 'The Rat Race and Internal Labor Markets', **8** *Bell Journal of Economics*, 1977, 394-418.

MOORE, William J., NEWMAN, Robert J. and THOMAS, R. William, 'Determinants of the Passage of Right-To-Work Laws: An Alternative Interpretation', **17** *Journal of Law and Economics*, 1974, 197-211.

MYHRMAN, Johan, 'Kontraktsrätt och löntagarfonder' [Contractual Rights and Labour Funds], *Ekonomisk Debatt*, 1981, No. 6.

PALOMBA, Neil A. and PALOMBA, Catherine A., 'Right-To-Work Laws: A Suggested Economic Rationale', **14** *Journal of Law and Economics*, 1971, 475-483.

PARDOLESI, Roberto, 'Invalidità temporanea del dipendente, illecito del terzo, 'rivalsa' del datore di lavoro (ovvero: l'analisi economica del diritto in cassazione)' [Temporary Disability of Employees, Tortious Conduct By Third Party, Employer's Remedies], *Foro italiano*, 1985, I, 2286-2291.

PETHIG, Rudiger, 'Eminent Domain: A New Industrial Policy Tool: Comment', **142** *Journal of Institutional and Theoretical Economics*, 1986, 44-51.

POSNER, Richard A., 'Some Economics of Labor Law', **51** *University of Chicago Law Review*, 1984, 988-1011.

POULMANS, G., 'Inkomensvorming en deregulering van de arbeidsmarkt: 1. Arbeidsflexibiliteit' [Income Formation and Deregulation in the Labour Market: Flexibility], in *18de Vlaams Wetenschappelijk Economisch Congres, Brussel 8 en 9 mei 1987, Sociaal-economische Deregulering*, Brussel, V.E.H.U.B., 1987, 229-248.

PRIEST, W. Curtiss, *Risks, Concerns, and Social Regulation: Forces that Led to Laws on Health, Safety, and the Environment*, Boulder, Westview Press, 1988, 204 p.

PRITCHARD, A.C., 'Note: Government Promises and Due Process: An Economic Analysis of the "New Property"', **77** *Virginia Law Review*, 1991, 1053-1090.

RADAY, Frances, 'Costs of Dismissal: An Analysis in Community Justice and Efficiency', **9** *International Review of Law and Economics*, 1989, 181-207.

REES, Albert and HAMILTON, Mary T., 'Postwar Movements of Wage Levels and Unit Labor Costs', **6** *Journal of Law and Economics*, 1963, 41-68.

ROSEN, Sherwin, 'Commentary: In Defense of the Contract at Will', **51** *University of Chicago Law Review*, 1984, 983-987.

ROWLEY, Charles K., 'Toward a Political Economy of British Labor Law', **51** *University of Chicago Law Review*, 1984, 1135-1160.

SAGOFF, Mark, *The Economy of the Earth: Philosophy, Law, and the Environment*, Cambridge, Cambridge University Press, 1988, 271 p.

SHULTZ, George P., 'Strategies for National Labor Policy', **6** *Journal of Law and Economics*, 1963, 1-9.

SMITH, Robert S., 'Compensating Wage Differentials and Public Policy: A Review', **32** *Industrial and Labour Relations Review*, 1979, 339-351.

SUNSTEIN, Cass R., 'Rights, Minimal Terms, and Solidarity: A Comment', **51** *University of Chicago Law Review*, 1984, 1041-1060.

TINBERGEN, J., 'Kan de economische wetenschap bijdragen tot de ontwikkeling van het recht?' [Can the Economic Science Contribute to Legal Development?], in *In Orde. Liber Amicorum Verloren van Themaat*, Deventer, Kluwer, 1982, 295-300.

TOLLEFSON, John O. and PICHLER, Joseph A., 'A Comment on Right-To-Work Laws: A Suggested Economic Rationale', **17** *Journal of Law and Economics*, 1974, 193-196.

TRAPANI, John M., III, 'Eminent Domain: A New Industrial Policy Tool: Comment', **142** *Journal of Institutional and Theoretical Economics*, 1986, 39-43.

VERKUIL, Paul R., 'Whose Common Law for Labor Relations?', **92** *Yale Law Journal*, 1983, 1409-1414.

VETTER, Jan, 'Commentary: Searching for the Right Questions', **75** *Virginia Law Review*, 1989, 285-294.

X, 'Note: Employer Opportunism and the Need for a Just Clause Standard', **103** *Harvard Law Review*, 1989, 510-529.

5410 Economics of Labor Contracts

ABOWD, John M. and CARD, David, 'Intertemporal Labor Supply and Long-Term Employment Contracts', **77** *American Economic Review*, 1987, 50-68.

AKERLOF, George A., 'Gift Exchange and Efficiency-Wage Theory: Four Views', **74** *American Economic Review. Papers and Proceedings*, 1984, 79-83.

ANTEL, John J., 'Costly Employment Contract Renegotiation and the Labor Mobility of Young Men', **75** *American Economic Review*, 1985, 976-991.

ARNOTT, Richard J., HOSIOS, Arthur J. and STIGLITZ, Joseph E., 'Implicit Contracts, Labor Mobility, and Unemployment', **78** *American Economic Review*, 1988, 1046-1066.

AZARIADIS, Costas, 'Implicit Contracts', in EATWELL, John, MILGATE, Murray and NEWMAN, Peter (eds.), *The New Palgrave: A Dictionary of Economics*, London, Macmillan, 1987, Volume 2, 733-737.

BALL, Laurence, 'Externalities from Contract Length', **77** *American Economic Review*, 1987, 615-629.

BARON, David P., 'Incentive Contracts and Competitive Bidding: Reply', **64** *American Economic Review*, 1974, 1072-1073.

BECKER, Gary S., *Human Capital*, New York, National Bureau of Economic Research, 1964.

BLAYDON, Colin C. and MARSHALL, Paul W., 'Incentive Contracts and Competitive Bidding: Comment', **64** *American Economic Review*, 1974, 1070-1071.

BULL, Clive, 'Implicit Contracts in the Absence of Enforcement and Risk Aversion',

73 *American Economic Review*, 1983, 658-671.

CANES, Michael E., 'The Simple Economics of Incentive Contracting: Note', **65** *American Economic Review*, 1975, 478-483.

CASTRONOVO, Carlo, 'Inattuazione della prestazione di lavoro e responsabilità del danneggiante' [Employee's Non-Performance and Tortfeasor's Liability], *Massimario di giurisprudenza del lavoro*, 1981, 370-377.

COOPER, Russell, 'Will Share Contracts Increase Economic Welfare?', **78** *American Economic Review*, 1988, 138-154.

DUDLEY, Leonard, 'Implicit Labor Contracts and Public Choice: A General Equilibrium Approach', **29** *Journal of Law and Economics*, 1986, 61-82.

DYE, Ronald A., 'Optimal Length of Labor Contracts', **26** *International Economic Review*, 1985, 251-270.

FLANAGAN, Robert J., 'Implicit Contracts, Explicit Contracts, and Wages', **74** *American Economic Review. Papers and Proceedings*, 1984, 345-349.

FREEMAN, Smith, 'Wage Trends as Performance Displays Productive Potential: a Model and Application to Academic Early Retirement', **8** *Bell Journal of Economics*, 1977, 419-443.

GOLDBERG, Victor P., 'A Relational Exchange Perspective on the Employment Relationship', in STEPHENS, Frank (ed.), *Organization and Labor*, 1984. Reprinted in GOLDBERG, Victor P. (ed.), *Readings in the Economics of Contract Law*, Cambridge, Cambridge University Press, 1989, 147-151.

GREENE, Kenneth V. and MOULTON, George D., 'Municipal Employee Residency Requirement Statutes: An Economic Analysis', **9** *Research in Law and Economics*, 1986, 185-204.

HALL, Robert E., 'The Importance of Lifetime Jobs in the U.S. Economy', **72** *American Economic Review*, 1982, 716-724.

HARRIS, Milton and HOLMSTROM, Bengt, 'On the Duration of Agreements', **28** *International Economic Review*, 1987, 389-406.

HARRIS, Milton and RAVIV, Artur, 'Some Results on Incentive Contracts with Applications to Education and Employment, Health Insurance, and Law Enforcement', **68** *American Economic Review*, 1978, 20-30.

HASHIMOTO, Masanori and YU, B.T., 'Specific Capital, Employment Contracts, and Wage Rigidity', **11** *Bell Journal of Economics*, 1980, 536-549.

HERTOG, Johan A. and KRAAMWINKEL, Margriet M., 'Pensioennadelen in het licht van de contracttheorie' [Pension Disadvantages in the Light of Contract Theory], *Economisch-statistische berichten*, 1991, 908-912.

HIRSCH, Werner Z., 'The Economics of Contracting Out: The Labor Cost Fallacy', **40** *Labor Law Journal*, 1989, 536-542.

ICKES, B.W. and SAMUELSON, L., 'Job Transfers and Incentives in Complex Organizations: Thwarting in the Ratchet Effect', **18** *Rand Journal of Economics*, 1987, 275-286.

IOANNIDES, Y.M. and PISSARIDES, C.A., 'Wages and Employment with Firm-Specific Seniority', **14** *Bell Journal of Economics*, 1983, 573-580.

KLEIN, Benjamin, 'Contract Costs and Administered Prices: An Economic Theory of Rigid Wages', **74** *American Economic Review. Papers and Proceedings*, 1984,

332-338.

LAZEAR, Edward P., 'Incentives and Wage Rigidity', **74** *American Economic Review. Papers and Proceedings*, 1984, 339-344.

LAZEAR, Edward P., 'Incentive Contracts', in EATWELL, John, MILGATE, Murray and NEWMAN, Peter (eds.), *The New Palgrave: A Dictionary of Economics*, London, Macmillan, 1987, Volume 2, 744-748.

LEWIS, Tracy R., 'Bonuses and Penalties in Incentive Contracting', **11** *Bell Journal of Economics*, 1980, 292-301.

MACDONALD, Glenn M. ' Specific Investments and Nonlabor Income', **13** *Bell Journal of Economics*, 1982, 225 ff.

MAGEE, R.P., 'Accounting Measurement and Employment Contracts: Current Value Reporting', **9** *Bell Journal of Economics*, 1978, 145-158.

MARTIN, Donald L., 'The Economics of Employment Termination Rights', **20** *Journal of Law and Economics*, 1977, 187-204.

McCALL, John, J., 'The Simple Economics of Incentive Contracting', **60** *American Economic Review*, 1970, 837-846.

MURPHY, Kevin J., 'Incentives, Learning, and Compensation: A Theoretical and Empirical Investigation of Managerial Labor Contracts', **17** *Rand Journal of Economics*, 1986, 59-76.

PLAUT, Steven E., 'Implicit Contracts in the Absence of Enforcement: Note', **76** *American Economic Review*, 1986, 257-258.

RASMUSEN, Eric and ZENGER, Todd, 'Diseconomies of Scale in Employment Contracts', **6** *Journal of Law, Economics, & Organization*, 1990, 65-92.

ROEMER, J., 'Divide and Conquer Microfoundations of a Marxian Theory of Wage Discrimination', **10** *Bell Journal of Economics*, 1979, 695-705.

ROSEN, Sherwin, 'Authority, Control, and the Distribution of Earnings', **13** *Bell Journal of Economics*, 1982, 311-323.

RUBIN, Paul H. and SHEDD, Peter, 'Human Capital and Covenants Not to Compete', **10** *Journal of Legal Studies*, 1981, 93-110.

SHADOWEN, Steve D. and VOYTEK, Kenneth, 'Note: Economic and Critical Analyses Of The Law Of Covenants Not To Compete', **72** *Georgetown Law Journal*, 1984, 1425-1450.

SIMON, Herbert A., 'A Formal Theory of the Employment Relationship', **19** *Econometrica*, 1951, 293-305.

SKLIVAS, S.D., 'The Strategic Choice of Managerial Incentives', **18** *Rand Journal of Economics*, 1987, 452-460.

TAYLOR, John B., 'Aggregate Dynamics and Staggered Contracts', **88** *Journal of Political Economy*, 1980, 1-23.

TOPEL, Robert H. and WELCH, Finis, 'Efficient Labor Contracts with Employement Risk', **17** *Rand Journal of Economics*, 1986, 490-507.

VOGEL, Kenneth, 'Analysis of Labour Contracts and their Administration Using Transaction Costs Economics', **5** *Law and Policy Quarterly*, 1983, 129-152.

WALDMAN, M. 'Job Assignments, Signalling, and Efficiency', **15** *Rand Journal of Economics*, 1984, 255-267.

WEITZMAN, Martin L., 'Efficient Incentive Contracts', **94** *Quarterly Journal of Economics*, 1980, 719-730.

WEITZMAN, Martin L., *The Share Economy. Conquering Stagflation*, Cambridge, Harvard University Press, 1984, 167 p.

WILLIAMSON, Oliver E., WACHTER, Michael L. and HARRIS, Jeffrey F., 'Understanding the Employment Relation: The Analysis of Idiosyncratic Exchange', **6** *Bell Journal of Economics*, 1975, 250-278.

WILLMAN, Paul, 'Opportunism in Labor Contracting: An Application of the Organizational Failures' Framework', **3** *Journal of Economic Behavior and Organization*, 1982, 83-98.

X, 'Note: Employer Opportunism and the Need for a Just Clause Standard', **103** *Harvard Law Review*, 1989, 510-529.

5420 Wage Control. Minimum Wages

ACKLEY, Gardner, 'Observations on Phase II Price and Wage Controls', **1** *Brookings Papers on Economic Activity*, 1972, 173-190.

AMES, Edward, 'The Consumer and Wage Price Controls', **30** *Journal of Economics and Business*, 1977, 15-22.

BROZEN, Yale, 'Minimum Wage Rates and Household Workers', **5** *Journal of Law and Economics*, 1962, 103-109.

BROZEN, Yale, 'The Effect of Statutory Minimum Wage Increases on Teen-Age Employment', **12** *Journal of Law and Economics*, 1969, 109-122.

BRUNNER, Karl and MELTZER, Allan H., 'The Economics of Price and Wage Controls: An Introduction', **2** *Journal of Monetary Economics*, 1976, 1-6.

COLBERG, Marshall R., 'Minimum Wage Effects on Florida's Economic Development', **3** *Journal of Law and Economics*, 1960, 106-117.

DARBY, Michael R., 'Price and Wage Controls: The First Two Years', **2** *Journal of Monetary Economics*, 1976, 235-263.

DARBY, Michael R., 'Price and Wage Controls: Further Evidence', **2** *Journal of Monetary Economics*, 1976, 269-271.

DAVIDSON, Lawrence S. and HOUSTON, Douglas, 'A Reexamination of the Nixon Wage Price Controls: An Application of Time Series Methods', **33** *Journal of Economics and Business*, 1981, 246-253.

DE BRUYNE, G., 'Inkomensvorming en deregulering van de arbeidsmarkt: 2. Indexering' [Income Formation and Deregulation in the Labour Market: Indexation], in *18de Vlaams Wetenschappelijk Economisch Congres, Brussel 8 en 9 mei 1987, Sociaal-economische Deregulering*, Brussel, V.E.H.U.B., 1987, 249-263.

EHEMANN, Christian, 'General Disequilibrium, Fiscal Policy, and a Wage Price Freeze', **12** *Economic Inquiry*, 1974, 35-52.

FIEDLER, Edgar R., 'The Price Wage Stabilization Program', **1** *Brookings Papers on Economic Activity*, 1972, 199-1206.

GITLOW, Abraham L., 'Are Peacetime Wage Price Controls Effective?', **23** *Rivista Internazionale di Scienze Economiche e Commerciali*, 1976, 722-739.

GORDON, Robert J., 'Wage Price Controls and the Shifting Phillips Curve', **2** *Brookings Papers on Economic Activity*, 1972, 385-421.

GORDON, Robert J., 'The Response of Wages and Prices to the First Two Years of Controls', **3** *Brookings Papers on Economic Activity*, 1973, 765-778.

HASHIMOTO, Masanori, 'The Minimum Wage Law and Youth Crimes: Time-Series Evidence', **30** *Journal of Law and Economics*, 1987, 443-464.

HEMPEL, George H., 'Wage and Price Controls for State and Local Governments: Their Effectiveness and the Potential Effects of Phase III', **21** *Public Policy*, 1973, 425-436.

KELLER, Robert R. and GRAY, S. Lee, 'A Neo Classical Argument for Wage Price Controls', **6(2)** *Intermountain Economic Review*, 1975, 46-54.

LEFFLER, Keith B., 'Minimum Wages, Welfare, and Wealth Transfers to the Poor', **21** *Journal of Law and Economics*, 1978, 345-358.

LIPSEY, Richard G., 'Wage Price Controls: How to do a Lot of Harm by Trying to do a Little Good', **3** *Canadian Public Policy*, 1977, 1-13.

McGRAW, Thomas K., 'Discussion [The Response of the Giant Corporations to Wage and Price Controls in World War II] 1[Planning for Peace: The Surplus Property Act of 1944].', **41(1)** *Journal of Economic History*, 1981, 136-137.

MITCHELL, Daniel J.B., 'The Future of American Wage Controls', **17(1)** *California Management Review*, 1974, 48-57.

MIYAGIWA, Kaz, 'Human Capital and Economic Growth in a Minimum Wage Economy', **30** *International Economic Review*, 1989, 187-202.

OI, Walter Y., 'On Measuring the Impact of Wage Price Controls: A Critical Appraisal', **2** *Journal of Monetary Economics*, 1976, 7-64.

OSTRY, Sylvia, 'Industrial Relations after Wage and Price Control: Panel Discussion', **4** *Canadian Public Policy*, 1978, 425-430.

PENCAVEL, John H., 'A Comment on the Papers at the Conference on Wage Price Controls', **2** *Journal of Monetary Economics*, 1976, 303-304.

POOLE, William, 'Wage Price Controls: Where Do We Go from Here?', **1** *Brookings Papers on Economic Activity*, 1973, 285-299.

POSSEN, Uri M., 'Wage and Price Controls in a Dynamic Macro Model', **46** *Econometrica*, 1978, 105-125.

REID, Frank, 'Control and Decontrol of Wages in the United States: An Empirical Analysis', **71** *American Economic Review*, 1981, 108-120.

ROCKOFF, Hugh, 'The Response of the Giant Corporations to Wage and Price Controls in World War II', **41** *Journal of Economic History*, 1981, 123-128.

ROCKOFF, Hugh, *Drastic Measures: A History of Wage and Price Controls in the United States*, Cambridge, Cambridge University Press, 1984, 289 p.

ROTTENBERG, Simon (ed.), *The Economics of Legal Mininum Wages*, Washington, American Entreprise Institute for Public Policy Research, 1981, 534 p.

SCHULTZ, George P. and DAM, Kenneth W., 'Reflections on Wage and Price

Controls', **30** *Industrial and Labor Relations Review*, 1977, 139-151.

SCHULTZ, George P. and DAM, Kenneth W., 'Further Reflections on Wage Controls: Reply', **31** *Industrial and Labor Relations Review*, 1978, 159-160.

SHALIT, Sol S. and BEN Zion, Uri, 'The Expected Impact of the Wage Price Freeze on Relative Shares', **64** *American Economic Review*, 1974, 904-914.

TAYLOR, Amy K., 'Government Health Policy and Hospital Labor Costs: The Effects of Wage and Price Controls on Hospital Wage Rates and Employment', **27** *Public Policy*, 1979, 203-225.

TREJO, Stephen J., 'The Effects of Overtime Pay Regulation on Worker Compensation', **81** *American Economic Review*, 1991, 719-740.

URI, Noel D. and MIXON, J. Wilson, Jr., 'An Economic Analysis of the Determinants of Minimum Wage Voting Behavior', **23** *Journal of Law and Economics*, 1980, 167-177.

VROMAN, Susan and VROMAN, Wayne, 'Money Wage Changes: Before, During and After Controls', **45** *Southern Economic Journal*, 1979, 1172-1187.

WAGSTAFF, Peter, 'A Benthamite Wages Policy', **42** *Review of Economic Studies*, 1975, 571-580.

WEBER, Arnold R., 'A Wage Price Freeze as an Instrument of Incomes Policy: Or the Blizzard of '71', **62** *American Economic Review*, 1972, 251-257.

WEBER, Arnold R. and MITCHELL, Daniel J.B., 'Further Reflections on Wage Controls: Comment', **31** *Industrial and Labor Relations Review*, 1978, 149-158.

WEIDENBAUM, Murray L., 'New Initiatives in National Wage and Price Policy', **54** *Review of Economics and Statistics*, 1972, 213-217.

WEILER, Paul, 'Industrial Relations after Wage and Price Control: Panel Discussion', **4** *Canadian Public Policy*, 1978, 433-442.

5430 Discrimination

BARBEZAT, Debra A., HUGHES, James W. and EVEN, William E., 'Sex Discrimination in Labor Markets: The Role of Statistical Evidence: Comments', **80** *American Economic Review*, 1990, 277 ff.

BECKER, Mary E., 'Barriers Facing Women in the Wage-Labor Market and the Need for Additional Remedies: A Reply to Fischel and Lazear', **53** *University of Chicago Law Review*, 1986, 934-949.

CHAMBERS, Julius L. and GOLDSTEIN, Barry, 'Title VII: The Continuing Challenge of Establishing Fair Employment Practices', **49(4)** *Law and Contemporary Problems*, 1986, 9-23.

CULP, Jerome M., 'Federal Courts and the Enforcement of Title VII', **76** *American Economic Review. Papers and Proceedings*, 1986, 355-358.

DEX, Shirley and SHAW, Lois B., *British and American Women at Work: Do Equal Opportunities Policies Matter?*, New York, St. Martin's Press, 1986, 159 p.

DONOHUE, John J., III, 'Is Title VII Efficient?', **134** *University of Pennsylvania Law Review*, 1986, 1411-1431.

DONOHUE, John J. III, 'Further Thoughts on Employment Discrimination Legislation: A Reply to Judge Posner', **136** *University of Pennsylvania Law Review*, 1987, 523-551.

DONOHUE, John J. III, 'Prohibiting Sex Discrimination in the Workplace: An Economic Perspective', **56** *University of Chicago Law Review*, 1989, 1337-1368.

EVANS, Sara M. and NELSON, Barbara J., *Wage Justice: Comparable Worth and the Paradox of Technocratic Reform*, Chicago, University of Chicago Press, 1989, 224 p.

FISCHEL, Daniel R. and LAZEAR, Edward P., 'Comparable Worth: A Rejoinder', **53** *University of Chicago Law Review*, 1986, 934-952.

FISCHER, Charles C., 'Toward a More Complete Understanding of Occupational Sex Discrimination', **21** *Journal of Economic Issues*, 1987, 113-138.

FISHBACK, Price V., 'Can Competition among Employers Reduce Governmental Discrimination? Coal Companies and Segregated Schools in West Virginia in the Early 1900s', **32** *Journal of Law and Economics*, 1989, 311-328.

FORMBY, John P. and MILLNER, E.L., '"Comparable Worth" and Rent Seeking', **7** *International Review of Law and Economics*, 1987, 65-78.

GUNDERSON, Morley, 'Male-Female Wage Differentials and Policy Responses', **27** *Journal of Economic Literature*, 1989, 46-72.

HOLZHAUER, James D., 'The Economic Possiblities of Comparable Worth', **53** *University of Chicago Law Review*, 1986, 919-933.

JOHNSON, George E. and SOLON, Gary R., 'The Attainment of Pay Equity Between the Sexes by Legal Means: An Economic Analysis', **20** *University of Michigan Journal of Law Reform*, 1986, 183 ff.

JOHNSON, William R., 'Racial Wage Discrimination and Industrial Structure', **9** *Bell Journal of Economics*, 1978.

JONES, Ethel B., 'ERA Voting: Labor Force Attachment, Marriage, and Religion', **12** *Journal of Legal Studies*, 1983, 157-168.

O'NEILL, June, BRIEN, Michael and CUNNINGHAM, James, 'Effects of Comparable Worth Policy: Evidence from Washington State', **79** *American Economic Review. Papers and Proceedings*, 1989, 305-309.

PETERSON, Janice, 'The Challenge of Comparable Worth: An Institutionalist View', **24** *Journal of Economic Issues*, 1990, 605-612.

POSNER, Richard A., 'An Economic Analysis of Sex Discrimination Laws', **56** *University of Chicago Law Review*, 1989, 1311-1335.

ROEMER, J., 'Divide and Conquer Microfoundations of a Marxian Theory of Wage Discrimination', **10** *Bell Journal of Economics*, 1979, 695-705.

ROTHSCHILD, Michael and WERDEN, Gregory J., 'Title VII and the Use of Employment Tests: An Illustration of the Limits of the Judicial Process', **11** *Journal of Legal Studies*, 1982, 261-280.

TULLOCK, Gordon, 'In Search of Exploited Workers: One Businessman's View of Comparable Worth', **9** *Harvard Journal of Law & Public Policy*, 1986, 95-97.

TURLEY, Jonathan, 'Transnational Discrimination and the Economics of Extraterritorial Regulation', **70** *Boston University Law Review*, 1990, 339-393.

5440 Occupational Safety and Health Regulation

ALDRICH, Mark, 'OSHA Fines and the Value of Saving a Life', **7** *Journal of Policy Analysis and Management*, 1988, 356-362.

BARTEL, Ann P. and THOMAS, Lacy Glenn, 'Direct and Indirect Effects of Regulation: A New Look at OSHA's Impact', **28** *Journal of Law and Economics*, 1985, 1-25.

BARTEL, Ann P. and THOMAS, Lacy Glenn, 'Predation through Regulation: The Wage and Profit Effects of the Occupational Safety and Health Administration and the Environmental Protection Agency', **30** *Journal of Law and Economics*, 1987, 239-264.

BARTH, Peter S., 'A Proposal for Dealing with the Compensation of Occupational Diseases', **13** *Journal of Legal Studies*, 1984, 569-586.

BARTRIP, P.W.J. and FENN, Paul T., 'Factory Fatalities and Regulation in Britain, 1878-1913', **25** *Explorations in Economic History*, 1988, 60-74.

BODEN, Leslie I. and JONES, Carl Adaire, 'Occupational Disease Remedies: The Asbestos Experience', in BAILEY, Elizabeth E. (ed.), *Public Regulation: New Perspectives on Institutions and Policies*, Cambridge (Mass.), MIT Press, 1987, 321-46.

CARLE, Susan D., 'A Hazardous Mix: Discretion to Disclose and Incentives to Suppress Under OSHA's Hazard Communication Standard', **97** *Yale Law Journal*, 1988, 581-601.

CARMICHAEL, H. Lorne, 'Reputations for Safety: Market Performance and Policy Remedies', **4** *Journal of Labor Economics*, 1986, 458-472.

CHELIUS, James R., 'The Control of Industrial Accidents: Economic Theory and Empirical Evidence', **38(4)** *Law and Contemporary Problems*, 1974, 700-729.

CURINGTON, William P., 'Safety Regulation and Workplace Injuries', **53** *Southern Economic Journal*, 1986, 51-72.

DEWEES, Donald N., *Controlling Asbestos in Buildings: An Economic Investigation*, 1986.

DEWEES, Donald N., 'Economic Incentives for Controlling Industrial Disease: The Asbestos Case', **15** *Journal of Legal Studies*, 1986, 289-319.

DEWEES, Donald N. and DANIELS, Ronald J., 'The Cost of Protecting Occupational Health: The Asbestos Case', **21** *Journal of Human Resources*, 1986, 381-396.

DEWEES, Donald N. with DANIELS, Ronald J., 'Prevention and Compensation of Industrial Disease', **8** *International Review of Law and Economics*, 1988, 51-72.

DICKENS, William T., 'Occupational Safety and Health Regulation and Economic Theory', in DARITY, William, Jr. (ed.), *Labor Economics: Modern Views*, Boston, Kluwer-Nijhoff, 1984, 133-173.

DICKENS, William T., 'Differences between Risk Premiums in Union and Nonunion Wages and the Case for Occupational Safety Regulation', **74** *American Economic Review. Papers and Proceedings*, 1984, 320-323.

ELDER, Harold W., 'An Economic Analysis of Factor Usage and Workplace Regulation: Reply', **53** *Southern Economic Journal*, 1987, 790 ff.

FEINSTEIN, Jonathan S., 'The Safety Regulation of U.S. Nuclear Power Plants: Violations, Inspections, and Abnormal Occurrences', **97** *Journal of Political Economy*, 1989, 115-154.

FISHBACK, Price V., 'Workplace Safety during the Progressive Era: Fatal Accidents in Bituminous Coal Mining, 1912-1923', **23** *Explorations in Economic History*, 1986, 269-298.

FISHBACK, Price V., 'Liability Rules and Accident Prevention in the Workplace: Empirical Evidence from the Early Twentieth Century', **16** *Journal of Legal Studies*, 1987, 305-328.

FRENCH, Michael Thomas, 'An Efficiency Test for Occupational Safety Regulation', **54** *Southern Economic Journal*, 1988, 675-693.

FRY, Clifford L. and LEE, Insup, 'OSHA Sanctions and the Value of the Firm', **24** *Financial Review*, 1989, 599-610.

FUESS, Scott M., Jr. and LOEWENSTEIN, Mark A., 'Further Analysis of the Theory of Economic Regulation: The Case of the 1969 Coal Mine Health and Safety Act', **28** *Economic Inquiry*, 1990, 354-389.

GRAY, Wayne B., 'The Cost of Regulation: OSHA, EPA and the Productivity Slowdown', **77** *American Economic Review*, 1987, 998-1006.

HERSCH, Philip L. and NETTER, Jeffrey M., 'The Impact of Early Safety Legislation: The Case of the Safety Appliance Act of 1893', **10** *International Review of Law and Economics*, 1990, 61-75.

HREZO, Margaret S. and HREZO, William E., 'Judicial Regulation of the Environment under Posner's Economic Model of the Law', **18** *Journal of Economic Issues*, 1984, 1071-1091.

HUGHES, John S., MAGAT, Wesley A. and RICKS, William E., 'The Economic Consequences of the OSHA Cotton Dust Standards: An Analysis of Stock Price Behavior', **29** *Journal of Law and Economics*, 1986, 29-59.

KAHN, Shulamit, 'Occupational Safety and Workers Preferences: Is There a Marginal Worker?', **69** *Review of Economics and Statistics*, 1987, 262-268.

LAVE, L.B., 'Viscusi's Risk by Choice: Regulating Health and Safety in the Workplace', **14** *Bell Journal of Economics*, 1983, 607-610.

LITAN, Robert E. and NORDHAUS, William D., 'Regulatory Reform and OSHA Policy: Comments', **5** *Journal of Policy Analysis and Management*, 1986, 467-481.

LOFGREN, Don, *Dangerous Premises: An Insider's View of OSHA Enforcement*, Ithaca, ILR Press, 1989, 244 p.

LYTTKENS, C.H., 'Workers' Compensation and Employees' Safety Incentives in Sweden', **8** *International Review of Law and Economics*, 1988, 181-185.

MARVEL, Howard P., 'Factory Regulation: A Reinterpretation of Early English Experience', **20** *Journal of Law and Economics*, 1977, 379-402.

McGOVERN, Francis E., 'Resolving Mature Mass Tort Litigation', **69** *Boston University Law Review*, 1989, 659-694.

MENDELOFF, John M., *The Dilemma of Toxic Substance Regulation: How Overregulation Causes Underregulation at OSHA*, Cambridge, MIT Press, 1988, 321 p.

MILLER, James C., III, 'Is Organized Labor Rational in Supporting OSHA?', **50** *Southern Economic Journal*, 1984, 881-885.

MOORE, Michael J. and VISCUSI, W. Kip, 'Promoting Safety Through Workers' Compensation: The Efficacy and Net Wage Costs of Injury Insurance', **20** *Rand Journal of Economics*, 1989, 499-515.

MORGENSTERN, Felice, 'Some Reflections on Legal Liability as a Factor in the Promotion of Occupational Safety and Health', **121** *International Labour Review*, 1982, 387-398.

NELSON, Jon P. and NEUMANN, George P., 'Comment on Beck and Alford: [Can Government Regulate Safety? The Coal Mine Example]', **76** *American Political Science Review*, 1982, 876-877.

NEUMANN, George R. and NELSON, Jon P., 'Safety Regulation and Firm Size: Effects of the Coal Mine Health and Safety Act of 1969', **25** *Journal of Law and Economics*, 1982, 183-199.

OI, Walter Y., 'On the Economics of Industrial Safety', **38(4)** *Law and Contemporary Problems*, 1974, 669-699.

OLSON, Dennis O. and SHIEH, Yeung Nan, 'An Economic Analysis of Factor Usage and Workplace Regulation: Comment', **53** *Southern Economic Journal*, 1987, 786-789.

PHILLIPS, J., 'Economic Deterrence and the Prevention of Industrial Accidents', **5** *Industrial Law Journal*, 1976, 148-163.

PHILLIPS, Jerry J., 'An Evaluation of the Federal Employers' Liability Act', **25** *San Diego Law Review*, 1988, 49-62.

PRIEST, George L., 'Law and Economics and Law Reform: Comment on Barth's Cancer Compensation Proposal', **13** *Journal of Legal Studies*, 1984, 587-592.

ROBERTS, Barry S. and KOSSEK, Regina, 'Implementation of Economic Impact Analysis: The Lessons of OSHA', **83** *West Virginia Law Review*, 1981, 449-470.

ROSENBERG, David, 'Comment: Of End Games and Openings in Mass Tort Cases: Lessons from a Special Master', **69** *Boston University Law Review*, 1989, 695-730.

RUBIN, Jeffrey, 'Economic Incentives and Safety Regulation: An Analytical Framework: Comments', **28(1)** *American Economist*, 1984, 25-26.

SCHROEDER, Elinor P. and SHAPIRO, Sidney A., 'Responses to Occupational Disease: The Role of Markets, Regulation, and Information', **72** *Georgetown Law Journal*, 1984, 1231-1309.

SHAPIRO, Sidney A. and McGARITY, Thomas O., 'Reorienting OSHA: Regulatory Alternatives and Legislative Reform', **6** *Yale Journal on Regulation*, 1989, 1-63.

SIDER, Hal, 'Economic Incentives and Safety Regulation: An Analytical Framework', **28(1)** *American Economist*, 1984, 18-24.

SMITH, Robert S., 'The Feasibility of an "Injury Tax" Approach to Occupational Safety', **38(4)** *Law and Contemporary Problems*, 1974, 730-744.

SMITH, Robert S., 'The Impact of OSHA Inspections on Manufacturing Injury Rates', **14** *Journal of Human Resources*, 1979, 145-170.

STATEN, Michael and UMBECK, John, 'A Study of Signaling Behavior in Occupational Disease Claims', **29** *Journal of Law and Economics*, 1986, 263-286.

VELJANOVSKI, Cento G., 'The Employment and Safety Effects of Employers' Liability', **29** *Scottish Journal of Political Economy*, 1982.

VISCUSI, W. Kip, 'The Impact of Occupational Safety and Health Regulation', **10** *Bell Journal of Economics*, 1979, 117-140.

VISCUSI, W. Kip, 'Structuring an Effective Occupational Disease Policy: Victim Compensation and Risk Regulation', **2** *Yale Journal on Regulation*, 1984, 53-81.

VISCUSI, W. Kip, 'Reforming OSHA Regulation of Workplace Risks', in WEISS, Leonard W. and KLASS, Michael W. (ed.), *Regulatory Reform: What Actually Happened*, Boston, Little Brown, 1986, 234-268.

VISCUSI, W. Kip, 'The Structure and Enforcement of Job Safety Regulation', **49(4)** *Law and Contemporary Problems*, 1986, 127-150.

VISCUSI, W. Kip, 'Regulatory Reform and OSHA Policy: The Status of OSHA Reform: A Comment on Mendeloff's Proposals', **5** *Journal of Policy Analysis and Management*, 1986, 469-475.

VISCUSI, W. Kip, 'The Impact of Occupational Safety and Health Regulation, 1973-1983', **17** *Rand Journal of Economics*, 1986, 567-580.

VISCUSI, W. Kip, 'The Interaction between Product Liability and Workers' Compensation as Ex Post Remedies for Workplace Injuries', **5** *Journal of Law, Economics, & Organization*, 1989, 185-210.

VISCUSI, W. Kip, 'Product and Occupational Liability', **5(3)** *Journal of Economic Perspectives*, 1991, 71-91.

WALTERS, Vivienne and HAINES, Ted, 'Workers' Use and Knowledge of the 'Internal Responsibility System': Limits to Participation in Occupational Health and Safety', **14** *Canadian Public Policy*, 1988, 411-423.

WEISS, Peter and MAIER, Gunther and GERKING, Shelby, 'The Economic Evaluation of Job Safety: A Methodological Survey and Some Estimates for Austria', **13** *Empirica*, 1986, 53-67.

WOODBURY, Stephen A., 'Occupational Safety and Health Regulation and Economic Theory: Comment', in DARITY, William, Jr., *Labor Economics: Modern Viewq*, Boston, Kluwer-Nijhoff, 1984, 269-278.

X, 'Note: Cost-Benefit Analysis and the Feasibility Requirement of the Occupational Noise Regulation', **55** *George Washington Law Review*, 1986, 123-151.

5450 Collective Bargaining and Worker Participation

ADAMS, G.W., 'Collective Bargaining by Salaried Professionals', in SLAYTON, Philip and TREBILCOCK, Michael J. (eds.), *The Professions and Public Policy*, Toronto, University of Toronto Faculty of Law, 1978.

ALBERT, Michael and HAHNEL, Robin, *The Political Economy of Participatory Economics*, Princeton, Princeton University Press, 1991, 132 p.

BACKHAUS, Jürgen, 'Wirtschaftliche Analyse der Entwicklungsmöglichkeiten mitbestimmter Wirtschaftssysteme' [Economic Analysis of Co-Determination], in KAPPLER, Ekkehard (ed.), *Unternehmensstruktur und Unternehmensentwicklung (Festschrift für Fritz Hodeige)*, Freiburg, Rombach, 1980, 266-289.

BACKHAUS, Jürgen, *Mitbestimmung im Unternehmen* [Co-Determination: A Legal and Economic Analysis], Göttingen, Vandenhoeck & Ruprecht, 1987, 306 p.

BACKHAUS, Jürgen G., 'The Emergence of Worker Participation: Evolution and Legislation Compared', **21** *Journal of Economic Issues*, 1987, 895-910.

COLJEE, P.D., 'Het economisch adviesrecht van de ondernemingsraad, quo vadis? Artikel 25 WOR nader beschouwd [The Workers Council Economic Right of Advice, Quo vadis? Section 25 Dutch Workers Council Act Reconsidered], in COLJEE, P.D., FRANKEN, H., HEERTJE, A. and KANNING, W. (eds.), *Law and Welfare Economics*, Symposium 24 October, VU Amsterdam, 77-99.

CROUCH, Colin, *Trade Unions: The Logic of Collective Action*, Glasgow, Fontana Paperbacks, 1982, 251 p.

DeBROCK, Lawrence M. and ROTH, A.E., 'Strike Two: Labor-Management Negotiations in Major League Baseball', **12** *Bell Journal of Economics*, 1981, 413-425.

DETMAN, Julius G., GOLDBERGH, Stephen B. and HERMAN, Jeanne B., 'The National Labor Relations Board Voting Study: A Preliminary Report', **1** *Journal of Legal Studies*, 1972, 233-258.

FRIED, Charles, 'Individual and Collective Rights in Work Relations: Reflections on the Current State of Labor Law and Its Prospects', **51** *University of Chicago Law Review*, 1984, 1012-1040.

GARELLO, Jacques, LEMENNICIER, Bertrand and LEPAGE, Henri, *Cinq questions sur les syndicats* [Five Questions on Labor Unions], Paris, PUF, 1990. (Subject Code: 5450)

GOLDBERG, Michael J., 'The Propensity to Sue and the Duty of Fair Representation: A Second Point of View [Tactical Use of the Union's Duty of Fair Representation: An Empirical Analysis]', **41** *Industrial and Labor Relations Review*, 1988, 456-461.

GUNDERSON, Morley, 'Economic Aspects of the Unionization of Salaried Professionals', in SLAYTON, P. and TREBILCOCK, Michael J., *The Professions and Public Policy*, Toronto, University of Toronto Faculty of Law, 1978.

HANSMANN, Henry B., 'When Does Worker Ownership Work? ESOPs, Law Firms, Codetermination, and Economic Democracy', **99** *Yale Law Journal*, 1990, 1749-1816.

HEDLUND, Jeffrey D., 'An Economic Case for Mandatory Bargaining over Partial Termination and Plant Relocation Decisions', **95** *Yale Law Journal*, 1986, 949-968.

HENDRICKS, Walter, 'The Effect of Regulation on Collective Bargaining in Electric Utilities', **6** *Bell Journal of Economics*, 1975, 451-465.

HUTT, W.H., 'The 'Power' of Labour Unions', in ANDERSON, Martin J. (ed.), *The Unfinished Agenda: Essays on the Political Economy of Government Policy in honour of Arthur Seldon*, London, I.E.A., 1986, 39-63.

KLEMM, Günter, *Ökonomische Analyse von Streik und Aussperrung im Rahmen einer marktwirtschaftlichen Ordnung* [Economic Analysis of Strike and Lock-out in the Context of a Market Economy], 1983, 214 p.

KNIGHT, Thomas R., 'The Propensity to Sue and the Duty of Fair Representation: Reply', **41** *Industrial and Labor Relations Review*, 1988, 461-464.

LANDE, Robert H. and ZERBE, Richard O. Jr., 'Reducing Unions' Monopoly Power: Costs and Benefits', **28** *Journal of Law and Economics*, 1985, 297-310. Reprinted in **29** *Corporate Practice Commentator*, 1987, 107-122.

LEEF, G.C., 'Legal Obstacles to a Market for Employee Representation Services', **9** *Cato Journal*, 1990, 663-687.

LESLIE, Douglas L., 'Multiemployer Bargaining Rules', **75** *Virginia Law Review*, 1989, 241-278.

LEVIN, William R., 'The False Promise of Worker Capitalism: Congress and the Leveraged Employee Stock Ownership Plan', **95** *Yale Law Journal*, 1985, 148-173.

LIVERNASH, E.R., 'The Relation of Power to the Structure and Process of Collective Bargaining', **6** *Journal of Law and Economics*, 1963, 10-40.

LURIE, Melvin, 'Government Regulation and Union Power : A Case Study of the Boston Transit Industry', **3** *Journal of Law and Economics*, 1960, 118-135.

MELTZER, Bernard D., 'Labor Unions, Collective Bargaining, and the Antitrust Laws', **6** *Journal of Law and Economics*, 1963, 152-223.

NUTZINGER, Hans G. and BACKHAUS, Jürgen (eds.), *Codetermination: A Discussion of Different Approaches*, Berlin, Springer, 1989, 309 p.

REES, Albert, 'Do Unions Cause Inflation?', **2** *Journal of Law and Economics*, 1959, 84-93.

REES, Albert, 'The Effects of Unions on Resource Allocation', **6** *Journal of Law and Economics*, 1963, 69-78.

ST.ANTOINE, Theodore J., 'Commentary on "Multiemployer Bargaining Rules": The Limitations of a Strictly Economic Analysis', **75** *Virginia Law Review*, 1989, 279-283.

STEINHERR, A., 'On the Efficiency of Profit Sharing and Labor Participation in Management', **8** *Bell Journal of Economics*, 1977, 545-555.

WACHTER, Michael L. and COHEN, George M., 'The Law and Economics of Collective Bargaining: An Introduction and Application to the Problems of Subcontracting, Partial Closure, and Relocation', **136** *University of Pennsylvania Law Review*, 1988, 1349-1417.

WALTERS, Vivienne and HAINES, Ted, 'Workers' Use and Knowledge of the 'Internal Responsibility System': Limits to Participation in Occupational Health and Safety', **14** *Canadian Public Policy*, 1988, 411-423.

WEBER, Arnold R., 'The Structure of Collective Bargaining and Bargaining Power:

Foreign Experiences', **6** *Journal of Law and Economics*, 1963, 79-151.

WOLFF, Christian, 'Comment: Share Ownership and Efficiency', in FAURE, Michael and VAN DEN BERGH, Roger (eds.), *Essays in Law and Economics. Corporations, Accident Prevention and Compensation for Losses*, Antwerpen, Maklu, 1989, 81-83.

ZIMAROWSKI, James B., 'A Primer on Power Balancing Under the National Labor Relations Act', **23** *University of Michigan Journal of Law Reform*, 1989, 47-104.

5500 CORPORATION LAW & REGULATION OF FINANCIAL MARKETS

Guy De Clercq

5500 Corporation Law: General

ALTMAN, E.I., 'Predicting Railroad Bankruptcies in America', **4** *Bell Journal of Economics*, 1973, 184-211.

ARETZ, Adward, 'Taxation and Incorporation: An Economic Analysis of Post-1992 Business Incorporations', in WEIGEL, Wolfgang (ed.), *Economic Analysis of Law - A Collection of Applications*, Vienna, Österreichischer Wirtschaftsverlag, 1991, 122-132.

ARRUÑADA, Benito, 'Control y propriedad: límites al desarrollo de la empresa española' [Property and Control: Limits of the Spanish Firms Development], *Información comercial Española*, 1990, n. 687, 67-88.

ARRUÑADA, Benito, *Control y regulación de la sociedad anónima* [Control and Regulation of Corporations], Madrid, Alianza Editorial, 1990.

ARRUÑADA, Benito, *Economía de la empresa: un enfoque contractual* [The Economics of the Firm: A Contractual Approach], Barcelona, Ariel, 1990.

BACKHAUS, Jürgen G., 'Public Policy Towards Corporate Structures: Two Chicago Approaches', **19** *Journal of Economic Issues*, 1985, 365-373.

BAIRD, Douglas G., 'Fraudulent Conveyances, Agency Costs, and Leveraged Buyouts', **20** *Journal of Legal Studies*, 1991, 1-24.

BEBCHUCK, Lucian Arye, 'Limiting Contractual Freedom in Corporate Law: The Desirable Constraints on Charter Amendments', **102** *Harvard Law Review*, 1989, 1820-1860.

BEBCHUCK, Lucian Ayre (ed.), *Corporate Law and Economic Analysis*, Cambridge, Cambridge University Press, 1990, 320 p.

BEBCHUK, Lucian Arye, 'Foreword: The Debate on Contractual Freedom in Corporate Law', **89** *Columbia Law Review*, 1989, 1395 ff.

BENNINGA, S. and MULLER, E., 'Majority Choice and the Objective Function of the Firm under Uncertainty', **10** *Bell Journal of Economics*, 1979, 670-682.

BENNINGA, S. and MULLER, E., 'Majority Choice and the Objective Function of the Firm under Uncertainty: Reply', **12** *Bell Journal of Economics*, 1981, 338-339.

BINDER, John J., 'Measuring the Effects of Regulation with Stock Price Data', **16** *Rand Journal of Economics*, 1985, 167-183.

BRAITHWAITE, John and MAKKAI, Toni, 'Testing an Expected Utility Model of Corporate Deterrence', **25** *Law and Society Review*, 1991, 7-39.

BRANSON, Douglas M., 'Indeterminacy: The Final Ingredient in an Interest Group Analysis of Corporate Law', **43** *Vanderbilt Law Review*, 1990, 85 ff.

BRINKMANN, Thomas and KÜBLER, Friedrich, 'Überlegungen zur Ökonomischen

Analyse im Unternehmensrecht' [Thoughts on an Economic analysis of Company Law], **137** *Zeitschrift fur die gesamte Staatswissenschaft* 1981, 681-688.

COHEN, Kalman J. and CONROY, Robert M., 'An Empirical Study of the Effect of Rule 19c-3', **33** *Journal of Law & Economics*, 1990, 277-305.

COLJEE, P.D., 'Het economisch adviesrecht van de ondernemingsraad, quo vadis? Artikel 25 WOR nader beschouwd [The Workers Council Economic Right of Advice, Quo vadis? Section 25 Dutch Workers Council Act Reconsidered], in COLJEE, P.D., FRANKEN, H., HEERTJE, A. and KANNING, W. (eds.), *Law and Welfare Economics*, Symposium 24 October, VU Amsterdam, 77-99.

CRAFTON, Steven M., 'An Empirical Test of the Effect of Usury Laws', **23** *Journal of Law and Economics*, 1980, 135-145.

CROSS, M.L., DAVIDSON, W.N., III and THORNTON, J.H., 'The Impact of Directors and Officers' Liability Suits on Firm Value', **56** *Journal of Risk and Insurance*, 1989, 128-136.

DEUTSCH, Jan G., 'Regulation and the United States Corporation: an Alternative to Law-and-order Economics', **9** *Cardozo Law Review*, 1988, 1463-1487.

HARMATHY, Attila, 'Vállalati gazdaságpolitika - szerződések' [Business Policy of the Company - Contracts], **4** *Allam- és Jogtudomány*, 1977, 528-567.

KIRCHNER, Christian, 'Ansatze zu einer ökonomischen Analyse des Konzernrechts' [Starting Point for an Economic Analysis of Large Companies Law], in BOETTCHER, Erik, HERDER-DORNEICH, Philipp and SCHENK, Karl-Ernst (eds.), **3** *Jahrbuch für Neue Politische Ökonomie*, Tübingen, J.C.B. Mohr, 1984, 223-251.

KRAAKMAN, Reinier H., 'The Economic Functions of Corporate Liability', in HOPT, Klaus J. and TEUBNER, Gunther (eds.), *Corporate Governance and Directors' Liabilities: Legal, Economic and Sociological Responsibility*, New York, de Gruyter, 1984, 178-207.

KÜBLER, Friedrich, MENDELSON, Morris and MUNDHEIM, Robert H., 'Die Kosten des Bezugsrechts - Eine rechtsökonomische Analyse des amerikanischen Erfahrungsmaterials [The Costs of the Subscription Right - A Legal Economic Analysis of the American Experience], *Die Aktiengesellschaft*, 1990, 461-475.

LEHN, Kenneth, 'Public Policy towards Corporate Restructuring', **25(2)** *Business Economics*, 1990, 26-31.

LUTTER, Marcus and WAHLERS, Henning W., 'Der Buyout: Amerikanische Fälle und die Regeln des deutschen Rechts' [The Buyout: American Cases and the German Rules], **34** *Die Aktiengesellschaft*, 1989, 1-17.

MACEY, Jonathan R., 'Externalities, Firm-Specific Capital Investments, and the Legal Treatment of Fundamental Corporate Changes', *Duke Law Journal*, 1989, 173-201.

MACEY, Jonathan R. and MILLER, Geoffrey P., 'Toward an Interest-Group Theory of Delaware Corporate Law', **65** *Texas Law Review*, 1987, 469-523.

MANNE, Henry G., 'Intellectual Styles and the Evolution of American Corporation Law', in RADNITZKY, Gerard and BERNHOLZ, Peter (eds.), *Economic Imperialism: The Economic Approach Applied Outside the Field of Economics*, New York, Paragon House, 1987, 219-241.

McCHESNEY, Fred S., 'Economics, Law, and Science in the Corporate Field: A Critique of Eisenberg', **89** *Columbia Law Review*, 1989, 1530 ff.

MEIER-SCHATZ, Christian, 'Über die Notwendigkeit gesellschaftsrechtlicher Aufsichtsregeln, Ein Beitrag zur Ökonomischen Analyse des Gesellschaftsrechts' [On the Necessity of Rules for the Supervision of Corporations, A Contribution to the Economic Analysis of Company Law], *Zeitschrift für schweizerisches Recht,* 1988, I, 191-241.

MEIER-SCHATZ, Christian, 'Europäische Harmonisierung des Gesellschafts- und Kapitalmarktrechts' [European Harmonization of Company and Capital Market Law], **41** *Wirtschaft und Recht*, 1989, 84-110.

METZGER, Michael R., 'Corporate Criminal Liability for Defective Products: Policies, Problems, and Prospects', **73** *Georgetown Law Journal*, 1984, 1-88.

PASHIGIAN, B. Peter, 'A Theory of Prevention and Legal Defense with an Application to the Legal Costs of Companies', **25** *Journal of Law and Economics*, 1982, 247-270.

PASTOR, Santos, 'Comment' [on Aretz, Taxation and Incorporation], in WEIGEL, Wolfgang (ed.), *Economic Analysis of Law - A Collection of Applications*, Vienna, Österreichischer Wirtschaftsverlag, 1991, 133-134.

PAZ-ARES, Cándido, 'Sobre la infracapitalización de las sociedades' [On Infra-Capitalization of Corporations], *Anuario de Derecho Civil*, 1983.

PAZ-ARES, Cándido, 'Seguridad jurídica y seguridad del tráfico' [Legal Certainty and Exhange Certainty], *Revista de Derecho Mercantil*, 1985.

POSNER, Richard A. and SCOTT, Kenneth E. (eds.), *Economics of Corporation Law and Securities Regulation*, Boston, Little Brown, 1980, 384 p.

PREITE, Disiano, 'In tema di sollecitazione del pubblico risparmio' [Enhancing Public Savings], *Giurisprudenza commerciale*, 1986, II, 217-245.

ROMANO, Roberta, 'Law as a Product: Some Pieces of the Incorporation Puzzle', **1** *Journal of Law, Economics, & Organization*, 1985, 225-283.

RUBIN, Paul H., *Business Firms and the Common Law. The Evolution of Efficient Rules*, New York, Praeger, 1983, 189 p.

SCHMIDT, Reinhard H. and KÜBLER, Friedrich, *Gesellschaftsrecht und Konzentration* [Company Law and Concentration], Schriften zur wirtschaftswissenschaftlichen Analyse des Rechts, Vol.3, Berlin, Duncker und Humblot, 1988, 225 p.

SCHMITZ-HERSCHEIDT, Friedhelm, 'Ansätze zu einer ökonomischen Theorie des Gesellschaftsrecht' [Initial Stages to an Economic Theory of Company Law], in BOETTCHER, Erik, HERDER-DORNEICH, Philipp and SCHENK, Karl-Ernst (eds.), 2 Jahrbuch für Neue Politische Ökonomie, Tübingen, J.C.B. Mohr, 1983, 181-211.

SCHÜLLER, Alfred, 'Property Rights, Unternehmerische Legitimation und Wirtschaftsordnung. Zum vermögenstheoretischen Ansatz einer allgemeinen Theorie der Unternehmung' [Property Rights, Entrepreneurial Legitimation and Economic System. On the Property Rights Approach of a General Theory of the Enterprise], in SCHENK, K.E. (ed.), *Ökonomische Verfügungsrechte und Allokationsmechanismen in Wirtschaftssystemen*, Schriften des Vereins für Socialpolitik, Vol. 97, N.F., 1978, 29-87.

SHUGHART, William F., II and TOLLISON, Robert D., 'Corporate Chartering: An

Exploration in the Economics of Legal Change', **23** *Economic Inquiry*, 1985, 585-599.

STRASSER, Kurt A., BARD, Robert L. and ARTHUR, H. Thomas, 'A Reader's Guide to the Uses and Limits of Economic Analysis with Emphasis on Corporation Law', **33** *Mercer Law Review*, 1982, 571-593.

SYMPOSIUM : 'The ALI's Corporate Governance Proposals: Law and Economics', **8** *Delaware Journal of Corporate Law*, Fall 1984.

TIMMERMAN, L., 'Onderneming en vennootschap' [Enterprise and Firm], in *Piercing Van Schilfgaarde*, Deventer, Kluwer, 1990, 3-11.

von WEIZSÄCKER, C.C., 'Der Markt für unternehmensgebundene Ressourcen' [The Market for Enterprise Restricted Resources], *Strukturwandel und Wirtschaftsordnung, Referate des XX.FIW-Symposiums - FIW Schriftenreihe*, Heft 126, 1987, 31-42.

X, 'Note: Liability of Parent Corporations for Hazardous Waste Cleanup and Damages', **99** *Harvard Law Review*, 1986, 986-1003.

5510 The Theory of the Firm

ALCHIAN, Armen A., 'Development of Economic Theory and Antitrust: A View From the Theory of the Firm', **147** *Journal of Institutional and Theoretical Economics*, 1991, 232-234.

ALCHIAN, Armen A. and DEMSETZ, Harold, 'Production, Information Costs, and Economic Organization', **62** *American Economic Review*, 1972, 777-795.

AOKI, Masahiko, *The Cooperative Game Theory of the Firm*, Oxford, Oxford University Press, 1984.

AOKI, Masahiko et al. (eds.), *The Firm as a Nexus of Treaties*, London, Sage, 1989, 358 p.

AOKI, Masahiko, 'Toward an Economic Model of the Japanese Firm', **28** *Journal of Economic Literature*, 1990, 1-27.

AVERCH, H. and JOHNSON, L.L., 'Behaviour of the Firm under Regulatory Constraints', **52** *American Economic Review*, 1962, 1052-1069.

BACKHAUS, Jürgen G., 'The Emergence of Worker Participation: Evolution and Legislation Compared', **21** *Journal of Economic Issues*, 1987, 895-910.

BAYSINGER, Barry D. and BUTLER, Henry N., 'The Role of Corporate Law in the Theory of the Firm', **28** *Journal of Law and Economics*, 1985, 179-191.

BERLE, Adolf A. and MEANS, Gardiner C., *The Modern Corporation and Private Property*, New York, Macmillan, 1932.

BJUGGREN, Per-Olof and SKOGH, Göran (eds.), *Företaget. En kontraktsekonomisk analys* [The Firm. A Contractual Approach], SNS Publishing company, 1990.

BLACK, Robert A., KREIDE, Rosalie S. and SULLIVAN, Mark, 'Critical Legal Studies, Economic Realism, and the Theory of the Firm', **43** *University of Miami Law Review*, 1988, 343-360.

BOND, Ronald S. and GREENBERG, Warren, 'Industry Structure, Market Rivalry, and Public Policy: A Comment', **19** *Journal of Law and Economics*, 1976, 201-204.

BOUDREAUX, Donald J. and HOLCOMBE, Randall G., 'The Coasian and Knightian Theories of the Firm', **10** *Managerial & Decision Economics*, 1989, 147-154.

BRATTON, William W., Jr., 'The New Economic Theory of the Firm: Critical Perspectives from History', **41** *Stanford Law Review*, 1989, 1471-1527.

BUTLER, Henry N., 'Nineteenth-Century Jurisdictional Competition in the Granting of Corporate Privileges', **14** *Journal of Legal Studies*, 1985, 129-166.

BUTLER, Henry N., 'General Incorporation in Nineteenth Century England: Interaction of Common Law and Legislative Processes', **6** *International Review of Law and Economics*, 1986, 169-188.

BUXBAUM, Richard M., 'Corporate Legitimacy, Economic Theory, and Legal Doctrine', **45** *Ohio State Law Journal*, 1984, 515-543.

CARR, Jack and MATHEWSON, Frank, 'The Economics of Law Firms: A Study in the Legal Organization of the Firm', **33** *Journal of Law & Economics*, 1990, 307-330.

CHEUNG, Steven N. S., 'The Contractual Nature of the Firm', **26** *Journal of Law and Economics*, 1983, 1-21.

COASE, Ronald H., 'The Nature of the Firm', **4** *Economica*, 1937, 386-405. Reprinted in KRONMAN, Anthony T. and POSNER, Richard A. (eds.), *The Economics of Contract Law*, Boston, Little Brown, 1979, 31-32.

COASE, Ronald H., *The Firm, the Market and the Law*, Chicago, University of Chicago Press, 1988, 217 p.

COFFEE, John C., Jr., 'Unstable Coalitions: Corporate Governance As a Multi-Player Game', **78** *Georgetown Law Journal*, 1990, 1495-1549.

CYERT, Richard M. and MARCH, James G., *A Behavioral Theory of the Firm*, Englewood Cliffs, N.J. Prentice Hall, 1963.

DAVENPORT, Herbert Joseph, *The Economics of Enterprise*, New York, Macmillan, 1913, 544 p.

DEMSETZ, Harold, 'The Structure of Ownership and the Theory of the Firm', **26** *Journal of Law and Economics*, 1983, 375-390.

DEMSETZ, Harold, 'The Theory of the Firm Revisited', **4** *Journal of Law, Economics, & Organization*, 1988, 141-161.

EASLEY, David and O'HARA, Maureen, 'Contracts and Asymmetric Information in the Theory of the Firm', **9** *Journal of Economic Behavior & Organization*, 1988, 229-246.

EASTERBROOK, Frank H. and FISCHEL, Daniel R., 'Close Corporations and Agency Costs', **38** *Stanford Law Review*, 1986, 271-301.

EISENBERG, Melvin Aron, 'Bad Arguments in Corporate Law', **78** *Georgetown Law Journal*, 1990, 1551-1558.

EKELUND, Robert B., Jr. and TOLLISON, Robert D., 'Mercantilist Origins of the Corporation', **11** *Bell Journal of Economics*, 1980, 715-720.

EKERN, S., 'On the Theory of the Firm in an Economy with Incomplete Markets: an Addendum', **6** *Bell Journal of Economics*, 1975, 388-393.

EKERN, S. and WILSON, R., 'On the Theory of the Firm in an Economy with Incomplete Markets', **5** *Bell Journal of Economics*, 1974, 171-180.

ENGEL, David L., 'An Approach to Corporate Social Responsability', **32** *Stanford Law Review*, 1979, 1 ff.

FAMA, Eugene F. and JENSEN, Michael C., 'Agency Problems and Residual Claims', **26** *Journal of Law and Economics*, 1983, 327-349.

FISHEL, Daniel R., 'The Corporate Governance Movement', **35** *Vanderbilt Law Review*, 1982, 1259 ff.

FRECH, H. Edward III, 'Property Rights, The Theory of the Firm, and Competitive Markets for Top Decision Makers', **2** *Research in Law and Economics*, 1980, 49-63.

FRECH, H. Edward III and GINSBURG, Paul B., 'Property Rights and Competition in Health Insurance: Multiple Objectives for Nonprofit Firms', **3** *Research in Law and Economics*, 1981, 155-171.

FURUBOTN, Eirik G. and PEJOVICH, Svetozar, 'Property Rights, Economic Decentralization and the Evolution of the Yugoslav Firm, 1965-1972', **16** *Journal of Law and Economics*, 1973, 275-302.

GATIGNON, Hubert and ANDERSON, Erin, 'The Multinational Corporation's Degree of Control over Foreign Subsidiairies: An Empirical Test of a Transaction Cost Explanation', **4** *Journal of Law, Economics, & Organization*, 1988, 305-336.

GIFFORD, Adam, Jr., 'A Constitutional Interpretation of the Firm', **68** *Public Choice*, 1991, 91-106.

GRANT, Wyn, 'Corporatism and the Public-Private Distinction', in LANE, Jan-Erik (ed.), *State and Market. The Politics of the Public and the Private*, London, Sage, 1985, 158-180.

HALPERN, Paul J. and TURNBULL, Stuart M., 'Legal Fees Contracts and Alternative Cost Rules: An Economic Analysis', **3** *International Review of Law and Economics*, 1983, 3-26.

HANSMANN, Henry B., 'The Organization of Insurance Companies: Mutual versus Stock', **1** *Journal of Law, Economics, & Organization*, 1985, 125-153.

HART, Oliver D., 'Incomplete Contracts and the Theory of the Firm', **4** *Journal of Law, Economics, & Organization*, 1988, 119-139.

HESSEN, Robert, 'A New Concept of Corporations: A Contractual and Private Property Model', **30** *Hastings Law Journal*, 1979, 1327-1350.

HOVENKAMP, Herbert J., 'Antitrust Policy, Federalism, and the Theory of the Firm: An Historical Perspective', **59** *Antitrust Law Journal*, 1990, 75-91.

JENSEN, Michael C. and MECKLING, William H., 'Theory of the Firm: Managerial Behaviour, Agency Costs and Ownership Structure', **3** *Journal of Financial Economics*, 1976, 305-360.

JOHN, George and WEITZ, Barton A., 'Forward Integration into Distribution: An Empirical Test of Transaction Cost Analysis', **4** *Journal of Law, Economics, & Organization*, 1988, 337-355.

JOSKOW, Paul L., 'Vertical Integration and Long-Term Contracts: The Case of Coal-Burning Electric Generating Plants', **1** *Journal of Law, Economics & Organization*, 1985, 33-80.

KROLL, Heidi, 'Property Rights and the Soviet Enterprise: Evidence from the Law of Contract', **13** *Journal of Comparative Economics*, 1989, 115-133.

LANDERS, Jonathan M., 'A Unified Approach to Parent, Subsidiairy and Affiliate Questions in Bankruptcy', **42** *University of Chicago Law Review*, 1975, 589-652.

LANGBEIN, John H., and POSNER, Richard, A., 'Social Investing and the Law of Trusts', **79** *Michigan Law Review*, 1980, 72-112.

MANNE, Henry G., 'Our Two Corporate Systems: Law and Economics', **53** *Virginia Law Review*, 1967, 259-284.

MARCUS, Alan J., 'Risk Sharing and the Theory of the Firm', **13** *Bell Journal of Economics*, 1982, 369-378.

MASTEN, Scott E., 'The Organisation of Production: Evidence from the Aerospace Industry', **27** *Journal of Law and Economics*, 1984, 403-417.

MASTEN, Scott E., 'A Legal Basis for the Firm', **4** *Journal of Law, Economics, & Organization*, 1988, 181-198.

MASTEN, Scott E. and MEEHAN, James W., Jr. and SNYDER, Edward A., 'Vertical Integration in the U.S. Auto Industry: A Note on the Influence of Transaction Specific Assets', **12** *Journal of Economic Behavior and Organization*, 1989, 265-273.

MASTEN, Scott E., MEEHAN, James W., Jr. and SNYDER, Edward A., 'The Costs of Organization', **7** *Journal of Law, Economics, & Organization*, 1991, 1-25.

McNULTY, Paul J. and PONTECORVO, G., 'Mercantilist Origins of the Corporation: Comment', **14** *Bell Journal of Economics*, 1983, 294-297.

MEANS, Gardiner C., 'Corporate Power in the Marketplace', **26** *Journal of Law and Economics*, 1983, 467-485.

NUTZINGER, Hans G. and BACKHAUS, Jürgen (eds.), *Codetermination: A Discussion of Different Approaches*, Berlin, Springer, 1989, 309 p.

O'HARA, Maureen, 'Property Rights and the Financial Firm', **24** *Journal of Law and Economics*, 1981, 317-332.

POSNER, Richard A., 'The Rights of Creditors of Affiliated Corporations', **43** *University of Chicago Law Review*, 1976, 499-526.

RICKETTS, Martin, *The New Industrial Economics: An Introduction to Modern Theories of the Firm*, New York, St. Martin's Press, 1987, 305 p.

RUBIN, Paul H., 'The Theory of the Firm and the Structure of the Franchise Contract', **21** *Journal of Law and Economics*, 1978, 223-233.

SAJó, András, 'Diffuse Rights in Search of an Agent: A Property Rights Analysis of the Firm in the Socialist Market Economy', **10** *International Review of Law and Economics*, 1990, 41-59.

SCHANZE, Erich, 'Der Beitrag von Coase zu Rechte und Ökonomie des Unternehmens' [Coase's Contribution to Law and Economics of Business Organizations], **137** *Zeitschrift für die gesamte Staatswissenschaft*, 1981, 694-701.

SCHANZE, Erich, 'Theorie des Unternehmens und Ökonomische Analyse des Rechts' [Theory of the Firm and Economic Analysis of Law], in BOETTCHER, Erik, HERDER-DORNEICH, Philipp and SCHENK, Karl-Ernst (eds.), **2** *Jahrbuch für Neue Politische Ökonomie*, Tübingen, J.C.B. Mohr, 1983, 161-180.

SCHANZE, Erich, 'Potential and Limits of Economic Analysis: The Constitution of the Firm', in DAINTITH, Terence and TEUBNER, Gunther (eds.), *Contract and Organisation. Legal Analysis in the Light of Economic and Social Theory*, Berlin, Walter de Gruyter, 1986, 204-218.

SCHÜLLER, Alfred, 'Theorie der Firma und wettbewerbliches Marktsystem' [Theory of the Firm and Competitive Market System], in SCHÜLLER, Alfred (ed.), *Property Rights und ökonomische Theorie*, WiSt Taschenbuch, München, Vahlen, 1983, 145-183.

SKLIVAS, S.D., 'The Strategic Choice of Managerial Incentives', **18** *Rand Journal of Economics*, 1987, 452-460.

TIROLE, Jean, 'Hierarchies and Bureaucracies: On the Role of Collusion in Organizations', **2** *Journal of Law, Economics, & Organization*, 1986, 181-214.

WEISMAN, Dennis L., 'Optimal Re-Contracting, Market Risk and the Regulated Firm in Competitive Transition', **12** *Research in Law and Economics*, 1989, 153-172.

WEISS, Elliott J., 'Economic Analysis, Corporate Law, and the ALI Corporate Governance Project', **70** *Cornell Law Review*, 1984, 1 ff.

WEST, Richard R., 'An Economist Looks at the ALI Proposals', **8** *Delaware Journal of Corporate Law*, Fall 1984.

WIGGINS, Steven N., 'The Comparitive Advantage of Long-Term Contracts and Firms', **6** *Journal of Law, Economics, & Organization*, 1990, 155-170.

WILLIAMSON, Oliver E., *Markets and Hierarchies: Analysis and Antitrust Implication: A Study in the Economics of Internal Organization*, New York, Free Press, 1975, 286 p.

WILLIAMSON, Oliver E., 'The Modern Corporation: Origins, Evolution, Attributes', **19** *Journal of Economic Literature*, 1981, 1537-1568.

WILLIAMSON, Oliver E., 'The Logic of Economic Organization', **4** *Journal of Law, Economics, & Organization*, 1988, 65-93.

WINTER, Ralph K., Jr., 'State Law, Shareholder Protection, and the Theory of the Corporation', **6** *Journal of Legal Studies*, 1977, 251-292.

WINTER, Sidney G., 'On Coase, Competence, and the Corporation', **4** *Journal of Law, Economics, & Organization*, 1988, 163-180.

5520 Limited Liability

ADAMS, Michael, 'Eigentum, Kontrolle und beschränkte Haftung' [Property, Control and Limited Liability], in OTT, Claus and SCHÄFER, Hans-Bernd (eds.), *Ökonomische Probleme des Zivilrechts*, Berlin, Springer, 1991, 193-225.

AMSLER, Christine E., BARTLETT, Robin L. and BOLTON, Craig J., 'Thoughts of Some British Economists on Early Limited Liability and Corporate Legislation', **13** *History of Political Economy*, 1981, 774-793.

ANDERSON, Gary M. and TOLLISON, Robert D., 'The Myth of the Corporation as a Creation of the State', **3** *International Review of Law and Economics*, 1983, 107-120.

BLUMBERG, Phillip L., 'Limited Liability and Corporate Groups', **11** *Journal of Corporation Law*, 1986, 573-631.

BORDERS, James R., 'Note: The Growth of Lender Liability: An Economic Perspective', **21** *Georgia Law Review*, 1987, 723 ff.

BRANDER, James A. and SPENCER, Barbara J., 'Moral Hazard and Limited Liability: Implications for the Theory of the Firm', **30** *International Economic Review*, 1989, 833-849.

BYAM, John I., 'The Economic Inefficiency of Corporate Criminal Liability', **73** *Journal of Criminal Law and Criminology*, 1982, 582-603.

CARR, Jack L. and MATHEWSON, G. Frank, 'Unlimited Liability as a Barrier to Entry', **96** *Journal of Political Economy*, 1988, 766-784.

DEMSETZ, Harold, 'A Commentary on Liability Rules and the Derivative Suit in Corporate Law', **71** *Cornell Law Review*, 1986, 352-356.

EASTERBROOK, Frank H. and FISCHEL, Daniel R., 'Limited Liability and the Corporation', **52** *University of Chicago Law Review*, 1985, 89-117.

FAIRBURN, James and KAY, John (eds.), *Mergers and Merger Policy*, Oxford, Oxford University Press, 1989, 356 p.

FISCHEL, Daniel R., 'The Economics of Lender Liability', **99** *Yale Law Journal*, 1989, 131-154.

FORBES, Kevin F., 'Limited Liability and the Development of the Business Corporation', **2** *Journal of Law, Economics, & Organization*, 1986, 163-177.

HALPERN, Paul J., TREBILCOCK, Michael J. and TURNBULL, Stuart M., 'An Economic Analysis of Limited Liability in Corporation Law', **30** *University of Toronto Law Journal*, 1980, 117-150.

HELLWIG, Martin F., 'Bankruptcy, Limited Liability, and the Modigliani-Miller Theorem', **71** *American Economic Review*, 1981, 155-170.

KATZ, Wilber G., 'Responsibility and the Modern Corporation', **3** *Journal of Law and Economics*, 1960, 75-85.

LAWRENCE, William H., 'Lender Control Liability: An Analytical Model Illustrated with Applications to the Relational Theory of Secured Financing', **62** *Southern California Law Review*, 1989, 1387-1447.

LEHMANN, Michael, 'Das Privileg der beschränkten Haftung und der Durchgriff im Gesellschafts- und Konzernrecht. Eine juristische und ökonomische Analyse' [The Privilege of Limited Liability and the Peircing of the Corporate Veil in Association and Trust Law], *Zeitschrift fur Unternehmens- und Gesellschaftsrecht*, 1986, Heft 3, 345-370.

OLD, J.L., 'Some Economic Considerations of Limited Liability', **19** *Law Teacher*, 1985, 84-89.

ROTH, Günter H., 'Zur "economic analysis" der beschränkten Haftung' [On the 'Economic Analysis' of Limited Liability], *Zeitschrift für Untemehmens- und*

Gesellschaftsrecht, 1986, Heft 3, 371-382.

ROTH, Günter H., 'Kommentar' [Comment] (On Adams, Eigentum, Kontrolle und beschränkte Haftung), in OTT, Claus and SCHÄFER, Hans-Bernd (eds.), *Ökonomische Probleme des Zivilrechts*, Berlin, Springer, 1991, 226-233.

SILICIANO, John A., 'Corporate Behavior and the Social Efficiency of Tort Law', **85** *Michigan Law Review*, 1987, 1820-1864.

5530 The Separation of Ownership and Control

ADAMS, Walter and BROCK, James W., 'Efficiency, Corporate Power, and the Bigness Complex', **21** *Journal of Economic Education*, 1990, 30-50.

ALCHIAN, Armen A., 'The Basis of Some Recent Advances in the Theory of Management of the Firm', **14** *Journal of Industrial Economics*, 1965, 30-41.

ALCHIAN, Armen A., 'Corporate Management and Property Rights', in MANNE, Henry G. (ed.), *Economic Policy and the Regulation of Corporate Securities*, Washington, American Enterprise Institute for Public Policy Research, 1969.

AMIHUD, Y. and LEV, B., 'Risk Reduction as a Managerial Motive for Conglomerate Mergers', **12** *Bell Journal of Economics*, 1981, 605-617.

BAB, Andrew Laurance, 'Debt Tender Offer Techniques and the Problem of Coercion', **91** *Columbia Law Review*, 1991, 846-890.

BAJT, Aleksander, 'Property in Capital and in the Means of Production in Socialist Economics', **11** *Journal of Law and Economics*, 1968, 1-4.

BAYSINGER, Barry D. and BUTLER, Henry N., 'Corporate Governance and the Board of Directors: Performance Effects of Changes in Board Composition', **1** *Journal of Law, Economics & Organization*, 1985, 101-124.

BAYSINGER, Barry D. and ZARDKOOHI, Asghar, 'Technology, Residual Claimants, and Corporate Control', **2** *Journal of Law, Economics, & Organization*, 1986, 339-349.

BEBCHUK, Lucian Arye and KAHAN, Marcel, 'A Framework for Analyzing Legal Policy Towards Proxy Contest', **78** *California Law Review*, 1990, 1071-1135.

BHAGAT, Sanjai and BRICKLEY, James A., 'Cumulative Voting: The Value of Minority Shareholder Voting Rights', **27** *Journal of Law and Economics*, 1984, 339-365.

BJUGGREN, Per-Olof, 'Ownership and Efficiency in Companies Listed on Stockhold Stock Exchange 1985', in FAURE, Michael and VAN DEN BERGH, Roger (eds.), *Essays in Law and Economics. Corporations, Accident Prevention and Compensation for Losses*, Antwerpen, Maklu, 1989, 71-79.

BOARDMAN, Anthony E. and VINING, Aidan R., 'Ownership and Performance in Competitive Environments: A Comparison of the Performance of Private, Mixed, and State-owned Enterprises', **32** *Journal of Law and Economics*, 1989, 1-33.

BRADLEY, Michael and ROSENZWEIG, Michael, 'Defensive Stock Repurchases', **99** *Harvard Law Review*, 1986, 1377-1430.

BRADLEY, Michael and ROSENZWEIG, Michael, 'Defensive Stock Repurchases and the Appraisal Remedy', **96** *Yale Law Journal*, 1986, 322-338.

BRICKLEY, James A., BHAGAT, Sanjai and LEASE, Ronald C., 'The Impact of Long-range Managerial Compensation Plans on Shareholder Wealth', **7** *Journal of Accounting and Economics*, 1985, 115-130.

BRUDNEY, Victor, 'Corporate Governance, Agency Costs, and the Rhetoric of Contract', **85** *Columbia Law Review*, 1985, 1403-1444.

BUNDY, Stephen M., 'Commentary: Rational Bargaining and Agency Problems', **75** *Virginia Law Review*, 1989, 335-365.

CHOI, Dosoung, KAMMA, Sreenivas and WEINTROP, Joseph, 'The Delaware Courts, Poison Pills, and Shareholder Wealth', **5** *Journal of Law, Economics, & Organization*, 1989, 375-393.

CLARCKSON, Kenneth W. and MARTIN, Donald L. (eds.), *The Economics of Nonproprietary Institutions*, Greenwich, JAI Press, *Supplement 1 to Research in Law and Economics*, 1979, 330 p.

CLARK, William, 'Production Costs and Output Qualities in Public and Private Employment Agencies', **31** *Journal of Law and Economics*, 1988, 379-393.

COFFEE, John C., Jr., 'Shareholders Versus Managers: The Strain in the Corporate Web', **85** *Michigan Law Review*, 1986, 1-109.

COOTER, Robert D. and RUBIN, Edward L., 'Orders and Incentives as Regulatory Methods: The Expedited Funds Availability Act of 1987', **35** *UCLA Law Review*, 1988, 1115-1186.

CUTLER, David M. and SUMMERS, Lawrence H., 'The Costs of Conflict Resolution and Financial Distress: Evidence from the Texaco-Pennzoil Litigation', **19** *Rand Journal of Economics*, 1988, 157-172.

DALLAS, Lynne L., 'Two Models of Corporate Governance: Beyond Berle and Means', **22** *University of Michigan Journal of Law Reform*, 1988, 19 ff.

DE ALESSI, Louis, 'Private Property and Dispersion of Ownership in Large Corporations', **28** *Journal of Finance*, 1973, 839-851.

DEMSETZ, Harold and LEHN, Kenneth, 'The Structure of Corporate Ownership: Causes and Consequences', **93** *Journal of Political Economy*, 1985, 1155 ff.

DENNIS, Roger J., 'Mandatory Disclosure Theory and Management Projections: A Law and Economics Perspective', **46** *Maryland Law Review*, 1987, 1197 ff.

DODD, Peter and LEFTWICH, Richard, 'The Market for Corporate Charters: "Unhealthy Competition" vs. Federal Regulation', **53** *Journal of Business*, 1980, 1-41.

EASTERBROOK, Frank H., 'Managers' Discretion and Investors' Welfare: Theories and Evidence', **9** *Delaware Journal of Corporate Law*, 1984, 540-571.

EASTERBROOK, Frank H. and FISCHEL, Daniel R., 'Voting in Corporate Law', **26** *Journal of Law and Economics*, 1983, 395-427.

EASTERBROOK, Frank H. and FISCHEL, Daniel R., 'Mandatory Disclosure and the Protection of Investors', **70** *Virginia Law Review*, 1984, 669-715.

ECKEL, Catherine C. and VERMAELEN, Theo, 'Internal Regulation: The Effects of Government Ownership on the Value of the Firm', **29** *Journal of Law and Economics*, 1986, 381-403.

FAMA, Eugene F., 'Agency Problems and the Theory of the Firm', **88** *Journal of Political Economy*, 1980, 288 ff.

FAMA, Eugene F. and JENSEN, Michael C., 'Separation of Ownership and Control', **26** *Journal of Law and Economics*, 1983, 301-325.

FAMA, Eugene F. and JENSEN, Michael C., 'Agency Problems and Residual Claims', **26** *Journal of Law and Economics*, 1983, 327-349.

GARTH, Bryant G. and NAGEL, Ilene H. and PLAGER, Sheldon J., 'Empirical Research and the Shareholder Derivative Suit: Toward a Better Informed Debate', **48(3)** *Law and Contemporary Problems*, 1985, 137-159.

HANSMANN, Henry B., 'Ownership of the Firm', **4** *Journal of Law, Economics, & Organization*, 1988, 267-304.

HANSMANN, Henry B., 'When Does Worker Ownership Work? ESOPs, Law Firms, Codetermination, and Economic Democracy', **99** *Yale Law Journal*, 1990, 1749-1816.

HINDLEY, Brian, 'Separation of Ownership and Control in the Modern Corporation', **13** *Journal of Law and Economics*, 1970, 185-221.

HOLDERNESS, Clifford G., 'Liability Insurers as Corporate Monitors', **10** *International Review of Law and Economics*, 1990, 115-129.

JANJIGIAN, Vahan and BOLSTER, Paul J., 'The Elimination of Director Liability and Stockholder Returns: An Empirical Investigation', **13** *Journal of Financial Research*, 1990, 53-60.

JENSEN, Michael C. and MECKLING, William H., 'Theory of the Firm: Managerial Behaviour, Agency Costs and Ownership Structure', **3** *Journal of Financial Economics*, 1976, 305-360.

JENSEN, Michael C. and MURPHY, Kevin J., 'CEO Incentives - It's Not How Much You Pay, But How', **68** *Harvard Business Review*, May-June, 1990, 138 ff.

JOSKOW, Paul L., 'Asset Specificity and the Structure of Vertical Relationship: Empirical Evidence', **4** *Journal of Law, Economics, & Organization*, 1988, 95-117.

KLEIN, Benjamin, 'Contracting Costs and Residual Claims: The Separation of Ownership and Control', **26** *Journal of Law and Economics*, 1983, 367-374.

KLEIN, Benjamin, 'Vertical Integration as Organizational Ownership: The Fisher Body-General Motors Relationship Revisited', **4** *Journal of Law, Economics, & Organization*, 1988, 199-213.

KRAAKMAN, Reinier H., 'Corporate Liability Strategies and the Costs of Legal Controls', **93** *Yale Law Journal*, 1984, 857-898.

LAMBERT, R. and LARCKER, D., 'Golden Parachutes, Executive Decision-making and Shareholder Wealth', **7** *Journal of Accounting and Economics*, 1985, 179-204.

LEHN, Kenneth, 'Majority-Minority Relationships - An Economic View', **13** *Canada-United States Law Journal*, 1988, 135-141.

LEVIN, William R., 'The False Promise of Worker Capitalism: Congress and the Leveraged Employee Stock Ownership Plan', **95** *Yale Law Journal*, 1985, 148-173.

LIEN, Da Hsiang Donald, 'Competition, Regulation and Bribery: A Note', **11** *Managerial and Decision Economics*, 1990, 127-130.

LIPTON, Martin and ROSENBLUM, Steven A., 'A New System of Corporate Governance: The Quinquennial Election of Directors', **58** *University of Chicago Law Review*, 1991, 187-253.

LYNK, William J., 'Regulatory Control of the Membership of Corporate Boards of Directors: The Blue Shield Case', **24** *Journal of Law and Economics*, 1981, 159-173.

MacAVOY, Paul W., et al., *Privatization and State-Owned Enterprises: Lessons from the United States, Great Britain and Canada*, Boston, Kluwer, 1989, 360 p.

MACE, Myles L., *Directors, Myth and Reality*, Boston, Harvard Business School, 1971.

MALATESTA, Paul H. and WALKLING, Ralph A., 'Poison Pill Securities: Stockholder Wealth, Profitability and Ownership Structure', *Journal of Financial Economics*, 1989.

MANNE, Henry G., 'Some Theoretical Aspects of Share Voting: An Essay in Honor of MERLE, Adolf A.', **64** *Columbia Law Review*, 1964, 1427-1444.

MARRIS, R., *The Economic Theory of Managerial Capitalism*, New York, Free Press, 1964.

MURDOCK, Charles W., 'The Evolution of Effective Remedies for Minority Shareholders and Its Impact upon Valuation of Minority Shares', **65** *Notre Dame Law Review*, 1990, 425-489.

MURPHY, Kevin J., 'Corporate Performance and Managerial Renumeration: An Empirical Analysis', *Journal of Accounting and Economics*, 1985, April, 11-42.

PORTER, Philip K. and SCULLY, Gerald W., 'Economic Efficiency in Cooperatives', **30** *Journal of Law and Economics*, 1987, 489-512.

POSNER, Richard A., 'The Rights of Creditors of Affiliated Corporations', **43** *University of Chicago Law Review*, 1976, 499-526.

POUND, John, 'Shareholder Activisme and Share Values: The Causes and Consequences of Countersolicitations against Management Antitakeover Proposals', **32** *Journal of Law and Economics*, 1989, 357-379.

PREITE, Disiano, *La destinazione dei risultati nei contratti associativi* [The Destination of the Results in Partnership Contracts], Milano, Giuffrè, 1988, 456 p.

RADNER, Roy, 'A Note of Unanimity of Stockholders' Preferences among Alternative Production Plans a Reformulation of the Ekern-Wilson Model', **5** *Bell Journal of Economics*, 1974, 181-184.

ROE, Mark J., 'A Political Theory of American Corporate Finance', **91** *Columbia Law Review*, 1991, 10-67.

ROMANO, Roberta, 'The Shareholder Suit: Litigation without Foundation?', **7** *Journal of Law, Economics, & Organization*, 1991, 55-87.

ROSS, Stephen A., 'The Determination of Financial Structure: the Incentive-Signalling Approach', **8** *Bell Journal of Economics*, 1977, 23-40.

RYAN, Patrick J., 'Strange Bedfellows: Corporate Fiduciaries and the General Law Compliance Obligation in Section 2.01(a) of the American Law Institute's

Principle of Corporate Governance', **66** *Washington Law Review*, 1991, 413-502.

SCHWARTZ, Alan, 'Products Liability, Corporate Structure, and Bankruptcy: Toxic Substances and the Remote Risk Relationship', **14** *Journal of Legal Studies*, 1985, 689-736.

SCHWARTZ, Alan, 'The Sole Owner Standard Reviewed', **17** *Journal of Legal Studies*, 1988, 231-235.

SHLEIFER, Andrei and VISHNY, Robert W., 'Greenmail, White Knights, and Shareholders' Interest', **17** *Rand Journal of Economics*, 1986, 293-309.

SHLEIFER, Andrei and VISHNY, Robert W., 'Large Shareholders and Corporate Control', **94** *Journal of Political Economy*, 1986, 461-488.

SLAGTER, Wiek J., *Macht en onmacht van de aandeelhouder* [Shareholders (Lack of) Power], Deventer, Kluwer, 1988, 47 p.

SLAGTER, Wiek J., *Schaarse rechten. Afscheidscollege Rotterdam* [Scarce Rights], Deventer, Kluwer, 1989, 42 p.

STANO, Miron, 'Monopoly Power, Ownership Control, and Corporate Performance', **7** *Bell Journal of Economics*, 1976, 672-679.

STANO, Miron, 'Executive Ownership Interests and Corporate Performance', **42** *Southern Economic Journal*, 1978, 272-278.

STÅHL, Ingemar, 'Ägande och makt i företagen - en debattinledning, Nationalekonomiska Föreningens Förhandlingar' [Ownership and Power in the Firms - An Introduction to Debate, The Economics Association's Negotiations], *Ekonomisk Debatt*, 1976, No. 1.

WATTS, Ross L. and ZIMMERMAN, Jerold L., 'Agency Problems, Auditing, and the Theory of the Firm: Some Evidence', **26** *Journal of Law and Economics*, 1983, 613-633.

WEISS, Elliott J. and WHITE, Lawrence J., 'Of Econometrics and Indeterminacy: A Study of Investors' Reactions to "Changes" in Corporate Law', **75** *California Law Review*, 1987, 551-607.

WILLIAMSON, Oliver E., 'Managerial Discretion and Business Behaviour', **53** *American Economic Review*, 1963, 1032-1057.

WILLIAMSON, Oliver E., 'The Economics of Internal Organization: Exit and Voice in Relation to Markets and Hierarchies', **66** *American Economic Review. Papers and Proceedings*, 1976, 369-377.

WILLIAMSON, Oliver E., 'Organization Form, Residual Claimants, and Corporate Control', **26** *Journal of Law and Economics*, 1983, 351-366.

WINTER, R.A., 'Majority Choice and the Objective Function of the Firm under Uncertainty: Note', **12** *Bell Journal of Economics*, 1981, 335-337.

WINTER, Ralph K., Jr., 'State Law, Shareholder Protection, and the Theory of the Corporation', **6** *Journal of Legal Studies*, 1977, 251-292.

ADAMS, Michael, 'Der Markt für Unternehmenskontrolle und sein Mißbrauch' [The Market of Corporate Control and Its Abuse], *Die Aktiengesellschaft*, 1989, October, 333-338.

ADAMS, Michael, 'Höchststimmrechte, Mehrfachstimmrechte und sonstige wundersame Hindernisse auf dem Markt für Unternehmenskontrolle' [Maximum Voting Right, Multiple Voting Right, and some Wonderfull Obstacles from the Market of Corporate Control], **35** *Die Aktiengesellschaft*, 1990, 63-78.

ASQUITH, P., 'Merger Bids, Uncertainty and Stockholder Returns', **11** *Journal of Financial Economics*, 1983, 51-83.

AUERBACH, Alan J. (ed.), *Corporate Takeovers*, Chicago, University of Chicago Press, 1991, 354 p.

BAYSINGER, Barry D. and BUTLER, Henry N., 'Antitakeover Amendments, Managerial Entrenchment, and the Contractual Theory of the Corporation', **71** *Virginia Law Review*, 1985, 1257-1303.

BEBCHUCK, Lucian Arye, 'The Case for Facilitating Competing Tender Offers', **2** *Journal of Law, Economics & Organization*, 1986, 253-271.

BEBCHUK, Lucian Arye, 'The Sole Owner Standard for Takeover Policy', **17** *Journal of Legal Studies*, 1988, 197-229.

BEBCHUK, Lucian Arye and KAHAN, Marcel, 'A Framework for Analyzing Legal Policy Towards Proxy Contest', **78** *California Law Review*, 1990, 1071-1135.

BERKOVITCH, Elazar, BRADLEY, Michael and KHANNA, Naveen, 'Tender Offer Auctions, Resistance Strategies, and Social Welfare', **5** *Journal of Law, Economics, & Organization*, 1989, 395-412.

BITTLINGMAYER, George, 'Shareholder Heterogeneity and the Gains from Merger', in FAURE, Michael and VAN DEN BERGH, Roger (eds.), *Essays in Law and Economics. Corporations, Accident Prevention and Compensation for Losses*, Antwerpen, Maklu, 1989, 49-70.

BOOTH, Richard A., 'State Takeovers Statutes Revisited', **88** *Michigan Law Review*, 1989, 120 ff.

BOOTH, Richard A., 'The Problem with Federal Tender Offer Law', **77** *California Law Review*, 1989, 707-776.

BOUKEMA, C.A., 'Economische en juridische aspecten van Hoofdstuk I Fusiecode' [Economic and Legal Aspects of Chapter I Dutch Merger Rules], in COLJEE, P.D., FRANKEN, H., HEERTJE, A. and KANNING, W. (eds.), *Law and Welfare Economics*, Symposium 24 October, VU Amsterdam, 49-58.

BRAAKMAN, A.J., 'Europees kartelrecht als strijdmiddel bij overnames' [European Anti-trust Law as Takeover Combat Mechanism], **73** *Economisch-Statistische Berichten*, 1988, 854-858.

BRADLEY, Michael, Interfirm Tender Offers and the Market for Corporate Control, *Journal of Business*, 1980, 1-55.

BRICKLEY, James A. and JAMES, Christopher M., 'The Takeover Market, Corporate Board Composition, and Ownership Structure: The Case of Banking', **30** *Journal of Law and Economics*, 1987, 161-180.

BROWNE, Lynn E. and ROSENGREN, Eric S., 'Are Hostile Takeovers Different?', in BROWNE, Lynn E. and ROSENGREN, Eric S. (ed.), *The Merger Boom:*

Proceedings of a Conference Held at Melvin Village, New Hampshire, October 1987, Boston, Federal Bank of Boston, 1987, 199-229.

BUCKLEY, F.H., 'When the Medium is the Message: Corporate Buybacks as Signals', **65** *Indiana Law Journal*, 1990, 493-547.

CAVES, Richard E., 'Mergers, Takeovers, and Economic Efficiency: Foresight vs. Hindsight', **7** *International Journal of Industrial Organization*, Special Issue, 1989, 151-174.

COFFEE, John C., Jr., 'Regulating the Market for Corporate Control: A Critical Assessment of the Tender Offer's Role in Corporate Governance', **84** *Columbia Law Review*, 1984, 1145-1296.

COFFEE, John C., Jr., 'Are Hostile Takeovers Different? Discussion', in BROWNE, Lynn E. and ROSENGREN, Eric S. (ed.), *The Merger Boom: Proceedings of a Conference Held at Melvin Village, New Hampshire, October 1987*, Boston, Federal Bank of Boston, 1987, 230-242.

COFFEE, John C., Jr., LOWENSTEIN, Louis and ROSE-ACKERMAN, Susan (eds.), *Knights, Raiders, and Targets: The Impact of the Hostile Takeover*, Oxford, Oxford University Press, 1988, 547 p.

COHEN, Lloyd R., 'Why Tender Offers? The Efficient Market Hypothesis, the Supply of Stock, and Signaling', **19** *Journal of Legal Studies*, 1990, 113-143.

COHEN, Lloyd, 'Holdouts and Free Riders', **20** *Journal of Legal Studies*, 1991, 351-362.

CRAMTON, Peter and SCHWARTZ, Alan, 'Using Auction Theory to Inform Takeover Regulation', **7** *Journal of Law, Economics, & Organization*, 1991, 27-53.

DeANGELO, Harry, DeANGELO, Linda and RICE, Edward M., 'Going Private: Minority Freezeouts and Stockholder Wealth', **27** *Journal of Law and Economics*, 1984, 367-401.

DENIS, Debra K. and McCONNELL, John J., 'Corporate Mergers and Security Returns', **16** *Journal of Financial Economics*, 1986, 143-187.

DODD, Peter, 'The Market for Corporate Control: A Review of the Evidence', in STERN, Joel M. and CHEW, Donald H. (eds.), *The Revolution in Corporate Finance*, Oxford, Blackwell, 1986.

EASTERBROOK, Frank H. and FISCHEL, Daniel R., 'The Proper Role of a Target's Management in Responding to a Tender Offer', **91** *Harvard Law Review*, 1981, 1161-1201.

EASTERBROOK, Frank H. and FISHEL Daniel R., 'Corporate Control Transactions', **91** *Yale Law Journal*, 1982, 698-737.

EPSTEIN, Richard A., 'The Pirates of Pennzoil: A Comic Opera Made Possible by a Grant from the Texaco Corporation', **9(6)** *Regulation*, 1985, 18-24, 42.

FISCHEL, Daniel R., 'Efficient Capital Market Theory, the Market for Corporate Control and the Regulation of Cash Tender Offers', **57** *Texas Law Review*, 1978, 1-46.

FISHMAN, Michael J., 'A Theory of Preemptive Takeover Bidding', **19** *Rand Journal of Economics*, 1988, 88-101.

FRANKS, Julian and MAYER, Colin, 'Takeovers: Capital Markets and Corporate

Control: A Study of France, Germany and the UK', **0(10)** *Economic Policy: A European Forum*, 1990, 189-231.

GORDON, Jeffrey N. and KORNHAUSER, Lewis A., 'Takeover Defense Tactics: A Comment on Two Models', **96** *Yale Law Journal*, 1986, 295-321.

GROSSMAN, Sanford J. and HART, Oliver D., 'Takeover Bids, the Free-Rider Problem, and the Theory of the Corporation', **11** *Bell Journal of Economics*, 1980, 42-64.

GUERIN-CALVERT, Margaret E., McGUCKIN, Robert H. and WARREN-BOULTON, Frederick R., 'State and Federal Regulation in the Market for Corporate Control', **32** *Antitrust Bulletin*, 1987, 661-691.

HACKL, Jo Watson and TESTANI, Rosa Anna, 'Second Generation State Takeover Statutes and Shareholder Wealth: An Empirical Study', **97** *Yale Law Journal*, 1988, 1193-1231.

HADDOCK, David D., MACEY, Jonathan R. and McCHESNEY, Fred, 'Property Rights in Assets and Resistance to Tender Offers', **73** *Virginia Law Review*, 1987, 701-746.

HAHN, Dieter, 'Takeover Rules in the European Community: An Economic Analysis of Proposed Takeover Guidelines and Already Issued Disclosure Rules', **10** *International Review of Law and Economics*, 1990, 131-148.

HILL, Alfred, 'The Sale of Controlling Shares', **70** *Harvard Law Review*, 1957, 986-1039.

HIRSCHEY, Mark, 'Mergers, Buyouts and Takeouts', **76** *American Economic Review. Papers and Proceedings*, 1986, 317-322.

HIRSCHLEIFER, David and TITMAN, Sheridan, 'Share Tendering Strategies and the Success of Hostile Takeover Bids', **98** *Journal of Political Economy*, 1990, 295-324.

HOLL, Peter, 'Control Type and the Market for Corporate Control in Large U.S. Corporations', **25** *Journal of Industrial Economics*, 1973, 259-273.

HUSSON, B., *Le prise de contrôle d'entreprises* [Takeovers], Paris, Presses Universitaires de France, 1987.

JAMES, Christopher, 'An Analysis of the Effect of State Acquisition Laws on Managerial Efficiency: The Case of the Bank Holding Company Acquisitions', **27** *Journal of Law and Economics*, 1984, 211-226.

JARRELL, Gregg A. and BRADLEY, Michael, 'The Economic Effects of Federal and State Regulations of Cash Tender Offers', **23** *Journal of Law and Economics*, 1980, 371-407.

JARRELL, Gregg A., 'The Wealth Effects of Litigation by Targets: Do Interests Diverge in a Merge ?', **28** *Journal of Law and Economics*, 1985, 151-179.

JARRELL, Gregg A., BRICKLEY, J.A. and NETTER, J.M., 'The Market for Corporate Control: The Empirical Evidence since 1980', **2** *Journal of Economic Perspectives*, 1988, Winter, 49-68.

JARRELL, Gregg A. and POULSEN, Annette B., 'Shark Repellents and Stock Prices: The Effects of Antitakeover Amendements since 1980', **19** *Journal of Financial Economics*, 1987, 127-168.

JENNINGS, Richard W., 'Trading in Corporate Control', **44** *California Law Review*,

1956, 1-39.

JENSEN, Michael C., 'Takeovers: Folklore and Science', *Harvard Business Review*, 1984, No.6 (Nov./Dec.), 109-121.

JENSEN, Michael C., 'Agency Costs and Free Cash Flow, Corporate Finance, and Takeovers', **76** *American Economic Review. Papers and Proceedings*, 1986, 323-329.

JENSEN, Michael C., 'Takeovers: Their Causes and Consequences', **2** *Journal of Economic Perspectives*, 1988, Winter, 21-48.

JENSEN, Michael C., 'The Takeover Controversy: Analysis and Evidence', in COFFEE, John, LOWENSTEIN, Louis and ROSE-ACKERMAN, Susan (eds.), *Takeovers and Contests for Corporate Control*, New York, Oxford University Press, 1989.

JENSEN, Michael C. and RUBACK, Richard S., 'The Market for Corporate Control: The Scientific Evidence', **11** *Journal of Financial Economics*, 1983, 5-50.

JOHNSON, Lyman and MYLON, David, 'Missing the Point About State Takeover Statutes', **87** *Michigan Law Review*, 1989, 846-857.

KACKL, Jo Watson and TESTANI, Rosa Anna, 'Note: Second Generation State Takeover Statutes and Shareholder Wealth: An Empirical Study', **97** *Yale Law Journal*, 1988, 1193 ff.

KAMIN, Jacob Y. and RONEN, Joshua, 'The Effects of Corporate Control on Apparent Profit Performance', **45** *Southern Economic Journal*, 1978, 181-191.

KATZ, Wilbur G., 'The Sale of Corporate Control', **38** *Chicago Bar Record*, 1957, 376-380.

KING, Mervyn and ROELL, Ailsa, 'The Regulation of Take overs and the Stock Market', *National Westminister Bank Quarterly Review*, February 1988, 2-14.

KYLE, Albert S. and VILA, Jean-Luc, 'Noise Trading and Takeovers', **22** *Rand Journal of Economics*, 1991, 54-71.

LEECH, Noyes, 'Transactions in Corporate Control', **104** *University of Pennsylvania Law Review*, 1956, 725-839.

LEVMORE, Saul, 'Monitors and Freeriders in Commercial and Corporate Settings', **92** *Yale Law Journal*, 1982, 49-83.

LUTTER, Marcus and WAHLERS, Henning W., 'Der Buyout: Amerikanische Fälle und die Regeln des deutschen Rechts' [The Buyout: American Cases and the German Rules], **34** *Die Aktiengesellschaft*, 1989, 1-17.

MACEY, Jonathan R., 'Takeover Defense Tactics and Legal Scholarship: Market Forces versus the Policymaker's Dilemma', **96** *Yale Law Journal*, 1986, 342-352.

MACEY, Jonathan R., 'State Anti-Takeover Legislation and the National Economy', *Wisconsin Law Review*, 1988, 467 ff.

MACEY, Jonathan R. and McCHESNEY, Fred S., 'A Theoretical Analysis of Corporate Greenmail', **95** *Yale Law Journal*, 1985, 13-61.

MALATESTA, P., 'The Wealth Effect of Merger Activity and the Objective Functions of the Merging Firms', **11** *Journal of Financial Economics*, 1983, 155-181.

MALONEY, Michael T. and McCORMICK, Robert E., 'Excess Capacity, Cyclical Production, and Merger Motives: Some Evidence from the Capital Markets', **31** *Journal of Law and Economics*, 1988, 321-350.

MANNE, Henry G., 'The Higher Criticism of the Modern Corporation', **62** *Columbia Law Review*, 1962, 399-432.

MANNE, Henry G., 'Mergers and the Market for Corporate Control', **73** *Journal of Political Economy*, 1965, 110-120.

MANNE, Henry G., 'In Defense of the Corporate Coup', **11** *Northern Kentucky Law Review*, 1984, 513-518.

MARGOTTA, Donald G., McWILLIAMS, Thomas P. and McWILLIAMS, Victoria B., 'An Analysis of the Stock Price Effect of the 1986 Ohio Takeover Legislation', **6** *Journal of Law, Economics, & Organization*, 1990, 235-251.

MAULE, C.J., 'Antitrust and the Takeover Activity of American Firms In Canada: A Rejoinder', **12** *Journal of Law and Economics*, 1969, 419-424.

MAULE, C.J., 'Antitrust and the Takeover Activity of American Firms in Canada: A Final Comment', **13** *Journal of Law and Economics*, 1970, 261.

McCHESNEY, Fred S., 'Assumptions, Empirical Evidence and Social Science Theory', **96** *Yale Law Journal*, 1986, 339-341.

McKEE, David L. (ed.), *Hostile Takeovers: Issues in Public and Corporate Policy*, New York, Greenwood Press, 1989, 179 p.

MEIER-SCHATZ, Christian, 'Unternehmenszusammenschlüsse mittels Übernahmeangebot [Mergers by Takeover Bid]', **39** *Wirtschaft und Recht*, 1987, 16-39.

MNOOKIN, Robert H. and WILSON, Robert B., 'Rational Bargaining and Market Efficiency: Understanding Pennzoil v. Texaco', **75** *Virginia Law Review*, 1989, 295-334.

MORCK, Randall, SHLEIFER, Andrei and VISHNY, Robert W., 'Characteristics of Targets of Hostile and Friendly Takeovers', in AUERBACH, A.J. (ed.), *Corporate Takeovers : Causes and Consequences*, Chicago, University of Chicago Press, 1988, 101-129.

MORCK, Randall, SHLEIFER, Andrei and VISHNY, Robert W., 'Alternative Mechanisms for Corporate Control', **79** *American Economic Review*, 1989, 842-852.

POUND, John, 'The Effects of Antitakeover Amendements on Takeover Activity: Some Direct Evidence', **30** *Journal of Law and Economics*, 1987, 353-367.

POUND, John, LEHN, Kenneth and JARRELL, Gregg, 'Are Takeovers Hostile to Economic Performance?', **10(1)** *Regulation*, 1986, 25-30, 55-56.

PUGH, W.N. and JAHERA, J.S., Jr., 'State Antitakeover Legislation and Shareholder Wealth', **13(3)** *Journal of Financial Research*, 1990, 221-231.

RAMSEYER, J. Mark, 'Takeovers in Japan: Opportunism, Ideology and Corporate Control', **35** *UCLA Law Review*, 1987, 1-64.

REUBER, Grant L., 'Antitrust and the Takeover Activity of American Firms In Canada: A Further Analysis', **12** *Journal of Law and Economics*, 1969, 405-417.

REUBER, Grant L., 'Antitrust and the Takeover Activity of American Firms in

Canada: A Reply', **13** *Journal of Law and Economics*, 1970, 257-259.

RIETKERK, G., 'Bestuursonvriendelijke onderneming: een countervailing power. Een economische analyse' [Management Unfriendly Take-over: A Countervailing Power. An Economic Analysis], **66** *De Naamloze Vennootschap*, 1988, 45-54.

ROLL, Richard, 'The Hubris Hypothesis of Corporate Takeovers', **59** *Journal of Business*, 1986, 197-216.

ROLL, Richard, 'Empirical Evidence on Takeover Activity and Shareholder Wealth', in COPELAND T.E. (ed.), *Modern Finance and Industrial Economics: Papers in Honor of J. Fred Weston*, New York, Blackwell, 1987.

ROMANO, Roberta, 'The Political Economy of Takeover Statutes', **73** *Virginia Law Review*, 1987, 111-199.

RONEN, Joshua, 'Sale of Controlling Interest: A Financial Economic Analysis of the Governing Law in the United States and Canada', **13** *Canada-United States Law Journal*, 1988, 263-298.

RYAN, Patrick J., 'Corporate Directors and the "Social Costs" of Takeovers - Reflections on the Tin Parachute', **64** *Tulane Law Review*, 1989, 3-70.

RYNGAERT, Michael and NETTER, Jeffry M., 'Shareholder Wealth Effects on the Ohio Antitakeover Law', **4** *Journal of Law, Economics, & Organization*, 1988, 373-383.

RYNGAERT, Michael and NETTER, Jeffry, 'Shareholder Wealth Effects of the 1986 Ohio Antitakeover Law Revisited: Its Real Effects', **6** *Journal of Law, Economics, & Organization*, 1990, 253-262.

SCHERER, F.M., 'Corporate Takeovers: The Efficiency Arguments', **2** *Journal of Economic Perspectives*, 1988, Winter, 69-82.

SCHÜLLER, Alfred, 'Eigentumsrechte, Unternehmenskontrollen und Wettbewerbsordnung' [Property Rights, Corporate Control and Competition], **30** *ORDO, Jahrbuch für die Ordnung von Wirtschaft und Gesellschaft*, 1979, Stuttgart, G. Fischer Verlag, 325-364.

SCHUMANN, Laurence, 'State Regulation of Takeovers and Shareholder Wealth: The Case of New York's 1985 Takeover Statutes', **19** *Rand Journal of Economics*, 1988, 557-567.

SCHWARTZ, Alan, 'Search Theory and the Tender Offer Auction', **2** *Journal of Law, Economics, & Organization*, 1986, 229-253.

SCHWARTZ, Alan, 'Bebchuck on Minimum Offer Periods', **2** *Journal of Law, Economics, & Organization*, 1986, 271-277.

SCHWARTZ, Alan, 'The Fairness of Tender Offer Prices in Utilitarian Theory', **17** *Journal of Legal Studies*, 1988, 165-196.

SCHWARTZ, Alan, 'Defensive Tactics and Optimal Search', **5** *Journal of Law, Economics, & Organization*, 1989, 413-424.

SHLEIFER, Andrei and VISHNY, Robert W., 'Value Maximization and the Acquisition Process', **2** *Journal of Economic Perspectives*, 1988, Winter, 7-20.

STAPLETON, R.C., 'Some Aspects of the Pure Theory of Corporate Finance: Bankruptcies and Take-Overs: Comment', **6** *Bell Journal of Economics*, 1975, 708-710.

STIGLITZ, Joseph E., 'Some Aspects of the Pure Theory of Corporate Finance:

Bankruptcies and Take-Overs', **3** *Bell Journal of Economics*, 1972, 458-482.

STIGLITZ, Joseph E., 'Some Aspects of the Pure Theory of Corporate Finance: Bankruptcies and Take-Overs: Reply', **6** *Bell Journal of Economics*, 1975, 711-714.

STOUT, Lynn A., 'Are Takeover Premiums Really Premiums? Market Price, Fair Value, and Corporate Law', **99** *Yale Law Journal*, 1990, 1235-1296.

STULZ, René M., 'Managerial Control of Voting Rights: Financing Policies and the Market for Corporate Control', **20** *Journal of Financial Economics*, 1988, 25-54.

TRIPP, Malcolm A., 'Note: Access, Efficiency, and Fairness in *Dirks v. SEC*', **60** *Indiana Law Journal*, 1984, 535-557.

VAN GERVEN, Yves, 'Regulering van vijandige overnames. De Amerikaanse ervaring' [Regulation of Hostile Takeovers: The American Experience], *Rechtskundig Weekblad*, 1990-91, 833-844.

WEIDENBAUM, Murray L. and CHILTON, Kenneth W. (eds.), *Public Policy toward Corporate Takeovers*, New Brunswick, Transaction Books, 1988, 176 p.

WINTROBE, Ronald, 'The Market for Corporate Control and the Market for Political Control', **3** *Journal of Law, Economics, & Organization*, 1987, 435-448.

5550 Insider Trading

ANABTAWI, 'Toward a Definition of Insider Trading', **41** *Stanford Law Review*, 1989, 377 ff.

AUSUBEL, Lawrence M., 'Insider Trading in a Rational Expectations Economy', **80** *American Economic Review*, 1990, 1022-1041.

BOWLES, Roger, 'Comment' [on Fenn, McGuire and Prentice, Insider Trading Regulation after 1992], in WEIGEL, Wolfgang (ed.), *Economic Analysis of Law - A Collection of Applications*, Vienna, Österreichischer Wirtschaftsverlag, 1991, 143-145.

BRUDNEY, Victor, 'Insiders, Outsiders and Informational Advantages under the Federal Securities Laws', **93** *Harvard Law Review*, 1979, 322-376.

CARLTON, Dennis W. and FISCHEL, Daniel R., 'The Regulation of Insider Trading', **35** *Stanford Law Review*, 1983, 857-895.

COX, James D., 'Insider Trading and Contracting: A Critical Response to the "Chicago School"', *Duke Law Journal*, 1986, 628-659.

DE GRAUWE, Paul, 'Financial Deregulation in Developing Countries', **32** *Tijdschrift voor Economie en Management*, 1987, 381-401.

DEMSETZ, Harold, 'Corporate Control, Insider Trading, and Rates of Return', **76** *American Economic Review. Papers and Proceedings*, 1986, 313-316.

DENNERT, Jürgen, 'Insider Trading', **44** *Kyklos*, 1991, 181-202.

DOOLEY, Michael P., 'Enforcement of Insider Trading Restrictions', **66** *Virginia Law Review*, 1980, 1-89.

DOORENBOS, D.R. and ROORDING, J.F.L., 'Rechtseconomie en strafrecht: een rechtseconomische analyse van de bestrijding van misbruik van voorwetenschap bij de handel in effecten' [Law-and-economics and Criminal Law: A Law-and-economics Analysis of Insider Trading in Securities], **39(10)** *Ars Aequi*, 1990, 733-742.

EASTERBROOK, Frank H. and FISCHEL, Daniel R., 'Mandatory Disclosure and the Protection of Investors', **70** *Virginia Law Review*, 1984, 669-715.

FENN, Paul, McGUIRE, Alistair and PRENTICE, Dan, 'Insider Trading Regulation after 1992: An Economic Analysis', in WEIGEL, Wolfgang (ed.), *Economic Analysis of Law - A Collection of Applications*, Vienna, Österreichischer Wirtschaftsverlag, 1991, 135-141.

FINNERTY, Joseph E., 'Insiders and Market Efficiency', **31** *Journal of Finance*, 1976, 1141-1148.

FISCHEL, Daniel R., 'An Economic Analysis of Dirks v. Securities and Exchange Commission', **13** *Hofstra Law Review*, 1984, 127 ff.

HADDOCK, David D. and MACEY, Jonathan R., 'A Coasian Model of Insider Trading', **80** *Nortwestern University Law Review*, 1986, 1449-1472.

HADDOCK, David D. and MACEY, Jonathan R., 'Controlling Insider Trading in Europe and America: The Economics of the Politics', in GRAF VON DER SCHULENBURG, J.-Matthias and SKOGH, Göran (eds.), *Law and Economics and The Economics of Legal Regulation*, Dordrecht, Kluwer, 1986, 149-167.

HADDOCK, David D. and MACEY, Jonathan R., 'Regulation on Demand: A Private Interest Model, with an Application to Insider Trading Regulation' **30** *Journal of Law and Economics*, 1987, 311-352.

JAFEE, Jeffrey F., 'The Effect of Regulation Changes on Insider Trading', **5** *Bell Journal of Economics*, 1974, 93-121.

JARRELL, Gregg A. and POULSEN, Annette B., 'Stock Trading Before the Announcement of Tender Offers: Insider Trading or Market Anticipation?', **5** *Journal of Law, Economics, & Organization*, 1989, 225-248.

KELLY, William A., Jr., NARDINELLI, Clark and WALLACE, Myles S., 'Regulation of Insider Trading: Rethinking SEC Policy Rules', **7** *Cato Journal*, 1987, 441-448.

LAFFONT, Jean-Jacques and MASKIN, Eric S., 'The Efficient Market Hypothesis and Insider Trading on the Stock Market', **98** *Journal of Political Economy*, 1990, 70-93.

LANGEVOORT, Donald C., 'Insider Trading and the Fiduciary Principle: A Post-Chiarella Restatement', **70** *California Law Review*, 1982, 1-53.

LANGEVOORT, Donald C., 'Investment Analysts and the Law of Insider Trading', **76** *Virginia Law Review*, 1990, 1023-1054.

LORIE, James H. and NIEDERHOFFER, Victor, 'Predictive and Statistical Properties of Insider Trading', **11** *Journal of Law and Economics*, 1968, 35-53.

MANNE, Henry G., *Insider Trading and the Stock Market*, New York, Free Press, 1966, 189 p.

MANNE, Henry G., 'In Defence of Insider Trading', **44** *Harvard Business Review*, 1966, Nov./Dec., 113-122.

MANNE, Henry G., 'Insider Trading and the Law Professors', **23** *Vanderbilt Law Review*, 1969, 547 ff.

MANNE, Henry G., 'Insider Trading and Property Rights in New Information', in DORN, James A. and MANNE, Henry G. (eds.), *Economic Liberties and the Judiciary*, Fairfax, George Mason University Press, 1987, 317-327.

MITCHELL, P.L., *Directors' Duties and Insider Dealing*, London, Butterworths, 1982.

O'CONNOR, Marleen A., 'Toward a More Efficient Deterrence of Insider Trading: The Repeal of Section 16(b)', **58** *Fordham Law Review*, 1989, 309 ff.

RIDER, Barry A., 'Should Insider Trading Be Regulated? Some Initial Considerations', **94** *South African Law Journal*, 1977, 79-101.

SAMUELSSON, Per and SKOGH, Göran, 'Juridisk forskning i gränsområdet mot ekonomi - exemplet insiderhandel' [Legal Research and Economics - The Example of Insider Trading], in BASSE, Ellen Margrethe (ed.), *Regulering og styring - en juridisk teoriog metodebog*, 91-110.

SCHULTE, David J., 'Note: The Fraud on the Market Theory: Efficient Markets and the Defenses to an Implied 10b-5 Action', **70** *Iowa Law Review*, 1985, 975 ff.

SCOTT, Kenneth E., 'Insider Trading: Rule 10b-5, Disclosure, and Corporate Privacy', **9** *Journal of Legal Studies*, 1980, 801-818.

WOLFSON, Nicholas, 'Comment: Civil Liberties and Regulation of Insider Trading', in DORN, James A. and MANNE, Henry G. (eds.), *Economic Liberties and the Judiciary*, Fairfax, George Mason University Press, 1987, 329-334.

X, 'Note: Private Causes of Action for Option Investors Under SEC Rule 10b-5: A Policy, Doctrinal, and Economic Analysis', **100** *Harvard Law Review*, 1987, 1959-1978.

X (S.B.), 'Note: A Critique of the Insider Trading Sanctions Act of 1984', **71** *Virginia Law Review*, 1985, 455-498.

5560 Regulation of the Securities Market

ARROW, Kenneth J., 'The Role of Securities in the Optimal Allocation of Risk Bearing', **31** *Review of Economic Studies*, 1964, 91-96.

AYRES, Ian, 'Back to *Basics*: Regulating How Corporations Speak to the Market', **77** *Virginia Law Review*, 1991, 945-999.

BANOFF, Barbara Ann, 'Regulatory Subsidies, Efficient Markets, and Shelf Registration: An Analysis of Rule 415', **70** *Virginia Law Review*, 1984, 135-185.

BEAVER, William H., 'The Nature of Mandated Disclosure', in POSNER, Richard A. and SCOTT, Kenneth E. (eds.), *Economics of Corporation Law and Securities Regulation*, Boston, Little Brown, 1980.

BENSTON, George J., 'Required Disclosure and the Stock Market: An Evaluation of the Securities Exchange Act of 1934', **63** *American Economic Review*, 1973, 132-155.

BENSTON, George J., *Corporate Financial Disclosure in the U.K. and the U.S.A.*, 1976.

COFFEE, John C., Jr., 'Market Failure and the Economic Case for a Mandatory Disclosure System', **70** *Virginia Law Review*, 1984, 717 ff.

FISCHEL, Daniel R., 'Organized Exchanges and the Regulation of Dual Class Common Stock', **54** *University of Chicago Law Review*, 1987, 119-152.

FOX, Merritt B., 'Shelf Registration, Integrated Disclosure, and Underwriter Due Diligence: An Economic Analysis', **70** *Virginia Law Review*, 1984, 1005-1034.

FRIEND, Irwin and HERMAN, Edward S., *The SEC through a Glass Darkly*, **37** *Journal of Business*, 1964, 382-405.

FRIEND, Irwin and WESTERFIELD, Randolph, 'Required Disclosure and the Stock Market', **65** *American Economic Review*, 1975, 467-472.

GORDON, Jeffrey N., 'Ties That Bond: Dual Class Common Stock and the Problem of Shareholder Choice', **76** *California Law Review*, 1988, 1-85.

GORDON, Jeffrey N. and KORNHAUSER, Lewis A., 'Efficient Markets, Cstly Information, and Securities Research', **60** *New York University Law Review*, 1985, 761-849.

HADDOCK, David D., 'An Economic Analysis of the Brady Report: Public Interest, Special Interest, or Rent Extraction?', **74** *Cornell Law Review*, 1989, 841 ff.

HARDING, Don, 'Implications of the Efficient Market Hypothesis for Securities Regulation', in CRANSTON, Ross and SCHICK, Anne (eds.), *Law and Economics*, Canberra, Australian National University, 1982, 129-144.

INGRAM, Robert W. and CHEWNING, Eugene G., 'The Effect of Financial Disclosure Regulation on Security Market Behavior', **58** *Accounting Review*, 1983, 562-580.

JARRELL, Gregg A., 'The Economic Effects of Federal Regulation of the Market for New Security Issues', **24** *Journal of Law and Economics*, 1981, 613-675.

JARRELL, Gregg A., 'Change at the Exchange: The Causes and Effects of Deregulation', **27** *Journal of Law and Economics*, 1984, 273-312.

KIDWELL, David S., MARR, M. Wayne and THOMPSON, G. Rodney, 'Shelf Registration: Competition and Market Flexibility', **30** *Journal of Law and Economics*, 1987, 181-206.

KRIPKE, Homer, 'Can the SEC Make Disclosure Policy Meaningful', **31** *Business Lawyer*, 1975, 293-317.

LAX, David A., 'Commentary: Market Expectations of Bargaining Inefficiency and Potential Roles for External Parties in Disputes Between Publicly Traded Companies', **75** *Virginia Law Review*, 1989, 367-381.

LEE, M.H. and BISHARA, H., 'Securities Regulation and Market Efficiency', **5** *International Review of Law and Economics*, 1985, 247-254.

LEVMORE, Saul, 'Efficient Markets and Puzzling Intermediaries', **70** *Virginia Law Review*, 1984, 645-667.

LORIE, James H. and HAMILTON, Mary T., *The Stock Market: Theories and Evidence*, 1973.

LOSS, Louis, *Securities Regulation*, Boston, Little Brown, 1961.

LOSS, Louis, *Fundamentals of Securities Regulation*, Boston, Little Brown, 1983.

MACEY, Jonathan R. and HADDOCK, David D., 'Shirking at the SEC: The Failure of the National Market System', *University of Illinois Law Review*, 1985, 315 ff.

MACEY, Jonathan R. and MILLER, Geoffrey P., 'The Fraud-on-the-Market Theory Revisited', **77** *Virginia Law Review*, 1991, 1001-1016.

MACEY, Jonathan, MILLER, Geoffrey P., MITCHELL, Mark L. and NETTER, Jeffry M., 'Lessons from Financial Economics: Materiality, Reliance, and Extending the Reach of *Basic v. Levinson*, **77** *Virginia Law Review*, 1991, 1017-1049.

MANNE, Henry G., *Economic Policy and the Regulation of Corporate Securities*, 1969.

PALMER, Matthew S.R., 'The Economics of Law: the Sharebrokers Act 1908', **16** *Victoria University of Welington Law Review*, 1986, 277-301.

PILLE, G., 'Financiële instellingen en markten: 2. Secundaire effectenmarkt' [Financial Institutions and Markets: Secundary Securities Market], in *18de Vlaams Wetenschappelijk Economisch Congres, Brussel 8 en 9 mei 1987, Sociaal-economische Deregulering*, Brussel, V.E.H.U.B., 1987, 649-663.

ROE, Mark J., 'A Political Theory of American Corporate Finance', **91** *Columbia Law Review*, 1991, 10-67.

SAMUELSSON, Per, *Information och ansvar. Om BÔrsbolagens ansvar fór bristfällig informationsgiuning på aktiemarknaden* [Information and Remedies. Listed Companies and Their Responsibility for False and Misleading Information in the Stock Market], Stockholm, Norstedt, 1991.

SCHOLES, Myron S., 'The Market for Securities: Substitution versus Price Pressure Effects and the Effects of Information on Share Prices', **45** *Journal of Business*, 1972, 179-211.

SCHWERT, G. William, 'Public Regulation of National Securities Exchanges: A Test of the Capture Hypothesis', **8** *Bell Journal of Economics*, 1977, 128-150.

SCHWERT, G. William, 'Using Financial Data to Measure Effects of Regulation', **24** *Journal of Law and Economics*, 1981, 121-158. Reprinted in POSNER, Richard A. and SCOTT, Kenneth E. (eds.), *Economics of Corporation Law and Securities Regulation*, Boston, Little Brown, 1980.

SELIGMAN, Joel, Stock Exchange Rules Affecting Takeovers and Control Transactions', in COFFEE, John, LOWENSTEIN, Louis and ROSE-ACKERMAN, Susan (eds.), *Takeovers and Contests for Corporate Control*, New York, Oxford University Press, 1989, 465-498.

SIMON, Carol J., 'The Effect of the 1933 Securities Act on Investor Information and the Performance of New Issues', **79** *American Economic Review*, 1989, 295-318.

SLAIN, John J. and KRIPKE, Homer, 'The Interface between Securities Regulation and Bankruptcy: Allocating the Risk of Illegal Securities Issuance between Securityholders and the Issuer's Creditors', **48** *New York University Law Review*, 1973, 261-300.

STIGLER, George J., 'Public Regulation of the Securities Market', **37** *Journal of Business*, 1964, 117-142.

STOUT, Lynn A., 'The Importance of Being Efficient: An Economic Analysis of Stock Market Pricing and Securities Regulation', **87** *Michigan Law Review*, 1988, 613-709.

X, 'Note: Efficient Capital Market Hypothesis, Economic Theory and the Regulation of the Securities Industry', **29** *Stanford Law Review*, 1977, 1031-1076.

YOUNG, S. David, 'The Economic Theory of Regulation: Evidence from the Uniform CPA Examination', **63** *Accounting Review*, 1988, 283-291.

5570 Regulation of Financial Markets: General

ABRAHAM, J.P. a.o., *De overheidstussenkomst in het financiewezen: Effectief? Efficiënt?* [Government Intervention in Finance: Effective? Efficient?], *Bank-en Financiewezen*, Cahier 12/13, Brussel, 1981, 17-39.

ALTMAN, Edward I. and NAMMACHER, S.A., 'Anatomy and Portfolio Strategies of the High Yield Debt Market' in COPELAND, T.E. (ed.), *Modern Finance and Industrial Economics: Papers in Honor of J. Fred Weston*, New York, Blackwell, 1987, 168-199.

ARVAN, Lanny and BRUECKNER, Jan K., 'Efficient Contracts in Credit Markets Subject to Interest Rate Risk: An Application of Raviv's Insurance Model', **76** *American Economic Review*, 1986, 259-263.

BALTENSPERGER, Ernst, 'The Borrower-Lender Relationship, Competitive Equilibrium, and the Theory of Hedonic Prices', **66** *American Economic Review*, 1976, 401-405.

BARTH, James R., CORDES, Joseph J. and YEZER, Anthony M. J., 'Benefits and Costs of Legal Restrictions on Personal Loan Markets', **29** *Journal of Law and Economics*, 1986, 357-380.

BAXTER, William F., 'Bank Interchange of Transactional Paper: Legal and Economic Perspectives', **26** *Journal of Law and Economics*, 1983, 541-588.

BOWLES, Roger A. and PHILLIPS, Jennifer, 'Judgments in Foreign Currencies: An Economist's View (Notes of Cases)', **39** *Modern Law Review*, 1976, 196-201.

BOWLES, Roger A. and WHELAN, Christopher J., 'Judgments in Foreign Currencies: Extension of the Milangos Rule (Notes of Cases)', **42** *Modern Law Review*, 1979, 452-459.

BRADLEY, Michael D. and JANSEN, Dennis W., 'Deposit Market Deregulation and Interest Rates', **53** *Southern Economic Journal*, 1986, 478-489.

BRATTON, William W., Jr., 'The Economics and Jurisprudence of Convertible Bonds', *Wisconsin Law Review*, 1984, 667 ff.

BREALEY, Richard A., *An Introduction to Risk and Return from Common Stocks*, 1969.

BUNDT, Thomas and KEATING, Barry, 'Depository Institution Competition in the Deregulated Environment: The Case of the Large Credit Union', **20** *Applied Economics*, 1988, 1333-342.

BUSS, James A. and BUSS, William E., 'A Note on the Economic Impact from the

Financed Capitalist Plan', **3** *Research in Law and Economics*, 1981, 227-239.

CHEN, Andrew H. and MERVILLE, Larry J., 'An Analysis of Divestiture Effects Resulting from Deregulation', **41** *Journal of Finance*, 1986, 997-1010.

DALE, Richard (ed.), *Financial Deregulation: The Proceedings of a Conference Held by the David Hume Institute in May 1986*, Cambridge, Woodhead-Faulkner, 1986, 1-12.

DAUW, C., 'Financiële deregulering en financiering der investeringen' [Financial Deregulation and Financing of Investments], in *18de Vlaams Wetenschappelijk Economisch Congres, Brussel 8 en 9 mei 1987, Sociaal-economische Deregulering*, Brussel, V.E.H.U.B., 1987, 695-730.

DEMUTH, Christopher C., 'The Case against Credit Card Interest Rate Regulation', **3** *Yale Journal on Regulation*, 1986, 201-242.

DRUKARCZYK, Jochen, 'Ökonomische Analyse der Rechtsprechung des BGH zur Sittenwidrigkeit von Sanierungskrediten' [Economic Analysis of the Jurisprudence of the Bundesgerichtshof on the Immorality of Reorganization Credit], in *Kapitalmarkt und Finanzierung*, Jahrestagung des Vereins für Socialpolitik in München, 1987, 379-397.

DRUKARCZYK, Jochen, *Unternehmen und Insolvenz - Zur effizienten Gestaltung des Kreditsicherungs- und Insolvenzrechts* [Entrepreneurship and Insolvency - On the Efficient Shape of Safeguarding of Credits Law and Insolvency Law], Wiesbaden, Gabler Verlag, 1987, 424 p.

EKELUND, Robert B., Jr., HÉBERT, Robert F. and TOLLISON, Robert D., 'An Economic Model of the Medieval Church: Usury as a Form of Rent Seeking', **5** *Journal of Law, Economics, & Organization*, 1989, 307-331.

FAMA, Eugene F., 'Random Walks in Stock Market Prices', **21** *Financial Analysts Journal*, 1965, 55-99.

FAMA, Eugene F., 'Efficient Capital Markets: A Review of Theory and Empirical Work', **25** *Journal of Finance*, 1970, 383-417.

FAZIO, Antonio and CAPRIGLIONE, Francesco, 'Governo del credito e analisi economica del diritto' [Governing Credit and Economic Analysis of Law], *Banca, borsa, e titoli di credito*, 1983, I, 310-346.

FISCHEL, Daniel R., 'The Economics of Lender Liability', **99** *Yale Law Journal*, 1989, 131-154.

FOX, Eleanor M., 'Chairman Miller, the Federal Trade Commission, Economics, and Rashomon', **50(4)** *Law and Contemporary Problems*, 1987, 33-55.

FURNISH, Dale Back and BOYES, William J., 'Usury and the Efficiency of Market Control Mechanisms: A Comment on "Usury in English Law"', **1** *Arizona Journal of International and Comparitive Law*, 1982, 61-81.

GILSON, Ronald J. and KRAAKMAN, Reinier H., 'The Mechanisms of Market Efficiency', **70** *Virginia Law Review*, 1984, 549-644.

GORINSON, Stanley M., 'Depository Institution Regulatory Reform in the 1980s: The Issue of Geographic Restrictions', **28** *Antitrust Bulletin*, 1983, 227-254.

GOTTFRIES, Nils Torsten and PALMER, Edward, 'Regulation, Financial Buffer Stocks, and Short run Adjustment: An Econometric Case Study of Sweden, 1970-82', **33** *European Economic Review*, 1989, 1545-565.

HARAF, William S., 'Toward a Sound Financial System', **7** *Cato Journal*, 1988, 677-681.

HEREMANS, Dirk, 'The Complementary Nature of Competition and Regulation in the Financial Sector, Commission Revell', in VERHEIRSTRAETEN, A. (ed.), *Competition and Regulation in Financial Markets*, London, Macmillan, 1989, 32-34.

JAFEE, Jeffrey F. and LONG, J.B., Jr., 'Corporate Investment under Uncertainty and Pareto Optimality in the Capital Markets', **3** *Bell Journal of Economics*, 1972, 151-174.

JENSEN, Michael C., 'Risk, The Pricing of Capital Assets, and the Evaluation of Investment Portfolios', **42** *Journal of Business*, 1969, 167-247.

JOHNSON, Harry G., 'The International Monetary System and the Rule of Law', **15** *Journal of Law and Economics*, 1972, 277-292.

JUNOD, Charles-André, 'L'indexation des crédits hypothécaires pourrait-elle à la fois améliorer le fonctionnement du marché du logement et servir de correctif à l'inflation?' [Could the Indexation of Mortgage-debt Improve the Functioning of the Housing Market as Well as Serve as a Corrective for Inflation?], **40** *Wirtschaft und Recht*, 1988, 88-123.

KANE, Edward J., 'Technology and the Regulation of Financial Markets', in SAUNDERS, Anthony and WHITE, Lawrence J. (eds.), *Technology and the Regulaton of Financial Markets: Securities, Futures, and Banking*, Lexington, Lexington Books, 1986, 187-193.

KANE, Edward J., 'Interaction of Financial and Regulatory Innovation', **78** *American Economic Review. Papers and Proceedings*, 1988, 328-334.

KANE, Edward J., 'Changing Incentives Facing Financial Services Regulators', **2** *Journal of Financial Services Research*, 1989, 265-274.

KESSEL, Reuben A. and TRUMAN, A. Clark, 'A Study of Expectational Errors in the Money and Capital Markets, 1921-1970', **19** *Journal of Law and Economics*, 1976, 1-15.

KOHL, Helmut, KÜBLER, Friedrich, WALZ, W. Rainer and WÜSTRICH, Wolfgang, 'Abschreibungsgesellschaften, Kapitalmarkteffizienz und Publizitätszwang - Plädoyer für ein Vermögensanlagegesetz' [Tax Shelter Companies, Efficiency of Capital Markets and Information Regulation? - A Pleade for a Law Regulating the Public Offer of Investment Opportunities], **138** *Zeitschrift für das gesamte Handels- und Wirtschaftsrecht*, 1974, 1-49.

LANGBEIN, John H. and POSNER Richard A., 'Market Funds and Trust-investment Law', *American Bar Foundation Research Journal*, 1976, 1 ff.

LANGBEIN, John H. and POSNER Richard A., 'Market Funds and Trust-investment Law II', *American Bar Foundation Research Journal*, 1977.

LELAND, H.E. and PYLE, D.H., 'Information Asymmetries, Financial Structure and Financial Intermediation', **32** *Journal of Finance*, 1977, 371-387.

LESSER, William and MADHAVAN, Ananth, 'Economic Impacts of a National Deposit Law: Cost Estimates and Policy Questions', **21** *Journal of Consumer Affairs*, 1987, 122-140.

LITAN, Robert E., 'Evaluating and Controlling the Risks of Financial Product Deregulation', **3** *Yale Journal on Regulation*, 1985, 1-52.

MACEY, Jonathan R. and MILLER, Geoffrey P., 'Good Finance, Bad Economics: An Analysis of the Fraud-on-the-Market Theory', **42** *Stanford Law Review*, 1990, 1059-1092.

MEIER-SCHATZ, Christian, 'Europäische Harmonisierung des Gesellschafts- und Kapitalmarktrechts' [European Harmonization of Company and Capital Market Law], **41** *Wirtschaft und Recht*, 1989, 84-110.

MILLER Merton H. and MODIGLIANI Franco, 'The Cost of Capital, Corporate Finance and the Theory of Finance', **48** *American Economic Review*, 1958, 261 ff.

MOCHIZUKI, Hiroshi and MURATE, Satoshi, 'The Impact of Deregulation on Financial Markets in the United States and Japan: Is the Market Always Rights?', in FINN, Richard B. (ed.), *U.S.-Japan Relations: A Surpising Partnership*, Naw Brnswick, Transaction Books, 1987, 97-108.

MULHERIN, J. Harold and MULLER, Walter J., III, 'Volatile Interest Rates and the Divergence of Incentives in Mortgage Contracts', **3** *Journal of Law, Economics, & Organization*, 1987, 99-115.

MYHRMAN, Johan, HÖRNGREN, Lars, VIOTTI, Staffan and ELIASSON, Gunnar, *Kreditmarknadens spelregler* [The Rules of the Game on the Credit Market], SNS Publishing company, 1987.

NEAVE, Edwin H., 'Canada's Approach to Financial Regulation', **15** *Canadian Public Policy*, 1989, 1-11.

O'DRISCOLL, Gerald P., Jr., 'Deregulation and Monetary Reform', *Federal Reserve Bank of Dallas Economic Review*, July 1986, 19-31.

O'DRISCOLL, Gerald P., Jr., 'Deposit Insurance in Theory and Practice', **7** *Cato Journal*, 1988, 661-675.

PACOLET, J., 'Financiële instellingen en markten: 1. Deposito-instellingen' [Financial Institutions and Markets: Deposit Offices], in *18de Vlaams Wetenschappelijk Economisch Congres, Brussel 8 en 9 mei 1987, Sociaal-economische Deregulering*, Brussel, V.E.H.U.B., 1987, 623-647.

PINTO, Arthur R., 'The Third Abraham L. Pomerantz Lecture The First Amendment and Government Regulation of Economic Markets: The Nature of the Capital Markets Allows a Greater Role for the Government', **55** *Brooklyn Law Review*, 1989, 77 ff.

POLLEFLIET, E., '1992: regulering of deregulering van de financiële sector?' [1992: Regulation or Deregulation of the Financial Sector?], **42** *Economisch en Sociaal Tijdschrift*, 1988, 631-654.

PYLE, D.H., 'The Losses on Savings Deposits from Interest Rate Regulation', **5** *Bell Journal of Economics*, 1974, 614-622.

RIEBER, Michael, 'Bids Bid Patterns and Collusion in the Auction Market for Treasury Bills', **10** *Journal of Law and Economics*, 1967, 149-168.

RUBINSTEIN, M.E., 'Jan Mossin's Theory of Financial Markets', **4** *Bell Journal of Economics*, 1973, 693-699.

SALYZYN, Vladimir, 'Limitations on Asset Acquisition and the Competition for Savings Deposits', **5** *Journal of Law and Economics*, 1962, 93-102.

SCHANZE, Erich, *Investitionsverträge im internationalen Wirtschaftsrecht*

[Investment Contracts in International Economic Law], Frankfurt, Metzner, 1986, 305 p.

SCHÜRMANN, Leo, 'Konjunkturpolitik und freie Wechselkurse [Conjuncture Policy and Free Exchange Rate], in *Schweizerische Wirtschaftspolitik zwischen gestern und morgen*, Bern, Haupt, 1976, 265-277.

SKOGH, Göran, 'Vilken är den rättvisa räntan? Kritisk kommentar till förslag om räntelag' [What is the Fair Interest Rate? Critical Commentary on a Law Proposal Concerning Interest Rates], *Svensk Juristtidning*, 1975, 116-121.

SKOGH, Göran, 'Ett alternativ till den föreslagna konsumentkreditlagen' [An Alternative to the Proposed Consumer Credit Law], *Svensk Juristtidning*, 1976, 542-547.

SMITH, Vernon L., 'The Borrower-Lender Relationship', **66** *American Economic Review*, 1976, 406-407.

SPIERINGS, Renee, 'Reflections on the Regulation of Financial Intermediaries', **43** *Kyklos*, 1990, 91-109.

VAN CAYSEELE, Patrick and HEREMANS, Dirk, 'Legal Principles of Financial Market Integration in 1992: An Economic Analysis', **11** *International Review of Law and Economics*, 1991, 83-99.

VAN DEN BERGH, P., 'Deregulering van de internationale financiële stromen en valutastelsel' [Deregulation of the International Financial Flaws and Exchange System], in *18de Vlaams Wetenschappelijk Economisch Congres, Brussel 8 en 9 mei 1987, Sociaal-economische Deregulering*, Brussel, V.E.H.U.B., 1987, 845-878.

VARELA, Oscar and OLSON, Richard E., 'A General Equilibrium Analysis of Financial Regulation', **30** *Journal of Public Economics*, 1986, 329-340.

WALL, Richard A. and GORT, Michael, 'Financial Markets and the Limits of Regulation', **9(1)** *Managerial and Decision Economics*, 1988, 65-73.

WEST, Richard R., 'Bond Ratings, Bond Yields and Financial Regulation: Some Findings', **16** *Journal of Law and Economics*, 1973, 159-168.

5580 Regulation of Banking

ARONOWITZ, Daniel, 'Retracing the Antitrust Roots of Section 1972 of the Bank Holding Company Act', **44** *Vanderbilt Law Review*, 1991, 865-898.

BALTENSPERGER, E. and DERMINE, J., 'Banking Deregulation', *Economic Policy*, April 1987, 61-109.

BAXTER, William F., COOTNER Paul H. and SCOTT Kenneth E., *Retail Banking in the Electronic Age: The Law and Economics of Electronic Funds Tranfer*, 1977.

BENSTON, George J. et al., *Perspectives on Safe and Sound Banking: Past Present and Future*, Cambridge, MIT Press, 1986, 358 p.

BLACK, Fisher, MILLER, Merton H. and POSNER Richard A., 'An Approach to the Regulation of Bank Holding Companies', **51** *Journal of Business*, 1978,

379-412.

BURNHAM, James B., 'The Government Securities Act of 1986: A Case Study of the Demand for Regulation', **13(2)** *Regulation*, 1990, 78-84.

CABLE, John, 'Capital Market Information and Industrial Performance: The Role of West German Banks', **95** *Economic Journal*, 1985, 118-132.

COSENTINO, Fabrizio, 'Il contratto di servizio delle cassette di sicurezza: clausole di limitazione della responsabilità della banca e dichiarazione di valore' [The Contract for Services Related to Safety Deposit Boxes: Exemption Clauses for the Bank and Statement of Value], *Foro italiano*, 1990, I, 1292-1298.

DALE, R., *The Regulation of International Banking*, Cambridge, Woodhead-Faulkner, 1984.

EDWARDS, Linda N. and EDWARDS, Franklin R., 'Measuring the Effectiveness of Regulation: The Case of Bank Entry Regulation', **17** *Journal of Law and Economics*, 1974, 445-460.

EISENBEIS, Robert A., 'Expanding Banking Powers: The Present Debate', **7** *Cato Journal*, 1988, 763-769.

ENGLAND, Catherine, 'Agency Costs and Unregulated Banks: Could Depositors Protect Themselves?', **7** *Cato Journal*, 1988, 771-797.

FISCHEL, Daniel R., ROSENFIELD, Andrew M. and STILLMAN, Robert, 'The Regulation of Banks and Bank Holding Companies', **73** *Virginia Law Review*, 1987, 301-338.

FISCHER, Thomas G., GRAM, William H., KAUFMAN, George G. and MOTE, Larry R., 'The Securities Activities of Commercial Banks: A Legal and Economic Analysis', **51** *Tennessee Law Review*, 1984. 467 ff.

FRIEDER, Larry A., 'The Interstate Banking Landscape: Legislative Policies and Rationale', **6(2)** *Contemporary Policy Issues*, 1988, 41-66.

FRIEDMAN, Milton and SCHWARTZ Anna J., *A Monetary History of the United States, 1867-1960*, 1963, 299-419.

GOLEMBE, Carter H., 'Long term Trends in Bank Regulation', **2** *Journal of Financial Services Research*, 1989, 171-183.

GOODMAN, Laurie S., 'The Interface between Technology and Regulation in Banking', in SAUNDERS, Anthony and WHITE, Lawrence J. (ed.), *Technology and the Regulation of Financial Markets: Securities, Futures, and Banking*, Lexington, Lexington Books, 1986, 181-186.

HARAF, William S., 'Bank and Thrift Regulation', **12(3)** *Regulation*, 1988, 50-56.

HUERTAS, Thomas, 'Can Banking and Commerce Mix?', **7** *Cato Journal*, 1988, 743-762.

JOFFRION, Theresa and ROSE, Peter S., 'Savings and Loans' Response to Deregulation: Evidence from Multivariate Models and a National Survey', **6** *Housing Finance Review*, 1987, 17-38.

JONUNG, Lars, 'The Legal Framework and the Economics of Private Bank Notes in Sweden, 1831-1902', in SKOGH, Göran (ed.), *Law and Economics. Report from a Symposium in Lund, Sweden, 24-26 August 1977*, Lund, Juridiska Föreningen, 1978, 185-202.

KEELEY, Michael C. and FURLONG, Frederick T., 'Bank Regulation and the Public

Interest', **0(2)** *Federal Reserve Bank of San Francisco Economic Review*, 1986, 55-71.

KITCH, Edmund W., 'The Framing Hypothesis: Is It Supported by Credit Card Issuer Opposition to a Surcharge on a Crash Price?', **6** *Journal of Law, Economics, & Organization*, 1990, 217-233.

KOLLER, Ingo, 'Die Verteilung des Scheckfälschungsrisikos zwischen Kunde und Bank' [The Division of the False Cheque Risk Between Client and Bank], *Neue Juristische Wochenschrift*, 1981, 2433 ff.

LLEWELLYN, David T., 'Capital Regulatory Convergence: The Basle Regime', in WEIGEL, Wolfgang (ed.), *Economic Analysis of Law - A Collection of Applications*, Vienna, Österreichischer Wirtschaftsverlag, 1991, 146-162.

MEIGS, A. James, 'Evolution in Banking', **7** *Cato Journal*, 1988, 799-802.

MILLER, Stephen M., 'Counterfactual Experiments of Deregulation on Banking Structure', **28(4)** *Quarterly Review of Economics and Business*, 1988, 38-49.

NG, Kenneth, 'Free Banking Laws and Barriers to Entry in Banking, 1838-1860', **48** *Journal of Economic History*, 1988, 877-889.

O'DRISCOLL, Gerald P., Jr., 'The American Express Case: Public Good or Monopoly ?', **19** *Journal of Law and Economics*, 1976, 163-175.

ORDOVER, Janusz A. and WEISS, Andrew, 'Information and the Law: Evaluating Legal Restrictions on Competitive Contracts', **71** *American Economic Review. Papers and Proceedings*, 1981, 399-404.

PELTZMAN, Sam, 'Entry in Commercial Banking', **8** *Journal of Law and Economics*, 1965, 11-50.

PETTWAY, Richard H. and TAPLEY, T. Craig and YAMADA, Takeshi, 'The Impacts of Financial Deregulation upon Trading Efficiency and the Levels of Risk and Return of Japanese Banks', **23** *Financial Review*, 1988, 243-268.

RASMUSEN, Eric, 'Mutual Banks and Stock Markets', **31** *Journal of Law and Economics*, 1988, 395-421.

ROE, Mark J., 'A Political Theory of American Corporate Finance', **91** *Columbia Law Review*, 1991, 10-67.

SAUNDERS, Anthony and STROCK, Elizabeth and TRAVLOS, Nickolaos G., 'Ownership Structure, Deregulation, and Bank Risk Taking', **45** *Journal of Finance*, 1990, 643-654.

SHUGHART, William F., II, 'A Public Choice Perspective of the Banking Act of 1933', **7** *Cato Journal*, 1988, 595-613.

SHULL, Bernard, 'The Separation of Banking and Commerce: Origin, Development, and Implications for Antitrust', **28** *Antitrust Bulletin*, 1983, 255-279.

SMITH, Bruce D., 'Legal Restrictions, "Sunspots", and Peel's Bank Act: The Real Bills Doctrine Versus the Quantity Theory Reconsidered', **96** *Journal of Political Economy*, 1988, 3-19.

TAKIGAWA, Yoshio, 'Deregulation of Interest Rate and Bank Rate Policy', **0(32)** *Kobe University Economics Review*, 1986, 121-137.

THOMSON, James B. and TODD, Walker F., 'Rethinking and Living with the Limits of Bank Regulation', **9** *Cato Journal*, 1990, 579-600.

THUROW, Lester C., 'The Politics of Deregulation and Evolution of the Major Banks and the Financial Intermediaries in the U.S.A.', **3** *Review of the Economic Conditions in Italy*, 1985, 353-362.

VAN CAYSEELE, Patrick and HEREMANS, Dirk, 'Legal Principles of Financial Market Integration in 1992: An Economic Analysis', **11** *International Review of Law and Economics*, 1991, 83-99.

WEISBROD, Steven R., 'Regulation of International Banking: A Review Essay', **22** *Journal of Monetary Economics*, 1988, 347-352.

WHITE, Lawrence J., 'The Partial Deregulation of Banks and Other Depository Institutions', in WEISS, Leonard W. and KLASS, Michael W. (ed.), *Regulatory Reform: What Actually Happened*, Boston, Little Brown, 1986, 169-209.

WHITE, Lawrence J., 'The S&L Debacle: How It Happened and Why Further Reforms Are Needed', **13(1)** *Regulation*, 1990, 11-16.

X, 'Note: Consumer Protection and Payment Systems: Policy for the Technological Era', **98** *Harvard Law Review*, 1985, 1870-1889.

ZDRAHAL, Peter, 'Comment' [on Llewellyn, Capital Regulatory Convergence], in WEIGEL, Wolfgang (ed.), *Economic Analysis of Law - A Collection of Applications*, Vienna, Österreichischer Wirtschaftsverlag, 1991, 164-166.

5600 BANKRUPTCY PROCEEDINGS
Francisco Cabrillo

ALTMAN, Edward I., 'Bankrupt Firms Equity Securities as an Investment Alternative', **25** *Financial Analysts Journal*, 1969, 129-135.

ALTMAN, Edward I., 'A Further Empirical Investigation of the Bankruptcy Cost Question', **39** *Journal of Finance*, 1984, 1067 ff.

ANG, James S. and CHUA, Jess H., 'Coalitions, the Me-First Rule, and the Liquidation Decision', **11** *Bell Journal of Economics*, 1980, 355-359.

APILADO, Vincent P., DAUTEN, Joel J. and SMITH, Douglas E., 'Personal Bankruptcies', **7** *Journal of Legal Studies*, 1978, 371-392.

AUMANN, Robert J. and MASCHLER, Michael, 'Game Theoretic Analysis of a Bankruptcy Problem from the Talmud', **36** *Journal of Economic Theory*, 1985, 195-213.

BAIRD, Douglas G., 'The Uneasy Case for Corporate Reorganization', **15** *Journal of Legal Studies*, 1986, 127-147.

BAIRD, Douglas G., 'A World without Bankruptcy', **50(2)** *Law and Contemporary Problems*, 1987, 173-193.

BAIRD, Douglas G., 'Loss Distribution, Forum Shopping and Bankruptcy. A Reply to Warren', **54** *University of Chicago Law Review*, 1987, 815-834.

BAIRD, Douglas G. and JACKSON, Thomas H., 'Corporate Reorganizations and the Treatment of Diverse Ownership Interests: A Comment on Adequate Protection of Secured Creditors in Bankruptcy', **51** *University of Chicago Law Review*, 1984, 97-130.

BAIRD, Douglas G. and JACKSON, Thomas H., *Cases, Problems, and Materials on Security Interests in Personal Property*, Mineola, Foundation Press, 1987, 889 p.

BAIRD, Douglas G. and JACKSON, Thomas H., 'Bargaining after the Fall and the Contours of the Absolute Priority Rule', **55** *University of Chicago Law Review*, 1988, 738-789.

BAIRD, Douglas G. and PICKER, Ronald C., 'A Simple Noncooperative Bargaining Model of Corporate Reorganizations', **20** *Journal of Legal Studies*, 1991, 311-349.

BEBCHUCK, Lucian Arye, 'A New Approach to Corporate Reorganizations', **101** *Harvard Law Review*, 1988, 775-804.

BISDAL, Joaquím, *La empresa en crisis y el derecho de quiebras* [The Crisis of the Firm and Bankruptcy Law], Bolonia, Real Colegio de España, 1986, 383 p.

BOWERS, James W., 'Groping and Coping in the Shadow of Murphy's Law: Bankruptcy Theory and the Elementary Economics of Failure', **88** *Michigan Law Review*, 1990, 2097-2150.

BOYES, William J. and FAITH, Roger L., 'Some Effects of the Bankruptcy Reform Act of 1978', **29** *Journal of Law and Economics*, 1986, 139-149.

BRATTON, Dale, 'Note: The California Agricultural Producer's Lien, Processing Company Insolvencies, and Federal Bankruptcy Law: An Evaluation and

Alternative Methods of Protecting Farmers', **36** *Hastings Law Journal*, 1985, 609-644.

BRIMMER, Andrew, 'Economic Implications of Personal Bankruptcies', **35** *Personal Finance Law Quarterly Report*, 1981, 187-191.

BULOW, Jeremy I. and SHOVEN, John B., 'The Bankruptcy Decision', **9** *Bell Journal of Economics*, 1978, 437-456.

CABRILLO, Francisco, 'Adam Smith on Bankruptcy Law. New Law and Economics in the Glasgow Lectures?', **8** *History of Economics Society Bulletin*, 1986, 1 ff.

CABRILLO, Francisco, *Quiebra y liquidación de empresas* [Bankruptcy and Closing Down of Firms], Madrid, Unión editorial, 1989, 151 p.

CABRILLO, Franscisco, *Análisis económico de derecho concursal español* [An Economic Analysis of Spanish Bankruptcy Law], Madrid, Fundación Juan March, 1987, 53 p.

CARLSON, David Gray, 'Is Fraudulent Conveyance Law Efficient?', **9** *Cardozo Law Review*, 1987, 643-683.

CARLSON, David Gray, 'Philosophy in Bankruptcy', **85** *Michigan Law Review*, 1987, 1341-1389.

CHIANG, Raymond and FINKELSTEIN, John M., 'An Incentive Framework for Evaluating the Impact of Loan Provisions on Default Risk', **49** *Southern Economic Journal*, 1982, 962-969.

CHOW, Garland and GRITTA, Richard D., 'Estimating Bankruptcy Risks Facing Class I and II Motor Carriers: An Industry-Specific Approach', **55** *Transportation Practitioners Journal*, 1988, 352-363.

COOTER, Robert D., 'Defective Warnings, Remote Causes, and Bankruptcy: Comment on Schwartz', **14** *Journal of Legal Studies*, 1985, 737-750.

COUNTRYMAN, Vern, 'The Concept of Voidable Preference in Bankruptcy', **38** *Vanderbilt Law Review*, 1985, 713-828.

CURME, Michael and KAHN, Lawrence, 'The Impact of the Threat of Bankruptcy on the Structure of Compensation', **8** *Journal of Labor Economics*, 1990, 419-447.

DRUKARCZYK, Jochen, *Unternehmen und Insolvenz - Zur effizienten Gestaltung des Kreditsicherungs- und Insolvenzrechts* [Entrepreneurship and Insolvency - On the Efficient Shape of Safeguarding of Credits Law and Insolvency Law], Wiesbaden, Gabler Verlag, 1987, 424 p.

DYE, Ronald A., 'An Economic Analysis of Bankruptcy Statutes', **24** *Economic Inquiry*, 1986, 417-428.

EISENBERG, Theodore, 'Bankruptcy Law in Perspective', **28** *UCLA Law Review*, 1981, 953-999.

EISENBERG, Theodore, 'Bankruptcy in the Administrative State', **50(2)** *Law and Contemporary Problems*, 1987, 3-52.

EISENBERG, Theodore, 'Commentary on "On the Nature of Bankruptcy": Bankruptcy and Bargaining', **75** *Virginia Law Review*, 1989, 205-218.

FLETCHER, Ian F., 'Bankruptcy Notices: Perils and Perplexities', *Journal of Business Law*, 1984, 355-357.

GOLBE, D.L., 'The Effects of Imminent Bankruptcy on Stockholder Risk Preferences and Behavior', **12** *Bell Journal of Economics*, 1981, 321-328.

GOLDBERG, Victor P., 'Economic Aspects of Bankruptcy Law: Comment', **141** *Zeitschrift für die gesamte Staatswissenschaft*, 1985, 99-103.

GUATRI, Luigi, *Crisi e risanamento delle imprese* [Crisis and Reorganization of the Firms], Milano, Giuffrè, 1986, 339 p.

HARRIS, Richard, 'The Consequences of Costly Default', **16** *Economic Inquiry*, 1978, 477-496.

HARRIS, Steven L., 'A Reply to Theodore Eisenberg's Bankruptcy Law in Perspective', **30** *UCLA Law Review*, 327 ff.

HARRIS, Steven, 'A Reply to Theodore Eisenberg's Bankruptcy Law in Perspective', **30** *UCLA Law Review*, 1982, 327-365.

HAX, Herbert, 'Economic Aspects of Bankruptcy Law', **141** *Zeitschrift für die gesamte Staatswissenschaft*, 1985, 80-98.

HUDSON, John, 'The Corporate Bankruptcy Decision: Comment', **4** *Journal of Economic Perspectives*, 1990, 209-211.

IWICKI, Matthew L., 'Accounting for Relational Financing in the Creditors' Ex Ante Bargain: Beyond the General Average Model', **76** *Virginia Law Review*, 1990, 815-851.

JACKSON, Thomas H., 'Bankruptcy, Non-Bankruptcy Entitlements, and the Creditors' Bargain', **91** *Yale Law Journal*, 1982, 857-907.

JACKSON, Thomas H., 'Avoiding Powers in Bankruptcy', **36** *Stanford Law Review*, 1984, 725-787.

JACKSON, Thomas H., 'Translating Assets and Liabilities to the Bankruptcy Forum', **14** *Journal of Legal Studies*, 1985, 73-114.

JACKSON, Thomas H., 'The Fresh-Start Policy in Bankruptcy Law', **98** *Harvard Law Review*, 1985, 1393-1448.

JACKSON, Thomas H., *The Logic and Limits of Bankruptcy Law*, Cambridge, Harvard University Press, 1986, 287 p.

JACKSON, Thomas H., 'Of Liquidation, Continuation, and Delay: An Analysis of Bankruptcy Policy and Nonbankruptcy Rules', **60** *American Bankruptcy Law Journal*, 1986, 399-428.

JACKSON, Thomas H. and SCOTT, Robert E., 'On the Nature of Bankruptcy: An Essay on Bankruptcy Sharing and the Creditors' Bargain', **75** *Virginia Law Review*, 1989, 155-204.

JOHNSON, Steven B., 'Bankruptcy Reform and Its International Competitive Implications', **9** *Harvard Journal of Law & Public Policy*, 1986, 667-681.

KELLY, Thomas O. III, 'Compensation for Time Value as Part of the Adequate Protection during the Automatic Stay in Bankruptcy', **50** *University of Chicago Law Review*, 1983, 305-325.

KOROBKIN, Donald R., 'Rehabilitating Values: A Jurisprudence of Bankruptcy', **91** *Columbia Law Review*, 1991, 717-789.

LANDERS, Jonathan M., 'A Unified Approach to Parent, Subsidiairy and Affiliate Questions in Bankruptcy', **42** *University of Chicago Law Review*, 1975, 589-652.

LEFF, Arthur A., 'Injury, Ignorance and Spite - The Dynamics of Coercive Collection', **80** *Yale Law Journal*, 1970, 1-46. Reprinted in KRONMAN, Anthony T. and POSNER, Richard A. (eds.), *The Economics of Contract Law*, Boston, Little Brown, 1979, 175-181.

LOPUCKI, Lynn M., 'The Debtor in Full Control. Systems Failure notwithstanding Chapter 11 of the Bankruptcy Code?', **57(2-3)** *American Bankruptcy Law Journal*, 1983, 99-126 and 247-273.

McCOID, John C. II, 'Bankruptcy, Preferences, and Efficiency: An Expression of Doubt', **67** *Virginia Law Review*, 1981, 249-273.

MECKLING, William H., 'Financial Markets, Default and Bankruptcy: The Role of the State', **41(4)** *Law and Contemporary Problems*, 1977, 13-38.

MILLER, Merton H., 'The Wealth Transfers and Bankruptcy: Some Illustrative Examples', **41(4)** *Law and Contemporary Problems*, 1977, 39-46.

MORRIS, C. Robert, Jr., 'Bankruptcy Law Reform: Preferences, Secret Liens and Floating Liens', **54** *Minnesota Law Review*, 1970, 737-774.

NELSON, Philip B., 'Contracts Between a Firm and Its Constituents during Bankruptcy Crises', **13** *Journal of Economic Issues*, 1979, 583-604.

PETERSON, Richard L. and AOKI, Kiyomi, 'Bankruptcy Filings before and after Implementation of the Bankruptcy Reform Law', **36** *Journal of Economics and Business*, 1984, 95-105.

REA, Samuel A., Jr., 'Arm-breaking, Consumer Credit and Personal Bankruptcy', **22** *Economic Inquiry*, 1984, 188-208.

ROE, Mark, 'Bankruptcy and Debt: A New Model for Corporate Reorganization', **83** *Columbia Law Review*, 1983, 527-602.

ROE, Mark J., 'Commentary on "On the Nature of Bankruptcy": Bankruptcy, Priority, and Economics', **75** *Virginia Law Review*, 1989, 219-240.

ROSE-ACKERMAN, Susan, 'Risk Taking and Ruin: Bankruptcy and Investment Choice', **20** *Journal of Legal Studies*, 1991, 277-310.

SAYAG, Alain and SERBAT, Henri, *L'application du droit de la faillite. Eléments pour un bilan* [The Application of Bankruptcy Law. Data for an Evaluation], Paris, Librairies Techniques, 1982.

SCHMIDT, Reinhard H., *Ökonomische Analyse des Insolvenzrechts* [Economic Analysis of Insolvency Law], Wiesbaden, Gabler, 1981, 155 p.

SCHMIDT, Reinhardt H., 'Die ökonomische Grundstruktur der Insolvenz Recht' [The Economic Basic Structure of Bankruptcy Law], *Die Aktiengesellschaft*, 1981, 35-44.

SCHWARTZ, Alan, 'Security Interests and Bankruptcy Priorities: A Review of Current Theories', **10** *Journal of Legal Studies*, 1981, 1-37.

SCHWARTZ, Alan, 'Products Liability, Corporate Structure, and Bankruptcy: Toxic Substances and the Remote Risk Relationship', **14** *Journal of Legal Studies*, 1985, 689-736.

SCOTT, Robert E., 'Through Bankruptcy with the Creditors' Bargain Heuristic', **53** *University of Chicago Law Review*, 1986, 690-708.

SCOTT, Robert E., 'Sharing the Risks of Bankruptcy: Timbers, Ahlers, and Beyond', *Columbia Business Law Review*, 1989, 183-194.

SHEPARD, Lawrence, 'Personal Failures and the Bankruptcy Reform Act of 1978', **27** *Journal of Law and Economics*, 1984, 419-437.

SHIERS, Alden F. and WILLIAMSON, Daniel P., 'Nonbusiness Bankruptcies and the Law: Some Empirical Results', **21** *Journal of Consumer Affairs*, 1987, 277-292.

SLAIN, John J. and KRIPKE, Homer, 'The Interface between Securities Regulation and Bankruptcy: Allocating the Risk of Illegal Securities Issuance between Securityholders and the Issuer's Creditors', **48** *New York University Law Review*, 1973, 261-300.

STERN, Jeffrey, 'Note: Failed Markets and Failed Solutions: The Unwitting Formulation of the Corporate Reorganization Technique', **90** *Columbia Law Review*, 1990, 783 ff.

SULLIVAN, A. Charlene and WORDEN, Debra Drecnik, 'Rehabilitation or Liquidation: Consumers' Choices in Bankruptcy', **24** *Journal of Consumer Affairs*, 1990, 69-88.

SULLIVAN, Teresa A. and WARREN, Elizabeth and WESTBROOK, Jay Lawrence, 'The Use of Empirical Data in Formulating Bankruptcy Policy', **50(2)** *Law and Contemporary Problems*, 1987, 195-235.

SWARD, Ellen E., 'Resolving Conflicts between Bankruptcy Law and the State Police Power', *Wisconsin Law Review*, 1987, 403-453.

SYMPOSIUM : 'The Economics of Bankruptcy Reform', **41(4)** *Law and Contemporary Problems*, 1977, 206 p.

TARZIA, Giuseppe, 'Credito bancario e risanamento dell'impresa nella procedura di amministrazione straordinaria' [Credit and the Reorganization of the Firm], *Giurisprudenza commerciale*, I, 1983, 340-352.

TROST, J. Ronald, 'Corporate Bankruptcy Reorganization for the Benefit of Creditors or Stockholders?', **21** *UCLA Law Review*, 1973, 540-552.

TROST, J. Ronald, 'Business Reorganizations under Chapter 11 of the New Bankruptcy Code', **34** *Business Lawyer*, 1979, 1309-1346.

TUSSING, Dale A., 'The Case for Bank Failure', **10** *Journal of Law and Economics*, 1967, 129-147.

WARNER, Jerold B., 'Bankruptcy Costs: Some Evidence', **32** *Journal of Finance*, 1977, 337 ff.

WARNER, Jerold B., 'Bankruptcy Absolute Priority Rule and Pricing of Risky Debt Claims', **4** *Journal of Financial Economics*, 1977, 239-276.

WARREN, Elizabeth, 'Reducing Bankruptcy Protection for Consumers: A Response', **72** *Georgetown Law Journal*, 1984, 1333-1357.

WARREN, Elizabeth, 'Bankruptcy Policy', **54** *University of Chicago Law Review*, 1987, 775-814.

WEISTART, John C., 'The Costs of Bankruptcy', **41(4)** *Law and Contemporary Problems*, 1977, 107-122.

WESTON, J. Fred, 'Some Economic Fundamentals for an Analysis of Bankruptcy', **41(4)** *Law and Contemporary Problems*, 1977, 47-65.

WHITE, Michelle J., 'Public Policy toward Bankruptcy: Me-First and Other Priority Rules', **11** *Bell Journal of Economics*, 1980, 550-564.

WHITE, Michelle J., 'Personal Bankruptcy Under the 1978 Bankruptcy Code: An Economic Analysis', **63** *Indiana Law Journal*, 1987, 1-53.

WHITE, Michelle J., 'The Corporate Bankruptcy Decision', **3** *Journal of Economic Perspectives*, 1989, 129-151.

X, 'Note: "Adequate Protection" and the Availability of Postpetition Interest to Undersecured Creditors in Bankruptcy', **100** *Harvard Law Review*, 1987, 1106-1124.

5700 ANTITRUST LAW & COMPETITION LAW IN GENERAL (a selection)

Gerrit De Geest

ADAMS, Gregory B., 'European and American Antitrust Regulation of Pricing by Monopolists', **18** *Vanderbilt Journal of Transnational Law*, 1985, 1-70.

ADAMS, Walter and BROCK, James W., 'The "New Learning" and the Euthanasia of Antitrust', **74** *California Law Review*, 1986, 1515-1566.

ADAMS, Walter and BROCK, James W., 'Antitrust and Efficiency: A Comment', **62** *New York University Law Review*, 1987, 1116-1124.

ADAMS, Walter and BROCK, James W., 'Reaganomics and the Transmogrification of Merger Policy', **33** *Antitrust Bulletin*, 1988, 309-359.

ADAMS, Walter and BROCK, James W., 'Mergers and Economic Performance: The Experience Abroad', **5(2)** *Review of Industrial Organization*, 1990, 175-188.

ADAMS, William James, 'Comment' [on Jenny, Evolution of Anti-Trust Policies in France], **147** *Journal of Institutional and Theoretical Economics*, 1991, 60-65.

AELEN, L.O.M., 'De EEG-groepsvrijstelling voor franchise-overeenkomsten' [The EX Block Exemption for Franchise Agreements], **38** *Sociaal-Economische Wetgeving: Tijdschrift voor Europees en Economisch Recht*, 1990, 3-16.

ALCHIAN, Armen A., 'Development of Economic Theory and Antitrust: A View From the Theory of the Firm', **147** *Journal of Institutional and Theoretical Economics*, 1991, 232-234.

ALEJO, M. Enrique, 'La efectividad de la política de competencia' [The Effectiveness of Competition Policy], *Información Comercial Española*, 1987, n. 687, pp. 51-66.

ALLEN, Bruce T., 'Vertical Integration and Market Foreclosure: The Case of Cement and Concrete', **14** *Journal of Law and Economics*, 1971, 251-274.

ALLEN, Bruce T., 'Vertical Foreclosure in the Cement Industry: Reply', **15** *Journal of Law and Economics*, 1972, 467-471.

ALLEN, Bruce T., 'Industrial Reciprocity: A Statistical Analysis', **18** *Journal of Law and Economics*, 1975, 507-520.

ALSMÖLLER, Horst, *Wettbewerbspolitische Ziele und kooperationstheoretische Hvpothesen im Wandel der Zeit: Eine dogmengeschichtliche Untersuchung von Einstellungen zu Verbundsystemen und von Grunden für diese Einstellungen* [Competition Policy Purpose and Cooperation-Theoretical Hypotheses Through the Times: A Historical Investigation of the Institutions for Alliance Systems and for the Causes of these Institutions], Tübingen, J.C.B. Mohr, 1982, 337 p.

ANGOFF, Jay, 'Insurance against Competition: How the McCarran-Ferguson Act Raises Prices and Profits in the Property-Casualty Insurance Industry', **5** *Yale Journal of Regulation*, 1988, 397-415.

AREEDA, Phillip, 'Monopolization, Mergers, and Markets: A Century Past and the Future', **75** *California Law Review*, 1987, 959-981.

AREEDA, Phillip, 'A Second Century of the Rule of Reason', **59** *Antitrust Law Journal*, 1990, 143-150.

ARMENTANO, Dominick T., *Antitrust and Monopoly: Anatomy of a Policy Failure*, New York, Wiley, 1982, 292 p.

ARMENTANO, Dominick T., 'Comment: Efficiency, Liberty, and Antitrust Policy', in DORN, James A. and MANNE, Henry G. (eds.), *Economic Liberties and the Judiciary*, Fairfax, George Mason University Press, 1987, 309-316.

ARMENTANO, Dominick T., 'Antitrust and Insurance: Should the McCarran Act Be Repealed?', **8** *Cato Journal*, 1989, 729-749.

ARMENTANO, Dominick T., 'Time to Repeal Antitrust Regulation?', **35** *Antitrust Bulletin*, 1990, 311-328.

ARMENTANO, Dominick T., 'Rationalizing Antitrust: Reply', **35** *Antitrust Bulletin*, 1990, 345-347.

ARONOWITZ, Daniel, 'Retracing the Antitrust Roots of Section 1972 of the Bank Holding Company Act', **44** *Vanderbilt Law Review*, 1991, 865-898.

ASCH, Peter, 'The Determinants and Effects of Antitrust Activity', **18** *Journal of Law and Economics*, 1975, 575-581.

ASCH, Peter, 'Industrial Concentration, Efficiency and Antitrust Reform: Once Again: A Reply to Professor Liebeler', **12** *Southwestern University Law Review*, 1981, 405-411.

AUDRETSCH, David B., 'Divergent Views in Antitrust Economics', **33** *Antitrust Bulletin*, 1988, 135-160.

AUDRETSCH, David B., 'Comment' [on Jorde and Teece, Antitrust Policy and Innovation: Taking Account of Performance Competition and Competitor Cooperation], **147** *Journal of Institutional and Theoretical Economics*, 1991, 145-151.

AUERBACH, Paul, *Competition: The Economics of Industrial Change*, Basil Blackwell, Oxford, 1988, 339 p.

AYRES, Ian, 'Rationalizing Antitrust Cluster Markets', **95** *Yale Law Journal*, 1985, 109-125.

BADEN FULLER, C.W., 'Article 86: Economic Analysis of the Existence of a Dominant Position', **4** *European Law Review*, 1979, 423-441.

BADEN FULLER, C.W., 'Economic Issues Relating to Property Rights in Trademarks: Export Bans, Differential Pricing, Restrictions on Resale and Repackaging', **6** *European Law Review*, 1981, 162-179.

BAILEY, Elizabeth E. and BAUMOL, William J., 'Deregulation and the Theory of Contestable Markets', **2** *Yale Journal of Regulation*, 1984, 110-137.

BAIN, Joe S., *Barriers to New Competition: Their Character and Consequences in Manufacturing Industries*, Cambridge, Mass., Harvard University Press, 1956, 329 p.

BAIN, Joe S., *Industrial Organization*, New York, John Wiley & Sons, 1968 (2nd ed.), 678 p.

BAIN, Joe S., 'Structure versus Conduct as Indicators of Market Performance: The Chicago Attempts Revisited', **18** *Antitrust Law & Economics Review*, 1986, 17-50.

BAIN, Joe S., 'Structure Versus Conduct as Indicators of Market Performance: The Chicago-School Attempts Revisited', **18(2)** *Antitrust Law & Economics*

Review, 1986, 17-50.

BAKER, D.J. and BLUMENTHAL, W., 'The 1982 Guidelines and Preexisting Law', **71** *California Law Review*, 1983, 311-347.

BAKER, Jonathan B., 'Private Information and the Deterrent Effect of Antitrust Damage Remedies', **4** *Journal of Law, Economics, & Organization*, 1988, 385-408.

BAKER, Jonathan B., 'Identifying Cartel Policing under Uncertainty: the U.S. Steel Industry, 1933-1939', **32** *Journal of Law and Economics*, 1989, S47-S76.

BAKKER, Luit M. and RIDDER, Ronald K. de, 'Het EG-mededingingsbeleid en de samenwerking en concentratie binnen het Europese bankwezen' [EC Competition Policy and European Banking Cooperation and Concentration], **39(11)** *Bank- en Effectenbedrijf*, 1990, 42-46.

BALDRIGE, Malcolm, 'Two Areas of Antitrust Law in Need of Reform', *Detroit College of Law Review*, 1983, 1035-1043.

BALDWIN, W.L., 'Efficiency and Competition: The Reagan Administration's Legacy in Merger Policy', **5(2)** *Review of Industrial Organization*, 1990, 159-174.

BALDWIN, William L., 'The Feedback Effect of Business Conduct on Industry Structure', **12** *Journal of Law and Economics*, 1969, 123-153.

BALMER, Thomas A., 'One Step Forward, Two Steps Back: Economic Analysis and Political Considerations in Antitrust Law Revision', **31** *Antitrust Bulletin*, 1986, 981-1001.

BARENTS, R., 'Enige recente ontwikkelingen in het Europese mededingingsbeleid (1980-1985)' [Some Recent Developments in European Competition Policy], **29** *TVVS: Maandblad voor Ondernemingsrecht en Rechtspersonen*, 1986, 192-198.

BARNES, David W., 'Nonefficiency Goals in the Antitrust Law of Mergers', **30** *William & Mary Law Review*, 1989, 787 ff.

BARNES, David W., 'Revolutionary Antitrust: Efficiency, Ideology, and Democracy', **58** *University of Cincinnati Law Review*, 1989, 59 ff.

BAUER, Joseph P., 'Government Enforcement Policy of Section 7 of the Clayton Act: Carte Blanche for Conglomerate Mergers', **71** *California Law Review*, 1983, 348-375.

BAUMOL William J., 'Contestable Markets: An Uprising in the Theory of Industry Structure', **72** *American Economic Review*, 1982, 1-15.

BAUMOL, William J. and ORDOVER, Janusz A., 'Use of Antitrust to Subvert Competition', **28** *Journal of Law and Economics*, 1985, 247-265.

BAUMOL, William J., PANZER, John C. and WILLIG, Robert D., *Contestable Markets and the Theory of Industry Structure*, New York, Harcourt Brace Jovanovich, 1982.

BAUMOL, William J., PANZAR, John C. and WILLIG, Robert D., 'Reply', **73** *American Economic Review*, 1983, 491-496.

BAUMOL William J., PANZAR, John C. and WILLIG, Robert D., *Contestable Markets and the Theory of Industry Structure*, Orlando, 1988 (2nd ed.).

BAXTER, William F., 'Responding to the Reaction: The Draftman's Response', **71** *California Law Review*, 1983, 618-631.

BAXTER, William F., 'The Viability of Vertical Restraints Doctrine', **75** *California Law Review*, 1987, 933-950.

BECKENSTEIN, Alan R. and GABEL, H. Landis, 'Predation Rules: An Economic and Behavioral Analysis', **31** *Antitrust Bulletin*, 1986, 29-49.

BENJAMIN, Daniel K., 'The Effect of Monopolies and Cartels on Market Prices', **5** *Research in Law and Economics*, 1983, 1-15.

BENSON, Bruce L., GREENHUT, M.L. and HOLCOMBE, Randall G., 'Interest Groups and the Antitrust Paradox', **6** *Cato Journal*, 1987, 801-817.

BERN, Roger and TANSEY, Michael M., 'Proper Application of the Rule of Reason to Vertical Territorial Restraints: Debunking the "Intrabranding-Interbrand" and "Efficiencies" Deviations', **20** *American Business Law Journal*, 1983, 435-469.

BERNHARD, Richard C., 'English Law and American Law on Monopolies and Restraints of Trade', **3** *Journal of Law and Economics*, 1960, 136-145.

BERRY, Charles H., 'Corporate Growth and Diversification', **14** *Journal of Law and Economics*, 1971, 371-383.

BESANKO, David A. and SPULBER, Daniel F., 'Are Treble Damages Neutral? Sequential Equilibrium and Private Antitrust Enforcement', **80** *American Economic Review*, 1990, 870-887.

BICKEL, David R., 'The Antitrust Division's Adaption of a Chicago School Economic Policy Calls for Some Reorganization: But is the Division's New Policy Here to Stay?', **20** *Houston Law Review*, 1983, 1083-1127.

BINDER, John J., 'The Sherman Antitrust Act and the Railroad Cartels', **31** *Journal of Law and Economics*, 1988, 443-468.

BITTLINGMAYER, George, 'Decreasing Average Cost and Competition: A New Look at the Addyston Pipe Case', **25** *Journal of Law and Economics*, 1982, 201-229.

BITTLINGMAYER, George, 'Price-Fixing and the Addyston Pipe Case', **5** *Research in Law and Economics*, 1983, 57-130.

BITTLINGMAYER, George, 'Did Antitrust Policy Cause the Great Merger Wave?', **28** *Journal of Law and Economics*, 1985, 77-118.

BITTLINGMAYER, George, 'Chicago Credo', **143** *Journal of Institutional and Theoretical Economics*, 1987, 658-667.

BITTLINGMAYER, George, 'Die wettbewerbspolitische Vorstellungen der Chicago School' [Competition Policy According to the Chicago School], **37** *Wirtschaft und Wettbewerb*, 1987, 709-718.

BITTLINGMAYER, George, 'The Economic Problem of Fixed Costs and What Legal Research Can Contribute', **14** *Law & Social Inquiry*, 1989, 739-762.

BLAIR, John M., *Economic Concentration: Structure, Behavior and Public Policy*, Harcourt Brace Jovanovich, New York, 1972, 742 p.

BLAIR, Roger D. and FINCI, Jeffrey, 'The Individual Coercion Doctrine and Tying Arrangements: An Economic Analysis', **10** *Florida State University Law Review*, 1983, 531 ff.

BLAIR, Roger D. and KASERMAN, David L., *Law and Economics of Vertical Integration and Control*, New York, Academic Press, 1983, 211 p.

BLAIR, Roger D. and KASERMAN, David L., *Law and Economics of Vertical Integration and Control*, Harcourt Brace Jovanovich, New York, 1983, 211 p.

BLAKE, Harlan M. and JONES, William K., 'In Defense of Antitrust', **65** *Columbia Law Review*, 1965, 377-400.

BLAKE, Harlan M. and JONES, William K., 'Toward a Three-dimensional Antitrust Policy', **65** *Columbia Law Review*, 1965, 422-466.

BLAKENEY, Michael, 'Comment [on Williams]', in CRANSTON, Ross and SCHICK, Anne (eds.), *Law and Economics*, Canberra, Australian National University, 1982, 122-128.

BLEEKER, K.A.M., 'De geheimhoudingsplicht volgens art. 42 WEM in het licht van het EEG-Verdrag' [The Secrecy Duty According to s. 42 WEM in the Light of the EC Treaty], **37** *Sociaal-Economische Wetgeving: Tijdschrift voor Europees en Economisch Recht*, 1989, 714-722.

BLOCK, Michael K. and SIDAK, Joseph Gergory, 'The Cost of Antitrust Deterrence: Why Not Hang a Price Fixer Now and Then?', **68** *Georgetown Law Journal*, 1980, 1131-1139.

BODOFF, Jean, 'Competition Policies of the US and the EEC: An Overview', **5** *European Competition Law Review*, 1984, 51-81.

BOK, Derek C., 'Section 7 of the Clayton Act and the Merging of Law and Economics', **74** *Harvard Law Review*, 1960, 226-355.

BOLKESTEIN, Frits, *Vrijheid en regeling: Een liberale visie op de mededingingspolitiek* [Freedom and Regulation: A Liberal View on Competition Policy], 's-Gravenhage, 1985, 35 p.

BOLTON, Patrick and WHINSTON, Michael D., 'The "Foreclosure" Effects of Vertical Mergers', **147** *Journal of Institutional and Theoretical Economics*, 1991, 207-226.

BORCHERT, Manfred, und GROSSEKETTLER, H., *Preis- und Wettbewerbstheorie: Marktprozesse als analytisches Problem und ordnungspolitische Gestaltungsaufgabe* [Price Theory and Competition Theory: Market Processes as Analytical Problem and Policy Recommendations], Verlag W. Kohlhammer, 1985, 371 p.

BORK, Robert H., 'Contrasts in Antitrust Theory: I', **65** *Columbia Law Review*, 1965, 401-416.

BORK, Robert H., 'Legislative Intent and the Policy of the Sherman Act', **9** *Journal of Law and Economics*, 1966, 7-48.

BORK, Robert H., 'Antitrust and Monopoly: The Goals of Antitrust Policy', **57** *American Economic Review: Papers and Proceedings*, 1967, 242-253.

BORK, Robert H., *The Antitrust Paradox: A Policy at War with Itself*, New York, Basic Books, 1978, 468 p.

BORK, Robert H., 'The Role of the Courts in Applying Economics', **54** *Antitrust Law Journal*, 1985, 21-26.

BORK, Robert H. and BOWMAN, Ward S., 'The Goals of Antitrust: A Dialogue on Policy', **65** *Columbia Law Review*, 1965, 363-376.

BORRIE, Sir Gordon, 'Competition Policy in Britain: Retrospect and Prospect', **2** *International Review of Law and Economics*, 1982, 139-149.

BOS, P.V.F. and FIERSTRA, Marc A., *Europees mededingingsrecht* [European Competition Law], Deventer, Kluwer, 1989, 274 p.

BOS, P.V.F. and STUYCK, J.H.V., 'Concentratiecontrole naar EEG-recht' [Concentration Control in EC-Law], **37** *Sociaal- Economische Wetgeving: Tijdschrift voor Europees en Economisch Recht*, 1989, 300-404.

BOUCKAERT, Boudewijn, 'Is de prins een goede herder van de mededinging? Grondslagen van het internationaal Europees economisch recht' [Is the Prince a Good Shepherd for Competition? Basics of international European Economic Law], **15** *Rechtstheorie en Rechtsfilosofie*, 1986, 8-27.

BOWMAN, Ward S., 'Contrasts in Antitrust Theory: II', **65** *Columbia Law Review*, 1965, 417-421.

BOWMAN, Ward S., Jr., *Patent and Antitrust Law: A Legal and Economic Appraisal*, Chicago, University of Chicago Press, 1973.

BRAAKMAN, A.J., 'Europees kartelrecht als strijdmiddel bij overnames' [European Anti-trust Law as Takeover Combat Mechanism], **73** *Economisch-Statistische Berichten*, 1988, 854-858.

BRACE, Frederic F., Jr., WEBB, Dan K., JOSLIN, Rodney D. and WILDMAN, Max E., 'Opening Statements and Testimony: Ohio-Sealy et al. v. Sealy, Inc. et al.', **21(1)** *Antitrust Law & Economics Review*, 1989, 9-110.

BRADLEY, Robert L., Jr., 'On the Origins of the Sherman Antitrust Act', **9** *Cato Journal*, 1990, 737-742.

BRAEUTIGAM, Ronald R., 'Regulation of Multiproduct Enterprises by Rate of Return, Markup, and Operating Ratio', **3** *Research in Law and Economics*, 1981, 15-38.

BREIT, William, 'Resale Price Maintenance: What do Economists Know and When did They Know it?', **147** *Journal of Institutional and Theoretical Economics*, 1991, 72-90.

BREIT, William and ELZINGA, Kenneth G., 'Antitrust Enforcement and Economic Efficiency: The Uneasy Case for Treble Damages', **17** *Journal of Law and Economics*, 1974, 329-356.

BREIT, William and ELZINGA, Kenneth G., 'Private Antitrust Enforcement: The New Learning', **28** *Journal of Law and Economics*, 1985, 405-443.

BRENNAN, Timothy J., 'Mistaken Elasticities and Misleading Rules', **95** *Harvard Law Review*, 1982, 1849-1856.

BRESNAHAN, Timothy F. and SUSLOW, Valerie Y., 'Short-Run Supply with Capacity Constraints', **32** *Journal of Law and Economics*, 1989, S11-S42.

BREYER, Stephen G., 'Antitrust, Deregulation and the Newly Liberated Marketplace', **75** *California Law Review*, 1987, 1005-1047.

BRICKLEY, James A., DARK, Frederick H. and WEISBACH, Michael S., 'The Economic Effects of Franchise Termination Laws', **34** *Journal of Law and Economics*, 1991, 101-132.

BRITTAN, Leon, 'The Law and Policy of Merger Control in the EEC', **15** *European Law Review*, 1990, 351-357.

BROCK, William A., 'Contestable Markets and the Theory of Industry Structure: A Review Article', **91** *Journal of Political Economy*, 1983, 1055-1066.

BRODLEY, Joseph F., 'Potential Competition under the Merger Guidelines', **71** *California Law Review*, 1983, 377-401.

BRODLEY, Joseph F., 'The Economic Goals of Antitrust: Efficiency, Consumer Welfare, and Technological Progress', **62** *New York University Law Review*, 1987, 1020-1053.

BRODLEY, Joseph F., 'The Economic Goals of Antitrust: Efficiency, Consumer Welfare, and Technological Progress', **62** *New York University Law Review*, 1987, 1020-1053.

BRONSTEEN, Peter, 'Market Share and Market Power in the Domestic Lemon Industry', **9** *Research in Law and Economics*, 1986, 13-28.

BROZEN, Yale, 'The Antitrust Task Force Deconcentration Recommendation', **13** *Journal of Law and Economics*, 1970, 279-292.

BROZEN, Yale, 'Bain's Concentration and Rates of Return Revisited', **14** *Journal of Law and Economics*, 1971, 351-369.

BROZEN, Yale, 'Deconcentration Reconsidered: Comment', **14** *Journal of Law and Economics*, 1971, 489-491.

BROZEN, Yale, 'The Persistence of "High Rates of Return" in High-Stable Concentration Industries', **14** *Journal of Law and Economics*, 1971, 501-512.

BROZEN, Yale, *The Competitive Economy: Selected Readings*, Morristown, New Jersey, 1975.

BROZEN, Yale, 'The Antitrust Tradition: Entrepreneurial Restraint', **9** *Harvard Journal of Law & Public Policy*, 1986, 337-356.

BUTLER, Henry N., 'Restricted Distribution Contracts and the Opportunistic Pursuit of Treble Damages', **59** *Washington Law Review*, 1983, 27-60.

BUTLER, Henry N., LANE, W.J. and PHILLIPS, Owen R., 'The Futility of Antitrust Attacks on Tie-In Sales: An Economic and Legal Analysis', **36** *Hastings Law Journal*, 1984, 173-213.

BUXBAUM, Richard M., 'Enforcement of US Antitrust Laws during the Reagan Administration: Review and Prospects', **39** *Wirtschaft und Wettbewerb*, 1989, 566-578.

CABANELLLAS, Guillermo and ETZRORDT, Wolf, 'The New Argentine Law: Competition as an Economic Policy Instrument', **17** *Journal of World Trade Law*, 1983, 34-53.

CALKINS, Stephen, 'The New Merger Guidelines and the Herfindahl-Hirschman Index', **71** *California Law Review*, 1983, 402-429.

CALVANI, Terry and BERG, Andrew G., 'Resale Price Maintenance after Monsanto: A Doctrine Still at War with Itself', **84** *Duke Law Journal*, 1984, 1163-1204.

CALVANI, Terry and SIEGFRIED, John (eds.), *Economic Analysis and Antitrust*, Boston, Little Brown, 1979.

CAMPBELL, Thomas J., 'The Efficiency of the Failing Company Defense', **63** *Texas Law Review*, 1984, 251-283.

CAMPBELL, Thomas J., 'The Antitrust Record of the First Reagan Administration', **64** *Texas Law Review*, 1985, 353-369.

CAMPBELL, Thomas J., 'Predation and Competition in Antitrust: The Case of

Nonfungible Goods', **87** *Columbia Law Review*, 1987, 1625-1675.

CANN, Wesley A., Jr., 'Section 7 of the Clayton Act and the Pursuit of Economic "Objectivity": Is There Any Role for Social and Political Value in Merger Policy?', **60** *Notre Dame Law Review*, 1985, 273-317.

CARLTON, Dennis W., 'A Reexamination of Delivered Pricing Systems', **26** *Journal of Law and Economics*, 1983, 51-70.

CARLTON, Dennis W. and GERTNER, Robert, 'Market Power and Mergers in Durable-Good Industries', **32** *Journal of Law and Economics*, 1989, S203-S226.

CARSTENSEN, Peter C., 'Antitrust Law, Competition, and the Macroeconomy', **14** *University of Michigan Journal of Law Reform*, 1981, 173-203.

CARSTENSEN, Peter C., 'Commentary: Reflections on Hay, Clark, and the Relationship of Economic Analysis and Policy to Rules of Antitrust Law', *Wisconsin Law Review*, 1983, 953-988.

CARTER, John R., 'Collusion, Efficiency, and Antitrust', **21** *Journal of Law and Economics*, 1978, 435-444.

CASSELL, Paul G., 'Exemption of International Shipping Conferences from the American Antitrust Laws: An Economic Analysis', **20** *New England Law Review*, 1985, 1-30.

CAVANAGH, Edward D., 'Contribution, Claim Reduction, and Individual Treble Damage Responsibility: Which Path to Reform of Antitrust Remedies?', **40** *Vanderbilt Law Review*, 1987, 1277 ff.

CAVANAGH, Edward D., 'Detrebling Antitrust Damages: An Idea Whose Time Has Come?', **61** *Tulane Law Review*, 1987, 777-848.

CHAMBERLIN, Edward H. (ed.), *Monopoly, and Competition and Their Regulation*, New York, 1954, 549 p.

CHARD, J.S., 'The Economics of the Application of Article 85 to Selective Distribution Systems', **7** *European Law Review*, 1982, 83-102.

CIRACE, John, 'Schizophrenia in the Justice Department's Merger Guidelines', **19(4)** *Antitrust Law & Economics Review*, 1987, 73-79.

CLARK, David W., 'Ties That May Bind: Antitrust Liability for Exclusive Hospital-Physician Contracts after Jefferson Parish Hospital District v. Hyde', **54** *Mississippi Law Journal*, 1984, 1-42.

CLARKE, R.N., 'Collusion and the Incentives for Information Sharing', **14** *Bell Journal of Economics*, 1983, 383-394.

CLAYDON, Jeanne-Marie, 'Joint Ventures: An Analysis of Commission Decisions', **7** *European Competition Law Review*, 1986, 151-192.

CLONINGER, Dale O. and KANTZ, Terrance R., 'Price Fixing and Legal Sanctions: The Stockholder-Enrichment Motive' Strickland, Thomas H. **19(1)** *Antitrust Law & Economics Review*, 1987, 17-24.

COASE, Ronald H., 'Industrial Organization: A Proposal for Research', in FUCHS, Victor R. (ed.), *Policy Issues and Research Opportunities in Industrial Organization*, National Bureau of Economic Research, Washington DC, 1972, 59-73.

COASE, Ronald H., 'Durability and Monopoly', **15** *Journal of Law and Economics*, 1972, 143-149.

COATE, Malcolm B., 'An Analysis of Three Approaches to Market Definition', **9** *Research in Law and Economics*, 1986, 29-43.

COATE, Malcolm B., HIGGINS, Richard S. and McCHESNEY, Fred S., 'Bureaucracy and Politics in FTC Merger Challenges', **33** *Journal of Law & Economics*, 1990, 463-482.

COHLER, Charles B., 'The New Economics and Antitrust Policy', **32** *Antitrust Bulletin*, 1987, 401-414.

COMANOR, William S., 'Vertical Price-Fixing, Vertical Market Restrictions, and the New Antitrust Policy', **98** *Harvard Law Review*, 1985, 983-1002.

COMANOR, William S., 'Antitrust Enforcement Policies Towards Vertical Restraints', **19(3)** *Antitrust Law & Economics Review*, 1987, 41-47.

COMANOR, William, et al., *Competition Policy in Europe and North America: Economic Issues and Institutions*, New York, Harwood, 1991, 260 p.

CONE, Kenneth R. and DRANOVE, David, 'Why Did States Enact Hospital Rate-setting Laws ?', **29** *Journal of Law and Economics*, 1986, 287-302.

COOK, Carla Tolbert, 'Antitrust Action Against Milk Marketing Cooperatives - Shaking Up the milk Industry', **34** *Drake Law Review*, 1985, 493-513.

COOTER, Robert D., 'Passing on the Monopoly Overcharge: A Further Comment on Economic Theory', **129** *University of Pennsylvania Law Review*, 1981, 1523-1532.

CORREIA, Eddie, 'Antitrust Policy after the First Reagan Administration', **76** *Georgetown Law Journal*, 1976, 329-335.

COWLING, Keith and MUELLER, Dennis C., 'The Social Costs of Monopoly Power', **88** *Economic Journal*, 1978, 727-748.

CREW, Michael A. and ROWLEY, Charles K., 'Toward a Public Choice Theory of Monopoly Regulation', **57** *Public Choice*, 1988, 49-67.

CRUMP, David and MAXWELL, Larry A., 'Comment: Health Care, Cost Containment, and the Antitrust Laws: A Legal and Economic Analysis of the Pireno Case', **56** *Southern California Law Review*, 1983, 913 ff.

CUBBIN, John S., *Market Structure and Performance: The Empirical Research*, Chur, Harwood Academic, 1988, 79 p.

CUMMINGS, F. Jay and RUHTER, Wayne E., 'The *Northern Pacific* Case', **22** *Journal of Law and Economics*, 1979, 329-350.

CURRAN, William J. III, 'Beyond Economic Concepts and Categories: A Democratic Refiguration of Antitrust Law', **31** *Saint Louis University Law Journal*, 1987, 349-378.

CURRAN, William J. III, 'On Democracy and Economics', **33** *Antitrust Bulletin*, 1988, 753-777.

DALE, Richard, *Anti-Dumping Law in a Liberal Trade Order*, London, Macmillan, 1980, 237 p.

DANKBAAR, Ben, GROENEWEGEN, John and SCHENK, Hans (eds.), *Perspectives in Industrial Organization*, Dordrecht, Kluwer Academic, 1990, 311 p.

DARBY, Michael R. and LOTT, J.R., Jr., 'Qualitative Information, Reputation, and

Monopolistic Competition', **9** *International Review of Law and Economics*, 1989, 87-103.

DAVIDOW, J., 'The Worldwide Influence of U.S. Antitrust', **35** *Antitrust Bulletin*, 1990, 603-630.

DAVIDOW, Joel, 'Cartels, Competition Laws and the Regulation of International Trade', **15** *New York University Journal of International Law and Politics*, 1983, 351-376.

DAVIDSON, Kenneth M., 'The Competitive Significance of Segmented Markets', **71** *California Law Review*, 1983, 445-463.

DAVIES, S.W. and LYONS, B.R., *Economics of Industrial Organization*, London, 1988.

DeBOW, Michael E., 'What's Wrong With Price Fixing: Responding to the New Critics of Antitrust', **12(2)** *Regulation*, 1988, 44-50.

DeLONG, James V., FLYNN, John J., CLOWER, Robert W. and GOODWIN, Alfred T., 'Economic Analysis', **12** *Southwestern University Law Review*, 1981, 297-377.

DEMSETZ, Harold, 'Industry Structure, Market Rivalry, and Public Policy, **16** *Journal of Law and Economics*, 1973, 1-9.

DEMSETZ, Harold, 'Economics as A Guide to Antitrust Regulation', **19** *Journal of Law and Economics*, 1976, 371-384.

DEMSETZ, Harold, *Economic, Legal and Political Dimensions of Competition*, Amsterdam, North-Holland, 1982, 125 p.

DEWEY, Donald, *Monopoly in Economics and Law*, Chicago, Rand McNally & Co., 1959, 328 p.

DEWEY, Donald, 'Industrial Concentration and the Rate of Profit: Some Neglected Theory', **19** *Journal of Law and Economics*, 1976, 67-78.

DEWEY, Donald, 'Antitrust and Economic Theory: An Uneasy Friendship', **87** *Yale Law Journal*, 1978, 1516-1526.

DEWEY, Donald, 'Economists and Antitrust: The Circular Road', **35** *Antitrust Bulletin*, 1990, 349-371.

DICK, Andrew R., 'Learning by Doing and Dumping in the Semiconductor Industry', **34** *Journal of Law and Economics*, 1991, 133-159.

DiLORENZO, T.J., 'The Origins of Antitrust: An Interest-Group Perspective', **5** *International Review of Law and Economics*, 1985, 73-90.

DIPLOCK, Kenneth Sir, 'Antitrust and the Judicial Process', **7** *Journal of Law and Economics*, 1964, 27-43.

DORMAN, Roderick G., 'The Case for Compensation: Why Compensatory Components Are Required for Efficient Antitrust Enforcement', **68** *Georgetown Law Journal*, 1980, 1113-1120.

DRIJBER, B.J., 'Groepsvrijstelling know-how licenties: Rechtszekerheid of onduidelijkheid' [Block Exemption Know-How Licences: Legal Certainty or Vagueness], **37** *Sociaal Economische Wetgeving: Tijdschrift voor Europees en Economisch Recht*, 1989, 200-216.

DROHAN, John P., 'Antitrust: Tailoring More Efficient Summary Judgment

Standards in Antitrust Conspiracy Actions: Apex Oil Co. v. DiMauro', **54** *Brooklyn Law Review*, 1988, 347 ff.

DUNNE, Timothy, ROBERTS, Mark J. and SAMUELSON, Larry, 'Firm Entry and Postentry Performance in the U.S. Chemical Industries', **32** *Journal of Law and Economics*, 1989, S233-S271.

EASTERBROOK, Frank H., 'Antitrust and the Economics of Federalism', **26** *Journal of Law and Economics*, 1983, 23-50.

EASTERBROOK, Frank H., 'The Limits of Antitrust', **63** *Texas Law Review*, 1984, 1-40.

EASTERBROOK, Frank H., 'Detrebling Antitrust Damages', **28** *Journal of Law and Economics*, 1985, 445-467.

EASTERBROOK, Frank H., 'Workable Antitrust Policy', **84** *Michigan Law Review*, 1986, 1696 ff.

EASTERBROOK, Frank H., 'Allocating Antitrust Decisionmaking Tasks', **76** *Georgetown Law Journal*, 1987, 305-320.

EASTERBROOK, Frank H., 'Comparative Advantage and Antitrust Law', **75** *California Law Review*, 1987, 983-989.

EASTERBROOK, Frank H., 'Removing Intent and Cost in Predatory Pricing Cases: Power to Recoup as "Initial Hurdle"', **21(2)** *Antitrust Law & Economics Review*, 1989, 37-48.

EASTERBROOK, Frank H., LANDES, William M. and POSNER, Richard A., 'Contribution among Antitrust Defendants: A Legal and Economic Analysis', **23** *Journal of Law and Economics*, 1980, 331-370.

ECKBO, B. Espen and WIER, Peggy, 'Antimerger Policy under the Hart-Scott-Rodino Act: A Reexamination of the Market Power Hypothesis', **28** *Journal of Law and Economics*, 1985, 119-149.

EICHNER, Alfred S., 'Monopoly, The Emergence of Oligopoly and the Case of Sugar Refining: A Reply', **14** *Journal of Law and Economics*, 1971, 521-527.

EIS, Carl, 'The 1919-1930 Merger Movement in American Industry', **12** *Journal of Law and Economics*, 1969, 267-296.

EISENBERG, Barry S., 'Information Exchange among Competitors: The Issue of Relative Value Scales for Physicians' Services', **23** *Journal of Law and Economics*, 1980, 441-460.

ELZINGA, K.G., 'The Compass of Competition for Professional Services', in BLAIR, Roger D. and RUBIN, Stephen, *Regulating the Professions: A Public-Policy Symposium*, Lexington, Lexington Books, 1980.

ELZINGA, Kenneth G., 'The Antimerger Law: Pyrrhic Victories ?', **12** *Journal of Law and Economics*, 1969, 43-78.

ELZINGA, Kenneth G., 'Predatory Pricing: The Case of the Gunpowder Trust', **13** *Journal of Law and Economics*, 1970, 223-240.

ELZINGA, Kenneth G., 'The Goals of Antitrust: Other than Competition and Efficiency, What Else Counts?', **125** *University of Pennsylvania Law Review*, 1977, 1191-1213.

ELZINGA, Kenneth G., 'New Developments on the Cartel Front', **29** *Antitrust Bulletin*, 1984, 3-26.

ELZINGA, Kenneth G., 'The New International Economics Applied: Japanese Televisions and U.S. Consumers', **64** *Chicago-Kent Law Review*, 1988, 941 ff.

ELZINGA, Kenneth G. and BREIT, William, *The Antitrust Penalties: A Study in Law and Economics*, New Haven, Yale University Press, 1976, 160 p.

ELZINGA, Kenneth G. and HOGARTY, Thomas F., '*Utah Pie* and the Consequences of Robinson-Patman', **21** *Journal of Law and Economics*, 1978, 427-434.

EMONS, Winand, 'Comment' [on Gilbert, Legal and Economic Issues in the Commercialization of New Technology], **147** *Journal of Institutional and Theoretical Economics*, 1991, 182-184.

EMPEL, Martijn van, 'Merger Control in the EEC', **13** *World Competition: Law and Economics Review*, 1990, 6-22.

ERICKSON, W. Bruce, 'Antitrust Consulting and the 'Knowledge-Loss' Factor: Money, Time, and Confidentiality', **18(3)** *Antitrust Law & Economics Review*, 1986, 49-58.

FAITH, Roger L., LEAVENS, Donald R. and TOLLISON, Robert D., 'Antitrust Pork Barrel', **25** *Journal of Law and Economics*, 1982, 329-342.

FAMA, Eugene F. and JENSEN, Michael C., 'Separation of Ownership and Control', **26** *Journal of Law and Economics*, 1983, 301-325.

FAULL, Jonathan, 'Joint Ventures under the EEC Competition Rules', **5** *European Competition Law Review*, 1984, 358-374.

FEENSTRA, J.J., 'Fusiecontrole door de EEG na het Philip Morris arrest' [EC Merger Control after the Philip Morris Case], **66** *De Naamloze Vennootschap*, 1988, 60-67.

FEINBERG, Robert M., 'The Effects of European Competition Policy on Pricing and Profit Margins', **39** *Kyklos*, 1986, 267-287.

FEJØ, Jens, *Monopoly Law and Market: Studies of EC Competition Law with US American Antitrust Law as a Frame of Reference and Supported by Basic Market Economics*, Deventer, Kluwer, 1990, 416 p.

FELDMAN, Roger, COOTNER, P.H. and BAILEY, M.N., 'An Econometric Model of the World Copper Industry', **3** *Bell Journal of Economics*, 1972, 568-609.

FERGUSON, James M., 'Daily Newspaper Advertising Rates, Local Media Cross-Ownership, Newspaper Chains, and Media Competition', **26** *Journal of Law and Economics*, 1983, 635-654.

FERGUSON, Paul R., *Industrial Economics: Issues and Perspectives*, Basingstoke, Macmillan, 1988, 216 p.

FERRALL, Victor E., Jr., 'Quantity Discounts and Competition: Economic Rationality or Robinson-Patman', **3** *Journal of Law and Economics*, 1960, 146-166.

FIERSTRA, Marc A., 'Communautaire concentratiecontrole: Een nieuwe fase in een ontwikkeling' [Community Concentration Control: A New Development Stage], **38** *Sociaal-Economische Wetgeving: Tijdschrift voor Europees en Economisch Recht*, 1990, 330-350.

FINE, Frank L., 'The Philip Morris Judgment: Does Article 85 Now Extend to Mergers?', **8** *European Competition Law Review*, 1987, 333-343.

FINE, Frank L., *Mergers and Joint Ventures in Europe: The Law and Policy of the*

EEC, Graham & Trotman, London, 1989.

FINE, Frank L., 'Ec Merger Control: An Analysis of the New Regulation', **11** *European Competition Law Review*, 1990, 47-51.

FISCHER, Franklin M., 'The Social Costs of Monopoly and Regulation: Posner Reconsidered (Comment)', **93** *Journal of Political Economy*, 1985, 410-416.

FISHER, Alan A., JOHNSON, Frederick I. and LANDE, Robert H., 'Price Effects of Horizontal Mergers', **77** *California Law Review*, 1989, 777-827.

FISHER, Alan A. and LANDE, Robert H., 'Efficiency Considerations in Merger Enforcement', **71** *California Law Review*, 1983, 1582-1696.

FISHER, Alan A., LANDE, Robert H. and VANDAELE, Walter, 'Afterword: Could a Merger Lead to Both a Monopoly and a Lower Price?', **71** *California Law Review*, 1983, 1697-1706.

FISHER, Alan A. and SCIACCA, Richard, 'An Economic Analysis of Vertical Merger Enforcement Policy', **6** *Research in Law and Economics*, 1984, 1-133.

FISHER, Franklin M., 'Matsushita: Myth v. Analysis in the Economics of Predation', **64** *Chicago-Kent Law Review*, 1988, 969 ff.

FISHWICK, F., *Definition of the Relevant Market in Communitv Competition Policy*, Luxemburg, 1986, 175 p.

FLYNN, John J., 'Antitrust Jurisprudence: A Symposium on the Economic, Political and Social Goals of Antitrust Policy, Introduction', **125** *University of Pennsylvania Law Review*, 1977, 1182-1190.

FLYNN, John J., '"Reaganomics" and Antitrust Enforcement: A Jurisprudential Critique', *Utah Law Review*, 1983, 269-312.

FLYNN, John J., 'The Reagan Administration's Antitrust Policy: "Original Intent" and the Legislative History of the Sherman Act', **33** *Antitrust Bulletin*, 1988, 259-307.

FLYNN, John J., 'Legal Reasoning, Antitrust Policy and the Social "Science" of Economics', **33** *Antitrust Bulletin*, 1988, 713-743.

FLYNN, John J. and PONSOLDT, James F., 'Legal Reasoning and the Jurisprudence of Vertical Restraints: The Limitations of Neoclassical Economic Analysis in the Resolution of Antitrust Disputes', **62** *New York University Law Review*, 1987, 1125-1152.

FORTENBERRY, Joseph E., 'A History of the Antitrust Law of Vertical Practices', **11** *Research in Law and Economics*, 1988, 133-259.

FOX, Eleanor M., 'Monopoly and Competition: Tilting the Law Towards a More Competitive Economy', **37** *Washington and Lee Law Review*, 1980, 49-71.

FOX, Eleanor M., 'The New American Competition Policy: From Anti-Trust to Pro--Efficiency', **2** *European Competition Law Review*, 1981, 439-451.

FOX, Eleanor M., 'The Modernization of Antitrust: A New Equilibrium', **66** *Cornell Law Review*, 1981, 1140-1192.

FOX, Eleanor M., 'Introduction. The 1982 Merger Guidelines: When Economists Are Kings?', **71** *California Law Review*, 1983, 281-302.

FOX, Eleanor M., 'Monopolization and Dominance in the United States and the European Community: Efficiency, Opportunity, and Fairness', **61** *Notre Dame*

Law Review, 1986, 981 ff.

FOX, Eleanor M., 'The Politics of Law and Economics in Judicial Decision Making: Antitrust as a Window', **61** *New York University Law Review*, 1986, 554-588.

FOX, Eleanor M., 'Monopolization and Dominance in the US and the EC: Efficiency, Opportunity, and Fairness', **61** *Notre Dame Law Review*, 1986, 981-1020.

FOX, Eleanor M., 'Consumer Beware Chicago', **84** *Michigan Law Review*, 1986, 1714-1720.

FOX, Eleanor M., 'The Battle for the Soul of Antitrust', **75** *California Law Review*, 1987, 917-923.

FOX, Eleanor M., 'Antitrust, Economics, and Bias', **2** *Antitrust*, 1988, 6-10.

FOX, Eleanor M. and SULLIVAN, Lawrence A., 'Antitrust: Retrospective and Prospective, Where Are We Coming From? Where Are We Going?', **62** *New York University Law Review*, 1987, 937-988.

FOX, Eleanor M., WHITE, Lawrence J. and TOPKIS, Jay, 'Demonstration: Economic Analysis and Expert Testimony: Defendant's Economist', **52** *Antitrust Law Journal*, 1983, 799-814.

FOX, Pauline H., 'Anti-Antitrust Bias in the US Judiciary', **20(2)** *Antitrust Law & Economics Review*, 1988, 57-60.

FRAWLEY, Alfred C., 'Predatory Intent, Pricing Below AVC, and Oligopoly Market Power: Usurping the Jury's Function', **21(2)** *Antitrust Law & Economics Review*, 1989, 27-36.

FRAZER, Tim, *Monopoly. Competition and the Law: The Regulation of Business Activity in Britain. Europe and America*, Brighton, Wheatsheaf, 1988, 265 p.

FRAZER, Tim, 'Competition Policy after 1992: The Next Step', **53** *Modern Law Review*, 1990, 609-623.

FREY, Bruno S., 'Comment' [on Shughart and Tollison, The Employment Consequences of the Sherman and Clayton Acts], **147** *Journal of Institutional and Theoretical Economics*, 1991, 53-57.

FRÖHLICH, P., *Marktabgrenzung in der Wettbewerbspolitik: Die parametrisch Interdependenz als Kriterium der Abgrenzung des relevanten Marktes* [Market Definition in Competition Policy: The Parameter Interdepence as Criterion for the Definition of the Relevant Markets], Göttingen, 1975.

GAAY FORTMAN, Bastiaan de, *Theory of Competition Policy: A Confrontation of Economic. Political and Legal Principles*, Amsterdam, North-Holland, 1966, 341 p.

GALLHORN, Ernest A., 'The Practical Uses of Economic Analysis: Hope vs. Reality', **56** *Antitrust Law Journal*, 1987, 933-945.

GARLAND, Merrick B., 'Antitrust and State Action: Economic Efficiency and the Political Process', **96** *Yale Law Journal*, 1987, 486-519.

GELLHORN, Ernest A., *Antitrust Law and Economics*, St. Paul, West Pub., 1976, 472 p.

GELLHORN, Ernest A., 'The Practical Uses of Economic Analysis: Hope vs. Reality', **56** *Antitrust Law Journal*, 1987, 933-945.

GELLHORN, Ernest, et al., 'Has Antitrust Outgrown Dual Enforcement? A Proposal for Rationalization', **35** *Antitrust Bulletin*, 1990, 695-743.

GERBER, David J., 'International Competitive Harm and Domestic Antitrust Laws: Forms of Analysis', **10** *Northwestern Journal of International Law & Business*, 1989, 41-55.

GERHART, Peter M., 'The Supreme Court and Antitrust Analysis: The (Near) Triumph of the Chicago School', *Supreme Court Review*, 1982, 319-349.

GERLA, Harry S., 'A Micro-Microeconomic Approach to Antitrust Law: Games Managers Play', **86** *Michigan Law Review*, 1988, 892-929.

GEVURTZ, Franklin A., 'Using the Antitrust Laws to Combat Overseas Bribery by Foreign Companies: A Step to Even the Odds in International Trade', **27** *Virginia Journal of International Law*, 1987, 211-272.

GIBBONS, John J., 'Antitrust, Law & Economics, and Politics', **50 (4)** *Law and Contemporary Problems*, 1987, 217-224.

GILBERT, Richard J., 'Legal and Economic Issues in the Commercialization of New Technology', **147** *Journal of Institutional and Theoretical Economics*, 1991, 155-181.

't GILDE, A.P.J. and HAANK, D.J., *De praktijk van de Wet economische mededinging* [The Competition Act in Practice], SWOKA, Onderzoeksrapport nr. 37, 's-Gravenhage, 1985, 38 p.

GILLEY, O.W. and KARELS, G.V., 'The Competitive Effect in Bonus Bidding: New Evidence', **12** *Bell Journal of Economics*, 1981, 637-648.

GINSBURG, D.H., 'Rationalizing Antitrust: A Rejoinder', **35** *Antitrust Bulletin*, 1990, 329-343.

GINSBURG, Douglas H., 'Comment' [on Möschel, The Goals of Antitrust Revisited], **147** *Journal of Institutional and Theoretical Economics*, 1991, 24-30.

GOETZ, Charles J., GRANET, Lloyd and SCHWARTZ, Warren F., 'The Meaning of 'Subsidy' and 'Injury' in the Countervailing Duty Law', **6** *International Review of Law and Economics*, 1986, 17-32.

GOLDBERG, Lawrence G., 'The Effect of Conglomerate Mergers on Competition', **16** *Journal of Law and Economics*, 1973, 137-158.

GOLDBERG, Victor, 'Enforcing Resale Price Maintenance: The FTC Investigation of Lenox', **18** *American Business Law Journal*, 1980, 225-258.

GOLDSCHMID, Harvey J., 'Horizontal Restraints in Antitrust: Current Treatment and Future Needs', **75** *California Law Review*, 1987, 925-931.

GORT, Michael and HOGARTY, Thomas F., 'New Evidence on Mergers', **13** *Journal of Law and Economics*, 1970, 167-184.

GOTTHOLD, Jürgen, 'Neuere Entwicklungen der Wettbewerbstheorie: Kritische Bemerkungen zur neo-liberalen Theorie der Wettbewerbspolitik' [New Developments in Competition Theory: Critical Remarks on the Neo-Liberal Theory of Competition Policy], **145** *Zeitschrift für das gesamte Handelsrecht*, 1981, 286-340.

GRECO, Anthony J., 'A Profile of Private Antitrust Suits Filed in a Federal District Court', **17(2)** *Antitrust Law & Economics Review*, 1985, 55-59.

GRECO, Anthony J., 'State Fluid Milk Regulation: Antitrust and Price Controls', **32** *Antitrust Bulletin*, 1987, 165-188.

GRECO, Anthony J., 'Errors in Antitrust Economic Reasoning: 14 Appellate-Court Opinions of '87', **20(1)** *Antitrust Law & Economics Review*, 1988, 81-88.

GREEN, Nicholas, 'Article 85 in Perspective: Stretching Jurisdiction, Narrowing the Concept of a Restriction and Plugging a Few Gaps', **9** *European Competition Law Review*, 1988, 190-206.

GREENFIELD, Jay, 'Beyond Herfindahl: Non-Structural Elements of Merger Analysis', **53** *Antitrust Law Journal*, 1984, 229-254.

GROSSMAN, Gene M. and SHAPIRO, Carl, 'Research Joint Ventures: An Antitrust Analysis', **2** *Journal of Law, Economics, & Organization*, 1986, 315-337.

GROVES, Peter, 'Motor Vehicle Distribution: The Block Exemption', **8** *European Competition Law Review*, 1987, 77-87.

GULLAND, Eugene D., BYRNE, J. Peter and STEINBACH, Sheldon Elliot, 'Intercollegiate Athletics and Television Contracts: Beyond Economic Justifications in Antitrust Analysis of Agreements Among Colleges', **52** *Fordham Law Review*, 1984, 717 ff.

GYSELEN, Luc and KYRIAZIS, Nicholas, 'Article 86 EEC: The Monoply Measurement Issue Revisited', **11** *European Law Review*, 1986,134-148.

HALE, G.E., 'The Case of Coal: Should Alt Horizontal Mergers Be Held Illegal ?', **13** *Journal of Law and Economics*, 1970, 421-437.

HALE, Rosemary D., 'Cookware: A Study in Vertical Integration', **10** *Journal of Law and Economics*, 1967, 169-179.

HALE, Rosemary D., 'Cookware and Vertical Integration: A Rejoinder', **12** *Journal of Law and Economics*, 1969, 439-440.

HALE, Rosemary D. and HALE, G.E., 'More on Mergers', **5** *Journal of Law and Economics*, 1962, 119-130.

HALL, Margaret, 'EEC: Competition or Competition Policy? An Economist's Enquiry', **1** *European Competition Law Review*, 1980, 287-296.

HANREICH, Hanspeter, 'Verbraucherpolitik durch Wettbewerbsrecht' [Consumer Policy By Competition Law], in KORINEK, Karl (ed.), *Beiträge zum Wirtschaftsrecht*, Vienna, Orac Publishers, 1983, 539-560.

HANSMANN, Henry B., 'Unfair Competition and the Unrelated Business Income Tax', **75** *Virginia Law Review*, 1989, 605-635.

HARRIS, Barry C. and SIMONS, Joseph J., 'Focusing Market Definition: How Much Substitution is Necessary?', **12** *Research in Law and Economics*, 1989, 207-226.

HARRIS, Robert G. and JORDE, Thomas M., 'Market Definition in the Merger Guidelines: Implications for Antitrust Enforcement', **71** *California Law Review*, 1983, 464-496.

HARRIS, Robert G. and JORDE, Thomas M., 'Antitrust Market Definition: An Integrated Approach', **72** *California Law Review*, 1984, 3-67.

HARRIS, Robert G. and SULLIVAN, Lawrence A., 'Passing on the Monopoly Overcharge: A Response to Landes and Posner', **28** *University of Pennsylvania Law Review*, 1980, 1274-1292.

HARRIS, Robert G. and SULLIVAN, Lawrence A., 'More on Passing On: A Reply to Cooter and to Viton and Winston', **129** *University of Pennsylvania Law Review*, 1981, 1533-1540.

HAUSCHKA, Christoph E., 'Zielkonflikte zwischen Unternehmenkontrolle und Wirtschaftsförderung in den wettbewerbspolitischen Programmaussagen der EG--Kommission' [Conflict of Goals Between Enterprise Control and Economic Imperatives in the Competition Programme of the EC-Commission], **40** *Wirtschaft und Wettbewerb*, 1990, 205-216.

HAUSE, John C., 'Comment on Bresnahan and Suslow', **32** *Journal of Law and Economics*, 1989, S43-S46.

HAWK, Barry E., 'The American (Antitrust) Revolution: Lessons for the EEC?', **9** *European Competition Law Review*, 1988, 53-87.

HAY, Donald A. and MORRIS, Derek J., *Industrial Economics: Theory and Evidence*, Oxford, Oxford University Press, 1979, 649 p.

HAY, Donald A. and VICKERS, John, *The Economics of Market Dominance*, Oxford, Basil Blackwell, 1987, 172 p.

HAY, George H., 'Competition Policy', **1(3)** *Oxford Review of Economic Policy*, 1985, 39-63.

HAY, George A. and KELLEY, Daniel, 'An Empirical Survey of Price Fixing Conspiracies', **17** *Journal of Law and Economics*, 1974, 13-38.

HAZLETT, Thomas W., 'Is Antitrust Anticompetitive?', **9** *Harvard Journal of Law & Public Policy*, 1986, 277-336.

HEGGESTAD, Arnold A. and WOLKEN, John D., 'Mergers and Acquisitions in Commercial Banking: Economic and Financial Considerations', **18** *Layola of Los Angeles Law Review*, 1985, 1165-1193.

HELFAT, Constance E. and TEECE, David J., 'Vertical Integration and Risk Reduction', **3** *Journal of Law, Economics, & Organization*, 1987, 47-67.

HENDRICKS, Kenneth, PORTER, Robert H. and SPADY, Richard H., 'Random Reservation Prices and Bidding Bevahavior in OCS Drainage Auctions', **32** *Journal of Law and Economics*, 1989, S83-S106.

HENNIPMAN, P., *De taak van de mededingingspolitiek* [The Role of Competition Policy], Haarlem, Bohn, 1966, 41 p.

HERDZINA, Klaus, 'Marktentwicklung und Wettbewerbsverhalten' [Market Development and Competition Attitude], in BOMBACH, G., GAHLEN, B. and OTT, A.E. (eds.), *Industrieökonomik: Theorie und Empirie*, Tübingen, J.C.B. Mohr, 1985, 105-123.

HERDZINA, Klaus, *Wettbewerbspolitik* [Competition Policy], Stuttgart, Gustav Fischer, 1987 (2nd ed.), 237 p.

HERDZINA, Klaus, *Möglichkeiten und Grenzen einer wirtschaftstheoretische Fundierung der Wettbewerbspolitik* [Possibilities and Limits of an Economic Foundation of Competition Policy], Tübingen, Walter Eucken Institut, Vorträge und Aufsätze 116, 1988, 61 p.

HILL, C.W.L. and PICKERING, J.F., 'Conglomerate Mergers, Internal Organization and Competition Policy', **6** *International Review of Law and Economics*, 1986, 59-75.

HOLT, Charles A., 'The Exercise of Market Power in Laboratory Experiments', **32** *Journal of Law and Economics*, 1989, S107-S130.

HOPPMANN, Erich, 'Das Konzept der optimalen Wettbewerbsintensität' [The Concept of Optimal Competition Intensity], **180** *Jahrbuch für Nationalökonomie und Statistik*, 1966, 286-323.

HOPPMANN, Erich, 'Wettbewerb als Norm der Wettbewerbspolitik' [Competition as Norm for Competition Policy], **18** *Ordo: Jahrbuch für die Ordnung von Wirtschaft und Gesellschaft*, 1967, 77-94.

HOPPMANN, Erich, 'Die Funktionsfähigkeit des Wettbewerbs: Bemerkungen zu Kantzenbachs Erwiderung' [The Functionality of Competition: Remarks on Kantzenbach's Reaction], **181** *Jahrbuch fur Nationalökonomie und Statistik*, 1967, 251-264.

HOPPMANN, Erich, 'Zum Problem einer wirtschaftpolitischen praktikablen Definition des Wettbewerbs' [On the Problem of and Economic and Practical Definition of Competition], in SCHNEIDER, H.K. (ed.), *Grundlagen der Wettbewerbspolitik*, Berlin, 1968, 9-49.

HOPPMANN, Erich, 'Neue Wettbewerbspolitik: Vom Wettbewerb zur staatlichen Mikro-Steuerung: Bemerkungen zu einem "neuen Leitbild" der Wettbewerbspolitik' [New Competition Policy: From Competition to Governmental Micro-Steering: Remarks on a "New Example" of Competition Policy], **184** *Jahrbuch für Nationalökonomie und Statistik*, 1970, 397-416.

HOPPMANN, Erich, *Wirtschaftsordnung und Wettbewerb* [Economic Order and Competition], Baden-Baden, Nomos, 1988, 566 p.

HORNSBY, Stephen B., 'Competition Policy in the 80's: More Policy Less Competition?', **12** *European Law Review*, 1987, 79-101.

HORNSBY, Stephen B., 'National and Community Control of Concentrations in a Single Market: Should Member States Be Allowed to Impose Stricter Standards?', **13** *European Law Review*, 1987, 295-317.

HOVENKAMP, Herbert J., 'Antitrust Policy after Chicago', **84** *Michigan Law Review*, 1985, 213-284.

HOVENKAMP, Herbert J., 'Chicago and Its Alternatives', *Duke Law Journal*, 1986, 1014-1029.

HOVENKAMP, Herbert J., 'Rhetoric and Skepticism in Antitrust Argument', **84** *Michigan Law Review*, 1986, 1721-1729.

HOVENKAMP, Herbert J., 'Fact, Value and Theory in Antitrust Adjudication', *Duke Law Journal*, 1987, 897-914.

HOVENKAMP, Herbert J., 'Antitrust Policy, Restricted Distribution, and the Market for Exclusionary Rights', **71** *Minnesota Law Review*, 1987, 1293-1318.

HOVENKAMP, Herbert J., 'Treble Damages Reform', **33** *Antitrust Bulletin*, 1988, 233-258.

HOVENKAMP, Herbert J., 'Derek Bok and the Merger of Law and Economics', **21** *University of Michigan Journal of Law Reform*, 1988, 515-539.

HOVENKAMP, Herbert J., 'Antitrust's Protected Classes', **88** *Michigan Law Review*, 1989, 1-48.

HOVENKAMP, Herbert J., 'The Antitrust Movement and the Rise of Industrial

Organization', **68** *Texas Law Review*, 1989, 105-168.

HOVENKAMP, Herbert J., 'The Antitrust Movement and the Rise of Industrial Organization', **68** *Texas Law Review*, 1989, 105-168.

HOVENKAMP, Herbert J., 'The Sherman Act and the Classical Theory of Competition', **74** *Iowa Law Review*, 1989, 1019-1065.

HOVENKAMP, Herbert J., 'Antitrust Policy, Federalism, and the Theory of the Firm: An Historical Perspective', **59** *Antitrust Law Journal*, 1990, 75-91.

HOVENKAMP, Herbert J. and SCHWARTZ, Louis B., 'Treble Damages and Antitrust Deterrence: A Dialogue', **18(1)** *Antitrust Law & Economics Review*, 1986, 67-79.

HUERTA, E., 'Política de competencia y economía industrial en España' [Competition Policy and Industrial Economics in Spain], *Información Comercial Española*, 1987, October.

HUERTA, E., 'Análisis de la integración vertical de empresas en España' [An Analysis of Firms Vertical Integration in Spain], *Información comercial Española*, 1989, n. 39-40.

HUNTLEY, John A.K. and PITT, Douglas C., 'Judicial Policymaking: The Greeneing of US Telecommunications', **10** *International Review of Law and Economics*, 1990, 77-100.

HUTTON, Susan and TREBILCOCK, Michael J., 'An Empirical Study of the Application of Canadian Anti-Dumping Laws: A Search for Normative Rationales', **24** *Journal of World Trade*, 1990, 123-146.

JACQUEMIN, Alexis P. and JONG, Hendrik W. de, *European Industrial Organization*, London, Macmillan, 1977, 269 p.

JANICKI, Thomas, 'EG-Fusionskontrolle auf dem Weg zur praktischen Umsetzung' [EC Merger Control on the Way of Practical Realization], **40** Wirtschaft und Wettbewerb, 1990, 195-205.

JEWKES, John and JEWKES, Sylvia, 'A Hundred Years of Change in the Structure of the Cotton Industry', **9** *Journal of Law and Economics*, 1966, 115-134.

JOHNSEN, D. Bruce, 'Property Rights to Cartel Rents: The *Socony-Vacuum* Story', **34** *Journal of Law and Economics*, 1991, 177-203.

JOHNSON, Frederick I., 'Two Approaches to Market Definition Under the Merger Guidelines', **12** *Research in Law and Economics*, 1989, 227-234.

JOHNSON, Frederick I., 'Market Definition Under the Merger Guidelines: Critical Demand Elasticities', **12** *Research in Law and Economics*, 1989, 235-246.

JOHNSON, Ronald N. and PARKMAN, Allen M., 'Premerger Notification and the Incentive to Merge and Litigate', **7** *Journal of Law, Economics, & Organization*, 1991, 145-162.

JOHNSON, Sam D. and FERRILL, A. Michael, 'Defining Competition: Economic Analysis and Antitrust Decisionmaking', **36** *Baylor Law Review*, 1984, 585-621.

JOHNSTONE, Robert P., 'Innovation, Lower Costs, and Hard Price Competition: Rose Acre's American Success Story', **21(3)** *Antitrust Law & Economics Review*, 1989, 63-76.

JONES, J.C.H. and LAUDADIO, L., 'Risk, Profitability, and Market Structure:

Some Canadian Evidence on Structural and Behavioral Approaches to Antitrust', **28** *Antitrust Bulletin*, 1983, 349-379.

JONG, Hendrik W. de, 'Marktorganisatie, mededinging en prijsvorming' [Market Organisation, Competition and Price-Making], **66** *Economisch-Statistische Berichten*, 1981, 1268-1280.

JONG, Hendrik W. de, 'De Europese mededingingspolitiek: overzicht en beoordeling' [European Competition Policy: Overview and Assessment], *Beleid & Maatschappij*, 1982, 230-240.

JONG, Hendrik W. de, 'Fusies, overnames en beschermingsconstructies' [Mergers, Take-overs and Protective Devices], **73** *Economisch-Statistische Berichten*, 1988, 842-847 + 852.

JONG, Hendrik W. de, *Dynamische markttheorie* [Dynamic Market Theory], Leiden, Stenfert Kroese, 1989 (4th ed.), 334 p.

JONG, Hendrik W. de, 'Concurrentie en concentratie in de markteconomie' [Competition and Concentration in the Market Economy], **37** *Sociaal-Economische Wetgeving: Tijdschrift voor Europees en Economisch Recht*, 1989, 664-688.

JONG, Hendrik W. de, 'Concurrentie, concentratie en het Europese mededingingsbeleid' [Competition, Concentration and European Competition Policy], **74** *Economisch-Statistische Berichten*, 1989, 1182-1187.

JONG, Hendrik W. de, 'Nederland: Het kartelparadijs van Europa' [The Netherlands: European Anti-trust Paradise], **75** *Economisch-Statistische Berichten*, 1990, 244-248.

JORDE, Thomas M., 'Remarks on Acceptable Cooperation among Competitors in the Face of Growing International Competition', **58** *Antitrust Law Journal*, 1989, 519-527.

JORDE, Thomas M. and TEECE, David J., 'Acceptable Cooperation among Competitors in the Face of Growing International Competition', **58** *Antitrust Law Journal*, 1989, 529-556.

JORDE, Thomas M. and TEECE, David J., 'Antitrust Policy and Innovation: Taking Account of Performance Competition and Competitor Cooperation', **147** *Journal of Institutional and Theoretical Economics*, 1991, 118-144.

KAHN, Alfred E., 'Comment: Deregulatory Schizophrenia', **75** *California Law Review*, 1987, 1059-1068.

KAHN, Alfred E., 'Deregulatory Schizophrenia', **75** *California Law Review*, 1987, 1059-1068.

KALLFASS, Hermann H., 'Die Chicago School: Eine Skizze des "neuen" amerikanisches Ansatzes für die Wettbewerbspolitik' [The Chicago School: A Sketch of the "New" American Approach for Competition Policy], **30** *Wirtschaft und Wettbewerb*, 1980, 596-601.

KANTZENBACH, Erhard, 'Das Konzept der optimalen Wettbewerbsintensität: Eine Erwiderung auf den gleichnamigen Besprechungsaufsatz von Erich Hoppmann' [The Concept of Optimal Competition Intensity: A Reaction on Erich Hoppman's Comment of the Same Name], **181** *Jahrbuch für Nationalökonomie und Statistik*, 1967, 193-241.

KANTZENBACH, Erhard, 'Comment' [on Neuberger and Neumann, Banking and

Antitrust: Limiting Industrial Ownership by Banks?], **147** *Journal of Institutional and Theoretical Economics*, 1991, 200-201.

KANTZENBACH, Erhard and KRÜGER, Reinald, 'Zur Frage der richtigen Abgrenzung des sachlich relevanten Markten bei der wettbewerbspolitischen Beurteilung von Unternehmenszusammenschlüssen' [On the Question of the Correct Definition of the Relevant Market at the Judgment of Mergers], **40** *Wirtschaft und Wettbewerb*, 1990, 472481.

KAPLOW, Louis, 'The Accuracy of Traditional Market Power Analysis and a Direct Adjustment Alternative', **95** *Harvard Law Review*, 1982, 1817-1848.

KAPLOW, Louis, 'The Patent-Antitrust Intersection: A Reappraisal', **97** *Harvard Law Review*, 1984, 1815-1892.

KAPLOW, Louis, 'Antitrust, Law & Economics, and the Courts', **50 (4)** *Law and Contemporary Problems*, 1987, 181-216.

KARP, David C., 'A Consumer Oriented Approach to Market Definition Under the Antitrust Laws', **18** *University of San Francisco Law Review*, 1984, 221-251.

KAUFER, Erich, 'Kantzenbachs Konzept des funktionsfähigen Wettbewerbs: Ein Kommentar' [Kantenbach's Concept of Functional Competition: A Comment], **179** *Jahrbuch für Nationalökonomie und Statistik*, 1966, 481-492.

KAUFER, Erich, 'Das Konzept der optimalen Wettbewerbsintensität: Eine Replik' [The Concept of Optimal Competition Intensity: A Reply], **181** *Jahrbuch für Nationalökonomie und Statistik*, 1968, 242-250.

KAUPER, Thomas E., 'The Goals of United States Antitrust Policy: The Current Debate', **136** *Zeitschrift für die gesamte Staatswissenschaft*, 1980, 408-434.

KAUPER, Thomas E., 'The 1982 Horizontal Merger Guidelines: Of Collusion, Efficiency, and Failure', **71** *California Law Review*, 1983, 497-534.

KAUPER, Thomas E., 'The Role of Economic Analysis in the Antitrust Division Before and After the Establishment of the Economic Policy Office: A Lawyer's View', **29** *Antitrust Bulletin*, 1984, 111-132.

KAUPER, Thomas E., 'The Sullivan Approach to Horizontal Restraints', **75** *California Law Review*, 1987, 893-915.

KAYSEN, Carl and TURNER, Donald F., *Antitrust Policy: An Economic and Legal Analysis*, Cambridge, Harvard University Press, 1959, 345 p.

KENNEY, Roy W. and KLEIN, Benjamin, 'The Economics of Block Booking', **26** *Journal of Law and Economics*, 1983, 497-540.

KINGDON, John S., 'Economic Arguments Applied in Department of Justice and Federal Trade Commission Merger Investigations', **6** *European Competition Law Review*, 1985, 366-376.

KINGDON, John S., 'Economic Argument in Antitrust Cases: An American Litigator's Perspective', **8** *European Competition Law Review*, 1987, 371-385.

KIRCHNER, Christian, '"Ökonomische Analyse des Rechts" und Recht der Wettbewerbsbeschränkungen' ["Economic Analysis of Law" and Anti-trust Law], **144** *Zeitschrift für das gesamte Handels- und Wirtschaftsrecht*, 1980, 563-588.

KIRCHNER, Christian, 'Comment' [on von Weizsäcker, Antitrust and the Division of Labor], **147** *Journal of Institutional and Theoretical Economics*, 1991, 114-117.

KIRCHNER, Christian and PICOT, Arnold, 'Transaction Cost Analysis of Structural Changes in the Distribution System: Reflections on Institutional Developments in the Fe deral Republic of Germany', **143** *Journal of Institutional and Theoretical Economics*, 1987, 62-81.

KITCH, Edmund W., 'The Yellow Cab Antitrust Case', **15** *Journal of Law and Economics*, 1972, 327-336.

KLEIN, Benjamin, 'Transaction Cost Determinants of "Unfair" Contractual Arrangements', **70** *American Economic Review. Papers and Proceedings*, 1980, 356-362. Reprinted in GOLDBERG, Victor P. (ed.), *Readings in the Economics of Contract Law*, Cambridge, Cambridge University Press, 1989, 139-146.

KLEIN, Benjamin, CRAWFORD, Robert G. and ALCHIAN, Armen A., 'Vertical Integration, Appropriable Rents, and the Competitive Contracting Process', **21** *Journal of Law and Economics*, 1978, 297-326.

KLEIN, Benjamin and MURPHY, Kevin M., 'Vertical Restraints as Contract Enforcement Mechanisms', **31** *Journal of Law and Economics*, 1988, 265-297.

KLEIN, Cristopher C., 'Predation in the Courts: Legal Versus Economic Analysis in Sham Litigation Cases', **10** *International Review of Law and Economics*, 1990, 29-40.

KNIGHT, Frank H., *The Ethics of Competition and Other Essays*, London, Allen and Unwin, 1935.

KORAH, Valentine, 'EEC Competition Policy: Legal Form or Economic Efficiency', in RIDEOUT, R. and JONNELL J. (eds.), **36** *Current Legal Problems*, 85-109.

KORAH, Valentine, 'Critical Comments on the Commission's Recent Decisions Exempting Joint Ventures to Exploit Research that Needs Further Development', **12** *European Law Review*, 1987, 18-39.

KORAH, Valentine, 'Franchising and the Draft Group Exemption', **8** *European Competition Law Review*, 1987, 124-142.

KORAH, Valentine, The Control of Mergers under the EEC Competition Law', **8** *European Competition Law Review*, 1987, 239-255.

KORAH, Valentine and LASOK, Paul, 'Philip Morris and its Aftermath: Merger Control?', **25** *Common Market Law Review*, 1988, 333-368.

KOVACIC, William E., 'Federal Antitrust Enforcement in the Reagan Administration: Two Cheers for the Disappearance of the Large Firm Defendant in Nonmerger Cases', **12** *Research in Law and Economics*, 1989, 173-206.

KRAKOWSN, Michael, 'The Requirements for EEC Merger Control, *Intereconomics*, 1989, 120-126.

KRATTENMAKER, Thomas G., LANDE, Robert H. and SALOP, Steven C., 'Monopoly Power and Market Power in Antitrust Law', **76** *Georgetown Law Journal*, 1987, 241-269.

KRATTENMAKER, Thomas G. and SALOP, Steven C., 'Anticompetitive Exclusion: Raising Rivals' Costs to Achieve Power over Price', **96** *Yale Law Journal*, 1986, 209-293.

LACROIX, Sumner, MIKLIUS, Walter and MAK, James. 'The New Standards of Unfair Competition: an Economic Analysis of the Du Pont v. FTC Litigation', **9** *The University of Hawaii Law Review*, 1987, 457-486.

LAFUENTE, Alberto, 'Aspectos económicos de la definición de mercado' [Some Economic Aspects of the Market Definition], *Información Comercial Española*, 1987, October.

LAMBERS, H.W., 'Mededingingspolitiek' [Competition Policy], in ANDRIESSEN, J.E. and VAN MEERHAEGHE, M.A.G. (eds.), *Theorie van de Economische Politiek*, Leiden, Stenfert Kroese, 1962, 307-338.

LAMPE, Hanes-Eckhard, *Wettbewerb. Wettbewerbsbeziehungen. Wettbewerbsintensität* [Competition. Competition Relations, Competition Intensity], Baden-Baden, Nomos, 1979, 317 p.

LANDE, Robert H., 'Wealth Transfers as the Original and Primary Concern of Antitrust: The Efficiency Interpretation Challenged', **34** *Hastings Law Journal*, 1982, 67-151.

LANDE, Robert H., 'The Rise and (Coming) Fall Of Efficiency as the Ruler of Antitrust', **33** *Antitrust Bullein*, 1988, 429-466.

LANDES, William M., 'Optimal Sanctions for Antitrust Violations', **50** *University of Chicago Law Review*, 1983, 652-678.

LANDES, William M. and POSNER, Richard A., 'The Economics of Passing On: A Reply to Harris and Sullivan', **128** *University of Pennsylvania Law Review*, 1980, 1274-1279.

LANDES, William M. and POSNER, Richard A., 'Market Power in Antitrust Cases', **94** *Harvard Law Review*, 1981, 937-996.

LANGENFELD, J. and SCHEFFMAN, D.T., 'The FTC in the 1980s', **5(2)** *Review of Industrial Organization*, 1990, 79-98.

LANGENFELD, James, 'Comment on Baker', **32** *Journal of Law and Economics*, 1989, S77-S82.

LANGENFELD, James and SCHEFFMAN, David, 'Innovation and U.S. Competition Policy', **34** *Antitrust Bulletin*, 1989, 1-63.

LARSON, David A., 'An Economic Analysis of the Webb-Pomerene Act', **13** *Journal of Law and Economics*, 1970, 461-500.

LAUDATI, Laraine L., 'Economies of Scale: Weighing Operating Efficiency When Enforcing Antitrust Law', **49** *Fordham Law Review*, 1981, 771-801.

LAVEY, Warren G., 'Commentary: Focus of Antitrust Markets', **62** *Washington University Law Quarterly*, 1985, 671-679.

LE BOLZER, Jean-Marc, 'The New EEC Merger Control Policy After the Adoption of Regulation 4064/89', **14** *World Competition: Law and Economics Review 1991*, 33-47.

LEFFLER, Keith, 'Toward a Reasonable Rule of Reason: Comments', **28** *Journal of Law and Economics*, 1985, 381-386.

LEHMANN, Michael, 'Considerazioni di ordine economico nel diritto della concorrenza nella Republica Federale Tedesca' [Economic Considerations Concerning German Competition Law], in *Problemi attuali del diritto industriale, Volume celebrativo del XXV anno della Rivista di diritto industriale*, Milano, 1977, 689-699.

LEHMANN, Michael, 'Das Prinzip Wettbewerb' [The Principle of Competition], *Juristenzeitung*, 1990, (Heft 2), 61-67.

LEIGH, Guy I.F., 'EEC Law and Selective Distribution: Recent Developments', **7** *European Competition Law Review*, 1986, 419-436.

LEITZINGER, Jeffrey J. and TAMOR, Kenneth L., 'Foreign Competition in Antitrust Law', **26** *Journal of Law and Economics*, 1983, 87-102.

LEMLEY, Mark A., 'Bad Economics in the 9th Circuit, Northern District of California', **20(3)** *Antitrust Law & Economics Review*, 1988, 9-13.

LERNER, Abba P., 'The Concept of Monopoly and the Measurement of Monopoly Power', **1** *Review of Economic Studies*, 1934, 157-175.

LEVY, David T., 'The Transactions Cost Approach to Vertical Integration: An Empirical Examination', **67** *Review of Economics and Statistics*, 1985, 438-445.

LEVY, David T., 'Comment on Dunne, Roberts, and Samuelson', **32** *Journal of Law and Economics*, 1989, S273-S275.

LIEBELER, Wesley J., 'Industrial Concentration, Efficiency, and Antitrust Reform: Another View', **12** *Southwestern University Law Review*, 1981, 379-404.

LIEBELER, Wesley J., '1984 Economic Review of Antitrust Developments: Horizontal Restrictions, Efficiency, and the Per Se Rule', **33** *UCLA Law Review*, 1986, 1019-1062.

LIEBELER, Wesley J., 'What Are the Alternatives to Chicago?', *Duke Law Journal*, 1987, 879-898.

LIEBELER, Wesley J., 'Resale Price Maintenance and Consumer Welfare: Business Electronics Corp. v. Sharp Electronics Corp.', **36** *UCLA Law Review*, 1989, 889-913.

LIEBOWITZ, S.J., 'What Do Census Price-Cost Margins Measure?', **25** *Journal of Law and Economics*, 1982, 231-246.

LIEBOWITZ, S.J., 'The Measurement and Mismeasurement of Monopoly Power', **7** *International Review of Law and Economics*, 1987, 89-99.

LIESNER, Jeremy and GLYNN, Dermot, 'Does Anti-trust Make Economic Sense?', **8** *European Competition Law Review*, 1987, 344-370.

LINSSEN, G.J., 'De rol van de Commissie bij de toepassing van het Europese mededingingsrecht' [The Role of the Commission in Applying European Competition Law], in VERLOREN VAN THEMAAT, Pieter, et al., *Europees kartelrecht anno 1973*, Deventer, Kluwer, 1973, 23-45.

LINSSEN, G.J. 'De verhouding tussen het formele en het informele kartelbeleid in Nederland en de plaats van de Commissie Economische Mededinging' [The Interrelationship between the Formal and Informal Dutch Anti-trust Policy and the Position of the Committee on Economic Competition], **24** *TVVS: Maandblad voor Ondernemingsrecht en Rechtspersonen*, 1981, 255-259.

LITTLECHILD, S.C., 'Misleading Calculations of the Social Costs of Monopoly Power', **91** *Economic Journal*, 1981, 348-363.

LONG, William F., SCHRAMM, Richard and TOLLISON, Robert, 'The Economic Determinants of Antitrust Activity', **16** *Journal of Law and Economics*, 1973, 351-364.

LOPATKA, John E., 'State Action and Municipal Antitrust Immunity: An Economic Approach', **53** *Fordham Law Review*, 1984, 23 ff.

LORIE, James H. and HALPERN, Paul, 'Conglomerates: The Rhetoric and the Evidence', **13** *Journal of Law and Economics*, 1970, 149-166.

LUSTGARTEN, Steven, 'Gains and Losses from Concentration: A Comment', **22** *Journal of Law and Economics*, 1979, 183-190.

LYNK, William J. and MORRISEY, Michael A., 'The Economic Basis of *Hyde*: Are Market Power and Hospital Exclusive Contracts Related ?', **30** *Journal of Law and Economics*, 1987, 399-421.

MacAVOY, Paul W., McKIE, James W. and PRESTON, Lee E., 'High and Stable Concentration Levels, Profitability, and Public Policy: A Response', **14** *Journal of Law and Economics*, 1971, 493-499.

MacCRIMMON, Marilyn and SADANARD, Asha, 'Models of Market Behaviour and Competition Law: Exclusive Dealing', **27** *Osgoode Hall Law Journal*, 1989, 711-768.

MACKAY, Robert J., MILLER, James C., III and YANDLE, Bruce (eds.), *Public Choice and Regulation: A View form Inside the Federal Trade Commission*, Stanford, Hoover Institution Press, 1987, 363 p.

MacLEOD, William C., 'FTC Consumer Protection Activities', **57** *Antitrust Law Journal*, 1988, 163-167.

MAGOULAS, Georgios and SIMON, Jürgen (eds.), *Recht und Ökonomie beim Konsumentenschutz und Konsumentenkredit. Interdisziplinäre Studien zu den Problemen und Konzepten des Verbraucherschutzes* [Law and Economics of Consumer Protection and Consumer Credit. Interdisciplinary Studies on the Problems and Concepts of Consumer Protection], Baden-Baden, Nomos, 1985, 436 p.

MALINA, Michael, 'Comment: Some Thoughts on Monopoly, Markets, and Mergers', **75** *California Law Review*, 1987, 997-1003.

MANNE, Henry G., 'New Views on Antitrust: Summary Comments', **147** *Journal of Institutional and Theoretical Economics*, 1991, 235-239.

MARFELS, Christian, 'Economic Criteria for the Application of Antitrust - Overview and Assessment of the Fifth Report of the Monopolies Commission of the Federal Republic of Germany', **31** *Antitrust Bulletin*, 1986, 1067-1087.

MARKOVITS, Richard S., 'Predicting the Competitive Impact of Horizontal Mergers in a Monopolistically Competitive World: A Non-Market-Oriented Proposal and Critique of the Market Definition-Market Share-Market Concentration Approach', **56** *Texas Law Review*, 1978, 587-731.

MARKOVITS, Richard S., 'Monopolistic Competition, Second Best, and the Antitrust Paradox: A Review Article', **77** *Michigan Law Review*, 1979, 567-640.

MARKOVITS, Richard S., 'The Limits of Simplifying Antitrust: A Reply to Professor Eeasterbrook', **63** *Texas Law Review*, 1984, 41-87.

MARKOVITS, Richard S., 'An Ideal Antitrust Regime', **64** *Texas Law Review*, 1985, 251-352.

MARKOVITS, Richard S., 'The Functions, Allocative Efficiency, and Legality of Tie-ins: A Comment', **28** *Journal of Law and Economics*, 1985, 387-404.

MARKOVITS, Richard S., 'The American Antitrust Laws on the Centennial of the

Sherman Act: A Critique of the Statutes Themselves, Their Interpretation, and Their Operationalization', **38** *Buffalo Law Review*, 1990, 673-776.

MARTIN, Stephen, *Industrial Economics: Economic Analysis and Public Policy*, MacMillan, New York, 1988, 540 p.

MARVEL, Howard P., 'Exclusive Dealing', **25** *Journal of Law and Economics*, 1982, 1-25.

MARVEL, Howard P. and McCAFFERTY, Stephen, 'The Welfare Effects of Resale Price Maintenance', **28** *Journal of Law and Economics*, 1985, 363-379.

MARVEL, Howard P., NETTER, Jeffry M. and ROBINSON, Anthony M., 'Price Fixing and Civil Damages: An Economic Analysis', **40** *Stanford Law Review*, 1988, 561-575.

MASSEL, Mark S., *Competition and Monopoly*, Washington, Brookings Institution, 1962, 477 p.

MASTEN, Scott E. and SNYDER, Edward A., 'The Design and Duration of Contracts: Strategic and Efficiency Considerations', **52(1)** *Law and Contemporary Problems*, 1989, 63-85.

MATHEWSON, G. Frank, TREBILCOCK, Michael J. and WALKER, Michael (eds.), *The Law and Economics of Competition Policy*, Vancouver, Fraser Institute, 1990, 443 p.

MAULE, C.J., 'Antitrust and the Takeover Activity of American Firms In Canada: A Rejoinder', **12** *Journal of Law and Economics*, 1969, 419-424.

MAULE, C.J., 'Antitrust and the Takeover Activity of American Firms in Canada: A Final Comment', **13** *Journal of Law and Economics*, 1970, 261.

MAY, James, 'Antitrust in the Formative Era: Political and Economic Theory in Constitutional and Antitrust Analysis, 1880-1918', **50** *Ohio State Law Journal*, 1989, 257-395.

MAYER, Colin, 'The Assessment: Recents Developments in Industrial Economics and their Implications for Policy', **1(3)** *Oxford Review of Economic Policv*, 1985, 1985, 1-25.

MAYS, Andrea and GRECO, Anthony J., 'Dr. Greco on Beer Competition; Reply', **20(1)** *Antitrust Law & Economics Review*, 1988, 53-58.

McCALL, Charles W., 'The Administrative Feasibility of a Rule of Reason Predatory Pricing Standard', **16** *University of Toledo Law Review*, 1984, 91-122.

McCHESNEY, Fred S., 'On the Economics of Antitrust Enforcement', **68** *Georgetown Law Journal*, 1980, 1103-1111.

McDAVID, Janet L., 'Failing Companies and the Antitrust Laws', **14** *University of Michigan Journal of Law Reform*, 1981, 229-265.

McGEE, John S., 'Predatory Price Cutting: The Standard Oil (N.J.) Case', **1** *Journal of Law and Economics*, 1958, 137-169.

McGEE, John S., *In Defense of Industrial Concentration*, New York, Praeger Publi., 1971, 167 p.

McGEE, John S., 'Economies of Size in Auto Body Manufacture', **16** *Journal of Law and Economics*, 1973, 239-273.

McGEE, John S., 'Predatory Pricing Revisited', **23** *Journal of Law and Economics*,

1980, 289-330.

McGEE, John S., *Industrial Organization*, Englewood Cliffs, Prentice-Hall, 1988, 497 p.

McGEE, John S. and BASSETT, Lowell R., 'Vertical Integration Revisited', **19** *Journal of Law and Economics*, 1976, 17-38.

McGOWAN, John J., 'International Comparisons of Merger Activity', **14** *Journal of Law and Economics*, 1971, 233-250.

McNULTY, Paul J., 'Economic Theory and the Meaning of Competition', **82** *Quarterly Journal of Economics*, 1968.

McQUAID, Kim, 'The Corporate Counterattack: Fighting for the Levers of Power (II)', **17(2)** *Antitrust Law & Economics Review*, 1985, 61-72.

MEANS, Gardiner C., 'Corporate Power in the Marketplace', **26** *Journal of Law and Economics*, 1983, 467-485.

MEEHAN, James W. Jr., 'Vertical Foreclosure in the Cement Industry: A Comment', **15** *Journal of Law and Economics*, 1972, 461-465.

MEEHAN, James W. Jr., '*Berkey Photo, Inc. v. Eastman Kodak Co*: A Search for an Explanation of Kodak's Dominance of the Amateur Photographic Equipment Industry', **5** *Research in Law and Economics*, 1983, 131-165.

MENSCH, Elizabeth and FREEMAN, Alan, 'Efficiency and Image: Advertising as an Antitrust Issue', *Duke Law Journal*, 1990, 321 ff.

MESTMÄCKER, Ernst-Joachim, 'Competition Policy and Antitrust: Some Comparative Observations', **136** *Zeitschrift für die gesamte Staatswissenschaft*, 1980, 387-407.

MESTMÄCKER, Ernst-Joachim, 'Fusions kontrolle im Gemeinsamen Markt zwischen Wettbewerbspolitik und Industriepolitik' [Merger Control in the Common Market Between Competition Policy and Industrial Policy], *Europarecht*, 1988, 349-377.

METZENBAUM, Howard M., 'Overruling Monsanto and Sharp: S. 865 and the Per Se Rule Against Resale Price Fixing', **21(2)** *Antitrust Law & Economics Review*, 1989, 71-86.

MILES, John J., 'Antitrust, Hospital Staff Priviled Decisions and Hospital Joint Venture', **17** *University of Toledo Law Review*, 1986, 873-922.

MILLER, Edward M., 'Do Economies of Scale Attract Enry?', **25** *Antitrust Bulletin*, 1980, 583-587.

MILLER, Elizabeth, 'Note: Antitrust Restrictions on Trade Secret Licensing: A Legal Review and Economic Analysis', **52(1)** *Law and Contemporary Problems*, 1989, 183-209.

MILLER, James C., III and PAUTLER, Paul, 'Predation: The Changing View in Economics and the Law', **28** *Journal of Law and Economics*, 1985, 495-502.

MILLER, John P. (ed.), *Competition. Cartels and their Regulation*, North-Holland Publ. Co., Amsterdam, 1962.

MILLER, Roger LeRoy, 'Where Joe Bain, Mike Scherer, and Fritz Mueller 'Went Wrong': A Libertarian View', **14** *Antitrust Law and Economics Review*, 1982, 15-70.

MILLSTEIN, Ira M., 'The Impact of the Antitrust Laws on America's Ability to Restructure Its Industries and Proposals for Change', **47** *University of Pittsburgh Law Review*, 1986, 713-725.

MILLSTEIN, Ira M. and KESSLER, Jeffrey L., 'The Antitrust Legacy of the Reagan Administration', **33** *Antitrust Bulletin*, 1988, 505-541.

MINDA, Gary, 'Interest Groups, Political Freedom, and Antitrust: A Modern Reassessment of the Noerr-Pennington Doctrine', **41** *Hastings Law Journal*, 1990, 905-1028.

MOK, M.R., 'Kartelbeleid nu en in de toekomst' [Present and Future Anti-trust Policy], in MOK, M.R., et al., *Nieuwe ontwikkelingen in het Europese kartelrecht*, Kluwer, Deventer, 1976, 1-15.

MOK, M.R., '20 jaar WEM' [20 Years WEM], **26** *Sociaal-Economische Wetgeving: Tijdschrift voor Europees en Economisch Recht*, 1978, 737-760.

MOK, M.R., 'Het paard achter de wagen: Deregulering en kartelrecht' [The Cart Before the Horse: Deregulation and Anti-trust Law], **31** *Sociaal- Economische Wetgeving: Tijdschrift voor Europees en Economisch Recht*, 1983, 666-678.

MONTEVERDE, Kirk and TEECE, David J., 'Appropriable Rents and Quasi-Vertical Integration', **25** *Journal of Law and Economics*, 1982, 321-328.

MORRISON, Steven A. and WINSTON, Clifford, 'Empirical Implications and Tests of the Contestability Hypothesis', **30** *Journal of Law and Economics*, 1987, 53-66.

MÖSCHEL, Wernhard, 'Wettbewerb im Schnittfeld von Rechtswissenschaft und Nationalökonomie' [Competition at the Crossing of Legal Science and National Economy], *Wirtschaftwissenschaftliche Studien*, 1978, 351-357.

MÖSCHEL, Wernhard, 'Divergierende Entwicklungen im amerikanischen und europäischen Kartellrecht' [Conflicting Developments in American and European Antitrust Law], *Wirtschaftwissenschaftliche Studien*, 1983, 603-609.

MOSCHEL, Wernhard, 'International Restraints of Competition: A Regulatory Outline', **10** *Northwestern Journal of International Law & Business*, 1989, 76-83.

MÖSCHEL, Wernhard, 'The Goals of Antitrust Revisited', **147** *Journal of Institutional and Theoretical Economics*, 1991, 7-23.

MUELLER, Charles E., 'Developments in Industrial Organization and Antitrust Policy: An Overview', **17(4)** *Antitrust Law & Economics Review*, 1985, 79-94.

MUELLER, Charles E., 'Developments in Industrial Organization and Antitrust Policy: An Overview (IV)', **18(3)** *Antitrust Law & Economics Review*, 1986, 59-74.

MUELLER, Charles E., 'Developments in Industrial Organization and Antitrust Policy: An Overview (III)', **18(2)** *Antitrust Law & Economics Review*, 1986, 93-110.

MUELLER, Charles E., 'Developments in Industrial Organization and Antitrust Policy: An Overview (II)', **18(1)** *Antitrust Law & Economics Review*, 1986, 101-110.

MUELLER, Charles E., 'Roundtable on U.S. Antitrust Policy: Further Reflections and a Summing Up (II)', **19(3)** *Antitrust Law & Economics Review*, 1987, 81-96.

MUELLER, Charles E., 'Roundtable on U.S. Antitrust Policy: Further Reflections and a Summing Up (III)', **19(4)** *Antitrust Law & Economics Review*, 1987, 81-94.

MUELLER, Charles E., 'Economics, the Courts, and Antitrust Policy: A Roundtable Discussion (II)', **20(3)** *Antitrust Law & Economics Review*, 1988, 21-38.

MUELLER, Charles E., HIURA, Thomas M. and SCANLON, Paul D., 'Predatory "Recoupment" Cases in 3 U.S. Circuits: Jury Findings Versus Judicial "Economic" Theorizing' **21(3)** *Antitrust Law & Economics Review*, 1989, 1-10.

MUELLER, Dennis C., 'Das Antitrustrecht der Vereinigten Staaten am Scheideweg' [The Antitrust Law of the United States at the Parting of the Ways], **36** *Wirtschaft und Wettbewerb*, 1986, 533-555.

MUELLER, Willard F., 'A New Attack on Antitrust: The Chicago Case', **18** *Antitrust Law & Economics Review*, 1986, 29-66.

MUELLER, Willard F., 'A New Attack on Antitrust: The Chicago Case', **18(1)** *Antitrust Law & Economics Review*, 1986, 29-66.

MUELLER, Willard F., 'End of the Chicago-School's Free Ride on Sealy: The Free-Rider Theory Meets the Facts of Life', **20(4)** *Antitrust Law & Economics Review*, 1988, 17-38.

MUELLER, Willard F., 'The Threshold of Market Power in Economics: 4-Firm Share of 40% to 50%', **21(3)** *Antitrust Law & Economics Review*, 1989, 11-21.

MUELLER, Willard F., 'The Rose Acre Decision and Below-Cost Price Discrimination: Spoiled Economic Eggs in the 7th Circuit', **21(2)** *Antitrust Law & Economics Review*, 1989, 49-70.

MUELLER, Willard F., 'The Rose Acre Decision and Below-Cost Price Discrimination: Spoiled Economic Eggs in the 7th Circuit (II)', **21(3)** *Antitrust Law & Economics Review*, 1989, 77-87.

NEUBERGER, Doris and NEUMANN, Manfred, 'Banking and Antitrust: Limiting Industrial Ownership by Banks?', **147** *Journal of Institutional and Theoretical Economics*, 1991, 188-199.

NEWMARK, Craig M., 'Is Antitrust Enforcement Effective?', **96** *Journal of Political Economy*, 1988, 1315-1328.

NEWMARK, Craig M., 'Does Horizontal Price Fixing Raise Price? A Look at the Bakers of Washington Case', **31** *Journal of Law and Economics*, 1988, 469-484.

NIX, Joan, 'Fair Competition: An Unambiguous Policy Guide?', *Wisconsin Law Review*, 1990, 501-511.

NOLAND, James E., '$9 Million Jury Verdict "Against the Clear Weight of the Evidence"', **21(2)** *Antitrust Law & Economics Review*, 1989, 13-26.

NUTTER, G. Warren and MOORE, John H., 'A Theory of Competition', **19** *Journal of Law and Economics*, 1976, 39-65.

ORDOVER, Janusz A. and BAUMOL William J., 'Antitrust Policy and High--Technology Industries', **4** *Oxford Review of Economic Polcy*, 1988, No. 4, 13-

34.

ORDOVER, Janusz A., SYKES, Alan 0. and WILLIG, Robert D., 'Herfindahl Concentration, Rivalry, and Mergers', **95** *Harvard Law Review*, 1982, 1857-1874.

ORDOVER, Janusz A., SYKES, Alan O. and WILLIG, Robert D., 'Unfair International Trade Practices', **15** *New York University Journal of International Law and Politics*, 1983, 323-337.

ORDOVER, Janusz A. and WALL, Daniel M., 'Proving Entry Barriers: A Practical Guide to the Economics of New Entry', **2** *Antitrust*, 1988, 12-17.

ORDOVER, Janusz A. and WILLIG, Robert D., 'The 1982 Department of Justice Merger Guidelines: An Economic Assessment', **71** *California Law Review*, 1983, 535-574.

ORDOVER, Janusz A. and WILLIG, Robert D., 'Antitrust for High-Technology Industries: Assessing Research Joint Ventures and Mergers', **28** *Journal of Law and Economics*, 1985, 311-333.

OSTRY, Sylvia, 'Competition Policy and the Self-Regulating Professions', in SLAYTON, P. and TREBILCOCK, Michael J. (eds.), *The Professions and Public Policy*, Toronto, University of Toronto Faculty of Law, 1978.

PAGE, W.H., 'State Action and "Active Supervision": An Antitrust Anomaly', **35** *Antitrust Bulletin*, 1990, 745-770.

PAGE, William H., 'Interest Groups, Antitrust, and State Regulation: Parker v. Brown in the Economic Theory of Legislation', *Duke Law Journal*, 1987, 618-668.

PAGE, William H., 'The Chicago School and the Evolution of Antitrust: Characterization, Antitrust Injury, and Evidentiary Sufficiency', **75** *Virginia Law Review*, 1989, 1221-1308.

PAGE, William H., 'Optimal Antitrust Penalties and Competitors' Injury', **88** *Michigan Law Review*, 1990, 2151-2166.

PARSONS, Donald O. and RAY, Edward John, 'The United States Steel Consolidation: The Creation of Market Control', **18** *Journal of Law and Economics*, 1975, 181-219.

PASHIGIAN, B. Peter, 'Market Concentration in the United States and Great Britain', **11** *Journal of Law and Economics*, 1968, 299-319.

PAULE, C.L., 'Antitrust and the Takeover Activity of American Firms in Canada', **11** *Journal of Law and Economics*, 1968, 423-432.

PAUTLER, Paul A., 'A Guide to the Herfindahl Index for Antitrust Attorneys', **5** *Research in Law and Economics*, 1983, 167-190.

PAUTLER, Paul A., 'A Review of the Economic Basis for Broad-Based Horizontal-Merger Policy', **28** *Antitrust Bulletin*, 1983, 571-651.

PEEPERKORN, Luc, 'Mededingingsbeleid op klompen' [Competition Policy on Wooden Shoes], **10** *Tijdschrift voor Politieke Economie*, 1987, 57-75.

PEEPERKORN, Luc, 'Openbaarheid van kartels' [The Public Nature of Cartels], **73** *Economisch-Statistische Berichten*, 1988, 212-214.

PEEPERKORN, Luc, 'Het EG-mededingingsbeleid' [EC Competition Policy], **74** *Economisch-Statistische Berichten*, 1989, 1139-1142.

PEEPERKORN, Luc, 'Fusiecontrole in de EG' [EC Merger Control], **74** *Economisch-Statistische Berichten*, 1989, 1163-1165.

PELTMAN, Sam, 'Comment' [on Jorde and Teece, Antitrust Policy and Innovation: Taking Account of Performance Competition and Competitor Cooperation], **147** *Journal of Institutional and Theoretical Economics*, 1991, 152-154.

PELTZMAN, Sam, 'The Gains and Losses from Industrial Concentration', **20** *Journal of Law and Economics*, 1977, 229-263.

PELTZMAN, Sam, 'The Causes and Consequences of Rising Industrial Concentration: A Reply', **22** *Journal of Law and Economics*, 1979, 209-211.

PERITZ, Rudolph J., 'The Predicament of Antitrust Jurisprudenc: Econmics and the Monopolization of Price Discrimination', *Duke Law Journal*, 1984, 1205-1295.

PERITZ, Rudolph J., 'The "Rule of Reason" in Antitrust Law: Property Logic in Restraint of Competition', **40** *Hastings Law Journal*, 1989, 285-342.

PERITZ, Rudolph J., 'A Genealogy of Vertical Restraints Doctrine', **40** *Hastings Law Journal*, 1989, 511-576.

PETERMAN, John L., 'The Brown Shoe Case', **18** *Journal of Law and Economics*, 1975, 81-146.

PETERMAN, John L., 'The Federal Trade Commission v. Brown Shoe Company', **18** *Journal of Law and Economics*, 1975, 361-419.

PETERMAN, John L., 'The *International Salt* Case', **22** *Journal of Law and Economics*, 1979, 351-364.

PHILLIPS, Almarin, 'Market Concentration and Performance: A Survey of the Evidence', **61** *Notre Dame Law Review*, 1986, 1099-1145.

PHILLIPS, Bernard J., 'Comment' [on Breit, Resale Price Maintenance: What do Economists Know and When did They Know it?], **147** *Journal of Institutional and Theoretical Economics*, 1991, 91-93.

PHILLIPS, C.F., Jr., 'Industrial Market Structure and Economic Performance." **2** *Bell Journal of Economics*, 1971, 683-687.

PICOT, Arnold, 'Comment' [on Breit, Resale Price Maintenance: What do Economists Know and When did They Know it?], **147** *Journal of Institutional and Theoretical Economics*, 1991, 94-98.

PINDYCK, Robert S., 'The Measurement of Monopoly Power in Dynamic Markets', **28** *Journal of Law and Economics*, 1985, 193-222.

PITOFSKY, Robert, 'Does Antitrust Have a Future?', **76** *Georgetown Law Journal*, 1987, 321-327.

PITOFSKY, Robert, 'Antitrust in the Next 100 Years', **75** *California Law Review*, 1987, 817-833.

PITTMAN, R.W. and WERDEN, G.J., 'The Divergence of SIC Industries from Antitrust Markets: Indications from Justice Department Merger Cases', **33** *Economic Letters*, 1990, 283-286.

POLINSKY, A. Mitchell, 'Detrebling Versus Decoupling Antitrust Damages: Lessons from the Theory of Enforcement', **74** *Georgetown Law Journal*, 1986, 1231-1236.

POLINSKY, A. Mitchell and SHAVELL, Steven, 'Contribution and Claim

Reduction Among Antitrust Defendants: An Economic Analysis', **33** *Stanford Law Review*, 1981, 447-471.

PONSOLDT, James F., 'The Enrichment of Sellers as a Justification for Vertical Restraints: A Response to Chicago's Swiftian Modest Proposal', **62** *New York University Law Review*, 1987, 1166-1171.

POPPER, Andrew F., 'The Antitrust System: An Impediment to the Development of Negotiation Models', **32** *America University Law Review*, 1983, 283-334.

POSNER, Richard A., 'A Statistical Study of Antitrust Enforcement', **13** *Journal of Law and Economics*, 1970, 365-419.

POSNER, Richard A. 'A Program for the Antitrust Division', **38** *University of Chicago Law Review*, 1971, 500-536.

POSNER, Richard A., 'Exclusionary Practices and the Antitrust Law', **41** *University of Chicago Law Review*, 1974, 506-535.

POSNER, Richard A., 'The Social Costs of Monopoly and Regulation', **83** *Journal of Political Economy*, 1975, 807-827.

POSNER, Richard A., *Antitrust Law: An Economic Perspective*, Chicago, University of Chicago Press, 1976, 262 p.

POSNER, Richard A., 'The Chicago School of Antitrust Analysis', **127** *University of Pennsylvania Law Review*, 1979, 925-952. Reprinted in **22** *Corporate Practice Commentator*, 1981, 583-610.

POSNER, Richard A., 'The Insignificance of Macroeconomics in Patent Antitrust Law: A Comment on Millstein', **9** *Cardozo Law Review*, 1988, 1203-1207.

PRICHARD, J. Robert S., STANBURY, W.T. and WILSON, T.A. (eds.), *Canadian Competition Policy - Essays in Law and Economics*, Toronto, Butterworth, 1979.

PRIEST, George L., 'Antitrust Suits and the Public Understanding of Insurance', **63** *Tulane Law Review*, 1989, 999-1044.

PRIMEAUX, Walter J. Jr. and SMITH, Mickey C., 'Pricing Patterns and the Kinky Demand Curve', **19** *Journal of Law and Economics*, 1976, 189-199.

RADLER, Warren S., 'Rose Acre's Long-Term Predatory Price Discrimination: "Picked Off One at a Time"', **21(3)** *Antitrust Law & Economics Review*, 1989, 51-62.

RAPP, Richard T., 'The Application of Economic Argument in Antitrust Cases: Recent American Trends', **9** *European Competition Law Review 1988*, 207-226.

RAVENSCRAFT, David J. and SCHERER, F.M., *Mergers. Sell-Offs and Economic Efficiency*, Washington, Brookings Institution, 1987.

REAGAN, Patricia B., 'Resale Price Maintenance: A Re-examination of the Outlets Hypothesis', **9** *Research in Law and Economics*, 1986, 1-12.

REED, Randal L. and WALDMAN, Don E., 'Mergers and Air Fares: "Contestable Markets" in the Airline Industry', **20(3)** *Antitrust Law & Economics Review*, 1988, 15-20.

REENE, W.D., *Industrial Economics: A Critical Introduction to Corporate Enterprise in Europe and America*, Aldershot, Gower Publ., 1989.

REID, Gavin C., *Theories of Industrial Organization*, Oxford, Basil Blackwell, 1987,

234 p.

REIFFEN, David and KLEIT, Andrew N., 'Terminal Railroad Revisited: Foreclosure of an Essential Facility or Simple Horizontal Monopoly?', **33** *Journal of Law & Economics*, 1990, 419-438.

REISS, Peter C. and SPILLER, Pablo T., 'Competition and Entry in Small Airline Markets', **32** *Journal of Law and Economics*, 1989, S179-S202.

REUBER, Grant L., 'Antitrust and the Takeover Activity of American Firms In Canada: A Further Analysis', **12** *Journal of Law and Economics*, 1969, 405-417.

REUBER, Grant L., 'Antitrust and the Takeover Activity of American Firms in Canada: A Reply', **13** *Journal of Law and Economics*, 1970, 257-259.

REYNOLDS, Michael J., 'Extra-territorial Aspects of Mergers and Joint Ventures: The EEC Position', **6** *European Competition Law Review*, 1985, 165-184.

REYNOLDS, Robert J., 'An Overview of the Economics of Antitrust Enforcement: Theory and Measurement', **68** *Georgetown Law Journal*, 1980, 1121-1130.

RHOADES, S.A. and BURKE, J., 'Economic and Political Foundations of Section 7 Enforcement in the 1980's', **35** *Antitrust Bulletin*, 1990, 373-446.

RHOADES, Stephen A., 'The Decline and Possible Resurrection of Antitrust Policy Toward Mergers', **17(4)** *Antitrust Law & Economics Review*, 1985, 49-55.

RICKETTS, Martin, *The New Industrial Economics: An Introduction to Modern Theories of the Firm*, New York, St. Martin's Press, 1987, 305 p.

RIDYARD, Derek, 'An Economic Perspective on the EC Merger Regulation', **11** *European Competition Law Review*, 1990, 247-254.

ROCK, James M., 'Cookware: A Study in Vertical Integration -A Reexamination', **12** *Journal of Law and Economics*, 1969, 425-438.

ROCK, James M., 'Cookware and Vertical Integration: A Reply', **12** *Journal of Law and Economics*, 1969, 441-443.

ROGERS, C. Paul, 'The Limited Case for an Efficiency Defense in Horizontal Mergers', **58** *Tulane Law Review*, 1983, 503-542.

ROGOWSKY, Robert A., 'The Justice Department's Merger Guidelines: A Study in the Application of the Rule', **6** *Research in Law and Economics*, 1984, 135-166.

RÖPER, Bernd, *Die Mißbrauchaufsicht vor dem Hintergrund der Entwicklung der neueren Wettbewerbstheorie* [The Abuse Aspect as Background for the Development of a New Competition Theory], Berlin, Humboldt, 1982.

ROSENFIELD, Andrew M., 'The Use of Economics in Antitrust Litigation and Counseling', *Columbia Business Law Review*, 1986, 49-82.

ROSS, Howard N., 'Oligopoly Theory and Price Rigidity', **32** *Antitrust Bulletin*, 1987, 451-469.

ROSS, Thomas W., 'Winners and Losers under the Robinson-Patman Act', **27** *Journal of Law and Economics*, 1984, 243-271.

ROUND, D.K., 'Industry Structure, Market Rivalry and Public Policy: Some Australian Evidence', **18** *Journal of Law and Economics*, 1975, 273-281.

ROWE, Frederick M., *Price Discrimination under the Robinson-Patman Act*, Boston, Little Brown, 1962.

ROWE, Frederick M., 'The Decline of Antitrust and the Delusions of Models: The Faustian Pact of Law and Economics', **72** *Georgetown Law Journal*, 1984, 1511-1570.

ROWE, Frederick M., 'Market as a Mirage', **75** *California Law Review*, 1987, 991-996.

ROWLEY, Charles K., 'Mergers and Public Policy in Great Britain', **11** *Journal of Law and Economics*, 1968, 75-132.

ROWLEY, Charles K., *Antitrust and Economic Efficiency*, London, Macmillan, 1973, 95 p.

RUFFNER, Markus, *Neue Wettbewerbstheorie und schweizerisches Kartellrecht, Möglichkeit und Grenzen einer markt- und institutionentheoretischen Fundierung der Wettbewerbspolitik* [New Competition Theory and Swiss Antitrust Law, Possibilities and Limitations of a Market and Institutionalist Foundation of Competition Policy], Zurich, Schulthess, 1990.

RULE, Charles F. and MEYER, David L., 'An Antitrust Enforcement Policy to Maximize the Economic Wealth of all Consumers', **33** *Antitrust Bulletin*, 1988, 677-712.

RUPPELT, Hans-Joachim, 'Der Verordnungsentwurf für eine europäische Fusionskontrolle im EG-Ministerrat' [The Regulation Bill for a European Fusion Control in the EC-Cabinet Council], **39** *Wirtschaft und Wettbewerb*, 1989, 187-202.

SPITZER, Matthew L., 'Antitrust Federalism and Rational Choice Political Economy: A Critique of Capture Theory', **61** *Southern California Law Review*, 1988, 1293-1326.

SALANT, Stephen W., 'Treble Damages Awards in Private Lawsuits for Price Fixing', **95** *Journal of Political Economy*, 1987, 1326-1336.

SALOP, Steven C. and WHITE, Lawrence J., 'Economic Analysis of Private Antitrust Litigation', **74** *Georgetown Law Journal*, 1986, 1001-1064.

SANTANGELO, Jerry M., 'Changing Configurations of Antitrust Law: Judge Posner's Applications of His Economic Analysis to Antitrust Doctrine', **32** *De Paul Law Review*, 1983, 839-899.

SASS, Tim R. and GISSER, Micha, 'Agency Cost, Firm Size, and Exclusive Dealing', **32** *Journal of Law and Economics*, 1989, 381-400.

SAUTER, Herbert, 'Gruppenfreistellungs-Verordnung für Know-how-Vereinbarungen' [The Group Exemption Regulation for Know-How Agreements], **39** *Wirtschaft und Wetbewerb*, 1989, 383-391.

SCHANZE, Erich, 'Comment' [on Jenny, Evolution of Anti-Trust Policies in France], **147** *Journal of Institutional and Theoretical Economics*, 1991, 66-71.

SCHANZE, Erich, 'Evolution of Antitrust Policies in France. Comment', **147** *Journal of Institutional and Theoretical Economics*, 1991, 66-71.

SCHEFFMAN, David T. and SPILLER, Pablo T., 'Geographic Market Definition under the *U.S. Departement of Justice Merger Guidelines*', **30** *Journal of Law and Economics*, 1987, 123-147.

SCHEFFMAN, David T. and SPILLER, Pablo T., 'Introduction: Empirical Approaches to Market Power', **32** *Journal of Law and Economics*, 1989, S3-

S10.

SCHERER, F.M., 'The Posnerian Harvest: Separating Wheat from Chaff', **86** *Yale Law Journal*, 1977, 974-1002.

SCHERER, F.M., *Industrial Market Structure and Economic Performance*, Chicago, Rand McNally, 1980 (2nd ed.), 632 p.

SCHERER, F.M., 'Stand und Perspektiven der Industrieökonomik' [State and Perspectives of Industrial Economics], in BOMBACH, G., GAHLEN, B. and OTT, A.E., *Industrieökonomik: Theorie und Empirie*, Tübingen, J.C.B. Mohr, 1985, 3-19.

SCHERER, F.M. and ROSS David, *Industrial Market Structure and Economic Performance*, Boston, Houghton Mifflin, 1990 (3rd ed.), 713 p.

SCHERER, Frederic M., 'The Causes and Consequences of Rising Industrial Concentration: A Comment', **22** *Journal of Law and Economics*, 1979, 191-208.

SCHERER, Frederic M., 'Efficiency, Fairness, and the Early Contributions of Economists to the Antitrust Debate', **29** *Washburn Law Journal*, 1990, 243-255.

SCHLICHT, Ekkehart, 'Comment' [on Gilbert, Legal and Economic Issues in the Commercialization of New Technology], **147** *Journal of Institutional and Theoretical Economics*, 1991, 185-187.

SCHLIEPER, Ulrich, 'Comment' [on Shughart and Tollison, The Employment Consequences of the Sherman and Clayton Acts], **147** *Journal of Institutional and Theoretical Economics*, 1991, 58-59.

SCHMALENSEE, Richard, 'On the Use of Economic Models in Antitrust: The Ralemon Case', **127** *University of Pennsylvania Law Review*, 1979, 994-1050.

SCHMALENSEE, Richard, 'Commodity Bundling by Single-Product Monopolies', **25** *Journal of Law and Economics*, 1982, 67-71.

SCHMALENSEE, Richard, 'Another Look at Market Power', **95** *Harvard Law Review*, 1982, 1789-1816.

SCHMALENSEE, Richard, 'Industrial Economics: An Overview', **98** *Economic Journal*, 1988, 643-681.

SCHMALENSEE, Richard and WILLIG, Robert D., *Handbook of Industrial Organization*, 2 Volumes, Amsterdam, North-Holland, 1990, 1555 p.

SCHMIDT, Ingo L.O., *Wettbewerbspolitik und Kartellrecht: Eine Einführung* [Competition Policy and Antitrust Law: An Introduction], Stuttgart, G. Fischer Verlag, 1990 (3rd ed.), 330 p.

SCHMIDT, Ingo L.O. and RITTALER, Jan B., *A Critical Evaluation of the Chicago School of Antitrust Analysis*, Dordrecht, Kluwer Academic Press, 1989, 132 p.

SCHMIDT, Ingo L.O. and RITTALER, Jan B., *Die Chicago School of Antitrust Analysis: Wettbewerbstheoretische und -politische Analyse eines Credos* [The Chicago School of Antitrust Analysis: Competition Theoretical and Political Analysis of a Credo], Baden-Baden, Nomos, 1986, 119 p.

SCHMIDTCHEN, Dieter, *Wettbewerbspolitik als Aufgabe: Methodologische und systemtheoretische Grundlagen für eine Neuorientierung* [Competition Policy as Task: Methodological and System Theoretical Foundations for a

Reorientatation], Baden-Baden, Nomos, 1978.

SCHMIDTCHEN, Dieter, 'Property Rights, Freiheitsschutz und die Logik staatlicher Preisinterventionen: Kritische Analyse der theoretischen Grundlagen einer freiheitsgefährdenden Wettbewerbspolitik' [Property Rights, Protection of Liberty and the Logic of Governmental Price Control: A Critical Analysis of the Theoretical Basis of Liberty Menacing Competition Policy], in RÖPER, Bernd (ed.), *Die Mißbrauchsaufsicht vor dem Hintergrund der Entwicklungen der neueren Wettbewerbstheorie*, Schriften des Vereins für Socialpolitik, Vol. 124, Berlin, 1982, 11-43.

SCHMIDTCHEN, Dieter, *Property Rights, Freiheit und Wettbewerbspolitik* [Property Rights, Freedom and Competition Policy], Tübingen, J.C.B. Mohr, 1983, 71 p.

SCHMIDTCHEN, Dieter, 'Comment' [on Möschel, The Goals of Antitrust Revisited], **147** *Journal of Institutional and Theoretical Economics*, 1991, 31-37.

SCHÖDERMEIER, M., Collective Dominance Revisited: An Analysis of the EC Commission's New Concepts of Oligopoly Control', **11** *European Competition Law Review*, 1990, 28-34.

SCHÜLLER, Alfred, 'Eigentumsrechte, Unternehmenskontrollen und Wettbewerbsordnung' [Property Rights, Corporate Control and Competition], **30** *ORDO, Jahrbuch für die Ordnung von Wirtschaft und Gesellschaft*, 1979, Stuttgart, G. Fischer Verlag, 325-364.

SCHÜLLER, Alfred, 'Theorie der Firma und wettbewerbliches Marktsystem' [Theory of the Firm and Competitive Market System], in SCHÜLLER, Alfred (ed.), *Property Rights und ökonomische Theorie*, WiSt Taschenbuch, München, Vahlen, 1983, 145-183.

SCHÜRMANN, Leo, 'Der Wettbewerb im Urteil der Staatswissenschaft' [The Competition in the Judgment of Economics], **42** *Wirtschaft und Recht*, 1990, 35-41.

SCHWARTZ, Gary T., 'An Overview of the Economics of Antitrust Enforcement', **68** *Georgetown Law Journal*, 1980, 1075-1102.

SCHWARTZ, Louis, 'On the Uses of Economics: A Review of the Antitrust Treatises (Book Reviews)', **128** *University of Pennsylvania Law Review*, 1979, 244 ff.

SCHWARTZ, Louis B., 'The New Merger Guidelines: Guide to Governmental Discretion and Private Counseling or Propaganda for Revsion of the Antitrust Laws?', **71** *California Law Review*, 1983, 575-603.

SCHWARTZ, Louis B., 'Some Additional Safeguards for the Newly Liberated Marketplace: Deregulatory Schizophrenia', **75** *California Law Review*, 1987, 1049-1057.

SCHWEIZER, Urs, 'Comment' [on Bolton and Whinston, The "Foreclosure" Effects of Vertical Mergers], **147** *Journal of Institutional and Theoretical Economics*, 1991, 227-231.

SCOTT, Kenneth E., 'Comment' [on Neuberger and Neumann, Banking and Antitrust: Limiting Industrial Ownership by Banks?], **147** *Journal of Institutional and Theoretical Economics*, 1991, 202-206.

SEE, Harold F. and GUNTHER, William D., 'Limit Pricing and Predation in the Antitrust Laws: Economic and Legal Aspects', **35** *Alabama Law Review*, 1984, 211-239.

SHAPIRO, Carl, 'Comment on Carlton and Gertner', **32** *Journal of Law and Economics*, 1989, S227-S232.

SHARPE, Tom, 'Predation', **8** *European Competition Law Review*, 1987, 53-76.

SHENEFIELD, John J., 'Market Definition and Horizontal Restraints: A Response to Professor Areeda', **52** *Antitrust Law Journal*, 1983, 587-600.

SHENFIELD, Arthur, *Myth and Reality in Antitrust*, London, 1983.

SHEPARD, Lawrence, 'Cartelization of the California-Arizona Orange Industry, 1934-1981', **29** *Journal of Law and Economics*, 1986, 83-123.

SHEPHERD, William G., *Public Policies Toward Business*, Homewoo, Irwin, 1985, 541 p.

SHEPHERD, William G., *The Economics of Industrial Organization*, Homewood, Irwin, 1985 (2nd ed.), 1990, 566 p. (3rd ed.).

SHEPHERD, William G., 'Contestability vs. Competition', **74** *American Economic Review*, 1984, 572-587.

SHEPHERD, William G., 'The Twilight of Antitrust', **18(1)** *Antitrust Law & Economics Review*, 1986, 21-27.

SHEPHERD, William G., '14 Recent Antitrust Cases and Mainstream Industrial-Organization Economic Criteria', **19(4)** *Antitrust Law & Economics Review*, 1987, 35-43.

SHEPHERD, William G., '14 Recent Antitrust Cases and Mainstream Industrial-Organization Economic Criteria (Part 2)', **20(1)** *Antitrust Law & Economics Review*, 1988, 61-70.

SHEPHERD, William G., 'Three "Efficiency School" Hypotheses about Market Power', **33** *Antitrust Bulletin*, 1988, 395-415.

SHUGHART, William F., II, 'Don't Revise the Clayton Act, Scrap It!', **6** *Cato Journal*, 1987, 925-932.

SHUGHART, William F., II and TOLLISON, Robert D., 'The Positive Economics of Anti-Trust Policy: A Survey Article', **5** *International Review of Law and Economics*, 1985, 39-57.

SHUGHART, William F., II and TOLLISON, Robert D., 'The Employment Consequences of the Sherman and Clayton Acts', **147** *Journal of Institutional and Theoretical Economics*, 1991, 38-52.

SIEGFRIED, John J., 'The Determinants of Antitrust Activity', **18** *Journal of Law and Economics*, 1975, 559-574.

SKOGH, Göran, 'The Social Costs of Monopoly and Regulation: Some Comments', **84** *Journal of Political Economy*, 1976, 1319-1323.

SKOGH, Göran, 'Comment' [on Van den Bergh, Competition Law and European Integration], in WEIGEL, Wolfgang (ed.), *Economic Analysis of Law - A Collection of Applications*, Vienna, Österreichischer Wirtschaftsverlag, 1991, 118-121.

SMITH, Paul, 'The Wolf in Wolf's Clothing: The Problem with Predatory Pricing',

14 *European Law Review*, 1989, 209-222.

SMITH, Richard L., II, 'Franchise Regulation: An Economic Analysis of State Restrictions on Automobile Distribution', **25** *Journal of Law and Economics*, 1982, 125-157.

SNIJDERS, W.L., 'Misbruikstoezicht en verbodsbeginsel in het kartelrecht (I)' [Supervising Abuse and the Principle of Banning Orders in Anti-trust Law (I)], **40** *Maandschrift Economie*, 1975, 133-154.

SNIJDERS, W.L., 'Misbruikstoezicht en verbodsbeginsel in het kartelrecht (II)' [Supervising Abuse and the Principle of Banning Orders in Anti-trust Law (II)], **40** *Maandschrift Economie*, 1975, 206-227.

SNIJDERS, W.L., 'Het optreden tegen economische machtsposities op grond van de Wet economische mededinging' [The Action against Economic Position of Powers on the Basis of the Economic Competition Act], in *In Orde: Liber Amicorum Pieter Verloren van Themaat*, Kluwer, Deventer, 1982, 267-293.

SNYDER, Edward A., 'Efficient Assignment of Rights to Sue for Antitrust Damages', **28** *Journal of Law and Economics*, 1985, 469-482.

SNYDER, Edward A., 'The Effect of Higher Criminal Penalties on Antritrust Enforcement', **33** *Journal of Law & Economics*, 1990, 439-462.

SOAMES, Trevor, 'The Community Dimension in the EEC Merger Regulation: The Calculation of the Turnover Criteria', **11** *European Competition Law Review*, 1990, 213-225.

SPENCE, A. Michael, 'Contestable Markets and the Theory of Industry Structure: A Review Article', **21** *Journal of Economic Literature*, 1983, 981-990.

SPILLER, Pablo T., 'On Vertical Mergers', **1** *Journal of Law, Economics, & Organization*, 1985, 285-312.

SPIVACK, Gordon B., 'The Chicago School Approach to Single Firm Exercises of Monopoly Power: A Response', **52** *Antitrust Law Journal*, 1983, 651-674.

SPULBER, Daniel F., *Regulation and Markets*, Cambridge, Cambridge University Press, 1989.

STEELE, Henry, 'Monopoly and Competition in the Ethical Drugs Market', **5** *Journal of Law and Economics*, 1962, 131-163.

STEINER, Peter O., 'Review "Antitrust Law: An Economic Perspective"', **44** *University of Chicago Law Review*, 1977, 873-894.

STELZER, Irving M., 'Economic Defences in Antitrust Litigation', **4** *European Competition Law Review*, 1983, 253-267.

STEUER, R.M., 'The Turning Points in Distribution Law', **35** *Antitrust Bulletin*, 1990, 467-536.

STIGLER, George J., 'Perfect Competition, Historically Contemplated', **65** *Journal of Political Economy*, 1957, 1-17.

STIGLER, George J., 'The Dominant Firm and the Inverted Umbrella', **8** *Journal of Law and Economics*, 1965, 167-171.

STIGLER, George J., 'The Economic Effects of the Antitrust Laws', **9** *Journal of Law and Economics*, 1966, 225-258.

STIGLER, George J., *The Organization of Industry*, Chicago, 1968.

STIGLER, George J., 'The Economists and the Problem of Monopoly', **72** *American Economic Review: Papers and Proceedings*, 1982, 1-11.

STIGLER, George J., 'The Origin of the Sherman Act', **14** *Journal of Legal Studies*, 1985, 1-12.

STIGLER, George J. and FRIEDLAND, Claire, 'The Literature of Economics: The Case of Berle and Means', **26** *Journal of Law and Economics*, 1983, 237-268.

STIGLER, George J. and SHERWIN, Robert A., 'The Extent of the Market', **28** *Journal of Law and Economics*, 1985, 555-585.

SULLIVAN, Daniel, 'Monopsony Power in the Market for Nurses', **32** *Journal of Law and Economics*, 1989, S135-S178.

SULLIVAN, E. Thomas, 'The Economic Jurisprudence of the Burger Court's Antitrust Policy: The First Thirteen Years', **58** *Notre Dame Law Review*, 1982, 1-59.

SULLIVAN, E. Thomas, 'On Nonprice Competition: An Economic and Marketing Analysis', **45** *University of Pittsburgh Law Review*, 1984, 771 ff.

SULLIVAN, Lawrence A., 'Economics and More Humanistic Disciplines: What Are the Sources of Wisdom for Antitrust', **125** *University of Pennsylvania Law Review*, 1977, 1214-1243.

SULLIVAN, Lawrence A., 'Antitrust, Microeconomics, and Politics: Reflections on Some Recent Relationships', **68** *California Law Review*, 1980, 1-12.

SULLIVAN, Lawrence A., 'U.S. Policy in a Mixed World Economy', **15** *New York University Journal of International Law and Politics*, 1983, 309-321.

SULLIVAN, Lawrence A., 'The New Merger Guidelines: An Afterword', **71** *California Law Review*, 1983, 632-648.

SULLIVAN, Lawrence A., 'The Viability of the Current Law on Horizontal Restraints', **72** *California Law Review*, 1987, 835-891.

SWAN, Peter L., 'The Durability of Goods and Regulation of Monopoly', **2** *Bell Journal of Economics*, 1971, 347-357.

SWANN, Dennis, *Competition and Industrial Policy in the European Community*, London, 1983.

SYMPOSIUM : 'Empirical Approaches to Market Power', **32** *Journal of Law and Economics*, 1989, S1-S275.

SYMPOSIUM : 'Symposium on New Views on Antitrust', **147(1)** *Journal of Institutional and Theoretical Economics*, 1991, 1-239.

TAFFETT, Richard S., 'Appendix A: Summary of Facts for the Demonstration of Economic Analysis and Expert Testimony', **52** *Antitrust Law Journal*, 1983, 819-821.

TELSER, Lester G., 'Why Should Manufacturers Want Fair Trade?', **3** *Journal of Law and Economics*, 1960, 86-105.

TELSER, Lester G., 'Cutthroat Competition and the Long Purse', **9** *Journal of Law and Economics*, 1966, 259-277.

TELSER, Lester G., 'Cooperation, Competition, and Efficiency', **28** *Journal of Law and Economics*, 1985, 271-295.

TELSER, Lester G., 'Why Should Manufacturers Want Fair Trade II?', **33** *Journal of*

Law & Economics, 1990, 409-417.

TELSER, Lester G., BEST, William, EGAN, John W. and HIGINBOTHAM, Harlow N., 'The Theory of Supply with Applications to the Ethical Pharmaceutical Industry', **18** *Journal of Law and Economics*, 1975, 449-478.

THOMPSON, D.R., 'Adjusting Attorney Fee Awards Through Multiplieres in Antitrust Class Actions', **21** *Houston Law Review*, 1984, 801-853.

TOLLISON, Robert D., '"Efficiency", "Cost Benefit" an Other Key Words - The Practical Uses of Economics at the FTC', **51** *Antitrust Law Journal*, 1982, 581-588.

TOLLISON, Robert D., 'Public Choice and Antitrust', in DORN, James A. and MANNE, Henry G. (eds.), *Economic Liberties and the Judiciary*, Fairfax, George Mason University Press, 1987, 289-300.

TOLLISON, Robert D., 'Comment on Holt', **32** *Journal of Law and Economics*, 1989, S131-S133.

TURNER, D.F., 'The Virtues and Problems of Antitrust Law', **35** *Antitrust Bulletin*, 1990, 297-310.

TURNER, Donald F., 'The Durability, Relevance and Future of American Antitrust Policy', **75** *California Law Review*, 1987, 797-815.

TYE, William B., 'Post-Merger Denials of Competitive Access and Trackage Rights in the Rail Industry', **53** *Transportation Practitioners Journal*, 1986, 413-427.

UITERMARK, P.J., 'Het Nederlandse mededingingspolitieke regime: Over de verhouding tussen verbod, misbruik, misstand en casuïstisch beleid' [Dutch Competition Policy: On the Interrelationship between Banning, Abuse, Wrongs and Case-to-Case Policy], **29** *TVVS Maandblad voor Ondernemingsrecht en Rechtspersonen*, 1986, 108-115.

UITERMARK, P.J., 'Over economische mededinging' [On Economic Competition], **35** *Sociaal-Economische Wetgeving: Ttijdschrift voor Europees en Economisch Recht*, 1987, 339-372.

UITERMARK, P.J., 'Over informeel mededingingsbeleid' [On Informal Competition Policy], **2** *Recht der Werkelijkheid*, 1988, 30-53.

UITERMARK, P.J., *Economische Mededinging en Algemeen Belang: Een onderzoek naar de economisch-theoretische fundering van de mededingingspolitiek* [Economic Competition and Public Interest: An Investigation into the Economic-theoretical Foundations of Competition Policy], Groningen, Wolters Noordhoff, 1990, 475 p.

URI, Noel D. and COATE, Malcolm B., 'The Department of Justice Merger Guidelines: The Search for Empirical Support', **7** *International Review of Law and Economics*, 1987, 113-120.

VAN DEN BERGH, Roger, 'Competition Law and European Integration: Will Free Riders Become the Heroes of the Internal Market?', in WEIGEL, Wolfgang (ed.), *Economic Analysis of Law - A Collection of Applications*, Vienna, Österreichischer Wirtschaftsverlag, 1991, 107-117.

VÀTH, Andreas, *Die Wettbewerbskonzeption des Europäischen Gerichtshofs: Eine wettbewerbstheoretische Analyse der Rechtsprechung des höchsten europäischen Gerichts anhand ausgewählter Entscheidungen* [The Competition Concept of the European Court of Justice: A Competition Theoretical Analysis of the

Jurisprudence of the Highest European Court on the Basis of Selected Decisions], Bayreuth, P.C.O.-Verlag, 1987, 298 p.

VENIT, J.E., 'The "Merger" Control Regulation: Europe Comes of Age ... or Caliban's Dinner?', **27** *Common Market Law Review*, 1990, 7-50.

VERLOREN VAN THEMAAT, Pieter, 'Het wetsontwerp-Lubbers tot wijziging van de Wet economische mededinging' [The Lubbers Bill on a Change of the Economic Competition Act], **26** *Sociaal-Economische Wetgeving: Tijdschrift voor Europees en Economisch Recht*, 1978, 178-192.

VERLOREN VAN THEMAAT, Pieter, 'Nieuw leven in de Wet economische mededinging of terug naar Abtsweg?' [New Life in the Economic Competition Act or Back to Abtsweg?], **36** *Sociaal-Economische Wetgeving: Tijdschrift voor Europees en Economisch Recht*, 1988, 4-15 and 60-77.

VON WEIZSÄCKER, Carl-Christian, 'Antitrust and the Division of Labor', **147** *Journal of Institutional and Theoretical Economics*, 1991, 99-113.

VUARIDEL, Roger, 'L'objet et le niveau de la concurrence dans la théorie économique et dans la jurisprudence' [The Object and Level of Competition in Economic Theory and in Jurisprudence], **20** *Wirtschaft und Recht*, 1986, 111-128.

WACHTER, Susan M., 'Residential Real Estate Brokage: Rate Uniformity and Moral Hazard', **10** *Research in Law and Economics*, 1987, 189-210.

WALDMAN, D.E., *The Economics of Antitrust: Cases and Analysis*, Boston, Little Brown, 1986.

WALTERS, Stephen J. K., 'Reciprocity Reexamined: The Consolidated Foods Case', **29** *Journal of Law and Economics*, 1986, 423-438.

WARREN-BOULTON, Frederick R., 'Implications of U.S. Experience with Horizontal Mergers and Takeovers for Canadian Competition Policy', in MATHEWSON, Frank, TREBILCOCK, Michael and WALKER, Michael (eds.), *The Law and Economics of Competition Policy*, Vancouver, Fraser Institute, 1990, 337-368.

WEIJDEN, Carel J. van der, *Toegang en toetreding: facetten van de mededinging* [Entry and Entrance: Aspects of Competition], Den Haag, 1962.

WEIJDEN, Carel J. van der, 'Toestaan of verbieden? Een beschouwing rond de Wet economische mededinging' [Allowing or Banning? Considerations about the Economic Competition Act], **66** *Economisch-Statistische Berichten*, 1981, 12-81-1284.

WEIJDEN, Carel J. van der, 'Werkzame mededinging' [Workable Competition], **72** *Economisch-Statistische Berichten*, 1987, 1194-1199.

WEISS, Leonard W., 'The Structure-Conduct-Performance Paradigm and Antitrust', **127** *University of Pennsylvania Law Review*, 1979, 1104-1140.

WEISS, Leonard W., 'The Extent and Effects of Aggregate Concentration', **26** *Journal of Law and Economics*, 1983, 429-455.

WENDERS, John T., 'Deconcentration Reconsidered', **14** *Journal of Law and Economics*, 1971, 485-488.

WERDEN, Gregory J., 'A Closer Analysis of Antitrust Markets', **62** *Washington University Law Quarterly*, 1985, 647-669.

WERDEN, Gregory J. and SCHWARTZ, Marius, 'Illinois Brick and the Deterrence of Antitrust Violations - An Economic Analysis', **35** *Hastings Law Journal*, 1984, 629-668.

WERTHEIMER, H.W. De Europese Concentratiecontrole in de revisie' [European Concentration Control in Revision], **31** *Sociaal-Economische Wetgeving: Tijdschrift voor Europees en Economisch Recht*, 1983, 66-84.

WHITE, David L., 'Shaping Antitrust Enforcement: Greater Emphasis on Barriers to Entry', *Brigham Young University*, 1989, 823-851.

WILEY, John Shepard, Jr., 'A Capture Theory of Antitrust Federalism', **99** *Harvard Law Review*, 1986, 713-789.

WILEY, John S., 'After Chicago: An Exaggerated Demise?, *Duke Law Journal*, 1986, 1003-1029.

WILEY, John Shepard, Jr., 'Antitrust and Core Theory', **54** *University of Chicago Law Review*, 1987, 556-589.

WILEY, John Shepard, Jr., 'Reciprocal Altruism as a Felony: Antitrust and the Prisoner's Dilemma', **86** *Michigan Law Review*, 1988, 1906-1928.

WILEY, John Shepard, Jr., 'A Capture Theory of Antitrust Federalism: Reply to Professors Page and Spitzer', **61** *Southern California Law Review*, 1988, 1327-1341.

WILLEKE, Frans-Ullrich, *Wettbewerbspolitik* [Competition Policy], Tübingen, J.C.B. Mohr, 1980.

WILLIAMS, Philip L., 'The Problem of Proving 'Arrangement or Understanding' under Section 45 A of the Trade Practices Act', in CRANSTON, Ross and SCHICK, Anne (eds.), *Law and Economics*, Canberra, Australian National University, 1982, 112-121.

WILLIAMSON, Oliver E., *Markets and Hierarchies: Analysis and Antitrust Implication: A Study in the Economics of Internal Organization*, New York, Free Press, 1975, 286 p.

WILLIAMSON, Oliver E., 'Vertical Merger Guidelines: Interpreting the 1982 Reforms', **71** *California Law Review*, 1983, 604-617.

WILLIAMSON, Oliver E., 'Delimiting Antitrust', **76** *Georgetown Law Journal*, 1987, 271-303.

WILLIAMSON, Oliver E., *Antitrust Economics: Mergers, Contracting and Strategic Behavior*, Oxford, Blackwell, 1989, 363 p.

WILLIAMSON, Oliver E. (ed.), *Industrial Organization*, Aldershot, Edward Elgar, 1990, 500 p.

WILLS, Robert L., 'Economists and Competition Policy: A Case Study', in WILLS, Robert L. and CASWELL, Julie A. and CULBERTSON, John D. (eds.), *Issues after a Century of Federal Competition Policy*, Lexington, Lexington Books, 1987, 3-8.

WILLS, Robert L., CASWELL, Julie A. and CULBERTSON, John D. (eds.), *Issues after a Century of Federal Competition Policy*, Lexington, Lexington Books, 1987, 387 p.

WINN, Daryl N. and LEABO, Dick A., 'Rates of Return, Concentration and Growth - Question of Disequilibrium', **17** *Journal of Law and Economics*, 1974, 97-115.

WOLLENBERG, Keith K., 'Note: An Economic Analysis of Tie-In Sales: Re-examining the Leverage Theory', **39** *Stanford Law Review*, 1987, 737-760.

WOODS, R. Kyle, 'Comment: Functional Discounts and Integrated Distribution under the Robinson-Patman Act', **37** *Emory Law Journal*, 1988, 799 ff.

WOUDE, M.H. van der, 'Kartelrechtelijke beschikkingen EG-Commissie 1985-1987' [EC Commission Anti-trust Orders 1985-1987], **37** *Sociaal Economische Wetgeving: Tijdschrift voor Europees en Economisch Recht*, 1989, 2-27.

X, 'Adverse Effects of Free-Riding and Intrabrand Competition: Ohio-Sealy v. Sealy, Inc.', **18(2)** *Antitrust Law & Economics Review*, 1986, 51-74.

X, 'Antitrust and Small Business: Killing the Business-Is-Better Myth (II)', **17(3)** *Antitrust Law & Economics Review*, 1985, 39-66.

X, 'Antitrust and International Competition: Courting the 'Cartel Malignancy' (II)', **17(2)** *Antitrust Law & Economics Review*, 1985, 41-54.

X, 'Antitrust, Large Corporations and the Innovation-Entrepreneurship Problem: A "Satellite" Approach', **17(3)** *Antitrust Law & Economics Review*, 1985, 67-97.

X, 'Antitrust and Capitol Hill: Industrial Policy, Foreign Competition, and the 'Siege' Syndrome', **17(2)** *Antitrust Law & Economics Review*, 1985, 73-96.

X, 'Antitrust and Small Business: Killing the Big-Is-Better Myth', **17(2)** *Antitrust Law & Economics Review*, 1985, 97-110.

X, 'Antitrust and Industrial Organization: The Loss of Idealism and Leadership (II)', **18(4)** *Antitrust Law & Economics Review*, 1986, 43-66.

X, 'Antitrust and Industrial Organization: The Loss of Idealism and Leadership (Part 1)', **18(3)** *Antitrust Law & Economics Review*, 1986, 75-94.

X, 'Antitrust, Economic Consulting, and the Public Interest: Deposition of the Economic Expert in the Settlement Process (Part 1)', **18(4)** *Antitrust Law & Economics Review*, 1986, 83-92.

X, 'Antitrust and International 'Competitiveness': The European Experience (Part 1)', **18(4)** *Antitrust Law & Economics Review*, 1986, 93-110.

X, 'Antitrust and Industrial Organization: The Loss of Idealism and Leadership (III)', **19(1)** *Antitrust Law & Economics Review*, 1987, 25-44.

X, 'Antitrust and International 'Competitiveness': The European Experience (IV)', **19(3)** *Antitrust Law & Economics Review*, 1987, 49-64.

X, 'Antitrust, Economic Consulting, and the Public Interest: Deposition of the Economic Expert in the Settlement Process (III)', **19(2)** *Antitrust Law & Economics Review*, 1987, 59-78.

X, 'Antitrust, Economic Consulting, and the Public Interest: Deposition of the Economic Expert in the Settlement Process (II)', **19(1)** *Antitrust Law & Economics Review*, 1987, 65-84.

X, 'Antitrust and International 'Competitiveness': The European Experience (III)', **19(2)** *Antitrust Law & Economics Review*, 1987, 79-97.

X, 'Antitrust and International 'Competitiveness': The European Experience (II)', **19(1)** *Antitrust Law & Economics Review*, 1987, 85-110.

X, 'Antitrust, Economics, and the 'Social' Issues: Fairness Is Good Economics (II)', **19(4)** *Antitrust Law & Economics Review*, 1987, 95-110.

X, 'Antitrust, Economics, and the 'Social' Issues: Fairness Is Good Economics', **19(3)** *Antitrust Law & Economics Review*, 1987, 97-110.

X, 'Antitrust Economics in the Courts: Theory Versus Empiricism (II)', **20(3)** *Antitrust Law & Economics Review*, 1988, 53-94.

X, 'Antitrust Economics and the Courts: The "When" and "How" of Judicial Miseducation (II)', **20(4)** *Antitrust Law & Economics Review*, 1988, 95-110.

X, 'Antitrust Economics and the Courts: The "When" and "How" of Judicial Miseducation', **20(3)** *Antitrust Law & Economics Review*, 1988, 95-110.

X, 'Antitrust, Economics, and the 'Social' Issues: Fairness Is Good Economics (Part 3)', **20(1)** *Antitrust Law & Economics Review*, 1988, 103-110.

X, 'Bad Antitrust Economics in the US Supreme Court: Business Electronics v. Sharp', **20(2)** *Antitrust Law & Economics Review*, 1988, 35-56.

X, 'Economists and Antitrust Policymaking: The 'Communications' Gap (II)', **18(4)** *Antitrust Law & Economics Review*, 1986, 67-82.

X, 'Economists and Antitrust Policymaking: The 'Communications' Gap (Part 1)', **18(3)** *Antitrust Law & Economics Review*, 1986, 95-110.

X, 'Economists and Antitrust Policymaking: The 'Communications' Gap (III)', **19(1)** *Antitrust Law & Economics Review*, 1987, 45-64.

X, 'Entry, Recoupment, and Higher Prices: Irrelevance of High Market Shares in Predatory Pricing', **21(3)** *Antitrust Law & Economics Review*, 1989, 89-110.

X, 'Foreword: Chicago Economics, the FTC, and the Education of the Federal Judiciary', **15** *Antitrust Law and Economics Review*, 1983, 1-8.

X, 'Foreword: Brennan, Marshall, and Sealy's 30% Higher Price Without Intrabrand Competition', **20(4)** *Antitrust Law & Economics Review*, 1988, 1-16.

X, 'Judges Versus Juries in Antitrust: Rush to Summary Judgment', **20(2)** *Antitrust Law & Economics Review*, 1988, 1-34.

X, 'Mergers, Tacit Collusion, and Import Protection: The Case for Hard Competition (II)', **17(4)** *Antitrust Law & Economics Review*, 1985, 57-77.

X, 'Mergers, Tacit Collusion, and Import Protection: The Case for Hard Competition', **17(3)** *Antitrust Law & Economics Review*, 1985, 99-110.

X, 'Monopoly, Unemployment, and the Welfare Burden: The Deindustrialization of America', **17(4)** *Antitrust Law & Economics Review*, 1985, 95-110.

X, 'Monopoly, Unemployment, and the Welfare Burden: The Deindustrialization of America (II)', **18(1)** *Antitrust Law & Economics Review*, 1986, 81-100.

X, 'No Anti-Antitrust 'Bias' at the Law and Economics Center: Federal Judges Can't Be 'Brainwashed'', **14** *Antitrust Law and Economics Review*, 1982, 15-70.

X, 'Note: An Economic Analysis of the 1982 Justice Department Guidelines for Horizontal Mergers', **67** *Minnesota Law Review*, 1983, 749-792.

X, 'Vertical Restraints and Market Power: Killing Price Competition in Court (II)', **20(3)** *Antitrust Law & Economics Review*, 1988, 39-52.

X, 'Vertical Restraints and Market Power: Killing Price Competition in Court (III)', **20(4)** *Antitrust Law & Economics Review*, 1988, 79-94.

YAMEY, Basil S., 'Predatory Price Cutting: Notes and Comments', **15** *Journal of*

Law and Economics, 1972, 129-142.

YAMEY, Basil S., 'Monopolistic Price Discrimination and Economic Welfare', **17** *Journal of Law and Economics*, 1974, 377-480.

YAMEY, Basil S., 'The New Anti-Trust Economics' in ANDERSON, Martin J. (ed.), *The Unfinished Agenda: Essays on the Political Economy of Government Policy in honour of Arthur Seldon*, London, I.E.A., 1986, 65-79.

ZERBE, Richard O., Jr., 'The American Sugar Refinery Company, 1887-1914: The Story of a Monopoly', **12** *Journal of Law and Economics*, 1969, 339-375.

ZERBE, Richard O., Jr., 'Monopoly, the Emergence of Oligopoly and the Case of Sugar Refining', **13** *Journal of Law and Economics*, 1970, 501-515.

ZERBE, Richard O., Jr., 'An Empirical and Theoretical Comparison of Alternative Predation Rules', **61** *Texas Law Review*, 1982, 655-715.

ZERBE, Richard O., Jr., 'The Chicago Board of Trade Case, 1918', **5** *Research in Law and Economics*, 1983, 17-55.

ZERBE, Richard O., Jr. (ed.), 'Symposium: Antitrust and Regulation', **6** *Research in Law and Economics*, 1984, 292 p.

ZIJLSTRA, Jelle and GOUDZWAARD, Bob, *Economische politiek en concurrentieproblematiek in de EEG en de lidstaten* [Economic Policy and Competition Problems in the EC and the Member States], Serie Concurrentie Nr. 2, Brussel, 1966.

ZIMMERMAN, Edwin M., 'Section 7 and the Evolving Role of Economics', **35** *Antitrust Bulletin*, 1990, 447-465.

5800 REGULATION OF NATURAL MONOPOLIES & PUBLIC UTILITIES (a selection)

Gerrit De Geest

FOR TRANSPORT REGULATION: SEE 5930

FOR TELECOMMUNICATIONS: SEE 5950

ABDEL KHALIK, A. Rashad, 'Incentives for Accruing Costs and Efficiency in Regulated Monopolies Subject to ROE Constraint', **26** *Journal of Accounting Research*, Supplement, 1988, 144-174.

ADIE, Douglas K., 'Abolishing the Postal Monopoly: A Comment', **5** *Cato Journal*, 1985, 657-661.

ALBON, Robert P., 'The Welfare Costs of the Australian Telecommunications Pricing Structure', **64** *Economic Record*, 1988, 102-112.

ARMSTRONG, Christopher and NELLIS, Henry Vivian, *Monopoly's Moment: The Organization and Regulation of Canadian Utilities, 1830-1930*, Toronto, University of Toronto Press, 1986, 393 p.

ATKINSON, Scott E. and HALVORSEN, Robert, 'Tests of Allocative Efficiency in Regulated Multi product Firms', **12** *Resources and Energy*, 1990, 65-77.

ATKINSON, Scott E. and KERKVLIET, Joe, 'Dual Measures of Monopoly and Monopsony Power: An Application to Regulated Electric Utilities', **71** *Review of Economics and Statistics*, 1989, 250-257.

BABILOT, George and FRANTZ, Roger and GREEN, Louis, 'Natural Monopolies and Rent: A Georgist Remedy for X Inefficiency among Publicly Regulated Firms', **46** *American Journal of Economics and Sociology*, 1987, 205-217.

BACA, Alvin, 'FERC $50 ERA: Issues in Natural Gas Regulation', **27** *Natural Resources Journal*, 1987, 815-822.

BAISH, Richard O., 'The Role of the California Public Utilities Commission in Western Gas', **27** *Natural Resources Journal*, 1987, 805-810.

BALDWIN, John R., *Regulatory Failure and Renewal: The Evolution of the Natural Monopoly Contract*, Ottawa, Supply and Services Canada, 1989, 122 p.

BARON, David P. and BESANKO, David, 'Regulation and Information in a Continuing Relationship', **1(3)** *Information Economics and Policy*, 1984, 267-302.

BARON, David P. and BESANKO, David, 'Regulation, Asymmetric Information, and Auditing', **15** *Rand Journal of Economics*, 1984, 447-470.

BEESLEY, Michael E. and LITTLECHILD, S.C., 'The Regulation of Privatized Monopolies in the United Kingdom', **20** *Rand Journal of Economics*, 1989, 454-472.

BERG, Sanford V. and TSCHIRHART, John, *Natural Monopoly Regulation: Principles and Practice*, Cambridge, Cambridge University Press, 1988, 564 p.

BERNARD, Jean Thomas and CAIRNS, Robert D., 'On Public Utility Pricing and Forgone Economic Benefits', **20** *Canadian Journal of Economics*, 1987, 152-163.

BERRY, S. Keith, 'Rate of Return Regulation and Demand Uncertainty with a Symmetric Regulatory Constraint', **31(2)** *American Economist*, 1987, 8-12.

BERRY, S. Keith, 'The Ratepayer and the Stockholder under Alternative Regulatory Policies: Comment', **63** *Land Economics*, 1987, 201-205.

BERRY, S. Keith, 'The Allocation of Risk between Stockholders and Ratepayers in Regulated Utilities', **64** *Land Economics*, 1988, 114-124.

BESEN, Stanley M., 'The Economics of the Cable Television "Consensus"', **17** *Journal of Law and Economics*, 1974, 39-51.

BLACKSTONE, Erwin A. and FUHR, Joseph P., Jr., 'The Economics of Public Utility Regulation: Review Article', **17(2)** *Atlantic Economic Journal*, 1989, 68-73.

BOLD, Frederick C., 'Responses to Energy Efficiency Regulations', **8** *Energy Journal*, 1987, 111-123.

BOWMAN, Ward, 'The New Haven, A Passenger Railroad for Nonriders', **9** *Journal of Law and Economics*, 1966, 49-59.

BOYES, William J. and McDOWELL, John M., 'The Selection of Public Utility Commissioners: A Reexamination of theImportance of Institutional Setting', **61** *Public Choice*, 1989, 1-13.

BRADLEY, Ian and PRICE, Catherine, 'Partial and Mixed Regulations of Newly Privatized U.K. Monopolies', in WEIGEL, Wolfgang (ed.), *Economic Analysis of Law - A Collection of Applications*, Vienna, Österreichischer Wirtschafts-verlag, 1991, 212-220.

BRAEUTIGAM, Ronald R., 'Regulatory Reform: Lessons for Natural Gas Pipelines', **8** *Contemporary Policy Issues*, 1990, 122-141.

BRAEUTIGAM, Ronald R. and HUBBARD, R. Glenn, 'Natural Gas: The Regulatory Transition', in WEISS, Leonard W. and KLASS, Michael W. (ed.), *Regulatory Reform: What Actually Happened*, Boston, Little Brown, 1986, 137-168.

BRAEUTIGAM, Ronald R. and PANZAR, John C., 'Diversification Incentives Under "Price-Based" and Cost-Based" Regulation', **20** *Rand Journal of Economics*, 1989, 373-391.

BROADMAN, Harry G., 'Natural Gas Deregulation: The Need for Further Reform', **5** *Journal of Policy Analysis and Management*, 1986, 496-516.

BROADMAN, Harry G. and KALT, Joseph P., 'How Natural Is Monopoly? The Case of Bypass in Natural Gas Distribution Markets', **6** *Yale Journal on Regulation*, 1989, 181-208.

BROWN, Donald J. and HEAL, Geoffrey M., 'Ramsey Pricing in Telecommunications Markets with Free Entry', in CREW, Michael A. (ed.), *Regulating Utilities in an Era of Deregulation*. New York, St. Martin's Press, 1987, 77-83.

BROWN, Lorenzo, 'Modelling Diversified Utilities and Cross Subsidization', **10** *Resources and Energy*, 1988, 213-224.

BUELL, Stephe, G. and GUERARD, John B., Jr., 'An Econometric Analysis of the Formal Regulatory Process', in BROWN, Roy Chamberlain (ed.), *Quantity and Quality in Economic Research*, Volume 1, Lanham, University Press of America, 1985, 15-38.

BULCKE, J., 'Industrie en energie: 3. Electriciteit' [Industry and Energy: Electricity], in *18de Vlaams Wetenschappelijk Economisch Congres, Brussel 8 en 9 mei 1987, Sociaal-economische Deregulering*, Brussel, V.E.H.U.B., 1987, 421-440.

BUNN, Derek and VLAHOS, Kiriakos, 'Evaluation of the Long term Effects on UK Electricity Prices following Privatisation', **10(4)** *Fiscal Studies*, 1989, 104-116.

CAILLAUD, B., 'Regulation, Competition, and Asymmetric Information', **52** *Journal of Economic Theory*, 1990, 87-110.

CHEN, Andrew H. and SANGER, Gary C., 'An Analysis of the Impact of Regulatory Change: The Case of Natural Gas Deregulation', **20(1)** *Financial Review*, 1985, 36-54.

CHEN, Paul, 'Prices vs. Quantities and Delegating Price Authority to a Monopolist', **57** *Review of Economic Studies*, 1990, 521-529.

COASE, Ronald H., 'The British Post Office and the Messenger Companies', **4** *Journal of Law and Economics*, 1961, 12-65.

COASE, Ronald H., 'The Interdepartment Radio Advisory Committee', **5** *Journal of Law and Economics*, 1962, 17-47.

COASE, Ronald H., 'The Auction System and North Sea Gas: A Comment', **13** *Journal of Law and Economics*, 1970, 45-47.

COMANOR, William S. and MITCHELL, Bridger M., 'The Costs of Planning: The FCC and Cable Television', **15** *Journal of Law and Economics*, 1972, 177-206.

COSTELLO, Kenneth W., 'The Struggle Over Electricity Transmission Access', **8** *Cato Journal*, 1988, 107-124.

COSTELLO, Kenneth W. and HEMPHILL, Ross C., 'Competitive Pricing in the Electric Industry', **12** *Resources and Energy*, 1990, 49-63.

COTE, Daniel O., 'Firm Efficiency and Ownership Structure: The Case of U.S. Electric Utilities Using Panel Data', **60** *Annals of Public and Co operative Economy*, 1989, 431-450.

COURSEY, Don L., ISAAC, R. Mark and SMITH, Vernon L., 'Natural Monopoly and Contested Markets: Some Experimental Results', **27** *Journal of Law and Economics*, 1984, 91-113.

COX, James C. and ISAAC, R. Mark, 'Mechanisms for Incentive Regulation: Theory and Experiment', **18** *Rand Journal of Economics*, 1987, 348-359.

CRAIN, W. Mark and EKELUND, Robert B., Jr., 'Chadwick and Demsetz on Competition and Regulation', **19** *Journal of Law and Economics*, 1976, 149-162.

CRANDALL, Robert W., 'Surprises form Telephone Deregulation and the AT&T Divestiture', **78** *American Economic Review. Papers and Proceedings*, 1988, 323-327.

CREW, Michael A. (ed.), *Analyzing the Impact of Regulatory Change in Public Utilities*, Lexington, Lexington Books, 1985.

CREW, Michael A. (ed.), *Regulating Utilities in an Era of Deregulation*, New York, St. Martin's Press, 1987, 201 p.

CREW, Michael A. (ed.), *Deregulation and Diversification of Utilities*, Dordrecht, Kluwer Academic, 1989, 206 p.

CREW, Michael A. (ed.), *Competition and the Regulation of Utilities*, Dordrecht, Kluwer Academic Publishers, 1991, 224 p.

CREW, Michael A. and KLEINDORFER, Paul R., 'Governance Costs of Rate of Return Regulation', **141** *Zeitschrift für die gesamte Staatswissenschaft*, 1985, 104-123.

CREW, Michael A. and KLEINDORFER, Paul R., 'Governance Structures for Natural Monopoly: A Comparative Institutional Assessment', **14** *Journal of Behavioral Economics*, 1985, 117-140.

CREW, Michael A. and KLEINDORFER, Paul R., *The Economics of Public Utility Regulation*, Cambridge, MIT Press, 1986, 304 p.

CREW, Michael A. and KLEINDORFER, Paul R., 'Productivity Incentives and Rate-of-Return Regulation', in CREW, Michael A. (ed.), *Regulating Utilities in an Era of Deregulation*. New York, St. Martin's Press, 1987, 7-23.

CREW, Michael A., KLEINDORFER, Paul R. and SCHLENGER, Donald L., 'Governance Costs of Regulation for Water Supply', in CREW, Michael A. (ed.), *Regulating Utilities in an Era of Deregulation*. New York, St. Martin's Press, 1987, 43-62.

CREW, Michael A. and ROWLEY, Charles K., 'Toward a Public Choice Theory of Monopoly Regulation', **57** *Public Choice*, 1988, 49-67.

CROCKER, Keith J. and MASTEN, Scott E., 'Mitigating Contractual Hazards: Unilateral Options and Contract Length', **19** *Rand Journal of Economics*, 1988, 327-343.

CROCKETT, J.H., Jr., 'Differential Pricing and Interconsumer Efficiency in the Electric Power Industry', **7** *Bell Journal of Economics*, 1976, 293-298.

CULBERTSON, William Patton, Jr., 'A Redistributive Effect of Natural Gas Price Regulation', **16(4)** *Nebraska Journal of Economics and Business*, 1977, 91-95.

DAM, Kenneth W., 'Oil and Gas Licensing and the North Sea', **8** *Journal of Law and Economics*, 1965, 51-75.

DAM, Kenneth W., 'The Pricing of North Sea Gas in Britain', **13** *Journal of Law and Economics*, 1970, 11-44.

DAM, Kenneth W., 'Implementation of Import Quotas: The Case of Oil', **14** *Journal of Law and Economics*, 1971, 1-60.

DAM, Kenneth W., 'The Evolution of North Sea Licensing Policy in Britain and Norway', **17** *Journal of Law and Economics*, 1974, 213-263.

DANIELSEN, Albert L. and KAMERSCHEN, David R. and KEENAN, Donald C., 'Third Best Pricing Rules for Regulated Utilities', **56** *Southern Economic Journal*, 1990, 628-638.

DE ALESSI, Louis, 'Private Ownership and Limits to Retroactive Regulation of Utility Rates', **37** *University of Miami Law Review*, 1983, 433 ff.

DeBROCK, Lawrence M. and SMITH, J.L., 'Joint Bidding, Information Pooling, and the Performance of Petroleum Lease Auctions', **14** *Bell Journal of Economics*, 1983, 395-404.

DELANEY, J.B. and HONEYCUTT, T.C., 'Determinants of Research and Development Activity by Electric Utilities: Comment', **7** *Bell Journal of Economics*, 1976, 722-725.

DELLA VALLE, Anna P., 'Short run versus Long run Marginal Cost Pricing', **10** *Energy Economics*, 1988, 283-286.

DEMSETZ, Harold, 'Why Regulate Utilities', **11** *Journal of Law and Economics*, 1968, 55-65.

DOPPEGIETER, J.J. and HAMMAN, W.D. and LAMBRECHTS, I.J., 'Tariff Policies for Public Utilities: The Accounting Cost Approach', **13(2)** *Journal for Studies in Economics and Econometrics*, 1989, 49-57.

DREYFUS, Daniel A., 'Deregulation of Utilities: The Natural Gas Experience', **24(2)** *Business Economics*, 1989, 41-47.

ECKEL, Catherine C., 'Customer Class Price Discrimination by Electric Utilities', **39** *Journal of Economics and Business*, 1987, 19-33.

EICKHOF, Norbert, 'Versorgungswirtschaft und Wettbewerbsordnung' [Public Utilities and the Competitive System], in EUCKEN, Walter and BOHM, Franz (eds.), *Ordo: Jahrbuch fur die Ordnung von Wirtschaft und Gesellschaft. Band 37*, Stuttgart, Fischer, 1986, 201-218.

EINHORN, Michael A., 'Optimality and Sustainability: Regulation and Intermodal Competition in Telecommunications', **18** *Rand Journal of Economics*, 1987, 550-563.

EINHORN, Michael A., 'Purchasing Power for the Grid: A Social Contract Approach', **12** *Resources and Energy*, 1990, 33-48.

ETZIONI, Amitai, 'Does Regulation Reduce Electricity Rates? A Research Note', **19(4)** *Policy Sciences*, 1986, 349-357.

EVANS, Lewis and GARBER, Steven, 'Public-Utility Regulators Are Only Human: A Positive Theory of Rational Constraints', **78** *American Economic Review*, 1988, 444-462.

FABELLA, Raul V., 'Monopoly Deregulation in the Presence of Tullock Activities', **62** *Public Choice*, 1989, 287-293.

FANARA, Philip, Jr. and SWEET, David M., 'What Do Regulated Firms Maximize? Some Empirical Evidence from the Natural Gas Pipeline Industry', **28(1)** *American Economist*, 1984, 44-48.

FARE, Rolf, GROSSKOPF, S. and LOGAN, James, 'The Relative Performance of Publicly Owned and Privately Owned Electric Utilities', **26** *Journal of Public Economics*, 1985, 89-106.

FARE, Rolf and LOGAN, James, 'Regulation, Scale and Productivity: A Comment', **27** *International Economic Review*, 1986, 777-781.

FERRIS, Stephen P. and JOHNSON, Dana J. and SHOME, Dilip K., 'Regulatory Environment and Market Response to Public Utility Rate Decisions', **9** *Journal of Financial Research*, 1986, 313-318.

FINSINGER, Jörg and VOGELSANG Ingo, 'Alternative Institutional Frameworks for Price Incentive Mechanisms', **34** *Kyklos*, 1981, 388-404.

FITZPATRICK, Dennis B. and SETTLE, John W. and PETRY, Glenn H., 'An Empirical Examination of Rate of Return Regulation in the ElectricUtility Industry: 1971 1982', **40** *Journal of Economics and Business*, 1988, 27-44.

FOREMAN Peck, J. S., 'Natural Monopoly and Railway Policy in the Nineteenth Century', **39** *Oxford Economic Papers*, 1987, 699-718.

FOX PENNER, Peter S., 'Regulating Independent Power Producers: Lessons of the PURPA Approach', **12** *Resources and Energy*, 1990, 117-141.

FOX, William F. and HOFLER, Richard A., 'Using Homothetic Composed Error Frontiers to Measure Water Utility Efficiency', **53** *Southern Economic Journal*, 1986, 461-477.

FOX-PENNER, Peter S., 'Cogeneration after PURPA: Energy Conservation and Industry Structure', **33** *Journal of Law & Economics*, 1990, 517-552.

FREEMAN, S. David, 'Electric Utility Conservation Programs: Progress and Problems: Comments', in SAWHILL, John C. and COTTON, Richard (eds.), *Energy Conservation: Successes and Failures*, Washington, Brookings Institution, 1986, 160-162.

FUHR, Joseph P., Jr., 'Vertical Integration and Regulation in the Electric Utility Industry', **24** *Journal of Economic Issues*, 1990, 173-187.

GATHON, Henry Jean, 'La distribution de l'eau en Belgique: Prix, coût et efficacité' [The Distribution of Water in Belgium: Price, Cost and Efficiency], **0(119)** *Cahiers Economiques de Bruxelles*, 1988, 371-384.

GEDDES, R. Richard and GRIFFES, Peter H., 'The Electric Utility Industry: New Challenges and Old Questions', **12** *Resources and Energy*, 1990, 1-15.

GERBER, David J., 'Rethinking the Monopolist's Duty to Deal: A Legal and Economic Critique of the Doctrine of "Essential Facilities"', **74** *Virginia Law Review*, 1988, 1069-1113.

GERWIG, Robert W., 'Natural Gas Production: A Study of Costs of Regulation', **5** *Journal of Law and Economics*, 1962, 69-92.

GILLIGAN, Thomas W., MARSHALL, William J. and WEINGAST, Barry R., 'Regulation and the Theory of Legislative Choice: The Interstate Commerce Act of 1887', **32** *Journal of Law and Economics*, 1989, 35-61.

GOLDBERG, Victor, 'Marginal Cost Pricing, Investment Theory and CATV: Comment', **14** *Journal of Law and Economics*, 1971, 513-516.

GOLDBERG, Victor P., 'Protecting the Right to be Served by Public Utilities', **1** *Research in Law and Economics*, 1979, 145-156.

GOLEC, Joseph, 'The Financial Effects of Fuel Adjustment Clauses on Electric Utilities', **63** *Journal of Business*, 1990, 165-186.

GORDON, Richard L., 'Timidity in Electric Utility Deregulation', **12** *Resources and Energy*, 1990, 17-32.

GORMLEY, William and HOADLEY, John and WILLIAMS, Charles, 'Potential Responsiveness in the Bureaucracy: Views of Public Utility Regulation', **77** *American Political Science Review*, 1983, 704-717.

GORT, Michael and WALL, Richard A., 'Foresight and Public Utility Regulation', **96** *Journal of Political Economy*, 1988, 177-188.

GRANDY, Christopher, 'Can Government Be Trusted to Keep Its Part of a Social Contract?: New Jersey and the Railroads, 1825-1888', **5** *Journal of Law, Economics, & Organization*, 1989, 249-269.

GREENBERG, Edward, 'Wire Television and the FCC's Second Report and Order on CATV Systems', **10** *Journal of Law and Economics*, 1967, 181-192.

GRIFFIN, James M. and MAYOR, Thomas H., 'The Welfare Gain from Efficient

Pricing of Local Telephone Services', **30** *Journal of Law and Economics*, 1987, 465-487.

HARTLEY, Peter and TRENGOVE, Chris, 'Who Benefits from Public Utilities?', **62** *Economic Record*, 1986, 163-179.

HAYASHI, Paul M., SEVIER, Melanie and TRAPANI, John M., 'An Analysis of Pricing and Production Efficiency of Electric Utilities by Mode of Ownership', in CREW, Michael A. (ed.), *Regulating Utilities in an Era of Deregulation*. New York, St. Martin's Press, 1987, 111-36.

HAZLETT, Thomas W., 'Wiring the Constitution for Cable', **12(1)** *Regulation*, 1988, 30-34.

HELBLING, Hans H. and TURLEY, James E., 'Oil Price Controls: A Counterproductive Effort', **57(11)** *Federal Reserve Bank of St. Louis Review*, 1975, 2-6.

HELM, Dieter, 'Regulating the Electricity Supply Industry', **9(3)** *Fiscal Studies*, 1988, 86-105.

HENDERSON, J. Stephen, 'The Effect of Regulation on Nonuniform Electricity Price Schedules inthe United States', **29** *Journal of Public Economic*, 1986, 317-332.

HENDRICKS, Walter, 'The Effect of Regulation on Collective Bargaining in Electric Utilities', **6** *Bell Journal of Economics*, 1975, 451-465.

HILLMAN, Jordan Jay and BRAEUTIGAM, Ronald R., *Price Leval Regulation for Diversified Public Utilities: An Assessment*, Dordrecht, Kluwer Academic, 1989, 141 p.

HILTON, George W., 'The Consistency of the Interstate Commerce Act', **9** *Journal of Law and Economics*, 1966, 87-113.

HOLLAS, Daniel R. and FRIEDLAND, Thomas S., 'Price Discrimination in the Municipal Electric Industry', **2** *Research in Law and Economics*, 1980, 181-198.

HOLLAS, Daniel R. and STANSELL, Stanley R., 'Regulation, Interfirm Rivalry, and the Economic Efficiency of Natural Gas Distribution Facilities', **28(4)** *Quarterly Review of Economics and Business*, 1988, 21-37.

HOLLAS, Daniel R. and STANSELL, Stanley R., 'An Examination of the Effect of Ownership Form on Price Efficiency: Proprietary, Cooperative and Municipal Electric Utilities', **55** *Southern Economic Journal*, 1988, 336-350.

HOTELLING, H., 'The General Welfare in Relation to Problems of Taxation and Railway and Utility Rates', **6** *Econometrica*, 1938, 242-269.

HOVENKAMP, Herbert J., 'Regulatory Conflict in the Gilded Age: Federalism and the Railroad Problem', **97** *Yale Law Journal*, 1988, 1017-1072.

HUETTNER, David A., 'The Effect of the Public Utility Regulatory Policy Act on the Electric Utility Industry', in PACHAURI, R.K. (ed.), *Global Energy Interactions*, Riverdale, Riverdale, 1987, 189-203.

HUGHES, Joseph P., 'Profit Maximizing Input Demand under Rate of Return Regulation: Pathological Substitution and Output Effects', **12** *Resources and Energy*, 1990, 79-95.

ISAAC, R. Mark, 'Petroleum Price Controls When Information Is a Joint Product', **56** *Land Economics*, 1980, 181-187.

JACOBSON, Charles, 'Same Game, Different Players: Problems in Urban Public Utility Regulation, 1850 1987', **26** *Urban Studies*, 1989, 13-31.

JARRELL, Gregg A., 'The Demand for State Regulation of the Electric Utility Industry', **21** *Journal of Law and Economics*, 1978, 269-295.

JEWKES, John, 'British Monopoly Policy 1944-56', **1** *Journal of Law and Economics*, 1958, 1-19.

JONES, Douglas N., 'Regulatory Concepts, Propositions, and Doctrines: Casualties and Survivors', **22** *Journal of Economic Issues*, 1988, 1089-0-108.

JONES, L.R. and THOMPSON, Frederick, 'Incremental vs. Comprehensive Reform of Economic Regulation: Predictable Outcomes and Unintended Consequences', **43** *American Journal of Economics and Sociology*, 1984, 1-17.

JORDAN, William A., 'Producer Protection, Prior Market Structure and the Effects of Government Regulation', **15** *Journal of Law and Economics*, 1972, 151-176.

JORGENSON, Dale W. and SLESNICK, Daniel T., 'General Equilibrium Analysis of Natural Gas Price Regulation', in BAILEY, Elizabeth E. (ed.), *Public Regulation: New Perspectives on Institutions and Policies*, Cambridge (Mass.), MIT Press, 1987, 153-90.

JOSKOW, Paul L., 'Inflation and Environmental Concern: Structural Change in the Process of Public Utility Price Regulation', **17** *Journal of Law and Economics*, 1974, 291-327.

JOSKOW, Paul L. and SCHMALENSEE, Richard, *Markets for Power: An Analysis of Electric Utility Deregulation*, Cambridge, MIT Press, 1983, 269 p.

JUREWITZ, John L., 'Deregulation of Electricity: A View from Utility Management', **6(3)** *Contemporary Policy Issues*, 1988, 25-241.

KAUFER, Erich, 'The Transaction Costs of Rate of Return Regulation: Comment', **141** *Zeitschrift für die gesamte Staatswissenschaft*, 1985, 124-126.

KEARL, J.R., 'Rules, Rule Intermediaries and the Complexity and Stability of Regulation', **22** *Journal of Public Economics*, 1983, 215-226.

KELLY, Kevin, et al., *Some Economic Principles for Pricing Wheeled Power*, Columbus, National Regulatory Research Institute, 1987, 361 p.

KELLY, Suedeen G., 'Regulatory Reform of the U.S. Natural Gas Industry: A Summing Up', **27** *Natural Resources Journal*, 1987, 841-863.

KENDRICK, J.W., 'Efficiency Incentives and Cost Factors in Public Utility Automatic Revenue Adjustment Clauses', **6** *Bell Journal of Economics*, 1975, 299-313.

KESHAVA, G. P., 'A Review of the Theory of Electricity Pricing', **34(2)** *Indian Economic Journal*, 1986, 71-86.

KIM, Jae Cheol and AHN, Byong Hun, 'On the Economics of Cogeneration: Pricing and Efficiency in Government Owned Utilities', **11** *Energy Journal*, 1990, 87-99.

KITCH, Edmund W., 'Regulation of the Field Market for Natural Gas by the Federal Power Commission', **11** *Journal of Law and Economics*, 1968, 243-280.

KLING, Robert W., 'General Equilibrium Effects of Regulation', **33(2)** *American Economist*, 1989, 53-59.

KOLLER, Roland H. II, 'Why Regulate Utilities? To Control Price Discrimination', **16** *Journal of Law and Economics*, 1973, 191-192.

KRYZANOWSKI, Lawrence and JALILVAND, Abolhassan, 'Statistical Tests of the Accuracy of Alternative Forecasts: Some Results for U.S. Utility Betas', **21** *Financial Review*, 1986, 319-335.

LABER, Gene, 'Regulators' Decisions on Rates of Return: Recent Experience in the Telephone Industry', **27(2)** *Quarterly Journal of Business and Economics*, 1988, 3-22.

LAFFONT, Jean-Jacques and TIROLE, Jean, 'Using Cost Observation to Regulate Firms', **94** *Journal of Political Economy*, 1986, 614-641.

LERNER, Abba P., 'Conflicting Principles of Public Utility Price Regulation', **7** *Journal of Law and Economics*, 1964, 61-70.

LESSER, Jonathan A., 'The Economics of Preference Power', **12** *Research in Law and Economics*, 1989, 131-151.

LEWIS, Tracy R. and SAPPINGTON, David E.M., 'Regulating a Monopolist with Unknown Demand and Cost Functions', **19** *Rand Journal of Economics*, 1988, 438-457.

LEWIS, Tracy R. and SAPPINGTON, David E.M., 'Regulating a Monopolist with Unknown Demand', **78** *American Economic Review*, 1988, 986-998.

LEWIS, Tracy R. and SAPPINGTON, David E.M., 'Regulatory Options and Price-Cap Regulation', **20** *Rand Journal of Economics*, 1989, 405-416.

LIPARTITO, Kenneth, 'System Building at the Margin: The Problem of Public Choice in the Telephone Industry', **49** *Journal of Economic History*, 1989, 323-336.

LOEB, Martin and MAGAT, Wesley A., 'A Decentralized Method for Utility Regulation', **22** *Journal of Law and Economics*, 1979, 399-404.

LOGAN, John W. and MASSON, Robert T. and REYNOLDS, Robert J., 'Efficient Regulation with Little Information: Reality in the Limit?', **30** *International Economic Review*, 1989, 851-861.

LYON, Thomas P., 'Natural Gas Policy: The Unresolved Issues', **11(2)** *Energy Journal*, 1990, 23-49.

MacAVOY, Paul W., 'The Regulation-Induced Shortage of Natural Gas', **14** *Journal of Law and Economics*, 1971, 167-199.

MacAVOY, Paul W., SPULBER, Daniel F. and STANGLE, Bruce E., 'Is Competitive Entry Free? Bypass and Partial Deregulation in Natural Gas Markets', **6** *Yale Journal on Regulation*, 1989, 209-247.

MAGAT, Wesley A., 'Regulation and the Rate and Direction of Induced Technical Change', **7** *Bell Journal of Economics*, 1976, 478-496.

MAKHIJA, Anil K. and SPIRO, Michael H., 'Determinants of Earned Rates of Return on Equity of U.S. Electric Utilities, 1976 1984', **30** *Economic Letters*, 1989, 367-371.

MALONEY, Michael T., McCORMICK Robert E. and TOLLISON, Robert D., 'Economic Regulation, Competitive Governments, and Specialised Resources', **27** *Journal of Law and Economics*, 1984, 329-338.

MANN, Patrick C., 'User Power and Electricity Rates', **17** *Journal of Law and*

Economics, 1974, 433-443.

MANN, Patrick C., 'The Dynamics of Traditional Rate Regulation', **1** *Research in Law and Economics*, 1979, 195-212.

MARX, Jane, 'Regulation of Electric Utilities and Affiliated Coal Companies Determining Reasonable Expenses: Comment', **26** *Natural Resources Journal*, 1986, 851-869.

MATHIOS, Alan D. and ROGERS, Robert P., 'The Impact of Alternative Forms of State Regulation of AT&T on Direct-Dial, Long-Distance Telephone Rates', **20** *Rand Journal of Economics*, 1989, 437-453.

MAYER, Robert N. and ZICK, Cathleen D. and BURTON, John R., 'Consumer Representation and Local Telephone Rates', **23** *Journal of Consumer Affairs*, 1989, 267-284.

MAYO, John W. and FLYNN, Joseph E., 'The Effects of Regulation on Research and Development: Theory and Evidence', **61** *Journal of Business*, 1988, 321-336.

McCONNELL, Michael W., 'Public Utilities' Private Rights: Paying for Failed Nuclear Power', **12(2)** *Regulation*, 1988, 35-43.

McNICOL, David L., 'Price Discrimination and Peak-load Pricing Subject to Rate of Return Constraint', **1** *Research in Law and Economics*, 1979, 213-238.

MEGDAL, Sharon B., 'On Regulation, Deregulation, and Economics', **10(3)** *Energy Journal*, 1989, 181-195.

MELODY, William H., 'Efficiency and Social Policy in Telecommunication: Lessons from the U.S. Experience', **23** *Journal of Economic Issues*, 1989, 657-688.

MICHAELS, Robert J., 'Reorganizing Electricity Supply in New Zealand: Lessons for the United States', **7(4)** *Contemporary Policy Issues*, 1989, 73-90.

MILLWARD, Robert and WARD, Robert, 'The Costs of Public and Private Gas Enterprises in Late 19th Century Britain', **39** *Oxford Economic Papers*, 1987, 719-737.

MINASIAN, Jora R., 'Television Pricing and the Theory of Public Goods', **7** *Journal of Law and Economics*, 1964, 71-80.

MOORHOUSE, John C. (ed.), *Electric Power: Deregulation and the Public Interest*, San Francisco: Pacific Research Institute for Public Policy, 1986.

MUNROE, Tapan, 'Electric Utility Competition: Lessons from Others', **12(2)** *Journal of Energy and Development*, 1987, 203-214.

NAUGHTON, Michael C., 'The Efficiency and Equity Consequences of Two Part Tariffs in Electricity Pricing', **68** *Review of Economics and Statistics*, 1986, 406-414.

NAUGHTON, Michael C., 'The Determinants of Regulators' Preferences: Discrimination in Electricity Pricing', **17** *Journal of Behavioral Economics*, 1988, 279-294.

NAUGHTON, Michael C., 'Regulatory Preferences and Two Part Tariffs: The Case of Electricity', **55** *Southern Economic Journal*, 1989, 743-758.

NELSON, Jon P., ROBERTS, MArk J; and TROMP, Emsley P., 'An Analysis of Ramsey Pricing in Electric Utilities', in CREW, Michael A. (ed.), *Regulating*

Utilities in an Era of Deregulation. New York, St. Martin's Press, 1987, 85-109.

NELSON, Jon P. and ROBERTS, Mark J., 'Ramsey Numbers and the Role of Competing Interest Groups in Electric Utility Regulation', **29(3)** *Quarterly Review of Economics and Business*, 1989, 21-42.

NELSON, Randy A., 'The Effects of Regulation on Capacity Utilization: Evidence from the Electric Power Industry', **29(4)** *Quarterly Review of Economics and Business*, 1989, 37-48.

NELSON, Randy A., 'The Effects of Competition on Publicly Owned Firms: Evidence from the Municipal Electric Industry in the U.S.', **8** *International Journal of Industrial Organization*, 1989, 37-51.

NEUFELD, John L., 'Price Discrimination and the Adoption of the Electricity Demand Charge', **47** *Journal of Economic History*, 1987, 693-709.

NG, Yew Kwang, 'Equity, Efficiency and Financial Viability: Public Utility Pricing with Special Reference to Water Supply', **79** *Australian Economic Review*, 1987, 21-35.

NISKANEN, William A., 'Natural Gas Price Controls: An Alternative View', **10(2)** *Regulation*, 1986, 46-50.

NORTON, Seth W., 'Regulation and Systematic Risk: The Case of Electric Utilities', **28** *Journal of Law and Economics*, 1985, 671-686.

NORTON, Seth W., 'In Search of Regulatory Lag', **26(4)** *Quarterly Journal of Business and Economics*, 1987, 3-16.

NORTON, Seth W., 'Regulation, the OPEC Oil Supply Shock, and Wealth Effects for Electric Utilities', **26** *Economic Inquiry*, 1988, 223-238.

NOWOTNY, Kenneth, 'Transmission Technology and Electric Utility Regulation', **22** *Journal of Economic Issues*, 1988, 555-562.

ODELL, P., 'The Deregulation of Oil: The International Oil Market Framework', in *18de Vlaams Wetenschappelijk Economisch Congres, Brussel 8 en 9 mei 1987, Sociaal-economische Deregulering*, Brussel, V.E.H.U.B., 1987, 455-471.

OREN, S.S. and SMITH, S.A., 'Criticial Mass and Tariff Structure in Electronic Communications Markets', **12** *Bell Journal of Economics*, 1981, 467-487.

PACE, Joe D. and LANDON, John H., 'Introducing Competition into the Electric Utility Industry: An Economic Appraisal', **3** *Energy Law Journal*, 1982, 1-65.

PARK, Rolla Edward, 'Cable Television, UHF Broadcasting, and FCC Regulatory Policy', **15** *Journal of Law and Economics*, 1972, 207-231.

PATTERSON, Cleveland S. and URSEL, Nancy D., 'Public Utility Equity Financing Practices: A Test of Market Efficiency', in CREW, Michael A. (ed.), *Regulating Utilities in an Era of Deregulation*. New York, St. Martin's Press, 1987, 63-76.

PAUL, Chris and SCHOENING, Niles, 'Regulation and Rent-Seeking: Prices, Profits, and Third-Party Transfers', **68** *Public Choice*, 1991, 185-194.

PELTZMAN, Sam, 'Pricing in Public and Private Enterprises: Electric Utilities in the United States', **14** *Journal of Law and Economics*, 1971, 109-147.

PENN, David W., 'Electric Supply Industry Regulation - Leadership or Retreat?', **24** *Journal of Economic Issues*, 1990, 545-553.

PETTWAY, Richard H. and JORDAN, Bradford D., 'APT vs. CAPM Estimates of the Return Generating Function Parameters for Regulated Public Utilities', **10** *Journal of Financial Research*, 1987, 227-238.

PIERCE, Richard J., Jr., 'Reconsidering the Roles of Regulation and Competition in the Natural Gas Industry', **97** *Harvard Law Review*, 1983, 345-385.

PIERCE, Richard J., Jr., 'A Proposal to Deregulate the Market for Bulk Power', **72** *Virginia Law Review*, 1986, 1183-1235.

POOLE, Robert W., Jr. (ed.), *Unnatural Monopolies: The Case for Deregulating Public Utilities*, Lexington, Lexington Books, 1985, 224 p.

POSNER, Richard A., 'Natural Monopoly and Its Regulation', **21** *Stanford Law Review*, 1969, 548-643.

PRIMEAUX, Walter J., Jr. et al., 'Determinants of Regulatory Policies toward Competition in the Electric Utility Industry', **43** *Public Choice*, 1984, 173-186.

PRIMEAUX, Walter J., Jr., 'What Can Regulators Regulate? The Case of Electric Utility Rates of Return', **9(2)** *Managerial and Decision Economics*, 1988, 145-152.

QUANDT, Richard E., 'Complexity in Regulation', **22** *Journal of Public Economics*-, 1983, 199-214.

RAFFIEE, Kambiz and WENDEL, Jeanne, 'The Effects of Alternative Regulatory Policies on Utility Investment Strategies', **54** *Southern Economic Journal*, 1988, 840-854.

RASHID, Salim, 'Public Utilities in Egalitarian LDC's: The Role of Bribery in Achieving Pareto Efficiency', **34** *Kyklos*, 1981, 34, 448-460.

RASSENTI, S.J., SMITH, V.L. and BULFIN, R.L., 'A Combinatorial Auction Mechanism for Airport Time Slot Allocation', **13** *Bell Journal of Economics*, 1982, 402-417.

REECE, D.K., 'Competitive Bidding for Offshore Petroleum Leases', **9** *Bell Journal of Economics*, 1978, 369-384.

REECE, D.K., 'An Analysis of Alternative Bidding Systems for Leasing Offshore Oil', **10** *Bell Journal of Economics*, 1979, 659-669.

RIORDAN, Michael H. and SAPPINGTON, David E.M., 'Awarding Monopoly Franchises', **77** *American Economic Review*, 1987, 375-387.

ROZEK, Richard P., 'Competitive Bidding in Electricity Markets: A Survey', **10(4)** *Energy Journal*, 1989, 117-138.

SALAUN, Fabienne, 'Privatisation et reglementation: le cas du British gas' [Privatization and Regulation: The Case of British Gas], **24** *Economies et Sociétés*, 1990, 53-469.

SALTZMAN, Sidney and SCHULER, Richard E., 'Electricity's Future: Sharpening the Debates', in SALTZMAN, Sidney and SCHULER, Richard E. (eds.), *The Future of Electrical Energy: A Regional Perspective of an Industry in Transition*, New York, Greenwood Press, 1986, 348-362.

SAPPINGTON, D., 'Strategic Firm Behavior under a Dynamic Regulatory Adjustment Process', **11** *Bell Journal of Economics*, 1980, 360-372.

SCHAP, David, *Municipal Ownership in the Electric Utility Industry: A Centennial View*, New York, Greenwood Press, 1986, 128 p.

SCHMIDT, Ronald H., 'Deregulating Electric Utilities: Issues and Implications', *Federal Reserve Bank of Dallas Economic Review*, September 1987, 13-226.

SCHNEIDER, Friedrich und BARTEL, Rainer, *Gemeinwirtschaft versus Privatwirtschaft* [Collective Economics versus Private Economics], Vienna, Manz Publishers, 1989, 315 p.

SCHOLTES, Philippe R., 'Dual v Uniform Prices An Application', **12(1)** *Energy Economics*, 1990, 18-26.

SCULLION, Patrick J., 'Electric Utility Conservation Programs: Progress and Problems: Comments', in SAWHILL, John C. and COTTON, Richard (eds.), *Energy Conservation: Successes and Failures*, Washington, Brookings Institution, 1986, 159-160.

SELDON, Zena A. and SELDON, James R., 'Natural Monopolies versus Desirable Monopolies and Regulation in the Public Interest: Two Quibbles and a Policy Note', **23(2)** *Quarterly Journal of Business and Economics*, 1984, 58-71.

SHARKEY, William W., 'A Decentralized Method for Utility Regulation: A Comment', **22** *Journal of Law and Economics*, 1979, 405-407.

SHARKEY, William W., *The Theory of Natural Monopoly*, Cambridge, Cambridge University Press, 1982, 229 p.

SHLEIFER, Andrei, 'A Theory of Yardstick Competition', **16** *Rand Journal of Economics*, 1985, 319-327.

SIBLEY, David, 'Asymmetric Information, Incentives and Price-Cap Regulation', **20** *Rand Journal of Economics*, 1989, 392-404.

SING, Merrile, 'Are Combination Gas and Electric Utilities Multiproduct Natural Monopolies?', **69** *Review of Economics and Statistics*, 1987, 392-398.

SMITH, Vernon L., 'Currents of Competition in Electricity Markets', **11(2)** *Regulation*, 1987, 23-29.

SPENCE, A. Michael, 'Monopoly, Quality and Regulation', **6** *Bell Journal of Economics*, 1975, 417-429.

SPULBER, Daniel F., 'Second-Best Pricing and Cooperation', **17** *Rand Journal of Economics*, 1986, 239-250.

STEWART, Marion B. (ed.), *Energy Deregulation and Economic Growth: Proceedings of the First Annual Conference on Energy Policy in the Middle Atlantic States*, New Brunswick, Rutgers, Bureau of Economic Research, 1987, 27-32.

STIGLER, George J., 'The Economics of Scale', **1** *Journal of Law and Economics*, 1958, 54-71.

STIGLER, George J. and FRIEDLAND, Claire, 'What Can Regulators Regulate? The Case of Electricity', **5** *Journal of Law and Economics*, 1962, 1-16.

STRASSER, Kurt A. and KOHLER, Kohler, Mark F., *Regulating Utilities with Management Incentives: A Strategy for Improved Performance*, Westport, Greenwood Press, 1989, 197 p.

TAGGART, Robert A., Jr., 'Effects of Regulation on Utility Financing: Theory and Evidence', **33** *Journal of Industrial Economics*, 1985, 257-276.

TAM, Mo Yin S., 'A Mechanism to Induce Ramsey Pricing for Natural Monopoly Firms', **6** *International Journal of Industrial Organization*, 1988, 247-261.

TAWADA, Makoto and KATAYAMA, Sei Ichi, 'On the Technical Efficiency under Regulation: A Case for the Japanese Electric Power Industry', **41** *Economic Studies Quarterly*, 1990, 34-47.

TEEPLES, Ronald and FEIGENBAUM, Susan and GLYER, David, 'Public versus Private Water Delivery: Cost Comparisons', **14** *Public Finance Quarterly*, 1986, 351-366.

THOMPSON, Howard E., 'Regulatory Policy under Uncertainty: How Should the Earned Rate of Return for a Public Utility Be Controlled?', in CREW, Michael A. (ed.), *Regulating Utilities in an Era of Deregulation*. New York, St. Martin's Press, 1987, 25-41.

THOMPSON, Howard E., *Regulatory Finance: Finacial Foundations of Rate of Return Regulation*, Dordrecht, Kluwer Academic Publishers, 1991, 256 p.

TISHLER, Asher, 'The Response of Large Firms to Different Schemes of Time of Use Pricing When the Production Function is Quadratic', **10(2)** *Energy Journal*, 1989, 69-90.

TRAIN, Kenneth E. and McFADDEN, Daniel L. and GOETT, Andrew A., 'Consumer Attitudes and Voluntary Rate Schedules for Public Utilities', **69** *Review of Economics and Statistics*, 1987, 383-391.

TRAIN, Kenneth E. and TOYAMA, Nate, 'Pareto Dominance through Self selecting Tariffs: The Case of TOU Electricity Rates for Agricultural Customers', **10(1)** *Energy Journal*, 1989, 91-109.

TREBING, Harry M., 'Public Utility Regulation: A Case Study in the Debate over Effectiveness of Economic Regulation', **18** *Journal of Economic Issues*, 1984, 223-250.

TREBING, Harry M., 'Apologetics of Deregulation in Energy and Telecommuniciations: An Institutionalist Assesment', **20** *Journal of Economic Issues*, 1986, 613-632.

VERMOES, J., 'De programmaovereenkomst: regulering of deregulering?' [Programme Contract: Regulation or Deregulation?], in *18de Vlaams Wetenschappelijk Economisch Congres, Brussel 8 en 9 mei 1987, Sociaal-economische Deregulering*, Brussel, V.E.H.U.B., 1987, 441-454.

VOGELSANG, Ingo, 'A Little Paradox in the Design of Regulatory Mechanisms', **29** *International Economic Review*, 1988, 467-476.

VOGELSANG, Ingo and FINSINGER, Jörg, 'A Regulatory Adjustment Process for Optimal Pricing by Multiproduct Monopoly Firms', **10** *Bell Journal of Economics*, 1979, 157-171.

VOLKONSKII, V. A. and KUZOVKIN, A. I., 'Marginal Costs and Optimal Electricity Tariffs', **24** *Matekon*, 1987, 43-69.

WALD, Patricia M., 'Judicial Review of Economic Analysis', **1** *Yale Journal on Regulation*, 1983, 43-62.

WALL, Richard A. and GORT, Michael, 'An Empirical Test of Feedbacks in Public Utility Regulation', **12(1)** *Resources and Energy*, 1990, 107-116.

WATERSON, Michael, 'Issues in the Regulation of Cable TV', **4** *International Review of Law and Economics*, 1984, 67-82.

WATERSON, Michael, *Regulation of the Firm and Natural Monopoly*, Oxford,

Blackwell, 1988, 164 p.

WATTLES, George M., 'The Rates and Costs of the United States Postal Service', **16** *Journal of Law and Economics*, 1973, 89-117.

WILSON, James Q. and RICHARDSON, Louise, 'Public Ownership Vs. Energy Conservation: A Paradox of Utility Regulation', **9(5)** *Regulation*, 1985, 13-17, 36-38.

WILSON, Robert B., 'Efficient and Competitive Rationing', **57** *Econometrica*, 1989, 1-40.

WOLFF, Nancy, *Income Redistribution and the Social Security Program*, Ann Arbor, UMI Research Press, 1987, 181 p.

WOODBURY, J.R., BESEN, S.M. and FOURNIER, G.M., 'The Determinants of Network Television Program Prices: Implicit Contracts, Regulation, and Bargaining Power', **14** *Bell Journal of Economics*, 1983, 351-365.

YUCEL, Mine Kuban, 'A Dynamic Model of Natural Gas Deregulation', **12(1)** *Energy Economics*, 1990, 35-47.

ZUPAN, Mark A., 'The Efficacy of Franchise Bidding Schemes in the Case of Cable Television: Some Systematic Evidence', **32** *Journal of Law and Economics*, 1989, 401-456.

ZUPAN, Mark A., 'On Cream Skimming, Coase and the Sustainability of Natural Monopolies', **22** *Applied Economics*, 1990, 487-492.

5900 REGULATION OF OTHER SECTORS (a selection)

Gerrit De Geest

5900 Regulation of Other Sectors: General

BLAIR, Roger D. and RUBIN, Stephen (eds.), *Regulating the Professions: A Public-Policy Symposium*, Lexington, Lexington Books, 1980, 328 p.

COMANOR, William S., 'The Political Economy of the Pharmaceutical Industry', **24** *Journal of Economic Literature*, 1986, 1178-1217.

DEMIN, P., 'Industrie en energie: 1. Industrie' [Industry and Energy: Industry], in *18de Vlaams Wetenschappelijk Economisch Congres, Brussel 8 en 9 mei 1987, Sociaal-economische Deregulering*, Brussel, V.E.H.U.B., 1987, 387-398.

DINGWALL, R. and FENN, Paul, '"A Respectable Profession"? Sociological and Economic Perspectives on the Regulation of Professional Services', **7** *International Review of Law and Economics*, 1987, 51-64.

FOLEY, Patrick, SHAKED, Avner and SUTTON, John, *The Economics of the Professions. An Introductory Guide to the Literature*, London, London School of Economics, 1981, 107 p.

GOFF, Brian L. and SHUGHART, William F. II and TOLLISON, Robert D., 'Disqualification by Decree: Amateur Rules as Barriers to Entry', **144** *Journal of Institutional and Theoretical Economics*, 1988, 515-523.

KLEIT, Andrew N. and STROUP, Richard L., 'Blackout at Bonneville Power', **11(2)** *Regulation*, 1987, 30-36.

MAIJOOR, Steven J., *The Economics of Accounting Regulation*, Maastricht, Datawyse, 1991, 213 p.

RICHLI, Paul, 'Handels- und Gewerbefreiheit contra Energiepolitik' [Freedom of Trade and Industry versus Energy Policy], **86** *Schweizerisches Zentralblatt für Staats- und Verwaltungsrecht*, 1985, 1-14.

S'JEGERS, R., FAES, P. en SEGEBARTH, K., 'Deregulering van de handels-en dienstenstromen en van de rechtstreekse investeringen: 3. Dienstverlening' [Deregulation of Trade and Service Flows and of Direct Investments: Service], in *18de Vlaams Wetenschappelijk Economisch Congres, Brussel 8 en 9 mei 1987, Sociaal-economische Deregulering*, Brussel, V.E.H.U.B., 1987, 797-839.

TOMA, Eugenia Froedge, 'Institutional Structures, Regulation, and Producer Gains in the Education Industry', **26** *Journal of Law and Economics*, 1983, 103-116.

VUCHELEN, J. en PRAET, P., 'Diensten en vrije beroepen' [Services and Free Professions], in *18de Vlaams Wetenschappelijk Economisch Congres, Brussel 8 en 9 mei 1987, Sociaal-economische Deregulering*, Brussel, V.E.H.U.B., 1987, 507-541.

WEST, E.G., 'The Political Economy of American Public School Legislation', **10** *Journal of Law and Economics*, 1967, 101-128.

5910 Legal Professions

ALLEN, Ronald J., GRADY, Mark F., POLSBY, Daniel D. and YASHKO, Michael S., 'A Positive Theory of the Attorney-Client Privilege and the Work Product Doctrine', **19** *Journal of Legal Studies*, 1990, 359-397.

ARNOULD, Richard J., 'Pricing Professional Services : A Case Study of the Legal Services Industry', **38** *Southern Economic Journal*, 1972, 38, 495-507.

BOWLES, Roger A. and PHILLIPS, Jennifer, 'Solicitors' Renumeration: A Critique of Recent Developments in Conveyancing', **40** *Modern Law Review*, 1977, 639-650.

BOWLES, Roger A. and SKOGH, Göran, 'Reputation, Monitoring and the Organisation of the Law Firm', in FAURE, Michael and VAN DEN BERGH, Roger (eds.), *Essays in Law and Economics. Corporations, Accident Prevention and Compensation for Losses*, Antwerpen, Maklu, 1989, 33-47.

CALVANI, Terry, LANGENFELD, James and SHUFORD, Gordon, 'Attorney Advertising and Competition at the Bar', **41** *Vanderbilt Law Review*, 1988, 761-788.

CARR, Jack and MATHEWSON, Frank, 'The Economics of Law Firms: A Study in the Legal Organization of the Firm', **33** *Journal of Law & Economics*, 1990, 307-330.

CLERMONT, K.N. and CURRIVAN, J.D., 'Improving on the Contingent Fee', **63** *Columbia Law Review*, 1973, 529-639.

COFFEE, John C., Jr., 'The Regulation of Entrepreneurial Litigation: Balancing Fairness and Efficiency in the Large Class Action', **54** *University of Chicago Law Review*, 1987, 877-937.

DOMBERGER, Simon and SHERR, Avrom, 'Economic Efficiency in the Provision of Legal Services: The Private Practitioner and the Law Centre', **1** *International Review of Law and Economics*, 1981, 29-49.

DOMBERGER, Simon and SHERR, Avrom, 'Competition in Conveyancing: An Analysis of Solicitors' Charges 1983 85', **8(3)** *Fiscal Studies*, 1987, 17-28.

FREEMAN, Richard B., 'Legal Cobwebs: a Recursive Model of the Market for New Lawyers', **62** *Review of Economics and Statistics*, 1975, 171-179.

FRIEDMAN, Milton and KUZNETS, S., *Income from Independent Professional Practice*, New York, National Bureau of Economic Research, 1945.

GALANTER, Marc and PALAY, Thomas M., 'Why the Big Get Bigger: The Promotion-to-Partner Tournament and the Growth of Large Law Firms', **76** *Virginia Law Review*, 1990, 747-811.

GROSS, Leonard E., 'Contractual Limitations on Attorney Malpractice Liability: An Economic Approach', **75** *Kentucky Law Journal*, 1986, 793 ff.

HAZARD, Geoffrey C., Jr., PEARCE, Russell G. and STEMPEL, Jeffrey W., 'Why Lawyers Should Be Allowed to Advertise: A Market Analysis of Legal Services', **58** *New York University Law Review*, 1983, 1084-1113.

HOLEN, Arlene S., 'Effects of Professional Licensing Arrangements on Interstate Labor Mobility and Resource Allocation', **73** *Journal of Political Economy*, 1965, 492-498.

HUDEC, Albert J. and TREBILCOCK, Michael J., 'Lawyer Advertising and the Supply of Information in the Market for Legal Services', **20** *University of Western Ontario Law Review*, 1982, 53-99.

JOSEPH, M., *The Conveyancing Fraud*, London, M. Joseph, 1976, ??? p.

JULIN, J.R., 'The Legal Profession: Education and Entry', in BLAIR, Roger D. and RUBIN, Stephen (eds.), *Regulating the Professions: A Public-Policy Symposium*, Lexington, Lexington Books, 1980, ???-???

KLEPPER, Steven, MAZUR, Mark and NAGIN, Daniel, 'Expert Intermediaries and Legal Compliance: The Case of Tax Preparers', **34** *Journal of Law and Economics*, 1991, 205-229.

KWON, J.K., 'A Model of the Law Firm', **45** *Southern Economic Journal*, 1978, 63-74.

LEES, D.S., *The Economic Consequences of the Professions*, London, Institute of Economic Affairs, 1966, 48 p.

McCHESNEY, Fred S., 'Team Production, Monitoring, and Profit Sharing in Law Firms: An Alternative Hypothesis', **11** *Journal of Legal Studies*, 1982, 379-393.

MICELI, Thomas J. and SEGERSON, Kathleen, 'Contingent Fees for Lawyers: The Impact on Litigation and Accident Prevention', **20** *Journal of Legal Studies*, 1991, 381-399.

MITCHELL, Daniel J.B. and SCHWART, M.L., 'Theoretical Implications of Contingent Legal Fees', **12** *Quarterly Review of Economics and Business*, 1972, 69-76.

MULVEY, C., 'Rate of Return to the Legal Profession in Scotland', **27** *Scottish Journal of Political Economy*, 1980, 250-259.

MUREIKO, William R., 'Note: A Public Goods Approach to Calculating Reasonable Fees Under Attorney Fee Shifting Statutes', *Duke Law Journal*, 1989, 438 ff.

MURIS, Timothy J. and McCHESNEY, Fred S., 'Advertising and the Price and Quality of Legal Services: The Case for Legal Clinics', **1** *American Bar Foundation Research Journal*, 1979, 179-207.

PASHIGIAN, B. Peter, 'The Market for Lawyers: The Determinants of the Demand for and Supply of Lawyers', **20** *Journal of Law and Economics*, 1977, 53-85.

PASHIGIAN, B. Peter, 'Occupational Licensing and the Interstate Mobility of Professionals', **22** *Journal of Law and Economics*, 1979, 1-25.

SMITH, Janet Kiholm and COX, Steven R., 'The Pricing of Legal Services: A Contractual Solution to the Problem of Bilateral Opportunism', **14** *Journal of Legal Studies*, 1985, 167-183.

TAMAN, L., 'The Emerging Legal Paraprofessionals', in SLAYTON, Philip and TREBILCOCK, Michael J. (eds.), *The Professions and Public Policy*, Toronto, University of Toronto Faculty of Law, 1978.

THOMASON, Terry, 'Are Attorneys Paid What They're Worth? Contingent Fees and the Settlement Process', **20** *Journal of Legal Studies*, 1991, 187-223.

VELJANOVSKI, Cento G. and WHELAN, Christopher J., 'Professional Negligence and the Quality of Legal Services - An Economic Perspective', **46** *Modern Law Review*, 1983, 700-718.

WILSON, Robert A., 'Rates of Return to Entering the Legal Profession: Some Further Evidence', **34** *Scottish Journal of Political Economy*,1987, 174-191.

WOLFRAM, Charles W., 'The Second Set of Players: Lawyers, Fee Shifting, and the Limits of Professional Discipline', **47(1)** *Law and Contemporary Problems*, 1984, 293-320.

5920 Medical Professions

ARNOULD, Richard J. and VAN VORST, Charles B., 'Supply Responses to Market and Regulatory Forces in Health Care', in MEYER, Jack A. (ed.), *Incentives vs. Controls in Health Policy: Broadening the Debate*, Washington, American Enterprise Institute for Public Policy Research, 1985, 107-131.

ARROW, Kenneth J., 'Uncertainty and the Welfare Economics of Medical Care', **53** *American Economic Review*, 1963, 941-973.

BENHAM, Lee, MAURIZI, A. and REDER, M.W., 'Migration, Location and Remuneration of Medical Personnel: Physicians and Dentists', **50** *Review of Economics and Statistics*, 332-347.

BERLANT, J.L., *Profession and Monopoly: A Study of Medicine in the United States and Great Britain*, Berkeley, University of California Press, 1975.

CONRAD, Douglas A. and WATTS, Carolyn A., 'A Note on Measuring the Extent of Competition in the Physicians' Services Market: An Alternative Approach', **3** *Research in Law and Economics*, 1981, 241-249.

DANZON, Patricia M., PAULY, Mark V. and KINGSTON, Raynard S., 'The Effects of Malpractice Litigation on Physicians' Fees and Income', **80** *American Economic Review. Papers and Proceedings*, 1990, 122-127.

DeVANY, Arthur S., GRAMM, Wendy L., SAVING, Thomas R. and SMITHSON, Charles W., 'The Impact of Input Regulation: The Case of the U.S. Dental Industry', **25** *Journal of Law and Economics*, 1982, 367-381.

DOLAN, A.K., 'Occupational Licensure and Obstruction of Change in the Health Care Delivery System: Some Recent Developments', in BLAIR, Roger D. and RUBIN, Stephen (eds.), *Regulating the Professions: A Public-Policy Symposium*, Lexington, Lexington Books, 1980.

EISENBERG, Barry S., 'Information Exchange among Competitors: The Issue of Relative Value Scales for Physicians' Services', **23** *Journal of Law and Economics*, 1980, 441-460.

EVANS, R.G., 'Does Canada Have Too Many Doctors? - Why Nobody Loves an Immigrant Physician', **11** *Canadian Public Policy*, 1976, 147-159.

EVANS, R.G., PARISH, E.M.A. and SULLY, F., 'Medical Productivity, Scale Effects and Demand Generation', **6** *Canadian Journal of Economics*, 1973, 376-393.

FEIN, Rashi, *The Doctor Shortage: An Economic Diagnosis*, Washington, The Brookings Institution, 1967, 199 p.

FELDMAN, P.H., 'The Impact of Third-Party Payment on Professional Practice: Lessons from the Medical Profession', in BLAIR, Roger D. and RUBIN,

Stephen (eds.), *Regulating the Professions: A Public-Policy Symposium*, Lexington, Lexington Books, 1980.

FELDSTEIN, Martin S., 'The Rising Price of Physicians' Services', **52** *Review of Economics and Statistics*, 1970, 121-133.

FELDSTEIN, P.J., *Health Associations and the Demand for Legislation: The Political Economy of Health*, Cambridge Mass., Ballinger Publishing, 1977.

FRECH, H. Edward III, 'Occupational Licensure and Health Care Productivity: The Issues and the Literature', in RAFFERTY, J. (ed.), *Health Manpower and Productivity*, Lexington, Lexington Books, 1974, chapter 6.

FRIEDMAN, Milton and KUZNETS, S., *Income from Independent Professional Practice*, New York, National Bureau of Economic Research, 1945.

GOLDSMITH, Art, 'Dental Hygienists' Wages: The Role of Human Capital and InstitutionalFactors', **29(2)** *Quarterly Review of Economics and Business*, 1989, 56-67.

HALL, Thomas D. and LINDSAY, Cotton M., 'Medical Schools: Producers of What? Sellers to Whom?', **23** *Journal of Law and Economics*, 1980, 55-80.

HOLEN, Arlene S., 'Effects of Professional Licensing Arrangements on Interstate Labor Mobility and Resource Allocation', **73** *Journal of Political Economy*, 1965, 492-498.

KESSEL, Reuben A., 'Price Discrimination in Medicine', **1** *Journal of Law and Economics*, 1958, 20-53.

KESSEL, Reuben A., 'The A.M.A. and the Supply of Physicians', **35** *Law and Contemporary Problems*, 1970, 267-283.

KESSEL, Reuben A., 'Higher Education and the Nation's Health: A Review of the Carnegie Commission Report on Medical Education', **15** *Journal of Law and Economics*, 1972, 115-127.

LEFFLER, Keith B., 'Physician Licensure: Competition and Monopoly in American Medicine', **21** *Journal of Law and Economics*, 1978, 165-186.

LINDSAY, C.M., 'Real Returns to Medical Education', **8** *Journal of Human Resources*, 1973, 331-348.

LYNK, William J., 'Physician Price Fixing under the Sherman Act: An Indirect Test of the Maricopa Issues', **7** *Journal of Health Economics*, 1988, 95-109.

MENNEMEYER, S.T., 'Really Great Returns to Medical Education?', **13** *Journal of Human Resources*, 1978, 75-90.

NEWHOUSE, Joseph P., WILLIAMS, Albert P., BENNETT, Bruce W. and SCHWARTZ, William B., 'Does the Geographical Distribution of Physicians Reflect Market Failure?' **13** *Bell Journal of Economics*, 1982, 493-505.

NOETHER, Monica, 'The Effect of Government Policy Changes on the Supply of Physicians: Expansion of a Competitive Fringe', **29** *Journal of Law and Economics*, 1986, 231-262.

PSACHAROPOULOS, G., *Earnings and Education in OECD Countries*, Paris, OECD, 1975, Chapter 5 ('Monopoly Elements in Earnings from Education').

RIZZO, John A. and ZECKHAUSER, Richard J., 'Advertising and Entry: The Case of Physician Services', **98** *Journal of Political Economy*, 1990, 476-500.

SHEPARD, Lawrencc, 'Licensing Restrictions and the Cost of Dental Care', **21** *Journal of Law and Economics*, 1978, 187-201.

SLOAN, Frank A. and STEINWALD, Bruce, 'Effects of Regulation on Hospital Costs and Input Use', **23** *Journal of Law and Economics*, 1980, 81-109.

WEINGAST, Barry R., 'Physicians, DNA Research Scientists, and the Market for Lemons', in BLAIR, Roger D. and RUBIN, Stephen (eds.), *Regulating the Professions: A Public-Policy Symposium*, Lexington, Lexington Books, 1980.

WHITE, William D., 'The Impact of Occupational Licensure of Clinical Laboratory Personnel', **13** *Journal of Human Resources*, 1978, 91-102.

WHITE, William D., 'Dynamic Elements of Regulation: The Case of Occupational Licensure', **1** *Research in Law and Economics*, 1979, 15-33.

WHITE, William D., 'The Introduction of Professional Regulation and Labor Market Conditions Occupational Licensure of Registered Nurses', **20** *Policy Sciences*, 1987, 27-51.

X, 'Note: Restrictive Licensing of Dental Paraprofessionals', **83** *Yale Law Journal*, 1974, 806-826.

5930 Transportation

ACKER, Mary H., 'Assessing the Impact of Regulation of Trucking Firms', **11** *Eastern Economic Journal*, 1985, 135-143.

AYRES, Ian, 'Determinants of Airline Carrier Conduct', **8** *International Review of Law and Economics*, 1988, 187-202.

BABCOCK, Michael W. and GERMAN, H. Wade, 'The Impact of Deregulation on Rail TOFC Carloadings', **20** *Logistics and Transportation Review*, 1984, 205-212.

BAILEY, Elizabeth E., 'Airline Deregulation in the United States: The Benefits Provided and the Lessons Learned', **12(2)** *International Journal of Transport Economics*, 1985, 119-144.

BAILEY, Elizabeth E. and WILLIAMS, Jeffrey R., 'Sources of Economic Rent in the Deregulated Airline Industry', **31** *Journal of Law and Economics*, 1988, 173-202.

BARLA, Philippe and PERELMAN, Sergio, 'Technical Efficiency in Airlines under Regulated and Deregulated Environments', **60** *Annals of Public and Co-operative Economy*, 1989, 103-124.

BARNEKOV, Christopher C., 'The Track Record', **11(1)** *Regulation*, 1987, 19-27.

BARNEKOV, Christopher C. and KLEIT, A. N., 'The Efficiency Effects of Railroad Deregulation in the United States', **17** *International Journal of Transport Economics*, 1990, 21-36.

BEESLEY, Michael E. and GLAISTER, Stephen G., 'Information for Regulating: The Case of Taxis', **93** *Economic Journal*, 1983, 594-615.

BEILOCK, Richard, 'Are Truckers Forced to Speed?', **21** *Logistics and Transportation Review*, 1985, 277-291.

BEILOCK, Richard and FREEMAN, James, 'The Effect on Rate Levels and Structures of Removing Entry and Rate Controls on Motor Carriers', **21** *Journal of Transport Economics and Policy*, 1987, 167-188.

BENNETT, Randall W. and BOYER, Kenneth D., 'Inverse Price/Quality Tradeoffs in the Regulated Airline Industry', **24** *Journal of Transport Economics and Policy*, 1990, 35-47.

BLAIR, Roger D. and KASERMAN, David L. and McCLAVE, James T., 'Motor Carrier Deregulation: The Florida Experiment', **68** *Review of Economics and Statistics*, 1986, 159-164.

BLAIR, Roger D. and KASERMAN, David L. and MCCLAVE, James T., 'Competition on Trial: Florida Deregulates Trucking', **30(4)** *Challenge*, 1987, 60-64.

BLAUWENS, Gust and VAN DE VOORDE, Eddy, 'Onderzoek naar de Economische Kost van de Regulering van het Goederenvervoer in België' [An Investigation of the Economic Cost of the Regulation of the Transport of Goods in Belgium], **40** *Economisch en Sociaal Tijdschrift*, 1986, 575-592.

BLAUWENS, Gust and VAN DE VOORDE, Eddy, 'Deregulering en de vraag naar luchtvervoer' [Deregulation and the Demand for Air Transport], **32** *Tijdschrift voor Economie en Management*, 1988, 127-142.

BLONK, W.A.G., 'Vervoer' [Transport], in *18de Vlaams Wetenschappelijk Economisch Congres, Brussel 8 en 9 mei 1987, Sociaal-economische Deregulering*, Brussel, V.E.H.U.B., 1987, 543-560.

BLUMESTOCK, James W. and THOMCHICK, Evelyn A., 'Deregulation and Airline Labor Relations', **22** *Logistics and Transportation Review*, 1986, 389-403.

BOHLANDER, George W. and FARRIS, Martin T., 'Collective Bargaining in Trucking The Effects of Deregulation', **20** *Logistics and Transportation Review*, 1984, 223-238.

BONGAERTS, Jan C. and VAN SCHAIK, A.S., 'The Demand for Regulation: The Case of Dutch Inland Shipping', **4** *International Review of Law and Economics*, 1984, 199-212.

BORENSTEIN, Severin and ZIMMERMAN, Martin B., 'Market Incentives for Safe Commercial Airline Operation', **78** *American Economic Review*, 1988, 913-935.

BOYER, Kenneth D., 'The Costs of Price Regulation: Lessons from Railroad Deregulation', **18** *Rand Journal of Economics*, 1987, 408-416.

BREEN, Denis A., 'The Monopoly Value of Household-Goods Carrier Operating Certificates', **20** *Journal of Law and Economics*, 1977, 153-185.

BRUNING, Edward R. and TEHRANIAN, Hassan, 'Stock Market Reactions to Motor Carrier Regulatory Reform', **15** *International Journal of Transport Economics*, 1988, 7-27.

BUCKLEY, Patricia, 'The Deregulation of Urban Taxicab Markets: A Note', **26** *American Economist*, 1982, 73-76.

BUTTON, Kenneth J., 'Liberalising the Canadian Scheduled Aviation Market', **10(4)** *Fiscal Studies*, 1989, 19-52.

BUTTON, Kenneth J., 'Economic Theories of Regulation and the Regulation of the

United Kingdom's Bus Industry', **34** *Antitrust Bulletin*, 1989, 489-515.

BUTTON, Kenneth J., *Airline Deregulation: International Experiences*, New York, New York University Press, 1990, 191 p.

BUTTON, Kenneth J. and SWANN, Dennis, 'European Community Airlines Deregulation and Its Problems', **27** *Journal of Common Market Studies*, 1989, 259-282.

CARD, David, 'The Impact of Deregulation on the Employment and Wages of Airline Mechanics', **39** *Industrial and Labor Relations Review*, 1986, 527-538.

CAVES, D.W., CHRISTENSEN, L.R. and SWANSON, J.A., 'Economic Performance in Regulated and Unregulated Environments: A Comparison of U.S. and Canadian Railroads', **66** *Quarterly Journal of Economics*, 1981, 559-581.

CAVES, D.W., CHRISTENSEN, L.R., TRETHEWAY, M.W. and WINDLE, Robert J., 'An Assessment of the Efficiency Effects of U.S. Airline Deregulation via an International Comparison', in BAILEY, E.E. (ed.), *Public Regulation: New Perspectives on Institutions and Policies*, Cambridge, Mass., MIT Press, 1987, 285-320.

COASE, Ronald H., 'The British Post Office and the Messenger Companies', **4** *Journal of Law and Economics*, 1961, 12-65.

COLEGATE, Raymond, 'Airline Deregulation in the United States Eight Years On: Review Article', **9** *World Economy*, 1986, 441-444.

CORDES, Joseph J. and GOLDFARB, Robert S., 'Alternate Rationales for Severence Pay Compensation under Airline Deregulation', **41** *Public Choice*, 1983, 351-369.

CORDES, Joseph J. and GOLDFARB, Robert S. and JOHNSON, Richard L., 'Design and Implementation of Job Loss Compensation Provisions: Lessons from the Airline Deregulation Experience', **16** *International Journal of Transport Economics*, 1989, 35-55.

CREW, Michael A. and KLEINDORFER, Paul R. (eds.), *Competition and Innovation in Postal Services*, Dordrecht, Kluwer Academic Publishers, 1991, 304 p.

CRUM, Michael R., 'U.S. Transportation Management Developments since Deregulation', **16** *International Journal of Transport Economics and Policy*, 1989, 263-295.

DAICOFF, Darwin W., 'Deregulation and Motor Carrier Safety', **24** *Logistics and Transportation Review*, 1988, 175-184.

DARDIS, Rachel, GARKEY, Janet and ZHANG, Zhiming, 'Deregulation of Trucking in the United States - Implications for Consumers', **12** *Journal of Consumer Policy*, 1989, 19-38.

DAUGHETY, Andrew F. and NELSON, Forrest D., 'An Econometric Analysis of Changes in the Cost and Production Structure of the Trucking Industry, 1953-1982', **70** *Review of Economics and Statistics*, 1988, 67-75.

DAVIDSON, Wallace N., III and CHANDY, P. R. and WALKER, Mike, 'The Stock Market Effects of Airline Deregulation', **23(4)** *Quarterly Journal of Business and Economics*, 1984, 31-45.

DAVIES, David G., 'Property Rights and Economic Efficiency - The Australian Airlines Revisited', **20** *Journal of Law and Economics*, 1977, 223-226.

DAWSON, D. A. and PARENT, L. P., 'Positive Steps in Transport Deregulation The Prairies', **13(1)** *Canadian Public Policy*, 1987, 86-96.

DERTHICK, Martha and QUIRK, Paul J., *The Politics of Deregulation*, Washington D.C., The Brookings Institution, 1985, 265 p.

DIONNE, Georges and GAGNE, Robert, 'Models and Methodologies in the Analysis of Regulation Effects in Airline Markets', **15** *International Journal of Transport Economics*, 1988, 291-312.

DIVELY, Dwight, 'Applications of Regulatory Theory to the Trucking Industry', **6** *Research in Law and Economics*, 1984, 211-226.

DODGSON, J.S. and KATSOULACOS, Y., 'Quality Competition in Bus Services: Some Welfare Implications of Bus Deregulation', **22** *Journal of Transport Economics and Policy*, 1988, 263-281.

DOUGLAS, G.W. and MILLER, J.C., *Economic Regulation of Domestic Air Transport: Theory and Policy*, Washington, Brookings Institution, 1974.

DUNBAR, Frederick C. and MEHRING, Joyce S., 'Coal Rail Prices during Deregulation: A Hedonic Price Analysis', **26** *Logistics and Transportation Review*, 1990, 17-34.

EADS, George C., 'Airline Competitive Conduct in a Less Regulated Environment: Implications for Antitrust', **28** *Antitrust Bulletin*, 1983, 159-184.

ECKERT, Ross D. and HILTON, George W., 'The Jitneys', **15** *Journal of Law and Economics*, 1972, 293-325.

EVANS, Andrew, 'Hereford: A Case Study of Bus Deregulation', **22** *Journal of Transport Economics and Policy*, 1988, 283-306.

FINDLAY, Christopher C., 'Effects of Australian International Air Transport Regulation', **34** *Journal of Industrial Economics*, 1985, 199-216.

FORSYTH, Peter, 'Airlines and Airports: Privatisation, Competition, and Regulation', **5(1)** *Fiscal Studies*, 1984, 61-75.

FRANKEL, E.G., 'Economic and Commercial Implications of the U.S. Shipping Act of 1984', **22(2)** *Logistics and Transportation Review*, 1986, 99-114.

FRANKENA, Mark W. and PAUTLER, Paul A., 'Taxicab Regulation: An Economic Analysis', **9** *Research in Law and Economics*, 1986, 129-165.

FREW, James R., 'The Existence of Monopoly Profits in the Motor Carrier Industry', **24** *Journal of Law and Economics*, 1981, 289-315.

FRIEDLANDER, Ann F. and DE NEUFVILLE, Richard, 'The Political Rationality of Federal Transportation Policy', **1** *Research in Law and Economics*, 1979, 97-114.

GAGNE, Robert and DIONNE, Georges, 'Qu'en est-il des rendements d'echelle dans les industries quebecoises et ontariennes de transport par camion' [What is True About the Economics of Scale in the Quebec and Ontario Trucking Industry], **64** *L'actualité économique*, 1988, 380-395.

GALLICK, Edward C. and SISK, David E., 'A Reconsideration of Taxi Regulation', **3** *Journal of Law, Economics, & Organization*, 1987, 117-128.

GARROD, P.V. and MIKLIUS, W., '"Captive Shippers" and the Success of Railroads in Capturing Monopoly Rent', **30** *Journal of Law and Economics*, 1987, 423-442.

GIL, Avishai, 'Air Transport Deregulation and Its Implications for Flight Attendants', **129** *International Labour Review*, 1990, 317-331.

GILLEN, David W. and OUM, Tae H. and TRETHEWAY, Michael W., 'Entry Barriers and Anti competitive Behaviour in a Deregulated Airline Market: The Case of Canada', **15** *International Journal of Transport Economics*, 1988, 29-41.

GILLEN, David W., OUM, Tae H. and TRETHEWAY, Michael W., 'Privatization of Air Canada: Why It Is Necessary in a Deregulated Environment', **15** *Canadian Public Policy*, 1989, 285-299.

GIORDANO, James N., 'A Trucker's Dilemma: Managerial Behavior under an Operating Ratio Standard', **10** *Managerial and Decision Economics*, 1989, 241-251.

GOLBE, Devra L., 'Product Safety in a Regulated Industry: Evidence from the Railroads', **21** *Economic Inquiry*, 1983, 39-52.

GRAHAM, David R. and KAPLAN, Daniel P. and SIBLEY, David S., 'Efficiency and Competition in the Airline Industry', **14** *Bell Journal of Economics*, 1983, 118-138.

GREENHUT, John, NORMAN, George and GREENHUT, M.L., 'Financial-Economic Aspects of Airline Deregulation', **18** *International Journal of Transport Economics*, 1991, 3-30.

GRIMM, Curtis M. and CORSI, Thomas M. and JARRELL, Judith L., 'U.S. Motor Carrier Cost Structure under Deregulation', **25** *Logistics and Transportation Review*, 1989, 231-249.

GRIMM, Curtis M. and SMITH, Ken G., 'The Impact of Rail Regulatory Reform on Rates, Service Quality, and Management Performance: A Shipper Perspective', **22** *Logistics and Transportation Review*, 1986, 57-68.

GURIA, Jagadish C., 'Effects of the Recent Road Transport Deregulation on Rail Freight Demands in New Zealand', **15** *International Journal of Transport Economics*, 1988, 169-187.

GURIA, Jagadish C., 'An Assessment of the Effects of Road Freight Transport Regulations in Developing Countries', **16** *International Journal of Transport Economics*, 1989, 237-262.

GWILLIAM, Ken M., 'Setting the Market Free: Deregulation of the Bus Industry', **23** *Journal of Transport Economics and Policy*, 1989, 29-43.

HARBESON, Robert W., 'Toward Better Resource Allocation in Transport', **12** *Journal of Law and Economics*, 1969, 321-338.

HARDAWAY, Robert M., 'Comment: Transportation Deregulation (1976-1984): Turning the Tide', **14** *Transport Law Journal*, 1985, 101 ff.

HARMATUCK, Donald J., 'Economies of Scale and Scope in the Motor Carrier Industry: An Analysis of the Cost Functions of Seventeen Large LTL Common Motor Carriers', **25** *Journal of Transport Economics and Policy*, 1991, 135-151.

HARPER, Donald V. and JOHNSON, James C., 'The Potential Consequences of Deregulation of Transportation Revisited', **63** *Land Economics*, 1987, 137-146.

HAYASHI, Paul M. and TRAPANI, John M., 'An Analysis of the Objectives of Domestic Airline Firms under CAB Regulation', **15** *Applied Economics*, 1983, 603-617.

HIRSCH, Barry T., 'Trucking Regulation, Unionization, and Labor Earnings: 1973 85', **23** *Journal of Human Resources*, 1988, 296-319.

HWANG, Ming Jeng and MANN, Patrick C., 'Deregulation and Efficiency in the Rail Industry', **15(2)** *Atlantic Economic Journal*, 1987, 47-52.

JAFFER, Sue M. and THOMPSON, David J., 'Deregulating Express Coaches: A Reassessment', **7(4)** *Fiscal Studies*, 1986, 45-68.

JANIS, Russell A., 'A Law and Economics Study of Rail Freight Rate Regulation: Traditional Standards, Ramsey Prices, and a Case of Neither', **15** *Transport Law Journal*, 1986, 31 ff.

JANSONIUS, John V. and BROUGHTON, Kenneth E., 'Coping with Deregulation: Reduction of Labor Costs in the Airline Industry', **19** *Journal of Air Law and Commerce*, 1984, 501-593.

JOHNSON, Nancy Brown and SAMBHARYA, Rakesh B. and BOBKO, Philip, 'Deregulation, Business Strategy, and Wages in the Airline Industry', **28** *Industrial Relations*, 1989, 419-430.

JORDAN, William A., 'Results of U.S. Airline Deregulation: Evidence from the Regulated Canadian Airlines', **22** *Logistics and Transportation Review*, 1986, 297-337.

JORDON, William D., 'Airline Performance under Regulation: Canada vs. the United States', **1** *Research in Law and Economics*, 1979, 35-79.

KAHN, Alfred E., 'I Would Do It Again', **12(2)** *Regulation*, 1988, 22-28.

KAHN, Alfred E., 'Surprises of Airline Deregulation', **78** *American Economic Review. Papers and Proceedings*, 1988, 316-322.

KEASEY, K. and MULLEY, C., 'Deregulation and Privatisation of Local Buses in the United Kingdom', **13** *International Journal of Transport Economics*, 1986, 153-175.

KEELER, Theodore E., 'Public Policy and Productivity in the Trucking Industry: Some Evidence on the Effects of Highway Investments, Deregulation, and the 55MPH Speed Limit', **76** *American Economic Review. Papers and Proceedings*, 1986, 153-158.

KEELER, Theodore E., 'Deregulation and Scale Economies in the U.S. Trucking Industry: An Econometric Extension of the Survivor Principle', **32** *Journal of Law and Economics*, 1989, 229-253.

KIM, Moshe, 'The Beneficiaries of Trucking Regulation, Revisited', **27** *Journal of Law and Economics*, 1984, 227-241.

KITCH, Edmund W., 'The Yellow Cab Antitrust Case', **15** *Journal of Law and Economics*, 1972, 327-336.

KITCH, Edmund W., ISAACSON, Marc and KASPER, Daniel, 'The Regulation of Taxicabs in Chicago', **14** *Journal of Law and Economics*, 1971, 285-350.

KLING, Robert W., 'Trucking Deregulation: Evolution of a New Power Structure', **22** *Journal of Economic Issues*, 1988, 1201-1211.

KYLE, Reuben, III and PHILLIPS, Laurence T., 'Airline Deregulation: Did

Economists Promise Too Much or Too Little?', **21** *Logistics and Transportation Review*, 1985, 3-25.

LEE, Tenpao and KIM, Tae Kyun and BAUMEL, C. Phillip, 'Impact of Deregulation on the Financial Performance of the Class I Railroads: Heuristic Models of Pooled Time Series and Cross Sectional Data', **24** *Logistics and Transportation Review*, 1988, 281-296.

LEE, Tenpao and KIM, Tae Kyun and BAUMEL, C. Phillip, 'Impact of Deregulation on the Financial Performance of the Class I Railroads: Errata', **25** *Logistics and Transportation Review*, 1989, 91-94.

LEVINE, Michael E., 'Regulating Airmail Transportation', **18** *Journal of Law and Economics*, 1975, 317-359.

LEVINE, Michael E., 'Revisionism Revised? Airline Deregulation and the Public Interest', **44(1)** *Law and Contemporary Problems*, 1981, 179-195.

LEVINE, Michael E., 'Airline Competition in Deregulated Markets: Theory, Firm Strategy, and Public Policy', **4** *Yale Journal on Regulation*, 1987, 393-494.

LEWISCH, Peter, *Erwerbsfreiheit und Bedarfsprüfung* [The Freedom to Earn one's Living as Subjected to Regulations Concerning Needs], Vienna, Marktwirtschaftliche Schriften des Carl Menger Institutes, 1989, 47 p.

LEWISCH, Peter, 'The Political Economy of Barriers to Entry: The Example of the Amendment for Taxicab Regulation in Austria', in WEIGEL, Wolfgang (ed.), *Economic Analysis of Law - A Collection of Applications*, Vienna, Österreichischer Wirtschaftsverlag, 1991, 222-234.

MACDONALD, James M., 'Railroad Deregulation, Innovation, and Competition: Effects of the Staggers Act on Grain Transportation', **32** *Journal of Law and Economics*, 1989, 63-95.

McCARTHY, Patrick S. and OESTERLE, William, 'The Deterrent Effects of Stiffer DUI Laws: An Empirical Study', **23** *Logistics and Transportation Review*, 1987, 353-371.

McFARLAND, Henry, 'Did Railroad Deregulation Lead to Monopoly Pricing? An Application of q*', **60** *Journal of Business*, 1987, 385-400.

McGOWAN, Francis and SEABRIGHT, Paul, 'Deregulating European Airlines', **0(9)** *Economic Policy: A European Forum*, 1989, 283-344.

McKENZIE, Richard B. and SHUGHART, William F. II, 'Deregulation and Air Travel Safety', **11(3/4)** *Regulation*, 1987, 42-47.

McMULLEN, B. Starr and STANLEY, Linda R., 'The Impact of Deregulation on the Production Structure of the Motor Carrier Industry', **26** *Economic Inquiry*, 1988, 299-316.

McSHAN, Scott and WINDLE, Robert, 'The Implications of Hub and Spoke Routing for Airline Costs and Competitiveness', **25** *Logistics and Transportation Review*, 1989, 209-230.

MEYER, J.R. and OSTER, C.V. (eds.), *Airline Deregulation: The Early Experience*, Boston, Auburn House, 1981.

MEYER, John R., OSTER, Clinton V., Jr. and STRONG, John S., 'The U.S. Experience with Airline Deregulation: The Effect on Travelers: Fares and Service', in MEYER, John, R. and OSTER, Clinton V., Jr. (eds.), *Deregulation and the Future of Intercity Passenger Travel*, Cambridge (Mass.), MIT Press, 1987, 109-124.

MICHEL, Allen and SHAKED, Israel, 'Trucking Deregulation and Motor Carrier Performance: The Shareholders' Perspective', **22** *Financial Review*, 1987, 295-311.

MILLER, James C., III, 'Airline Market Shares vs. Capacity Shares and the Possibility of Short-Run Loss Equilibria', **1** *Research in Law and Economics*, 1979, 81-96.

MITCHELL, Mark L. and MALONEY, Michael T., 'Crisis in the Cockpit? The Role of Market Forces in Promoting Air Travel Safety', **32** *Journal of Law and Economics*, 1989, 329-355.

MOORE, Thomas G., *Trucking Regulation. Lessons from Europe*, Washington, A.E.I.P.P.R., 1976, 148 p.

MOORE, Thomas G., 'The Beneficiaries of Trucking Regulation', **21** *Journal of Law and Economics*, 1978, 327-343.

MOORE, Thomas G., 'U.S. Airline Deregulation: Its Effects on Passengers, Capital, and Labor', **29** *Journal of Law and Economics*, 1986, 1-28.

MOORE, Thomas G., 'Transportation Policy', **12(3)** *Regulation*, 1988, 57-62.

MORRISON, Steven and WINSTON, Clifford, *The Economic Effects of Airline Deregulation*, Washington D.C., Brookings, 1986, 84 p.

MORRISON, Steven A. and WINSTON, Clifford, 'The Dynamics of Airline Pricing and Competition', **80** *American Economic Review. Papers and Proceedings*, 1990, 389-393.

MOSES, Leon N. and SAVAGE, Ian (eds.), *Transportation Safety in an Age of Deregulation*, Oxford, Oxford University Press, 1989, 368 p.

NELSON, James C., 'Politics and Economics in Transport Regulation and Deregulation A Century Perspective of the ICC's Role', **23** *Logistics and Transportation Review*, 1987, 5-32.

NETTER, Jeffry M., POULSEN, Annette B. and HERSCH, Philip L., 'Insider Trading: The Law, the Theory, the Evidence', **6(3)** *Contemporary Policy Issues*, 1988, 1-13.

OLSON, C. Vincent and TRAPANI III, John M., 'Who Has Benefited from Regulation of the Airline Industry ?', **24** *Journal of Law and Economics*, 1981, 75-93.

OUM, T.H., STANBURY, W.T. and TRETHEWAY, M.W., 'Airline Deregulation in Canada and its Economic Effects', in HAYASHI, T. (ed.), *New Dimensions for Public Utilities*, Osaka, Osaka University Press, 1990.

OUM, Tae Hoon and TRETHEWAY, Michael W., 'Reforming Canadian Airline Regulation', **20** *Logistics and Transportation Review*, 1984, 261-284.

OUM, Tae Hoon and ZHANG, Yimin, 'Utilisation of Quasi-Fixed Inputs and Estimation of Cost Functions: An Application to Airline Costs', **25** *Journal of Transport Economics and Policy*, 1991, 121-134.

PANZAR, John C., 'Regulatory Theory and the U.S. Airline Experience', **139** *Zeitschrift für die gesamte Staatswissenschaft*, 1983, 490-4505.

PEETERS, Ch., VERBEKE, A. and WINKELMANS, W., 'Een geïntegreerd overheidsbeleid voor de Belgische binnenvaartsector' [An Integrated Governmental Policy for the Belgian Inland Shipping], **32** *Tijdschrift voor Economie en Management*, 1987, 19-37.

PERA, Alberto, 'Deregulation and Privatisation in an Economy Wide Context', **0(12)** *OECD Economic Studies*, 1989, 159-204.

PETERSON, Rodney, 'SYMPOSIUM: An Economic Analysis of Statutory Changes in Rail Carrier Entry and Exit', *Transportation Law Journal*, 1984, 189 ff.

PHILLIPS, Karen Borlaug and PHILLIPS, Laurence T., 'Research, Politics, and the Dynamics of Policy Development: A Case Study of Motor Carrier Regulatory Reform', **17** *Policy Sciences*, 1984, 367-384.

PLOURDE, André, 'On the Role and Status of Canadian Natural Gas Carriers under Deregulation', **13(1)** *Journal of Energy and Development*, 1987, 1-25.

PRAGER, Robin A., 'Using Stock Price Data to Measure the Effects of Regulation: The Interstate Commerce Act and the Railroad Industry', **20** *Rand Journal of Economics*, 1989, 280-290.

PRIEST, George L., 'The History of the Postal Monopoly in the United States', **18** *Journal of Law and Economics*, 1975, 33-80.

PUSTAY, Michael W., 'Liberalization of U.S. International Aviation Policy: A Preliminary Assessment', **29(2)** *Quarterly Review of Economics and Business*, 1989, 15-26.

RAKOWSKI, James P., 'Marketing Economics and the Results of Trucking Deregulation in the Less-Than-Truckload Sector', **27** *Transportation Journal*, 1988, 11-22.

REISS, Peter C. and SPILLER, Pablo T., 'Competition and Entry in Small Airline Markets', **32** *Journal of Law and Economics*, 1989, S179-S202.

ROSE, Nancy L., 'The Incidence of Regulatory Rents in the Motor Carrier Industry', **16** *Rand Journal of Economics*, 1985, 299-318.

ROSE, Nancy L., 'Labor Rent Sharing and Regulation: Evidence from the Trucking Industry', **95** *Journal of Political Economy*, 1987, 1146-1178.

SACASAS, Rene and GLASKOWSKY, Nicholas A., Jr., 'Motor Carrier Deregulation: A Decade of Legal and Economic Conflict', **18** *Transport Law Journal*, 1990, 189 ff.

SAMUELS, George E., 'Airline Deregulation: Its Effects and the Competitive Environment', **17** *International Journal of Transport Economics*, 1990, 131-146.

SARWAR, Ghulam and ANDERSON, Dale G., 'Railroad Rate Deregulation and Uncertainty of Farm Level Prices for Corn', **71** *American Journal of Agricultural Economics*, 1989, 883-891.

SCHIPPER, Katherine, THOMPSON, Rex and WEIL, Roman L., 'Disentangling Interrelated Effects of Regulatory Changes on Shareholders Wealth: The Case of Motor Carrier Deregulation', **30** *Journal of Law and Economics*, 1987, 67-100.

SICKLES, Robin C. and GOOD, David and JOHNSON, Richard L., 'Allocative Distortions and the Regulatory Transition of the U.S. Airline Industry', **33** *Journal of Econometrics*, 1986, 143-163.

SPILLER, Pablo T., 'The Differential Impact of Airline Regulation on Individual Firms and Markets: An Empirical Analysis', **26** *Journal of Law and Economics*,

1983, 655-689.

STANBURY, W.T. and TRETHEWAY, Michael W., 'Airline Deregulation: A Bibliography', **22** *Logistics and Transportation Review*, 1986, 449-489.

TALLEY, Wayne K. and SCHWARZ Miller, Ann, 'The Demand for Air Services Provided by Air Passenger Cargo Carriers in a Deregulated Environment', **15** *International Journal of Transport Economics*, 1988, 159-168.

TAYLOR, D. Wayne, 'The Economic Effects of the Direct Regulation of the Taxicab Industryin Metropolitan Toronto', **25** *Logistics and Transportation Review*, 1989, 169-182.

TEHRANIAN, Hassan and BRUNING, Edward R., 'Deregulation and Investor Perception of Motor Carrier Securities', **20** *Logistics and Transportation Review*, 1984, 165-186.

THOMAS, Janet M. and CALLAN, Scott J., 'Constant Returns to Scale in the Post Deregulatory Period and THE Case of Specialized Motor Carriers', **25** *Logistics and Transportation Review*, 1989, 271-288.

TRETHEWAY, Michael W., 'Airline Deregulation: Introduction', **22** *Logistics and Transportation Review*, 1986, 293-296.

TUCCI, Gianrocco, 'Regulation and "Contestability' in Formulating an Air Transport Policy for the European Community', **76** *Rivista di Politica Economica*, 1985, 219-239.

TULLOCK, Gordon, 'The Case of Dutch Inland Shipping: Comment', **6** *International Review of Law and Economics*, 1986, 139-140.

TYE, William B., 'The Postal Service: Economics Made Simplistic', **3** *Journal of Policy Analysis and Management*, 1983, 62-73.

TYE, William B., *Encouraging Cooperation among Competitors: The Case of Motor Carrier Deregulation and Collective Ratemaking*, New York, Greenwood Press, 1987, 202 p.

VAN SCYOC, Lee J., 'Effects of Airline Deregulation on Profitability', **25** *Logistics and Transportation Review*, 1989, 39-251.

VETSUYPENS, Michael R. and HELMUTH, John A., 'Airline Deregulation: Additional Evidence from the Capital Markets', **27(2)** *Quarterly Journal of Business and Economics*, 1988, 117-138.

WHITE, Evan D., 'Economic Regulation of Oregon Intrastate Trucking: A Policy Evaluation', **17** *Transp. Law Journal*, 1989, 179 ff.

WILLIAMS, George, 'Achieving a Competitive Environment for Europe's Airline Industry', *National Westminister Bank Quarterly Review*, May 1990, 2-14.

WILLIG, Robert D. and BAUMOL, William J., 'Using Competition as a Guide', **11(1)** *Regulation*, 1987, 28-35.

WOODBURY, John R. and BESEN, Stanley M. and FOURNIER, Gary M., 'The Determinants of Network Television Program Prices: Implicit Contracts, Regulation, and Bargaining Power', **14** *Bell Journal of Economics*, 1983, 351-365.

YING, John S., 'The Inefficiency of Regulating a Competitive Industry: Productivity Gains in Trucking Following Reform', **72** *Review of Economics and Statistics*, 1990, 191-201.

YING, John S., 'Regulatory Reform and Technical Change: New Evidence of Scale Economies in Trucking', **56** *Southern Economic Journal*, 1990, 996-1009.

ZIMMERMAN, Martin B., 'Rent and Regulation in Unit-Train Rate Determination', **10** *Bell Journal of Economics*, 1979, 271-281.

5940 Agriculture

CAMPBELL, H.F. and LINDNER, R.K., 'The Production of Fishing Effort and the Economic Performance of Licence Limitation Programs', **66** *Land Economics*, 1990, 56-66.

JOHNSON, D. Gale, 'Government and Agriculture: Is Agriculture a Special Case?', **1** *Journal of Law and Economics*, 1958, 122-135.

RUCKER, Randal R. and THURMAN, Walter N., 'The Economic Effect of Supply Controls: The Simple Analytics of the U.S. Peanut Program', **33** *Journal of Law & Economics*, 1990, 483-515.

SQUIRES, Dale, 'Public Regulation and the Structure of Production in Multiproduct Industries: An Application to the New England Otter Trawl Industry', **18** *Rand Journal of Economics*, 1987, 232-247.

TROJAN, C., 'Landbouw' [Agriculture], in *18de Vlaams Wetenschappelijk Economisch Congres, Brussel 8 en 9 mei 1987, Sociaal-economische Deregulering*, Brussel, V.E.H.U.B., 1987, 475-504.

ULRICH, Alvin, FURTAN, William H. and SCHMITZ, Andrew, 'The Cost of a Licensing System Regulation: An Example from Canadian Prairie Agriculture', **95** *Journal of Political Economy*, 1987, 160-178.

WILCOX, Christopher J., 'Social Costs of Regulation of Primary Industry: An Application to Animal Welfare Regulation of the Victorian Pig Industry', **33** *Australian Journal of Agricultural Economics*, 1989, 187-202.

5950 Telecommunications

BALDWIN, R., CAVE, M. and JONES, T.H., 'The Regulation of Independent Local Radio and Its Reform', **7** *International Review of Law and Economics*, 1987, 177-191.

BAXTER, William F., 'Regulation and Diversity in Communications Media', **64** *American Economic Review. Papers and Proceedings*, 1974, 392-399.

BEESLEY, Michael E. and LAIDLAW, Bruce, *The Future of Telecommunications: An Assessment of the Role of Competition in UK Policy*, London, Institute of Economic Affairs, 1989, 96 p.

BEESLEY REPORT, *Liberalization of the Use of British Telecommunications Network*, London, HMSO, 1981.

BESEN, Stanley M. and WOODBURY, John R., 'Regulation, Deregulation, and

Antitrust in the Telecommunications Industry', **28** *Antitrust Bulletin*, 1983, 39-68.

BLANKART, Charles B. and KNIEPS, Gunter, 'What Can We Learn from Comparative Institutional Analysis? The Case of Telecommunications', **42** *Kyklos*, 1989, 579-598.

BOTEIN, Michael and PEARCE, Alan, 'The Competitiveness of the U.S. Telecommunications Industry: A New York Case Study', **6** *Cardozo Arts & entertainment Law Journal*, 1988, 233-325.

BROCK, Gerald W., 'The Regulatory Change in Telecommunications: The Dissolution of AT&T', in WEISS, Leonard W. and KLASS, Michael W. (ed.), *Regulatory Reform: What Actually Happened*, Boston, Little Brown, 1986, 210-233.

CARTER, Richard, 'Le Canada est-il entraine dans la dereglementation: le cas des communications' [Is Canada Deregulating? The Case of Telecommunications], **10** *Canadian Public Policy*, 1984, 10-24.

COASE, Ronald H., 'The Federal Communications Commission', **2** *Journal of Law and Economics*, 1959, 1-40.

COASE, Ronald H., 'The Interdepartment Radio Advisory Committee', **5** *Journal of Law and Economics*, 1962, 17-47.

COASE, Ronald H., 'Payola in Radio and Television Broadcasting', **22** *Journal of Law and Economics*, 1979, 269-328.

COMANOR, William S. and MITCHELL, Bridger M., 'The Costs of Planning: The FCC and Cable Television', **15** *Journal of Law and Economics*, 1972, 177-206.

COPELAND, Basil L., Jr. and SEVERN, Alan, 'Price Theory and Telecommunications Regulation: A Dissenting View', **3** *Yale Journal on Regulation*, 1985, 53-85.

CRANDALL, Robert W., 'The Economic Effect of Television-Network Program "Ownership"', **14** *Journal of Law and Economics*, 1971, 385-412.

CRANDALL, Robert W., 'Telecommunications Policy in the Reagan Era', **12(3)** *Regulation*, 1988, 28-33.

CRANDALL, Robert W. and FLAMM, Kenneth (eds.), *Changing the Rules: Technological Change, International Competition and Regulation in Communications*, Washington, Brookings Institution, 1988, 424 p.

CUDE, Brenda J., 'Consumer Response to Telecommunications Deregulation: The Equal Access Decision', **23** *Journal of Consumer Affairs*, 1989, 285-300.

d'ALCANTARA, G., 'Telecommunicatie. Economische aspecten' [Telecommunication: Economic Aspects], in *18de Vlaams Wetenschappelijk Economisch Congres, Brussel 8 en 9 mei 1987, Sociaal-economische Deregulering*, Brussel, V.E.H.U.B., 1987, 565-579.

DALY, George and MAYOR, Thomas, 'Estimating the Value of a Missing Market: the Economics of Directory Assistance', **23** *Journal of Law and Economics*, 1980, 147-166.

DE FONTENAY, Alain, SHUGARD, Mary H. and SIBLEY, David S. (eds.), *Telecommunications Demand Modelling: An Integrated View*, Amsterdam, North Holland, 1990, 479 p.

DYK, Timothy B., 'Full First Amendment Freedom for Broadcasters: The Industry as Elizaon the Ice and Congress as the Friendly Overseer', **5** *Yale Journal on Regulation*, 1988, 299-329.

ECKEL, Russel, 'Industrial Relations and High Technology: The Transformation of Telecommunications through Deregulation', in CHILD, John and BATE, Paul (ed.), *Organization of Innovation: East-West Perspectives*, Berlin, De Gruyter, 1987, 173-189.

EINHORN, Michael A. (ed.), *Price Caps and Incentive Regulation in Telecommunications*, Dordrecht, Kluwer Academic, 1991, 244 p.

ENCAOUA, David and KOEBEL, Philippe, 'Réglementation et déréglementation des télécommunications: Leçons anglo-saxonnes et perspectives d'évolution en France' [Regulation and Deregulation of the Telecommunication Industry: From the American and British Experiences to a Possible Evolution in France], **38** *Revue Economique*, 1987, 475-520.

ENCAOUA, David and MOREAUX, Michel, 'L'analyse théorique des problemes de tarification et d'allocation des coûts dans les télécommunications' [The Theoretical Approach to Pricing and Cost Allocation for Telecommunication Services], **38** *Revue Economique*, 1987, 375-413.

FAULHABER, Gerald R., *Telecommunications in Turmoil: Technology and Public Policy*, Cambridge, Harper and Row, 1987, 186 p.

FISHER, Franklin M., 'The Financial Interest and Syndication Rules in Network Television: Regulatory Fantasy and Reality', in FISHER, Franklin M. (ed.), *Antitrust and Regulation: Essays in Memory of John J. McGowan*, Cambridge, MIT Press, 1985, 263-298.

FOURNIER, Gary M., 'Nonprice Competition and the Dissipation of Rents from Television Regulation', **51** *Southern Economic Journal*, 1985, 754-765.

FUHR, Joseph P., Jr., 'Maintaining Universal Telephone Service under Deregulation', **5** *Journal of Policy Analysis and Management*, 1986, 583-590.

GELLER, Henry, 'The Role of Future Regulation: Licensing, Spectrum Allocation, Content, Access, Common Carrier and Rates', in NOAM, Eli H. (ed.), *Video Media Competition: Regulation, Economics, and Technology*, New York, Columbia University Press, 1985, 283-310.

GLAISTER, Stephen, 'Regulation through Output Related Profits Tax', **35** *Journal of Industrial Economics*, 1987, 281-296.

HAHN, Robert W. and KROSZNER, Randall S., 'Lost in Space: U.S. International Satellite Communications Policy', **13(2)** *Regulation*, 1990, 57-66.

HAZLETT, Thomas W., 'Competition vs. Franchise Monopoly in Cable Television', **4(2)** *Contemporary Policy Issues*, 1986, 80-97.

HAZLETT, Thomas W., 'Wiring the Constitution for Cable', **12(1)** *Regulation*, 1988, 30-34.

HAZLETT, Thomas W., 'Should Telephone Companies Provide Cable TV?', **13(1)** *Regulation*, 1990, 72-80.

HAZLETT, Thomas W., 'Regulation and Competition in Cable Television: Reply', **7** *Yale Journal on Regulation*, 1990, 141-148.

HUGHES, Gordon and VINES, David (eds.), *Deregulation and the Future of*

Commercial Television, Glasgow, Aberdeen University Press, 1989, 139 p.

HUNTLEY, John A.K. and PITT, Douglas C., 'Judicial Policymaking: The Greeneing of US Telecommunications', **10** *International Review of Law and Economics*, 1990, 77-100.

KALVEN, Harry Jr., 'Broadcasting, Public Policy, and the First Amendment', **10** *Journal of Law and Economics*, 1967, 15-49.

KASERMAN, David L. and MAYO, John W., 'The Ghosts of Deregulated Telecommunications: An Essay by Exorcists', **6** *Journal of Policy Analysis and Management*, 1986, 84-92.

KNIEPS, Gunter, 'Is Technological Revolution a Sufficient Reason for Changing the System of Regulation? The Case of Telecommunications', **139** *Zeitschrift für die gesamte Staatswissenschaft*, 1983, 578-597.

LEVIN, Harvey J., 'Federal Control of Entry in the Broadcast Industry', **5** *Journal of Law and Economics*, 1962, 49-67.

MACAULEY, Molly K., 'Out of Space? Regulation and Technical Change in Communications Satellites', **76** *American Economic Review. Papers and Proceedings*, 1986, 280-284.

MELODY, William H., 'Efficiency and Social Policy in Telecommunication: Lessons from the U.S. Experience', **23** *Journal of Economic Issues*, 1989, 657-688.

MINASIAN, Jora R., 'The Political Economy of Broadcasting in the 1920's', **12** *Journal of Law and Economics*, 1969, 391-403.

NATIONAL ECONOMIC RESEARCH ASSOCIATES, *Telecommunications in a Competitive Environment: Proceedings of the Third Biennial Telecommunications Conference, Marriott's Camelback Inn, Scottsdale, Arizona, April 12-15, 1989*, White Plains, N.E.R.A., 1989, 233 p.

NOLL, Roger G., 'The Twisted Pair: Regulation and Competition in Telecommunications', **11(3/4)** *Regulation*, 1987, 15-22.

NOO, Roger G., 'State Regulatory Responses to Competition and Divestiture in the Telecommunications Industry', in GRIESON, Ronald E. (ed.), *Antitrust and Regulation*, Lexington, Lexington Books, 1986, 165-200.

OHLS, James C., 'Marginal Cost Pricing, Investment Theory and CATV', **13** *Journal of Law and Economics*, 1970, 439-460.

OHLS, James C., 'Marginal Cost Pricing, Investment Theory and CATV: A Reply', **14** *Journal of Law and Economics*, 1971, 517-519.

OLSEN, Ole Jess, 'Deregulation and Reorganisation: The Case of the Danish Telecommunications', **60** *Annals of Public and Co operative Economy*, 1989, 251-258.

OWEN, Bruce M. and GOTTLIEB, Paul D., 'The Rise and Fall and Rise of Cable Television Regulation', in WEISS, Leonard W. and KLASS, Michael W. (ed.), *Regulatory Reform: What Actually Happened*, Boston, Little Brown, 1986, 78-104.

PACEY, Patricia L., 'Cable Television in a Less Regulated Market', **34** *Journal of Industrial Economics*, 1985, 81-91.

PERA, Alberto, 'Deregulation and Privatisation in an Economy Wide Context',

0(12) *OECD Economic Studies*, 1989, 159-204.

PERRAKIS, Stylianos and SILVA Echenique, Julio, 'The Profitability and Risk of CATV Operations in Canada', **15** *Applied Economics*, 1983, 745-758.

PETERMAN, John L., 'The Structure of National Time Rates in the Television Broadcasting Industry', **8** *Journal of Law and Economics*, 1965, 77-131.

PETERMAN, John L., 'The Clorox Case and the Television Rate Structures', **11** *Journal of Law and Economics*, 1968, 321-422.

PICARD, Pierre, 'La tarification optimale des télécommunications: une présentation synthetique' [Optimal Pricing for Telecommunications: An Overview], **0(12)** *Annales d'économie et de statistique*, 1988, 27-62.

RICHTER, Wolfram F. and WEIMANN, Joachim, 'Ramsey Pricing the Telephone Services of the Deutsche Bundespost', **141** *Zeitschrift für die gesamte Staatswissenschaft*, 1985, 516-524.

SAMUELSON, Paul A., 'Public Goods and Subscription TV: Correction of the Record', **7** *Journal of Law and Economics*, 1964, 81-83.

SARDINAS, Joseph L., Jr., 'Regulation of International Data Communications and the Effect upon Multinational Corporations', in MOST, Kenneth S. (ed.), *Advances in International Accounting*, Volume 1, Greewich, JAI Press, 1987, 305-315.

SCHMANDT, Jurgen, WILLIAMS, Frederick and WILSON, Robert H. (eds.), *Telecommunications Policy and Economic Development: The New State Role*, New York, Greenwood Press, 1989, 299 p.

SHEDD, M.S., WILMAN, Elizabeth A. and BURCH, R. Douglas, 'An Economic Analysis of Canadian Content Regulations and a New Proposal', **16** *Canadian Public Policy*, 1990, 60-72.

SMILEY, Albert K., 'Regulation and Competition in Cable Television', **7** *Yale Journal on Regulation*, 1990, 121-139.

SNOW, Marcellus S., *Marketplace for Telecommunications: Regulation and Deregulation in Industrialized Democracies*, New York, Longman, 1986, 304 p.

SNOW, Marcellus S., 'The State as Stopgap: Social Economy and Sustainability of Monopoly in the Telecommunications Sector', **46** *Review of Social Economy*, 1988, 1-23.

SNOW, Marcellus S. and JUSSAWALLA, Meheroo, *Telecommunications Economics and International Regulatory Policy: An Annotated Bibliography*, New York, Greenwood, 1986, 216 p.

TESKE, Paul E., 'Rent-Seeking in the Deregulatory Environment: State Telecommunications', **68** *Public Choice*, 1991, 235-243.

TREBING, Harry M., 'Apologetics of Deregulation in Energy and Telecommuniciations: An Institutionalist Assesment', **20** *Journal of Economic Issues*, 1986, 613-632.

VIETOR, Richard H. K. and DAVIDSON, Dekkers L., 'Economics and Politics of Deregulation: The Issue of Telephone Access Charges', **5** *Journal of Policy Analysis and Management*, 1985, 3-22.

VON WEIZSACKER, C. Christian, 'Free Entry into Telecommunications?', **1(3)** *Information Economics and Policy*, 1984, 197-216.

WEISMAN, Dennis L., 'Default Capacity Tariffs: Smoothing the Transitional Regulatory Asymmetries in the Telecommunications Market', **5** *Yale Journal on Regulation*, 1988, 149-178.

WENDERS, John T., *The Economics of Telecommunications: Theory and Policy*, Cambridge, Harper and Row, 1987, 284 p.

ZUPAN, Mark A., 'Non-price Concessions and the Effect of Franchise Bidding Schemes on Cable Company Costs', **21** *Applied Economics*, 1989, 305-323.

5960 International Trade

DAVIDSON, Russell et al., 'On the Welfare Effects of Anti discrimination Regulations in the EC Car Market', **7** *International Journal of Industrial Organization*, 1989, 205-230.

DOUGAN, William R., 'Tariffs and the Economic Theory of Regulation', **6** *Research in Law and Economics*, 1984, 187-210.

FARRAN, Andrew, 'The Interplay of Law and Economics in International Trade Regulation', in SNAPE, R.H. (ed.), *Issues in World Trade Policy: GATT at the Crossroads. Papers presented at a conference of the Centre of Policy Studies, Monash University, Australia*, New York, St. Martin's Press, 1986, 193-217.

FREY, Bruno S., 'Regulations by Consensus: The Practice of International Investment Agreements: Comment', **144** *Journal of Institutional and Theoretical Economics*, 1988, 176-179.

GERBER, David J., 'The United States Sugar Quota Program: A Study in the Direct Congressional Control of Imports', **19** *Journal of Law and Economics*, 1976, 103-147.

GODEK, Paul E., 'Industry Structure and Redistribution through Trade Restrictions', **28** *Journal of Law and Economics*, 1985, 687-703.

KALT, Joseph P., 'Exhaustible Resource Price Policy, International Trade, and Intertemporal Welfare', **17** *Journal of Environmental Economics and Management*, 1989, 109-126.

KELLY, Kenneth, 'Can Imports Injure a Domestic Industry When They Decline?', **12** *Research in Law and Economics*, 1989, 119-129.

KNOLL, Michael S., 'Legal and Economic Framework for the Analysis of Injury by the U.S. International Trade Commission', **23(3)** *Journal of World Trade*, 1989, 95-107.

KRAUSS, Melvyn B., *The New Protectionism. The Welfare State and International Trade*, New York, New York University Press, 1978, 179 p.

NAVARRO, Peter, 'Creating and Destroying Comparative Advantage: The Role of Regulation in International Trade', **13** *Journal of Comparative Economics*, 1989, 205-226.

NISKANEN, William A., 'U.S. Trade Policy', **12(3)** *Regulation*, 1988, 34-42.

PHEGAN, Colin, 'The Interplay of Law and Economics in International Trade Regulation: Comment', in SNAPE, R.H. (ed.), *Issues in World Trade Policy:*

GATT at the Crossroads. Papers presented at a conference of the Centre of Policy Studies, Monash University, Australia, New York, St. Martin's Press, 1986, 218-221.

PINDYCK, Robert S. and ROTEMBERG, Julio J., 'Are Imports to Blame? Attribution of Injury under the 1974 Trade Act', **30** *Journal of Law and Economics*, 1987, 101-122.

ROUSSLANG, D.J., 'Import Injury in U.S. Trade Law: An Economic View', **8** *International Review of Law and Economics*, 1988, 117-122.

SCHANZE, Erich, 'Untemehmensrechtliche Koordination von Staat und Wirtschaft bei internationalen GroßProjekten in Entwicklungsländern' [Corporate Coordination of State and Economy Concerning Project Investment in Developing Countries], **6** *Jahrbuch fur neue Politische Ökonomie*, Tübingen, J.C.B. Mohr, 1986, 269-287.

SCHANZE, Erich, *Investitionsverträge im internationalen Wirtschaftsrecht* [Investment Contracts in International Economic Law], Frankfurt, Metzner, 1986, 305 p.

SOLOMON, Lewis D. and DICKER, Howard B., 'The Crash of 1987: A Legal and Public Policy Analysis', **57** *Fordham Law Review*, 1988, 191 ff.

SYKES, Alan O., 'Protectionism as a "Safeguard": A Positive Analysis of the GATT "Escape Clause" with Normative Speculations', **58** *University of Chicago Law Review*, 1991, 255-305.

VOUSDEN, Neil, *The Economics of Trade Protection*, Cambridge, Cambridge University Press, 1990, 305 p.

6000 TAX LAW
Gerrit De Geest and Ludwig Van den Hauwe

6000 Tax Law: General

BIZER, David S. and JUDD, Kenneth L., 'Taxation and Uncertainty', **79** *American Economic Review. Papers and Proceedings*, 1989, 331-336.

BUCOHETSKY, Sam, 'Choosing Tax Rates and Public Expenditure Levels Using Majority Rule', **46** *Journal of Public Economics*, 1991, 113-131.

CAANEN, Ch. and ESSERS, P.H.J., 'Rechtseconomie en belastingrecht' [Law-and-economics and Taxation Law], **39(10)** *Ars Aequi*, 1990, 677-681.

COLLARD, David (ed.), *Fiscal Policy: Essays in Honour of Cedric Sandford*, Aldershot, Gower, Avebury, 1989, 173 p.

COOPER, Graeme S., 'Income Tax Law and Contributive Justice: Some Thoughts on Defining and Expressing a Consistent Theory of Tax Justice and Its Li mitations', **3** *Australian Tax Forum*, 1986, 297-332.

DIAMOND, Stephen, 'The Death and Transfiguration of Benefit Taxation: Special Assessments in Nineteenth-Century America', **12** *Journal of Legal Studies*, 1983, 201-240.

GRAETZ, Michael J. and WILDE, Louis L., 'The Economics of Tax Compliance: Fact and Fantasy', **38** *National Tax Journal*, 1985, 355-363.

GRAETZ, Michael J., REINGANUM, Jennifer F. and WILDE, Louis L., 'The Tax Compliance Game: Toward and Interactive Theory of Law Enforcement', **2** *Journal of Law, Economics, & Organization*, 1986, 1-32.

HETTICH, Walter and WINER, Stanley L., 'Economic and Political Foundations of Tax Structure', **78** *American Economic Review*, 1988, 701-712.

INMAN, Robert P. and FITTS, Michael A., 'Political Institutions and Fiscal Policy: Evidence from the U.S. Historical Record', **6** *Journal of Law, Economics, & Organization*, 1990, S79-S132.

JACKMAN, Richard, 'The Economic Effects of Tax Based Incomes Policy', in COLANDER, David C. (ed.), *Incentive based incomes policies: Advances in TIP and MAP*, Cambridge, Mass., Harper and Row, 1986, 95-109.

KAY, J.A. and KING, M.A., *The British Tax System*, Oxford, Oxford University Press, 1986, 261 p.

KIESLING, Herbert J., 'Economic and Political Foundations of Tax Structure: Comment', **80** *American Economic Review*, 1990.

McCAFFERY, Edward J., 'The Holy Grail of Tax Simplification', *Wisconsin Law Review*, 1990, 1267-1322.

MUSGRAVE, Richard A. and MUSGRAVE, Peggy B., *Public Finance in Theory and Practice*, Tokyo, MacGraw-Hill, 1985, 824 p.

PEACOCK, Alan and FORTE, Francesco (eds.), *The Political Economy of Taxation*, Oxford, Blackwell, 1981, 211 p.

PECHMAN, Joseph A., *Federal Taw Policy*, Washington, Brookings Institution, 1987, 430 p.

PECHMAN, Joseph A., 'The Future of Income Tax', **80** *American Economic Review*, 1990, 1-20.

PECHMAN, Joseph A., *Tax Reform, the Rich and the Poor*, Washington, Brookings Institution, 1989, 211 p.

REINGANUM, Jennifer F. and WILDE, Louis L., 'Equilibrium Enforcement and Compliance in the Presence of Tax Practitioners', **7** *Journal of Law, Economics, & Organization*, 1991, 163-181.

ROIN, Julie, A., 'United they Stand, Divided they Fall: Public Choice Theory and the Tax Code', **74** *Cornell Law Review*, 1988, 62-134.

SHAVIRO, Daniel N., 'Beyond Public Choice and Public Interest: A Study of the Legislative Process as Illustrated by Tax Legislation in the 1980s', **139** *University of Pennsylvania Law Review*, 1990, 1-123.

TIEBOUT, Charles M., 'A Pure Theory of Local Government Expenditures', **64** *Journal of Political Economy*, 1956, 416-424.

TILLMAN, Georg, *Equity, Incentives, and Taxation*, Berlin, Springer, 1989, 132 p.

VANBERG, Viktor and BUCHANAN, James M., 'Organization Theory and Fiscal Economics: Society, State and Public Debt', **2** *Journal of Law, Economics, & Organization*, 1986, 215-227.

WALZ, W. Rainer, 'Rechtssicherheit und Risikozuweisung bei Steuerrechtsänderungen - Verbotene Rückwirkung, gebotene Übergangsregelung, richterliche Vertragsanpassung' [Legal Certainty and Risk Allocation for Changes in Tax Law - Illegal Retroaction, Transitional Rules, Judicial Adjustment of Contract], in FINSINGER, Jörg and SIMON, Jürgen, (eds.), *Recht und Risiko*, 1988, München, Florentz, 252-286.

WHITE, P.D., 'Realization, Recognition, Reconciliation, Rationality and the Structure of the Federal Income Tax System', **88** *Michigan Law Review*, 1990, 2034-2096.

ZELINSKY, Edward A., 'Efficieny and Income Taxes: The Rehabilitation of Tax Incentives', **64** *Texas Law Review*, 1986, 973-1037.

6010 Macro Aspects

ALEXANDER, J. Davidson, 'The Political Economy of Tax Based Incomes Policy: Wealth Effects of Post Keynesian TIP', **23** *Journal of Economic Issues*, 1989, 135-146.

BACKHAUS, Jürgen G., 'Taxation and Entrepreneurship: An Austrian Approach to Public Finance', **16(2)** *Journal of Economic Studies*, 1989, 5-22.

BANKMAN, Joseph and GRIFFITH, Thomas, 'Social Welfare and the Rate Structure: A New Look at Progressive Taxation', **75** *California Law Review*, 1987, 1905-1967.

BAUM, Donald N., 'Economic Effects of Including Services in the Sales Tax Base:

An Applied General Equilibrium Analysis', **19(2)** *Public Finance Quarterly*, 1991, 166-192.

BERNSTEIN, Jeffrey I., *Research and Development, Tax Incentives, and the Structure of Production and Financing*, Toronto, University of Toronto Press, 1986, 107 p.

BIORN, E., *Taxation, Technology and the User Cost of Capital*, Amsterdam, North-Holland, 1989, 325 p.

BOVENBERG, A. Lans, 'The Effects of Capital Income Taxation on International Competitiveness and Trade Flows', **79** *American Economic Review*, 1989, 10511064.

BROWNING, Edgar K., 'On the Marginal Welfare Cost of Taxation', **77** *American Economic Review*, 1987, 11-23.

BUCHHOLZ, Wolfgang, 'Tax Effect in General Equilibrium Models with Uncertainty: A Generalization', **45** *Journal of Public Economics*, 1991, 397-399.

CHARI, V.V. and KEHOE, Patrick J., 'International Coordination of Fiscal Policy in Limiting Economies', **98** *Journal of Political Economy*, 1990, 617-636.

DAVIDSON, Carl and MARTIN, Lawrence, 'Tax Incidence in a Simple General Equilibrium Model with Collusion and Entry', **45** *Journal of Public Economics*, 1991, 161-190.

FLOWERS, Marilyn R., 'Public Choice and the Flat Tax', **5** *Cato Journal*, 1985, 625-628.

FRIEDMAN, Milton, 'Interest Rates and the Demand for Money', **9** *Journal of Law and Economics*, 1966, 71-85.

GRBICH, Yuri, 'Towards a More Substantial Jurisprudence to Replace Legalism: a Welfare Economics Model of Decision-Making in Tax Cases', in CRANSTON, Ross and SCHICK, Anne (eds.), *Law and Economics*, Canberra, Australian National University, 1982, 192-205.

HOTELLING, H., 'The General Welfare in Relation to Problems of Taxation and Railway and Utility Rates', **6** *Econometrica*, 1938, 242-269.

KINGSTON, Geoffrey, 'Should Marginal Tax Rates Be Equalized through Time', *Quarterly Journal of Economics*, August 1991.

KOCH, Walter A.S., 'Negative Einkommensteuern und Konjunkturpolitik' [Negative Income Taxes and Stabilization Policy], **30** *Konjunkturpolitik*, 1984, 348-373.

PISSARIDES, Christopher A., 'Equilibrium Effects of Tax Based Incomes Policies', in COLANDER, David C. (ed.), *Incentive based incomes policies: Advances in TIP and MAP*, Cambridge, Mass., Harper and Row, 1986, 111-127.

REYNOLDS, Alan, 'Some International Comparisons of Supply-Side Tax Policy', **5** *Cato Journal*, 1985, 543-569.

SIEGFRIED, John J. and SMITH, Paul A., 'The Distributional Effects of a Sales Tax on Services', **44(1)** *National Tax Journal*, 1991, 41-54.

VEDDER, Richard, 'Tiebout Taxes, and Economic Growth', **10** *Cato Journal*, 1991, 91-108.

6020 Tax Evasion and the Underground Economy

ALLINGHAM, M.G. and SANDMO, A., 'Income Tax Evasion: A Theoretical `Analysis', **1** *Journal of Public Economics*, 1972, 323-338.

BENJAMINI, Yael and MAITAL, Shlomo, 'Optimal Tax Evasion and Optimal Tax Evasion Policy: Behavioral Aspects', in GAERTNER, Wulf and WENIG, Alois (eds.), *The Economics of the Shadow Economy: Proceedings of the International Conference on the Economics of the Shadow Economy Held at the University of Bielefeld, West Germany, October 10-14, 1983*, Berlin, Springer, 1985, 245-264.

BROWN, C. V., et al., 'Tax Evasion and Avoidance on Earned Income: Some Survey Evidence', **5(3)** *Fiscal Studies*, 1984, 1-22.

COWELL, Frank A., 'Public Policy and Tax Evasion: Some Problems', in GAERTNER, Wulf and WENIG, Alois (eds.), *The Economics of the Shadow Economy: Proceedings of the International Conference on the Economics of the Shadow Economy Held at the University of Bielefeld, West Germany, October 10-14, 1983*, Berlin, Springer, 1985, 273-84.

COWELL, Frank A., 'The Economic Analysis of Tax Evasion', in HEY, John D. and LAMBERT, Peter J. (eds.), *Surveys in the Econmics of Uncertainty*, Oxford, Blackwell, 1987, 173-203.

COWELL, Frank A., 'The Economic Analysis of Tax Evasion', **37** *Bulletin of Economic Research*, 1985, 163-193.

CRANE, Steven E. and NOURZAD, Farrokh, 'Time Value of Money and Income Tax Evasion under Risk averse Behavior: Theoretical Analysis and Empirical Evidence', **40** *Public Finance*, 1985, 481-494.

CRANE, Steven E. and NOURZAD, Farrokh, 'Federal Income Tax Evasion', in LINDHOLM, Richard W. (ed.), *Examination of Basic Weaknesses of Income as the Major Federal Tax Base*, New York, Greenwood, 1986, 140-162.

DUBIN, Jeffrey A., GRAETZ, Michael J. and WILDE, Louis L., 'Are We a Nation of Tax Cheaters? New Econometric Evidence on Tax Compliance', **77** *American Economic Review. Papers and Proceedings*, 1987, 240-245.

FEIGE, Edgar L., 'A Re-examination of the "Underground Economy' in the United States: A Comment', **33** *International Monetary Fund Staff Papers*, 1986, 768-781.

FEIGE, Edgar L. (ed.), *The Underground Economies: Tax Evasion and Information Distortion*, Cambridge, Cambridge University Press, 1989, 378 p.

FEINSTEIN, Jonathan S., 'An Econometric Analysis of Income Tax Evasion and its Detection', **22** *Rand Journal of Economics*, 1991, 14-35.

FELDMAN, J. and KAY, John A., 'Tax Avoidance', in BURROWS, Paul and VELJANOVSKI, Cento G. (eds.), *The Economic Appraoch to Law*, London, Butterworths, 1981, 320-333.

FLUET, Claude, 'Fraude fiscale et offre de travail au noir' [Tax Evasion and the Supply of Unofficial Labour], **63** *L'actualité économique*, 1987, 225-242.

GORDON, James P.F., 'Individual Morality and Reputation Costs as Deterrents to

Tax Evasion', **33** *European Economic Review*, 1989, 797-805.

GREENBERG, Joseph, 'Avoiding Tax Avoidance: A (Repeated) Game Theoretic Approach', **32(1)** *Journal of Economic Theory*, 1984, 1-13.

HANSSON, Ingemar, 'Tax Evasion and Government Policy', in GAERTNER, Wulf and WENIG, Alois (eds.), *The Economics of the Shadow Economy: Proceedings of the International Conference on the Economics of the Shadow Economy Held at the University of Bielefeld, West Germany, October 10-14, 1983*, Berlin, Springer, 1985, 285-300.

KESSELMAN, Jonathan R., 'Income Tax Evasion: An Intersectoral Analysis', **38** *Journal of Public Economics*, 1989, 137-182.

KLEPPER, Steven and NAGIN, Daniel, 'The Autonomy of Tax Evasion', **5** *Journal of Law, Economics, & Organization*, 1989, 1-24.

KOSKELA, Erkki, 'A Note on Progression, Penalty Schemes and Tax Evasion', **22** *Journal of Public Economics*, 1983, 127-133.

MARRELLI, M., 'The Economic Analysis of Tax Evasion: Empirical Aspects', in HEY, John D. and LAMBERT, Peter J. (eds.), *Surveys in the Econmics of Uncertainty*, Oxford, Blackwell, 1987, 204-228.

POMMEREHNE, Werner W., 'Steuerhinterziehung und Schwarzarbeit als Grenzen der Staatstatigkeit' [Tax Evasion and Underground Activities as Limits of Government's Growth], **119** *Schweizerische Zeitschrift fur Volkswirtschaft und - Statistik*, 1983, 261-284.

PYLE, David J., *Tax Evasion and the Black Economu*, New York, St. Martin's Press, 1989, 212 p.

RUSSELL, A.M. and RICKARD, J.A., 'A Model of Tax Evasion Incorporating Income Variation and Retroactive Penalities', **26** *Australian Economic Papers*, 1987, 254-264.

SAMUELSON, Paul A., 'The Pure Theory of Public Expenditure', **36** *Review of Economics and Statistics*, 1954, 387-389.

SKINNER, Jonathan and SLEMROD, Joel, 'An Economic Perspective on Tax Evasion', **38** *National Tax Journal*, 1985, 345-353.

SMITH, Rodney T., 'The Legal and Illegal Markets for Taxed Goods: Pure Theory and Application to State Governement Taxation of Distilled Spirits', **19** *Journal of Law and Economics*, 1976, 393-429.

WECK-HANNEMANN, Hannelore and POMMEREHNE, Werner W., 'Einkommensteuerhinterziehung in der Schweiz: Eine empirische Analyse' [Income Tax Evasion in Switzerland: An Empirical Analysis], **125** *Schweizerische Zeitschrift fur Volkswirtschaft und Statistik*, 1989, 515-556.

YANIV, Gideon, 'Fraudulent Collection of Unemployment Benefits: A Theoretical Analysis with Reference to Income Tax Evasion', **30** *Journal of Public Economics*, 1986, 369-383.

AUERBACH, Alan J. and HINES, James R. Jr., 'Investment Tax Incentives and Frequent Tax Reforms', **78** *American Economic Review. Papers and Proceedings*, 1988, 211-216.

BARNETT, Richard, BARROW, Michael and SMITH, Peter, 'Representation without Taxation: An Empirical Assessment of the Validity of the Accountability Argument Underlying the Reform of Local Government Finance in England, **12(3)** *Fiscal Studies*, 1991, -46.

BOSSONS, John, 'The Value of a Comprehensive Tax Base as a Tax Reform Goal', **13** *Journal of Law and Economics*, 1970, 327-363.

BROWNING, Edgar K. and BROWNING, Jacquelene M., 'Why Not a True Flat Rate Tax?', **5** *Cato Journal*, 1985, 629-650.

BUCHANAN, James M., 'Tax Reform in Constitutional Perspective', in SKOGH, Göran (ed.), *Law and Economics. Report from a Symposium in Lund, Sweden, 24-26 August 1977*, Lund, Juridiska Föreningen, 1978, 103-120.

CUTLER, David M., 'Tax Reform and the Stock Market: An Asset Price Approach', **78** *American Economic Review*, 1988, 1107-1117.

DAVIS, Karen, 'National Health Insurance: A Proposal', **79** *American Economic Review. Papers and Proceedings*, 1989, 349-352.

DYE, Thomas R., 'Impact of Federal Tax Reform on State-Local Finances', **5** *Cato Journal*, 1985, 597 ff.

EDEN, Lorraine, 'Free Trade, Tax Reform, and Transfer Pricing', **39(1)** *Canadian Tax Journal*, 1991, 90-112.

FANE, George, 'Piecemeal Tax Reforms and the Compensated Radial Elasticities of Tax Bases', **45** *Journal of Public Economics*, 1991, 263-270.

GEPHARDT, Richard, 'The Economics and Politics of Tax Reform', **5** *Cato Journal*, 1985, 455-464.

GERGEN, Mark P., 'The Case for a Charitable Contributions Deduction', **74** *Virginia Law Review*, 1988, 1393-1450.

GORDON, James P.F., 'Tax Reform and Uniformity: Explaining the Hatta Result', **45(2)** *Journal of Public Economics*, 1991, 161-190.

GRAETZ, Michael J., 'Assessing the Distributional Effects of Income Tax Revision: Some Lessons from Incidence Analysis', **4** *Journal of Legal Studies*, 1975, 351-368.

HAMILTON, Bob and KUO, Chun-Yan, 'Reforming the Canadian Sales Tax System: A Regional General Equilibrium Analysis', **39(1)** *Canadian tax Journal*, 1991, 113 ff.

HANSEN, Susan B., 'Tax Reform: Sound Economics or Power Politics? Comment on Dye', **5** *Cato Journal*, 1985, 609-612.

LABOVITZ, John R., 'The Impact of the Private Foundation Provisions of the Tax Reform Act of 1969: Early Empirical Measurements', **3** *Journal of Legal Studies*, 1974, 63-105.

McCOMBS, J.B., 'Refining the Itemized Deduction for Home Property Tax Payments', **44** *Vanderbilt Law Review*, 1991, 317-338.

MINTZ, Jack and WHALLEY, John (eds.), *The Economic Impacts of Tax Reform*, Toronto, Canadian Tax Foundation, 1989, 463 p.

PETERSON, Pamela P., 'Lingering Questions About Tax Reform: Comment on Browning and Browning', **5** *Cato Journal*, 1985, 651-656.

ROGERS, Carol Ann, 'A Simple Model of Endogenous Tax Reform', **46** *Journal of Public Economics*, 1991, 91-111.

SHUGHART, William F., II, 'Durable Tax Reform', **7** *Cato Journal*, 1987, 273-281.

STEPHAN, Paul B. III, 'Disaggregation and Subchapter C: Rethinking Corporate Tax Reform', **76** *Virginia Law Review*, 1990, 655-711.

VEDDER, Richard, 'Federal Tax Reform: Lessons from the States', **5** *Cato Journal*, 1985, 571-590.

WIBAUT, Serge, *Tax Reform in Disequilibrium Economies*, Cambridge, Cambridge University Press, 1989, 113 p.

ZELENAK, Lawrence, 'When Good Preferences Go Bad: A Critical Analysis of the Anti-Tax Shelter Provisions of the Tax Reform Act of 1986', **67** *Texas Law Review*, 1989, 499 ff.

6040 Policy Aspects: General

ALM, James, 'Uncertain Tax Policies, Individual Behavior, and Welfare', **78** *American Economic Review*, 1988, 237-245.

BITTKER, Boris I., 'Income Tax Deductions, Credits, and Subsidies for Personal Expenditures', **16** *Journal of Law and Economics*, 1973, 193-213.

BOHANON, Cecil E. and VAN COTT, T. Norman, 'Product Quality and Taxation: A Reconciliation', **19** *Public Finance Quarterly*, 1991, 233-237.

BROWN, John Prather and HOLAHAN, William L., 'Taxes and Legal Rules for the Control of Externalities When There Are Strategic Responses', **9** *Journal of Legal Studies*, 1980, 165-178.

CANZONERI, Matthew B. and ROGERS, Carol Ann, 'Is the European Community an Optimal Currency Area? Optimal Taxation Versus the Cost of Multiple Currencies', **80** *American Economic Review*, 1990, 419-433.

CHIRINKO, Robert S., 'A Further Comment on "Would Tax Shifting Undermine the Tax Based Incomes Policy?"', **15** *Journal of Economic Issues*, 1981, 177-181.

DEVEREUX, Michael and FREEMAN, Harold, 'A General Neutral Profits Tax', **12(3)** *Fiscal Studies*, 1991, 2 ff.

DOWNS, Thomas W. and TEHRANIAN, Hassan, 'Predicting Stock Price Responses to Tax Policy Changes', **78** *American Economic Review*, 1988, 1118-1130.

FAZZARI, Steven, HUBBARD, R. Glenn and PETERSEN, Bruce, 'Investment, Financing Decisions, and Tax Policy', **78** *American Economic Review. Papers and Proceedings*, 1988, 200-205.

FELDSTEIN, Martin S., 'Tax Policy for the 1990s: Personal Saving, Business Investment, and Corporate Debt', **79** *American Economic Review. Papers and Proceedings*, 1989, 108-112.

HALL, Mark A. and COLUMBO, John D., 'The Caritable Status of Nonprofit

Hospitals: Toward a Donative Theory of Tax Exemption', **66** *Washington Law Review*, 1991, 307-411.

HENDERSHOTT, Patric H., 'The Long-Run Impact on Federal Tax Revenues and Capital Allocation of a Cut in the Capital Gains Tax Rate', **19(1)** *Public Finance Quarterly*, 1991, 3-21.

HOLLAND, D.M., 'An Evaluation of Tax Incentives for on-the-Job Training of the Disadvantaged', **2** *Bell Journal of Economics*, 1971, 293-327.

JOHNSON, Calvin H., 'Why Have Anti-Tax Legislation? A Response to Professor Zelenak', **67** *Texas Law Review*, 1989, -625.

JOHNSON, Manuel H., 'President Reagan's Modified Flat Tax: Analysis and Comparison', **5** *Cato Journal*, 1985, 499-520.

KAY, John, and KEEN, Michael, 'Product Quality Under Specific and Ad Valorem Taxation', **19** *Public Finance Quarterly*, 1991, 238-247.

LEE, Dwight R. (ed.), *Taxation and the Deficit Economy: Fiscal Policy and Capital Formation in the United States*, San Francisco, Pacific Research Institute for Public Policy, 1986, 554 p.

LINDSEY, Lawrence, *The Growth Experiment: How the New Tax Policy is Transforming the U.S. Economy*, New York, Basic Books, 1990, 260 p.

MANSFIELD, Edwin, 'The R&D Tax Credit and Other Technology Policy Issues', **76** *American Economic Review. Papers and Proceedings*, 1986, 191-197.

MARTINELLO, F. and WEST, E.G., 'Education Budget Reductions via Tax Credits: Some Further Considerations', **19** *Public Finance Quarterly*, 1991, 355-368.

McCALEB, Thomas S., 'Public Choice Perspectives on the Flat Tax Follies', **5** *Cato Journal*, 1985, 613-624.

McCUBBINS, Mathew D., 'Note: Budget Policy-making and the Appearance of Power', **6** *Journal of Law, Economics, & Organization*, 1990, S133-S153.

MOOKHERJEE, Dilip and PNG, Yvan P.L., 'Enforcement Costs and the Optimal Progressivity of Income Taxes', **6** *Journal of Law, Economics, & Organization*, 1990, 411-431.

PACI, Pierella, 'Tax Based Incomes Policies: Will They Work? Have They Worked?', **9(2)** *Fiscal Studies*, 1988, 81-94.

PETERSON, Wallace C., *Transfer Spending, Taxes, and the American Welfare State*, Dordrecht, Kluwer Academic Publishers, 1991, 192 p.

ROGERSON, William P., 'Comment on "Political Institutions and Fiscal Policy: Evidence from the U.S. Historical Record', **6** *Journal of Law, Economics, & Organization*, 1990, S155-S166.

RUSSELL, R. Robert, 'Tax Based Incomes Policies: Some Skeptical Remarks', **in** COLANDER, David C. (ed.), *Incentive based incomes policies: Advances in TIP and MAP*, Cambridge, Mass., Harper and Row, 1986, 159-175.

SAFFER, Henry and GROSSMAN, Michael, 'Beer Taxes, the Legal Drinking Age, and Youth Motor Vehicle Fatalities', **16** *Journal of Legal Studies*, 1987, 351-374.

SALTER, Sarah W., 'Value Added: Economic Concepts in Tax Policy Analysis', in CRANSTON, Ross and SCHICK, Anne (eds.), *Law and Economics*, Canberra,

Australian National University, 1982, 175-189.

SCHMALBECK, Richard, 'Income Averaging After Twenty Years: A Failed Experiment in Horizontal Equity', *Duke Law Journal*, 1984, 509-580.

SCHMALBECK, Richard L. and MYERS, Gary, 'A Policy Analysis of Fee-Shifting Rules under the Internal Revenue Code', *Duke Law Journal*, 1986, 970-1002.

SCHOLES, Myron S. and WOLFSON, Mark A., 'The Effects of Changes in Tax Laws on Corporate Reorganization Activity', **63** *Journal of Business*, Part 2, 1990, S141-164.

STEIN, Herbert, 'Pre-Revolutionary Fiscal Policy: The Regime of Herbert Hoover', **9** *Journal of Law and Economics*, 1966, 189-223.

STEUERLE, C. Eugene, *Who Should Pay for Collecting Taxes? Financing the IRS*, Washington, American Enterprise Institute for Public Policy Research, 1986, 75 p.

TREBILCOCK, Michael J. and ENGELHART, Kenneth, 'A Tax Credit for Public Interest Groups', **3** *Canadian Taxation: A Journal of Tax Policy*, 1981, 29-33.

WILSON, John Douglas, 'On the Optimal Tax Base for Commodity Taxation', **79** *American Economic Review*, 1989, 1196-1206.

YOHE, Gary W., 'Improving Tax based Incomes Policies: The Lessons of the Environmental Literature', **13** *Public Finance Quarterly*, 1985, 183-205.

YORIO, Edward, 'Federal Income Tax Rulemaking: An Economic Approach, **51** *Fordham Law Review*, 1982, 1 ff.

YORIO, Edward, 'The President's Tax Proposals: A Major Step in the Right Direction', **53** *Fordham Law Review*, 1985, 1255 ff.

ZOLT, Eric M., 'Deterrence via Taxation: A Critical Analysis of Tax Penalty Provisions', **37** *UCLA Law Review*, 1989, 343 ff.

6050 Income versus Consumption Tax

AARON, Henry J., GALPER, Harveu and PECHMAN, Joseph A. (eds.), *Uneasy Compromise: Problems of a Hybrid Income-Consumption Tax*, Washington, Brookings Institution, 1988, 441 p.

LINDHOLM, Richard W. (ed.), *Examination of Basic Weaknesses of Income as the Major Federal Tax Base*, New York, Greenwood, 1986.

PARSONS, Ross W., 'Income Taxation An Institution in Decay?', **3** *Australian Tax Forum*, 1986, 233-266.

WILDASIN, David, 'R.M. Haig: Pioneer Advocate of Expenditure Taxation?', **28** *Journal of Economic Literature*, 1990, 649-654.

6060 Other

ABRAMS, Howard E., 'Rethinking Tax Trasitions: A Reply to Dr. Shachar', **98** *Harvard Law Review*, 1985, 1809-1889.

ANDREONI, James, 'The Desirability of a Permanent Tax Amnesty', **45** *Journal of Public Economics*, 1991, 161-190.

ARETZ, Adward, 'Taxation and Incorporation: An Economic Analysis of Post-1992 Business Incorporations', in WEIGEL, Wolfgang (ed.), *Economic Analysis of Law - A Collection of Applications*, Vienna, Österreichischer Wirtschaftsverlag, 1991, 122-132.

BATINA, Raymond G., 'Equity and the Time Consistent Taxation of Income', **93(3)** *Scandinavian Journal of Economics*, 1991, 407-419.

BELL, Edward B., BODENHORN, Diran and TAUB, Allan J., 'Taxes and Compensation for Lost Earnings', **12** *Journal of Legal Studies*, 1983, 181-194.

BELL, Edward B., BODENHORN, Diran and TAUB, Allan J., 'Taxes and Compensation for Lost Earnings: Reply', **14** *Journal of Legal Studies*, 1985, 457-458.

BENSON, Bruce L., 'Interstate Tax Competition, Incentives to Collude, and Federal Influences', **10(1)***Cato Journal*, 1991, 75-90.

BRACEWELL-MILNES, Barry, *The Wealth of Giving: Every One in his Inheritance*, London, Institute of Economic Affairs, 1989, 112 p.

BRUCE, Christopher J., 'An Efficient Technique for Determining the Compensation of Lost Earnings', **13** *Journal of Legal Studies*, 1984, 375-378.

BURKE, John F. Jr. and ROSEN, Harvey S., 'Taxes and Compensation for Lost Earnings: A Comment', **12** *Journal of Legal Studies*, 1983, 195-200.

BURNS, Arthur Edward, 'The Tax Court and Profit Renegotiation', **13** *Journal of Law and Economics*, 1970, 307-326.

CHEN, Charng Yi, 'Risk-Preferences and Tax-Induced Dividend Clienteles: Evidence from the Insurance Industry', **57** *Journal of Risk & Insurance*, 1990, 199-219.

COATES, Dennis, 'Endogenous Capital Utilization and Taxation of Corporate Capital', **44** *National Tax Journal*, 1991, 79-92.

CREEDY, J., 'Taxation and Compensation to Dependents of Accident Victims', **8** *International Review of Law and Economics*, 1988, 85-95.

CROSS, Mark L., DAVIDSON, Wallace N. III and THORNTON, John H., 'Taxes, Stock Returns ad Captive Insurance Subsidiaries', **55** *Journal of Risk & Insurance*, 1988, 331-338.

DYE, Richard F. and McGUIRE, Therese J., 'Growth and Variability of State Individual Income and General Sales Taxes', **44(1)** *National Tax Journal*, 1991, 55-66.

EATON, Jonathan, 'Foreign-Owned Land', **78** *American Economic Review*, 1988, 76-88.8

EVANS, Thomas L., 'The Taxation of Multi-Period Projects: An Analysis of Competing Models', **69(5)** *Texas Law Journal*, 1991, 1109 ff.

FELLOWS, Mary Louise, 'A Comprehensive Attack on Tax Deferral', **88** *Michigan Law Review*, 1990, 722-811.

FREY, Donald E., 'Optimal-Sized Tuition Tax Credits Reconsidered: Comment',

19(3) *Public Finance Quarterly*, 1991, 347-354.

GILLETTE, Clayton P. and HOPKINS, Thomas D., 'Federal User Fees: A Legal and Economic Analysis', **67** *Boston University Law Review*, 1987, 795-874.

GORDON, Roger H. and WILSON, John Douglas, 'Measuring the Efficiency Cost of Taxing Risky Capital Income', **79** *American Economic Review*, 1989, 427-439.

GRAETZ, Michael J., 'Retroactivity Revisited', **98** *Harvard Law Review*, 1985, 1820-1841.

GRAVELLE, Jane G. and KOTLIKOFF, Laurence J., 'The Incidence and Efficiency Costs of Corporate Taxation When Corporate and Noncorporate Firms Produce the Same Good', **97** *Journal of Political Economy*, 1989, 749-780.

HANSMANN, Henry B., 'Condominium and Cooperative Housing: Transactional Efficiency, Tax Subsidies, and Tenure Choice', **20** *Journal of Legal Studies*, 1991, 25-71.

HANSMANN, Henry B., 'Unfair Competition and the Unrelated Business Income Tax', **75** *Virginia Law Review*, 1989, 605-635.

HENDERSHOTT, Patric H., TODER, H. and WON YUNHI, 'Effects of Capital Gains Taxes on Revenue and Economic Efficiency', **44(1)** *National Tax Journal*, 1991, 21-40.

HULTEN, Charles R. and SCHWAB, Robert M., 'A Haig-Simons-Tiebout Comprehensive Income Tax', **44(1)** *National Tax Journal*, 1991, 67-78.

INTERNATIONAL FISCAL ASSOCIATION (ed.), *Administrative and Compliance Costs of Taxation*, Deventer, Kluwer Law and Taxation, 1989, 650 p.

ISACHSEN, Arne Jon and STRØM, Steinar, *Skattefritt. Svart Sektor i Vekst* [Taxfree. The Growth of the Black Sector], Oslo, Universitetsforlaget, 1981.

JONES, A.M. and POSNETT, J.W., 'The Impact of Tax Deductibility on Charitable Giving by Covenant in the U.K.', **101** *Economic Journal*, 1991, 1117-1129.

KANDA, Hideki and LEVMORE, Saul, 'Taxes, Agency Costs, and the Price of Incorporation', **77** *Virginia Law Review*, 1991, 211-256.

KLEIN, William A., 'Timing in Personal Taxation', **6** *Journal of Legal Studies*, 1977, 461-481.

KLEPPER, Steven, MAZUR, Mark and NAGIN, Daniel, 'Expert Intermediaries and Legal Compliance: The Case of Tax Preparers', **34** *Journal of Law and Economics*, 1991, 205-229.

KORNHAUSER, Marjorie E., 'The Rhetoric of the Anti-Progressice Income Tax Movement: A Typical Male Reaction', **86** *Michigan Law Review*, 1987, 465-523.

MADDOCK, Rodney, 'Comment', in CRANSTON, Ross and SCHICK, Anne (eds.), *Law and Economics*, Canberra, Australian National University, 1982, 190-191.

MADDOCK, Rodney, 'Comment', in CRANSTON, Ross and SCHICK, Anne (eds.), *Law and Economics*, Canberra, Australian National University, 1982, 206-207.

MADEO, Silvia A., SCHEPANSKI, Albert and UECKER, Wilfred C., 'Modeling Judgments of Taxpayer Compliance', **62** *Accounting Review*, 1987, 323-342.

MALIK, Arun S., 'The Economics of Tax Amnesties', **46** *Journal of Public Economics*, 1991, 29-49.

MIESZKOWSKI, Peter and ZODROW, George R., 'Taxation and the Tiebout Model: The Differential Effects of Head Taxes, Taxes in Land Rents, and Property Taxes', **27** *Journal of Economic Literature*, 1989, 1098-1146.

NADEAN, Serge and STRAUSS, Robert P., 'Tax Policies and the Real and Finacial Decisions of the Firm: The Effects of the Tax Reform Act of 1986', **19** *Public Finance Quarterly*, 1991, 251-292.

NORMAN, Neville, 'The Economics of Tax Ploision and Corporate Tax Integration', **2** *Australian Tax Forum*, 1985, 71-77.

PASTOR, Santos, 'Comment' [on Aretz, Taxation and Incorporation], in WEIGEL, Wolfgang (ed.), *Economic Analysis of Law - A Collection of Applications*, Vienna, Österreichischer Wirtschaftsverlag, 1991, 133-134.

PAULY, Mark V., 'Taxation, Health Insurance, and Market Failure in the Medical Economy', **24** *Journal of Economic Literature*, 1986, 629-675.

PITT, Mark M. and SLEMROD, Joel, 'The Compliance Cost of Itemizing Deductions: Evidence from Individual Tax Returns', **79** *American Economic Review*, 1989, 1224-1232.

POGUE, Thomas F. and SGONTZ, Larry G., 'Taxing to Control Social Costs: The Case of Alcohol', **79** *American Economic Review*, 1989, 235-243.

POTERBA, James, 'Lifetime Incidence and the Distributional Burden of Excise Taxes', **79** *American Economic Review. Papers and Proceedings*, 1989, 325-330.

RAMSEYER, J. Mark and NAKAZATO, Minoru, 'Tax Transitions and the Protection Racket: A Reply to Professors Graetz and Kaplow', **75** *Virginia Law Review*, 1989, 1155-1175.

ROSS, Thomas W., 'Store Wars: The Chain Tax Movement', **29** *Journal of Law and Economics*, 1986, 125-137.

SALINAS, Javier, *Economía política del federalismo fiscal español* [The Political Economy of Spanish Fiscal Federalism], Madrid, Instituto de Estudios Fiscales, 1990.

SHACHAR, Avishai, 'The Importance of Considering Liabilities in Tax Transitions', **98** *Harvard Law Review*, 1985, 1842-1868.

SHAVIRO, Daniel N., 'Selective Limitations on Tax Benefits', **56** *University of Chicago Law Review*, 1989, 1189-1260.

SPINNEWYN, F., 'Inkomensvorming en deregulering van de arbeidsmarkt: 4. Sociale Zekerheid' [Income Formation and Deregulation of the Labour Market: Social Security], in *18de Vlaams Wetenschappelijk Economisch Congres, Brussel 8 en 9 mei 1987, Sociaal-economische Deregulering*, Brussel, V.E.H.U.B., 1987, 305-320.

SURREY, Stanley S., 'The United States Taxation of Foreign Income', **1** *Journal of Law and Economics*, 1958, 72-96.

WEBB, V.C., 'The Taxation Rulings System - A Helpful Child or a Potential Bully?', **7(2)** *Australian Tax Forum*, 1990, 217-252.

WILSON, John Douglas, 'Optimal Public Good Provision with Limited Lump-Sum Taxation', **81** *American Economic Reviuew*, 1991, 153-166.

WOOD, John C., 'Alfred Marshall and the Tariff-Reform Campaign of 1903', **23**

Journal of Law and Economics, 1980, 481-495.

6100 SOCIAL SECURITY (a selection)
Gerrit De Geest

AARON, Henry J. (ed.), *Social Security and the Budget: Proceedings of the First Conference of the National Academy of Social Insurance*, Lanham, University Press of America, 1990, 151 p.

AARON, Henry J., BOSWORTH, Barry P. and BURTLESS, Gary T., *Can America Afford to Grow Old? Paying for Social Security*, Washington, Brookings Institution, 1989, 144 p.

ANDERSON, Martin, *Welfare. The Political Economy of Welfare Reform in the United States*, Stanford, Hoover Press, 1978, 251 p.

ARROW, Kenneth J., 'Uncertainty and the Welfare Economics of Medical Care', **53** *American Economic Review*, 1963, 941-973.

ATKINSON, Anthony B., *Poverty and Social Security*, New York, Simon and Schuster, 1989, 379 p.

ATKINSON, Anthony B. and MICKLEWRIGHT, John, *Unemployment Benefits and Unemployment Duration: A Study of Men in the United Kingdom in the 1970s*, London, London School of Economics and Political Science, 1985, 282 p.

BALASSA, Bela, 'The Economic Consequences of Social Policies in the Industrial Countries', **120** *Weltwirtschaftliches Archiv*, 1984, 213-227.

BALASSA, Bela, 'The Economic Consequences of Social Policies in the Industrial Countries', in BALASSA, Bela, *Change and Challenge in the World Economy*, New York, St. Martin's Press, 1985, 44-59.

BALLARD, Charles L., 'The Marginal Efficiency Cost of Redistribution', **78** *American Economic Review*, 1988, 1019-1033.

BEENSTOCK, Michael and BRASSE, Valerie, *Insurance for Unemployment*, London, Allen and Unwin, 1986, 106 p.

BEENSTOCK, Michael and BRASSE, Valerie, *Insurance for Unemployment*, London, Allen & Unwin, 1986, 107 p.

BERKOWITZ, Edward D. (ed.), *Social Security after Fifty: Successes and Failures*, New York, Greenwood Press, 1987, 168 p.

BERNHEIM, B. Douglas and LEVIN, Lawrence, 'Social Security and Personal Saving: An Analysis of Expectations', **79** *American Economic Review. Papers and Proceedings*, 1989, 97-102.

BERNSTEIN, Merton C. and BERNSTEIN, Joan Brodshaug, *Social Security: The System That Works*, New York, Basic Books, 1988, 321 p.

BLACK, Dan A., 'The Social Security System, the Provision of Human Capital, and the Structure of Compensation', **5** *Journal of Labor Economics*, 1987, 242-254.

BLACKORBY, Charles and DONALDSON, David, 'Cash Versus Kind, Self-Selection, and Efficient Transfers', **78** *American Economic Review*, 1988, 691-700.

BODIE, Zvi, 'Pensions as Retirement Income Insurance', **28** *Journal of Economic Literature*, 1990, 28-49.

BODIE, Zvi, SHOVEN, John B. and WISE, David A. (eds.), *Issues in Pension*

Economics, Chicago, University of Chicago Press, 1987, 376 p.

BODKIN, Ronald G. (ed.), *Unemployment Insurance. Global Evidence of its Effects on Unemployment*, s.l., Fraser Institute, 1978, 388 p.

BORJAS, George J., 'Discrimination in HEW: Is the Doctor Sick or Are the Patients Healthy ?', **21** *Journal of Law and Economics*, 1978, 97-110.

BOWLES, Roger A. and JONES, Philip, 'Medical Indemnity Insurance in the UK: a Public Choice Approach', **15** *Geneva Papers on Risk and Insurance*, 1990, 27-40.

BROWN, Eleanor and KAUFOLD, Howard, 'Human Capital Accumulation and the Optimal Level of Unemployment Insurance Provision', **6** *Journal of Labor Economics*, 1988, 493-514.

BROWNING, Edgar K., 'Social Insurance and Intergenerational Transfers', **16** *Journal of Law and Economics*, 1973, 215-237.

BROWNING, Edgar K. and JOHNSON, William R., 'The Cost of Reducing Economic Inequality', **6** *Cato Journal*, 1986, 85-109.

BUCHANAN, James M., *The Inconsistencies of the National Health Service*, London, Institute of Economic Affairs, Occasional Paper No. 7, 1964.

BURGESS, Paul L. and KINGSTON, Jerry L., *An Incentives Approach to Improving the Unemployment Compensation System*, Kalamazoo, Upjohn Institute for Employment Research, 1987, 273 p.

BUTLER, Richard J. and WORRALL, John D., 'The Costs of Workers' Compensation Insurance: Private versus Public', **29** *Journal of Law and Economics*, 1986, 329-356.

CAMPBELL, Colin D., 'Social Insurance in the United States: A Program in Search of an Explanation', **12** *Journal of Law and Economics*, 1969, 249-265.

CASSEN, Robert, *Does Aid Work ? Report to an Intergovernemental Task Force*, Oxford, Clarendon, 1986, 381 p.

CASTLES, Francis G., *Australian Public Policy and Economic Vulnerability: A Comparative and Historical Perspective*, Winchester, Allen and Unwin, 1988, 184 p.

CLARK, William, 'Production Costs and Output Qualities in Public and Private Employment Agencies', **31** *Journal of Law and Economics*, 1988, 379-393.

CONE, Kenneth R. and DRANOVE, David, 'Why Did States Enact Hospital Rate-setting Laws ?', **29** *Journal of Law and Economics*, 1986, 287-302.

CULYER, A.J., WISEMAN, J. and WALKER, A., *An Annotated Bibliography of Health Economics*, London, Martin Robertson, 1977.

DARITY, William A. Jr and MYERS, Samuel L., Jr., 'Do Transfer Payments Keep the Poor in Poverty?', **77** *American Economic Review. Papers and Proceedings*, 1987, 216-222.

DILNOT, Andrew, *The Economics of Social Security*, Oxford, Oxford University Press, 1989, 287 p.

DURMAN, Eugene C., 'The Impact of the Elimination of Residency Laws on Public Assistance Rolls', **4** *Journal of Legal Studies*, 1975, 199-218.

FELDSTEIN, Martin S., 'Should Social Security Benefits Be Means Tested?', **95**

Journal of Political Economy, 1987, 468-484.

FENN, Paul, 'The Law and Economics of the Misconduct Rule of Unemployment Insurance', in BURROWS, Paul and VELJANOVSKI, Cento G. (eds.), *The Economic Appraoch to Law*, London, Butterworths, 1981, 307-319.

FRANK, Richard G. and LAVE, Judith R., 'A Comparison of Hospital Responses to Reimbursement Policies for Medicaid Psychiatric Patients', **20** *Rand Journal of Economics*, 1989, 588-600.

FRANKFORD, David M., 'Creating and Dividing the Fruits of Collective Economic Activity: Referrals among Health Care Providers', **89** *Columbia Law Review*, 1989, 1861 ff.

FUCHS, Victor R., 'From Bismarck to Woodcock: The "Irrational" Pursuit of National Health Insurance', **19** *Journal of Law and Economics*, 1976, 347-359.

GAERTNER, W. and PATTANAIK, P.K., *Distributive Justice and Inequality: A Selection of Papers Given at a Conference, Berlin, May 1986*, New York, Springer, 1988, 171 p.

GRAMLICH, Edward M., 'Economist's View of the Welfare System', **79** *American Economic Review. Papers and Proceedings*, 1989, 191-196.

GUNDERSON, Morley and PESANDO, James, 'The Case for Allowing Mandatory Retirement', **14** *Canadian Public Policy*, 1988, 32-39.

GUSTAFSSON, B.A. and KLEVMARKEN, N. Anders (eds.), *The Political Economy of Social Security*, Amsterdam, North-Holland, 1989, 240 p.

GUSTMAN, Alan L. and STEINMIER, Thomas L., 'The Effects of Pensions and Retirement Policies on Retirement in Higher Education', **81** *American Economic Review. Papers and Proceedings*, 1991, 111-115.

HANSSON, Ingemar and STUART, Charles, 'Social Security as Trade Among Living Generations', **79** *American Economic Review*, 1989, 1182-1195.

HART, P.E. (ed.), *Unemployment and Labour Markets Policies*, Aldershot, Gower, 1986, 198 p.

HOCHMAN, Harold M. and PETERSON, George E. (eds.), *Redistribution through Public Choice*, New York, Columbia Univ. Press, 1974, 341 p.

HOLEN, Arlene S. and HORWITZ, Stanley A., 'The Effect of Unemployment Insurance and Eligibility Enforcement on Unemployment', **17** *Journal of Law and Economics*, 1974, 403-431.

HONIG, Marjorie and REIMERS, Cordelia, 'Is It Worth Eliminating the Retirement Test?', **79** *American Economic Review. Papers and Proceedings*, 1989, 103-107.

HOWITT, Peter and SINN, Hans-Werner, 'Gradual Reforms of Capital Income Taxation', **79** *American Economic Review*, 1989, 106-124.

HURD, Michael D., 'Research on the Elderly: Economic Status, Retirement, and Consumption and Saving', **28** *Journal of Economic Literature*, 1990, 565-637.

IPPOLITO, Richard A., 'The Economic Function of Underfunded Pension Plans', **28** *Journal of Law and Economics*, 1985, 611-651.

IPPOLITO, Richard A., 'Pension Security: Has ERISA Had Any Effect?', **11(2)** *Regulation*, 1987, 15-22.

IPPOLITO, Richard A., 'A Study of the Regulatory Effect of the Employee

Retirement Income Security Act', **31** *Journal of Law and Economics*, 1988, 85-125.

IPPOLITO, Richard A., *The Economics of Pension Insurance*, Homewood, Irwin for the University of Pennsylvania, Wharton School, Pension Research Council, 1989, 270 p.

JOHNSON, William R., 'Income Redistribution as Human Capital Insurance', **22** *Journal of Human Resources*, 1987, 269-280.

KAKWANI, Nanak, Analyzing Redistribution Policies: A Study Using Australian Data, Cambridge, Cambridge University Press, 1986, 293 p.

KALB, Paul E., 'Controlling Health Care Costs by Controlling Technology: A Private Contractual Approach', **99** *Yale Law Journal*, 1990, 1109-1126.

KEATING, Daniel, 'Pension Insurance, Bankruptcy, and Moral Hazard', *Wisconsin Law Review*, 1991, 65-108.

KODRAS, Janet E., 'The Spatial Perspective in Welfare Analysis', **6** *Cato Journal*, 1986, 77-83.

KOTLIKOFF, Laurence J., 'On the Contribution of Economics to the Evaluation and Formation of Social Insurance Policy', **79** *American Economic Review. Papers and Proceedings*, 1989, 184-190.

KRASHINSKY, Michael, 'The Case for Eliminating Mandatory Retirement: Why Economics and Human Rights Need Not Conflict', **14** *Canadian Public Policy*, 1988, 40-51.

LE BLANC, L.J.C.M., 'Bismarck als Benchmark. Enkele rechtseconomische beschouwingen over publieke sector en sociale zekerheid in Nederland' [Bismarck as Benchmark. Some Law-and-economics Considerations on the Public Sector and Social Welfare in the Netherlands], **39(10)** *Ars Aequi*, 1990, 654-659.

LEE, Dwight R. and McKENZIE, Richard B., 'Second Thoughts on the Public-Good Justification for Government Poverty Programs', **19** *Journal of Legal Studies*, 1990, 189-202.

LEES, D.S., 'The Logic of the British National Health Service', **5** *Journal of Law and Economics*, 1962, 111-118.

MAYO, John W. and McFARLAND, Deborah A., 'Regulation, Market Structure, and Hospital Costs', **55** *Southern Economic Journal*, 1989, 559-569.

MEYER, Charles W. (ed.), *Social Security: A Critique of Radical Reform Proposals*, Lexington, Lexington Books, 1987, 153 p.

MILLER, James C., III and YANDLE, Bruce (eds.), *Benefit-Cost Analysis of Social Regulation*, Washington, American Enterprise Institute, 1979.

MYRDAL, Gunnar, *Beyond the Welfare State*, Westport, Greenwood Press, 1965, 287 p.

NASH, Gerald D., PUGACH, Noel H. and TOMASSON, Richard F. (eds.), *Social Security: The First Half-Century*, Albuquerque, University of New Mexico Press, 1988, 344 p.

NIESWIADOMY, Michael, HAYES, K. and SLOTTJE, D.J., 'An Analysis of the Relationship between Various Redistributive Programs and Poverty', **68** *Public Choice*, 1991, 175-184.

O'CONNELL, Jeffrey, 'Must Health and Disability Insurance Subsidize Wasteful

Injury Suits?', **41** *Rutgers Law Review*, 1989, 1055-1065.

O'NEIL, June and KODRAS, Janet E., 'Transfers and Poverty: Cause and/or Effect?', **6** *Cato Journal*, 1986, 55-76.

OLSON, Mancur, 'Why Some Welfare-State Redistribution to the Poor is a Great Idea', in ROWLEY, Charles K. (ed.), *Democracy and Public Choice: essays in Honor of Gordon Tullock*, Oxford, Blackwell, 1987, 191-222.

PASOUR, E.C., Jr., 'Marginal Cost Pricing: Implications for Public Utility Regulation', **5** *Economia delle Scelte Pubbliche/Journal of Public Finance and Public Choice*, 1987, 45-251.

PAULY, Mark V., 'Taxation, Health Insurance, and Market Failure in the Medical Economy', **24** *Journal of Economic Literature*, 1986, 629-675.

PAULY, Mark V., 'Relational Contracting, Transaction Cost Economics and the Governance of HMOs', **59** *Temp. Law Quarterly*, 1986, 927 ff.

PAULY, Mark V., 'Competition in Health Insurance Markets', **51(2)** *Law and Contemporary Problems*, 1988, 237-271.

PETERSON, Wallace C., *Transfer Spending, Taxes, and the American Welfare State*, Dordrecht, Kluwer Academic Publishers, 1991, 192 p.

POSNETT, J. and SANDLER, T., 'Transfers, Transaction Costs and Charitable Intermediaries', **8** *International Review of Law and Economics*, 1988, 145-160.

PRITCHARD, A.C., 'Note: Government Promises and Due Process: An Economic Analysis of the "New Property"', **77** *Virginia Law Review*, 1991, 1053-1090.

RAHMSDORF, Detlev W., 'Zur Renaissance der Sozialvertragstheorien in den Wirtschaftswissenschaften und ihrer interdisziplinären Relevanz' [The Renaissance of the Social Contract in Political Economies and their Interdisciplinary Significance], *Der Staat*, 1986, Heft 2, 269-284.

REINHARDT, Uwe E., 'Economists in Health Care: Saviors, or Elephants in a Porcelain Shop?', **79** *American Economic Review. Papers and Proceedings*, 1989, 337-342.

RICARDO-CAMPBELL, Rita and LAZEAR, Adward P. (eds.), *Issues in Contemporary Retirement*, Stanford, Hoover Institution Press, 1988, 427 p.

RICE, Dorothy P., 'Health and Long-Term Care for the Aged', **79** *American Economic Review. Papers and Proceedings*, 1989, 343-348.

RINGEN, Stein, *The Possibility of Politics: A Study in the Political Economy of the Welfare State*, Oxford, Clarendon, 1987, 303 p.

ROBERTS, Russell D., 'Recipient Preferences and the Design of Governement Transfer Programs', **28** *Journal of Law and Economics*, 1985, 27-54.

ROTTENBERG, Simon, 'Unintended Consequences: The Probable Effects of Mandated Medical Insurance', **13(2)** *Regulation*, 1990, 21-28.

ROWLEY, Charles K. and PEACOCK, Alan T., *Welfare Economics: A Liberal Restatement*, London, Martin Robertson, 1975, 198 p.

SAWHILL, Isabel V., 'Poverty in the U.S.: Why Is It So Persistent?', **26** *Journal of Economic Literature*, 1988, 1073-1119.

SCHMAHL, Winfried (ed.), *Redefining the Process of Retirement: An International Perspective*, London, Springer, 1989, 179 p.

SCHULENBURG, J.-Matthias Graf von der, *Essays in Social Security Economics: Selected Papers of a Conference of the Internationa Institute of Management, Berlin, Wissenschaftszentrum*, Berlin, Springer, 1986, 222 p.

SCULLY, Gerald W., 'Rights, Equity, and Economic Efficiency', **68** *Public Choice*, 1991, 195-215.

SEMKOW, B.W., 'Social Insurance and Tort Liability', **5** *International Review of Law and Economics*, 1985, 153-171.

SMITH, Sharon P., 'Ending Mandatory Retirement in the Arts and Sciences', **81** *American Economic Review. Papers and Proceedings*, 1991, 106-110.

STIGLER, George J., 'Director's Law of Public Income Redistribution', **13** *Journal of Law and Economics*, 1970, 1-10.

STRAUSS, Peter J., WOLF, Robert and SHILLING, Dana, *Aging and the Law*, Chicago, Commerce Clearing House, 1990, 892 p.

TOBIN, James, 'On Limiting the Domain of Inequality', **13** *Journal of Law and Economics*, 1970, 263-277.

TOPEL, Robert H., 'Experience Rating of Unemployment Insurance and the Incidence of Unemployment', **27** *Journal of Law and Economics*, 1984, 61-90.

TULLOCK, Gordon, 'Subsidized Housing in a Competitive Market: Comment', **61** *American Economic Review*, 1971, 218-219.

TULLOCK, Gordon, *Economics of Income Redistribution*, Boston, Kluwer-Nijhoff, 1983, 208 p.

TULLOCK, Gordon, *The Economics of Wealth and Poverty*, New York, Columbia University Press, 1986, 210 p.

VISCUSI, W. Kip, *Welfare for the Elderly: An Economic Analysis and Policy Prescription*, New York, Wiley, 1979, 251 p.

VISCUSI, W. Kip, MAGAT, Wesley A. and HUBER, Joel, 'An Investigation of the Rationality of Consumer Valuations of Multiple Health Risks', **18** *Rand Journal of Economics*, 1987, 465-479.

WACHTER, Susan M. (ed.), *Social Security and Private Pensions: Providing for Retirement in the Twenty-First Century*, Lexington, Lexington Books, 1988, 232 p.

WAGNER, Richard E., *To Promote the General Welfare: Market Processes vs. Political Transfers*, San Francisco: Pacific Research Institute for Public Policy, 1989, 239 p.

WEST, E.G., 'An Economic Analysis of the Law and Politics of Non-Public School "Aid"', **19** *Journal of Law and Economics*, 1976, 79-101.

WHINSTON, Michael D., 'Moral Hazard, Adverse Selection, and the Optimal Provision of Social Insurance', **22** *Journal of Public Economics*, 1983, 49-71.

WICKSTRÖM, Bengt-Arne, 'The Norwegian Social-Security System: Present State and Future Prospects', in FAURE, Michael and VAN DEN BERGH, Roger (eds.), *Essays in Law and Economics. Corporations, Accident Prevention and Compensation for Losses*, Antwerpen, Maklu, 1989, 163-184.

6200 TAKINGS
Gerrit De Geest

BLUME, Lawrence E. and RUBINFELD, Daniel L., 'Compensation for Takings: An Economic Analysis', **72** *California Law Review*, 1984, 569-628. Reprinted in **10** *Research in Law and Economics*, 1987, 53-103.

BURROWS, Paul, 'Getting a Stranglehold with the Eminant Domain Clause', **9** *International Review of Law and Economics*, 1989, 129-147.

DURHAM, James Geoffrey, 'Efficient Just Compensation as a Limit on Eminent Domain', **69** *Minnesota Law Review*, 1985, 1277 ff.

EPSTEIN, Richard A., *Takings: Private Property and the Power of Eminent Domain*, Cambridge, Harvard University Press, 1985, 362 p.

FISCHEL, William A. and SHAPIRO, Perry, 'A Constitutional Choice Model of Compensation for Takings', **9** *International Review of Law and Economics*, 1989, 115-128.

FISHEL, William A. and SHAPIRO, Perry, 'Takings, Insurance and Michelman: Comments on Economic Interpretations of "Just Compensation" Law', **17** *Journal of Legal Studies*, 1988, 269-293.

GECKER, Frances F., 'Comment: The Recovery of Opportunity Costs as Just Compensation: A Takings Analysis of Adequate Protection', **81** *Northwestern University Law Review*, 1987, 953-1025.

GOLDBERG, Victor P., MERRILL, Thomas W. and UNUMB, Daniel, 'Bargaining in the Shadow of Eminent Domain: Valuing and Apportioning Condemnation Awards Between Landlord and Tenant', **34** *UCLA Law Review*, 1987, 1083-1137.

KNETSCH, Jack L. and BORCHERDING, T.E., 'Expropriation of Private Property and the Basis for Compensation', **29** *University of Toronto Law Journal*, 1979, 237-252.

LEVMORE, Saul and STUNTZ, William J., 'Remedies and Incentives in Private and Public Law: A Comparitive Essay', *Wisconsin Law Review*, 1990, 483-499.

LODISE, John P., 'Retroactive Compensation and the Illusion of Economic Efficiency: An Analysis of the First English Decision', **35** *UCLA Law Review*, 1988, 1267-1290.

MACKAAY, Ejan J.P., 'Le paradoxe des droits acquis' [The Paradox of Acquired Rights], in *De "l'ancienne" à la "nouvelle" économie. Essais à l'occasion de la dixième université d'été de la nouvelle économie. Aix-en-Provence 1978-87*, Aix-en-Provence, Librairie de l'université, 1987, 205-219.

McKENZIE, Richard B., 'Eminent Domain: A New Industrial Policy Tool', **142** *Journal of Institutional and Theoretical Economics*, 1986, 27-38.

MICHELMAN, Frank I., 'Property, Utility and Fairness: Comments on the Ethical Foundations of "Just Compensation" Law', **80** *Harvard Law Review*, 1967, 1165-1258. Reprinted in ACKERMAN, Bruce A., *Economic Foundations of Property a Law*, Boston, Little Brown, 1975, 100 ff.

MUNCH, Patricia, 'An Economic Analysis of Eminent Domain', **84** *Journal of Political Economy*, 1976, 473-497.

PAUL, Ellen Frankel, 'Public Use: A Vanishing Limitation on Governmental Takings', in DORN, James A. and MANNE, Henry G. (eds.), *Economic Liberties and the Judiciary*, Fairfax, George Mason University Press, 1987, 357-373.

ROSE, Carol M., 'Mahon Reconstructed: Why the Takings Issue is Still a Muddle', **57** *Southern California Law Review*, 1984, 561 ff.

SAMUELS, Warren J., 'Commentary: An Economic Perspective on the Compensation Problem', **21** *Wayne Law Review*, 1974, 113-134. Reprinted in SAMUELS, Warren J. and SCHMID, A. Allen (eds.), *Law and Economics: An Institutional Perspective*, Boston, Kluwer-Nijhoff, 1981, 188-209.

SAMUELS, Warren J. and MERCURO, Nicholas, 'The Role and Resolution of the Compensation Principle in Society: Part One - The Role', **1** *Research in Law and Economics*, 1979, 157-194.

SAMUELS, Warren J. and MERCURO, Nicholas, 'The Role and Resolution of the Compensation Principle in Society: Part Two The Resolution', **2** *Research in Law and Economics*, 1980, 103-128.

SAX, Joseph, 'Takings and the Police Power', **74** *Yale Law Journal*, 1964, 36-76.

SAX, Joseph L., 'Takings, Private Property and Public Rights', **81** *Yale Law Journal*, 1971, 149-186. Reprinted in ACKERMAN, Bruce A., *Economic Foundations of Property a Law*, Boston, Little Brown, 1975, 146-158.

SYMPOSIUM : 'Symposium on Takings', **88** *Columbia Law Review*, 1988, 1581-1794.

WERIN, Lars, 'Expropriation - en studie i lagstiftningsmotiv och ersättningsrättsliga grundprinciper' [Expropriation - A Study in Legislative Motives and Compensatory Basic Principles], *Svensk Juristtidning*, 1978, 81-120.

6300 ADMINISTRATIVE PROCESS
Jürgen G. Backhaus

6300 Administrative Law: General

BACKHAUS, Jürgen G., *Public Enterprise: Forms and Functions*. (1st ed. 1977). Haag & Herchen, 1977 (1st ed.), 441 p, 1980 (2nd ed.), 535 p.

BACKHAUS, Jürgen G., 'How to Write an Economic Analysis of a Legal problem,' in HOLZHAUER, Rudi W., TEIJL, Rob et al., *Inleiding Rechtseconomie* [Introduction to Law-and-Economics], Gouda Quint, Arnhem, 1989, 345 p.

BACKHAUS, Jürgen G., 'Law: Cooperation between Lawyers and Economists; Common Denominator, **45(10)** *Wirtschaftswoche*, 1991, 149-150.

BERGE, J.B.J.M. ten, 'Rechtseconomie en staatsrecht/bestuursrecht' [Law-and-economics and Constitutional/Administrative Law], in *Rechtseconomie en Recht*, Zwolle, Tjeenk Willink, 1991, 149-162.

BISHOP, William, 'A Theory of Administrative Law', **19** *Journal of Legal Studies*, 1990, 489-530.

CALABRESI, Guido, *The Costs of Accidents: A Legal and Economic Analysis*, New Haven, Yale University Press, 1970, 340 p.

CLARCKSON, Kenneth W. and MARTIN, Donald L. (eds.), *The Economics of Nonproprietary Institutions*, Greenwich, JAI Press, *Supplement 1 to Research in Law and Economics*, 1979, 330 p.

FARBER, Daniel A. and FRICKEY, Philip P., 'Integrating Public Choice and Public Law: A Reply to DeBow and Lee', **66** *Texas Law Review*, 1988, 1013-1019.

HARMATHY, Attila, 'Allami támogatások jogi kérdéseiröl' [Legal Questions on State Subsidies], **1** *Allam- és Jogtudomány*, 1980, 33-61.

HARMATHY, Attila, *Szerzödések, államigazgatás, gazdaságirányitás* [Contract, Administration, Business Governing], Budapest, Akadémiai Kiadó, 1983, 210 p.

HONDIUS, E.H., SCHIPPERS, J.J. and SIEGERS, J.J., *Law and Economics: Getting to Know the New Subject Area*, Zwolle, W.E.J. Tjeenk Willink, 1991, 201 p.

HOWSE, Robert, PRICHARD, J. Robert S. and TREBILCOCK, Michael J., 'Smaller or Smarter Government?', **40** *University of Toronto Law Journal*, 1990, 498-541.

LANE, J.-E., *State and Market; The Politics of the Public and the Private*, London, Sage Publications, 1985, 304 p.

MASHAW, Jerry L., 'Explaining Administrative Process: Normative, Positive, and Critical Stories of Legal Devopment', **6** *Journal of Law, Economics, & Organization*, 1990, S267-S298.

OMMEREN, F.J. van, 'Bestuurscompensatie, draagkracht en rechtseconomie' [Administrative Compensation, Financial Capacity and Economic Analysis of Law], **39(10)** *Ars Aequi*, 1990, 682-691.

PREITE, Disiano, 'Sovrapprezzo, aste competitive e mercato mobiliare' [Overpricing, Competitive Auctions and Security Market], *Giurisprudenza commerciale*, 1987, I, 882-924.

SUNSTEIN, Cass R., 'Is Cost-Benefit Analysis a Panacea for Administrative Law?', **29** *The Law School Record*, 1983, 19-21.

SUNSTEIN, Cass R., 'Political Economy, Administrative Law: A Comment', **6** *Journal of Law, Economics, & Organization*, 1990, S299-S306.

SUPPER, Meinhard, ' Das niederösterreichische Landesrecht und die ökonomische Analyse des Rechts' [The Law of the Province of Lower Austria and the Economic Analysis of Law], in FUNK, Bernd-Christian (project management), *Deregulierung und Entbürokratisierung am Beispiel von Niederösterreich*, Vienna, Austrian economic Publishing Comp., 1988, 43-48.

6310 Substantive Administrative Law and Economics

MARTIN, Dolores Tremewan and WAGNER, Richard E., 'The Institutional Framework for Municipal Incorporation: An Economic Analysis of Local Agency Formation Commissions in California', **21** *Journal of Law and Economics*, 1978, 409-425.

MASHAW, Jerry L., 'Prodelegation: Why Administrators Should Make Political Decisions', **1** *Journal of Law, Economics, & Organization*, 1985, 81-100.

PEETERS, Bruno, *De continuïteit van het overheidsondernemen: een begrippenanalyse en een kritiek op de uitvoeringsimmuniteit* [The Continuity Principle of Governmental Activities: A Concept Analysis and a Critique on the Execution Immunity], Antwerpen, Maklu, 1989, 559 p.

ROSE-ACKERMAN, Susan, 'Progressive Law and Economics - and the New Administrative Law', **98** *Yale Law Journal*, 1988, 341-368.

6320 Basic Institutes

HACKNEY, James R., Jr., 'A Proposal for State Funding of Municipal Tort Liability', **98** *Yale Law Journal*, 1988, 389-407.

KRAMER, Larry and SYKES, Alan O., 'Municipal Liability under Section 1983: A Legal and Economic Analysis', *Supreme Court Review*, 1987, 249-301.

6330 Public Organizations

AUSTER, Richard D. and SILVER, Morris, *The State as a Firm: Economic Forces in Political Development*, Den Haag, Martinus Nijhoff, 1979, 178 p.

CLARCKSON, Kenneth W. and TOLLISON, Robert, 'Toward a Theory of

Government Advertising', **1** *Research in Law and Economics*, 1979, 131-143.

DeSOUZA, Patrick J., 'Regulating Fraud in Military Procurement: A Legal Process Model', **95** *Yale Law Journal*, 1985, 390-413.

GREENE, Kenneth V. and MOULTON, George D., 'Municipal Employee Residency Requirement Statutes: An Economic Analysis', **9** *Research in Law and Economics*, 1986, 185-204.

JOHNSON, Ronald N. and LIBECAP, Gary D., 'Bureaucratic Rules, Supervisor Behavior, and the Effect on Salaries in the Federal Government', **5** *Journal of Law, Economics, & Organization*, 1989, 53-82.

VAN DER KROGT, T.P.W.M. et.al. (ed.), 'Municipal Cooperation', in *Big is Beautiful? Schaalveranderingen in overheid en samenleving*, Den Haag, 1987, 127-148.

VICKEY, W., 'The City as a Firm' in FELDSTEIN, M.S. and INMAN, R.S. (eds.), *The Economics of Public Services*, London, Macmillan, 1980, 334-343.

6340 Regulatory Administration

AUDRETSCH, D.B., SLEUWAEGEN, L. and YAMAWAKI, H., *The Convergence of International and Domestic Markets*, Amsterdam, North-Holland, 1989, 317 p.

BACKHAUS, Jürgen G., 'On Censoring and Persuading', **14 (7/8/9)** *International Journal of Social Economics*, 1987, 99-114.

BORJAS, George J., 'The Politics of Employment Discrimination in the Federal Bureaucracy', **25** *Journal of Law and Economics*, 1982, 271-299.

DE KRAAN, D.J., 'Deregulering' [Deregulation], **62** *Economische Statistische Berichten*, 1982, 692-696.

DE KRAAN, D.J., 'Deregulering: een Begripsbepaling' [Deregulation: A Definition], **9** *Beleid en Maatschappij*, 1982, 177-181.

KÜNNEKE, R.W., 'Privatisation of Municipal Utilities', **18(5)** *Openbare Uitgaven*, 1986, 218-228.

ROGERSON, William P., 'Profit Regulation of Defense Contractors and Prizes for Innovation', **97** *Journal of Political Economy*, 1989, 1284-1305.

STEWART, Richard B., 'Regulation, Innovation, and Administrative Law: A Conceptual Framework', **69** *California Law Review*, 1981, 1256-1377.

ZALM, G., 'Deregulation', **67** *Economische Statistische Berichten*, 1982, 692-696.

6350 Administrative Service

BOARDMAN, Anthony E. and VINING, Aidan R., 'Ownership and Performance in Competitive Environments: A Comparison of the Performance of Private, Mixed, and State-owned Enterprises', **32** *Journal of Law and Economics*, 1989,

1-33.

NEELEN, G.H.J.M., 'Creditmanagement', Universiteit Twente, Enschede, 1988.

NEELEN, G.H.J.M., 'Efficiency differences between Organizations within the Public Sector: The Dutch Social housing Sector', **2** *Tinbergen Institute Research Bulletin*, 1990, 33-41.

6360 Administrative Procedure

DIVER, Colin S., 'The Optimal Precision of Administrative Rules', **93** *Yale Law Journal*, 1983, 65-109.

FINKELSTEIN, M.O., 'Regression Models in Administrative Proceedings', **86** *Harvard Law Review*, 1973, 1442-1475.

McCUBBINS, Mathew D., NOLL, Roger G. and WEINGAST, Barry R., 'Administrative Procedures as Instruments of Political Control', **3** *Journal of Law, Economics, & Organization*, 1987, 243-277.

McCUBBINS, Mathew D., NOLL, Roger G. and WEINGAST, Barry R., 'Positive and Normative Models of Procedural Rights: An Integrative Approach to Administrative Procedures', **6** *Journal of Law, Economics, & Organization*, 1990, S307-S332.

SCHWARTZ, Bernard, 'Cost-Benefit Analysis in Administrative Law: Does It Make Priceless Procedural Right Worthless?', **37** *Administrative Law Review*, 1985, 1-14.

7000 CIVIL AND CRIMINAL PROCEDURE
Patrick Wallaert

7000 Procedure: General

BAILY, Mary Ann and CIKINS, Warren I. (eds.), *The Effects of Litigation on Health Care Costs*, Washington, Brookings Institution, 1985.

BEIER, Martin D., 'Economics Awry: Using Access Fees for Caseload Diversion', **138** *University of Pennsylvania Law Review*, 1990, 1175-1207.

BLANKENBURG, E., 'Naar een planeconomie voor de rechtshulp' [Towards a Planned Economy for Legal Aid], *Nederlands Juristen Blad*, 1990, 879-882.

BOWLES, Roger A., 'Economic Aspects of Legal Procedure', in BURROWS, Paul and VELJANOVSKI, Cento G. (eds.), *The Economic Appraoch to Law*, London, Butterworths, 1981, 191-209.

BOWLES, Roger A. and WHELAN, Christopher J., 'Judgement Awards and Simple Interest Rates', **1** *International Review of Law and Economics*, 1981, 111 ff.

BOWLES, Roger A. and WHELAN, Christopher J., 'Judicial Responses to Exchange Rate Instability', in BURROWS, Paul and VELJANOVSKI, Cento G. (eds.), *The Economic Appraoch to Law*, London, Butterworths, 1981, 253-272.

BRAEUTIGAM, Ronald R. and OWEN, Bruce M. and PANZAR, John C., 'An Economic Analysis of Alternative Fee Shifting Systems', **47(1)** *Law and Contemporary Problems*, 1984, 173-185.

BROWN, John Prather, 'Alternatives to the Present System of Litigation for Personal Injury', in BAILY, Mary Ann and CIKINS, Warren I. (eds.), *The Effects of Litigation on Health Care Costs*, Washington, Brookings Institution, 1985, 69-79.

BUNDY, Stephen McG. and ELHAUGE, Einer Richard, 'Do Lawyers Improve the Adversary System? A General Theory of Litigation Advice and Its Regulation', **79** *California Law Review*, 1991, 313-420.

CALFEE, John E. and CRASWELL, Richard, 'Some Effect of Uncertainty on Compliance with Legal Standards', **70** *Virginia Law Review*, 1984, 965-1003.

CARROLL, Sidney L. and GASTON, Robert J., 'A Note on the Quality of Legal Services: Peer Review and Disciplinary Service', **3** *Research in Law and Economics*, 1981, 251-260.

CHURCH, T.W. and HEUMANN, M., 'The Underexamined Assumptions of the Visible Hand: Monetary Incentives as Policy Instruments', **8** *Journal of Policy Analysis and Management*, 1989, 641-657.

CONFERENCE : 'Conference on the Law and Economics of Procedure', **3** *Journal of Law, Economics, & Organization*, 1987, 143-372.

COOTER, Robert D. and RUBINFELD, Daniel L., 'Economic Analysis of Legal Disputes and Their Resolution', **27** *Journal of Economic Literature*, 1989, 1067-1097.

CRASWELL, Richard and CALFEE, John E., 'Deterrence and Uncertain Legal

Standards', **2** *Journal of Law, Economics, & Organization*, 1986, 279-303.

DANZON, Patricia M., 'Contingent Fees for Personal Injury Litigation', **14** *Bell Journal of Economics*, 1983, 213-224.

DAVIS, Otto A., 'Public and Private Characteristics of a Legal Process: A Comment', **8** *Journal of Legal Studies*, 1979, 285-293.

DENZAU, Arthur, 'Litigation Expenditures as Private Determinants of Judicial Decisions: A Comment', **8** *Journal of Legal Studies*, 1979, 295-302.

DOMBERGER, Simon and SHERR, Avrom, 'The Impact of Competition on Pricing and Quality of Legal Services', **9** *International Review of Law and Economics*, 1989, 41-56.

EASTERBROOK, Frank H., LANDES, William M. and POSNER, Richard A., 'Contribution among Antitrust Defendants: A Legal and Economic Analysis', **23** *Journal of Law and Economics*, 1980, 331-370.

EBNER, P., *Reducing Pretrial Delay... A Look at What State and Local Courts Are Doing to Break the Logjam*, Santa Monica, Rand Institute of Civil Justice, 1982.

ENGELMANN, Kathleen and CORNELL, Bradford, 'Measuring the Cost of Corporate Litigation: Five Case Studies', **17** *Journal of Legal Studies*, 1988, 377-399.

EPSTEIN, Richard A., 'Judicial Review: Reckoning on Two Kinds of Error', in DORN, James A. and MANNE, Henry G. (eds.), *Economic Liberties and the Judiciary*, Fairfax, George Mason University Press, 1987, 39-46.

FEELEY, Malcolm, *Court Reform on Trial: Why Simple Solutions Fail*, New York, Basic Books, 1983, 251 p.

GAMBARO, Antonio, *La legittimazione passiva alle azioni possessorie* [Standing to Be Sued in Ownership Litigation], Milano, Giuffrè, 1979, 163 p.

GAY, Gerald D., GRACE, Martin F., KALE, Jayrant R. and NOE, Thomas H., 'Noisy Juries and the Choice of Trial Mode in a Sequential Signalling Game: Theory and Evidence', **20** *Rand Journal of Economics*, 1989, 196-213.

GETMAN, Julius G., 'A Critique of the Report of the Shreveport Experiment', **3** *Journal of Legal Studies*, 1974, 487-497.

GOLDMAN, Jerry and MARKS, Kenneth S., 'Diversity Jurisdiction and Local Bias: A Preliminary Empirical Inquiry', **9** *Journal of Legal Studies*, 1980, 93-104.

GOOD, I.J. and TULLOCK, Gordon, 'Judicial Errors and a Proposal for Reform', **13** *Journal of Legal Studies*, 1984, 289-298.

GRAVELLE, Hugh S.E., 'Judicial Review and Public Firms', **3** *International Review of Law and Economics*, 1983, 187-205.

GRAVELLE, Hugh S.E., 'Default Risk and the Optimal Pricing of Court Enforcement Services', in GRAF VON DER SCHULENBURG, J.-Matthias and SKOGH, Göran (eds.), *Law and Economics and The Economics of Legal Regulation*, Dordrecht, Kluwer, 1986, 85-112.

GRAVELLE, Hugh S.E., 'Rationing Trials by Waiting: Welfare Implications', **10** *International Review of Law and Economics*, 1990, 255-270.

HALLAUER, Robert Paul, 'The Shreveport Experiment in Prepaid Legal Services', **2** *Journal of Legal Studies*, 1973, 223-242.

HALPERN, Paul J. and TURNBULL, Stuart M., 'An Economic Analysis of Legal Fee Contracts', in EVANS, R.M. and TREBILCOCK, Michael J. (eds.), *Lawyers and the Consumer Interest*, Toronto, Butterworths, 1981.

HANKE, Steve H., 'Comment: Compatibility of Legal Rules and Cost-Benefit Analysis', in DORN, James A. and MANNE, Henry G. (eds.), *Economic Liberties and the Judiciary*, Fairfax, George Mason University Press, 1987, 245-247.

HASKELL, Thomas L., 'Litigation and Social Status in Seventeenth-Century New Haven', **7** *Journal of Legal Studies*, 1978, 219-241.

HAZARD, Geoffrey C., Jr., 'Rationing Justice', **8** *Journal of Law and Economics*, 1965, 1-10.

HYLTON, Keith N., 'The Influence of Litigation Costs on Deterrence under Strict Liability and under Negligence', **10** *International Review of Law and Economics*, 1990, 161-171.

JOHNSON, Ronald N. and PARKMAN, Allen M., 'Premerger Notification and the Incentive to Merge and Litigate', **7** *Journal of Law, Economics, & Organization*, 1991, 145-162.

KAPLOW, Louis and SHAVELL, Steven, 'Legal Advice about Acts Already Committed', **10** *International Review of Law and Economics*, 1990, 149-159.

KATZ, Avery, 'Measuring the Demand for Litigation: Is the English Rule Really Cheaper?', **3** *Journal of Law, Economics, & Organization*, 1987, 143-176.

KATZ, Avery, 'Judicial Decisionmaking and Litigation Expenditure', **8** *International Review of Law and Economics*, 1988, 127-143.

KLEIN, Cristopher C., 'Predation in the Courts: Legal Versus Economic Analysis in Sham Litigation Cases', **10** *International Review of Law and Economics*, 1990, 29-40.

KOPPEN, P.J. van, 'Cassatieadvocaten en de selectiekamer' [Cassation Lawyers and the Chamber of Selection], *Nederlands Juristen Blad*, 1990, 14-26.

KRITZER, Herbert, SARAT, Austin, TRUBEK, David, BUMILLER, Kristin and McNICHOL, Elizabeth, 'Understanding the Cost of Litigation: The Case of the Hourly-Fee Lawyer', **3** *American Bar Foundation Research Journal*, 1984, 559-604.

LANDES, William M. and POSNER, Richard A., 'Adjudication as a Private Good', **8** *Journal of Legal Studies*, 1979, 235-284.

LEIBOWITZ, Arleen and TOLLISON, Robert, 'Earning and Learning in Law Firms', **7** *Journal of Legal Studies*, 1978, 65-81.

LEVMORE, Saul, 'Strategic Delays and Fiduciary Duties', **74** *Virginia Law Review*, 1988, 863-913.

LEWIS, Donald E., 'Economic Aspects of the Parole Decision', **22** *Australian Economic Papers*, 1983, 259-279.

MALSCH, Marijke, *Advocaten voorspellen de uitkomst van hun zaken* [Lawyers' Predictions of Judicial Decisions: A Study on Calibration of Experts], Lisse, Swets & Zeitlinger, 1990, 109 p.

McLAUCHLAN, William P., 'An Empirical Study of the Federal Summary Judgment Rule', **6** *Journal of Legal Studies*, 1977, 427-459.

MELUMAD, Nahum D. and THOMAN, Lynda, 'On Auditors and the Courts in an Adverse Selection Setting', **28** *Journal of Accounting Research*, 1990, 77-120.

MICELI, Thomas J. and SEGERSON, Kathleen, 'Contingent Fees for Lawyers: The Impact on Litigation and Accident Prevention', **20** *Journal of Legal Studies*, 1991, 381-399.

MILLER, Arthur R., 'The Adversary System: Dinosaur or Phoenix', **69** *Minnesota Law Review*, 1984, 1-37.

MILLER, Geoffrey P., 'Comment: Some Thoughts on the Equilibrium Hypothesis', **69** *Boston University Law Review*, 1989, 561-568.

NEDERLANDS JURISTEN BLAD: *Tussen kwaliteit en efficiency in de rechtspraak* [Between Quality and Efficiency in Case Law], Special Issue, 1987, (a number of articles).

NEDERLANDS JURISTEN BLAD: *Rechtshulp anno 1990*, Special Issue, 1990, (a number of articles).

NESSON, Charles R., 'Correspondence: Kaplow and Shavell on Legal Advice in Litigation', **103** *Harvard Law Review*, 1990, 2082-2084.

OGUS, Anthony I., 'Quantitative Rules and Judicial Decision Making', in BURROWS, Paul and VELJANOVSKI, Cento G. (eds.), *The Economic Appraoch to Law*, London, Butterworths, 1981, 210-225.

ORDOVER, Janusz A., 'Costly Litigation in the Model of Single Activity Accidents', **7** *Journal of Legal Studies*, 1978, 243-261.

ORDOVER, Janusz A., 'On the Consequences of Costly Litigation in the Model of Single Activity Accidents: Some New Results', **10** *Journal of Legal Studies*, 1981, 269-291.

PASHIGIAN, B. Peter, 'A Theory of Prevention and Legal Defense with an Application to the Legal Costs of Companies', **25** *Journal of Law and Economics*, 1982, 247-270.

PASTOR, Santos, 'El análisis económico del acceso a la justicia' [The Economics of Access to Justice], *Información Comercial Española*, 1990, n. 687, 23-42.

PATELL, James, M., WEIL, Roman L. and WOLFSON, Mark A., 'Accumulating Damages in Litigation: The Roles of Uncertainty and Interest Rates', **11** *Journal of Legal Studies*, 1982, 341-364.

PLOTT, Charles R., 'Legal Fees: A Comparison of the American and English Rules', **3** *Journal of Law, Economics, & Organization*, 1987, 185-192.

PNG, Ivan P.L., 'Litigation, Liability, and Incentives for Care', **34** *Journal of Public Economics*, 1987, 61-85.

POLINSKY, A. Mitchell and RUBINFELD, Daniel L., 'The Welfare Implications of Costly Litigation for the Level of Liability', **17** *Journal of Legal Studies*, 1988, 151-164.

POLINSKY, A. Mitchell and SHAVELL, Steven, 'Contribution and Claim Reduction Among Antitrust Defendants: An Economic Analysis', **33** *Stanford Law Review*, 1981, 447-471.

POLINSKY, A. Mitchell and SHAVELL, Steven, 'Legal Error, Litigation, and the Incentive to Obey the Law', **5** *Journal of Law, Economics, and Organization*, 1989, 99-108.

POSNER, Richard A., 'An Economic Approach to Legal Procedure and Judicial Administration', **2** *Journal of Legal Studies*, 1973, 399-458.

POSNER, Richard A., 'Toward and Economic Theory of Federal Jurisdiction', **6** *Harvard Journal of Law & Public Policy*, 1982, 41-50.

POSNER, Richard A., 'The Summary Jury Trial and Other Methods of Alternative Dispute Resolution: Some Cautionary Observations', **53** *University of Chicago Law Review*, 1986, 366-393.

POSNER, Richard A., 'Comment: Responding to Gordon Tullock', **2** *Research in Law and Policy Studies*, 1988, 29-33.

PRIEST, George L., 'Measuring Legal Change', **3** *Journal of Law, Economics, & Organization*, 1987, 193-225.

ROWE, Thomas D., 'Predicting the Effects of Attorney Fee Shifting', **47(1)** *Law and Contemporary Problems*, 1984, 139-171.

SCHMALBECK, Richard L. and MYERS, Gary, 'A Policy Analysis of Fee-Shifting Rules under the Internal Revenue Code', *Duke Law Journal*, 1986, 970-1002.

SPURR, Stephen J., 'An Economic Analysis of Collateral Estoppel', **11** *International Review of Law and Economics*, 1991, 47-61.

SYMPOSIUM : 'Attorney Fees Shifting', **47(1)** *Law and Contemporary Problems*, 1984, 1-354.

SYMPOSIUM : 'Conference on the Law and Economics of Procedure', **3** *Journal of Law, Economics, and Organization*, 1987, 143-447.

TRIBE, Laurence H., 'Trial by Mathematics Precision and Ritual in the Legal Process', **84** *Harvard Law Review*, 1971, 1329-1393.

TRUBECK, David M., SARAT, Austin, FELSTINER, William L.F., KRITZER, Herbert M. and GROSSMAN, Joel B., 'The Cost of Ordinary Litigation', **31** *UCLA Law Review*, 1983, 72 ff.

TULDER, Frank van, 'Over fietsen en recht' [On Bicycles and Law], **66** *Nederlands Juristenblad*, 1991, 444-445.

TULDER, Frank van, 'Rechtshulp in economisch perspectief' [Legal Aid from an Economic Perspective], **39(10)** *Ars Aequi*, 1990, 692-705.

TULDER, Frank van, and JANSSEN, S., 'De prijselasticiteit van het recht' [The Price Elasticity of Law], **73** *Economisch-Statistische Berichten*, 1988, 19-22.

TULDER, Frank van, and JANSSEN, S., 'De prijs van de weg naar het recht' [The Price of the Road to the Law], *Sociaal Cultureel Planbureau*, Stukwerk no. 45, 1988.

TULLOCK, Gordon, 'On Effective Organization of Trials', **28** *Kyklos*, 1975, 745-762.

TULLOCK, Gordon, *Trials on Trial - The Pure Theory of Legal Procedure*, New York, Columbia University Press, 1980, 255 p.

TULLOCK, Gordon, 'Defending the Napoleontic Code over the Common Law', **2** *Research in Law and Policy Studies*, 1988, 3-27.

WOLFRAM, Charles W., 'The Second Set of Players: Lawyers, Fee Shifting, and the Limits of Professional Discipline', **47(1)** *Law and Contemporary Problems*, 1984, 293-320.

YUNKER, J.A., 'The Effect of Decision Time and Argument Complexity on Legal Judgment', **3** *International Review of Law and Economics*, 1983, 161-178.

ZEMANS, Frances Kahn, 'Fee Shifting and the Implementation of Public Policy', **47(1)** *Law and Contemporary Problems*, 1984, 187-1210.

7100 Evidence

BUNDY, Stephen McG. and ELHAUGE, Einer Richard, 'Do Lawyers Improve the Adversary System? A General Theory of Litigation Advice and Its Regulation', **79** *California Law Review*, 1991, 313-420.

EASTERBROOK, Frank H., 'Comment: Discovery as Abuse', **69** *Boston University Law Review*, 1989, 635-648.

ELLIOTT, E. Donald, 'Toward Incentive-Based Procedure: Three Approaches for Regulating Scientific Evidence', **69** *Boston University Law Review*, 1989, 487-511.

FAIRLEY, William B., 'Probabilistic Analysis of Identification Evidence', **2** *Journal of Legal Studies*, 1973, 493-513.

FIENBERG, Stephen E. (ed.), *The Evolving Role of Statistical Assessments as Evidence in the Courts*, New York, Springer, 1989, 357 p.

GIBBONS, T. and HUTCHINSON, A.C., 'The Practice and Theory of Evidence Law - A Note', **2** *International Review of Law and Economics*, 1982, 119-126.

GROSS, Samuel R., 'Loss of Innocence: Eyewitness Identification and Proof of Guilt', **16** *Journal of Legal Studies*, 1987, 395-453.

HUBER, Peter, 'A Comment on 'Toward Incentive-Based Procedure: Three Approaches for Regulating Scientific Evidence' by E. Donald Elliott', **69** *Boston University Law Review*, 1989, 513-516.

KAPLOW, Louis and SHAVELL, Steven, 'Legal Advice About Information to Present in Litigation: Its Effects and Social Desirability', **102** *Harvard Law Review*, 1989, 565-615.

KAPLOW, Louis and SHAVELL, Steven, 'Legal Advice about Acts Already Committed', **10** *International Review of Law and Economics*, 1990, 149-159.

LEVMORE, Saul and STUNTZ, William J., 'Remedies and Incentives in Private and Public Law: A Comparitive Essay', *Wisconsin Law Review*, 1990, 483-499.

RUBINFELD, Daniel L. and SAPPINGTON, David E.M., 'Efficient Awards and Standards of Proof in Judicial Proceedings', **18** *Rand Journal of Economics*, 1987, 308-315.

SCHWARTZ, Robert L., 'There is no Archbishop of Science - A Comment on Elliott's Toward Incentive-Based Procedure: Three Approaches for Regulating Scientific Evidence', **69** *Boston University Law Review*, 1989, 517-525.

SETEAR, John K., 'The Barrister and the Bomb: The Dynamics of Cooperation, Nuclear Deterrence, and Discovery Abuse', **69** *Boston University Law Review*, 1989, 569-633.

SHAVELL, Steven, 'Legal Advice about Contemplated Acts: The Decision to Obtain Advice, Its Social Desirability, and Protection of Confidentiality', **17** *Journal of Legal Studies*, 1988, 123-150.

SHAVELL, Steven, 'Optimal Sanctions and the Incentive to Provide Evidence to Legal Tribunals', **9** *International Review of Law and Economics*, 1989, 3-11.

SOBEL, Joel, 'An Analysis of Discovery Rules', **52(1)** *Law and Contemporary Problems*, 1989, 133-159.

SPIOTTO, James E., 'Search and Seizure: An Empirical Study of the Exclusionary Rule and Its Alternatives', **2** *Journal of Legal Studies*, 1973, 243-278.

TULLOCK, Gordon, 'Defending the Napoleontic Code over the Common Law', **2** *Research in Law and Policy Studies*, 1988, 3-27.

WEINSTEIN, Jack B., 'What Discovery Abuse? A Comment on John Setear's The Barrister and the Bomb', **69** *Boston University Law Review*, 1989, 649-657.

X, 'Note: The Theoretical Foundation of the Hearsay Rules', **93** *Harvard Law Review*, 1980, 1786-1815.

7200 Civil Procedure

7200 Civil Procedure: General

ABRAHAM, Kenneth S. and JEFFRIES, John C. Jr., 'Punitive Damages and the Rule of Law: The Role of Defendant's Wealth', **18** *Journal of Legal Studies*, 1989, 415-425.

ADAMS, Michael, *Ökonomische Analyse des Zivilprozesses* [Economic Analysis of Civil Procedure], Königstein/Ts, Athenäum, 1981, 130 p.

ADAMS, Michael, 'Eine wohlfahrtstheoretische Analyse des Zivilprozesses und der Rechtsschutzversicherungen' [An Economic Analysis of Civil Procedure and Legal Aid Insurance], **139** *Zeitschrift für Schweizerisches Recht*, 1983, 187-208.

ADAMS, Michael, 'Der Zivilprozeß als Folge strategischen Verhaltens' [On Civil Procedure as a Consequence of Strategic Behavior], **7** *Zeitschrift für Rechtssoziologie*, 1986, 212-225.

ANDERSON, Gary M. and HIGGINS, R.S., 'Substantive Due Process Review and the Extent of Government Regulation', **7** *International Review of Law and Economics*, 1987, 101-111.

BRODER, Josef M., 'Citizen Participation in Michigan District Courts', in RANDALL, Allan (ed.), *Citizen Participation in Natural Resource Decision Making*, North Central Research Strategy Committee for Natural Resources, Departement of Agricultural Economics, University of Kentucky, 1978. Reprinted in SAMUELS, Warren J. and SCHMID, A. Allen (eds.), *Law and Economics: An Institutional Perspective*, Boston, Nijhoff, 1981, 166-178.

BRUNET, Edward, 'Measuring the Costs of Civil Justice', **83** *Michigan Law Review*, 1985, 916-938.

CHIORAZZI, Michael et al., 'Empirical Studies in Civil Procedure: A Selected Annotated Bibliography', **51(3)** *Law and Contemporary Problems*, 1988, 87-207.

EASTERBROOK, Frank H., 'Comment: Discovery as Abuse', **69** *Boston University Law Review*, 1989, 635-648.

ELLIOTT, E. Donald, 'Toward Incentive-Based Procedure: Three Approaches for Regulating Scientific Evidence', **69** *Boston University Law Review*, 1989, 487-511.

EPSTEIN, Richard A., 'The Temporal Dimension in Tort Law', **53** *University of Chicago Law Review*, 1986, 1175-1218.

FLANAGAN, Robert J., *Labor Relations and the Litigation Explosion*, Washington D.C., Brookings Institution, 1987, 122 p.

GALANTER, Marc, 'The Day After the Litigation Explosion', **46** *Maryland Law Review*, 1986, 3 ff.

GROSS, Samuel R., 'The American Advantage: The Value of Inefficient Litigation', **85** *Michigan Law Review*, 1987, 734 ff.

HAZARD, Geoffrey C., Jr., 'Authority in the Dock', **69** *Boston University Law Review*, 1989, 469-476.

HUBER, Peter, 'A Comment on 'Toward Incentive-Based Procedure: Three Approaches for Regulating Scientific Evidence' by E. Donald Elliott', **69** *Boston University Law Review*, 1989, 513-516.

KAUFMANN, Patrick J. and STERN, Louis W., 'Relational Exchange Norms, Perceptions of Unfairness, and Retained Hostility in Commercial Litigation', **32** *Journal of Conflict Resolution*, 1988, 534-552.

KENNEDY, Duncan, 'Form and Substance in Private Law Adjudication', **89** *Harvard Law Review*, 1976, 1685-1778. Reprinted in KRONMAN, Anthony T. and POSNER, Richard A. (eds.), *The Economics of Contract Law*, Boston, Little Brown, 1979, 100-107.

McLAUCHLAN, William P., 'An Empirical Study of Civil Procedure: Directed Verdicts and Judgments Notwithstanding Verdict', **2** *Journal of Legal Studies*, 1973, 459-468.

MILLER, Geoffrey P., 'An Economic Analysis of Rule 68', **15** *Journal of Legal Studies*, 1986, 93-125.

MILLER, Geoffrey P., 'Comment: Some Thoughts on the Equilibrium Hypothesis', **69** *Boston University Law Review*, 1989, 561-568.

PASTOR, Santos, 'Informe sobre la litigación, recursos y acceso de los cuidadanos a la Justicie' [Report on Litigation, Courts Inputs and Access to Justice], in MINISTERIO DE JUSTICIA, *Materiales para una reforma Procesal*, Madrid, 1991.

PRIEST, George L., 'Private Litigants and the Court Congestion Problem', **69** *Boston University Law Review*, 1989, 527-559.

PRIEST, George L., 'Private Litigants and the Court Congestion Problem', **69** *Boston University Law Review*, 1989, 527-559.

SAROKIN, H. Lee, 'A Comment on Geoffrey Hazard's *Authority in the Dock*', **69** *Boston University Law Review*, 1989, 477-479.

SCHWARTZ, Murray L. and MITCHELL, D.J.B., 'An Economic Analysis of the Contingent Fee in Personal Injury Litigation', **22** *Stanford Law Review*, 1970, 1125-1162.

SCHWARTZ, Robert L., 'There is no Archbishop of Science - A Comment on Elliott's Toward Incentive-Based Procedure: Three Approaches for Regulating Scientific Evidence', **69** *Boston University Law Review*, 1989, 517-525.

SCHWARZER, William W., 'Rule 11 Revisited', **101** *Harvard Law Review*, 1988, 1013-1025.

SEMINAR : 'Private Alternatives to the Judicial Process', **8(2)** *Journal of Legal Studies*, 1979, 231-418.

SETEAR, John K., 'The Barrister and the Bomb: The Dynamics of Cooperation, Nuclear Deterrence, and Discovery Abuse', **69** *Boston University Law Review*, 1989, 569-633.

SNYDER, Edward A. and HUGHES, James W., 'The English Rule for Allocating Legal Costs: Evidence Confronts Theory', **6** *Journal of Law, Economics, & Organization*, 1990, 345-380.

SPILLER, Pablo T., 'Treble Damages and Optimal Suing Time', **9** *Research in Law and Economics*, 1986, 45-56.

SYMPOSIUM : 'Issues in Civil Procedure: Advancing the Dialogue', **69** *Boston University Law Review*, 1989, 467-779.

WEINSTEIN, Jack B., 'What Discovery Abuse? A Comment on John Setear's The Barrister and the Bomb', **69** *Boston University Law Review*, 1989, 649-657.

WHITE, Lawrence J., 'Litigation and Economic Incentives', **11** *Research in Law and Economics*, 1988, 73-90.

YEAZELL, Stephen C., 'The Salience of Salience: A Comment on Professor Hazard's *Authority in the Dock*', **69** *Boston University Law Review*, 1989, 481-486.

7210 Settlement. Arbitrage.
Disposal of Proceedings without Trial

BEBCHUK, Lucian Ayre, 'Litigation and Settlement under Imperfect Information', **15** *Rand Journal of Economics*, 1984, 404-415.

BEBCHUK, Lucian Arye, 'Suing Solely to Extract a Settlement Offer', **17** *Journal of Legal Studies*, 1988, 437-450.

BLANKENBURG, E. and VERWOERD, J.R.A., 'Vermijden en benutten van civielrechtelijke procedures in Nederland en omringende landen' [The Use and Avoidance of Private Law Proceedings in the Netherlands and Surrounding Countries], *Justitiële Verkenningen*, 1987/2, 20-35.

BLOOM, David E. and CAVANAGH, Christopher L., 'An Analysis of The Selection of Arbitrators', **76** *American Economic Review*, 1986, 408-422.

BOWLES, Roger A., 'Settlement Range and Cost Allocation Rules: A Comment on Avery Katz's Measuring the Demand for Litigation', **3** *Journal of Law, Economics & Organization*, 1987, 177-184.

BRUNET, Edward, 'Questioning the Quality of Alternate Dispute Resolution', **62** *Tulane Law Review*, 1987, 1-23.

BUNDY, Stephen M., 'Commentary: Rational Bargaining and Agency Problems', **75** *Virginia Law Review*, 1989, 335-365.

CARRINGTON, Paul D., 'Adjudication as a Private Good: A Comment', **8** *Journal of Legal Studies*, 1979, 303-317.

CONFERENCE : 'Private Alternatives to the Judicial Process. Proceedings of a seminar sponsored by the Liberty Fund and administered by the Law and Economics Center of the University of Miami School of Law', **8** *Journal of Legal Studies*, 1979, 231-415.

CORNELL, Bradford, 'The Incentive to Sue: An Option-Pricing Approach', **19** *Journal of Legal Studies*, 1990, 173-187.

CRYSTAL, Nathan M., 'An Empirical View of Relational Contracts under Article Two of the Uniform Commercial Code', *Annual Survey of American Law*, 1988, 293-306.

DANZON, Patricia M., 'On "Bargaining Behavior by Defendant Insurers: An Economic Model"', **15** *Geneva Papers on Risk and Insurance*, 1990, 53-54.

DANZON, Patricia M. and LILLARD, Lee A., 'Settlement out of Court: The Disposition of Medical Malpractice Claims', **12** *Journal of Legal Studies*, 1983, 345-377.

DAVIS, Otto A., 'Public and Private Characteristics of a Legal Process: A Comment', **8** *Journal of Legal Studies*, 1979, 285-293.

EISENBERG, Theodore, 'Testing the Selection Effect: A New Theoretical Framework with Empirical Tests', **19** *Journal of Legal Studies*, 1990, 337-358.

FENN, Paul and VLACHONIKOLIS, Ioannis, 'Bargaining Behaviour by Defendant Insurers: An Economic Model', **15** *Geneva Papers on Risk and Insurance*, 1990, 41-52.

FLANAGAN, Robert J., *Labor Relations and the Litigation Explosion*, Washington D.C., Brookings Institution, 1987, 122 p.

FOURNIER, Gary M. and ZUEHLKE, Thomas W., 'Litigation and Settlement: An Empirical Approach', **71** *Review of Economics and Statistics*, 1989, 189-195.

GOLDBERG, Victor P. (ed.), 'Discussion by Seminar Participants', **8** *Journal of Legal Studies*, 1979, 323-398.

HARRIS, Donald and VELJANOVSKI, Cento G., 'Remedies For Breach Under Contract Law: Designing Rules to Facilitate Out-of-Court Settlements', **5** *Law and Policy Quarterly*, 1983, 97-127.

HAUSE, John C., 'Indemnity, Settlement, and Litigation, or I'll Be Suing You', **18** *Journal of Legal Studies*, 1989, 157-179.

HERSCH, Philip L., 'Indemnity, Settlement, and Litigation: Comment and Extension', **19** *Journal of Legal Studies*, 1990, 235-241.

HOLZHAUER, Rudi W. and TEIJL, Rob, 'Geschillenbeslechting als economisch alternatief' [Dispute Settlement as Economic Alternative], in SNIJDERS, H.J., et al. (eds.), *Overheidsrechter gepasseerd*, Arnhem, Gouda Quint, 1988, 489-499.

KAPLOW, Louis, 'Private versus Social Costs in Bringing Suit', **15** *Journal of Legal Studies*, 1986, 371-385.

KATZ, Avery, 'The Effect of Frivolous Lawsuits on the Settlement of Litigation', **10** *International Review of Law and Economics*, 1990, 3-27.

KERKMEESTER, H.O. and MULDER, R.V. de, 'Beslissingstheoretische criteria voor de beslechting van een juridisch geschil door een onafhankelijke derde' [Theoretical Decisionmaking Criteria in Settling a Legal Dispute by a Third Party], in SNIJDERS, H.J. et al. (eds.), *Overheidsrechter gepasseerd*, Arnhem, Gouda Quint, 1988, 501-511.

KING, Allan G., 'The Economics of Structured Settlements', **45** *Texas Bar Journal*, 1982, 301-304.

KLEIN, Christopher C., 'Strategic Sham Litigation: Economic Incentives in the Context of the Case Law', **6** *International Review of Law and Economics*, 1986, 241-253.

KOPPEN, P.J. van, 'Risk-taking in Civil Law Negotiations', **14** *Law and Human Behaviour*, 1990, 151-165.

KOPPEN, P.J. van, RICHTERS, H.W. and TEN KATE, J., *Schikken of procederen:*

Psychologische kanttekeningen bij de economie van civielrechtelijke geschillen [Settlement vs. Trial: Psychological Notes on the Economy of Private Law Disputes], Rapport aangeboden aan de Minister van Justitie, 1989.

LANDES, William M. and POSNER, Richard A., 'Adjudication as a Private Good', **8** *Journal of Legal Studies*, 1979, 235-284.

LANGENFELD, James and ROGOWSKY, Robert A., 'Settlement vs. Litigation in Antitrust Enforcement', in MACKAY, Robert J., MILLER, James C., III and YANDLE, Bruce (eds.), *Public Choice and Regulation: A View form Inside the Federal Trade Commission*, Stanford, Hoover Institution Press, 1987, 205-219.

LANGERWERF, Etienne, 'De sociaal-economische ontwikkeling en de procesvoeringsratio's van de burgerlijke rechtbanken tussen 1950 en 1980' [The Social and Economic Development and the Litigation Ratio's of the Civil Courts Between 1950 en 1980], **40** *Economisch en Sociaal Tijdschrift*, 1986, 87-102.

LINDER, Douglas O., 'Some Doubts Concerning the Selection Hypothesis of George Priest', **37** *University of Kansas Law Review*, 1989, 319-347.

MENELL, Peter S., 'A Note on Private Versus Social Incentives to Sue in a Costly Legal System', **12** *Journal of Legal Studies*, 1983, 41-52.

MEURER, Michael J., 'The Settlement of Patent Litigation', **20** *Rand Journal of Economics*, 1989, 77-91.

MILLER, Geoffrey P., 'Some Agency Problems in Settlement', **16** *Journal of Legal Studies*, 1987, 189-215.

MILLER, Geoffrey P., 'Comment: Some Thoughts on the Equilibrium Hypothesis', **69** *Boston University Law Review*, 1989, 561-568.

PHILLIPS, Jenny and HAWKINS, Keith O., 'Some Economic Aspects of the Settlement Process: A Study of Personal Injury Claims', **39** *Modern Law Review*, 1976, 497-515

PHILLIPS, Jenny, HAWKINS, Keith O. and FLEMING, J., 'Compensation for Personal Injury', **85** *Economic Journal*, 1975, 129-134.

PNG, Ivan P.L., 'Strategic Behavior in Suit, Settlement, and Trial', **14** *Bell Journal of Economics*, 1983, 539-550.

POLINSKY, A. Mitchell and RUBINFELD, Daniel L., 'The Deterrent Effects of Settlements and Trials', **8** *International Review of Law and Economics*, 1988, 109-116.

POLINSKY, A. Mitchell and RUBINFELD, Daniel L., 'A Note on Optimal Public Enforcement with Settlements and Litigation Costs', **12** *Research in Law and Economics*, 1989, 1-8.

PRIEST, George L., 'Reexamining the Selection Hypothesis: Learning from Wittman's Mistakes', **14** *Journal of Legal Studies*, 1985, 215-243.

PRIEST, George L., 'Private Litigants and the Court Congestion Problem', **69** *Boston University Law Review*, 1989, 527-559.

PRIEST, George L. and KLEIN, Benjamin, 'The Selection of Disputes for Litigation', **13** *Journal of Legal Studies*, 1984, 1-55.

RAMSEYER, J. Mark and NAKAZATO, Minoru, 'The Rational Litigant: Settlement Amounts and Verdict Rates in Japan', **18** *Journal of Legal Studies*,

1989, 263-290.

REINGANUM, Jennifer F. and WILDE, Louis L., 'Settlement, Litigation, and the Allocation of Litigation Costs', **17** *Rand Journal of Economics*, 1986, 557-566.

RICHTERS, H.W., *Schikkingen en Proceskansen* [Settlements and Expected Proceeding Outcome], diss. Rotterdam, 1991, 171 p.

ROB, Rafael, 'Pollution Claim Settlements under Private Information', **47** *Journal of Economic Theory*, 1989, 307-333.

ROSE-ACKERMAN, Susan and GEISTFELD, Mark, 'The Divergence between Social and Private Incentives to Sue: A Comment on Shavell, Menell, and Kaplow', **16** *Journal of Legal Studies*, 1987, 483-491.

ROSENBERG, David and SHAVELL, Steven, 'A Model in which Suits are Brought for their Nuisance Value', **5** *International Review of Law and Economics*, 1985, 3-13.

ROSENFIELD, Andrew, 'An Empirical Test of Class-Action Settlement', **5** *Journal of Legal Studies*, 1976, 113-120.

SCHWEIZER, Urs, 'Litigation and Settlement under Two Sided Incomplete Information', **56** *Review of Economic Studies*, 1989, 163-177.

SHAVELL, Steven, 'Suit, Settlement and Trial: A Theoretical Analysis under Alternative Methods for the Allocation of Legal Costs', **11** *Journal of Legal Studies*, 1982, 55-81.

SHAVELL, Steven, 'The Social versus the Private Incentive to Bring Suit in a Costly Legal System', **11** *Journal of Legal Studies*, 1982, 333-339.

SHAVELL, Steven, 'Sharing of Information Prior to Settlement or Litigation', **20** *Rand Journal of Economics*, 1989, 183-195.

SNYDER, Edward A. and HUGHES, James W., 'The English Rule for Allocating Legal Costs: Evidence Confronts Theory', **6** *Journal of Law, Economics, & Organization*, 1990, 345-380.

SOBEL, Joel, 'An Analysis of Discovery Rules', **52(1)** *Law and Contemporary Problems*, 1989, 133-159.

STANLEY, Linda R. and COURSEY, Don L., 'Empirical Evidence on the Selection Hypothesis and the Decision to Litigate or Settle', **19** *Journal of Legal Studies*, 1990, 145-172.

TEN KATE, J., 'Schikkingen tijdens civielrechtelijke geschillen' [Settlements in Private Law Disputes], in *Recht der Werkelijkheid*,'s-Gravenhage, VUGA, 1989, 63-79.

THOMASON, Terry, 'Are Attorneys Paid What They're Worth? Contingent Fees and the Settlement Process', **20** *Journal of Legal Studies*, 1991, 187-223.

TULLOCK, Gordon, 'Negotiated Settlement', in GRAF VON DER SCHULENBURG, J.-Matthias and SKOGH, Göran (eds.), *Law and Economics and The Economics of Legal Regulation*, Dordrecht, Kluwer, 1986, 39-50.

VISCUSI, W. Kip, 'Product Liability Litigation with Risk Aversion', **17** *Journal of Legal Studies*, 1988, 101-121.

WHITE, Jim, 'Evaluating Article 2 of the Uniform Commercial Code: A Preliminary Empirical Expedition', **75** *Michigan Law Review*, 1977, 1262 ff.

WITTMAN, Donald, 'Is the Selection of Case for Trial Biased?', **14** *Journal of Legal Studies*, 1985, 185-214.

WITTMAN, Donald, 'Dispute Resolution, Bargaining, and the Selection of Cases for Trial: A Study of the Generation of Biased and Unbiased Data', **17** *Journal of Legal Studies*, 1988, 313-352.

7220 Class Actions. Representative Proceedings

BERNSTEIN, Roger, 'Judicial Economy and Class Actions', **7** *Journal of Legal Studies*, 1978, 349-370.

BRUNT, Maureen and FELS, Alan, 'Economics of Class Actions: A Research Design', in CRANSTON, Ross and SCHICK, Anne (eds.), *Law and Economics*, Canberra, Australian National University, 1982, 1-9.

BUCKLEY, Colin Hugh, 'Note: A Suggested Remedy for Toxic Injury: Class Actions, Epidemiology, and Economic Efficiency', **26** *William & Mary Law Review*, 1985, 497 ff.

COFFEE, John C., Jr., 'Understanding the Plaintiff's Attorney: the Implications of Economic Theory for Private Enforcement of Law through Class and Derivative Actions', **86** *Columbia Law Review*, 1986, 669-727.

COFFEE, John C., Jr., 'The Regulation of Entrepreneurial Litigation: Balancing Fairness and Efficiency in the Large Class Action', **54** *University of Chicago Law Review*, 1987, 877-937.

DAM, Kenneth W., 'Class Actions: Efficiency, Compensation, Deterrence, and Conflict of Interest', **4** *Journal of Legal Studies*, 1975, 47-73.

DEWEES, Donald N., PRICHARD, J. Robert S. and TREBILCOCK, Michael J., 'An Economic Analysis of Cost and Fee Rules for Class Actions, **10** *Journal of Legal Studies*, 1981, 155-185.

GEORGE, Edward I. and WECKER, William E., 'Estimating Damages in a Class Action Litigation', **3** *Journal of Business and Economic Statistics*, 1985, 132-139.

GOLDBERG, Michael J., 'The Propensity to Sue and the Duty of Fair Representation: A Second Point of View [Tactical Use of the Union's Duty of Fair Representation: An Empirical Analysis]', **41** *Industrial and Labor Relations Review*, 1988, 456-461.

HARTMAN, Raymond S. and DOANE, Michael J., 'The Use of Hedonic Analysis for Certification and Damage Calculations in Class Action Complaints', **3** *Journal of Law, Economics, & Organization*, 1987, 351-372.

JENSEN, Michael C., MECKLING, William H. and HOLDERNESS, Clifford G., 'Analysis of Alternative Standing Doctrines', **6** *International Review of Law and Economics*, 1986, 205-216.

KNIGHT, Thomas R., 'The Propensity to Sue and the Duty of Fair Representation: Reply', **41** *Industrial and Labor Relations Review*, 1988, 461-464.

LYNK, William J., 'The Courts and the Market: An Economic Analysis of Contingent Fees in Class-Action Litigation', **19** *Journal of Legal Studies*, 1990,

247-260.

MACEY, Jonathan R. and MILLER, Geoffrey P., 'The Plaintiffs' Attorney's Role in Class Action and Derivative Litigation: Economic Analysis and Recommendations', **58** *University of Chicago Law Review*, 1991, 1-118.

McGOVERN, Francis E., 'Resolving Mature Mass Tort Litigation', **69** *Boston University Law Review*, 1989, 659-694.

ROSENBERG, David, 'Comment: Of End Games and Openings in Mass Tort Cases: Lessons from a Special Master', **69** *Boston University Law Review*, 1989, 695-730.

ROSENFIELD, Andrew, 'An Empirical Test of Class-Action Settlement', **5** *Journal of Legal Studies*, 1976, 113-120.

7300 Criminal Procedure

ADELSTEIN, Richard P., 'The Plea Bargain in Theory: A Behavioral Model of the Negotiated Guilty Plea', **44** *Southern Economic Journal*, 1978, 488-503.

ADELSTEIN, Richard P., 'Institutional Function and Evolution in the Criminal Process', **76** *Northwestern University Law Review*, 1981, 1-99.

ADELSTEIN, Richard P., 'The Plea Bargain in England and America: A Comparitive Institutional View', in BURROWS, Paul and VELJANOVSKI, Cento G. (eds.), *The Economic Appraoch to Law*, London, Butterworths, 1981, 226-252.

ALSCHULER, Albert W., 'Implementing the Criminal Defendant's Right to Trial: Alternatives to the Plea Bargaining System', **50** *University of Chicago Law Review*, 1983, 931-1050.

BOWLES, Roger A., 'Juries, Incentives and Self-selection', *British Journal of Criminology*, 1980, 368-376.

CASPER, Gerhard and ZEISEL, Hans, 'Lay Judges in the German Criminal Courts', **1** *Journal of Legal Studies*, 1972, 135-191.

CHU, C.Y. Cyrus, 'Note: An Economic Analysis of the Criminal Proceedings in Civil-Law Countries', **11** *International Review of Law and Economics*, 1991, 111-116.

EASTERBROOK, Frank H., 'Criminal Procedure as a Market System', **12** *Journal of Legal Studies*, 1983, 289-332.

ELDER, Harold W., 'Trials and Settlements in the Criminal Courts: An Empirical Analysis of Dispositions and Sentencing', **18** *Journal of Legal Studies*, 1989, 191-208.

FORST, Brian and BROSI, Kathleen, 'A Theoretical and Empirical Analysis of the Prosecutor', **6** *Journal of Legal Studies*, 1977, 177-191.

GENTRY, James Theodore, 'The Panopticon Revisited: The Problem of Monitoring Private Prisons', **96** *Yale Law Journal*, 1986, 353-375.

GROSSMAN, Gene M. and KATZ, Michael L., 'Plea Bargaining and Social Welfare', **73** *American Economic Review*, 1983, 749-757.

LANDES, William M., 'Legality and Reality: Some Evidence on Criminal Procedure', **3** *Journal of Legal Studies*, 1974, 287-337.

LEVIN, Martin A., 'Delay in Five Criminal Courts', **4** *Journal of Legal Studies*, 1975, 83-131.

MICELI, Thomas J., 'Optimal Prosecution of Defendants Whose Guilt is Uncertain', **6** *Journal of Law, Economics, & Organization*, 1990, 189-201.

MICELI, Thomas J., 'Optimal Criminal Procedure: Fairness and Deterrence', **11** *International Review of Law and Economics*, 1991, 3-10.

NOAM, Eli M., 'A Cost-benefit Model of Criminal Courts', **3** *Research in Law and Economics*, 1981, 173-183.

PALMER, J., 'An Economic Analysis of the Right to a Jury Trial', **4** *International Review of Law and Economics*, 1984, 29-53.

PASTOR, Santos, 'Economìa de la Justicia (I) y (II)' [Economics of the Judicature], *Revista de Economìa Pública*, 1990, Nr. 5 and 6.

PASTOR, Santos, 'Informe sobre la litigación, recursos y acceso de los cuidadanos a la Justicie' [Report on Litigation, Courts Inputs and Access to Justice], in MINISTERIO DE JUSTICIA, *Materiales para una reforma Procesal*, Madrid, 1991.

POLINSKY, A. Mitchell and SHAVELL, Steven, 'The Optimal Tradeoff between the Probability and Magnitude of Fines', **69** *American Economic Review*, 1979, 880-891.

POLINSKY, A. Mitchell and SHAVELL, Steven, 'The Optimal Use of Fines and Imprisonment', **24** *Journal of Public Economics*, 1984, 89-99.

POSNER, Richard A., 'Excessive Sanctions for Governmental Misconduct in Criminal Cases' (transcript), **57** *Washington Law Review*, 1982, 635-646.

REINGANUM, Jennifer F., 'Plea Bargaining and Prosecutorial Discretion', **78** *American Economic Review*, 1988, 713-728.

RHODES, William M., 'A Study of Sentencing in the Hennepin County and Ramsey County District Courts, **6** *Journal of Legal Studies*, 1977, 333-353.

SCHULHOFER, Stephen J., 'Criminal Justice Discretion as a Regulatory System', **17** *Journal of Legal Studies*, 1988, 43-82.

STEENHUIS, D.W., 'Strafrechtelijk optreden: stapje terug en een sprong voorwaarts' [Criminal Policy: A Step Backwards and a Jump Ahead], in *Delikt en Delinkwent*, Arnhem, Gouda Quint, 1984/5, 1984/6.

STUNTZ, William J., 'Warrants and Fourth Amendment Remedies', **77** *Virginia Law Review*, 1991, 881-943.

TIFFANY, Lawrence P., AVICHAI, Yakov and PETERS, Geoffrey W., 'A Statistical Analysis of Sentencing in Federal Courts: Defendants Convicted After Trial, 1967-1968', **4** *Journal of Legal Studies*, 1975, 369-390.

VELJANOVSKI, Cento G., 'The Economics of Criminal Law and Procedure', **23** *Coexistence*, 1986, 137-153.

WITTMAN, Donald, 'Two Views of Procedure', **3** *Journal of Legal Studies*, 1974, 249-256.

7400 Judicial Administration

BARNARD, David, *The Civil Court in Action*, Butterworths, London, 1977, 350 p.

BOWLES, Roger A., 'Juries, Incentives and Self-Selection', **20** *British Journal of Criminology*, 1980, 368-376.

CASPER, Gerhard and POSNER, Richard A., 'A Study of the Supreme Court's Caseload', **3** *Journal of Legal Studies*, 1974, 339-375.

CASPER, Gerhard and POSNER, Richard A., *The Workload of the Supreme Court*, Chicago, American Bar Foundation, 1976.

CASPER, Gerhard and ZEISEL, Hans, 'Lay Judges in the German Criminal Courts', **1** *Journal of Legal Studies*, 1972, 135-191.

COHEN, Mark A., 'Explaining Judicial Behavior or What's "Unconstitutional" about the Sentencing Commission?', **7** *Journal of Law, Economics, & Organization*, 1991, 183-199.

EBNER, P., *Reducing Pretrial Delay... A Look at What State and Local Courts Are Doing to Break the Logjam*, Santa Monica, Rand Institute of Civil Justice, 1982.

FEELEY, Malcolm, *Court Reform on Trial: Why Simple Solutions Fail*, New York, Basic Books, 1983, 251 p.

FRIEDMAN, David, 'Private Creation and Enforcement of Law: A Historical Case', **8** *Journal of Legal Studies*, 1979, 399-415.

GELY, Rafael and SPILLER, Pablo T., 'A Rational Choice Theory of Supreme Court Statutory Decisions with Applications to the *State Farm* and *Grove City* Cases', **6** *Journal of Law, Economics, & Organization*, 1990, 263-300.

GILLESPIE, Robert W., 'The Production of Court Services: An Analysis of Scale Effects and Other Factors', **5** *Journal of Legal Studies*, 1976, 243-265.

GOLDMAN, Jerry, HOOPER, Richard L. and MAHAFFEY, Judy, 'Caseload Forecasting Models for Federal District Courts', **5** *Journal of Legal Studies*, 1976, 201-242.

GREENBERG, Paul E. and HALEY, James A., 'The Role of the Compensation Structure in Enhancing Judicial Quality', **15** *Journal of Legal Studies*, 1986, 417-426.

GRIFFITHS, J., 'De rechtbank als fietsenfabriek' [The Court as Bicycle Manufacturer], **66** *Nederlands Juristenblad*, 1991, 129-130, 445.

KLEVORICK, Alvin K., 'Jury Composition: An Economic Approach', in SIEGAN, Bernard H. (ed.), *The Interactions of Economics and the Law*, Lexington, Lexington Books, 1977.

KLEVORICK, Alvin K. and ROTHSCHILD, Michael, 'A Model of the Jury Decision Process', **8** *Journal of Legal Studies*, 1979, 141-164.

KORNHAUSER, Lewis A. and SAGER, Lawrence G., 'Unpacking the Court', **96** *Yale Law Journal*, 1986, 82-117.

LANDES, William M., 'An Economic Analysis of the Courts', **14** *Journal of Law and Economics*, 1971, 61-107.

LEVIN, Martin A., 'Delay in Five Criminal Courts', **4** *Journal of Legal Studies*,

1975, 83-131.

MILLER, Arthur R., 'The Adversary System: Dinosaur or Phoenix', **69** *Minnesota Law Review*, 1984, 1-37.

MILLER, Geoffrey P., 'Comment: Some Thoughts on the Equilibrium Hypothesis', **69** *Boston University Law Review*, 1989, 561-568.

NOAM, Eli M., 'A Cost-benefit Model of Criminal Courts', **3** *Research in Law and Economics*, 1981, 173-183.

PASTOR, Santos, 'Economìa de la Justicia (I) y (II)' [Economics of the Judicature], *Revista de Economìa Pública*, 1990, Nr. 5 and 6.

PASTOR, Santos, 'Economìa de la Justicia en España' [The Spanish Courts and the Economic Analysis], *Revista de Economìa*, 1990, 4.

PASTOR, Santos, 'Informe sobre la litigación, recursos y acceso de los cuidadanos a la Justicie' [Report on Litigation, Courts Inputs and Access to Justice], in MINISTERIO DE JUSTICIA, *Materiales para una reforma Procesal*, Madrid, 1991.

POSNER, Richard A., 'An Economic Approach to Legal Procedure and Judicial Administration', **2** *Journal of Legal Studies*, 1973, 399-458.

POSNER, Richard A., 'Will the Federal Courts of Appeals Survive until 1984? An Essay on Delegation and Specialization of the Judicial Function', **56** *Southern California Law Review*, 1983, 761-791.

POSNER, Richard A., 'The Meaning of Judicial Self-Restraint', **59** *Indiana Law Journal*, 1984, 1-24.

POSNER, Richard A., *The Federal Courts: Crisis and Reform*, Harvard University Press, Cambridge, 1985, 365 p.

POSNER, Richard A., 'Coping with the Caseload: A Comment on Magistrates and Masters', **137** *University of Pennsylvania Law Review*, 1989, 2215-2218.

PRIEST, George L., 'Private Litigants and the Court Congestion Problem', **69** *Boston University Law Review*, 1989, 527-559.

SCHEINER, Alan Howard, 'Judicial Assessment of Punitive Damages, the Seventh Amendment, and the Politics of Jury Power', **91** *Columbia Law Review*, 1991, 142-226.

SHANLEY, Michael G., 'The Distribution of Posttrial Adjustments to Jury Awards', **20** *Journal of Legal Studies*, 1991, 463-481.

SOCIAAL CULTUREEL PLANBUREAU, *Doelmatig Rechtspreken* [Efficient Administration of Justice], S.C.P., Cahier no. 88, 's-Gravenhage, Staatsdrukkerij, 1990, 74 p.

STRAUSSMAN, Jeffrey D., 'Courts and Public Purse Strings: Have Portraits of Budgeting Missed Something?', **4** *Public Administration Review*, 1986, 315-351.

8000 CRIMINAL LAW, ECONOMICS OF CRIME & LAW ENFORCEMENT

Michael Faure

ADELSTEIN, Richard P., 'Informational Paradox and the Pricing of Crime: Capital Sentencing Standards in Economic Perspective', **70** *Journal of Criminal Law and Criminology*, 1979, 281-298.

ADELSTEIN, Richard P., 'Institutional Function and Evolution in the Criminal Process', **76** *Northwestern University Law Review*, 1981, 1-99.

AKINS, Nancy, 'New Direction in Sacred Lands Claims: Lyng v. Northwest Indian Cemetery Protective Association', **29** *Natural Resources Journal*, 1989, 593-605.

ALTROGGE, Phyllis and SHUGHART, William F., 'The Regressive Nature of Civil Penalties', **4** *International Review of Law and Economics*, 1984, 55-66.

ANDERSON, Lee G. and LEE, Dwight R., 'Optimal Governing Instrument, Operation Level, and Enforcement in Natural Resource Regulation: The Case of the Fishery', **68** *American Journal of Agricultural Economics*, 1986, 678-690.

ANDERSON, R.W ., *The Economics of Crime*, London, Macmillan, 1976, 71 p.

ANDREANO, Ralph and SIEGFRIED, John J. (eds.), *The Economics of Crime*, Cambridge, Schenkman, 1980, 426 p.

ANDVIG, Jens Christian, 'Korrupsjon i Utviklingsland' [Corruption in Developing Countries] **23** *Nordisk Tidsskrift för Politisk Ekonomi*, 1989, 51-70.

ARLACCHI, Pino, 'Effects of the New Anti-Mafia Law on the Proceeds of Crime and on the Italian Economy', in ALESSANDRINI, Sergio and DALLAGO, Bruno (eds.), *The Unofficial Economy: Consequences and Perspectives in Different Economic Systems*, Aldershot, Gower, 1987, 247-255.

ASCH, Peter and LEVY, David T., 'The Drinking Age and Traffic Safety', **11(2)** *Regulation*, 1987, 48-52.

ASCH, Peter and LEVY, David T., 'Does the Minimum Drinking Age Affect Traffic Fatalities?', **6** *Journal of Policy Analysis and Management*, 1987, 180-192.

ATKINSON, Scott E., SANDLER, Todd and TSCHIRHART, John, 'Terrorism in a Bargaining Framework', **30** *Journal of Law and Economics*, 1987, 1-21.

AVIO, Kenneth L., 'Clemency in Economic and Retributive Models of Punishment', **7** *International Review of Law and Economics*, 1987, 79-88.

AVIO, Kenneth L., 'Measurement Errors and Capital Punishment', **20** *Applied Economics*, 1988, 1253-1262.

AVIO, Kenneth L., 'Retribution, Wealth Maximization, and Capital Punishment: A Law and Economics Approach', **19** *Stetson Law Review*, 1990, 373-409.

BACKHAUS, Jürgen G., 'Defending Organized Crime? A Note', **8** *Journal of Legal Studies*, 1979, 623-631.

BADFORD, R.S., 'Going to the Island: A Legal and Economic Analysis of the Medieval Icelandic Duel', **67** *Southern California Law Review*, 1989, 615-644.

BALDRY, Jonathan C., 'Positive Economic Analysis of Criminal Behaviour', in CEUJLER, A.J. (ed.), *Economic Policies and Social Goals*, London, Martin

Robertson, 1974.

BALDRY, Jonathan C., 'Crimes Punishable by Imprisonment: A Note', **9** *Journal of Legal Studies*, 1980, 617-619.

BANFIELD, Edward C., 'Corruption as a Feature of Governemental Organization', **18** *Journal of Law and Economics*, 1975, 587-605.

BARNETT, Randy E. and HAGEL, John III, *Assessing the Criminal. Restitution, Retribution, and the Legal Process*, Cambridge, Ballinger, 1977, 403 p.

BARTEL, Ann P., 'An Analysis of Firm Demand for Protection Against Crime', **4** *Journal of Legal Studies*, 1975, 443-478.

BARTHOLD, Thomas A. and HOCHMAN, Harold M., 'Addiction as Extreme Seeking', **26** *Economic Inquiry*, 1988, 89-106.

BARTLING, Hartwig, 'Zur Ökonomie der Kriminalitätsbekämpfung. Eine Integration der Resozialisierung in die Kriminalökonomie' [On the Economics of Criminal Policy: An Integration of Resocializing in Criminal Economics], *Zeitschrift für Wirtschafts- und Sozialwissenschaften*, 1974, 313-333.

BAUDENBACHER, Carl, *Rechtsverwirklichung als ökonomisches Problem? Zur Überlastung der Zivilgerichte* [Enforcement of Law as an Economic Problem? On the Overload of the Civil Courts], Zurich, Schulthess, 1985.

BECCARIA-BONESARA, C., *An Essay on Crime and Punishment* (1764), New York, Oceania Pub., 1958.

BECKER, Gary S., 'Irrational Behavior and Economic Theory', **70** *Journal of Political Economy*, 1962, 1-13.

BECKER, Gary S., 'Crime and Punishment: An Economic Approach', **76** *Journal of Political Economy*, 1968, 169-217.

BECKER, Gary S. and LANDES, William M. (eds.), *Essays in the Economics of Crime and Punishment*, New York, Columbia University Press, 1974, 268 p.

BECKER, Gary S. and STIGLER, George J., 'Law Enforcement, Malfeasance, and Compensation of Enforcers', **3** *Journal of Legal Studies*, 1974, 1-18.

BENSON, Bruce L., 'Corruption in Law Enforcement: One Consequence of "The Tragedy of the Commons" Arising with Public Allocation Processes', **8** *International Review of Law and Economics*, 1988, 73-84.

BENSON, Bruce L. and BADEN, John, 'The Political Economy of Governmental Corruption: The Logic of Underground Governement', **14** *Journal of Legal Studies*, 1985, 391-410.

BERGSTROM, T., 'On the Economics of Crime and Confiscation', **4(3)** *Journal of Economic Perspectives*, 1990, 171-178.

BERON, Kurt J., 'Applying the Economic Model of Crime to Child Support Enforcement: A Theoretical and Empirical Analysis', **70** *Review of Economics and Statistics*, 1988, 382-390.

BESANKO, David A. and SPULBER, Daniel F., 'Delegated Law Enforcement and Noncooperative Behavior', **5** *Journal of Law, Economics, & Organization*, 1989, 25-52.

BLADES, Derek W., 'Crime: What Should Be Recorded in the National Accounts; and What Difference Would It Make', in GAERTNER, Wulf and WENIG, Alois (ed.), *The Economics of the Shadow Economy: Proceedings of the International*

Conference on the Economics of the Shadow Economy Held at the University of Bielefeld, West Germany, October 10-14, 1983, New York, Springer, 1985, 45-58.

BLOCK, Michael K. and LIND, Robert C., 'Crime and Punishment Reconsidered', **4** *Journal of Legal Studies*, 1975, 241-247.

BLOCK, Michael K. and LIND, Robert C., 'An Economic Analysis of Crimes Punishable by Imprisonment', **4** *Journal of Legal Studies*, 1975, 479-492.

BLUMSTEIN, A., 'Cost-Effectiviness Analysis in the Allocation of Police Resources', in KENDALL, M.G. (ed.) *Cost-benefit Analysis*, London, English Universities Press, 1971.

BLUMSTEIN, J. et al. (eds.), *Deterrence and Incapacitation: Estimating the Effects of Criminal Sanctions on Crime Rates*, Washington, National Academy of Science, 1978.

BONE, J., 'On Substituting a Socially Costless Penalty for Costly Crime', **5** *International Review of Law and Economics*, 1985, 239-246.

BOWLES, Roger A., 'Juries, Incentives and Self-selection', *British Journal of Criminology*, 1980, 368-376.

BOWLES, Roger A., *Law and the Economy*, Oxford, Martin Robertson, 1982, 54-86.

BRADEN, John B. et al., 'A Displacement Model of Regulatory Compliance and Costs', **63** *Land Economics*, 1987, 323-336.

BRAITHWAITE, John, 'Consumers as Victims of Corporate Crime', in WHEELWRIGHT, Ted (ed.), *Consumers, Transnational Corporations and Development*, Sydney, University of Sydney, Transnational Corporations Research Project, 1986, 331-342.

BROTMAN, B.A. and FOX, P., 'The Impact of Economic Conditions on the Incidence of Arson: Comment', **55** *Journal of Risk and Insurance*, 1988, 751-754.

BUCK, Andrew J., et al., 'The Deterrence Hypothesis Revisited', **13** *Regional Science and Urban Economics*, 1983, 471-486.

BUTLER, Richard V. and HUSTON, John H., 'Airline Service to Non hub Airports Ten Years after Deregulation', **26** *Logistics and Transportation Review*, 1990, 3-16.

BYAM, John I., 'The Economic Inefficiency of Corporate Criminal Liability', **73** *Journal of Criminal Law and Criminology*, 1982, 582-603.

CADOT, Olivier, 'Corruption as a Gamble', **33** *Journal of Public Economics*, 1987, 223-244.

CAMERON, S., 'Victim Compensation Does Not Increase the Supply of Crime', **16** *Journal of Economic Studies*, 1989, 52-59.

CAMERON, S., 'On the Welfare Economics of Capital Punishment', **28** *Australian Economic Papers*, 1989, 253-266.

CAMERON, Samuel, 'An Empirical Study of Malicious False Fire Alarm Calls', **6** *International Review of Law and Economics*, 1986, 33-44.

CAMERON, Samuel, 'A Disaggregated Study of Police Clear Up Rates for England and Wales', **16(4)** *Journal of Behavioral Economics*, 1987, 1-18.

CAMERON, Samuel, 'Substitution between Offence Categories in the Supply of Property Crime: Some New Evidence', **14(11)** *International Journal of Social Economics*, 1987, 48-60.

CAMERON, Samuel, 'The Economics of Crime Deterrence: A Survey of Theory and Evidence', **41** *Kyklos*, 1988, 301-323.

CAMERON, Samuel, 'Determinants of the Prison Population: An Empirical Analysis', **16(8)** *International Journal of Social Economics*, 1989, 17-25.

CAMERON, Samuel, 'Police Cost Function Estimates for England and Wales', **21** *Applied Economics*, 1989, 1279-289.

CARLIN, Paul and SANDY, Robert, 'The Value of Time and the Effect of Fines on Child Car Safety Seat Usage', **22** *Applied Economics*, 1990, 463-476.

CARR-HILL, R.A. and STERN, H.H., *Crime, The Police and Criminal Statistics*, London, Academic Press, 1979.

CHALMERS, J.A. and SHELTON, R.B., 'An Economic Analysis of Riot Participation', **13** *Economic Inquiry*, 1975, 322-336.

CHRESSANTHIS, George A., 'Capital Punishment and the Deterrent Effect Revisited: Recent Time Series Econometric Evidence', **18(2)** *Journal of Behavioral Economics*, 1989, 81-97.

CLARF, Stevens H., FREEMAN, Jean L. and KOCH, Gary G., 'Bail Risk: A Multivariate Analysis', **5** *Journal of Legal Studies*, 1976, 341-385.

CLONINGER, Dale O., 'Capital Punishment and Deterrence: A Revision', **16(4)** *Journal of Behavioral Economics*, 1987, 55-57.

CLONINGER, Dale O., 'Lethal Police Response as a Crime Deterrent: 57-City Study Suggests a Decrease in Certain Crimes', **50** *American Journal of Economics and Sociology*, 1991, 59-69.

CLOTFELTER, Charles T., 'Public Services, Private Substitutes, and the Demand for Protection Against Crime', **67** *American Economic Review*, 1977, 867-877.

COATE, Douglas and GROSSMAN, Michael, 'Effects of Alcoholic Beverage Prices and Legal Drinking Ages on Youth Alcohol Use', **31** *Journal of Law and Economics*, 1988, 145-171.

COCHRAN, Philip L. and NIGH, Douglas, 'Illegal Corporate Behavior and the Question of Moral Agency: An Empirical Examination', in FREDERICK, William C. (ed.), *Empirical Studies of Business Ethics and Values. Vol. 9*, Greenwich, JAI Press, 1987, 73-91.

COELEN, Stephen P. and McINTYRE, Robert J., 'An Econometric Model of Pronatalist and Abortion Policies', **94** *Journal of Political Economy*, 1986, 1077-1101.

COFFEE, John C., Jr., 'Corporate Crime and Punishment: A Non-Chicago View of the Economics of Criminal Sanctions', **17** *American Criminal Law Review*, 1980, 419-476.

COFFEE, John C., Jr., 'Understanding the Plaintiff's Attorney: the Implications of Economic Theory for Private Enforcement of Law through Class and Derivative Actions', **86** *Columbia Law Review*, 1986, 669-727.

COHEN, Mark A., 'Optimal Enforcement Strategy to Prevent Oil Spills: An Application of a Principal-Agent Model with Moral Hazard', **30** *Journal of Law* *and Economics*, 1987, 23-51.

COHEN, Mark A., 'A Note on the Cost of Crime to Victims', **27** *Urban Studies*, 1990, 139-146.

COLEMAN, Jules L., 'Crime, Kickers and Transaction Structures', in PENNOCK, J. Ronald and CHAPMAN, John W., *Nomos XXVII: Criminal Justice*, 1984.

COOK, Philip J., 'Punishment and Crime: A Critique of Current findings Concerning the Preventative Effects of Punishment', **41(1)** *Law and Contemporary Problems*, 1977, 164-209.

COOK, Philip J., 'The Relationship Between Victim Resistance and Injury in Noncommercial Robbery', **15** *Journal of Legal Studies*, 1986, 405-416.

COOK, Philip J. and TAUCHEN, George, 'The Effect of Minimum Drinking Age Legislation on Youthful Auto Fatalities, 1970-1977', **13** *Journal of Legal Studies*, 1984, 169-190.

COOK, Philip J. and ZARKIN, Gary A., 'Crime and the Business Cycle', **14** *Journal of Legal Studies*, 1985, 115-128.

COOTER, Robert D., 'Prices and Sanctions', **84** *Columbia Law Review*, 1984, 1523-1560.

CORMAN, Hopz and JOYCE, Theodore, 'Urban Crime Control: Violent Crimes in New York City', **71** *Social Science Quarterly*, 1990, 567-584.

CORMAN, Hope and JOYCE, Theodore and LOVITCH, Norman, 'Crime, Deterrence and the Business Cycle in New York City: A VAR Approach', **69** *Review of Economics and Statistics*, 1987, 695-700.

COVER, James Peery and THISTLE, Paul D., 'Time Series, Homicide, and the Deterrent Effect of Capital Punishment', **54** *Southern Economic Journal*, 1988, 615-622.

CRAIG, Steven G., 'The Deterrent Impact of Police: An Examination of a Locally Provided Public Service', **21** *Journal of Urban Economics*, 1987, 298-311.

CRAIG, Steven G. and HEIKKILA, Eric J., 'Urban Safety in Vancouver: Allocation and Production of a Congestible Public Good', **22** *Canadian Journal of Economics*, 1989, 867-884.

CRASWELL, Richard and CALFEE, John E., 'Deterrence and Uncertain Legal Standards', **2** *Journal of Law, Economics, & Organization*, 1986, 279-303.

CURRAN, Christopher and DWYER, Gerald, 'The Effect of the Double Nickel Speed Limit on Death Rates', in FAURE, Michael and VAN DEN BERGH, Roger (eds.), *Essays in Law and Economics. Corporations, Accident Prevention and Compensation for Losses*, Antwerpen, Maklu, 1989, 117-156.

DANIEL, S., 'Social Science and Death Penalty Cases', **1** *Law and Policy Quarterly*, 1979, 336-372.

DAU-SCHMIDT, Kenneth G., 'An Economic Analysis of the Criminal Law as a Preference-Shaping Policy', *Duke Law Journal*, 1990, 1-38.

DAVIS, Michael L., 'Time and Punishment: An Intertemporal Model of Crime', **96** *Journal of Political Economy*, 1988, 383-390.

DE ALBUQUERQUE, Klaus, 'A Comparative Analysis of Violent Crime in the Caribbean', **33(3)** *Social and Economic Studies*, 1984, 93-142.

DEUTSCH, Joseph, HAKIM, Simon and WEINBLATT, J., 'A Micro Model of the Criminal's Location Choice', **22** *Journal of Urban Economics*, 1987, 198-208.

DEUTSCH, Joseph and HAKIM, Simon and SPIEGEL, Uriel, 'The Effects of Criminal Experience on the Incidence of Crime', **49** *American Journal of Economics and Sociology*, 1990, 1-5.

DEY, Harendra Kanti, 'The Genesis and Spread of Economic Corruption: A Microtheoretic Interpretation', **17** *World Development*, 1989, 503-511.

DEYAK, Timothy A. and SMITH, V. Kerry, 'The Economic Value of Statute Reform: The Case of Liberalised Abortion', **84** *Journal of Political Economy*, 1976, 83-99.

DICKENS, William T., 'Crime and Punishment Again: The Economic Approach with a Psychological Twist', **30** *Journal of Public Economics*, 1986, 97-107.

DICKENS, William T. et al., 'Employee Crime and the Monitoring Puzzle', **7** *Journal of Labor Economics*, July 1989, 331-347.

DIJK, J.J.M. van, 'Financieel economische aspecten van misdaad en misdaadbestrijding' [Financial Economic Aspects of Crime and Prevention], **69** *Economisch-Statistische Berichten*, 1984, 1248-1252.

DIJK, J.J.M. van, 'Over de wenselijkheid van overheidsinterventies op de markt van recht en orde. Preadvies voor de 35e jaarvergadering van de Nederlandse Orde van Advocaten' [On the Desirability of Governmental Intervention on the Market for Law and Order], *Advocatenblad*, Tjeenk Willink, 1987, 343-352.

DIJK, J.J.M. van and ROELL, A., 'Criminaliteit in tal en last' [Criminality], *Justitiële verkenningen*, Arnhem, Gouda Quint, 1988, Nr. 2, 7-33.

DIVER, Colin S., 'A Theory of Regulatory Enforcement', **28** *Public Policy*, 1980, 257-299.

DOORENBOS, D.R. and ROORDING, J.F.L., 'Rechtseconomie en strafrecht: een rechtseconomische analyse van de bestrijding van misbruik van voorwetenschap bij de handel in effecten' [Law-and-economics and Criminal Law: A Law-and-economics Analysis of Insider Trading in Securities], **39(10)** *Ars Aequi*, 1990, 733-742.

DOSSER, D., 'Notes for Standards for Distribution of a Free Governmental Service: Crime Prevention', **19** *Public Finance*, 1964, 375-401.

DUBIN, Jeffrey A., GRAETZ, Michael J. and WILDE, Louis L., 'Are We a Nation of Tax Cheaters? New Econometric Evidence on Tax Compliance', **77** *American Economic Review. Papers and Proceedings*, 1987, 240-245.

DU BOIS, W.E.B., 'The Negro Criminal', **16(1-2)** *Review of Black Political Economy*, 1987, 17-31.

DUMOUCHEL, William, WILLIAMS, Allan F. and ZADOR, Paul, 'Raising the Alcohol Purchase Age: It's Effects on Fatal Motor Vehicle Crashes in Twenty-six States', **16** *Journal of Legal Studies*, 1987, 249-266.

EASTERBROOK, Frank H., 'Criminal Procedure as a Market System', **12** *Journal of Legal Studies*, 1983, 289-332.

EHRLICH, Isaac, 'The Deterrent Effect of Criminal Law Enforcement', **1** *Journal of Legal Studies*, 1972, 259-276.

EHRLICH, Isaac, 'Participation in Illegitimate Activities: A Theoretical and

Empirical Investigation', **80** *Journal of Political Economy*, 1972, 521-565.

EHRLICH, Isaac, 'The Deterrent Effect of Capital Punishment: A Question of Life and Death', **65** *American Economic Review*, 1975, 397-417.

EHRLICH, Isaac, 'The Economic Approach to Crime - A Preliminary Assessment' in MESSINGER, S.L. and BRITTINER, E. (eds.), *Criminological Review Yearbook, vol. 1* Beverley Hills, Sage Publications, 1979.

EHRLICH, Isaac, 'On the Usefulness of Controlling Individuals: An Economic Analysis of Rehabilitation, Incapacitation and Deterrence', **71** *American Economic Review*, 1981, 307-332.

EHRLICH, Isaac, 'The Market For Offences and the Public Enforcement of Laws: An Equilibrium Analysis', **21** *British Journal of Psychology*, 1982.

EHRLICH, Isaac, 'The Optimum Enforcement of Laws and the Concept of Justice: A Positive Analysis', **2** *International Review of Law and Economics*, 1982, 3-27.

EHRLICH, Isaac, 'On Positive Methodology, Ethics, and Polemics in Deterrence Research', **22** *British Journal of Criminology*, 1982, 124-139.

EHRLICH, Isaac and GIBBONS, Joel C., 'On the Measurement of the Deterrent Effect of Capital Punishment and the Theory of Deterrence', **6** *Journal of Legal Studies*, 1977, 35-50.

EHRLICH, Isaac and RANDALL, Mark, 'Fear of Deterrence: A Critical Evaluation of the "Report of the Panel on Research on Deterrent and Incapacitative Effects"', **6** *Journal of Legal Studies*, 1977, 293-316.

EHRLICH, Isaac and RANDALL, Mark, 'Deterrence and Economics: A Perspective on Theory and Evidence', in YINGER, J.M. and CUTLER, S.J. (eds.), *Major Social Issues*, New York, 1978, 172-188.

ELDER, Harold W., 'Property Rights Structures and Criminal Courts: An Analysis of State Criminal Courts', **7** *International Review of Law and Economics*, 1987, 21-32.

ELZINGA, Kenneth G. and BREIT, William, *The Antitrust Penalties: A Study in Law and Economics*, New Haven, Yale University Press, 1976, 160 p.

EPPLE, Dennis and VISSCHER, Michael, 'Environmental Pollution: Modelling Occurrence, Detection, and Deterrence', **27** *Journal of Law and Economics*, 1984, 29-60.

EPSTEIN, Richard A., 'Intentional Harms', **4** *Journal of Legal Studies*, 1975, 391-442.

FADAEI TEHRANI, Reza, 'The Costs of Crime: Unemployment and Poverty', **16(12)** *International Journal of Social Economics*, 1989, 34-243.

FAITH, Roger L. and TOLLISON, Robert D., 'The Pricing of Surrogate Crime and Law Enforcement', **12** *Journal of Legal Studies*, 1983, 401-411.

FAURE, Michael G., 'De verzekering van geldboeten bij zeewaterverontreiniging door olie' [The Insurance of Fines with Respect to the Oil-Pollution of Seawater], in *Grensoverschrijdend strafrecht. Opstellen*, Arnhem, Gouda Quint, 1990, 203-221.

FEINSTEIN, Jonathan S., 'Detection Controlled Estimation', **33** *Journal of Law & Economics*, 1990, 233-276.

FENN, Paul and VELJANOVSKI, Cento G., 'A Positive Economic Theory of

Regulatory Enforcement', **98** *Economic Journal*, 1988, 1055-1070.

FISCHER, Charles C., 'Forensic Economics and the Wrongful Death of a Household Producer: Current Practices, Methodological Biases and Alternative Solutions of Losses', **46** *American Journal of Economics and Sociology*, 1987, 219-228.

FISHER, Sethard, 'Economic Development and Crime: Two May Be Associated as an Adaptation to Industrialism in Social Revolution', **46** *American Journal of Economics and Sociology*, 1987, 17-34.

FLEISHER, Arthur A. III et al., 'Crime or Punishment? Enforcement of the NCAA Football Cartel', **10** *Journal of Economic Behavior and Organization*, 1988, 433-451.

FLEISHER, B., *The Economics of Delinquency*, New York, Quadrangle, 1966.

FLETCHER, George P., 'A Transaction Cost Theory of Crime?', **85** *Columbia Law Review*, 1985, 921-930.

FORST, Brian and BROSI, Kathleen, 'A Theoretical and Empirical Analysis of the Prosecutor', **6** *Journal of Legal Studies*, 1977, 177-191.

FRANK, Jürgen, 'Ökonomische Modelle der Abschreckung' [Economic Models of Deterrence], *Kriminologisches Journal*, 1987, Heft 1, 55-65.

FRANKEN, Hans, 'Economische analyse van het strafrecht' [Economic Analysis of Criminal Law], *Bij deze stand van zaken. Opstellen aangeboden aan A.L. Melai*, Arnhem, Gouda Quint, 1983, 117-131.

FRANKEN, Hans, 'Voorkomen is beter dan genezen' [Prevention is Better Than Cure], *RMThemis*, 1987, 469-471.

FRANKEN, Hans, 'Rechtseconomie en strafrecht' [Law-and-Economics and Criminal Law], in *Rechtseconomie en Recht*, Zwolle, Tjeenk Willink, 1991, 163-179.

FREEMAN, Richard B., 'The Relation of Criminal Activity to Black Youth Employment', **16(1-2)** *Review of Black Political Economy*, 1987, 99-107.

FREY, Bruno S., 'Fighting Political Terrorism by Refusing Recognition', *Journal of Public Policy*, 1988, 179-188.

FREY, Bruno S. and BUHOFER, Heinz, 'Prisoners and Property Rights', **31** *Journal of Law and Economics*, 1988, 19-46.

FRIEDMAN, David, 'Private Creation and Enforcement of Law: A Historical Case', **8** *Journal of Legal Studies*, 1979, 399-415.

FRIEDMAN, David D., 'Reflections on Optimal Punishment or: Should the Rich Pay Higher Fines ?', **3** *Research in Law and Economics*, 1981, 185-205.

FRIEDMAN, David D., 'Impossibility, Subjective Probability, and Punishments for Attempts', **20** *Journal of Legal Studies*, 1991, 179-186.

FRIEDMAN, Joseph, HAKIM, Simon and SPIEGEL, Uriel, 'The Effects of Community Size on the Mix of Private and Public Use of Security Services', **22** *Journal of Urban Economics*, 1987, 230-241.

FRIEDMAN, Joseph, HAKIM, Simon and SPIEGEL, Uriel, 'The Difference between Short and Long Run Effects of Police Outlays on Crime: Policing Deters Criminals Initially, but Later They May', **48** *American Journal of Economics and Sociology*, 1989, 177-191.

FURLONG, William J., 'A General Equilibrium Model of Crime Commission and

Prevention', **34** *Journal of Public Economics*, 1987, 87-103.

GALASI, Péter and KERTESI, Gábor, 'Korrupció és tulajdon, Tanulmány a tulajdonjogok közgazdaságtanának köreböl' [Corruption and Property], **4** *Közgazdasági Szemle*, 1990, 389-425.

GANDER, James P., 'Highway Speed and Uncertainty of Enforcement: The Traveling Salesman(or Trucker) Case', **22** *Logistics and Transportation Review*, 1986, 43-55.

GEYIKDAGI, Yasar M. and GEYIKDAGI, Necla V., 'The Economics of Street Crime', **33** *Rivista Internazionale di Scienze Economiche e Commerciali*, 1986, 813-818.

GHALI, Moheb, et al., 'Economic Factors and the Composition of Juvenile Property Crimes', **15** *Applied Economics*, 1983, 267-281.

GIBBONS, T., 'The Utility of Economic Analysis of Crime', **2** *International Review of Law and Economics*, 1982, 173-191.

GIBBS, J., 'Crime, Punishment and Deterrence', **48** *Southwestern Social Science Quarterly*, 1968, 515-530.

GIBBS, J., *Crime, Punishment and Deterrence*, New York, Elsevier, 1975.

GIERTZ, J. Fred and NARDULLI, Peter F., 'Prison Overcrowding', **46** *Public Choice*, 1985, 71-78.

GOEL, Rajeev K. and RICH, Daniel P., 'On the Economic Incentives for Taking Bribes', **61** *Public Choice*, 1989, 269-275.

GOOD, David H. and PIROG GOOD, Maureen A., 'Employment, Crime, and Race', **5(4)** *Contemporary Policy Issue* and, 1987, 91-104.

GOOD, David H. and PIROG GOOD, Maureen A., 'A Simultaneous Probit Model of Crime and Employment for Black and White Teenage Males', **16(1-2)** *Review of Black Political Economy*, 1987, 109-127.

GRAETZ, Michael J., REINGANUM, Jennifer F. and WILDE, Louis L., 'The Tax Compliance Game: Toward and Interactive Theory of Law Enforcement', **2** *Journal of Law, Economics, & Organization*, 1986, 1-32.

GRAPENDAAL, M., 'De paradox en het dilemma. Effecten van politieoptreden op de Zeedijk' [Paradox and Dilemma. Effects of Police Action at the Zeedijk], **39(10)** *Ars Aequi*, 1990, 714-720.

GRAVES, Philip E., LEE, Dwight R. and SEXTON, Robert L., 'Statutes versus Enforcement: The Case of the Optimal Speed Limit', **79** *American Economic Review*, 1989, 932-936.

GRAVES, Philip E., LEE, Dwight R. and SEXTON, Robert L., 'A Note on Drinking, Driving and Enforcement Costs', **56** *Southern Economic Journal*, 1990, 793-796.

GRAY, Tara and OLSON, Kent W., 'A Cost-Benefit Analysis of the Sentencing Decision for Burglars', **70** *Social Science Quarterly*, 1989, 708-722.

GREENBERG, Stephanie W. and ROHE, William M., 'Informal Social Control and Crime Prevention in Modern Urban Neighborhoods', in TAYLOR, Ralph B. (ed.), *Urban Neighborhoods: Research and Policy*, New York, Praeger, 1986, 79-118.

GRIESON, Ronald E. and SINGH, Nirvikar, 'Regulating Externalities through

Testing', **41** *Journal of Public Economics*, 1990, 369-387.

GROGGER, Jeffrey, 'The Deterrent Effect of Capital Punishment: An Analysis of Daily Homicide Counts', **85** *Journal of the American Statistical Association*, 1990, 295-303.

GYAPONG, Anthony O. and GYIMAH BREMPONG, Kwabena, 'Factor Substitution, Price Elasticity of Factor Demand and Returns toScale in Police Production: Evidence from Michigan', **54** *Southern Economic Journal*, 1988, 863-878.

GYIMAH BREMPONG, Kwabena, 'Empirical Models of Criminal Behavior: How Significant a Factor Is Race?', **15** *Review of Black Political Economy*, 1986, 27-43.

GYIMAH BREMPONG, Kwabena, 'Economies of Scale in Municipal Police Departments: The Case of Florida', **69** *Review of Economics and Statistics*, 1987, 352-356.

GYIMAH BREMPONG, Kwabena, 'Functional Substitution among Crimes: Some Evidence', **15** *Eastern Economic Journal*, 1989, 129-140.

HANNAN, Timothy H., 'Bank Robberies and Bank Security Precautions', **11** *Journal of Legal Studies*, 1982, 83-92.

HARRIS, Milton and RAVIV, Artur, 'Some Results on Incentive Contracts with Applications to Education and Employment, Health Insurance, and Law Enforcement', **68** *American Economic Review*, 1978, 20-30.

HASHIMOTO, Masanori, 'The Minimum Wage Law and Youth Crimes: Time-Series Evidence', **30** *Journal of Law and Economics*, 1987, 443-464.

HAWKINS, Keith O., *Environment and Enforcement*, Oxford, Oxford University Press, 1982, 253 p.

HEERTJE, A. and WABEKE, J.W., 'Het dreigende faillissement van justitie en politie' [The Near Bankrupcty of Prosecution and Police], **74** *Economisch-Statistische Berichten*, 1989, 1152-1155.

HEINEKE, J.M. (ed.), *Economic Models of Criminal Behaviour*, Amsterdam, North Holland, 1978, 391 p.

HELLAMAN, D.A., *The Economics of Crime*, New York, St. Martins Press, 1980.

HELLMAN, Daryl A. and ALPER, Neil O., *Economics of Crime: Theory and Practice*, Needham Heights, Simon and Schuster, Ginn Press, 1990, 226 p.

HERSCH, Philip L. and NETTER, Jeffrey M., 'The Effects of Crime Rates on Time Served in Prison: An Empirical Analysis', **39** *Public Finance*, 1984, 314-320.

HERSCH, Philip L. and NETTER, Jeffrey M., 'State Prohibition of Alcohol: An Application of Diffusion Analysis to Regulation', **12** *Research in Law and Economics*, 1989, 55-70.

HERSHBARGER, R.A. and MILLER, R.K., 'The Impact of Economic Conditions on the Incidence of Arson: A Reply', **55** *Journal of Risk and Insurance*, 1988, 755-757.

HILL, John K. and PEARCE, James E., 'The Incidence of Sanctions against Employers of Illegal Aliens', **98** *Journal of Political Economy*, 1990, 28-44.

HIRSCH, Werner Z. and RUFOLO, Anthony M., 'Economic Effects of Residence Laws on Municipal Police', **17** *Journal of Urban Economics*, 1985, 335-348.

HOLLER, P., 'Probleme der utilitaristischen Strafrechtfertigung' [Problems of Utilitarian Criminal Law Making], *Zeitschrift für die Gesamte Strafrechtswissenschaften*, 1979, 45-95.

HOOGENBOOM, B., 'Rechtseconomie en particuliere beveiliging: "Policing for profits" als voorloper van strafrechtelijke hervormingen' [Law-and-Economics and Private Security: "Policing for Profit" as Precursor of Criminal Reform], **39(10)** *Ars Aequi*, 1990, 721-732.

HOVENKAMP, Herbert J., 'Antitrust's Protected Classes', **88** *Michigan Law Review*, 1989, 1-48.

HOWSEN, Roy M. and JARRELL, Stephen B., 'Some Determinants of Property Crime: Economic Factors Influence Criminal Behavior but Cannot Completely Explain the Syndrome', **46** *American Journal of Economics and Sociology*, 1987, 445-457.

ICHNIOWSKI, Casey and PRESTON, Anne, 'The Persistence of Organized Crime in New York City Construction: An Economic Perspective', **42** *Industrial and Labor Relations Review*, 1989, 549-565.

IM, Eric Iksoon, CAULEY, Jon and SANDLER, Todd, 'Cycles and Substitutions in Terrorist Activities: A Spectral Approach', **40** *Kyklos*, 1987, 238-255.

ISAAC, Ehrlich and BROWER, George D., 'On the Issue of Causality in the Economic Model of Crime and Law Enforcement: Some Theoretical Considerations and Experimental Evidence', **77** *American Economic Review*, 1987, 99-106.

JARRELL, S.B. and HOWSEN, R.M., 'Transient Crowding and Crime: The More 'Strangers' in an Area, the More Crime Except for Murder, Assault and Rape', **49** *American Journal of Economics and Sociology*, 1990, 483-494.

JENNINGS, William P., Jr., 'A Note on the Economics of Organized Crime', **10** *Eastern Economic Journal*, 1984, 315-321.

JOHNSON, Burce M., *Taking Care of Business: The Economics of Crime by Heroin Abusers*, Lexington, Lexington Books, 1985, 278 p.

JONES, Carol Adaire, 'Standard Setting with Incomplete Enforcement Reviewed', **8** *Journal of Policy Analysis and Management*, 1989, 72-87.

KADISH, 'Some Observations on the Use of Criminal Sanctions in Enforcing Economic Regulations', *University of Chicago Law Review*, 1963, 423 ff.

KAPLAN, L.J. and KESSLER, P. (eds.), *An Economic Analysis of Crime: Selected Readings*, Springfield, Charles Thomas, 1976.

KAPLOW, Louis, 'Optimal Deterrence, Uninformed Individuals, and Acquiring Information about Whether Acts Are Subject to Sanctions', **6** *Journal of Law, Economics, & Organization*, 1990, 93-128.

KAPLOW, Louis, 'A Note on the Optimal Use of Nonmonetary Sanctions', **42** *Journal of Public Economics*, 1990, 245-247.

KAYE, David and AICKIN, Mikel, 'A Comment on Causal Apportionment', **13** *Journal of Legal Studies*, 1984, 191-208.

KENAN, Donald C. and RUBIN, Paul H., 'Criminal Violations and Civil Violations', **11** *Journal of Legal Studies*, 1982, 365-377.

KLEIMAN, Mark A.R., *Marijuana: Costs of Abuse, Costs of Control*, Westport,

Greenwood Press, 1989, 197 p.

KLEVORICK, Alvin K., 'On the Economic Theory of Crime', in PENNOCK, J. Roland and CHAPMAN, John W. (eds.), *Nomos XXVII: Criminal Justice*, 1985.

KLEVORICK, Alvin K., 'Legal Theory and the Economic Analysis of Torts and Crimes', **85** *Columbia Law Review*, 1985, 905-920.

KLITGAARD, Robert, *Controlling Corruption*, Berkeley, University of California Press, 1988, 220 p.

KNOEBER, Charles R., 'Penalties and Compensation for Auto Accidents', **7** *Journal of Legal Studies*, 1978, 263-278.

KOMESAR, Neil K., 'A Theoretical and Empirical Study of Victims of Crime', **2** *Journal of Legal Studies*, 1973, 301-321.

KRAAKMAN, Reinier H., 'Gatekeepers: The Anatomy of a Third-Party Enforcement Strategy', **2** *Journal of Law, Economics, & Organization*, 1986, 53-104.

LANDES, William M., 'The Bail System: An Economic Approach', **2** *Journal of Legal Studies*, 1973, 79-105.

LANDES, William M., 'An Economic Study of U.S. Aircraft Hijacking, 1961-1976', **21** *Journal of Law and Economics*, 1978, 1-31.

LANG, Kevin and BELL, Duran, 'An Economic Model of the Intake Disposition of Juvenile Offenders', **32** *Journal of Public Economics*, 1987, 79-99.

LANGBEIN, John H., 'The Historical Origins of the Sanction of Imprisonment for Serious Crime', **5** *Journal of Legal Studies*, 1976, 35-60.

LAVE, Charles A., 'Speeding, Coordination, and the 55 MPH Limit', **75** *American Economic Review*, 1985, 1159-1164.

LAVE, Charles A., 'Speeding, Coordination, and the 55 MPH Limit: Reply', **79** *American Economic Review*, 1989, 926-931.

LAYSON, Stephen K., 'Homicide and Deterrence: Another View of the Canadian Time Series Evidence', **16** *Canadian Journal of Economics*, 1983, 52-73.

LAYSON, Stephen K., 'Homicide and Deterrence: A Reexamination of the United States Time Series Evidence', **52** *Southern Economic Journal*, 1985, 68-89.

LAYTON, Allan P., 'The Impact of Increased Penalties on Australian Drink/Driving Behaviour', **19** *Logistics and Transportation Review*, 1983, 261-266.

LEE, Dwight R., 'On Substituting a Socially Costless Penalty for Costly Detection', **3** *International Review of Law and Economics*, 1983, 179-185.

LEE, Dwight R., 'Policing Cost, Evasion Cost, and the Optimal Speed Limit', **52** *Southern Economic Journal*, 1985, 34-45.

LEMPERT, Richard O., 'Desert and Deterrence: An Assessment of the Moral Basis for Capital Punishment', **79** *Michigan Law Review*, 1981, 1177-1231.

LEVINE, Daniel, STOLOFF, Peter and SPRUILL, Nancy, 'Public Drug Treatment and Addict Crime', **5** *Journal of Legal Studies*, 1976, 435-462.

LEVY, David T. and ASCH, Peter, 'Speeding, Coordination, and the 55 MPH Limit: Comment', **79** *American Economic Review*, 1989, 913-915.

LEWIN, Jeff L. and TRUMBULL, William N., 'The Social Value of Crime?', **10**

International Review of Law and Economics, 1990, 271-284.

LIEBERMANN, Yehoshua and SYRQUIN, M., 'On the Use and Abuse of Rights: An Economic View', **4** *Journal of Economic Behavior and Organization*, 1983, 25-40.

LINDER, Stephen H. and MCBRIDE, Mark E., 'Enforcement Costs and Regulatory Reform: The Agency and Firm Response', **11** *Journal of Environmental Economics and Management*, 1984, 327-346.

LINDNER, G.L., 'Arreststraf of geldboete' [Detention or Fine], diss. Rijks Universiteit Leiden, 1985.

LIU, Yih Wu and BEE, Richard H., 'Modeling Criminal Activity in an Area in Economic Decline: Local Economic Conditions Are a Major Factor in Local Property Crimes', **42** *American Journal of Economics and Sociology*, 1983, 385-392.

LOTT, John R., Jr., 'Should the Wealthy Be Able to "Buy Justice"?', **95** *Journal of Political Economy*, 1987, 1307-1316.

LOTT, John R., Jr., 'Juvenile Delinquency and Education: A Comparison of Public and Private Provision', **7** *International Review of Law and Economics*, 1987, 163-175.

LOTT, John R., Jr., 'Getting Tough on White-Collar Criminals', **13(1)** *Regulation*, 1990, 18-19.

LOTT, John R., Jr., 'A Transaction-Costs Explanation for Why the Poor Are More Likely to Commit Crime', **19** *Journal of Legal Studies*, 1990, 243-245.

LOTT, John R., Jr., 'The Effect of Conviction on the Legitimate Income of Criminals', **34** *Economic Letters*, 1990, 381-385.

LOTT, John R., Jr. and ROBERTS, Russell D., 'Why Comply: One-sided Enforcement of Price Controls and Victimless Crime Laws', **18** *Journal of Legal Studies*, 1989, 403-414.

LUI, Francis T., 'A Dynamic Model of Corruption Deterrence', **31** *Journal of Public Economics*, 1986, 215-236.

LUKSETICH, William and WHITE, Michael, *Crime and Public Policy: An Economic Approach*, 1982.

MACRAE, John, 'Underdevelopment and the Economics of Corruption: A Game Theory Approach', **10** *World Development*, 1982, 677-687.

MAGADDINO, Joseph P. and MEDOFF, Marshall H., 'A Reanalysis of Deterrence and Gun Control', **10(2)** *Atlantic Economic Journal*, 1982, 50-53.

MALES, Mike A., 'The Minimum Purchase Age for Alcohol and Young-Driver Fatal Crashes: A Long-Term View', **15** *Journal of Legal Studies*, 1986, 181-211.

MALIK, Arun S., 'Avoidance, Screening and Optimum Enforcement', **21** *Rand Journal of Economics*, 1990, 341-353.

MARTIN, Donald L., 'The Economics of Jury Conscription', **80** *Journal of Political Economy*, 1972, 680-702.

MATHIESON, Donald and PASSELL, Peter, 'Homicide and Robbery in New York City: An Economic Model', **5** *Journal of Legal Studies*, 1976, 83-98.

McALEER, Michael and VEALL, Michael R., 'How Fragile Are Fragile Inferences?

A Re-evaluation of the Deterrent Effect of Capital Punishment', **71** *Review of Economics and Statistics*, 1989, 99-106.

McCORMICK, Robert E. and TOLLISON, Robert D., 'Crime on the Court', **92** *Journal of Political Economy*, 1984, 223-235.

McCORMICK, Robert E. and TOLLISON, Robert D., 'Crime and Income Distribution in a Basketball Economy', **6** *International Review of Law and Economics*, 1986, 115-124.

McPHETERS, Lee R. and STRANGE, W.B. (eds.), *The Economics of Crime and Law Enforcement*, Springfield, Charles R. Thomas, 1976.

McPHETERS, Lee R., MANN, Robert and SCHLAGENHAUF, Don, 'Economic Response to a Crime Deterrence Program: Mandatory Sentencing for Robbery with a Firearm', **22** *Economic Inquiry*, 1984, 550-570.

MEESTER, G. and WESEMANN, P., 'Kosten-baten analyse en strafrecht' [Cost Benefit Analysis and Criminal Law], *Portret van de juridische faculteit Rotterdam 12 1/2*, Deventer, Kluwer, 1976, 217-228.

MEINBERG, Volker, 'Empirische Erkentnissen zum Vollzug des Umweltstrafrechts' [Empirical Insights Concerning the Enforcement of Environmental Criminal Law], **100** *Zeitschrift für die gesamte Strafrechtswissenschaft*, 1988, 112-157.

MELAI, A.L., 'De straf en het gezichtspunt van de econometristen' [Punishment and the Econometrist Perspective], in *Speculum Langemeyer*, Zwolle, Tjeenk Willink, 1973, 315-331.

MELOSSI, Dario, 'Political Business Cycles and Imprisonment Rates in Italy: Report on a Work in Progress', **16(1-2)** *Review of Black Political Economy*, 1987, 211-218.

METZGER, Michael R., 'Corporate Criminal Liability for Defective Products: Policies, Problems, and Prospects', **73** *Georgetown Law Journal*, 1984, 1-88.

MICHAELS, Robert J., 'Noncriminal Deviance and Mental Hospitalization: Economic Theory and Evidence, **5** *Journal of Legal Studies*, 1976, 387-433.

MICHAELS, Robert J., 'Addiction, Compulsion, and the Technology of Consumption', **26** *Economic Inquiry*, 1988, 75-288.

MIKESELL, John and PIROG GOOD, Maureen A., 'State Lotteries and Crime: The Regressive Revenue Producer Is Linked with a Crime Rate Higher by 3 Percent', **49** *American Journal of Economics and Sociology*, 1990, 7-19.

MIRON, Jeffrey A. and ZWIEBEL, Jeffrey, 'Alcohol Consumption During Prohibition', **81** *American Economic Review. Papers and Proceedings*, 1991, 242-247.

MOERLAND, H. and RODERMOND, J.G., 'Ontwikkelingen in het afschrikkingsonderzoek'[Developments in Deterrence Research], *Panopticon*, 1987, 59-75.

MOERLAND, H. and RODERMOND, J.G., 'Winkeldiefstal, een (te) riskante zaak? Onderzoek naar een mogelijke samenhang tussen het plegen van winkeldiefstal en de verwachte gevolgen' [Theft in Shops, a (too) Risky Business? Investigation of a Possible Relationship between Theft in Shops and the Expected Consequences], *Panopticon*, 1987, 335-349.

MORGAN, Rod and BOWLES, Roger A., 'Fines: The Case for Review', *Criminal*

Law Review, 1981, 203-214.

MORRIS, John Richard, 'Enforcement of Property Rights and the Provision of Public Good Attributes', **3(2)** *Information Economics and Policy*, 1988, 91-108.

MORRIS, Norval, *The Future of Imprisonment*, Chicago, University of Chicago Press, 1974, 144 p.

MORRIS, Norval and HAWKINS, Gordon, *Letter to the President on Crime Control*, Chicago, University of Chicago Press, 1974, 144 p.

MYERS, Samuel L., Jr., 'The Economics of Bail Jumping', **10** *Journal of Legal Studies*, 1981, 381-396.

MYERS, Samuel L., Jr., 'Do Better Wages Reduce Crime? A Research Note', **43** *American Journal of Economics and Sociology*, 1984, 191-195.

MYERS, Samuel L., Jr., 'Race and Punishment: Directions for Economic Research', **74** *American Economic Review*, 1984, 288-292.

NARDULLI, Peter F., 'The Misalignment of Penal Responsibilities and State Prison Crises: Costs, Consequences, and Corrective Actions', *University of Illinois Law Review*, 1984, 365 ff.

NASH, John, 'To Make the Punishment Fit the Crime: The Theory and Statistical Estimation of a Multi-Period Optimal Deterrence Model', **11** *International Review of Law and Economics*, 1991, 101-109.

NEDERLANDS ECONOMISCH INSTITUUT, *Naar een economische benadering van criminaliteit en veiligheidszorg* [Towards an Economic Approach of Delinquency and Security Provision], Rotterdam, Nederlands Economisch Instituut, 1989.

NENTJES, Andries, 'De welvaartseffecten van het strafrecht' [Welfare Effects of Criminal Law], *Justitiële Verkenningen*, Arnhem, Gouda Quint, 1988, n. 2, 34-52.

NENTJES, Andries, 'Enforcement of Environmental Regulation', in WEIGEL, Wolfgang (ed.), *Economic Analysis of Law - A Collection of Applications*, Vienna, Österreichischer Wirtschaftsverlag, 1991, 54-65.

NICKERSON, Gary W., 'Analytical Problems in Explaining Criminal Behavior: Neoclassical and Radical Economic Theories and an Alternative Formulation', **15(4)** *Review of Radical Political Economy*, 1983, 1-23.

NORTON, Desmond A. G., 'On the Economic Theory of Smuggling', **55** *Economica*, 1988, 107-118.

OPP, Karl Dieter, 'The Economics of Crime and the Sociology of Deviant Behaviour: A Theoretical Confrontation of Basic Propositions', **42** *Kyklos*, 1989, 405-430.

OTTO, Hans-Jochen, *Generalprävention und externe Verhaltenskontrolle, Wandel vom sociologischen zum ökonomischen Paradigma in der Nordamerikanischen Kriminologie?* [General Prevention and External Control of Behavior, Evolution from Sociological to Economic Paradigm in the North American Criminology?], Freiburg, Max-Planck-Institut für ausländisches internationales Strafrecht, 1982, 323 p.

OZENNE, Tim, 'The Economics of Bank Robbery', **3** *Journal of Legal Studies*, 1974, 19-51.

PACKER, Herbert L., *The Limits of the Criminal Sanction*, Stanford, Stanford University Press, 1968, 366 p.

PALMER, J., 'Economic Analysis of the Deterrent Effect of Punishment: A Review', **14** *Journal of Research in Crime and Delinquency*, 1977, 4-21.

PASHIGIAN, B. Peter, 'On the Control of Crime and Bribery', **4** *Journal of Legal Studies*, 1975, 311-326.

PASTOR, Santos, 'Derecho penal, política criminal y economía: un intento de generalizaci6n' [Criminal Law, Criminal Policy and Economics], in *Homenaje al Professor Jiménez de Asúa*, Revista de la Facultad de Derecho de la UCM, 1986, n. 11.

PASTOR, Santos, 'Heroína y Política Criminal: Un enfoque alternativo' [Heroin and Criminal Policy: An Alternative Approach], in *La problemática de la droga en España; análisis y propuestas político-criminales*, Madrid, IUC y Edersa, 1986.

PASTOR, Santos, 'Liberty versus Security: Should Drugs Be Illegal?', in ROLSTON, B. and TOMLINSON, M. (eds.), *Civil Rights, Public Opinion and the State*, Belfast, European Group for the Study of Deviance and Social Control, 1987.

PASTOR, Santos, 'Economìa de la Justicia (I) y (II)' [Economics of the Judicature], *Revista de Economìa Pública*, 1990, Nr. 5 and 6.

PASTOR, Santos, 'Informe sobre la litigaci6n, recursos y acceso de los cuidadanos a la Justicie' [Report on Litigation, Courts Inputs and Access to Justice], in MINISTERIO DE JUSTICIA, *Materiales para una reforma Procesal*, Madrid, 1991.

PAYNE, M. and FURNHAM, A., 'Perceptions of Crime and Delinquency in Barbados', **39** *Social and Economic Studies*, 1990, 135-150.

PHILLIPS, D., 'The Deterrent Effect', *American Journal of Sociology*, 1980-81, 139-148.

PHILLIPS, Llad, 'The Criminal Justice System: Its Technology and Inefficiencies', **10** *Journal of Legal Studies*, 1981, 363-380.

PHILLIPS, Llad, 'Race and Crime: Comments', **16** *Review of Black Political Economy*, 1987, 219-221.

PHILLIPS, Llad and VOTEY, Harold L., Jr., 'An Economic Analysis', **63** *Journal of Criminal Law, Criminology and Police Science*, 1972, 330-342.

PHILLIPS, Llad and VOTEY, Harold L., Jr., 'Crime Control in California', **4** *Journal of Legal Studies*, 1975, 327-349.

PHILLIPS, Llad and VOTEY, Harold L., Jr., 'Black Women, Economic Disadvantage, and Incentives to Crime', **74** *American Economic Review*, 1984, 293-297.

PHILLIPS, Llad and VOTEY, Harold L., Jr., 'Crimes by Youth: Deterrence and Moral Compliance with the Law', **5(4)** *Contemporary Policy Issues*, 1987, 73-90.

PHILLIPS, Llad and VOTEY, Harold L., Jr., 'Rational Choice Models of Crimes by Youth', **16** *Review of Black Political Economy*, 1987, 129-187.

PHILLIPS, Llad, VOTEY, Harold L., Jr. and HOWELL, John, 'Handguns and Homocide: Minimizing Losses and the Costs of Control', **5** *Journal of Legal*

Studies, 1976, 463-478.

PNG, Ivan P.L., 'Optimal Subsidies and Damages in the Presence of Judicial Error', **6** *International Review of Law and Economics*, 1986, 101-105.

POLINSKY, A. Mitchell, 'Private versus Public Enforcement of Fines', **9** *Journal of Legal Studies*, 1980, 105-127.

POLINSKY, A. Mitchell and RUBINFELD, Daniel L., 'A Note on Optimal Public Enforcement with Settlements and Litigation Costs', **12** *Research in Law and Economics*, 1989, 1-8.

POLINSKY, A. Mitchell and SHAVELL, Steven, 'The Optimal Tradeoff between the Probability and Magnitude of Fines', **69** *American Economic Review*, 1979, 880-891.

POLINSKY, A. Mitchell and SHAVELL, Steven, 'The Optimal Use of Fines and Imprisonment', **24** *Journal of Public Economics*, 1984, 89-99.

POLINSKY, A. Mitchell and SHAVELL, Steven, 'Legal Error, Litigation, and the Incentive to Obey the Law', **5** *Journal of Law, Economics, and Organization*, 1989, 99-108.

POLINSKY, A. Mitchell and SHAVELL, Steven, 'A Note on Optimal Fines when Wealth Varies Among Individuals', **81** *American Economic Review*, 1991, 618-621.

POSNER, Richard A., 'Retribution and Related Concepts of Punishment', **9** *Journal of Legal Studies*, 1980, 71-92.

POSNER, Richard A., 'Optimal Sentences for White-Collar Criminals', **17** *American Criminal Law Review*, 1980, 409-418.

POSNER, Richard A., 'Excessive Sanctions for Governmental Misconduct in Criminal Cases' (transcript), **57** *Washington Law Review*, 1982, 635-646.

POSNER, Richard A., 'An Economic Theory of the Criminal Law', **85** *Columbia Law Review*, 1985, 1193-1231.

PRINZINGER, Joseph M., 'The Effect of the Repeal of Helmet Use Laws on Motorcycle Fatalities', **10(2)** *Atlantic Economic Journal*, 1982, 36-39.

PRISCHING, Manfred, 'Sozioökonomische Bedingungen der Kriminalität. Über empirische Divergenzen und theoretische Kontroversen' [Socio-economic Conditions of Criminality. On Empirical Divergencies and Theoretical Controversies], **65** *Monatsschrift für Kriminologie und Strafrechtsreform*, 1982, Heft 3, 163-176.

PYLE, David J., *The Economics of Crime and Law Enforcement: A Selected Bibliography*, SSRC Public Sector Study Group, Bibliography Series No. 1, 1979, 216 p. (Supplement 1980)

PYLE, David J., 'Crime Rates and Police Expenditure', in MAUNDER, P. (ed.), *Case Studies in the Economics of Social Issues*, Heinemann, London, 1979.

PYLE, David J., *The Economics of Crime and Law Enforcement*, London, MacMillan, 1983, 216 p.

RADFORD, R.S., 'Going to the Island: A Legal and Economic Analysis of the Medieval Icelandic Duel', **62** *Southern California Law Review*, 1989, 615 ff.

RAMSEYER, J. Mark, 'Indentured Prostitution in Imperial Japan: Credible Commitments in the Commercial Sex Industry', **7** *Journal of Law, Economics,*

& Organization, 1991, 89-116.

REDER, M.W., 'Citizen Rights and the Cost of Law Enforcement', **3** *Journal of Legal Studies*, 1974, 435-455.

REINGANUM, Jennifer F., 'Plea Bargaining and Prosecutorial Discretion', **78** *American Economic Review*, 1988, 713-728.

REUTER, Peter, *Disorganized Crime: The Economics of the Visible Hand*, London, MIT Press, 1983, 233 p.

RHODES, William M., 'The Economics of Criminal Courts: A Theoretical and Empirical Investigation', **5** *Journal of Legal Studies*, 1976, 311-340.

RIZZO, Mario J., 'The Cost of Crime to Victims: An Empirical Analysis', **8** *Journal of Legal Studies*, 1979, 177-205.

ROBERT, Philippe and GODEFROY, Thierry, *Le coût du crime ou l'économie poursuivant le crime* [The Cost of Crime or Economics Prosecuting Crime], Genève, Masson, 1977, 225 p.

ROGERS, A.J., *The Economics of Crime*, Illinois, Dryden Press, 1973.

ROSS, H. Laurence, 'Deterrence Regained: The Cheshire Constabulary's "Breathalyser Blitz"', **6** *Journal of Legal Studies*, 1977, 241-249.

ROSS, H. Laurence and BLUMENTHAL, Murray, 'Sanctions for the Drinking Driver: An Experimental Study', **3** *Journal of Legal Studies*, 1974, 53-61.

ROSS, H. Laurence and LaFREE, Gary D., 'Deterrence in Criminology and Social Policy', in SMELSER, Neil J. and GERSTEIN, Dean R. (eds.), *Behavioral and Social Science: Fifty Years of Discovery*, Washington D.C., National Academy Press, 1986, 129-152.

ROSS, Laurence H., 'The Scandinavian Myth: The Effectiveness of Drinking-and-Driving Legislating in Sweden and Norway', **4** *Journal of Legal Studies*, 1975, 285-310.

ROTTENBERG, Simon (ed.), *The Economics of Crime and Punishment*, Washington, American Enterprise Institute for Public Policy Research, 1973, 232p.

ROVENS, R. and PRINSEN, P.J., 'Extra politie-inzet en rijden onder invloed' [More Police and Drunken Driving], *WODC reeks*, no. 52, 's-Gravenhage, Staatsuitgeverij, 1984.

RUBIN, Paul H., 'Costs and Benefits of a Duty to Rescue', **6** *International Review of Law and Economics*, 1986, 273-276.

RUBIN, Paul H. and ZWIRH Robert, 'The Economics of Civil RICO', **20** *U.C. Davis Law Review*, 1987, 883-917.

RYAN, Patrick J., 'Strange Bedfellows: Corporate Fiduciaries and the General Law Compliance Obligation in Section 2.01(a) of the American Law Institute's *Principle of Corporate Governance*', **66** *Washington Law Review*, 1991, 413-502.

SAFFER, Henry and CHALOUPKA, Frank, 'Breath Testing and Highway Fatality Rates', **21** *Applied Economics*, 1989, 901-912.

SAFFER, Henry and GROSSMAN, Michael, 'Beer Taxes, the Legal Drinking Age, and Youth Motor Vehicle Fatalities', **16** *Journal of Legal Studies*, 1987, 351-374.

SAFFER, Henry and GROSSMAN, Michael, 'Drinking Age Laws and Highway Mortality Rates: Cause and Effect', **25** *Economic Inquiry*, 1987, 403-417.

SANDELIN, Bo and SKOGH, Göran, 'Property Crimes and the Police: An Empirical Analysis of Swedish Data', **88** *Scandinavian Journal of Economics*, 1986, 547-561.

SANSARRICQ, Frank, 'Crime and Economic Development in a Small, Open Economy', **27** *Keio Economic Studies*, 1990, 41-49.

SCHELLING, Thomas C., 'Economic Analysis of Organized Crime', in KAPLAN, L.J. and KESSLER, D. (eds.), *An Economic Analysis of Crime: Selected Readings*, Springfield, Charles Thomas, 1976.

SCHMIDT, Peter and WITTE, Ann D., *An Economic Analysis of Crime and Justice: Theory, Methods, and Applications*, New York, Academic Press, 1984, 416 p.

SCHMIDT, Peter and WITTE, Ann D., 'Predicting Criminal Recidivism Using 'Split Population' Survival Time Models', **40** *Journal of Econometrics*, 1989, 141-159.

SCHNEIDER, A.L. and ERVIN, L., 'Specific Deterrence, Rational Choice, and Decision Heuristics: Applications in Juvenile Justice', **71** *Social Science Quarterly*, 1990, 585-601.

SCHÖCH, Heinz, 'Empirische Grundlagen der Generalprävention' [Empirical Foundations of General Prevention], in VOGLER, T. (ed.), *Festschrift für Hans-Heinrich Jescheck zum 70. Geburtstag*, vol. II, Berlin, Duncker & Humblot, 1985, 1081-1105.

SCHULHOFER, Stephen J., 'Criminal Justice Discretion as a Regulatory System', **17** *Journal of Legal Studies*, 1988, 43-82.

SCHWARTZ, Warren F., BAXTER, Keith and RYAN, David, 'The Duel: Can These Gentlemen Be Acting Efficiently ?', **13** *Journal of Legal Studies*, 1984, 321-335.

SEIDMAN, Louis Michael, 'Soldiers, Martyrs, and Criminals: Utilitarian Theory and the Problem of Crime Control', **94** *Yale Law Journal*, 1984, 315-349.

SHAVELL, Steven, 'Criminal Law and the Optimal Use of Nonmonetary Sanctions as a Deterrent', **85** *Columbia Law Review*, 1985, 1232-1262.

SHAVELL, Steven, *Economic Analysis of Accident Law*, Cambridge, Harvard University Press, 1987, 277-290 (ch.12).

SHAVELL, Steven, 'A Model of Optimal Incapacitation', **77** *American Economic Review*, 1987, 107-110.

SHAVELL, Steven, 'The Optimal Use of Nonmonetary Sanctions as a Deterrent', **77** *American Economic Review*, 1987, 584-592.

SHAVELL, Steven, 'Optimal Sanctions and the Incentive to Provide Evidence to Legal Tribunals', **9** *International Review of Law and Economics*, 1989, 3-11.

SHAVELL, Steven, 'Deterrence and the Punishment of Attempts', **19** *Journal of Legal Studies*, 1990, 435-466.

SISK, David E., 'Police Corruption and Criminal Monopoly: Victimless Crimes', **11** *Journal of Legal Studies*, 1982, 395-403.

SKOGH, Göran, *Staffrätt och samhällsekonomi* [Criminal Law and the Economy], Lund Economic Studies, 1973.

SKOGH, Göran, 'A Note of Gary Becker's "Crime and Punishment: An Economic Approach"', **75** *Swedish Journal of Economics*, 1973, 305-311.

SKOGH, Göran, *Priser, skadestånd och straff* [Prices, Damages and Penalties], Malmö, Liber, 1977.

SKOGH, Göran, 'Straffvärdering enligt välfärdsekonomiska principer' [Penalty Assessment According to Welfare-economic Principles], in *Påföljdsval, Straffmätning och Straffvärde*, Brottsförebyggande rådet. Rapport 1980:2.

SKOGH, Göran, 'Public Insurance and Accident Prevention', **2** *International Review of Law and Economics*, 1982, 67-80.

SKOGH, Göran and STUART, Charles, 'A Contractarian Theory of Property Rights and Crime', **84** *Scandinavian Journal of Economics*, 1982, 27-40.

SKOGH, Göran and STUART, Charles, 'An Economic Analysis of Crime Rates, Punishments and the Consequences of Crime', **38** *Public Choice*, 1982, 171-179.

SNYDER, Edward A., 'The Effect of Higher Criminal Penalties on Antritrust Enforcement', **33** *Journal of Law & Economics*, 1990, 439-462.

SOLOMAN, H., 'Economists Perspectives on Economic Crime', **14** *American Criminal Law Review*, 1977, 641-649.

SOLOW, R.M., 'Leff's Swindling and Selling the Spanish Prisoner & Other Bargains', **8** *Bell Journal of Economics*, 1977, 627-629.

SOMMERS, Paul M., 'Deterrence and Gun Control: A Reply', **10(2)** *Atlantic Economic Journal*, 1982, 54-57.

SOMMERS, Paul M., 'The Effect of Gun Control Laws on Suicide Rates', **12(1)** *Atlantic Economic Journal*, 1984, 67-69.

SOMMERS, Paul M., 'Drinking Age and the 55 MPH Speed Limit', **13(1)** *Atlantic Economic Journal*, 1985, 43-48.

STEENHUIS, D.W., 'Strafrechtelijk optreden: stapje terug en een sprong voorwaarts' [Criminal Policy: A Step Backwards and a Jump Ahead], in *Delikt en Delinkwent*, Arnhem, Gouda Quint, 1984/5, 1984/6.

STEVANS, Lonnie K., 'An Empirical Model of Property Crime: Deterrence versus Redistribution', **10** *Journal of Post Keynesian Economics*, 1988, 572-584.

STIGLER, George J., 'The Optimum Enforcement of Law', **78** *Journal of Political Economy*, 1970, 526-536.

STITH, Kate, 'The Risk of Legal Error in Criminal Cases: Some Consequences of the Asymmetry in the Right to Appeal', **57** *University of Chicago Law Review*, 1990, 1-61.

SULLIVAN, R.F., 'The Economics of Crime: An Introduction to the Literature', **19** *Crime and Delinquency*, 1973, 138-149.

SUTINEN, Jon G. and ANDERSEN, Peder, 'The Economics of Fisheries Law Enforcement', **61** *Land Economics*, 1985, 387-397.

SWANSON, Timothy M., 'Enforcement of Environmental Regulation', in WEIGEL, Wolfgang (ed.), *Economic Analysis of Law - A Collection of Applications*, Vienna, Österreichischer Wirtschaftsverlag, 1991, 67-78.

TABAAZ, T.F., *Toward an Economics of Prisons*, Lexington, Heath, 1975.

TEMPLEMAN, Joseph, 'The Effect of Gun Control Laws on Suicide Rates: A Comment', **12(4)** *Atlantic Economic Journal*, 1984, 71.

THEROUX, Richard and UMBECK, John, 'Drunken Driving, Hit-and-Runs, and Bribery', **11(2)** *Regulation*, 1987, 44-47.

THOMPSON, James W. and CATALDO, James, 'Market Incentives for Criminal Behavior: Comment', in FREEMAN, Richard B. and HOLZER, Harry J. (eds.), *The Black Youth Employment Crisis*, Chicago, University of Chicago Press, 1986, 347-351.

THUROW, L., 'Equity vs. Efficiency in Law Enforcement', **18** *Public Policy*, 1970, 451-459.

TIETZEL, Manfred, 'Zur ökonomischen Theorie des Betrügens und Fälschens' [On the Economic Theory of Fraud and Counterfeiting], **204** *Jahrbuch für Nationalökonomie und Statistik*, 1988, 17-34.

TRUMBULL, William N., 'Estimations of the Economic Model of Crime Using Aggregate and Individual Level Data', **56** *Southern Economic Journal*, 1989, 423-439.

TULDER, Frank van, *Criminaliteit, pakkans en politie* [Criminality, Chance of Being Caught and Police], Sociaal Cultureel Planbureau, Cahier no. 45, 's-Gravenhage, Staatsdrukkerij, 1985.

TULDER, Frank van, 'Kosten en baten van twee vormen van criminaliteitsbestrijding' [Costs and Benefits of Two Types of Crime Combat], **71** *Economisch-Statistische Berichten*, 1986, 172-179.

TULLOCK, Gordon, 'The Welfare Costs of Tariffs, Monopolies and Theft', **5** *Western Economic Review*, 1967, 224-232.

TULLOCK, Gordon, 'An Economic Approach to Crime', **50** *Social Science Quarterly*, 1969, 59-71.

TULLOCK, Gordon, *The Logic of Law*, New York, Basic Books, 1971, 151-249.

TULLOCK, Gordon, 'Does Punishment Deter Crime?', *The Public Interest*, 1974, 103-111.

USHER, Dan, 'Police, Punishment, and Public Goods', **41** *Public Finance*, 1986, 96-115.

USHER, Dan, 'Theft as a Paradigm for Departures from Efficiency', **39** *Oxford Economic Papers*, 1987, 235-252.

VANBERG, Viktor, *Verbrechen, Strafe und Abschreckung, die Theorie der Generalprävention im Lichte der neueren sozialwissenschaftslichen Diskussion* [Crime, Sanction and Deterrence: The Theory of General Prevention in the Light of the New Discussion in Social Science], Tübingen, J.C.B. Mohr, 1982, 50 p.

VELJANOVSKI, Cento G., 'Regulatory Enforcement - An Economic Case Study of the British Factory Inspectorate', **4** *Law and Policy Quarterly*, 1982.

VELJANOVSKI, Cento G., 'The Market for Regulatory Enforcement', *Economic Journal*, Supplement March 1983, 123-129.

VELJANOVSKI, Cento G., 'The Economics of Regulatory Enforcement', in HANKINS, Keith and THOMAS, John M. (eds.), *Enforcing Regulation*, Boston, Kluwer-Nijhoff, 1984, 169-188.

VELJANOVSKI, Cento G., 'The Economics of Criminal Law and Procedure', **23**

Coexistence, 1986, 137-153.

VIRÉN, M., 'A Note on Finnish Property Criminality', **17** *International Journal of Social Economics*, 1990, 55-59.

VISCUSI, W. Kip, 'Market Incentives for Criminal Behavior', in FREEMAN, Richard B. and HOLZER, Harry J. (eds.), *The Black Youth Employment Crisis*, Chicago, University of Chicago Press, 1986, 301-346.

VISCUSI, W. Kip, 'The Risks and Rewards of Criminal Activity: A Comprehensive Test of Criminal Deterrence', **4** *Journal of Labor Economics*, Part 1, 1986, 317-340.

VOTEY, Harold L., Jr., *Economic Crimes: Their Generation, Deterrence and Control*, Washington, U.S. Department of Commerce, 1969.

VOTEY, Harold L., Jr., 'Detention of Heroin Addicts, Job Opportunities, and Deterrence', **8** *Journal of Legal Studies*, 1979, 585-606.

VOTEY, Harold L. Jr., 'Scandinavian Drinking-Driving Control: Myth or Intuition ?', **11** *Journal of Legal Studies*, 1982, 93-116.

VOTEY, Harold L. Jr. and PHILLIPS Llad, 'Police Effectiveness and the Production Function for Law Enforcement, **1** *Journal of Legal Studies*, 1972, 423-436.

WAGSTAFF, Adam and MAYNARD, Alan, *Economic Aspects of the Illicit Drug Market and Drug Enforcement Policies in the United Kingdom*, London, Her Majesty's Stationary Office, 1988, 156 p.

WALTHER, Sylvia R.B., 'Eigen schuld slachtoffer en schadevergoedingsmaatregel. Een civielrechtelijke verdeelsleutel in het strafrecht' [Victims Fault and Damage Orders. A Civil Law Distributive Code in Criminal Law], **66** *Nederlands Juristenblad*, 1991, 90-94.

WARD, Peter M. (ed.), *Corruption, Development and Inequality: Soft Touch or Hard Graft?*, London, Routlegde, 1989, 191 p.

WEICHMAN, Dennis, GREEN, Gary and BAE, Ronald, 'The Death Penalty: A Study in General Deterrence', **1** *Research in Law and Policy Studies*, 1987, 187-194.

WEINBLATT, J., et al., 'Crime Prevention Policies and Externalities: A Theoretical Analysis', **38** *Public Finance*, 1983, 110-131.

WICKSTRÖM, Bengt-Arne, 'Comment: The Speed Limit as Life Saver', in FAURE, Michael and VAN DEN BERGH, Roger (eds.), *Essays in Law and Economics. Corporations, Accident Prevention and Compensation for Losses*, Antwerpen, Maklu, 1989, 157-161.

WILKINSON, James T., 'Reducing Drunken Driving: Which Policies Are Most Effective?', **54** *Southern Economic Journal*, 1987, 322-334.

WILLIAMS, Allan F., 'Comment on Males', **15** *Journal of Legal Studies*, 1986, 213-217.

WILLIAMS, Allan F., RICH, Robert F., ZADOR, Paul L., and ROBERTSON, Leon S., 'The Legal Minimum Drinking Age and Fatal Motor Vehicle Crashes', **4** *Journal of Legal Studies*, 1975, 219-239.

WILLIAMS, Allan F., ZADOR, Paul L., HARRIS, Sandra S. and KARPF, Ronald S., 'The Effect of Raising the Legal Minimum Drinking Age on Involvement in Fatal Crashes', **12** *Journal of Legal Studies*, 1983, 169-179.

WILLIS, K. G., 'Spatial Variations in Crime in England and Wales: Testing an Economic Model', **17** *Regional Studies*, 1983, 261-272.

WITHERS, Glenn, 'Crime, Punishment and Deterrence in Australia: An Empirical Investigation', **60** *Economic Record*, 1984, 176-185.

WITTMAN, Donald, 'Efficient Rules in Highway Safety and Sports Activity', **72** *American Economic Review*, 1982, 78-90.

WLADIMIROFF, M., 'Rechtseconomie en strafrecht: enige kritische kanttekeningen' [Law-and-Economics and Criminal Law: Some Critical Remarks], in *Rechtseconomie en Recht*, Tjeenk Willink, Zwolle, 1991, 181-186.

WOLPIN, K.I., 'Capital Punishment and Homicide in England: A Summary of Results', **68** *American Economic Review. Papers and Proceedings*, 1978, 422-427.

WOLPIN, K.I., 'An Economic Analysis of Crime and Punishment in England and Wales, 1894-1967', **86** *Journal of Political Economy*, 1978, 815-840.

YANIV, Gideon, 'Crime and Punishment: A Note on Instrumental Violence', **17** *Journal of Behavioral Economics*, 1988, 143-148.

YOHE, Gary W., 'Fines as Economic Incentives - An Alternative Variable Control', **2** *International Review of Law and Economics*, 1982, 95-109.

ZIMRING, Franklin E., 'The Medium Is the Message: Firearm Caliber as a Determinant of Death from Assault', **1** *Journal of Legal Studies*, 1972, 97-123.

ZIMRING, Franklin E., 'Firearms and Federal Law: The Gun Control Act of 1968', **4** *Journal of Legal Studies*, 1975, 133-198.

ZIMRING, Franklin E., 'Determinants of the Death Rate from Robbery: A Detroit Time Study', **6** *Journal of Legal Studies*, 1977, 317-323.

ZIMRING, Franklin E., 'Youth Homicide in New York: A Preliminary Analysis', **13** *Journal of Legal Studies*, 1984, 81-99.

ZIMRING, Franklin E. and ZUEHL, James, 'Victim Injury and Death in Urban Robbery: A Chicago Study', **15** *Journal of Legal Studies*, 1986, 1-40.

ZOLT, Eric M., 'Deterrence via Taxation: A Critical Analysis of Tax Penalty Provisions', **37** *UCLA Law Review*, 1989, 343 ff.

9000 PRODUCTION OF LEGAL RULES
Pierre Coulange

9000 Production of Legal Rules: General

BACKHAUS, Jürgen G., 'De eis tot correctie van ondoelmatig recht' [The Need to Correct Inefficient Law], **39(10)** *Ars Aequi*, 1990, 660-665.

BERGE, J.B.J.M. ten, 'Rechtseconomie en staatsrecht/bestuursrecht' [Law-and-economics and Constitutional/Administrative Law], in *Rechtseconomie en Recht*, Zwolle, Tjeenk Willink, 1991, 149-162.

COULANGE, Pierre, 'La production de droit' [The Production of Legal Rules], **3** *Journal des Economistes et des Etudes Humaines*, 1990, 277-302.

COULANGE, Pierre, *Analyse économique de la production de droit* [Economic Analysis od the Production of Legal Rules], Ph.D., Aix-en-Provence, Université d'Aix-Marseille III, Faculté d'Economie Appliquée, 1990.

CULP, Jerome M., 'Foreword', **50 (4)** *Law and Contemporary Problems*, 1987, 1-16.

DIVER, Colin S., 'The Optimal Precision of Administrative Rules', **93** *Yale Law Journal*, 1983, 65-109.

EASTERBROOK, Frank H., 'Method, Result and Authority: A Reply', **98** *Harvard Law Review*, 1985, 622-629.

GEELHOED, L.A., *De interveniërende staat* [The Intervening State], 's-Gravenhage, Staatsuitgeverij, 1983.

HEINER, Ronald A., 'Rule-Governed Behavior in Evolution and Human Society', **1** *Constitutional Political Economy*, 1990, 19-46.

KENNEDY, Duncan, 'Legal Formality', **2** *Journal of Legal Studies*, 1973, 351-398.

KERKMEESTER, H.O., *Recht en speltheorie* [Law and Game Theory] (diss. Rotterdam), 1989, 212 p.

KOMESAR, Neil K., 'Legal Change, Judicial Behavior, and the Diversity Jurisdiction: A Comment', **9** *Journal of Legal Studies*, 1980, 387-397.

LANDES, William M. and POSNER, Richard A., 'Legal Change, Judicial Behavior, and the Diversity Jurisdiction', **9** *Journal of Legal Studies*, 1980, 367-386.

O'DRISCOLL, Gerald P., Jr. and RIZZO, Mario J., 'Subjectivism, Uncertainty, and Rules', in KIRZNER, Israel M. (ed.), *Subjectivism, Intelligibility and Economic Understanding. Essays in Honor of Ludwig M. Lachmann on his Eightieth Birthday*, London, Macmillan, 1986, 252-267.

OGUS, Anthony I., 'Social Costs in a Private Law Setting', **3** *International Review of Law and Economics*, 1983, 27-44.

OGUS, Anthony I., 'Comment' [on Staaf and Yandle, Collective and Private Choice; Constitutions, Statutes and the Common Law], in WEIGEL, Wolfgang (ed.), *Economic Analysis of Law - A Collection of Applications*, Vienna, Österreichischer Wirtschaftsverlag, 1991, 267-269.

PRICHARD, J. Robert S., 'A Systemic Approach to Comparative Law: The Effect of Cost, Fee, and Financing Rules on the Development of the Substantive Law', **17** *Journal of Legal Studies*, 1988, 451-475.

ROSE-ACKERMAN, Susan, 'Comment on Ferejohn and Shipan's "Congressional Influence on Bureaucracy"', **6** *Journal of Law, Economics, & Organization*, 1990, S21-S27.

RU, H.J. de, *Staat, markt en recht* [The State, the Market and the Law], Zwolle, Tjeenk Willink, 1987, 93 p.

SAMUELS, Warren J., 'Some Considerations Which May Lead Lawmakers to Modify a Policy When Adopting It as Law: Comment', **141** *Zeitschrift für die gesamte Staatswissenschaft*, 1985, 58-61.

SCHANZE, Erich, 'Regulation by Consensus: The Practice of International Mining Agreements', **144** *Journal of Institutional and Theoretical Economics*, 1988, 152-171.

SCHMIDTCHEN, Dieter and SCHMIDT-TRENZ, H.-J., 'The Division of Labor is Limited by the Extent of the Law. A Constitutional Economics Approach to International Private Law', **1(3)** *Constitutional Political Economy*, 1990, 49-71.

SCHWARTZ, Warren F. and TULLOCK, Gordon, 'The Costs of a Legal System', **4** *Journal of Legal Studies*, 1975, 75-82.

SHAVELL, Steven, *Economic Analysis of Accident Law*, Cambridge, Harvard University Press, 1987, 277-290 (ch.12).

SLOT, P.J., *Regelen en ontregelen. Oratie Leiden* [Regulating and De-regulating], Kluwer, Deventer, 1983.

STAAF, Robert and YANDLE, Bruce, 'Collective and Private Choice: Constitutions, Statutes and the Common Law', in WEIGEL, Wolfgang (ed.), *Economic Analysis of Law - A Collection of Applications*, Vienna, Österreichischer Wirtschaftsverlag, 1991, 254-265.

SUMMERS, Robert S., 'Some Considerations Which May Lead Lawmakers to Modify a Policy When Adopting It as Law', **141** *Zeitschrift für die gesamte Staatswissenschaft*, 1985, 41-57.

TULLOCK, Gordon, 'Defending the Napoleontic Code over the Common Law', **2** *Research in Law and Policy Studies*, 1988, 3-27.

9100 Constitution

ACKERMAN, Bruce A., 'Constitutional Politics/Constitutional Law', **99** *Yale Law Journal*, 1989, 453-547.

BACKHAUS, Jürgen G., 'Een economische analyse van het constitutionele recht' [An Economic Analysis of Constitutional Law], in *Rechtseconomie en Recht*, Zwolle, Tjeenk Willink, 1991, 107-148.

BORNER, Silvio, 'Wirtschafts- Sozial- und Eigentumsordnung um Verfassungsentwurf: Ein Diskussionsbeitrag aus ökonomischer Sicht' [Economic, Social and Property Structure in the Constitutionial Bill: A Contribution to the Discussion from an Economic Viewpoint], **98** *Zeitschrift für schweizerisches Recht*, 1979, 463-479.

BUCHANAN, James M., 'Justification of the Compound Republic: The Calculus in Retrospect', **7** *Cato Journal*, 1987, 305-312.

BUCHANAN, James M., 'Contractarian Political Economy and Constitutional Interpretation', **78** *American Economic Review. Papers and Proceedings*, 1988, 135-139.

BUCHANAN, James M., 'The Domain of Constitutional Economics', **1** *Constitutional Political Economy*, 1990, 1-18.

BUCHANAN, James M. and TULLOCK, Gordon, *The Calculus of Consent. Logical Foundations of Constitutional Democracy*, Ann Arbor, University of Michigan Press, 1962. University of Michigan Press (Arm Arbor Paperbacks), 1971, 361 p.

BUND, Dorothee, *Die Ökonomische Theorie der Verfassung* [The Economic Theory of the Constitution], Baden-Baden, Nomos, 1984, 96 p.

CRAIN, W. Mark and TOLLISON, Robert D., 'The Executive Branch in the Interest-Group Theory of Government', **8** *Journal of Legal Studies*, 1979, 555-567.

DYE, Thomas R., 'The Politics of Constitutional Choice', **7** *Cato Journal*, 1987, 337-344.

FARBER, Daniel A. and FRICKEY, Philip P., *Law and Public Choice: A Critical Introduction*, Chicago, University of Chicago Press, 1991, 159 p.

GWARTNEY, James D. and WAGNER, Richard E. (eds.), *Public Choice and Constitutional Economics*, Greenwhich, JAI Press, 1988, 422 p.

JANSSEN, Martin and HUMMLER, Konrad, 'Bundesverfassung und Verfassungsentwurf, Eine ökonomisch-rechtliche Analyse [Constitution and Revision of the Constitition, An Economic and Legal Analysis], *Schriften des Schweizerischen Aufklärungs-Dienstes*, 1979.

LEVINSON, Sanford, 'Some Reflections on the Posnerian Constitution', **56** *George Washington Law Review*, 1987, 39-49.

LEVY, David, 'The Statistical Basis of Athenian-American Constitutional Theory', **18** *Journal of Legal Studies*, 1989, 79-103.

MACEY, Jonathan R., 'Competing Economic Views of the Constitution', **56** *George Washington Law Review*, 1987, 50-80.

MACEY, Jonathan R., 'Transaction Costs and the Normative Elements of the Public Choice Model: An Application to Constitutional Theory', **74** *Virginia Law*

Review, 1988, 471-518.

MICHELMAN, Frank I., 'Constitutions, Statutes, and the Theory of Efficient Adjudication', **9** *Journal of Legal Studies*, 1980, 431-461.

NORTH, Douglass C. and WEINGAST, Barry R., 'Constitutions and Commitment: The Evolution of Institutions Governing Public Choice in Seventeenth Century England', **49** *Journal of Economic History*, 1989, 803-832.

POSNER, Richard A., 'Economics, Politics and the Reading of Statutes and the Constitution', **49** *University of Chicago Law Review*, 1982, 263-291.

POSNER, Richard A., 'The Constitution as an Economic Document', **56** *George Washington Law Review*, 1987, 4-38.

PRITCHARD, A.C., 'Note: Government Promises and Due Process: An Economic Analysis of the "New Property"', **77** *Virginia Law Review*, 1991, 1053-1090.

SAJó, András, 'Az alkotmányosság lehetöségei a gazdaságban, különös tekintettel a környezetvédelemre, mint gazdaságilag releváns tevékenységre' [Constitutionalism and its Possibilities in the Economy with Special Attention to the Environment as an Economicly Relevant Activity], **3-4** *Allam- és Jogtudomány* 1987-88, 474-511.

SEIDMAN, Louis Michael, 'Public Principle and Private Choice: The Uneasy Case for a Boundary Maintenance Theory of Constitutional Law', **96** *The Yale Law Journal*, 1987, 1006-1059.

TOLLISON Robert D. and CRAIN, W. Mark, 'Constitutional Change in an Interest-Group Perspective', **8** *Journal of Legal Studies*, 1979, 165-175.

TRIBE, Laurence H., 'Constitutional Calculus: Equal Justice or Economic Efficiency', **98** *Harvard Law Review*, 1985, 592-621.

VANDERVEEREN, Christine, VAN ROMPUY, Paul, HEREMANS, Dirk en HEYLEN, E., *De economische en monetaire unie in de Belgische staatshervorming: juridische en economische aspecten* [The Economic and Monetary Union in the Belgian State Reform: Legal and Economic Aspects], Antwerpen, Maklu, 1987, 250 p.

WAGNER, Richard E., 'Courts, Legislatures, and Constitutional Maintenance', **7** *Cato Journal*, 1987, 323-329.

WILSON, James G., 'Constraints of Power: The Constitutional Opinions of Judges Scalia, Bork, Posner, Easterbrook, and Winter', **40** *University of Miami Law Review*, 1986, 1171-1266.

9200 Legislation. Statutory Interpretation

ADAMS, James D. and KENNY, Lawrence W., 'Optimal Tenure of Elected Public Officials', **29** *Journal of Law and Economics*, 1986, 303-328.

ALPA, Guido, PULITINI, Francesco, RODOTA', Stefano and ROMANI, Franco, *Interpretazione giuridica e analisi economica* [Legal Interpretation and Economic Analysis], Milano, Giuffrè, 1982, 662 p.

ANDERSON, Gary M., ROWLEY, Charles K. and TOLLISON, Robert D., 'Rent Seeking and the Restriction of Human Exchange', **17** *Journal of Legal Studies*, 1988, 83-100.

ARANSON, Peter H., 'Judicial Control of the Political Branches: Public Purpose and Public Law', in DORN, James A. and MANNE, Henry G. (eds.), *Economic Liberties and the Judiciary*, Fairfax, George Mason University Press, 1987, 47-110.

ASHWORTH, John and PAPPS, Ivy, 'Should Environmental Legislation Set the Rules Constraining Polluters?', in WEIGEL, Wolfgang (ed.), *Economic Analysis of Law - A Collection of Applications*, Vienna, Österreichischer Wirtschaftsverlag, 1991, 83-88.

BARON, David P., 'Regulation and Legislative Choice', **19** *Rand Journal of Economics*, 1988, 467-477.

BECKER, Gary S., 'Public Policies, Pressure Groups, and Dead Weight Costs', **28** *Journal of Public Economics*, 1985, 329-347.

BECKER, Gary S., 'The Public Interest Hypothesis Revisited: A New Test of Peltzman's Theory of Regulation', **49** *Public Choice*, 1986, 223 ff.

BENSON, Bruce L. and ENGEN, Eric M., 'The Market for Laws: An Economic Analysis of Legislation', **54** *Southern Economic Journal*, 1988, 732-745.

BENSON, Bruce L. and FAMINOW, M.D., 'The Incentives to Organize and Demand Regulation: Two Ends against the Middle', **24** *Economic Inquiry*, 1986, 473-484.

BLUME, Lawrence E. and RUBINFELD, Daniel L., 'The Dynamics of Legal Process', **11** *Journal of Legal Studies*, 1982, 405-419.

BUCHANAN, James M. and TULLOCK, Gordon, *The Calculus of Consent. Logical Foundations of Constitutional Democracy*, Ann Arbor, University of Michigan Press, 1962. University of Michigan Press (Arm Arbor Paperbacks), 1971, 361 p.

BUCHANAN, James M., TOLLISON, Robert D. and TULLOCK, Gordon (eds.), *Toward a Theory of the Rent Seeking Society*, College Station, Texas A & M University Press, 1980.

CRAIN, W. Mark, 'Cost and Output in the Legislative Firm', **8** *Journal of Legal Studies*, 1979, 607-621.

CRAIN, W. Mark and TOLLISON, Robert D., 'The Executive Branch in the Interest-Group Theory of Government', **8** *Journal of Legal Studies*, 1979, 555-567.

DE CLERCQ, Marc and NAERT, Frank, *De politieke markt* [The Political Market], Antwerpen, Kluwer, 1985, 163 p.

DE GEEST, Gerrit, 'Public Choice en rechtseconomie' [Public Choice and Law &

Economics], **39** *Ars Aequi*, 1990, 666-673.

DiLORENZO, T.J., 'The Domain of Rent-Seeking Behaviour: Private or Public Choice?', **4** *International Review of Law and Economics*, 1984, 185-197.

DiLORENZO, T.J., 'Property Rights, Information Costs, and the Economics of Rent Seeking', **144** *Journal of Institutional and Theoretical Economics*, 1988, 318-322.

EASTERBROOK, Frank H., 'Statutes' Domains', **50** *University of Chicago Law Review*, 1983, 533-552.

EHRLICH, Isaac and POSNER, Richard A., 'An Economic Analysis of Legal Rulemaking', **3** *Journal of Legal Studies*, 1974, 257-286.

EKELUND, Robert B., Jr. and TOLLISON, Robert D., *Mercantilism as a Rent Seeking Society: Economic Regulation in Historical Perspective*, College Station, Texas A&M University Press, 1981, 169 p.

ESKRIDGE, William N., Jr., 'Interpreting Legislative Inaction', **87** *Michigan Law Review*, 1988, 63-137.

ESKRIDGE, William N., Jr., 'Politics without Romance: Implications of Public Choice Theory for Statutory Interpretation', **74** *Virginia Law Review*, 1988, 275-338.

FARBER, Daniel A., 'Statutory Interpretation, Legislative Inaction, and Civil Rights', **87** *Michigan Law Review*, 1988, 1-19.

FARBER, Daniel A. and FRICKEY, Philip P., *Law and Public Choice: A Critical Introduction*, Chicago, University of Chicago Press, 1991, 159 p.

FEREJOHN, John and SHIPAN, Charles, 'Congressional Influence on Bureaucracy', **6** *Journal of Law, Economics, & Organization*, 1990, S1-S20.

FLOWERS, Marilyn R., 'Rent Seeking and Rent Dissipation: A Critical View', **7** *Cato Journal*, 1987, 431-440.

FORMBY, John P., KEELER, James P. and THISTLE, Paul D., 'X-Efficiency, Rent-Seeking, and Social Costs', **57** *Public Choice*, 1988, 115-126.

FORMBY, John P., KEELER, James P. and THISTLE, Paul D., 'X-Efficiency, Rent-Seeking and Social Costs: Reply', **68** *Public Choice*, 1991, 267-271.

GOULD, John P., 'The Economics of Legal Conflicts', **2** *Journal of Legal Studies*, 1973, 279-300.

HUTTER, Michael, *Die Produktion von Recht. Eine selbstreferentielle Theorie der Wirtschaft, angewandt auf den Fall des Arzneimittelpatentrechts* [The Production of Law. A Selfreferential Theory of the Economy, applied to the Case of Pharmaceutical Patent Law], Tübingen, Mohr, 1989, 213 p.

KALT, Joseph P. and ZUPAN, Mark A., 'Capture and Ideology in the Economic Theory of Politics', **74** *American Economic Review*, 1984, 279-300.

KALT, Joseph P. and ZUPAN, Mark A., 'The Apparent Ideological Behavior of Legislators: Testing for Principal-Agent Slack in Political Institutions', **33** *Journal of Law & Economics*, 1990, 103-131.

KAU, James B. and RUBIN, Paul H., 'Self-Interest, Ideology, and Logrolling in Congressional Voting', **22** *Journal of Law and Economics*, 1979, 365-384.

KERWIN, Cornelis M., 'Assessing the Effects of Consensual Processes in

Regulatory Programs: Methodological and Policy Issues', **32** *American University Law Review*, 1983, 401 ff.

KRUEGER, Anne O., 'The Political Economy of the Rent-Seeking Society', **64** American Economic Review, 1974, 291-303.

LEHMANN, Michael, 'Umwelthaftungsrecht dient der Internalisierung negativer Extemalitäten, Kommentar' [Environmental Liability Law Is to Internalize Negative Externalities. A Comment] (on Panther, Zivilrecht und Umweltschutz), in OTT, Claus and SCHÄFER, Hans-Bernd (eds.), *Ökonomische Probleme des Zivilrechts*, Berlin, Springer, 1991, 290-294.

MACEY, Jonathan R., 'Promoting Public-Regarding Legislation Through Statutory Interpretation: An Interest Group Model', **86** *Columbia Law Review*, 1986, 223-268.

McARTHUR, John and MARKS, Stephen V., 'Constitutent Interest vs. Legislator Ideology: The Role of Political Opportunity Cost', **26** *Economic Inquiry*, 1988, 461-470.

McCHESNEY, Fred S., 'Rent Extraction and Rent Creation in the Economic Theory of Regulation', **16** *Journal of Legal Studies*, 1987, 101-118.

MICHELMAN, Frank I., 'Political Markets and Community Self Determination: Competing Judicial Models of Local Government Legitimacy', **53** *Indiana Law Journal*, 1977, 145-206.

MICHELMAN, Frank I., 'Constitutions, Statutes, and the Theory of Efficient Adjudication', **9** *Journal of Legal Studies*, 1980, 431-461.

NAERT, Frank, 'De politieke economie van pressiegroepen' [The Political Economy of Pressure Groups], **69** *Economisch-Statistische Berichten*, 1984, 56-61.

NAERT, Frank, 'Overheidsuitgaven en pressiegroepen in België', **32** *Tijdschrift voor Economie en Management*, 1987, 165-187.

NEUMANN, Manfred J.M. et al., 'The Appropriate Level of Regulation in Europe: Local, National or Community Wide? A Roundtable Discussion', **0(9)** *Economic Policy: A European Forum*, 1989, 467-481.

PAGE, William H., 'Interest Groups, Antitrust, and State Regulation: Parker v. Brown in the Economic Theory of Legislation', *Duke Law Journal*, 1987, 618-668.

PELTZMAN, Sam, 'Constituent Interest and Congressional Voting', **27** *Journal of Law and Economics*, 1984, 181-210.

POSNER, Richard A., 'Economics, Politics and the Reading of Statutes and the Constitution', **49** *University of Chicago Law Review*, 1982, 263-291.

POSNER, Richard A., 'Comment: Responding to Gordon Tullock', **2** *Research in Law and Policy Studies*, 1988, 29-33.

PRIEST, W. Curtiss, *Risks, Concerns, and Social Regulation: Forces that Led to Laws on Health, Safety, and the Environment*, Boulder, Westview Press, 1988, 204 p.

PRITCHARD, A.C., 'Note: Government Promises and Due Process: An Economic Analysis of the "New Property"', **77** *Virginia Law Review*, 1991, 1053-1090.

RICE, Edward M. and ULEN, Thomas S., 'Rent Seeking and Welfare Loss', **3** *Research in Law and Economics*, 1981, 53-65.

RIZZO, Mario J., 'Rules versus Cost-Benefit Analysis in the Common Law', **4** *Cato Journal*, 1985, 865-884. Reprinted in DORN, James A. and MANNE, Henry G. (eds.), *Economic Liberties and the Judiciary*, Fairfax, George Mason University Press, 1987, 225-244.

RIZZO, Mario J. and ARNOLD, Frank S., 'An Economic Framework for Statutory Interpretation', **50 (4)** *Law and Contemporary Problems*, 1987, 165-180.

ROMANO, Roberta, 'Law as a Product: Some Pieces of the Incorporation Puzzle', **1** *Journal of Law, Economics, & Organization*, 1985, 225-283.

ROSE-ACKERMAN, Susan, 'Progressive Law and Economics - and the New Administrative Law', **98** *Yale Law Journal*, 1988, 341-368.

ROSE-ACKERMAN, Susan, 'Comment on Ferejohn and Shipan's "Congressional Influence on Bureaucracy"', **6** *Journal of Law, Economics, & Organization*, 1990, S21-S27.

ROWLEY, Charles K., TOLLISON, Robert D. and TULLOCK, Gordon (eds.), *The Political Economy of Rent-Seeking*, Boston, Kluwer Academic Publishers, 1988.

RU, H.J. de, *Prijst de wet zich uit de markt?* [Does the Law Price Itself Out of the Market?] Inaugural Lecture, Zwolle, Tjeenk Willink, 1988.

RUBIN, Paul H., 'Common Law and Statute Law', **11** *Journal of Legal Studies*, 1982, 205-223.

SHAVIRO, Daniel N., 'Beyond Public Choice and Public Interest: A Study of the Legislative Process as Illustrated by Tax Legislation in the 1980s', **139** *University of Pennsylvania Law Review*, 1990, 1-123.

SHUGHART, William F., II and TOLLISON, Robert D., 'On the Growth of Government and the Political Economy of Legislation', **9** *Research in Law and Economics*, 1986, 111-127.

TOLLISON, Robert D., 'Rent-Seeking: a Survey', **35** *Kyklos*, 1982, 575-602.

TULLOCK, Gordon, 'Efficient Rent Seeking', in BUCHANAN, James M., TOLLISON, Robert D. and TULLOCK, Gordon (eds.), *Toward a Theory of the Rent-Seeking Society*, College Station, Texas A&M Press, 1980. Reprinted in GOLDBERG, Victor P. (ed.), *Readings in the Economics of Contract Law*, Cambridge, Cambridge University Press, 1989, 35-42.

TULLOCK, Gordon, 'The Costs of Rent-Seeking: A Metaphysical Problem', **57** *Public Choice*, 1988, 15-24.

TULLOCK, Gordon, *The Economics of Special Privilege and Rent Seeking*, Boston, Kluwer, 1989, 104 p.

WATERS, Melissa and MOORE, William J., 'The Theory of Economic Regulation and Public Choice and the Determinants of Public Sector Bargaining Legislation', **66** *Public Choice*, 1990, 161-175.

WENDERS, John T., 'On Perfect Rent Dissipation', **77** *American Economic Review*, 1987, 456-459.

YANDLE, Bruce, *The Political Limits of Environmental Regulation: Tracking the Unicorn*, Westport, Greenwood Press, 1989, 180 p.

9300 Judge Made Law. Precedents

ANDERSON, Gary M., SHUGHART, William F. II and TOLLISON, Robert D., 'On the Incentives of Judges to Enforce Legislative Wealth Transfers', **32** *Journal of Law and Economics*, 1989, 215-228.

BOND, Ronald S. and MITLER, James C., Jr., 'Voting Patterns of FTC Commissioners', in MACKAY, Robert J., MILLER, James C., III and YANDLE, Bruce (eds.), *Public Choice and Regulation: A View from Inside the Federal Trade Commission*, Stanford, Hoover Institution Press, 1987, 322-330.

BOWLES, Roger A. and WHELAN, Christopher J., 'Judicial Responses to Exchange Rate Instability', in BURROWS, Paul and VELJANOVSKI, Cento G. (eds.), *The Economic Appraoch to Law*, London, Butterworths, 1981, 253-272.

BRUCE, Christopher J., 'The Adjudication of Labor Disputes as a Private Good', **8** *International Review of Law and Economics*, 1988, 3-19.

CALVERT, Randall L., MORAN, Mark J. and WEINGAST, Barry R., 'Congressional Influence over Policy Making: The Case of the FTC', in McCUBBINS, Mathew D. and SULLIVAN, Terry (eds.), *Congress: Structure and Policy*, Cambridge, University Press, 1987, 493-522.

CARRINGTON, Paul D., 'Adjudication as a Private Good: A Comment', **8** *Journal of Legal Studies*, 1979, 303-317.

CHRISTAINSEN, Gregory B., 'Law as a Discovery Procedure', **9** *Cato Journal*, 1990, 497-530.

CHUBB, Larry L., 'Economic Analysis in the Courts: Limits and Constraints', **64** *Indiana Law Journal*, 1989, 769-801.

COHEN, George M., 'Posnerian Jurisprudence and Economic Analysis of Law: The View from the Bench', **133** *University of Pennsylvania Law Review*, 1985, 1117-1166.

COHEN, Mark A., 'Explaining Judicial Behavior or What's "Unconstitutional" about the Sentencing Commission?', **7** *Journal of Law, Economics, & Organization*, 1991, 183-199.

COOTER, Robert D., 'The Objectives of Private and Public Judges', **41** *Public Choice*, 1983, 107-132.

COOTER, Robert D., KORNHAUSER, Lewis A. and LANE, D., 'Liability Rules, Limited Information, and the Role of Precedent', **10** *Bell Journal of Economics*, 1979, 366-373.

COOTER, Robert D. and KORNHAUSER, Lewis A., 'Can Litigation Improve the Law without the Help of Judges ?', **9** *Journal of Legal Studies*, 1980, 139-163.

CRAMTON, Roger C., 'The Supreme Court and the Decline of State Power', **2** *Journal of Law and Economics*, 1959, 175-189.

CULP, Jerome M., 'Judex Economicus', **50 (4)** *Law and Contemporary Problems*, 1987, 95-140.

DAVIS, Otto A., 'Public and Private Characteristics of a Legal Process: A Comment', **8** *Journal of Legal Studies*, 1979, 285-293.

DAYNARD, Richard A., 'Use of Social Policy in Judicial Decision-Making', **56** *Carnell Law Review*, 1971, 919-950.

DE Alessi, Louis, 'Property Rights and the Judiciary', **4** *Cato Journal*, 1985, 805-811. Reprinted in DORN, James A. and MANNE, Henry G. (eds.), *Economic Liberties and the Judiciary*, Fairfax, George Mason University Press, 1987, 175-181.

DICKE, Hugo and HARTUNG, Hans, *Externe Kosten von Rechtsvorschriften* [External Effects of Legal Rules], Möglichkeiten und Grenzen der ökonomischen Gesetzesanalyse, Tübingen, J.C.B. Mohr, 1986, 123 p.

EASTERBROOK, Frank H., 'The Supreme Court, 1983 Term, Foreword: The Court and the Economic System', **98** *Harvard Law Review*, 1984, 4-60.

EISENBERG, Melvin Aron, *The Nature of the Common Law*, Cambridge (Mass.), Harvard University Press, 1988, 204 p.

EPSTEIN, Richard A., 'Judicial Review: Reckoning on Two Kinds of Error', in DORN, James A. and MANNE, Henry G. (eds.), *Economic Liberties and the Judiciary*, Fairfax, George Mason University Press, 1987, 39-46.

FOX, Eleanor M., 'The Politics of Law and Economics in Judicial Decision Making: Antitrust as a Window', **61** *New York University Law Review*, 1986, 554-588.

GELY, Rafael and SPILLER, Pablo T., 'A Rational Choice Theory of Supreme Court Statutory Decisions with Applications to the *State Farm* and *Grove City* Cases', **6** *Journal of Law, Economics, & Organization*, 1990, 263-300.

GERHART, Peter M., 'The Supreme Court and Antitrust Analysis: The (Near) Triumph of the Chicago School', *Supreme Court Review*, 1982, 319-349.

GOLBERT, J.P. and LOWENSTEIN, Paul, 'The Court and the Marketplace: Who Should Regulate Whom?', **34** *Baylor Law Review*, 1982, 39-65.

GOLDBERG, Victor P. (ed.), 'Discussion by Seminar Participants', **8** *Journal of Legal Studies*, 1979, 323-398.

GREENWALT, Kent, 'Policy, Rights and Judicial Decision', **11** *Georgia Law Review*, 1977, 991-1053.

HARRIS, Peter, 'Difficult Cases and the Display of Authority', **1** *Journal of Law, Economics, & Organization*, 1985, 209-221.

HEINER, Ronald A., 'Imperfect Decisions and the Law: On the Evolution of Legal Precedent and Rules', **15** *Journal of Legal Studies*, 1986, 227-261.

HIGGINS, Richard S. and RUBIN, Paul H., 'Judicial Discretion', **9** *Journal of Legal Studies*, 1980, 129-138.

HOLMES, Oliver Wendell, *The Common Law*, Boston, Little Brown, 1880.

KAPLOW, Louis, 'Antitrust, Law & Economics, and the Courts', **50 (4)** *Law and Contemporary Problems*, 1987, 181-216.

KATZ, Avery, 'Judicial Decisionmaking and Litigation Expenditure', **8** *International Review of Law and Economics*, 1988, 127-143.

KORNHAUSER, Lewis A., 'An Economic Perspective of Stare Decisis', **65** *Chicago-Kent Law Review*, 1989, 63-92.

KORNHAUSER, Lewis A., 'Response to Macey', **65** *Chicago-Kent Law Review*, 1989, 115-122.

LANDES, William M., 'An Economic Analysis of the Courts', **14** *Journal of Law and Economics*, 1971, 61-107.

LANDES, William M. and POSNER, Richard A., 'The Independent Judiciary in an Interest-Group Perspective', **18** *Journal of Law and Economics*, 1975, 875-901.

LANDES, William M. and POSNER, Richard A., 'Legal Precedent: A Theoretical and Empirical Analysis', **19** *Journal of Law and Economics*, 1976, 249-307.

LANDES, William M. and POSNER, Richard A., 'Adjudication as a Private Good', **8** *Journal of Legal Studies*, 1979, 235-284.

LATIN, Howard, 'Legal and Economic Considerations in the Decisions of Judge Breyer', **50(4)** *Law and Contemporary Problems*, 1987, 57-86.

LIEBELER, Wesley J., 'A Property Rights Approach to Judicial Decision Making', **4** *Cato Journal*, 1985, 783-804. Reprinted in DORN, James A. and MANNE, Henry G. (eds.), *Economic Liberties and the Judiciary*, Fairfax, George Mason University Press, 1987, 153-174.

LINDER, Douglas O., 'Some Doubts Concerning the Selection Hypothesis of George Priest', **37** *University of Kansas Law Review*, 1989, 319-347.

MACEY, Jonathan R., 'The Internal and External Costs and Benefits of Stare Decisis', **65** *Chicago-Kent Law Review*, 1989, 93-113.

MAGAT, Wesley A., 'Howard Latin's Analysis of the Legal and Economic Considerations in the Decisions of Judge Breyer', **50(4)** *Law and Contemporary Problems*, 1987, 87-93.

MENDELSON, Wallace, 'The Politics of Judicial Supremacy', **4** *Journal of Law and Economics*, 1961, 175-185.

POLINSKY, A. Mitchell and RUBINFELD, Daniel L., 'The Deterrent Effects of Settlements and Trials', **8** *International Review of Law and Economics*, 1988, 109-116.

POLLOCK, Stewart G., 'Economic Analysis at Work in Judicial Decision-Making', *Annual Survey of American Law*, 1988, 133-136.

POSNER, Richard A., *The Federal Courts: Crisis and Reform*, Harvard University Press, Cambridge, 1985, 365 p.

PRIEST, George L., 'Selective Characteristics of Litigation', **9** *Journal of Legal Studies*, 1980, 399-421.

RIZZO, Mario J. (ed.), 'Symposium: Change in the Common Law: Legal and Economic Perspectives. A Symposium Sponsored by The Institute for Humane Studies and the Liberty Fund', **9** *Journal of Legal Studies*, 1980, 189-427.

RIZZO, Mario J., 'Can There Be a Principle of Explanation in Common Law Decisions? A Comment on Priest', **9** *Journal of Legal Studies*, 1980, 423-427.

RIZZO, Mario J., 'Rules versus Cost-Benefit Analysis in the Common Law', **4** *Cato Journal*, 1985, 865-884. Reprinted in DORN, James A. and MANNE, Henry G. (eds.), *Economic Liberties and the Judiciary*, Fairfax, George Mason University Press, 1987, 225-244.

ROWLEY, Charles K., 'Comment: A Public Choice Perspective on Judicial Pragmactivism', in DORN, James A. and MANNE, Henry G. (eds.), *Economic Liberties and the Judiciary*, Fairfax, George Mason University Press, 1987, 219-224.

RUBIN, Paul H., 'Common Law and Statute Law', **11** *Journal of Legal Studies*, 1982, 205-223.

SAMUELS, Warren J. and MERCURO, Nicholas, 'Posnerian Law and Economics on the Bench', **4** *International Review of Law and Economics*, 1984, 107-130.

SAMUELS, Warren J. and MERCURO, Nicholas, 'Wealth Maximization and Judicial Decision-Making: The Issues Further Clarified', **6** *International Review of Law and Economics*, 1986, 133-137.

SHAPIRO, Martin, 'Toward a Theory of Stare Decisis', **1** *Journal of Legal Studies*, 1972, 125-134.

SINDER, Janet, 'Economists as Judges: A Selective, Annotated Bibliography', **50** **(4)** *Law and Contemporary Problems*, 1987, 279-286.

TOMA, Eugenia Froedge, 'Congressional Influence and the Supreme Court: The Budget as a Signaling Device', **20** *Journal of Legal Studies*, 1991, 131-146.

VARAT, Jonathan D., 'Review Essay: Economic Ideology and the Federal Judicial Task (Review of The Federal Courts: Crisis and Reform by Richard A. Posner), **74** *California Law Review*, 1986, 649-674.

WALD, Patricia M., 'Limits on the Use of Economic Analysis in Judicial Decisionmaking', **50(4)** *Law and Contemporary Problems*, 1987, 225-244.

WHICHARD, Willis P., 'A Common Law Judge's View of the Appropriate Use of Economics in Common Law Adjudication', **50(4)** *Law and Contemporary Problems*, 1987, 253-263.

WILLIAMS, Stephen F., 'The Static Conception of the Common Law: A Comment', **9** *Journal of Legal Studies*, 1980, 277-289.

WILSON, James G., 'Justice Diffused: A Comparison of Edmund Burke's Conservatism with the Views of Five Conservative, Academic Judges', **40** *University of Miami Law Review*, 1986, 913-975.

X, 'Note: Judge Frank H. Easterbrook: A Faithful Adherent of the Law & Economics Approach Advocates by Professor Frank H. Easterbrook', **50** **(4)** *Law and Contemporary Problems*, 1987, 265-277.

9400 Agencies

BREYER, Stephen G., 'Economists and Economic Regulation', **47** *University of Pittsburgh Law Review*, 1985, 205-218.

ECKERT, Ross D., 'The Life Cycle of Regulatory Commissioners', **24** *Journal of Law and Economics*, 1981, 113-120.

FEREJOHN, John and SHIPAN, Charles, 'Congressional Influence on Bureaucracy', **6** *Journal of Law, Economics, & Organization*, 1990, S1-S20.

FIORINA, Morris P., 'Legislative Choice of Regulatory Forms: Legal Process or Administrative Process?', **39** *Public Choice*, 1982, 33-66.

FIORINA, Morris P., 'Legislator Uncertainty, Legislative Control, and the Delegation of Legislative Power, **2** *Journal of Law, Economics, & Organization*, 1986, 33-51.

FOX, Eleanor M., 'Chairman Miller, the Federal Trade Commission, Economics, and Rashomon', **50(4)** *Law and Contemporary Problems*, 1987, 33-55.

FUCHS, Edward Paul and ANDERSON, James, 'Institutinalizing Cost-Benefit Analysis in Regulatory Agencies', in NAGEL, Stuart S. (ed.), *Research in Public Policy Analysis and Management*, Volume 4, Greenwich, JAI Press, 1987, 187-211.

GELY, Rafael and SPILLER, Pablo T., 'A Rational Choice Theory of Supreme Court Statutory Decisions with Applications to the *State Farm* and *Grove City* Cases', **6** *Journal of Law, Economics, & Organization*, 1990, 263-300.

HORN, Murray J. and SHEPSLE, Kenneth A., 'Commentary: Administrative Process and Organizational Form as Legislative Responses to Agency Costs', **75** *Virginia Law Review*, 1989, 499-508.

LAFFONT, Jean-Jacques and TIROLE, Jean, 'The Politics of Government Decision Making: Regulatory Institutions', **6** *Journal of Law, Economics, & Organization*, 1990, 1-31.

LANDY, Marc K., ROBERTS, Marc J. and THOMAS, Stephen R., *The Environmental Protection Agency: Asking the Wrong Questions*, Oxford, Oxford University Press, 1990, 309 p.

MACKAY, Robert J., MILLER, James C., III and YANDLE, Bruce (eds.), *Public Choice and Regulation: A View form Inside the Federal Trade Commission*, Stanford, Hoover Institution Press, 1987, 363 p.

MAGAT, Wesley A., KRUPNICK, A. and HARRINGTON, W., *Rules in the Making: A Statistical Analysis of Regulatory Agency Behavior*, Washington, Resources for the Future, 1986.

MASHAW, Jerry L., 'Prodelegation: Why Administrators Should Make Political Decisions', **1** *Journal of Law, Economics, & Organization*, 1985, 81-100.

McCUBBINS, Mathew D., NOLL, Roger G. and WEINGAST, Barry R., 'Structure and Process, Politics and Policy: Administrative Arrangements and the Political Control of Agencies', **75** *Virginia Law Review*, 1989, 431-482.

McCUBBINS, Mathew D. and PAGE, T., 'The Congressional Foundations of Agency Performance', **51** *Public Choice*, 1986, 173-190.

MILLER, James C., III., *The Economist as Reformer: Revamping the FTC, 1981-*

1985, Washington D.C., American Enterprise Institure for Public Policy Research, 1989, 110 p.

MURIS, Timothy J., 'Regulatory Policymaking at the Federal Trade Commission: The Extent of Congressional Control', **94** *Journal of Political Economy*, 1986, 884-889.

POSNER, Richard A., 'The Behavior of Administrative Agencies', **1** *Journal of Legal Studies*, 1972, 305-347.

ROBINSON, Glen O., 'Commentary: Political Uses of Structure and Process', **75** *Virginia Law Review*, 1989, 483-498.

ROSE-ACKERMAN, Susan, 'Comment on Ferejohn and Shipan's "Congressional Influence on Bureaucracy"', **6** *Journal of Law, Economics, & Organization*, 1990, S21-S27.

SPITZER, Matthew L., 'Antitrust Federalism and Rational Choice Political Economy: A Critique of Capture Theory', **61** *Southern California Law Review*, 1988, 1293-1326.

SPITZER, Matthew L. 'Extensions of Ferejohn and Shipan's Model of Administrative Agency Behavior', **6** *Journal of Law, Economics, & Organization*, 1990, S29-S43.

STALON, Charles G., 'Analysis and Synthesis in Quasi-Judical Multimember Regulatory Agencies', in SALTZMAN, Sidney and SCHULER, Richard E. (eds.), *The Future of Electrical Energy: A Regional Perspective of an Industry in Transition*, New York, Greenwood Press, 1986, 330-339.

WEINGAST, Barry R., 'Regulation, Reregulation, and Deregulation: The Political Foundations of Agency Clientele Relationships', **44** *Law and Contemporary Problems*, 1981, 147-177.

WEINGAST, Barry R. and MORAN, Mark J., 'Bureaucratic Discretion or Congressional Control? Regulatory Policymaking by the Federal Trade Commission', **91** *Journal of Political Economy*, 1983, 765-800. Reprinted in MACKAY, Robert J., MILLER, James C., III and YANDLE, Bruce (eds.), *Public Choice and Regulation: A View form Inside the Federal Trade Commission*, Stanford, Hoover Institution Press, 1987, 30-62.

WEINGAST, Barry R. and MORAN, Mark J., 'Congress and Regulatory Agency Choice: Reply', **94** *Journal of Political Economy*, 1986, 890-894.

WILEY, John Shepard, Jr., 'A Capture Theory of Antitrust Federalism', **99** *Harvard Law Review*, 1986, 713-789.

WILEY, John Shepard, Jr., 'A Capture Theory of Antitrust Federalism: Reply to Professors Page and Spitzer', **61** *Southern California Law Review*, 1988, 1327-1341.

9500 Self-Regulation

BARKENBUS, Jack N., 'Is Self-Regulation Possible?', **2** *Journal of Policy Analysis and Management*, 1983, 576-588.

BENHAM, Lee and BENHAM, Alexandra, 'Regulating Through the Professions: A Perspective on Information Control', **18** *Journal of Law and Economics*, 1975, 421-447.

BLAIR, Roger D. and KASERMAN, David L., 'Preservation of Quality and Sanctions within the Professions', in BLAIR, Roger D. and RUBIN, S. (eds.), *Regulating the Professions: A Public-Policy Symposium*, Lexington, Lexington Books, 1980.

FRIEDMAN, Milton and KUZNETS, S., *Income from Independent Professional Practice*, New York, National Bureau of Economic Research, 1945.

GORTON, Gary and MULLINEAUX, Donald J., 'The Joint Production of Confidence: Endogenous Regulation and Nineteenth Century Commercial Bank Clearinghouses', **19** *Journal of Money, Credit, and Banking*, 1987, 457-468.

HAUG, Marie, 'The Sociological Approach to Self-Regulation', in BLAIR, Roger D. and RUBIN, Stephen (eds.), *Regulating the Professions: A Public-Policy Symposium*, Lexington, Lexington Books, 1980.

HOLCOMBE, Randall G. and HOLCOMBE, Lora P., 'The Market for Regulation', **142** *Journal of Institutional and Theoretical Economics*, 1986, 684-696.

HOROWITZ, Ira, 'The Economic Foundations of Self-Regulation in the Professions', in BLAIR, Roger D. and RUBIN, Stephen (eds.), *Regulating the Professions: A Public-Policy Symposium*, Lexington, Lexington Books, 1980.

KISSAM, P.C., 'Anti-Trust Law, The First Amendment, and Professional Self-Regulation of Technical Quality', in BLAIR, Roger D. and RUBIN, Stephen (eds.), *Regulating the Professions: A Public-Policy Symposium*, Lexington, Lexington Books, 1980.

LEES, D.S., *The Economic Consequences of the Professions*, London, Institute of Economic Affairs, 1966, 48 p.

LIEBERMAN, J.K., 'Some Reflections on Self-Regulation', in SLAYTON, P. and TREBILCOCK, Michael J., *The Professions and Public Policy*, Toronto, University of Toronto Faculty of Law, 1978.

MAURIZI, Alex R., 'Occupational Licensing and the Public Interest', **82** *Journal of Political Economy*, 1974, 399-413.

MILLER, James C., III, 'The FTC and Voluntary Standards: Maximizing the Net Benefits of Self-Regulation', **4** *Cato Journal*, 1985, 897-903. Reprinted in DORN, James A. and MANNE, Henry G. (eds.), *Economic Liberties and the Judiciary*, Fairfax, George Mason University Press, 1987, 281-287.

MOORE, Thomas G., 'The Purpose of Licensing', **4** *Journal of Law and Economics*, 1961, 93-117.

OLLEY, R.E., 'The Future of Self-Regulation: a Consumer Economist's Viewpoint', in SLAYTON, P. and TREBILCOCK, Michael J., *The Professions and Public Policy*, Toronto, University of Toronto Faculty of Law, 1978.

OSTRY, Sylvia, 'Competition Policy and the Self-Regulating Professions', in

SLAYTON, P. and TREBILCOCK, Michael J. (eds.), *The Professions and Public Policy*, Toronto, University of Toronto Faculty of Law, 1978.

PLOTT, Charles R., 'Occupational Self-Regulation: A Case-Study of the Oklahoma Dry Cleaners', **8** *Journal of Law and Economics*, 1965, 195-222.

SHAKED, Avner and SUTTON, John, 'Heterogeneous Consumers and Product Differentiation in a Market for Professional Services', **15** *European Economic Review*, 1981, 159-177.

SHAKED, Avner and SUTTON, John, 'The Self-Regulating Profession', **47** *Review of Economic Studies*, 1981, 217-234.

SHEPPARD, Claud-Armand, 'Enforcing Continuing Competence', in SLAYTON, Philip and TREBILCOCK, Michael J. (eds.), *The Professions and Public Policy*, Toronto, University of Toronto Faculty of Law, 1978.

TUOHY, Carolyn and WOLFSON, Alan, 'Self-Regulation: Who Qualifies?', in SLAYTON, Philip and TREBILCOCK, Michael J. (eds.), *The Professions and Public Policy*, Toronto, University of Toronto Faculty of Law, 1978.

WEINGAST, Barry R., 'Physicians, DNA Research Scientists, and the Market for Lemons', in BLAIR, Roger D. and RUBIN, Stephen (eds.), *Regulating the Professions: A Public-Policy Symposium*, Lexington, Lexington Books, 1980.

YOUNGER, J.W., 'Competition Policy and the Self-Regulating Professions', in SLAYTON, Philip and TREBILCOCK, Michael J. (eds.), *The Professions and Public Policy*, Toronto, University of Toronto Faculty of Law, 1978.

9600 Spontaneous Emergence of Law

BENSON, Bruce L., 'Legal Evolution in Primitive Societies', **144** *Journal of Institutional and Theoretical Economics*, 1988, 772-788.

BENSON, Bruce L., 'The Spontaneous Evolution of Commercial Law', **55** *Southern Economic Journal*, 1989, 644-661.

FRIEDMAN, David, 'Private Creation and Enforcement of Law: A Historical Case', **8** *Journal of Legal Studies*, 1979, 399-415.

MACKAAY, Ejan J.P., 'L'ordre spontane comme fondement du droit - un survol des modèles de l'émergence des règles dans une société civile' [Spontaneous Order as Foundation of Law - A Survey of Models of the Emergence of Rules in a Civil Society], **22** *Revue Juridique Themis*, 1988, 347-383.

O'DRISCOLL, Gerald P., Jr. and RIZZO, Mario J., 'Subjectivism, Uncertainty, and Rules', in KIRZNER, Israel M. (ed.), *Subjectivism, Intelligibility and Economic Understanding. Essays in Honor of Ludwig M. Lachmann on his Eightieth Birthday*, London, Macmillan, 1986, 252-267.

POSNER, Richard A., 'A Theory of Primitive Society, with Special Reference to Primitive Law', **23** *Journal of Law and Economics*, 1980, 1-53.

POSNER, Richard A., *The Economics of Justice*, Cambridge (Mass.), Harvard University Press, 1981, 415 p.

PRIEST, George L., 'The New Scientism in Legal Scholarship: A Comment on Clark and Posner', **90** *Yale Law Journal*, 1981, 1284-1295.

RUBIN, Paul H., *Business Firms and the Common Law. The Evolution of Efficient Rules*, New York, Praeger, 1983, 189 p.

VERSTEEG, J. Russell, 'Law and the Security of Homeric Society (A Response to Richard A. Posner)', **10** *Journal of Legal History*, 1989, 265-284.

WARREN, Elizabeth, 'Trade Usage and Parties in the Trade: An Economic Rationale for an Inflexible Rule', **42** *University of Pittsburg Law Review*, 1981, 515 ff.

9700 Legal Evolution. Tradition. Legal Culture

ACKERMAN, Bruce A., 'Law, Economics and the Problem of Legal Culture', *Duke Law Journal*, 1986, 929-947.

BELL, John W., 'Averting a Crisis in Product Liability : An Evolutionary Process of Socioeconomic Justice', **65** *Illinois Bar Journal*, 1977, 640-648.

BENSON, Bruce L., 'Legal Evolution in Primitive Societies', **144** *Journal of Institutional and Theoretical Economics*, 1988, 772-788.

BENSON, Bruce L., 'The Spontaneous Evolution of Commercial Law', **55** *Southern Economic Journal*, 1989, 644-661.

BROMLEY, Daniel W., 'Institutional Change and Economic Efficiency', **23** *Journal of Economic Issues*, 1989, 735-759.

CHRISTAINSEN, Gregory B., 'Law as a Discovery Procedure', **9** *Cato Journal*, 1990, 497-530.

CLARK, Robert C., 'The Interdisciplinary Study of "Legal Evolution"', **90** *Yale Law Journal*, 1981, 1238-1274.

ELLIOTT, E. Donald, 'Holmes and Evolution: Legal Process as Artificial Intelligence', **13** *Journal of Legal Studies*, 1984, 113-146.

ELLIOTT, E. Donald, ACKERMAN, Bruce A. and MILLIAN, John C., 'Toward a Theory of Statutory Evolution: The Federalization of Environmental Law', **1** *Journal of Law, Economics, & Organization*, 1985, 313-340.

EPSTEIN, Richard A., 'The Static Conception of the Common Law', **9** *Journal of Legal Studies*, 1980, 253-275.

FRIED, Charles, SUMMERS, Robert S., TULLOCK, Gordon and ARROW, Kenneth J., 'Commentary on Hirschleifer Paper', **4** *Research in Law and Economics*, 1982, 61-208.

GALANTER, Marc, 'Conceptualizing Legal Change and Its Effect: A Comment on George Priest's "Measuring Legal Change"', **3** *Journal of Law, Economics, & Organization*, 1987, 235-241.

GOLDBERG, Victor P., 'Institutional Change and the Quasi-Invisible Hand', **17** *Journal of Law and Economics*, 1974, 461-492. Reprinted in GOLDBERG, Victor P. (ed.), *Readings in the Economics of Contract Law*, Cambridge, Cambridge University Press, 1989, 169-173.

GOODMAN, John C., 'An Economic Theory of the Evolution of the Common Law', **7** *Journal of Legal Studies*, 1978, 393-406.

HESSE, Günter, 'Der Property-Rights-Ansatz. Eine ökonomische Theorie der Veränderung des Rechts?' [The Property Rights Approach. An Economic Theory of Legal Evolution?], **195** *Jahrbuch für Nationalökonomie und Statistik*, 1980, 481 ff.

HESSE, Günter, 'Zur Erklärung der Änderung von Handlungsrechten mit Hilfe der ökonomischen Theorie' [The Explanation of the Change of Property Rights with the Help of the Economic Theory], in SCHÜLLER, A. (ed.), *Property Rights und ökonomische Theorie*, München, Vahlen, 1983, 79-109.

HIRSHLEIFER, Jack, 'Evolutionary Models in Economics and Law: Cooperation versus Conflict Strategies', **4** *Research in Law and Economics*, 1982, 1-60.

HOLMES, Oliver Wendell, *The Common Law*, Boston, Little Brown, 1880.

HOVENKAMP, Herbert J., 'The Economics of Legal History', **67** *Minnesota Law Review*, 1983, 645-697.

KENNEDY, Duncan, 'Cost-Reduction Theory as Legitimation', **90** *Yale Law Journal*, 1981, 1275-1283.

KUBASEK, N., 'The Artificiality of Economic Models as a Guide for Legal Evolution', **33** *Cleveland State Law Review*, 1984-85, 505-512.

LEHMANN, Michael, 'Ökonomie, Sozialbiologie - Humanwissenschaften. Über die Notwendigkeit und Möglichkeit einer interdisziplinären Grundlagenforschung' [Economics, Social Biology - Human Sciences. About the Necessity and Possibility of a Interdisciplinary Fundamental Research], *Der Betriebs-Berater*, 1982, 1997-2004.

LEHMANN, Michael, 'Evolution in Biologie, Ökonomie und Jurisprudenz' [Evolution in Biology, Economics and Jurisprudence], **17** *Rechtstheorie*, 1986, 463-477.

LIBECAP, Gary D., 'Economic Variables and the Development of the Law: The Case of Western Mineral Rights', **38** *Journal of Economic History*, 1978, 338-362.

PRIEST, George L., 'The New Scientism in Legal Scholarship: A Comment on Clark and Posner', **90** *Yale Law Journal*, 1981, 1284-1295.

PRIEST, George L., 'Measuring Legal Change', **3** *Journal of Law, Economics, & Organization*, 1987, 193-225.

REESE, David A., 'Does the Common Law Evolve?', **12** *Hamline Law Review*, 1989, 321-353.

RIZZO, Mario J. (ed.), 'Symposium: Change in the Common Law: Legal and Economic Perspectives. A Symposium Sponsored by The Institute for Humane Studies and the Liberty Fund', **9** *Journal of Legal Studies*, 1980, 189-427.

RUBIN, Paul H. (ed.), 'Symposium: Evolutionary Models in Economics and Law', **4** *Research in Law and Economics*, 1982, 218 p.

SHUGHART, William F., II and TOLLISON, Robert D., 'Corporate Chartering: An Exploration in the Economics of Legal Change', **23** *Economic Inquiry*, 1985, 585-599.

SIMPSON, A.W.B., 'The Horwitz Thesis and the History of Contracts', **46** *University of Chicago Law Review*, 1979, 533-601.

SMITH, James Charles, 'Book Review of Morton J. Horwitz *The Transformation of American Law*, 1780-1860', *Wisconsin Law Review*, 1977, 1253-1276.

TERREBONNE, R. Peter, 'A Strictly Evolutionary Model of Common Law', **10** *Journal of Legal Studies*, 1981, 397-407.

WILLIAMS, Stephen F., 'The Static Conception of the Common Law: A Comment', **9** *Journal of Legal Studies*, 1980, 277-289.

9800 Intertemporal Law. Retroactivity

ABRAMS, Howard E., 'Rethinking Tax Transitions: A Reply to Dr. Shachar', **98** *Harvard Law Review*, 1985, 1809-1889.

ALM, James, 'Uncertain Tax Policies, Individual Behavior, and Welfare', **78** *American Economic Review*, 1988, 237-245.

BIZER, David S. and JUDD, Kenneth L., 'Taxation and Uncertainty', **79** *American Economic Review. Papers and Proceedings*, 1989, 331-336.

GRAETZ, Michael J., 'Retroactivity Revisited', **98** *Harvard Law Review*, 1985, 1820-1841.

KAPLOW, Louis, 'An Economic Analysis of Legal Transitions', **99** *Harvard Law Review*, 1986, 509-617.

MUNZER, Stephen R., 'Retroactive Law', **6** *Journal of Legal Studies*, 1977, 373-397.

QUINN, John and TREBILCOCK, Michael J., 'Compensation, Transition Costs, and Regulatory Change', **32** *University of Toronto Law Journal*, 1982, 117-175.

RAMSEYER, J. Mark and NAKAZATO, Minoru, 'Tax Transitions and the Protection Racket: A Reply to Professors Graetz and Kaplow', **75** *Virginia Law Review*, 1989, 1155-1175.

RUSSELL, A.M. and RICKARD, J.A., 'A Model of Tax Evasion Incorporating Income Variation and Retroactive Penalities', **26** *Australian Economic Papers*, 1987, 254-264.

SCHWARTZ, Gary T., 'New Products, Old Products, Evolving Law, Retroactive Law', **58** *New York University Law Review*, 1983, 796-852.

SHACHAR, Avishai, 'The Importance of Considering Liabilities in Tax Transitions', **98** *Harvard Law Review*, 1985, 1842-1868.

SKOGH, Göran, Rättssäkerhet i marknadsekonomin [Legal Certainty in the Market Economy], in *Rättssäkerhet och Demokrati*, Ratios förlag, 1985.

VAN DEN BROEK, Peter, 'Retrospectivity and Transitional Relief in Tax Law', **6** *Australian Tax Forum*, 1989, 201-216.

WALZ, W. Rainer, 'Rechtssicherheit und Risikozuweisung bei Steuerrechtsänderungen - Verbotene Rückwirkung, gebotene Übergangsregelung, richterliche Vertragsanpassung' [Legal Certainty and Risk Allocation for Changes in Tax Law - Illegal Retroaction, Transitional Rules, Judicial Adjustment of Contract], in FINSINGER, Jörg and SIMON, Jürgen, (eds.), *Recht und Risiko*, 1988, München, Florentz, 252-286.

WEISS, Elliott J. and WHITE, Lawrence J., 'Of Econometrics and Indeterminacy: A Study of Investors' Reactions to "Changes" in Corporate Law', **75** *California Law Review*, 1987, 551-607.

9900 Efficiency of the (Common) Law

ARANSON, Peter H., 'Economic Efficiency and the Common Law: A Critical Survey', in GRAF VON DER SCHULENBURG, J.-Matthias and SKOGH, Göran (eds.), *Law and Economics and The Economics of Legal Regulation*, Dordrecht, Kluwer, 1986, 51-84.

ARMITAGE, Thomas C., 'Economic Efficiency as a Legal Norm', **7** *Research in Law and Economics*, 1985, 1-27.

BACKHAUS, Jürgen G., 'Efficient Statute Law', in FAURE, Michael and VAN DEN BERGH, Roger (eds.), *Essays in Law and Economics. Corporations, Accident Prevention and Compensation for Losses*, Antwerpen, Maklu, 1989, 23-32.

BRUCE, Christopher J., 'Testing the Hypothesis of Common Law Efficiency: The Doctrine of Informed Consent', **6** *Research in Law and Economics*, 1984, 227-265.

BUCHANAN, James M., 'Law and the Invisible Hand', in SIEGAN, Bernard H., *The Interaction of Economics and the Law*, Lexington, Lexington Books, 1978.

CARRINGTON, Paul D., 'Adjudication as a Private Good: A Comment', **8** *Journal of Legal Studies*, 1979, 303-317.

CLARK, Robert C., 'The Interdisciplinary Study of "Legal Evolution"', **90** *Yale Law Journal*, 1981, 1238-1274.

COOTER, Robert D., 'Liberty, Efficiency, and Law', **50 (4)** *Law and Contemporary Problems*, 1987, 141-163.

CREW, Michael A. and TWIGHT, Charlotte, 'On the Efficiency of Law: A Public Choice Perspective', **66** *Public Choice*, 1990, 15-136.

DENZAU, Arthur, 'Litigation Expenditures as Private Determinants of Judicial Decisions: A Comment', **8** *Journal of Legal Studies*, 1979, 295-302.

DICKE, Hugo and HARTUNG, Hans, *Externe Kosten von Rechtsvorschriften* [External Effects of Legal Rules], Möglichkeiten und Grenzen der ökonomischen Gesetzesanalyse, Tübingen, J.C.B. Mohr, 1986, 123 p.

ELLICKSON, Robert C., 'A Hypothesis of Wealth-Maximizing Norms: Evidence from the Whaling Industry', **5** *Journal of Law, Economics, & Organization*, 1989, 83-97.

EPSTEIN, Richard A., 'The Static Conception of the Common Law', **9** *Journal of Legal Studies*, 1980, 253-275.

EPSTEIN, Richard A., 'The Social Consequences of Common Law Rules', **95** *Harvard Law Review*, 1982, 1717-1751.

FRIEDMAN, David, 'Private Creation and Enforcement of Law: A Historical Case', **8** *Journal of Legal Studies*, 1979, 399-415.

GOLDBERG, Victor P. (ed.), 'Discussion by Seminar Participants', **8** *Journal of Legal Studies*, 1979, 323-398.

HAZARD, Geoffrey C., Jr., 'Adjudication as a Private Good: A Comment', **8** *Journal of Legal Studies*, 1979, 319-321.

KENNEDY, Duncan, 'Cost-Reduction Theory as Legitimation', **90** *Yale Law*

Journal, 1981, 1275-1283.

KENNY, Paul, 'Economic Analysis and Efficiency in the Common Law', in CRANSTON, Ross and SCHICK, Anne (eds.), *Law and Economics*, Canberra, Australian National University, 1982, 42-58.

KORNHAUSER, Lewis A., 'A Guide to the Perplexed Claims of Efficiency in the Law', **8** *Hofstra Law Review*, 1980, 591-639.

KÜBLER, Friedrich, ' Effizienz als Rechtsprinzip - Überlegungen zum rechtspraktischen Gebrauch ökonomischer Argumente' [Efficiency als Legal Principle - Considerations for the Legal Practice Use of Economic Arguments], in BAUR, Jürgen F., HOPT, Klaus J. and MAILÄNDER, Peter K. (eds.), *Festschrift für Ernst Steindorff*, 1990, Berlin, de Gruyter, 687-704.

LANDES, William M. and POSNER, Richard A., 'Adjudication as a Private Good', **8** *Journal of Legal Studies*, 1979, 235-284.

LIEBERMANN, Yehoshua, 'Economic Efficiency and Making of the Law: The Case of Transaction Costs in Jewish Law', **15** *Journal of Legal Studies*, 1986, 387-404.

LINDER, Douglas O., 'Some Doubts Concerning the Selection Hypothesis of George Priest', **37** *University of Kansas Law Review*, 1989, 319-347.

MICHELMAN, Frank I., 'Norms and Normativity in the Economic Theory of Law', **62** *Minnesota Law Review*, 1978, 1015-1048.

MILLER, Geoffrey P., 'Comment: Some Thoughts on the Equilibrium Hypothesis', **69** *Boston University Law Review*, 1989, 561-568.

PARSONS, Wes (Student Contribution), 'The Inefficient Common Law', **92** *Yale Law Journal*, 1983, 863-887.

POLLOCK, Stewart G., 'Economic Analysis at Work in Judicial Decision-Making', *Annual Survey of American Law*, 1988, 133-136.

POSNER, Richard A., 'The Ethical and Political Basis of the Efficiency Norm in Common Law Adjudication', **8** *Hofstra Law Review*, 1980, 487-507.

POSNER, Richard A., 'A Reply to Some Recent Criticisms of the Efficiency Theory of the Common Law', **9** *Hofstra Law Review*, 1981, 775 ff.

POSNER, Richard A., 'The Present Situation in Legal Scholarship', **90** *Yale Law Journal*, 1981, 1113-1130.

PRIEST, George L., 'The Common Law Process and the Selection of Efficient Rules', **6** *Journal of Legal Studies*, 1977, 65-82.

PRIEST, George L., 'The New Scientism in Legal Scholarship: A Comment on Clark and Posner', **90** *Yale Law Journal*, 1981, 1284-1295.

RICHTER, Rudolf, 'The Efficiency of the Common Law: A New Institutional Economics Perspective: Comment', in PETHIG, Rudiger and SCHLIEPER, Ulrich (eds.), *Efficiency, Institutions, and Economic Policy: Proceedings of a Workshop Held by the Sonderforschungsbereich 5 at the University of Mannheim, June 1986*, New York, Springer, 1987, 123-125.

RIZZO, Mario J., 'Uncertainty, Subjectivity and the Economic Analysis of Law', in RIZZO, Mario J. (ed.), *Time, Uncertainty and Disequilibrium*, Lexington, Lexington Books, 1979, 71-89.

ROBERTS, Neal A., 'Beaches: The Efficiency of the Common Law and Other Fairy

Tales', **28** *UCLA Law Review*, 1980, 169-196.

ROSE-ACKERMAN, Susan, 'Tullock and the Inefficiency of the Common Law', in ROWLEY, Charles K. (ed.), *Democracy and Public Choice: essays in Honor of Gordon Tullock*, Oxford, Blackwell, 1987, 181-185.

ROWLEY, Charles K. and BROUGH, Wayne, 'The Efficiency of the Common Law: A New Institutional Economics Perspective', in PETHIG, Rudiger and SCHLIEPER, Ulrich (eds.), *Efficiency, Institutions, and Economic Policy: Proceedings of a Workshop Held by the Sonderforschungsbereich 5 at the University of Mannheim, June 1986*, New York, Springer, 1987, 103-121.

RUBIN, Paul H., 'Why is the Common Law Efficient?', **6** *Journal of Legal Studies*, 1977, 51-63.

RUBIN, Paul H., *Business Firms and the Common Law. The Evolution of Efficient Rules*, New York, Praeger, 1983, 189 p.

SAJó, András, 'A gazdaság jogi szabályozásának egy lehetséges útja' [A Possible Way of Legal Regulation of the Economy], **4** *Jogtudományi Közlöny*, 1981, 297-308.

SAJó, András, 'A jog a gazdaság szabályozástechnikái közt' [Law as One of the Regulating Means of the Economy], **3** *Jogtudományi Közlöny*, 1987, 126-132.

SAMUELS, Warren J. and MERCURO, Nicholas, 'Posnerian Law and Economics on the Bench', **4** *International Review of Law and Economics*, 1984, 107-130.

SAMUELS, Warren J. and MERCURO, Nicholas, 'Wealth Maximization and Judicial Decision-Making: The Issues Further Clarified', **6** *International Review of Law and Economics*, 1986, 133-137.

SCHÄFER, Hans-Bernd, 'Allokationseffizienz als Grundprinzip des Zivilrechts' [Allocative Efficiency as Basic Principle of Civil Law], in OTT, Claus and SCHÄFER, Hans-Bernd (eds.), *Allokationseffizienz in der Rechtsordnung*, Berlin, Springer, 1989, 1-24.

SCHEPPELE, Kim Lane, *Legal Secrets, Equality and Efficiency in the Common Law*, Chicago, University of Chicago Press, 1988, 363 p.

SIMPSON, A.W.B., 'The Horwitz Thesis and the History of Contracts', **46** *University of Chicago Law Review*, 1979, 533-601.

SMITH, Steven D., 'Rhetoric and Rationality in the Law of Negligence', **69** *Minnesota Law Review*, 1984, 277-323.

VELJANOVSKI, Cento G., 'The Role of Economics in the Common Law', **7** *Research in Law and Economics*, 1985, 41-64.

WITTMAN, Donald, 'Why Democracies Produce Efficient Results', **97** *Journal of Political Economy*, 1989, 1395-1424.

PART II:

LAW & ECONOMICS IN EUROPE: NATIONAL SURVEYS OF NON-ENGLISH PUBLICATIONS

LAW & ECONOMICS IN AUSTRIA
Wolfgang Weigel

BÖHM, Stephan, 'Handlungsrechte, Wettbewerb und Privatisierung' [Property Rights, Competition and Privatization], **34** *Wirtschaftspolitische Blätter*, 1987, 576-583. (Subject Code: 0650, 2100)

BYDLINSKI, Franz, *Fundamentale Rechtsgrundsätze* [Fundamental Principles of Law], Vienna-New York, Springer Publishers, 1988, 133-290 (ch.III). (Subject Code: 0300, 0650)

CLEMENZ, Gerhard and INDERST, Alfred, *Ökonomische Analyse der Ladenöffnungszeiten* [Economic Analysis of Shop Opening Hours], Vienna, Manz Publishers, 1989, 128 p. (Subject Code: 5250)

GENSER, Bernd (ed.), *Abfertigungsregeln im Spannungsfeld der Wirtschaftspolitik* [Rules of Indemnification as a Current Problem in Economic Policy], Vienna, Manz Publishers, 1987, 272 p. (Subject Code: 5400)

HAFNER, Gerhard, *Seerechtliche Verteilung von Nutzungsrechten* [The Assignment of Property Rights on the Sea], Vienna-New York, Springer Publishers, 1987, 533 p. (Subject Code: 0650, 3500)

HANREICH, Hanspeter, 'Verbraucherpolitik durch Wettbewerbsrecht' [Consumer Policy By Competition Law], in KORINEK, Karl (ed.), *Beiträge zum Wirtschaftsrecht*, Vienna, Orac Publishers, 1983, 539-560. (Subject Code: 5200, 5700)

LEWISCH, Peter, *Erwerbsfreiheit und Bedarfsprüfung* [The Freedom to Earn one's Living as Subjected to Regulations Concerning Needs], Vienna, Marktwirtschaftliche Schriften des Carl Menger Institutes, 1989, 47 p. (Subject Code: 5240, 5930)

MATAJA, Victor, *Das Recht des Schadenersatzes vom Standpunkte der Nationalökonomie* [The Law of Compensation from the Standpoint of Economics], Leipzig, 1888. (Subject Code: 0020, 3000)

MUSGER, Gottfried, 'Ökonomische Analyse der Umwelthaftung' [Economic Analysis of Environmental Liability], in HALREICH, Hanspeter and SCHWARZER, Stephan (project management), *Umwelthaftung*, Vienna, Austrian Economic Publishers, 1991, 22-41. (Subject Code: 3800)

PRISCHING, Manfred, 'Ökonomische Rechtslehre? Über die Prämissen und Grenzen des "Economic Approach" im Recht' [Economic Jurisprudenz? On the Premisses and Limits of the Economic Approach to Law], in FREISITZER, Kurt, HOLZER, Hans Ludwig, MANTL, Wolfgang and HÖFLECHNER, Walter (eds.), *Reformen des Rechts. Festschrift zur 200-Jahr-Feier der Rechtswissenschaftlichen Fakultät der Universität Graz*, Graz, Akademische Druck u.Verlagsanstalt, 1979, 995-1020. (Subject Code: 0010, 0300)

PRISCHING, Manfred, 'Sozioökonomische Bedingungen der Kriminalität. Über empirische Divergenzen und theoretische Kontroversen' [Socio-economic Conditions of Criminality. On Empirical Divergencies and Theoretical Controversies], **65** *Monatsschrift für Kriminologie und Strafrechtsreform*, 1982, Heft 3, 163-176. (Subject Code: 8000)

PRISCHING, Manfred, 'Über die Karriere einer Handlungstheorie. Der ökonomische Weg auf dem Weg durch die Sozialwissenschaften' [On the Career of a Behavioral Theory. The Economic Way on the way through the Social Sciences], **37** *Zeitschrift für philosophische Forschung*, 1983, 256 -274. (Subject Code: 0300)

PRISCHING, Manfred, 'Regeln für das Handeln. Soziale Entscheidungsmechanismen im Modernisierungsprozeß' [Rules for Behavior. Social Decision Mechanisms in Modernization Process], **18** *Rechtstheorie. Zeitschrift für Logik, Methodenlehre, Kybernetik und Soziologie des Rechts*, 1987, Heft 2, 151-181. (Subject Code: 0300)

ROTH, G., 'Der Schutzzweck richterlicher Kontrolle von AGB' [The Protection Goal of the Judicial Control of Standard Term Clauses], **4(2)** *Österreichische Zeitschrift für Wirtschaftsrecht*, 1977, 32-37. (Subject Code: 4200)

SCHNEIDER, Friedrich und BARTEL, Rainer, *Gemeinwirtschaft versus Privatwirtschaft* [Collective Economics versus Private Economics], Vienna, Manz Publishers, 1989, 315 p. (Subject Code: 5800)

SUPPER, Meinhard, ' Das niederösterreichische Landesrecht und die ökonomische Analyse des Rechts' [The Law of the Province of Lower Austria and the Economic Analysis of Law], in FUNK, Bernd-Christian (project management), *Deregulierung und Entbürokratisierung am Beispiel von Niederösterreich*, Vienna, Austrian economic Publishing Comp., 1988, 43-48. (Subject Code: 0010, 6300)

WEIGEL, Wolfgang, 'Ökonomie und Recht - Eine Einführung' [Economics and Law - An Introduction], **31(3/4)** *Das öffentliche Haushaltswesen in Österreich*, 1990, 169-198. (Subject Code: 0010, 0300)

WEIGEL, Wolfgang, 'Grenzen der Wettbewerbspolitik' [The Limits of Competition Policy], **37(6)** *Wirtschaftspolitische Blätter*, 1990, 560-566. (Subject Code: 5100)

WEIGEL, Wolfgang, 'Ökonomie und Recht - Eine Einführung' [Law and Economics, a Primer], in WEIGEL, Wolfgang (project management) and AUSTRIAN ECONOMIC CHAMBER (ed.), *Economic Analysis of Law - a Collection of Applications*, Vienna, Austrian Economic Publishing Compl., 1991, 13-37. (Subject Code: 0010)

WEIGEL, Wolfgang (project management) and AUSTRIAN ECONOMIC CHAMBER (ed.), *Economic Analysis of Law - a Collection of Applications*, Vienna, Austrian Economic Publishing Compl., 1991, 295 p. (Subject Code: 0040

LAW & ECONOMICS IN BELGIUM
Gerrit De Geest

18de Vlaams Wetenschappelijk Economisch Congres, Brussel 8 en 9 mei 1987, Sociaal-economische Deregulering, Brussel, V.E.H.U.B., 1987, 892 p. (Subject Code: 0040, 5000)

ABRAHAM, J.P. a.o., *De overheidstussenkomst in het financiewezen: Effectief? Efficiënt?* [Government Intervention in Finance: Effective? Efficient?], *Bank-en Financiewezen*, Cahier 12/13, Brussel, 1981, 17-39. (Subject Code: 5570)

ANDERSEN, Cecilia, 'Het Octrooirecht ten dienste van Kleine en Middelgrote Ondernemingen' [Patent Law to the Use of Small and Middle Size Companies], **40** *Economisch en Sociaal Tijdschrift*, 1986, 613-629. (Subject Code: 2930)

BAECK, L., ONGENA, H. and COOLS, J.P., 'Begripsbepaling en situering van het dereguleringsverschijnsel in de geschiedenis van het economisch denken' [Definition and Sketch of the Deregulation Phenomenon in the History of Economic Thought], in *18de Vlaams Wetenschappelijk Economisch Congres, Brussel 8 en 9 mei 1987, Sociaal-economische Deregulering*, Brussel, V.E.H.U.B., 1987, 29-47. (Subject Code: 5000)

BLAUWENS, Gust and VAN DE VOORDE, Eddy, 'Onderzoek naar de Economische Kost van de Regulering van het Goederenvervoer in België' [An Investigation of the Economic Cost of the Regulation of the Transport of Goods in Belgium], **40** *Economisch en Sociaal Tijdschrift*, 1986, 575-592. (Subject Code: 5930)

BLAUWENS, Gust and VAN DE VOORDE, Eddy, 'Deregulering en de vraag naar luchtvervoer' [Deregulation and the Demand for Air Transport], **32** *Tijdschrift voor Economie en Management*, 1988, 127-142. (Subject Code: 5930)

BLONK, W.A.G., 'Vervoer' [Transport], in *18de Vlaams Wetenschappelijk Economisch Congres, Brussel 8 en 9 mei 1987, Sociaal-economische Deregulering*, Brussel, V.E.H.U.B., 1987, 543-560. (Subject Code: 5930)

BONGAERTS, Jan C., 'Inleiding tot de economische analyse van het recht met toepassing op het contractenrecht en het aansprakelijkheidsrecht, inzonderheid de milieuramp te Bhopal' [Introduction to Economic Analysis of Law, with Applications to Contract and Tort Law, and in Particular to the Environmental Disaster in Bhopal], in VAN DEN BERGH, Roger (ed.), *Verslagboek Eerste Werkvergadering recht en Economie*, Antwerpen, Handelshogeschool, 1986, 5-20. (Subject Code: 0010)

BONGAERTS, Jan C., 'Milieubeleid : Regulering of Aansprakelijkheidsregel?' [Environmental Policy: Regulation or Liability?], *Vlaams Jurist Vandaag*, 1987, nr. 1, 17-22. (Subject Code: 3800)

BOUCKAERT, Boudewijn, *Recht op Zoek naar Economie? Prolegomena tot een Economische Analyse van het Recht* [Law in Search for Economics? Introduction to Economic Analysis of Law], Gent, Story-Scientia, 1984, 49 p. (Subject Code: 0000)

BOUCKAERT, Boudewijn, 'Efficiëntie of rechtvaardigheid: het onvermijdelijk dilemma?' [Efficiency or Justice: the Unavoidable Dilemma?], **29** *Tijdschrift voor Sociale Wetenschappen*, 1984, 101-133. (Subject Code: 0010, 0400)

BOUCKAERT, Boudewijn, 'Is de prins een goede herder van de mededinging? Grondslagen van het internationaal Europees economisch recht' [Is the Prince a Good Shepherd for Competition? Basics of international European Economic Law], **15** *Rechtstheorie en Rechtsfilosofie,* 1986, 8-27. (Subject Code: 5700)

BOUCKAERT, Boudewijn, 'Het aansprakelijkheidsrecht tussen rechtvaardigheid en efficiëntie' [Liability Law between Justice and Efficiency], *Vlaams Jurist Vandaag*, 1987, Nr. 1, 23-26. (Subject Code: 3000)

BOUCKAERT, Boudewijn, 'L'analyse économique du droit: vers un renouveau de la science juridique?' [Economic Analysis of Law: Towards a Renewal of Legal Science?], **18** *Revue interdisciplinaire d'études juridiques*', 1987-88, 47-61. (Subject Code: 0010)

BOUCKAERT, Boudewijn, 'Economische analyse van het stadsverval in België: naar een geïntegreerd stadsrenovatiebeleid?' [Economic Analysis of City Decline in Belgium: Towards an Integrated City Renovation Policy?], *Planologische Discussiebijdragen*, 1988, 53-61. (Subject Code: 3600)

BOUCKAERT, Boudewijn, 'Eigendomsrechten vanuit rechtseconomisch perspectief' [Property Rights from an Economic Perspective], **39** *Ars Aequi*, 1990, 777-786. (Subject Code: 2000, 3600)

BOUCKAERT, Boudewijn, 'Zin of Onzin van Planning' [Sense or Nonsense of Planning], *Ruimtelijke Planning*, 1990, Afl. 25, II.D.1.b., 19 p. (Subject Code: 3600)

BOURGOIGNIE, Th., 'Overheid en bedrijfsleven/3 La reglementation des prix en Belgique' [Price Regulation in Belgium], **27** *Economisch en Sociaal Tijdschrift*, 1973, 387-400. (Subject Code: 5100)

BRACKE, F., 'Deregulering en algemeen belang: 1. Bronnen en doelstellingen' [Deregulation and General Interest: Sources and Purposes], in *18de Vlaams Wetenschappelijk Economisch Congres, Brussel 8 en 9 mei 1987, Sociaal-economische Deregulering*, Brussel, V.E.H.U.B., 1987, 101-122. (Subject Code: 5000)

BULCKE, J., 'Industrie en energie: 3. Electriciteit' [Industry and Energy: Electricity], in *18de Vlaams Wetenschappelijk Economisch Congres, Brussel 8 en 9 mei 1987, Sociaal-economische Deregulering*, Brussel, V.E.H.U.B., 1987, 421-440. (Subject Code: 5800)

COUSY, Herman, 'Produktenaansprakelijkheid. Proeve van een juridisch-economische analyse' [Product Liability. Attempt of a Legal-Economic Analysis], *Tijdschrift voor Privaatrecht*, 1976, 995-1035. (Subject Code: 5300)

DAEMS, H. and DE GRAUWE, Paul, 'Determinanten van de overheidsreglementering' [Determinants of Government Regulation], in, *Overheidsinterventies, Effectiviteit en Efficiëntie. Vijftiende Vlaams wetenschappelijk Economisch Congres*, Leuven, Departement Toegepaste Economische Wetenschappen, 1981, 25-41. (Subject Code: 5000)

d'ALCANTARA, G., 'Telecommunicatie. Economische aspecten' [Telecommunication: Economic Aspects], in *18de Vlaams Wetenschappelijk Economisch Congres, Brussel 8 en 9 mei 1987, Sociaal-economische Deregulering*, Brussel, V.E.H.U.B., 1987, 565-579. (Subject Code: 5950)

DAUW, C., 'Financiële deregulering en financiering der investeringen' [Financial Deregulation and Financing of Investments], in *18de Vlaams Wetenschappelijk*

Economisch Congres, Brussel 8 en 9 mei 1987, Sociaal-economische Deregulering, Brussel, V.E.H.U.B., 1987, 695-730. (Subject Code: 5570)

DE BONDT, R. and VAN HERCK, G., 'Prijsbeleid en economische efficiëntie' [Price Policy and Economic Efficiency], in *15de Vlaams Wetenschappelijk Economisch Congres*, Leuven, Universitaire Pers, 1981, 253-278. (Subject Code: 5100)

DE BRUYNE, G., 'Inkomensvorming en deregulering van de arbeidsmarkt: 2. Indexering' [Income Formation and Deregulation in the Labour Market: Indexation], in *18de Vlaams Wetenschappelijk Economisch Congres, Brussel 8 en 9 mei 1987, Sociaal-economische Deregulering*, Brussel, V.E.H.U.B., 1987, 249-263. (Subject Code: 5420)

DE CLERCQ, Marc, 'Liberaal milieubeleid' [Liberal Environmental Policy], **69** *Economisch-Statistische Berichten*, 1984, 488-493. (Subject Code: 3500)

DE CLERCQ, Marc and NAERT, Frank, *De politieke markt* [The Political Market], Antwerpen, Kluwer, 1985, 163 p. (Subject Code: 0020, 9200)

DEGADT, J., 'Het Leefmilieu: relevantie van economische analyses voor een doelmatig overheidsbeleid in het geregionaliseerde België' [The Environment: Relevance of Economic Analyses for an Effective Governmental Policy in Federalized Belgium], **30** *Tijdschrift voor Economie en Management*, 1985, 367-386. (Subject Code: 3500)

DE GEEST, Gerrit, 'James Buchanan, Nobelprijswinnaar economie 1986' [James Buchanan, Nobel Laureate Economics 1986], *De Vlaamse Gids*, 1987, 44-49. (Subject Code: 0200)

DE GEEST, Gerrit, 'Public Choice, mensbeeld en ideologie' [Public Choice, Model of Man and Ideology], **19** *Rechtsfilosofie en Rechtstheorie*, 1990, 109-122. (Subject Code: 0300, 0400)

DE GEEST, Gerrit, 'Public Choice en rechtseconomie' [Public Choice and Law & Economics], **39** *Ars Aequi*, 1990, 666-673. (Subject Code: 0010, 0300, 2600, 9200)

DE KOCK, S., 'De vervuiler betaalt: slogan of noodzaak?' [The Polluter Pays: Slogan or Necessity?], **23** *Tijdschrift voor Economie en Management*, 1978, 99-124. (Subject Code: 3500)

DEMIN, P., 'Industrie en energie: 1. Industrie' [Industry and Energy: Industry], in *18de Vlaams Wetenschappelijk Economisch Congres, Brussel 8 en 9 mei 1987, Sociaal-economische Deregulering*, Brussel, V.E.H.U.B., 1987, 387-398. (Subject Code: 5990)

D'URSEL, Laurent, 'L'analyse économique du droit des contrats' [Economic Analysis of Contract Law], **14** *Revue interdisciplinaire d'études juridiques*, 1985, 45-88. (Subject Code: 4000)

FAURE, Michael, 'Commentaar bij de paper van Dr.Jan C. Bongaerts: Coase en Produktenaansprakelijkheid' [Comment on the paper of Dr. Jan C. Bongaerts: Coase and Product Liability], in VAN DEN BERGH, Roger (ed.), *Verslagboek Eerste Werkvergadering recht en Economie*, Antwerpen, Handelshogeschool, 1986, 31-37. (Subject Code: 0630, 5300)

FAURE, Michael and VAN BUGGENHOUT, Willy, 'Produktenaansprakelijkheid. De Europese richtlijn: harmonisatie en consumentenbescherming? (tweede deel en slot)' [The European Directive Concerning Product Liability, Harmonization and Consumer Protection?], **51** *Rechtskundig Weekblad*, 1987-88, 33-49. (Subject

Code: 5300)

FAURE, Michael and VAN DEN BERGH, Roger, 'Efficiënties van het foutcriterium in het Belgisch aansprakelijkheidsrecht' [Efficiencies of the Fault Criterion in Belgian Liability Law], **51** *Rechtskundig Weekblad*, 1987-88, 1105-1119. (Subject Code: 3000)

FAURE, Michael and VAN DEN BERGH, Roger, *Objectieve aansprakelijkheid, verplichte verzekering en veiligheidsregulering* [Strict Liability, Mandatory Insurance and Safety Regulation], Antwerpen, Maklu, 1989, 386 p. (Subject Code: 0020, 3000, 3800)

GATHON, Henry Jean, 'La distribution de l'eau en Belgique: Prix, coût et efficacité' [The Distribution of Water in Belgium: Price, Cost and Efficiency], **0(119)** *Cahiers Economiques de Bruxelles*, 1988, 371-384. (Subject Code: 5800)

GERMAIN, Marc , 'Externalités, taxation et traitement de la pollution dans le cadre d'un duopole de Cournot' [Externalities, Taxation and Dealing with Pollution in the Case of a Cournot Duopoly], **55** *Recherches Economiques de Louvain*, 1989, 273-292. (Subject Code: 3700)

HOLDERBEKE, F., PERNOT, A. and DENYS, J., 'Inkomensvorming en deregulering van de arbeidsmarkt: 3. Arbeidsvoorwaarden' [Income Formation and Deregulation of the Labour Market: Labour Conditions], in *18de Vlaams Wetenschappelijk Economisch Congres, Brussel 8 en 9 mei 1987, Sociaal-economische Deregulering*, Brussel, V.E.H.U.B., 1987, 265-303. (Subject Code: 5400)

HUYSE, Luc, 'Deregulering en algemeen belang: 2. Deregulering als maatschappelijke reconstructie' []Deregulation and General Interest: Deregulation as Social Reconstruction], in *18de Vlaams Wetenschappelijk Economisch Congres, Brussel 8 en 9 mei 1987, Sociaal-economische Deregulering*, Brussel, V.E.H.U.B., 1987, 123-140. (Subject Code: 5000)

KRUITHOF, Robert, 'Leven en dood van het contract' [Life and Death of Contract], **49** *Rechtskundig Weekblad*, 1985-86, 2761-2768. (Subject Code: 0300)

KRUITHOF, Robert, 'Naschrift' [Afterword], **50** *Rechtskundig Weekblad*, 1986-87, 1669-1680. (Subject Code: 0300)

LANGERWERF, Etienne, 'De sociaal-economische ontwikkeling en de procesvoeringsratio's van de burgerlijke rechtbanken tussen 1950 en 1980' [The Social and Economic Development and the Litigation Ratio's of the Civil Courts Between 1950 en 1980], **40** *Economisch en Sociaal Tijdschrift*, 1986, 87-102. (Subject Code: 7210)

LEUNIS, J. and DE VOS, G., 'De Wet betreffende de Handelsvestigingen: De Eerste 10 Jaar' [The Licensing Law: The First 10 Years], **31** *Tijdschrift voor Economie en Management*, 1986, 309-333. (Subject Code: 5240)

MACKAAY, Ejan, 'La règle juridique observée par le prisme de l'économiste. Une histoire stylisée du mouvement de l'analyse économique du droit' [The Legal Rule Seen Through and Economist's Eyes], *Revue internationale de droit économique*, 1986, 43-88. (Subject Code: 0010)

MEYERS, Jan and STEENBERGEN, Jacques, 'Deregulering, Europese eenmaking en bescherming van het nationaal belang' [Deregulation, European Unification and Protection of National Interest], in *18de Vlaams Wetenschappelijk Economisch Congres, Brussel 8 en 9 mei 1987, Sociaal-economische Deregulering*, Brussel,

V.E.H.U.B., 1987, 51-75. (Subject Code: 5000)

MICHIELSSEN, F. and VAN HECKE, M., 'Prijsbeleid' [Price Policy], in *11de Vlaams Wetenschappelijk Economische Congres. De overheid in de gemengde economie*, Leuven, Universitaire Pers, 1973, 189-223. (Subject Code: 5100)

NAERT, Frank, 'De politieke economie van pressiegroepen' [The Political Economy of Pressure Groups], **69** *Economisch-Statistische Berichten*, 1984, 56-61. (Subject Code: 9200)

NAERT, Frank, 'Overheidsuitgaven en pressiegroepen in België', **32** *Tijdschrift voor Economie en Management*, 1987, 165-187. (Subject Code: 9200)

PACOLET, J., 'Financiële instellingen en markten: 1. Deposito-instellingen' [Financial Institutions and Markets: Deposit Offices], in *18de Vlaams Wetenschappelijk Economisch Congres, Brussel 8 en 9 mei 1987, Sociaal-economische Deregulering*, Brussel, V.E.H.U.B., 1987, 623-647. (Subject Code: 5570)

PEETERS, Bruno, *De continuïteit van het overheidsondernemen: een begrippenanalyse en een kritiek op de uitvoeringsimmuniteit* [The Continuity Principle of Governmental Activities: A Concept Analysis and a Critique on the Execution Immunity], Antwerpen, Maklu, 1989, 559 p. (Subject Code: 6310)

PEETERS, Ch., VERBEKE, A. and WINKELMANS, W., 'Een geïntegreerd overheidsbeleid voor de Belgische binnenvaartsector' [An Integrated Governmental Policy for the Belgian Inland Shipping], **32** *Tijdschrift voor Economie en Management*, 1987, 19-37. (Subject Code: 5930)

PILLE, G., 'Financiële instellingen en markten: 2. Secundaire effectenmarkt' [Financial Institutions and Markets: Secundary Securities Market], in *18de Vlaams Wetenschappelijk Economisch Congres, Brussel 8 en 9 mei 1987, Sociaal-economische Deregulering*, Brussel, V.E.H.U.B., 1987, 649-663. (Subject Code: 5560)

POLLEFLIET, E., 'Prijsvorming en mededingingsbeleid: 1. Economische aspecten' [Price Formation and Competition Policy: Economic Aspects], in *18de Vlaams Wetenschappelijk Economisch Congres, Brussel 8 en 9 mei 1987, Sociaal-economische Deregulering*, Brussel, V.E.H.U.B., 1987, 145-170. (Subject Code: 5100)

POLLEFLIET, E., '1992: regulering of deregulering van de financiële sector?' [1992: Regulation or Deregulation of the Financial Sector?], **42** *Economisch en Sociaal Tijdschrift*, 1988, 631-654. (Subject Code: 5570)

POULMANS, G., 'Inkomensvorming en deregulering van de arbeidsmarkt: 1. Arbeidsflexibiliteit' [Income Formation and Deregulation in the Labour Market: Flexibility], in *18de Vlaams Wetenschappelijk Economisch Congres, Brussel 8 en 9 mei 1987, Sociaal-economische Deregulering*, Brussel, V.E.H.U.B., 1987, 229-248. (Subject Code: 5400)

RAES, Koen, 'Onrechtmatige daad en de markt van pijn en smart' [Tort and the Market for Pain and Sorrow], *Recht en Kritiek*, 1988, 102-125. (Subject Code: 0300, 3200)

RAES, Koen, 'Recht en neo-klassieke economie' [Law and Neo-classical Economics], **17** *Rechtsfilosofie en Rechtstheorie*, 1988, 29-30. (Subject Code: 0300)

RAES, Koen, 'Het recht van de schaarste' [The Law of Scarcity], *Recht en kritiek*, 1990, 380-394. (Subject Code: 0300)

ROSIERS, Marc, 'De Effecten van Leegstand op de Huisvesting' [The Effects of Unoccupied Houses on Housing], **40** *Economisch en Sociaal Tijdschrift*, 1986, 67-85. (Subject Code: 3600)

S'JEGERS, R., FAES, P. en SEGEBARTH, K., 'Deregulering van de handels-en dienstenstromen en van de rechtstreekse investeringen: 3. Dienstverlening' [Deregulation of Trade and Service Flows and of Direct Investments: Service], in *18de Vlaams Wetenschappelijk Economisch Congres, Brussel 8 en 9 mei 1987, Sociaal-economische Deregulering*, Brussel, V.E.H.U.B., 1987, 797-839. (Subject Code: 5900)

SPINNEWYN, F., 'Inkomensvorming en deregulering van de arbeidsmarkt: 4. Sociale Zekerheid' [Income Formation and Deregulation of the Labour Market: Social Security], in *18de Vlaams Wetenschappelijk Economisch Congres, Brussel 8 en 9 mei 1987, Sociaal-economische Deregulering*, Brussel, V.E.H.U.B., 1987, 305-320. (Subject Index: 6060)

STROWEL, Alain, 'Utilitarisme et approche économique dans la théorie du droit. Autour de Bentham et de Posner' [Utilitarianism and Economic Approach in Legal Theory. On Bentham and Posner], **18** *Revue Interdisciplinaire d'Etudes Juridiques*, 1987, 1-45. (Subject Code: 0010, 0400)

STROWEL, Alain, 'A la recherche de l'intérêt en économie. De l'utilitarisme à la science économique néo-classique' [Searching for Interest in Economics. From Utilitarianism to Neo-Classical Economics], in GERARD, Philippe, OST, François, et VAN DE KERCHOVE, Michel (eds.), *Droit et intérêt*, Bruxelles, Fac. Univ. St-Louis, 1990, Vol. I, 37-87. (Subject Code: 0500)

TROJAN, C., 'Landbouw' [Agriculture], in *18de Vlaams Wetenschappelijk Economisch Congres, Brussel 8 en 9 mei 1987, Sociaal-economische Deregulering*, Brussel, V.E.H.U.B., 1987, 475-504. (Subject Code: 5940)

VAN DEN BERGHE, Lutgart, 'Financiële instellingen en markten: 3. Verzekeringen' [Financial Institutions and Markets: Insurance], in *18de Vlaams Wetenschappelijk Economisch Congres, Brussel 8 en 9 mei 1987, Sociaal-economische Deregulering*, Brussel, V.E.H.U.B., 1987, 665-692. (Subject Code: 4600)

VAN DEN BERGH, P., 'Deregulering van de internationale financiële stromen en valutastelsel' [Deregulation of the International Financial Flaws and Exchange System], in *18de Vlaams Wetenschappelijk Economisch Congres, Brussel 8 en 9 mei 1987, Sociaal-economische Deregulering*, Brussel, V.E.H.U.B., 1987, 845-878. (Subject Code: 5570)

VAN DEN BERGH, Roger, 'Over de mededingingsbeperkende werking van de Wet Handelspraktijken of het verhaal van concurrenten die tegen de concurrentie beschermd willen worden' [On the Competition Limiting Effect of the Law on Trade Practices or the Story of Competitors Who Want to Be Protected Against Competition], **34** *Economisch en Sociaal Tijdschrift*, 1980, 421-446. (Subject Code: 5230)

VAN DEN BERGH, Roger, 'De economische reguleringstheorie en de Belgische vestigingswetgeving voor kleine en middelgrote handels- en ambachtsondernemingen' [The Economic Theory of Regulation and the Belgian Licensing Law for Small and Middle Size Companies], in VAN DEN BERGH, Roger (ed.), *Verslagboek Eerste Werkvergadering recht en Economie*, Antwerpen, Handelshogeschool, 1986, 38-49. (Subject Code: 5240)

VAN DEN BERGH, Roger (ed.), *Verslagboek Eerste Werkvergadering recht en Economie* [Conference Volume First Workshop in Law and Economics], Antwerpen, Leerstoel A. Van Melkebeke, Handelshogeschool, 1986, 72 p. (Subject Code: 0040)

VAN DEN BERGH, Roger, 'Le droit civil face à l'analyse économique du droit' [Civil Law Facing Economic Analysis of Law], *Revue internationale de droit économique*, 1988, 229-254. (Subject Code: 0010)

VAN DEN BERGH, Roger, 'Economische analyse van het consumentenrecht' [Economic Analysis of Consumer Protection Law], **39** *Ars Aequi*, 1990, 787-793. (Subject Code: 5200)

VAN DEN BERGH, Roger, 'Wat is rechtseconomie?' [What is Law and Economics?], in HONDIUS, E.H., SCHIPPERS, J.J. and SIEGERS, J.J. (eds.), *Rechtseconomie en Recht,* Zwolle, Tjeenk Willink, 1991, 9-49. (Subject Code: 0010)

VAN DEN BERGH, Roger and FAURE, Michael G., 'De invloed van verzekering op de civiele aansprakelijkheid, een rechtseconomische analyse' [The Influence of Insurance on Tort Liability, an Economic Analysis], in *Preadviezen uitgebracht voor de Vereniging voor Burgerlijk Recht*, Lelystad, Vermande, 1990, 9-53. (Subject Code: 3000)

VAN DEN BERGH, Roger and HEREMANS, Dirk, 'Over krommen en rechten. Een reactie op de kritiek van Kruithof ten aanzien van de economische analyse van het recht' [On Curves and Lines: A Reaction on the Critique of Kruithof on Economic Analysis of Law], **50** *Rechtskundig Weekblad*, 1986-87, 1649-1668. (Subject Code: 0010, 0300)

VAN DEN BERGH, Roger and HEREMANS, Dirk, 'Recht en economie' [Law and Economics], **32** *Tijdschrift voor Economie en Management*, 1987, 139-164. (Subject Code: 0010, 0300)

VAN GERVEN, Yves, 'Regulering van vijandige overnames. De Amerikaanse ervaring' [Regulation of Hostile Takeovers: The American Experience], *Rechtskundig Weekblad*, 1990-91, 833-844. (Subject Code: 5540)

VAN GERVEN, Walter, 'Herijken van economische wetgeving (over reguleren en dereguleren)' [Re-Stamping of Economic Regulation (on Regulating and Deregulating)], **49** *Rechtskundig Weekblad*, 1985-86, 289-308. (Subject Code: 5000)

VAN HULLE, K., 'Informatie en markttransparantie' [Information and Market Transparency], in *18de Vlaams Wetenschappelijk Economisch Congres, Brussel 8 en 9 mei 1987, Sociaal-economische Deregulering*, Brussel, V.E.H.U.B., 1987, 79-97. (Subject Code: 5000)

VAN OEVELEN, Aloïs, 'Enige bedenkingen van een jurist bij de economische analyse van het aansprakelijkheidsrecht' [Some Considerations of a Jurist on Economic Analysis of Tort Law], in VAN DEN BERGH, Roger (ed.), *Verslagboek Eerste Werkvergadering recht en Economie*, Antwerpen, Handelshogeschool, 1986, 21-30. (Subject Code: 3000)

VANBUGGENHOUT, Willy, 'De economische benadering van het recht. Haar nut en grenzen voor de praktijk(bedrijfs)jurist' [The Economic Approach of Law: Its Use and Limits for a (Company) Lawyer], *Vlaamse Jurist Vandaag*, 1987, Nr.1, 27-30. (Subject Code: 0300)

VANDERVEEREN, Christine, VAN ROMPUY, Paul, HEREMANS, Dirk en

HEYLEN, E., *De economische en monetaire unie in de Belgische staatshervorming: juridische en economische aspecten* [The Economic and Monetary Union in the Belgian State Reform: Legal and Economic Aspects], Antwerpen, Maklu, 1987, 250 p. (Subject Code: 9100)

VANWILDEMEERSCH, J., 'Industrie en milieu' [Industry and Environment], in *18de Vlaams Wetenschappelijk Economisch Congres, Brussel 8 en 9 mei 1987, Sociaal-economische Deregulering*, Brussel, V.E.H.U.B., 1987, 399-405. (Subject Code: 3500)

VERMOES, J., 'De programmaovereenkomst: regulering of deregulering?' [Programme Contract: Regulation or Deregulation?], in *18de Vlaams Wetenschappelijk Economisch Congres, Brussel 8 en 9 mei 1987, Sociaal-economische Deregulering*, Brussel, V.E.H.U.B., 1987, 441-454. (Subject Code: 5800)

VUCHELEN, J. en PRAET, P., 'Diensten en vrije beroepen' [Services and Free Professions], in *18de Vlaams Wetenschappelijk Economisch Congres, Brussel 8 en 9 mei 1987, Sociaal-economische Deregulering*, Brussel, V.E.H.U.B., 1987, 507-541. (Subject Code: 5900

LAW & ECONOMICS IN FRANCE

Bertrand Lemennicier

ACKERMAN, Bruce A., 'Deux sortes de recherche "en droit et économie"' [Two Sorts of Research in Law & Economics], *Revue de la Recherche Juridique*, 1986, Nr. 1. (Subject Code: , F, 0300)

ATIAS, Christian, 'La distinction du patrimonial et de l'extra-patrimonial et l'analyse économique du droit: un utile face à face' [The Distinction Between Patrimonial and Extra-Patrimonial Rights and the Economic Analysis of Law], *Revue de la Recherche Juridique*, 1986, Nr. 1. (Subject Code: 2200)

BIENAYME, A., 'Défense et illustration d'une réflexion juridique intégrant l'économie' [Defense and Illustration of a Legal Reflexion Integrating Economics], **64(6)** *La Semaine Juridique*, 33-35. (Subject Code: 0010)

CENTI, Jean-Pierre, 'Quel critère d'efficience pour l'analyse économique du droit' [Which Efficiency Criterion for Economic Analysis of Law], *Revue de la Recherche Juridique*, 1987, Nr. 2. (Subject Code: 0400, 0620)

CHEROT, Jean-Yves, 'Elements pour une théorie de la réglementation' [Elements for a Theory of Regulation], *Revue de la Recherche Juridique*, 1987, Nr. 2. (Subject Code: 5000)

CHEROT, Jean-Yves, 'Trois thèses sur l'analyse économique du droit - Quelques usages de l'approche économique des règles juridiques' [Three Theses on Economic Analysis of Law - Some Uses of the Economic Approach to Legal Rules], *Revue de la Recherche Juridique*, 1987, nr.2, réédité *Problèmes économiques*, La Documentation française, 10 février 1988, nr. 2061. (Subject Code: 0010)

COULANGE, Pierre, 'La production de droit' [The Production of Legal Rules], **3** *Journal des Economistes et des Etudes Humaines*, 1990, 277-302. (Subject Code: 9000)

COULANGE, Pierre, *Analyse économique de la production de droit* [Economic Analysis od the Production of Legal Rules], Ph.D., Aix-en-Provence, Université d'Aix-Marseille III, Faculté d'Economie Appliquée, 1990. (Subject Code: 9000)

DUHARCOURT, Pierre, '"Théories" et "concept" de la régulation' [Regulation as a Theory and as a Concept], **22(5)** *Economies et Sociétés*, 1988, 135-161. (Subject Code: 5000)

ENCAOUA, David and KOEBEL, Philippe, 'Réglementation et déréglementation des téléommunications: Leçons anglo-saxonnes et perspectives d'évolution en France' [Regulation and Deregulation of the Telecommunication Industry: From the American and British Experiences to a Possible Evolution in France], **38** *Revue Economique*, 1987, 475-520. (Subject Code: 5950)

ENCAOUA, David and MOREAUX, Michel, 'L'analyse théorique des problemes de tarification et d'allocation des coûts dans les télécommunications' [The Theoretical Approach to Pricing and Cost Allocation for Telecommunication Services], **38** *Revue Economique*, 1987, 375-413. (Subject Code: 5950)

FLUET, Claude, 'Fraude fiscale et offre de travail au noir' [Tax Evasion and the Supply of Unofficial Labour], **63** *L'actualité économique*, 1987, 225-242.

(Subject Code: 6020)

FLUET, Claude, 'L'analyse économique du droit' [Economic Analysis of Law], **43(3)** *Economie Appliquée*, 1990, 53-66. (Subject Code: 0010)

GARELLO, Jacques, LEMENNICIER, Bertrand and LEPAGE, Henri, *Cinq questions sur les syndicats* [Five Questions on Labor Unions], Paris, PUF, 1990. (Subject Code: 5450)

HANNEQUART, Achille and GREFFE, Xavier, *Economie des interventions sociales* [Economics of Social Interventions], Paris, Economica, 1985, 264 p. (Subject Code: 5000)

HUSSON, B., *Le prise de contrôle d'entreprises* [Takeovers], Paris, Presses Universitaires de France, 1987. (Subject Code: 5540)

KORNHAUSER, Lewis A., L'analyse économique du droit' [The Economic Analysis of Law], *Revue de Synthese*, 1985, Nr.118-119, 313 ff. (Subject Code: 0010)

LEMENNICIER, Bertrand, *Le Marché du Mariage et de la Famille* [The Marriage Market and the Family], Collection Libre Echange, Paris, PUF, 1988. (Subject Code: 1000, 1100)

LEMENNICIER, Bertrand, 'La spécialisation des rôles conjugaux les gains du mariage et la perspective du divorce', *Consommation*, 1980, n. 1. (Subject Code: 1100)

LEMENNICIER, Bertrand, 'Les déterminants de la mobilité matrimoniale' [The Determinants of Matrimonial Mobility], *Consommation*, 1982, n. 2. (Subject Code: 1100)

LEMENNICIER, Bertrand, 'Indemnités de licenciement: assurances tous risques, réparation d'un préjudice ou impôt sur la liberté de contracter' [Damages of Licensing: All Risk Insurance, Retrieving a Loss or Taxation on the Freedom of Contract], in *Droit Prospectif Revue de la Recherche Juridique*, Aix-Marseille, PUF, 1987. (Subject Code: 4600)

LEMENNICIER, Bertrand, 'Bioéthique et liberté' [Bio-Ethics and Liberty], **13** *Droits: revue française de théorie juridique*, 1990, 111-122. (Subject Code: 1000)

LEMENNICIER, Bertrand, *Economie du Droit* [Economics of Law], Paris, Ed. Cujas, 1991, 177 p. (Subject Code: 0000)

LEMENNICIER, Bertrand et LEVY-GARBOUA, 'L'arbitrage autarcie-marché: une explication du travail féminin' [Arbitration Autarchy-Market: An Explanation of Female Labour], *Consommation*, 1981, n. 2. (Subject Code: 1100)

LEPAGE, Henri, *Pourquoi la propriété* [Why Property?], Paris, 1984. (Subject Code: 0020, 2000)

MACKAAY, Ejan J.P., 'La règle juridique observée par le prisme de l'économiste. Une histoire stylisée du mouvement de l'analyse économique du droit' [The Legal Rule Observed Through the Glasses of the Economist. A History of the Law & Economics Movement], *Revue Internationale de Droit Economique*, 1986, 43-83. (Subject Code: 0200)

MACKAAY, Ejan J.P., 'Le paradoxe des droits acquis' [The Paradox of Acquired Rights], in *De "l'ancienne" à la "nouvelle" économie. Essais à l'occasion de la dixième université d'été de la nouvelle économie. Aix-en-Provence 1978-87*, Aix-en-Provence, Librairie de l'université, 1987, 205-219. (Subject Code: 5000, 6200)

MACKAAY, Ejan J.P., 'Les droits intellectuels - entre propriété et monopole' [Intellectual Property Rights - Between Property and Monopoly], **1** *Journal des Economistes et des Etudes Humaines*, 1989-1990. (Subject Code: 2900)

NAUDET, Jean-Yves and SERMENT, Laurent, 'Le droit de propriété garanti par la Convention européenne des droits de l'homme face à l'analyse économique' [Property Law Guaranteed by the European Convention of Human Rights, in the Light of Economic Analysis], **15** *Revue de la Recherche Juridique Droit Perspectif*, 1990, 15-50. (Subject Code: 1500, 2000)

PICARD, Pierre, 'La tarification optimale des télécommunications: une présentation synthétique' [Optimal Pricing for Telecommunications: An Overview], **0(12)** *Annales d'économie et de statistique*, 1988, 27-62. (Subject Code: 5950)

POINT, Patrick, 'Entreprises, normes d'environnement et incitations à reduire les delais de mise en conformité' [Firms, Environmental Standards and Incentives to Promote Compliance], **100** *Revue d'économique politique*, 1990, 260-282. (Subject Code: 3500)

POUGHON, Jean-Michel, 'Une constante doctrinale: l'approche économique du contract', **12** *Droits. Revue française de théorie juridique*, 1990, 47-59. (Subject Code: 4000)

RIBOUD, M., 'Altruisme au sein de la famille, croissance économique et démographie' [Altriusm in the Family, Economic Growth and Demography], *Revue Economique*, 1988, janvier. (Subject Code: 1000)

ROSA, J.J., 'Deréglementation et théorie du droit' [Deregulation and Legal Theory], *Politique Economique*, 1984, Nr. 33. (Subject Code: 5000)

SALAUN, Fabienne, 'Privatisation et reglementation: le cas du British gas' [Privatization and Regulation: The Case of British Gas], **24** *Economies et Sociétés*, 1990, 53-469. (Subject Code: 5800)

SAYAG, Alain and SERBAT, Henri, *L'application du droit de la faillite. Eléments pour un bilan* [The Application of Bankruptcy Law. Data for an Evaluation], Paris, Librairies Techniques, 1982. (Subject Code: 5600)

SCHWEITZER, Serge, 'De "l'ancienne" à la "nouvelle" économie: Comment passe-t-on d'un paradigme à l'autre' [From "Old" to "New" Economics: How One Goes From One Paradigme to Another], in *De "l'ancienne" à la "nouvelle" économie. Essais à l'occasion de la dixième université d'été de la nouvelle économie. Aix-en-Provence 1978-87*, Aix-en-Provence, Librairie de l'université, 1987, 257-274. (Subject Code: 0300)

SEUROT, François, 'Analyse économique de la liberté des contrats' [Economic Analysis of Freedom of Contracts], in *De "l'ancienne" à la "nouvelle" économie. Essais à l'occasion de la dixième université d'été de la nouvelle économie. Aix-en-Provence 1978-87*, Aix-en-Provence, Librairie de l'université, 1987, 275-281. (Subject Code: 4000)

SOFER, C., *La Division du Travail entre Hommes et Femmes* [The Division of Labour Between Men and Women], Paris, Economica, 1985. (Subject Code: 1100)

THÉRET, B., 'La place de l'État dans les théories économiques françaises de la régulation: éléments critiques et repositionnement à la lumière de l'histoire' [The Place of the State in French Economic Theories of Regulation; Critical Arguments and New Posture Brought to Light by History], **43(2)** *Économie*

Appliquée, 1990, 43-81. (Subject Code: 5000

LAW & ECONOMICS IN GERMANY
Patrick Burow

ADAMS, Michael, *Ökonomische Analyse des Sicherungsrechte* [Economic Analysis of Security Law], Königstein/Ts, Athenäum, 1980, 322 p. (Subject Code: 0020, 2800)

ADAMS, Michael, *Ökonomische Analyse des Zivilprozesses* [Economic Analysis of Civil Procedure], Königstein/Ts, Athenäum, 1981, 130 p. (Subject Code: 0020, 7200)

ADAMS, Michael, 'Ist die Ökonomie eine imperialistische Wissenschaft? Über Nutz und Frommen der Ökonomische Analyse des Rechts' [Is Economics an Imperialistic Science? On the Utility of Economic Analysis of Law], in *Juristische Ausbildung*, 1984 (Heft 7), 337-349. (Subject Code: 0300, 0400)

ADAMS, Michael, 'Ökonomische Analyse des Gesetzes zur Regelung des Rechts der Allgemeinen Geschäftsbedingungen' [Economic Analysis of Laws on Standard Term Clauses], in NEUMANN, M. (ed.), *Ansprüche, Eigentums- und Verfügungsrechte*, Schriften des Vereins für Socialpolitik, Vol. 140, 1983, 655-680. (Subject Code: 4200)

ADAMS, Michael, 'Zur Behandlung von Irrtümern und Offenbarungspflichten im Vertragsrecht' [On Mistake and Information Revelation Duties in Contract Law], **186** *Archiv für die civilistische Praxis*, 1986, 453-489. (Subject Code: 4200)

ADAMS, Michael, *Ökonomische Analyse des Gefährdungs- und Verschuldenshaftung* [Economic Analysis of Strict and Fault Liability], Heidelberg, R.v Decker's/C.F. Müller, 1985, 310 p. (Subject Code: 0020, 3000)

ADAMS, Michael, 'Der Zivilprozeß als Folge strategischen Verhaltens' [On Civil Procedure as a Consequence of Strategic Behavior], **7** *Zeitschrift für Rechtssoziologie*, 1986, 212-225. (Subject Code: 7200)

ADAMS, Michael, 'Zur Aufgabe des Haftungsrechts im Umweltschutz' [On the Task of Liability Law for the Protection of the Environment], **99** *Zeitschrift für Zivilprozeß*, 1986, 129-165. (Subject Code: 3000)

ADAMS, Michael, 'Produkthaftung - Wohltat oder Plage - Eine ökomische Analyse' [Product Liability - Benefit or Plague - An Economic Analysis], *Der Betriebsberater*, 1987, Beilage 20 zu Heft 31, 24 p. (Subject Code: 5300)

ADAMS, Michael, 'Ökonomische Analyse der Produkthaftung' [Economic Analysis of Product Liability], *Der Betriebs- Berater*, 1987, Beilage 20, 11/87. (Subject Code: 5300)

ADAMS, Michael, 'Warum kein Ersatz von Nichtvermögensschäden?' [Why No Damages for Nonpecuniary Losses?], in OTT, Claus and SCHÄFER, Hans-Bernd (eds.), *Allokationseffizienz in der Rechtsordnung*, Berlin, Springer, 1989, 210-217. (Subject Code: 3200)

ADAMS, Michael, 'Der Markt für Unternehmenskontrolle und sein Mißbrauch' [The Market of Corporate Control and Its Abuse], *Die Aktiengesellschaft*, 1989, October, 333-338. (Subject Code: 5540)

ADAMS, Michael, 'Das Verursacherprinzip als Leerformel' [The Polluter Pays

Principe as Empty Formula], *Juristenzeitung,* 1989, 789-790. (Subject Code: 3500)

ADAMS, Michael, 'Ökonomische Begründung des AGB-Gesetzes - Verträge bei asymetrischer Information' [The Economic Basis of the German Unfair Contract Terms Act in Case of Asymmetric Information], in *Der Betriebs-Berater*, 1989, 781-788. (Subject Code: 5300)

ADAMS, Michael, 'Höchststimmrechte, Mehrfachstimmrechte und sonstige wundersame Hindernisse auf dem Markt für Unternehmenskontrolle' [Maximum Voting Right, Multiple Voting Right, and some Wonderfull Obstacles from the Market of Corporate Control], **35** *Die Aktiengesellschaft*, 1990, 63-78. (Subject Code: 5540)

ADAMS, Michael, 'Eigentum, Kontrolle und beschränkte Haftung' [Property, Control and Limited Liability], in OTT, Claus and SCHÄFER, Hans-Bernd (eds.), *Ökonomische Probleme des Zivilrechts*, Berlin, Springer, 1991, 193-225. (Subject Code: 5520)

ALSMÖLLER, Horst, *Wettbewerbspolitische Ziele und kooperationstheoretische Hvpothesen im Wandel der Zeit: Eine dogmengeschichtliche Untersuchung von Einstellungen zu Verbundsystemen und von Grunden für diese Einstellungen* [Competition Policy Purpose and Cooperation-Theoretical Hypotheses Through the Times: A Historical Investigation of the Institutions for Alliance Systems and for the Causes of these Institutions], Tübingen, J.C.B. Mohr, 1982, 337 p. (Subject Code: 5700)

ASSMANN, Heinz-Dieter, 'Entwicklungstendenzen der Prospekthaftung' [Tendencies of Liability for Misleading Information Included in Prospectuses], *WM*, 1983, 138-144. (Subject Code: 5220)

ASSMANN, Heinz-Dieter, *Prospekthaftung* [Liability for Misleading Information Included in Prospectuses], Köln, Heymann, 1985, 456 p. (Subject Code: 5220)

ASSMANN, Heinz-Dieter, 'Multikausale Schäden im deutschen Haftungsrecht' [Multicausal Injuries in German Tort Law], in FENYVES, Attila and WEYERS, Hans-Leo (eds.), *Multikausale Schäden im modernen Haftungsrechten*, Frankfurt a.M., Metzner, 1988, 99-151. (Subject Code: 3100)

ASSMANN, Heinz-Dieter, 'Kommentar' (on Ott, Allokationseffizienz, Rechtsdogmatik und Rechtsprechung), in OTT, Claus and SCHÄFER, Hans-Bernd (eds.), *Allokationseffizienz in der Rechtsordnung*, Berlin, Springer, 1989, 45-49. (Subject Code: 0010, 0300)

ASSMANN, Heinz-Dieter, 'Privatrechtliche Tatbestände der Umwelthaftung in ökonomischer Analyse' [Economic Analysis of Civil Liability for Pollution], in WAGNER, Gerd Rainer (ed.), *Unternehmung und ökologische Umwelt*, München, Vahlen, 1990, 201-219. (Subject Code: 3500)

ASSMANN, Heinz-Dieter, KIRCHNER, Christian and SCHANZE, Erich (eds.), *Ökonomische Analyse des Rechts* [Economic Analysis of Law], Kronberg, Athenäum, 1978, 369 p. (Subject Code: 0050)

BACKHAUS, Jürgen G., 'Wirtschaftliche Analyse der Entwicklungsmöglichkeiten mitbestimmter Wirtschaftssysteme' [Economic Analysis of Co-Determination], in KAPPLER, Ekkehard (ed.), *Unternehmensstruktur und Unternehmensentwicklung (Festschrift für Fritz Hodeige)*, Freiburg, Rombach, 1980, 266-289. (Subject Code: 5450)

BACKHAUS, Jürgen G., *Mitbestimmung im Unternehmen* [Co-Determination: A Legal and Economic Analysis], Göttingen, Vandenhoeck & Ruprecht, 1987, 306 p. (Subject Code: 5450)

BARTLING, Hartwig, 'Zur Ökonomie der Kriminalitätsbekämpfung. Eine Integration der Resozialisierung in die Kriminalökonomie' [On the Economics of Criminal Policy: An Integration of Resocializing in Criminal Economics], *Zeitschrift für Wirtschafts- und Sozialwissenschaften*, 1974, 313-333. (Subject Code: 8000)

BAUM, Herbert, 'Das Stabilisierungspotential staatlich administrierter Preise' [On the Stabilization Effects of Public Regulated Prices], **190** *Jahrbucher fur Nationalokonomie und Statistik*, 1976, 349-376. (Subject Code: 5100)

BAUM, Herbert, 'Verteilungswirkungen der staatlichen Preispolitik' [Effects of Public Regulated Prices on Distribution of Income], **193** *Jahrbucher fur Nationalokonomie und Statistik*, 1978, 220-243. (Subject Code: 5100)

BEHRENS, Peter, 'Aspekte einer ökonomischen Theorie des Rechts' [Aspects of an Economic Theory of Law], **12** *Rechtstheorie*, 1981, 472-490. (Subject Code: 0010, 0300)

BEHRENS, Peter, *Die ökonomischen Grundlagen des Rechts* [The Economic Foundations of Law], Tübingen, Mohr, 1986, 386 p. (Subject Code: 0000)

BEHRENS, Peter, 'Über das Verhältnis der Rechtswissenschaft zur Nationalökonomie: Die ökonomischen Grundlagen des Rechts' [On the Interrelationship between Law and Economics: The Economic Foundations of Law], in BOETTCHER, Erik, HERDER-DORNEICH, Philipp and SCHENK, Karl-Ernst (eds.), **7** *Jahrbuch für neue Politische Ökonomie*, Tübingen, J.C.B. Mohr, 1988, 209-228. (Subject Code: 0010)

BEHRENS, Peter, 'Die Bedeutung der ökonomischen Analyse des Rechts für das Arbeitsrecht' [The Importance of Economic Analysis of Law for Labour Law], **20** *Zeitschrift für Arbeitsrecht*, 1989, 209-238. (Subject Code: 5400)

BEIER, Friedrich-Karl, 'Die Bedeutung des Patentsystems für den technischen, wirtschaftlichen und sozialen Fortschritt' [The Significance of Patent Law for the Technical, Economic and Social Evolution], *Gewerblicher Rechtsschutz und Urheberrecht - Internationaler teil*, 1979, 227-235. (Subject Code: 2930)

BITTLINGMAYER, George, 'Die wettbewerbspolitische Vorstellungen der Chicago School' [Competition Policy According to the Chicago School], **37** *Wirtschaft und Wettbewerb*, 1987, 709-718. (Subject Code: 5700)

BÖBEL, Ingo, *Eigentum, Eigentumsrechte und Institutioneller Wandel* [Property, Property Rights and Institutional Change], Berlin, Springer Verlag, 1988, 360 p. (Subject Code: 0650, 2000)

BONGAERTS, Jan C. and HEINRICHS, Dirk, 'Deutsche Umweltschutzgesetze und Umweltschutzinvestitionen des produzierenden Gewerbes' [German Environmental Protection Legislation and Environmental Investment by West German Manufacturing Industries], **32(3)** *Konjunkturpolitik*, 1986, 151-163. (Subject Code: 3500)

BONGAERTS, Jan C., MEYERHOFF, Jürgen, THOMASBERGER, Claus and WITTKE, Anja, *Lösungsansätze für ein ganzheitliches System von Umweltsteuern und Sonderabgaben in der Bundesrepublik Deutschland* [A Solution for a Total Environmental System and Special Taxes in the Federal Republic of Germany], Berlin, Schriftenreihe des Instituts für Oekologische

Wirtschaftsforschung Nr. 31, 1989. (Subject Code: 3500, 3700)

BORCHERT, Manfred, und GROSSEKETTLER, H., *Preis- und Wettbewerbstheorie: Marktprozesse als analytisches Problem und ordnungspolitische Gestaltungsaufgabe* [Price Theory and Competition Theory: Market Processes as Analytical Problem and Policy Recommendations], Verlag W. Kohlhammer, 1985, 371 p. (Subject Code: 5700)

BRINKMANN, Thomas and KÜBLER, Friedrich, 'Überlegungen zur Ökonomischen Analyse im Unternehmensrecht' [Thoughts on an Economic analysis of Company Law], **137** *Zeitschrift fur die gesamte Staatswissenschaft* 1981, 681-688. (Subject Code: 5500)

BRÜGGEMEIER, Gert, 'Die Gefährdungshaftung der Produzenten nach der EG-Richtlinie - ein Fortschritt der Rechtsentwicklung?' [Strict Liability of Producers according to the EC-Directive - An Improvement in Legal Development?], in OTT, Claus and SCHÄFER, Hans-Bernd (eds.), *Allokationseffizienz in der Rechtsordnung*, Berlin, Springer, 1989, 228-247. (Subject Code: 5300)

BUHBE, Matthes, *Ökonomische Analyse von Eigentumsrechten - Der Beitrag der economics of property rights zur Theorie der Institutionen* [Economic Analysis of Property Rights - The Contribution of the Property Rights Approach to the Theory of Institutions], Frankfurt am Main, Peter D. Lang, 1980, 185 p. (Subject Code: 0650, 2000)

BUND, Dorothee, *Die Ökonomische Theorie der Verfassung* [The Economic Theory of the Constitution], Baden-Baden, Nomos, 1984, 96 p. (Subject Code: 9100)

DICKE, Hugo and HARTUNG, Hans, *Externe Kosten von Rechtsvorschriften* [External Effects of Legal Rules], Möglichkeiten und Grenzen der ökonomischen Gesetzesanalyse, Tübingen, J.C.B. Mohr, 1986, 123 p. (Subject Code: 9300, 9900)

DRUKARCZYK, Jochen, 'Ökonomische Analyse der Rechtsprechung des BGH zur Sittenwidrigkeit von Sanierungskrediten' [Economic Analysis of the Jurisprudence of the Bundesgerichtshof on the Immorality of Reorganization Credit], in *Kapitalmarkt und Finanzierung*, Jahrestagung des Vereins für Socialpolitik in München, 1987, 379-397. (Subject Code: 5570)

DRUKARCZYK, Jochen, *Unternehmen und Insolvenz - Zur effizienten Gestaltung des Kreditsicherungs- und Insolvenzrechts* [Entrepreneurship and Insolvency - On the Efficient Shape of Safeguarding of Credits Law and Insolvency Law], Wiesbaden, Gabler Verlag, 1987, 424 p. (Subject Code: 4600, 5570, 5600)

EGER, Thomas, 'Einführung in die Ökonomische Analyse des Rechts' [Introduction to the Economic Analysis of Law], in NAGEL, B. (ed.), *Wirtschaftsrecht II*, München, Oldenborg, 1989, 18-35 (Eigentumsrecht), 51-62 (Deliktrecht), 150-158 (Vertragsrecht) (Subject Code: 0010)

EGER, Thomas, 'Kommentar' [Comment] (On Finsinger and von Randow, Neue Akivitäten und Haftungsregeln), in OTT, Claus and SCHÄFER, Hans-Bernd (eds.), *Ökonomische Probleme des Zivilrechts*, Berlin, Springer, 1991, 109-114. (Subject Code: 3000)

EGER, Thomas, NAGEL, Bernhard, and WEISE, Peter, 'Effizienz und Menschenwürde - Ein Gegensatz?' [Efficiency and Human Dignity - An Opposition?], in OTT, Claus and SCHÄFER, Hans-Bernd (eds.), *Ökonomische Probleme des Zivilrechts*, Berlin, Springer, 1991, 18-34. (Subject Code: 0610, 0620)

EGGERSTEDT, Harald, 'Wettbewerb and Regulierung auf Versicherungsmarkten' [Competition and Regulation in Insurance Markets], **107** *Zeitschrift fur Wirtschafts und Sozialwissenschaften*, 1987, 397-416. (Subject Code: 4600)

EGGERSTEDT, Harald, 'Uber Regulierung und Deregulierung von Versicherungsmarkten. Eine Replik' [On Regulation and Deregulation of Insurance Markets. A Reply], **58** *Zeitschrift fur Betriebswirtschaft*, 1988, 704-707. (Subject Code: 4600)

EICKHOF, Norbert, 'Versorgungswirtschaft und Wettbewerbsordnung' [Public Utilities and the Competitive System], in EUCKEN, Walter and BOHM, Franz (eds.), *Ordo: Jahrbuch fur die Ordnung von Wirtschaft und Gesellschaft. Band 37*, Stuttgart, Fischer, 1986, 201-218. (Subject Code: 5800)

ENDRES, Alfred, 'Das Coase-Theorem bei langfristiger Betrachtung' [The Coase Theorem in a Long Term Perspective], **27** *Jahrbuch für Sozialwissenschaft*, 1976, 430-433. (Subject Code: 0630)

ENDRES, Alfred, 'Die Coase-Kontroverse' [The Coase Controversy], **133** *Zeitschrift für die gesamte Staatswissenschaft*, 1977, 637-651. (Subject Code: 0630)

ENDRES, Alfred, *Umwelt- und Ressourcenökonomie* [Environmental and Resources Economics], Darmstadt, 1985, 193 p. (Subject Code: 3500)

ENDRES, Alfred, 'Allokationswirkungen des Haftungsrechts' [Allocative Effects of Liability Law], in **40(1)** *Jahrbuch für Sozialwissenschaft*, 1989, 115-129. (Subject Code: 3000, 4400)

ENDRES, Alfred and GAFGEN, Gerard, 'Wettbewerb und Regulierung auf dem bundesdeutschen Lebensversicherungsmarkt' [Competition and Regulation in the W. German Life Insurance Market], **205** *Jahrbucher fur Nationalokonomie und Statistik*, 1988, 11-29. (Subject Code: 4600)

ENDRES, Alfred and GÄFGEN, Gerard, 'Regulierung und Versicherungswirtschaft - Die ökonomische Perspektive' [Regulation and the Insurance Industry - The Economic Perspective], in Forschungsgesellschaft für Wettbewerb und Unternehmensorganisation - FWU (eds.), *Versicherungsmärkte im Wettbewerb*, Baden-Baden, 1989, 11-42. (Subject Code: 4600)

ENDRES, Alfred and SCHWARZE, Reimund, 'Allokationswirkungen einer Umwelt-Haftpflichtversicherung' [Allocative Effects of an Environmental Liability Insurance], in **14** *Zeitschrift für Umweltpolitik und Umweltrecht*, 1991, 1-25. (Subject Code: 3500, 4600)

ENGELHARDT, Günther, 'Strafzuschlag zum Schadensersatz, Kommentar' [Punitive Damages, Comment] (On Köndgen, Immaterialschadensersatz, Gewinnabschöpfung oder Genugtuung in Geld bei vorsätzlichen Vertragsbruch?), in OTT, Claus and SCHÄFER, Hans-Bernd (eds.), *Ökonomische Probleme des Zivilrechts*, Berlin, Springer, 1991, 183-190. (Subject Code: 4440)

ESCHENBURG, Rolf, 'Vertragstheoretisches Denken in der Ökonomie' [Contractual Theory in Economics], **23** *Hamburger Jahrbuch zur Wirtschafts- und Gesellschaftspolitik*, 1978, 221-236. (Subject Code: 0400)

ESCHENBURG, Rolf, 'Mikroökonomische Aspekte von Property Rights' [Microeconomic Aspects of Property Rights], in SCHENK, K.E. (ed.), *Ökonomische Verfügungsrechte und Allokationsmechanismen in Wirtschaftssystemen*, Schriften des Vereins für Socialpolitik, Vol. 97, N.F., 1978, 9-27. (Subject Code: 0650, 2000)

FARNY, Dieter, 'Uber Regulierung und Deregulierung von Versicherungsmarkten' [On Regulating and Deregulating Insurance Markets], **57** *Zeitschrift fur Betriebswirtschaft*, 1987, 1001-023. (Subject Code: 4600)

FEZER, Karl-Heinz, 'Aspekte einer Rechtskritik an der economic analysis of law und am property rights approach' [Aspects of a Legal Critique on Law & Economics and the Property Rights Approach], *Juristenzeitung*, 1986, 817-824. (Subject Code: 0300, 0650)

FEZER, Karl-Heinz, 'Nochmals: Kritik an der ökonomischen Analyse des Rechts' [Once More: Critique on the Economic Analysis of Law], *Juristenzeitung*, 1988, 223-228. (Subject Code: 0300)

FINSINGER, Jörg, *Verbraucherschutz auf Versicherungsmärkten* [Consumer Protection in Insurance Markets], München, Florentz, 1988, 219 p. (Subject Code: 4600, 5200)

FINSINGER, Jörg, 'Zur Deregulierung von Versicherungsmarkten' [On the Deregulation of Insurance Markets], **58** *Zeitschrift fur Betriebswirtschaft*, 1988, 698-703. (Subject Code: 4600)

FINSINGER, Jörg, 'Kommentar' [Comment] (on Lehmann, Die Zivilrechtliche Haftung für Werbeangaben bei der Vertragsanbahnung als Problem der Allokationseffizienz), in OTT, Claus and SCHÄFER, Hans-Bernd (eds.), *Allokationseffizienz in der Rechtsordnung*, Berlin, Springer, 1989, 185-187. (Subject Code: 5220)

FINSINGER, Jörg and SIMON, Jürgen, 'Vertragsbruch und Schadensersatz' [Breach of Contract and Damages], **2** *Kritische Vierteljahresschrift für Gesetzgebung und Rechtswissenschaft*, 1987, 262-274. (Subject Code: 4400)

FINSINGER, Jörg and SIMON, Jürgen, *Eine ökonomische Bewertung der EG-Produkthaftungsrichtlinie und des Produkthaftungsgesetzes* [An Economic Appreciation of the EC-Product Liability Directive and the Product Liability Laws], Arbeitsbericht Hochschule Lüneburg, Fachbereich Wirtschafts- und Sozialwissenschaften, 1988, 44 p. (Subject Code: 5300)

FINSINGER, Jörg and SCHULENBURG, J. Matthias Graf von der, 'Der Sonntagsverkauf' [The Effects of Sunday Trading], **109** *Zeitschrift fur Wirtschafts und Sozialwissenschaften*, 1989, 119-128. (Subject Code: 5250)

FINSINGER, Jörg and VON RANDOW, Phillip, 'Neue Aktivitäten und Haftungsregeln - Zugleich ein Beitrag zur ökonomischen Analyse des privaten Nachbarrechts' [New Activities and Liability Rules - Also a Contribution to the Economic Analysis of Private Neighbour Law], in OTT, Claus and SCHÄFER, Hans-Bernd (eds.), *Ökonomische Probleme des Zivilrechts*, Berlin, Springer, 1991, 87-108. (Subject Code: 3000)

FRANK, Jürgen, 'Die "Rationalität" einer ökonomischen Analyse des Rechts' [The "Rationality" of an Economic Analysis of Law], **2** *Zeitschrift für Rechtssoziologie*, 1986, 191-211. (Subject Code: 0300)

FRANK, Jürgen, 'Ökonomische Modelle der Abschreckung' [Economic Models of Deterrence], *Kriminologisches Journal*, 1987, Heft 1, 55-65. (Subject Code: 8000)

FRANK, Jürgen, Kollektive oder Individuelle Steuerung der Umwelt?' [Collective or Individual Control of the Environment?], *Kritische Justiz*, 1989, Heft 1, 36-55. (Subject Code: 3500)

FRÖHLICH, P., *Marktabgrenzung in der Wettbewerbspolitik: Die parametrisch Interdependenz als Kriterium der Abgrenzung des relevanten Marktes* [Market Definition in Competition Policy: The Parameter Interdepence as Criterion for the Definition of the Relevant Markets], Göttingen, 1975. (Subject Code: 5700)

FUCHS, Maximilian, 'Die Behandlung von Ehe und Scheidung in der "Ökonomischen Analyse des Rechts"' [The Treatment of Marriage and Divorce in the "Economic Analysis of Law"], **7** *Zeitschrift für das gesamte Familienrecht*, 1979, 553-557. (Subject Code: 1100)

GÄFGEN, Gérad, 'Entwicklung und Stand der Theorie der Property Rights. Eine kritische Bestandsaufnahme' [Development and Actual Situation of the Property Rights Theory. A Critical Element], in NEUMANN, M. (ed.), *Ansprüche, Eigentums- und Verfügungsrechte*, Schriften des Vereins für Socialpolitik, Vol. 140, 1983, 43-62. (Subject Code: 0650)

GOTTHOLD, Jürgen, 'Zur ökonomischen "Theorie des Eigentums". Eine kritische Einfuhrung' [The Economic Theory of Property - A Critical Introduction] **144** *Zeitschrift für das gesamte Handels- und Wirtschaftsrecht*, 1980, 545-562. (Subject Code: 0650, 2000)

GOTTHOLD, Jürgen, 'Neuere Entwicklungen der Wettbewerbstheorie: Kritische Bemerkungen zur neo-liberalen Theorie der Wettbewerbspolitik' [New Developments in Competition Theory: Critical Remarks on the Neo-Liberal Theory of Competition Policy], **145** *Zeitschrift für das gesamte Handelsrecht*, 1981, 286-340. (Subject Code: 5700)

GREIPEL, E. und TAEGER, U., *Auswirkungen des Patentschutzes und der Lizenzvergabepraxis auf den Wettbewerb in ausgewählten Wirtschaftsbereichen unter besonderer Berücksichtigung der Marktsituation kleiner und mittlerer Unternehmen* [Effects of Patent Protection and License Practice Activity on Competition in Specific Areas of Economic Activity with Special Reference to the Market Position of Small and Middle Size Companies], Gutachten erstellt für das Bundeswirtschaftsministerium in Bonn, München, Ifo-Institut, 1981. (Subject Code: 2965)

HAUSCHKA, Christoph E., 'Zielkonflikte zwischen Unternehmenkontrolle und Wirtschaftsförderung in den wettbewerbspolitischen Programmaussagen der EG--Kommission' [Conflict of Goals Between Enterprise Control and Economic Imperatives in the Competition Programme of the EC-Commission], **40** *Wirtschaft und Wettbewerb*, 1990, 205-216. (Subject Code: 5700)

HENNING-BODEWIG, Frauke, 'Die Qualitätsfunktion der Marke im Amerikanischen Recht' [The Quality Function of Trademarks in American Law], **7** *GRUR Int.*, 1985, 445-453. (Subject Code: 2940)

HENNING-BODEWIG, Frauke, *Marke und Verbraucher* [Trademark and Consumer], Weinheim, VCH Verlagsgesellschaft, 1988, 127-168, 258-268. (Subject Code: 2940)

HERDZINA, Klaus, 'Marktentwicklung und Wettbewerbsverhalten' [Market Development and Competition Attitude], in BOMBACH, G., GAHLEN, B. and OTT, A.E. (eds.), *Industrieökonomik: Theorie und Empirie*, Tübingen, J.C.B. Mohr, 1985, 105-123. (Subject Code: 5700)

HERDZINA, Klaus, *Wettbewerbspolitik* [Competition Policy], Stuttgart, Gustav Fischer, 1987 (2nd ed.), 237 p. (Subject Code: 5700)

HERDZINA, Klaus, *Möglichkeiten und Grenzen einer wirtschaftstheoretische Fundierung der Wettbewerbspolitik* [Possibilities and Limits of an Economic Foundation of Competition Policy], Tübingen, Walter Eucken Institut, Vorträge und Aufsätze 116, 1988, 61 p. (Subject Code: 5700)

HESSE, Günter, 'Der Property-Rights-Ansatz. Eine ökonomische Theorie der Veränderung des Rechts?' [The Property Rights Approach. An Economic Theory of Legal Evolution?], **195** *Jahrbuch für Nationalökonomie und Statistik*, 1980, 481 ff. (Subject Code: 0650, 9700)

HESSE, Günter, 'Zur Erklärung der Änderung von Handlungsrechten mit Hilfe der ökonomischen Theorie' [The Explanation of the Change of Property Rights with the Help of the Economic Theory], in SCHÜLLER, A. (ed.), *Property Rights und ökonomische Theorie*, München, Vahlen, 1983, 79-109. (Subject Code: 0650, 9700)

HOLLER, P., 'Probleme der utilitaristischen Strafrechtfertigung' [Problems of Utilitarian Criminal Law Making], *Zeitschrift für die Gesamte Stafrechtswissenschaften*, 1979, 45-95. (Subject Code: 8000)

HOPPMANN, Erich, 'Das Konzept der optimalen Wettbewerbsintensität' [The Concept of Optimal Competition Intensity], **180** *Jahrbuch für Nationalökonomie und Statistik*, 1966, 286-323. (Subject Code: 5700)

HOPPMANN, Erich, 'Wettbewerb als Norm der Wettbewerbspolitik' [Competition as Norm for Competition Policy], **18** *Ordo: Jahrbuch für die Ordnung von Wirtschaft und Gesellschaft*, 1967, 77-94. (Subject Code: 5700)

HOPPMANN, Erich, 'Die Funktionsfähigkeit des Wettbewerbs: Bemerkungen zu Kantzenbachs Erwiderung' [The Functionality of Competition: Remarks on Kantzenbach's Reaction], **181** *Jahrbuch fur Nationalökonomie und Statistik*, 1967, 251-264. (Subject Code: 5700)

HOPPMANN, Erich, 'Zum Problem einer wirtschaftpolitischen praktikablen Definition des Wettbewerbs' [On the Problem of and Economic and Practical Definition of Competition], in SCHNEIDER, H.K. (ed.), *Grundlagen der Wettbewerbspolitik*, Berlin, 1968, 9-49. (Subject Code: 5700)

HOPPMANN, Erich, 'Neue Wettbewerbspolitik: Vom Wettbewerb zur staatlichen Mikro-Steuerung: Bemerkungen zu einem "neuen Leitbild" der Wettbewerbspolitik' [New Competition Policy: From Competition to Governmental Micro-Steering: Remarks on a "New Example" of Competition Policy], **184** *Jahrbuch für Nationalökonomie und Statistik*, 1970, 397-416. (Subject Code: 5700)

HOPPMANN, Erich, *Wirtschaftsordnung und Wettbewerb* [Economic Order and Competition], Baden-Baden, Nomos, 1988, 566 p. (Subject Code: 5700)

HORN, Norbert, 'Zur ökonomischen Rationalität des Privatrechts. Die privatrechts theoretische Verwertbarkeit der "Economics Analysis of Law"' [On the Economic Rationality of Private Law. On the Utility of the Economic Analysis of Law for Private Law Theory], **176** *Archiv für die Civilistiche Praxis*, 1976, 307-333. (Subject Code: 0300)

HUMMEL-BERGER, *Die volkswirtschaftliche Bedeutung von Kunst und Kultur* [The Economic Significance of Art and Culture], München, 1988. (Subject Code: 2900)

HUTTER, Michael, *Die Gestaltung von Property Rights als Mittel gesellschaftlich-*

wirtschaftlicher Allokation [The Structure of Property Rights as a Means of Social-Economic Allocation], Göttingen, Vandenhoeck & Ruprecht, 1979, 245 p. (Subject Code: 0650, 2000)

HUTTER, Michael, 'Über eine Alternative zur neoklassischen ökonomischen Analyse des Rechts' [On An Alternative for Neo-classical Economic Analysis of Law], **144** *Zeitschrift für das gesamte Handels- und Wirtschaftsrecht*, 1980, 642-651. (Subject Code: 0300)

HUTTER, Michael, *Die Produktion von Recht. Eine selbstreferentielle Theorie der Wirtschaft, angewandt auf den Fall des Arzneimittelpatentrechts* [The Production of Law. A Selfreferential Theory of the Economy, applied to the Case of Pharmaceutical Patent Law], Tübingen, Mohr, 1989, 213 p. (Subject Code: 2930, 9200)

ISAY, H., *Die Funktion der Patente im Wirtschaftskampf* [Patent Functions in Economic Battle], Franz Vahlen Verlag, Berlin, 1927. (Subject Code: 2930)

JANICKI, Thomas, 'EG-Fusionskontrolle auf dem Weg zur praktischen Umsetzung' [EC Merger Control on the Way of Practical Realization], **40** *Wirtschaft und Wettbewerb*, 1990, 195-205. (Subject Code: 5700)

KALLFASS, Hermann H., 'Die Chicago School: Eine Skizze des "neuen" amerikanisches Ansatzes für die Wettbewerbspolitik' [The Chicago School: A Sketch of the "New" American Approach for Competition Policy], **30** *Wirtschaft und Wettbewerb*, 1980, 596-601. (Subject Code: 5700)

KANTZENBACH, Erhard, 'Das Konzept der optimalen Wettbewerbsintensität: Eine Erwiderung auf den gleichnamigen Besprechungsaufsatz von Erich Hoppmann' [The Concept of Optimal Competition Intensity: A Reaction on Erich Hoppman's Comment of the Same Name], **181** *Jahrbuch für Nationalökonomie und Statistik*, 1967, 193-241. (Subject Code: 5700)

KANTZENBACH, Erhard and KRÜGER, Reinald, 'Zur Frage der richtigen Abgrenzung des sachlich relevanten Markten bei der wettbewerbspolitischen Beurteilung von Unternehmenszusammenschlüssen' [On the Question of the Correct Definition of the Relevant Market at the Judgment of Mergers], **40** *Wirtschaft und Wettbewerb*, 1990, 472481. (Subject Code: 5700)

KAUFER, Erich, 'Kantzenbachs Konzept des funktionsfähigen Wettbewerbs: Ein Kommentar' [Kantenbach's Concept of Functional Competition: A Comment], **179** *Jahrbuch für Nationalökonomie und Statistik*, 1966, 481-492. (Subject Code: 5700)

KAUFER, Erich, 'Das Konzept der optimalen Wettbewerbsintensität: Eine Replik' [The Concept of Optimal Competition Intensity: A Reply], **181** *Jahrbuch für Nationalökonomie und Statistik*, 1968, 242-250. (Subject Code: 5700)

KIRCHNER, Christian, '"Ökonomische Analyse des Rechts" und Recht der Wettbewerbsbeschränkungen' ["Economic Analysis of Law" and Anti-trust Law], **144** *Zeitschrift für das gesamte Handels- und Wirtschaftsrecht*, 1980, 563-588. (Subject Code: 5700)

KIRCHNER, Christian, 'Ansatze zu einer ökonomischen Analyse des Konzernrechts' [Starting Point for an Economic Analysis of Large Companies Law], in BOETTCHER, Erik, HERDER-DORNEICH, Philipp and SCHENK, Karl-Ernst (eds.), **3** *Jahrbuch für Neue Politische Ökonomie*, Tübingen, J.C.B. Mohr, 1984, 223-251. (Subject Code: 5500)

KIRCHNER, Christian, 'Kommentar' [Comment] (On Brüggemeier, Die Gefährdungshaftung der Produzenten nach der EG-Richtlinie), in OTT, Claus and SCHÄFER, Hans-Bernd (eds.), *Allokationseffizienz in der Rechtsordnung*, Berlin, Springer, 1989, 248-253. (Subject Code: 5300)

KIRCHNER, Christian, 'Kommentar' [Comment] (On Eger, Nagel and Weise, Effizienz und Menschenwürde), in OTT, Claus and SCHÄFER, Hans-Bernd (eds.), *Ökonomische Probleme des Zivilrechts*, Berlin, Springer, 1991, 35-38. (Subject Code: 0610, 0620)

KLAUS, J., ' Umweltökonomie und Umweltpolitik' [Environmental Economics and Environmental Politics], in WENZ, E., ISSING, O. and HOFMANN, H. (eds.), *Oekologie, Oekonomie und Jurisprudenz*, München, Florentz, 1987. (Subject Code: 3500)

KLEMM, Günter, *Ökonomische Analyse von Streik und Aussperrung im Rahmen einer marktwirtschaftlichen Ordnung* [Economic Analysis of Strike and Lock-out in the Context of a Market Economy], 1983, 214 p. (Subject Code: 5450)

KOBOLDT, Christian, ' Kommentar' [Comment] (On Schanze, Stellvertretung und ökonomische Agentur-Theorie), in OTT, Claus and SCHÄFER, Hans-Bernd (eds.), *Ökonomische Probleme des Zivilrechts*, Berlin, Springer, 1991, 76-86. (Subject Code: 0670, 4200)

KOCH, Hans-Joachim, 'Die wirtschaftliche Vertretbarkeit nachträglicher Anordnungen' [The Economic Justification of Additional Orders], *Wirtschaft und Verwaltung*, 1983, 158-173. (Subject Code: 3500)

KOCH, Harald, 'Die Ökonomie der Gestaltungsrechte. Möglichkeiten und Grenzen der ökonomische Analyse des Rechts am Beispiel von Kündiging und Anfechtung' [The Economics of Dispositive Right. Possibilities and Limits of the Economic Analysis of Law by the Example of Notion of Termination and Dispute], in BERNSTEIN, H., DROBNIG, U. and KÖTZ, H. (eds.), *Festschrift für Konrad Zweigert zum 70. Geburtstag*, Tübingen, J.C.B. Mohr, 1981, 851-877. (Subject Code: 0300, 4200, 5400)

KOCH, Walter A.S., 'Negative Einkommensteuern und Konjunkturpolitik. (Negative Income Taxes and Stabilization Policy. With English summary.)', **30** *Konjunkturpolitik*, 1984, 348-373. (Subject Index: 6010)

KOHL, Helmut, 'Das Allgemeine Persönlichkeitsrecht als Ausdruck oder Grenze des Effizienzdenkens im Zivilrecht?' [The General Right of Privacy as Expression or Limitation of Efficiency Thinking in Civil Law?], in OTT, Claus and SCHÄFER, Hans-Bernd (eds.), *Ökonomische Probleme des Zivilrechts*, Berlin, Springer, 1991, 41-51. (Subject Code: 1900)

KOHL, Helmut, KÜBLER, Friedrich, WALZ, W. Rainer and WÜSTRICH, Wolfgang, 'Abschreibungsgesellschaften, Kapitalmarkteffizienz und Publizitätszwang - Plädoyer für ein Vermögensanlagegesetz' [Tax Shelter Companies, Efficiency of Capital Markets and Information Regulation? - A Pleade for a Law Regulating the Public Offer of Investment Opportunities], **138** *Zeitschrift für das gesamte Handels- und Wirtschaftsrecht*, 1974, 1-49. (Subject Code: 5220, 5570)

KÖHLER, Helmut, 'Vertragsrecht und "Property Rights"-Theorie, Zur Integration ökonomischer Theorien in das Privatrecht' [Contract Law and Property Rights Theory - On the Integration of Economic Theory into Private Law], **144** *Zeitschrift für das gesamte Handels- und Wirtschaftsrecht*, 1980, 589-607.

(Subject Code: 0650, 2000, 4000)

KÖHLER, Helmut, 'Zur ökonomischen Analyse der Regeln über die Geschäftsgrundlage' [On the Economic Analysis of the Rules of the Implicit Basis of a Contract], in OTT, Claus and SCHÄFER, Hans-Bernd (eds.), *Allokationseffizienz in der Rechtsordnung*, Berlin, Springer, 1989, 148-162. (Subject Code: 4000)

KOLLER, Ingo, *Die Risikozurechnung bei Vertragsstörungen in Austauschverträgen* [The Risk Allocation of Contract Disturbances in Bilateral Contracts], München, C.H. Beck, Münchener Universitätsschriften, Vol. 39, 1979, 474 p. (Subject Code: 4100, 4300)

KOLLER, Ingo, 'Die Verteilung des Scheckfälschungsrisikos zwischen Kunde und Bank' [The Division of the False Cheque Risk Between Client and Bank], *Neue Juristische Wochenschrift*, 1981, 2433 ff. (Subject Code: 4420, 5580)

KÖNDGEN, Johannes, 'Ökonomische Aspekte des Schadensproblems. Bemerkungen zur Kommerzialisierungsmethode des Bundesgerichtshofes' [Economic Aspects of the Damage Problem. Remarks on the 'Commercializing Method' of the Bundesgerichtshofes], **177** *Archiv für civilistische Praxis*, 1977, 1-34. (Subject Code: 3200)

KÖNDGEN, Johannes, 'Immaterialschadenersatz, Gewinnabschöpfung oder Genugtuung in Geld bei vorsätzlichen Vertragsbruch?' [Damages for Nonpecuniary Losses, Skimming-off of Extra-Profits or Satisfaction in Money in Case of Intentional Breach of Contract?], in OTT, Claus and SCHÄFER, Hans-Bernd (eds.), *Ökonomische Probleme des Zivilrechts*, Berlin, Springer, 1991, 169-182. (Subject Code: 4440)

KÖNDGEN, Johannes and VON RANDOW, Philipp, 'Sanktionen bei Vertragsverletzung' [Sanctions for Breach of Contract], in OTT, Claus and SCHÄFER, Hans-Bernd (eds.), *Allokationseffizienz in der Rechtsordnung*, Berlin, Springer, 1989, 122-140. (Subject Code: 4400)

KOSLOWSKI, Peter, 'Grenzen der Verkehrsfähigkeit und der Privatrechtsautonomie in der Verfügung über den menschlichen Leib - Kommentar' [Limits of the Marketability and Private Autonomy in the Disposition over the Human Body - Comment], in OTT, Claus and SCHÄFER, Hans-Bernd (eds.), *Allokationseffizienz in der Rechtsordnung*, Berlin, Springer, 1989, 115-119. (Subject Code: 2700, 4000)

KÖTZ, Hein, 'Haftungsausschlussklauseln, Eine juristisch-ökonomische Analyse' [Exemption Clauses, a Legal-Economic Analysis], *25 Jahre Karlsruher Forum. Beiheft zu Versicherungsrecht*, 1983, 145-152. (Subject Code: 4420)

KÖTZ, Hein, 'Haftungsausschluß der Chemischreiniger' [Exemption Clauses in Cleaning Contracts, Legal Validity and Economic Efficiency], in WALZ, W. Rainer and RASCHER-FRIESENHAUSEN, Heinrich (eds.), *Sozialwissenschaften im Zivilrecht: Fälle und Lösungen in Ausbildung und Prüfung*, Neuwied, Luchterhand, 1983, 76-88. (Subject Code: 4420)

KÖTZ, Hein, 'Zivilrechtliche Haftung aus ökonomischer Sicht' [Civil Liability from an Economic Perspective], in SCHÄFER, Hans-Bernd and WEHRT, Klaus (eds.), *Die Ökonomisierung der Sozialwissenschaften: Sechs Wortmeldungen*, 1989, 149-167. (Subject Code: 3000)

KÖTZ, Hein, 'Zur Effizienz von Haftungsausschlußklauseln' [On the Efficiency of

Exemption Clauses], in OTT, Claus and SCHÄFER, Hans-Bernd (eds.), *Allokationseffizienz in der Rechtsordnung*, Berlin, Springer, 1989, 189-200. (Subject Code: 4420)

KÖTZ, Hein, 'Ziele des Haftungsrechts' [Purposes of Civil Liability], in BAUR, Jürgen F., HOPT, Klaus J. and MAILÄNDER, Peter K. (eds.), *Festschrift für Ernst Steindorff*, Berlin, de Gruyter, 1990, 643-666. (Subject Code: 3000)

KÖTZ, Hein and SCHÄFER, Hans-Bernd, 'Schadensverhütung durch ökonomische Anreize. Eine empirische Untersuchung' [Damage Prevention by Economic Incentives. An Empirical Investigation], **189** *Archiv für die civilistische Praxis*, 1989, 501-525. (Subject Code: 3000)

KRÜSSELBERG, Hans-Günter, 'Property Rights-Theorie und Wohlfartsökonomik' [Property Rights Theory and Welfare Economics], in SCHÜLLER, Alfred (ed.), *Property Rights und ökonomische Theorie*, München, Vahlen, 1983, 45-75. (Subject Code: 0650)

KÜBLER, Friedrich, 'Was leistet die Konzeption der Property Rights für aktuelle rechtspolitische Probleme?' [What is the Use of the Conception of Property Rights for Actual Legal-Political Problems?], in NEUMANN, M. (ed.), *Ansprüche, Eigentums- und Verfügungsrechte*, Schriften des Vereines für Socialpolitik, Vol. 140, 1983, 105-122. (Subject Code: 0650)

KÜBLER, Friedrich, 'Schlußwort: Vergleichende Überlegungen zur rechtspraktischen Bedeutung der ökonomischen Analyse' [Closing Word; Comparitive Considerations on the Meaning of Economic Analysis for Legal Practice], in OTT, Claus and SCHÄFER, Hans-Bernd (eds.), *Allokationseffizienz in der Rechtsordnung*, Berlin, Springer, 1989, 293-306. (Subject Code: 0300)

KÜBLER, Friedrich, ' Effizienz als Rechtsprinzip - Überlegungen zum rechtspraktischen Gebrauch ökonomischer Argumente' [Efficiency als Legal Principle - Considerations for the Legal Practice Use of Economic Arguments], in BAUR, Jürgen F., HOPT, Klaus J. and MAILÄNDER, Peter K. (eds.), *Festschrift für Ernst Steindorff*, 1990, Berlin, de Gruyter, 687-704. (Subject Code: 0620, 9900)

KÜBLER, Friedrich, MENDELSON, Morris and MUNDHEIM, Robert H., 'Die Kosten des Bezugsrechts - Eine rechtsökonomische Analyse des amerikanischen Erfahrungsmaterials [The Costs of the Subscription Right - A Legal Economic Analysis of the American Experience], *Die Aktiengesellschaft*, 1990, 461-475. (Subject Code: 5500)

KUNZ, Harald, 'Kommentar' [Comment] (on Tietzel, Probleme der asymmetrischen Informationsverteilung beim Güter- und Leistungstausch), in OTT, Claus and SCHÄFER, Hans-Bernd (eds.), *Allokationseffizienz in der Rechtsordnung*, Berlin, Springer, 1989, 64-69. (Subject Code: 0670)

LAMPE, Hanes-Eckhard, *Wettbewerb. Wettbewerbsbeziehungen. Wettbewerbsintensität* [Competition. Competition Relations, Competition Intensity], Baden-Baden, Nomos, 1979, 317 p. (Subject Code: 5700)

LEHMANN, Michael, 'Die Untersuchungs- und Rügepflicht des Käufers in BGB und HGB. Rechtsvergleichender Überblick - ökonomische Analyse' [The Duty to Examine and Notify a Defect in the German Civil and Commercial Code. A Comparitive Survey - Economic Analysis],in *Wertpapiermitteilungen*, 1980, Bd.II, 1162-1169. (Subject Code: 4200)

LEHMANN, Michael, *Vertragsanbahnung durch Werbung* [Contract Preparing through Promotion], München, C. H. Beck, 1981. (Subject Code: 4200, 5220)

LEHMANN, Michael, 'Die bürgerlich-rechtliche Haftung für Werbeangaben. Culpa in contrahendo als Haftungsgrundlage für vertragsanbahnende Erklärungen' [Civil Liability for Advertising Statements. Culpa in Contrahendo as Liability Ground for Statements which Precede a Contract], *Neue Juristische Wochenschrift*, 1981, 1233-1242. (Subject Code: 4400)

LEHMANN, Michael, 'Die UWG-Novelle sollte nicht sterben. Zur wirschaftlichen Bedeutung der Bereitstellung von ökonomisch relevanten Sanktionen' [The UWG-Novelle Should Not Die. The Economic Importance of Relevant Civil Sanctions from an Economic Point of View], **36** *Der Betriebsberater*, 1981, 1717-1726. (Subject Code: 5230)

LEHMANN, Michael, 'Ökonomie, Sozialbiologie - Humanwissenschaften. Über die Notwendigkeit und Möglichkeit einer interdisziplinären Grundlagenforschung' [Economics, Social Biology - Human Sciences. About the Necessity and Possibility of a Interdisciplinary Fundamental Research], *Der Betriebs-Berater*, 1982, 1997-2004. (Subject Code: 9700)

LEHMANN, Michael, 'Patentrecht und Theory der Property Rights, eine ökonomische und juristische Analyse' [Patent Law and Property Rights Theory, an Economic and Legal Analysis], in *Festschrift für R. Franceschelli*, Mailand, 1983, 35-51. (Subject Code: 0650, 2930)

LEHMANN, Michael, 'Eigentum, geistiges Eigentum, gewerbliche Schutzrechte, Property Rights als Wettbewerbsbeschränkungen zur Förderung des Wettbewerbs' [Property, Intellectual Property, Commercial Rights of Protection, Property Rights as Restraints of Competition to Promote the Competition], in *Gewerblicher Rechtsschutz und Urheberrecht, Internationaler Teil (Festschrift für E.Ulmer)*, 1983, 356-362. (Subject Code: 0650, 2000)

LEHMANN, Michael, 'Die mißglückte Probefahrt. Vertragsrecht, Quasivertragsrecht, Deliktrecht. Ökonomische Analyse des Rechts' [The Failed Excursion. Contract Law, Quasi-Contract Law, Economic Analysis of Law], in WALZ, W. Rainer and RASCHER-FRIESENHAUSEN, Heinrich (eds.), *Sozialwissenschaften im Zivilrecht: Fälle und Lösungen in Ausbildung und Prüfung*, Neuwied, Luchterhand, 1983, 35-51. (Subject Code: 3000, 4400)

LEHMANN, Michael, *Bürgerliches Recht und Handelsrecht - eine juristische und ökonomische Analyse ausgewählter Probleme für Wirtschaftswissenschaftler und interdisziplinär interessierte Juristen unter besonderer Berücksichtigung der "Ökonomischen Analyse des Rechts" und der "Theorie der Property Rights"* [Civil Law and Commercial Law - a Legal and Economic Analysis of Selected Problems for Lawyers with an Economic and Interdisciplinary Interest with a Special Attention for the "Economic Analysis of Law" and the "Theory of Property Rights"], Stuttgart, Poeschel, 1983, 329 p. (Subject Code: 0020)

LEHMANN, Michael, 'Theorie der Property Rights und Schutz des geistigen und gewerblichen Eigentums - Wettbewerbsbeschränkungen zur Förderung des Wettbewerbs' [Property Rights Theory and the Protection of Intellectual and Commercial Property], in *Ansprüche, Eigentums- und Verfügungsrechte Schriften des Vereins für Socialpolitik*, Band 140, Berlin, Duncker & Humblot, 1984, 519-535. (Subject Code: 0650, 2900)

LEHMANN, Michael, 'Das Privileg der beschränkten Haftung und der Durchgriff im Gesellschafts- und Konzernrecht. Eine juristische und ökonomische Analyse'

[The Privilege of Limited Liability and the Peircing of the Corporate Veil in Association and Trust Law], *Zeitschrift fur Unternehmens- und Gesellschaftsrecht*, 1986, Heft 3, 345-370. (Subject Code: 5520)

LEHMANN, Michael, 'Evolution in Biologie, Ökonomie und Jurisprudenz' [Evolution in Biology, Economics and Jurisprudence], **17** *Rechtstheorie*, 1986, 463-477. (Subject Code: 9700)

LEHMANN, Michael, 'Die UWG-Neuregelungen 1987 - Erläuterungen und Kritik' [The New UWG Unfair Competition Rules - Explanations and Critique], **89** *Gewerblicher Rechtsschutz und Urheberrecht*, 1987, 199-214. (Subject Code: 5230)

LEHMANN, Michael, 'Juristisch-ökonomische Kriterien zur Berechnung des Verletzergewinns bzw. des entgangenen Gewinns' [Legal-economic Criteria for the Calculation of the Profit of the Injurer Respectively the Lost Profit], **25** *Der Betriebs-Berater*, 1988, 1680-1687. (Subject Code: 3200)

LEHMANN, Michael, 'Die Zivilrechtliche Haftung für Werbeangaben bei der Vertragsanbahnung als Problem der Allokationseffizienz' [Civil Liability for Advertising as a Problem of Allocative Efficiency], in OTT, Claus and SCHÄFER, Hans-Bernd (eds.), *Allokationseffizienz in der Rechtsordnung*, Berlin, Springer, 1989, 169-184. (Subject Code: 5220)

LEHMANN, Michael, 'Just in time: Handels- und ABG-rechtliche Probleme' [Just in Time: Problems in the Law of Commerce and of Unfair Contract Terms], **27** *Der Betriebs-Berater*, 1990, 1849-1855. (Subject Code: 4100)

LEHMANN, Michael, 'Das Prinzip Wettbewerb' [The Principle of Competition], *Juristenzeitung*, 1990, (Heft 2), 61-67. (Subject Code: 5700)

LEHMANN, Michael, 'Umwelthaftungsrecht dient der Internalisierung negativer Extemalitäten, Kommentar' [Environmental Liability Law Is to Internalize Negative Externalities. A Comment] (on Panther, Zivilrecht und Umweltschutz), in OTT, Claus and SCHÄFER, Hans-Bernd (eds.), *Ökonomische Probleme des Zivilrechts*, Berlin, Springer, 1991, 290-294. (Subject Code: 3000, 3500, 9200)

LEVMORE, Saul and STUNTZ, William J., 'Rechtsfolgen im Privatrecht und im öffentlichen Recht: Rechtsvergleichung unter einem Law-and-Economics Blickwinkel' [Legal Consequences in Private and Public Law: Comparitive Law from a Law and Economics Viewpoint], in OTT, Claus and SCHÄFER, Hans-Bernd (eds.), *Ökonomische Probleme des Zivilrechts*, Berlin, Springer, 1991, 297-314. (Subject Code: 3000, 3300)

LUTTER, Marcus and WAHLERS, Henning W., 'Der Buyout: Amerikanische Fälle und die Regeln des deutschen Rechts' [The Buyout: American Cases and the German Rules], **34** *Die Aktiengesellschaft*, 1989, 1-17. (Subject Code: 5500, 5540)

MAGOULAS, Georgios, 'Zur ökonomischen Analyse des Konsumentenschutzes - unter besonderer Berücksichtigung informations- und risikobezogener Probleme von Konsumentenmärkten' [On the Economic Analysis of Consumer Protection - With Special Attention for Information and Risk-Related Problems of Consumer Markets], in MAGOULAS, Georgios and SIMON, Jürgen (eds.), *Recht und Ökonomie beim Konsumentenschutz und Konsumentenkredit*, Baden-Baden, Nomos, 23-57. (Subject Code: 5200)

MAGOULAS, Georgios, 'Ökonomische Probleme und Funktionen finanzierter Abzahlungsgeschäfte und vermittelter Konsumentenkredite' [Economic Problems and Functions of Instalment Sales and Mediated Consumer Loans], in MAGOULAS, Georgios and SIMON, Jürgen (eds.), *Recht und Ökonomie beim Konsumentenschutz und Konsumentenkredit*, Baden-Baden, Nomos, 1985, 265-292. (Subject Code: 5200)

MAGOULAS, Georgios, 'Ökonomische Bemerkungen zum Problem eines "Sondermarktes" im Rahmen rechtlicher Sittenwidrigkeitsprüfung' [Economic Remarks on the Problem of a "Special Market" in the Context of the Legal Rule of Public Policy], in MAGOULAS, Georgios and SIMON, Jürgen (eds.), *Recht und Ökonomie beim Konsumentenschutz und Konsumentenkredit*, Baden-Baden, Nomos, 1985, 293-308. (Subject Code: 5200)

MAGOULAS, Georgios, 'Ökonomische Funktionen und Probleme der Haustürgeschäfte als Instrument direkter Vertriebsstrategien' [Economic Functions and Problems of Door-to-Door Selling as an Instrument of Direct Sales Strategies], in MAGOULAS, Georgios and SIMON, Jürgen (eds.), *Recht und Ökonomie beim Konsumentenschutz und Konsumentenkredit*, Baden-Baden, Nomos, 1985, 391-401. (Subject Code: 5230)

MAGOULAS, Georgios, 'Privatrechtlicher Immissionsschutz, Wucher und ökonomische Analyses des Rechts' [Civil Law Protection against Harmfull Effects on the Environment, Usury and Economic Analysis of Law], in SIMON, Jürgen (ed.), *Regulierungsprobleme im Wirtschaftsrecht*, Neuwied und Darmstadt, Luchterhand, 1986, 1-24. (Subject Code: 0300, 3500)

MAGOULAS, Georgios, 'Verbraucherschutz als Problem asymmetrischer Informationskosten' [Consumer Protection as a Problem of Asymmetric Information Costs], in OTT, Claus and SCHÄFER, Hans-Bernd (eds.), *Allokationseffizienz in der Rechtsordnung*, Berlin, Springer, 1989, 70-80. (Subject Code: 5200)

MAGOULAS, Georgios and SIMON, Jürgen (eds.), *Recht und Ökonomie beim Konsumentenschutz und Konsumentenkredit. Interdisziplinäre Studien zu den Problemen und Konzepten des Verbraucherschutzes* [Law and Economics of Consumer Protection and Consumer Credit. Interdisciplinary Studies on the Problems and Concepts of Consumer Protection], Baden-Baden, Nomos, 1985, 436 p. (Subject Code: 0050, 5200, 5700)

MAGOULAS, Georgios and SCHWARTZE, Andreas, 'Das Gesetz über den Widerruf von Haustürgeschäften und ähnlichen Geschäften: Eine rechtliche und ökonomische Analyse' [The Law Regarding Revocation of Door-to-Door Dealings and Similar Transactions: A Legal and Economic Analysis], **18(5)** *Jüristische Arbeitsblätter*, 1986, 225-235. (Subject Code: 5230)

MEINBERG, Volker, 'Empirische Erkentnissen zum Vollzug des Umweltstrafrechts' [Empirical Insights Concerning the Enforcement of Environmental Criminal Law], **100** *Zeitschrift für die gesamte Strafrechtswissenschaft*, 1988, 112-157. (Subject Code: 3500, 8000)

MERAN, Georg, 'Zur Kontroverse uber die Wettbewerbswirkungen eines Umweltlizenzmarktes' [The Controversy on the Competition on a Market for Environmental Licenses], **108** *Zeitschrift fur Wirtschafts und Sozialwissenschaften*, 1988, 439-450. (Subject Code: 3800)

MESTMÄCKER, Ernst-Joachim, 'Fusions kontrolle im Gemeinsamen Markt zwischen Wettbewerbspolitik und Industriepolitik' [Merger Control in the Common Market Between Competition Policy and Industrial Policy], *Europarecht*, 1988, 349-377. (Subject Code: 5700)

MEYER, Dirk, 'Rent Seeking durch Rationalisierungsschutz oder die Wohlfahrtsverluste einer Kostensenkungssteuer' [Rent Seeking through Regulations Protecting Human Capital from Devaluation Due to Technological Innovation], **35** *Konjunkturpolitik*, 1989, 188-1200. (Subject Code: 5400)

MÖSCHEL, Wernhard, 'Wettbewerb im Schnittfeld von Rechtswissenschaft und Nationalökonomie' [Competition at the Crossing of Legal Science and National Economy], *Wirtschaftwissenschaftliche Studien*, 1978, 351-357. (Subject Code: 5700)

MÖSCHEL, Wernhard, 'Divergierende Entwicklungen im amerikanischen und europäischen Kartellrecht' [Conflicting Developments in American and European Antitrust Law], *Wirtschaftwissenschaftliche Studien*, 1983, 603-609. (Subject Code: 5700)

MUELLER, Dennis C., 'Das Antitrustrecht der Vereinigten Staaten am Scheideweg' [The Antitrust Law of the United States at the Parting of the Ways], **36** *Wirtschaft und Wettbewerb*, 1986, 533-555. (Subject Code: 5700)

NAGEL, Bernhard, 'Kommentar' [Comment] (On Wehrt, Die Qualitätshaftung des Verkäufers aus ökonomischer Sicht), in OTT, Claus and SCHÄFER, Hans-Bernd (eds.), *Ökonomische Probleme des Zivilrechts*, Berlin, Springer, 1991, 260-264. (Subject Code: 4420)

NEUMEYER, F., 'Patent und Beschränkung des Wettbewerbs' [Patent and Limitation of Competition], **12** *Wirtschaft und Recht*, 1969, 240-251. (Subject Code: 2930)

OBERENDER, Peter and RUTER, Georg, 'Innovationsforderung: Einige grundsatzliche ordnungspolitische Bemerkungen' [The Promotion of Innovation: Some Basic Remarks on Policies], in LENEL, Hans Otto at al. (ed.), *ORDO: Jahrbuch fur die Ordnung von Wirtschaft und Gesellschaft*, Band 38, Stuttgart, Fischer, 1987, 143-54. (Subject Code: 2900)

OPPENLÄNDER, K.H., (ed.), *Patentwesen, technischer Fortschritt und Wettbewerb* [Patents, Technical Progress and Competition], Göttingen, Verlag Otto Schwartz, 1974. (Subject Code: 2930)

OTT, Claus, 'Allokationseffizienz, Rechtsdogmatik und Rechtsprechung - die immanente ökonomische Rationalität des Zivilrechts' [Allocative Efficiency, Legal Dogmatics and Jurisprudence - The Implicit Economic Rationality of Civil Law], in OTT, Claus and SCHÄFER, Hans-Bernd (eds.), *Allokationseffizienz in der Rechtsordnung*, Berlin, Springer, 1989, 25-44. (Subject Code: 0010, 0300)

OTT, Claus, 'Vorvertragliche Aufklärungspflichten im Recht des Güter- und Leistungsaustausches' [Precontractual Obligation to Provide Information in the Sale of Goods and Services Act], in OTT, Claus and SCHÄFER, Hans-Bernd (eds.), *Ökonomische Probleme des Zivilrechts*, Berlin, Springer, 1991, 142-162. (Subject Code: 0640, 4200)

OTT, Claus and SCHÄFER, Hans-Bernd, 'Begründung und Bemessung des Schadensersatzes wegen entganger Sachnutzung' [Foundation and Rating of the Compensation for Damage Because of Lost Utility of Property], **7** *Zeitschrift für*

Wirtschaftsrecht, 1986, 613-624. (Subject Code: 3200)

OTT, Claus and SCHÄFER, Hans-Bernd, 'Die ökonomische Analyse des Rechts. Irrweg oder Chance wissenschaftlicher Rechtserkenntnis?' [The Economic Analysis of Law. Wrong Track or Chance for a Scientific Legal Knowledge?], *Juristenzeitung*, 1988, 213-223. (Subject Code: 0010, 0300)

OTT, Claus and SCHÄFER, Hans-Bernd (eds.), *Allokationseffizienz in der Rechtsordnung. Beiträge zum Travemünder Symposium zur ökonomischen Analyse des Zivilrechts 23.-26. März 1988* [Allocative Efficiency in Legal Order. Contributions to the Travemünder Symposium on Economic Analysis of Civil Law], Berlin, Springer, 1989, 306 p. (Subject Code: 0040)

OTT, Claus and SCHÄFER, Hans-Bernd (eds.), *Ökonomische Probleme des Zivilrechts. Beiträge zum 2. Travemünder Symposium zur ökonomischen Analyse des Rechts, 21. - 26. März 1990* [Economic Problems of Civil Law. Contributions to the Second Travemünder Symposium on Economic Analysis of Law], Berlin, Springer, 1991, 347 p. (Subject Code: 0040)

OTTO, Hans-Jochen, *Generalprävention und externe Verhaltenskontrolle, Wandel vom sociologischen zum ökonomischen Paradigma in der Nordamerikanischen Kriminologie?* [General Prevention and External Control of Behavior, Evolution from Sociological to Economic Paradigm in the North American Criminology?], Freiburg, Max-Planck-Institut für ausländisches internationales Strafrecht, 1982, 323 p. (Subject Code: 0020, 8000)

PANTHER, Stephan, 'Zivilrecht und Umweltschutz' [Civil Law and Environmental Protection], in OTT, Claus and SCHÄFER, Hans-Bernd (eds.), *Ökonomische Probleme des Zivilrechts*, Berlin, Springer, 1991, 267-289 (Subject Code: 3000, 3500)

PROSI, G., *Ökonomische Theorie des Buches. Volkswirtschaftliche Aspekte des Urheber- und Verlegerschutzes* [The Economic Theory of Books, Copyright and Publisher's Rights], Düsseldorf, 1971. (Subject Code: 2910, 2920)

RAHMSDORF, Detlev W., 'Zur Renaissance der Sozialvertragstheorien in den Wirtschaftswissenschaften und ihrer interdisziplinären Relevanz' [The Renaissance of the Social Contract in Political Economies and their Interdisciplinary Significance], *Der Staat*, 1986, Heft 2, 269-284. (Subject Code: 6100)

RAHMSDORF, Detlev W., 'Ökonomische Analyse des Rechts, Utilitarismus und die klassische deutsche Philosophie' [Economic Analysis of Law, Utilitarianism and the Classical German Philosophy], in *Rechtstheorie*, 1987, Heft 4, 487-501. (Subject Code: 0400, 0500)

RAHMSDORF, Detlev W. and SCHÄFER, Hans-Bernd, 'Ökonomische Analyse des Rechts - Ein Gegentrend? [Economic Analysis of Law - A Controversy?]', in VOIGT, R. (ed.), *Verrechtlichung*, Köningstein/Ts., Athenäum, 1980, 94-108. (Subject Code: 0010)

RAHMSDORF, Detlev W. and SCHÄFER, Hans-Bernd (eds.), *Ethische Fragen der Wirtschaftspolitik und des Rechts* [Ethical Questions of Political Economics and Law], Berlin, Dietrich-Reimer-Verlag, 1988, 219 p. (Subject Code: 0400)

RÖPER, Bernd, *Die Mißbrauchaufsicht vor dem Hintergrund der Entwicklung der neueren Wettbewerbstheorie* [The Abuse Aspect as Background for the Development of a New Competition Theory], Berlin, Humboldt, 1982. (Subject

Code: 5700)

ROTH, Günter H., 'Zur "economic analysis" der beschränkten Haftung' [On the 'Economic Analysis' of Limited Liability], *Zeitschrift für Untemehmens- und Gesellschaftsrecht*, 1986, Heft 3, 371-382. (Subject Code: 5520)

ROTH, Günter H., 'Kommentar' [Comment] (On Adams, Eigentum, Kontrolle und beschränkte Haftung), in OTT, Claus and SCHÄFER, Hans-Bernd (eds.), *Ökonomische Probleme des Zivilrechts*, Berlin, Springer, 1991, 226-233. (Subject Code: 5520)

RUPPELT, Hans-Joachim, 'Der Verordnungsentwurf für eine europäische Fusionskontrolle im EG-Ministerrat' [The Regulation Bill for a European Fusion Control in the EC-Cabinet Council], **39** *Wirtschaft und Wettbewerb*, 1989, 187-202. (Subject Code: 5700)

SALJE, Peter, *Ökonomische Analyse des Rechts aus deutscher Sicht* [Economic Analysis of Law from a German Point of View], **15 (3)** *Rechtstheorie*, 1984, 277-312. (Subject Code: 0010)

SAUTER, Herbert, 'Gruppenfreistellungs-Verordnung für Know-how-Vereinbarungen' [The Group Exemption Regulation for Know-How Agreements], **39** *Wirtschaft und Wetbewerb*, 1989, 383-391. (Subject Code: 5700)

SCHÄFER, Hans-Bernd, 'Allokationseffizienz als Grundprinzip des Zivilrechts' [Allocative Efficiency as Basic Principle of Civil Law], in OTT, Claus and SCHÄFER, Hans-Bernd (eds.), *Allokationseffizienz in der Rechtsordnung*, Berlin, Springer, 1989, 1-24. (Subject Code: 0400, 9900)

SCHÄFER, Hans-Bernd, 'Ökonomische Analyse von Aufklärungspflichten' [Economic Analysis of the Duty to Provide Information], in OTT, Claus and SCHÄFER, Hans-Bernd (eds.), *Ökonomische Probleme des Zivilrechts*, Berlin, Springer, 1991, 117-141. (Subject Code: 0670)

SCHÄFER, Hans-Bernd and OTT, Claus, *Lehrbuch der ökonomischen Analyse des Zivilrechts* [Handbook of Economic Analysis of Civil Law], Berlin, Springer, 1986, 367 p. (Subject Code: 0000)

SCHÄFER, Hans-Bernd and OTT, Claus, 'Schmerzengeld bei Körperverletzungen. Eine Ökonomische Analyse' [Damages for Pain and Suffering], *Juristenzeitung*, 1990, 563-573. (Subject Code: 3200)

SCHÄFER, Hans-Bernd and STRUCK, Gerhard, 'Schlammbeseitigung auf der Bundesstraße. Geschäftsführung ohne Auftrag, Deliktsrecht, negatorische Haftung. Ökonomische Analyse des Rechts' [The Case of the Mud Removal at the Federal Highway], in WALZ, W. Rainer and RASCHER-FRIESENHAUSEN, Heinrich (eds.), *Sozialwissenschaften im Zivilrecht: Fälle und Lösungen in Ausbildung und Prüfung*, Neuwied, Luchterhand, 1983, 119-132. (Subject Code: 0100, 3000, 4700)

SCHÄFER, Hans-Bernd and WEHRT, Klaus (eds.), *Die Ökonomisierung der Sozialwissenschaften: Sechs Wortmeldungen* [Economics in Social Sciences: Six Contributions], Frankfurt am Main, Campus Verlag, 1989, 182 p. (Subject Code: 0050)

SCHÄFER, Hans-Bernd and WEHRT, Klaus, 'Ökonomische Analyse des Schadensrechts. Ein Überblick' [Economic Analysis of Tort Law. A Survey], **34** *Hamburger Jahrbuch für Wirtschaft und Gesellschaftspolitik*, 1989, 81-106. (Subject Code: 3000)

SCHANZE, Erich, 'Ökonomische Analyse des Rechts in den U.S.A. / Verbindungslinien zur realistischen Tradition' [Economic Analysis of Law in the U.S.A. - Origins and Relations to Legal Realism], in ASSMANN, Heinz-Dieter, KIRCHNER, Christian and SCHANZE, Erich (eds.), *Ökonomische Analyse des Rechts*, Kronberg, 1978, 3-19. (Subject Code: 0010, 0200)

SCHANZE, Erich, 'Der Beitrag von Coase zu Rechte und Ökonomie des Unternehmens' [Coase's Contribution to Law and Economics of Business Organizations], **137** *Zeitschrift für die gesamte Staatswissenschaft*, 1981, 694-701. (Subject Code: 0200, 5510)

SCHANZE, Erich, 'Rechtsnorm und ökonomisches Kalkül' [Legal Norm and Economic Calculus], **138** *Zeitschrift für die gesamte Staatswissenschaft*, 1982, 297-312. (Subject Code: 0010, 0300)

SCHANZE, Erich, 'Theorie des Unternehmens und Ökonomische Analyse des Rechts' [Theory of the Firm and Economic Analysis of Law], in BOETTCHER, Erik, HERDER-DORNEICH, Philipp and SCHENK, Karl-Ernst (eds.), **2** *Jahrbuch für Neue Politische Ökonomie*, Tübingen, J.C.B. Mohr, 1983, 161-180. (Subject Code: 5510)

SCHANZE, Erich, 'Unternehmensrechtliche Koordination von Staat und Wirtschaft bei internationalen GroßProjekten in Entwicklungsländern' [Corporate Coordination of State and Economy Concerning Project Investment in Developing Countries], **6** *Jahrbuch fur neue Politische Ökonomie*, Tübingen, J.C.B. Mohr, 1986, 269-287. (Subject Code: 5960)

SCHANZE, Erich, *Investitionsverträge im internationalen Wirtschaftsrecht* [Investment Contracts in International Economic Law], Frankfurt, Metzner, 1986, 305 p. (Subject Code: 5570, 5960)

SCHANZE, Erich, 'Stellvertretung und ökonomische Agentur-Theorie - Probleme und Wechselbezüge' [The Law of Agency and Agency Theory - Problems and Relations], in OTT, Claus and SCHÄFER, Hans-Bernd (eds.), *Ökonomische Probleme des Zivilrechts*, Berlin, Springer, 1991, 60-75. (Subject Code: 0670, 4200)

SCHENK, Karl-Ernst, *"Institutional Choice" und Ordnungstheorie* ["Institutional Choice" and Theory of Order], Walter Eucken Institut, Vorträge und Aufsätze, Tübingen, J.C.B. Mohr, Bd. 82, 1982, 39 p. (Subject Code: 0020)

SCHENK, Karl-Ernst, 'Property Rights und Theorie der Institutionen' [Property Rights and Theory of Institutions], in **17(4)** *Das Wirtschaftsstudium*, 1988, 226-231. (Subject Code: 0650)

SCHERER, F.M., 'Stand und Perspektiven der Industrieökonomik' [State and Perspectives of Industrial Economics], in BOMBACH, G., GAHLEN, B. and OTT, A.E., *Industrieökonomik: Theorie und Empirie*, Tübingen, J.C.B. Mohr, 1985, 3-19. (Subject Code: 5700)

SCHMIDT, Ingo L.O., *Wettbewerbspolitik und Kartellrecht: Eine Einführung* [Competition Policy and Antitrust Law: An Introduction], Stuttgart, G. Fischer Verlag, 1990 (3rd ed.), 330 p. (Subject Code: 5700)

SCHMIDT, Ingo L.O. and RITTALER, Jan B., *Die Chicago School of Antitrust Analysis: Wettbewerbstheoretische und -politische Analyse eines Credos* [The Chicago School of Antitrust Analysis: Competition Theoretical and Political Analysis of a Credo], Baden-Baden, Nomos, 1986, 119 p. (Subject Code: 5700)

SCHMIDT, Reinhardt H., 'Die ökonomische Grundstruktur der Insolvenz Recht' [The Economic Basic Structure of Bankruptcy Law], *Die Aktiengesellschaft*, 1981, 35-44. (Subject Code: 5600)

SCHMIDT, Reinhard H., *Ökonomische Analyse des Insolvenzrechts* [Economic Analysis of Insolvency Law], Wiesbaden, Gabler, 1981, 155 p. (Subject Code: 5600)

SCHMIDT, Reinhard H. and KÜBLER, Friedrich, *Gesellschaftsrecht und Konzentration* [Company Law and Concentration], Schriften zur wirtschaftswissenschaftlichen Analyse des Rechts, Vol.3, Berlin, Duncker und Humblot, 1988, 225 p. (Subject Code: 5500)

SCHMIDTCHEN, Dieter, *Wettbewerbspolitik als Aufgabe: Methodologische und systemtheoretische Grundlagen für eine Neuorientierung* [Competition Policy as Task: Methodological and System Theoretical Foundations for a Reorientatation], Baden-Baden, Nomos, 1978. (Subject Code: 5700)

SCHMIDTCHEN, Dieter, 'Property Rights, Freiheitsschutz und die Logik staatlicher Preisinterventionen: Kritische Analyse der theoretischen Grundlagen einer freiheitsgefährdenden Wettbewerbspolitik' [Property Rights, Protection of Liberty and the Logic of Governmental Price Control: A Critical Analysis of the Theoretical Basis of Liberty Menacing Competition Policy], in RÖPER, Bernd (ed.), *Die Mißbrauchsaufsicht vor dem Hintergrund der Entwicklungen der neueren Wettbewerbstheorie*, Schriften des Vereins für Socialpolitik, Vol. 124, Berlin, 1982, 11-43. (Subject Code: 5700)

SCHMIDTCHEN, Dieter, *Property Rights, Freiheit und Wettbewerbspolitik* [Property Rights, Freedom and Competition Policy], Tübingen, J.C.B. Mohr, 1983, 71 p. (Subject Code: 0650, 5700)

SCHMIDTCHEN, Dieter, 'Evolutorische Ordnungstheorie oder: die Transaktionskosten und das Unternehmertum' [The Theory of Evolutionary Order, or: Transaction Costs and Entrepreneurship], *ORDO (Jahrbuch für die Ordnung von Wirtschaft und Gesellschaft)*, Stuttgart, G. Fischer Verlag, 1989, 161-182. (Subject Code: 0640)

SCHMIDTCHEN, Dieter, 'Jenseits von Maximierung, Gleichgewicht und Effizienz: Neuland für die ökonomische Analyse des Rechts?' [Beyond Maximization, Balance and Efficiency: New Land for the Economic Analysis of Law?], in OTT, Claus and SCHÄFER, Hans-Bernd (eds.), *Ökonomische Probleme des Zivilrechts*, Berlin, Springer, 1991, 316-343. (Subject Code: 0200, 0300)

SCHMITZ-HERSCHEIDT, Friedhelm, 'Ansätze zu einer ökonomischen Theorie des Gesellschaftsrecht' [Initial Stages to an Economic Theory of Company Law], in BOETTCHER, Erik, HERDER-DORNEICH, Philipp and SCHENK, Karl-Ernst (eds.), **2** *Jahrbuch für Neue Politische Ökonomie*, Tübingen, J.C.B. Mohr, 1983, 181-211. (Subject Code: 5500)

SCHÖCH, Heinz, 'Empirische Grundlagen der Generalprävention' [Empirical Foundations of General Prevention], in VOGLER, T. (ed.), *Festschrift für Hans-Heinrich Jescheck zum 70. Geburtstag*, vol. II, Berlin, Duncker & Humblot, 1985, 1081-1105. (Subject Code: 8000)

SCHÜLLER, Alfred, 'Property Rights, Unternehmerische Legitimation und Wirtschaftsordnung. Zum vermögenstheoretischen Ansatz einer allgemeinen Theorie der Unternehmung' [Property Rights, Entrepreneurial Legitimation and Economic System. On the Property Rights Approach of a General Theory of the

Enterprise], in SCHENK, K.E. (ed.), *Ökonomische Verfügungsrechte und Allokationsmechanismen in Wirtschaftssystemen*, Schriften des Vereins für Socialpolitik, Vol. 97, N.F., 1978, 29-87. (Subject Code: 0650, 5500)

SCHÜLLER, Alfred, 'Eigentumsrechte, Unternehmenskontrollen und Wettbewerbsordnung' [Property Rights, Corporate Control and Competition], **30** *ORDO, Jahrbuch für die Ordnung von Wirtschaft und Gesellschaft*, 1979, Stuttgart, G. Fischer Verlag, 325-364. (Subject Code: 0650, 5540, 5700)

SCHÜLLER, Alfred, 'Theorie der Firma und wettbewerbliches Marktsystem' [Theory of the Firm and Competitive Market System], in SCHÜLLER, Alfred (ed.), *Property Rights und ökonomische Theorie*, WiSt Taschenbuch, München, Vahlen, 1983, 145-183. (Subject Code: 5510, 5700)

SCHÜLLER, Alfred, 'Zur Ökonomik der Property Rights' [On the Economics of Property Rights], **14(5)** *Das Wirtschaftsstudium*, 1985, 259-265. (Subject Code: 0650)

SCHULZ, Andreas, 'Überlegungen zur ökonomischen Analyse des Haftungsrechts' [Considerations on the Economic Analysis of Liability Law], **35** *Versicherungsrecht*, 1984, 608-618. (Subject Code: 3000)

SCHUMANN, Joachim, '"Neue Mikroökonomik" und Theorie des Eigentumsrechte. Ansätze zur Ergänzung der mikroökonomischen Theorie' ['New Microeconomics' and Property Rights Theory. An Introduction to the Completion of Microeconomic Theory], **7** *Wirtschaftswissenschaftliches Studium*, 1978, 307-311. (Subject Code: 0650)

SCHWARTZE, Andreas, 'Die Beseitigung des Wegfalls der Geschäftsgrundlage: Zur wirtschaftlichen Effizienz und zur juristischen Konsistenz eines ökonomischen Modells' [The Abolition of the Frustration of Contract: On Economic Efficiency and Legal Consistency of an Economic Model], in FINSINGER, Jörg and SIMON, Jürgen (eds.), *Recht und Risiko*, München, Florentz, 1988, 155-170. (Subject Code: 4000)

SEIDL, Christian, 'Kommentar' [Comment] (On Kötz, Zur Effizienz von Haftungsausschlußklauseln), in OTT, Claus and SCHÄFER, Hans-Bernd (eds.), *Allokationseffizienz in der Rechtsordnung*, Berlin, Springer, 1989, 201-207. (Subject Code: 4420)

SEIDL, Christian, 'Kommentar' [Comment] (On Kohl, Das Allgemeine Persönlichkeitsrecht als Ausdruck oder Grenze des Effizienzdenkens im Zivilrecht), in OTT, Claus and SCHÄFER, Hans-Bernd (eds.), *Ökonomische Probleme des Zivilrechts*, Berlin, Springer, 1991, 52-57. (Subject Code: 1900)

SINN, Hans-Werner, 'Kommentar' [Comment] (on Magoulas, Verbraucherschutz als Problem asymmetrischer Informationskosten), in OTT, Claus and SCHÄFER, Hans-Bernd (eds.), *Allokationseffizienz in der Rechtsordnung*, Berlin, Springer, 1989, 81-90. (Subject Code: 5200)

SULLIVAN, Lawrence A., 'Warenzeichen und Behinderungspratiken in den USA: Eine vorläufige Analyse' [Product Marks and Hindrance Practices in the USA: A Preliminary Analysis], **9** *GRUR int.*, 1983, 714-721. (Subject Code: 2940)

TAEGER, U.C., 'Untersuchung der Aussagefähigkeit von Patentstatistiken hinsichtlich technologischer Entwicklungen' [Research into the Informal Value of Patent Statistics with Respect to Technological Developments], **17** *Ifo-Studien zur Industriewirtschaft*, München, Ifo-Institut, 1979. (Subject Code:

2930, 2965)

TIETZEL, Manfred, 'Die Rationalitätsannahme in den Wirtschaftswissenschaften oder Der homo oeconomicus und seine Verwandten' [The Rationality Assumption in Economics or the Homo Oeconomicus and his Relatives], **32** *Jahrbuch für Sozialwissenschaften*, 1981, 115-136. (Subject Code: 0610)

TIETZEL, Manfred 'Die Ökonomie der Property Rights: Ein Überblick' [The Economics of Property Rights: A Survey], **30** *Zeitschrift für Wirtschaftspolitik*, 1981, 207-243. (Subject Code: 0650, 2000)

TIETZEL, Manfred, 'Zur ökonomischen Theorie des Betrügens und Fälschens' [On the Economic Theory of Fraud and Counterfeiting], **204** *Jahrbuch für Nationalökonomie und Statistik*, 1988, 17-34. (Subject Code: 8000)

TIETZEL, Manfred, 'Probleme der asymmetrischen Informationsverteilung beim Güter- und Leistungstausch' [Problems of Asymmetric Information in the Trade of Goods and Services], in OTT, Claus and SCHÄFER, Hans-Bernd (eds.), *Allokationseffizienz in der Rechtsordnung*, Berlin, Springer, 1989, 52-63. (Subject Code: 0650)

TIETZEL, Manfred, 'Kommentar' [Comment] (on Schäfer, Ökonomische Analyse von Aufklärungspflichten and Ott, Vorvertragliche Aufklärungspflichten), in OTT, Claus and SCHÄFER, Hans-Bernd (eds.), *Ökonomische Probleme des Zivilrechts*, Berlin, Springer, 1991, 163-166. (Subject Code: 0670)

TODT, Horst, 'Freiheit und Utilitarismus' [Freedom and Utilitarianism], in OTT, Claus and SCHÄFER, Hans-Bernd (eds.), *Ökonomische Probleme des Zivilrechts*, Berlin, Springer, 1991, 1-17. (Subject Code: 0550)

TRIMARCHI, Pietro, 'Die Regelung der Vertragshaftung aus ökonomischer Sicht' [The Regulation of Contractual Liability from an Economic Point of View], **136** *Zeitschrift fur das gesamte Handelsrecht und Wirtschaftsrecht*, 1972, 118-138. (Subject Code: 4400)

TRIMARCHI, Pietro, 'Der Wegfall der Geschäftsgrundlage aus allokativer Sicht - Kommentar' [The Frustration of Contract from an Allocative Sight], in OTT, Claus and SCHÄFER, Hans-Bernd (eds.), *Allokationseffizienz in der Rechtsordnung*, Berlin, Springer, 1989, 163-167. (Subject Code: 4300)

VÀTH, Andreas, *Die Wettbewerbskonzeption des Europäischen Gerichtshofs: Eine wettbewerbstheoretische Analyse der Rechtsprechung des höchsten europäischen Gerichts anhand ausgewählter Entscheidungen* [The Competition Concept of the European Court of Justice: A Competition Theoretical Analysis of the Jurisprudence of the Highest European Court on the Basis of Selected Decisions], Bayreuth, P.C.O.-Verlag, 1987, 298 p. (Subject Code: 5700)

VANBERG, Viktor, *Verbrechen, Strafe und Abschreckung, die Theorie der Generalprävention im Lichte der neueren sozialwissenschaftslichen Diskussion* [Crime, Sanction and Deterrence: The Theory of General Prevention in the Light of the New Discussion in Social Science], Tübingen, J.C.B. Mohr, 1982, 50 p. (Subject Code: 0020, 8000)

von RANDOW, Philipp, 'Kommentar' [Comment] (On Adams, Warum kein Ersatz von Nichtvermögensschäden), in OTT, Claus and SCHÄFER, Hans-Bernd (eds.), *Allokationseffizienz in der Rechtsordnung*, Berlin, Springer, 1989, 218-225. (Subject Code: 3200)

von WEIZSÄCKER, Carl-Christian, 'Was leistet die Property Rights Theorie für aktuelle wirtschaftspolitische Fragen?' [What Brings the Property Rights Theory for Economic Policy Questions?], in NEUMANN, M. (ed.), *Ansprüche, Eigentums- und Verfügungsrechte*, Schriften des Vereins für Socialpolitik, Vol. 140, Berlin, Dunker u. Humblot, 1984, 123-152. (Subject Code: 0650)

von WEIZSÄCKER, C.C., 'Der Markt für unternehmensgebundene Ressourcen' [The Market for Enterprise Restricted Resources], *Strukturwandel und Wirtschaftsordnung, Referate des XX.FIW-Symposiums - FIW Schriftenreihe*, Heft 126, 1987, 31-42. (Subject Code: 5500)

WALZ, W. Rainer, 'Marktbezogener Umweltschutz und privatrechtlicher Immissionsschutz - Kann Umweltökonomie einen Beitrag zur Funktionsbestimmung privatrechtlicher Immissionsschutzregeln leisten?' [Market Related Environmental Protection and Private Law Protection against Noxious Substances - Can Environmental Economics Offer a Contribution concerning the Function of Private Law Protection against Noxious Substances Rules?], in BAUR, P., ESSER, J., KÜBLER, F. and STEINDORFF, E.(eds.), *Funktionswandel der Privatrechtsinstitutionen, Festschrift für Ludwig Raiser*, Tübingen, 1974, 185-222. (Subject Code: 3500)

WALZ, W. Rainer (ed.), *Sozialwissenschaften im Zivilrecht, Fälle und Lösungen in Ausbildung und Prüfung* [Social Science in Civil Law, Cases and Answers in Education and Examination], Neuwied, 1983. (Subject Code: 0100)

WALZ, W. Rainer, 'Sachenrecht für Nichtsachen? Kritik einer Systemanalogie' [Property Law for Immaterial Goods? Critique on a System Analogy], **1** *Kritische Vierteljahresschrift für Gesetzgebung und Rechtswissenschaft*, 1986, 131-164. (Subject Code: 2000)

WALZ, W. Rainer, 'Rechtssicherheit und Risikozuweisung bei Steuerrechtsänderungen - Verbotene Rückwirkung, gebotene Übergangsregelung, richterliche Vertragsanpassung' [Legal Certainty and Risk Allocation for Changes in Tax Law - Illegal Retroaction, Transitional Rules, Judicial Adjustment of Contract], in FINSINGER, Jörg and SIMON, Jürgen, (eds.), *Recht und Risiko*, 1988, München, Florentz, 252-286. (Subject Code: 6000, 9800)

WALZ, W. Rainer, 'Ökonomische und rechtssystematische Überlegungen zur Verkehrsfähigkeit von Gegenständen' [Economic and Legal Dogmatic Considerations in Marketability of Objects], in OTT, Claus and SCHÄFER, Hans-Bernd (eds.), *Allokationseffizienz in der Rechtsordnung*, Berlin, Springer, 1989, 93-114. (Subject Code: 4000)

WALZ, W. Rainer, 'Sachenrechtliches Systemdenken im Wandel - Die ökonomischen Determinanten des Verfügungstatbestandes' [Property Law System Thinking in Change - The Economic Determinants of the Disposition General Findings], **5** *Kritische Vierteljahresschrift für Gesetzgebung und Rechtswissenschaft*, 1990, 374-405. (Subject Code: 2000)

WALZ, W. Rainer and WIENSTROH, Claas, 'Die Fehlgeschlagene Investition' [The Case of the Investment Failure], in WALZ, W. Rainer and RASCHER-FRIESENHAUSEN, Heinrich (eds.), *Sozialwissenschaften im Zivilrecht: Fälle und Lösungen in Ausbildung und Prüfung*, Neuwied, Luchterhand, 1983, 52-75. (Subject Code: 0100, 0300)

WEGEHENKEL, Lothar, *Coase Theorem und Marktsystem* [Coase Theorem and the Market System], Tübingen, J.C.B. Mohr, 1980, 138 p. (Subject Code: 0630)

WEGEHENKEL, Lothar, *Transaktionskosten, Wirtschaftssystem und*

Unternehmertum [Transaction Costs, Economic System and Entrepreneurship], 1980, Tübingen, J.C.B. Mohr, 1980, 77 p. (Subject Code: 0640)

WEGEHENKEL, Lothar, 'Kommentar' [Comment] (on Köndgen and van Randow, Sanktionen bei Vertragsverletzung), in OTT, Claus and SCHÄFER, Hans-Bernd (eds.), *Allokationseffizienz in der Rechtsordnung*, Berlin, Springer, 1989, 141-145. (Subject Code: 4400)

WEHRT, Klaus, 'Die Qualitätshaftung des Verkäufers aus ökonomischer Sicht' [The Quality Liability of Sellers from an Economic Point of View], in OTT, Claus and SCHÄFER, Hans-Bernd (eds.), *Ökonomische Probleme des Zivilrechts*, Berlin, Springer, 1991, 235-259. (Subject Code: 4420)

WILLEKE, Frans-Ullrich, *Wettbewerbspolitik* [Competition Policy], Tübingen, J.C.B. Mohr, 1980. (Subject Code: 5700)

LAW & ECONOMICS IN HUNGARY

András Sajó and Kinga Pétervári

GALASI, Péter and KERTESI, Gábor, 'Korrupció és tulajdon, Tanulmány a tulajdonjogok közgazdaságtanának köreböl' [Corruption and Property], **4** *Közgazdasági Szemle*, 1990, 389-425. (Subject Code: 8000)

HANAK, András, 'Neoklasszicista Justitia' [Neo-classicist Justitia], **12** *Jogtudományi Közlöny*, 1979, 855-859. (Subject Code: 0400)

HARMATHY, Attila, 'Vállalati gazdaságpolitika - szerzödések' [Business Policy of the Company - Contracts], **4** *Allam- és Jogtudomány*, 1977, 528-567. (Subject Code: 5500)

HARMATHY, Attila, 'A gazdasági szabályozók és a Szerzödések kapcsolata' [The Connection between Economic Regulation and Contracts], **12** *Jogtudományi Közlöny*, 1979, 906-813. (Subject Code: 5000)

HARMATHY, Attila, 'Allami támogatások jogi kérdéseiröl' [Legal Questions on State Subsidies], **1** *Allam- és Jogtudomány*, 1980, 33-61. (Subject Code: 6300)

HARMATHY, Attila, *Szerzödések, államigazgatás, gazdaságirányitás* [Contract, Administration, Business Governing], Budapest, Akadémiai Kiadó, 1983, 210 p. (Subject Code: 6300)

SAJó, András, 'A gazdaság jogi szabályozásának egy lehetséges útja' [A Possible Way of Legal Regulation of the Economy], **4** *Jogtudományi Közlöny*, 1981, 297-308. (Subject Code: 9900)

SAJó, András, 'Közgazdaságtani vizsgálódások a jogról' [Analysis of Law from an Economic Point of View], in SáRKÖZY, Tamás, *Gazdasági Jogi Tanulmányok II*, Budapest, Közgazdasági és Jogi Könyvkiadó, 1984, 5-42. (Subject Code: 0010)

SAJó, András, 'A környezetszennyezés leküzdését célzó gazdasági jogi eszközök' [The Economic Law Devices in Order to Defeat the Pollution], **4** *Allam- és Jogtudomány*, 1986, 545-568. (Subject Code: 3500)

SAJó, András, 'Az alkotmányosság lehetöségei a gazdaságban, különös tekintettel a környezetvédelemre, mint gazdaságilag releváns tevékenységre' [Constitutionalism and its Possibilities in the Economy with Special Attention to the Environment as an Economicly Relevant Activity], **3-4** *Allam- és Jogtudomány* 1987-88, 474-511. (Subject Code: 9100)

SAJó, András, 'A jog a gazdaság szabályozástechnikái közt' [Law as One of the Regulating Means of the Economy], **3** *Jogtudományi Közlöny*, 1987, 126-132. (Subject Code: 0010, 9900).

SAJó, András, 'Allami változásipar és a jog stabilizáló ereje' [The State Changing Industry and the Stabilizing Effort of the Law], in HOPPAL, Mihály and SZECSKó, Tamás (eds.), *Értékek és változások I*, Budapest, Tömegkommunikációos Kutató Központ, 1987, 91-102. (Subject Code: 0010)

SAJó, András, 'Környezetvédelmi jogunk továbbfejlesztéséröl' [On the Improvement of Our Laws on the Protection of the Environment], **5** *Jogtudományi Közlöny*, 1987, 213-220. (Subject Code: 3500)

LAW & ECONOMICS IN ITALY
Roberto Pardolesi

ALPA, Guido, 'Colpa e responsabilità oggettiva nella prospettiva dell'analisi economica del diritto' [Negligence and Strict Liability in an EAL Perspective], *Politica del diritto*, 1976, 431-448. (Subject Code: 3000)

ALPA, Guido, 'Interpretazione economica del diritto' [Economic Interpretation of Law], *voce del Novissimo digesto italiano*, Appendice IV, Torino, UTET, 1983, 315-324. (Subject Code: 0010)

ALPA, Guido, 'Diritto e analisi economica (a proposito di un recente libro di R. Bowles)' [Law and Economic Analysis, With Regard to a Recent Book by R. Bowles], *Diritto dell'impresa*, 1984, 111-120. (Subject Code: 0010)

ALPA, Guido, PULITINI, Francesco, RODOTA', Stefano and ROMANI, Franco, *Interpretazione giuridica e analisi economica* [Legal Interpretation and Economic Analysis], Milano, Giuffrè, 1982, 662 p. (Subject Code: 0020, 9200)

APRILE, Ercole, 'Regolamentazione dei fenomeni economici e analisi economica degli strumenti giuridici: spunti per una riflessione' [Regulation of Economic Phenomena and Economic Analysis of Legal Instruments: Hints for a Reflection], *Nuovo diritto*, 1989, 505-521. (Subject Code: 0010)

BESSONE, Mario, 'Gli "standards" dei contratti di impresa e l'analisi economica del diritto' [The "Standards" in Contracts and Economic Analysis of Law], *Giurisprudenza di merito*, 1984, 982-987. (Subject Code: 4200)

CASTRONOVO, Carlo, 'Inattuazione della prestazione di lavoro e responsabilità del danneggiante' [Employee's Non-Performance and Tortfeasor's Liability], *Massimario di giurisprudenza del lavoro*, 1981, 370-377. (Subject Code: 3000, 5410)

COSENTINO, Fabrizio, 'Autonomia privata e paternalismo del legislatore nella prospettiva dell'analisi economica del diritto' [Individual Autonomy and the Paternalism of the Legislator: An EAL Perspective], *Riv. critica dir. priv.*, 1988, 473-511. (Subject Code: 0400)

COSENTINO, Fabrizio, 'Responsabilità da prodotto difettoso: appunti di analisi economica del diritto (nota a U.S. Supreme Court California, 31 marzo 1988, Brown c. Abbott Laboratories)' [Liability for Defective Products: An Economic Analysis of Law], *Foro Italiano*, 1989, IV, 137-143. (Subject Code: 5300)

COSENTINO, Fabrizio, 'Il contratto di servizio delle cassette di sicurezza: clausole di limitazione della responsabilità della banca e dichiarazione di valore' [The Contract for Services Related to Safety Deposit Boxes: Exemption Clauses for the Bank and Statement of Value], *Foro italiano*, 1990, I, 1292-1298. (Subject Code: 5580)

COSENTINO, Fabrizio, 'Analisi economica del diritto: ritorno al futuro?' [Economic Analysis of Law: Back to the Future?], *Foro it.*, 1990, V, 153-156. (Subject Code: 0010)

FAZIO, Antonio and CAPRIGLIONE, Francesco, 'Governo del credito e analisi economica del diritto' [Governing Credit and Economic Analysis of Law], *Banca, borsa, e titoli di credito*, 1983, I, 310-346. (Subject Code: 5570)

FERRARINI, G., *La locazione finanziaria* [Leasing], Milano, Giuffrè, 1977, 261 p. (Subject Code: 4000)

GAMBARO, Antonio, *La legittimazione passiva alle azioni possessorie* [Standing to Be Sued in Ownership Litigation], Milano, Giuffrè, 1979, 163 p. (Subject Code: 2000, 7000)

GUATRI, Luigi, *Crisi e risanamento delle imprese* [Crisis and Reorganization of the Firms], Milano, Giuffrè, 1986, 339 p. (Subject Code: 5600)

LEHMANN, Michael, 'Considerazioni di ordine economico nel diritto della concorrenza nella Republica Federale Tedesca' [Economic Considerations Concerning German Competition Law], in *Problemi attuali del diritto industriale, Volume celebrativo del XXV anno della Rivista di diritto industriale*, Milano, 1977, 689-699. (Subject Code: 5700)

MARINI, Giovanni, *Promessa ed affidamento nel diritto dei contratti*, [Promise and Reliance in Contract Law], Napoli, Jovene, 1990, 317 p. (Subject Code: 4000)

MATTEI, Ugo, 'I modelli nella tutela dell'ambiente' [The Models for the Protection of the Environment], *Rivista di diritto civile*, 1985, II, 389-427. (Subject Code: 3500)

MATTEI, Ugo, *Tutela inibitoria e tutela risarcitoria* [Inhibited Protection and Compensatory Protection], Milano, Giuffrè, 1987, 419 p. (Subject Code: 3000)

MATTEI, Ugo, 'Diritto e rimedio nell'esperienza italiana ed in quella statunitense: un primo approccio' [Law and Remedies Related to Italian and American Experiences: A First Approach], *Quadrimestre*, 1987, 341-359. (Subject Code: 4400)

MENGARONI, F., 'Analisi economica del diritto' [Economic Analysis of Law], *Enciclopedia giuridica*, Roma, Treccani, 1988, vol. I, 1-9. (Subject Code: 0010)

MONATERI, Pier Giuseppe, *Cumulo di responsabilità contrattuale ed extracontrattuale* [Overlap of Contractual and Extracontractual Liability], Padova, CEDAM, 1989, 315 p. (Subject Code: 4400)

PAGANELLI, Maurizio, 'Alla volta di Frankenstein: Biotecnologie e proprietà (di parti) del corpo' [Toward Frankenstein: Biotechnology and Property Rights in Body Parts], *Foro italiano*, 1989, IV, 417-441. (Subject Code: 2700)

PARDOLESI, Roberto, 'Azione reale e azione di danni nell'art. 844 c.c. Logica economica e logica giuridica nella composizione del conflitto tra usi incompatibili delle proprietà vicine' [Property Rule and Liability Rule in Article 844 Codice Civile: Economic Arguments, Legal Arguments and Litigation for Inconsistent Uses of Neighbours' Lands], *Foro italiono*, 1977, I, 1144-1154. (Subject Code: 2200, 3400)

PARDOLEI, Roberto, 'Luci ed ombre nell'analisi economica del diritto (appunti in margine ad un libro recente)' [Lights and Shadows in Law and Economics - Notes about a Recent Book], *Rivista di diritto civile*, 1982, II, 718-728. (Subject Code: 0010)

PARDOLESI, Roberto, 'Invalidità temporanea del dipendente, illecito del terzo, 'rivalsa' del datore di lavoro (ovvero: l'analisi economica del diritto in cassazione)' [Temporary Disability of Employees, Tortious Conduct By Third Party, Employer's Remedies], *Foro italiano*, 1985, I, 2286-2291. (Subject Code: 5400)

PARDOLESI, Roberto, *Una introduzione all' analisi economica del diritto con postfazione (Translation of A. Mitchell Polinsky' s "Introduction")*, Bologna, Zanichelli, 1986, 149 p. (Subject Code: 0000)

PARDOLESI, Roberto, 'Analisi economica del diritto' [Economic Analysis of Law], *Digesto civile*, vol. I, Torino, UTET, 1987, 309-320. (Subject Code: 0010)

PARDOLESI, Roberto, 'Tutela specifica e tutela per equivalente nella prospettiva dell'analisi economica del diritto' [Specific Performance and Damages: An EAL Perspective], *Quadrimestre*, 1988, 76-97. (Subject Code: 0010, 4410)

PARDOLESI, Roberto, 'Un moderno Minotauro: Law and Economics' [A Modern Minotaur: Law and Economics], *Economia, Società e Instituzioni*, 1989, 519-534. (Subject Code: 0010)

PASQUINI, Nello, 'Interpretazione giuridica e analisi economica - In margine ad un "reading" recente' [Legal Interpretation and Economic Analysis with Regard to a Recent "Reading"], *Rivista trimestrale di diritto e procedura civile*, 1983, 288-300. (Subject Code: 0010)

PREITE, Disiano, 'In tema di sollecitazione del pubblico risparmio' [Enhancing Public Savings], *Giurisprudenza commerciale*, 1986, II, 217-245.

PREITE, Disiano, 'Sovrapprezzo, aste competitive e mercato mobiliare' [Overpricing, Competitive Auctions and Security Market], *Giurisprudenza commerciale*, 1987, I, 882-924. (Subject Code: 6300)

PREITE, Disiano, *La destinazione dei risultati nei contratti associativi* [The Destination of the Results in Partnership Contracts], Milano, Giuffrè, 1988, 456 p. (Subject Code: 5530)

PULITINI, Francesco, 'Regole giuridiche e teoria economica' [Law and Economic Theory], *Politica del diritto*, 1967, 297-310. (Subject Code: 0010)

PULITINI, Francesco, 'Le "new properties" e il decentramento delle scelte pubbliche' [New Properties and Decentralization of Public Choices], in AA.VV., *Dalle res alle new properties*, Minalo, 1991, 67-80. (Subject Code: 2700)

RAITERI, Monica, 'Giustizia distributiva e funzione giudiziaria: qualche osservazione nella prospettiva della analisi economica del diritto' [Distributive Justice and the Judicial Function, Some Observations in an EAL Perspective], *Materiali storia cultura giur.*, 1988, 209-228. (Subject Code: 0010, 0400)

RODANO, Giorgio, 'Il giudice e l' efficienza del mercato. Riflessioni di un economista su un libro di diritto comparato' [The Judge and the Efficiency of the Market. An Economist's Thoughts about an Essay in Comparative Law], *Rivista critica del diritto privato*, 1989, 293-312. (Subject Code: 0010)

ROMANI, Franco, 'Appunti sull' analisi economica dei contratti' [Notes about the Economic Analysis of Contract Law], *Quadrimestre*, 1985, 15-29. (Subject Code: 4000)

ROSSELLO, Carlo, *Il danno evitabile. La misura della responsabilità tra diligenza ed efficienza* [Avoidable Damage: The Measure of Liability Between Due Care and Efficiency], Padova, CEDAM, 1990, 320 p. (Subject Code: 3100, 3200)

SANTINI, Gerardo, *Il commercio* [Trading], Bologna, Il Mulino, 1979, 364 p. (Subject Code: 0020)

SANTINI, Gerardo, *I servizi. Saggio di economia del diritto* [The Services: An Essay in Economics of Law], Bologna, Il Mulino, 1987, 562 p. (Subject Code: 0020)

TARZIA, Giuseppe, 'Credito bancario e risanamento dell'impresa nella procedura di amministrazione straordinaria' [Credit and the Reorganization of the Firm], *Giurisprudenza commerciale*, I, 1983, 340-352. (Subject Code: 5600)

TRICOLI, Clara, 'Per una teoria economica dell' espropriazione e dell' indennizzo' [An Economic Theory of Takings and Compensation], *Rivista di diritto commerciale*, 1981, I, 335-357. (Subject Code: 3000)

TRIMARCHI, Pietro, *Rischio e responsabilità oggettiva* [Risk and Strict Liability], Milano, Giuffrè, 1961, 383 p. (Subject Code: 0020, 3000)

TRIMARCHI, Pietro, 'Sul significato economico dei criteri di responsabilità contrattuale' [Economic Meaning of Contract-Liability Criteria], *Rivista trimestrale di diritto e procedura civile*, 1970, 512-531. (Subject Code: 4400)

TRIMARCHI, Pietro, 'L'analisi economica del diritto: tendenze e prospettive' [Economic Analysis of Law: Tendencies and Perspectives], *Quadrimestre*, 1987, 563-582. (Subject Code: 0010)

VILLA, Gianroberto, 'Errore riconosciuto, annullamento del contratto ed incentivi alla ricerca di informazioni' [Known Mistake, Contract Avoidance and Incentives To Gathering Information], *Quadrimestre*, 1988, 286-300. (Subject Code: 0650, 4200)

LAW & ECONOMICS IN THE NETHERLANDS

Rudi W. Holzhauer and Rob Teijl

ABN, *Kwekersrecht* [Plant Breeders Right], Alg. Bank Nederland, 1989, 12 p. (Subject Code: 2950)

ABN, *Octrooien en licenties* [Patents and Licences], Alg. Bank Nederland, 1989, 35 p. (Subject Code: 2965)

ABN, *Octrooien in het midden- en kleinbedrijf* [Patents in Middle-size and Small Companies], Alg. Bank Nederland, 1990, 11 p. (Subject Code: 2930)

AELEN, L.O.M., 'De EEG-groepsvrijstelling voor franchise-overeenkomsten' [The EC Block Exemption for Franchise Agreements], **38** *Sociaal-Economische Wetgeving: Tijdschrift voor Europees en Economisch Recht*, 1990, 3-16. (Subject Code: 5700)

ARS AEQUI, 'Special Issue on Law-and-Economics', **39(10)** *Ars Aequi*, October 1990, 603-804. (Subject Code: 0050)

ASSELT, Henk Th. van, 'Balanceren tussen innovatie en monopolie: octrooiduur en innovatie in de Geneesmiddelenindustrie' [Balancing Innovation and Monopoly: The Patent Term and Innovation in the Pharmaceutical Industry], **57** *Bijblad Intellectuele Eigendom*, 1989, 143-147. (Subject Code: 2930)

ASSELT, Henk Th. van, 'Octrooiduur & innovatie in de geneesmiddelenindustrie' [Patent Term and Innovation in the Pharmaceutical Industry], **32** *Management Report Series, Rotterdam School of Management*, 1989, 17 p. (Subject Code: 2930)

BAARSLAG, A.D., 'Octrooibeleid van de onderneming' [Patent Policy of the Firm], in *Octrooien in Nederland en Europa*, Kamer van Koophandel en Fabrieken voor Rotterdam en de Beneden-Maas, 22 mei 1990. (Subject Code: 2930)

BACKHAUS, Jürgen G., 'De eis tot correctie van ondoelmatig recht' [The Need to Correct Inefficient Law], **39(10)** *Ars Aequi*, 1990, 660-665. (Subject Code: 0300, 9000)

BACKHAUS, Jürgen G., 'Een economische analyse van het constitutionele recht' [An Economic Analysis of Constitutional Law], in *Rechtseconomie en Recht*, Zwolle, Tjeenk Willink, 1991, 107-148. (Subject Code: 9100)

BAKKER, Luit M. and RIDDER, Ronald K. de, 'Het EG-mededingingsbeleid en de samenwerking en concentratie binnen het Europese bankwezen' [EC Competition Policy and European Banking Cooperation and Concentration], **39(11)** *Bank- en Effectenbedrijf*, 1990, 42-46. (Subject Code: 5700)

BARENTS, R., 'Enige recente ontwikkelingen in het Europese mededingingsbeleid (1980-1985)' [Some Recent Developments in European Competition Policy], **29** *TVVS: Maandblad voor Ondernemingsrecht en Rechtspersonen*, 1986, 192-198. (Subject Code: 5700)

BERGE, J.B.J.M. ten, 'Rechtseconomie en staatsrecht/bestuursrecht' [Law-and-economics and Constitutional/Administrative Law], in *Rechtseconomie en Recht*, Zwolle, Tjeenk Willink, 1991, 149-162. (Subject Code: 6300, 9000)

BLANKENBURG, E., 'Naar een planeconomie voor de rechtshulp' [Towards a

Planned Economy for Legal Aid], *Nederlands Juristen Blad*, 1990, 879-882. (Subject Code: 7000)

BLANKENBURG, E. and VERWOERD, J.R.A., 'Vermijden en benutten van civielrechtelijke procedures in Nederland en omringende landen' [The Use and Avoidance of Private Law Proceedings in the Netherlands and Surrounding Countries], *Justitiële Verkenningen*, 1987/2, 20-35. (Subject Code: 7210)

BLEEKER, K.A.M., 'De geheimhoudingsplicht volgens art. 42 WEM in het licht van het EEG-Verdrag' [The Secrecy Duty According to s. 42 WEM in the Light of the EC Treaty], **37** *Sociaal-Economische Wetgeving: Tijdschrift voor Europees en Economisch Recht*, 1989, 714-722. (Subject Code: 5700)

BLOEMBERGEN, *Duizend botsingen: Een kwantitatieve analyse van civiele rechtbankvonnissen in verkeerszaken* [Thousand Accidents: A Quantitative Analysis of Civil Court Decisions on Traffic Matters], Deventer, Kluwer, 1972, 74 p. (Subject Code: 3000)

BOLKESTEIN, Frits, *Vrijheid en regeling: Een liberale visie op de mededingingspolitiek* [Freedom and Regulation: A Liberal View on Competition Policy], 's-Gravenhage, 1985, 35 p. (Subject Code: 5700)

BOOIJ, H., 'Nieuwe institutionele economie' [Neo-Institutional Economics], *Van alle markten thuis. Opstellen aangeboden aan J.R. Zuidema*, Universitaire Pers, Rotterdam, 1987, 90-96. (Subject Code: 0500)

BOS, P.V.F. and FIERSTRA, Marc A., *Europees mededingingsrecht* [European Competition Law], Deventer, Kluwer, 1989, 274 p. (Subject Code: 5700)

BOS, P.V.F. and STUYCK, J.H.V., 'Concentratiecontrole naar EEG-recht' [Concentration Control in EC-Law], **37** *Sociaal- Economische Wetgeving: Tijdschrift voor Europees en Economisch Recht*, 1989, 300-404. (Subject Code: 5700)

BOUKEMA, C.A., 'Economische en juridische aspecten van Hoofdstuk I Fusiecode' [Economic and Legal Aspects of Chapter I Dutch Merger Rules], in COLJEE, P.D., FRANKEN, H., HEERTJE, A. and KANNING, W. (eds.), *Law and Welfare Economics*, Symposium 24 October, VU Amsterdam, 49-58. (Subject Code: 5540)

BOVENS, M.A.P. and WITTEVEEN, W.J., 'Bruce Ackerman over sociale rechtvaardigheid, de rol van de rechter en "Law and Economics"' [Bruce Ackerman on Social Justice, the Role of the Judiciary and "Law and Economics"] (interview), *Staatkundig Jaarboek*, Nijmegen, Ars Aequi Libri, 1987, 255-278. (Subject Code: 0400)

BRAAKMAN, A.J., 'Europees kartelrecht als strijdmiddel bij overnames' [European Anti-trust Law as Takeover Combat Mechanism], **73** *Economisch-Statistische Berichten*, 1988, 854-858. (Subject Code: 5540, 5700)

BRINKHOF, Jan J., 'Over octrooirecht en economie' [On Patent Law and the Economy], **39(10)** *Ars Aequi*, 1990, 794-802. (Subject Code: 2930)

BROEK, Jan H.G. van den, 'Nieuwe instrumenten voor energiebesparing' [New Instruments for Energy Savings], in COLJEE, P.D., FRANKEN, H., HEERTJE, A. and KANNING, W. (eds.), *Law and Welfare Economics*, Symposium 24 October, VU Amsterdam, 59-76. (Subject Code: 3500)

CAANEN, Ch. and ESSERS, P.H.J., 'Rechtseconomie en belastingrecht' [Law-and-economics and Taxation Law], **39(10)** *Ars Aequi*, 1990, 677-681. (Subject

Code: 6000)

CASTERMANS, A.G., 'Schadevergoeding bij dwaling' [Damages for Misrepresentation], *Rechtsgeleerd Magazijn Themis*, 1989, 136-146. (Subject Code: 4200)

CASTERMANS, A.G. and NOTERMANS, R., 'Naar een economische analyse van de mededelingsplicht bij dwaling' [Towards an Economic Analysis of the Duty to Inform in Misrepresentation Law], *BW-krant jaarboek 1985, BW-NBW: twee sporen, één weg*, Leiden, Rijksuniversiteit Leiden, 1985, 141-155. (Subject Code: 4200)

CHAO-DUYVIS, M.A.B., 'Vergelding als schadevergoeding' [Retribution as Damages], *Nederlands Juristen Blad*, 1990, 513-520. (Subject Code: 3000)

COHEN JEHORAM, Herman, 'Industriële eigendom en innovatie' [Industrial Property and Innovation], *Nederlands Juristen Blad*, 1979, 609-612. (Subject Code: 2905)

COHEN JEHORAM, Herman, 'Het economisch belang van het auteursrecht en de gevaren daarvan' [The Economic Importance of Copyright and Its Dangers], **13** *Informatierecht AMI*, 1989, 91-95. (Subject Code: 2910)

COLJEE, P.D., 'Het economisch adviesrecht van de ondernemingsraad, quo vadis? Artikel 25 WOR nader beschouwd [The Workers Council Economic Right of Advice, Quo vadis? Section 25 Dutch Workers Council Act Reconsidered], in COLJEE, P.D., FRANKEN, H., HEERTJE, A. and KANNING, W. (eds.), *Law and Welfare Economics*, Symposium 24 October, VU Amsterdam, 77-99. (Subject Code: 5450, 5500)

COLIJN, P.J. et al. (ed.), *Economische eigendom* [Economic Ownership], Deventer, Kluwer, Stichting tot bevordering der notariële wetenschap, 1981, 92 p. (Subject Code: 2700)

CRAMER-MEIJERING-NIJSSEN, *De economische betekenis van het auteursrecht 1* [The Economic Importance of Copyright 1], Amsterdam, Stichting voor Economisch Onderzoek Universiteit van Amsterdam, 1986. (Subject Code: 2910)

CUELENAERE, L.M. and LEEN, A.R., 'Een rechtseconomisch aspect van de positie van de crediteur in een faillissement. Is afschaffing van de maximum rente een oplossing?' [A Law-and-economics Aspect of the Creditors Position in Bankruptcy. Is Abolishing the Maximum Interest Rate a Solution?], **38(10)** *Ars Aequi*, 1989, 834-836. (Subject Code: 2800)

DAM, C.C. van, *Zorgvuldigheidsnorm en aansprakelijkheid* [The Duty of Care and Liability] (diss. Utrecht), Kluwer, Deventer, 1989, 333 p. (Subject Code: 3000)

DEGENKAMP, J.Th. and HEYNEN, H.M., 'Juridische en economische eigendom. Een formele analyse' [Legal and Economic Ownership. A Formal Analysis],in *Tolvrije gedachten*, Deventer, Kluwer, 1980, 117-129. (Subject Code: 2000)

DE KRAAN, D.J., 'Deregulering' [Deregulation], **62** *Economisch-Statistische Berichten*, 1982, 692-696. (Subject Code: 6340)

DE KRAAN, D.J., 'Deregulering: een Begripsbepaling' [Deregulation: A Definition], **9** *Beleid en Maatschappij*, 1982, 177-181. (Subject Code: 6340)

DIJK, J.J.M. van, 'Financieel economische aspecten van misdaad en misdaadbestrijding' [Financial Economic Aspects of Crime and Prevention], **69** *Economisch-*

Statistische Berichten, 1984, 1248-1252. (Subject Code: 8000)

DIJK, J.J.M. van, 'Over de wenselijkheid van overheidsinterventies op de markt van recht en orde. Preadvies voor de 35e jaarvergadering van de Nederlandse Orde van Advocaten' [On the Desirability of Governmental Intervention on the Market for Law and Order], *Advocatenblad*, Tjeenk Willink, 1987, 343-352. (Subject Code: 8000)

DIJK, J.J.M. van and ROELL, A., 'Criminaliteit in tal en last' [Criminality], *Justitiële verkenningen*, Arnhem, Gouda Quint, 1988, Nr. 2, 7-33. (Subject Code: 8000)

DOORENBOS, D.R. and ROORDING, J.F.L., 'Rechtseconomie en strafrecht: een rechtseconomische analyse van de bestrijding van misbruik van voorwetenschap bij de handel in effecten' [Law-and-economics and Criminal Law: A Law-and-economics Analysis of Insider Trading in Securities], **39(10)** *Ars Aequi*, 1990, 733-742. (Subject Code: 5550, 8000)

DRIJBER, B.J., 'Groepsvrijstelling know-how licenties: Rechtszekerheid of onduidelijkheid' [Block Exemption Know-How Licences: Legal Certainty or Vagueness], **37** *Sociaal Economische Wetgeving: Tijdschrift voor Europees en Economisch Recht*, 1989, 200-216. (Subject Code: 5700)

FAURE, Michael G., 'Milieubescherming door aansprakelijkheidsrecht of regulering' [Protecting the Environment through Liability Law or Regulation], **39(10)** *Ars Aequi*, 1990, 759-769. (Subject Code: 3800)

FAURE, Michael G., 'De verzekering van geldboeten bij zeewaterverontreiniging door olie' [The Insurance of Fines with Respect to the Oil-Pollution of Seawater], in *Grensoverschrijdend strafrecht. Opstellen*, Arnhem, Gouda Quint, 1990, 203-221. (Subject Code: 4600, 8000)

FAURE, Michael G., 'Rechtseconomie en privaatrecht: Kunnen rechtsregels bijdragen tot de reductie van ongevalskosten' [Law-and-economics and Private Law: Can Legal Rules Contribute to Reducing Accident Costs], in *Rechtseconomie en Recht*, Zwolle, Tjeenk Willink, 1991, 51-93. (Subject Code: 3000)

FEENSTRA, J.J., 'Fusiecontrole door de EEG na het Philip Morris arrest' [EC Merger Control after the Philip Morris Case], **66** *De Naamloze Vennootschap*, 1988, 60-67. (Subject Code: 5700)

FIERSTRA, Marc A., 'Communautaire concentratiecontrole: Een nieuwe fase in een ontwikkeling' [Community Concentration Control: A New Development Stage], **38** *Sociaal-Economische Wetgeving: Tijdschrift voor Europees en Economisch Recht*, 1990, 330-350. (Subject Code: 5700)

FRANKEN, Hans, 'Economische analyse van het strafrecht' [Economic Analysis of Criminal Law], *Bij deze stand van zaken. Opstellen aangeboden aan A.L. Melai*, Arnhem, Gouda Quint, 1983, 117-131. (Subject Code: 8000)

FRANKEN, Hans, 'Voorkomen is beter dan genezen' [Prevention is Better Than Cure], *RMThemis*, 1987, 469-471. (Subject Code: 8000)

FRANKEN, Hans, 'Rechtseconomie en strafrecht' [Law-and-Economics and Criminal Law], in *Rechtseconomie en Recht*, Zwolle, Tjeenk Willink, 1991, 163-179. (Subject Code: 8000)

GEELHOED, L.A., *De intervenïerende staat* [The Intervening State], 's-Gravenhage, Staatsuitgeverij, 1983. (Subject Code: 9000)

GHERING, M., PUFFELEN, F. van and SCHILTHUIS, F., *De economische betekenis van het auteursrecht 2* [The Economic Importance of Copyright 2], Amsterdam, Stichting voor Economisch Onderzoek Universiteit van Amsterdam, 1989, 58 p. (Subject Code: 2910)

GIER, H.G. de, 'Heeft het arbeidsrecht een toekomst? Een verhandeling over de invloed van de economie op het arbeidsrecht' [Has Labour Law a Future? An Essay on the Influence of Economics on Labour Law], in COLJEE, P.D., FRANKEN, H., HEERTJE, A. and KANNING, W. (eds.), *Law and Welfare Economics*, Symposium 24 October, VU Amsterdam, 101-113. (Subject Code: 5400)

't GILDE, A.P.J. and HAANK, D.J., *De praktijk van de Wet economische mededinging* [The Competition Act in Practice], SWOKA, Onderzoeksrapport nr. 37, 's-Gravenhage, 1985, 38 p. (Subject Code: 5700)

GRAPENDAAL, M., 'De paradox en het dilemma. Effecten van politieoptreden op de Zeedijk' [Paradox and Dilemma. Effects of Police Action at the Zeedijk], **39(10)** *Ars Aequi*, 1990, 714-720. (Subject Code: 8000)

GRIFFITHS, J., 'De rechtbank als fietsenfabriek' [The Court as Bicycle Manufacturer], **66** *Nederlands Juristenblad*, 1991, 129-130, 445. (Subject Code: 7400)

GROENEWEGEN, J., 'Transactiekosten' [Transactions Costs], *Tijdschrift voor politieke economie*, 1990, 50-76. (Subject Code: 5400)

GROSHEIDE, F.W. and FREQUIN, M.J., 'Uitgeversrecht' [Publishers Right], **14** *Informatierecht AMI*, 1990, 43-47. (Subject Code: 2920)

HEERTJE, A., 'Conflictstof voor juristen en economen' [Conflict Material for Lawyers and Economists], **15** *Ars Aequi*, 1966, 14-16. (Subject Code: 0400)

HEERTJE, A., 'Speltheorie als economische analyse van het recht' [Game Theory as Economic Analysis of Law], in MARIS, C.W. et al. (eds.), *Recht, Rechtvaardigheid en Doelmatigheid*, Arnhem, Gouda Quint, 1990, 90-100. (Subject Code: 0670)

HEERTJE, A. and WABEKE, J.W., 'Het dreigende faillissement van justitie en politie' [The Near Bankruptcy of Prosecution and Police], **74** *Economisch-Statistische Berichten*, 1989, 1152-1155. (Subject Code: 8000)

HENNIPMAN, P., *De taak van de mededingingspolitiek* [The Role of Competition Policy], Haarlem, Bohn, 1966, 41 p. (Subject Code: 5700)

HERTOG, Johan A. and KRAAMWINKEL, Margriet M., ‘Pensioennadelen in het licht van de contracttheorie’ [Pension Disadvantages in the Light of Contract Theory], *Economisch-statistische berichten*, 1991, 908-912. (Subject Code: 5410)

HESSEL, B., 'De mogelijke rol van de rechtseconomie in een moderne rechtsstaat' [The Possible Role of Law-and-Economics in a Modern Constitutional State], **39(10)** *Ars Aequi*, 1990, 645-653. (Subject Code: 0300)

HOL, A.M., 'Efficiëntie als instrument en als norm. Enkele rechtstheoretische kanttekeningen bij de economische analyse van het recht' [Efficiency as Instrument and Norm: Some Remarks from Legal Theory on the Economic Analysis of Law], **39(10)** *Ars Aequi*, 1990, 632-644. (Subject Code: 0400)

HOL, A.M., ‘Rechten en doeleinden. Enkele morele aspecten van juridische aansprakelijkheid' [Rights and Goals. Some Moral Aspects of Legal Liability], in *Dilemma's van aansprakelijkheid*, Zwolle, Tjeenk Willink, 1991, 127-142. (Subject Code: 0400)

HOLZHAUER, Rudi W. and TEIJL, Rob, 'Geschillenbeslechting als economisch alternatief' [Dispute Settlement as Economic Alternative], in SNIJDERS, H.J., et al. (eds.), *Overheidsrechter gepasseerd*, Arnhem, Gouda Quint, 1988, 489-499. (Subject Code: 7210)

HOLZHAUER, Rudi W., TEIJL, Rob et al., *Inleiding Rechtseconomie* [Introduction to Law-and-Economics], Gouda Quint, Arnhem, 1989, 345 p. (Subject Code: 0000)

HOLZHAUER, Rudi W. and TEIJL, Rob, 'Rechtseconomie in Nederland' [Law-and-Economics in the Netherlands], **38(4)** *Ars Aequi*, 1989, 248-252. (Subject Code: 0100)

HONDIUS, E.H., 'Rechtseconomie en privaatrecht: enige kanttekeningen' [Law-and-Economics and Private Law: Some Remarks], in *Rechtseconomie en Recht*, Tjeenk Willink, Zwolle, 1991, 95-105. (Subject Code: 0300)

HONDIUS, E.H., SCHIPPERS, J.J. and SIEGERS, J.J. (eds.), 'Rechtseconomie: Brug tussen twee disciplines' [Law-and-Economics: Bridge between two Disciplines], in *Rechtseconomie en Recht*, Tjeenk Willink, Zwolle, 1991, 1-7 p. (Subject Code: 0010)

HOOGENBOOM, B., 'Rechtseconomie en particuliere beveiliging: "Policing for profits" als voorloper van strafrechtelijke hervormingen' [Law-and-Economics and Private Security: "Policing for Profit" as Precursor of Criminal Reform], **39(10)** *Ars Aequi*, 1990, 721-732. (Subject Code: 8000)

HULS, N.J.H., *Van liquidatie tot rehabilitatie* [From Liquidation to Rehabilitation], 's-Gravenhage, Ministerie van Economische Zaken, 1988, 106 p. (Subject Code: 5600)

HULST, W.G.J. van and WILLEMS, J.G.L.M., *Externe organisatie: Een kennismaking met het ondernemingsgedrag in markteconomische stelsels* [External Organisation: An Introduction to Firm Behaviour in Market Systems], Leiden, Stenfert Kroese, 1989, 284 p. (Subject Code: 5700)

JONG, Hendrik W. de, 'Marktorganisatie, mededinging en prijsvorming' [Market Organisation, Competition and Price-Making], **66** *Economisch-Statistische Berichten*, 1981, 1268-1280. (Subject Code: 5700)

JONG, Hendrik W. de, 'De Europese mededingingspolitiek: overzicht en beoordeling' [European Competition Policy: Overview and Assessment], *Beleid & Maatschappij*, 1982, 230-240. (Subject Code: 5700)

JONG, Hendrik W. de, 'Fusies, overnames en beschermingsconstructies' [Mergers, Take-overs and Protective Devices], **73** *Economisch-Statistische Berichten*, 1988, 842-847 + 852. (Subject Code: 5700)

JONG, Hendrik W. de, *Dynamische markttheorie* [Dynamic Market Theory], Leiden, Stenfert Kroese, 1989 (4th ed.), 334 p. (Subject Code: 5700)

JONG, Hendrik W. de, 'Concurrentie en concentratie in de markteconomie' [Competition and Concentration in the Market Economy], **37** *Sociaal-Economische Wetgeving: Tijdschrift voor Europees en Economisch Recht*, 1989, 664-688. (Subject Code: 5700)

JONG, Hendrik W. de, 'Concurrentie, concentratie en het Europese mededingingsbeleid' [Competition, Concentration and European Competition Policy], **74** *Economisch-Statistische Berichten*, 1989, 1182-1187. (Subject Code: 5700)

JONG, Hendrik W. de, 'Nederland: Het kartelparadijs van Europa' [The Netherlands: European Anti-trust Paradise], **75** *Economisch-Statistische Berichten*, 1990, 244-248. (Subject Code: 5700)

KANNING, W., 'Een non-cooperatieve benadering van het Coase-theorema' [A Non Cooperative Approach to the Coase Theorem]', in COLJEE, P.D., FRANKEN, H., HEERTJE, A. and KANNING, W. (eds.), *Law and Welfare Economics*, Symposium 24 October, VU Amsterdam, 39-48. (Subject Code: 0630)

KAUFMANN, Peter J. and WIJNBERG, N.M., 'Het Decca arrest: bescherming van prestatie en imitatie' [The Decca Case: Protecting Activities and Imitation], *Intellectuele eigendom en reclamerecht*, 1990, 77-81. (Subject Code: 2995)

KAUFMANN, Peter J., 'Verwarringsgevaar of verwateringsgevaar in het Europese merkenrecht anno 1991: artikel 13 A.1 Benelux Merkenwet mag niet blijven!' [Confusion or Dilution in European Trademark Law 1991: Section 13 A.1 Benelux Trademark Act Cannot Continue to Exist!], *Qui Bene Distinguit Bene Docet*, Arnhem, Gouda Quint, 1991, 175-190. (Subject Code: 2940)

KERKMEESTER, H.O., *Recht en speltheorie* [Law and Game Theory] (diss. Rotterdam), 1989, 212 p. (Subject Code: 9000)

KERKMEESTER, H.O. and MULDER, R.V. de, 'Beslissingstheoretische criteria voor de beslechting van een juridisch geschil door een onafhankelijke derde' [Theoretical Decisionmaking Criteria in Settling a Legal Dispute by a Third Party], in SNIJDERS, H.J. et al. (eds.), *Overheidsrechter gepasseerd*, Arnhem, Gouda Quint, 1988, 501-511. (Subject Code: 7210)

KNEPPERS-HEYNERT, E.M., *Een economische en juridische analyse van franchising tegen de achtergrond van een property rights- en transactiekosten benadering* [An Economic and Legal Analysis of Franchising in the Light of a Property and Transaction Costs Approach] (diss. Groningen), Groningen, Van Denderen, 1988, 268 p. (Subject Code: 4140)

KOOPMANS, T., 'Mini-monopolies' [Mini-monopolies], *Rechtsgeleerd Magazijn Themis*, 1983, 342-344. (Subject Code: 2900)

KOPPEN, P.J. van, 'Cassatieadvocaten en de selectiekamer' [Cassation Lawyers and the Chamber of Selection], *Nederlands Juristen Blad*, 1990, 14-26. (Subject Code: 7000)

KOPPEN, P.J. van, RICHTERS, H.W. and TEN KATE, J., *Schikken of procederen: Psychologische kanttekeningen bij de economie van civielrechtelijke geschillen* [Settlement vs. Trial: Psychological Notes on the Economy of Private Law Disputes], Rapport aangeboden aan de Minister van Justitie, 1989. (Subject Code: 7210)

LAMBERS, H.W., 'Mededingingspolitiek' [Competition Policy], in ANDRIESSEN, J.E. and VAN MEERHAEGHE, M.A.G. (eds.), *Theorie van de Economische Politiek*, Leiden, Stenfert Kroese, 1962, 307-338. (Subject Code: 5700)

LE BLANC, L.J.C.M., 'Bismarck als Benchmark. Enkele rechtseconomische beschouwingen over publieke sector en sociale zekerheid in Nederland' [Bismarck as Benchmark. Some Law-and-economics Considerations on the Public Sector and Social Welfare in the Netherlands], **39(10)** *Ars Aequi*, 1990, 654-659. (Subject

Code: 6100)

LINDNER, G.L., 'Arreststraf of geldboete' [Detention or Fine], diss. Rijks Universiteit Leiden, 1985. (Subject Code: 8000)

LINNEMAN, M.J.T., 'Sportrechten, artikel 15 en marktopdeling' [Sports Rights, Section 15 and Splitting up the Market], **14** *Informatierecht AMI*, 1990, 63-66. (Subject Code: 2920)

LINSSEN, G.J., 'De rol van de Commissie bij de toepassing van het Europese mededingingsrecht' [The Role of the Commission in Applying European Competition Law], in VERLOREN VAN THEMAAT, Pieter, et al., *Europees kartelrecht anno 1973*, Deventer, Kluwer, 1973, 23-45. (Subject Code: 5700)

LINSSEN, G.J. 'De verhouding tussen het formele en het informele kartelbeleid in Nederland en de plaats van de Commissie Economische Mededinging' [The Interrelationship between the Formal and Informal Dutch Anti-trust Policy and the Position of the Committee on Economic Competition], **24** *TVVS: Maandblad voor Ondernemingsrecht en Rechtspersonen*, 1981, 255-259. (Subject Code: 5700)

MACKAAY, Ejan J.P., 'Veranderingen in het stelsel van vergoeding en verhaal van schade' [Changes in the System of Compensation and Recoupment of Damages], **55** *Nederlands Juristen Blad*, 1980, 813-825. Reprinted in *Schade lijden en schade dragen*, Zwolle, Tjeenk Willink, Nederlands Juristenblad Boekenreeks No. 6, 1981. (Subject Code: 3000)

MACKAAY, Ejan J.P., 'De hersenschim als rustig bezit. Moet alle informatie voorwerp van eigendom zijn?' [Chimera as Quiet Possession. Should All Information Be Owned?], *Computerrecht*, 1985, 12-16. (Subject Code: 2900)

MACKAAY, Ejan J.P., 'Het recht bezien door de bril van de economist - Een gestyleerd overzicht van de rechtseconomie' [Law Seen Through an Economists Glasses: An Overview of Law-and-economics], *Rechtsgeleerd Magazijn Themis*, 1988, 411-452. (Subject Code: 0010, 0300)

MACKAAY, Ejan J.P., 'Het aansprakelijkheidsrecht' [Liability Law], **39(10)** *Ars Aequi*, 1990, 743-749. (Subject Code: 3000)

MACKAAY, Ejan J.P., 'Verschuivingen in de rechtseconomie' [Shifts in Law-and-Economics], **66** *Nederlands Juristenblad*, 1991, 1505-1521. (Subject Code: 0010, 0500)

MALSCH, Marijke, *Advocaten voorspellen de uitkomst van hun zaken* [Lawyers' Predictions of Judicial Decisions: A Study on Calibration of Experts], Lisse, Swets & Zeitlinger, 1990, 109 p. (Subject Code: 7000)

MEESTER, G. and WESEMANN, P., 'Kosten-baten analyse en strafrecht' [Cost Benefit Analysis and Criminal Law], *Portret van de juridische faculteit Rotterdam 12 1/2*, Deventer, Kluwer, 1976, 217-228. (Subject Code: 8000)

MEIJS, Paul and JANSEN, Wim, *Eigendom tussen politiek en economie* [Ownership between Politics and Economy], Groningen, Wolters-Noordhoff, 1989, 195 p. (Subject Code: 2000)

MELAI, A.L., 'De straf en het gezichtspunt van de econometristen' [Punishment and the Econometrist Perspective], in *Speculum Langemeyer*, Zwolle, Tjeenk Willink, 1973, 315-331. (Subject Code: 8000)

MINISTERIE VAN JUSTITIE, *Rapport van de Studiegroep Verkeersaansprakelijk-*

heid, Deel I, Vergoeding van schade door dood en letsel [Report of the Commission Traffic Liability, Part I, Compensation of Damages through Death and Injury], 's-Gravenhage, Staatsuitgeverij, 1978. (Subject Code: 3200)

MINISTERIE VAN JUSTITIE, *Rapport van de Studiegroep Verkeersaansprakelijkheid, Deel II, Vergoeding van zaakschade* [Report of the Commission Traffic Liability, Part I, Compensation of Damages Caused to Things], 's-Gravenhage, Staatsuitgeverij, 1980. (Subject Code: 3200)

MOERLAND, H. and RODERMOND, J.G., 'Ontwikkelingen in het afschrikkingsonderzoek'[Developments in Deterrence Research], *Panopticon*, 1987, 59-75. (Subject Code: 8000)

MOERLAND, H. and RODERMOND, J.G., 'Winkeldiefstal, een (te) riskante zaak? Onderzoek naar een mogelijke samenhang tussen het plegen van winkeldiefstal en de verwachte gevolgen' [Theft in Shops, a (too) Risky Business? Investigation of a Possible Relationship between Theft in Shops and the Expected Consequences], *Panopticon*, 1987, 335-349. (Subject Code: 8000)

MOK, M.R., 'Kartelbeleid nu en in de toekomst' [Present and Future Anti-trust Policy], in MOK, M.R., et al., *Nieuwe ontwikkelingen in het Europese kartelrecht*, Kluwer, Deventer, 1976, 1-15. (Subject Code: 5700)

MOK, M.R., '20 jaar WEM' [20 Years WEM], **26** *Sociaal-Economische Wetgeving: Tijdschrift voor Europees en Economisch Recht*, 1978, 737-760. (Subject Code: 5700)

MOK, M.R., 'Het paard achter de wagen: Deregulering en kartelrecht' [The Cart Before the Horse: Deregulation and Anti-trust Law], **31** *Sociaal- Economische Wetgeving: Tijdschrift voor Europees en Economisch Recht*, 1983, 666-678. (Subject Code: 5700)

NAGELKERKE, J.J., 'Beschouwingen over economische wetenschap en haar betekenis voor de rechtsvorming' [Considerations about Economic Science and its Use in the Formation of Law], *RMThemis*, 1979, 356-385. (Subject Code: 0300)

NEDERLANDS ECONOMISCH INSTITUUT, *Naar een economische benadering van criminaliteit en veiligheidszorg* [Towards an Economic Approach of Delinquency and Security Provision], Rotterdam, Nederlands Economisch Instituut, 1989. (Subject Code: 8000)

NEDERLANDS ECONOMISCH INSTITUUT, *Verhuur- en leenrecht EG. Commentaar op het SEO-rapport "Naar een verhuur- en leenrecht in de Europese Gemeenschap* [EC Rental and Lending Rights. Commentary on the SEO-report "Towards a Rental and Lending Right in the European Community], Rotterdam, Nederlands Economisch Instituut, 1991, 24 p. (Subject Code: 2920)

NEDERLANDS JURISTEN BLAD: *Tussen kwaliteit en efficiency in de rechtspraak* [Between Quality and Efficiency in Case Law], Special Issue, 1987, (a number of articles). (Subject Code: 7000)

NEDERLANDS JURISTEN BLAD: *Rechtshulp anno 1990*, Special Issue, 1990, (a number of articles). (Subject Code: 7000)

NENTJES, Andries, *De economie van het recht* [The Economy of the Law], oratie Groningen, s.l., 1987, 18 p. (Subject Code: 0010)

NENTJES, Andries, 'De welvaartseffecten van het strafrecht' [Welfare Effects of Criminal Law], *Justitiële Verkenningen*, Arnhem, Gouda Quint, 1988, n. 2, 34-52. (Subject Code: 8000)

NENTJES, A., 'Van wie is het milieu?' [Who Owns the Environment?], **39(10)** *Ars Aequi*, 1990, 706-713. (Subject Code: 3500)

NIEUWENHUIS, J.H., 'Recht en belang' [Law and Interests], *Flores Debitorem*, Zwolle, Tjeenk Willink, 1984, 65-74. (Subject Code: 0400)

NIEUWENHUIS, J.H., 'Ieder het zijne' [Each His Own], *RMThemis*, 1988, Nr. 2, 73-84. (Subject Code: 0400)

NIEUWENHUIS, J.H., 'Blinddoek en balans in het milieurecht. Drie manieren om belangen af te wegen' [Blindfold and Balance in Environmental Law. Three Ways of Balacing Interests], in *Dilemma's van aansprakelijkheid*, Zwolle, Tjeenk Willink, 1991, 37-51. (Subject Code: 0300)

OMMEREN, F.J. van, 'Bestuurscompensatie, draagkracht en rechtseconomie' [Administrative Compensation, Financial Capacity and Economic Analysis of Law], **39(10)** *Ars Aequi*, 1990, 682-691. (Subject Code: 6300)

PEEPERKORN, Luc, 'Mededingingsbeleid op klompen' [Competition Policy on Wooden Shoes], **10** *Tijdschrift voor Politieke Economie*, 1987, 57-75. (Subject Code: 5700)

PEEPERKORN, Luc, 'Openbaarheid van kartels' [The Public Nature of Cartels], **73** *Economisch-Statistische Berichten*, 1988, 212-214. (Subject Code: 5700)

PEEPERKORN, Luc, 'Het EG-mededingingsbeleid' [EC Competition Policy], **74** *Economisch-Statistische Berichten*, 1989, 1139-1142. (Subject Code: 5700)

PEEPERKORN, Luc, 'Fusiecontrole in de EG' [EC Merger Control], **74** *Economisch-Statistische Berichten*, 1989, 1163-1165. (Subject Code: 5700)

PERRON, Edgar du, 'De rechtseconomische analyse van het verbintenissenrecht' [A Law-and-economics Analysis of the Law of Obligations], **39(10)** *Ars Aequi*, 1990, 770-776. (Subject Code: 4000)

RESIUS, F.J., 'Uitgeversbescherming' [The Protection of Publishers], 14 *Informatierecht AMI*, 1990, 67-69. (Subject Code: 2920)

RICHTERS, H.W., *Schikkingen en Proceskansen* [Settlements and Expected Proceeding Outcome], diss. Rotterdam, 1991, 171 p. (Subject Code: 7210)

RIETKERK, G., 'Bestuursonvriendelijke onderneming: een countervailing power. Een economische analyse' [Management Unfriendly Take-over: A Countervailing Power. An Economic Analysis], **66** *De Naamloze Vennootschap*, 1988, 45-54. (Subject Code: 5540)

ROVENS, R. and PRINSEN, P.J., 'Extra politie-inzet en rijden onder invloed' [More Police and Drunken Driving], *WODC reeks*, no. 52, 's-Gravenhage, Staatsuitgeverij, 1984. (Subject Code: 8000)

RU, H.J. de, *Staat, markt en recht* [The State, the Market and the Law], Zwolle, Tjeenk Willink, 1987, 93 p. (Subject Code: 9000)

RU, H.J. de, *Prijst de wet zich uit de markt?* [Does the Law Price Itself Out of the Market?] Inaugural Lecture, Zwolle, Tjeenk Willink, 1988. (Subject Code: 9200)

SCHILFGAARDE, E. van, 'Economische analyse van het Nederlands aansprakelijkheidsrecht uit onrechtmatige daad' [Economic Analysis of Dutch Tort Liability Law], **39(10)** *Ars Aequi*, 1990, 750-758. (Subject Code: 3000)

SEO, *De economische betekenis van het auteursrecht in Nederland: 1982* [The

Economic Importance of Copyright in the Netherlands: 1982], Amsterdam, Stichting voor Economisch Onderzoek, 1986. (Subject Code: 2920)

SEO, *De economische betekenis van de professionele kunsten in Amsterdam* [The Economic Importance of Professional Art in Amsterdam], Amsterdam, Stichting voor Economisch Onderzoek, 241 p. (Subject Code: 2920)

SEO, *De economische betekenis van het auteursrecht 2: Rapportage 1989* [The Economic Importance of Copyright in the Netherlands 2: Report 1989], Amsterdam, Stichting voor Economisch Onderzoek, 1989. (Subject Code: 2910)

SEO, *Naar een verhuur- en leenrecht in de Europese gemeenschap* [Towards a Rental and Lending Rights in the European Community], Amsterdam, Stichting voor Economisch Onderzoek, 1989, 203 p. (Subject Code: 2920)

SLAGTER, Wiek J., *Macht en onmacht van de aandeelhouder* [Shareholders (Lack of) Power], Deventer, Kluwer, 1988, 47 p. (Subject Code: 5530)

SLAGTER, Wiek J., *Schaarse rechten. Afscheidscollege Rotterdam* [Scarce Rights], Deventer, Kluwer, 1989, 42 p. (Subject Code: 2000, 5530)

SLAGTER, Wiek J., *Juridische en economische eigendom* [Legal and Economic Ownership], Deventer, Kluwer, 1968, 66 p. (Subject Code: 2000)

SLOT, P.J., *Regelen en ontregelen. Oratie Leiden* [Regulating and De-regulating], Kluwer, Deventer, 1983. (Subject Code: 9000)

SNIJDERS, H.J., 'Prijzig recht, kwetsbaar recht. Preadvies voor de 35e jaarvergadering van de Nederlandse Orde van Advocaten' [Expensive Law, Vulnerable Law], *Advocatenblad*, 1987, 325-342. (Subject Code:)

SNIJDERS, W.L., 'Misbruikstoezicht en verbodsbeginsel in het kartelrecht (I)' [Supervising Abuse and the Principle of Banning Orders in Anti-trust Law (I)], **40** *Maandschrift Economie*, 1975, 133-154. (Subject Code: 5700)

SNIJDERS, W.L., 'Misbruikstoezicht en verbodsbeginsel in het kartelrecht (II)' [Supervising Abuse and the Principle of Banning Orders in Anti-trust Law (II)], **40** *Maandschrift Economie*, 1975, 206-227. (Subject Code: 5700)

SNIJDERS, W.L., 'Het optreden tegen economische machtsposities op grond van de Wet economische mededinging' [The Action against Economic Position of Powers on the Basis of the Economic Competition Act], in *In Orde: Liber Amicorum Pieter Verloren van Themaat*, Kluwer, Deventer, 1982, 267-293. (Subject Code: 5700)

SOCIAAL CULTUREEL PLANBUREAU, *Doelmatig Rechtspreken* [Efficient Administration of Justice], S.C.P., Cahier no. 88, 's-Gravenhage, Staatsdrukkerij, 1990, 74 p. (Subject Code: 7400)

SOETENHORST, W.J., 'Wettelijke bescherming van de uitgeefprestatie in Nederland, Duitsland, Zwitserland en Groot-Brittannië' [Legal Protection of Publishers Activities in the Netherlands, Germany, Switzerland and Great-Britain], **13** *Informatierecht*, 1989, 55-57. (Subject Code: 2920)

SPITTJE, Petra J., 'De hinderwetgeving' [Nuisance Legislation], in COLJEE, P.D., FRANKEN, H., HEERTJE, A. and KANNING, W. (eds.), *Law and Welfare Economics*, Symposium 24 October, VU Amsterdam, 115-132. (Subject Code: 3400)

STEENHUIS, D.W., 'Strafrechtelijk optreden: stapje terug en een sprong voorwaarts' [Criminal Policy: A Step Backwards and a Jump Ahead], in *Delikt en*

Delinkwent, Arnhem, Gouda Quint, 1984/5, 1984/6. (Subject Code: 7300, 8000)

TEIJL, Rob and HOLZHAUER, Rudi W., 'Pluriformiteit in de rechtseconomie: een verkenning van scholen' [Multiformity in Law-and-economics: an Exploration of Schools], **39(10)** *Ars Aequi*, 1990, 617-631. (Subject Code: 0500)

TEIJL, Rob and HOLZHAUER, Rudi W. (eds.), *Teksten Rechtseconomie* [Readings in Law-and-Economics], Arnhem, Gouda Quint, 1990/1991, 549 p. (Subject Code: 0060)

TEIJL, Rob and HOLZHAUER, Rudi W., 'De toenemende complexiteit van het intellectuele eigendomsrecht. Een economische analyse' [The Growing Complexity of Intellectual Property Law. An Economic Analysis], in *Rechtseconomische Verkenningen Deel 1*, Arnhem, Gouda Quint, 1991. (Subject Code: 2900)

TEN KATE, J., 'Schikkingen tijdens civielrechtelijke geschillen' [Settlements in Private Law Disputes], in *Recht der Werkelijkheid*,'s-Gravenhage, VUGA, 1989, 63-79. (Subject Code: 7210)

THEEUWES, Jules J.M., VAN VELTHOVEN, B.C.J., WINTERS, J.K. e.a., *Recht en Economie* [Law and Economics], Amsterdam, Addison-Wesley, 1989, 294 p. (Subject Code: 0050)

TIMMERMAN, L., 'Onderneming en vennootschap' [Enterprise and Firm], in *Piercing Van Schilfgaarde*, Deventer, Kluwer, 1990, 3-11. (Subject Code: 5500)

TINBERGEN, J., 'Kan de economische wetenschap bijdragen tot de ontwikkeling van het recht?' [Can the Economic Science Contribute to Legal Development?], in *In Orde. Liber Amicorum Verloren van Themaat*, Deventer, Kluwer, 1982, 295-300. (Subject Code: 5400)

TULDER, Frank van, *Criminaliteit, pakkans en politie* [Criminality, Chance of Being Caught and Police], Sociaal Cultureel Planbureau, Cahier no. 45, 's-Gravenhage, Staatsdrukkerij, 1985. (Subject Code: 8000)

TULDER, Frank van, 'Kosten en baten van twee vormen van criminaliteitsbestrijding' [Costs and Benefits of Two Types of Crime Combat], **71** *Economisch-Statistische Berichten*, 1986, 172-179. (Subject Code: 8000)

TULDER, Frank van, 'Rechtshulp in economisch perspectief' [Legal Aid from an Economic Perspective], **39(10)** *Ars Aequi*, 1990, 692-705. (Subject Code: 7000)

TULDER, Frank van, 'Over fietsen en recht' [On Bicycles and Law], **66** *Nederlands Juristenblad*, 1991, 444-445. (Subject Code: 7000)

TULDER, Frank van, and JANSSEN, S., 'De prijselasticiteit van het recht' [The Price Elasticity of Law], **73** *Economisch-Statistische Berichten*, 1988, 19-22. (Subject Code: 7000)

TULDER, Frank van, and JANSSEN, S., 'De prijs van de weg naar het recht' [The Price of the Road to the Law], *Sociaal Cultureel Planbureau*, Stukwerk no. 45, 1988. (Subject Code: 7000)

UITERMARK, P.J., 'Maximumprijzen: een vergeten hoofdstuk?' [Maximum Prices: A Forgotten Chapter?], **36** *Maandschrift Economie*, 1972, 465-484. (Subject Code: 5100)

UITERMARK, P.J., 'Het Nederlandse mededingingspolitieke regime: Over de verhouding tussen verbod, misbruik, misstand en casuïstisch beleid' [Dutch Competition Policy: On the Interrelationship between Banning, Abuse, Wrongs and Case-to-Case Policy], **29** *TVVS Maandblad voor Ondernemingsrecht en Rechtspersonen*, 1986, 108-115. (Subject Code: 5700)

UITERMARK, P.J., 'Over economische mededinging' [On Economic Competition], **35** *Sociaal-Economische Wetgeving: Tijdschrift voor Europees en Economisch Recht*, 1987, 339-372. (Subject Code: 5700)

UITERMARK, P.J., 'Over informeel mededingingsbeleid' [On Informal Competition Policy], **2** *Recht der Werkelijkheid*, 1988, 30-53. (Subject Code: 5700)

UITERMARK, P.J., *Economische Mededinging en Algemeen Belang: Een onderzoek naar de economisch-theoretische fundering van de mededingingspolitiek* [Economic Competition and Public Interest: An Investigation into the Economic-theoretical Foundations of Competition Policy], Groningen, Wolters Noordhoff, 1990, 475 p. (Subject Code: 5700)

VERLOREN VAN THEMAAT, Pieter, 'Het wetsontwerp-Lubbers tot wijziging van de Wet economische mededinging' [The Lubbers Bill on a Change of the Economic Competition Act], **26** *Sociaal-Economische Wetgeving: Tijdschrift voor Europees en Economisch Recht*, 1978, 178-192. (Subject Code: 5700)

VERLOREN VAN THEMAAT, Pieter, 'Nieuw leven in de Wet economische mededinging of terug naar Abtsweg?' [New Life in the Economic Competition Act or Back to Abtsweg?], **36** *Sociaal-Economische Wetgeving: Tijdschrift voor Europees en Economisch Recht*, 1988, 4-15 and 60-77. (Subject Code: 5700)

VERLOREN VAN THEMAAT, Pieter, 'Economie, gezien door juristen' [Economics, Seen by Lawyers], *Koninklijke Nederlandse Akademie van Wetenschappen*, Noord-Hollandsche Uitgevers Maatschappij, 1988, 229-258. Reprinted as 'L'économie à travers le prisme du juriste', *Revue internationale de droit économique*, 1989, 133-162. (Subject Code: 0010)

WALTHER, Sylvia R.B., 'Eigen schuld slachtoffer en schadevergoedingsmaatregel. Een civielrechtelijke verdeelsleutel in het strafrecht' [Victims Fault and Damage Orders. A Civil Law Distributive Code in Criminal Law], **66** *Nederlands Juristenblad*, 1991, 90-94. (Subject Code: 8000)

WASSENAER VAN CATWIJCK, A.J.O. Baron van, *Verkeersverzekering* [Traffic Insurance], Zwolle, Tjeenk Willink, 1977, 78 p. (Subject Code: 3000, 4600)

WASSENAER VAN CATWIJCK, A.J.O. Baron van, 'Verkeersverzekering in Noord--Amerika' [Traffic Insurance in North-America: No-fault in Action], *Het Verzekerings-Archief*, 's-Gravenhage, Verbond van Verzekeraars in Nederland, 1988, 321-377. (Subject Code: 3000, 4600)

WASSENAER VAN CATWIJCK, A.J.O. Baron van, 'Op zeker spelen. Invloeden van zekerheden in het NBW op het financieringsbedrijf' [Play it Safe. Influence of Dutch New Civil Code Security on Financing Practice], in COLJEE, P.D., FRANKEN, H., HEERTJE, A. and KANNING, W. (eds.), *Law and Welfare Economics*, Symposium 24 October, VU Amsterdam, 133-150. (Subject Code: 2800)

WEIJDEN, Carel J. van der, *Toegang en toetreding: facetten van de mededinging* [Entry and Entrance: Aspects of Competition], Den Haag, 1962. (Subject Code: 5700)

WEIJDEN, Carel J. van der, 'Toestaan of verbieden? Een beschouwing rond de Wet economische mededinging' [Allowing or Banning? Considerations about the Economic Competition Act], **66** *Economisch-Statistische Berichten*, 1981, 12-81-1284. (Subject Code: 5700)

WEIJDEN, Carel J. van der, 'Werkzame mededinging' [Workable Competition], **72** *Economisch-Statistische Berichten*, 1987, 1194-1199. (Subject Code: 5700)

WERTHEIMER, H.W. De Europese Concentratiecontrole in de revisie' [European Concentration Control in Revision], **31** *Sociaal-Economische Wetgeving: Tijdschrift voor Europees en Economisch Recht*, 1983, 66-84. (Subject Code: 5700)

WICHERS HOETH, L., 'Mini-monopolies: Een reactie' [Mini-monopolies: A Response], *Rechtsgeleerd Magazijn Themis*, 1984, 356-357. (Subject Code: 2900)

WIERSMA, D., *De efficiëntie van een marktconform milieubeleid* [The Efficiency of an Environmental Policy in Accordance with Market Principles], diss. Groningen, 1989. (Subject Code: 3500)

WINDEN, Frans van, 'De economie van de politieke besluitvorming', *ESB*, Nederlands Economisch Instituut, Vol. 73, 1988. 'The Economic Theory of Political Decision Making: A Survey and Perspective', in VAN DEN BROECK, J., *Public Choice*, Kluwer, Dordrecht, 9-42. (Subject Code: 0720)

WLADIMIROFF, M., 'Rechtseconomie en strafrecht: enige kritische kanttekeningen' [Law-and-Economics and Criminal Law: Some Critical Remarks], in *Rechtseconomie en Recht*, Tjeenk Willink, Zwolle, 1991, 181-186. (Subject Code: 0300, 8000)

WOUDE, M.H. van der, 'Kartelrechtelijke beschikkingen EG-Commissie 1985-1987' [EC Commission Anti-trust Orders 1985-1987], **37** *Sociaal Economische Wetgeving: Tijdschrift voor Europees en Economisch Recht*, 1989, 2-27. (Subject Code: 5700)

ZIJLSTRA, Jelle and GOUDZWAARD, Bob, *Economische politiek en concurrentieproblematiek in de EEG en de lidstaten* [Economic Policy and Competition Problems in the EC and the Member States], Serie Concurrentie Nr. 2, Brussel, 1966. (Subject Code: 5700)

LAW & ECONOMICS IN NORWAY

Alf Erling Risa

ANDVIG, Jens Christian, 'Korrupsjon i Utviklingsland' [Corruption in Developing Countries] **23** *Nordisk Tidsskrift för Politisk Ekonomi*, 1989, 51-70. (Subject Code: 8000)

EIDE, Erling, 'Kapitaliseringsrente ved Personskadeerstatning. Kritikk av en Dom i Høyesterett' [Capitalization Interest Rates in Personal Injury Compensation. A Critique of a Supreme Court Verdict], *Lov og Rett. Norsk Juridisk Tidsskrift*, 1982, 30-42. (Subject Code: 3200)

EIDE, Erling, 'Renter og Verdisikring av Pengekrav' [Interest Rates and Security against Inflation in Monetary Claims], **97** *Tidsskrift for Rettsvitenskap*, 1984, 477-533. (Subject Code: 3200)

EIDE, Erling, 'Ekspropriasjonserstatning i en Inflasjonstid: Valg av Kapitaliseringsrente' [Compensation for Expropriation in Inflationary Times: The Choice of Capitalization Interest Rates], *Lov og Rett. Norsk Juridisk Tidsskrift*, 1987, 165-177. (Subject Code: 3200)

HEYERDAHL, H. Cristopher, *En Økonomisk Analyse av de Ulovfestede Ansvarsreglene i Erstatningsretten, for Risikonøytrale Aktører* [An Economic Analysis of Common Law Liability Rules in Tort Law for Risk-Neutral Agents], Unpublished thesis, Department of Economics, University of Bergen, 1991. (Subject Code: 3000)

ISACHSEN, Arne Jon and STRØM, Steinar, *Skattefritt. Svart Sektor i Vekst* [Taxfree. The Growth of the Black Sector], Oslo, Universitetsforlaget, 1981. (Subject Code: 6000)

WILHELMSEN, Trine-Lise, *Egenrisiko i Skadeforsikring* [Residual Risk in Accident Insurance], Oslo, Sjørettsfondet, 1989. (Subject Code: 4600)

LAW & ECONOMICS IN SPAIN

Santos Pastor

ALEJO, M. Enrique, 'La efectividad de la política de competencia' [The Effectiveness of Competition Policy], *Información Comercial Española*, 1987, n. 687, pp. 51-66. (Subject Code: 5700)

ARRUÑADA, Benito, *Control y regulación de la sociedad anónima* [Control and Regulation of Corporations], Madrid, Alianza Editorial, 1990. (Subject Code: 5500)

ARRUÑADA, Benito, *Economía de la empresa: un enfoque contractual* [The Economics of the Firm: A Contractual Approach], Barcelona, Ariel, 1990. (Subject Code: 5500)

ARRUÑADA, Benito, 'Control y propriedad: límites al desarrollo de la empresa española' [Property and Control: Limits of the Spanish Firms Development], *Información comercial Española*, 1990, n. 687, 67-88. (Subject Code: 5500)

BARBERA, Salvador, 'Los derechos individuales en el análisis económico' [Individual Rights and Economic Analysis], **38** *Economistas*, 1989. (Subject Code: 0010)

BISBAL, Joaquím, 'La Responsabilidad Extracontractual y la Distribución de los Costes del Progreso' [Liability Rules and Development Cost Allocation], *Rivista de Derecho Mercantil*, 1983, enero-junio. (Subject Code: 3000)

BISDAL, Joaquím, *La empresa en crisis y el derecho de quiebras* [The Crisis of the Firm and Bankruptcy Law], Bolonia, Real Colegio de España, 1986, 383 p. (Subject Code: 2800, 5600)

CABRILLO, Francisco, '¿Por qué un análisis económico del derecho?' [Why an Economic Analysis of Law?], *Revista de Occidente*, 1987, 58. (Subject Code: 0010)

CABRILLO, Franscisco, *Análisis económico de derecho concursal español* [An Economic Analysis of Spanish Bankruptcy Law], Madrid, Fundación Juan March, 1987, 53 p. (Subject Code: 5600)

CABRILLO, Francisco, *Quiebra y liquidación de empresas* [Bankruptcy and Closing Down of Firms], Madrid, Unión editorial, 1989, 151 p. (Subject Code: 5600)

CABRILLO, Francisco, 'Una nueva frontera: el análisis económico del Derecho' [A New Border: The Economic Analysis of Law], *Información Comercial Española*, 1990, n. 687, 9-22. (Subject Code: 0010)

ECONOMISTAS (Journal), *Los derechos de propriedad en el análisis económico* [Property Rights in Economic Analysis], **38** *Economistas*, Special Issue, 1989. (Subject Code: 0050)

GOMEZ-POMAR, Fernando, 'Reglas de transacción y derechos de propriedad intelectual'[Transaction Rules and Intellectual Property Rights], **38** *Economistas*, 1989. (Subject Code: 2900)

GOMEZ-POMAR, Fernando, 'Copias, fotocopias y derechos de autor' [Copies, Photocopies and Copyrights], *Revista de la Facultad de Derecho de la Universidad Complutense*, 1990. (Subject Code: 2910)

GOMEZ-POMAR, Fernando, 'Tutela de la apariencia y reglas de responsabilidad: los arts. 1164 y 1527 del código civil' [Protection of Appearance and Liability Rules: Articles 1164 and 1527 of the Civil Code], *Rivista de Derecho Privado*, 1990. (Subject Code: 3000)

GOMEZ-POMAR, Fernando, 'La producción de copias y los derechos de autor: el caso de la fotocopiadora' [Copy Production and Copyright: The Photocopy-Machine Case], *Información comercial Española*, 1990, n. 687, 43-50. (Subject Code: 2910)

GOMEZ-POMAR, Fernando and PASTOR, Santos, 'El derecho de accidentes y la responsabilidad civil: Un análisis jurídico y económico' [Accident Law and Liability Rules: A Legal and Economic Analysis], *Anuario de Derecho Civil*, 1989. (Subject Code: 3000)

HUERTA, E., 'Política de competencia y economía industrial en España' [Competition Policy and Industrial Economics in Spain], *Información Comercial Española*, 1987, October. (Subject Code: 5700)

HUERTA, E., 'Análisis de la integración vertical de empresas en España' [An Analysis of Firms Vertical Integration in Spain], *Información comercial Española*, 1989, n. 39-40. (Subject Code: 5700)

LAFUENTE, Alberto, 'Aspectos económicos de la definición de mercado' [Some Economic Aspects of the Market Definition], *Información Comercial Española*, 1987, October. (Subject Code: 5700)

LEHMANN, Michael, 'La teoría de los "Property Rights" y la protección de la propriedad intelectual e industrial' [The Property Rights Theory and the Protection of Intellectual and Industrial Property], *Revista General de Derecho*, 1990, n. 544-545, 265-281. (Subject Code: 2900)

PASTOR, Santos, 'Derecho penal, política criminal y economía: un intento de generalización' [Criminal Law, Criminal Policy and Economics], in *Homenaje al Professor Jiménez de Asúa*, Revista de la Facultad de Derecho de la UCM, 1986, n. 11. (Subject Code: 8000)

PASTOR, Santos, 'Heroína y Política Criminal: Un enfoque alternativo' [Heroin and Criminal Policy: An Alternative Approach], in *La problemática de la droga en España; análisis y propuestas político-criminales*, Madrid, IUC y Edersa, 1986. (Subject Code: 8000)

PASTOR, Santos, 'Estado, mercado, eficiencia y equidad' [The Market, the State, Efficiency and Equity], in CORCUERA, J. and GARCIA HERRERA, M.A. (eds.), *Derecho y economía en el estado social*, Tecnos & Gobierno Vasco, 1988. (Subject Code: 5000)

PASTOR, Santos, 'Derechos de propriedad y análisis económico: ¿nuevas luces a viejas sombras?' [The Economics of Property Rights: Enlightening Old Shades?], **38** *Economistas*, 1989. (Subject Code: 1500, 2000)

PASTOR, Santos, *Economía y Sistema Jurídico. Una Introducción al Anàlisis Económico del Derecho* [Economics and the Legal System. An Introduction to Economic Analysis of Law], Madrid, Tecnos, 1989. (Subject Code: 0010)

PASTOR, Santos, 'Economìa de la Justicia en España' [The Spanish Courts and the Economic Analysis], *Revista de Economìa*, 1990, 4. (Subject Code: 7400)

PASTOR, Santos, 'Economìa de la Justicia (I) y (II)' [Economics of the Judicature], *Revista de Economìa Pública*, 1990, Nr. 5 and 6. (Subject Code: 7300, 7400, 8000)

PASTOR, Santos, 'El análisis económico del acceso a la justicia' [The Economics of Access to Justice], *Información Comercial Española*, 1990, n. 687, 23-42. (Subject Code: 7000)

PASTOR, Santos, 'Informe sobre la litigación, recursos y acceso de los cuidadanos a la Justicie' [Report on Litigation, Courts Inputs and Access to Justice], in MINISTERIO DE JUSTICIA, *Materiales para una reforma Procesal*, Madrid, 1991. (Subject Code: 7200, 7300, 7400, 8000)

PAZ-ARES, Cándido, 'La Economía Política como Jurisprudencia racional. Aproximación a la Teoría Económica del Derecho' [The Political Economy as Rational Jurisprudence. An Introduction to Law and Economics], *Anuario de Derecho Civil*, 1981, julio/septiembre. (Subject Code: 0010)

PAZ-ARES, Cándido, 'Sobre la infracapitalización de las sociedades' [On Infra-Capitalization of Corporations], *Anuario de Derecho Civil*, 1983. (Subject Code: 5500)

PAZ-ARES, Cándido, 'Seguridad jurídica y seguridad del tráfico' [Legal Certainty and Exhange Certainty], *Revista de Derecho Mercantil*, 1985. (Subject Code: 0010, 5500)

SALINAS, Javier, *Economía política del federalismo fiscal español* [The Political Economy of Spanish Fiscal Federalism], Madrid, Instituto de Estudios Fiscales, 1990. (Subject Index: 6060)

TORRES, Juan, 'Tradición y resultados de una disciplina novedosa: la Economía del Derecho. Una orientación bibliográfica' [Tradition and Outcome of a New Discipline: The Economics of Law. A Guide to the Literature], **5** *Revista de la Facultad de Derecho de la Universidad de Granada*, 1987. (Subject Code: 0010)

TORRES, Juan, *Análisis económico del derecho. Panorama doctrinal* [Economic Analysis of Law: An Overview], Madrid, Tecnos, 1987. (Subject Code: 0000)

VASQUEZ, Pablo, 'Grupos de interés en la Comunidad Económica Europea. Apuntes sobre un regulación actual' [The Regulation of Interest Groups in the European Community], *Información Comercial Española*, 1990, n. 689, 89-102. (Subject Code: 5000)

LAW & ECONOMICS IN SWEDEN

Göran Skogh

BJUGGREN, Per-Olof and SKOGH, Göran (eds.), *Företaget. En kontraktsekonomisk analys* [The Firm. A Contractual Approach], SNS Publishing company, 1990. (Subject Code: 5510)

HANNESSON, Rögnvaldur, 'Varför fiskegränserna bör utvidgas' [Why the Fishing Borders Have to Be Expanded], *Ekonomisk Debatt*, 1974, Nr. 5. (Subject Code: 2700)

HELLNER, Jan, *Rättsekonomi, avbeställning och Coase-teorem* [Law and Economics, Cancellation and Coase Theorem], Juridiska föreningen i Lund, No. 24, 1978, 101 p. (Subject Code: 0630)

HÖGLUND, Bengt, *Spelet om Resurserna i den Svenska Blandekonomin* [The Swedish Mixed Economy], Lund, Dialogos, 1984. (Subject Code: 5000)

ISACHSEN, Arne Jon and STRØM, Steinar, *Skattefritt. Svart Sektor i Vekst* [Taxfree. The Growth of the Black Sector], Oslo, Universitetsforlaget, 1981. (Subject Code: 6060)

LUNDGREN, Nils and LÖNN, H., 'Gör hyresrätt till bostadsrätt' [Transform Rent Contract to Ownership], *Ekonomisk Debatt*, 1980, Nr. 4. (Subject Code: 2000)

MYHRMAN, Johan, 'Kontraktsrätt och löntagarfonder' [Contractual Rights and Labour Funds], *Ekonomisk Debatt*, 1981, No. 6. (Subject Code: 5400)

MYHRMAN, Johan, 'Äganderätt och samhällssystem' [Property Rights and Social Structure], in *Äganderätt och egendomsskydd* [Property Right and Property Protection], Svenska Arbetsgivareföreningen, 1985. (Subject Code: 2000)

MYHRMAN, Johan, HÖRNGREN, Lars, VIOTTI, Staffan and ELIASSON, Gunnar, *Kreditmarknadens spelregler* [The Rules of the Game on the Credit Market], SNS Publishing company, 1987. (Subject Code: 5570)

MYHRMAN, Johan, PETRÉN, Gustav and STRÖMHOLM, Stig, *Marknadsekonomins rättsliga grundvalar* [The Legal Foundations of the Market Economy], Timbro, 1987. (Subject Code: 0020)

ROOS, Carl Martin, *Ersättningsrätt och ersättningssystem* [Compensation Right and Compensation System], Nordstedts, Stockholm, 1990. (Subject Code: 3000)

SAMUELSSON, Per, *Information och ansvar. Om BÔrsbolagens ansvar fór bristfällig informationsgiuning på aktiemarknaden* [Information and Remedies. Listed Companies and Their Responsibility for False and Misleading Information in the Stock Market], Stockholm, Norstedt, 1991.

SAMUELSSON, Per and SKOGH, Göran, 'Juridisk forskning i gränsområdet mot ekonomi - exemplet insiderhandel' [Legal Research and Economics - The Example of Insider Trading], in BASSE, Ellen Margrethe (ed.), *Regulering og styring - en juridisk teoriog metodebog*, 91-110. (Subject Code: 5550)

SKOGH, Göran, *En samhällsekonomisk mål-medel-analys av butikssnatterier* [An Economic Analysis of Shop-liftings], Statens offentliga utredning 'Snatteri', SOU 1971:10, suppl. 9. (Subject Code: 5200)

SKOGH, Göran, *Staffrätt och samhällsekonomi* [Criminal Law and the Economy],

Lund Economic Studies, 1973. (Subject Code: 8000)

SKOGH, Göran, 'Vilken är den rättvisa räntan? Kritisk kommentar till förslag om räntelag' [What is the Fair Interest Rate? Critical Commentary on a Law Proposal Concerning Interest Rates], *Svensk Juristtidning*, 1975, 116-121. (Subject Code: 5570)

SKOGH, Göran, 'Ett alternativ till den föreslagna konsumentkreditlagen' [An Alternative to the Proposed Consumer Credit Law], *Svensk Juristtidning*, 1976, 542-547. (Subject Code: 5570)

SKOGH, Göran, *Priser, skadestånd och straff* [Prices, Damages and Penalties], Malmö, Liber, 1977. (Subject Code: 8000)

SKOGH, Göran, 'Konsumentlagstiftningen i Rättsekonomisk Belysning' [The Consumer Legislation from a Law and Economics Perspective], in *Festskrift till Per Stiernquist*, Juridiska Föreningen i Lund, No. 24, 1978. (Subject Code: 5200)

SKOGH, Göran, 'Kontraktsteoretisk översikt' [Contractual-theoretical Survey], *Statsökonomisk tidskrift*, 1979, No. 1. (Subject Code: 4000)

SKOGH, Göran, 'Straffvärdering enligt välfärdsekonomiska principer' [Penalty Assessment According to Welfare-economic Principles], in *Påföljdsval, Straffmätning och Straffvärde*, Brottsförebyggande rådet. Rapport 1980:2. (Subject Code: 8000)

SKOGH, Göran, *Marknadens villkor* [The Terms of the Market], Stockholm, Timbro, 1982. (Subject Code: 5000)

SKOGH, Göran, 'Den osynliga handen och lagens långa arm' [The Invisible Hand and the Law's Long Arm], *Ekonomisk Debatt*, 1982, No. 8. (Subject Code: 0010)

SKOGH, Göran (ed.), *Vem skall bestämma över skog och mark?* [Who is Going to Decide Over Forest and Land?], Lund, Distr. Dialogos, 1984. (Subject Code: 2700)

SKOGH, Göran, Rättssäkerhet i marknadsekonomin [Legal Certainty in the Market Economy], in *Rättssäkerhet och Demokrati*, Ratios förlag, 1985. (Subject Code: 9800)

SKOGH, Göran, 'Äganderätten och Lagstiftningen om Markresurserna' [The Property Right and the Legislation on the Land Resources], *Svensk Juristtidning*, February 1985. (Subject Code: 2700)

SKOGH, Göran, 'Äganderättens ekonomi och politik' [The Economics and Politics of Property Rights], *Politiskt-Filosofiska Sällskapets årsskrift*, 1988. (Subject Code: 2000)

SKOGH, Göran and SAMUELSSON, Per, *Splittring eller sammanhållning i svensk försäkring? En ekonomisk och rättslig analys av marknadsföringsöverenskommelse m.m* [Disruption or Unity in Swedish Insurance? An Economic and Legal Analysis of the Marketing Agreements etc], Lund, Dialogos, 1985. (Subject Code: 4600)

SKOGH, Göran and SAMUELSSON, Per, *Konsumentpolitik* [Consumer Policy], Stiftelsen Marknadsekonomiskt Alternativ för Sverige, 1985. (Subject Code: 5200)

SOERIA-ATMADJA, S., 'Handlar konsumentombudsmannen alltid i konsumenternas intresse?' [Do the Consumers' Representatives Always Protect the Consumers'

Interests?], *Ekonomisk Debatt*, 1982, No. 4. (Subject Code: 5200)

STÅHL, Ingemar, 'Ägande och makt i företagen - en debattinledning, Nationalekonomiska Föreningens Förhandlingar' [Ownership and Power in the Firms - An Introduction to Debate, The Economics Association's Negotiations], *Ekonomisk Debatt*, 1976, No. 1. (Subject Code: 5530)

WERIN, Lars, 'Expropriation - en studie i lagstiftningsmotiv och ersättningsrättsliga grundprinciper' [Expropriation - A Study in Legislative Motives and Compensatory Basic Principles], *Svensk Juristtidning*, 1978, 81-120. (Subject Code: 6200)

WERIN, Lars, Ekonomi och rättssystem [Economy and Legal System], Malmö, Liber, 1982 (2nd ed.). (Subject Code: 0000)

WIJKMAN, P.M., 'Kampen om jordens allmänningar' [The Struggle for the Common Land on Earth], *Ekonomisk Debatt*, 1974, No. 6. (Subject Code: 2000)

LAW & ECONOMICS IN SWITZERLAND
Gerrit De Geest

ADAMS, Michael, 'Eine wohlfahrtstheoretische Analyse des Zivilprozesses und der Rechtsschutzversicherungen' [An Economic Analysis of Civil Procedure and Legal Aid Insurance], **139** *Zeitschrift für Schweizerisches Recht*, 1983, 187-208. (Subject Code: 4600, 7200)

ADAMS, Michael, *Ökonomische Analyse des Gefährdungs- und Verschuldenshaftung* [Economic Analysis of Strict and Fault Liability] (Habilitationsschrift at the University of Bern), Heidelberg, R.v Decker's/C.F. Müller, 1985, 310 p. (Subject Code: 3000)

ADAMS, Michael, 'Der Irrtum über "künftige Sachverhalte": Anwendungsbeispiel und Einführung in die ökonomische Analyse des Rechts' [The Mistake on Future States: Example and Introduction into the Economic Analysis of Law], **4** *Recht*, 1986, 14-23. (Subject Code: 0010)

BAUDENBACHER, Carl, *Wirtschafts- schuld- und verfahrens-rechtliche Grundprobleme der Allgemeinen Geschäftsbedingungen* [Standard Term Clauses: Basic Problems of Economic, Liability and Procedural Law], Zurich, Schulthess, 1983. (Subject Code: 4200)

BAUDENBACHER, Carl, *Rechtsverwirklichung als ökonomisches Problem? Zur Überlastung der Zivilgerichte* [Enforcement of Law as an Economic Problem? On the Overload of the Civil Courts], Zurich, Schulthess, 1985. (Subject Code: 8000)

BORNER, Silvio, 'Wirtschafts- Sozial- und Eigentumsordnung um Verfassungsentwurf: Ein Diskussionsbeitrag aus ökonomischer Sicht' [Economic, Social and Property Structure in the Constitutionial Bill: A Contribution to the Discussion from an Economic Viewpoint], **98** *Zeitschrift für schweizerisches Recht*, 1979, 463-479. (Subject Code: 9100)

EISEN, Roland, 'Wettbewerb und Regulierung in der Versicherung Die Rolle asymmetrischer Information' [Competition and Regulation in Insurance: The Role of Asymmetrical Information], **122** *Schweizerische Zeitschrift fur Volkswirtschaft und Statistik*, 1986, 339-358. (Subject Code: 4600)

FELDER, St., 'Sind Externalitäten in jeden Fall zu internalisieren?' [Are Externalities Always to Internalize?], **125** *Schweizerische Zeitschrift für Volkswirtschaft und Statistik*, 1989, 189-193. (Subject Code: 3500)

FREY, Bruno S., *Ökonomie ist Sozialwissenschaft. Die Anwendung der Ökonomie auf neue Gebiete* [Economics is a Social Science. The Use of Economics in New Domains], München, Vahlen, 1990. (Subject Code: 0020)

FREY, Rene L., 'Wirtschaftswachstum und Umweltqualitat: Auf der Suche nach einer neuen Wachstumspolitik' [Economic Growth and Environmental Quality: In Search of a New Growth Policy], **123** *Schweizerische Zeitschrift fur Volkswirtschaft und Statistik*, 1987, 289-315. (Subject Code: 3500)

FREY, René L. and LEU, Robert E., 'Waldsterben: von der naturwissenschaftlichen Analyse zur Umweltpolitik' [The Death of the Forest: From a Natural Sciences Analysis to Environmental Policy], **39** *Wirtschaft und Recht*, 1987, 58-72.

(Subject Code: 3500)

HOTZ, Beat, 'Ökonomische Analyse des Rechts - eine skeptische Betrachtung' [Economic Analysis of Law - A Sceptical Reflection], **34** *Wirtschaft und Recht*, 1982, 293-314. (Subject Code: 0010, 0300)

ITEN, R., MAGGI, R., SCHELBERT-SYFRIG, Heidi and ZIMMERMAN, Andreas J., 'There is no such thing as a free lunch', **125** *Schweizerische Zeitschrift für Volkswirtschaft und Statistik*, 1989. (Subject Code: 3500)

JANSSEN, Martin and HUMMLER, Konrad, 'Bundesverfassung und Verfassungsentwurf, Eine ökonomisch-rechtliche Analyse [Constitution and Revision of the Constitition, An Economic and Legal Analysis], *Schriften des Schweizerischen Aufklärungs-Dienstes*, 1979. (Subject Code: 9100)

JUNOD, Charles-André, 'L'indexation des crédits hypothécaires pourrait-elle à la fois améliorer le fonctionnement du marché du logement et servir de correctif à l'inflation?' [Could the Indexation of Mortgage-debt Improve the Functioning of the Housing Market as Well as Serve as a Corrective for Inflation?], **40** *Wirtschaft und Recht*, 1988, 88-123. (Subject Code: 5570)

KLEINEWEFERS, Henner, 'Ökonomische Theorie des Rechts, Über Unterschiede zwischen dem ökonomischen und dem juristischen Denken' [Economic Theory of Law, On the Differences between Economic and Legal Thinking], in *Staat und Gesellschaft, Festschrift für Leo Schürmann zum 70. Geburtstag*, Fribourg, Universitätsverlag, 1987, 83-116. (Subject Code: 0010, 0300)

KRAMER, Ernst A., 'Konsumentenschutz als neue Dimension des Privat- und Wirtschaftsrecht' [Consumer Protection as a New Dimension of Private and Economic Law], **98** *Zeitschrift für schweizerisches Recht*, 1979, I, 49-92. (Subject Code: 5200)

MEIER-SCHATZ, Christian, 'Unternehmenszusammenschlüsse mittels Übernahmeangebot [Mergers by Takeover Bid]', **39** *Wirtschaft und Recht*, 1987, 16-39. (Subject Code: 5540)

MEIER-SCHATZ, Christian, 'Über die Notwendigkeit gesellschaftsrechtlicher Aufsichtsregeln, Ein Beitrag zur Ökonomischen Analyse des Gesellschaftsrechts' [On the Necessity of Rules for the Supervision of Corporations, A Contribution to the Economic Analysis of Company Law], *Zeitschrift für schweizerisches Recht,* 1988, I, 191-241. (Subject Code: 5500)

MEIER-SCHATZ, Christian, *Wirtschaftsrecht und Unternehmenspublizität* [Economic Legislation and Enterprise Publicity], Zurich, Schulthess, 1989. (Subject Code: 5000)

MEIER-SCHATZ, Christian, 'Europäische Harmonisierung des Gesellschafts- und Kapitalmarktrechts' [European Harmonization of Company and Capital Market Law], **41** *Wirtschaft und Recht*, 1989, 84-110. (Subject Code: 5500, 5570)

POMMEREHNE, Werner W., 'Steuerhinterziehung und Schwarzarbeit als Grenzen der Staatstatigkeit' [Tax Evasion and Underground Activities as Limits of Government's Growth], **119** *Schweizerische Zeitschrift fur Volkswirtschaft und - Statistik*, 1983, 261-284. (Subject Code: 6020)

RICHLI, Paul, 'Handels- und Gewerbefreiheit contra Energiepolitik' [Freedom of Trade and Industry versus Energy Policy], **86** *Schweizerisches Zentralblatt für Staats- und Verwaltungsrecht*, 1985, 1-14. (Subject Code: 5900)

ROBERT, Philippe and GODEFROY, Thierry, *Le coût du crime ou l'économie poursuivant le crime* [The Cost of Crime or Economics Prosecuting Crime], Genève, Masson, 1977, 225 p. (Subject Code: 0020, 8000)

RUFFNER, Markus, *Neue Wettbewerbstheorie und schweizerisches Kartellrecht, Möglichkeit und Grenzen einer markt- und institutionentheoretischen Fundierung der Wettbewerbspolitik* [New Competition Theory and Swiss Antitrust Law, Possibilities and Limitations of a Market and Institutionalist Foundation of Competition Policy], Zurich, Schulthess, 1990. (Subject Code: 5700)

SCHELBERT-SYFRIG, Heidi, LANG, Th., BUSE, I., HENZMAN, J., MAGGI, R., ITEN, R. and NIELSEN, C., *Wertvolle Umwelt* [Valuable Environment], Zurich, Schriftenreihe Wirtschaft und Gesellschaft der Zürcher Kantonalbank, September 1988. (Subject Code: 3500)

SCHELBERT-SYFRIG, Heidi and ZIMMERMANN, Andreas J., 'Konkurrenz und Umweltschutz. Wald und Holzwirtschaft zwischen Okonomie und Okologie' [Competition and Environment Protection. Forest and Forestry Between Economics and Ecology], **124** *Schweizerische Zeitschrift fur Volkswirtschaft und Statistik*, 1988, 289-302. (Subject Code: 3500)

SCHÜRMANN, Leo, 'Konjunkturpolitik und freie Wechselkurse [Conjuncture Policy and Free Exchange Rate], in *Schweizerische Wirtschaftspolitik zwischen gestern und morgen*, Bern, Haupt, 1976, 265-277. (Subject Code: 5570)

SCHÜRMANN, Leo, 'Der Wettbewerb im Urteil der Staatswissenschaft' [The Competition in the Judgment of the Economics], **42** *Wirtschaft und Recht*, 1990, 35-41. (Subject Code: 5700)

SIEBER, Hugo, 'Wirtschaftsfreiheit und Wirtschaftspolitik' [Economic Freedom and Economic Policy], in *Recht als Prozess und Gefüge* (Festschrift für Hans Huber zum 80. Geburtstag), Bern, 1981, 447-465. (Subject Code: 5000)

STOLZ, Peter, 'Das wiedererwachte Interesse der Ökonomie an rechtlichen und politischen Institutionen. [The Renewed Interest of Economics in Legal and Political Institutions. With English summary.]', **119** *Schweizerische Zeitschrift fur Volkswirtschaft und Statistik*, 1983, 49-67. (Subject Code: 0010)

VUARIDEL, Roger, 'L'objet et le niveau de la concurrence dans la théorie économique et dans la jurisprudence' [The Object and Level of Competition in Economic Theory and in Jurisprudence], **20** *Wirtschaft und Recht*, 1986, 111-128. (Subject Code: 5700)

WECK-HANNEMANN, Hannelore and POMMEREHNE, Werner W., 'Einkommensteuerhinterziehung in der Schweiz: Eine empirische Analyse' [Income Tax Evasion in Switzerland: An Empirical Analysis], **125** *Schweizerische Zeitschrift fur Volkswirtschaft und Statistik*, 1989, 515-556. (Subject Code: 6020)

WIEGANG, Wolfgang, ' Die Rezeption amerikanischen Rechts' [The Reception of American Law], in *Die schweizerische Rechtsordung in ihren internationalen Bezügen*, Bern, Haupt, 1988, 229-262. (Subject Code: 0100)

NAME INDEX

SUBJECT INDEX